SOUTH-WESTERN
ADMINISTRATIVE
OFFICE
MANAGEMENT

ELEVENTH EDITION

B. Lewis Keeling
Professor Emeritus
Bucks County Community College
Newtown, Pennsylvania

Norman F. Kallaus
The University of Iowa
Iowa City, Iowa

Contributing Authors

Dr. Kent Burnham
Eastern Washington University
Chaney, WA

Mary Ruprecht
Office Automation Consultant
Duluth, MN

Consulting Editor
Dr. Sharon Massen
Clarks Summit, PA

Software Consultant
Marly Bergerud
Saddleback Community College

South-Western Educational Publishing

Editor-in-Chief:	Robert E. First
Marketing Manager:	Al S. Roane
Developmental Editor:	Inell Bolls
Consulting Editor:	Sharon Massen
Senior Production Editor:	Jane Congdon
Production Editor:	Diane Bowdler
Art Director:	John Robb
Staff Designer:	Nicola Hardy
Cover Design:	Ben Ross, Ross Design
Photography Coordinator:	Devore Nixon
Photo Editors:	Kathryn A. Russell, Fred Middendorf

ISBN: 0-538-71127-2

3 4 5 6 7 8 D1 02 01 00 99 98 97 96

Printed in the United States of America

Library of Congress Cataloging-in-Publication Data

Keeling, B. Lewis (Billy Lewis)
   Administrative office management / B. Lewis Keeling ; contributing authors, Kent R. Burnham, Mary M. Ruprecht. —11th ed.
      p. cm.
   Rev. ed. of: Administrative office management / Norman F. Kallaus.
10th ed. ©1991
   Includes bibliographical references and index.
   ISBN 0-538-71127-2
   1. Office management.   I. Burnham, Kent R.   II. Ruprecht, Mary M.
III. Kallaus, Norman Francis, 1924-   Administrative office management.   IV. Title.
HF5547.K43 1996
651.3—dc20   94-30408
                                                                                  CIP

I(T)P

International Thomson Publishing
South-Western Educational Publishing is a division of International Thomson Publishing Inc. The ITP trademark is used under license.

Brief Contents

Part One

Developing Basic Concepts in Administrative Office Management   1

    1 Managing Offices in Our Global Economy   2
    2 Applying Basic Management Principles   26
    3 Developing Problem-Solving Skills   55
    4 Administering Office Systems   82
    5 Communicating in the Office   105

Part Two

Managing a Culturally Diverse Workforce   129

    6 Recruiting and Orienting the Workforce   130
    7 Supervising the Office Staff   158
    8 Training, Appraising, and Promoting Office Personnel   184
    9 Analyzing Office Jobs   212
    10 Administering Office Salaries   238
    11 Providing Employee Benefits   262
    12 Examining Workplace Issues   287

Part Three

Managing Administrative Services   321

    13 Managing Office Space   322
    14 Planning an Ergonomically Sound Office Environment   356
    15 Selecting Office Furniture and Equipment   384
    16 Automating the Office   407
    17 Understanding Text/Word Processing Systems   440
    18 Distributing Information: Telecommunication and Mailing Systems   471
    19 Managing Records   506
    20 Managing Microimage and Reprographic Systems   543

Part Four

Controlling Administrative Services   571

    21 Improving Administrative Office Systems   572
    22 Improving Office Productivity   603
    23 Budgeting Administrative Expenses   634

Glossary   657

Index   683

Contents

Part One

Developing Basic Concepts in Administrative Office Management   1

1 Managing Offices in Our Global Economy   2

Administrative Office Management Defined • The Functions of Management • The Functions of Administrative Office Management • The Administrative Office Manager • Schools of Management Thought

2 Applying Basic Management Principles   26

Basic Principles of Management • Forms of Organization • Centralizing/Decentralizing Managerial Authority • Leadership Styles of the Administrative Office Manager

3 Developing Problem-Solving Skills   55

Administrative Office Managers as Problem Solvers • The Problem-Solving Process • Barriers in Solving Office Problems • A Case Illustration of Problem Solving

4 Administering Office Systems   82

The Administrative Office Systems Function • Basic Systems Concepts • Conducting Systems Studies • Organizing the Systems Function • The Human System in the Office

5 Communicating in the Office   105

The Communication Process • Communication Networks • The Flow of Communication • Barriers to Effective Communication • Nonverbal Communication • Report-Writing Principles

iv

Part Two

Managing a Culturally Diverse Workforce 129

6 Recruiting and Orienting the Workforce 130

Background Information About the Workforce Problem • Sources of Office Workers • Selecting Office Workers • Preemployment Testing • Orienting the Office Staff • Government Regulations Affecting the Employment Process • Other Federal Regulations Affecting the Employment Process

7 Supervising the Office Staff 158

The Office Supervision Process • Motivating the Workforce • Ethics and Value Systems

8 Training, Appraising, and Promoting Office Personnel 184

Training • Entry-Level Training • Supervisory Training and Management Development (STMD) • Appraising the Office Worker's Performance • Promoting • Terminating the Office Worker's Services

9 Analyzing Office Jobs 212

Uses of Office Job Analysis • Gathering and Analyzing Job Information • Job Descriptions • Job Specifications • Job Evaluation

10 Administering Office Salaries 238

Objectives of Office Salary Administration • Factors to Consider in Determining Office Salaries • Pricing Office Jobs • Variable Pay Plans

11 Providing Employee Benefits 262

Why Companies Provide Employee Benefits • Nature and Extent of Employee Benefits • Developing and Implementing a Cost-Effective Employee Benefits Program

12 Examining Workplace Issues 287

The Workers' Physical and Mental Well-Being • Job Attendance and Work Schedules • Unionization of Office Workers

Part Three

Managing Administrative Services   321

13   Managing Office Space   322

Space in the Administrative Office
System • The Space Management
Program • Space Needs in the Office
• Office Design Plans • Space Plan-
ning in Workcenters • Principles of
Space Management • Relocating the
Office • The Workplace of the Fu-
ture

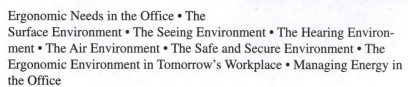

14   Planning an Ergonomically Sound
Office Environment   356

Ergonomic Needs in the Office • The
Surface Environment • The Seeing Environment • The Hearing Environment • The Air Environment • The Safe and Secure Environment • The
Ergonomic Environment in Tomorrow's Workplace • Managing Energy in
the Office

15   Selecting Office Furniture and Equipment   384

Selecting Office Furniture and Equipment • Procuring Office Equipment •
Maintaining Office Equipment • Replacing Office Equipment • Centralizing the Control of Office Equipment

16   Automating the Office   407

The Nature and Purpose of Computers • Computer Systems Technology •
The Automated Office • Applications of Automated Systems • Managing
Automated Office Systems

17   Understanding Text/Word Processing Systems   440

Written Communications in the Office • Text/Word Processing (T/WP)
Systems • Manual T/WP Systems • Automated T/WP Systems • Management of T/WP Systems

18   Distributing Information: Telecommunication and Mailing Systems   471

Telecommunication Systems • The Tools of Telecommunication Systems •
Telecommunication Services • Managing Telecommunication Systems •
Managing Mailing Systems

19   Managing Records   506

The Records Management Function in the Organization • The Records
Life Cycle • Paper Forms and Records Systems • Managing the Records
Life Cycle with Manual Systems • Managing the Records Life Cycle with
Automated Systems • Administration of the Records Management Pro-
gram

20   Managing Microimage and Reprographic Systems   543

Microimage Technology • Management of Microimage Systems • Reprographic Technology • Management of Reprographic Systems

Part Four

Controlling Administrative Services   571

21   Improving Administrative Office Systems   572

Why Systems Must Change • The Systems Improvement Process • Defining Objectives, Surveying the Present System, and Proposing Changes for Systems Improvement • Major Studies in Administrative Office Systems • Designing, Installing, and Evaluating the Improved System

22   Improving Office Productivity   603

Work Measurement and Work Standards • Preparing for the Work Measurement Program • Methods of Measuring Routine Office Work and Setting Standards • Performance Standards for Nonroutine Office Jobs • Improving Office Productivity Through Quality Management

23   Budgeting Administrative Expenses   634

The AOM's Role in Budgetary Control • Principles of Preparing Administrative Expenses Budgets • The Administrative Expenses Budget • Cost-Analysis Problems Related to Budgetary Control

Glossary   657

Index   683

Photo Credits   701

Preface

Today, we view the office as both the *information function* and the *information center*—a place where information-related operations occur. As we anticipate a national information infrastructure—the so-called "information superhighway"—we see that changes in information technology are accelerating rapidly. Along with these changes, many office employees must meet the challenge of working in a newly competitive global environment. This means that students preparing for business careers, as well as workers on the job seeking positions in management, need to be on the "cutting edge" of technology and human relations to maximize the use of information tools and procedures in their work.

OUR AUDIENCE

We have designed our textbook mainly to service two groups: (1) students using the book in their administrative office management courses and (2) managers and supervisors using it as a handbook in the daily management of their offices. Both of these groups will find a thorough discussion of the theory and current practice of administrative office systems.

THE BOOK AT A GLANCE

In the Eleventh Edition, we have followed the logical organization plan of its predecessor, but with substantial updating and strengthening of content. In doing so, we continue to emphasize the overriding importance of *human resources*. It is *people* who make decisions and who plan, organize, direct, and control the administrative process. In other words, *it is people who manage.* Further, since all employees have some decision-making responsibilities, *all employees manage,* to some degree, even if it is only their individual work assignments.

Here is a brief highlight of each part of the textbook:

Part 1

In this opening part, we introduce students to the fundamentals of effective management. These fundamentals include the basic principles of management, problem solving, systems thinking, and communications needed to administer the office function.

Part 2

This part stresses *people* and their role in using the tools of information technology required in the battle to increase productivity.

viii

Part 3

In this part, we highlight the main concepts needed to understand the services used by successful office administrators—computers, text/word processing, telecommunications, records management, microimage and reprographic systems, and the ergonomic environment required for the new networking technology.

Part 4

This final part provides a "control" setting that explains how office managers evaluate the productivity of their office systems and the "bottom-line" importance of living within their budgets.

Throughout this new edition, we continue to emphasize systems. This emphasis aids students in understanding the interaction of the main elements in the process of administrative office management. Also, the systems "way of thinking" helps students apply the concepts involved in discussing the questions posed and in solving the case problems presented at the end of each chapter. Thus, we provide a strong management-based background so that students may assume responsibilities later as members of the management team.

WHAT ARE THE NEW FEATURES?

To update and further strengthen our coverage of the office management field, we provide these new features in the Eleventh Edition:

- The effects of downsizing and re-engineering in the flattening of traditional organization structures, with the emergence of new features such as broadbanding, matrix organizations, and self-managed work teams.
- An expanded coverage of career opportunities in offices of all sizes and the steps taken by organizations to work with employees in planning their career goals.
- A discussion of critical human relations issues, such as meeting the needs of a *diverse workforce: employee empowerment* as a tool for increasing employee participation; providing workers with requisite skills by means of training techniques such as *multimedia* and *virtual reality*; evaluating new aspects of salary compensation programs, including *broadbanding* and *skill-based pay systems*; providing cost-effective *health care* and *flexible benefits* programs; and formulating contingency plans in the event of *violence in the workplace.*
- A description of the *workplace of the future*, paying particular attention to the use of computer-aided design in laying out offices and the effects of a firm's restructuring upon its ergonomic environment.
- The latest developments in *information technology*, including (a) word processing and text management; (b) information distribution, encompassing telecommunication and mailing systems; (c) microimage systems; and (d) the integration of automated services.
- The role played by *total quality management* in improving office productivity as we examine continuous improvement, benchmarking, downsizing, work teams, and outsourcing.

WHAT "OLD" FEATURES ARE RETAINED?

Resisting the temptation to change solely for the sake of change, we have kept many features of the prior edition, such as the following, which have proven to be well received:

- The *personal, informal writing style* that effectively communicates with readers.
- Retention of *general management principles*, augmented by the contributions of practitioners such as Drucker, Deming, and Juran.
- *Profiles of managers* who describe their jobs, explain their methods of solving human and technical problems in the office, and provide personal information about their education and work experience. Termed *Dialog from the Workplace*, these profiles give students practical information from managers and supervisors presently on the "firing line."

END-OF-CHAPTER ACTIVITIES

At the end of each chapter, you will find the following activities:

- *For Your Review*: These questions, arranged in the same sequence as the textual material, are answered specifically in the chapter.
- *For Your Discussion*: Designed to stretch the reader's thinking, these questions interrelate the chapter content to the reader's philosophy, value system, and work experience.
- *Cases for Critical Thinking*: The three case problems are designed to improve the readers' problem-solving skills by requiring them to think critically about the problems and develop workable solutions. Many of the problems were drawn from the authors' on-the-job experiences, while others are adaptations of problems facing other managers in the office.
- *Computer Option*: The third case in each chapter is a Computer Option which emphasizes problem solving with the aid of a computer. The Computer Option is new in the Eleventh Edition. Instructions for using the Computer Option activities are given on the template diskette available from the publisher.

SUPPORT MATERIALS

The following supplementary items are available:

- **Practical Experience Assignments**. The activities in this workbook enable students to participate more directly in their study of office management by offering a variety of projects that simulate on-the-job office experiences. In addition, the workbook provides supplementary readings, self-test review questions, and a new item, *Computer Hands-On*. Instructions for using the Computer Hands-On projects are found on the template diskette available from the publisher.
- **Template diskette**. The diskette, available from the publisher, contains instructions for the textbook Computer Option problems and the workbook Computer Hands-On projects. These problems and projects provide applications in word processing, spreadsheet, and database management.

ACKNOWLEDGMENTS

The Eleventh Edition of *Administrative Office Management* represents our combined teaching, research, and consulting experience. This experience has been strengthened materially by the valuable contributions of the following persons:

Ms. Fran Blade, Longview Community College

Dr. Anna Burford, Middle Tennessee State University

Dr. Della L. Cooper, Jackson State University

Dr. C. Steven Hunt, Tennessee State University

Dr. Gerald Jernigan, Corinth, TX

Ms. Ella W. Jones, Trenholm State Technical College

Ms. Mary Ruprecht, Duluth, MN

Dr. Marguerite Shane-Joyce, California State University

Karon L. Tomerlin, Southwest Missouri State University

Dr. Kathryn G. Woolard, Beaufort County Community College

In addition, office managers, students, colleagues, including users of earlier editions of the textbook, and a highly competent editorial staff have contributed many useful suggestions. Good luck in your study of administrative office management and much success as you start (or continue) your work in the office!

B. L. K.
N. F. K.

B. LEWIS KEELING

August 1, 1926–August 15, 1994

In memory of a great leader—teacher, editor, author, father, and friend. A man of patience, love, courage, and understanding—a true visionary with the highest of ideals. He will be missed by all.

DEVELOPING BASIC CONCEPTS IN ADMINISTRATIVE OFFICE MANAGEMENT

1 • *Managing Offices in Our Global Economy*

2 • *Applying Basic Management Principles*

3 • *Developing Problem-Solving Skills*

4 • *Administering Office Systems*

5 • *Communicating in the Office*

MANAGING OFFICES IN OUR GLOBAL ECONOMY

GOALS FOR THIS CHAPTER

After completing this chapter, you should be able to:

1. Define the functions of management and indicate the managerial levels at which these functions may be carried out.
2. Describe some typical office activities performed in each of the functional areas of administrative office management.
3. Show how the information-handling responsibilities of the administrative office manager may vary according to the size of the organization.
4. Identify the skills needed by administrative office managers.
5. Compare the career opportunities for office managers in small and large companies.
6. Describe the goals of the International Office Management Association and the Certified Administrative Manager program sponsored by the Academy of Administrative Management.
7. Identify briefly the major contributions of each of the schools of management thought.

Standing at the edge of the twenty-first century, we see that the Information Revolution is in full bloom as the powers of computer networks and communications systems are merged. Yesterday it was the Industrial Revolution that divided jobs into their component parts and created rigid, hierarchical organizations that tightly controlled workers. Today, many organizations are giving way to looser, more decentralized arrangements that provide workers with greater autonomy and responsibility. In these firms, the flow of information is no longer local or national, but global. In our offices, we network via the computer with our associates, suppliers, and customers in far-flung locations both at home and abroad. It is as if geographic boundaries have evaporated when we send and receive information among offices around the globe. With this Information Revolution have come new opportunities for employment in firms striving to gain the competitive edge. So, let's examine the career opportunities in one of the most essential and satisfying professions in business—administrative office management.

ADMINISTRATIVE OFFICE MANAGEMENT DEFINED

Before commencing an in-depth study of this subject, we shall take a look at each of the words in the name *Administrative Office Management* in order to learn more about the complex nature of this field.

Administrative is related to the word *administration,* which describes the performance of, or carrying out of, assigned duties. *Administration* is also used to refer to a group of persons who execute these duties, such as the governing board of your school or the top-level executives of a corporation. We shall soon see that administration is essential in every aspect of business operations.

Office is a term used by many to refer to the *place* where information is processed, such as a credit office, a lawyer's office, or an office in the home. Others may use the word *office* when referring to the *people* working in that location. For example, we may hear, "The employment office left work Monday at 3:30." Today, we commonly look upon the office as a *function,* where interdependent systems of technology, procedures, and people are at work to manage one of the firm's most vital resources—*information.* In these workplaces, the focus is not on "high-tech" machines and equipment but on *systems* within which information is produced at the lowest possible cost.

Management is the art or skill used by those who blend together the *six M's*—Manpower, Materials, Money, Methods, Machines, and Morale—in order to set and achieve the goals of the organization. The word *management* is also commonly used to refer to a *group of persons,* such as top management, who collectively direct or manage the organization. In the process of blending the six M's, those in charge of the organization are greatly involved with directing people of diverse cultures and coordinating the use of economic resources.

Before putting all three of these words together and learning about this exciting field of administrative office management, let's examine the duties or functions of management in general.

THE FUNCTIONS OF MANAGEMENT

Any form of group endeavor (an **organization**), whether it is a social club, a governmental unit, an educational institution, or a business firm, requires leadership and direction at various levels in order to realize its goals. To achieve its goals as an organization, a firm must be well managed. Thus, the functions of **management** involve the planning, organizing, and controlling of all resources and the leading or directing of people to attain the goals of a productive, unified organization.

The functions of management are performed by persons called **managers** at several levels in any organization, from the president to a supervisor. The titles held by managers vary considerably depending on the nature of the work assigned, the responsibilities delegated to the position, and the type and size of organization. Traditionally, the managerial levels have been divided as shown in Figure 1–1. However, as we shall see later, many business firms have reduced the number of their managerial levels, which, in turn, provides a "flatter" organization structure.

THE FUNCTIONS OF ADMINISTRATIVE OFFICE MANAGEMENT

What has been said about management in general also applies to those responsible for managing the office and for making decisions that concern the day-to-day operations of the office. (Such decisions are often called **operational decisions** or *administrative decisions*.) **Administrative office management** is the process of planning, organizing, and controlling all the *information-related activities* and of leading or directing people to attain the objectives of the organization.

Traditionally, the administrative office management functions were limited to basic clerical services and to office personnel. However, with the passage of time came an accompanying increase in government regulations, a larger and more culturally diverse workforce, a global economy, and the development of new information technologies. All of these factors brought about the Information Revolution—an increased demand for more information in order to make intelligent decisions at greatly accelerated rates. Management began to place more reliance upon office personnel and well-designed work systems as the new technology created greater information-processing power. The "one-department office" concept gradually gave way to a broader, company-wide information management concept in which the administrative office manager became responsible for an expanded area of work in the information age.

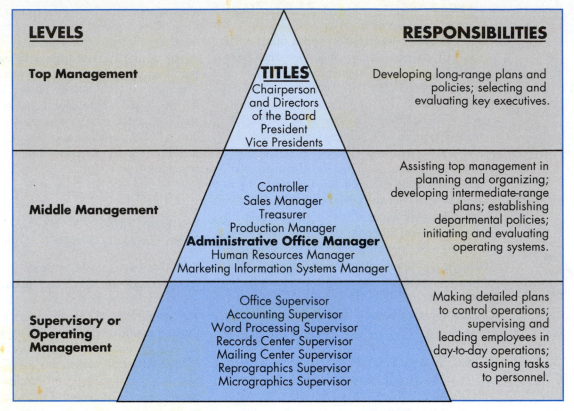

Figure 1–1
Traditional
Managerial
Levels, Titles,
and Respon-
sibilities

THE ADMINISTRATIVE OFFICE MANAGER

The person who heads up the company-wide information management function may have one of several titles, such as administrative office manager; office manager; manager, administrative services; information manager; manager, information services; manager of office services; or administrative manager. Throughout this textbook, the person responsible for planning, organizing, and controlling the information-processing activities and for leading people in attaining the organization's objectives is called the **administrative office manager** or *office manager.* Because of the high frequency with which these two titles are used, they will often be abbreviated—AOM or OM—much like the common usage of CEO for chief executive officer.

Responsibilities of the AOM

The scope and responsibilities of the AOM are identified in this section, and each of the managerial functions is analyzed as it applies to office activities. The logical sequence of these functions and their related activities is outlined in Figure 1–2.

Although similarities exist in the job content of OMs, no two have exactly the same job responsibilities. In a small firm, often the OM is an accountant who has been assigned the added supervision of correspondence, mailing, filing, and other general administrative services. In another firm, the OM assumes the additional responsibility of human resources manager or credit manager with miscellaneous supervisory activities. In still another company, the OM is an office services executive who supervises support services,

Illustration 1–1 Large banks rely on the AOM to keep business running smoothly so they can provide efficient service to customers.

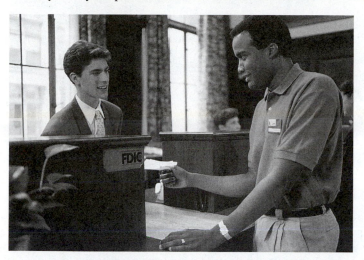

which meet the needs of users in all office divisions. Such support services include mailing, records management, word processing, messenger service, communications, copying, office security, and maintenance.

The differences in responsibilities assigned to AOMs are due to several factors, the most important of which is the size of the organization. Many large banks, for example, employ several thousand office workers, and major insurance companies employ 10,000 or more. Naturally, an AOM is needed to direct the volume of services in such organizations where the collection and production of information are the main responsibilities of the office staff. The job description in Figure 1–3 lists the typical responsibilities that may be assigned to a manager of administrative services in large and medium-size organizations. In small organizations, factory workers may be the primary source of business activity; hence, the office force is not so great in number. In such firms, the office service activities may be supervised directly by an accountant, the controller, the treasurer, the credit manager, or the human resources manager (formerly called the personnel manager).

In this section, we shall briefly examine three very challenging areas in which AOMs have

great responsibilities: the information cycle, the management information system, and office automation. Each of these areas of responsibility will be discussed in more detail in later chapters.

The Information Cycle

AOMs have a company-wide responsibility for managing the **information cycle**—the collecting, processing, storing, retrieving, and distributing of information for internal and external use. Each of these sequential phases of the information cycle is shown in Figure 1–4. Administrative office management is looked upon as a process of converting information into action. Organizations view information as a critical economic resource—an asset that is as valuable as any physical property owned, such as a building or office equipment. AOMs are aware that the competitive positions of their companies depend on their abilities to produce timely and reliable information and to use that information productively. Like all other resources, information must be managed.

At all levels of management, there is a growing interest in improving the quality of decision making. To do so, AOMs must make decisions based on relevant, accurate, and timely information. To provide information that meets these qualifications, management information systems have been developed.

Management Information Systems

A **management information system (MIS)** is an organizational process that supplies timely information to managers for use in drawing conclusions, making predictions, recommending courses of action, and in some cases, making decisions in order to take action. Thus, an MIS is directly tied into the productivity of any business enterprise.

At the heart of an MIS is the computer, which performs many of the functions that make up the information cycle. For example, the computer is used for collecting, processing, and storing business information, and, when the need arises, the computer retrieves information to assist in decision making. The computer also aids managers in making plans for the future by analyzing the con-

Figure 1–2
Managerial
Functions and
Related Office
Activities

MANAGERIAL FUNCTIONS	OFFICE ACTIVITIES
Planning: analyzing relevant information from both the past and the present and assessing probable developments of the future so a course of action—the *plan*—may be determined that will enable the firm to meet its goals.	*Developing policies and objectives for the various information-processing services,* such as communications, records management, mailing, and reprographics or copymaking; procuring a suitable office site; equipping the work areas with modern, functional office furniture, machines, and equipment; staffing the office with qualified employees so the work will flow smoothly and quickly.
Organizing: bringing together all economic resources (the work, the workplace, the information, and the workers) to form a controllable (manageable) unit—the *organization*—to accomplish specific objectives.	*Applying basic principles of organization in determining the working relationships among employees,* who are equipped with the best physical facilities and workflows, to achieve the maximum productivity.
Leading: motivating and directing the workers so the objectives of the organization will be successfully achieved.	*Directing and supervising effectively the office activities;* adopting and implementing workable personnel policies that maintain a desirable level of morale; training, orienting, counseling, promoting, and compensating office personnel; providing static-free communication lines between employees and employer.
Controlling: ensuring that operating results conform as closely as possible to the plans made for the organization.	*Developing, installing, and improving administrative office systems and procedures* to be followed when completing each major phase of office work; supervising the procurement, preparation, and use of office forms and other supplies; measuring the work done and setting standards for its accomplishment; reducing the costs of administrative services; preparing budgets, reports, and office manuals as means whereby costs are reduced and controlled.

tents of its extensive historical files. In an MIS, automated machines do not perform all the activities in the information cycle; the MIS is controlled by people who play an active part in each step in decision making as well as in developing solutions to all types of problems.

In large organizations, such as banks, financial services, airlines, and insurance companies, a management specialist with the title **information manager** or *chief information officer (CIO)* is often responsible for all information-handling activities. In addition to having expertise in managing administrative services, the information manager has some of the training and experience required of a systems analyst, a data processing manager, and a communication specialist. Such broad experience and education are required to understand and to manage the information-related activities in the organization.

AOMs have always been managers of facts and information. They have had the responsibility for developing and maintaining good systems, efficient personnel, and reliable equipment. With the advent of office automation, as discussed on the next page, the AOM's sphere of responsibility has been further extended throughout the company.

Figure 1–3
Job Description Showing Responsibilities of Manager, Administrative Services

Manager, Administrative Services

1. Supervises administrative services such as word processing, telecommunications, records storage and retrieval, printing and/or copying, mailing, reception, and messenger.

2. Secures office supplies, furniture, and equipment, and contracts for maintenance and repairs of office equipment.

3. Controls interoffice communications, maintaining directories and communication systems.

4. Conducts special studies to determine equipment performance and costs, and meets with sales representatives to evaluate new equipment.

5. Coordinates with operating departments to establish new and to modify existing administrative office systems.

6. Supervises the orientation and training of office employees.

Figure 1–3 Job Description Showing Responsibilities of Manager, Administrative Services

Office Automation

Of all the changes that have occurred in offices, none has more dramatically affected the AOM's responsibilities than office automation. According to John Naisbitt, writing in *Megatrends*, the official transition of the United States from an industrial economy into an information economy occurred in 1956.[1] For the first time in our history,

white-collar workers in technical, managerial, and clerical positions outnumbered blue-collar workers; *for the first time, most of us worked with information rather than producing goods.*

As you saw earlier, all organizations are faced with the challenge of developing high-quality yet cost-effective information systems. Office automation offers the most promising approach for meeting this need. **Office automation (OA)** is an MIS process that aims to maximize the productivity of managing information through the integration of skilled personnel, powerful technology, and sophisticated

[1] John Naisbitt, *Megatrends* (New York: Warner Communications, 1982), Chaps. 5 and 8.

Figure 1–4
The Information Cycle

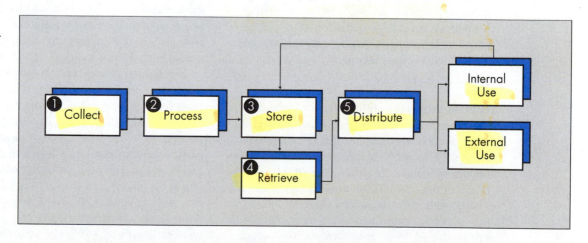

systems. The components of OA—*people, technology,* and *systems*—make up an interdependent team, none of which stands alone or apart from the rest.

Before the trend toward OA within an information society began in the 1950s, most offices were collections of independent entities such as *a* telephone system, *a* duplicating system, *a* data processing system, and *a* workforce. Today, however, OA views these same entities as essential components of the information system—all *interrelated,* all *interdependent,* and all *interconnected* by communications systems.

Skills of the AOM

The AOM must be a skillful innovator—a creative manager—to administer the changes occurring in the organization's information-handling activities. The three types of skills needed by creative managers—*conceptual, human,* and *technical*—are discussed below.

Conceptual Skill

Conceptual skill is the ability to use existing knowledge in order to acquire additional knowledge. One example of conceptual skill is the ability to view an entity as a whole and see how a change in one of its parts affects all other parts or functions. Thus, an AOM is using conceptual skill when evaluating the need to install an automated system for storing company records. In making a decision, the AOM displays conceptual skills by questioning, exploring, and probing to see how such a change will affect all other phases of the information cycle, especially the processing and retrieving of records.

Human Skill

Human skill is the ability to use knowledge and understanding of people as they interact with others. Such knowledge and understanding enable the AOM to identify, comprehend, and solve human problems. To do so, the AOM must be aware of the cultural and ethnic diversity of individuals and understand how these factors affect the workers' attempts to attain their goals. As a result, the AOM is able to sense the workers'

needs and drives, to empathize with diverse values and lifestyles, to lead a group of workers, to work effectively as a member of the team, and to obtain cooperation from all team members.

AOMs exhibit their human skills when leading and directing workers and interrelating with peers and top management. As an example, assume that you are appointed to serve as head of a labor-management team that is investigating a change in work schedules. In this role you exhibit your human skills by being sensitive to the feelings and needs of others and by creating an environment in which workers freely express themselves and offer suggestions for improvement.

Technical Skill

Technical skill is the ability to understand a specific function, with its specialized knowledge, and to use efficiently the tools and techniques related to that function or activity. At the middle-management level, fewer technical skills are required because persons at this level do not need in-depth technical know-how. As we move down the organization ladder, however, we find that technical supervisors need more specialized technical skills than conceptual skills.

As an example of the use of technical skill, assume that you are updating the salary compensation plan for your office personnel. To develop a fair compensation plan, you must know how to undertake a salary survey and be currently informed of government regulations that affect the payment of wages and salaries. Some of the methods used to adjust salaries may require that you have expertise in charting current and proposed salary rates or in using mathematical techniques to determine salary rates and ranges.

Throughout this textbook, you will be aided in learning more about the skills needed by AOMs. For example, in the *Dialog from the Workplace,* Lisbeth K. Green of Intel Corporation speaks of the skills and competencies that have helped her most in her rise to success. By solving the critical thinking cases and the optional computer problem at the end of each chapter, you will be able to sharpen your own skills. Also, you will have additional opportunity to improve your management skills while you work in your chosen career.

Illustration 1–2 The ability to communicate effectively is a human skill vitally needed by the administrative office manager.

Thus, by means of academic courses and on-the-job training, you increase your competency as an office manager. In the next section, we shall examine some of the opportunities for professional development in the field of administrative office management.

Careers in Administrative Office Management

Let's take a look at some of the possible career paths that you may follow. As we discussed earlier, the job titles, job content, and responsibilities of the positions in administrative office management vary, mainly due to differences in the size of organizations.

Career Paths in Small and Medium-Size Firms

In small and medium-size firms, you may find that, as the office manager, you are often responsible for functions such as accounting and human resources in addition to your company's administrative support services. You may have

been employed as an accountant or credit manager. However, with the passage of time, additional responsibilities were delegated to you, with the result that your job grew into one that included the management of all office services. In other instances, you might have first held an information-related job such as word processing operator, records librarian, or executive assistant. Then, as you gained more experience, sharpened your skills, and expanded your competencies, you were promoted to a supervisory post and later to the OM position. Thus, we see that, in many small and medium-size firms, usually there is no clear-cut path of promotion to the position of OM that we generally find in larger organizations.

Career Paths in Large Firms

In a large firm, depending upon your education and experience, you might have been employed as a word processing operator, payroll clerk, or administrative assistant. In companies that restructured by reducing the number of their employees, especially middle managers, we find

DIALOG FROM THE WORKPLACE

LISBETH K. GREEN

*Controller, Corporate Employee
Information Services
Intel Corporation
Santa Clara, California*

With more than 17 years of experience in payroll and benefits, Ms. Lisbeth K. Green currently holds the position of controller, corporate employee information services, at Intel Corporation in Santa Clara, California. Intel has approximately 18,000 domestic employees working in more than 40 states as well as 10,000 international employees.

Ms. Green received her B.A. from the University of California at Santa Barbara in 1968 and her M.B.A. from Golden State University in 1983. She was named president of the American Payroll Association (APA) in 1993. As a member of APA, Ms. Green has presented both year-end and effective payroll manager classes for the association, contributed articles to *PaytecH,* and served on the certification board for the Certified Payroll Professional and the board of advisors for the Bureau of National Affairs.

Active in her local APA chapter, Ms. Green has served as chapter president as well as a participant in many workshops, such as the California Payroll Conference, of which she was the director in 1991.

QUESTION: Take a look back, Ms. Green, and think about your rise to success. What skills and competencies have helped you most? What advice do you offer those who are starting their careers in management?

RESPONSE: Success is certainly a relative term, and I honestly don't know if I'm a "success," but I do feel confident and comfortable with my chosen profession. I have always had a love of learning. I was fortunate to attend excellent schools that stimu-

lated young minds and made learning "fun," and luckily the "fun" of learning never left me.

I enjoy reading and currently subscribe to many technical publications. Even though the information may be duplicated, the nuances from several articles help me grasp the overall flavor of the information. In addition, there's a bit of stubbornness in me, too, for I want to make sure information is correct, and if I see it more than once, I feel better! I tend to take notes on my reading, which helps me in retaining the information.

Another aspect that I feel has helped me accomplish some of my objectives has been my ability to keep an open mind and try to stay flexible. It's obvious how true the cliché "the only constant we know is change" is! I feel comfortable with change and embrace it as a natural evolution.

I also make it a point to meet with all the different groups I interface with at work in order to establish effective business partnerships. I really believe honest, open communication is the number one ingredient in any successful relationship.

It's important to be able to stay focused and organized, and I do that by using a good planning and scheduling tool. Currently for planning I am using MBO (management by objectives), and for scheduling I use a Franklin planner. I have my time scheduled for as much as a year in advance, and I schedule everything, including my personal strategic time. This approach really works very well for me.

As far as giving advice to someone just starting in management, I would encourage them to:

Listen well. Stay well informed. Keep an open mind. Take advantage of every training opportunity. Always ask "why." Choose a "successful" manager as a personal mentor. Develop a good network. Read, read, read!

highly skilled administrative assistants taking over many managerial and supervisory duties. For example, technical administrative assistants may perform duties once assigned to middle managers—selecting new technology, budgeting, training, and supervising clerical staff. The Labor Department expects that more than half a million administrative assistant jobs will be created by the year 2005. The average salaries paid these administrative assistants are: entry-level, $16,000–$20,000; mid-level, $26,000–$32,000; and top-level, $50,000.[2]

As you gained experience and demonstrated your managerial skills and competencies, you were promoted to a supervisory position in one of the firm's departments, such as administrative services, accounting, or the records center. Based upon the career paths available in your firm, the next stage of your career development may be a junior management post, such as administrative services manager, controller, or manager of human resources. Your company's management training and development program may show that next you will be assigned to a senior executive (a *mentor*), who will help groom you for promotion to a top-management position, such as vice president of information systems or chief information officer. (Training and development programs for supervisors and managers are discussed in more detail in Chapter 8.)

Salaries

You will find that the salaries paid office managers vary a great deal, depending on factors such as type and size of business, annual gross sales, geographic location, responsibilities assigned the position, and the manager's years of education and experience. For example, in a survey of *average annual salaries* paid *nontraining* managers (personnel managers and managers not responsible for training), *Training* magazine reported:[3]

1. Average annual salary, $55,157.
2. By number of employees on payroll:

Fewer than 500—$53,066 to 2,500 or more—$60,704.
3. By sex: Males—$61,541; females—$44,312.
4. By educational level:
From $52,135 for no college degree to $57,347 for a Master's degree.
5. By age:
From $33,589 for under 30 to $62,579 for 45 or older.

The preceding information may be helpful to you in learning about the salaries that managers command. However, as we shall see in Chapter 10, the results of any salary survey must be accepted with caution. If you are comparing the results of a recent survey with the salary offered you by a prospective employer, you must examine more than the two job titles. For example, are the job responsibilities of the two positions comparable? Are the companies under consideration of similar size? in the same recruiting area? in the same industry? with similar operations?

Professional Organizations for the AOM

Your skills and competencies as an AOM are further strengthened by joining and actively participating in various professional organizations. You may wish to become associated with one or more of the following organizations:

American Management Association (AMA)

Association for Information and Image Management (AIIM)

Association for Systems Management (ASM)

Association of Information Managers (AIM)

Association of Records Managers and Administrators (ARMA)

Data Processing Management Association (DPMA)

Society for Advancement of Management (SAM)

Society for Human Resources Management (SHRM)

International Office Management Association (IOMA)

---

[2]"Hot Tracks in 20 Professions," *U.S. News & World Report* (October 26, 1992), p. 108.

[3]"Salary Survey, 1992," *Training* (November, 1992), p. 26.

Illustration 1–3 Attending and participating in management conferences and seminars contribute to the professional development of the office manager.

The International Office Management Association (IOMA) was formed to meet the changing demands of the profession by providing its members with opportunities for learning and development in the office management field. IOMA serves professional office managers and those individuals who aspire to a career in office management. The organization is committed to promoting the profession of office management, techniques of sound management in an office environment, education in current office technology, and recognizing excellence in office management. Membership in IOMA enables you to take advantage of the Certified Administrative Management program, discussed below, and to purchase the publications and annual salary surveys of the Administrative Management Society Foundation.[4]

---

[4]Until the end of 1992, the Administrative Management Society (AMS) was one of the major professional organizations for AOMs. However, because of a continuing loss in membership, AMS was dissolved. The dissolution did not directly affect the activities of the Academy of Administrative Management or the AMS Foundation since these two organizations are separate legal entities.

As a means of recognizing managers as "professionals," the Academy of Administrative Management sponsors the **Certified Administrative Manager (C.A.M.)** program. To achieve the C.A.M. designation and to gain membership in the Academy, you must meet the following five program standards:

1. Have at least three years of management experience.
2. Possess high standards of personal and professional conduct.
3. Exhibit leadership ability.
4. Have made a contribution to administrative management effectiveness.
5. Pass the C.A.M. examinations covering five content areas (management concepts, personnel management, finance, administrative services, and information systems) and a case study analysis.

This certification program is further evidence of the broadening scope and important responsibilities of the manager in today's office.

Like today's C.A.M. who might walk through a museum of natural history to learn more about the evolutionary process, we are going back in history in the following section. There, we shall examine some philosophies of management that laid the foundation for contributions being made today by professional managers, educators, and other practitioners.

SCHOOLS OF MANAGEMENT THOUGHT

Because of their diverse personal philosophies, office managers follow different lines of thinking in managing the information function. For example, some OMs view the management process primarily as the *science* of managing—knowing what the principles are and how they should work. Others look upon management mainly as an *art*—knowing when, how, and why to apply a given principle in a particular situation. Like the question, "Which came first—the chicken or the egg?" no precise answer is available for resolving the question of whether management is a science or an art.

Science and art are two sides of the same management coin, and it would be pointless to support an approach based solely on either science or art. In their decision-making processes, OMs use the scientific method of problem solving (discussed later in this chapter and in Chapter 3); but the skill and the ability of OMs as they use this method represent the art side of the coin. As a science, the study of management develops many basic assumptions upon which decisions are based and presents proven theories that make up the basis of management education. However, many successful OMs are unable to spell out these theories even though, as a result of their "practicing management," they use the theories. Plans must be scientifically developed; but their implementation may be disastrous if the art of management, which involves working with and through people to accomplish the aims of the plans, is not practiced. Although the science of management can be predicted in many of its aspects, no one has scientifically determined how people will behave as they become emotionally involved in those plans.

The efficient office reflects a *perceptive* or *intuitive* manager—one who by training, experience, and intuition has sensed the need for improvement and has taken steps to bring about change. Managers who know or perceive, as a result of their intuition, are much in demand since by their training and experience they have proven themselves able to lead people effectively toward the firm's objectives. As we shall see in Chapter 3, highly intuitive managers form the most innovative and creative pool of talent in their organizations. These persons are the **intrapreneurs**—those managers who create innovation of any kind *within their organizations.*[5] Unfortunately, however, many of us are not gifted with such powerful intuition. Therefore, we turn to education to learn about the conceptual, human, and technical skills required to manage a firm's economic and human resources.

Over the years, various functions in the management process have been identified and attempts have been made to classify the approaches used by management theorists and practitioners. In this discussion, we have divided the divergent streams of management thought into five schools—*classical, behavioral, management science, quality management,* and *systems.* Each school of thought emphasizes a somewhat different approach to management and draws separate, though related, conclusions as to the most significant factors in the management process. These differing conclusions have become basic to the management process and over the years have been looked upon as principles of management, which are presented in the following chapter. Although as students of administrative office management, you may not find the specific answers you desire in the literature of these schools, you will discover principles that will serve as guidelines for any actions you take and as aids in better understanding the information management concept.

The Classical School

In the eighteenth and early nineteenth centuries, the Industrial Revolution brought about the mass production of goods and created the modern industrial organization. The new companies with their great potential for production were little understood, and the need for knowledge about the management of such firms soon became apparent. Hence, it is not surprising that the early approaches to the study of management concerned themselves with the major characteristic of the newly formed businesses—production. The early theorists emphasized the essential nature of management and its relationship to the production process.

Intertwined in the development of classical management theory were two views toward the management of work and of organizations—scientific management and total entity management. These views and several of the leaders who espoused them are briefly discussed in the following paragraphs.

---

[5]Weston H. Agor, "Nurturing Executive Intrapreneurship with a Brain-Skill Management Program," *Business Horizons* (May–June, 1988), pp. 12–15. Also in this same issue, see W. Jack Duncan et al., "Intrapreneurship and the Reinvention of the Corporation," pp. 16–21.

Scientific Management

Scientific management evolved in order to solve two major problems: how to increase the output of the average worker and how to improve the efficiency of management. Scientific management has been called doing that which is most logical, that is, using common sense to make decisions. What is required in scientific management, however, is a higher order of common sense involving the careful definition of problems and the development of plausible solutions. The **scientific method of problem solving,** which characterizes scientific management, involves the use of logical, systematic steps to develop effective solutions to problems. These steps are explained fully in Chapter 3.

Frederick W. Taylor. Taylor is looked upon as the father of scientific management. In the 1880s, using his engineering background, Taylor studied work standards and the relationship of output to wages. He emphasized management at the shop level rather than general management and was concerned mainly with the efficiency of workers and managers in actual production.

Taylor considered each worker as a separate economic person motivated by financial needs. He believed that workers tended to restrict their output because of their fear of displacement. To minimize this fear, Taylor suggested that workers be educated to understand that their economic salvation lay in producing more units of work at a lower cost. The effectiveness of his argument could be proved to workers by placing them on a piecework system; thus by producing more, they would earn more. Underlying Taylor's entire approach to scientific management was the conviction that there is *one best way* of doing everything, whether it be using a shovel or filing a piece of paper.[6]

Taylor saw several new functions emerge for managers: the replacement of rule-of-thumb methods with scientific determination of each element of a person's job; the scientific selection and training of workers; the need for cooperation between management and labor to accomplish work in accordance with the scientific method; and a more equal division of responsibility between managers and workers, with managers planning and organizing the work.

Frank and Lillian Gilbreth. In the early 1900s, the husband-and-wife team of Frank and Lillian Gilbreth furthered the development of scientific management thought. The Gilbreths invented devices and introduced techniques to aid workers in developing their fullest potential through training, tools, environment, and work methods. Their accomplishments included the use of motion pictures to study and improve motion sequences, the development of charts and diagrams to record work-process and workflow patterns, the exploration of worker fatigue and its effect on health and productivity, and the application of principles of management and motion study to self-management.

Max Weber. Weber (pronounced Vāber) was a German sociologist who developed the concept of an ideal model or pure form of organizational design. The term **bureaucracy** is used to describe Weber's pure form of organization, which is formal, impersonal, and governed by rules rather than by people. Weber's bureaucratic model was identified by features such as:

[6]Frederick W. Taylor, *The Principles of Scientific Management* (New York: Harper & Bros., 1911).

Illustration 1–4 Assembly line work is an example of Max Weber's bureaucratic model of organizational design.

1. A clear-cut division of labor in which complex jobs are broken down into simple, repetitive operations, with each specialized operation being performed by one worker.
2. A well-defined hierarchy with a fixed chain of command.
3. A system of abstract rules for controlling operations.
4. Administrative acts, decisions, and rules recorded in writing to provide permanent files.
5. Employment and promotion based on technical qualifications.
6. Employee protection against arbitrary dismissal.

Weber made great contributions to the understanding of organization structure and management. However, we would expect to find very few features of his pure form of bureaucracy in today's well-managed offices.

William H. Leffingwell. Leffingwell, looked upon as the father of office management, was credited with applying the principles of scientific management to office work. His book, *Scientific Office Management,* published in 1917, was the forerunner of all modern studies in office managment.

Leffingwell developed the *Five Principles of Effective Work.* Since these principles are related to the proper management of *all* work, they may be easily applied to the office, as shown below:

1. *Plan the work.* Any OM must plan what work must be done; how, when, and where it must be done; and how fast it can be done.
2. *Schedule the work.* By recognizing a total office plan of organization and product development, the OM can coordinate the efforts of all workers, machines, and information to formulate a proper work schedule to agree with the plan.

3. *Execute the work.* Proper operating systems and procedures, record-keeping practices, and methods for executing the work must be developed. The work must be done skillfully, accurately, rapidly, and without unnecessary effort and delay.

4. *Measure the work.* With the effective development of measurements, standards, and layouts for getting the work done, it must then be measured as to quantity, quality, the workers' potential, and past records.

5. *Reward the worker.* Perhaps of most importance, the OM must select, train, motivate, compensate, and promote employees to keep their interests and those of the firm at an optimum level.

Total Entity Management

The followers of the total entity management school of thought emphasized an *overall* approach to the administrative problems of management. Thus, they searched for effective means of directing the business firm as a whole, or as an entity.

Henri Fayol. In his book *General and Industrial Management,*[7] Fayol presented his concept of the universal nature of management, developed the first comprehensive theory of management, and stressed the need for teaching management in schools and colleges.

Fayol was the first management author to state a series of management principles that would provide guidelines for successful coordination. He looked upon the elements of management as its functions—planning, organizing, commanding, coordinating, and controlling. In his writings, he stressed over and over that these elements apply not only to business but also *universally* to political, religious, philanthropic, military, and other organizations. His thesis was that since all enterprises require management, the formulation of a theory of management is necessary to provide for the effective teaching of management.

Mary Parker Follett. Follett was a political philosopher, social reform critic, and creative problem solver in the field of motivation and group processes. Her work spanned the gap between Taylor's scientific management and the new social psychology of the 1920s that promoted better human relations in industry, a first concern of modern management.

Follett called for a revolutionary new concept of association. This concept was found in her one principle, which stated that *group organization* was to be the new method in politics, the basis for the future industrial system, and the foundation of international order. In her penetrating study of human relations, Follett was perhaps the first to promote what she termed "togetherness" and "group thinking."

Many of the later developments in management thought were anticipated by Follett: the application of behavioral science to problems of organization, the constructive uses of conflict, the psychology of power, the nature of horizontal communications, and, above all, the social responsibilities of management.

The early classicists emphasized the structure and the formal relationships in business firms but did not ignore the human element. They developed an extensive body of knowledge and logically related concepts, many of which form the basis for the organization of this book and, more specifically, the discussion of managerial principles in Chapter 2.

The Behavioral School

Scientific management is still used as the basis for solving business problems, but coupled with it is an even greater concern for the human element.

---

[7]Henri Fayol, *General and Industrial Management* (New York: Pitman Publishing, 1949, translated from French; originally published in 1916).

Today there is a clear-cut recognition that, as workers, we are interested in more than money. We have social, psychological, and physiological needs that are of great importance to us.

Having become interested in the human element within the organization, managers began to conceive two main approaches that placed increased emphasis upon the members of the organization. The early approach to worker behavior—the **human relations approach**—calls attention to the importance of the individual within the organization. The modern approach to worker behavior—the **behavioral science approach**—cuts across the fields of psychology, sociology, and anthropology to emphasize interpersonal relations and democratic actions on the part of workers.

Human Relations Approach to Worker Behavior

In the 1920s and 1930s, the idea emerged that people are important considerations in management since objectives are set and achieved by individuals. Representative of this early approach to the development of human relations is Elton Mayo, whose Hawthorne experiments are briefly discussed below.

Elton Mayo. The human relations approach was stimulated by a group of researchers from Harvard University who conducted studies from 1927 to 1932 among a group of women workers at the Hawthorne plant of Western Electric in Chicago.[8] The research team, headed by Elton Mayo, a Harvard University professor, was formed to study the effects of the physical environment upon worker productivity.

The Hawthorne Experiments. In one of the Hawthorne experiments, Mayo's research team examined changes in the amount of light available in the work area. The results were confusing at first. When the lighting was increased, output rose; on the other hand, when the lighting was decreased, output still rose. An analysis of this and other such puzzling results showed that the workers were highly motivated not only by the amount of light provided but also by their feelings of importance. It mattered to them that they were really making a contribution to company operations by participating in the study.

The research team also examined other effects of change in the work environment. They varied the working conditions such as rest periods, hot lunches, and working hours; used interviews to determine attitudes; and analyzed the social organization among workers. During the studies, it was found that changes in the work environment had little long-term effect upon worker productivity. The explanation offered was that the workers were made to feel like more than just cogs in a machine and that management realized their importance. Since management had asked for their opinions on working conditions, the workers felt that their relationships with management were no longer impersonal. The workers felt that they had achieved status and some degree of respect. The Hawthorne experiments proved that the road to more effective worker effort lay in recognizing the emotional as well as the physical well-being of the employees, explaining to them the reasons for management decisions, and making them aware that management appreciated the importance of their work.

The Hawthorne study placed new emphasis upon the social, psychological, and physiological factors in the study of work. As a result of this concern with human relations, a new direction—the behavioral science approach—was given to the study of management.

The Behavioral Science Approach to Worker Behavior

Early theories of behavior tended to explain all behavior on the basis of a single need, such as the need to assert one's ego. Modern behaviorists typically list several needs ranging from 3 (physi-

[8]See Elton Mayo, *The Human Problems of an Industrial Civilization* (Cambridge: Harvard University Press, 1933) and F. J. Roethlisberger and William J. Dickson, *Management and the Worker* (Cambridge: Harvard University Press, 1939).

cal, social, and egoistic) to 15 in number. Managers cannot *see* their own human needs or those of their workers but must *infer* their pattern from a study of human behavior. Therefore, it is expected that there will be different theories about human needs, as explained below.

Abraham Maslow. One classification of human needs came from Maslow, a psychologist who developed a theory of human motivation.[9] At the core of his theory is the concept that we are motivated by fulfilling a hierarchy of needs. The hierarchy of needs shows that as our lower-level needs are satisfied, they are no longer motivating factors. At this point, our higher-level needs become dominant. A need at one level does not have to be completely satisfied before the next need emerges, however. Since very few of us ever fully realize the fulfillment of our higher-level needs, there is always a basis for motivation. (The hierarchy of needs is illustrated and further discussed in Chapter 7.)

The AOM must recognize that the needs pattern of each worker is different and should not assume that a single approach can be used to motivate all workers toward the accomplishment of the organization's objectives. Further, AOMs should be aware that well-satisfied needs do not motivate. After obtaining a reasonable satisfaction of their needs, workers will be stimulated to direct their actions toward satisfying higher-level needs.

Douglas McGregor. The nature of people, with all their apparent contradictory feelings and emotions, has long puzzled philosophers. Some see us as having a capacity for tenderness, sympathy, and love, with little need for external regulation. Others see us as having tendencies toward cruelty, hate, and destruction, with the need for close control and reg-

imentation for the good of society. This *dual nature* of people was introduced into management theory by Douglas McGregor, who explored the human side of organizations and defined the traditional and the current views of worker behavior.[10] These views, which McGregor labeled Theory X and Theory Y, are explained in Part 2.

Frederick Herzberg. The research conducted by Herzberg and his associates at the Psychological Service in Pittsburgh resulted in the **motivation-hygiene theory.**[11] According to this theory, we work in an environment where the following two kinds of factors are present:

1. **Motivators,** which result from experiences that create positive attitudes toward work and arise from the job content itself. Examples are those incidents associated with the feelings of self-improvement, recognition, achievement, and desire for and acceptance of greater responsibility.

2. **Hygienic** (or maintenance) **factors,** which are related to productivity on the job but are external to the job itself. Examples are pay, working conditions (such as heating, lighting, and ventilation), company policy, and quality of supervision.

Herzberg found that when, as workers, we feel the hygienic factors are inadequate, they function

[9]Abraham Maslow, *Motivation and Personality* (New York: Harper & Bros., 1954).

[10]Douglas McGregor, *The Human Side of Enterprise* (New York: McGraw-Hill, 1960), pp. 33–57.

[11]Frederick Herzberg, Bernard Mausner, and Barbara B. Snyderman, *The Motivation to Work,* 2nd ed. (New York: John Wiley & Sons, 1959). See also Frederick Herzberg, *Work and the Nature of Man* (Cleveland: World Publishing, 1966).

as *dissatisfiers.* On the other hand, when the hygienic factors *are* present, they do not necessarily motivate us to greater productivity; instead, they make it possible for the motivators to function.

The motivation-hygiene theory is discussed further in Part 2, along with other motivational approaches such as job enrichment, participative management, management by objectives, goal setting, and expectancy theory.

Peter F. Drucker. Known to millions in U.S. business and economics, Drucker has authored more than 20 books dealing with management, economics, politics, and society. In one of his early books, *The Practice of Management,* Drucker introduced the concept of management by objectives, a technique long associated with George S. Odiorne.[12] In **management by objectives (MBO),** objectives are set forth for every area where performance and results directly and vitally affect the survival and prosperity of the organization. For example, as we shall see in later chapters, MBO may be used to appraise and reward performance, train to improve performance levels, and motivate workers to do better.

Writing about the "knowledge society" in *Managing for the Future: The 1990s and Beyond,* Drucker describes how large business and government organizations operate on the flow of information.[13] To equip students to become members of this knowledge society, Drucker stresses their need to be equipped with the following skills: the ability to present ideas orally and in writing; the ability to work with people; and the ability to shape and direct one's own work, contribution, and career.

---

[12]For the development and presentation of the concept of management by objectives, see Peter F. Drucker, *The Practice of Management* (New York: Harper & Brothers, 1954). Also see George S. Odiorne, "How to Succeed in MBO Goal Setting," *Personnel Journal* (August, 1978), pp. 427–429, 451. Also, George S. Odiorne, "MBO: A Backward Glance," *Business Horizons* (October, 1978), pp. 14–24.

[13]Peter F. Drucker, *Managing for the Future: The 1990s and Beyond* (New York: Truman Talley Books/Dutton, 1992).

The Management Science School

Management science, also known as *quantitative business methods,* makes use of engineering and mathematical skills to solve complex decision-making problems. Simply stated, **decision making** is consciously choosing between two or more alternative courses of action. While this definition is readily understandable, the selection of such courses of action—that is, how a decision is made—is more complex. We do know, however, that *sound* decision making depends on the accuracy and timeliness of relevant information upon which to base the decisions.

Management science, aided by the advances in mathematics and computer technology, can be applied to many business problems, such as how to conserve energy and effectively use natural and human resources. Managers are able to collect volumes of data to perform precise mathematical analyses as substitutions for their intuition. Examples of the mathematical techniques for making decisions include: (1) *work sampling,* where a number of random samples are taken in order to supply information for use in setting work standards; (2) *waiting-line,* or *queuing, theory,* in which a study is made of the behavior of persons waiting in line, such as customers lining up at a bank teller's window; and (3) *forecasting,* which is used to plan capital expenditures for new plant and equipment. Many mathematical techniques of decision making use higher-level mathematics and are dependent upon the rapid calculating ability and accuracy of the computer.

The Quality Management School

Quality management, or *total quality management (TQM),* is both a philosophy and a set of principles used to guide the entire organization in *continuous improvement.* To achieve this goal, TQM uses quantitative methods along with the organization's human and capital resources to improve (1) all processes, (2) performance in every functional area, and (3) the degree to which the organization meets the needs of present and future customers and suppliers. A few of the quality management tools that we shall examine in later chapters include brainstorming, goal setting, quality circles, statistical measurement, work team techniques, and workflow analysis. In this section, we shall summarize the contributions of three persons mainly concerned with quality improvement programs.

W. Edwards Deming. The leading exponent of quality management and a pioneer in statistical analysis, Deming taught American companies during World War II to improve their production of high-quality goods and services. Following the war, however, most of Deming's lessons were forgotten. During the early 1950s, Deming was invited to Japan to advise its business leaders on quality, a move that sparked Japan's postwar recovery and its economic rise in global markets. While there, he taught the Japanese how to use statistics to find out what any system would do and then to design improvements that would make the system yield the best results. The basics of Deming's method are contained in a list of objectives that he calls "the 14 points."[14]

In the 1970s, companies in the United States began to "import" and modify certain features of Deming's quality improvement program such as quality circles and employee participation groups. As a result, today more and more American companies are adopting his concepts, with the hope that Deming's contributions will do as much for us as they did for our competition in Japan.

Joseph M. Juran. Juran, the elder statesman of total quality control, found a loyal following in Japan in the mid-1950s. Over the years, like Dem-

ing, Juran taught the Japanese how to apply total quality control to everyone, from managers to clerical staff. Regarding worker participation, Juran believes that, due to the dramatic rise in worker education, it is now possible to delegate to self-directing teams of workers many functions that were formerly carried out by planners and supervisors.[15]

William Ouchi. As noted earlier, American companies have become very interested in the Japanese management system and its techniques for increasing productivity. Managers in the United States are aware that the Japanese believe high quality to be the key to increased productivity and greater profits. The attitude of Japanese management toward work and workers is contained in Theory Z. *Theory Z management* is a term coined by Professor William Ouchi, who spent years researching Japanese companies and examining American companies with Theory Z management styles.[16] We shall further explore the nature of Theory Z management in Part 2.

The Systems School

In most modern approaches to the study of the management process, the systems concept is used as a means of describing the total organization. A **system** is a group of parts that are interrelated in such a manner that they form a unified whole and

[14]For a summary of Deming's 14 points, see Bruce Brocka and M. Suzanne Brocka, *Quality Management: Implementing the Best Ideas of the Masters* (Homewood, IL: Business One Irwin, 1992), pp. 65–68. A very fine insight into Deming's lifetime accomplishments provided by one of his students appears in Rafael Aguayo, *Dr. Deming: The American Who Taught the Japanese About Quality* (New York: A Lyle Stuart Book published by Carol Publishing Group, 1990).

[15]Juran's structured approach to quality improvement was first set forth in his book, Joseph M. Juran, *Managerial Breakthrough* (New York: McGraw-Hill, 1964).

[16]William G. Ouchi, *Theory Z: How American Business Can Meet the Japanese Challenge* (Reading, MA: Addison-Wesley, 1981).

work together to attain a definite objective. Thus, a business firm—the total system—is made up of the following major systems: *marketing, finance, human resources, production, accounting, purchasing,* and *administrative office.* Each of these major systems, in turn, is made up of lower-level subsystems that are responsible for accomplishing specialized functions. For example, the administrative office system consists of subsystems such as communication, data processing, word processing, records management, reprographics, micrographics, and administrative personnel management.

As developed in detail later in the text, systems are given boundaries for the purpose of analysis. However, there are no systems that are completely independent of other systems. For example, when administrative office systems are being analyzed, many environmental factors must be taken into consideration. When OMs plan, they must take into account such external factors as technology, social forces, laws, and regulations. When OMs work with others in designing an organizational system to help their people perform, they cannot avoid being influenced by the cultural diversity and code of ethics that people bring to their jobs from a variety of external situations. Thus, perceptive OMs see their problems and operations as a network of interrelated elements having daily interactions with environments inside and outside their organizations.

SUMMARY

1. The functions of management involve the planning, organizing, and controlling of all resources and the leading or directing of people to attain the goals of the organization. These functions are carried out at several levels in the organization, from the president to a supervisor.

2. Although no two AOMs have exactly the same duties and responsibilities, they represent the major party in the operation of the information cycle—collecting, processing, storing, retrieving, and distributing information. AOMs are often assigned responsibility for developing, implementing, and supervising the firm's management information system. In addition, many organizations delegate to the AOM full responsibility for office automation. Thus, by shouldering these responsibilities, the AOM often becomes the company's chief information officer.

3. Today's AOMs must be creative persons with conceptual, human, and technical skills. By means of formal courses, on-the-job training, and active membership in professional organizations, AOMs are able to improve their skills so that the competencies needed for effective office administration are at their peak.

4. The International Office Management Association (IOMA) serves professional office managers and those who aspire to a career in office management. IOMA promotes the profession of office management, techniques of sound management, and education in current office technology, and recognizes excellence in office management.

The Certified Administrative Manager program, sponsored by the Academy of Administrative Management, awards the C.A.M. certificate and membership in the Academy to those office managers who meet its program standards.

5. As a student of administrative office management, you can profit greatly from the experiences of management theorists and practitioners of the past and the present. By studying and evaluating the management principles and practices of the several schools of management—classical, behavioral, management science, quality management, and systems—you gain insight into theories and practices that will aid you in better understanding and working in today's offices in our global economy.

FOR YOUR REVIEW

1. Briefly define each of the words in the name *Administrative Office Management*.

2. List the six M's that must be blended through the management process in order to ensure business success.

3. Summarize the office activities that are related to each of the functions of management.

4. List the several phases of the information cycle in their proper sequence.

5. What are the major characteristics of a management information system?

6. Describe the three types of skills needed by AOMs.

7. What are the requirements for achieving the C.A.M. designation?

8. Explain the statement: "The efficient office reflects a perceptive or intuitive manager."

9. What were the major contributions made by Taylor, the father of scientific management?

10. Why is Leffingwell looked upon as the father of office management?

11. In what way are Fayol's concepts of management related to total entity management?

12. What were the major contributions made by Mayo and his research team to the development of the behavioral school of management thought?

13. What are the implications of Maslow's theory of motivation for today's AOM?

14. How are motivator factors and hygienic factors related to Herzberg's motivation theory?

15. Explain how the management science approach aids in the decision-making process.

16. How does total quality management guide a company in its program of continuous improvement?

17. What are the major systems that make up the *total* system of an organization?

FOR YOUR DISCUSSION

1. In writing about tomorrow's workplace, an author and teacher states that the concept of the office as a "place" will be challenged in the 1990s as new computer and communication technologies allow the office to be "wherever you are."[17] What do you believe this writer means by "wherever you are"?

---

[17]Leonard B. Kruk, "Office 2000: A Glimpse into Tomorrow's Workplace," *The Balance Sheet* (September–October, 1992), p. 10.

c
o
n
t

2. Some businesspeople use the words *manager* and *leader* interchangeably. Do you believe the two terms are the same, or can you clearly distinguish between them?

3. Stanley Gault, CEO of Goodyear Tire & Rubber Company, tells how his firm has discontinued using the word "employee" and replaced it with "associate."[18] What reasons can you offer for referring to employees as associates?

4. In its study of how the nature of work and the workplace in the United States are being reshaped, the Hudson Institute notes that a structural shift in our economy is occurring, away from producing goods and toward service-based industries. The number of jobs is projected to increase by twenty-five million by the year 2000, mostly in management, administrative support, sales, and service.[19] What implications does this projection have as you consider the advances in computer technology, global competition, and workplace literacy?

5. In some companies we find a chief information officer (CIO). This position often requires the CIO to bridge the gap between the nontechnical people on the board of directors and the heads of the management information systems. Generally, CIOs concentrate on long-term planning and report directly to a high-ranking executive, such as the chief executive officer or chairperson. If your firm were planning to create the new position of CIO, in which functional areas of your company would you search for CIO candidates? Which of the three skills—conceptual, human, technical—would you rank highest in your search for a CIO candidate? Why?

6. An office worker in one of the major computer manufacturing firms was asked to describe the qualifications required of a good office manager. The worker's answer indicated, among other things, that the person must be a self-starter, a highly motivated individual with the ability to see what is needed and the capacity to make plans and follow through. The worker concluded the answer by saying that if the right person is in the job, he or she will take orders from the situation. What is meant by "the situation"? Do these statements apply equally well to all middle managers, including the office manager? If the right office manager is in the job, how is he or she able to take orders from the situation?

7. Taylor's scientific principles set the stage for a revolution in management and the organization of work. However, one writer observed that the experience of the last 20 years has taught managers that, in our new business environment, such "scientific" principles are a recipe for disaster.[20] What is your reaction to this writer's comments?

8. During the past several years, many articles have appeared that stress the importance of *intuition* in management decision making. Some schools of business incorporate the development of intuitive management skills within their courses. How do you account for a rather sudden interest in intuition as a tool of management?

[18]"Leaders of Corporate Change," *Fortune* (December 14, 1992), pp. 104–105.

[19]*Workforce 2000: Work and Workers for the Twenty-first Century* (Indianapolis, IN: Hudson Institute, June, 1987), pp. 58–59.

[20]David H. Freedman, "Is Management Still a Science?" *Harvard Business Review* (November–December, 1992), p. 28.

c
o
n
t

9. A top-ranking executive with more than 50 years of experience in the business world made the following statements in an article dealing with management theories and styles:[21]

   a. Like fads and fashions, business theories tend to come and go. They are the talk of the town one year, gone and forgotten the next.

   b. The trouble with these neat theories, however, is that no company I know of is run in strict accordance with either Theory X or Theory Y.

   c. I do not envision a future in which American working men and women will turn to the Japanese style of corporate paternalism, starting each working day singing songs in praise of General Motors, ITT or any of the old component parts of the Bell System.

   d. No Theory X, Y, or Z will give us simple answers to complex problems.

   Let us accept that these statements are fairly typical of those made by men and women at the helm of today's business organizations in the United States. Why, then, should you, as students of administrative office management, be expected to learn about the various management theories and styles of yesterday and today?

CASES FOR CRITICAL THINKING

Good office managers are good problem solvers. Therefore, at the end of each chapter in this textbook, two cases are presented so you will be able to gain experience in critical thinking and problem solving as you work individually or in small groups. The cases play a vital part in learning about the process of administrative office management—its theories, principles, and practices. However, effective problem solving requires proper instruction in the techniques of problem solving. Before you are introduced to these techniques in Chapter 3, you will want to know exactly what this subject, administrative office management, is all about. Also, you will want to be introduced to workable principles of management prior to tackling a full-fledged case. Therefore, the first two chapters of this textbook have been designed to provide you with background knowledge that will be of benefit to you in solving your first cases in Chapter 3.

At this time, you will examine two relatively short cases with the purpose of aiding you in developing a proper attitude toward critical thinking and problem solving. After you have studied each of the cases, answer the questions that follow. Later, after you have studied Chapter 3, your instructor may ask you to return to one or both of these cases and engage in more intensive problem solving.

Case 1–1 Developing a Problem-Solving Attitude—A

When recently downsizing its home-office operations, the Valeria Company laid off eight of its employees in the order processing and records management departments. One of the workers, Bob Azilla, brought the dismissed workers together and told them that they have a good case against the company. Azilla explained to them, "See? Right here in the policy manual it says that if there is a layoff, senior workers with acceptable work records will be given preferential treatment."

---

[21]Harold S. Geneen, "Theory G," *United* (November, 1984), pp. 60–68.

c
o
n
t

Maria Torres, age 45 with eight years' experience in order processing, replied, "Preferential treatment? Ha! They let us go and kept all the young ones. Let's show those big shots that they violated their own policy and we are going to nail 'em."

Spearheaded by Azilla, the workers met with Tim O'Connor, the human resources manager. O'Connor cautioned them, "Just forget it. We didn't violate any company policy. Read it again. The policy states that only senior workers with acceptable performance are covered. You people were dismissed because of your poor performance."

Azilla burst out, "Well, we'll see about this. This is the first time we've heard anything about our poor performance!" His coworkers applauded and yelled, "Right on, Bob!"

1. In a few words, what is the real problem in this case?

2. Did Azilla make any mistakes? If so, what is the nature of his mistakes?

3. Did O'Connor make any mistakes? If so, what is the nature of his mistakes?

Case 1–2 Developing a Problem-Solving Attitude—B

Barbara Kato heads up the customer services division of San Francisco Data Processing, a firm that processes the payrolls for hundreds of West Coast companies. One of the systems analysts who reports directly to Kato is Ralph Martens, who has been with the firm for ten years. During the past several months, Martens has become irritable and sometimes antagonizes customers. Kato realizes that she should speak to Martens about his relationship with the customers, but for some reason she has been reluctant to do so.

Today Kato gets wind of another "run-in" that Martens had with a customer. She sits back, sighs, and reflects: "I really must sit down and talk with Martens. But I am fearful that he may quit. He handles all this technical stuff so very well, and I know that it would be difficult to find a replacement. But, yes, he is kind of touchy. I'll just put it off a little longer. Maybe he's having some personal problems at home."

1. What is the real problem involved in this case?

2. Can you identify clearly the specific nature of the problem?

 ## Case 1–3 Outline: Computer Option (available on disk)

2

APPLYING BASIC MANAGEMENT PRINCIPLES

GOALS FOR THIS CHAPTER

After completing this chapter, you should be able to:

1. Describe the basic principles of management as applied to the office.
2. Show how the organization chart is an important tool for the administrative office manager.
3. Describe the different kinds of formal and informal organization.
4. Distinguish between centralization and decentralization of managerial authority.
5. Identify the main characteristics of the various leadership styles.

Principles are broad, general statements that are considered to be true and that accurately reflect real-world conditions in all walks of life. Thus, you find principles of ethics, principles of sociology, principles of accounting, to name a few. Over the years, new principles are developed. Old principles are questioned and, in some cases, changed or discarded if they no longer serve useful purposes.

When we group sets of principles into a general framework that explains the basic relationships among them, we have created a **theory.** Thus, the sets of principles included in this chapter are classified and grouped into a managerial framework and can be thought of as **management theory.** By applying these principles under carefully controlled conditions, you should be able to predict accurately the outcomes of management operations. In this way, the AOM can put theory to practical use.

In this chapter, you will first examine the basic principles that apply to any specialized area of management, such as administrative office management. Next, you will study the kinds of organizations in which these principles are applied and examine a related issue—whether to centralize or decentralize office operations. We close the chapter by taking a look at the role of leadership in the effective office.

BASIC PRINCIPLES OF MANAGEMENT

To manage the office with minimum physical and mental effort, and at the lowest possible cost, the AOM must consider many persons. Within a corporation, these persons include stockholders, the board of directors, managers and supervisors, and workers. In less complex, small firms, the manager-owners, supervisors, and workers need to be considered. Outside each firm, customers, suppliers, the government, and many others must also receive the attention of management.

On the job, managers and workers apply management principles using various techniques to complete their work. Figure 2–1 outlines the main principles associated with good management along with examples of practical application techniques used by managers and workers. The effectiveness of these principles is measured by the performance of people in achieving the desired results, which is the ultimate test of good management.

PRINCIPLE 1

Define Objectives

The objectives of an organization and all of its divisions must be clearly defined and understood.

An **objective** is a desired goal—a target or an aim. Objectives range from broad, general statements about an organization to specific, narrow statements about a department or an employee's activities. For example, company-wide objectives are commonly stated in this way:

To earn a fair return on investment for our stockholders.

To improve our share of the market.

To provide the best possible service to our customers.

More specific objectives, which are easier to understand and to measure, may be stated as:

To increase the productivity of word processing operators by 8 percent during the current year (department goal).

Figure 2–1 Management Principles and Techniques for Applying Principles	Summary of Management Principles	Techniques Used in Applying Management Principles
	1. Objectives clearly defined and understood	**Develop** and explain policies, objectives, and budgets to workers in meetings and organization manuals.
	2. Responsibility for proper organization of work	**Analyze** functional needs of the organization and create a sound structure, including an organization chart in line with the objectives.
	3. Unity of functions	**Emphasize** in meetings and group projects the interrelationships among the functional areas in the firm.
	4. Use of specialization	**Assign** work to persons with highest levels of aptitude, interest, work experience, and education.
	5. Delegation of authority	**Schedule** meetings involving managers, supervisors, and workers to clarify the responsibilities assigned to each level.
	6. Unity of command	**Explain** flow of authority to workers and identify the person from whom they will receive instructions.
	7. Span of control	**Study** the work being performed and the organization chart to determine how many persons report to each supervisor.
	8. Centralization or decentralization of managerial authority	**Centralize** all highly complex or technical responsibilities, such as computer operations, in one location. **Decentralize** all simpler responsibilities, such as copying systems, in each department.

Illustration 2–1 Outstanding customer service is a broadly defined company objective.

To reduce by 12 percent the costs of operating the mailing center (department goal).

To improve attendance on the job (individual worker's goal).

Objectives are often established as part of the planning process for one- and five-year periods. Objectives are revised both on a regular basis and in response to major unexpected changes. For example, objectives may be altered because of reduced earnings from sales or an increase in the prime interest rate.

In progressive firms, top management is responsible for setting quantifiable (measurable), attainable objectives and then directing the organization toward meeting these objectives. First introduced in the opening chapter, this effective management technique—management by objectives—is fully explained in Chapter 7.

For each of the organization's objectives, a **policy**—a broad guideline for operating the organization—should be developed. A common policy in most firms stresses the continual need to maximize profits in a just, reasonable manner. As a result, the corresponding objective of such a firm would be to earn the greatest possible profits by increasing sales, an objective that, in turn, determines how the operations of the sales department are carried out. A related objective of the manufacturing division is to produce the right amount of goods at the lowest cost to fill the increased sales orders. A main objective of the administrative office management function is to coordinate and communicate the information activities of each of the organization's main divisions so that unit costs of production may be reduced and productivity increased. Here, administrative office management provides a support service for all other functions.

PRINCIPLE 2

Accept Responsibility

Responsibility for organizing work exists with managers at all levels, beginning with top-level managers and extending to first-line supervisors.

Responsibility is the obligation and accountability for properly performing work that is assigned. At the top level, the CEO determines the major work functions and has responsibility for organizing each division that performs the assigned work. At this same level, the company's long-range plans and objectives are formulated. Sound organization is necessary if these plans and objectives are to be achieved. Thus, top management must identify and accept the many responsibilities that accompany such high-level work.

In the same way, each succeeding level of management in the organization must accept an appropriate amount of responsibility. In order to do so, each level should first:

1. Identify its major objectives.
2. Determine the activities necessary to attain these objectives.
3. Develop the most logical pattern of organization to carry out its activities and to meet the needs of its workers.
4. Assign responsibility to workers for accomplishing these objectives. Where similar but not identical assignments are given to several individuals, carefully explain the similarities and differences to prevent misunderstanding.
5. Establish proper communication channels among all responsible parties to unify efforts and to develop team spirit.

These same steps are used at every level of management throughout the company. The only difference in their use lies within the scope of authority and responsibility of the job and the supervision of detailed work. **Authority** is the right to command and to give orders and the power to make decisions. Figure 2–2 shows that as you move up the levels in a company, there is more authority and responsibility but less supervision of detailed work. As you move down, the reverse is true.

PRINCIPLE 3

Unify Functions

All organizations are composed of various functions that must be effectively integrated so they can work together as a unit to achieve their major objectives.

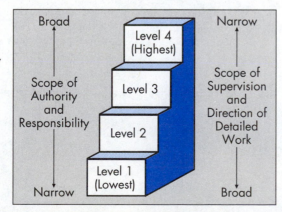

Figure 2–2 Comparing Authority and Responsibility with Supervision of Detailed Work

As indicated in Chapter 1, an organization may be thought of as a system. Thus, each of the four functions of a business organization—production, marketing, finance, and human resources administration—may be regarded as a subsystem or subdivision. Since these functional subsystems are interrelated, the effectiveness of any one subsystem depends on, as well as affects, the operations of the other three subsystems. Each of these subsystems, in turn, must be considered in relation to the other parts of the system. For example, the operations in a subsystem may need to be expanded or reduced in order to satisfy the overall objectives of the business.

The unity-of-functions principle has the following requirements:

1. The various functions must be in *proper balance* in keeping with the importance of their contributions to meeting the firm's objectives. For example, if a firm's objectives require increased sales of 9 percent, then production capacity must be expanded accordingly. Also, enough funds must be made available to purchase additional equipment, and the workers needed for the increased production volume must be recruited, oriented, trained, and supervised.
2. A reasonable amount of *stability* in human resources must be maintained. This allows an organization anticipating a lengthy decline in sales revenue to provide for a stable workforce by reducing the number of hours each office employee works during the week.
3. *Flexibility* must be ensured to meet seasonal or economic changes. For example, in many offices the workers are trained to perform more than one kind of job so that during rush periods the workers may be transferred from job to job as the need arises. Flexibility also means providing for expansion or contraction in order to adjust easily to the firm's future needs. As explained in a later chapter, one way an AOM effectively adjusts either to expansion or contraction of office operations is by installing furniture, equipment, and lighting systems that can be quickly and inexpensively moved about.

The successful administrative office system provides support services for every functional area in the organization. These service activities are so closely interrelated that none can be considered without examining their effect upon the others. For example, the services offered by word processing must be related to the needs of the persons writing letters, to records management, to the mailing function, and to office supervision. Also, the activities of the human resources function must relate to each of the activities just mentioned. In addition, the managers of other functions, such as production and marketing, must work with the AOM, because in various ways their activities are interdependent. Similarly, as the office organization expands by adding more supervisors and administrative assistants, all must work together as a unit or team under the AOM's direction. The AOM must keep this integration of functions constantly in mind because it improves productivity and reduces the cost of the work. The result is an increase in the efficiency of the information function, which is a major objective of the AOM.

PRINCIPLE 4

Utilize Specialization

An organization should utilize specialization to achieve efficiency. The more specialized the work assigned to individuals within the limits of human tolerance, the greater the opportunity for efficient performance.

A **specialist** is a person who masters or becomes expert at doing a certain type of work. Usually such expertise comes from extended periods of training, good work experience, or some combination of the two.

Illustration 2–2 Learning a specialized skill such as cooking involves personalized training with an experienced chef.

Specialization has made possible much of our economic and social progress. Workers with expert skills can be found everywhere—welders on the automotive assembly lines, chefs in restaurants, sales agents in the insurance industry, and computer programmers in offices. When people specialize, the quality of their work is higher, they are usually more accurate and adaptable, they learn new tasks faster, and they can do more work in a given time period. Hence, such workers are more productive than those without specialized skills.

Specialization, however, can be overdone. When the work becomes too narrow in scope or too repetitious, workers may become bored, and the quality and quantity of work may suffer. To attack this common problem, AOMs may experiment with several techniques of motivation, such as job enlargement and job enrichment discussed in Chapter 7.

PRINCIPLE 5

Delegate Authority

Authority must be delegated to individuals in the organization in keeping with the responsibility assigned them so that they can be held accountable for performing their duties properly.

Delegation is the process of entrusting work to employees who are qualified to accept responsibility for doing the work. We should think of delegation as a three-part process that involves:

1. *Assigning responsibility* to complete a task, which may range from preparing a report to keeping morale at a high level.
2. *Granting authority* to do the job, such as giving a department manager the power to hire and fire.
3. *Creating accountability* to carry out the task assigned.

When work is being delegated, the delegators and their assistants must mutually understand the results to be accomplished. In order for delegation to work well, there must be a clear-cut flow of authority from the top to the bottom of the organization. If this is accomplished, functions will

be carried out effectively, and duplication and overlapping of work assignments will be minimized. As a result, management goals will be achieved.

A common complaint is that managers and supervisors fail to delegate authority. As will be pointed out in Chapter 7, some supervisors never learn to delegate; instead, they insist on handling many work details themselves. Also, in many cases, managers assign their assistants responsibilities but little or no authority.

To manage their departments successfully, office supervisors must delegate enough authority to get the work done, to allow their key workers to take initiative, and to keep work flowing in the supervisors' absence. Of course, the people to whom authority and responsibility are delegated must be willing to accept their obligations and be competent in those areas for which they are being held accountable.

PRINCIPLE 6

Report to One Supervisor

Each employee should receive orders from, and be responsible to, only one supervisor.

Reporting to one supervisor is often called the principle of **unity of command.** When employees receive orders from more than one supervisor, often they do not know from whom they should receive orders or what work should be done first. When two supervisors share the responsibility for one department, one supervisor may not know where his or her authority stops and the other's begins. The result may be confusion among workers and a breakdown in morale and discipline. By reporting to one supervisor only, which is the main theme of the unity-of-command principle, employees should know exactly what work is expected of them, and supervisors should know exactly who reports to them.

Each office employee should report directly to the one person named as the primary supervisor on a specific job or project. In one firm, the AOM may report to the controller because of conditions existing in that company; in another firm where administrative services are sales oriented, the OM may report to the vice president of sales. Who reports to whom depends on the organization structure, the objectives, and existing conditions within each company. With today's emphasis on matrix organization, we find that middle managers and staff personnel often report to several individuals—one with primary authority and others with secondary authority. (This arrangement is discussed later in this chapter.)

PRINCIPLE 7

Limit Span of Control

For effective supervision and leadership, the number of employees reporting to one supervisor should be limited to a manageable number.

Span of control, also known as the *span of management,* refers to the number of employees who are directly supervised by one person. When the span of control is narrow, a great opportunity exists for close supervision and regimentation. In such cases, the number of levels or layers in the organization is usually great, which creates a tall pyramid-shaped structure, as shown in Figure 2–3. As the span is broadened, the degree of freedom for employees becomes greater because the organization has fewer levels, as shown in Figure 2–4. The heavy lines in each chart show the **chain of command,** which is the means of transmitting authority from the top level (the chief ex-

Figure 2–4
Broad Span of Control (two levels)

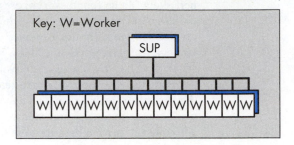

ecutive officer) through successive levels of management to the workers at the lowest operative level.

Early management theorists felt that the span of control at the *top level* should be no more than five or six persons whose work is closely related. Today, among salaried jobs (such as the manager of human resources), the average span is three.[1] At lower levels in an organization, some management authorities consider 12 to 20 workers to be the ideal span. In firms having company-wide computerized information systems, many workers at the same level often perform the same or very similar kinds of work. Thus, it becomes possible through internal control systems to increase the number of persons being supervised by one person.

Many large high-technology firms, such as the Ford Motor Company and the Xerox Corporation, have reduced the size of their workforce by layoffs, attrition, or other means. In this process, known as **downsizing,** or *rightsizing,* the number of organization levels was reduced by eliminating large numbers of middle managers. The resulting effect was to widen the senior managers' spans of control and thus provide "leaner" and "flatter" organization structures. The American Management Association reports that while middle managers were only about 5 to 8 percent of the workforce at more than 800

Figure 2–3
Narrow Span of Control (five levels)

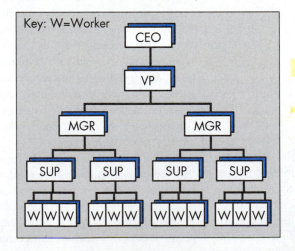

---

[1]Robert E. Sibson, *Strategic Planning for Human Resources Management* (New York: American Management Association, 1992), p. 230.

companies it surveyed, they accounted for 22 percent of the layoffs in 1992.[2] The reasons offered for the elimination of middle managers relate to their traditional functions—supervising people and gathering, processing, and transmitting information—which are now being taken over by self-managed teams and computerized operations.

PRINCIPLE 8

Centralize or Decentralize Managerial Authority

Wherever possible, centralize managerial authority and responsibility for all highly complex or technical functions in one location and decentralize the responsibility for all simpler functions throughout the organization.

The word *center* is widely used in our society. Typically, you will find a computer center, a learning resources center (or library), and an audiovisual center on college campuses. In most large communities, you will find a medical center (hospital), the financial center (representing banking and lending institutions), and one or more shopping centers. In each case, certain specialized functions are located in one place; that is, the functions are *centralized*. In a similar way, managerial authority may be centralized in an organization.

In organizations with **centralized authority,** similar functions are carried out in one place, and decisions tend to be made at or near the top of the organization. This is true of large computerized information systems as well as the human resources and payroll functions. If, on the other hand, much authority is delegated to lower levels in the organization, **decentralized authority** exists. In a firm with decentralized authority, fewer levels of management exist, and the prevailing philosophy is that decisions should be made at the lowest levels possible.

FORMS OF ORGANIZATION

A basic responsibility of management is to develop an effective organization structure. The term **organization structure** refers to the arrangement of functions—the framework—that must be constructed in order to achieve the organization's goals. However, a good structure does not guarantee sound organizational health. In the words of Peter F. Drucker, "The test of a healthy business is not the beauty, clarity, or perfection of its organization structure. *It is the performance of people.*"[3]

The best organization structure is the simplest one that will do the job. The simpler the structure, the more easily office workers will understand the organization of work. With a simple form of organization, the interrelationships among workers become clearer, and there are fewer problems. To create a simple form of office organization, the key activities or functions needed to produce the desired results must be identified and provided. Thus, in designing a sound organization structure, the OM serves as an architect who must keep in mind the basic purposes for which the office exists.

C. Northcote Parkinson. One critical set of problems to avoid in organizing the office is known as **Parkinson's Law,** a condition that exists at times in all companies. C. Northcote Parkinson, who originated this "law," found that the following serious problems can be expected in firms that lack good organization structures:

1. Work expands to fill the time available for its completion with little regard for the volume or usefulness of the tasks to be carried out.
2. Work expands to fit the organization that is designed to perform that work.

[2]"Upswing in Downsizings to Continue," *Management Review* (February, 1993), p. 5. Also see Brian Dumaine, "The New Non-Manager Managers," *Fortune* (February 22, 1993), p. 80.

[3]Peter F. Drucker, *Management: Tasks, Responsibilities, Practices* (New York: Harper & Row, 1974), p. 602.

3. Each unit in an organization tends to build up its importance by expanding the number of its personnel.[4]

When these conditions are found, too many workers get bogged down in useless red tape, which brings about inefficiency and excessive costs.

Organization structures are usually planned on a functional basis, that is, according to the basic functions of business—production, marketing, finance, and human resources. Within each of these groupings, the functions may be further subdivided. As you saw in Chapter 1, the administrative services function, which includes office activities, may be a subgroup under finance or another major function, general administration. In addition to examining the functionally planned formal organization in this section, you will learn about the informal organization, which is found worldwide in all sizes and types of firms.

Formal Organization

The plan of organization depicted in an organization chart is called the **formal organization.** A formal organization is designed to plan work, to assign responsibility, to supervise work, and to measure results. The formal organization also recognizes the existence of, and works alongside, the informal organization in the firm. To understand the nature of the formal organization, a knowledge of departmentation, organization charts, and various types of formal organizations must be mastered.

Departmentation

The process of organizing work into distinct areas based on some common characteristic is called **departmentation.** Most frequently, we find this arrangement based on functional lines with a separate department for each of the main functions, such as sales, production, and finance. Service departments, such as word processing, public relations, and research and development, may also be organized for managing the work.

Although each of the areas is often called a *department,* some firms prefer the term *division;* others use *section* or *branch.* For example, there may be a purchasing department in one firm, while in another company the same function is called a purchasing division. In other firms, the use of each term implies a hierarchy of organization. For example, reading from the top of a traditional organization chart to the bottom, a vice president may head a division, a manager may head each of the several departments in the division, and a supervisor may be in charge of each section in each department. This type of structure is commonly found in government organizations and in many large corporations. Effective AOMs develop and maintain up-to-date organization charts for reasons noted in the following paragraphs.

Charting the Formal Organization

An **organization chart** is a graphic picture that shows how the functional units of a firm are tied together along the principal lines of authority. The charts are management tools that indicate the flow of work, the span of control, and the major responsibilities for work in each functional area or department. In order to keep an organization chart simple and easy to understand, unnecessary detail should be avoided, and, if needed, several charts may be prepared to give a complete guide to a company's organization.

No matter how well organized the firm, people must understand the structure in order to make the organization plan work. In this respect, charts help workers understand basic reporting relationships, which is important in developing teamwork and in reducing buck-passing and duplication of work effort. Having available an up-to-date chart aids the AOM in identifying the lines of decision-making authority which, in turn, helps to disclose inconsistencies and overly complex work assignments. Then, too, charts are especially useful to managers who are orienting new employees since charts tie together the entire organization structure.

Having a chart available, however, is no assurance that good organization exists. Since they show only the present structure, with little regard

---

[4]C. Northcote Parkinson, *Parkinson's Law* (Boston: Houghton-Mifflin, 1957).

for the future, many charts quickly become obsolete, and, when they are not updated, charts become relatively useless. Most charts are criticized because they show only the formal relationships within a firm and not *how much authority* has been delegated at any point in the structure. Most charts also ignore informal relationships, which are discussed in a later section.

Figure 2–5 lists ten suggestions for preparing conventional organization charts.[5] These suggestions are not hard-and-fast rules, because charts should be modified when the occasion demands. Specialized charting software enables you to select symbols such as boxes and choose from a variety of different ways to connect lines. If you relocate a box, the lines automatically adjust. To simplify the task of creating charts, some software programs produce charts automatically from a written outline.[6]

Organization charts are often housed in the **organization manual.** This manual explains in narrative form the organization, duties, and responsibilities of the departments and all other functional areas of the firm. Charts for each of the main forms of organization are shown in the following section.

---

[5]Adapted from J. Clifton Williams, Andrew J. DuBrin, and Henry L. Sisk, *Management and Organization,* 5th ed. (Cincinnati: South-Western Publishing Co., 1985), p. 283.

[6]Kathryn Alesandrini, *Survive Information Overload* (Homewood, IL: Business One Irwin, 1992), pp. 48–51. Also see "Outlining and Diagraming Software" in the Resource Directory, pp. 248–249.

Figure 2–5
Suggestions for Preparing Conventional Organization Charts

1. Identify the chart by showing the name of the company, date of preparation, and title of person or department responsible for preparation. If the chart is for one division only, include such information as part of the title.

2. Start at the top of the organization structure and identify the major functions (divisions, departments, etc.). Next, chart the secondary functions.

3. Use a rectangular box to show either an organization unit or a person. Use one box for several executives who function as a committee.

4. Arrange boxes vertically to show relative positions in the hierarchy; however, due to space limitations, you may show the line units one level below the staff units. (See Figure 2–8.)

5. Make all the boxes in each horizontal row the same size and include only those positions having the same organizational rank.

6. Use vertical and horizontal solid lines to show the flow of line authority; use dotted lines to show functional and staff authority.

7. Show lines of authority as entering at the top center of a box and leaving at the bottom center. Exception: The line of authority to a staff assistant or an assistant-to may enter the center of one side of the box. (See Figure 2–8.) Do not draw lines through the boxes.

8. Place the title of each position in the box. Titles should be consistent; if necessary, revise titles so they are both consistent and descriptive.

9. Include the name of the person currently holding the position unless turnover is so great that revising the chart is burdensome.

10. Keep the chart as simple as possible; if necessary, include a legend to explain any special notations.

Traditional Types of Formal Organization

As you will see in the following discussion, many types of formal organizations have evolved based upon the specific needs of management.

Line Organization. The earliest and simplest form of organization structure is the **line organization,** also known as the *scalar* or *military* type. In a line organization, authority is passed down from top management to middle managers in charge of particular activities and from them down to supervisors who are directly in charge of workers at the operative level. As shown in Figure 2–6, authority flows in an unbroken chain of command from the president to the individual office worker.

The line organization is simple and easy to understand. The division of authority and responsibility and the corresponding duties to be performed are clearly identified. In turn, the performance of duties can be easily traced to a worker and to the person supervising that worker. In the line organization, decision making is completed with a minimum of red tape, thus enabling action to be taken quickly. On the other hand, each super-visor is responsible for a wide variety of duties and may not be expert in all these areas. Thus, specialization may be lacking at the supervisory level.

The line organization is found in government agencies, in military organizations, and in some small business firms. However, few business offices follow a "pure" line organization, although some phases of work in large firms may follow a line-organization plan.

Functional Organization. The concept of **functional organization** was developed by Frederick W. Taylor to provide for specialized skills at the supervisory level in a plant. To handle the mental and physical aspects of production, a clerical force consisting of a time and cost clerk, an instruction card clerk, an order of work and route clerk, and a shop disciplinarian was provided.[7]

---

[7]Taylor's contributions to the classical school of management thought are described in Chapter 1. From 1880 through 1890, Taylor formulated fundamental principles, called duties of management, that challenged the traditional methods of management. See Frederick W. Taylor, *Scientific Management* (New York: Harper & Bros., 1947).

Figure 2–6
Partial Organization Chart Showing Line Organization

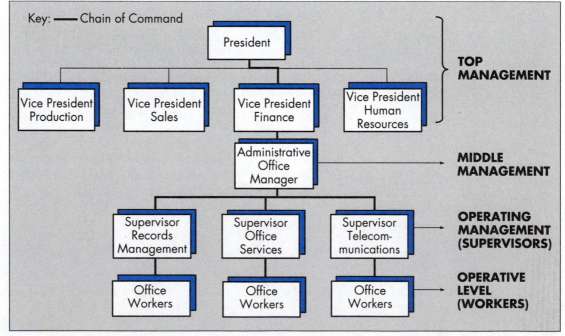

The objective of the functional organization was to provide specialists at the supervisory level who would be in charge of the work related to their specialities in departments other than their own.

When applied to an office, the functional organization might appear as shown in Figure 2–7. Instead of one large general office that provides administrative services for the entire firm, four divisions, each headed by a vice president, are provided. Furthermore, a staff of office workers is maintained in each division. Notice that each of the main functions has line authority (the solid lines) over the office staff. At the same time, the office staff in each division is supervised by a specialist in employee training, with the dotted lines in Figure 2–7 representing the functional authority. (Many other specialties exist in larger firms.) Thus, each of the office workers has two supervisors, with the exception of the employee training area, where line authority exists between the employee training supervisor and the office staff. Such a "two-boss" arrangement represents a violation of the unity-of-command principle cited earlier in this chapter. At the same time, however, such a structure may be defended on the basis of its being an application of the principle of specialization also discussed earlier.

In the functional organization, each supervisor devotes time to only one phase of work. Such specialization provides for increased efficiency because the workers are given expert and skilled supervisory attention. However, with the development of so many kinds of independent specialists, confusion can result due to overlapping of authority and a lack of fixed lines of responsibility. As a result, the functional form lends itself to "buck-passing." Since the workers must report to two or more supervisors, conflicting instructions are often given, which result in friction. Because of all its disadvantages, a "pure" functional organization, like the line form, is rarely found in business. As we see in the following discussion, however, the workable principles of the line form and the functional form have been brought together in the commonly used line-and-staff organization.

Line-and-Staff Organization. In a **line-and-staff organization,** policies and practices at the top-management level are carried out on a *line plan.* Further down the line of authority and responsibility, the work is carried out on a *functional* basis, department by department. The *staff* feature emerges when a group of experts assists management as advisers to all the various depart-

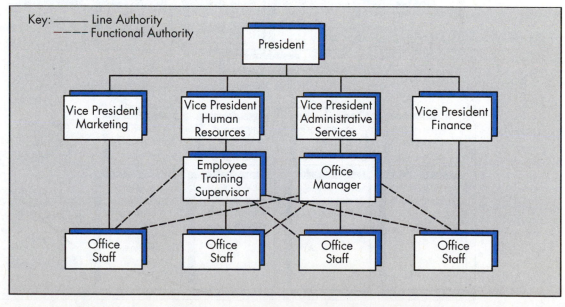

Figure 2–7
Partial Organization Chart Showing Functional Organization

Key: —— Line Authority
‑ ‑ ‑ ‑ Functional Authority

President

Vice President Marketing   Vice President Human Resources   Vice President Administrative Services   Vice President Finance

Employee Training Supervisor   Office Manager

Office Staff   Office Staff   Office Staff   Office Staff

ments. In many organizations, the AOM is a line officer who is responsible for certain business activities but acts as a staff specialist. In this case, the AOM offers expert advice to the functional departments that require administrative services such as records management, word processing, and reprographics.

As shown in the line-and-staff organization chart in Figure 2–8, a clear-cut flow of authority and responsibility exists from the top to the bottom of the organization. Operating efficiency through specialization is achieved because middle managers, such as the AOM, directly control the employees under them and are held responsible for specific activities. Supervisors, such as the head of administrative services, report through the AOM to the controller. The supervisors, however, are not burdened with all the varied duties that they would have under a line organization.

The personnel in the staff positions shown in Figure 2–8 (internal auditing, systems and procedures, human resources, budgets, and reports) act as advisers and provide services for line managers throughout the organization. (In Figure 2–8, only the relationship of the staff positions to the controller is illustrated by the dotted lines.)

An **assistant-to,** or *administrative assistant,* serving as a personal assistant to his or her supervisor, is often found in many firms. The assistant-to president, as shown in Figure 2–8, is a form of staff authority whose duties vary widely from one firm to another and may vary from time to time within the same company. No specific line authority is associated with the position since authority is granted only for the completion of each individual assignment. Assistants-to do not act in their own behalf; rather, they act as personal representatives of their supervisors.

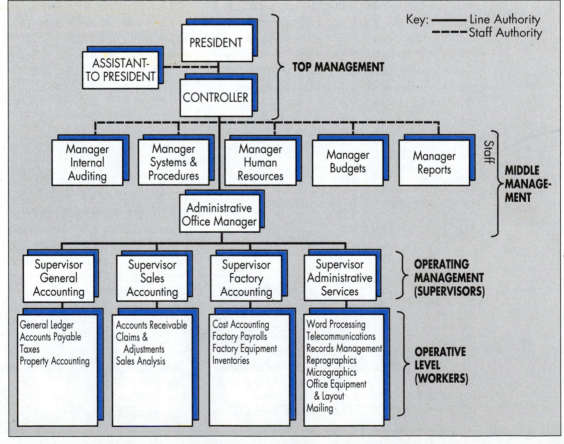

Figure 2–8
Partial Organization Chart Showing Line-and-Staff Organization

Illustration 2–3 Task forces draw on employee expertise from many functional areas for special studies and problem analysis.

Staff managers usually have the necessary line authority to supervise their own departments, but their basic responsibilities are to provide expert advice and to render services for the line managers. Traditionally, staff managers do not give orders directly to line personnel outside their departments, nor do they ordinarily have the authority to put their recommendations into action. *The authority and responsibility for executing operations rests with the line managers.*

Today, however, as a result of the increased complexity of business operations and the development of new concepts in technology, we find that the traditional distinction between line and staff has become blurred. Danger arises when specialists are added to the staff without any clear understanding of how their activities interact with those of the line personnel. Disagreements arise and friction occurs when staff departments wrongfully assume line authority and exert this authority over individuals and departments in line positions. Line managers, in turn, may hesitate to accept accountability and may abdicate their authority. We should not forget, however, that line managers are users of the services rendered by staff personnel, whose job is to make the line operations more productive at lower costs.

Alternatives to the line-and-staff organization, which by its very nature may create problems with interpersonal relationships, are presented in the following sections.

Committee Organization. With the growth of larger and more complex organizations, the need for interaction and coordination among personnel at all levels has increased. To meet this need, the **committee organization** provides a structure where authority and responsibility are jointly held by a group of individuals rather than by a single manager. The committee organization is usually employed in conjunction with, or as a modification of, the line-and-staff structure.

At Texas Instruments, a policy committee was formed as a joint venture between two *teams* of management—human resources managers and operating managers—to establish human resources policies for the organization. Every business division in the organization is represented on the teams, and representation is global. The presidents of the European, Asian, and Japanese operations are all members of the committee. In the *Dialog from the Workplace*, Chuck Nielson, vice president of human resources, tells how this committee ensures that the policies and programs meet the needs of the organization.

Kinds of Committee Organization. Several different kinds of committee organization are described below.

- *Task force.* This type of committee, consisting of representatives of several departments or functional areas, is responsible for coordinating a study or other efforts involving departmental units.
- *Staff group.* The primary purpose of this group is to integrate a basic management activity, such as company-wide planning.

DIALOG FROM THE WORKPLACE

CHARLES F. NIELSON

*Vice President of
Human Resources
Texas Instruments, Inc.
Dallas, Texas*

In 1992, Texas Instruments won a *Personnel Journal* Optimas Award, which was created to foster an increased awareness of human resources in the general business community. TI's award in the *Service* category honors departments that have developed a program or policy in an effort to support another constituency within the organization.

Charles F. "Chuck" Nielson received a B.S. degree from Brigham Young University in sociology with minors in psychology and economics. Mr. Nielson did graduate work at the University of Utah and Utah State University.

Nielson's work experience began at Thiokol Chemical Corporation in Brigham City, Utah, where he was involved in the employment and supervisor training function. His next experience was with Fairchild-Hiller Corporation in St. Augustine, Florida, where he supervised the industrial relations function. Nielson joined Texas Instruments in 1965. He has had a variety of personnel responsibilities, including personnel director—Curaçao, Netherlands Antilles; personnel director, consumer group—Lubbock, Texas; and U.S. personnel manager. He is currently vice president of human resources.

Nielson was appointed by President Bush to the President's Drug Advisory Council, which advised and assisted the President and the Director of the Office of National Drug Control Policy on ways to mobilize the private sector against illegal drugs. Nielson is a member of The Business Roundtable Employee Relations Committee (ERC), which is comprised of the top human resources executives at the leading Roundtable companies. The ERC plays an active role in legislation affecting the relationship between employees, employers, and the government. Nielson is also a member of the board of directors of the Labor Policy Association. This group is composed of corporate human resources executives concerned exclusively with the development of the nation's human resources and employment policies.

QUESTION: We have read about the formation of your policy committee that represents a joint venture between two teams of management—the operating people on one team and the human resources (HR) people on the other. How has this policy committee aided in ensuring that Texas Instruments' policies and programs are responsive to the needs of your organization?

RESPONSE: It is becoming very evident that what differentiates one company from another is the effectiveness of the people. To provide an environment that enables the best performance from each individual requires policies which are insightful from a human resources perspective and which add value from an operating manager perspective.

The true significance of the current situation in TI can best be understood by looking at how things used to be. In the past many times HR views and operating views were poles apart. HR viewed the operating perspective as being punitive and insensitive; operating managers viewed the HR perspective as soft.

The Policy Committee has accomplished a synergistic relationship between HR professionals and key operating managers. HR policies are now, in fact, aimed at enhanced performance, and ownership of the policy is jointly held by both HR managers and operating managers.

- *Codetermination.* Within this committee organization, the employees participate in decision making at upper-management levels, sometimes with appointment to the board of directors.
- *Labor-management committee.* The objective of this committee is to ease the collective bargaining process by finding solutions to labor problems before the union contract expires.

Advantages of Committee Organization. Those favoring group decision making point out the following advantages of committee organization:

- People often accept a group decision rather than the dictates of one person.
- Members of the group actively participate in their interactions. This provides better teamwork, and supervisors think of their organization more as a cohesive unit than in terms of their own individual departments.
- Broader understandings of the decision are developed because the group examines the overall conduct of the organization, discusses problems that affect more than one unit of the company's organization, and learns the reasoning behind the selection of a particular course of action.
- Plans developed by the group may be executed more easily because all members participate in pooling their knowledge and experience to develop the plans. For example, the quality communications committee at Lincoln Electric consists of members drawn from a variety of areas—quality assurance, receiving, and so forth—so that each member is aware of possible communication problems that may arise in the planning for parts inventory, scheduling, and manpower.[8]

Disadvantages of Committee Organization. Others who have served on committees and experienced group decision making point out the following negative features of this form of organization:

- The group is slower in reaching decisions than is one person, although admittedly snap judgments are eliminated.

- No one individual is fully responsible for any decisions made by the group since the majority rules. As a result, compromise decisions that may not be of the best quality are sometimes made.
- Group meetings consume much valuable time, and too often the committee is faced with time-consuming problems that could be handled more efficiently by individual executives.

Nontraditional Types of Organization

Facing an urgent need to improve their competitive position, to increase employee motivation, and to overcome a hierarchical structure that has an inherent tendency toward growth, many companies have restructured or re-engineered their traditional forms of organization. The goals of these new structures include:[9]

1. Moving the workforce closer to the customer.
2. Empowering each worker: giving each worker the authority to do more for the customer without asking management.
3. Shrinking the decision chain: when decisions must be referred to management, making the path followed by each decision as short as possible.

The hub-and-spokes chart in Figure 2–9 shows how a company might re-engineer its organization in keeping with the previous goals. No longer do employees see their goal as climbing to the top of a pyramidal structure; instead, the employees focus their attention upon the goal lying at the hub of the organizational wheel—*customer satisfaction.* The employees see how the company earns a profit by learning how each of the spokes—a job function—operates in tandem and focuses upon customers. With the objective of promoting more direct contact between customers and all workers, the circle of customer service surrounds the internal operations. Thus, the customer service employees see their coworkers as customers who deliver and exchange information with the line employees. Lying within the outside circle are the chief executive officer and the chief operating officer, the two leaders who represent the corporation to its customers.

[8]Chris Lee, "Followership: The Essence of Leadership," *Training* (January, 1991), p. 31.

[9]Daniel Morris and Joel Brandon, *Re-Engineering Your Business* (New York: McGraw-Hill, 1993), pp. 223–224.

Figure 2–9
Hub-and-
Spokes Chart
Showing the
Organization's
Goal—Cus-
tomer Satis-
faction

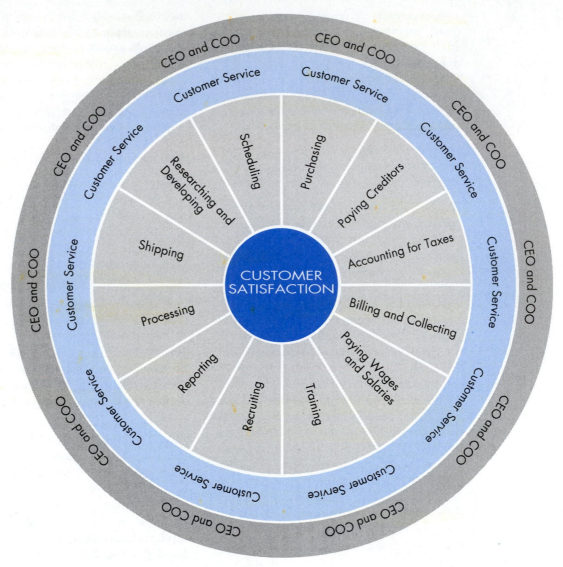

Several of the newer, nontraditional forms of organization are discussed below.

Work Team. Today, with the goal of tapping their workers' knowledge to improve productivity and their own competitive position, companies such as Ford, General Motors, Motorola, and Cummins Engine have reorganized around teams of workers. A **work team,** either a permanent or temporary organization structure, is created to improve lateral relations and to solve problems throughout the organization. As you will learn in Chapter 12, management must be concerned about the extent of its "domination" of the team and with the range of topics being discussed.[10]

---

[10]In 1992, the National Labor Relations Board (NLRB) ruled that the labor-management teams formed at Electromation Inc., in Elkhart, Indiana, violated federal labor law. The teams, each consisting of two managers and about five nonmanagement employees, studied such issues as absenteeism, smoking, and pay levels. The NLRB ruled that the work teams at Electromation, a nonunion company, constituted an attempt to negotiate wages and working conditions with workers, which made the teams illegal.

Common types of work teams include:

Problem-solving. This team usually consists of 5 to 12 volunteers who meet several hours each week to discuss ways of improving quality, efficiency, and the work environment. The team does not implement its ideas.

Special-purpose. This team may design and introduce work reforms or new technology or meet with suppliers and customers. In union shops, labor and management collaborate at all levels.

Self-managed or *self-directed.* About 5 to 15 workers learn all production tasks and rotate from job to job. The team performs managerial duties such as scheduling work, preparing budgets, and ordering materials.

Matrix Organization. Matrix organization, sometimes called *project organization,* combines both vertical authority relationships and horizontal or diagonal work relationships in order to deal with complex work projects. The objective of matrix organization is to obtain a higher degree of coordination than can be obtained in the conventional organization structures discussed earlier. Work is organized around several ongoing projects rather than around the specialized departments or functional areas found in the line or the line-and-staff organizations.

As you can see in the simple matrix organization depicted in Figure 2–10, four functional managers, with their vertical authority relationships, are positioned along the vertical axes. The managers of the three projects are placed along the horizontal axes. The functional managers and the project managers have dual authority over those working in the matrix unit. At the top of the matrix, or grid, is the president or the CEO, who is responsible for balancing the power between the functional managers and the project managers. Each work group (represented by a square on the matrix) is held uniquely accountable to two supervisors—one functional manager in the department where the employee regularly works and one special project manager who uses the employee's services for a varying period of time. Thus, the matrix organization seemingly violates the unity-of-command principle discussed earlier. Because of the conflicts that may occur when personnel have two supervisors, matrix organizations are difficult to manage. Each matrix man-

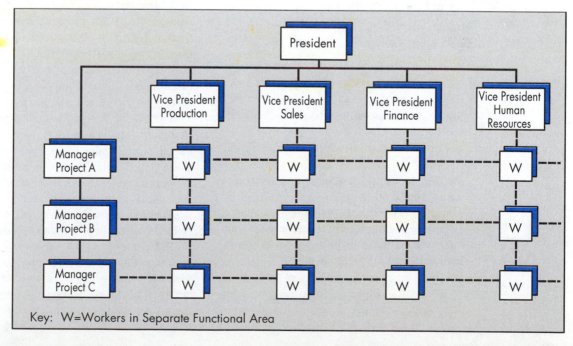

Figure 2–10
Matrix Organization

ager appears to have overlapping, and often conflicting, roles of authority and responsibility.

Along with being difficult to manage, the matrix organization is faced with added pressures to share its human resources. For example, in Figure 2–10, assume that the manager of Project A is responsible for installing and operating a new management information system. At various stages of the project manager's work, team members are drawn upon from the functional areas as needed. This allows the project manager to obtain expertise from systems and procedures analysts, computer center personnel, financial analysts, and administrative services support personnel as well as advice from outside vendors of forms, equipment, and furniture. When the project is completed, the personnel return to their various departments or cost centers for assignment to new projects.

Broadbanding. In **broadbanding,** employees are loosely organized into a few broad job categories called *bands*. As you have seen, many corporations have become smaller by downsizing the number of their middle-management positions. It is expected that such organizations are likely to move toward horizontal structures like broadbanding. For example, the Scott Paper Company in Philadelphia has restructured its 30 or more traditional job categories into a few broad bands. Some expected benefits from broadbanding include:

1. Managers will have increased flexibility to relate workers' pay to performance since each salary range will be wider as a result of more job classifications having been bundled within one band.
2. Employees will be provided more opportunity to develop skills and make *lateral* moves instead of focusing on whether their next job is a move up or down.
3. Managers will become more important to their employees' career paths because each manager will be more responsible for salary adjustments and job assignments.[11]

---

[11]Mary Rowland, "Sidestepping Toward Success," *The New York Times* (January 24, 1993), p. F17.

Informal Organization

The **informal organization** refers to the interpersonal relationships that do not appear on the formal organization chart. An informal, or *unwritten,* organization develops over time to meet the workers' human needs, such as their needs for recognition and socialization, which are not explicitly provided for in the formal organization plan.

The typical informal organization is composed of two or more persons who, by design or chance, develop mutually useful interaction concerning personal and job-related matters. For example, during work breaks, group assignments, or routine work activities, a closeness develops among certain individuals because of their common interests. Such people may extend their job associations to after-hour activities in the community, including participation in professional meetings where the employees "talk shop." Thus, ample opportunity is provided for people to air their attitudes and feelings, an important psychological outlet for healthy employees.

One of the most important values of the informal organization is its capability for efficiently sending and receiving communications in the office. The **grapevine,** which is discussed in Chapter 5, describes the informal oral communication network that helps employees learn more about what is happening in the organization and how they, in turn, might be affected by it. This informal channel is often more effective than the formal line in passing information, obtaining feedback, solving problems, and revising procedures.

Because the informal organization is constantly changing and in many cases is undefined, we find that it is often abused. A common example of abuse is the "buddy system" in which workers find "opportunities" to work together even though no such work assignments have been made. Also, workers may agree informally not to comply with official changes in policies and procedures.

The perceptive OM knows that the informal organization complements the formal plan. In fact, no company can exist without people interacting at all levels. Rather than try to eliminate the informal organization, the effective manager observes carefully the typical interactions of his or her office staff in order to identify such informal groups. The OM can then work closely with such groups who will feel an added sense of belonging and, ultimately, job satisfaction, even though their names do not appear on the company's organization chart.

CENTRALIZING/DECENTRALIZING MANAGERIAL AUTHORITY

One of the basic organizational decisions that managers make relates to the question, "Shall we centralize or decentralize our operations?" This topic, which appears as Principle 8 earlier in the chapter, usually involves two basic issues: (1) centralizing or decentralizing the firm's functions, such as the human resources department; and (2) centralizing or decentralizing the location in which the company's operations are performed.

If a large firm with 50 departments sets up a human resources department that does the hiring and firing of workers for all departments, we have an example of *functional centralization*. On the other hand, if each department is permitted to do its own hiring and firing, we have an example of *functional decentralization*.

If this same firm has 15 branch offices located throughout the United States and each branch is permitted its own human resources, sales, finance, and production units, the firm practices *geographic decentralization*. When the firm locates all its operating units in one place, it uses *geographic centralization* in its organization plan. Therefore, the answer to the question asked at the beginning of this section depends on a thorough study of the benefits of both centralization and decentralization.

Benefits of Centralization

A firm with centralized authority may realize the following benefits: (1) the actions taken are in strict accord with policies, (2) there is a reduction in the risk of errors made by workers who lack either information or ability, (3) the skills of specialized experts are used, and (4) close control may be exercised over operations. As a rule, an organization that is still in the hands of its original owner is likely to retain centralized authority.

Benefits of Decentralization

Firms having decentralized authority often cite the following benefits: (1) decisions are more speedily made; (2) action can be taken on the spot without consulting higher levels of management; (3) decisions can be adapted to local conditions, such as in branch offices; (4) employees to whom authority and responsibility have been delegated show a great deal of interest and enthusiasm in their work; and (5) top-level executives can better use their time by setting policies as well as planning and organizing the firm's goals.

Generally, the degree of centralization depends upon factors such as the nature, size, and complexity of the business; its products and markets; the extent of automated operations; and the managerial styles and skills of those involved. Large, diversified, and mature companies tend to benefit from the advantages of both centralized and decentralized authorities.

Centralization of Office Operations

Centralizing the management of information and the administration of office services fixes responsibility, lessens the investment in machines and equipment, permits effective supervision, and balances the distribution of the workload. Thus, the bulk of office operations is often centralized under an AOM, who delegates to assistants the authority and responsibility for supervising the support services such as word processing, filing, mailing, and reprographics. These support services, each under the direction and control of a person accountable to the AOM, can be provided at minimum cost and with expert supervision. In addition, in large companies some decentralized office work is often performed by administrative assistants, executive secretaries, and others who maintain their own personal or confidential files.

An example of centralization found in some firms is the **satellite administrative services** center, or *substation*. The substation is a compact workstation that handles information processing and general office services which are usually scattered throughout a number of offices. Thus, we may find a substation that supplies a minimum number of services such as mail, stationery supplies, and fast copies, in a defined area which serves operations in close proximity. As the substation proves successful in meeting the users' needs, additional services may be provided in a sort of building-block plan. Ideally, each of the substations is linked with one another, with the central services unit, and with the computer center.

Physical Decentralization of Office Operations

Do not confuse the decentralization of authority with the *physical decentralization,* or *geographic dispersion,* of a company's management or of any office operations. In large organizations, the home-office managers may be geographically separated from the division or branch managers. If desired, the delegation of authority can be limited, however. Under such conditions, the firm is highly centralized even though the activities of the organization are decentralized geographically.

When a firm maintains plants and offices in several locations, many of the information-processing activities and administrative support services are often decentralized to permit more efficient operations. As a result, a certain amount of duplication of supervision and investment in equipment occurs. Often, we find that the administrative services are decentralized because of branch offices in many locations. However, with today's telecommunication systems, the accounting operations may be centralized in one location, such as the home office. Centralizing the accounting function is not only less costly but also more efficient. The work is done more accurately, and, by means of timely reports, management can make better use of the accounting and statistical information.

The operation of branch offices varies with different firms. In many firms, the branch office is a sales office under the direction of a branch sales manager who is provided as much clerical and accounting assistance as necessary. Under this arrangement, the AOM in the home office provides little guidance and control except, perhaps, to issue office procedures manuals developed by the home office. The rest of the work is ordinarily directed by the branch sales manager.

Some branches are established on a somewhat independent basis, with each branch acting as a separate unit. In such a branch, the OM is assigned the same duties and responsibilities as any other OM. In some firms, too, there is a greater volume of office work than in others. For example, in life insurance companies, banks, and brokerage firms, the amount of information processing is much greater than in manufacturing or retail organizations. Based on this information, you can see that the question of centralized versus decentralized authority tends to become an individual problem to be solved by each firm.

LEADERSHIP STYLES OF THE ADMINISTRATIVE OFFICE MANAGER

The success with which the AOM applies the principles of management discussed earlier depends largely upon effective leadership. In this section, we shall briefly consider the nature of leadership and leadership styles.

Nature of Leadership

Leadership is a purely human process of influencing people to work willingly and enthusiastically to attain organizational objectives. Research has shown that there is no one best leadership behavior, although for many decades it was believed that all great leaders possessed certain traits. A widely held view is that leaders have high intelligence, broad social interests and maturity, strong motivation to accomplish, and great respect for, and interest in, people.

Contingency Theory of Leadership

Research on leadership has gone beyond identifying personal traits to emphasize (1) the *tasks to be performed* (i.e., the work to be completed) and (2) the *human relationships in the workplace.* Illustrating this last school of research is the work of Fred E. Fiedler, who developed the **contingency theory of leadership effectiveness.** Fiedler's studies suggest that the *situation* confronting the leader and the workers determines the leadership behavior that will be successful in the firm. More specifically, Fiedler found that leadership behavior—either task-oriented or relationship-oriented—is contingent upon a combination of three variables:

1. *Quality of leader-worker relations* (good or poor)—the degree to which the workers support the leader.
2. *Degree of task structure* (high or low)—the extent to which the task goals, procedures, and guidelines are clearly spelled out.
3. *Amount of position power* (strong or weak)— the degree to which the position gives the leader power to reward and punish workers.

Fiedler observed that task-oriented leaders are most successful in either very favorable (high control) or very unfavorable (low control) situations; relationship-oriented leaders are most successful in situations of moderate control. Continuing to work on his contingency model of leadership, Fiedler has advanced a *cognitive resource theory,* which states that the more task-relevant a leader's competencies, intelligence, and experience are, the more directive the leader can be. Otherwise, a more participative style works best.[12]

Transactional Leadership

Exhibiting **transactional leadership** behavior, the leader sees job performance as a series of task-oriented and/or people-oriented "transactions" with the workers. By means of these transactions, the leader helps the workers meet their needs and those of the organization in mutually satisfactory ways. The leader's main task is to influence workers by using a leadership style that best fits the situation and causes workers to apply themselves to meet the performance objectives. Rewards are exchanged for services rendered, and punishment is given for inadequate performance.

Transformational Leadership

The leader who follows a **transformational leadership** approach inspires the workers to achieve outstanding performance by influencing their beliefs, values, and goals. After the leader has diagnosed a situation and adopted a leadership style that meets the demands of the situation, next comes the need for a powerful display of inspiration, charisma, and contagious enthusiasm that will create "transformations." As a result of these transformations, workers shift into new and high-performance patterns as they convert their own self-interest into the interest of the group.

Drucker's Practical Leadership.

In his book, *Managing for the Future: The 1990s and Beyond,* Peter Drucker presents a very pragmatic approach to leadership, which he states, ". . . is all the rage now." Developing the thesis that leadership has little to do with personality qualities, traits, and charisma, Drucker concludes that the essence of leadership is performance. Drucker's requirements for effective leadership are summarized as follows:[13]

1. *Define and establish the organization's mission.* Here, the leader sets goals and priorities and maintains standards.
2. *Accept leadership as a responsibility rather than a rank or a privilege.* Effective leaders encourage and push but do not fear a display of strength in their associates. However, when things go wrong, the leaders know that they are ultimately reponsible for their associates' mistakes.

---

[12]For a very fine discussion of several contingency theories of leadership and other leadership models, see John R. Schermerhorn, Jr., *Management for Productivity* (New York: John Wiley & Sons, 1993), Chap. 12.

[13]Peter F. Drucker, *Managing for the Future: The 1990s and Beyond* (New York: Truman Talley Books/Dutton, 1992), pp. 119–123.

Illustration 2–4 The diplomatic leadership style uses tactful, open dialogue to effectively handle conflicts and problems.

3. *Earn and keep the trust of followers.* A leader is someone who has followers—those who trust that the leader has integrity and means what is said.

Now, let's see how these leadership theories and behaviors are reflected in the *styles* of leadership that we may encounter in today's workplace.

Leadership Styles

When a consistent pattern of behavior is found in a leader, a **leadership style** is said to exist. As Figure 2–11 shows, there is a wide range of leadership styles, each involving managers and workers to varying degrees in the decision-making process.

The effective OM will carefully study the strengths and weaknesses of each of the leadership styles discussed below. The best leadership style, which may be a mix of several styles, depends on the following factors: (1) the manager's personality; (2) the kinds of workers reporting to the OM, especially their expectations and their willingness to assume responsibility; (3) the type of work performed; (4) the philosophies and lead-ership styles prevailing at the top level of the company; and (5) the particular situation or problem being explored.

Autocratic

An **autocratic leader,** or *authoritarian leader,* rules with unlimited authority. This is the OM who "tells" rather than "sells" or "consults." The autocratic manager has little confidence or trust in those reporting to him or her. Thus, the autocratic manager controls the bulk of power and influence in the decision-making process. As a result, those who report to the autocrat are given little, if any, motivation to engage in problem solving or in decision making. Rather, they often work under the threat of punishment with only a few rewards.

When decisions must be made quickly, such as during emergencies, the "telling" style of leadership is effective and efficient. Such a style is workable when dealing with office employees who do not seek freedom of action on their jobs and who are very secure working under close supervision. On the other hand, this management style emphasizes one-way communication; there is little, if any, feedback from the office workers. As a result, misunderstandings occur often and result in costly mistakes and wasteful office practices.

Bureaucratic

The **bureaucratic leader** sets and follows fixed rules, a hierarchy of authority, and narrow, rigid, formal routines. The OM viewed as a bureaucrat "tells" the office workers what to do. The bases for the OM's orders are the policies, procedures, and rules of the organization rather than the force of the leader's personality, as is true of the autocratic leader.

Office workers who report to a bureaucratic OM know that the firm's policies and procedures will be consistently interpreted for them and that the OM will be fair and impartial. However, the bureaucratic style is marked by inflexibility when exceptions to the rules must be made to meet the needs of a particular situation. Also, when situations arise that are not covered by a policy or a rule or when the rules may be ambiguous, the

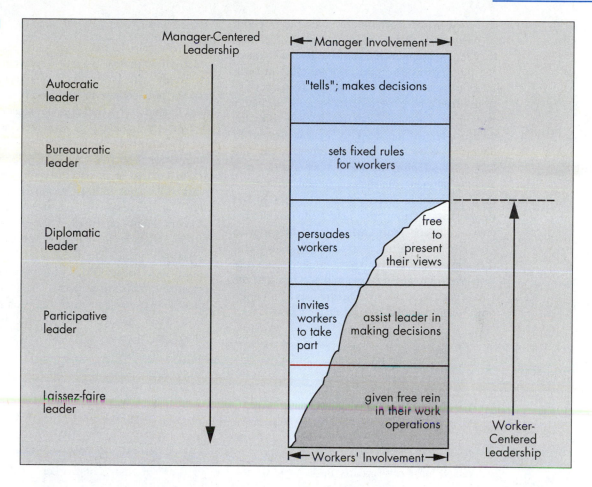

Figure 2–11
Leadership
Styles

Manager-Centered
Leadership

◄— Manager Involvement —►

Autocratic
leader — "tells"; makes decisions

Bureaucratic
leader — sets fixed rules
for workers

Diplomatic
leader — persuades
workers — free
to
present
their views

Participative
leader — invites
workers
to take
part — assist leader in
making decisions

Laissez-faire
leader — given free rein
in their work
operations

Worker-
Centered
Leadership

◄— Workers' Involvement —►

---

workers may become annoyed and frustrated because they do not know what to do. Consequently, office workers may become resentful and resist the OM's attempts to lead them.

Diplomatic

The **diplomatic leader** is skillful in helping people to solve their problems or to meet the needs of a particular situation. This manager is expert in using tact and conciliation and rarely arouses hostility among the workers. The diplomatic OM, who prefers "selling" rather than "telling" people, manages by persuasion and individual motivation. The office workers are usually provided some freedom to react, to question, to discuss, and even to present arguments that support their views.

The diplomatic OM gains the cooperation and enthusiasm of his or her workers by taking time to explain the reasons for following particular procedures. When this style of leadership fails to sell the workers on the "why" of decisions that have been made, a diplomatic manager must resort to giving orders ("telling"). As a result, the workers may then see the diplomat's style as hypocritical and weak.

Participative

The **participative leader** openly invites the workers to join in and take part in making decisions, setting policies, and analyzing methods of operation. Some participative OMs are democratic and let their workers know in advance that the group's decision, usually arrived at by consensus or majority vote, will be binding.

When office workers are given the freedom to participate and help form a plan of action, they tend to support it and strive harder to make the plan work. The participative OM, in turn, benefits by obtaining the workers' best information, ideas, and experiences. As a result, better worker attitudes are created and productivity increases. The office workers are encouraged to develop, grow, and rise in the organization, and they have a feeling of personal satisfaction and accomplishment. On the other hand, because of the time spent in meetings between the OM and the workers, participative leadership can be time consuming, and some OMs may use this style as a means of avoiding responsibility. Further, if the workers' ideas and recommendations are consistently rejected or ignored as a result of the OM's misuse of the participative style, a breakdown of managerial control may occur.

Free-Rein

The **free-rein leader** sets goals and develops clear guidelines for the workers, who then operate freely with no further direction unless they ask for help. However, the free-rein or *laissez-faire* ("hands-off") OM does not abandon all control since the manager is ultimately accountable for the actions (or lack of actions) of the office employees. The free-rein OM delegates to the greatest extent in an effort to motivate the office workers to their fullest. However, the free-rein style can be disastrous for the manager if the workers are not qualified to accept the responsibilities and authority that are delegated.

As indicated earlier, there is no one best leadership style for an OM. In the various forms of organization discussed in this chapter, OMs may effectively use characteristics of each managerial style. Such managers are flexible in deciding what style of leadership is needed to solve their existing problems.

SUMMARY

1. AOMs must rely greatly upon basic principles of management in their daily activities. These principles are designed to provide a healthy organizational climate in which human resources are effectively used to produce results. As we observed in this chapter, these principles pertain to the objectives of the organization, scope and assignment of responsibilities, unity of functions, use of specialization, delegation of authority and responsibility, unity of command, span of control, and centralization or decentralization of managerial authority.

2. The different kinds of *formal* organization include:

   a. *Line organization,* the simplest form of organization, where authority is passed down from top management to supervisors who are in charge of workers at the operative level.

   b. *Functional organization,* which provides specialists at the supervisory level who are in charge of the work related to their specialties in departments other than their own.

   c. *Line-and-staff organization,* where policies and practices at the top-management level are carried out on a line plan, and further down the line of authority and responsibility, work is carried out on a functional basis.

   d. *Committee organization,* a structure where authority and responsibility are jointly held by a group of individuals. Examples include the task force, staff group, codetermination, and labor-management committee.

   e. *Work team,* a permanent or temporary organization structure, created to improve lateral relations and to solve problems throughout the organization. Examples include problem-solving, special-purpose, and self-managed teams.

f. *Matrix organization,* which combines both vertical authority relationships and horizontal or diagonal work relationships in order to deal with complex work projects.

g. *Broadbanding,* a structure that loosely organizes employees into a few broad job categories.

Informal organization refers to the interpersonal relationships that do not appear on the organization chart. Probably the most common type of informal organization is the *grapevine.*

3. Managerial authority may be *centralized,* where similar functions are carried out in one place, or *decentralized,* where considerable authority is delegated to many lower levels in the organization.

4. In putting the management principles to work, AOMs select a style of leadership that mirrors their individual personalities, philosophies, and behavioral traits. The main characteristics of the leadership styles are:

a. *Autocratic*—ruling with unlimited authority; "telling" rather than "selling."

b. *Bureaucratic*—setting and following fixed rules, a hierarchy of authority, and formal routines.

c. *Diplomatic*—persuading by use of tact and conciliation; "selling" rather than "telling."

d. *Participative*—inviting workers to join in and take part in making decisions, setting policies, and analyzing methods of operation.

e. *Free-rein*—setting goals and developing guidelines for workers who then operate freely with no further direction unless requested.

FOR YOUR REVIEW

1. Of what value are the principles of management to an administrative office manager?
2. What are the main characteristics of objectives?
3. For what reasons does a business firm develop policies?
4. Distinguish between authority and responsibility.
5. Explain how a business organization may be looked upon as a system.
6. What conditions must be met in an organization for the unity-of-functions principle to operate effectively?
7. What are the three parts involved in the process of delegation?
8. Why should an office worker receive orders from and be responsible to only one supervisor?
9. How does downsizing generally affect the span of control in an organization?
10. Show how an organization chart serves as an important management tool for the administrative office manager.
11. Describe the line-and-staff form of organization.

c
o
n
t

12. What advantages and disadvantages are associated with committee organizations?

13. Explain how a matrix organization might function in undertaking a new project—relocating the home office from the center of the city to the suburbs.

14. What benefits may be realized by a firm with centralized authority? With decentralized authority?

15. List Drucker's requirements for effective leadership.

16. Contrast the characteristics of the autocratic leadership style with those of the participative leadership style.

FOR YOUR DISCUSSION

1. Before his company began downsizing last summer, Andrew Whitaker had ten people reporting to him, five of whom were middle managers who had people reporting to them. After the restructuring, which eliminated an entire layer of management, Whitaker wound up with 20 people. It is now one month later and here is what Whitaker has to say: "I feel overworked. I work hard, but quite honestly sometimes I don't enjoy it anymore. I consider myself a good manager. But it's just a lot of work." What steps can top management take to help Whitaker?

2. Marie Dippolito, supervisor of the records management center, has tried on several occasions during the past three months to make improvements in her office's filing and retrieval methods. Whenever she offers recommendations for change, her superior, Carol Shaw, responds with remarks such as, "It's always been done this way. Your suggestions were tried once before but without success." Dippolito feels these are not satisfactory answers and would like to bypass Shaw and go to a higher level of authority for approval of her ideas. Discuss how you feel Dippolito should solve her problem.

3. A survey of men and women leaders, undertaken by the Leadership Foundation of the International Women's Forum, found little similarity between men and women when they describe their leadership performance and how they usually influence those with whom they work.[14] Would you expect women to describe themselves in ways that characterize *transformational* leadership or *transactional* leadership? Explain.

4. Over the years the Velez Company has added new administrative services units, such as word processing, automated records retrieval, and desktop publishing, in the main office in San Jacinto, California. Each of these units is headed by a manager who is responsible for all such service activities in the main office and who, in turn, reports to you, the administrative services director. Next year the firm plans to expand its operations to the Mission Viejo, Redondo Beach, and Glendale areas within the state. If the new branch plan works out satisfactorily, it is planned to set up branch offices in adjacent states. As the director of administrative services, you wonder what plans should be made, or what discussions should take place, regarding the need for continued centralization of these activities or possibly the need to decentralize this work. Prepare a list of important questions that should be asked in a forthcoming planning meeting.

5. Explain the significance of the following statement made by a practical-minded student of administrative office management: "All this theory about management is unnecessary. What I really need is a lot of facts about how to run an office."

[14]Judy B. Rosener, "Ways Women Lead," *Harvard Business Review* (November–December, 1990), pp. 119–125.

c
o
n
t

6. "The delegation of decision making, which is sometimes known as decentralization, is a current fad. Many apparently believe that all problems would dissolve if only the boss would delegate and decentralize." What are your reactions to these comments made by a former chairperson of the board of a large insurance company?

7. Bob Yukimura, supervisor of corporate records for an electronics company, finds himself involved in many operational details even though he does everything necessary to delegate responsibility. In spite of defining authority, delegating to competent people, spelling out the delegation, keeping control, and coaching, he is still burdened with a mass of detailed work. What reasons can you advance for Yukimura's overinvolvement in details of his daily work?

8. Elaine Trimble is seen by her associates as a person concerned mainly with her effectiveness. She strives to do the right things, develop the proper vision, and establish a workable atmosphere that encourages her workers to live up to their full potential. She is very innovative, creative, and receptive to change. Trimble is looked upon as being in charge. From this limited portrait of Trimble, would you label her an administrator, a manager, or a leader? Explain.

CASES FOR CRITICAL THINKING

The following two cases will help you prepare for the problem-solving activities that commence at the end of Chapter 3.

Case 2–1 Developing a Problem-Solving Attitude—A

Victor Gomez has served as supervisor of the accounts payable section of his firm for the past eight years. Gomez takes great pains to see that all invoice details are checked twice by his accounting clerks. Unknown to his clerks, Gomez manually spot-checks 10 to 15 percent of their work, which he is required to initial for approval. Other aspects of his supervisory style seem unique. For example, he insists that all employees keep neat desk areas (which he monitors each week). Also, from 8:50 to 9:10 A.M. each day, Gomez positions himself near the office entrance to check on his workers' punctuality.

None of Gomez's five clerks have objected to his supervisory style. In fact, he is very popular with the group. He keeps records of their birthdays and other important anniversaries in order to remember them in some special way. Also, he seems to be very sympathetic to their personal needs for time off from work when the occasion demands it.

Gomez's section has an excellent record of productivity. Largely for this reason, he has been chosen to "move up" to the position of office manager. In this position, he will be responsible for five sections, each headed by a supervisor who, in turn, is responsible for the work of eight to ten persons, depending on the section involved.

As he starts his new job, Gomez has a good talk with himself in which he looks back approvingly at the success of his work as accounts payable supervisor. Thus, he believes he can effectively manage the entire office using the same leadership style.

1. What important problem(s) would you anticipate in this case?

2. Considering Gomez's work history, how would you expect him to delegate work? Does it appear that he has applied equally well the principles of management discussed at the beginning of this chapter?

3. How do you classify Gomez's leadership style? Do you feel that his past leadership style will be effective in his relationship with the five supervisors? Explain.

Case 2–2 Developing a Problem-Solving Attitude—B

The Osaka Company is a Japanese-owned firm, located in northern California, which manufactures computers. The company has expanded steadily over the past ten years and recently received several large orders from the government for laptop and notebook computers. The expansion of the office activities has taken place under three vice presidents, each of whom is in charge of one of the main functions of manufacturing, marketing, and finance. However, no one person in the company has been assigned responsibility for administrative office services.

The three functional vice presidents maintain their own records storage, secretarial, mailing, and reprographics departments. Supervisors are in charge of the functional activities under each of the vice presidents. Part of the organization chart indicates that in the manufacturing area, supervisors are in charge of purchasing, receiving, storing, accounts payable, factory payroll, cost accounting, and shipping. Under the heading of marketing, supervisors are in charge of sales, advertising, credit, and accounts receivable. Under the direction of the vice president in charge of finance, there are supervisors of financial accounting, taxes, government reports, and office payroll.

Many of these supervisors have been shifted into supervisory positions with little knowledge of systems or methods. The supervisors find it difficult to complete their work because of inefficiency, lack of knowledge, and needless duplication of records and work. Office equipment is ordered periodically and placed where it is thought it will be used later.

The president of the company, Sumio Osaka, has recently been overwhelmed by the difficulty of obtaining information needed to manage the firm. Whenever information is needed, several different sources must be contacted, and much time is wasted locating the information. Osaka is also beginning to notice idle equipment in the offices and delays in the preparation of important operating reports.

Last week Osaka held a conference with the vice presidents and indicated his dissatisfaction. The three executives feel they cannot change any of their work routines or give up any of their personnel.

1. What major problem areas do you see in this case?

2. Are there any principles of management being violated by the officers of the company? Explain.

3. Under which form of organization is the company presently operating? Do you find any evidence of decentralized managerial authority? Explain.

Case 2–3 Organizational Chart: Computer Option (available on disk)

3

DEVELOPING PROBLEM-SOLVING SKILLS

GOALS FOR THIS CHAPTER

After completing this chapter, you should be able to:

1. Describe the relationships among problem solving, decision making, and choice making.
2. Explain the concept of productivity and its dependence on adequate problem solving.
3. List the main factors in the problem-solving environment and their interrelationships.
4. Outline the essential features of each step in the problem-solving process.
5. Discuss the typical barriers to problem solving.

As you saw in the first two chapters, management is a complex process with many organizational functions to coordinate. At the very core of the management process is problem solving, which requires that managers (1) identify problems to be solved and (2) delegate the solving of problems to the most qualified individuals. Usually these are the people who will need as little information, time, and money as possible to make the best decisions.

Figure 3–1 shows that problem solving, decision making, and choice making are closely related. **Problem solving,** the broadest of the three concepts, is the process of recognizing or identifying a discrepancy (or gap) between an actual and a desired state of affairs and then taking action to resolve the discrepancy (i.e., to close the gap).

Decision making, on the other hand, includes those problem-solving activities that range from the recognition of a problem through the choice of a preferred solution. Thus, decision making in its broadest context is a central part of the problem-solving process. The third activity—and the narrowest in scope—shown in Figure 3–1 is **choice making,** which represents the process of evaluating and selecting among alternatives available for solving a problem. Much of the remainder of this chapter is built upon a correct understanding of these three terms and a clear appreciation of the basic universal problem facing each organizational manager: *finding an effective way to meet the organization's objectives.*

In the last quarter of this century, which has been characterized by unsettling changes in our global economy, the management profession has focused on the topic of productivity improvement as its primary objective. Because of the widespread need to understand problems so that managers can become better problem solvers, this chapter discusses in detail the entire problem-solving process. Included are an explanation of

Figure 3–1
Activities Involved in Problem Solving, Decision Making, and Choice Making

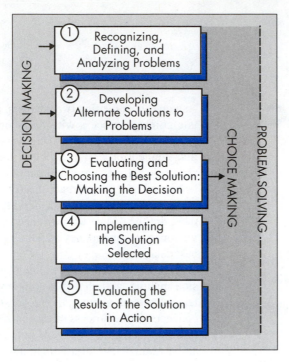

Problem solving is a managerial skill. It involves an understanding of the nature and types of responsibilities facing managers. Further, problem solving requires a person's ability to tie together organizational goals with the abilities to plan, organize, and use the many resources needed to meet those goals. In turn, these problem-solving skills must be coordinated among people and departments, which requires the ability to understand, communicate, and cooperate with people. Without these various abilities and the skill to use them to produce workable solutions, managers cannot solve problems.

Typically, AOMs face operating problems that put into action the policies made by top management. Such problems generally fall into two categories: (1) *routine problems* that are well structured and that occur regularly with the operation of the business and (2) *nonroutine problems* that are unique and that require creative solutions. Typical routine, or programmed, problems are the reordering of office supplies and the recruiting of office employees. Common nonroutine, or unprogrammed, problems include setting up a new branch office, converting from a manual to a computerized filing system, selecting appropriate software, and dealing with an unexpected drop in office productivity. All types of managers—whether they are problem avoiders, problem solvers, or problem seekers who routinely search for problems to solve—can benefit from a study of the problem-solving process, which begins by defining the concept of *problem*.

the office manager's responsibilities for problem solving; a discussion of the concept of productivity as an important problem in the office; guidelines for solving human, systems, and economic problems; and a summary of common problem areas to which the OM must be alert.

ADMINISTRATIVE OFFICE MANAGERS AS PROBLEM SOLVERS

Each of the managerial functions of planning, organizing, leading, and controlling may be regarded in a broad way as a *problem* area. Administrative office managers are responsible for solving many basic functional problems, such as the following:

1. Setting the right objectives.
2. Organizing the employees, equipment, and space to meet these objectives.
3. Directing and supervising the workforce in a productive manner.
4. Putting into place controls over systems and procedures to ensure that high levels of productivity are maintained.

Definitions of *Problem*

To understand the concept of *problem,* which has both general and specific meanings, let's examine two common definitions:

1. In a specific sense, a **problem** is a *question to be answered.* Examples of such a question are:

   How can the accuracy of word processing operators be improved?

   How well is management communicating to the employees?

   In what departments can operating costs be trimmed?

2. In a general, academic sense, a **problem** is considered as the difference between *what is* (the present condition) and *what should be* (the goal). In a similar way, a problem may be considered as the difference between *that which is known* and *that which is unknown but desired.* (See Figure 3–2, which shows in very general form a broad definition of a problem.) Examples of this broad view of a problem are:

The difference between the actual number of letters produced in the office and the production standard (or quota) set by the OM.

The difference between the present turnover of office employees in the firm (a known fact) and the turnover of this group in competing firms (unknown but desired information).

Most people regard Definition 1—a question to be answered—as simple and easy to use. For this reason, problem statements such as those found in Definition 2 are often revised into question form. For instance, the first example for Definition 2 can easily be changed into a question such as:

What is the difference between the number of letters produced in the office and the number expected of average word processing operators?

A word processing operator might state the problem to be solved in a more personal question form:

How many more letters must I complete in order to meet my quota?

Such problem-questions can be answered by obtaining production records and by comparing these amounts with the standards set by the office manager. The difference between the two amounts represents the *extent of the problem.* A much more difficult problem to solve—again stated in question form—is, "How can the office manager motivate the word processors to increase their production in order to meet their work quotas with accuracy?" or, "How can the OM be certain that the standards set for the workers are fair?"

Office problems usually fall into two categories. The first category involves the destruction, removal, or containment of *something present but not desired,* such as absenteeism, noise, inaccurate accounting work, or poor morale. The second category of office problems involves acquiring *something not present but desired.* Examples of this category are: creating good working relationships, achieving a high performance rating as an office supervisor, or receiving a promotion. All of the problems identified in this textbook fall into one or the other of these two categories, as do all the problems in today's offices.

Practical office managers consider problems as present or anticipated sources of dissatisfaction for which more desirable alternatives exist. If managers are faced with a number of undesirable circumstances *over which they have no control,* such as the high cost of acquiring badly needed space, then no problem exists. Such circumstances are a part of the external environment of the firm, and managers should not waste their time on conditions they cannot change.

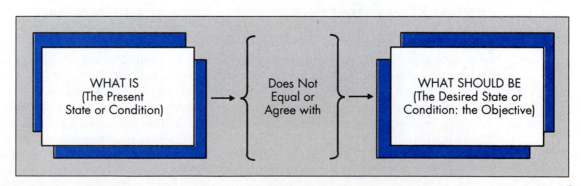

Figure 3–2
A General Definition of a Problem

WHAT IS (The Present State or Condition)   Does Not Equal or Agree with   WHAT SHOULD BE (The Desired State or Condition: the Objective)

Problem Solving and Productivity

Problems in the office have a direct bearing on the *quantity* and the *quality* of work produced by the office staff. For this reason, office productivity has become a major factor in the economic struggle against inflation and the mounting costs of office operations.

Productivity refers to the ratio between the resources (inputs) used by a business firm (hours of labor, capital, machinery and equipment, raw materials such as information, and energy) and what the firm realizes from using those resources. Or, as economists define it, productivity is the net wealth created after subtracting the inputs (those resources mentioned above) and throughputs (the activities required to process work) from the outputs or final results.

The office productivity concept is illustrated in Figure 3–3. It defines the productive office as one in which the value of the output produced outweighs the costs of the inputs and the costs of the throughputs, or processing activities.

Within the past few decades, the activities of office personnel have shifted dramatically from manual clerical work to computer processing services. With this shift have come higher salaries, which raise the costs of office operations unless workers increase output. At the same time, space and energy costs have skyrocketed and more government regulations have been imposed, increasing the amount of paperwork and office costs.

Measuring the output of an office staff is difficult because much of the work is mental and hence intangible in nature. However, most surveys show that the output of each labor hour in the office has declined as the cost of that labor increases. *This means that office workers produce less while earning higher salaries.* To a lesser extent, this situation exists in the factory, where prices for goods and services must be raised to cover the increasing costs of production. If, however, productivity levels can be improved—that is, if more units of work can be produced in a given period of time relative to the prices of resources in the economy—then productivity will have increased. This, in turn, will lower labor costs and, before long, will also lower the prices asked for products and services.

Alone, the AOM has little control over some resources used in the office. For example, energy costs are set outside the firm; prices of furniture and equipment are also set by the manufacturers and vendors; and salaries of some office workers are directly influenced by prevailing rates in the community. However, the AOM has the power to solve low-productivity problems within the office and thus exert a positive effect on the costs of producing goods and services.

To assist AOMs, major efforts are needed to improve productivity. In the United States, many not-for-profit centers have been created to study productivity and the quality of work life. The most prestigious is the *American Productivity Center (APC),* in Houston, Texas, which is funded by many blue-ribbon U.S. firms. The APC engages in research on productivity improvement and distributes information on its findings through short courses and publications.

Figure 3–3
The Office Productivity Concept

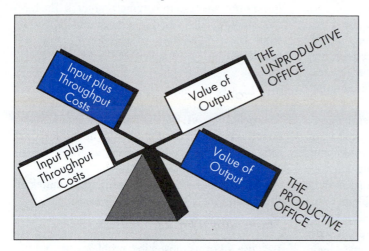

In one landmark study, the APC investigated the problems of white-collar productivity, a major concern of AOMs. In this nationwide study, 1,000 office workers and managers from 122 firms were asked to answer the question, "How can white-collar productivity be increased without sacrificing the quality of work life?"[1] While the findings of this study are noteworthy, space limitations prevent their being included. What is more important for this chapter, however, is the set of conclusions drawn by the APC before starting the study. Figure 3–4 outlines the main conclusions drawn by the APC along with the principal features of each. Such a list offers useful guidelines for the AOM who is studying productivity problems in the office.

THE PROBLEM-SOLVING PROCESS

Solving problems is a universal occupation. On and off the job, we face small and large problems; personal and social problems; and cultural, economic, and political problems, many of

---

[1]The reader is referred to the full study, *White-Collar Productivity: The National Challenge,* compiled by the American Productivity Center and sponsored by Steelcase, Inc., Grand Rapids, MI 49501.

Figure 3–4
Conclusions Drawn in the APC Study of White-Collar Productivity

Conclusions Drawn About White-Collar Productivity	Main Factors Considered in the Conclusion
1. Productivity improvement depends on the integration of people, tools, and places.	Human resource development, automated office systems, and environmental design.
2. Work means more than titles. It is the nature of the work that is important.	Interdependence of people, the routine or variation in the work, and the extent to which the work involves information.
3. Improved productivity means better delivery of products and services.	Quality of output that results from coordinating the work of managers, supervisors, and subordinates is more important than individual efficiency.
4. Productivity results from a balance between efficiency and effectiveness.	Effectiveness centered on such factors as timeliness and quality of services provided; efficiency centered on cost reduction.
5. Productivity relates to the quality of work life.	Work satisfaction depends upon office surroundings, and job performance depends on how the workers feel at the end of the workday.

Source: *White-Collar Productivity: The National Challenge,* compiled by the American Productivity Center and sponsored by Steelcase, Inc.

which are interrelated. For example, experienced workers agree that office politics account for many personal problems on the job, some of which can be traced to conditions in the home. And problems with achieving high levels of clarity in composing written communications may stem from the office employees' lack of interest, poor attitudes, inadequate skills, or a combination of these factors.

Usually, problems do not "arrive" at the OM's desk in a prearranged, ready-to-be-solved form. Instead, the OM finds an unorganized, unarranged, conflicting situation involving sensitive employee feelings and information that may be both relevant and irrelevant to the problem. There will be factual data as well as biased points of view about the ways that office procedures work or fail to work. Because of such typical conditions surrounding most problems, we must take a systematic, logical, and unbiased approach to solve problems. With such an approach, we can bring our best and fairest thinking on a problem and thus ensure that the most appropriate solution will result.

On the surface, it appears that there are many different types and forms of problems; however, in reality only the context or environment in which they occur is different. Thus, the general characteristics of most problems are very similar. For example, too high a cost of producing copies of reports for a department over a one-year period has many of the same general characteristics as the problem of too little office space available for comfortable, efficient work performance. When we carefully study both situations, we find that the *present conditions* fail to meet the *desired conditions*. Therefore, we must determine the extent of the differences between the present and the desired states. Once we have accomplished this, we can search for specific means of closing the gap between these conditions.

Simply stated, the *process* of solving problems remains the same for these two situations as well as for all other problem-solving situations. First, we must understand the nature of the problem before that understanding can be turned into action as details about the specific problem are clarified. Thus, a systematic approach to solving problems

is required, keeping in mind the environment within which problems occur and the frequent difficulties we face in solving problems. Each of these topics is discussed in this section along with some basic guidelines to solving all types of problems.

The Problem-Solving Environment

The **problem-solving environment** includes the conditions surrounding the problem and the specific factors directly involved in its solution. Some of these factors can be controlled by the AOM and others cannot. The principal features of this environment are discussed below.

Multicultural Backgrounds

Because all of us must solve problems, our multicultural backgrounds play important roles in problem solving. Persons born and reared in rural areas often develop values very different from those of people living in metropolitan areas. Ethnic groups with widely differing backgrounds bring widely different attitudes and values to the workplace. To illustrate, U.S. business firms and governmental agencies as well as colleges and universities are seeking to develop closer working ties with their counterparts in the Middle East and in the Orient. Students of intercultural communication point out the widely differing values held by the people in these areas—values relating to the home and family, to their elders, to their religious convictions, to their use of time, and to their concepts of fairness and equity in the workplace.

For example, an Israeli manufacturer of semiconductors notes how its organizational culture and management style differ greatly from those of its parent company in the United States. The Israeli culture, influenced by the cultures of both Eastern Europe and Islam, places emphasis on the *group*. The individual worker acts primarily within and as part of a group. The American culture, on the other hand, with its foundations in the Protestant ethos of Western societies, concentrates on private enterprise. Here, the emphasis is on the *individual worker,* not on the group. The goal of the Israeli firm is to integrate the strengths of its culture with those of its parent company to form a decision-making process that suits its needs best.[2]

As another example, we find that conducting an office interview with a Japanese executive calls for the U.S. participant to understand the many cultural differences existing between the two people. Failure to observe some of the important interview protocols (who enters the room first, the time and nature of the handshake, and the times of arrival and departure) can quickly make such an interview ineffective and the interviewer viewed as uncaring or even insulting.

Human Attitudes

Our diverse cultural backgrounds are responsible for developing attitudes that each of us brings to our jobs. Included in this important problem-solving factor are our attitudes toward ourselves; our attitudes toward other workers, including supervisors and coworkers; and our attitudes toward the work. Attitudes are complex mental outlooks that we develop and strengthen through the years and, as a result, are difficult to change.

One of the most common—and serious—human attitudes in problem solving is a resistance to change. Studies show that resisting change is almost instinctive—that doing things differently upsets comfortable ways of thinking and of doing work. In addition, change involves risks, especially the risk of failure. The following comments, often made in problem-solving situations in the office, illustrate this resistance-to-change attitude:

That's a great idea for some firms, but not for us.

We've never done it that way.

It just won't work.

We haven't the time now to consider that idea.

The budget won't permit it.

We're not quite ready for such an idea yet.

Not a bad idea, but our office is different.

That's too academic; we're practical-minded here.

That idea involves too much paperwork.

It's against company policy.

We're too small (or too big) for that.

Let's form a committee to study the idea.

Generally, the use of such expressions represents an excuse to veto an idea and procrastinate or even avoid action that would lead to changes in personnel, work organization, or work procedures in the office. Such negative attitudes effectively stop progress because they are serious barriers to problem solving. On the other hand, positive attitudes stemming from open minds that are willing to consider suggestions for change will lead to improved productivity, which is vital to all office functions. Positive attitudes are discussed in more detail later in this chapter.

Basic Elements of the Problem

Before we can define a problem in clear form, let alone solve it, we must identify all the basic elements of the problem. The principal elements causing problems in the office are (1) *human resources,* including the decision maker responsible for solving the problem; (2) *space* in which the office work is done; (3) *machines and equipment;* (4) *time* required for completing the work; (5) *systems and procedures* needed to perform the work; and (6) *other resources,* including *capital,* the *psychophysiological environment,* and the *information* available for performing the work. An understanding of these elements as well as a knowledge of the present state, the desired state, and related factors is needed to solve office problems effectively.

The Present State

As we mentioned earlier in our definition of *problem,* a problem to be solved can be viewed as a state or condition that requires improvement (as in the case of an existing system, a procedure, or a worker's attitude). Or, the problem may require obtaining valid information on a subject about which information is lacking. Common examples of the *present state,* that is, the current office problems, are:

[2]Eli Lazar, "Values Must Blend in Overseas Operations," *Personnel Journal* (February, 1993), p. 67.

Illustration 3–2 Limited time and resources are basic elements of many problems in the workplace.

1. Low morale of key office workers.
2. Unequal distribution of work within the office.
3. Difficulties in accessing records requested from the electronic files.
4. Workers bored by so-called dull paper-filing tasks.
5. Too much work for the size of the staff.
6. Failure of the staff to work at a reasonable pace, leading to lower-than-expected productivity.
7. Inability of supervisors to delegate tasks.
8. Little or no measurement of office work and, hence, problems in compensating workers for their contributions to the work done.
9. Overemphasis on the values of office automation and at the same time underemphasis on the human factors in an automated setting.
10. Lack of coordination by the office manager regarding the various functions under his or her jurisdiction.

Each of these conditions is considered as a problem when it is compared with the desired state discussed in the next section.

The Desired State

Usually, the *desired state* or condition of an office operation is described in the statements of objectives, goals, or expected outcomes toward which all office work is directed. (The planning function, which includes setting organizational objectives, was discussed at length in Chapter 2.) Examples of general objectives include the following:

1. Increasing productivity.
2. Reducing office expenses.
3. Decreasing absenteeism.

To be useful, such general objectives must be converted into more specific objectives against which the office work can be measured. For example, an AOM along with the office supervisors may convert the above objectives into these specific goals:

1. Increasing production of customers' billings by 10 percent without a corresponding increase in employees.

2. Reducing office overtime expense by 25 percent.
3. Decreasing absenteeism in the computer center by 5 percent.

If, for example, an AOM has set a specific objective of reducing departmental telephone expenses by 15 percent, a problem will exist if at the end of the period such expenses have *increased* by 8 percent. The present state would then exceed the desired state by 23 percent. This is the amount representing the difference between the *present state* (an increase of 8 percent) and *what is desired* (a decrease of 15 percent). Such a problem can be considered as solved only when this difference is reduced to zero.

Some personnel problems, such as personality conflicts and low morale, do not lend themselves to solutions stated in quantitative terms. This is true because neither the present state of personnel nor the desired state is easily measured, which accounts for much of the AOM's difficulty in solving human problems.

Controllable and Uncontrollable Factors

When buying an automobile, we can control such items as the make and model to buy, which accessories to choose, and what financing plan to select. Such factors may be either quantitative, such as the number of doors or cylinders, or qualitative, such as the type of seat covering. OMs, too, have control over many factors in their environments, such as which workers are hired, to whom work is delegated, what procedures to design for performing the work, what makes and models of machines to buy, and whether or not to purchase service agreements on these machines.

In many cases, however, some of the factors may *not* be controllable by the OM. Some firms have policies requiring that all office machines be placed under service agreements or that such machines be purchased exclusively from one vendor. Working hours that are specified by top management and over which the OM has no control may also affect the office personnel and contribute to office problems. Closely related to these uncontrollable factors are limitations that

are imposed on the office function. For example, the size of the budget for salaries may limit how many new staff members are hired to help reduce a steady backlog of work or how much renovation of badly needed space is permitted. Too, when top management allows three full workdays for the preparation of a major report that realistically requires one week, a time "bind" exists that must be carefully managed if the work is to be completed on schedule.

Problem-Solving Abilities

The problem solver needs both knowledge of the problem and a broad background concerning its possible causes. In addition, an effective problem solver needs three types of human abilities: creative, logical, and intuitive, which are discussed in this section.

Creative Ability

Creativity is our ability to apply imagination and ingenuity as we develop a novel approach or a unique solution to a problem. Many people can apply the word *creativity* more easily to art than to business. However, creativity is not restricted to the artist. On the contrary, creativity exists in every worker and is an absolute requirement for the innovative manager and the office staff. The creative office worker is one who can develop useful ideas for solving problems. Such a person is able to suggest many alternate options as possible solutions for the problem in question. And when creative individuals work together, each adding to the supply of new ideas, one worker can often "hitchhike" on the others' ideas, which enriches the whole problem-solving process.

Although managers and supervisors cannot demand creativity from their workers, they can provide a climate which encourages creativity. We find that various techniques, such as those discussed below, are used by managers and supervisors to develop creativity.

Brainstorming. Brainstorming is a group technique for creating a large quantity of ideas by freewheeling contributions made without criticism. A small problem-solving group may generate dozens of ideas in a few minutes. (Fifty ideas in five minutes is not an uncommon number during a brainstorming session.) Brainstorming requires that four rules be followed:

1. Defer judgments; that is, initially the group does not stop to decide whether the ideas are worthwhile or not.
2. Freewheel or "hang loose" without concern for the ideas of others.
3. Do not wait for an idea to come but rather develop another idea out of the last one given (the so-called hitchhiking process).
4. Aim for a quantity of ideas as a goal; it can be decided in a later evaluation session which ideas are valuable and which are not.

The main idea behind brainstorming is the more ideas generated, the greater the opportunity for good ideas. Brainstorming is especially useful in creating alternate solutions in problem solving, such as when your class works on a solution to this problem:

> In our high-rise office building, a man comes to work each morning. He boards the elevator, presses the 10th floor button, gets out, and walks to his office on the 15th floor. At closing time, he boards the elevator on the 15th floor, pushes the ground floor (lobby) button, rides to the lobby, and gets out. What is the man up to?[3]

Idea Quota. The **idea quota** is another technique for stimulating the creation of ideas in which a fixed number of new ideas is required in a stated period of time, thus forcing extreme concentration by participants. To use this technique in a meeting, you as a manager may ask each of the employees to write down:

> Five ways to reduce proofreading errors, in one minute.

> Six ways to improve spelling awareness in correspondence, in two minutes.

Seven ways to make performance appraisal procedures more useful, in three minutes.

Forced Relationship. A third technique, **forced relationship,** requires problem solvers to consider in a new way something that is already known. Familiar topics are everywhere if the workers only take time to see them in a new light. For example, a group of workers is given the following question: "What would be the result if you were to combine an office desk with a four-drawer file?" In answering this question, the workers are forced to see a new relationship (a desk connected to a file cabinet) made up of familiar items (a desk and a file cabinet). From an intensive study of such relationships, alternate points of view are developed which, in turn, become alternate solutions to the problem.[4]

Nominal Group Technique (NGT). A variation of brainstorming, the **nominal group technique (NGT),** is particularly useful for solving problems related to office productivity improvement. NGT is distinguished from other group processes in that the participants work alone, silently, in small *noninteraction* groups of five to nine persons. One by one, each member of the group responds in writing with possible solutions to a problem, such as how to obtain more cost-effective use of copying equipment and facsimile (FAX) machines. Later, guided by a facilitator, the members read their ideas aloud, but with no discussion or criticism. Next, the ideas are recorded, discussed, and clarified as needed. Finally, the participants individually and silently rate or rank all alternative solutions in priority order.

---

[3]Harvey J. Brightman, *Problem Solving: A Logical and Creative Approach* (Atlanta: Business Publishing Division, Georgia State University, 1980), p. 84.

[4]There is a large body of literature available on developing creativity and understanding its role in decision making. At the outset, you should consider the many contributions of Alex F. Osborn, *the* pioneer in developing creative thinking, and the growing list of publications from the Center for Creative Leadership, 5000 Laurinda Drive, Greensboro, NC 27402-1660. For an excellent discussion of many useful techniques for generating and evaluating ideas, see Arthur B. VanGundy, *Techniques of Structured Problem Solving,* 2nd ed. (New York: Van Nostrand Reinhold, 1988), Chaps. 4–7.

Logical Ability

Creativity and logic work together in the difficult task of problem solving. The effective use of logic requires us to collect relevant, current facts; to use them in an orderly, unbiased way; and to reason in a systematic, analytical manner with an open mind to solve the problem at hand.

The logical person does not have preconceived ideas that impede a fair answer to the problem in question. Rather, such a person uses the mind to weigh carefully all information; to get as much assistance as possible from competent, unbiased persons; and to use such information while working toward a fair solution. For example, the creative employee might develop a number of artistic ideas for making the office area more attractive in appearance. On the other hand, the logical worker would compare the cost of such recommendations with the available budget and might come to the conclusion that most of the ideas are too expensive to implement. Perhaps the most common example of logical ability in problem solving is found in programming a computer, which is discussed later in the text.

Intuitive Ability

While the literature on business problem solving has historically emphasized creative and logical abilities, we find that a third ability—intuitive ability—is stressed by experienced managers. As the name suggests, intuitive ability is made up of intuition, the emotional feelings and judgment that managers develop based on long years of experience using methods that have worked well for them. When managers say, "I've got a gut feeling this is going to work for us," they are using their intuitive ability. Intuitive thinkers use hunch, a "sixth sense," and unspoken or unverbalized messages (discussed as nonverbal communications in Chapter 5).

By using fewer people to make decisions than the logical, systematic problem solvers, intuitive thinkers can move quickly to consider more simplified solutions than other types of problem solvers. In doing so, however, such intuitive thinkers run the risk of ignoring and failing to consider all aspects of a problem. Managers, in-

cluding AOMs, use creative and logical abilities to solve problems, but frequently they fall back on their intuition about what seems right and wrong in a decision-making situation, especially when time is limited.[5]

Steps in Problem Solving

Generally, people solve problems in one of two ways. People with considerable common sense, much work experience, and a good feel for the situation often solve simple problems in an *informal,* intuitive way without specifically considering the steps outlined in this chapter. Other people, however, use a more *formal* approach to problem solving, especially if the problems are unusually complex or of long duration. This latter approach is emphasized in this section and outlined in Figure 3–5. It shows in logical, sequential order the steps required to *state* (define and analyze) the problem and then to *solve* it, an approach that is especially useful in problem solving. Each step in this process is discussed briefly in this section. Later in the chapter, all steps are combined in a case that illustrates the complete problem-solving cycle.

Step 1: Recognize the Problem

To solve a problem, we must first recognize the problem, which is not as easy as it seems. Too often, we mistake problems for **symptoms,** which are signs indicating that a problem may exist. An ailing patient, for example, may complain of a lack of appetite, which, in turn, seems to be responsible for weight loss. Yet the physician, who is trained to differentiate between problems and symptoms, recognizes these "problems" as symptoms of the real problem, cancer, and accordingly takes steps to treat the real problem.

---

[5]A valuable source of information on the role of intuition in management is Weston H. Agor. Two of his useful publications are *Intuitive Management: Integrating Left and Right Brain Management Skills* (Englewood Cliffs, NJ: Prentice-Hall, 1984) and *The Logic of Intuitive Decision Making: A Research-Based Approach for Top Management* (Westport, CA: Greenwood Press, 1986).

Figure 3–5
Steps in the
Problem-
Solving
Process

STATE THE PROBLEM		SOLVE THE PROBLEM	
Step No.	Process Steps	Step No.	Process Steps
1	Recognize the problem	5	Develop alternate solutions to the problem
2	Define the problem	6	Choose the best solution
3	Collect relevant information	7	Implement the solution
4	Analyze relevant information	8	Evaluate the results

In an office, a common symptom may be the high turnover of personnel. This can be traced to a condition of low morale, which may lead to the more basic problem, the manager's inability to lead and delegate. Poor productivity may be a symptom of inefficient workflow, which may then be traced to the root problem of overcrowded working conditions. Typical sources of problems are the personal dissatisfactions of employees, poor working conditions, insufficient compensation, and inefficient work methods.

Step 2: Define the Problem

Answering the question, "What is the problem?" requires that we first carefully define the problem. At the outset, each of us as a problem solver brings to the situation insight that comes from the sum total of our experiences. From available information, we then seek to determine the goals that were given to the worker or department and the apparent reasons for not achieving those goals. Thus, *defining* means *deciding* what the main issues of the problem are and clarifying the differences between the major goals and the actual operating results. The use of relevant information, therefore, is very important in defining the problem. In haste, some problem solvers mistakenly assume that the difficulties found in the office are obvious; therefore, the definition phase is bypassed, which usually results in inadequate solutions. For this reason, the axiom "The problem well defined is half solved" is good advice.

Step 3: Collect Relevant Information[6]

While this step in the problem-solving process is listed as Step 3 in Figure 3–5, actually the collection of relevant information is not limited to just this one step. Information is collected throughout the problem-solving cycle.

If we are to be efficient information collectors, we must be good questioners in seeking useful information to solve the problem. To assist in the process of data collection, you will find this simple questioning framework invaluable:

1. WHAT is the real problem, and what are the principal components or elements, including symptoms, that make up the problem?
2. WHERE did the problem occur? WHY did it occur there?
3. WHEN did the problem occur? WHY did it occur at that time?
4. HOW did the problem occur? WHY did it occur in that way?
5. To WHOM did the problem occur? WHY did it occur to him or her (or them)?
6. WHO should make the final decision for solving the problem?

---

[6]In the computer systems field, two terms—data and information—are commonly used. In this context, *data* refer to alphabetic and numeric characters that serve as the raw material to be processed into the finished form, *information*. In this chapter, however, we use the term *information* in a broad, generic sense that includes *data*.

No easy set of guidelines is available for collecting information. Rather, a thorough knowledge of the problem and its setting, plus good judgment, will point the way to gathering information.

Step 4: Analyze Relevant Information

After the information has been gathered, we are able to analyze the main aspects of the problem, piecing together as much information as possible to ensure an accurate picture of the situation. In the process of analysis, many complex mental activities are involved, during which time the majority of our real learning about the problem takes place.

To analyze a problem means to examine each element and its relationship to the other elements and to the whole problem; to discover interrelationships and patterns; to compare the problem with other situations; and to sort, sequence, or order the problem. In general, to analyze a problem means to search for insight within the problem, similar to the way an X-ray provides an "insight" into the human body.

An illustration of analytical thinking about an office problem shows how questioning, further questioning, and comparing of processes are necessary. For example, suppose a male office supervisor in the purchasing department suddenly starts coming in late for work and is being harassed by his peers. The work of his entire section continues to decline. The supervisor has been an efficient worker for the past 10 years. He has an employed wife and three teenage children.

To analyze this problem, we must answer such questions as:

1. What is the real problem? What are only symptoms?
2. Who can help me solve this problem?
3. Who are the supervisor's closest associates?
4. What is the total scope of the supervisor's responsibilities?
5. Which factors in the problem can be controlled and which cannot?
6. How does the supervisor's personal life relate to his work on the job?
7. What does the supervisor himself have to say about the problem? Does he have a reasonable explanation for it?
8. What are the viewpoints of the supervisor's associates (his coworkers and those reporting directly to him)?
9. How extensive or important does the problem seem? Is there agreement about its severity?

By asking such questions during the analysis stage, we can obtain answers that are useful in developing solutions to the problem.

Step 5: Develop Alternate Solutions to the Problem

This is the creative phase of the problem-solving process. At this time, a useful set of **hypotheses** or alternate solutions to the problem is developed. This phase involves finding better ways or means for reaching goals, developing useful options, and uncovering possible choices, thus providing various possibilities for action. For example, an insurance office manager faced the problem of insufficient staff to handle a greatly enlarged workload. The three key alternate solutions brainstormed by the problem-solving group were: (1) hire three well-qualified workers, (2) schedule the present staff to work overtime on a regular basis, and (3) obtain workers from a temporary help service. Frequently, a **decision tree,** as shown in Figure 3–6, is used to chart the alternate courses of action for solving the problem and some of the probable consequences stemming from each course of action.

In one office workflow problem, analysis showed that many conditions were blocking the smooth flow of work. When a group of workers sought to solve this problem, they used the following questions to develop possible solutions to the problem:

1. *Elimination.* What procedures, forms and reports, and office positions can we eliminate?
2. *Rearrangement.* Can we resequence the work or the job assignments, or rearrange the office layout? If so, how?
3. *Modification.* What new form, shape, or "twist" can we give to the work procedures? Can we assign more work to some employees and less to others? Can we include more or less work in the procedures themselves?
4. *Substitution.* Can we substitute certain work-

Figure 3–6
A Decision Tree Showing Alternate Solutions to a Problem

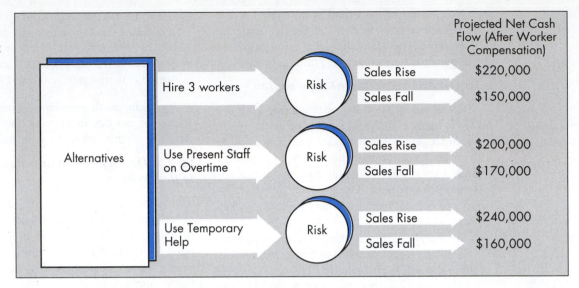

					Projected Net Cash Flow (After Worker Compensation)
	Hire 3 workers	Risk	Sales Rise		$220,000
			Sales Fall		$150,000
Alternatives	Use Present Staff on Overtime	Risk	Sales Rise		$200,000
			Sales Fall		$170,000
	Use Temporary Help	Risk	Sales Rise		$240,000
			Sales Fall		$160,000

ers for others? Can we substitute machines for workers?

5. *Combination.* Can we combine certain procedures, such as those for creating forms, records, and other paperwork?
6. *Enlargement.* What work/workers should we add? Should we allow more time for completing work? Can we place the filed materials in higher, longer, or deeper cabinets?
7. *Reduction.* What work/workers should we subtract? Should we allocate less time for completing work? Can we reduce the quantity of filed materials and still provide adequate information?

Using the adage, "Two heads are better than one," managers have found that small groups of workers with common interests, backgrounds, and motivations can create more solutions to problems than persons working alone. *Work teams,* discussed in the previous chapter, illustrate one effective means for group problem solving. The main advantages cited for using a work team, rather than an individual, in decision making include: (1) more information and knowledge are available, (2) more alternatives are likely to be generated, (3) more acceptance of the final decision is likely, (4) improved communication of the decision may occur, and (5)

more accurate decisions generally result. In the *Dialog from the Workplace,* John M. Carney, a director of human resources, tells of the benefits his workers receive as a result of the emphasis his organization places upon the team approach to problem solving.

On the other hand, the team approach typically takes longer than individuals making decisions, so it is costlier. Often, too, groups may compromise, which makes their actions indecisive and, hence, ineffective. Many times one person dominates the group; in other cases, groupthink sets in. **Groupthink** occurs when the group's desire for consensus and cohesiveness overcomes its desire to reach the best possible decisions. In such cases, the team may arrive at decisions that are not in the best interest of the group or the organization.

Step 6: Choose the Best Solution (Make the Decision)

For various reasons, experience tells us that one of the several alternatives developed in Step 5 will usually be considered better than the others. Typical reasons why we decide to choose one solution over the others are as follows:

1. It takes less time.
2. It will be more effective.

DIALOG FROM THE WORKPLACE

JOHN M. CARNEY

Director of Human Resources
Bancroft, Inc.
Haddonfield, New Jersey

John M. Carney manages the human resources function of Bancroft, Inc., a diverse, not-for-profit human services corporation of more than 600 employees. Now heading a team of five human resources professionals, Carney has had several years of previous experience as a director of human resources in the private, for-profit sector in both union and nonunion settings.

Carney received his B.A. in psychology from the University of Delaware. He did graduate work at Temple University in the field of vocational guidance. Carney is nationally certified as a senior professional in human resources (SPHR).

QUESTION: What methods or techniques of motivation have you found most effective in working with your subordinates?

RESPONSE: My basic belief is that the vast majority of employees want to be productive and do a good job. Therefore, they bring a lot of self-motivation with them to the workplace. What happens once they get there to decrease motivation usually involves the effect of the working environment, in particular the supervisory/management "climate" of the office.

While most situations are somewhat different, over the years I've tried to follow some basic management principles that seem to help maintain the basic self-motivation a person brings to the job. I try to establish clear job expectations for each individual on my team, taking into consideration their skills and abilities, and making sure we both understand what these expectations entail. By doing this, performance criteria are established up front. These expectations become the basis for regular candid feedbacks about performance, a way to recognize employees for good performance and to provide information if corrective action is needed. To me, setting clear job expectations and providing timely feedback form the basis of how employees feel about their jobs. It answers the two questions most employees are always asking in one way or another: What do you want me to do? and How am I doing?

I believe that employees want to be a part of what's happening in their work environment. So, I place a great deal of emphasis on the "team" approach. I try to involve each employee in the planning and goal-setting process that affects our department. Listening to and responding to the ideas of employees makes them feel they are contributing and are an important part of the group.

Also, what has helped me to motivate employees is to review regularly the department's performance as a team. When we honestly look at how we are performing as members of a team and openly discuss what is working or not working, we can make the changes necessary to improve performance. However, the focus has to be on *performance* and not on personality or attitude differences. When this honest climate is developed, employees feel that support is available from their supervisor or from the other employees in the department.

I've also found it helpful for employees to understand how their work contributes to the end results by showing them the importance of their job to the department and the organization. Here I aim to explain how their job or project fits into the "bigger" picture and why the assignment is being given. Just explaining to an employee the reason why something needs to be done is a positive motivator.

Finally, I believe that treating the people you supervise with dignity and respect is a great motivator. Showing a personal interest in how they are doing and where they want to go—their personal goals—sends a message that you as a supervisor are aware of them and have a general interest in them as human beings.

3. It will be preferred by employees (or by management).
4. It will result in greater productivity.
5. Intuition tells me it's the thing to do.
6. It meets the company's ethical and moral standards.
7. It will serve our customers' needs better.
8. It will help to reduce operating costs.

In times of continuing inflation and rising costs, this last reason provides a powerful argument for solving problems in the office. In any case, the solution chosen should be a realistic one.

Step 7: Implement the Solution

Implementing means putting the selected solution to work. By the time we reach this stage, all the reorganizing and other necessary work have been completed. If the problem involves the selection of a new computer for the office, implementing is the step in which the computer is installed and put into operation. If the decision involves the hiring of a new administrative assistant, implementing is the step in which the

Illustration 3–3 Theft of company property is a tangible example of an economic problem that can destroy business profits and information security.

new worker appears for work, is oriented, and begins work.

Step 8: Evaluate the Results

After the solution has been put into operation for a reasonable time, the OM evaluates the results of the solution. In the evaluation process, two factors are considered: (1) *quantity* (how much work is produced) and (2) *quality* (how satisfactory or how convenient is the new operation). The sum of the two factors (quantity and quality) represents the total value of the solution measured against the objectives to be met. As a result of putting a new solution into operation, were the employees more productive? Did the costs of operating the office decrease? Was there a more satisfactory level of morale?

Evaluating involves many complex studies: self-criticism of a group's solution, reviewing present work processes in order to do better in the future, and objectively rating how well the solution removes or decreases the seriousness of the problem. Also, an evaluation may show some unforeseen benefits or some negative side effects that are minor in nature. Or, it may show that the solution was not satisfactory. In the last case, the entire problem-solving process must be repeated, beginning with the definition step.

BARRIERS IN SOLVING OFFICE PROBLEMS

The problem-solving process discussed in this chapter is a **general problem-solving model,** which means it is useful for solving all types of office problems. While all office problems ultimately affect productivity, we know from experience that each problem has certain features that must be recognized if an acceptable solution is to be found. For this reason, you need to understand the common types of office problems and the typical barriers to problem solving that constitute a major portion of the discussion in this textbook. Figure 3–7 outlines the major types of problems encountered by the AOM and the main barriers to solving each type of problem.

Figure 3–7
Major Problems in the Office and Barriers to Their Solution

TYPE OF PROBLEM AND BARRIERS TO ITS SOLUTION		EXAMPLES OF BARRIERS
1. Human	Barrier: Subjective, intangible, emotional human nature	Misperceptions Negative attitudes Attitudes of personnel Interpersonal conflict
2. Systems	Barrier: Inability to achieve higher levels of productivity	Poor working conditions Inefficient use of machines Weak procedures Inadequate training
3. Economic	Barrier: Poor use of available funds and resources	Poor use of time by office workers Theft of company property Failure to develop a sense of cost cutting

Human Problems

Human problems comprise the first and most important set of problems facing the AOM. Such problems deal with individual perceptions, which are often defined as a person's view of the world and his or her fears of failure in it. Some of these problems relate to (1) the attitudes and biases that have evolved during our years of human development; (2) our ethical concepts and value systems; (3) our motivation and interest in our jobs; (4) the fears that many of us have of being laid off or losing the respect of supervisors and coworkers; and (5) our personal skills, such as the effective use of time and the ability to organize, write, and speak effectively. Supervisors and managers also face these problems and additional ones common to the level of their work. Such problems include their inability to set priorities and delegate work, failure to assume assigned responsibilities, reluctance to discipline employees, limited views of their spheres of work, and lack of vision regarding the future needs of their units.

Human problems must be resolved first since people are responsible for all aspects of the office operation. Figure 3–7 illustrates this point clearly, for it shows that human traits, such as those listed below, cause barriers to effective problem solving:

1. We have very limited memories with a capacity to use only a few pieces of information at a time.
2. Of the information we retain, we can process only a limited amount simultaneously since people are basically serial processors of information (item 1, then item 2, then item 3, rather than all three items being processed at one time).
3. Unlike computers, we have limited computational ability and care about the outcomes of our problem solving.
4. We are greatly influenced by the group to which we belong and often make decisions that we think the group would look upon favorably. Similarly, as problem solvers, we are strongly influenced by the organizational environment. Thus, if the organization rewards cautious decisions, the OM's decisions might well be cautious ones, playing it safe.
5. As problem solvers and decision makers, we must often act under considerable stress, which makes it difficult to make decisions in a rational manner.[7]

[7]Ramon J. Aldag and Timothy M. Stearns, *Management,* 2nd ed. (Cincinnati: South-Western Publishing Co., 1991), p. 678.

The major difficulty in dealing with human problems is our subjective, intangible, and emotional nature. This many-sided human quality makes problem solving more difficult because the achievement of objectives is harder to measure. Consequently, the qualities of trust, fair-mindedness, patience, good judgment, and common sense are basic qualifications for persons responsible for solving human problems.

Systems Problems

A second major category of office problems deals with the many facets of systems that are set up to accomplish the assigned work. Examples of this type of problem are overly expensive costs of machine operations; frequent machine breakdown; poor working conditions, including cramped work areas, too little light, and the ineffective operation of air conditioners; inadequate training and inefficient procedures for performing the work; poorly designed forms for recording information; disorganized filing systems; and lack of good control over all phases of the office operation.

Systems problems are much more objective and measurable than human problems. As a result, we can solve systems problems in a more straightforward manner. However, the solutions to such problems still depend on an understanding of the problem and acceptance of the solutions by people.

Economic Problems

Money is doubtless the basic means by which all organizations—profit and not-for-profit—continue to operate, and the misuse of money is a common economic barrier, as shown in Figure 3–7. Office workers face a host of problems rooted in practical economics, including high energy costs in the office, too much time required to do assigned work (remember that "time is money"), lowered productivity, theft of company property, and exceeded office budgets. The typical economic problem we find in offices is that too much money is being spent for the resulting amount of output. Economic problems can be stated in tangible terms (hours of work to be saved or numbers of forms to be eliminated), but the solution to cutting costs still depends on the attitudes and interests of the office staff and the effectiveness of the supervisor and manager in leading the group toward such a goal.

A CASE ILLUSTRATION OF PROBLEM SOLVING

Most real-life problems faced by the AOM are complex. These problems are composed of many facts, details, and relationships that take time and considerable study to understand. In this textbook, problems are presented in case form. For solving these case problems, you should follow these suggestions:

1. Question what is going on—or what has happened—and attempt to determine why the problem occurred.
2. Carefully identify each of the individuals involved and study their backgrounds, work assignments, and motivations.
3. Search for the underlying causes of the problem. Also, make an effort to determine what could have been done to prevent the problem from occurring.
4. Suggest procedures that might be used to prevent a recurrence of the problem.

The following practical case shows the relationships between each of the elements in a problem and how the steps in the problem-solving process are used. The case also provides an example of a report that summarizes the results of the solution to the case problem.

Basic Elements of the Case Problem

In this section, each of the basic elements in the case is discussed so that sufficient background is provided to help you understand the problem and the solution recommended.

The Firm

Village Realty sells real estate—private homes, commercial establishments, farms, and acreages.

Located in a medium-size midwestern city, the firm has long been a member of the local multiple-listing association of realtors that has fifteen member firms. In this association, each member firm is automatically informed of, and has an opportunity to sell, the property listings of all other member firms. On the average, the Village Realty office maintains listings of more than 300 homes, over 100 commercial firms, and 60 to 70 farms and acreages.

The Office Staff

The Village Realty office staff consists of three persons: two salespersons (the owner-manager, Joyce Bryant, and a part-time person, both of whom are paid from commissions on sales) and a full-time secretary. The secretary coordinates the schedules and appointments of the sales staff but does no actual sales work. The part-time salesperson receives 50 percent of the 7 percent commission charged for selling property, a rate agreed upon by all association members.

In such a small-office setting, there is little opportunity for work specialization; thus, each of the workers gets involved in all phases of the operation. This may account for the main source of difficulty—that is, the real problem: *The files on real estate listings are not kept up to date and therefore are not immediately available to salespersons and customers.*

Main Factors to Be Considered

The following factors—some controllable and others uncontrollable—relate directly to the problem. Each is discussed briefly in this section.

Controllable Factors. With better management, Bryant, as owner-manager, believes she could have a reasonable amount of control over most of the following factors:

1. Customers call or come into the office and ask for a certain type of house (ranch style, three-bedroom, brick construction) or ask for a listing of all houses in the $95,000–$125,000 price range in the northeast section of the city. Because Village Realty does not file listings by type of house or price, the office staff has trouble identifying such houses quickly. This

situation causes the most difficulty during the busy season (April through August), but it occurs five to ten times daily throughout the year.

2. Much time is required to match the customers' interests with available properties.

3. Each of the listings is recorded on a multiple-listing association form, filed by property location, and cross-referenced by owner name. Within the association, each real estate firm sets up its own record classification system from the copy of the listing that is provided several times a week by the association coordinator.

4. In the Village Realty office, one set of records for each type of listing is filed in a three-ring notebook. Bryant often works from her home and needs a complete set of listings there also. The office space (30 feet by 28 feet) can accommodate additional files and is large enough that each staff member has a workstation (desk) with a telephone. This arrangement permits consultation with customers but often creates simultaneous demands for the listings file.

5. Because of the frequent changes in listings, a backlog of unfiled listings is a constant problem. These listings include new properties on the market as well as listings to be deleted because of sales or because the listing time has expired. (Both conditions are largely uncontrollable.)

Uncontrollable Factors. In contrast to the factors discussed in the preceding section, the following factors are largely beyond the control of the Village Realty office staff:

1. Customers call in asking about listings, but they do not furnish their names, thereby robbing the firm of follow-up for future sales. Many, in fact, refuse to give their names when asked.

2. Some customers want to buy property but cannot do so until they sell their home or business, thereby using as a down payment on the new property the equity held in the property to be sold.

Objectives of the Village Realty Office

The office staff members have become frustrated by the obsolete-listings problem and the effect it has had on their ability to provide efficient service. As a beginning step in solving the problem cited, staff members have decided to clarify the objectives the records system should meet so that the office can provide good service to its customers. The objectives are listed as follows:

1. To provide ready access to any listing of the multiple-listing service from which information is requested by customers. This information includes price range; property location; type of home; type of commercial business; and farm information that includes size, type of soil, and records of crop yields.
2. To match quickly the real estate interests of potential customers with the available listings.
3. To increase the number of sales and listings without adding to the costs of operating the office or adding to the staff.

Limitations

The achievement of these objectives is not automatic because of typical limitations that are placed on the staff. For example, little time is presently available to revise the records system, and the present office employees would not have the expertise to do so if time permitted. In addition, all records must be available at all times in the office. Therefore, the files cannot be taken out of the office to be studied in order to create a new filing system. Further, the office budget does not permit the acquisition of an automated records retrieval system, but Bryant has made $1,000 available to improve office operations.

Key Questions to Be Answered

The problem with the records system as well as the objectives and limitations of the office require careful study by the Village Realty office staff. Before starting this study and solving the problem, office employees have identified the following questions that need to be answered:

1. What changes in the record systems can be made in order that the listings file will be up to date at all times and available to all the office staff when needed?
2. How can the retrieval of information be speeded up so the listing information requested by customers will be immediately accessible?
3. To what extent can the multiple-listing association assist its members in improving their filing systems? Can all of the association member offices be connected through computer networks? Or can access to the multiple-listing association database be available to members?
4. Is it possible to make sufficient changes in the present manual system so the records system will function more efficiently?
5. What time and cost considerations are involved in any changes made? Will the benefits anticipated from such changes more than offset the costs of making changes in the system?

Possible Solutions

After dealing with the records problems outlined in this case and considering the questions stated above, the three members of the Village Realty staff met on several occasions to search for solutions to the problems cited. The work sheet, shown in Figure 3–8 was used to separate relevant facts from irrelevant facts and also to identify possible causes of, and solutions to, the problem. Two possible solutions to the problem emerged:

1. Install small computers on a trial basis in all multiple-listing association member offices that are connected to a service bureau. Thus, for a modest monthly fee, the service bureau would be responsible for the technical operations of the computer network. Each office would enter all its listings into the computer and thus all multiple-listing information would be immediately available to all salespersons. If laptop or notebook computers were also used, Bryant and others could use

Figure 3–8
A Problem
Solver's Work
Sheet

STEP 1—SPECIFY THE PROBLEM

	Relevant Facts	Irrelevant Facts
What is it?	No adequate category of listings. Listings difficult to find in categories requested by customers. Changes in listings so frequent that the office file is never up to date.	One salesperson works part time. Salespersons are paid from sales commissions while the secretary is paid from profits of the firm.
Where is it?	Records problems occur at the real estate office and at the residence of the owner-manager.	Size of the office space (30 feet by 28 feet).
When does it occur?	Five to ten times daily during busy periods.	Time of day.
How extensive is it?	Retrieval of records and matching customer interests with listings occur daily for each salesperson and for all association member offices.	

STEP 2—ANALYZE RELEVANT INFORMATION

1. There is no central source of all listings arranged by most-requested categories.
2. Multiple-listing association has not developed a standard classification of listings.
3. Each worker needs access to total file of listings concurrent with other workers.
4. Files of listings are never up to date because of delay in categorizing and the time needed to make additions and cancellations to the listings each week.

STEP 3—DETERMINE MOST LIKELY CAUSE OF PROBLEM

1. No approved standardized classification for listings.
2. No efficient filing/retrieval system in association member offices.
3. No set of priorities in the office, such as completing all listing file updates by the end of each workday.

STEP 4—LIST POSSIBLE SOLUTIONS

1. Ask association to develop and approve a standard classification scheme for all listings. Revise the Village Realty office files using this classification plan. Provide one copy of all listings to each Village Realty office staff member. Require that all new/canceled listings be posted by the end of the day received.
2. Consider an association-promoted system of automating all listings on a computer installed in each member office. Updating could be done centrally, but the updated files would be immediately available to all association members.

them while working "in the field" and at home.

2. Revise the present filing system, maintaining at least two copies of notebooks for each type of listing. The future filing tasks could be simplified if the multiple-listing association agreed on a classification scheme for all listings and then marked all new listings and listings to be removed from the file by classification code for easy storage in the appropriate file.

In order to communicate the results of the complete problem-solving process, some type of report was considered necessary. Figure 3–9 illustrates the format and a portion of the content of an informal memorandum report. Longer, more formal written reports may also be used along with an oral presentation defending the recommendations made. Chapter 5 expands upon the subject of such communication, as used by the AOM.

Figure 3–9
An Informal Memorandum Report

VILLAGE REALTY

To: Anthony V. Beane, President, Multiple-Listing Association
From: Joyce Bryant, Manager, Village Realty
Date: October 17, 19--
Subject: Suggestions for Improving the Multiple-Listing Files

At each of the last four association meetings, discussion centered on the problems that we are having with the maintenance of our listings files. Providing ready access to the information in these files has become a critical problem that calls for immediate action. Here are the results of a study of the problem in the Village Realty office.

Purpose

The purpose of our study was to pinpoint the main operating problems in our office as they relate to (1) keeping the listings files up to date and (2) providing ready access to listings information on a concurrent basis for all three members of our staff. We believe that a further objective of our study was to provide assistance to other association members who have indicated they are having the same types of problems.

Summary and Recommendations

Many times each day our office receives requests for listings information but cannot quickly locate the information because the files are not up to date. Usually the main drawback to immediate filing is the lack of standard classification. Our staff suggests that the association develop a classification plan that will establish uniform codes which will speed up the maintenance of the listings files. Since access to such files is concurrently required by each staff member, the association should furnish multiple copies of each listing. At the end of each workday, all updates of listings should be completed.

We have found much busywork regarding the listings files. If funds are available, a feasibility study should be conducted to determine if the association should purchase (or lease) a computer to handle listings. Thus, all changes to the files could be handled centrally as soon as they occur; and all association member offices equipped with computers would have the benefit of this uniform classification and immediate, concurrent access to the file.

Discussion of the Problem

Village Realty continues to have problems keeping its listings files up to date. Presently, we receive only one complete copy, and several times daily our staff members need the files at the same time. Retrieval of records is slow, especially when many offerings are needed to provide alternative suggestions to customers who have specific buying interests. We are losing customers and income in the process. Further, we believe that the association has a responsibility to help its members improve their method of operation.

SUMMARY

1. In the interrelationship among the three activities—problem solving, decision making, and choice making—*problem solving* is the broadest. Problem solving is the process of recognizing or identifying a discrepancy between an actual and a desired state of affairs and then taking action to resolve the discrepancy. *Decision making,* a central part of the problem-solving process, includes those steps ranging from the recognition of a problem through the choice of a preferred solution. *Choice making,* the narrowest activity, is the process of evaluating and selecting among alternatives available for solving a problem.

2. *Productivity* is defined as the ratio between the resources (inputs) used by a business firm and what the firm realizes from using those resources (outputs). The problem of measuring office productivity is difficult because much of the work is mental and, hence, intangible in nature. However, if we can improve productivity levels by producing more units of work in a given period of time relative to the prices of resources in the economy, then we will have increased productivity.

3. The problem-solving environment is made up of those conditions surrounding the problem and the specific factors directly involved in its solution. The main features of this environment are our diverse multicultural backgrounds, which are responsible for the human attitudes we bring to the workplace.

4. The steps in the problem-solving process are:

   a. *Recognize the problem*—making sure we are not mistakenly looking at symptoms.

   b. *Define the problem*—deciding what the main issues are and clarifying the differences between the major goals and the actual operating results.

   c. *Collect relevant information*—undertaking this step throughout the problem-solving cycle.

   d. *Analyze relevant information*—examining each element, discovering interrelationships and patterns, comparing the problem with other situations, and so forth.

   e. *Develop alternate solutions*—finding better ways for reaching goals, developing useful options, and uncovering possible choices that provide possibilities for action.

   f. *Choose the best solution*—selecting the alternative that takes less time, is more effective, results in greater productivity, and so on.

   g. *Implement the solution*—putting the solution to work.

   h. *Evaluate the results*—considering quantity and quality in relation to the objectives to be met.

5. Typical barriers to problem solving include: (a) *human*--our subjective, intangible, emotional human nature; (b) *systems*—our inability to achieve higher levels of productivity; and (c) *economic*—our poor use of available funds and other resources.

FOR YOUR REVIEW

1. Explain how problem solving, decision making, and choice making are closely related.

2. In what two ways can we define the concept of *problem?*

3. In what general ways does the productive office differ from the unproductive office?

4. Even though each problem has many characteristics that are unique, is it possible that a common approach can be used to solve all office problems? Explain.

5. Why is a knowledge of the cultural background of problem solvers an important part of the problem-solving environment?

6. What roles do the present state and the desired state play in solving problems?

7. Identify controllable and uncontrollable factors in solving office problems. How important is the latter group to office managers since they have no influence over those factors?

8. Compare the functions of creativity, logic, and intuition in the problem-solving process.

9. List the steps taken in solving problems by the formal approach. How does this approach differ from the informal, intuitive approach?

10. Why are human problems more difficult to solve than other types of problems in the office?

11. Cite several common systems problems. Are these problems related in any way to human problems? Explain.

12. Are economic problems in the office separate and distinct from human and systems problems, or are they closely interrelated? Discuss.

FOR YOUR DISCUSSION

1. Charlie Brown is credited with saying that no problem is so large or so complex that it can't be run away from. Discuss the significance of this philosophy to the solving of problems in office management.

2. Ever since its founding 20 years ago, the Tri-Dent Company has paid the full cost of the premiums for its employees' hospital and medical insurance. During the past few years, health-care costs have skyrocketed, and the company is now searching for ways to reduce and hold the line on these costs. With the guidance of your instructor, form groups of five to ten members each who will brainstorm the problem of mounting health-care costs and the approaches that the company might take to reduce and contain these costs.

3. Refer to the scenario described in Question 2. Divide into small groups and use the nominal group technique (NGT) to solve the problem of mounting health-care costs. (If brainstorming and NGT were both used by your groups, spend some time in comparing the relative effectiveness of each as a technique for generating ideas.)

4. A practical-minded business executive, speaking to a college class in administrative office management, asserted flatly that, "Problem solving as discussed in management textbooks is a lot of poppycock; problem solving, when you get down to brass tacks, is mainly hunch and good intuition. It's having a 'feel' for the situation." What is your reaction to these comments?

5. In her presentation of guidelines on leadership diversity in the United States, Ann M. Morrison, author of *The New Leaders,* states: "Finding and understanding the most significant problems in your organization (or in your part of the organization) is a basic first step in making headway on diversity issues."[8] What reasons can you give for investigating current issues in your company and uncovering problems on your own?

6. Everyone is creative, but some people are more so than others. That idea was recently mentioned by a visitor to your campus. To prove this point—that each member of your class is creative—you are asked to do the following:

   a. List ten other uses for a metal paper clip.

   b. Suggest how waste paper can be "reclaimed" for use in the office without spending any money.

   c. Recommend a way of using the shavings that accumulate in the pencil sharpeners in an office.

   d. Discuss ways of using personal accessories on office desks (photographs, plants, and the like) that will provide a uniformly attractive appearance for the entire office area.

   e. Assume your stapler has other uses. List five.

   f. Find a way of retrieving books from the top shelf of a seven-foot bookcase without the use of a ladder or step stool.

7. Your instructor has given you a sheet with nine dots arranged in the form of a square, as follows:

   You are asked to place a pencil on one of the dots and draw four straight lines without lifting the pencil so that all nine dots are covered by the lines. Complete this assignment and indicate how this miniproject is useful to managerial problem solvers.

---

[8]Ann M. Morrison, *The New Leaders* (San Francisco: Jossey-Bass Publishers, 1992), p. 164.

CASES FOR CRITICAL THINKING

In each of the preceding chapters, you had an opportunity to study case problems in order to identify problems and appreciate their complexities. That introduction will now assist you in effectively dealing with the heart of the problem-solving process—*developing the solution.*

At this point in your study of administrative office management, it will be helpful if you:

1. Review the components of the problem-solving attitude you developed in studying the cases in Chapters 1 and 2.

2. Re-examine the guidelines for solving problems discussed previously in this chapter, especially the section *Steps in Problem Solving.* Once you understand the logical flow of thought outlined in these guidelines, you are ready to begin problem solving in earnest. You may now wish to return to the cases in Chapters 1 and 2, this time to apply systematically the problem-solving principles in order to solve one or more of the cases. You are then prepared to solve the problems in Chapter 3 and the remainder of the cases in this textbook.

In order that you may retain a sound, problem-solving attitude and become adept in applying the principles of problem solving, you should periodically review the contents of Chapter 3. Doing so will assist you in becoming an effective problem solver throughout this course and in later life.

Case 3–1 Basking in the Florida Sun for Three Weeks? For Two Weeks? For No Weeks?

One Friday in early January, Beth Rogers and Amy Shaw, computer operators for Flex-Shoes, Inc., were discussing their plans to get some sun and attend the NCAA basketball play-offs in Orlando, Florida. Rogers said that their hotel reservations had been made and that she was now waiting for flight confirmations. Excitedly, Shaw commented: "I'm sure glad we saved those five vacation days from last year. Come March, that gives us three whole weeks in sunny Florida."

As Rogers and Shaw left work that day, they noticed that their supervisor, Hal Moser, was still at his desk, checking time sheets for the week. "Guess we'd better clear our vacation plans with Hal," Rogers said to Shaw. The conversation continued:

Shaw: Hal, Beth and I have decided to take the first three weeks in March for our vacation. You'll remember that we still have five days due us from last year.

Moser: (flustered at being interrupted in his work) I remember. Go ahead with your plans. Just give me a note to remind me of your vacation dates. See you Monday—have a good weekend!

On Monday afternoon, after Moser read the note indicating Rogers and Shaw's vacation dates, he broke into their work to say: "Hey, you two! You know you can't carry your vacation time over from year to year. You should have used up those five days before this year began!"

Rogers: (stunned) But, Hal, you can't do that to us. On Friday you told us to go ahead with our plans. Don't you remember? We've made our hotel reservations and Saturday we paid for the airline tickets. If we cancel our flight plans now, we'll be stuck with a fat penalty!

Moser: Guess I wasn't thinking too clearly Friday. I sympathize with you; I really do. But, look here in the employee handbook. See? It says that all vacation time must be taken during the calendar year. Employees cannot accumulate vacation time from year to year.

1. Identify the real problem in this case.

2. What is your solution to the problem you have defined?

c
o
n
t

Case 3–2 Assessing the Potential of a Minority Employee

Shortly after migrating to the United States from Haiti six months ago, Ana Ramos joined your sales office staff. Her duties involve typing correspondence and reports and serving as a backup receptionist to assist in handling the many customers coming to the office. Ramos has excellent writing skills stemming from seven years of English language study in her homeland; however, owing to lack of practice, her oral language skills are not yet well developed. This has created problems, because the longer she is on the job, the more she is expected to answer the telephone and help in receiving customers, which requires making introductions and giving extensive oral instructions and directions. Coupled with this problem is Ramos's personality. Although she is very pleasant and well liked, she is unusually shy, making her reluctant to speak out and gain the speaking experience she needs. As time goes on, her typing work improves, but she has "gone into a shell," as the supervisor, Helen Masters, mentions.

Masters has discussed the problem with you, her assistant, and the other office supervisors, who feel that Ramos is making progress and that in time she will overcome the language barrier. Masters, on the other hand, does not agree, indicating that she is strongly considering terminating Ramos's employment because of her inability to perform the job for which she was hired. Only because of a physical handicap (Ramos lost the use of one leg in a childhood accident) has Masters delayed making a decision earlier.

Using the problem-solving process outlined in this chapter,

1. Define the problem and constraints. Determine the controllable and uncontrollable factors important to its solution.

2. What sources would you consult before making a decision? Why?

3. What alternate solutions would you recommend to Masters?

Case 3–3 Memorandum: Computer Option (available on disk)

4

ADMINISTER-ING OFFICE SYSTEMS

GOALS FOR THIS CHAPTER

After completing this chapter, you should be able to:

1. Explain the purpose of administrative office systems in the modern organization.
2. Identify the basic systems concepts and explain their value in understanding administrative office systems.
3. Discuss the steps involved in conducting systems studies and the relationship of such studies to the management and problem-solving processes.
4. Compare the various methods of organizing the systems function and the advantages and disadvantages of each method.
5. Describe the basic role of the human system in the office.

Today's use of the term *system* has increased to the point where it has become a central concept in general management and administrative office studies. In all areas of daily life, references are frequently made to systems—to circulatory and nervous systems in medicine; to free-enterprise and socialistic systems in government; and, as discussed throughout this textbook, to accounting, communication, and computer systems in business and industry. A worker is often described as having a good system for performing work or as being *systematic* by nature.

The systems school of management presented in Chapter 1 was the latest in a series of major viewpoints regarding the nature of the management process. At that point, the *systems* concept was introduced from an *organization-wide* perspective and is usually called a *management information system (MIS)*. In this chapter, on the other hand, the concept of system is defined in a more *specific, work-related* manner. Keeping this in mind, *system* refers to a *set* of *related elements* that are *linked together* according to a *plan* for achieving a specific *objective*. However, all levels of systems share the same basic components shown in italics in this definition; each system depends on the proper coordination and operation of all its elements in order to achieve its assigned goals.

The information function is carried out through **administrative office systems (AOS).**[1] These specialized systems are responsible for planning, organizing, operating, and controlling all phases of the information cycle in order to meet the main systems objective—*to provide appropriate information and service for management's use in making decisions.* Increasingly

---

[1]To communicate more effectively with the reader, the term *administrative office systems* is represented by the initials *AOS*. This practice is consistent with the use of *AOM* and *OM* to represent the terms *administrative office manager* and *office manager,* respectively, throughout this textbook.

Figure 4–1
Key Elements
in Administrative Office
Systems

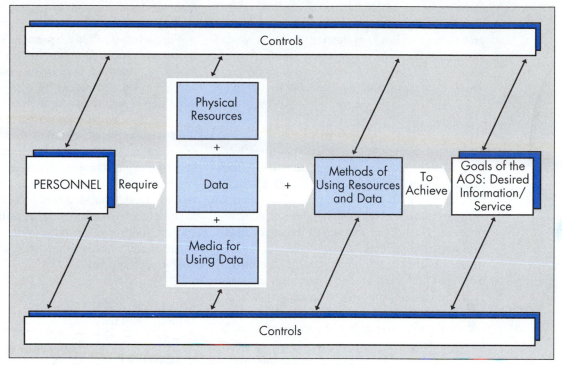

greater impetus has been given to AOS with the expanding use of the computer and related automated information processes.

Since all sizes and types of firms depend on AOS, managers and their employees must understand systems concepts in order to perform their jobs efficiently. This chapter identifies the major AOS and discusses basic concepts needed to create, operate, and evaluate systems. Special attention is devoted to the human factor in making each system function properly. The specific techniques by which personnel analyze, operate, and evaluate AOS are covered later in the text.

THE ADMINISTRATIVE OFFICE SYSTEMS FUNCTION

Through effective leadership, the work to be accomplished in an organization must be carefully planned, organized, and controlled. Each department manager is in effect an administrator who must apply Leffingwell's Principles of Effective

Work, which were discussed in Chapter 1. In systems terms, this requires making decisions on *what* work is to be done; *how* it is to be done; *who* will do the work; *when* the work will be done; and, after the work has been completed, determining *how well* the work has been done. To the extent that the effective performance of the work depends largely on the use of information, *each department manager is also an information manager.*

The key elements in the AOS function are shown in systems terms in Figure 4–1. This figure emphasizes the primary role of *personnel* in managing, supervising, and doing the work. Such work must be done through the use of *physical resources,* such as office furniture, machines and supplies, and the space necessary for housing these resources and personnel. *Data* must be available for processing into information using efficient *methods* (manual, mechanical, and automated) for completing the work. And *media,* such as forms and related records for storing, retrieving, and using data, must be provided. All of these elements are regulated by a set of *controls*—policies, rules, objectives, procedures, computer programs, and various evaluation techniques—to ensure that the system achieves its *goals*. And as we know, *all systems depend completely on adequate support to ensure their effective operations.*

Major Administrative Office Systems

The major administrative functions of purchasing, sales, production, finance, accounting, and human resources are found in all business organizations. In addition, we usually see a separate administrative function that handles the general-office services. Even so, each of the major-function departments may have added to its regular responsibilities a certain amount of administrative operations so that each department manager is in effect an information manager, as stated earlier. For example, even though separate human resources and purchasing departments exist, a large production department may handle some of its own personnel and purchasing responsibilities. If a decentralized plan is in operation, each department also maintains its own correspondence and record systems, which may be controlled by the department manager. Or, the maintenance of correspondence and records may be placed under the central responsibility of the administrative office manager. Figure 4–2 illustrates a firm's main systems and **subsystems,** which are lower-level subdivisions of systems responsible for accomplishing specialized functions of the total system (the firm). Note, however, that any subsystem has all the same systems features as its "parent."

In the operation of each department, the manager develops a number of procedures for completing the work. A **procedure** is a planned sequence of operations for handling recurring transactions uniformly and consistently. For example, in a purchasing system, various procedures are set up to complete the required work in each of the subsystems. To request a desired machine, an office worker must obtain the necessary information to place the order, fill out a purchase requisition, compute the total cost of the desired item, obtain approval of the requesting depart-

ment head, and forward the requisition to the purchasing department head for final approval.

For each step within the procedure, we note that a method is required to accomplish that phase of the work. A **method** represents a manual, mechanical, or automated means by which each procedural step is performed. As shown in the previous example, in a purchasing system the department head may use one of several methods of obtaining or transmitting information. The manager may talk in person to an employee, write a letter to a distant vendor, or use a telephone or facsimile transmission to expedite the shipment of a rush order. The nature of the system's needs, the skills and preferences of the workers, and the cost and availability of the equipment determine the various methods used in each system.

Objectives of Administrative Office Systems

"If you don't know where you're going, any road will take you there." As organizations grow larger and more complex, so does their need for considering "where they are going"; that is, deciding on the *objectives* of their administrative office systems. The personnel responsible for the AOS function are expected to achieve this broad organizational goal: *to plan, design, operate, and control systems that result in the highest levels of productivity at the lowest possible cost.* In turn, the office manager or the head of the AOS unit is responsible for achieving more specific objectives that include all of the important phases of the system. Typically, the following tangible objectives are identified:

1. Furnish the best information, in the right format, to the right people at an appropriate time, at the least cost, and in the right amount so improved decision making results.
2. Eliminate unnecessary work or the duplication of work.
3. Design systems that ensure safer, less fatiguing work.
4. Automate repetitive, routine tasks where possible when automatic equipment will do the work more quickly, more accurately, more

Figure 4–2

Major Systems and Subsystems in a Business Firm

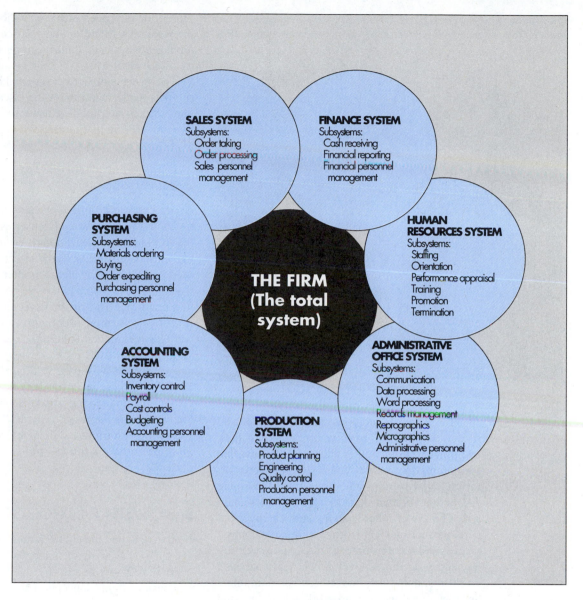

economically, and more reliably. Such a system should be as flexible as possible to meet the users' present requirements and still be able to accommodate changes in future requirements without the need for major systems revisions.

5. Establish an efficient, uniform procedure to follow for each similar transaction.

6. Determine responsibility for satisfactory work performance.

7. Provide adequate training for employees and supervisors to ensure top-level work performance.

8. Gain the acceptance and support of all systems users.

Because such objectives relate to all phases of the system, many systems studies are required. One of the basic studies is the **feasibility study,** a planning method that seeks to find out whether

Illustration 4–1 Supervisors are responsible for providing adequate training to meet the established objectives of their administrative office systems.

specific systems operations can be improved and if the addition of new resources (machines, equipment, personnel) is economically justified for making these improvements. (The steps followed in a feasibility study are outlined in Figure 4–3 and are further discussed later in this chapter.) These and other systems studies cover paperwork management (forms design and control, records and reports control, correspondence studies, and procedures development and analysis), workflow, data flow, quality control, equipment and personnel usage, and work scheduling and evaluation. A comprehensive systems study of such magnitude requires high-level skills and broad work experience of the office manager, for it not only affects all the technical work processes but also, more important, the basic attitudes of people toward themselves, their supervisors, and their work. To be effective, a systems study must promote change toward better working conditions and more efficient work per–formance through a concentrated, analytical approach to problem solving. Such an ongoing

search for improved office operations eliminates the weakness found in many offices—because a job has always been done a certain way, that way is still satisfactory.

The systems objectives outlined in this section serve as the foundation for the discussion of systems studies later in this chapter. In essence, *each objective is directed toward finding the best way to perform each office job.*

Systems Problems

As we know, each office manager must be realistic about the operation, effectiveness, and cost of the AOS in the organization. If each of the objectives discussed earlier were consistently attained, there would be no systems problems. In the real world, however, such is not the case. Hence, it is important that the principal systems problems be identified so that the office staff can take steps toward achieving their solution.

In general, AOS problems may be classified and illustrated as shown in Figure 4–4 on page 88. Each of these problems is typical of the difficulties encountered by office managers as well as many other managers in general. Such problems can be solved or reduced in intensity if the proper problem-solving attitude—positive thinking—is present.

BASIC SYSTEMS CONCEPTS

If you are to understand the nature and purpose of systems in all areas of management—but especially in AOS—you must be able to identify several basic systems concepts. These concepts are:

1. The general systems model that explains the overall operation of any system.
2. The organization of systems within the firm.
3. The various systems levels that we find in operation, ranging from the manual to the automated and expert type of systems.

In the discussion of systems in this textbook, emphasis is placed on general systems and the needs of the small office for improving its system. This type of basic systems thinking will simplify your efforts in learning about all types of

Figure 4–3
Steps in Making a Feasibility Study

Steps in Making a Feasibility Study

1. *Define the nature and scope of the problem as well as the objectives to be achieved by the study.* Examples of such objectives include (a) reduce administrative office costs, (b) speed up processing operations, (c) increase the productivity of present personnel or equipment, (d) develop management information for more efficient and effective operations, (e) introduce new management methods, (f) determine the relative merits of various types of systems or equipment, and (g) attain greater prestige and a more progressive image.

2. *Gather data on current operations.* Through personal interviews and questionnaires, find answers to such questions as:
   a. What information is available and what additional information is needed? What documents (forms, correspondence, and reports) are received, from what sources, and how often? What files are kept to support operations?
   b. What personnel are involved in the operations and what are their assignments and skill levels?
   c. What machines and equipment are used in the system, for what purpose, and for how long?
   d. What output is required of the system, and how is such output evaluated?
   e. What are the time and cost requirements for completing an operations cycle? (Note direct or tangible costs, such as personnel, equipment, and floor space, and indirect or intangible costs, such as customer dissatisfaction and employee morale.)

3. *Analyze the data collected.* Study work/data flows, including space assignments; the unique characteristics of managerial, supervisory, and work personnel as well as the equipment used; the number of hours worked in a week on each assignment; and the costs and benefits of performing systems operations.

4. *Develop an approach for solving the problem.* Include factual information that logically defends the approach. Examples of such information include documenting how to eliminate personnel, equipment, time, space, or paperwork; balanced facts on the costs and benefits of the present system as well as reasonable methods for improving the system.

5. *Present the completed feasibility study to management for their consideration and action.*

systems—from the manual systems that still play important roles in modern offices to the automated systems discussed in the remaining parts of this textbook.

The General Systems Model

Models are used to an increasing degree in problem solving and management planning. In one sense, a model represents an *ideal* form of operation, such as a model office or a model worker. More commonly in systems work, a **model** explains in simplified, *general* form the complex interrelationships and activities of an organization or its parts. Thus, the model is free of the many specific details that would prevent an easy understanding of the total or overall system.

To study AOS, a **general systems model** is used to represent a broad explanation of the system (or any of its subsystems) to which more concrete details can be added as needed. Figure 4–5 outlines the principal phases of a system arranged in the sequential order in which each phase functions. Throughout the use of this model, the AOM and other managers can more readily understand the changes that occur within their operations in each system.

Systems are usually divided into two classes: open and closed. An **open system** interacts with its environment, as we see in Figure 4–5, in order to attain its goals. A business firm is an open system, because it is affected by many factors, such as tax laws, its competition, and the quality of its workers. A **closed system,** on the other hand, op-

Figure 4–4
Administrative
Office Sys-
tems Problems
and Examples

Types of Problems	Examples
1. Organizational	High costs, low productivity levels, excessive waste, decreasing profits, poor organization structure.
2. Managerial	Ineffective delegation of work, difficulties in assigning responsibility, infrequent interaction with workers, inappropriate or unknown goals, poor organization, failure or inability to lead.
3. Personnel	Poor motivation, tardiness and absenteeism, low morale, and increasingly serious interpersonal problems on the job.
4. Information systems	Poor use of space, inefficient workflow, poorly designed forms, lack of control over records creation and disposition, lack of knowledge about information needs of the firm, failure to control costs, poor selection of equipment, poor use and care of equipment, inability to identify and measure production levels, late completion of work, and excessive overtime work.

Figure 4–5
The General
Systems
Model

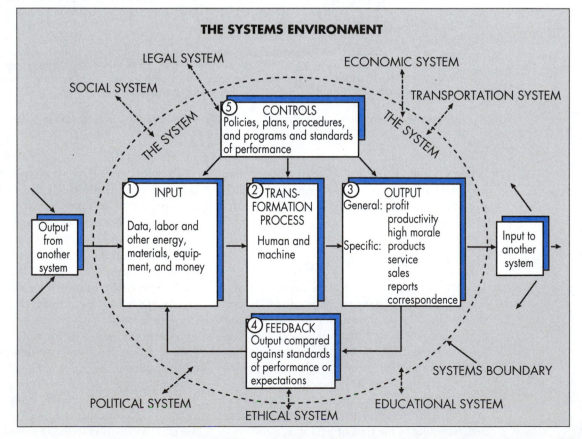

Illustration 4–2A and 4–2B An interactive business environment such as this shopping mall is an example of an open system. This farm, because it produces its own food and is self-sustaining, is an example of a closed system.

erates as a self-regulating unit; hence, it does not interact with its environment. A monastery is probably the best example today of a closed system. Even then, a monastery must depend on outside sources for additional members of the order. For all practical purposes, AOMs deal only with open systems in the business firm. In this section, each of the phases of the open system is briefly discussed and numbered to correspond with the numbers in Figure 4–5.

Systems Phase 1: Input

Input is the first phase of any system in which data, labor and other energy, materials, equipment, and money are received from another system. Examples of input are raw materials introduced into a manufacturing operation, the arrival of the morning mail, the skill needed by a word processing operator to produce a letter, or telephone calls coming into the office. (As discussed later, feedback also furnishes information that becomes input for further operations of the system.) Other examples of input are shown in Figure 4–6.

Systems Phase 2: Transformation Process

That phase of the system that changes or transforms input into a desired form is called the **transformation process,** often shortened to *process*. (Sometimes, too, this phase of the system is called *processor* because a worker or a machine combined with an efficient procedure is involved.) Common examples of transformation processing activities dealing with information are classifying, sorting, storing, retrieving, and computing; additional examples frequently found in other types of systems are shown in Figure 4–6.

Systems Phase 3: Output

Output is the ultimate goal of a system, that which results after the input has been changed in some way during the second phase—the transformation process—to a desired form. Thus, unprocessed sales data (the system's input) are converted (transformed) into a finished sales report (the system's output) by certain processing procedures. In so doing, the process phase adds

Figure 4–6
Common Sys-
tems Exam-
ples

COMMON SYSTEMS	SYSTEMS PHASES				
	1 Input	**2** Transformation Process	**3** Output	**4** Feedback	**5** Controls
A. Production system	Raw materials Labor Energy Blueprints	Assembling Construction Welding	Automobile Box of cereal Telephone service	Customer evaluation of product or service	Policies Procedures Plans Federal Communications Commission
B. Sales system	Sales data Feedback (complaints from customers)	Classifying Sorting Storing Billing Filling orders	Invoices to customers Sales reports	The results of comparing sales with sales quotas	Policies Procedures Plans Competition
C. College student (human system)	Money Attitudes Abilities Food Rumor Class lectures	Advising Studying Testing Using the brain as a processor	Course grades Changed attitudes Knowledge College degree	Employer evaluation of graduates Graduates' reactions to courses	Parents Social customs Finances Laws

value to the input, which makes it more useful to the firm. Common examples of output in the AOS are correspondence, reports, accounting statements, budgets, advertising brochures, and invoices. More general forms of output in other types of systems are listed in Figure 4–6.

Systems Phase 4: Feedback

In the AOS, **feedback** is the regulating force that compares the system's output (*what was produced*) with the standards of performance set for the system (*what should have been produced*). Notice how this feedback definition compares with the definition of *problem* in Chapter 3. Thus, if the actual output levels are lower than the levels desired, a message is "fed back" to the input phase of the system specifying how the next operating cycle of the system involving all five systems phases must be modified in order to attain its goals. Several types of feedback are shown in Figure 4–6.

Systems Phase 5: Control

While the previous four systems phases usually function in 1, 2, 3, 4 sequential order, the control phase operates in a different manner. **Control** is the systems phase that dictates what can and cannot be done in each of the other phases of the AOS. As a result, controls are placed over the input phase, the transformation process phase, the output phase, and the feedback phase. Examples of control inside the firm include plans, procedures, programs, and standards of employee performance. The dotted lines in Figure 4–5 represent the **systems boundary,** which defines the scope or limits of an open system and at the same time separates a system from its environment. (If the dotted lines were replaced by a solid line, a closed system would be illustrated.) Outside the firm (i.e., outside the dotted lines shown in Figure 4–5) is the **systems environment,** which sets up controls that affect the operations of the firm. Government (legal) regulations on taxes, working conditions, and labor relations, as well as the economic, political, social, transportation, educational, and ethical systems in existence, impose controls that affect the behavior of any firm and the people within it.

Examples of several common systems are shown in Figure 4–6. The third example illustrates the human being as a system. Here, the brain is the main agent that processes information received as input through the five senses. This example qualifies as a system because it includes all the elements found in the general systems model. The human system in the office will be discussed later in the chapter.

Systems Structure

Because of the complex set of management information needs, an equally complex set of AOM systems is required. Thus, a *systems structure,* or systems hierarchy, somewhat related to the structure appearing on an organization chart, evolves as the form of organization for providing a wide variety of systems services to the firm. Several of the most important systems relationships in the structure are discussed in this section.

Total System–Subsystems Relationships

As we see in Figure 4–2, various key systems are needed to meet the goals of any firm. When all of these systems are combined into a **total system,** they form a company-wide information network. In this respect, we note that the physician regards the human body as a total system made up of many major systems. Each of these main systems is, in turn, divided into a number of subsystems. The communication system operates in a similar manner as a subsystem of the broader AOS just as the cardiac, or heart, system acts as a subsystem of the broader cardiovascular system in the human body. However, all three levels of system—total, major, and subsystem—have the same general makeup and follow the same operating phases outlined in Figure 4–6.

Each system is related to the other systems and in a sense "leans" on the others so that the total system can fulfill its mission. In a business firm, for example, the human resources system is responsible for hiring workers, the production system is responsible for assigning the workers their duties, and the accounting system is responsible for paying the workers. In an interdependent manner, these systems and their subsystems support the main objective of the firm—to sell at a profit the products or services made available by the firm.

Information Systems

The information function defined in Chapter 1 operates through a system that controls the many activities making up the *information cycle* (collecting, processing, storing, retrieving, and distributing information). Thus, management typically considers each of its major systems as an **information system** and the total set as a *management information system.* At the heart of such a system is the computer, which performs many of the functions making up the information cycle. For example, the computer is used for collecting, processing, and storing business information, and when the need arises, it retrieves and distributes information to assist in decision making. The computer also aids managers in formulating plans for the future by analyzing the contents of its extensive historical files and thus acting as a knowledge-based or expert system.

Database

A **database** is a central master file containing company-wide information from the major systems of the firm. Or, on a smaller scale, we find departments setting up databases that consolidate their own automated records. The ideal database represents a total collection of information from such areas as accounting, engineering, marketing, human resources, production, and research and development in one large computerized library. It also provides organization-wide access to the master file via computer terminals. Information to be used in the database is "captured" and stored only once. As a result, total file space is reduced since duplicate files, previously maintained by individual departments, can be eliminated. Because transactions come into the system at one point only, updating of the files is facilitated.

The database concept becomes possible with the use of large computers or with small networked computers to provide additional storage power. However, many firms or departments within firms automate only portions of their files. Departments or individuals within departments are often reluctant to release certain information to a centralized unit responsible for maintaining the database because they fear unauthorized access to the files or accidental destruction or removal of the stored information. However, code words (passwords) that limit access to data have lessened this fear somewhat in using computer systems.

Systems Levels

Systems may be classified in terms of processing power and thus in terms of the degree of automation involved. In this section, we note three levels of systems: (1) manual, (2) mechanical (sometimes called electromechanical), and (3) computer.

Figure 4–7

A Common Office Workplace Illustrating a Manual System

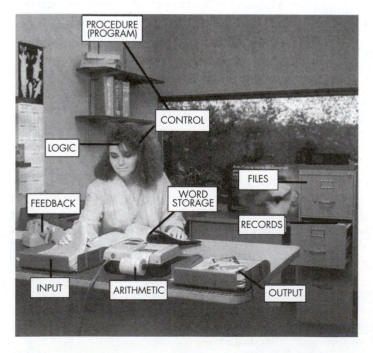

Manual Systems

With all the emphasis given to computers in today's society, we naturally find it difficult to remember the millions of manual systems still in existence. However, we have only to study a manual system such as shown in Figure 4–7 to realize that there are many systems in which manual or hand processing of information is commonplace.

In a **manual system,** the *earliest and still commonplace type of system,* the human being is the data processor. We can illustrate such a system by considering the preparation of paychecks in small firms, such as antique or woodworking shops or service stations and garages. In such firms with manual payroll systems, the person preparing the payroll receives input data through the senses, usually the eyes and ears, from the information appearing on time cards or time sheets and related oral communications. The data are then sent via the nervous system to the brain for storage, with the brain acting as the control unit. The brain may also act as a processing unit by performing such processing operations as arithmetic calculations; storing the results; comparing one number or word with others (as in the case of proofreading); and finally producing output such as paychecks, payroll registers, and tax reports. Output in the manual system is provided by the set of instructions or "program" stored in the payroll clerk's brain or perhaps contained in a procedures manual.

In the earliest manual systems, all tools for processing data (pencils and pens) and the journals and ledgers for storing information were operated by hand. Under such a system, information appears in a human-readable form, and changes or corrections are easily made. Such manual methods may be quickly adapted to various working conditions and to the exercise of judgment in making decisions from the data. However, we find certain weaknesses in manual systems. The human mind is subject to fatigue and boredom, which frequently cause from 5 to 10 percent error in computations and related clerical tasks. Too, our minds are slow in performing arithmetic calculations, and, because of the im-

Illustration 4–3 Even though technology has automated many areas, manual tasks such as proofreading still play an important role in business.

pact of emotions, we may have difficulty applying the rules of logic. The final output in a manual system can be no better than our human conditions—both psychological and physical—will permit.

Mechanical Systems

For most of the past century, simple machines have assisted in the operation of the manual system. For many of us, simple machines such as typewriters, adding and calculating machines. dictation and transcribing machines, and the telephone have become routine office tools, with each performing a single processing function. Compared with performing all office work by hand, such electromechanical machines offer great speed and accuracy; but, at the same time, their use is limited to the skill, experience, and control of human beings.

Punched-card records, a higher-level **mechanical system,** served for many decades as the mainstay of information processing by machine. Later, as the computer age dawned, punched cards became important input documents for au-

tomated systems. However, because electro-mechanical systems are too slow and costly for processing information in today's high-speed processing world, punched-card systems have greatly diminished in number and importance. However, we still find punched-card records often used for time cards, invoices, and other common applications that can be linked to the computer.

Computer Systems

The **computer system,** familiar by name to most of us, is made up of a group of interconnected machines, including the computer, that process data at the speed of light and that perform many other information-handling functions. Unlike earlier machines, the computer is able to store in its internal "memory" both the data to be processed and the instructions (or **program**) to process the data. A computer system depends upon a code, or machine language, for representing data within the machine. Alphabetic and numeric data recorded in coded form on diskettes, magnetic tape, punched paper tape, punched cards, or some other input are sources of data for computer systems.

The coded data and the instructions for their processing are in the form of magnetic codes for use in the computer's processing system. Computations are performed, and summaries and various types of output reports are prepared according to the stored instructions. Processed data appear on the terminal screen for later storage or are printed out of the computer on punched cards, magnetic tape, magnetic disk, or business documents (such as invoices, reports, paychecks, journals, and ledgers). We know from observation that the computer system also uses many manual systems whenever the systems functions cannot be performed by machines. Examples are the human functions, such as customer relations, keyboarding of information, proofreading source documents, solving human relations problems, and making decisions from data based on intuition, judgment, and common sense. *Hence, we must not forget that people serve as the main control element in this highest level of system as in other levels of systems.*

CONDUCTING SYSTEMS STUDIES

Generally, we call the process of improving systems a **systems study.** Other names used are systems analysis, systems and procedures analysis, methods analysis, systems engineering, or work simplification. Whatever the label used, a systems study is closely related to the processes of management and problem solving discussed earlier in Part 1. In fact, senior managers, looking back on long, successful business careers, describe success in management in terms of satisfactory problem solving and the ability to make sound decisions. *Thus, we can conclude that effective office management is solving problems that occur in the systems and procedures of the office.*

The staff in charge of AOS must be alert to internal problems throughout the systems, as well as to those problems that involve the external environment (the business community and the customers or clients). A well-planned program of systems studies should be developed by the staff unit that specializes in systems work. Of special importance in such a program is the mental attitude of the analyst. Systems studies require of the analyst a keen, analytical skill and an objective viewpoint that sets aside preconceived ideas about the area of study and that places personal considerations in the background. For these reasons, each problem must be carefully defined, clear-cut objectives formulated, and the systems approach to problem solving carefully followed. In this section, each of the required steps in the systems study cycle is discussed briefly. Typical areas of application in AOS are then treated in the following section of this chapter.

The Systems Approach

In this age of systems, we still use widely the scientific method for solving office problems discussed in Chapter 3. This problem-solving technique centers on the careful definition of a problem and the development of reasonable solutions to the problem. Since the primary objective of systems analysis is problem solving, analysts have taken the scientific method, adapted it to

their needs, and called it the **systems approach** to problem solving. When they use the systems approach, analysts apply the scientific method in addition to these unique systems steps:

1. *Identify the work problem and all its components, noting the interrelationships of all parts and how each contributes to the total work system.* Frequently, this all-components approach is called "seeing the big picture." Systems studies are far more concerned with interrelationships in the work system than were the early scientific management problem-solving studies.
2. *Clarify the objectives for which the system is designed.* Systems analysts emphasize the great need for developing and writing objectives or unit goals so all workers involved understand what is expected of them.
3. *Note the effect of synergism in the system.* (**Synergism** describes the fact that interrelated parts produce a total effect greater than the sum of each of the parts working independently. An example would be a symphony orchestra playing in concert or a successful football team playing on the field.) What this means in the office is that more can be accomplished through creativity and teamwork than through working as individuals.
4. *Consider all problems from a systems point of view,* that is, consider the input, transformation processing, output, feedback, and control factors involved in any problem.

The effect of any proposed changes in AOS must be weighed carefully because of the large or long-term investment involved. By working together to improve AOS, the office staff has reinforced again and again a basic systems concept—*interrelatedness.* Usually, one change in a system, no matter how small, results in a series of other changes. An office manager may purchase an expensive machine only to realize later that it cannot handle the load for which it was designed. As a result, considerably more worker retraining, maintenance costs, and space than considered at the outset are required, thus affecting the human resources department, as well as maintenance and facilities management. Such a disaster might have been avoided if a feasibility study had been made prior to the purchase.

This and other types of organizational studies use the steps in the systems study cycle discussed in the next section.

The Systems Study Cycle

As we saw earlier, systems studies are problem-solving activities designed to improve productivity in the office. The conduct of such studies involves the **systems study cycle,** a set of sequential, problem-solving steps required to improve the systems function.

Typically a systems study begins whenever a recurring problem of some importance is recognized by the information user. Usually such a study covers three major steps: (1) analysis of the present system, (2) design of a new or improved system, and (3) installation of the improved system.

To put these *general* steps into action, several *specific* activities are performed. Six of these activities, outlined in Figure 4–8, are discussed in this section.

Figure 4–8

Steps in the Systems Study Cycle

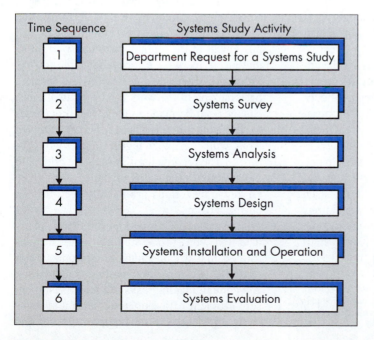

Time Sequence	Systems Study Activity
1	Department Request for a Systems Study
2	Systems Survey
3	Systems Analysis
4	Systems Design
5	Systems Installation and Operation
6	Systems Evaluation

Step 1: Department Request for a Systems Study

Recognizing that a systems problem may be the cause of reduced productivity, a department head may request that a systems study be conducted. The systems staff (or the office manager) may then conduct a feasibility study to determine the probable value of such a study. During this time, the problem is redefined and objectives (such as lowering costs, improving the data flow, strengthening operating controls, improving customer relations, or automating a phase of the office system) are established. The study is broken down into major phases (human resources, equipment, space layout, and procedures), and a timetable is developed for completing each phase of the study.

Step 2: Systems Survey

After the department request for a systems study has been approved by the systems unit or the office manager, data must be collected concerning all aspects of the problem. During this phase of a study, it is important to explain to the employees in the department involved why the study is being done and what data are needed from them. The facts are recorded on questionnaires, preferably during personal interviews. Frequently, charts, such as organization charts and charts showing workflow, space utilization, worker motions, work sequence, and travel time involved, are used to pinpoint the task assignments of all workers involved. Experienced analysts may visit other companies having similar information needs and get advice from systems specialists and equipment vendors having expertise in solving the type of problem under study.

Step 3: Systems Analysis

One of the most important phases in the systems study involves the analysis of the data collected. During this phase, the analyst considers the objectives of the system and notes the special causes, effects, and interrelationships of problems and systems elements. The analyst often discusses the facts collected with members of the department under study in order that the accuracy of the data may be determined and the possible solutions to the problems may be explained.

Step 4: Systems Design

Based upon the information obtained during the systems analysis, a new system is designed (or a proposal for revising an existing system is developed). Such a design proposal is usually a joint effort stemming from suggestions of the department personnel involved and managers who understand the nature of the problem. The proposal must consider the possible effects on (1) employees (whether anyone will be laid off, how much retraining will be required, or what interdepartmental transfers may be suggested by the study); (2) profits (how the proposed system may affect salaries, space, material and supplies, overhead costs, cost of capital, and profits earned on capital invested as well as on equipment required); (3) work schedules and data flow; and (4) customer service. While no set rule for answering these kinds of questions is available, we find that experienced analysts frequently use a checklist covering each of the many elements of systems studies in their systems-design efforts.[2]

Step 5: Systems Installation and Operation

Good planning and persuasion are required to sell a departmental staff on making a change in its systems operation, because the jobs and personal security of the workers are at stake. An effective approach for selling the new system is for the analyst to work with department personnel during the entire study period, thereby gaining their confidence. The report presenting the proposal should be carefully prepared in clear-cut form and made available to all personnel concerned. Emphasis should be placed on the anticipated savings, advantages, and the expected results related to the profits to be realized. If a large-scale study is involved, sometimes parallel operations are conducted, which allows the old, scaled-down system to operate alongside the new system, until

all of the problems or "bugs" have been removed. At that time, the old system can be phased out.

Step 6: Systems Evaluation

One of the important control activities in AOS is the evaluation of systems operations. Periodically, the office manager studies systems to determine how effectively they are meeting their goals. Such studies include (1) appraising the performance of human resources, the use of equipment, furniture, and space, and the allocation of financial resources and (2) determining the overall benefits and costs of the system. In addition, a full-fledged systems evaluation seeks to find out what changes should be made in the system so that future operations of the system will be more effective.

Typical Areas for Systems Studies

From long-term studies of office work, we find that the same general types of systems problems occur in most offices although the specific details of each differ. Thus, the systems steps discussed in the previous section are commonly followed in studying these typical problem areas:

1. *Workflow.* The study of workflow in the system involves the effective use of furniture and space as well as the flow and frequency of movement of the workers who transport information (paperwork) throughout the office. From such studies, wasted motion and needless backtracking of the work can be spotted. Thus, changes can be made in the office procedures to shorten the time required for completing the work, which results in higher productivity.

2. *Forms.* The records used in AOS are critical to the effective operations of the systems since all key transactions are usually recorded on business forms.

3. *Equipment use.* Throughout the office, many data and word processing activities are performed that use mechanical equipment. For example, sorting, keyboarding, calculating, and communicating tasks use machines to ensure efficient office operations. In a systems study, an analysis of the equipment needs and

---

[2]Useful systems analysis and design checklists can be found in the systems analysis textbooks available in college and university libraries.

the comparative costs and advantages of the various methods of performing work (manual or machine) should be undertaken.

4. *Personnel use.* Before any system is analyzed, the role of personnel in the department under study should be given the highest priority, for the workers can "make or break" the system. Studying the human resources involves such areas as job analysis and evaluation, work incentives, motion economies, work distribution among employees, personnel policies, attitudes, training programs, and employee performance appraisal.

5. *Systems costs.* Systems studies focus strongly on the control of office costs, such as the costs of moving equipment and people, renovating costs (repainting, relocating telephones and electrical outlets), furniture costs, and the costs of converting the files to a new system and removing the current system.

After the costs of operating the present and proposed systems have been pinpointed, the benefits anticipated from the improved systems should be determined. Some of the benefits may be measured in dollars. However, other benefits, such as better public relations, more prompt deliveries to customers, and higher employee morale, although not measurable in dollars, provide benefits that ultimately have a strong influence on the firm's profit picture.

ORGANIZING THE SYSTEMS FUNCTION

The most common approaches for organizing the systems functions are:

1. Employing a firm of management consultants or systems analysts to make special studies of AOS, procedures, and methods.
2. Developing in the large firm an internal staff of systems analysts whose services are available to the entire organization.
3. Assigning the responsibility for systems improvement in the small firm to the office manager.

The organizational approach used for studying and improving systems is determined by

the size of the office, the skills of the staff, and the attitude of management toward this phase of work. Whatever the subdivision of office work may be, the office manager must realize that the analysis of AOS requires the support and approval of top management if new or improved systems are to be successfully installed and operated.

The program of systems studies must be recognized not only by top management, but also by the company as a whole. The entire company must participate in recognizing, defining, analyzing, and solving systems problems and in implementing the recommended changes that are aimed at increasing company profits. Through the issuance of company regulations or instructions, proposals for systems improvement must be "sold" to the employees. In this way, employees will understand that in most instances they will not lose their jobs, that their skills and abilities will be used more effectively, and that they will not receive less pay.

Use of Outside Consultants

A number of consulting firms engage in systems analysis. Many firms specialize in general systems analysis, which involves layout, equipment, furniture, and personnel use, and interdepartmental information flows. Others specialize in the study of office automation, word processing, and communications. Consultants are hired in much the same way a company hires auditors or lawyers to provide expert advice.

Outside consultants bring certain advantages to a firm. Such consultants:

1. Provide special counsel and offer new ideas because of their experience with other firms.
2. Are outsiders and thus can study the client's systems with an objectivity that the internal consultant does not possess.
3. Often carry more weight than an internal consultant who may have become a part of the firm's political network.

On the other hand, the use of outside consultants creates certain disadvantages for the firm, such as:

1. The consultant's lack of familiarity with the firm, especially its strong informal organization, discussed in Chapter 2.
2. The relatively high cost of consultants' services.
3. The negative reaction of many workers to the so-called efficiency expert, as a person who may eliminate many jobs within the firm and who may not care about the best interests of individual workers.

As a rule, the *advantages* of using outside consultants may be considered as *disadvantages* of using internal consultants. Similarly, the *disadvantages* of using outside consultants can be translated into *advantages* of using internal consultants, as discussed in the next section.

The Systems Function in Large Firms

Large firms with highly specialized staffs find the use of an internal systems staff a necessity as the systems become more complex. If the firm is especially large with many branches, such as General Electric Company and the Ford Motor Company, a centralized systems staff may be set up to coordinate the work of the decentralized staffs, which can deal more effectively with the systems found in each division. On the other hand, firms that are served by a corporate staff in one central location view the organization as an entity and maintain adequate systems service for each of the individual departments. In either case, systems personnel should meet the standards set by the Institute for Certification of Computer Professionals (ICCP). Persons passing the requirements of the Institute are certified as Certified Computing Professionals with specialization in either management, systems development, or procedural programming. Recertification is required every three years.[3]

There is no set rule that dictates the size of an internal staff. Some corporate managers estimate that an adequate systems staff is 1 percent of the office personnel employed by the firm. Others believe that there should be one analyst for approximately every 200 office workers. The size of the systems staff should be determined by the results expected of its work—ensuring high productivity in the organization by supplying management with better information and at the same time producing sufficient savings to justify its existence.

To ensure that a company-wide perspective is maintained, in most firms the systems staff reports to a high-level administrator, such as the president, the controller, or the treasurer. Regardless of its organizational placement, the systems staff should be available to all departments in the firm for assistance in improving working conditions and levels of work performance.

The Systems Function in Small Firms

In the typical small firm, we find that the office manager is *the* specialist in information management. Thus, the OM is responsible for systems work since the main goal of systems work is the improvement of information flow. To fulfill this responsibility, the office manager must possess these attributes of an effective systems analyst: a logical, probing, perceptive mind; an inventive, imaginative, creative nature; sound judgment; and a thorough understanding of the firm and its information needs. As a part-time analyst, the office manager offers an inexpensive means of systems improvement that can be used by small as well as large offices. Also, the office manager is usually more familiar with the work than anyone else. On the other hand, he or she may be so busy with routine duties that the systems work may be neglected. On occasion, too, the employees reporting to the office manager may resent the office manager's efforts more than those of a separate staff unit or an independent consulting firm.

For the enterprising office manager who handles the bulk of the firm's systems duties, considerable assistance is available at little or no cost. Memberships in such organizations as the Association for Systems Management (ASM) and the

---

[3]For additional information, contact the Institute for Certification of Computer Professionals (ICCP), 2200 East Devon Avenue, Suite 268, Des Plaines, IL 60018, (708) 299-4227.

Association of Records Managers and Administrators (ARMA) give office managers access to worthwhile meetings, conventions, and useful publications dealing with systems subjects. Additional advice can be obtained from many firms, such as Standard Forms, Inc., and Moore Business Forms, Inc., that specialize in the design and control of business forms. Also, representatives of office machine and equipment manufacturers will aid in the design or adaptation of systems to their equipment. Through contact with such firms, many office managers are able to adapt the systems used by other firms and thereby improve their own office productivity.

THE HUMAN SYSTEM IN THE OFFICE

One overriding thought we must never forget: *People and their needs must receive first and last consideration in any systems study.* The success of an AOS program is closely tied to the effective participation and harmonious work relationships that exist between department personnel and the systems staff. The staff must rely on the managers of the departments under study to provide the knowledge and information for developing effective policies, procedures, and methods in the operating departments. On the other hand, the managers need the expertise of the systems personnel for analyzing the systems and developing new and improved designs.

The most important element in the office is the human system, that is, the expectations, behavior, and performance of the people responsible for the system. The office manager and the office staff represent the key input to any office job; accordingly, this group has the greatest impact on the output of the office. Managers and their employees bring *individual inputs,* such as their skills, knowledge, motives, needs, attitudes, and values, to any task. Similarly, collections of individuals bring *group inputs,* such as group cohesiveness, group norms and ideas, and group conduct regarding what is acceptable behavior, to their work. For example, office managers can have a very positive effect on their staffs by the manner in which they direct the staffs. Similarly, a group of keyboard specialists in a word processing center, if unhappy with the type of supervision provided, may reduce their daily output of correspondence to show their dissatisfaction.

By understanding and applying the philosophies of the behavioral and the systems schools of management thought discussed in Chapter 1, effective managers consider employee goals and company goals in systems planning. Thus, job satisfaction for the worker and profit making for the firm are basic, compatible objectives of effective AOS.

Ms. Josephine Sessa, director of the International School of Naples, realizes the importance of the interrelationships involved in the total system. In the *Dialog from the Workplace,* she comments on some of her responsibilities and shows how the individual and group inputs work together to solve problems in this international organization.

DIALOG FROM THE WORKPLACE

JOSEPHINE SOVIERO SESSA

Director, International School
of Naples
Naples, Italy

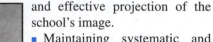

The International School of Naples, Naples, Italy, has an enrollment of 185 students and a staff of 28. Ms. Josephine Sessa, director, received her B.A. degree from Hunter College, CUNY. Her M.Ed. is from Framingham State College. In her position as director, she has many responsibilities and duties. Working with the personnel and overseeing the smooth functioning of the total system are important aspects of her job.

QUESTION: What are your responsibilities in the total system in which you are involved? What types of problems do you experience in working with such a diverse group of people in your organization? How do you solve these problems?

RESPONSE: My responsibilities in the functioning of the total system of the International School of Naples include:

- Coordinating the activities of the school administration and through them the activities of all employees.
- Maintaining high academic standards through the periodic review of curricula and methodology.
- Recruiting and selection of personnel.
- Ensuring evaluation of all personnel.
- Overseeing and coordinating the short- and long-range planning of the school, including responsibility for the building program and participation in fund-raising activities.
- Stimulating, supervising, and evaluating the school's entire program in relation to school objectives, Board policies, community desires, and the best current educational practices.
- Representing the school and seeing to the proper and effective projection of the school's image.
- Maintaining systematic and open communication with the Board of Governors and all constituencies.
- Preparing the annual budget and long-term financial plan for the school.
- Recommending appropriate policy additions and changes to facilitate the fair and smooth functioning of the school.

Breakdowns in communication are inevitable in an international environment. The fact that my staff is made up of people from diverse backgrounds, customs, and cultures has contributed to this breakdown.

Initially I find that teachers are reluctant to suggestions of change in their classroom management and teaching styles because they feel such suggestions imply inadequacy in their performance. Often, standard methods practiced "back home" are not always valid in this type of organization. Many times, teachers do not take into consideration that they are working at an international school in a foreign country and that their colleagues come from as diverse a background as their students.

I have tried to overcome these obstacles in a variety of ways. Peer coaching has proved to be a very effective method of bringing new ideas into the classroom without the negative effects of supervisory observations. In addition to this, I have allowed teachers to take on the responsibility of trying new methods and techniques to increase overall achievement. This empowerment of responsibility makes them feel more confident in their job. They share in the decision-making process at the school. They share their ideas with colleagues at weekly staff meetings and play a vital role in the overall functioning of the school on an organizational level. All of this heightens their interest and cooperation level and helps eliminate possible communication problems.

SUMMARY

1. Administrative office systems (AOS) are organized in business firms to meet the information needs of those organizations. Each system contains these common elements: human resources; physical resources, such as furniture, machines, space, and equipment; data; methods for completing the work; media, such as forms and records; and controls for ensuring that these elements are properly regulated to meet the system's goals. General models of systems have been created to describe the sequential phases of a system's operation: input, transformation process, output, feedback, and control.

2. Systems work is performed at all levels of an organization. Although most recognition is given to computer systems, two other levels of systems are found: manual and mechanical in which manual labor is combined with electrical machines, such as copiers, calculators. and typewriters, to perform the required work.

3. Systems studies begin when a department head requests that the operations be studied because of plaguing problems. Following the approval of such a request, a logical set of "study" steps is followed. The system is surveyed, the data from such a survey analyzed, and a new system designed. Upon approval of the design, the new system is installed and later evaluated for its effectiveness.

4. Large firms maintain their own internal staff of systems personnel, while small firms typically assign systems work to the office manager. Frequently, companies of all sizes obtain the services of outside consultants whose objectivity and broad experience offer many advantages for improving the systems function.

5. In all systems studies and in the office, the most important element is the human factor.

FOR YOUR REVIEW

1. Discuss the purpose of an administrative office system.

2. What are the main elements in an administrative office system? Cite several of the main administrative office systems in which these elements operate.

3. What are the major administrative functions found in all business organizations?

4. Explain the relationship that exists among a system, a procedure, and a method.

5. What are the principal objectives of administrative office systems?

6. What are the steps you should follow in conducting a feasibility study?

7. Identify several of the most important problems found in administrative office systems. How can these problems be solved or reduced in intensity?

8. Describe the control phase of an administrative office system. How is it different from other phases?

9. Describe the advantages of a database. How practical is such a concept for present-day business firms?

10. What is the systems approach? How does it differ from the use of the scientific method in the solution of administrative problems?

11. List the principal steps in the systems study cycle. Indicate why the office manager should be familiar with these systems analysis responsibilities.

12. What role can the office manager play in handling the systems responsibilities of the small office?

13. Why is the human factor considered the key to the effective operation of any system?

FOR YOUR DISCUSSION

1. Consider and explain your office management class as an administrative office system. What limitations and strengths does your class system possess in helping you understand fully a system?

2. Your class recently toured a large new office building occupied by the Dextor Corporation. In the systems department of the firm, the following slogans were framed and hung on the wall of each workstation:

    a. There is nothing quite so useless as doing with great efficiency something that should not be done at all.

    b. Where am I going? How do I get there? How do I know when I've arrived?

    Explain why systems personnel would find these slogans relevant to their work.

3. Because the work of data-entry operators and file personnel is tangible, it can be measured and efficiently designed in an administrative office system. On the other hand, the work of supervising and managing these employees is intangible and thus difficult to measure. Because of these differences in the type and level of work, how can a systems analyst design an effective system which assures that both types of workers will make equitable contributions?

4. The *total* administrative office system of the Manmouth Manufacturing Company (a carpet company) includes these main systems for accomplishing the goals of the firm:

    a. Purchasing raw materials and semifinished goods.

    b. Receiving purchased items.

    c. Sales.

    d. Production (manufacturing the firm's products for sale).

    e. Collection (receipt) of sales revenues.

    f. Billing (invoicing) customers.

    g. Delivery of products sold.

    Using the systems approach, define the purpose of each main system and identify the principal subsystems likely to be found in each main system. Then arrange each system and its subsystems in a logical sequence that reflects the order of each in the total system's operations. The use of a modified organization chart would help to show the interrelationships that exist among the main systems of the firm.

c
o
n
t

5. You have been asked to help an office manager, Shelley Thomas, decide on the better method of handling systems-improvement projects in her office. The question is whether to use outside consultants or to assign this responsibility to an assistant office manager on a continuing basis. What approach would you recommend be taken to resolve this problem? What aspects of the problem are mainly objective in nature, and what aspects seem mainly subjective? How should Thomas proceed?

6. Your office management class is planning to take an "observation tour"—visiting legal, medical, and city government offices in your community. Since the main intent of these visits is to *observe* common systems in action, what type of guidelines should be in place before taking this visit?

7. You are responsible for making recommendations to solve personnel systems problems in your company (see Figure 4–4). How would your methods for solving personnel problems be different from solving managerial problems?

CASES FOR CRITICAL THINKING

Case 4–1 Identifying Systems Concepts in a College Registration System

After a class discussion of the main concepts found in administrative office systems, your instructor asks you to observe the operating procedures of a "real-world" organization in order to understand better the functions of office systems. As a practical and timely way of completing the assignment, you have selected the registration system of your college as you are about to complete your registration for five three-hour courses for your next and last semester in college.

After obtaining the *apparent* approval of your adviser, you take the required registration form to the registrar's office to complete your computerized registration. The assistant registrar (A/R) takes your form, keys the information, and obtains feedback information on the computer screen. Shortly thereafter, this conversation takes place:

A/R: I'm sorry, but Advanced Cost Accounting 455 and Management of Change and Conflict 499 are both closed.

You: But these are required courses for my major. If I don't complete these courses by the end of next semester, I'll have to stay in school an additional semester. Isn't there anything I can do—maybe put my name on a waiting list?

A/R: I'm sorry. All I do here is operate the computer and tell you whether you are registered or not. The registrar has told me to tell students with this problem to contact their department advisers or check with the heads of the departments concerned. Of course, if you want to go higher, you can always appeal your case to the dean of the college. Maybe the department heads will waive the course requirements for you. By the way, I noticed that your adviser failed to initial the five courses listed on your schedule, so they aren't officially approved. You'll have to get these initialed before I can complete your registration on the computer.

Feeling frustrated and angry, you leave the registrar's office.

1. What is the systems structure (from total system to subsystems) involved in this administrative office system?

c
o
n
t

2. What specific controls are built into such a system? Using as a guide the general systems model (see Figure 4–5), construct a registration systems model that includes all the phases of this open system.

3. How are human beings and human relationships an integral part of the system(s) issues raised here?

Case 4–2 Conducting Systems Studies

The financial vice president of your company, Harve Jones, has asked you to help develop a systems study because of low productivity in processing collection claims/letters for overdue accounts. Many accounts reach overdue status of 90–100 days before a collection attempt is made. Jones feels that a study of the present system needs to be completed and a new automated system designed and installed immediately. Jones asks you for a prompt report on what you plan to do.

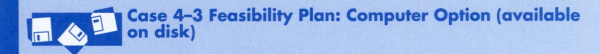 ## Case 4–3 Feasibility Plan: Computer Option (available on disk)

5

COMMUNI-CATING IN THE OFFICE

GOALS FOR THIS CHAPTER

After completing this chapter, you should be able to:

1. Discuss the communication process and the purposes for which communication is transmitted.
2. Explain how formal and informal communication networks are used in the organization.
3. Describe the flow of communication and the channels used to transmit messages.
4. Identify the major barriers to communication.
5. Explain the importance of the different kinds of nonverbal communication in the messages transmitted and received by office managers or supervisors.
6. Summarize the effective report-writing principles.

The Latin word *communis,* which means "common," is the origin of our word **communication.** Communication describes the process by which managers establish a degree of "commonness" (i.e., common understanding) with employees and the public. As such, communication is the process by which information and human attitudes are exchanged with others. Simply stated, communication is the "glue" that holds business together. When communication breaks down, an organization invariably goes into decline; without communication, the managerial functions of planning, organizing, leading, and controlling cannot be performed.

This chapter begins with a discussion of the communication process upon which all effective office administration depends. Next, communication networks, which represent the flow of communication as it ties together all persons in the firm, are described. Later, the barriers to effective communication are discussed with suggestions for their elimination. Finally, principles of effective report writing are identified to assist AOMs in coordinating their overall communication responsibilities.

THE COMMUNICATION PROCESS

In this section, a communication model will be used to explain the manner in which communication occurs in the office. Understanding this concept of communication (often referred to as *communication theory*) will assist you in designing and operating effective office communication systems.

The Communication Process Model

The **communication process** is the transmission of a message as intended from one person (the *sender*) to another person (the *receiver*). In automated systems, the sender may be a computer operator and the receiver another computer. As shown in Figure 5–1, the process begins when the sender's senses (sight, hearing, touch), experiences, skills, attitudes, and emotional needs are combined with information to form an idea. The idea (or ideas) generated will become the content of the *message*. The idea is encoded, or organized, into a series of symbols (words, numbers, etc.) that are used for transmitting the message to the receiver through a selected *channel*. At the receiving end, the receiver decodes, or interprets, the message and takes action (or nonaction) as revealed by the feedback. *Feedback mechanisms* are used to send another message from the receiver to the sender saying that the original message has been received and understood or not. Below, we shall

take a look at a very common feedback mechanism—the question-and-answer session at the end of a meeting.

To see how the communication process operates in a typical office situation, let's sit in on a monthly department meeting. Susan Radcliff, supervisor of credit processing (the *sender*), has talked (the *channel*) about the new procedure (the *message*) to her workers (the *receivers*) for processing credit applications. Following her presentation, Radcliff answers several of the workers' questions (the *feedback*) and discusses with them how their present methods will be affected by the change. With accurate feedback, Radcliff is able to make an objective and realistic evaluation of her presentation and to detect any potential prob-

Figure 5–1
A Model of the Communication Process

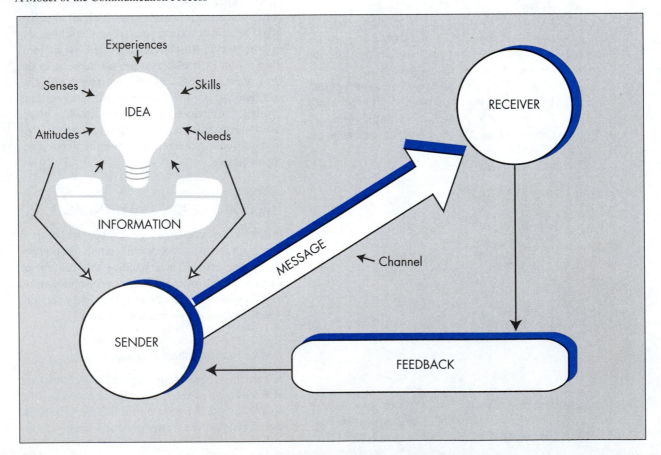

lems that may affect the implementation of the new procedure.

Verbal Communication

In the communication process, the most basic form of communication is verbal. **Verbal communication** consists of words—spoken or written. This form of communication is discussed in this section.

In spoken communication, usually called **oral communication,** your tone of voice or emotional state influences the message as significantly as the words you use. In the office, oral communication consists of one-to-one conversations, conferences and meetings of all kinds, telephone conversations, and messages transmitted through public address systems, television, radio, and film. Equally important in oral communication is the emotional state of the listeners, because their reception and understanding of the message are greatly influenced by their preconceived opinions, personal relationship with the speaker, and general outlook toward the organization.

When very important messages are involved, the sender often avoids oral communication and, instead, relies upon **written communication.** Examples of written communication transmitted in the office are the letters, reports, memos, invoices, paychecks, and facsimiles that may be handwritten, printed out on a typewriter, or keyed on a word processor or computer. When using written communication to transmit messages, the AOM has tangible evidence of what the employees have been asked to do. Also, since the messages can be stored permanently, the AOM is able to refer to them as needed in order to evaluate the actions taken by workers.

Purposes of Communication

The purposes for which oral and written communication are transmitted in the office and some of the media commonly used for their transmission are presented in Figure 5–2. Messages such as those listed in this figure may be transmitted through formal or informal communication networks, which are described in the following section.

COMMUNICATION NETWORKS

A **communication network** is the pattern of channels used to communicate messages to and from, or among, a group of people. These networks may be classified as formal or informal.

Formal Communication Network

The formal communication network is based on the chain of command, and its line of authority flows from the top of the organization down. The formal communication network is shown on the organization chart in Figure 5–3. In this formal network, messages are transmitted up and down the structure through the channels identified with heavy lines.

The formal communication network is used to transmit official messages, policies, procedures, directives, and job instructions. For example, in Figure 5–3, a new directive pertaining to hours of work would flow from the vice president of administrative services to each manager who might hold small group meetings to present the changes to the office workers. Although the formal network is used mainly for communicating downward in the organization, provision is usually made for formal upward communication such as attitude surveys, grievances, suggestions, and performance appraisals.

Informal Communication Network

As any office manager knows, office workers transmit many messages every day that do not flow through a formal network. Instead, the workers use an informal communication network that is mainly oral. Many of the messages transmitted informally are not vital to office operations since they do not affect the completion of work assignments. This information is often referred to as *scuttlebutt* (so named after a drinking fountain aboard ship or at a naval installation where the crew congregates to pass along rumors or gossip).

Much informal communication occurs when office employees socialize and pass along information that they believe their coworkers may not

Figure 5–2
Purposes of Communication and Commonly Used Media

Purpose of Communication	Communication Media
1. To Inform	1–1 Interoffice memo announcing a meeting 1–2 Telephone call in which a customer is quoted a price and shipping date for goods ordered 1–3 Insert for employee handbook explaining a new benefit 1–4 Sales meeting to present new products to marketing staff 1–5 Press release announcing the selection of a new CEO
2. To Persuade	2–1 Personal conversation in which a coworker is requested to serve as a volunteer in a fund-raising effort 2–2 Fax announcing benefits gained by the extension of a contract time period 2–3 Report to management on the need to purchase new word processors
3. To Evaluate	3–1 Performance appraisal records 3–2 Quality control report summarizing the output of word processing center 3–3 Budget performance report that compares amounts budgeted with expenses incurred
4. To Instruct	4–1 Instruction manual for operating a personal computer 4–2 Directions given orally to coworkers for reconciling a bank statement 4–3 Instructions given by vendor to mail room personnel on proper use of postage equipment
5. To Meet Human and Cultural Needs	5–1 "Small talk" ("Hello, how are you today?" "Have a good weekend?" "Are you free to bowl tonight?") before, during, and after business hours 5–2 Note inviting workers to participate in annual fitness run for charity 5–3 Announcement of free World Series tickets to be given as incentive to improve attendance record

have. For example, consider the opportunities that workers have for informally communicating when they commute in carpools, work out together at a health center, or spend work breaks together. On occasions such as these, information is freely transmitted among workers at various levels in the organization. Those receiving the messages are in a position to transmit the information to others directly above or below them in the formal communication network. Thus, the effect of the informal communication network becomes very extensive, as evidenced by the operation of the grapevine.

The grapevine is an informal communication network in which messages are rapidly transmitted, usually orally on a one-to-one basis. Like a grapevine, the tendrils of the informal network wander in and out of the organization and attach themselves to any willing listener without regard to the formal organization structure and its channels. Rumors about company matters such as a proposed merger, relocation of the headquarters office, or a cutback in the workforce are often spread by means of the grapevine. The effects of the messages transmitted can cripple productivity and seriously disturb the climate of the organiza-

Figure 5–3
A Formal
Communica-
tion Network

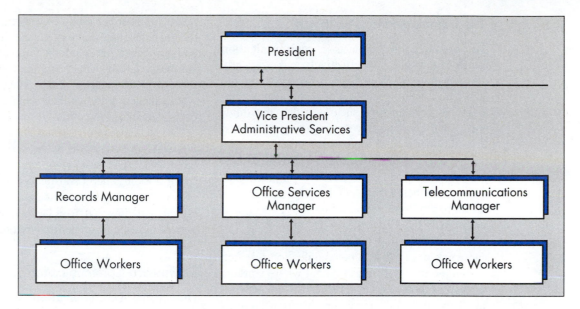

tion. For this reason, the grapevine is often viewed negatively by managers and employees since the messages transmitted are either groundless or have been distorted in some way.

Illustration 5–1 Employees share information with each other during breaks via an informal communication network.

On the other hand, the grapevine provides office managers with an excellent means of finding out what their workers think and feel. Workers associate informally on the job, have a natural desire to communicate with each other, and wish to be aware of the latest happenings in the firm. As a very informal way of quickly spreading information, the grapevine provides workers with a means of finding answers to their questions and aids in filling communication voids.

Office managers should accept the fact that the grapevine cannot be eliminated, even if it were desirable to do so. Instead, an attempt should be made to analyze and understand any rumors being circulated and then take positive steps to prevent their recurrence. OMs should be aware of the grapevine and "feed" accurate information only to those "leading grapes" or key employees who can be relied upon to transmit information without embellishment or distortion. As a result, OMs may find the grapevine working favorably for the firm. For example, the grapevine can clarify and publicize a company directive often in more understandable language and far more rapidly than the formal communication network.

The Communication Audit

An organization conducts a **communication audit** to evaluate how effectively and efficiently its communication system is working. In the audit, an inventory is taken of all the firm's communication activities, such as group meetings, hiring and exit interviews, company publications, bulletin boards, and supervisor-worker meetings. These activities are then analyzed and appraised to determine whether the firm's communications policies are being followed.

As part of its communication audit, the organization may use network analysis to study its formal and informal communication networks. **Network analysis** is a communication research technique that is used to find out where workers go to get their needed information. In network analysis, the informal communication patterns are studied to learn how they compare with the relationships expected if the formal communication network were used. Such studies aid OMs in evaluating the present formal network and adopting new policies and procedures that will better satisfy the needs of all workers.

THE FLOW OF COMMUNICATION

In the flow of communication, the office supervisor serves as a "linking pin," since he or she is the main person in the formal channel that links together the downward and upward communication. As shown in Figure 5–4, the office supervisor is a leader in his or her group of workers and a subordinate in the other group of middle managers. As a person "caught in the middle," the office supervisor must carefully select communication channels that will clearly transmit the messages to receivers whose feedback shows their clear understanding of the contents of the message.

To be successful, communication must be two-way—*up* and *down* between supervisors and employees. The supervisor must take into account not only the upward and downward flows of communication in an organization but also the lateral and diagonal flows. Each of these four communication flows is discussed in this section.

Downward Communication

Downward communication flows vertically from the top of the organization to one or more levels below and carries the messages that translate top-management planning and decision making into orders that direct office employees. Much of the downward communication transmitted by OMs and their supervisors involves:

1. Informing employees of their job responsibilities.
2. Enlisting the understanding and support of employees about management objectives and company goals.
3. Instructing employees on how to improve their productivity.
4. Relaying to employees the results of their job performance.

When communicating downward with employees, the key is *openness*. OMs should not be so formal that employees are afraid to approach them. To see if you, as an office manager or supervisor, are effectively communicating downward, answer each of the questions in Figure 5–5. If you can *honestly* check seven or eight Yeses, you are an exceptionally effective communicator!

Most messages are transmitted downward through several formal channels such as face-to-face meetings, conferences and committees, and in written materials. Informal channels often contain memoranda, phone calls, notes, as well as face-to-face meetings and other written commu-

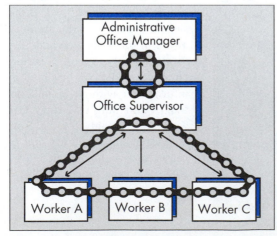

Figure 5–4
The Office Supervisor as a Linking Pin in Downward and Upward Communication

Administrative Office Manager

Office Supervisor

Worker A   Worker B   Worker C

Figure 5–5
A Checklist for Effective Downward Communication

	Yes	No
Study each question carefully, answer it honestly, and see how many "Yes" check marks you have. If you have fewer than 7 "Yes" check marks, you need to improve your downward communication skills.		
• Do I keep my workers informed about planned changes in company policies and procedures?..	___	___
• When I am faced with problems that affect my workers and their productivity, do I freely consult with them?.............................	___	___
• Are my workers aware of how I feel about their on-the-job problems?......	___	___
• Do I initiate steps to become informed of my workers' personal interests?	___	___
• Am I familiar with and try to advance the career goals of my employees?	___	___
• Do I often have private talks with my workers?................................	___	___
• Do I try to squelch any unfounded rumors about company policies and practices?...	___	___
• Do I hold meetings during which employees may freely raise questions?	___	___
• When I give an employee a directive, do I explain it and offer reasons for my decision?...	___	___
• Do I plan and schedule performance appraisals so that my workers are not taken by surprise?..	___	___

nications. Although the use of more than one channel brings about a certain amount of repetition, a combination of oral and written communication channels ensures that information will be received and understood.

When deciding which channels of downward communication to use, the OM should consider the following factors:

1. *Speed of transmission.* Some channels provide faster transmission than others. For example, the OM can explain changes in company practice such as new work schedules more quickly at a group meeting than by announcing the new schedules in the company newspaper. A message sent by computer to all workstations can be immediately received and read.

2. *Appropriateness to employee level.* The complex features of a firm's retirement plan may be adequately explained by means of a memo to all supervisors. However, to ensure that all workers understand how the retirement plan affects them individually, each manager may plan to hold question-and-answer sessions at small group meetings. The managers may decide to reinforce the discussion at the group meetings by inserting a question-and-answer column in each issue of the company newspaper.

3. *Perception of authority.* Office workers view some channels of downward communication as more authoritative than others. The president of the organization exercises more authority and has more power than the AOM. However, office workers may attach more importance and trust to the AOM's oral explanation of changes in the salary compensation program than the president's announcement of the changes in a formal letter received at their homes.

4. *Nature of information to be transmitted—good news or bad news.* Most messages transmitted to office workers are likely to be viewed either positively or negatively. The favorable results of an employee appraisal and an accompanying salary increase are usually positively received by an office worker. Such good news is often transmitted by informal oral communication—a personal chat—between the employee and the manager or supervisor. On the other hand, bad news, such as a reduction in working hours because of a decline in sales, is often communicated in a group meeting. At the meeting, all employees' questions can be answered, and future prospects for returning to a normal workweek schedule can be explored.

5. *Need for feedback.* When transmitting many kinds of messages, the AOM needs to find out to what extent the employees have understood and accepted the communication. For example, consider an AOM who is explaining the company's change in its year of operations for accounting purposes. The AOM must make sure by means of question-and-answer sessions that all employees clearly understand how their departmental operations will be affected and what steps must be taken to implement the changes. If, on the other hand, the office is shutting down at noon today because of inclement weather, the AOM's announcement over the public address system requires no feedback!

The previous factors, which are considered when selecting channels for transmitting messages, are further described in the following examination of several channels of downward communication.

Meetings

Formal meetings with managers and workers should be regularly scheduled to convey the importance of keeping the lines of communication open. In small group meetings, two-way communication is facilitated; employees can ask questions, freely discuss information, and receive answers. Thus, feedback is immediately obtained. Office managers or supervisors should

also be urged to hold *informal* discussions with their employees. In such settings of mutual trust and respect, employees are more at ease and seem to relate their true feelings more freely. This approach has a very positive effect on the morale of employees; and, at the same time, managers learn what the workers think and how they feel.

Company Publications

Company publications, such as newsletters and newspapers, are used to keep workers informed of the operations, plans, and changes in the firm. Also commonly found in company publications are good-news items such as promotions, retirements, hiring of new employees, births, weddings, and anniversaries. In addition, the publications describe off-work experiences of employees, announce cultural and recreational activities, and explain various safety and health practices.

Pamphlets, booklets, manuals, and posters are used to inform workers of changes in company policies and methods, new products or services, and future plans. Letters from the president or other officers of the company to the employee's home are especially effective when a new policy or procedure is to be implemented or when a new product or service is being offered.

Bulletin Boards

Bulletin boards are used by nearly all organizations as a means of keeping employees informed. Bulletin boards may be used for posting rules and regulations; announcements of recreation and social events; safety records; job openings; attendance records; suggestion system awards; new product announcements; vacation schedules; lost-and-found notices; personal announcements of illness, births, weddings, and deaths; educational opportunities; and press releases. To be an effective communication channel, bulletin boards should be sufficient in number and properly located to attract the attention of all workers. The communications posted on the boards should be kept current, and both managers and workers should be encouraged to use the boards.

Illustration 5–2 Bulletin boards are a source of company and employee information for all personnel.

Upward Communication

Upward communication flows vertically from one level in the organization to one or more levels above. An effective flow of upward communication aids in motivating office workers to perform their jobs in the most efficient manner possible. The establishment of effective upward communication channels between the office manager and the employees is one of the most important and demanding problems of human relations affecting business offices. As offices become larger, the problem of maintaining adequate communication becomes more difficult.

Leonard D. Troy, senior manager, network operations, discusses changes in communications at MCI Telecommunications Corp. He notes an explosion in the amount of computer-based technology being applied to communication tasks and problems. In the *Dialog from the Workplace,* Mr. Troy describes communication problems and solutions resulting from a major aspect of this technology.

In many organizations, the problem of keeping the upward communication lines open and providing feedback is so important that attitude sur-

veys (discussed in Chapter 7) are conducted periodically to find out how workers feel about their firm, its products or services, and its supervisors and managers.

In a comprehensive survey of the U.S. workplace, the National Study of the Changing Workforce by the Families and Work Institute found that 65 percent of the respondents felt open communication was a very important reason in deciding to take their current jobs.[1]

Upward communication channels are used in the office mainly:

1. To provide the OM or supervisor with feedback indicating whether the messages transmitted downward have been received and understood.
2. To transmit information needed for higher-level decision making.
3. To pass along suggestions for systems improvements and changes in policies.
4. To give office employees an opportunity to ask questions, to make complaints, and to express satisfaction or dissatisfaction with the way office activities are being managed.

Generally you will find that the most effective channels for upward communication are the informal discussions that occur between you and your supervisor or manager. In these discussions, a major problem in communications is the unwillingness or inability of your supervisor to encourage feedback of your viewpoints and reactions. If supervisors or managers lack empathy, they are unable to put themselves in your position and see things through your eyes and mind. Or, the organization may have failed to provide managers and supervisors with an adequate understanding of the importance of communication and sufficient training in developing a high level of communication skill. Thus, upward communication is often haphazard and unreliable.

Another problem in upward communication is associated with the hierarchy found in most busi-

---

[1]Sue Shellenbarger, "Work-Force Study Finds Loyalty Is Weak, Divisions of Race and Gender Are Deep," *The Wall Street Journal* (September 3, 1993), p. B1.

DIALOG FROM THE WORKPLACE

LEONARD D. TROY

*Senior Manager, Network Operations
MCI Telecommunications Corp.,
Central Division
Cincinnati, Ohio*

Mr. Troy attended Purdue University where he received a B.S. in math. His M.B.A. was awarded from Xavier University. Beginning at MCI in Kansas City, Missouri, in 1978 as a switch technician, Mr. Troy moved rapidly into a Washington, DC, position as a circuit engineer. From there, he moved to Cincinnati in 1980 as a supervisor. After a promotion to manager, Cincinnati-Dayton, in 1984, he was promoted in 1991 to his present position of senior manager, Southern Ohio, Cincinnati-Dayton-Columbus.

QUESTION: What changes have you seen at MCI in communication activities? Have you seen any changes in the amount and/or levels of communication problems both from upward and downward communications?

RESPONSE: The last ten years have seen an explosion in the amount of computer-based technology being applied to communication tasks and problems. These technologies include personal computers, electronic phone systems, electronic mail systems, voice mail systems, voice and video conference systems, pagers, cellular phones, etc. All of these have been geared to make communications easier, faster, and more complete.

At MCI, the single technology that has made the largest impact on the way we communicate has been our MCI Mail electronic mail system that we originally developed and deployed in the early 1980s. Currently, there are many public and private electronic mail systems throughout the world. These systems are interconnected to allow the easy exchange of messages between the systems. This allows anybody on any one of the systems to communicate with virtually anybody else in the world who has a computer, FAX machine, telex terminal, or other type of electronic communications device on a near real-time basis. At MCI, virtually all written communications, including memos, reports, data files, etc., are transported from one person to another by the electronic mail system. In a large, growing company like MCI, having the ability to rapidly move critical information to the people who need it is a key problem to have solved.

Electronic mail systems present some issues concerning the security and control of information. Information can be easily misdirected and could end up in the hands of people who should not have the information. Since the electronic mail systems are interconnected and shared, an unintended recipient could be someone outside the organization.

When information is presented to people, there is no guarantee that the people will absorb the information and use it. Getting people to read memos and reports was a problem before electronic mail and remains a problem. Here the communication problem is not in the message or the medium, but with the people themselves who are involved in the communication. Simply changing the medium to an electronic format has no effect on this issue.

On the whole, MCI has found the electronic mail system to be a very useful communications tool that has assisted the company to grow and prosper. With a little care, the problems are controllable and not a major concern. This also sums up the experience that other organizations have had with electronic mail systems. These systems will not totally replace written documents as a form of communication in the near future, but they have proven their usefulness and will continue to grow and to be enhanced.

ness organizations. For example, your supervisor or department head may stifle your complaints or block your reports of dissatisfaction. Some of the fault may be yours, especially when you tend to tell your supervisors only what they want to hear. Or, your manager may be a poor listener and hear only what he or she wants to hear. As a result, the organization may attempt to minimize these problems by creating formal upward communication channels that flow around the supervisor. This is true, for example, of employee suggestion systems and grievance-handling procedures which are described briefly below.

Employee Suggestion Systems

An **employee suggestion system** is a channel of upward communication in which employees offer ideas that result in cost reduction and the elimination of inefficiency and waste. Suggestion systems are used as a means of building morale among office workers and of getting workers to think more seriously about their jobs.

Most employees are eligible to participate in the suggestion system. However, the officers of the company are usually excluded from participation. Supervisors ordinarily receive awards only for ideas not connected directly with their own departments or fields of activity. The disadvantage of having both workers and supervisors submit suggestions is that the workers and supervisors come into competition with one another. As a result, conflicts may arise. Also, the workers may think their ideas are being "stolen" by the supervisors.

Some companies pay a flat amount for each suggestion accepted. Other firms pay a percentage of the savings that result from implementing the suggestion. When determining the amount of the award, AOMs should consider whether the idea involves recurring or nonrecurring savings and the possibility that the idea may be later supplanted by another suggestion that would bring forth still greater savings.

Grievance-Handling Procedure

In unionized offices, we find that specific rules for handling grievances are provided within the union contract. In nonunion offices that do not have a formal arrangement for handling employee grievances, a definite procedure should be provided for their settlement. Having an established procedure for handling grievances facilitates the office workers' upward communication and improves their morale. Also, by having a grievance-handling procedure, the organization recognizes that complaints do exist in the office and that they should be considered a normal part of supervising office work.

Lateral Communication

Organizations often see the need for lateral (horizontal) communication, as well as downward and upward communication. **Lateral communication** occurs among personnel at the same level. Provision for lateral communication is essential in order to coordinate the activities of coworkers and to facilitate their interactions as they perform their jobs.

For example, the job assignment of a worker in the records management department may require periodic consultation with a worker in office services. As shown by the heavy lines in Figure 5–6, the formal network requires that the records management employee communicate through the records manager to the vice president, administrative services and then to the office services manager and finally to the coworker in office services. For purposes of efficiency in practice, however, lateral communication, shown by the broken line in Figure 5–6, is encouraged as long as it has been authorized by both managers.

Diagonal Communication

Diagonal communication occurs when employees communicate with other workers at higher or lower levels in the organization using communication networks other than those formally shown on the organization chart. For example, the broken lines in Figure 5–7 show a records manager who communicates diagonally with the vice presidents of sales and human resources in addition to communicating upward with the vice president of ad-

Lateral Communication Between Office Workers in Two Departments

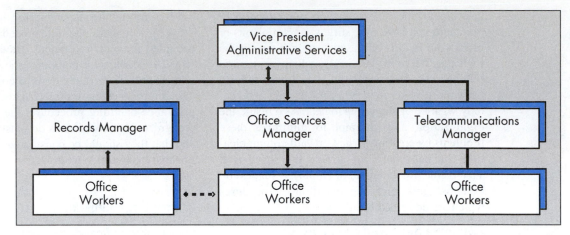

ministrative services. Such diagonal communication regarding routine office operations is encouraged by most organizations to aid in efficiently solving problems involving two or more segments of the organization.

Both diagonal and lateral communication enable employees to plan jointly when establishing policies and procedures that affect several departments, to share information, and to resolve conflicts. Diagonal and lateral communication provide for the direct exchange of messages more quickly and with less distortion than when the senders and receivers are required to use formal upward and downward communication. Thus, the communication barriers described in the following section may be avoided.

BARRIERS TO EFFECTIVE COMMUNICATION

In any type of communication—downward, upward, lateral, or diagonal—there are inherent difficulties or barriers that we should recognize and overcome. A common breakdown in communication occurs when we, as senders, fail to transmit the message intended for those who should receive it. In turn, many people for whom a message is intended either do not receive it or receive a distorted version. As a result, the effective operation of the communication system is hampered or blocked. This section examines several barriers to effective communication and points out ways to reduce communication breakdown.

Figure 5–7
Diagonal Communication Between the Records Manager and Two Vice Presidents

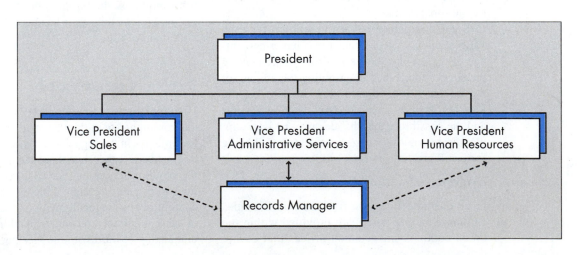

Illustration 5–3 Good listening skills develop at an early age and require intense concentration on what another person is saying.

Barrier l: Differences in Perception

Each office worker is unique and brings to the job a unique **perception**—a way of interpreting situations based on the individual's personal experiences. Thus, the employees' perceptions determine the manner in which they interpret whatever they see or hear. For example, Fred Lemieux, a mail clerk, perceives his manager, Sarah Jagoe, as a "parent figure." Lemieux may accept or reject most of what Jagoe says, depending upon Lemieux's personal experiences at home. In Jagoe, Lemieux may see his quiet, submissive mother and thus react with eagerness to please. On the other hand, Lemieux may see in Jagoe's actions and words those of his loud, abusive former employer; as a result, Lemieux may rebel against Jagoe's authority.

When office employees sense they have been "let down" by a former employer, they are likely to view the replacement with distrust. Because of their differing value systems, older office workers are often unable to "tune in" on the younger workers' "wavelength" and thus experience difficulty in communicating.

As an office manager, you must learn enough about each employee to know what meaning will be attached to your messages and what emotional overtones may be expected. Here, the key to effective, open communication is feedback. Means should be provided for the sender of the message to verify its receipt and understanding through some feedback process or two-way interaction. Although two-way communication is more time-consuming and not feasible for all kinds of messages, it is viewed as more accurate and more satisfying to the parties involved than one-way written communication.

Listening is probably the most important and yet the most neglected dimension of communication. By *listening,* office managers can learn much about how employees perceive the office environment and the emotional states they may be experiencing. To understand the worker's perceptions, the office manager should try to listen to the entire message before evaluating its contents. For example, Lawrence Ogletree, head of the statistical reports division, informs his boss, Jon Mendez, that there is no way to meet the deadline for producing the year-end reports unless more help is made available. Mendez hears only the first part of the message—no way to meet the deadline—and quickly perceives how top management will react to the delay and its effect upon his performance.

Check your perception! Do you see an old lady? A young lady? Both?

Here, Mendez seems more interested in immediately evaluating a part of the message than listening to the entire communication. Had he listened to the whole story, without evaluation, Mendez might have understood Ogletree's frame of reference and effectively worked with him in mutually solving the problem.

You know that there is a great difference between "hearing" and "listening." Most of us have the capacity to receive sounds—to *hear*—but how many of us really *listen* by "tuning in" and paying attention to those sounds? Do we listen intensely and absorb into our consciousness what the other person is saying? How many times in class or on the job have you "come to" with a start and asked yourself what the speaker said during the last several minutes? Have you experienced any major setbacks because you were not listening? Did the other person with whom you were conversing perceive that you were hearing only the words? Have you recently taken inventory of your skill (or bad habits) regarding listening? Here are some guidelines for you to consider as you evaluate and sharpen your listening skill:

While I am listening:

1. I pay close attention by looking at the speaker. I do not daydream, doodle on my notepad, or shuffle papers.
2. I suspend judgment of the speaker and the message by being open-minded to differences of opinion.
3. I try to understand the speaker's purpose.
4. I separate facts from opinions.
5. I focus on the main points, evaluate carefully, and avoid jumping to conclusions.
6. I listen carefully before asking questions or offering comments.
7. I take notes at meetings and during my instructor's lectures, but I don't let note taking become a substitute for listening.

Illustration 5–4 Daydreaming and lack of eye contact demonstrate very poor listening habits.

Barrier 2: Differences in Semantics

Semantics is the study of word meanings and their effect upon human behavior. How often have you heard statements such as "Don't worry about it; it's just a matter of semantics" or "The difficulty is that we have a problem in semantics"?

Since the meaning of words may be interpreted differently by the sender and the receiver, a barrier to communication may be created. Often there is no connection between the *symbol* (the word) and *what is being symbolized* (the meaning). Thus, a message may be received very differently than was intended. For example, let's say you tell a worker, "Please fold this contract as little as possible." Will the worker fold it until it is very small, or will the worker fold it as few times as possible before fitting it in the envelope? In selecting words, you must carefully consider the receiver of the message and the likely interpretation of the words being used.

Barrier 3: Differences in Status

Status, or the level of individuals in the organization structure, influences the quality of communication. Differences in status create barriers to communication since generally it is easier for persons of equal rank than for a manager and a worker to share information and their feelings.

When communicating downward, some managers believe that workers should not receive all the information. Therefore, the managers "dilute" or "water down" the messages. In other cases, workers may be given information that is not relevant to their needs or is not received in time to be useful. The OM should make every effort to reduce any unnecessary dilution of downward communication so that workers receive as much timely information as possible.

In upward communication, workers often dilute messages by giving their employers only partial information. Workers may also "color" or distort events in order to conceal news that may be unpleasant. The conscious manipulation of facts in order to distort events is called **slanting.** A worker often slants communication in order to appear competent in the eyes of the employer. For example, Betsy Monahan, an office manager, "toned down" one of her worker's cost-reduction suggestions in the publicity release for the company's newspaper. The newspaper article was slanted so that most credit for the savings would be attributed to Monahan rather than to the worker. Monahan felt that the cost-savings ideas should have originated with her because of her supervisory position. Thus, she did not want any communication "leaks" to reflect negatively upon her own performance.

At the highest status level in the organization, managers are often faced with information overload. **Information overload** is the communication of an excessive number of details about company operations and personnel activities. The computer, with its tremendous information-producing capability, adds greatly to the problem of information overload in many organizations. However, this same computer can be used in information-distribution systems that are designed to channel information only to those persons who need it. Thus, it is possible to provide information "on call" by means of terminals that are linked with computerized libraries to supply information on various subjects. Top-level managers must decide what information is really needed for decision making and how often that information must be updated. However, in their programs of reducing information overload, managers must make certain that all crucial messages get through. With the enormous capacity of computers today, firms often develop large databases. Managers must guard against the urge to create information and store it simply for information's sake. The databases must serve a purpose for the decision-making needs of the people who have access to them.

Barrier 4: Differences in Preconceived Judgment or Opinion (Bias)

Bias, or prejudice, is the highly personal judgment or opinion formed by an individual before the facts are known. Bias, like prejudice, is both a positive and a negative word. For example, as employees we may be biased *against* or biased *in favor of* a particular company executive, the color selected for the general offices, the dress code adopted by the company, and so forth. As we shall see, bias is a barrier in face-to-face communication as well as in written communication.

Bias may be found when an interviewer obtains background information from a job applicant. Often the interviewer, possibly subconsciously but because of bias, selects a person who has similar interests, hobbies and personal experiences. **Stereotyping,** which is closely related to bias, is the formation of a commonly held mental picture of how people of a particular sex, religion, or race appear, think, feel, and act. Like bias, stereotyping is a barrier in face-to-face communication. For example, the sales manager loses the attention of some of the male and female sales force when at the monthly meeting reference is constantly being made to "My sales*men.*" Or, consider the interviewer who is searching for a male to fill a management position with a starting salary of $60,000 and a female to fill the job of executive secretary at a salary of $20,000!

Bias is often created in written communication when the reader's perception of the message is tilted in one direction or another. Studies have been made that relate the appearance of the sender to the receiver's interpretation of oral and written communication. It has been found that the sender's picture greatly influences how the receiver evaluates the quality of communication.[2]

For example, with the insertion of the author's picture alongside this paragraph, he can expect the message to be interpreted differently by you, the reader, depending on how you are influenced by the picture. Some readers will be biased by the strength of character appearing in the lines of the face and attach much importance to the words; others may see in the picture a lack of sincerity and therefore attach little significance to the content of the message.

In written communications, readers are also greatly influenced by the different faces and styles of type that are used. For example, how did you react to the content of the preceding paragraphs, which are printed in a color other than black and which have been set in a typeface and type size that differ from those used in other parts of the book?

Barrier 5: Differences in Organization Climate

Some organizations encourage workers to express their opinions openly and to participate in important decision-making activities. In these firms, the climate is one of mutual trust and respect between management and employees. As a result, even very controversial messages can be easily transmitted. On the other hand, some managers are authoritarian and discourage the participation of employees and their freedom of expression. As might be expected, the messages transmitted in these organizations are highly diluted and slanted. In both types of organizations, managers at all levels exert considerable influence on communication by the kind of climate they create.

Barrier 6: Business Jargon

Oral and written communication often become ineffective because of the use of jargon. **Jargon** consists of technical terms and idioms that are peculiar to a special group or activity such as business. When the receivers of messages containing business jargon do not recognize and understand the terms, the messages become merely a collection of words that are confusing and unintelligible.

Here is a memo sent by a manager to the employees: "*It is anticipated that our forthcoming meeting will provide considerable opportunities to generate viable alternatives and sufficient interface for resolving the continuing conflict existent in our department. Group interaction should facilitate and expedite problem solutions.*" By eliminating the jargon and words of many syllables, the manager could have sent the following memo, which would have been clearly understood by all workers: "*At our meeting we will discuss different ways for quickly solving the problems in our department.*"

---

[2]For additional studies on photographs and on interview bias, see John T. Molloy, *New Dress for Success* (New York: Warner Books, 1988), pp. 25, 348–349.

Spoken and written messages are also misunderstood if they contain words of many syllables or use long, complex sentences. *A loss in mental perception and acuity is less likely to transpire if the materials presented have no deficiencies in grammatical expression and structural cohesiveness that might contribute to a diminution of clarity.* See what we mean? This type of writing (or speaking) has been labeled "gobbledygook" and should be eliminated in all written and oral communication. Through training and experience in plain talking and writing, you can convert the previous italicized sentence into something like this: *"Misunderstanding is less likely to occur when the materials presented are clear."*

Many organizations hire consultants to teach employees how to write and speak clearly. Some companies send their managers to one-day communication-improvement classes, while other firms bring in coaches for seminars that may last several days. These companies realize that messages loaded with jargon, somewhat like static in a radio broadcast, waste time and money and cause much vital information to wind up in the waste basket.

Barrier 7: Poor Reading Skills

Some office workers have deficiencies in their reading skills and thus are unable to understand and take action on the messages received. Such deficiencies can be detected through tests, and reading-improvement programs may be conducted to improve the skill levels. With training, even good readers can learn to read faster and with greater comprehension. Many organizations encourage their employees to attend such training sessions as part of their communication-improvement program.

Other Barriers to Effective Communication

Other barriers that bring about faulty transmission and reception of messages in the office include:

1. *Time pressure,* as evidenced by the overly busy office manager who does not have time to see all workers or talk with them as fully as might be desired. Employees, also working under time pressure, often do not take the time to read thoroughly the messages received.
2. *Noise,* such as telephones, operation of machines and equipment, and workers' conversations, especially in open areas where employees are trying to talk and hear each other.
3. *Physical distance* between the sender and the receiver, such as the several feet over which the office manager in a private office must loudly call to a secretary located in a nearby cubicle.

The interpersonal communication process discussed up to this point relies upon verbal (oral or written) symbols. However, in face-to-face communication, another kind of communication—nonverbal communication—is occurring at the same time as, or in place of, the spoken words. We shall explain this form of communication in the following section.

NONVERBAL COMMUNICATION

Probably the oldest human communication process, **nonverbal communication** consists of any information not spoken or written that is perceived by our senses. Thus, everything we see, touch, smell, taste, or hear that is not structured into a formal verbal message is considered nonverbal communication. Examples of nonverbal communication are gestures, facial expressions, mannerisms, touching, tones of voice, body positions, uniforms, hairstyles, and other nonverbal stimuli used by the sender and the receiver. Since nonverbal communication may last only a fleeting moment, it cannot be easily remembered or written down for future recall like spoken words.

Several kinds of nonverbal communication and their importance to administrative office managers and workers are discussed in the next sections.

Body Language

Body language refers to our gestures, expressions, and body positions. This nonverbal form of communication conveys to us as senders and as receivers the attitudes and feelings of the other and is just as important to the communication

Illustrations 5–5A and 5-5B Stiff posture, minimal eye contact, and body positioning behind furniture impede effective communication. Improved body language creates a more positive communicated message.

process as the words being spoken. Body language may be consistent with the words we speak, or it may contradict our oral message. In the latter case, body language may become a more accurate expression of the situation and thus reduce the credibility of what we say.

For example, Jana Tompkins, an office manager, is explaining a new departmental regulation to her workforce. While casually reading the message, she shrugs her shoulders, lets a smirk appear on her face, and avoids any eye-to-eye contact with her workers. Although Tompkins' workers may hear what she is saying, it is unlikely they will pay much attention or take any favorable action regarding the newly issued rule. The workers have perceived the rule as one in which Tompkins has little faith and one she plans not to enforce. Thus, when transmitting oral communication, we must be very concerned with our body language and how it will be perceived by those receiving the message.

Research into the field of **kinesics**—the study of the relationship between body motions and communication—shows the importance of recognizing the emotional attitudes of people who are sending and receiving messages since these attitudes are often communicated nonverbally.

Therefore, we should learn how to monitor nonverbal communication and act upon it to our advantage. For example, when trying to present an open attitude to our workers, we should guard against the use of any gesture, such as folding our arms across our chest, which may reveal a closed mind. We usually find it easy to portray attitudes that are considered to be positive. It is much less easy, however, to control those nonverbal signals that should be concealed.

Physical Space

The distance that we maintain with others is related to our feelings toward those persons, indicates something about the relationships, and determines the kind of communication that takes place. The study of **proxemics** examines how individuals use physical space in their interactions with others and how physical space influences behavior.[3] Proxemics has identified three basic zones of physical space—intimate, personal, and social.

---

[3]The term *proxemics* was introduced by Edward T. Hall, the noted anthropologist, who first systematically studied the human use of space. See Edward T. Hall, *The Hidden Dimension* (Garden City, NY: Doubleday, 1966).

An understanding of proxemics helps us in planning and controlling the territorial space in which communication occurs. For example, the AOM will find that the success of a small group meeting is affected by the amount of available space. When meeting in small offices or conference rooms, the employees tend to become more argumentative and more difficult to control. The small space also intensifies conflict. Therefore, to hold a more efficient meeting and reduce potential conflict, the AOM should seat everyone around a large table in a spacious room.

Paralanguage

Paralanguage consists of those aspects of oral communication such as voice qualities and vocalizations that are free of words. Voice qualities include pitch, rhythm, resonance, and tempo; vocalizations are nonlanguage sounds such as laughing, whispering, and "nonwords" such as "uh-huh" and "uh-uh" (standing for yes and no, respectively).

Often more meaning is communicated by paralanguage than by the words we speak. Through training, we can learn to vary our voice qualities and vocalizations to convey a wide range of emotions such as enthusiasm, disappointment, sincerity, interest, or disinterest.

You have now seen how important verbal and nonverbal communication skills are in the problem-solving process, which was fully explained in Chapter 3. When tentative solutions to problems are developed and one is selected, discussion, persuasion, and acceptance occur, which involve both oral and written communication. One communication skill that is basic to all phases of work performance but especially important to the solution of office problems is the writing of reports. Report writing is the topic of the closing section of this chapter.

REPORT-WRITING PRINCIPLES

Reports are prepared to transmit many kinds of messages. For example, reports are written to reflect past, present, and future financial positions or operating results; to summarize the appraisal of employee performance; to present details of productivity-improvement programs; and to verify progress on projects. Reports are used by AOMs to make decisions, since the facts and opinions included in the reports are sound bases for action. Each report states problems and recommends solutions as discussed in Chapter 3.

The size and structure of the organization determine the type and frequency of reports. In a small company, monthly reports prepared from accounting records usually suffice to describe the firm's financial condition. As the company grows, however, we find that the work becomes more specialized and departments are provided with supervisory staff. Therefore, it becomes necessary to keep all levels of management informed by reports that are prepared more frequently. The following discussion provides a set of general principles that is useful for preparing all types of business reports.

PRINCIPLE OF SOUND PURPOSE

The report must have a sound and specific purpose that may be translated into effective business management by the decision maker.

The main reason for writing a report is to transmit information in the hope that action will be taken based on the conclusions reached in the report. Generally, a report serves managers in two ways: (1) it forms the basis for a discussion of the facts and for recommendations, and (2) it serves as a historical record of that phase of the business activity.

Persons preparing reports for management must determine the minimum information requirements of each manager in relation to his or her needs in the decision-making process. Often, managers may not know their needs exactly and may request more information "to play it safe." In turn, managers become burdened with information overload, as discussed earlier in the chapter. Thus, those responsible for report preparation must make sure that they are meeting the needs, as opposed to the wants, of management.

PRINCIPLE OF EFFECTIVE ORGANIZATION

The report should be well planned and well organized.

Since business reports differ widely in content, their organization also varies. For example, a report of operations is usually an accounting report supported by financial statements and schedules. Other reports are statistical, while still others are surveys or investigations that present answers to specific questions. The organization of most reports includes these sections that are usually arranged in this order:

1. *Purpose.* The introduction states the reason for writing the report, the information it contains, and the method employed in collecting the data.
2. *Summary.* The summary contains the conclusions reached and the recommendations made. Many managers prefer the summary at the beginning of the report since placing it first saves them time in reading the entire report. If necessary, they can examine the supporting details later.
3. *Problems and solution.* The body of the report consists of a logical development of the subject matter. For example, a report dealing with the retrieval of information from the files might show the present method and cost of manually retrieving documents, the average cost of each document retrieved, a description of the proposed automated method of retrieval, the expected costs under this method, the advantages and disadvantages of each method, and recommendations.
4. *Recommendations.* Whenever a report results in recommendations for action, the recommendations should be stated positively, clearly, and completely. They may be stated in the form of a summary at the end of each section, or they may be part of the summary at the beginning of the report.
5. *Appendix.* Exhibits should be included whenever the narrative of the report needs more detailed explanation. Appendix items may be in the form of supporting letters, memorandums, charts, layouts, tabulations, or statistics.

A very long formal report may include additional sections, such as preliminary pages consisting of the title page, copyright page (if appropriate), foreword, acknowledgments, table of contents, and list of tables and charts; bibliography; and sometimes an index. A letter of transmittal (sometimes called a cover letter) should be attached to the report to inform the reader about the nature and purpose of the report.

PRINCIPLE OF BREVITY

The report should be kept as short as possible.

The old adage, "If I had more time, I would have written less" applies to report writing. The reader's attention can be quickly captured by reducing or eliminating much introductory material.

Reports should be reasonably brief because (1) they are expensive to prepare; (2) long reports are complicated, are difficult to analyze, and usually indicate poor planning; (3) verbosity usually indicates too much emphasis on minor details or irrelevant matters; and (4) unnecessary length evokes criticism about efficiency.

PRINCIPLE OF CLARITY

Simple language should be used for easy understanding.

When writing reports, we should avoid long, involved sentences. We should select words carefully so that our intended meaning is clearly communicated to our readers. New, technical terms that may create misunderstanding should be defined in order to eliminate communication "static," which may detract from the purpose of our message.

PRINCIPLE OF TIMELY SCHEDULING

Reports should be scheduled so they can be well prepared without undue burden on the staff.

The interval between compiling the data and completing the report should not be so long that the content is obsolete by the time it is presented. With the availability of personal computers, managers are greatly aided in the timely scheduling and preparing of business reports.

PRINCIPLE OF JUSTIFIED COST

The benefits received from the preparation and use of a report should exceed its cost.

With today's high-speed computer printers, many managers are flooded with useless reports that are sent out under the guise of useful information. Therefore, someone should be assigned the responsibility of evaluating the reporting needs of the firm to determine whether the cost of preparing and using the reports justifies their continuance. Such a study is aimed at determining the essential information needs of all managers, discontinuing any unneeded and questionable copies of reports, and revising reports to omit information not sufficiently useful to warrant the costs of collection and reporting. Definite procedures should be established and maintained for a cost-control study throughout the year so that the preparation of any new reports is properly authorized.

SUMMARY

1. The communication process is the transmission of a message from the sender to the receiver.

2. In many instances, the lack of good communication lies not in the network or channel selected but in the communicator—the sender of the message. The sender must transmit messages that are understood by the receiver so that desired action is taken as evidenced by feedback. Importantly, too, the sender must be concerned with the emotional reactions, attitudes, and feelings of those who receive the messages.

3. Communication is not a one-way street between the office manager and the employees, or vice versa. Successful communication flows not only downward and upward but also laterally and diagonally. In each of these flows, there is potential for a communication breakdown unless the sender is aware of barriers relating to perception, semantics, status, bias, organization climate, jargon, and the receiver's reading skills. The sender must also be concerned with nonverbal communication, such as body language, which is just as important to the oral and written communication processes as the spoken and written words.

4. Much of the written communication in offices is transmitted by formal reports, which are often used in decision making. Successful business reports have a sound purpose and are well planned and organized, brief, easily understood, timely scheduled, and cost justified.

FOR YOUR REVIEW

1. How does the communication process begin?

2. Why are written rather than spoken words recommended when important messages are to be transmitted?

3. Distinguish between the formal and the informal communication network.

4. How can an office manager effectively use the grapevine?

c
o
n
t

5. What is the purpose of a communication audit?

6. What factors should be considered by the office manager when deciding which channel of downward communication to use?

7. Of what value are bulletin boards to a business?

8. What are the main uses of upward communication channels?

9. Why is there need for lateral and diagonal communication in the office?

10. How do differences in perception become barriers to effective communication?

11. When communicating upward, why do workers dilute or slant their messages?

12. Explain how the climate of an organization may affect the communication process.

13. What is business jargon?

14. Since nonverbal communication cannot be easily remembered or written down, why is it important in the communication process?

15. What is the significance of proxemics to the communication process?

16. Of what does paralanguage consist?

17. In what order do the sections of most business reports appear?

18. What are the principles of good report preparation?

FOR YOUR DISCUSSION

1. Some authorities strongly advocate that managers should *never* use the grapevine to disseminate information. Do you agree with these authorities? Why? If you disagree with them, under what conditions could you effectively use the grapevine?

2. How can diagonal communication become so complex that it becomes a barrier to good communication?

3. The administrative manager for Johnson Telegraphics, Randy McLemore, has created a communication climate so well liked by his workers that they drop into his office very often merely to chat. McLemore does not want to react negatively to his workers and "turn them off," since he does not want to be avoided when they have information he needs. However, McLemore is very much concerned about the amount of time being wasted every day in idle chitchat. What approach can you recommend he use to reduce the number of "drop-ins"?

4. Anna Sessa prides herself on her supervisory abilities and often tells visitors and clients that she has "good communications" in the office. As a visitor receiving this message, explain what you think Sessa means by her statement.

5. Steven Williams is the newly hired office manager of Madrid Fibers, Inc. Only 25 years old and relatively inexperienced, Williams is aware of his number one deficiency—very poor listening skills. Do you believe Williams can hope to function effectively with this deficiency? Explain.

CASES FOR CRITICAL THINKING

Case 5–1 Creating Effective Downward Communication

Your organization has recently promoted several area managers. The employees in your company have been experiencing difficulty in understanding communications from these area managers. The vice president, Pat Montesanto, has asked you to develop a short checklist to orient managers on good downward communication. She plans to have a training session soon. What items will you present on your checklist?

Case 5–2 Writing More Clearly

Georgia Moschou, vice president of office services at Mint Savings and Loan, believes that many of the reports prepared by the department managers are so poorly written that the messages become garbled in transmission. As a result, those receiving the messages have difficulty in determining what action, if any, they are to take. Moschou's beliefs are confirmed by samples of her manager's reports that have been collected and analyzed over the past six months. Some of the findings of Moschou's audit are given below:

1. Words and phrases to be simplified. What short, simple words can the managers use instead?

    a. afford an opportunity   f. interrogate

    b. prioritize   g. utilization

    c. voluminous   h. finalize

    d. consummate   i. profitwise

    e. automatization   j. substantial portion

2. A few "static-loaded" sentences. How can these sentences be revised to communicate more clearly by using simple words?

    a. The antiquated electronic calculator housed in my office is ineffectual for solving the sophisticated mathematical problems I encounter.

    b. It is imperative that all unwarranted absenteeism be adequately investigated so reminders can be promulgated to the parties at fault.

    c. The customer's dilatory actions precipitated the necessity for our loan people to respond with exiguous information.

Give Moschou a helping hand by answering the questions she has raised in 1 through 2.

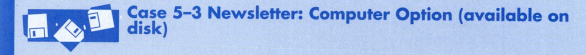 ## Case 5–3 Newsletter: Computer Option (available on disk)

MANAGING A CULTURALLY DIVERSE WORKFORCE

6 • Recruiting and Orienting
the Workforce

7 • Supervising the
Office Staff

8 • Training, Appraising, and
Promoting Office Personnel

9 • Analyzing Office Jobs

10 • Administering
Office Salaries

11 • Providing Employee
Benefits

12 • Examining Workplace
Issues

6

RECRUITING AND ORIENT- ING THE WORKFORCE

GOALS FOR THIS CHAPTER

After completing this chapter, you should be able to:

1. Identify the sources of human resources that the AOM may use in recruiting office workers.
2. Describe the procedures used by small and large companies to select office personnel.
3. Classify and state the purposes of the pre-employment tests used in selecting office workers.
4. Describe an effective orientation program for newly employed office workers.
5. Summarize those government regulations that directly influence the employment process.

Human resources with all its diversity—the most valuable asset in the office—is the theme of this second part of the textbook. As you saw in Chapter 1, determining the needs for human resources is one of the office manager's major activities in the planning function. Today, to meet those needs, more and more companies rely upon hiring *contingent* employees—temporary workers, independent contractors, and part-timers—rather than recruiting full-time, permanent workers. When taken together, temporary, contract, and part-time workers made up about 25 percent of the workforce in early 1993.[1]

How do we account for this trend toward the increased popularity of a so-called "disposable," contingent workforce? Companies answer this question by citing their need to downsize and restructure in order to remain globally competitive, to avoid the growing burdens imposed by employment rules and antidiscrimination laws, and to reduce the skyrocketing costs of health-care and pension plans.[2] As you continue your study of Part 2, you will find that this move toward the use of contingent office workers signals an end to the security and sense of loyalty and dedication that for so many years have traditionally characterized full-time office workers. Thus, in many firms, today's AOM is faced with a brand-new pressing problem: *How do I plan and organize an effective, efficient workforce composed of full-time and contingent employees?* Having stated and defined the problem, the AOM can aim for its solution by next gathering and analyzing information relevant to the recruiting and orienting activities.

---

[1]Clare Ansberry, "Workers Are Forced to Take More Jobs with Few Benefits," *The Wall Street Journal* (March 1, 1993), p. A1.

[2]Janice Castro, "Disposable Workers," *Time* (March 29, 1993), pp. 43–47.

BACKGROUND INFORMATION ABOUT THE WORKFORCE PROBLEM

In many small and medium-size offices, recruiting and orienting office workers are major phases of the administrative office manager's job. In large offices, the responsibility for recruiting and orienting office personnel may be assigned to a specialist in the human resources department. Or, the orientation may be combined with the initial training program under the jurisdiction of the training department or the AOM.

Regardless of who selects and orients office workers, every effort must be made to keep and promote qualified workers. For a fair day's work, an office employee must be paid a fair day's salary. Salary costs are at their highest level in history and represent an increasing percentage of the cost of products and services. Further, in 1991, the cost of employee benefits (fringe benefits) for *salaried* employees was 37.1 cents of every payroll dollar. This means that, in addition to regular pay, employers spent an average of $15,996 that year for each *salaried* employee's benefits.[3]

Another element that adds to increased staffing costs is the creating and processing of employee records. For example, federal, state, and local governments have greatly increased their record-keeping and reporting requirements for equal opportunity compliance, legally required insurance and compensation claims, performance analyses, and job evaluations. All of these record-keeping and forms-completion activities involve costly administrative labor time and thus create substantial charges against a firm's profits.

Figure 6–1 shows that recruiting, selecting, and retaining qualified employees for office positions involve knowing the sources of supply; interviewing and testing the applicants; maintaining personnel records, such as personnel requisitions and application forms, required by business and government; properly introducing the new office workers to their jobs; and keeping abreast of the government regulations and agency guidelines that affect employee recruitment. Each of these topics is discussed in this chapter. Supervising, training, appraising, promoting, and compensating office personnel are discussed in the following chapters.

SOURCES OF OFFICE WORKERS

Selecting the sources of office employees is based on these criteria: interviewing a minimum number of applicants to save the employer's time; carefully screening reliable sources to reduce turnover; and creating a workforce that is cooperative, progressive, productive, and happy.

Public Employment Services and Private Employment Agencies

When recruiting office personnel, many employers make use of public employment services and private employment agencies. These organizations put an employer in contact with a selected number of prospective workers.

Public Employment Services

The largest **public employment service** is the United States Employment Service (USES), which is supervised by the Department of Labor. Each state has an employment service, sometimes called an employment commission or an employment security agency, which is affiliated with USES. The state placement service is usually called *Job Service*. Job Service, located in every metropolitan area, requires no fees from the jobseekers or the employers who use its services.

Some of the services provided by Job Service include:

1. Locating qualified workers through a nation-wide recruitment service.
2. Selecting qualified workers through valid interviewing and testing techniques.

---

[3]*Employee Benefits (1992 Edition),* Survey Data from Benefit Year 1991 (Washington, DC: U.S. Chamber Research Center, 1992), p. 11. The percentage of payroll allocated to benefits for *hourly paid* employees was 39.6 percent of payroll, with an annual dollar value of benefits totaling $12,814.

Figure 6–1
Recruiting,
Selecting, and
Retaining the
Workforce

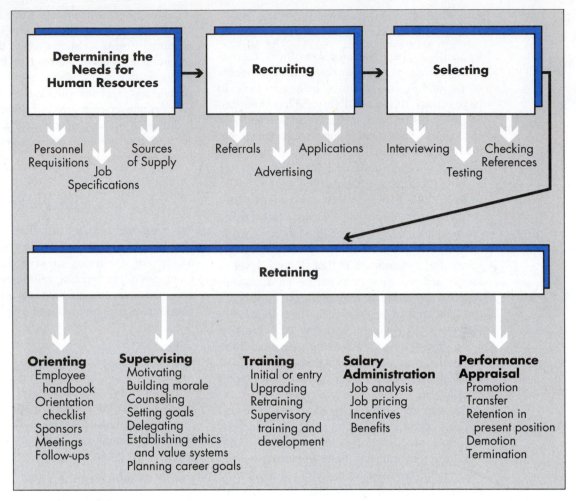

3. Testing and counseling people about the fields of work for which their aptitudes and interests best suit them.
4. Providing guidance in solving problems of turnover and absenteeism.
5. Developing training courses to help alleviate existing shortages of qualified workers and meet expected needs for additional trained workers.
6. Aiding veterans by relating their service training to civilian job openings.
7. Developing special programs for recruiting older workers, the disabled, and members of minority groups.

Private Employment Agencies

Private employment agencies, also known as *placement firms,* charge a fee for their selection and placement services. This fee, depending upon local or state law, may range from a week's pay to possibly 15 percent of the employee's first-year pay. Practices vary as to whether the job applicant or the employer pays the fee. For example, when an executive recruiting agency is hired to search for a senior executive or manager, the employer commonly pays the fee.

In selecting a private employment agency, the AOM should make sure that the agency is professionally qualified to do its job. The AOM can determine that an agency subscribes to professional and ethical standards by checking to see that the agency has membership in its state and national employment agency association. More information about the agency's standing and reputation in the community may be obtained from the Better Business Bureau, the chamber of commerce, and consumer protection bureaus.

Temporary Office Help Services

Temporary office help services "rent out" office workers for varying periods of time, such as a day, a week, several months, or longer. Temporary workers, an integral part of the labor force, have been used for years as emergency fill-ins to reduce work overloads during peak periods, to assist with special projects, and to fill in for vacationing employees. Today, however, as we noted earlier, the restructuring of organizations has changed the nature of employment. Thus, we find companies using temporary workers as long-term employees.

Among the nationally known temporary office help services are Accountemps, Kelly Services, Manpower, Inc., Olsten Corporation, Talent Tree Personnel Services, TempForce, and Western Temporary Services. The five types of jobs for which the services most often provide temporary help, arranged according to frequency of use, are clerical/filing, secretarial, data processing, word processing, and accounting/finance.[4]

In using the services of temporary workers, the employer commonly pays a flat fee to the temporary office help service. The temporary employee is interviewed, trained, and paid by the service. The employee's bonding, social security records, tax deductions, accident and sickness insurance, and vacation, if earned, are all obligations of the service. The client-company realizes its savings in the areas of record-keeping costs, payroll taxes, workers' compensation, vacation and sick time, and use of the employee only when needed. Because of the tremendous increase in the cost of employee benefits, companies realize

considerable savings by using temporary help. The National Planning Association estimates that temporary and part-time workers are paid 20 to 40 percent less than their full-time counterparts.[5]

The following guidelines are offered to the AOM who is considering the use of temporary office help:

1. Determine in advance the number of clerical hours needed in the department requiring help. Compare the cost of part-time help on the company's own payroll with the cost of using temporary helpers (sometimes called *temporaries* or *temps*).
2. When seeking workers, provide the service with a current and complete job description for each position to be filled. Thus, if a payroll clerk is needed, the service will not refer a person who has the skills of only a data-entry clerk.
3. Have the work ready prior to the arrival of the temporary worker by planning complete step-by-step job instructions.
4. Make sure the permanent workers understand in advance that the temporary is being brought in for special needs only and not to complete their work. Ask the permanent workers to be helpful and cooperative in whatever way possible.
5. Make sure that the office equipment to be used is in good working order, supplies are on hand, and space is adequate for the temporary's needs.
6. Appoint one person to meet the temporary worker, to introduce the worker to others in the department, and to orient the worker to the locations of the lounge, the cafeteria, and the workstation.
7. Make sure the temporary understands the step-by-step job instructions.
8. If possible, employ the temporary a day in advance so he or she can become familiar with the job duties. Company practices regarding time for lunch and work breaks and

---

[4]"Temporary Help: The Need Is Still There," *The Office* (October, 1992), p. 36.

[5]Julia Lawlor, "Cutbacks Fuel Contingent Workforce," *USA Today* (March 3, 1993), p. 2B.

procedures for handling personal incoming and outgoing calls should be reviewed.

9. If a temporary's work is not satisfactory, contact the service and explain the situation. Usually, the temporary can be released after the first few hours, and the worker will be replaced by the service.

10. Review with the temporary the overall performance on each job so that ways may be discovered to do the job better and at a lower cost.

Employee Leasing Services

Some firms obtain employees from leasing companies that assign workers to the client firms under a contract to provide on-the-job services. In contrast to a temporary help service, an **employee leasing service** places workers on a permanent, or fairly permanent, basis.

In a typical employee leasing arrangement, an employer discharges his or her workers (or certain groups of workers), who then are hired by the leasing service. The leasing service, in turn, prepares a leasing agreement and assigns the same employees back to their original employer. The original employer still determines who works for the firm, who receives how much compensation, who gets promotions, who gets time off, and who is discharged.

Because a leasing firm represents employees of many companies, it obtains lower group rates on workers' compensation, unemployment compensation, and health insurance. Some leasing services base their fees on a percentage of the client-firm's total payroll. This fee, which varies with the number of employees and their pay, may range from 2 to 10 percent of a company's total payroll. Other leasing services quote a flat annual fee, depending upon the size of the client-firm.

Business firms enter into this type of "lease-back" arrangement in order to reduce the costs of administering their human resources function. The employee leasing service often offers full personnel administration services and provides employee benefits such as health- and dental-care insurance and pension plans. Thus, by leasing its employees, a small firm is better able to compete with a larger company in providing high-quality benefits. When

it can offer a broader array of benefits, a small firm may often experience a higher morale level and a lower turnover rate. The leasing service is also responsible for computing the payroll and paying the employees, maintaining payroll records, and preparing employee-related reports.

Local Community Agencies

Sources of office personnel include local community agencies operated by minority groups; veterans' organizations; churches; charitable organizations; fraternal lodges and clubs; trade associations; and institutions for rehabilitation of physically and mentally disabled persons, drug addicts, and ex-prisoners. Generally, such agencies refer only members of their own groups and do not charge the applicant or employer a fee for the services rendered.

Advertising

Before placing help-wanted advertisements, the AOM should carefully study the most effective form of advertising and the most appropriate advertising medium. The type of position to be filled will influence the selection of a medium, and a little experimentation will show which is the most satisfactory. Care must be exercised when placing help-wanted advertisements to make sure the wording of the advertisements does not conflict with fair employment practices laws, which are discussed later in this chapter.

One disadvantage of placing help-wanted advertisements in newspapers is that a large number of responses may be received when time and resources permit the interviewing of only a few applicants. This method proves suitable, however, for the firm that has a human resources department adequately staffed to screen, interview, and test applicants.

Referrals

A firm often obtains qualified employees through **referrals** by present employees, company officers, and customers. (Showing favoritism in the employment of relatives, a practice called *nepotism,* is discussed in Chapter 12.) Great care must be exercised when using such referrals, however. If a customer or an officer of the firm recommends a person who is not suitable or qualified for the job, it may cause the firm some embarrassment if the applicant is not hired or is not retained for any length of time.

Some firms encourage their workers to recommend friends as possible employees because it adds to the prestige of present employees and creates a good psychological effect. Firms may offer incentives, such as cash payments, U.S. savings bonds, and company merchandise, for referrals after the newly employed worker has been on the job for a stipulated period of time.

Educational Institutions

Many large business firms send representatives to college and school campuses to interview students, such as you, about possible employment after graduation. If it is not possible to send representatives to college campuses, a firm may write to the placement office of the college, describe the types of job openings available, and ask you to submit your resumé (personal data sheet).

Many private business schools maintain a placement service for their students, some of whom have had office experience. A number of high schools, vocational schools, junior colleges, community colleges, and universities cooperate with industry by setting up internship and cooperative work-study programs. In these programs, students may attend school part time and work part time or alternate full-time work and full-time school terms. Some companies sponsor summer-hire programs in which students work for the companies during the summer months of their junior and senior years. If the students' work proves satisfactory, they are asked to return the following summer at an appropriate salary increase. Such cooperative training programs develop many good trainees who later become full-time employees of the participating companies.

Other Sources of Office Employees

Additional recruiting sources available to the AOM include:

1. *Walk-ins,* those who walk in from the street to apply for a position.
2. *Unsolicited letters of application.*
3. *Manufacturers of office equipment* who have established training schools and placement agencies to supply you, their customer, with well-trained, efficient operators of their equipment.
4. *Career conferences and job fairs,* where you and your staff screen qualified job applicants.
5. *Resumé databases* containing students' resumés that you can evaluate to provide a list of schools to visit and names of those to interview.[6]
6. *Resumé-search services* that search through thousands of current resumés in their databases, looking for specific skills. The search firms generally charge less than "headhunters," and they guarantee qualified candidates.[7]
7. *Advertising job openings on The Career Television Network (TCTN),* a nationwide job opportunity video network. Here, you can announce your job openings and plan a program that includes interviews of people currently employed and the advantages and benefits of working in your firm.[8]
8. *Former employees* who had good work records. Relying upon a pool of experienced, familiar workers who can come to work on very short notice is sometimes called *just-in-time hiring.* Just-in-time employers try to maintain their competitive position by reducing the time spent recruiting qualified workers who can quickly commence contributing to the firm's profitability.

---

[6]Bill Leonard, "Resumé Databases to Dominate Field," *HR Magazine* (April, 1993), pp. 59–60.

[7]"Hiring Through Resumé Databases," *INC.* (May, 1993), p. 30.

[8]Bill Leonard, "Looking for a Job? Then Turn on Your TV," *HR Magazine* (April, 1993), pp. 58–59.

Illustration 6–1 Properly designed application forms solicit only data relevent to the job requirements.

9. *Previous job applicants* who were not hired because there were no openings at the time of application. To aid you in your search, you may want to use a computer program that provides a job applicant database which lets you track applicants by: personal information (name, address, telephone number, etc.), position applied for, disability, veteran status, skills, education level, referrals, and so forth.

10. *Retirees.* Many organizations find a fertile field of labor supply among those who have found retirement boring or expensive and now look for on-the-job socialization and extra cash. Often, you may find that the retirees have the required skills, knowledge, and experience and may exhibit more drive, ambition, and ingenuity than your younger workers.

SELECTING OFFICE WORKERS

You will find that the employee selection procedure in small offices is very simple compared to that in offices having large staffs. In small offices, an interview is usually all that is necessary, followed by a statement that within a few days you will be informed if you have been offered the position. In this way, no decision need be reached until a sufficient number of applicants have been interviewed. In large offices, however, the procedure becomes more formal and complex since the larger the office staff, the more necessary the record-keeping requirements become.

Federal, state, and local laws affecting the employment process stimulate the need for complete and detailed records of job applicants and employees. For small and medium-size offices, the employment records should include, as a minimum, the application form and the record of employment. In a firm large enough to have a human resources department, the following additional forms may be used to establish definite procedures and adequate control over employee selection.

Personnel Requisition Form

To many people, the application is probably the first and most important office employment record. Its use in large offices, however, is sometimes preceded by the **personnel requisition** prepared by a department head. This form specifies the number of persons required and the kind of work to be done. If job specifications have been prepared, they are studied in order to obtain specific information concerning the job requirements.[9] This study is completed before any search for a job applicant begins.

Application Form

Probably the most frequently used form in the selection process is the **application form.** Careful use of application forms permits a preliminary screening of applicants for a position, thus saving the interviewer's time.

The information called for on an application form is usually grouped under the headings of personal information, education, business experience, references, and general remarks. In designing application forms, employers should request only data that are useful in predicting job-relevant behavior. Employers should not ask questions that

---

[9]The preparation of job specifications, as part of a company's program of job analysis, is fully discussed in Chapter 9.

may become the basis for charges of discrimination under the fair employment practices regulations. For example, questions that request your sex and religion are clearly inappropriate unless it can be shown that they are bona fide ("good faith") occupational qualifications (discussed later in this chapter). Questions about age, race, marital status, and national origin are also unacceptable. Questions about intimate subjects, such as your sexual orientation or personal characteristics, are doubly dangerous. These questions not only are illegal on the basis of their relevance to the job requirements, but also represent an invasion of your privacy.

State departments of labor examine application forms to make sure they are prepared within the meaning of the law. Whenever there are inconsistencies between federal requirements and state laws, federal requirements may take precedence. For example, in many states the fair employment practices legislation makes it illegal to identify your race on your personnel record. However, federal agencies have found it useful to have this information to detect possible discrimination in a firm. The federal government may, therefore, request that certain companies maintain such records, with the stipulation that the information is not to be used for unfair discrimination.

The Interview

Let's say you are interviewing a job applicant for the position of administrative assistant in your firm. By studying the jobseeker's application or resumé, you can select specific areas to discuss or to clarify during the interview. You should guard against arriving at hasty conclusions regarding the applicant's personality, intelligence, skills, abilities, and motivations. Instead, you should try to remain as objective as possible and resist drawing conclusions about the applicant until the interview is well under way and you have obtained enough evidence to justify your feelings.

During the interview, you can evaluate the applicant's personal appearance in relation to the job opening and to any dress codes (regulations) your firm may have established. In many firms, dress codes are flexible depending upon the job and the extent to which the jobholder meets the public. For example, your company may require its male employees to wear dress shirts, ties, and jackets if they meet and work with the public in

Illustrations 6–2A and 6-2B Although dress codes vary between companies and for different jobs, a professional and well-groomed personal appearance is essential when going on an interview.

DIALOG FROM THE WORKPLACE

TONY NORRIS

PC Specialist
Sears Merchandise Group
Hoffman Estates, Illinois

In 1968, Tony Norris joined Sears in California. He was later promoted to the Chicago home office and by 1980 he had become a shoe buyer for the retail chain and its catalog.

In 1986, a spinal tumor paralyzed Norris from the neck down, forcing him to leave Sears and a job he dearly loved. In 1988, after a coma and a 20-month hospital stay, his former boss called, asking if he would like to come back to work at Sears. Norris accepted and currently works as a PC specialist, planning and budgeting, for Sears shoe departments in some 800 stores across the country.

QUESTION: Tony, think about today's management students who tomorrow may be interviewing job candidates who have disabilities. What suggestions can you offer that will aid in reducing job bias during the interview?

RESPONSE: I never tell people ahead of time that I'm in a wheelchair. They shouldn't do anything different for me than they'd do for anybody else—and it's no different for a job interview. I don't put that information on my resumé either. I just concentrate on my qualifications and I hope the interviewer will do the same.

My advice to new interviewers would be to never prejudge *any* applicant, especially one with a disability. Keep an open mind and focus on capabilities, not disabilities.

If I were applying for a position, I'd want the interviewer to tell me what the job description requires and then leave it up to me as to how I'd meet those requirements. In other words, focus on the final outcome, not how the person actually performs the task.

It's probably human nature to say, "Gee, if I were in that person's shoes, I could never do this job." But an unbiased interviewer won't fall into that trap. Don't underestimate a person with a disability and don't try to second guess what his or her abilities are.

It always irritates me when I go into a restaurant and the waitress asks my nurse, "What would *he* like for dinner?" Don't let that scenario happen on the job. If, for example, you're interviewing someone who is deaf, always address the applicant, *not* the interpreter. The interpreter is just the go-between. It's the job applicant that you want to get to know.

I don't know why people do this, but many times they'll be overly nice to me simply because I'm in a wheelchair. Sometimes I think they're going to reach out and pat me on the head like a little child. Perhaps they're uncomfortable or just uninformed, but I'd prefer that they see me as a professional in a business environment.

What I want from a work situation is to be treated as an equal—whether it's an interview or just an average day on the job. Just because I've got splints on my hands doesn't mean you shouldn't offer to shake hands with me.

As your company's recruiter, it's your job to ask all the tough questions, evaluate each candidate fairly, and select the best person for the company. I'm sure you'll make the right decision if you keep this one thing in mind: There's no relationship between the disability and the capabilities of a person.

the course of their workday. However, in some departments of your firm, such as the computer center, sports shirts without ties and jackets may be acceptable.

In arriving at an opinion about the applicant's suitability for the job opening, you should strive to preserve the applicant's sense of dignity and self-respect. At the close of the interview, the applicant should be able to leave with a positive feeling toward the company. For some job openings, you may schedule a second interview to check impressions gained during the first meeting and to ensure that the applicant still displays interest in the position. During the second interview, senior members of the firm may be called upon to interview the applicant to make sure that the individual is well qualified for the position.

You can use several different kinds of interviews, or approaches, to obtain information from the job applicant about education, training, and experience. Three common types of interviews—direct, indirect, and patterned—are briefly described in Figure 6–2.

Record of Interview

The **record of interview** contains in an organized format all the information acquired during the interview. The record aids you, as an interviewer, in remembering all the facts and in making a thorough analysis regarding an applicant's employment. If the personal interview was favorable and there is a possibility of employment, you may schedule a follow-up interview during which you use the interview record.

Reference Checks and Letters of Recommendation

Many office managers find that the value of reference checks is limited since job applicants naturally list as references those persons who can be relied upon to provide positive comments. Persons giving reference information must guard against supplying information that may be looked upon as discriminatory or slanderous and thus open the door to costly litigation. For this reason, a former employer named as a reference may provide only information such as dates of employment, the person's job title, location of job site, and possibly the salary. Some employers require permission from former employees before supplying such information. Thus, these employers are protected against a claim of having invaded the privacy of their former employees.

Telephone calls are an excellent means of checking references when time is of the essence and thorough information is essential. When checking references, try to talk with the applicant's former supervisor, who may be more forthright than a person in the human resources department. The telephone call will be effective if, as an interviewer, you establish good rapport with the reference and ask carefully phrased questions. In the conversation, you should follow up on every clue about the applicant's past work performance, or there is a risk of your accepting biased information and making a poor hiring decision.

Office managers find that letters of recommendation, like reference checks, are only fairly effective. First, as you might expect, job applicants name those persons who are likely to write favorable letters of recommendation. Second, fearful of potential lawsuits, many persons decline to give information to a prospective employer unless that information is favorable. As a result, letters of recommendation are often vague, noncommittal, or incredibly glowing. Finally, requests for information from the references supplied by the job applicant may not be answered.

Record of Employment

The **record of employment,** typically maintained in the human resources department of medium-size and large companies, consists of the employee's resumé and a history of employment with the firm. In addition to providing personal data and other information usually found on the application, the record of employment is kept up to date by recording such information as the employee's absences, promotions, transfers, and salary increases. Much of the information kept on the record of employment is needed at the time of employee appraisal and also for preparing statistical reports required by government agencies.

Figure 6–2
Three Com-
mon Types of
Interviews

DIRECT INTERVIEW

The interviewer asks job applicants direct questions related to their qualifications and ability to fill the job.

Sample Questions Asked by Interviewer
1. What is your keyboarding rate?
2. What hours of work do you prefer? Why?
3. Do you like to work overtime?
4. Do you work better in a group or alone?
5. Do you like our work schedule? Why?

The interview is completed relatively quickly because a concise answer is required for each specific question. The direct interview is commonly used to screen applicants for routine office jobs.

The amount of information obtained during the interview is limited. Often no more is learned than specific "yes" or "no" answers, which may not provide enough information to make a hiring decision. Applicants may have pertinent information to pass along but are not given the opportunity to do so.

INDIRECT INTERVIEW

The interviewer asks open-ended questions in order to stimulate the applicants to talk about themselves. The questions asked are designed to solicit opinions and ideas from the applicants, to learn about their attitudes, and to obtain insight into their value systems.

Sample Questions Asked by Interviewer
1. Why are you interested in obtaining a position in our company?
2. What are your long-range goals?
3. What are your plans for furthering your education?
4. What are your major strengths and weaknesses?
5. What is most important to you about your job?

By listening carefully, the interviewer learns much as the applicants elaborate on important points, such as why they left their former jobs. During this time, the interviewer sees how well the applicants demonstrate their qualifications and observes their self-expression, along with other factors such as manners, poise, and self-confidence.

The indirect interview is time-consuming and requires an interviewer who is skilled at listening and observing, who can keep applicants from digressing too far from the subject at hand, and who can effectively interpret the answers.

PATTERNED INTERVIEW

Each interviewer uses a standard printed form or questionnaire containing specific key questions like the following:

Sample Questions Asked by Interviewer
1. How many years experience do you have?
2. What languages do you speak fluently?
3. What weekly salary do you expect to receive when starting on this job?
4. What days or evenings during the week would you not be available for overtime work?
5. How soon will you be able to start work?

As the questions are asked during the interview, the interviewer records the applicant's answers. This type of interview is especially effective when many people are being screened to fill a number of jobs. Time is saved by obtaining the same type of information from all applicants so the responses may be compared. Also, more than one interviewer may be used at the same time, and the questionnaire answers can then be compared and reviewed by a senior executive, such as the human resources administrator.

Illustration 6–3 Employers may conduct one of several types of interviews (direct, indirect, or patterned) with prospective job applicants.

1. Employees may be required to inspect records on their own time.
2. Employees may be required to fill out a written form requesting access to their personnel files and stating either the purpose of the inspection or the specific records they want to see.
3. Employers may require that inspection of the files be done in the presence of a management-level employee.
4. Inspections may be limited to once a year for each employee, unless an employee has "reasonable cause" to inspect the file more than once.

The Pennsylvania law permits note taking, but not copying of records. Employees are allowed to place in their files any counterstatements of disagreement with any of the material kept on file. However, inspection rights do not apply to criminal or grievance procedure records, letters of reference, medical records, or staff planning information.

Employment Records and Employee Privacy

Many workers are greatly concerned about threats to their personal privacy and thus question the use of the information kept in their employment files. At the federal level, the **Privacy Act of 1974** regulates the collection and use of personal data by the government. This act is designed to protect your right to privacy by permitting you to exercise some control over the information the government keeps about you. Some companies have voluntarily set up informal record-keeping procedures to meet the concern of workers about their personal privacy. These procedures attempt to discourage the misuse of information contained in employees' medical and insurance records, although they do provide for computer printouts of records for employee verification.

Some states have enacted laws relating to the keeping of employee records and the inspection rights of workers. For example, in Pennsylvania, all employees have the right to inspect their individual personnel files. Employers, however, may use the following guidelines when applying the law:

PREEMPLOYMENT TESTING

The use of tests in selecting office workers is based on these two principles:

1. Tests for selecting, placing, evaluating, and promoting office employees must be administered and interpreted in an unbiased, objective manner.
2. Tests are not exclusive devices but *supplemental* tools in the total assessment of personnel.

Testing practices that have a discriminatory effect upon job applicants are prohibited. As a result of the U.S. Supreme Court ruling in the *Griggs v Duke Power* case, "Any test must measure the person for the job, and not the person in the abstract."[10] The Supreme Court decision was designed not to abolish job tests but, rather, to

---

[10]In 1971, the U.S. Supreme Court unanimously declared that practices which act to exclude applicant groups artificially because of race or other factors and that cannot be shown to bear a predictive relationship to job performance violate the law. Nothing in the ruling prevents employers from excluding minority members, but if they do, they must be able to demonstrate a substantial relationship between the test scores and critical job performance.

make sure the tests are "job related." The word *test* is interpreted broadly to include any paper-and-pencil or performance measure used as a basis for any employment decision. Thus, included in the concept of testing are not only traditional kinds of tests but also personal history questions, scored application forms, scored interviews, and interviewers' rating scales.

All aspects of employee selection are open to examination for possible discriminatory personnel practices. Employers must be able to validate, or justify, any selection procedure that adversely affects members of any race, sex, or ethnic group by showing that the procedure is job related. The validation procedures, contained in the *Uniform Guidelines on Employee Selection Procedures,* apply to all aspects of the employee selection process—interviews, tests, reviews of experience or education from application forms, work samples, physical requirements, and evaluations of performance. The guidelines apply not only to hiring but also to other employment decisions such as promotion, demotion, retention, and selection for training or transfer.[11]

Major Kinds of Preemployment Tests

The major kinds of preemployment tests are classified and briefly described in Figure 6–3. Some professional testers maintain that a group (or battery) of tests is necessary in order to test the variety of abilities required for a specific job. Others feel that every job can be categorized into certain basic skills and abilities that can be discovered by a single test.

Whether the testing program should be administered by someone within the company, such as the office manager, or handled by an outside professional organization depends upon the number of workers who must be hired from time to time.

The cost of tests and trained personnel to administer and interpret the tests is more than some firms choose to spend.

Large companies may purchase published tests. For example, the AOM may select a software package designed to screen and prequalify prospective employees. The features of one package program are as follows:[12]

1. The job applicant, seated at a computer, undergoes a preliminary evaluation by completing an on-screen application form.
2. Next, the applicant is led through evaluation exercises that determine (a) the skill level on the computer programs used by the employing company, (b) job knowledge of the position being applied for, and (c) personality traits desirable for the position.
3. After viewing the exercise scores, the interviewer decides whether to interview the applicant personally. Thus, the interviewer spends time only with qualified applicants.
4. The program is designed to generate personalized letters to those who do not qualify for the position, letting them know that the employer appreciates their interest in working for the company.
5. The office module portion of the program covers the major office positions—secretary, administrative assistant, office manager, receptionist, bookkeeper, and manager.

Other large organizations may develop their own tests, or have them designed by a consulting firm of professional testers. Some firms experiment by using published tests and those of their own creation until they find a combination of testing practices and procedures that is valid and reliable. Whether a firm selects tests developed by test publishers or creates its own, the factors of reliability and validity should be considered.

---

[11]The *Uniform Guidelines on Employee Selection Procedures* were issued jointly with the Department of Labor, Office of Personnel Management, and the Department of Justice. Charges filed with the Equal Employment Opportunity Commission regarding employee selection procedures are investigated using these guidelines.

[12]Detailed information about this program, *The Interviewer,* and a demonstration disk may be obtained by contacting Global Publishing Corp., 2255 North University Parkway Station 15, Provo, UT 84604-9921.

Figure 6–3
Types of Pre-
employment
Tests

Type of Test and Its Purpose	Examples of Published Tests*
1. **Intelligence tests**—designed to measure mental and reasoning ability.	Wonderlic Personnel Test Wechsler Adult Intelligence Scale Otis Self-Administering Test of Mental Ability SRA (Science Research Associates) Verbal Thurstone Test of Mental Alertness
2. **Aptitude tests**—designed to measure the ability to perform a particular kind of task (such as facility with numerical concepts) and to predict future performance on the job or in training.	Minnesota Assessment Battery Wolfe-Spence Programming Aptitude Test Fogel Word Processing Operator Test Systems Programming Aptitude Test Hay Aptitude Test Battery Wonderlic Personnel Test ADA (Americans with Disabilities Act) Hiring Kit
3. **Achievement tests**—designed to measure the degree of proficiency in a given type of work such as typewriting and related clerical skills.	SRA Typing Skills Test Typing Skill Test Seashore-Bennett Stenographic Proficiency Test Wolfe Programming Language Test: COBOL Wonderlic's Automated Skills Assessment Program QWIZ Automated Office Skills Assessment System
4. **Personality and psychological tests**—designed to measure abstract concepts such as aggressiveness, honesty, integrity, independence, conformity, and passivity.	Minnesota Multiphasic Personality Inventory Survey of Interpersonal Values Thurstone Temperament Schedule Jackson Personality Inventory Myers-Briggs Type Indicator California Personality Inventory
5. **Interest tests**—designed to identify a person's likes and dislikes to aid in career counseling.	Strong-Campbell Interest Inventory Kuder Preference Record Strong Vocational Interest Blank

* A directory of test publishers that gives a listing of tests, critical evaluations of the tests, and the names and addresses of the publishers are contained in Buros' *Mental Measurements Yearbook* series. The *Yearbook* series may be obtained from Gryphon Press, Highland Park, NY 08904, and in many public and university or college libraries.

Reliability

A test used in selecting office workers should have a high degree of **reliability;** that is, the test should measure *consistently* the items it is designed to measure. This means that the same general score can be expected if the test is given to the same person more than once. The publishers of reputable, standardized tests include within their instruction manuals information on the reliability of their tests.

Validity

A test has **validity** if it can be shown to serve the purpose for which it was intended. For example, the validity of an employment test depends on whether a score on the test accurately predicts a level of performance on the job. If the test accurately predicts performance at a particular level, the test is valid. If the test does not accurately predict performance at that level, the test is not valid. Tests that have been professionally constructed and can be shown to measure an important aspect of the job, such as typewriting and keyboarding tests, are usually accepted as valid.

Other Types of Preemployment Testing and Screening

In addition to using one or more of the preemployment tests described above, employers often test and screen job applicants with reference to drug and alcohol abuse, criminal record, and honesty. Results from tests such as these enable employers to make hiring decisions aimed at decreasing absenteeism and tardiness, improving productivity, and decreasing accidents. To prevent discriminatory testing practices, however, federal and state laws limit what kind of information may be solicited in these types of screening. Thus, to avoid potential lawsuits, the person in charge of preemployment testing and screening must ask applicants only for information that is directly related to their ability to perform the job they seek.

Drug and Alcohol Abuse

The screening of job applicants for drug and alcohol use is not prohibited by federal law. Nor does federal legislation prohibit private employers from refusing to hire an applicant who currently uses illegal drugs and/or alcohol. According to the 1992 American Management Association survey on workplace drug testing, more and more companies are testing employees and jobseekers for controlled or illegal substance use. For the first time, more than half of the 1,200 surveyed firms reported testing newly hired workers.[13]

Generally the courts have ruled that a jobseeker's right to privacy is second in importance to public safety. Thus, the courts usually permit the testing of job applicants for drugs and alcohol when the job opening is directly involved with public safety. Also, the courts generally grant employers more freedom to test job applicants than to test employees who are presently working for the company. However, some states have passed laws that limit the situations in which private employers may test job applicants and present employees for drug use. Because of rapidly changing legislation, those in charge of applicant-screening procedures should check their state and local laws.

Criminal Record

Regulations issued by the Equal Employment Opportunity Commission prohibit an employer from asking a job applicant to disclose information about an arrest or detention that did not result in a conviction. An employer may, however, ask the job applicant whether he or she has ever been *convicted* of a criminal offense. The courts have generally held that asking questions about a job applicant's arrest record is discriminatory against minorities. Further, the courts find no evidence that past arrests tell the interviewer anything about how the applicant is likely to perform on the job. However, questions may be raised about pending indictments, since the answer could be relevant to job performance. For example, suppose a jobseeker has been charged with the theft of a social security check from a neighbor's mailbox, a crime directly related to the job being applied for in the mailing room. When the job applicant has been charged with such a criminal offense, the interviewer may want to postpone a hiring decision until it is known that the applicant will be cleared of the charge.

In some states, you, as an employer, are permitted to ask job applicants whether they have ever been convicted of a crime. However, you cannot follow a blanket policy of refusing to hire all persons who have ever been convicted. In evaluating applicants convicted of a crime, you should determine the severity of the crime, how long ago the applicant was convicted, evidence of rehabilitation, and the presence of any mitigating circumstances.

Honesty and Integrity

In this section, we shall examine three preemployment devices designed to evaluate a prospective worker's honesty and integrity—credit reports, polygraph tests, and paper-and-pencil honesty tests.

---

[13]Barbara Ettorre, "Drug Testing Made Easier," *Management Review* (July, 1992), p. 8.

Credit Reports. Faced with the task of recruiting honest, reliable employees, many employers include credit reports as part of their background checks. The **Fair Credit Reporting Act of 1968** governs the use of credit and investigative agencies that supply information about a person's character, general reputation, and lifestyle. You may use such reports, often referred to as **investigative consumer reports,** to verify the information provided by job applicants. When using investigative consumer reports, you must notify the applicant or the present employee in writing that you are requesting such a report. Also, you must notify the applicant or employee that he or she may request information from you about the nature and type of information being sought. In the event you deny employment because of the consumer report information, you must inform the applicant that this was the reason or part of the reason for denying employment. Further, you must furnish the applicant with the name and address of the consumer reporting agency that made the report.

Polygraph Tests. Another prescreening device is the polygraph (lie detector) test, which has caused much controversy even with the passage of legislation that has virtually eliminated its use. The **Employee Polygraph Protection Act of 1988** bars *private* employers from requiring that most job applicants and current employees be given polygraph tests. Among those who may use polygraph testing are federal, state, and local governments and any political subdivision of a state or local government. Polygraph tests may also be administered for national defense or security reasons. In addition, polygraph testing is permitted in connection with investigations that involve theft at the workplace or other injury or loss to an employer's business.

Among the exemptions contained in the act is the preemployment testing of security guards and employees who will have direct access to controlled substances. Questions regarding religious, political, racial, and union beliefs, as well as questions relating to sexual behavior, are prohibited in the polygraph tests. Those giving the tests are required to present all questions to the examinee in writing before the test, and the examinee is entitled to review the results of any test and to terminate a test at any time.

Paper-and-Pencil Honesty Tests. With the use of the polygraph prohibited except in very restricted situations, many paper-and-pencil honesty tests have been published. Several of these personality tests, designed to measure characteristics such as honesty and integrity, are listed in Figure 6–3. In 1990, the U.S. Office of Technology Assessment reported on integrity tests and concluded that there was little scientific justification for their use. One year later, the American Psychological Association (APA) issued findings that were inconsistent with those of the government. The APA claimed that honesty tests used in selecting personnel should be viewed no differently than other instruments designed for that purpose; that is, if there is research evidence of validity, then an employer would be justified in using the tests.[14] Another study of paper-and-pencil integrity tests, conducted at the University of Iowa, reported that the tests can have substantial success in predicting and screening out behaviors that cause disciplinary problems, chronic tardiness, and excessive absenteeism. The study indicated that employers can optimize their selection of the most productive employees by using integrity tests along with mental ability tests.[15]

The differing findings support the need for further research on the validity of paper-and-pencil tests that claim to measure personality characteristics such as honesty and integrity. Also, the studies support our previous assertion that preemployment decisions should not be based exclusively on the results of honesty and integrity tests but should be viewed as supplementary in the broader context of interviews and background checks.

ORIENTING THE OFFICE STAFF

Orientation refers to a carefully planned, systematic, and effective introduction of new workers to their jobs so they may start working with a

---

[14]Elliot D. Lasson, "How Good Are Integrity Tests?" *Personnel Journal* (April, 1992), pp. 35–38.

[15]"Searching for Integrity," *Fortune* (March 8, 1993), p. 140.

minimum of delay, misunderstanding, and error. Orientation covers many topics such as those listed in Figure 6–4, which shows the contents of a typical handbook given to all new office employees. In addition to providing employees with essential information, the **employee handbook** aids in establishing a warm relationship between management and employees at the beginning of the employment experience.

The Orientation Checklist

Supplementing the employee handbook is the **orientation checklist,** which contains items to be covered by the person who is introducing new employees to the firm and their jobs. The checklist is one of the most effective means of making sure that new employees are properly introduced to the firm and to their jobs.

The two-page checklist shown in Figure 6–5 provides for an orientation program extending over a period of eleven days. This carefully planned program leaves a lasting impression of the firm's interest in its workers and is very effective for "breaking in" new employees. Furthermore, using this checklist properly ensures a complete orientation in all the details of the firm's policies and procedures.

The Sponsor System

Many companies find that the sponsor system is an effective technique for orienting new office employees. Under the **sponsor system,** you, as a new employee, are assigned to a worker who acquaints you with the duties of the job and answers your questions. The sponsor system relieves a supervisor or department head of part of the orientation procedure. It also gives the sponsors an added sense of responsibility and participation and aids in their own self-improvement. The sponsor selected to orient you should have a job similar to the one you are assuming, a complete knowledge of company policies and department operations, a pleasant outgoing personality, an interest in people and their problems, and the desire to be a sponsor.

GOVERNMENT REGULATIONS AFFECTING THE EMPLOYMENT PROCESS

To solve today's problems of fair employment and, at the same time, to comply with relevant labor relations laws and company requirements, AOMs must thoroughly understand federal, state, and local regulations. The most important of these regulations affecting the employment process are described in this section.

Civil Rights Act of 1964

Nearly half of the pages contained in the **Civil Rights Act of 1964** affect AOMs and their responsibilities for staffing the office. The act contains sections dealing with voting rights; prohibition of discrimination on the basis of race, color, religion, or national origin by hotels, restaurants, and certain other facilities; and the creation of new federal agencies. However, of most significance to the OM is Title VII, known as **Equal Employment Opportunity.** This section of the act affects the hiring practices not only of business firms but also of unions and employment agencies and defines certain actions (or inactions) as unlawful employment practices. For the purposes of the Civil Rights Act, as amended in 1972, an *employer* is defined as a person who is engaged in an industry that affects interstate commerce and who has 15 or more workers. With the passage of the **Equal Employment Opportunity Act of 1972,** state and local governments became subject to the provisions against employment discrimination contained in the Civil Rights Act. The 1972 act also obligated the federal government to undertake all of its employment practices without discrimination.

As a result of the Civil Rights Act and its amendments and executive orders, if you, as an employer, refuse to hire job applicants because of their race, color, religion, national origin, or sex, your action is looked upon as an unlawful employment practice. It is also unlawful for you to discharge individuals or discriminate against them with respect to their compensation or any terms, conditions, or privileges of employment because of their race, color, religion, nationality,

Figure 6–4
Contents Page
of an Employee Hand-
book

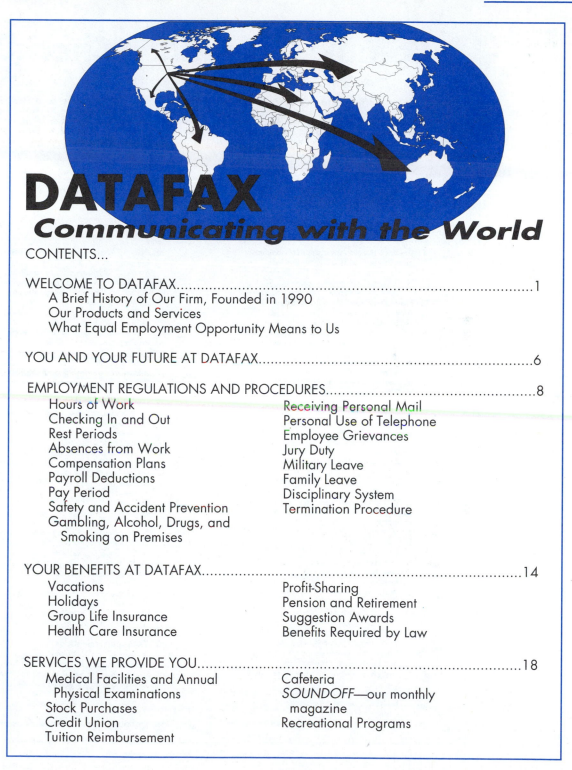

DATAFAX
Communicating with the World

CONTENTS...

WELCOME TO DATAFAX..1
    A Brief History of Our Firm, Founded in 1990
    Our Products and Services
    What Equal Employment Opportunity Means to Us

YOU AND YOUR FUTURE AT DATAFAX...6

EMPLOYMENT REGULATIONS AND PROCEDURES..................................8

Hours of Work   Receiving Personal Mail
Checking In and Out   Personal Use of Telephone
Rest Periods   Employee Grievances
Absences from Work   Jury Duty
Compensation Plans   Military Leave
Payroll Deductions   Family Leave
Pay Period   Disciplinary System
Safety and Accident Prevention Termination Procedure
Gambling, Alcohol, Drugs, and
    Smoking on Premises

YOUR BENEFITS AT DATAFAX..14

Vacations   Profit-Sharing
Holidays   Pension and Retirement
Group Life Insurance   Suggestion Awards
Health Care Insurance   Benefits Required by Law

SERVICES WE PROVIDE YOU..18

Medical Facilities and Annual   Cafeteria
   Physical Examinations   *SOUNDOFF*—our monthly
Stock Purchases   magazine
Credit Union   Recreational Programs
Tuition Reimbursement

Figure 6–5
Orientation
Checklist
(page 1)

Sample Orientation Checklist

FOR USE BY SUPERVISORS AS A GUIDE IN ORIENTING NEW EMPLOYEES

One of the most effective tools that can be used in orienting new workers is the orientation checklist. Its primary value lies in the fact that it spreads orientation over a number of days, giving the new employees a chance to absorb and digest the various facts, figures, rules, and policies they

should know. With the use of a checklist like this one, the employer can be certain that the new workers are getting all the information about the company they need in order to do a good job. And it helps the supervisor present the information in a logical, orderly manner.

Supervisor _____   Date _____

For Employee _____   Dept. _____

BEFORE WORKER ARRIVES

Check when completed

____ 1. **Prepare Future Associates** (by individual or group conference) **If**
  a. The job is different
  b. The person is different
  c. Someone could have been promoted from within

____ 2. **Have Desk and Supplies Ready**

____ 3. **Alert Job Instructor**

____ 4. **Arrange for Luncheon Escort**
  Escort will explain location of employee lounge and other facilities (show employee)

FIRST DAY

____ 1. **Review the Job**
  a. Confidential aspects
  b. Stimulate job enthusiasm and satisfaction in a job well done
  c. Explain work in other sections (give copy of job description and organization manual)
    1. The way work originates
    2. Where it goes
    3. Relation of the job to other jobs in section
    4. Relation of the section to division
    5. Relation of the division to company
    6. Let employee know you are depending on him or her
    7. Give assurance employee will learn quickly

____ 2. **Explain Hours of Work** (give copy of company personnel manual)
  a. Starting and quitting time
  b. Hours per week
  c. Break periods
  d. Lunch period

____ 3. **Review Compensation**
  a. Amount
  b. When paid
  c. Cost of living allowance
  d. Mention deductions
    1. Income taxes (federal and state)
    2. Social security taxes
    3. Retirement (if applicable)
  e. If applicable, review company's retirement plan (give copy of retirement plan)
  f. Emphasize value of employee benefits paid by company
  g. Salaries must be kept confidential
  h. Explain thoroughly the electronic transfer of employee's net pay
  i. Right reserved to deduct for absence

Check when completed

____ 4. **Discuss Attendance Requirements and Records**
  a. Filling out time card (show card and demonstrate)
  b. Method of reporting tardiness (stress honor system)
  c. How and to whom absence is reported
  d. Stress punctuality
  e. Explain effect of good attendance and punctuality on employee's record

____ 5. **Has the Employee Any Questions?** (ask)

____ 6. **Explain Orientation Quiz**
  Voluntary; will be given if employee chooses at end of first 10 days

____ 7. **Introduce to Immediate Associates**
  In department and supervisors and others in related departments

____ 8. **Introduce to Workplace**
  a. Workplace to be in order as employee is expected to keep it
  b. Stress good housekeeping

____ 9. **Have Chair Adjusted**

____ 10. **Give Job Instruction** (use job breakdowns or manuals if available; have a trainer well prepared and temperamentally suited to teach)
  a. Prepare
  b. Tell
  c. Show
  d. Practice
  e. Check
  f. Explain what to do about any idle time
    1. Report to supervisor for more work
    2. Emphasize this is not a reflection on employee but responsibility of management

____ 11. **Discuss Work Instructions**
  a. Majority will come from supervisor
  b. Occasionally from department head
  c. Question any orders received from fellow workers—check with supervisor
  d. Stress that all instructions should be clearly understood

____ 12. **Explain Learning Aids**
  a. Examples of work (show employee)
  b. Job instruction breakdown, if available
  c. Special terms used, including abbreviations

____ 13. **Encourage Employee to Ask Questions**
  a. They aid in learning
  b. They help to develop judgment

____ 14. **Explain where to store work overnight** (show)

Figure 6–5
Orientation
Checklist
(page 2)

SECOND DAY

Check when
completed
____ **1. Explain Performance Review** (show the form
and illustrate with examples)
  a. Important to employee
  b. Raises depend upon work, attitude, length of
    service
____ **2. Explain Quality and Quantity of Work**
  a. Production standards, if any
  b. Importance of accuracy
  c. Quality before quantity
  d. Speed will come with experience

THIRD DAY

____ **1. Explain Telephone Technique If Employee
Conducts Company Business on Telephone**
(give copy of telephone company booklet)
  a. Speak clearly
  b. Give your name when answering
  c. Take messages in writing for those not present
  d. Deliver messages before you forget
  e. Find numbers in company directory
____ **2. Give Reasons for Rules, Policies, and Plans**
  a. To make cooperation easier
  b. To result in greater efficiency
  c. To avoid duplication of effort
____ **3. Explain Voluntary Disability Plan and
Company's Group Insurance Plan** (give copy,
if not already included in company manual)
____ **4. Has Employee Any Questions?** (ask)

FOURTH DAY

____ **1. Give Employee Opportunity to Say How He
or She Is Getting Along**
____ **2. Explain Use of Medical Facilities**
____ **3. Discuss Suggestion System** (show current
scoreboard on bulletin board)
  a. How it encourages initiative and ideas
  b. How awards are made
  c. How to submit
  d. Should be well-thought-out ideas
  e. Must sign suggestion form
  f. All suggestions are thoroughly considered
____ **4. Explain Messenger Service**
  a. Messengers work on regular schedule (show
    message carrier envelope and illustrate how to
    fill out)
  b. Don't expect special service
  c. Don't make a messenger of yourself

FIFTH DAY

____ **1. Discuss Personal Telephone Calls**
  a. Can be made during working hours if urgent
  b. Incoming calls only when urgent
____ **2. Explain Policy on Donations**
  a. No solicitors allowed in building
  b. Start no subscriptions for company without
    approval
____ **3. Discuss Departmental Policies That Are in
Addition to (But Not in Conflict with) Overall
Company Policy**
____ **4. Has the Employee Any Questions?** (ask)

SIXTH DAY

Check when
completed
____ **1. Explain How to Get Additional Supplies**
  a. On requisition, on approval of department head
  b. Don't visit supply department
  c. Explain conservation of supplies
____ **2. Discuss Personal Mail**
  a. Best to have sent to home
  b. Deposit outgoing letter in box outside building (or
    in lobby)
  c. Company does not pay postage
  d. Can get stamps from cashier
  e. Do not write personal letters on company time

SEVENTH DAY

____ **1. Explain Change of Address**
  a. Company must have complete record
  b. Notify human resources department of changes
  c. Same for telephone number
____ **2. Explain Company Educational Program** (give
copy of plan)
____ **3. Explain Company Security System**

EIGHTH DAY

____ **1. Explain the Employees' Association**
  a. Membership advantages
  b. Dues
  c. How collected
____ **2. Explain Company Library**
  a. Free to use it
  b. Where located
____ **3. Describe Company Magazine** (give copy of
latest issue)

NINTH DAY

____ **1. Describe Vacation Plan** (show copy of schedules)
  a. Explain vacation system
  b. How length of vacation is determined
  c. The part seniority plays
  d. The part convenience to section plays
  e. Time selected must be approved by department
    head
  f. Subject to change for good of company
____ **2. Explain Company's Bulletin Boards**
  a. Do not post anything without approval
  b. Watch for current announcements

TENTH DAY

____ **1. Explain That Patience and Understanding
Are Important Qualities to Develop** (give
examples)
Employee will work with widely diverse associates as
to age, ethnic and cultural background, training,
education, and experience.
____ **2. Encourage Employee to Talk Things Over with
Immediate Supervisor**
____ **3. Talk Things Over with Department Manager
When Necessary with Knowledge of
Immediate Supervisor**
____ **4. Administer Orientation Quiz** (get written answers)
____ **5. Review Employee's Public Relations Influence**

ELEVENTH DAY

____ **1. Review Quiz Results**
Employee's Orientation Completed:...
Department Manager Signature

Instructions: Upon completion of this checklist, return it to the human resources department for inclusion in the employee's personnel file.

or sex. Further, you are prohibited from segregating or classifying employees for the reasons given above if doing so deprives them of employment opportunities or adversely affects their status as employees.

Bona Fide Occupational Qualifications

Employers are still permitted to hire and train persons on the basis of their race, religion, or sex when these are **bona fide occupational qualifications (BFOQ)** necessary to the normal operations of the business. Thus, if it can be shown that the sex of applicants for a job, such as modeling men's swimwear, would prevent them from performing successfully on the job (a BFOQ), this qualification may be used as a basis for recruiting job applicants. Also, for reasons of national or state security, information about the applicant's national origin and creed may be a BFOQ. However, the task of demonstrating that a discriminatory requirement constitutes a BFOQ rests with the employer.

Employers may not place help-wanted advertisements that specify any preference, limitation, specification, or discrimination based on sex unless sex is a BFOQ. This provision has been interpreted to mean that the content of classified ads must be free of such preferences. For example, an ad stating, "WANTED: Young, attractive woman to be secretary to young male executive" directly violates Title VII. Also, the placement of ads in separate male and female columns is in violation of Title VII when sex is not an occupational qualification for the advertised job.

Employers may continue to apply different standards of compensation or different terms and conditions of employment provided such differences are not the result of an intention to discriminate on account of race, color, religion, national origin, or sex. Therefore, employers may set their hiring and work standards as high as they please, but they may not enforce them in a discriminatory manner.

Pregnancy Discrimination Act of 1978

The **Pregnancy Discrimination Act of 1978,** an amendment to the Civil Rights Act, makes it unlawful for an employer to fire or refuse to hire a woman because she is pregnant. Employers may not force the female employee to leave work at an arbitrarily established time if she is still willing and able to work. Further, all health care and disability benefits provided by the employer must be the same for pregnant employees as for sick or disabled employees. Employers are given the option of excluding from the benefits program any coverage for nontherapeutic abortions. However, if employers elect to exclude this condition, they are still required to furnish benefits for medical complications due to abortion, provided that medical benefits are also extended to other employees for non-job-related disabilities.

Equal Employment Opportunity Commission

Under the Civil Rights Act, the **Equal Employment Opportunity Commission (EEOC)** was created to enforce the law. The EEOC tries to obtain voluntary compliance with the law before a court action for an injunction is filed. The EEOC may seek a temporary restraining order or other preliminary relief when a preliminary investigation determines that prompt action is needed to carry out the purposes of the act. If the EEOC cannot reach an acceptable agreement with the party within 30 days, it can file suit in a federal

Illustration 6–4 The Pregnancy Discrimination Act of 1978 protects the rights of pregnant women.

district court. However, where a state or local law forbids discriminatory practices, relief must first be sought under the state or local law before a complaint is filed with the EEOC.

The EEOC may also institute court proceedings for an injunction if there is reason to believe that any person or group of persons is not complying with the law. The court may find that employers have intentionally engaged in an unlawful employment practice. In such cases, the court can order the employers to stop such practices, to reinstate employees, to pay back wages, and to take other appropriate action to eliminate existing discrimination and prevent its recurrence.

Affirmative Action and Executive Orders

Employers not subject to Title VII coverage discussed above may come within the scope of the Civil Rights Act by reason of a contract or subcontract involving federal funds. In a series of executive orders, the federal government has banned, in employment on government contracts, discrimination that is based on race, color, religion, national origin, or sex. More significantly, these orders have been held to require that contractors take affirmative action to ensure equal opportunity.

Affirmative Action

The concept of affirmative action was developed to clarify in a concrete, positive way what firms seeking to conduct business with the federal government must do to be equal opportunity employers. An **affirmative action plan** is a program designed to eliminate, limit, or prevent discriminatory treatment on the basis of race, ethnic group, and sex. Some plans are required by law, while others are developed voluntarily. The affirmative action plan is often designed to remedy the effects of past discrimination and prevent its recurrence. Usually the plan involves an analysis of the use of the workforce; the establishment of attainable results-oriented goals and timetables for recruiting, hiring, training, and promoting any underrepresented classes; an explanation of the methods to be used to eliminate discrimination; and the establishment of responsibility for implementing the program.

Executive Orders

By means of **executive orders,** the executive branch of the federal government strives to require equal employment opportunities in firms doing business with the government. Executive Order 11246 requires equal employment opportunity and affirmative action by contractors and subcontractors having contracts with the federal government. Each contract amounting to $10,000 or more must contain an equal employment opportunity clause that is binding on the contractor or subcontractor for the life of the contract. Nonconstruction contractors and subcontractors who have at least 50 employees and a contract exceeding $50,000 must establish affirmative action plans. The plans must include goals and timetables for the increased use of minority persons and women.

Other executive orders deal with age discrimination in the performance of federal government contracts, the offering of work to business enterprises owned by racial minority persons, and the creation of a national policy and program for women's business enterprises.

State and Local Fair Employment Practices Laws

The fair employment practices laws enacted by the states do not replace Title VII of the Civil Rights Act since the purpose of the federal law was to encourage the states to adopt such laws. Generally, the state fair employment practices laws are aimed at employers, employment agencies, and unions. Employers are forbidden to discriminate in their hiring and firing practices, and unions and employment agencies are forbidden to aid or cause such discrimination.

Cities, too, have enacted ordinances that prohibit discriminatory practices in the employment process. One of the most comprehensive and enlightened laws of its kind is the Human Rights Law of the District of Columbia. This law covers discrimination by reason of race, color, religion, national origin, sex, age, marital status, personal appearance, sexual orientation, family responsibilities, physical handicap, matriculation (formal education completed), and political affiliation.

Illustration 6–5 People cannot be discriminated against due to age under the Age Discrimination in Employment Act of 1967.

OTHER FEDERAL REGULATIONS AFFECTING THE EMPLOYMENT PROCESS

There are several other laws in addition to the Civil Rights Act, as amended, with which the AOM should have a working knowledge. These regulations are summarized in Figure 6–6.

Wages and Hours Regulations

The wages and salaries paid and the hours worked by office employees are regulated under federal law by a number of statutes. The Fair Labor Standards Act, commonly known as the Federal Wage-Hour Law, has broadest application for the AOM. The major provisions of this law concern minimum wages, overtime pay, restrictions upon the employment of children, and record-keeping requirements. Under the Equal Pay Act of 1963, an amendment to the Fair Labor Standards Act, an employer is forbidden to discriminate solely on the basis of sex in setting wage rates for men and women doing equal work under similar working conditions. These regulations, and others affecting compensation practices, are discussed in more detail in Chapter 10.

Figure 6–6
Other Federal
Regulations
Affecting the
Employment
Process

Age Discrimination in Employment Act of 1967

Purpose: To promote employment of older persons based on ability rather than age, to prohibit arbitrary age discrimination in employment, and to help employers and workers find ways of solving problems arising from the impact of age.

Coverage: Private businesses employing 20 or more workers; federal, state, and local government employees not covered by Civil Service.

Details:
1. Employers, employment agencies, and labor unions may not discriminate on the basis of age against those over the age of 40.
2. Employees may not be forced to retire if they are otherwise able to perform duties of their jobs. Exception: highly paid executives and policymakers.
3. Federal employees are permitted to work as long as they wish.

Vocational Rehabilitation Act of 1973

Purpose: To provide employment opportunities for qualified physically and mentally handicapped individuals and to eliminate employment discrimination based on physical or mental handicaps.

Coverage: Employers having federal contracts exceeding $2,500.

Details:
1. Employers must take affirmative action to provide hiring, placement, and advancement opportunities.
2. Handicapped persons are defined as those having a mental or physical condition that substantially affects their ability to perform "life activities" (caring for one's self, performing manual tasks, walking, seeing, hearing, speaking, learning, and working).
3. Courts have held that obesity, suicidal tendencies, diabetes, and sensitivity to tobacco smoke are examples of handicaps protected by federal or state law.

Vietnam Era Veterans' Readjustment Assistance Act of 1974

Purpose: To employ and advance in employment qualified veterans of the Vietnam era and disabled veterans of all wars.

Coverage: Employers having federal contracts exceeding $10,000.

Details:
1. Employers must take affirmative action to provide hiring and advancement opportunities.
2. Employers must list employment openings with local employment service, which then gives referral priority to veterans.

Immigration Reform and Control Act of 1986

Purpose: To verify the employment eligibility of all newly hired persons and thus bar the hiring of aliens unauthorized to work in the United States.

Coverage: All employers.

Details: Employer must examine the employees' work-eligibility documents (U.S. passport, certificate of naturalization, resident alien card with photo, birth certificate, Social Security card, driver's license, etc.) and complete employment eligibility verification form to attest that the documents are genuine.

Americans with Disabilities Act of 1990 (ADA)

Purpose: To protect from discrimination those persons who suffer any physical or mental disability that substantially limits their major life activities.

Coverage: Employers of 25 or more workers were covered by equal-employment rules in July, 1992; employers of 15 or more workers were covered in July, 1994.

Details:
1. Protection also extended to persons with less obvious impairments such as Acquired Immune Deficiency Syndrome (AIDS) and contagious diseases so long as they do not pose direct threat to coworkers.
2. ADA also covers rehabilitated drug abusers and alcoholics, obese persons, and those with cosmetic disfigurements.
3. Along with outlawing discrimination, ADA requires employers to make necessary "reasonable accommodations" for disabled workers who are qualified to handle "essential functions" of a job.
4. Employers may refuse to make necessary accommodations if they impose undue financial hardship on the business.
5. Preemployment medical tests and medical questionnaires are prohibited.
6. Interviewers may not ask applicants if they have a disability that would prevent them from performing the job tasks.

S U M M A R Y

1. Among the sources of office workers available to the AOM are public employment services, private employment agencies, temporary office help services, leasing services, local community agencies, advertising, employee referrals, and educational institutions.

2. In small offices, the employee selection procedure may consist of an interview, followed by a statement that within a few days the applicant will be informed of the employer's decision. In large offices, the procedure becomes more formal and complex. In addition to one or more interviews, reference checks, and letters of recommendation, the following records and forms are often used: personnel requisition, application form, record of interview, and record of employment.

3. Preemployment tests may be classified as (a) *intelligence*—designed to measure mental and reasoning ability; (b) *aptitude*—designed to measure the ability to perform a particular kind of task and to predict future performance on the job or in training; (c) *achievement*—designed to measure the degree of proficiency in a given type of work such as typewriting; (d) *personality and psychological*—designed to measure abstract concepts such as aggressiveness, honesty, integrity, independence, conformity, and passivity; and (e) *interest*—designed to identify a person's likes and dislikes to aid in career counseling.

4. The orientation program should provide the newly hired office worker with an effective introduction to the job by covering topics such as the following: detailed review of the job and job instructions, hours of work, compensation, attendance requirements, introduction to associates and workplace, performance review, quality and quantity standards, telephone technique, company rules and policies, employee benefits, medical facilities, messenger service, personal telephone calls and personal mail, employee assistance program, company library, vacation scheduling, and bulletin board postings.

5. The major government regulations that directly influence the employment process include the (a) Civil Rights Act, as amended, and the Equal Employment Opportunity Act, which prohibit discrimination on the basis of race, color, religion, national origin, or sex; (b) Pregnancy Discrimination Act, which prohibits the firing or refusal to hire a woman because she is pregnant; (c) Age Discrimination in Employment Act, which prohibits age discrimination against people over 40 years of age; (d) Immigration Reform and Control Act, which requires employers to verify the employment eligibility of all newly hired persons; (e) Americans with Disabilities Act, which protects from discrimination those persons who suffer physical or mental disability; and (f) wages and hours legislation, which covers minimum wages, overtime pay, and employment of children.

FOR YOUR REVIEW

1. For what reasons do companies recruit contingent employees to meet their needs for office personnel?

2. What are some of the services that Job Service offers AOMs who are recruiting office employees?

3. What steps should the AOM take to make sure that the private employment agency selected is professionally qualified?

4. In what ways does the use of temporary office workers bring about savings for employers?

c
o
n
t

5. Describe the operation of a typical employee leasing service.

6. Why must special care be taken by employers in designing their application forms?

7. What are the advantages and disadvantages of using (a) the direct interview and (b) the indirect interview?

8. Why do many office managers place relatively little confidence in reference checks and letters of recommendation?

9. What two basic principles should guide the AOM in using tests as a tool in selecting office workers?

10. Describe the major kinds of preemployment tests and state for what purpose each type is designed.

11. Distinguish between these two factors: test reliability and test validity.

12. Identify the preemployment devices available for evaluating a prospective employee's honesty and integrity.

13. Explain how an orientation checklist is used in an orientation program.

14. What provision in the Civil Rights Act of 1964, as amended, has the most significance for the AOM?

15. For what purposes does a company develop an affirmative action plan?

16. What are the major provisions of the (a) Age Discrimination in Employment Act and (b) Americans with Disabilities Act?

FOR YOUR DISCUSSION

1. At age 55, Leslie Koss finds himself swept up in the early-retirement program as part of his former employer's downsizing efforts. Koss has worked as office manager and head administrator at the firm for 15 years but has now lost hope of finding another job. He sees no way back into the workforce because companies have shut their doors to older workers. As a counselor talking with Koss about how to obtain a position, what advice can you offer?

2. Consult your state's human relations commission, fair employment practices agency, or comparable organization to determine which of the following questions may legally be used on the application form:

    a. Will you be taking time off from work to observe Passover?

    b. What is the birthplace of your parents?

    c. Have you ever been convicted of any crime?

    d. When did you graduate from high school?

    e. Do you have children?

f. How did you learn to speak and read Russian?

g. Do you have any disability that will interfere with your doing the work?

h. Are you HIV-positive?

3. Before anyone is hired at Wyler, Inc., the human resources department has a handwriting analyst examine the jobseeker's writing in order to develop a personality profile. Do you believe that handwriting analysis (graphology) is an indicator of personality? Can graphology be used to screen persons who have a drug or alcohol problem? What evidence can you offer to defend the validity of handwriting analysis?

4. Debbie Woo is employed by an activist group to pose as a job applicant to uncover alleged discriminatory practices at companies. Discuss the legality and validity of this employment testing practice.

5. John Perez has just completed reproducing his two-page resumé, which he plans to mail to several companies that have advertised job openings in the daily newspaper. After you read Perez's resumé, you ask, "Where is your cover letter?" Perez replies that he does not plan to write a cover letter or letter of transmittal, because he would repeat in such a letter the data contained in his resumé. What suggestions have you for Perez about the need for a cover letter? What are your recommendations for the contents of a cover letter?

6. In a desperate moment three years ago, you misrepresented your educational background when you completed the application form at your present place of employment. Ever since, that little lie has been like a time bomb ticking away in your personnel file. Tomorrow you face an employee appraisal and a review of your qualifications for promotion. Today you are in a quandary. What should you do? Ask for your personnel file and delete the "padded" degree? Live with the lie and keep your mouth shut? Or what?

7. You have narrowed down the candidates for a supervisory position in your company to three persons who have outstanding supervisory experience. One candidate, Steven Cox, is clearly the favorite because of his present position with a company competing in your international market. When you check the background reports on all three candidates, you find that when he was 16, Cox served a short prison term for illegal possession of a controlled substance. All other information on Cox and the other two candidates is beyond reproach. What would you do?

CASES FOR CRITICAL THINKING

Case 6–1 Discriminating on the Basis of Accent

As part of her preemployment screening, Tien Ho scored in the top 2 percent on the two-hour battery of tests. In fact, her performance on the mathematical skills tests yielded the best score in the history of the Colony Finance Company. However, during her interview with Mark Hope, assistant controller, she found herself facing a brick wall. The interview ended something like this:

Hope: I congratulate you, Tien, on your outstanding scores on all the written tests. You surely have a fine grasp of mathematics.

Ho: You are very kind. Thank you, Mr. Hope.

Hope: (struggling to understand Ho's words) What's that? Oh, yes. As you know, Tien, this job requires you to work closely with clients on a one-to-one basis every day. And these people come from all walks of life. I'm afraid that, like me, most of our clients will not be able to understand your accent. During our interview, I found it hard to understand you sometimes, and we can't have that. So, Tien, we shall be unable to hire you. I do thank you for thinking of us . . . .

Ho left the office, feeling that Colony Finance just did not want a foreigner on the job and that the company rejected her application solely because of her accent.

1. Has Colony Finance illegally discriminated in its rejection of Ho's application for employment?

2. Would your answer be the same if Ho had applied for a "behind-the-scene" job such as data-entry clerk?

Case 6–2 Moving from Temporary to Full Time

Friday afternoon Marjorie Rivo, office supervisor of Lee's Software, called a local temporary help service and requested a payroll clerk for several days' work during the end-of-the-year rush. Monday morning Alan Stein reported for work. After two days, Rivo found that Stein was a highly competent worker, got along well with his department head and coworkers, and took on responsibility as if he had been with the firm for years and expected to be there for years to come. Toward the end of Stein's first week, a permanent vacancy occurred in the accounting department and Rivo approached him with a full-time job offer. She was pleased to find that Stein liked the company and would like to become a full-time employee.

1. Was Rivo unethical in approaching Stein with an offer of full-time employment?

2. What steps should Rivo now take to obtain Stein's services on a full-time basis?

3. What are the ethics and business practices involved in hiring a temporary worker on a permanent basis?

 ## Case 6–3 Cost Comparison: Computer Option (available on disk)

7

SUPERVISING THE OFFICE STAFF

GOALS FOR THIS CHAPTER

After completing this chapter, you should be able to:

1. Give examples of the office supervisor's responsibilities in the business organization.
2. Identify the skills supervisors must develop to work with today's diverse workforce.
3. Describe how office supervisors discipline and counsel workers and plan career goals.
4. Show how the theories of motivation help office supervisors better understand what motivates human behavior.
5. Explain how the ethics and value systems of office workers relate to effective supervision.

One of the major changes we noted in Chapter 2 is a flattening of the classic pyramid-like organization structure, with more decisions being made at the supervisory or operating management level. This means that the people who can manage information most effectively are making more key decisions and judgments about administrative services and other internal operations such as marketing and accounting. Thus, more power and authority are flowing downward from the top of the organization to the supervisory level. In adapting to such changes, today's office supervisors strive to become proficient in using office technology and in achieving excellence as they accept new responsibilities for managing human resources.

Up to this point in the text, we have been concerned mostly with *managers,* those members of the organization who plan, organize, lead, and control the work of others. *First-line managers,* or *supervisors,* as they are usually called, directly supervise the *nonmanagement* employees in the organization. Although every person who has managerial responsibilities can be looked upon as a supervisor, the term *supervisor* is generally applied to the first level of managerial responsibility. It is from this point of view that we shall study the role of office supervisors in this chapter.

THE OFFICE SUPERVISION PROCESS

As you examine the process of supervision, you can see how each of the managerial functions is carried out. Office supervisors *plan* and *organize* their work experiences to meet their firms' needs for effective and efficient operations and their employees' needs for job satisfaction. To meet both kinds of needs, an organization must be created in which employees make major contributions to the organization's goals and at the same time attain their own personal objectives.

158

Supervision also involves *leading,* which is concerned with motivating the workers so that the objectives of the organization will be attained. In exercising the leadership function, supervisors place special emphasis on human resources, for it is only through people that things happen. Office supervisors find that optimum productivity is obtained when they plan and organize their information activities around the workers' needs and talents. Supervisors find, too, that productivity is improved when the workers are led—not pushed—into doing their best. To attain the goals jointly established by the office supervisor and the workers, the supervisor must create an environment in which the workers grow both personally and professionally.

Finally, supervision involves *control*—obtaining actual performance that matches as closely as possible the desired performance. The practical aspects of supervising involve the performance of a certain job by the *best method* and by the *best person* in order to obtain the *best results.* A well-trained office supervisor is therefore needed to assure the accomplishment of these three aspects of carrying out a job.

Responsibilities of Office Supervisors

In the small office, we usually find that an office manager directs all the information-processing activities. As the office work and the staff expand, a centralized department for word processing may be developed under a trained supervisor. Further expansion may require the appointment of supervisors for centralized departments such as records management, computer operations, mailing services, and reprographics. Whatever the organization or the number of supervisors, the jobs of office supervision are essentially the same. The jobs require *working with people* at all levels to develop and carry out the plans of office work, to establish systems and procedures that include the measurement of work, and to improve the systems wherever possible.

All supervisory positions involve responsibility, which flows in several directions—*upward* to higher management, *horizontally* to peers (supervisors of equal rank), and *downward* to subordinates (workers at the operative level). Other responsibilities include *coordinating* the office work to be done and *self-development* as the supervisor prepares for growth and promotion in the organization. An outline of each of the office supervisor's key responsibilities and its direction is provided in Figure 7–1.

To carry out these responsibilities effectively, office supervisors must first be able to manage their own time. Many office supervisors spend the bulk of their time on projects that produce few benefits. In order to get the most benefit out of their working hours, these supervisors must realize that they probably cause most of their own time problems. Thus, the need emerges for office supervisors to undertake a program of **time management,** as described in a later chapter. In such a program, supervisors use all resources, including time, in order to achieve their important professional and personal goals.

Supervising Today's Diverse Workforce

We do not become supervisors merely because we are the best workers and know intimately the operations of our departments. Although these requisites are important, as supervisors we must use the *human approach.* This means that we must become specialists in working with a **diverse workforce**—employees who differ not only in their gender, age, race, and culture but also in other ways, such as religion, education, lifestyle, and sexual orientation. In working with a diverse workforce, supervisors are continually being appraised as to their genuine value as leaders. Determining the work to be done and how to do it is the easiest task of supervision because it deals with the *objective,* or *tangible,* phase of the position. Most important, and more difficult, however, is the *subjective,* or *human,* phase of supervision. Herein lies the secret of motivating and leading a diverse workforce, which we shall examine in the following section.

Diversity

Supervising diversity is the process of accepting, understanding, and appreciating differences among employees and creating an environment that allows *all* kinds of people to reach their full

Figure 7–1
The Office
Supervisor's
Responsibili-
ties
(page 1)

SUPERVISOR'S RESPONSIBILITIES TO OTHERS IN THE ORGANIZATION

Upward responsibilities to higher management:
1. Finding out what top-level managers want done and then following their directives.
2. Keeping management informed of what is being done in the department and passing along ideas for improving productivity.
3. Accepting full responsibility and accountability for the work in the department without "passing the buck."
4. Referring matters requiring management's attention promptly without bothering management unnecessarily.
5. Interpreting the employees' needs to management, and vice versa.

Horizontal responsibilities to peers (supervisors of equal rank):
1. Cooperating with peers in the same manner that subordinates are expected to cooperate with each other.
2. Helping coordinate the work of the department with that of other supervisors for the good of the firm.
3. Supporting the transfer and/or promotion of good workers among departments.

Downward responsibilities to workers at the operative level:
1. Aiding in selecting, orienting, and training new workers.
2. Motivating workers to assume greater responsibilities.
3. Assisting workers to learn what to do and how to do it and checking the results.
4. Evaluating workers periodically and recommending promotions, salary adjustments, transfers, retraining, and dismissals.
5. Delegating authority and responsibility in order to develop understudies.
6. Developing harmony, cooperation, and teamwork.
7. Building and maintaining employee morale and handling grievances promptly and fairly.
8. Maintaining discipline and controlling absenteeism and tardiness.
9. Taking a personal interest in workers without showing partiality
10. Using courtesy, tact, and consideration in treating workers as human beings.

potential in pursuit of company and personal objectives. We can anticipate increased diversity among our workers by looking ahead to the year 2005 and a labor force that will have grown to 151 million. Demographers (scientists who study vital and social statistics of a population) have studied the period 1990–2005 and project the following percentage increases in our labor force:[1]

1. *Sex.* Women will increase by 26 percent; men, an increase of 16 percent.
2. *Age.* Young people (ages 16 to 24 years) will increase by 13 percent; ages 25 to 54, an increase of 19 percent; age 55 and over, an increase of 44 percent.
3. *Race.* African Americans will increase by 32 percent; Asian and others (including Pacific Islanders, native Americans, and Alaskan natives), an increase of 74 percent; Hispanics, an increase of 75 percent.

Figure 7–2 shows how these projected increases will be reflected in the makeup of our workforce.

To view employee diversity as a vital organization resource, supervisors need to develop the skills required to:[2]

[1]Howard N. Fullerton, Jr., "Labor Force Projections: The Baby Boom Moves On," *Monthly Labor Review* (November, 1991), pp. 31–44.

[2]Marilyn Loden and Judy B. Rosener, *Workforce America! Managing Employee Diversity as a Vital Resource* (Homewood, IL: Business One Irwin, 1991), p. 5.

Figure 7–1
The Office
Supervisor's
Responsibili-
ties
(page 2)

Responsibilities for **coordinating** the office work:
1. Planning the systems, procedures, and methods.
2. Distributing the workload fairly.
3. Coordinating the work of different units, as necessary.
4. Seeing that the work is done correctly and on time.
5. Anticipating difficulties and peak loads in the work.
6. Maintaining the quality of the work by setting standards.
7. Developing new methods and evaluating equipment that will reduce and control costs.
8. Training understudies so that absences, overload, and other interferences with the workflow may be handled efficiently.

Responsibilities for **self-development:**
1. Constantly analyzing and attempting to improve self-control, analytical ability, ability to instill confidence within others, initiative, punctuality, courtesy, leadership, fair play, and personal appearance.
2. Studying the firm's organization and human resources to develop the maximum departmental cooperation, train understudies, and prepare for the next job in the line of promotion.
3. Assuming membership and actively participating in professional organizations.
4. Studying up-to-date literature that will aid in improving the work in present and future positions
5. Continuing formal education in the areas that will aid in work performance.
6. Developing an effective time-management program in which all resources, including time, are efficiently used to achieve important professional and personal goals.

1. *Communicate effectively* with employees from diverse cultural backgrounds.
2. *Coach and develop people* who are diverse along many dimensions including age, education, ethnicity, gender, physical ability, race, sexual/affectional orientation, and so on.
3. *Provide objective performance feedback* that is based on substance rather than on style.
4. *Help create organizational climates* that nurture and utilize the rich array of talents and perspectives that diversity can offer.

Office supervisors must possess certain personal qualities to command the respect and loyalty from their diverse employees and to ensure maximum efficiency. Foremost among these attributes listed in Figure 7–3 is the ability to treat subordinates as human beings.

Discipline

The words **discipline** and *disciple* can be traced to the same root, meaning "to teach so as to mold." Nevertheless, many people think of disciplining as reprimanding or punishing rather than teaching or molding. To be effective, however, true discipline should teach at the same time it

corrects. Discipline should be constructive and consistent and should enable employees to learn so their behavior and performance in the future will be changed. Consider the following comments made by two supervisors as they talk to a worker returning from lunch 25 minutes late:

Supervisor A: (rushing from her desk to confront a tardy employee as he enters the work area) Rob, you're 25 minutes late! So, you can just make it up after quitting time today.

Supervisor B: (calling the tardy employee, Rob, into her office) Rob, what happened that caused you to be late in returning from lunch? Alice has been waiting for you to get back so you two could process the orders you were pricing. You know, Rob, each of us needs to be on time in order to meet our quotas and earn that bonus! Will you and Alice be able to pick up the slack in the next hour to make up for your tardiness?

It is obvious that Supervisor B is the one who looks upon Rob as a human being and is able to discipline effectively.

Illustration 7–1 Supervising diversity requires today's office supervisor to create an environment that enables all workers to attain their full potential.

Figure 7–2
Percentage
Distribution of
the Civilian
Labor Force
by Sex, Age,
Race, and His-
panic Origin,
Moderate
Growth Pro-
jection to 2005

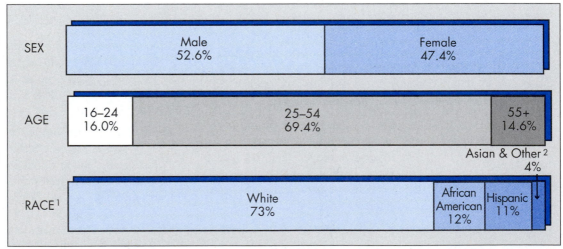

Notes: 1. Persons of Hispanic origin may be of any race.

2. The "Asian and other" group includes Asians, Pacific Islanders, native Americans, and Alaskan natives.

Source: Howard N. Fullerton, Jr., "Labor Force Projections: The Baby Boom Moves On," *Monthly Labor Review* (November, 1991), pp. 31–44.

Figure 7–3

A Checklist of
Qualities That
Make for
Excellence
in Office
Supervision

A PROFILE OF SUCCESSFUL OFFICE SUPERVISORS

Regardless of their age, sex, or race, or the size, location, and structure of their organizations, successful office supervisors possess the following qualities:

1. *Ability to treat subordinates as human beings.* Supervisors strive to be "one of the employees" without sacrificing any dignity of the position. Supervisors cannot be too intimate because with intimacy often comes leniency, and with leniency comes loss of respect and confidence. Similarly, supervisors cannot be cold, aloof, or arrogant. The goal of office supervisors is to be sensitive to the needs of others by achieving a workable blending of human relations skills.

2. *Attitude of leader rather than of boss.* Office supervisors win the utmost cooperation by being willing to coach subordinates and work constructively with them to develop desirable performance levels. Innovation and new ideas are encouraged.

3. *Fairness and open-mindedness.* In all dealings with workers, supervisors are candid, honest, and direct. Supervisors are willing to see both sides of problems and to solve them fairly and reasonably so that no resentment remains in those against whom a decision goes.

4. *Willingness to be available for advice.* Supervisors are available for counseling and are patient and understanding when dealing with workers and their personal problems. Effective supervisors display a high level of integrity and trust that is respected by subordinates.

5. *Dependability in keeping promises and providing support.* Supervisors keep all promises made to workers and support them when dealing with other departments and top management. Supervisors follow up on important issues and provide feedback to subordinates on how they are doing.

6. *Objectivity.* Supervisors are fair and unbiased in their relationships with subordinates. Supervisors avoid playing favorites among employees and also avoid giving the appearance of doing so.

7. *Ability to delegate responsibility and authority effectively.* Supervisors involve subordinates in the establishment of mutually agreed upon goals. Clear direction is provided by stating goals and standards clearly and by delegating responsibility and authority.

Need for Discipline. The need for discipline is closely related to such problems as absenteeism, tardiness, low productivity, and poor quality of output. Behavioral scientists believe that such problems are associated with employees' boredom and disinterest, which result from their abilities not being fully used. These specialists look upon human talent as a valuable resource like any other capital resource such as the building housing the workers. They suggest that, when human resources are underutilized, the end result is costly and inefficient operations. Some behavioral scientists feel that we dedicate ourselves to our work in relation to how well the work meets our needs for satisfaction and self-worth. Thus, if work and the work environment do not support our needs, we hold back on our energies. This means that our lack of action severely reduces the organization's cost effectiveness.

Developing a Disciplinary System. Not all violations of office rules and conduct deserve the same treatment. For example, in one company, the office supervisor may orally warn a worker who has been tardy twice during the workweek. However, this same supervisor may recommend the immediate termination of a worker who is caught trying to sell cocaine to a coworker. Therefore, a system of *progressive* disciplinary actions should be designed so that employees are informed of each kind of misconduct and its penalty. The progressive disciplinary actions often follow a four-step process, as outlined below:

1. *Oral reprimand or warning.* This formal discussion between employee and supervisor should be documented, with the supervisor retaining the paperwork.
2. *Written reprimand.* Following this formal, documented discussion, the write-up is placed in the worker's personnel file along with the paperwork from Step 1.
3. *Time off without pay or a probationary period.* At this stage, the employee must be made aware that if the problem continues, termination will result.
4. *Termination.*

Counseling

In the office, our personal problems often affect our efficiency. Therefore, a supervisor should be available to talk with workers as the need arises. Or, the supervisor should refer troubled workers to the appropriate person either within or outside the company. Some firms that are unable to support a staff counselor maintain contact with an outside professional counselor whose services are called upon as needed. Small firms often pool their resources so they can share the services and the cost of such a consultant.

Many medium-size and large organizations have developed employee assistance programs that specialize in providing aid and counseling. An **employee assistance program (EAP)** provides specially trained persons who diagnose and offer help in solving personal problems that affect employees' job performance and attendance.

Employees are aided in solving problems such as alcoholism, family or marital distress, financial troubles, nervous or emotional disorders, poor physical health, drug abuse, and legal matters. In firms having an EAP, supervisors can refer their troubled workers directly to the EAP. Thus, the supervisors are freed from becoming involved in the personal lives of their employees. Instead, the employees' personal problems are handled with the utmost confidentiality and competency by professionally trained counselors.

Office supervisors should note any emotional disturbances among workers in their departments and know how to react. The supervisor should watch for symptoms of emotional difficulties, such as a marked change in a worker's behavior pattern, as when a punctual worker suddenly develops a high tardiness record. A worker who persistently complains of headaches and nausea may be showing signs of psychosomatic illness (physical symptoms with an emotional base). A worker who has a series of minor accidents is probably troubled, for such accidents may often be the result of inattention, and inattention is a sign of preoccupation. A bigger problem than any of these, however, is alcoholism, which may indicate a deeply rooted emotional problem that workers are unable to handle alone. In these cases, the office supervisor is responsible for helping workers recognize their problems and for urging them to seek proper professional help before they are dismissed from the company.[3]

How far supervisors should go in talking with employees about their personal problems or personal relations with coworkers depends upon the perception, sympathy, judgment, training, and counseling experience of the supervisors themselves. In counseling, supervisors should listen sympathetically; only through such listening can they come to understand their workers' problems and learn why these problems are affecting productivity. The supervisor can sometimes help a disturbed worker by granting a leave of absence or suggesting where assistance may be found. But the supervisor should avoid assuming the

---

[3]The topic of alcoholism is discussed in further detail in Chapter 12.

role of psychologist or human relations counselor in problems unrelated to the job.

When employees seek help, however, on how to improve performance or how to prepare for career advancement, supervisors should freely pass along their opinions and recommendations. Supervisors have a responsibility to provide their workers with guidance not only on how to prepare themselves to meet performance standards but also on how to acquire the skills and knowledge to advance their careers. In the *Dialog from the Workplace,* Ms. Noel A. Kreicker, president and founder of International Orientation Resources, enumerates the skills and knowledge needed by overseas managers while advancing their careers and meeting the challenges faced during their assignments abroad.

Career Goal Planning

Office workers may look to their supervisors for help in formulating clear, practical career goals. Many office workers ask questions about the firm's promotional opportunities, such as, "What are the prospects of my being promoted to department head or supervisor?" "What steps should I now be taking to prepare for the new position?" Although most workers cannot be guaranteed a specific organizational slot in the future, the su-

pervisor, fully supported by top management, can aid workers in planning their career goals.

In **career goal planning,** the supervisor works with the employees to assess their personal strengths, weaknesses, preferences, and values; to select and formulate career goals; to develop action plans so the workers can carry out their goals; and to put their action plans to work. In this role, the supervisor serves as a coach by getting the workers to take responsibility for developing their abilities to make an expanded contribution to the company. To help employees become the best performers, the supervisor should provide direction in career management and offer guidelines such as those listed in Figure 7–4.

Performance Appraisal

Much of the office supervisor's counseling and career goal planning is concerned with **performance appraisal,** in which the employee's work is evaluated and constructively criticized. In appraising the performance of subordinates, supervisors must measure (1) how well the employees have done the work assigned, (2) how well they can do work that may be more demanding, and (3) to what extent they can be depended upon to carry out directions if no one is available to provide close supervision. Such constructive appraisal of employee perfor-

Figure 7–4
Career Management Guidelines

CAREER MANAGEMENT GUIDELINES	
1. Assess.	People managing their careers should know themselves as well as possible. What are their strengths, weaknesses, shortcomings?
2. Investigate.	Has the employee examined and discovered all the needs, challenges, and opportunities his or her division or department can offer?
3. Match.	Employees should match their self-assessments with the needs and challenges that are available.
4. Choose.	Have the employees, upon careful examination of their needs and their opportunities, chosen the proper targets?
5. Manage.	Employees need a development plan that can lead to the achievement of their goals.

Reprinted, by permission of publisher, from *Supervisory Management,* November, 1990, © 1990. American Management Association, New York. All rights reserved.

DIALOG FROM THE WORKPLACE

NOEL A. KREICKER

President and Founder
International Orientation
Resources (IOR)
Northbrook, Illinois

Noel A. Kreicker is president and founder of IOR, an international training and consulting company. IOR provides cross-cultural training, global business briefings, language, and on-site worldwide orientation services to over 100 *Fortune* 1,000 companies. Ms. Kreicker was a teacher in the Philippines as a Peace Corps volunteer from 1967 to 1969; an expatriate in Bogotá, Colombia, in 1978; and travels overseas extensively. She writes and publishes articles on various aspects of cross-cultural training, communication, and leadership. In addition, she leads workshops for various international training associations.

QUESTION: What are the most important skills for success as global managers and what advice do these managers have for their successors?

RESPONSE: To determine what characteristics are necessary for overseas management in today's global economy, IOR surveyed 125 expatriate managers from around the world. The survey asked experienced international businesspeople about skills needed for and challenges faced during assignments abroad.

Four *skills* were considered essential: flexibility, patience, the ability to listen well, and interest in learning foreign languages. One manager's comment is typical: "Patience, listening and learning skills, and the ability to adapt strategies to fit local circumstances are most important, as is having enthusiasm for local foods, drinks, and traditions."

Expatriates face *challenges* at home as well as at work. Common responses included loneliness and lack of established roots. This is exacerbated when expatriates work long hours and have little family time. Repatria-tion—fitting in back home professionally—was a concern of many.

Managers working overseas become aware of the value differences which may impede *cultural understanding*. These include their own personal values, values of their native culture, and values of the host culture. Awareness of the first two helps in understanding the host culture.

U.S. citizens find that their inherent cultural assumptions, such as individualism, privacy, equality, and control over time, are not operative in most of the world. In Japan, for example, the welfare of the group comes before that of the individual. In China, there is no word for "privacy." Latin Americans believe that good interpersonal relationships are more important than arriving on time or adhering to a fixed schedule.

When asked what *demands* expatriates will face in the future, the global managers responded:

Learning to think on a global scale rather than on a U.S.-market scale.

Coping with a rapidly changing political environment, particularly in Eastern Europe and the Middle East.

Accepting that the age of American superiority is over.

Others included helping headquarters understand the reduced level of productivity that cultural differences can cause, finding qualified successors who possess the cross-cultural communication skills necessary to succeed in a foreign environment, and ensuring that expatriates are employed effectively upon repatriation.

While technical knowledge is important to success anywhere, cross-cultural understanding and communication skills are critical for success in a foreign environment. Future managers will no longer be able to operate effectively unless they understand other cultures.

mance is a valuable tool used by office supervisors to strengthen the supervisor–subordinate relationship. Employee appraisal is discussed in detail in the following chapter.

MOTIVATING THE WORKFORCE

One of the major downward responsibilities of office supervisors is to **motivate**—to create the kind of environment in which workers are enthusiastic and have a desire to work. This is best accomplished by treating workers as human beings, not as machines that are turned on and off automatically. In addition to possessing desirable personal qualities, supervisors must see that the necessary psychological conditions, as well as material satisfactions, exist in their departments.

In this section, we will discuss some of the factors that aid in creating an environment of worker enthusiasm and desire to work. Interwoven throughout the discussion are several theories of motivation that were briefly mentioned in Chapter 1. We shall also examine *expectancy theory,* which, along with the others, guides the office supervisor to an understanding of what motivates human behavior.

Building and Maintaining Morale

Morale refers to our mental and emotional attitudes toward the tasks expected of us by our group and our loyalty to that group. A high level of morale, or *esprit de corps,* exists when we perform our work with satisfaction and enjoyment. Such an attitude creates a feeling of enthusiasm and happiness during and after working hours. The desires, interests, and feelings of most human beings are somewhat alike, and when supervisors help to satisfy them for us, our morale is improved. Improved morale results in our doing more and better work and enjoying life at the same time.

Unless a proper level of morale is built and maintained, a growing distrust and dissatisfaction may develop among employees. The company and its interest in its workers must be "sold" to the workers by a sincere and continuous effort that takes into consideration their needs, as illustrated in Figure 7–5. This hierarchy of needs, as

identified by the psychologist Abraham Maslow, shows that human beings have two sets of needs—primary and secondary.

Primary Needs

Primary needs consist of basic *physiological needs* (food, water, clothing, shelter, rest, air, etc.) and *safety needs* (security, protection against physical and mental dangers and future deprivation). One thread of continuity tying together both kinds of needs is *security,* of which job security and personal security are fundamental.

Job Security. As employees, we want to know that our jobs are necessary and permanent and that we will be provided a basic salary with pay increases based on performance, promotional opportunities, and seniority. However, when the number of layoffs and downsizings increases, *fear* is instilled in the minds of many workers. In fact, a Gallup Poll shows that only 35 percent of employees are satisfied with their job security; this figure represents a 10 percent reduction in the satisfaction level since 1989.[4] In another survey of more than 900 firms that had downsized, 72 percent of the employees still on the job did not think the newly revamped company was a better place to work; 70 percent felt insecure about their future with the firm.[5] Such reports of job dissatisfaction and insecurity require that office managers and supervisors work toward maintaining morale both *before and after* any workforce reduction.

One effective means of maintaining morale and meeting the workers' needs for job security lies in the area of *communications.* Here, supervisors have an obligation to make the company's intentions clear to employees and to keep them informed of conditions that may affect the firm and their jobs. In such a communications program, some effective tools are: company-wide or departmental meetings, small face-to-face group meetings, personalized letters to employees, outplacement assistance manuals, bulletin board an-

---

[4]Jeffrey E. Myers, "Downsizing Blues: How to Keep Up Morale," *Management Review* (April, 1993), p. 28.

[5]Larry Reynolds, "America's Work Ethic: Lost in Turbulent Times?" *Management Review* (October, 1992), p. 23.

Figure 7–5
Maslow's
Hierarchy of
Needs

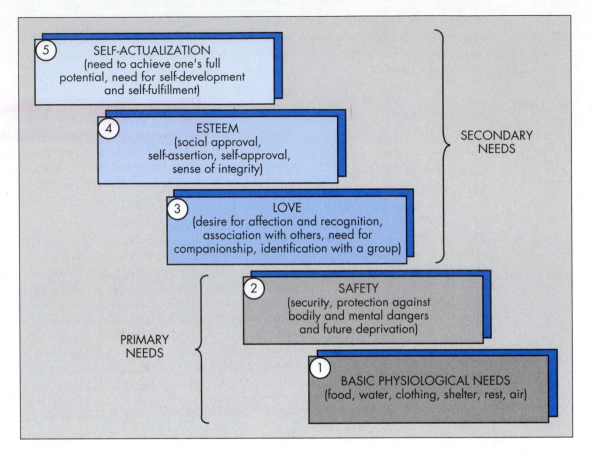

nouncements, company newsletters, and other media described in Chapter 5.

Wages and Salaries. Of prime importance to morale is the existence of fair and uniform wage and salary rates. Workers are interested in their own rates of pay. However, they are also interested in the salaries being received by workers doing similar work in other offices and by those doing the same kind of work for about the same length of time in their own departments. As discussed later in the text, the pay rates for each job classification should be made available to employees so they know how far they can rise within any given classification. Workers should be told how standards were developed; nothing is so demoralizing to the workers in a department as a belief that pay rates are determined arbitrarily, that employees doing similar work are being paid

widely divergent salaries, and that the pay rates are not commensurate with the earnings of the company.

Sharing Equity. With the goals of increasing productivity, improving job performance, and appealing to the workers' needs for job security, some companies share with their employees an *equity,* or interest, in the ownership of the business. Companies usually share equity by offering items such as options to buy stock or participation in a stock ownership plan. A poll sponsored by Xerox found that when equity is offered to employees, over two-thirds of the respondents stated that the employees are most likely to work harder and become better team players.[6]

---

[6]"Whose Company Is It, Anyway?" *INC.* (January, 1993), p. 16.

Personal Security. Certain contingencies in life exist for which almost all of us try to prepare. Among these contingencies are our health, employment, retirement, and death. Business firms, either by choice or through the stimulation of union efforts and contracts, try to recognize these contingencies and do what they can to improve their employees' situations. Many firms attempt to meet the safety needs of their workers through employee benefits, such as hospitalization insurance, medical services, life insurance, pension plans, and guidance and counseling.

Maslow theorized that once the primary needs have been well satisfied, they no longer motivate. It is then that the secondary needs stimulate the worker.

Secondary Needs

As you see in Figure 7–5, secondary needs consist of *love* (desire for affection, association with others, need for companionship, identification with a group), *esteem* (social approval, self-assertion, self-approval, and sense of integrity), and *self-actualization* (need to achieve one's full potential and need for self-development and self-fulfillment).

According to Maslow's theory of motivation, a *secondary* need does not have to be completely satisfied before the next need emerges. The needs pattern differs from one office worker to the next. Thus, supervisors cannot assume that only one approach can be used to motivate their subordinates toward attaining the firm's objectives.

Love. Here, when we speak of the *love and affection need,* we are referring to the unselfish loyalty and warm attachment that one person has for another. When our need to feel important and do something worthwhile is recognized and fulfilled, a high level of morale is established. Employees should know and feel the importance of their jobs and their work to the firm. Explaining the "why of the job" and showing employees how their efforts contribute to attaining the company goals are also helpful in creating a feeling of importance. Recognition should be constantly stressed and, if possible, should be emphasized by developing group projects and teamwork.

Poor supervision can cause us, as employees, to lose our identity and give us a feeling of unimportance. We feel our lack of importance if we are unable to express ourselves in connection with our work. Poor supervision becomes evident when our supervisor criticizes us in front of our coworkers, plays favorites, becomes unfriendly, and shows a lack of understanding of basic human relationships.

Supervisors must recognize their employees' exceptional work and length of service if the love and affection need is to be met. As far as exceptional work is concerned, some companies prefer to pay bonuses established on one of several bases, such as units produced or time saved. Other firms use merit ratings, whereby outstanding performance is rewarded either by a pay increase within a given job classification or by promotion to a higher classification. Other companies favor incentive wage systems, of which there are many basic types and numerous variations, such as piece rate and guaranteed base wage plus piece rate.

Length of service is usually recognized by an annual increase in salary, by an annual bonus tied in with the length of employment, or by a combination of the two. Some businesses reward long and faithful service by distributing company stock or by giving employees a share in the profits.

Esteem. This need includes both *self-esteem and esteem by others.* It is shown in our desire for achievement and freedom of thought and in our search for status, prestige, and reputation in the eyes of others. Some behavioral scientists feel that management sometimes fails to create jobs that utilize fully the employees' talents and skills. As a result, the work becomes less satisfying than it would otherwise be. Thus, for many persons, work becomes a boring time in their lives.

Self-Actualization. The opportunity for *self-actualization*—the achievement of our full potential—is only part of our feeling important on the job and in the firm. It is also part of our personal self-development. In the management theories contributed by behavioral scientists, workers are viewed as having great potential and constantly searching for significant ways to develop themselves. Office workers bring this aspect of themselves to their jobs, and thus they desire work and work-related experiences that will contribute to meeting this self-actualization need.

Motivation-Maintenance Theory

Money is the oldest motivator, and most companies still rely heavily on salaries and employee benefits as a motivating force. However, some behaviorists compare the giving of more and more money with heroin—it takes more and more to produce less and less effect.

According to the *motivation-maintenance theory* developed by Frederick Herzberg, environmental conditions such as heating, lighting, and ventilation; quality of supervision; and pay are examples of *hygienic (maintenance) factors.*[7] We know that pay is related to productivity, but it is external, or peripheral, to the job itself. That is, pay is not an intrinsic part of the job but, instead, is an element that lies outside the work and the workplace. When a hygienic factor, such as pay, is felt by workers to be inadequate, it functions as a *dissatisfier.* This means that it has only the potential to affect performance negatively. When the pay factor is adequate, however, it does not motivate workers to greater productivity. Instead, it makes it possible for the other set of factors, the *motivators,* to function. Included in the set of motivators are opportunities for workers to say how their jobs are to be done, recognition of the workers and their accomplishments, and a feeling that the workers are using their talents and developing as individuals.

The positive feelings that may be aroused as a result of hygienic work conditions, such as a supervisor's word of encouragement, last only a short time. When employees are highly motivated and find their jobs interesting and challenging, they are able to tolerate considerable dissatisfaction with the hygienic factors. Although the hygienic factors cannot be ignored or slighted, a full measure of all of them does not make jobs interest-

ing or bring about the attainment of the firm's goals. The task of the supervisor is to increase the use of such motivator factors as achievement, recognition, the work itself, responsibility, and advancement. Thus, we find at the core of Herzberg's theory the concept that the factors which cause employee dissatisfaction are different from those which cause employee satisfaction. Supervisors must therefore work on both sets of factors to avoid discontent and to provide the best conditions for employee motivation.

Job Enrichment

Motivation theory includes the assumption that we want to do a good job, but we need to be challenged. Herzberg believed that, if employees are to be motivated, meaningful changes must be made in their jobs. The workers must be given challenging and interesting work through which they can assume responsibility. By means of **job enrichment,** a job is *redesigned* by building into it higher-level responsibilities and authorities and more challenging content. This gives the worker an opportunity for achievement, recognition, and growth. In turn, this makes the job a satisfying and a meaningful experience at which the worker is motivated to perform well. The individual's accountability for his or her own work is increased as a complete, natural unit of work is assigned to the employee. The worker is then granted additional authority as new and more difficult tasks are introduced to the job.

To see how job enrichment works, let us say that 75 employees are working in the accounting-policyholder services section of an insurance company. In the past, these workers operated in separate groups to perform three phases of information processing: (1) coding the changes to be made in policy contents, (2) recording the receipt of premium payments, and (3) reviewing the accounts to check upon the accuracy of the recorded information. Each of the three functions was performed in sequence (serially) by different groups of workers. As a result of redesigning the jobs, the three separate functions were combined into a single job called an "account analyst." Thus, instead of performing only one part of the

---

[7]See Chapter 1, page 18.

service for a large number of accounts, each analyst becomes responsible for the entire procedure for a smaller number of accounts. With such job redesign, the firm can anticipate increased productivity since the delays that occurred as the information-processing work flowed from one workstation to another have been eliminated.

As a result of redesigning the work in order to enrich jobs, companies expect to improve quality, increase productivity, raise levels of job satisfaction, reduce absenteeism and turnover, and possibly reduce the size of the workforce. However, opposite results may occur. For example, when more responsibilities are added to a job, the worker may immediately ask for more money. The redesign of several tasks into a new, more complex job may lead to increased requirements for floor space and the duplication of office furniture and equipment. Outside consultants may have to be hired to design and execute the work-related changes. Also, considerable time and money may have to be spent to train the workforce to perform the new work satisfactorily. Herzberg himelf said that "the greater efficiency of enriched jobs in the long term will lead to a

competitive edge and more jobs only if we invest in essential training and retraining."[8] Therefore, firms should weigh the possible benefits to be gained from a job enrichment program against the potential increased costs of (1) wages and salaries, (2) required changes in facilities, (3) implementing the new work design, and (4) training and retraining employees to perform the newly expanded jobs.

Delegating

As we saw in Chapter 2, *delegating* is the process of entrusting work to others who are qualified to accept responsibility for doing the work. Implied in the process of delegating is the granting of sufficient authority to get the work done and an understanding by all concerned of the results to be accomplished. Office supervisors have a responsibility to themselves and to their subordinates to delegate effectively the authority and responsibility for the work to be done.

By strengthening the confidence of their subordinates and developing their initiative and capability, supervisors look for more efficient operation of their departments. Supervisors have a responsibility to their company to inspire their workers to assume new responsibilities and to explore new methods on their own. Supervisors must realize that to a great extent the future of their company lies in the hands of those who report to them. By effectively delegating work, supervisors can help their subordinates prepare for advancement to higher-level positions in the firm.

Unfortunately, however, many supervisors are unable to delegate because they do not fully understand their role. Some mistrust their subordinates' abilities to do the job and feel that the work will not be done properly unless they do it themselves. Others enjoy doing a task so much they are reluctant to let someone else handle it. Supervisors also fail to delegate because of psychological reasons—the fear of competition, the fear of losing credit and recognition, and the

Illustration 7–2 Supervisors who effectively delegate work increase office efficiency and prepare subordinates for taking on greater responsibilities.

---

[8]"Letters to the Editor," *Harvard Business Review* (November–December, 1992), p. 142.

fear that their own shortcomings and weaknesses will be exposed. Many times these fears cause poor work, low productivity, and a serious breakdown in morale among the workers in a department.

Similar feelings of insecurity and lack of motivation may account for a subordinate's resistance to accepting more power and responsibility, as evidenced in Douglas McGregor's views of worker behavior.

Authoritarian Versus Participative Organizations

After studying traditional managers, McGregor concluded that their approaches to managing workers and their work were based on the assumptions that he labeled Theory X and Theory Y.[9]

Theory X

According to **Theory X,** the traditional view of supervising workers and of working, subordinates dislike work and avoid it if they can. Being irresponsible and lacking ambition, they prefer to be led rather than lead. Managers and supervisors who evaluate worker behavior from this point of view conclude that restrictive controls are necessary. An example of such restriction is the supervisor who exercises "tight" control over all aspects of employee performance. Those who adhere to Theory X believe in a work-centered organization that relies on the traditional concept of authority—the right to command. Because such organizations are so dependent upon authority, they are often called **authoritarian organizations.**

Theory Y

Supervisors operating under **Theory Y** view their subordinates as willing to work and accept responsibility. Capable of self-direction and self-control, the workers are able to use their imagination and originality. The assumptions of Theory Y represent the behaviorist's faith in the capacity and potential of workers. This, in turn, leads supervisors to create conditions under which all workers have the opportunity to achieve their full potential. Those who adhere to Theory Y emphasize democratic relations in their organizations, which are often called **participative organizations.**

Supervisors must be willing to share their knowledge and experience with their subordinates so that they may more actively participate. In fact, qualified subordinates should be trained to step into their supervisors' jobs as a result of their supervisors having delegated the work. As supervisors free themselves of work through delegation, they become available to assume new, higher-level responsibilities, which may lead to new job opportunities for them.

Participative Management

Subordinates who accept responsibility for the work delegated to them gain practical experience in **participative management.** Using this technique, supervisors give workers a voice in determining what they are to do, how they are to do it, and how they are to be appraised. A great motivating force comes into play when workers are (1) put in charge of a portion of the department's work, (2) given the authority to make decisions that spell success or failure, and (3) rewarded for what is accomplished. In this way, when subordinates become involved in identifying and solving office problems, more of their personal needs—especially status, recognition, and self-actualization—are met.

Participative management, therefore, increases employee motivation because workers identify more closely with the company, develop greater team spirit, and, most important, work harder to achieve the goals they helped to establish. To reflect this spirit of participation, some companies no longer refer to their workforce as "employees"; instead, in these firms, we find "partners," "associates," "stakeholders," and "team members."

In their search for ways to improve productivity, companies use a variety of motivational techniques designed to involve their employees.

---

[9]Douglas McGregor, *The Human Side of Enterprise* (New York: McGraw-Hill Book Company, 1960).

Various formal programs of employee participation are found—from the task forces, problem-solving committees, and self-directed teams described earlier to management by objectives and employee attitude surveys presented in this chapter. (In our discussion of productivity improvement in a later chapter, we shall examine another participation program—the quality circle.)

In today's workplace, a popular means of increasing employee participation is **empowerment**—delegating to others the authority to act and to make decisions on their own. As a result of this process, employees gain power and become more influential within the organization. For example, by involving workers in selecting their work assignments and deciding which methods they will use to do the work, office supervisors help empower others. This, in turn, aids in instilling confidence and maintaining high morale. In empowering employees to make informed operational decisions, some companies communicate relevant financial information to workers at all levels. Thus, the workers come to understand the linkage between finance and operations. The payoff appears when workers focus their attention upon those activities that will enhance the firm's financial performance.[10]

Even with the availability of employee participation programs, we may question the effectiveness of the programs and to what extent companies make use of the motivation techniques at their disposal. For example, the Hay Group, an international management consulting group, studied employee involvement by asking: Does your immediate supervisor encourage you to provide suggestions for improvements? Do you have a chance to put your ideas into use? As you examine some of the answers to these questions, you may question the effectiveness of employee empowerment in solving problems related to morale, job security, and job satisfaction:

1. Of the *middle managers,* 58 percent responded positively when asked if their supervisors encouraged suggestions; 59 percent said they had a chance to see their suggestions implemented.
2. Of the *professional/technical employees,* one-half said managers encouraged them to make suggestions; 35 percent saw their ideas put to use.
3. Of the *clerical workers,* 48 percent said they were encouraged to make suggestions; only 22 percent saw their ideas put to use.[11]

Although participation programs hold promise as a means of motivating employees, such programs are sure to fail when supervisors resist their establishment. Many supervisors, concerned solely with their own self-interest, see no benefit for themselves in the programs. They worry about their jobs and resent any loss of power and control when worker involvement increases. In one way or another, these supervisors fall into a pattern of passive resistance. To overcome this problem, top management needs to increase the involvement of supervisors in upper-level planning sessions. Thus, supervisors will be able to more actively participate in decision making and improve their own managerial skills. In turn, such participation will aid supervisors in learning how to define their own goals and to manage people more effectively.

Theory Z Organizations

In Chapter 1, *Theory Z management* was introduced to explain the nature of a management style formulated by William Ouchi. In his study of companies in Japan and a comparative analysis of those in the United States, Ouchi identified firms that lean toward a Theory Z organization.

The **Theory Z organization,** which resembles the Japanese style of management, relies greatly upon long-range planning; strong, mutual worker-

[10]William L. Christison, "Pushing Financial Information Down the Organization," *Management Review* (January, 1993), pp. 43–44.

[11]"Empowered Employees: Rhetoric or Reality?" *Personnel* (September, 1991), p. 19.

Figure 7–6
Characteristics
of the Theory
Z Organiza-
tion

THE THEORY Z ORGANIZATION PROVIDES:

- *Stable, long-term employment* where employees expect to stay on the job for their lifetime, under no assumption they will be laid off.

- *Moderately specialized careers* and rotation of workers through different kinds of jobs.

- *Slow evaluation and promotion* to ensure that no one is advanced into a position of responsibility until complete job commitment occurs.

- *Decision making by consensus,* a natural result of workers having become completely socialized in the culture of their organization.

- *Individual responsibility,* which results from collective decision making and a commonly shared culture.

- *Strong emotional well-being* among workers who believe in collective responsibility and action.

- *Concern for each subordinate* as a functioning whole person, with emphasis placed upon the working relationships among people.

employer loyalty and trust; and those elements listed in Figure 7–6. Ouchi stresses that the special abilities of the individual worker are more important than the contents of the job description. According to Theory Z, workers should be hired for their talents. Further, jobs should be designed around the workers' talents rather than trying to fit workers into preset job descriptions. In firms that have experimented with the theory by adopting flexible work schedules, for example, workers are given a great deal of freedom to make their own decisions about work. Rather than relying upon technological change in itself to bring about increased productivity, Theory Z calls for managers and supervisors to redirect their attention to human relations.

In contrasting the organizations of the United States and Japan, Ouchi notes that Japan's homogeneous structure, a fairly uniform culture, encourages mutual trust and cooperation. This, in turn, allows collective enterprises like large corporations to form a strong paternalistic bond between workers and their firms. However, not all Japanese management practices can be transplanted into American life. For example, Americans place a high value on their mobility and have cultural values that do not agree with the practice of lifelong employment. However,

Ouchi found that some firms in the United States exhibit characteristics of the Theory Z organization and have used some of the Theory Z practices, such as problem solving by collective project teams, reducing working hours for all employees during a recession, and permitting self-directed teams to govern their own jobs to improve productivity.

Management by Objectives and Goal Setting

First mentioned in Chapter 1, *management by objectives (MBO)* is a motivational technique that brings subordinates and their supervisors together to agree mutually upon practical goals to be achieved. To be realistic, the goals must be attainable and challenging enough to require effort for their accomplishment. The goals should also motivate the workers to use their talents and skills to the fullest to improve personal performance.

Under guidelines set by the supervisor, the workers set specific targets for their own objectives (such as arriving five minutes early each morning), commit themselves to the attainment of these targets, and evaluate themselves with respect to their performance in meeting the objectives. Thus, individual workers are encouraged to assume greater responsibility for planning as well as for appraising and measuring their contributions in meeting organizational objectives. This in turn aids in meeting the ego and self-development needs of the workers that might otherwise have been ignored.

Feedback must be provided so the employees' progress toward each of their goals may be monitored by the supervisor. For example, each mutually agreed upon goal is evaluated by the supervisor during a periodic performance review. At that time, subordinates are given the opportunity to discuss any problems they might be having. At the time of the performance review, new goals may mutually be set for the next time period. Thus, the performance review might emphasize a concrete, measurable goal, such as a 25 percent reduction in the cost of wasted office supplies.

Expectancy Theory of Motivation

The expectancy theory of motivation was developed by psychologists who see workers as *thinking* persons who have beliefs and anticipations about future events in their lives. According to **expectancy theory,** our motivational force to perform depends upon the expectancy that we have concerning future outcomes and the value that we place on these outcomes. Victor H. Vroom defines an expectancy as a "momentary belief concerning the likelihood that a particular act will be followed by a particular outcome."[12] Thus, your belief that "working overtime will improve your image in the boss's mind" is an expectancy. For you, such an expectancy serves as a guideline by which you can plan to fulfill your personal needs. The theory suggests that you have managed your personal motivation depending upon what you expect in terms of the three-way relationship among (1) effort, (2) performance, and (3) rewards for performance. If you had seen little relationship among the three factors and were faced with a backup of work at the end of the day, you may have decided, "Why bother? Forget it!"

For the office supervisor, the expectancy theory provides yet another basis for trying to explain the direction of employee behavior and to evaluate those environmental factors that affect behavior. Thus, this theory, along with all the others described in this chapter, aids the supervisor in learning what motivates employees and in understanding the relationships among effort, performance, and reward.

ETHICS AND VALUE SYSTEMS

As individuals differ, so do their ethical concepts and value systems. Personal guidelines or policies for everyday ethical conduct are needed in the office. Like all policies, a code of ethics must be capable of being enforced. Many problems facing today's office supervisors suggest clashing or poorly understood value systems. These problems come about in an attempt to apply traditional supervisory methods to employees who have a different work ethic. To manage effectively, office supervisors must adapt their means for achieving organizational goals to the value systems of their workers.

Ethics

In a Harris/Steelcase survey, office workers were asked what they considered the most important characteristics of their office environments. Of the workers interviewed, 89 percent said that "management that is honest, upright, and ethical in its dealings with employees and the community" is very important; however, only 41 percent said that this description characterizes their current employers.[13] What do we mean by "ethical conduct"? Let's take a few minutes to examine this word *ethics.*

Ethics is a systematic study of that part of science and philosophy which deals with moral con-

---

[12]Victor H. Vroom, *Work and Motivation* (New York: John Wiley & Sons, 1964), p. 170.

[13]"Office Talk," *Personnel* (October, 1988), p. 12. The survey of 1,031 office workers and 150 top-level executives from around the country was conducted by Louis Harris and Associates and sponsored by Steelcase, Inc., an office furniture manufacturer in Grand Rapids, Michigan.

duct, duty, and judgment. Your concept of what is and is not ethically and morally right stems from your religious convictions, personal philosophy, and motives. Look at the list of office practices shown in Figure 7–7 and decide which of them are or are not ethically and morally right.

The inspiration for ethical behavior must originate at the top level of management and filter down to permeate the entire business organization. Today we find many companies taking great pains to create an atmosphere of credibility and responsibility by adding an ethics officer position. In a survey of *Fortune* 1,000 companies, one-third of the respondents reported having an ethics officer, who holds a title ranging from director to vice president.[14] Among the ethics officer's responsibilities are: providing information and advice on ethics to top management, disseminating a code of conduct, and investigating and answering questions about any alleged ethics violations.

The best guarantee of high standards of morality is that subordinates work under the direction of men and women who themselves have high standards. Consider the code of ethics developed during the Great Depression by Herbert J. Taylor, a Chicago Rotarian, for the conduct of his company, Club Aluminum:[15]

THE FOUR-WAY TEST
of the Things We Think, Say, or Do

1. Is it the TRUTH?
2. Is it FAIR to all concerned?
3. Will it build GOODWILL and BETTER FRIENDSHIPS?
4. Will it be BENEFICIAL to all concerned?

Ask yourself: Now, some 60 years later, can the Four-Way Test work in today's society? Is it "sophisticated" enough to guide office supervisors and their workers in these fast-paced times?

For at least one-third of each working day, supervisors enter into social relationships with their employees. During the remaining two-thirds of each day, the attitudes, ideals, and beliefs that the employees have formed while at work in the office are being carried back and relayed to society—the families and friends of the employees. Thus, supervisors have a social responsibility to set a good example for their employees. The ethical and moral conduct of supervisors, as leaders, must rise above their own personal and individual motives and needs.

In communicating with upper management, supervisors should strive to report all facts honestly, accurately, and objectively. Supervisors must train themselves and their workers to avoid distorting the facts in order to fill a psychological need; all too often communication lines become warped by the biases of the sender. In reaching decisions, the goal of supervisors should be to discipline their thinking into a logical, orderly process, rather than to jump to conclusions impulsively. In working with subordinates, supervisors may find it easy to abuse their authority, with the result that employees feel "let down" and unsupported in their actions. To gain employees who will work with him or her, a supervisor must work with them; be kind, fair, and just; and sincerely praise the workers' satisfactory performance.

Basic to ethical and moral conduct is *loyalty*. Without this fundamental quality, no supervisor, no office, and no business firm can perform at the peak of potential capability. When supervisors are unable to give allegiance to the authority of their firms, they find themselves in a position of conflict, which in turn hinders them from being loyal to either themselves or their companies. The only workable solution to the problem of office supervisors who cannot abide by the policies and principles set forth by their firm is for them to seek employment in companies where they can be loyal.

Value Systems

A **value system** is the sum of our moral and social perceptions of those things that are intrinsically desirable or valuable. As a result of our experi-

[14]"Ethics: A New Profession in American Business," *HR Focus* (May, 1993), p. 22.

[15]"The 4-Way Test: Can It Work in Today's Society?" *The Rotarian* (October, 1992), p. 39.

Figure 7–7
Determining
an Office
Ethics Quo-
tient (OEQ)

WHAT IS YOUR OFFICE ETHICS QUOTIENT (OEQ)?

As you examine each of the office practices described below, indicate with a check (✓) on the scale at the right how you judge the ethics and morality of the practice. After you have evaluated all 12 practices, add your points to obtain your OEQ. An interpretation of your OEQ is given at the bottom of the form.

OFFICE PRACTICE	ETHICS SCALE		
	(A) Unethical or Immoral	(B) Possibly Unethical or Immoral	(C) Ethical and Moral
1. Employee A, knowing he will be arriving late, asks B to punch in for him at the time clock.			
2. C leaves her workstation (a nonsmoking area) and goes outside about ten times each day to smoke a cigarette.			
3. D occasionally leaves his desk in the morning and the afternoon to go to the company lounge, where he sips a little vodka from the flask in his locker.			
4. E puts a few ballpoint pens and a box of paper clips in her purse before leaving the office.			
5. During the lunch hour, F sits in his car in the company parking lot and smokes pot.			
6. G places weekly long-distance calls to her grandmother and reports them as business calls to the accounting department.			
7. H, who does not want to be bothered with incoming calls or visitors, tells his secretary, I, to inform all callers that he is not in.			
8. Each time J passes the desk of K, K whistles at her.			
9. To obtain her job with the company, L exaggerated her educational background on the application form to show she had a two-year associate degree.			
10. M, working in accounts receivable, "borrows" some of the incoming receipts in the form of cash, with the intention of repaying the "borrowed" amount next payday.			
11. N, a data-entry operator in the medical department, supplies the psychological file of a worker to a manager who wants to see if the worker might crack under stress.			
12. O, a payroll clerk, leaks information about present salaries earned by company personnel and the increases planned for these workers.			

Determine you OEQ and its interpretation by assigning the following value to each check mark: Column A, 5 points; Column B, 2 points; Column C, 1 point. Add the point values of all check marks to obtain your OEQ.

OEQ	Interpretation
42 to 60 points	You adhere to an exceptionally high level of morality and ethics in the office. Your supervisor looks upon you as morally and ethically right.
24 to 41 points	You often hedge on issues and feel fairly secure and safe by being inconsistent. Your supervisor sizes you up as a fence straddler, one from whom it is difficult to obtain a clear-cut yes-or-no answer.
fewer than 24 points	Your low level of ethical and moral conduct in the office differs significantly from the norm. Your supervisor is obligated to impose strict controls upon your job performance and work habits.

Illustration 7–3 Job satisfaction depends largely on how interesting and challenging employees find their jobs.

ences and education and the customs and traditions of our culture, we develop values that will satisfy our personal needs. If office workers can look upon their working lives as a real contribution not only to their coworkers and the firm but also to society, they may find opportunities to satisfy their love, esteem, and self-actualization needs. If, on the other hand, office workers view themselves as being saddled with boring, unchallenging work, the opportunities to find satisfaction and happiness and meet their needs are practically nil.

Many workers, as a result of their increased educational economic status, find that having an interesting job is nearly as important as the economic benefits derived from the job. In a survey conducted by the Gallup Poll, the factor, interesting work, was ranked by more than three-fourths of the respondents as very important. However, only 41 percent of this group were satisfied with this factor in their current jobs.[16] A similar finding

was announced in a global survey of office workers, the *1991 Worldwide Office Environment Index.* This survey found that 43 percent of the office workers in the United States were very satisfied with their jobs. (Interestingly, only 17 percent of the Japanese office workers were satisfied with their jobs; 39 percent, in Canada; and 28 percent, in the European Community.)[17]

High income, good health insurance, and other benefits are still very important, but they must support an adequate standard of living and be perceived as equitable. However, high pay and a broad employee benefits program alone do not lead to job (or life) satisfaction. As Peter F. Drucker so aptly observed, "To make a living is no longer enough. Work also has to make a life."[18]

The preceding survey results confirm that supervisors must try to understand their workers' value systems and involve them in providing input, such as their recommendations for redesigning the firm's systems and procedures. One approach that may be used to learn more about the workers' value systems, their attitudes, and their work frustrations is to conduct attitude surveys and climate surveys, as discussed next.

Attitude Surveys

An **attitude survey** is a polling of workers to determine their moods and feelings toward supervisory treatment, salaries and employee benefits, their jobs, and the firm. For example, a company may ask its workers to rank on a scale of 1 to 5 ("very poor" to "outstanding") how they view elements such as the following:

Your company:
1. As a place to work.
2. Provisions for job security.
3. Wages and salaries paid.
4. Employee benefits offered.

[16]Christopher Caggiano, "What Do Workers Want?" *INC.* (November, 1992), p. 101.

[17]"Satisfaction in the USA, Unhappiness in Japanese Offices," *HR Focus* (January, 1992), p. 8.

[18]Peter F. Drucker, *Management: Tasks, Responsibilities, Practices* (New York: Harper & Row, Publishers, Inc., 1974), p. 179.

Your management:
1. Ability of top management.
2. Ability of immediate supervisor.
3. Cooperation among departments.

Your job:
1. Opportunity to take part in decision making.
2. Challenges provided by the work.
3. Level of interest in the work.
4. Amount of pay received.
5. Relationship between job performance and salary increases.

By surveying employees at regular intervals and comparing their responses to the questions raised, the supervisor can spot changes in employee opinions and gain insight into the workers' wants and needs. With little investment in time and money, the company, and especially its supervisors, can obtain very significant results that can go a long way toward improving employee motivation.

Climate Surveys

In a similar vein, companies may conduct a **climate survey** to determine "weather conditions" by identifying among the workers any prevailing winds of discontent, impending storms, temperatures reaching the boiling point, and so on. The climate survey is a "no-holds barred," two-way feedback process—an interpersonal exchange between supervisors and subordinates in which unwarranted employee gripes can be explained and legitimate ones discussed. Thus, in feedback sessions, supervisors are obligated to face up to and correct any unpleasant situations. Of course, the success of such feedback sessions hinges on the willingness of supervisors and managers to submit themselves to close scrutiny by their subordinates.

Attitude surveys and climate surveys aid supervisors in learning what employees expect since the surveys raise basic questions that most workers usually ask themselves about their work situations. Most employees want answers to questions such as, "What's in it for me?" "How important to me are the rewards for working at this job?" "If I try harder, will it really make a difference in my performance?" "Am I really rewarded for what I produce?" "If I improve my performance level, will I receive an increase in rewards?" "If I don't improve, what will be the consequences?"

SUMMARY

1. In their planning, organizing, leading, and controlling, office supervisors assume the following specific responsibilities: (a) *upward* to higher management, (b) *horizontally* to peers (supervisors of equal rank), and (c) *downward* to subordinates (workers at the operative level). The supervisor also has responsibilities for *coordinating* the work to be done and for *self-development* by preparing for growth and promotion.

2. To work with today's diverse workforce, supervisors must develop the skills required to (a) communicate effectively, (b) coach and develop people having great diversity, (c) provide objective performance feedback, and (d) help create organizational climates that nurture and utilize the diverse workers' talents and perspectives.

3. In disciplining, office supervisors often follow a four-step process: (a) oral reprimand or warning, (b) written reprimand, (c) time off without pay or a probationary period, and (d) termination.

To provide counsel, supervisors aim to be available to talk with workers as the need arises; to refer them to trained persons, such as professionals in the firm's employee assistance program (EAP); or to recommend the services of an outside professional consultant.

cont

In career goal planning, supervisors work with the employees to assess their personal strengths, weaknesses, preferences, and values; to select and formulate career goals; to develop action plans so the workers can carry out their goals; and to put their action plans to work.

4. In using the human approach in supervision, office supervisors need to understand the theories of motivation such as the hierarchy of needs; motivation-maintenance; job enrich-

ment; Theories X, Y, and Z; participative management; management by objectives and goal setting; and expectancy.

5. To create the kind of office atmosphere that affects worker performance positively and enables effective leadership, supervisors must acknowledge the ethics and diverse value systems of today's office workers. Above all, the office supervisor, by example, must set the standard for moral and ethical conduct and loyalty.

FOR YOUR REVIEW

1. Describe the five types of supervisory responsibilities.

2. Explain the relationship between the projected increase in the labor force and its effect upon the diversity of workers by the year 2005.

3. List the qualities that characterize successful office supervisors.

4. What are the four steps that make up a progressive disciplinary system?

5. How are employees and their supervisors aided by the company's employee assistance program?

6. What role does the office supervisor play in planning the workers' career goals?

7. What is morale? How is morale related to the needs of workers?

8. Describe the different kinds of primary and secondary needs found in Maslow's hierarchy of needs.

9. How may a company provide job security as it tries to meet the primary needs of its workers?

10. Explain the relevance of Herzberg's motivation-maintenance theory to the concept that the major motivator of workers is the size of their paychecks.

11. How does job enrichment serve as a means of motivation?

12. What are the underlying reasons why many supervisors do not delegate or delegate ineffectively?

13. Contrast the underlying assumptions of McGregor's Theories X and Y of worker behavior.

14. Explain how empowerment may serve as a motivating force.

15. For what reasons do office supervisors sometimes resist the establishment of employee participation programs?

16. Describe the main features of the Theory Z organization that distinguish it from the traditional type of organization found in the United States.

17. Explain how management by objectives may be used as a motivational technique.

18. What is the best guarantee of high standards of morality in the business world?

19. Explain how attitude surveys and climate surveys may be used by an organization to learn more about its employees' value systems.

FOR YOUR DISCUSSION

1. When Ilona Marsh passes the mailing center on the way to her workstation, she often drops several unstamped pieces of personal mail in the outgoing mail slot. Marsh feels that her company owes her this "little benefit" to compensate for all her years of service. As Marsh's supervisor, what action would you take when you learn about the company's subsidizing her postage bill?

2. Carlos Torres, supervisor of records management at Dawn Products, asked Tom Garcia, the records librarian, to step into his office. Torres began to discuss Garcia's poor attendance record. While his time reports for the past month were being reviewed, Garcia began to cry. How would you, as Torres, handle the situation?

3. Penny Ash, assistant manager of accounts payable in a large accounting department, was helping Sylvia Baum, a data-entry operator, with some month-end reports. Ash uncovered a mathematical error made by Baum and called it to her attention. Being confronted with her mistake, Baum yelled at Ash: "You're embarrassing me in front of all my coworkers. How can you do this?" As Ash, how would you respond to the screaming Baum?

4. You have just learned that one of your workers, Amy Duffy, has gone over your head and taken her complaint to your boss, Hal Temple. Later, when Temple comes into your office, he informs you that Duffy is very upset that you will not reschedule her vacation. What steps can you take to make sure that your effectiveness as a supervisor will not be undermined by any future breach in the line of authority?

5. As the instructor continues with the lecture on motivational techniques, a neighboring student turns to you and remarks, "I think a lot of this motivation stuff is for the birds. We all know that motivation comes from within—you either have it or you don't." What is your reaction to this student's statements?

6. While attending a three-day seminar on "Improving Office Productivity," Jon Rupert calls his office four times each day, punctually at 10:00 A.M., 12:30 P.M., 2:00 P.M., and 3:30 P.M. As the supervisor in charge of communications, Rupert feels obligated to check in with his workers at least four times each day to see if things are running smoothly in his absence. What do you see as the most pressing problem facing Rupert in his supervisory relations with his subordinates? What solution can you offer to solve this problem?

cont

7. You have been asked to design a disciplinary system which recognizes that not all infractions deserve the same treatment and that each penalty should fit the violation. Of the following list of employee infractions, which do you consider serious enough to justify either suspension or discharge with the first offense? Be prepared to defend your answers.

   a. Taking an unexcused absence.

   b. Stealing.

   c. Gambling on company premises.

   d. Falsifying the petty cash records.

   e. Smoking in a smoking-prohibited area.

   f. Working while under the influence of drugs.

   g. Achieving less than satisfactory job performance.

   h. Sleeping on the job.

CASES FOR CRITICAL THINKING

Case 7–1 Solving a Morale Problem

Last week you said farewell to the supervisor of your word processing center who took advantage of your firm's early retirement policy. You have hired Pamela Chou, age 24 with a master's degree, as the replacement. The first several days of Chou's orientation roll along very well. At the end of the week, however, one of the operators, Betty Irwin (age 53 with no degree), tells you she will no longer take orders from Chou—"that new, young kid on the block." One of your assistants also informs you that Irwin is trying to cause friction among Chou and the other workers. How would you handle the situation?

Case 7–2 Improving the Status of Office Supervisors Who Are Misfits

One afternoon as Adele Hanks, an administrative manager, was returning from the company lounge to her office, she happened to overhear one of her supervisors, Matt Breyer, talking with a department head, Jeremy Stahl. Although the voices were muffled, Hanks caught the gist of their conversation, which was something like this:

Breyer: . . . I would go back to my old job of auditing freight bills any day if I wouldn't lose out on the bucks and my status. . . .

Stahl: I'm just as unhappy in my supervisory job as you. I just don't feel fit for my job. You'll never know how many days I wish I were back operating that terminal!

Back in her office Hanks wonders about other supervisors and department heads who may feel they are misfits. She questions to what extent such dissatisfaction may account for the increased loss of productivity in the office. She sits back and begins to think about what she, as administrative manager, can do to solve the problem of supervisors who are unhappy on the job and who feel they are misfits.

c
o
n
t

Assume the role of Hanks and prepare a proposal for a remedial program for top management to consider. Your objective is to improve the quality of supervision by selecting supervisory personnel who will fit the jobs and be happy with the quality of their daily work.

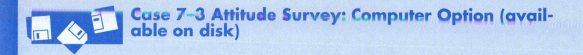

Case 7–3 Attitude Survey: Computer Option (available on disk)

8

TRAINING, APPRAISING, AND PROMOT- ING OFFICE PERSONNEL

After completing this chapter, you should be able to:

1. Describe how the principles of office training are applied in an effective training program.
2. Identify the psychological factors that must be provided when developing a training program.
3. List the outcomes to be realized from an effective training program.
4. Describe the methods and techniques commonly used in conducting an entry-level training program.
5. Identify the instruction methods and techniques used in supervisory training and management development programs.
6. List the purposes for undertaking employee performance appraisal and describe the methods of conducting such appraisals.
7. Describe the characteristics of a successful promotion plan.
8. Identify the factors to be considered in developing a termination procedure.

In addition to learning specific tasks, office workers often need basic education to improve their knowledge and retraining of their skills in order to become productive on the job. For example, in a survey of skills needed and training offered, it was found that four out of five companies feel that employees' writing skills need enhancing; however, only one out of five firms offer any training in writing skills. Further, 75 percent of the companies cited the need for employees with stronger interpersonal communication skills; only 42 percent offer training in this area.[1] Supervisors and managers also need to sharpen their skills and to keep up to date regarding modern management practices and technological changes occurring in their fields.

Office workers must be provided with opportunities for continuing growth and development so they can acquire the needed skills, knowledge, and attitudes in order to prepare themselves for more advanced positions in the firm. Training and development programs must also meet the needs of the workers' present activities and responsibilities. Thus, such programs should lessen the need for training after promotion and provide for smoother transition upward.

In this chapter, we shall examine the nature of training programs, along with employee appraisal and promotion. Also, we shall see the need for AOMs and office supervisors to follow a well-planned termination procedure when discontinuing the employment of workers.

TRAINING

Training is the process of providing individuals with an organized series of experiences and materials that comprise opportunities to learn. What

---

[1] "Skills for Success," The Olsten Forum on Human Resource Issues and Trends (Westbury, NY: The Olsten Corporation, 1992).

Illustration 8–1 Companies invest in training programs to help achieve organizational objectives of increasing productivity and improving employee work habits.

takes place within the individuals—that is, what changes occur in their behavioral patterns and attitudes—is known as **learning.** The money that a company spends for training pays dividends as a result of fewer errors, greater productivity, and less turnover.

Like any business activity, training has no value unless it aids in achieving the goals of the organization by contributing to better performance. Training should help a firm attain goals *directly* by increasing productivity, improving the quality of work, and reducing costs; and *indirectly* by improving the skills, attitudes, and work habits of employees and by increasing their knowledge and experiences.

Objectives of Office Training Programs

Before any training program can be undertaken, we must answer the question, "What are the goals of the training to be offered?" As shown in the model illustrated in Figure 8–1, we must clearly identify the objectives of the training program, its courses, and its instructional content in order to

show their relation to the objectives of the firm. Included among the broad goals of office training programs are provisions for:

1. **Entry-level,** or *initial,* **training** by which employees qualify for entry-job assignments.
2. **Remedial training** to remedy or correct deficiencies in work habits, attitudes, knowledge, skills, or job performance.
3. **Retraining** of workers whose jobs have changed, have become obsolete, or are no longer required.
4. **Cross-training** to develop multiskilled workers who can adapt to changes in job requirements and advancing technology and thus become ready to assume more responsible or more demanding positions.
5. **Diversity training** to share information about the changing demographics of the workforce, new approaches to managing the workforce, the dynamics of stereotyping and its effects upon teamwork, and the workers' changing cultural and ethical values.
6. **Supervisory training and management development (STMD)** to qualify workers for the added responsibilities and challenges of higher positions.

Principles of Office Training

We may look upon the office training program as a subsystem of the major business system, human resources, discussed earlier in the text. Along with the other subsystems of human resources—hiring, orienting, appraising, and terminating—the effectiveness of office training depends upon the extent to which management is committed to support the program; the proper assignment of responsibility to line managers; and the care and skill with which the training program is planned, implemented, and evaluated.

In Chapter 2, you read about several principles that underlie efficient management and healthy organization. How effectively these principles are applied, like the principles of office training described below, is measured by the performance of

Figure 8–1
Model for an
Office Train-
ing Program

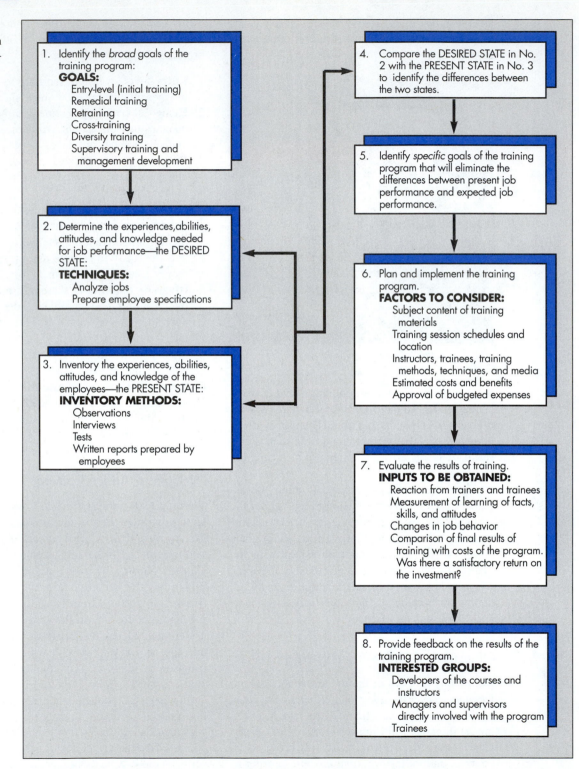

1. Identify the *broad* goals of the
   training program:
   GOALS:
   Entry-level (initial training)
   Remedial training
   Retraining
   Cross-training
   Diversity training
   Supervisory training and
   management development

2. Determine the experiences, abilities,
   attitudes, and knowledge needed
   for job performance—the DESIRED
   STATE:
   TECHNIQUES:
   Analyze jobs
   Prepare employee specifications

3. Inventory the experiences, abilities,
   attitudes, and knowledge of the
   employees—the PRESENT STATE:
   INVENTORY METHODS:
   Observations
   Interviews
   Tests
   Written reports prepared by
   employees

4. Compare the DESIRED STATE in No.
   2 with the PRESENT STATE in No. 3
   to identify the differences between
   the two states.

5. Identify *specific* goals of the training
   program that will eliminate the
   differences between present job
   performance and expected job
   performance.

6. Plan and implement the training
   program.
   FACTORS TO CONSIDER:
   Subject content of training
   materials
   Training session schedules and
   location
   Instructors, trainees, training
   methods, techniques, and media
   Estimated costs and benefits
   Approval of budgeted expenses

7. Evaluate the results of training.
   INPUTS TO BE OBTAINED:
   Reaction from trainers and trainees
   Measurement of learning of facts,
   skills, and attitudes
   Changes in job behavior
   Comparison of final results of
   training with costs of the program.
   Was there a satisfactory return on
   the investment?

8. Provide feedback on the results of the
   training program.
   INTERESTED GROUPS:
   Developers of the courses and
   instructors
   Managers and supervisors
   directly involved with the program
   Trainees

people in achieving results. As you study these principles, see how they are applied in the model shown in Figure 8–1.

PRINCIPLE OF COMMITMENT

Management must be committed to providing an organizational climate that stimulates continued learning and growth.

Without the support of top management, office training efforts are likely to have little lasting impact. The quality of the training program is greatly influenced by top management, which sets the policies designed to support the training effort. The goal of such policies is to create a climate that will lead to the healthy personal and professional development of all office workers who participate in the training program.

PRINCIPLE OF RESPONSIBILITY

Line managers must be assigned responsibility for organizing and administering the office training program in their own departments.

As line managers, office managers must accept as one of their prime responsibilities the training and development of their workers. Also, they must be willing to be evaluated on how well they carry out this responsibility. Although OMs may aid in planning, organizing, conducting, and evaluating the training activity, their greatest contribution lies in helping their workers apply to their jobs what they have learned from training.

In large firms, the OM is usually provided staff assistance to help administer the office training program. Staff training personnel may aid in planning and coordinating the various aspects of the training program and in training the instructors and the trainees. In smaller firms, an office supervisor is usually personally responsible for training workers in acquiring the skills and knowledge needed to perform their jobs. Often the supervisor does not have the assistance of a training specialist. If help is needed, the supervisor may call upon another supervisor, a representative from the human resources department, or a specialist outside the company.

PRINCIPLE OF PLANNING AND IMPLEMENTATION

The organization must accurately identify its training needs and specify clearly how the objectives of training are to be implemented.

With its investment in an office training program, a company expects that the funds budgeted for training will be spent on the right people in the right positions and that the resources will be used to achieve the goals of the firm. Thus, effective planning and implementation require that adequate emphasis upon training be properly placed within the organization.

The specific experiences, abilities, attitudes, and knowledge needed for the successful performance of each job should be determined and clearly stated by undertaking a program of job analysis, as explained in the following chapter. Next, an inventory of the workers' present experiences, abilities, attitudes, and knowledge may be determined through observations, interviews, tests, and written reports prepared by the workers. The needs of the jobs are then compared with the present inventory of worker experiences, abilities, attitudes, and knowledge. As a result, the differences can be identified and specific training objectives, oriented toward meeting the needs of the trainees, can be stated. Thus, the training objectives express the gap that needs to be bridged between present performance and expected performance.

The person responsible for developing the office training program should prepare a plan that considers each of the factors listed in Step 6 of the model in Figure 8–1. In estimating the costs of planning and implementing the training program, the following factors should be included:

1. *Time costs*—time lost when employees and in-house instructors are off the job.
2. *Instruction costs*—salaries of instructors as well as development, publication, and use of training materials by the instructors.

3. *Transportation costs*—bringing personnel together for training.
4. *Facilities costs*—rental, food, and lodging.

PRINCIPLE OF EVALUATION

A sound office training program should provide for periodic evaluation and measurement of its effectiveness.

The results of any office training program must be evaluated in order to determine the extent to which the objectives of the training function were achieved. For certain office tasks, such as data entry, billing, and filing, the volume and accuracy of work produced serve as measures of the skill level attained. Or, production figures may be used that are based on the percentage of workers who meet job standards or accomplish the task within the time required to do the job. Performance standards, discussed in a later chapter, are created through a work measurement program and serve as one means by which the effectiveness of new office employees and their rates of learning may be measured. By means of standards, it is possible to determine at what point in the training process trainees should be able to handle a normal workload on a full-time basis.

Indirect measures of the effectiveness of training include the savings realized as a result of error reduction, less absenteeism, and decreased employee turnover. However, difficulty arises when evaluating the effectiveness of training in human relations or social skills. The outcomes of desirable attitude development and modification of behavioral patterns are not easily identified, let alone reviewed and measured.

To measure and evaluate the effectiveness of an office training program, the person in charge of the program should follow the steps listed in Figure 8–2.

PRINCIPLE OF FEEDBACK

The results of the training program should be effectively communicated to all groups needing feedback.

Those who designed the training program and the instructors need feedback in order to make improvements that will assure better results in the future. The managers and supervisors directly involved with the program are often charged with making decisions about future training programs. Therefore, they need to know the results of the training program in order to

Figure 8–2
Steps in Measuring and Evaluating the Effectiveness of an Office Training Program

1. Establish standards of learning time against which the progress of trainees may be checked.

2. Test trainees on the abilities, skills, attitudes, and knowledge acquired.

3. Rate each trainee at the beginning, during, and at the end of the training program.

4. Keep records on each trainee's progress.

5. Develop data on trainee performance before, during, and after training.

6. Obtain feedback from the trainees about what they liked and disliked in the training program, and their suggestions for improvement. This information may be obtained by having the trainees fill out questionnaires at the end of the course or program. Another approach uses small teams of trainees who think about and evaluate what has been learned.

7. Check the results of the training program against its objectives.

8. Follow up on the trainees by periodically observing the long-range effects of their training.

decide how much money should be allocated to future programs. Finally, the trainees need to learn how well they did in the program and how their performance compared with that of their coworkers.

Psychological Factors in the Learning Situation

To develop an effective office training program, we need to examine several psychological factors in the learning situation. Often a well-planned training program suffers simply because one or more of these factors was overlooked or not adequately provided.

As we saw earlier in this chapter, learning is any change that occurs in the behavioral patterns and attitudes of the trainees. The product of such learning is called a **habit.** The psychological factors discussed in this section surround the learning situation, which leads to the development of desirable work habits.

Motivation

Office workers are motivated by certain needs, but workers differ from one another in the relative importance of these needs at any given time. Among those needs that can be satisfied through training activities are the needs for safety, recognition, esteem, and self-actualization. Thus, those responsible for training must recognize the workers' needs and use them as a basis for motivating the employees.

In motivating office workers, the trainer must set performance standards that are realistic and attainable during the training sessions. For example, in the word processing center of a company, an average, fully qualified word processing operator can keyboard original text at a rate of 5.25 pages each hour. However, during a program of upgrading the word processing employees, the trainer incorrectly adopted a standard of 6.5 pages each hour. By trying to meet such an unrealistic performance standard, the trainees became frustrated, anxious, and confused, all of which caused stress and hindered learning.

Knowledge of Results

Knowledge of results is a strong incentive at all stages of the learning process. However, such feedback is especially needed after the initial enthusiasm of the learning situation has diminished. The person in charge of training should inform the new learners that their rates of improvement during the practice sessions on a complex task are not expected to be steady. At first, improvement is rapid, with a considerable portion of the total task being mastered in the first few trial sessions. However, each of the following trial sessions contributes decreasingly to the learning process.

The trainees should also anticipate those occasions in many learning situations, especially in the development of skills, when progress does not occur. On these occasions, the trainees are said to have reached a **plateau**—a period of time or a level of learning where no observable improvement occurs or where the rate of increase in learning levels off. Trainees should understand the nature and function of a plateau so that while it lasts, their discouragement and anxiety will be reduced. Reaching a plateau may result from ineffective work methods, or it may come about because of reduced motivation. With proper guidance by the trainer, the real cause of the plateau may be found.

Reinforcement

Reinforcement is a condition following a response that results in an increase in the strength of that response. Examples of reinforcers include:

1. Approval and recognition from the trainer.
2. The trainee's personal feeling of accomplishment that follows good performance.
3. Self-satisfaction in arriving at a correct answer to a problem.
4. Information about one's progress and achievement on the job.
5. Additional assistance or support provided by the trainer to the trainee.
6. Monetary rewards for attaining and exceeding quantity and quality standards.

Once the desired behavior occurs, it should be reinforced so that the chances of its recurring will be increased. Reinforcement is generally most effective if it occurs immediately after a correct response has been made, such as the proper performance of a task.

Practice

Few, if any, office trainees would hope to learn how to keyboard by merely reading a book on the subject. Most know that the development of keyboarding skill depends upon practice. Office trainees should be given frequent opportunity to practice their job tasks with relevant learning materials and in the same manner that they will finally be expected to perform their work. For example, the payroll clerk who is being taught to operate a computer should have ample opportunity to practice keyboarding while using payroll problem exercises. The practice exercises may be instructor-directed or computer-based experiences, and the materials should indicate possible pitfalls the trainee should guard against.

Massed Training Versus Spaced Training

In planning the courses of instruction for an office training program, instructors must decide whether the training sessions will be massed or spaced. An example of a *massed* training session is two highly concentrated three-hour periods. A *spaced* (or distributed) training session might be six one-hour periods. Usually, practice sessions that are spaced out over several time periods, with rest or other activities intervening, result in more rapid learning and more permanent retention than if the same amount of practice is concentrated in a single period.

Whole Versus Part Learning

To determine whether learning by parts or by the whole is the most efficient approach to learning a task, the nature of the task must be studied. If the task can be broken down successfully into component parts, it probably should be broken down to facilitate learning. Otherwise, the task probably should be taught as a unit.

Often the trainer is an experienced worker who may think of the task in larger units than the trainee can readily grasp. A good trainer knows how to break down the units of information into sizes appropriate for the learner. The trainer must then arrange the units of information into their proper, logical sequence. In a small office, the supervisor-trainer may present some phase of his or her job in the order in which the supervisor performs that job. However, an entry-level worker does not learn in that same order and thus may become frustrated and confused. A good supervisor-trainer knows how to organize the information into a logical learning sequence by proceeding from the known to the unknown and from the simple to the complex. This means that the training should begin where the trainee is at present and not where the trainer has determined the trainee should be.

Individual Differences

The extent of individual differences among trainees affects the type and amount of instruction as well as the training methods and techniques used to present the learning materials. To provide for individual differences, trainees are sometimes grouped according to their capacity to learn as determined by scores on their preemployment tests. The test scores provide a basis for offering a different or an extended type of instruction to meet the varying needs of the groups. For example, the trainer may find that in teaching one group of workers how to master a complex skill, the language level must be kept relatively simple, the skill broken down into easy learning segments, or the training spread out over a relatively long period of time.

Outcomes of Effective Office Training

The principles of office training and the factors at work in the learning situation are directly related to the major objective of the training program—to develop office personnel who have learned to improve performance and are using the new learning on the job. With the attainment of this goal, the following outcomes will become evident.

An Improved Competitive Position for the Firm

Office workers who have participated in training and development programs aid in maximizing the company's profits and improving its competitive position. The training experience helps the workers satisfy their own needs to do a good job and reach a high level of productivity. Thus, production is increased and costly errors are reduced. As a result of the improved performance of its employees, a firm realizes additional economies in the production of its goods or services.

Better Preparation of Employees for Promotion

Supervisory training and development programs that utilize the best available methods and techniques prepare office personnel to take advantage of promotional opportunities in their firms. Thus, when there is a change in business conditions, such as expansion, qualified workers are available to fill the newly created positions. Also, if employees are well trained, the illness, death, reassignment, or resignation of other workers will have little effect upon the smooth operation of the business.

More Self-Confident Office Employees

Well-trained, confident office workers lessen the need for close supervision. Training increases the self-confidence of workers, which means that well-trained employees will have fewer questions to ask and will cooperate more readily with their coworkers. As a result, the supervisor's burden is reduced and worker morale is improved.

More Effective Employee Performance Appraisal

Training that is relevant to the real world and geared to the individual needs of office workers enables supervisors to appraise employees' capabilities more effectively. As pointed out later in this chapter, employee performance appraisal, in turn, helps to ensure proper placement of employees in the organization. Therefore, turnover caused by unsatisfactory adjustment to the job should be reduced. Also, employee interest in the job should be increased because of a more thorough understanding of the work and its relation to that of other employees.

ENTRY-LEVEL TRAINING

As we saw earlier, *entry-level training* is designed to qualify employees for their initial job assignments. The following discussion pertaining to the instructional staff and the methods and techniques of entry-level training applies equally to remedial training, retraining, and cross-training.

Instructional Staff

Instructors responsible for entry-level training should possess *human relations ability, leadership ability,* and *technical ability.* Those in charge of training, whether a first-line supervisor or a training director, must know enough about human nature, behavioral patterns, and attitudes to realize that trainees should be accepted as they are. In trying to adapt new employees to work situations, even the most skilled trainer cannot completely remold personalities or greatly alter the behavioral patterns of the employees. The trainer can, however, create the kind of environment in which employees accept the need to change their attitudes.

The trainer should have had experience in planning, organizing, leading, and controlling in order to develop the skills, attitudes, and work habits of the trainees. The trainer must be technically competent in order to command the respect of trainees and to impart to them the knowledge and skills required to qualify them to produce a quality product or service.

Conducting the Training Program

In-house training programs are conducted by a variety of persons. In large firms with formal training programs, instructors or specialists on the company staff are frequently used to conduct the training. Some typical position titles and total median annual compensation include:[2]

Corporate Training Director	$63,940
Training & Organizational Development Supervisor	47,400
Corporate Training Supervisor	39,612
Training & Organizational Development Specialist	33,280
Classroom Instruction Specialist (General)	29,112
Training Material Developer (Computer)	28,320

Sometimes outside specialists, such as college or university professors and training consultants, are called upon to provide the entry-level training. Qualified line managers and first-line supervisors are also often assigned the training responsibility.

In many small firms, the responsibility for training rests with the first-line supervisor. In firms having a training department, that department may provide assistance to the supervisor, who often conducts the training. The responsibility of the supervisor goes beyond conducting courses, however. It is the supervisor's job to be alert to the training needs of workers and to opportunities for meeting these needs. The supervisor's job is to see that training which cannot be provided personally is obtained from some other source and to follow up on the training when it has been completed.

Training Methods and Techniques

Of major concern in the selection of any training method or technique is the kind of change the training is intended to bring about. The purpose of the training, whether to increase knowledge, to improve skills, or to influence attitudes and change behavior, strongly influences the method or technique to be selected. Other factors must be

considered when selecting a particular training method or technique. These include the number of trainees and their location; their similarities and differences in education, experience, abilities, functions, and occupational levels; the abilities of the trainers; the instructional space, equipment, and media available for the training program; and the cost of the method selected in relation to the results expected.

The training methods described in this section are as follows: on the job, lecture, company courses of study, job rotation, and vestibule training. In conjunction with these training methods, entry-level training makes use of computer-based instruction, videotapes and films, teleconferencing, videoconferencing, multimedia, and virtual reality. Each of these techniques is briefly described below.

On-the-Job Training (OJT)

The most common method of training entry-level office employees is on-the-job training. **On-the-job training (OJT)** provides the office trainee with the knowledge and skills needed to perform a job while using the actual equipment and materials required by the job. By means of OJT, a new office worker learns about the job by working on a one-to-one basis under the direction of a coworker, a first-line supervisor, or a department head. Along with teaching the needed knowledge and skills, the trainer often discusses problem areas peculiar to the department and may delegate certain responsibilities to the trainee. This trainer-trainee relationship also provides an opportunity for close and continuous shaping of behavior within the work environment. However, the value to be gained from OJT depends upon the teaching or coaching ability of the trainer to whom the new worker is assigned.

On-the-job training is well suited for teaching many office operations, such as opening and sorting incoming mail, billing customers, posting to customers' and vendors' accounts, and operating the switchboard.

Lecture

A **lecture** is a nonparticipative, one-way communication technique in which an instructor imparts

[2]"For Your Information," *Personnel Journal* (February, 1993), p. 18.

Illustration 8–2 Operating the switchboard is one office operation requiring on-the-job training to properly learn how to use the telephone equipment.

factual information to a group in a relatively short period of time. The lecture may be supplemented with demonstrations, either in person or on film, transparencies, or videotape. For example, a lecture and demonstration may be used to explain how to take a physical inventory of office supplies, how to reconcile the monthly bank statement with the bank account balance, and how to process an incoming sales order.

Of all training methods, the lecture is probably the least expensive, easiest to use, and most universally used and understood. However, the lecture, whether presented in person, on film, or by television, is limited in its ability to influence attitudes and shape behavior since the method cannot discriminate among the needs of trainees. Further, trainees receive little motivation because they are unable to participate actively in practicing what they are taught.

Company Courses of Study

Company courses of study may be provided by the firm either during or outside work hours. Many large firms have their own educational facilities for entry-level training. Such in-house training, in spite of its expense, may be the best solution for firms that require large numbers of office workers. In other companies, entry-level training may be provided in conjunction with public institutions, such as high schools, vocational schools, junior and community colleges, and four-year colleges and universities; and in cooperation with private institutions, such as business colleges. For example, a firm may enter into a partnership with local high schools and provide work-study courses in computer operations. The students are paid while training at the company and are given competency certificates from their employers along with their diplomas from their high schools when they graduate.

Job Rotation

In the **job rotation** method, trainees learn a number of functions in a relatively short period of time as they rotate through the various departments of the company or sections of a department. Trainees may be assigned to jobs solely as observers. Or, they may be assigned specific job responsibilities so they become personally involved in the operations and learn a set of skills as they move from one job to the next. For example, when recruiting general office and secretarial workers, one company does not hire employees for a specific job but instead assigns them to a training center. The new employees are assigned to various temporary jobs from one department to another. However, they always return to the center for further training until positions for which they are qualified become available.

Vestibule Training

Vestibule training, used primarily for skills development, takes place in an area away from the site where the job is usually performed. In this area, the trainee's future workstation, including a duplicate of any equipment to be used, is simulated. Vestibule training is often used in those situations where the trainees have little knowledge of the jobs to be performed such as the information processing activities handled by a retail sales associate, or where there are strict demands on the accuracy and quality of work such as that performed by a bank teller.

Computer-Based Training (CBT)

By means of **computer-based training (CBT),** trainees have simultaneous access to a computer, usually through terminal input-output units. The lessons consist of explanations or lectures with questions and quizzes programmed on the computer with an immediate response or reinforcement furnished by the computer. Some CBT systems use sound and pictures (on slides, film, or videodisc) in addition to computer screens to present information.

CBT may be used, for example, to teach how to compute wages and salaries and to prepare a payroll. The computer informs the trainees if their answers are accurate, tells where and how to proceed next, and informs trainees as to how well they are doing. Further, in most CBT systems, trainees can easily go back and repeat a section until they have mastered it. Generally, it takes longer and costs more to develop a CBT course than it does a classroom program; however, it will cost less to *deliver* the CBT course.[3]

Videotapes and Films

Videotapes and films offer many advantages in the development of office training programs. Video cameras and camcorders can be used easily and transported to various locations for use. Videotapes may be re-edited and updated to meet changing training requirements and erased and used again. Videotapes and films bring into the learning situation scenes and other audiovisual materials not possible in the usual lecture approach. Also, the training sessions can be repeated at various times during the day or evening. Several companies may share the cost of producing a training program that meets their common needs and therefore be able to obtain outstanding instructors who otherwise would be unable to come to the individual firms to participate in training sessions. However, before deciding to use television and films as supplemental training aids, all cost factors—equipment, trained personnel, and installation—should be carefully evaluated and compared with the benefits expected.

The effectiveness of training by videotapes and films depends upon how closely the program content is related to the specific learning objectives established. Further, the program content must be directly related to the viewer reactions or behaviors that are expected or desired by the instructor planning the audiovisual program.

Teleconferencing

By means of **teleconferencing** (audio only), as we shall see in a later chapter, three or more peo-

---

[3]Nina Adams, "CBT or Not CBT?" *Training* (May, 1993), p. 73.

ple at two or more separate locations are tied together by telephone. With the high cost of travel, some companies have found teleconferencing to be a cost-effective means of presenting their training courses. Besides traditional lecture-type training sessions, management seminars may be held over telephone lines.

Videoconferencing

Videoconferencing uses a combination of audio and video equipment to join two or more distant groups. It allows people in one city or country to communicate live with people in another—or with groups in several other cities. In 1991, about 10 percent of organizations with more than 100 employees used this medium for some sort of training-related purpose. However, the heaviest users of videoconferencing as a training medium are universities, which broadcast live programs to large groups of students at remote campuses.[4]

Multimedia

By combining audio, video, text, graphics, still images, and animation, **multimedia** enables the trainer to present learning materials in a computer-based setting that calls upon the trainee's senses of sight, sound, and touch. When compared with classroom instruction, textbook, and video training, multimedia training offers benefits such as these:

1. The training is brought to students, instead of their traveling to a centralized training center.
2. By means of relatively short, self-contained, modular lessons, multimedia training fits in with the students' work schedules.
3. The training can be offered on an individual basis as needed, without a minimum class size.
4. Multimedia allows for consistent delivery of training materials and self-paced learning and demands more student involvement and interaction than classroom or video training. The training requires students to interact immediately by answering every question and to cor-

rect any missed question. This feedback provides highly effective reinforcement of concepts and contents.
5. Travel and lodging costs are eliminated, thus providing savings that may be greater than the cost involved in multimedia training.

Virtual Reality

Sometimes called *artificial reality* or *cyberspace*, **virtual reality** is a computer-created sensory experience that immerses the participant so completely that it is difficult to distinguish the "virtual" experience from a real one.[5] For example, one software manufacturer has created a graphic representation of a typical office that is viewed by a user who wears goggles containing liquid-crystal display screens. When the user turns his or her head, a tracking sensor signals the computer to display a different view of the office, a view consistent with the person's head position. The user feels as if he or she is walking through an office, complete with all the sights, sounds, and feelings ordinarily obtained from touching wall surfaces or floor coverings. By manipulating variables in the computer software, the user can "experience" traffic flows, rearrange desks and partitions, alter lighting systems, and so on, without having set foot in the actual office available for rent or in an office building under construction. Likely to become even more significant, virtual reality offers to trainers the ultimate method of simulation.

SUPERVISORY TRAINING AND MANAGEMENT DEVELOPMENT (STMD)

Supervisory training (ST) provides experiences, education, and development that helps promising employees qualify for supervision, the first tier of management. **Management development (MD)** provides training, education, and development for those employees who aspire to—or are already functioning in—the manage-

---

[4]Michael Emery and Margaret Schubert, "A Trainer's Guide to Videoconferencing," *Training* (June, 1993), pp. 59–63.

[5]Mark Fritz, "The World of Virtual Reality," *Training* (February, 1991), pp. 45–50.

ment ranks.[6] Having a definite plan for supervisory training and management development (STMD) improves the morale in all departments. Nothing is more discouraging to conscientious employees who have worked many years for a company than to learn that persons outside the organization were given preferred consideration when promotions were made.

A major part of STMD programs is conducted by organizations *outside* the company. Training outside the company includes attendance at professional or trade association meetings, career seminars, and university development programs. Many companies provide *in-house* training and development programs. In most of these firms, the training programs are scheduled on a regular basis, such as four hours a week for six weeks or one day a month for six months. In some instances, the programs are scheduled as needed, while in the largest companies, management training programs may be presented on a continuing basis.

Diversity Training

As part of their STMD programs, many organizations provide *diversity training,* which, as we saw earlier, focuses on: (1) how to deal with *diversity in the work environment;* (2) *awareness* (informing workers about stereotypes, assumptions, and biases); and (3) *sensitivity* to individual needs without violating any requirements for fair or equal treatment. Much of this training aims at creating an environment that is conducive to retaining and promoting a diverse workforce that has experienced significant changes. Some of the changes that have occurred in the workforce composition over the last decade are shown in Table 8–1.

To ensure successful diversity training, two consultants who specialize in diversity training services offer the following guidelines:[7]

1. Distinguish between *education* and *training,* and build both into the program.

2. Make training part of the overall strategy for managing diversity, not an end in itself.

3. Do not start training prematurely simply to meet the need to "do something."

4. Conduct a thorough needs analysis, as would be done with any other training or organization development initiative.

5. Include diverse input into the design process to increase relevance.

6. Test the program thoroughly before implementation to reduce risk and to generate enthusiasm.

7. Use a mix of internal and external resources to enhance efficiency and credibility.

8. Incorporate diversity education and training into the core curriculum so that it becomes an ongoing organizational way of life.

Instructional Staff

In companies having in-house training programs, the person usually responsible for the program is a training/development manager or a human resources officer. In other firms, line managers, assisted by staff personnel, are in charge of the training program. The training program should be carefully planned and organized so that potential supervisors and managers obtain full knowledge of the work to be done and its place in the total organization. A knowledge of what work is to be done and how it is to be done can be obtained by work experience in the departments, by a study of the operations manuals that many firms have developed, or by working on studies with the firm's systems and procedures department. Information relating to company policies, promotion paths, authority, and responsibility may be obtained from company manuals, organization charts, and personal consultations with senior executives.

---

[6]William J. Rothwell and H. C. Kazanas, *The Complete AMA Guide to Management Development* (New York: AMACOM, a division of the American Management Association, 1993), Chapter 1.

[7]Ann Perkins Delatte and Larry Baytos, "Guidelines for Successful Diversity Training," *Training* (January, 1993), pp. 55–60.

Group	Percentage Increase
Women	69.1
African-Americans	59.1
Hispanics	49.4
Asians	44.4
Older workers	43.0
Employees with disabilities	33.2
Employees with literacy problems	22.7
Gay men/Lesbians	15.1
White males	10.4

Reproduced with permission from *1993 Society for Human Resource Management/Commerce Clearing House Survey,* published and copyrighted by Commerce Clearing House, Inc., 4025 W. Peterson Ave., Chicago, IL 60646.

Training Methods and Techniques

Supervisory training and development may be provided by many kinds of formal education. As indicated above, supervisory training may be carried out entirely in house by the company. Or, the company may cooperate with nearby educational institutions in providing evening classes in areas such as financial management, business communications, ethics, and basic computer concepts. Supervisors may take advantage of home-study courses and executive development programs offered by professional organizations such as the American Management Association. Some firms engage management consultants to conduct such intensive courses.

The one-on-one training methods and techniques used in entry-level training programs, described previously, are also found in STMD programs. However, other methods and techniques of instruction have been designed to deal with the more complex topics and concepts found in training prospective office supervisors and managers. Several of these methods and techniques are described below.

In-House Seminars and Workshops

At in-house seminars and workshops, a discussion leader may instruct the trainees, or the leader may guide the trainees to reach a decision partially or entirely by themselves. Seminars and workshops are effectively used in training prospective supervisors and managers in human relations and in modifying group attitudes and behaviors by using case histories. Some organizations use seminars and workshops to train their managers in understanding cultural diversity. For example, the Gannett Company is widely recognized for its success in recruiting, hiring, and advancing women and minorities through its "Partners in Progress" program. As you see in the *Dialog from the Workplace,* Gannett relies upon in-house and outside seminars, management development programs, and workshops in attaining its goal of developing a workforce that reflects the diverse makeup of the communities in which the firm operates.

Mentoring

Mentoring is a training arrangement whereby senior managers (*mentors*) impart their expertise to younger managers and supervisors (*protégés*) in the company. Experienced mentors pass along their knowledge of the values, culture, and management styles of the organization; help new managers and supervisors to get along with people; and teach specific job skills. Successful mentoring depends upon the interaction skills of both the mentor and the protégé. Therefore, it is crucial that the mentor be carefully matched to the protégé. For this reason, the protégé may be asked to interview several mentors before choosing one to serve as a coach.

Some firms allow several years for their formal mentoring programs, while other companies limit the formal activities to about six months. After this time, the participants are encouraged to continue their relationships informally; often,

DIALOG FROM THE WORKPLACE

MADELYN P. JENNINGS

Senior Vice President of Personnel
Gannett Company
Arlington, Virginia

Madelyn Pulver Jennings is senior vice president of personnel for the Gannett Company, a news and information company that publishes 81 daily newspapers, including *USA Today*. Gannett also has television and radio stations in major markets across the country and operates the largest outdoor advertising company in North America.

Madelyn joined Gannett in 1980. She previously held executive positions at Standard Brands and General Electric. She has a bachelor's degree in business and economics from Texas Woman's University.

Madelyn serves on many boards of directors and committees, including the American Press Institute, Emory Business School's Center for Leadership and Career Studies Board of Advisors, George Washington University's School of Business and Public Management Associates Council, the Conference Board's Advisory Council on Human Resource Management, the University of Illinois' Institute of Labor and Industrial Relations Advisory Committee, and UCLA's Human Resources Outlook Panel.

QUESTION: I understand that your company uses the Standard Metropolitan Statistical Area (SMSA) figures as one criterion when setting the advancement goals for your operating unit's workforce. How has the diverse ethnic and gender mix reflected in the SMSA figures affected your career-advancement program?

RESPONSE: Our goal is that our workforce reflects the makeup of the communities where we operate.

To do that, we focus on the top four of the nine EEO categories—managers, professionals, technicians, and sales jobs, the positions with the most economic clout. We compare the SMSA minority and female labor force percentages for each of those categories as well as the total labor force percentage as indicators of available people. For jobs recruited on a regional or national basis, we use those labor force statistics for comparisons. Managers' compensation is based in part on achieving employment parity in each job category with the labor force availability.

This method has served to focus our efforts using an easily understood goal. Beyond that, we periodically review our ranks from an organizational standpoint to make sure minorities and women are fairly represented throughout, from the board room to the mailroom.

Each year, we review our progress to see how we're doing. We analyze the number of openings which occurred. When you have an opening, that's your opportunity for outreach efforts which enable you to help make change happen. Of all the openings which occurred, we look to see how many minorities and women were selected. If a unit's employee population is not representative of the makeup of its community, we expend extra efforts to find diverse slates of candidates.

We make sure that once employees are hired, they have access to training and development opportunities locally through a satellite network of educational programs and through the corporate training and development library. We recently introduced a career development program called "Where Do I Go from Here," which is made available through workshops and for self-directed study.

The result of these programs is a diverse workforce which we're convinced represents a "competitive edge" for us . . . in attracting and retaining people of promise, and in the bottom line performance of our company.

lasting friendships are formed. The mentors are responsible for assigning challenging projects to the younger managers so that they are exposed to meaningful, real-life learning experiences. Mentors benefit by receiving *psychic income*—the personal satisfaction and peer recognition gained from passing on their experiences and knowledge in developing the talents of protégés.

Role Playing

Role playing, a training technique also known as *play acting* and *psychodrama,* calls upon potential supervisors and other trainees to act out their own parts or those of others under simulated conditions. The supervisor may assume the role of a high-level executive and "act out" a solution to problems that would face the executive on that level. Other trainees act as observers, and afterward their immediate supervisor or training specialist evaluates the performance.

Decision Simulation

Decision simulation, commonly known as *business games,* is based on a model that simulates the actual business or one of its functions. The objectives of the method are to furnish insights into organizational behavior, to promote teamwork among participants, and to teach at the behavioral level.

In playing a game, competing groups of supervisors or managers assume certain roles in managing a mythical company. They are given a description of the firm and asked to perform tasks and make organizational decisions, often with the aid of a computer. The decisions to be made may be related to improving the company's position by taking such actions as cutting costs, improving production, and increasing sales.

In-Basket Training

In the decision simulation technique referred to as **in-basket training,** the prospective office supervisor is given a brief description of a higher-ranking position. Next, the trainee is "promoted" to that job and given a representative sample of the problems—usually memos and correspondence—as they might arrive in the mail. Within a specified period of time, the trainee must make all decisions and solve all problems, ranging from taking action on reports and letters to settling conflicts among coworkers.

Case Study

When the **case study** is used, each trainee is given a written history of a problem or situation that exists or has existed in the business firm. After the background information available for decision making has been studied, each trainee presents a solution to the problem in class. The trainees then evaluate the decisions reached by each other and learn to relate the solutions to the enterprise as a whole and to perceive the interrelationships of people and events. After having evaluated their own decisions, the trainees may be told what actually took place in the business firm. As you have seen when solving the case problems in this textbook, there is rarely a single solution to a case problem; however, like you, trainees gradually develop insights into management behavior as a result of having analyzed and discussed several possible solutions.

Incident Process

In the **incident process,** a group of potential supervisors or managers is given a series of incidents that occur in a mythical company. However, only a minimum of related information is supplied. The participants themselves must obtain all additional data needed and then make the decisions. The objective of this training technique is to teach the trainee how to examine all facets of the incident and to engage in research by gathering data from many sources.

Assessment Centers

Assessment centers use simulation exercises similar to the kinds of work situations employees will find in higher-level jobs. The centers are also used to identify managerial talent among workers and sometimes as part of the appraisal process when promotions are being considered. A series of exercises is used to test the qualities most organizations consider important in management: organizational planning, problem analysis, judgment, ethical and moral conduct, decisiveness, leadership, interpersonal sensitivity, and initiative. Typical exercises include in-basket decision making, leaderless group discussion, simulated interviews, analysis problems, and fact-finding problems. The simulated exercises are observed by specially trained persons who work together as a team to pool their observations and arrive at a consensus evaluation of each participant. Some firms train their own managers to act as assessors, while other companies rely upon outside psychologists and consultants.

APPRAISING THE OFFICE WORKER'S PERFORMANCE

In **employee performance appraisal,** or *performance evaluation,* the relative value of an employee's traits, personal qualifications, attitudes, and behavior is appraised. You will want to remember that in performance appraisal, the evalu-

Illustration 8–3 Performance appraisal evaluations are used to decide salary increases, to identify training opportunities, and to recognize outstanding skills.

ator studies and analyzes the performance of the *employee,* not the job held by that employee. The evaluator may use the information obtained from performance appraisal for the following purposes:

1. To determine salary increases and to make decisions regarding promotion, transfer, and demotion.
2. To enhance the worker's morale, to contribute directly and indirectly to self-improvement, and to stimulate confidence in management's fairness.
3. To stimulate employees to improve their work.
4. To discover workers' needs for retraining and promotional training programs.
5. To uncover exceptional skills among employees.
6. To furnish a tangible basis for terminating unqualified or unfit employees.
7. To help assign work in accordance with the worker's ability by furnishing information for the proper placement, career counseling, and guidance of the worker.
8. To aid in validating the selection process, especially in the areas of interviewing and testing.
9. To help settle disputes in arbitration cases.

From this list, we can conclude that performance appraisal should provide a fair treatment of all employees, an objective rating, and a feeling by employees that they are not ignored or overlooked.

Methods of Appraising Employee Performance

Several commonly used methods of performance appraisal are briefly described in Figure 8–3. Some companies use two or more of these methods, or a modification of each, to design their appraisal programs. Companies that have installed a program of work measurement and work standards, as discussed later in the text, may use their work standards in conjunction with most appraisal methods. Since work standards are aimed at improving productivity, their use makes possible a more objective and accurate appraisal of the office worker's performance.

Figure 8–3
Methods of
Appraising
Employee Per-
formance

1. **Rating scales**, in which factors dealing with *quantity* and *quality* of work are listed and rated. A numeric value may be assigned each factor and an effort made to weight the factors in the order of their relative importance. The rating scale is a widely used method of evaluating performance because it is economical to develop and easily understood by the worker and the evaluator. A major weakness is that each evaluator is apt to interpret differently the factors (such as Knowledge of Work) and the degrees describing that factor that are marked off along the scale (such as Excellent, Good, Fair, Poor).

2. **Narrative** or **essay**, in which the evaluator provides a written paragraph or more covering such topics as an employee's strengths, weaknesses, and potential. The narrative method is often used in evaluating office workers although there is a disadvantage in the varying length and content of the narratives. Since the narratives touch on different aspects of performance and personal characteristics, they are difficult to combine for comparison purposes.

3. **Management by objectives (MBO)** or **goal setting**, in which a number of short-range goals or objectives that appear to be within the capabilities of the worker are established. The goals, agreed upon mutually by the employee and the supervisor, become the job performance standards by which the employee is evaluated for the period of time for which the goals are established.
   The method rests on the premise that the only real measure of how we perform is whether we achieve specific results. Thus, management by objectives, as discussed in Chapter 7, is *results oriented* rather than *trait oriented*. Although not practical for use at all levels and for all kinds of office work, the method provides for systematic goal setting and performance reviews that concentrate upon the work accomplished rather than upon problems related to personality traits and characteristics.

4. **Simple ranking** or **grading**, in which all employees are classified by rank as best, second best, third best, and so on throughout the entire employee group. Employees are evaluated on their overall usefulness and value to the firm, and no attempt is made to describe and evaluate their performances, traits, qualifications, or characteristics. The simple ranking method is useful only in very small companies with fewer than 25 employees where a suitable criterion has been established as the basis for the rating.

5. **Rank order** or **order of merit**, in which the evaluator ranks all employees in order from the best to the poorest on the merits of performance and specific factors such as quantity and quality of work. This method, which takes considerable time and is very subjective, is successful to the extent that employees accept the criteria used for the rankings and respect their rater's honesty.

6. **Forced distribution**, in which employees are rated on only two characteristics: *job performance* and *promotability*. A five-point job performance scale is used, and the supervisor is asked to allocate 10 percent of the workers to the best rating, 20 percent to the next best, 40 percent to the middle group, 20 percent to the group next to the lowest, and 10 percent to the lowest group.
   The method forces the rater not to rank too many workers on the highest or the middle scale. Also, the rater will not appraise the poorest workers as medium or fair since they must be placed among the lowest 10 percent.

7. **Paired comparison**, in which each employee is paired with every other employee in the group. For example, by comparing each pair of workers in the order processing and billing department, the rater decides which of the two workers is more valuable. When making each comparison, the supervisor underlines the name of the preferred worker on a specially prepared form. The employee's score is obtained by counting the number of times his or her name is underlined. After all workers in the group have been thus compared, a list is prepared to show the rank of each employee in order of merit, according to the number of times his or her name was underlined.
   The paired comparison method is workable only in very small groups of 10 to 12 employees; in larger groups, the job of rating becomes overly burdensome and time consuming.

8. **Factor comparison**, in which numerous phrases or questions referring to specific factors are listed, such as those in Figure 8–4. The rater checks the statement or answers the question "yes" or "no" to describe the appropriate characteristic of the worker being appraised. A numeric value is provided for each statement or question, and the complete rating is obtained by totaling all statement values. Using this method, the rater thinks critically about the employee's performance in terms of each important factor and is able to make a study of the worker's specific strengths and weaknesses.

An Illustrative Performance Appraisal Form

The appraisal form in Figure 8–4 is well designed, with five degrees contained in the range for each of the eight factors to be evaluated. The rater is further aided by a brief but clear definition of each of the degrees.

On the second page, the form provides space for the rater to indicate an overall opinion of the employee and to record what improvement, if any, has taken place since the last appraisal. Space is also provided for the rater to record any other information that may aid in appraising the employee's performance. Provision is made for recording any comments the employee may offer about the evaluation. Finally, space is provided for both the employee and the rater to sign the form, indicating that the appraisal was discussed with the worker.

Weaknesses of Performance Appraisal Forms

When using any appraisal instrument, the rater should be concerned that the form provides information that aids in meeting the purposes listed previously. However, an examination of employee performance appraisal forms indicates that some contain certain weaknesses, such as the following, which should be avoided:

1. *Too many questions or characteristics to answer, check, or rate.* Only enough factors and degrees should be given to provide a fair and reasonable picture of the work being done and of the employee who is doing it. Too many questions take too much time and may cause careless or routine, superficial ratings. Probably six or eight factors, each with five or six degrees, are sufficient in most instances.

2. *Poor phrasing of questions.* Using detailed and descriptive phrases motivates the rater to exercise more careful judgment than if he or she has only to check general terms. Instead of using such words as "very good," "good," "fair," or "poor" to describe a factor, phrases such as the following might be used: (a) Shows a high level of intelligence in doing

work; (b) Shows some intelligence and initiative in performing work; (c) Understands simple routines and follows instructions; and (d) Little comprehension of work, needs constant instruction.

3. *A pattern in the arrangement of the descriptive phrases for each factor.* To provide for a less biased evaluation by the rater, the form should be arranged so that for some factors the highest rating degree appears first, and for others the highest rating degree appears last. Alternating or otherwise differentiating the order of the degrees requires the evaluator to make an individual appraisal of each factor.

Frequency of Performance Appraisal

The performance of workers is being informally appraised in a never-ending process by their supervisors who observe, evaluate, and coach them on a day-to-day basis. This kind of appraisal is one of the supervisor's downward responsibilities to aid workers in improving their performance, to heighten their motivation, and to solve job-performance and human-relations problems on the spot by "striking while the iron is hot." However, this continuing type of appraisal is not an adequate substitute for formal employee appraisal, which is discussed in this section.

In most companies, the performance of office workers is evaluated once each year; however, more frequent reviews can be arranged in the event of promotional openings, poor performance, or outstanding performance. Often, during an entry-level worker's probationary period or during the first year on a new job, appraisals are made more frequently. Thus, a firm with a probationary period of six months may evaluate the new office workers at the end of one month, three months, and six months; thereafter, the employee is placed on permanent status and reviews are scheduled annually on the anniversary of the employee's hiring date. Anniversary-date reviews are very important to employees; therefore, supervisors should not postpone the review of employee performance even if the reviews contain a great deal of negative criticism.

Figure 8–4
Performance
Appraisal
Form
(page 1)

EMPLOYEE PERFORMANCE APPRAISAL

Tim Bray	/	Finance	/	Sr. Accountant	/	7-15--
Employee's Name		Department		Position		Date

Instructions: For each of the following factors listed in the the left-hand column, place an X in the box that best describes the employee's performance.

QUANTITY OF WORK— volume of work produced consistently	Unsatisfactory output	Limited. Does just enough to get by	Average output	Above average output	Exceptional output
	☐	☐	☒	☐	☐

QUALITY OF WORK— accuracy and neatness	Very poor	Not entirely acceptable	Acceptable accuracy and neatness	Very neat and accurate	Exceptionally neat and accurate
	☐	☐	☐	☒	☐

COOPERATION— with associates and supervisors	Entirely uncooperative	Reluctant to cooperate	Adequately cooperative	Very cooperative	Unusually cooperative
	☐	☒	☐	☐	☐

DEPENDABILITY— amount of supervision required and application to work	Unreliable and inattentive	Needs frequent supervision	Generally reliable and attentive to work. Follows Instructions carefully	Very reliable and conscientious, needs little supervision	Extremely reliable and industrious
	☐	☐	☒	☐	☐

ABILITY TO LEARN— ability to understand and retain	Very limited	Requires repeated instructions	Learns reasonably well	Readily understands and retains	Unusual capacity
	☐	☒	☐	☐	☐

INITIATIVE— originality and resourcefulness	Lacking	Routine worker	Occasionally shows initiative	Better than average	Outstanding
	☐	☒	☐	☐	☐

JUDGMENT— ability to evaluate situations and make sound decisions	Poor	Not always reliable	Good in most matters	Reliable	Decisions most logical and well founded
	☐	☐	☒	☐	☐

LEADERSHIP— ability to gain cooperation, inspire confidence, and direct people	Very poor	Reluctant to lead	Average display of leadership	Above average leader	Exceptional leadership skills
	☐	☒	☐	☐	☐

(OVER)

Figure 8–4
Performance
Appraisal
Form
(page 2)

WHAT IS YOUR OVERALL OPINION OF THIS EMPLOYEE?

Unsatisfactory ☐
Poor ☐
Fair ☐
Good ☒
Very good ☐
Outstanding ☐

SINCE EMPLOYEE'S LAST APPRAISAL, EMPLOYEE HAS

Improved ☒
Made little or
   no change ☐
Slipped back ☐

REMARKS: Furnish any additional information that you believe may be helpful in evaluating this employee.

Tim continues to open up more around his coworkers. He feels that by serving as a sponsor the next three months, he will improve his leadership skills.

This appraisal has been discussed with the employee, who offers the following comments:

Plans to sit for CPA exams next spring. Now serving as vice president of local American Accounting Association chapter.

Tim Bray
Employee's Signature

7/15/--
Date

Sally H. Jaeger
Department Head or Supervisor

7/15/--
Date

FOR USE OF HUMAN RESOURCES DEPARTMENT

Who Should Appraise Employees?

In answering the question of who should appraise employees, it seems logical that the evaluation should be made by those who come in direct supervisory contact with the workers. In many large companies, you will find that the appraisal is made by the employee's immediate supervisor and is reviewed by both the next higher-level manager and the human resources department.

Generally, the appraisal is discussed with the employee, who in many companies must sign the appraisal form to indicate that it has been discussed with him or her. The appraisal then becomes part of the employee's permanent personnel record. Sometimes the office worker may be given a copy of the appraisal. In many instances, the office workers have the right to appeal or to protest the performance appraisal. State laws may provide for employees to place counterstatements in their personnel records. If the employees are represented by a union, the appeal may be made through the regular grievance procedure. In nonunion offices, the appeal procedure is informal. It may consist of the employees' noting their disagreement with the appraisal, either in discussion with the supervisor or a representative from the human resources department or in writing on the appraisal form.

PROMOTING

Successful promotion plans are definite, systematic, fair, and followed uniformly. The basis of promotion is the organization chart, developed after a systematic job analysis as described in the following chapter. Each employee should understand the responsibilities of his or her position, the line of promotion, the requirements for the next higher job, and the salary to be expected, which should not be less than the minimum salary for the higher classification or rank.

A promotion plan must have the confidence of the employees. To provide for promotions based upon objective data and not solely upon personal opinion and assessment, the human resources department should maintain a database of all personnel. These files should contain information such as

the following for each worker: age, education, experience, special abilities, physical condition, absences from work, tardiness, suggestions offered by the employee to the firm, any disciplinary action taken, and, most important, the periodic performance appraisals.

Commonly we find that promotions are granted as rewards for successful work done in a previous position. The firm senses that status and compensation can be increased only by moving a person up the organizational ladder. However, these firms must develop a greater awareness that each position requires different skills and attitudes and that success in one area does not, in itself, qualify a person for promotion to a higher position. Thus, promotions should be related to the specific requirements of the new position. As a result, individuals will not be promoted solely because of their success in previously held jobs, longevity, or their personal loyalty to the firm or to their superiors. Although these factors are important indicators of a person's overall contribution to the firm, they should be used only as part of the promotion criteria. Other criteria that are more indicative of success on the future job include a complete knowledge and understanding of the duties, responsibilities, and requirements of the new position; interviews and tests that have been checked for their validity and reliability; promotion trials, which, as explained later, give the prospective candidate an insight into some of the new duties, followed by an evaluation of performance; and participation in assessment centers, where the potential of the candidate for promotion is judged by a team of trained observers.

Publicizing Job Vacancies

Companies use several methods to inform office employees of job vacancies for which they may apply. A common method of publicizing job vacancies is to post notices on bulletin boards. Job posting is a procedure highly recommended by the Equal Employment Opportunity Commission and other agencies charged with enforcing equal employment opportunity laws and regulations. Generally, there is a limit on the length of time the notice must remain posted and the time during which employees may bid for the job. However, in many companies, employees may bid at any time until the job is filled.

Memos may also be sent by the human resources department to supervisors, who announce the job openings to their workers. For example, one firm issues to all its supervisors a weekly report that lists all current openings. Other approaches to publicizing job vacancies include listing the openings in employee publications and announcing any openings at supervisory meetings. Also, some firms operate a job preference system that gives employees an opportunity to indicate interest in certain types of jobs should openings occur.

Identifying Employees' Promotion Potential

Companies may use a skills inventory or human resources information system to provide names of employees who are eligible for promotion when vacancies occur. More frequently, however, companies make use of their performance appraisal system, which includes an evaluation of their employees' promotion potential.

Some firms seek outside professional help to evaluate their employees' potential for promotion. Management consulting firms may be called upon to test employees and to conduct interviews in an attempt to determine which employees possess the abilities and characteristics for promotion. For example, one management consulting firm gives personality tests to obtain a better understanding of the employees' attitudes and opinions and to help determine the employees' future benefit to the company.

In large companies, psychological testing is sometimes used to observe and to evaluate workers in order to locate future managerial ability. Also, we saw earlier that companies may use assessment centers to identify employees who are suited for higher positions.

Factors Considered in Promotion Decisions

Many companies take seniority, or length of service, into account when making promotion decisions concerning office jobs. However, seniority is rarely the *only* factor examined. When making promotion decisions for office jobs, the following factors are commonly given more consideration than seniority:

1. Ability to perform the work.
2. Previous work record.
3. Previous experience or education.
4. Recommendation of supervisor or department head.
5. Interview ratings.

Other firms, especially governmental offices and unionized companies, place more emphasis upon seniority when promoting office personnel. These firms feel that people who have served loyally for a long period merit recognition. The philosophy of basing promotions upon seniority tends to stabilize employment and to reduce turnover. Seniority should not be adhered to rigidly, however, since it may become an arbitrary check on younger workers. Also, promotion based solely upon seniority may result in a somewhat stagnant staff. New ideas and ability to perform the work must be given recognition, even at the expense of seniority. Otherwise the younger and perhaps more creative, aggressive employees will seek work with a competitor or maybe start in business themselves, with either action possibly being detrimental to the firm.

Probationary Periods

Many firms provide a probationary period for newly promoted employees to prove themselves on the new job. Most probationary periods last three months or 90 days. Some firms provide **promotion trials** for positions that have been vacated. Under this approach, promotion in position or change in responsibilities is made with the consent of the person being transferred. The promoted employees are given the option of returning to their previous jobs if they are unsuccessful or unhappy on the new job. The time limit for exercising such an option may range from one week to six months, with three months being a very common time limit. Often there is a stipulation that returning to the old job is not guaranteed unless it is still vacant or another suitable vacancy exists.

Horizontal Promotion

Employees may reach a level in their departments at which the future is not very promising because there is little turnover and the departments are not expanding. Therefore, consideration should be given to transferring such capable workers to other departments where promotional opportunities are greater. This type of transfer is really a form of promotion—a **horizontal promotion**—though there may be no increase in salary or rank. It is a promotion because in the new position there will be an earlier chance for advancement.

Transfers

Transfers and promotions are related, although not all transfers are promotions. For instance, a transfer may be necessary because an employee has been improperly matched to the job. As a result of the transfer, the employee is moved to a position for which he or she is better qualified and where the worker's capabilities will be challenged. Of course, such a transfer can be made only where the firm has a staff large enough to absorb the transferee.

The fundamental purpose of transferring employees is to stimulate them out of the monotony, and perhaps inefficiency, in which their long service may have placed them. Some firms believe in the practice of developing understudies and therefore have a regular schedule of transfers so resignations, promotions, reassignments, deaths, and illnesses of employees do not seriously affect the office work. There is always someone who can step in and do the work. This policy also stimulates the worker since few workers will feel that their services are indispensable or that "the firm cannot get along without them."

Other firms have rush and slack periods either during the month or during certain periods of the year. By having a series of employee transfers, workers obtain experience in a variety of positions, thus enabling the office manager to shift workers during the busy seasons.

The closing section of this chapter deals with another objective of employee appraisal—to furnish a tangible basis for terminating unqualified or unsatisfactory employees.

TERMINATING THE OFFICE WORKER'S SERVICES

In small and medium-size companies that have no human resources department, office supervisors are responsible for terminating the services of unqualified or unsatisfactory office workers. In larger firms, the responsibility for firing office workers is usually handled by the human resources department according to a standard procedure. Regardless of the size of the firm, few things in life are as traumatic for office workers as losing their jobs. Although firing may not be a pleasant task for the office supervisor, if it is done humanely, the supervisor can aid in creating a better organization in the long run.

Developing a Termination Procedure

Basic to the firing of any worker is the existence of a well-planned disciplinary system and termination procedure that satisfies the union agreement, if any, and government regulations, such as those described in Chapter 6. The termination procedure should be planned to ensure a fair hearing for the worker as well as legal protection for the employer. The disciplinary system and termination procedure should be carefully written and placed in the employee handbook, which is regularly reviewed and updated.

Personnel records must be objectively and consistently maintained to reflect up-to-date, accurate data so that the cause for termination is well documented. Firing should not come as a surprise to an office worker, although there may be an occasion when, for justifiable cause, a worker is fired on the spot. For example, most companies have a policy that if an office employee reports for work intoxicated, the worker is subject to immediate discharge. Prior to most terminations, however, the worker will have been forewarned by means of warnings and reprimands, performance appraisals, or in counseling sessions and meetings with the supervisor. Thus, as a result of actions taken earlier, the worker should know that he or she has not met the company's expectations.

The *exit interview* should be carefully planned and held in privacy. The interview may be scheduled near the end of the workday so that the terminated worker does not have to confront any peers in the office following the meeting. During the exit interview, the worker's unsatisfactory performance as compared with expectations should be objectively and candidly reviewed. The continued failure of the worker to meet goals should be clearly indicated. The worker's strengths and weaknesses can be spelled out by the supervisor, and, if possible, the worker may be aided by indicating where his or her strengths may be better utilized. The decision to fire the worker must be clearly stated along with the date upon which the worker's duties are to cease. The worker should be informed of the procedure to follow in obtaining his or her last paycheck. If the company plans to respond to reference checks about the fired worker, the worker should be so notified and both parties should agree on what will be cited as the reason for termination.

The person conducting the exit interview must avoid becoming emotionally involved with the worker, personally insulting him or her, or being highly critical of any personal qualities outside the worker's control. The interviewer should listen carefully for any feedback from the dismissed worker that will aid in improving future job performance in the department.

Employment and Termination at Will

Under the **employment-at-will** doctrine, the employee and the employer have the right to enter freely into the employment relationship and to sever this relationship at *any* time for *any* reason. Under this rule, the employer's power to discharge workers went unchallenged for many years, during which time many companies had little regard for their human resources. However, over the past 50 years, the employment-at-will doctrine has been gradually eroded. For example, unionized employees may be fired only for "cause" or "just cause." The *just-cause standard* requires that a job-related, valid reason must exist

for the discharge. Further, Civil Service rules protect from arbitrary dismissal the majority of employees working for the federal, state, or local government. Employees are also protected by a variety of state and federal statutes that prohibit discharge based on the employee's religion, national origin, race, sex, age, physical or mental disability, or union activity.

Today the courts are becoming more sensitive to the personal rights of workers and the growing awareness of the social need for job protection. Of course, employers have the right to fire employees who have poor safety records, refuse work orders, produce poor-quality work, are absent without excuse, or are unqualified to perform the work. However, the power of employers to terminate arbitrarily is being curbed more and more. The courts in most states have said that job-security promises may constitute legally binding contracts. States have ruled that employers cannot fire employees (union or nonunion) if the terminations are unfair. Therefore, in order to avoid costly lawsuits, companies have revised their employee handbooks, application forms, and advertising materials to make sure that there are no statements implying permanent employment or job security. Some companies have set up *alternative dispute-resolution systems,* such as arbitration, in an attempt to avoid possible lawsuits. More attention is being paid to the issuance of performance appraisals that show candid evaluations of employee performance. Disciplinary or critical discussions with employees are being carefully and completely documented and retained for a reasonable period of time, such as five years.

As a result of court rulings and the prospect of further state legislation that will affect employment at will, many companies have taken a closer look at their employee relations programs. Companies are also paying much closer attention to selecting, orienting, training, appraising, promoting, and terminating their employees. Office managers have become increasingly concerned with the adoption of an attitude of fairness in their dealings with the company's most valuable asset—its human resources.

SUMMARY

1. The office training program must be built upon sound principles of learning if office personnel, with their diverse needs, are to function efficiently. The program must provide for effective application of those psychological factors that create a meaningful learning situation.

2. In designing its training and development programs, the firm must carefully evaluate the wide array of training methods and techniques available. From these, the firm should select those that best meet the needs of the persons who plan and implement the programs and of those who will receive the training.

3. Office supervisors must know how to undertake performance appraisals so that all employees are fairly treated and objectively evaluated. In light of the eroding employment-at-will rule, supervisors must be familiar with the methods or techniques of conducting such appraisals to make sure that candid evaluations of employee performance are obtained and documented.

4. Proper employee performance appraisal aids the firm in developing and retaining employees who are self-confident, properly matched with the requirements of their present jobs, and prepared to meet the requirements of those jobs that lie ahead on the promotional ladder.

5. Since office employees may be found to be unqualified for their positions or performing unsatisfactorily, a well-planned termination procedure is needed to make sure that the workers to be discharged are given a fair hearing in which the rights of both the workers and the employer are protected.

FOR YOUR REVIEW

1. Distinguish between the concepts of *training* and *learning*.

2. Contrast the role of the office manager in a large firm to that of the office supervisor in a small company in organizing and administering the office training program.

3. How should the administrative office manager proceed in evaluating the effectiveness of the firm's office training program?

4. What kinds of reinforcers strengthen the desired responses in a learner's behavior?

5. Describe the outcomes of effective office training.

6. What advantages can be cited for on-the-job training as contrasted to vestibule training?

7. What benefits does multimedia training offer to the trainer and the trainee?

8. Describe how mentors are used in a supervisory training and management development program.

9. How is a rating scale used in appraising employee performance? What are the disadvantages of using this method of appraisal?

10. Briefly describe the procedure followed in using the management by objectives (MBO) method to appraise employees.

11. What steps can a company take to prevent its workers from being promoted solely because of their success in previously held jobs?

12. What factors are usually considered when decisions about promotions are being made?

13. What points should the office supervisor keep in mind when developing a termination procedure?

14. With the erosion of the employment-at-will rule, what steps have companies taken to protect themselves from lawsuits involving the possible unfair termination of workers?

FOR YOUR DISCUSSION

1. Many small companies do not have the time or money to set up a conventional in-house training program. How else can a small business train?

2. In some offices, the senior workers are assigned responsibility for entry-level training. What are the advantages of using a senior worker as a trainer? What kinds of problems may emerge when a company follows this approach?

3. In a national survey of management information systems executives, The Olsten Corporation found that three out of four executives agree that their employees' computer literacy skills have a major impact on their firms' overall operations. However, most companies do not offer continuous training or even test to verify that employees have these skills. Further, it was learned that only a third conduct hands-on exercises during prescreening to determine the computer skills of job applicants.[8] What steps can companies, regardless of their size, take to bridge this workplace literacy gap?

4. Rob Weiss, office supervisor at Naples Imports, asks you how he can adapt his training program to reflect the new employees he is seeing: the older worker, the illiterate worker, the foreign-born worker. What advice can you offer Weiss?

5. You have just learned from your boss that one of your workers and very best friend, Rita Flick, must be laid off as part of your firm's downsizing, which resulted from a takeover by a Japanese holding company. Flick has been with your firm for more than 20 years and during this time she has become like a "sister" to you. Is there a kind way to terminate Flick's services?

6. Last Friday when Anna Copello left work at the Doyle Company, she was an executive secretary. When she reports to work on Monday morning, she will be assuming a new position, supervisor of general office services. What kind of "people" problems may face Copello as she undertakes her new post? As her boss, what steps should you have taken prior to her promotion in order to alleviate any potential "people" problems for her?

7. Several common weaknesses of performance appraisal forms are listed on page 202. Using this list, evaluate the employee appraisal form in Figure 8–4.

8. When George Petri applied for a job at Cortez, Inc., he was told by an interviewer that he would be with the company as long as he did his job. Three months later, Petri was fired after a bitter disagreement with his supervisor. What are the implications of this happening in view of the attacks upon the employment-at-will doctrine? What precautions might Cortez take in order to avoid any possible lawsuits in which terminated employees claim they were unfairly discharged?

---

[8]"Training and Testing for Computer Skills Lag," *HR Magazine* (May, 1993), p. 74.

CASES FOR CRITICAL THINKING

Case 8–1 Finding Time for Performance Appraisals

When she arrives for work Monday morning, Shirley Ku, data-entry supervisor for Quik Service Bureau, examines her daily calendar. Looking ahead to next week, Ku notes that 14 annual employee appraisals are scheduled. Quickly she calculates that filling out a form for each worker and updating the files will require a minimum of 7 hours. Aware that it has been a problem to meet her production schedule the past several weeks, she wonders where she will find the extra hours needed for the appraisals. Ku figures that she will have to limit each interview to 15 minutes and get approval for enough overtime to catch up.

What recommendations can you offer to Ku so she can effectively and efficiently handle the performance appraisals?

Case 8–2 Planning a Training Program for Personnel in the Payroll Department

Paul Fiandaca has just graduated from high school and has accepted the job of payroll clerk in the home office of the Durand Oil Company. The job consists of auditing weekly time cards and entering variable payroll data (regular hours worked, overtime hours worked, updated wage and salary rates, etc.) for processing by the computer. This is Fiandaca's first job, and he has no business background other than one semester's cooperative work experience (clerk-typist) as part of his course requirements.

It is your plan, as supervisor of the payroll department, to have each new worker, such as Fiandaca, properly trained before actual employment begins. Your budget allows you to pay all new workers an hourly wage of $9.50 during the initial training period. After having successfully completed the entry-level training program, the new workers will be placed on an annual salary of $20,000 to $21,750 during the three-months' probationary period. The payroll department, with its 14 office workers, has had an annual turnover of 22 percent.

Outline a complete plan for training the entry-level office workers in your department.

Case 8–3 MBO Form: Computer Option (available on disk)

9

ANALYZING OFFICE JOBS

GOALS FOR THIS CHAPTER

After completing this chapter, you should be able to:

1. Indicate how the information obtained from a job analysis is used.
2. Describe the methods of gathering and analyzing job information.
3. Point out the characteristics of well-written job descriptions and job specifications.
4. Identify the major features of the job evaluation methods.

We analyze an office job to learn how the work may be done in the one best way by the best qualified person and at the fairest salary that will produce the largest volume of satisfactory work. Thus, office job analysis is a major problem-solving activity, where workable solutions lead to improved office productivity.

As you see in Figure 9–1, the activities involved in analyzing office jobs are:

1. **Job analysis**—the gathering of information about a specific job and determining the principal elements involved in performing it. As you will see later, the major means of gathering job information are questionnaires, interviews, and observations. Usually job analysis is performed as the first step prior to job evaluation.

   a. **Job description**—an outline of the information obtained from the job analysis, which describes the content and essential requirements of a specific job or position.

   b. **Job specification**—a detailed record of the minimum job requirements explained in relation to the job factors (skill, effort, responsibility, and working conditions).

2. **Job evaluation**—the process of appraising the value of each job in relation to other jobs in order to set a monetary value for each specific job.

3. **Work measurement and setting work standards**—the procedure for determining the time required to complete each job or task and for setting up criteria by which the degree of work performance may be measured.

The first two phases of job analysis are explained in this chapter. We shall examine the third phase, work measurement and setting work standards, in a later chapter.

Figure 9–1
Activities Involved in Analyzing Jobs

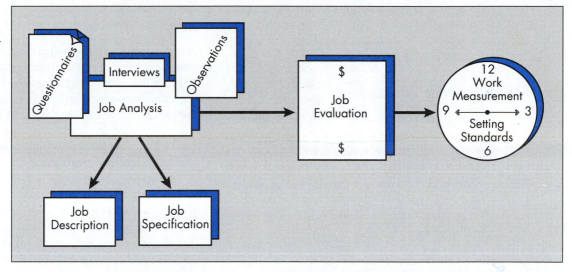

USES OF OFFICE JOB ANALYSIS

The information gathered during job analysis serves a wide variety of purposes, most of which relate closely to the use of the resulting job descriptions. One study revealed that the most common use of job analysis was in recruitment and selection, followed closely by the setting of equitable wage and salary levels.[1] The ongoing perfection of computerized data-gathering techniques has led, in turn, to increased uses of the job analysis information, as you will see in the following discussion.

Recruitment, Testing, and Selection

Job analysis is fundamental to the preparation of job descriptions and job specifications, which are used in recruiting, testing, and selecting office personnel. When properly undertaken, job analysis places a firm's personnel practices on a nondiscriminatory basis by meeting the requirements of federal legislation such as the Civil Rights Act, the Age Discrimination in Employment Act, and the Americans with Disabilities

Act. As you saw in Chapter 6, these acts require that job applicants and employees be accorded equal treatment, regardless of their race, color, religion, sex, national origin, age, and physical and mental disabilities.

The Uniform Guidelines on Employee Selection Procedure, discussed earlier, require employers to devote special attention to job analysis when justifying any selection procedure that has an impact on a certain race, sex, or ethnic group. When firms undertake a validity study of their employment practices, they find that an ongoing job analysis program is vital, especially when their employment practices are challenged in court. Job descriptions and specifications are also needed by those who prepare or select tests to make sure that the tests are a valid measure of the job content and requirements.

Orienting and Training

Office supervisors who orient and train employees find job descriptions and specifications a great help in spelling out the routines to emphasize in teaching work procedures and desirable performance levels. Distributing up-to-date job descriptions and specifications to employees enables them to understand better their specific duties.

---

[1]"Uses of Job Analysis," *How to Analyze Jobs: A Step-by-Step Approach* (Madison, CT: Business & Legal Reports, 1986), p. 10.

Thus, any misunderstandings concerning performance expectations will be reduced. Also, employees will be more likely to accept explanations as to how work grievances are handled.

Clarifying Relationships

Well-developed job descriptions clarify the relationships between jobs, job functions, and departments, and aid in establishing harmony and balance within the organization structure. Supervisors and their workers are provided a clear understanding of their job duties and thus are able to set goals that include standards for competent job performance.

Promotions and Career Counseling

A department promotion plan can be developed through use of job descriptions to show the differences between present jobs and those lying above in the promotion sequence. Thus, employees being groomed for promotion can learn about the qualifications they must possess in order to perform the new duties. By showing relationships among jobs and the education, experience, or skills needed to advance from one job to another, the descriptions are essential in discussing upward mobility when counseling workers.

Job Simplification

As a result of studying jobs, an analyst can facilitate the employees' work by identifying and eliminating wasted motions. For example, when filling in insurance claim forms, a clerk was found leaning far to the left and stretching 28 inches to grasp a blank form and insert it into the typewriter. In studying just this one phase of the task, the analyst found that by relocating the stack of blank forms, the clerk eliminated stretching and reduced the reach to 12 inches. Job analysis, therefore, brings about simplification and improvement of jobs, which allows workers to perform more efficiently and more economically. As a result, office employees spend a smaller amount of effort in order to accomplish greater results.

Job Standardization and Work Measurement

Job analysis leads to standardization of job content as revealed by the job title. For all employees holding the same title, the office supervisor has an accurate picture of what the employees do on the job; how and why they perform the work; the skills involved in work performance; and the physical demands, such as lifting and carrying, that are made upon employees.

Job standardization improves the supervisor's ability to control operations; once the job contents have been standardized, it is easier to measure the output of employees holding the same positions. The supervisor can measure the work produced on each job and set production standards, which, in turn, may be tied in with bonus payments or some other form of incentive for increased output. Also, supervisors are aided in assigning certain time-consuming tasks to lower-paid office personnel and in planning equitable workload assignments to make sure all essential work is accomplished.

Organizational Restructuring

For many organizations undergoing restructuring, downsizing, decentralization, or other structural change, job analysis becomes a basic management issue. To reflect such structural changes, existing job descriptions, especially those for the management ranks, must be overhauled. For example, the elimination of certain middle-management positions and their functions can have major effects on the remaining positions, which must be updated to show the added responsibilities or increased workloads. Job descriptions may also be used to pinpoint gaps in personnel needs as well as to identify overstaffed positions. Thus, for companies undergoing restructuring and redeployment of their human resources, the descriptions provide input for revising the organization structure.

Job Evaluation

The basic characteristics of jobs—education, experience, skills, working conditions, and health and safety requirements—directly affect the differences in jobs and their relative worth. These characteristics are identified through job analysis and then used in evaluating and pricing the jobs. Job evaluation, which is fully described later in this chapter, is undertaken to justify the payment of wages and salaries in relation to the relative worth of the jobs.

GATHERING AND ANALYZING JOB INFORMATION

The office manager, or the person charged with analyzing jobs, must decide which method of gathering job information will be most effective at minimal cost. Traditionally, job information has been obtained by questionnaires, interviews, observations, or a combined approach, as described in this section. Today, with the computer processing of data obtained from questionnaires, we can obtain information relatively quickly from jobholders and their supervisors at a relatively low cost.

Questionnaire Method

Under the **questionnaire method,** employees are often aided by their supervisors and the job analyst to describe their job duties and indicate the

Illustration 9–1 Job analysis questionnaires collect information about a position's daily, weekly, and monthly tasks.

minimum requirements for holding the job. A variety of questionnaires, or *job inventories,* is available for obtaining job information. Questionnaires may be designed by the firm's OM or job analyst to meet the special needs of the organization. Or, consultants, who design their own questionnaires or purchase them from various computer software suppliers, can be used to gather and analyze the job information. Whatever the form of questionnaire, its results must be analyzed and interpreted in the form of job descriptions and specifications that provide management with a knowledge of the job requirements.

Designing the Questionnaire

Relatively simple questionnaires may be designed for manual processing in small firms. On such questionnaires, two groups of questions are often found. In the first group of *general* questions, the employee is asked to provide information such as the following:

Description of duties.

Special knowledge required for the job.

Experience required to qualify for the job.

How much time must be spent on the job before the employee feels capable of working without supervision.

In the second group of *specific* questions about job routines and tasks, the employee is asked to indicate:

Routine tasks performed daily.

Tasks performed weekly.

Tasks performed monthly.

Special tasks performed.

Other job-related information.

To obtain data on the frequency or time spent on different tasks, employees may be asked to keep *work logs* or *diaries.* Work logs, often called *time logs,* are also used in connection with work measurement and the setting of standards.

If the office force is made up of a large number of employees, you will find a much more structured questionnaire used. A **structured questionnaire** requests information on whether specific tasks are part of the worker's job in order to learn the importance the jobholder attaches to each task. A structured questionnaire, such as the job information sheet illustrated in Figure 9–2, is given to employees so they may describe their jobs in accordance with the instructions on the form. Each employee's write-up is edited by the employee's immediate supervisor and submitted to a job analyst. The analyst follows up with the employees and their supervisors to obtain any additional information needed to complete the job analysis.

Techniques of Using Structured Questionnaires

Many job analysis techniques that rely heavily upon the use of structured questionnaires have been designed to provide special types of job information.[2] Brief descriptions of two techniques are given below.

Position Analysis Questionnaire (PAQ). PAQ, a very widely used computerized system, analyzes and documents only those activities performed by the worker. A few questions pertain to the employee's description of the job and the compensation received; the remaining questions examine the kind of worker behaviors required and the type of environmental factors surrounding the job. The questionnaires may be completed by an analyst during an interview with the jobholders or their supervisors or while observing the work as it is being performed. The questionnaire form is designed so that the results may be optically scanned and analyzed on a computer.

Comprehensive Occupational Data Analysis Programs (CODAP). This collection of computer software products is designed to analyze and report job information that has been collected through questionnaires called task inventories. The *task inventory* is designed to obtain information about the jobholder's education and training; major items of equipment, tools, and materials

used on the job; and the jobholder's assessment of the skills and abilities needed to perform the job. The rating of the task items is created by the job analyst, jobholder, supervisor or manager, and, where appropriate, a union representative. The task ratings are analyzed by computer to provide a variety of reports that give information in areas such as job classification, recruitment and selection, career planning, performance evaluation, and training.

Advantages and Disadvantages of Using the Questionnaire Method

Among the advantages of using the questionnaire method are:

1. Information is obtained rapidly, especially when compared with the time-consuming activity of personally interviewing each worker.
2. By means of computer programs, job information obtained by questionnaires may be quickly organized and analyzed, with printouts providing data to be used in a variety of applications. Programs are also available for checking statistically the validity of questionnaire results.

Several disadvantages characterize the questionnaire method of gathering job information:

1. It may be difficult to design or obtain a questionnaire that is sufficiently thorough to secure all the data required by the job analyst. Unless the questions are precisely and clearly worded, it may be difficult for jobholders to communicate the information requested and for the analyst to interpret the information supplied.
2. So many questions may be asked that the questionnaire becomes overly complex and confusing. As a result, the jobholders may give misleading or incomplete responses because they do not take time to complete the form correctly.
3. Some employees are not skilled in properly analyzing their jobs and thus may exaggerate the importance of their jobs. Or, they may underemphasize those phases of their jobs that require a fairly large percentage of their total work time.

---

[2]For detailed information about these techniques and others that may be used in analyzing office jobs, see Milton R. Rock and Lance A. Berger (editors in chief), *The Compensation Handbook* (New York: McGraw-Hill Book Company, 1991), Chapter 28.

4. The personal touch is lacking since the job-holders are called upon merely to fill out a questionnaire rather than discuss their job content with an interviewer.

5. In order to obtain reliable and valid results, the manual processing of completed questionnaires requires careful analysis and editing, all of which are a costly means of obtaining job information.

However, the questionnaire method does serve as a starting point in the job analysis program. Despite the disadvantages just given, you will find the questionnaire commonly used, often in conjunction with the interview and/or observation methods, which are discussed in the next sections.

Figure 9–2
Job Informa-
tion Sheet
(page 1)

JOB INFORMATION SHEET

Instructions
   Present Job Title—Enter the name by which the job is now called.
   Department—Enter the general office department in which the job is located.
   Description of Duties—This portion of the job description is to be a series of numbered statements, each of which describes a task or major step of your job.

   1. Introduce each task or major step with an action verb and follow it by a concise statement that tells what you are doing, and where appropriate, include an account of how the task or major step is done.

      If additional space is needed for the completion of your Job Description, please attach another sheet.

   2. Tasks or major steps are to be written in descending order of frequency of performance: i.e., the task on which the most time is spent is listed first, and the task on which the least time is spent is last.

   3. Minor steps or tasks are to be combined and written in one catch-all paragraph at the end of the Job Description.

Questions 1 through 14—Complete each of these questions as it relates to your job.

After completing the Job Information Sheet, give it to your supervisor.

Your Name *Bernard Amati*   Date Issued *4/16/--*
Present Job Title *Payroll Clerk*   Date Due *4/23/--*
Name of Your Supervisor *Janice Bradley*   Dept. *Payroll Accounting*
Description of Duties: *Verify time sheets; keyboard weekly payroll data into computer system; prepare bank deposits; reconcile bank statement and payroll account; distribute paychecks*

1. EDUCATION REQUIRED. Indicate the minimum schooling required for your job by check mark.
   No schooling required_____   2 yrs. high school_____   4 yrs. high school__✓__
   Technical high school_____   Special schooling_____   College_____
   Do you make any reports? No _✓_ Yes____ If yes, what are they?_____

2. EXPERIENCE. The minimum experience required for your job.
   Months: 1 _✓_ 2___ 3___ 4___ 5___ 6___ 7___ 8___ 9___ 10___ 11___ 12___
   Years: 1___ 2___ 3___ 4___ 5___ 6___ 7___ 8___

3. TRAINING.   The minimum training required for your job.
   Months: 1 _✓_ 2___ 3___ 4___ 5___ 6___ 7___ 8___ 9___ 10___ 11___ 12___
   Does your job require many skills? No__ Yes_✓_ If yes, enumerate and describe briefly._____
   Keyboarding on computer terminal; using 10-key printing calculator

   How often does your job repeat itself? Per Hour___ Per Day___ Per Week _1_ Per Month _4-5_

Figure 9–2
Job Informa-
tion Sheet
(page 2)

4. PHYSICAL DEMANDS. What kind of equipment do you use? *Terminal & calculator*
What is the maximum weight of your work in pounds? Lifting __*3-5 lbs.*__
Pulling__ Pushing__ The heaviest work is done___ percent of working time. Your work position is
Sitting ✓ Standing__ Walking ✓ Holding steadily__ Lifting overhead__ Bending__

5. MENTAL OR VISUAL DEMANDS. What accuracy is required on the job? __*100%*__
Are the hands and eyes constantly coordinated? *Yes*
Are operations automatic? No___ Partly ✓ Yes___

6. RESPONSIBILITY FOR EQUIPMENT. Are you responsible for any equipment? No___ Yes ✓
If yes, describe the equipment. *Terminal and calculator*
_____
_____
What is the cost of possible damage to equipment? No damage___ Minimum $ _25_ Maximum $ *1500*
Do you repair equipment? No ✓ Yes___ If yes, what kind? _____

7. RESPONSIBILITY FOR MATERIAL OR PRODUCT. Are you responsible for any materials? No ✓ Yes___
If yes, what are they?_____
How much spoilage may occur? Loss in dollars $____ What is required to avoid spoilage?_____
_____
Can the spoiled work be repaired? No___ Partly___ Completely_____
Enumerate and briefly describe various materials you have to recognize. _____
_____
_____
_____

8. RESPONSIBILITY FOR SAFETY OF OTHERS. How many people may be injured if carelessness would
occur? _1_ Are there hazards that may cause injury? No ✓ Yes___ If yes, what are they?_____
_____
_____
_____

9. RESPONSIBILITY FOR WORK OF OTHERS. Are you responsible for work of others? No ✓ Yes___
How Many?____ For new employees only?____ How Many?____

10. WORKING CONDITIONS. Are the working conditions Agreeable?____ Disagreeable? ✓
Which disagreeable conditions affect your job? Noise ✓ Fumes___ Cold___ Hot___
Changes in temperature___ Dirt___ Dust___ Oil___ Steam___ Too wet___ Glare ✓
Somewhat dark___ Drafty___ Others _____

11. UNAVOIDABLE HAZARDS. Which accidents may occur? Burns___ Shock___ Cuts___ Crushed Fingers___
Injury to Feet___ Eyes___ Ears___ Lungs___ Is your health affected? No ✓ Yes___ If yes, in what way?____
_____

12. SUPERVISION. Received from *Janice Bradley*
Weekly ✓ Daily___ Hourly___ Do you supervise? No ✓ Yes___ If yes, how many workers?____
Weekly___ Daily___ Hourly___ Do you make your own decisions? No___ Yes ✓ Do you inspect someone
else's job? No ✓ Yes___

13. Would you prefer to be transferred to another job? No ✓ Yes___ If yes, which job could you perform?____
_____

14. REMARKS. Give additional information which has not been covered and which may assist in a better
description of your job. *None* _____
_____
_____
_____
_____

Interview Method

The **interview method** requires the job analyst to spend time in meeting with the employee and the employee's supervisor in order to gather information about the job. Thus, this method is often costlier than the questionnaire method. However, for some types of job analyses, the interview may be conducted at the employee's workstation so the job may be observed at the same time.

The effectiveness of the interview method depends greatly upon the skill of the analyst, who must be trained to deal with people in order to receive their full cooperation. At the beginning of the interview, the analyst must establish rapport with the jobholder so that he or she is at ease and will not be hesitant in replying to the questions asked. When collecting information, the analyst must be objective so that personal bias does not influence the data being recorded. All information recorded should be read to the employee to confirm its correctness. Following the interview, the employee's supervisor should be consulted to verify the accuracy of the information obtained.

Observation Method

In addition to gathering job information by the questionnaire and the interview methods, the analyst may observe workers while they are performing their tasks. The **observation method** permits the analyst to obtain job information firsthand and to become acquainted with the working conditions, the equipment used, and the requirements for special skills, such as finger dexterity. For jobs that are relatively simple and repetitive, such as statistical keyboarding, the observation method may be effectively used. For other types of jobs, the analyst may select one of the other methods or a combination of methods.

Illustration 9–2 Direct observation by a trained analyst while the worker is engaged in performing job duties is a common method for obtaining job information.

In some large companies, you will find that the analyst obtains data about job-performance times from the industrial engineering department. The time-study engineer in such a department is concerned with observing and studying all aspects of the job, including skill requirements, physical and mental effort required, job environment needs, and flow of information, which may not be precisely stated in job descriptions. These factors are necessary, however, for preparing performance standards, as explained in a later chapter.

Combined Approach

The questionnaire, interview, and observation methods may be combined when undertaking a job analysis. Here are brief summaries of three techniques that involve a combination of the methods.

Critical Incident Technique (CIT)

Rather than provide a complete description of the job, this technique defines a job in terms of the specific *behaviors* necessary to perform the job successfully. By means of structured questionnaires, interviews, and observations, incidents are gathered from supervisors, jobholders, and analysts. These incidents describe behaviors that are observed to be critical to job performance and that reflect particularly outstanding or poor performance. The descriptions of the behaviors are then reviewed, edited, and grouped into categories of general behavior dimensions, such as "the ability to work in an environment that requires a moderate degree of trust" or "the ability to work in an environment that requires an exceptionally high degree of accuracy, tact, and diplomacy and a high degree of confidentiality."

Functional Job Analysis (FJA)

Using this approach to analyzing jobs, you would examine the *interactions among the work, the workers, and the organization*. The FJA technique centers upon:

1. Identifying the purposes and objectives of the organization.
2. Identifying and describing the tasks performed by workers.
3. Analyzing the workers' tasks.
4. Developing performance standards that describe the amount of time spent by workers on tasks at each functional level.
5. Developing training content related to the skills needed to perform the tasks.

To obtain all this information, analysts review background information on the present jobs, interview workers and supervisors, and directly observe the work as it is performed.

Job Element Method (JEM)

When using the JEM, you are concerned with identifying the *elements* that workers use in performing their jobs. Examples of job elements include knowledge, skills, abilities, and personal traits. Workers and supervisors meet in brainstorming sessions to identify and rate the elements used in performing jobs. The elements are rated as to whether they represent minimum, satisfactory, or outstanding levels of job performance. Next, the ratings are further defined and described in the form of *task statements,* which are analyzed to determine those requirements needed to perform the job. The task statements form the basis for preparing job descriptions, which are explained in the following section.

JOB DESCRIPTIONS

The results of job analysis are expressed in the job description, from which job specifications are separately developed or combined with the job description. Some firms prepare *position descriptions* in addition to their job descriptions. Generally in these organizations, position descriptions are prepared for the higher-level jobs (such as management jobs) while job descriptions are used for lower-level jobs. Position descriptions usually stress intangibles to a greater extent than job descriptions, and they emphasize results rather than specific job procedures.[3] For our purposes here, we shall restrict the discussion to *job* descriptions.

Analyzing jobs and preparing job descriptions may require a period of a year or more before you have refined the descriptions to the point where they become a valuable tool to be used by managers and supervisors in all departments. As a result of changes such as revisions in administrative systems, reduced need for human resources resulting from downsizing, and tightened budgetary control, you should review and revise the job descriptions regularly. You will want to provide office workers with easy access to the job descriptions so they can improve their performance, be fully aware of the dimensions of their jobs, know who in the firm can aid them in their work, see how their performance will be evaluated, and become aware of their opportunities for advancement.

Writing the Job Description

The job description must be clearly written, with all statements expressed as simply as possible. The terms used should be widely accepted or carefully defined since the descriptions will be used by several persons for different purposes, including wage and salary surveys. There is no prescribed amount of information that should be included in a job description. However, it should contain enough information to ensure that the job can be accurately evaluated. *The job—not the person holding the job—is to be described as it is; no modifications should be made in the description for what the job ought to be or may become in the future.*

The job titles and descriptions should compare as closely as possible with the standardized descriptions listed in the *Dictionary of Occupational Titles* (DOT) and the *Occupational Out-*

look Handbook.[4] Other sources of job information include organizations that conduct periodic wage and salary surveys, such as the American Payroll Association, American Management Association, Dartnell, Temp Force, and the Bureau of Labor Statistics.

A Typical Job Description

Figure 9–3 shows a job description for purchasing clerk, a *nonexempt* worker (entitled to overtime pay for hours worked over 40 during the workweek). Sometimes, the job specification, discussed in the following section, may be combined with the job description.

JOB SPECIFICATIONS

A *job specification* describes the minimum requirements of the job, such as the education, experience, and personal qualifications that you see listed in Figure 9–4. Job specifications are used mainly in job evaluation when rating jobs for wage and salary purposes. Often, job specifications are confused with **employee specifications,** which are the minimum qualifications a person must possess to be considered for employment. For example, on a *job* specification, we might read: "Requires keen vision." However, on the *employee* specification, we see: "Must have 20/20 vision." When the job specification and employee specification are brought together, an interviewer has accurate data for matching the job applicants with job openings.

---

[3]"Position Descriptions," *How to Write Job Descriptions—The Easy Way* (Madison, CT: Business & Legal Reports, Inc., 1991), p. 59.

[4]Both the *Dictionary of Occupational Titles* and the *Occupational Outlook Handbook* are available from the Superintendent of Documents, U.S. Government Printing Office, Washington, DC 20402, or the Bureau of Labor Statistics Sales Center, P.O. Box 2145, Chicago, IL 60690.

The *Handbook* gives information for some 250 occupations, including nature of the work; working conditions; employment, training, other qualifications, and advancement; job outlook; earnings; and related occupations. Also available from the Bureau of Labor Statistics is *Occupational Projections and Training Data,* which ranks occupations by employment growth, earnings, susceptibility to unemployment, separation rates, and part-time work.

Figure 9–3
Job Descrip-
tion for Pur-
chasing Clerk

JOB DESCRIPTION

Job Title Purchasing Clerk
Department Finance
Reports to Purchasing Manager

Date August 15, 19–
Status Nonexempt

Job Summary Under the purchasing manager's supervision, prepares purchase orders, checks receipt of purchases and approves payment, maintains stock of office supplies, prepares specifications for purchases of printed forms, and receives sales representatives of office equipment, services, and stationery.

Job Duties

1. Prepares purchase orders—receives and checks all departmental requisitions as to vendor, account numbers, and prices; keyboards purchase orders and distributes copies.

2. Checks receipt of purchases and initiates payment procedure.

3. Maintains stock of office supplies—purchases supplies, controls inventory levels, and prepares quarterly cost records for supplies used by each department.

4. Prepares specifications for purchases of printed forms—obtains samples from vendors, specifies color and weight of paper and number of copies, obtains price quotations and delivery dates; and places orders.

5. Receives sales representatives of office equipment, stationery and forms; evaluates offerings; coordinates equipment repair and maintenance services; and directs salespeople to other departments when appropriate.

6. Performs miscellaneous duties related to purchasing—assisting departments in preparing price quotations for equipment and services.

7. May assume some duties of the finance secretary, as assigned by the purchasing manager.

Job Responsibilities

For money, securities, and funds Can order up to $1,000 worth of supplies each month with purchasing manager's authorization. Does not deal directly with money, securities, or funds.

For confidential matters None

For getting along with others Has close contact with six coworkers in department. Extensive contact with members of all departments. External contacts maintained with numerous vendors of supplies and services.

For accuracy High degree of accuracy in keyboarding purchase orders. Errors in receipt of proper materials can result in great inconvenience, time loss, and overpayment of bills.

Figure 9–4
Job Specification for General Clerk A

JOB SPECIFICATION

Job Title: General Clerk A

Qualifications: Education—High school graduate.

Experience—Two or more years with company as General Clerk B.
Experience in office systems and procedures.

Personal—Speed and efficiency in handling volume of detail.
Ability to instruct others in clerical jobs.
Ability to supervise work of others.

Duties:
1. Handle mail and answer incoming correspondence.
2. Index and file important records and correspondence.
3. Process payroll records and prepare reports.
4. Summarize and tabulate cost information and records.
5. Receive, safeguard, and account for petty cash and office funds.
6. Supervise general clerks.

Promotional Opportunities: Advancement to accounting clerk after two years.

Salary Range: $1,325–$1,800 per month.

JOB EVALUATION

Job analysis and its components—the job description and the job specification—are needed before you can determine the relative value of each job. The aim of *job evaluation* is to develop an equitable payroll policy based on the estimated or measured worth of each job in relation to other jobs. The benefits to be gained from job evaluation are set forth by Robert J. Sahl, management consultant, in the *Dialog from the Workplace.* When jobs are properly evaluated, employees doing similar work under similar working conditions are paid about the same salary. However, worker experience and level of skill, the cost of living, the supply and demand of office workers, government regulations, collective bargaining agreements, and competitive conditions also influence the salaries paid office workers.

In this section of the chapter, we shall examine two methods of job evaluation—nonquantitative and quantitative. In the following chapter, you will read about the pricing of jobs and the determination of pay ranges.

Nonquantitative Methods

In the *nonquantitative methods* of job evaluation, jobs are evaluated according to their relative or estimated difficulty. The two methods that we shall examine are (1) ranking and (2) job classification.

Ranking Method

The **ranking method** is the simplest and oldest method of determining the economic value of a job. Using the ranking method, we analyze and rank the individual jobs according to the difficulty and the overall responsibility of each job. Jobs are ranked according to job titles from the most important to the least important (or vice versa) in relation to their contribution to the business. We assume that the salary increases as the job becomes more difficult. This is not always true, however, because sometimes a salary is determined by the working conditions, level and amount of responsibility, or experience involved. A simple ranking of office jobs is given in Table 9–1.

DIALOG FROM THE WORKPLACE

ROBERT J. SAHL

Founder and General Partner
WMS and Co., Inc.
King of Prussia, Pennsylvania

The management consulting firm, WMS and Co., Inc., provides broad-base consulting service to clients in many areas, including compensation plan design, performance appraisal, individual assessments, management development, and management succession planning. Dr. Robert J. Sahl is a general partner of the firm and directs its Applied Behavioral Sciences consulting.

Prior to founding WMS and Co., Dr. Sahl was a principal with Hay Associates, where he aided companies in the selection, placement, and development of management personnel through psychological assessment. His experiences include conducting management development seminars, formulating team-building programs, vocational guidance, and career path planning. Over the years, Dr. Sahl has been heavily involved in developing and installing base and incentive compensation programs for a number of organizations varying in size and nature of business. He has also conducted industry-specific compensation surveys.

Dr. Sahl's academic background is: B.S. in Psychology from Albright College, M.S. in Personnel Psychology from George Washington University, and Ph.D. in Industrial Psychology from Colorado State University.

QUESTION: When talking with a client about the need for evaluating office and clerical jobs, what benefits do you set forth?

RESPONSE: When an organization determines a need to evaluate its jobs, it is embarking on a process from which a number of benefits will be derived. First, the organization will end up with an internally equitable rank ordering of its positions. This will be based on the consistent application of the same measurement tool for measuring all jobs. This internally equitable rank ordering of jobs will get translated into a salary range for each job. These ranges will then be internally fair. This is essential for maintaining employee morale.

With this same set of data, the organization can relate its current pay practices to the marketplace and see how competitive they currently are. If a more (or less) competitive posture is desired, the salary ranges can be adjusted over time. In this manner another benefit is realized. The organization is now neither overpaying nor underpaying its people. This results in the optimal use of payroll dollars and can reduce turnover as people recognize they are fairly paid in the market.

Typically with this approach, each position ends up with a salary range. People may be moved through this range on the basis of their performance. Hence, a third benefit surfaces. The organization can now strengthen the relationship between pay and performance.

Sometimes organizations inadvertently promote people into a "smaller" job. Once jobs have been evaluated, however, this will not occur. It now becomes a relatively straightforward process to gauge the size and reasonableness of a promotion. This, then, becomes another benefit to be realized.

Rank Order	Job Title	Median Monthly Salary (Midpoint) Of Salary Range
1	Administrative Office Manager	$3,350
2	Systems Analyst	3,220
3	Programmer/Analyst	2,675
4	Programmer	2,290
5	Executive Secretary/Administrative Assistant	1,985
6	Computer Operator A	1,865
7	Secretary A	1,805
8	Lead Word Processing Operator	1,740
9	Computer Operator B	1,695
9	Accounting Clerk A	1,695
10	Secretary B	1,590
10	Word Processing Operator	1,590
11	General Clerk A	1,530
12	Accounting Clerk B	1,485
13	Data-Entry Operator A	1,480
14	Switchboard Operator/Receptionist	1,440
14	Clerk-Typist	1,440
15	General Clerk B	1,390
15	Data-Entry Operator B	1,390
16	File Clerk	1,270

Table 9–1 Simple Ranking of Office Jobs

Note: Titles and median salaries are illustrative and for comparison purposes only.

Often an evaluation committee consisting of supervisors and department heads ranks the jobs. They may do the ranking in terms of job titles alone or by combining titles, job content, and compensation rates. The number of ranks assigned will vary with the number of jobs or positions and the type of business organization. In Table 9–1, for example, the 20 jobs making up one activity field—office—are arranged in rank order from 1 through 16.

Two types of job-ranking methods sometimes used are *card ranking* and *paired comparison*. In both methods, the supervisors are asked to rank the jobs in the order of their importance from highest to lowest, or vice versa.

Card-Ranking Method. When using the card-ranking method, we place each job title on a 3″ × 5″ index card. Next, we arrange the cards in order of the relative importance of each job to the company, ignoring the present salary of the job, the historic position or status of the job in the company, and the performance of any particular employee holding that job. This approach to job evaluation provides an effective analysis of jobs without the influence of established, historical precedents and appears more like an independent survey based upon sound operations. If there are too many jobs to be thus ranked, it may be necessary to rank them first by groups of jobs and then to rank the jobs within each group.

Paired-Comparison Method. In the paired-comparison method, we rank each job against another job of comparable ranking on the basis of the total difficulty of the job. The greater number of times a job is ranked as more difficult, the more important the job becomes. One type of form used in the paired-comparison method is shown in Figure 9–5.

Advantages and Disadvantages of the Ranking Method. You may use the ranking method satisfactorily in very small offices where comparatively few jobs (fewer than 25) are to be evaluated and where the employees respect the employer's integrity in ranking jobs. One advantage of the method is its simplicity; it is easily understood. However, the rating is extremely subjective and often incorrectly based on the employee who is performing the job rather than on the job itself. Also, the relative ranking of jobs depends greatly on current salary and wage rates, which fluctuate with economic conditions.

The ranking method may be implemented without much expense. However, some grievances and loss of time may occur when the rater is unable to explain why one job is slotted above or below another because there are no objective studies to back up the established salary or wage rates. Then, too, the evaluation process often becomes unwieldy when there is a large number of jobs. Finally, it is unlikely that there is any one person who knows all the jobs and is thus qualified to evaluate them.

Job Classification Method

The **job classification method** is an outgrowth of the ranking method. This method has long been used by civil service authorities in evaluating office and clerical workers and in granting periodic salary increases. Before the jobs are classified, the analyst selects a number of predetermined classes or family groupings on the basis of common features, such as levels of responsibilities, abilities or skills, knowledge, and duties. The jobs are then analyzed and grouped into those

Figure 9–5
Form Used
in Paired-
Comparison
Method

Directions: Compare the first job in the first column with each job in the slant columns. If the job in the first column is considered to have greater value to the firm than the job in the slant column, place a check mark (✓) in the box below the job in the slant column. Repeat process until all jobs have been compared. Tally check marks to find rank of jobs.

JOBS	Secretary B	Secretary A	Executive Secretary	Data-Entry Operator	File Clerk	Total (checks)	Rank
Secretary B				✓	✓	2	3
Secretary A	✓			✓	✓	3	2
Executive Secretary	✓	✓		✓	✓	4	1
Data-Entry Operator					✓	1	4
File Clerk						0	5

specific classes in order of importance according to the job and the work performed. Thus, it is assumed that each job involves duties and responsibilities that fit into the respective graded classification.

One method of grouping jobs in a classification chart is shown in Table 9–2. The nature of the work is combined with the salary range to show that there is a direct relationship between the rating of the importance of the job and the salary paid. In this table, the four family groupings are clerical, secretarial, accounting, and data processing. Under each of these family groupings, the jobs are ranked according to their importance, which, in turn, is influenced by the salary range.

The General Schedule. The most common example of the job classification method is the **General Schedule** used by the federal government for virtually all of its civilian jobs (professional, scientific, clerical, administrative, and custodial). The General Schedule is composed of 18 job classes (GS-1 through GS-18) with the job classes differing in the levels of job difficulty, responsibilities, and qualification requirements of the work performed. The less difficult the job, the lower the job class number; the greater the responsibilities and qualifications needed to fill the job, the higher the job class number. For example, the entry level for most jobs is GS-3 or GS-4; junior management jobs tend to be in the GS-5 to GS-10 range; supervisory levels are usually GS-

Table 9–2
Breakdown of Job Classifications by Job Levels and Weekly Salary Ranges

Job Level	Weekly Salary Range	Mid-point	Clerical	Secretarial	Accounting	Data Processing
				FAMILY GROUPINGS		
1	$265–$315	$290	File Clerk	—	—	—
2	$290–$350	$320	General Clerk B	—	Order Clerk	—
3	$305–$365	$335	Clerk-Typist	—	Accounting Clerk B	Data-Entry Operator B
4	$325–$390	$355	General Clerk A	Secretary B	Accounting Clerk A	Data-Entry Operator A
5	$335–$395	$365	—	Word Processing Operator	Payroll Clerk	Computer Operator B
6	$380–$460	$420	—	Secretary A	—	Computer Operator A
7	$420–$500	$460	—	Executive Secretary	—	—
8	$410–$550	$480	—	—	Junior Accountant	—
9	$430–$570	$500	—	—	—	Programmer
10	$500–$650	$575	—	—	Chief Accountant	Programmer/ Analyst

Note: Titles and median salaries are illustrative and for comparison purposes only.

11 to GS-15. Most workers above GS-15 are in the Senior Executive Service.

Advantages and Disadvantages of the Job Classification Method. Like the ranking method, the job classification method is inexpensive to implement. Also, like the ranking method, the job classification method may be applied in small business firms or offices; only a small amount of time and few trained personnel are needed to use this method. Since there is usually a hierarchy already present in the office, this method of informally ranking employees may be easily accepted by the workers and serve as a good starting point for introducing a quantitative method of evaluating jobs, as discussed in the next section.

The job classification method has the disadvantage of its subjective grading. Also, the rating of jobs by their total content may create distrust among employees. In the same way, the very purpose of this method of job evaluation is defeated if outside influences, such as existing wage rates or qualifications of present jobholders, create a biased effect on the job classification rating.

Quantitative Methods

In the *quantitative methods* of job evaluation, jobs are grouped according to mental, physical, skill, and experience requisites. The two quantitative methods that we shall examine in this section are (1) factor-comparison and (2) point-factor.

Factor-Comparison Method

The **factor-comparison method** is also known as the *key-job system* and the *job-to-money method*. Using this method, you rate the jobs in terms of money according to the following five critical factors:

1. *Mental requirements* (education, judgment, initiative, ingenuity, versatility).
2. *Skill requirements* (use of equipment and materials, dexterity, precision).
3. *Physical requirements* (strength, endurance).
4. *Responsibility* (for safety of others; for equipment, materials, and processes; cost of error; extent of supervision exercised).
5. *Working conditions* (accident hazard, environment).

Illustration 9–3 The file clerk position is a common office job used as a benchmark in the factor-comparison method of quantitative job evaluation.

Using the Factor-Comparison Method. As the first step in using the factor-comparison method, along with a committee representing workers and management, select 10 to 20 benchmark jobs that represent a cross section of all the jobs that will be evaluated. A **benchmark job,** or *key job,* is one whose present rate is not subject to controversy and that is considered to be neither underpaid nor overpaid. You can easily identify such benchmark jobs, commonly found in many firms, by using salary surveys. Other criteria used to select benchmark jobs are:

1. The job titles should be immediately recognizable.
2. The job content should be precisely defined so that workers who are asked to provide job information are not confused about the jobs being analyzed.
3. The jobs should be performed in a more or less similar manner by most organizations. Thus, the jobs have about the same content and skill requirements wherever they are found.

4. The jobs should remain relatively unchanged so they can provide a basis for analysis and comparison with other jobs.

Some fairly common office and clerical jobs that are identified as benchmark include executive secretary, data-entry operator, file clerk, and messenger.

In identifying the benchmark jobs, the committee should select those that range from the lowest- to the highest-paid jobs. The benchmark jobs are next analyzed by each member of the committee. At this time, the committee must also agree on the definitions of the five critical factors so each person interprets each factor alike.

The committee next ranks the benchmark jobs according to the five factors, one factor at a time, in the order of their relative importance. The ranking should first be arranged numerically, as shown in Table 9–3. Note that in the factor column "Mental Requirements," the highest rank (1)

Table 9–3
Simple Ranking of Benchmark Jobs in the Factor-Comparison Method

Rank	Mental Requirements	Skill Requirements	Physical Requirements	Responsibility	Working Conditions
1	Senior Accounting Clerk	Executive Secretary	Messenger	Senior Accounting Clerk	Data-Entry Operator
2	Executive Secretary	Senior Accounting Clerk	File Clerk	Executive Secretary	Messenger
3	Executive Correspondence Secretary	Executive Correspondence Secretary	Executive Secretary	Switchboard Operator/ Receptionist	File Clerk
4	Correspondence Secretary	Correspondence Secretary	Executive Correspondence Secretary	Executive Correspondence Secretary	Switchboard Operator/ Receptionist
5	Senior Typist	Data-Entry Operator	Correspondence Secretary	Correspondence Secretary	Senior Typist
6	Switchboard Operator/ Receptionist	Senior Typist	Data-Entry Operator	Data-Entry Operator	General Clerk
7	Data-Entry Operator	Switchboard Operator/ Receptionist	Switchboard Operator/ Receptionist	General Clerk	Correspondence Secretary
8	General Clerk	General Clerk	Senior Typist	Senior Typist	Senior Accounting Clerk
9	File Clerk	File Clerk	Senior Accounting Clerk	Messenger	Executive Correspondence Secretary
10	Messenger	Messenger	General Clerk	File Clerk	Executive Secretary

is given to the job of Senior Accounting Clerk while the lowest rank (10) is assigned to the job of Messenger. In the factor column "Physical Requirements," the job of Senior Accounting Clerk is assigned the next to lowest rank (9), while the job of Messenger is assigned the highest rank (1).

Next, the committee establishes the *average* salary for all ranked benchmark jobs and divides the money value for each job among the five factors according to the importance of the respective factor to the job. Table 9–4 shows the average weekly salary apportioned to the five basic factors for three of the benchmark jobs ranked in Table 9–3. The assumed weekly salaries are distributed for each factor of the three jobs.

After the weekly salaries have been distributed to the benchmark jobs according to the ranked and evaluated factors, the committee takes the following steps:

1. Pool the rankings in a master reference table such as Table 9–5.
2. List the titles of the benchmark jobs in the first column from the highest- to the lowest-paid job.
3. Enter the average weekly salaries in the next column.
4. Record the monetary rates, representing the factor rankings for each job, as well as the rank numbers, under the five major factors.
5. Add horizontally the total distributed money

values for each factor to verify the established average weekly salary.
6. Study all jobs that can be compared with the benchmark jobs listed in Table 9–5.

Advantages and Disadvantages of the Factor-Comparison Method. The major advantage of the factor-comparison method in relation to the ranking and the job classification methods is that you evaluate each job on the basis of five factors basic to the job. Since you compare each job against a benchmark job, and factor against factor, you are able to obtain a fair degree of accuracy. Also, you can determine not only which job is worth more but also how much more. Thus, the method provides a tailor-made plan of job evaluation that meets a firm's own needs as a result of properly selecting and weighting the factors. Further, once established in a firm, the method can be taught relatively easily to union members and managers.

On the other hand, the factor-comparison method is difficult to explain and communicate to workers. Although the method provides for establishing comparable job factors within the firm, it is inflexible in dealing with salary rates outside the firm. Thus, if a salary level change for a job is brought about by a change in the outside labor market rate, changes must be made throughout the entire salary structure in order to maintain internal equity.

Table 9–4
Average Weekly Salaries Apportioned to Five Factors for Three Benchmark Jobs in the Factor-Comparison Method

BENCHMARK JOBS AND GRADED SALARIES			
Factor	Executive Secretary	Data-Entry Operator	File Clerk
Mental requirements	$140	$ 60	$ 35
Skill requirements	160	80	35
Physical requirements	85	70	110
Responsibility	120	70	25
Working conditions	30	110	85
Total weekly salary	$535	$390	$290

Note: Titles and median salaries are illustrative and for comparison purposes only.

Table 9–5
Job Rankings
and Salary
Rates in the
Factor-
Comparison
Method

Bench-mark Job	Average Weekly Salary	Mental Requirements Rank	Mental Requirements Rate	Skill Requirements Rank	Skill Requirements Rate	Physical Requirements Rank	Physical Requirements Rate	Responsibility Rank	Responsibility Rate	Working Conditions Rank	Working Conditions Rate
Executive Secretary	$535	2	$140	1	$160	3	$85	2	$120	10	$30
Senior Accounting Clerk	495	1	140	2	140	9	65	1	120	8	30
Executive Correspondence Secretary	450	3	135	3	125	4	80	4	80	9	30
Correspondence Secretary	425	4	120	4	115	5	70	5	80	7	40
Data-Entry Operator	390	7	60	5	80	6	70	6	70	1	110
Switchboard Operator/Receptionist	360	6	65	7	80	7	70	3	80	4	65
Senior Typist	350	5	75	6	80	8	70	8	60	5	65
General Clerk	340	8	60	8	80	10	65	7	70	6	65
File Clerk	290	9	35	9	35	2	110	10	25	3	85
Messenger	275	10	20	10	20	1	110	9	25	2	100

Note: Titles and median salaries are illustrative and for comparison purposes only.

Point-Factor Method

A survey by the Human Resources Management Association found that the most common approach to job evaluation is the point-factor method. Results of the study showed that the point-factor method is used for 45 percent of all exempt positions and 42 percent of all salaried nonexempt positions surveyed.[5] In the **point-factor method** of job evaluation, each of the basic factors is divided into degrees, and points are assigned to each factor and its degrees. No wage or salary rates are taken into consideration.

In evaluating most jobs, the four widely accepted factors used in the point-factor method are *skill, effort, responsibility,* and *job conditions.* Since these factors are broad and may be interpreted differently in different situations, each factor is divided into *subfactors* such as the following:

[5]Robert J. Sahl, "How to Install a Point-Factor Job-Evaluation System," *Personnel* (March, 1989), p. 38.

Skill
1. Education and Job Knowledge
2. Experience and Training
3. Initiative and Ingenuity

Effort
4. Physical Demand
5. Mental and/or Visual Demand

Responsibility
6. For Equipment or Tools
7. For Materials or Product
8. For Safety of Others
9. For Work of Others

Job Conditions
10. Working Conditions
11. Unavoidable Hazards

Each of the subfactors is divided into a number of *degrees* that serve as a scale for measuring the distinct levels of each factor. The degrees, in turn, are evaluated separately by a number of *points*. For example, the subfactor "Responsibility for Equipment or Tools" may be divided into degrees that are assigned points as shown in Figure 9–6. The sum of all the points for all subfactors represents the total score for the job. Thus, in a firm using the point-factor method, jobs with similar point values would be paid the same salary even though the points are related to different factors.

Advantages of the Point-Factor Method. You will find that the point-factor method is probably less subjective in its approach and provides more consistency of results than any other job evaluation method since each subfactor is clearly defined in terms of degrees. With each subfactor divided into several degrees, you are able to judge quickly and, at the same time, minimize discriminations and inequities. You are further aided by various computerized evaluation systems that easily manage the application of the method and the weighting of the different factors and degrees. Since the job is analyzed and rated in its entirety, independently of wage and salary rates, you are not influenced by pressure from unions, workers, or management. The number of points assigned to a job as the result of an equitable rating remains the same until the job is changed. Thus, bargaining for wage and salary rates can be easily accomplished because the job evaluation continues to serve its purpose as a measuring stick.

Disadvantages of the Point-Factor Method. Some critics of the point-factor method feel that it is inflexible or highly rigid because of the limited number of degrees and the fact that the largest number of points depends on, and is assigned to, the highest factor degree. Also, some feel that the point-factor method, with its elements of factors, degrees, and weighting, requires a great deal of time to develop and thus becomes very costly, especially in dynamic companies where job content changes or new jobs are added frequently. Further, use of the method may require the services of out-

Figure 9–6
Subfactor, Responsibility for Equipment or Tools, with Degrees and Points

	RESPONSIBILITY FOR EQUIPMENT OR TOOLS	
Degree	Amount of Responsibility	Points
1	Probability of damage is small. Uses equipment that is difficult to damage. Little or no care required for equipment.	5
2	Some care required to recognize trouble and shut down equipment to prevent or minimize danger. Uses equipment that is subject to damage.	11
3	Moderate care required to prevent damage to power-driven equipment.	18
4	Sustained high degree of care required to control rapidly changing conditions and prevent damage to expensive equipment.	25

side consultants to install the system and conduct ongoing audits. Then, too, the firm must train and support a large internal staff to administer the plan.

It is claimed that the details and weightings of the point-factor method are difficult to explain to employees. Thus, the staff in charge of administering the plan must educate workers about the nature of the job evaluation program. In one large firm, the job evaluation supervisor visits each plant at the request of the union or of management and conducts discussion sessions with the employees wherein the evaluation method is fully explained. Thus, a great deal of time and effort are required to implement the method, resulting in substantial costs.

Implementing the Job Evaluation Method

Many trade and professional associations have developed job evaluation plans to meet the needs of their own members, as we saw earlier in this chapter. However, most job evaluation experts recommend that a company not adopt in its entirety the method currently used by another firm. Any plan established and installed by another company or association must be modified to meet the individual needs of the firm involved. For example, the values that are significant to a high-tech computer manufacturer may not be major factors for a low-tech manufacturing firm. Some companies have installed the ranking, job classi-

fication, and factor-comparison methods but have discarded them in favor of the point-factor method, especially when the method is used as the basis for compensating rank-and-file workers. In other companies, two methods of job evaluation may be used concurrently, with each method keyed to different job families. Then, too, today's computer software packages help users to compare the results of various job evaluation methods against each other and thus aid in deciding which method, or combination of methods, is most appropriate for the company.

Regardless of the method or methods used to evaluate jobs, the firm should discuss with its workers the basis for its job evaluation method. As a result, the workers can see they are being treated equitably. The method or methods used in evaluating office jobs should be clearly set forth in employee handbooks. Also, special programs to explain the job evaluation plans should be provided for supervisors and workers. In addition, a formal procedure should be established in which the results of any job evaluation plan may be appealed. For example, in one large manufacturing company, the office supervisor may appeal a job evaluation to the person in charge of salary administration. The evaluation, based on additional data or interpretation supplied by the supervisor, is then reviewed by the salary administration officer who has the final authority to make any needed changes.

SUMMARY

1. The information gathered in the analysis of office jobs is assembled into job descriptions and job specifications. The descriptions and specifications accurately identify each job and its tasks and spell out the requirements the job makes upon the worker for successful performance.

2. Job information may be obtained by several methods—questionnaire, interview, and ob-

servation, or a combined approach. The use of computers greatly aids in organizing and analyzing job data quickly and in statistically validating the job information.

3. Job descriptions and job specifications provide the foundation upon which a company may establish a job evaluation program with the ultimate goal of designing an equitable wage and salary administration plan.

c
o
n
t
.

4. In developing an equitable wage and salary administration plan, the value of each office job in relation to all other jobs must be determined by job evaluation. The person in charge of evaluating the jobs must determine which of the basic methods—ranking, job classification, factor-comparison, or point-factor—should be used. A company must also decide whether to design its own evaluation plan or turn to outside professional associations or consultants for help in studying and evaluating jobs and implementing the selected method.

FOR YOUR REVIEW

1. How is the information obtained from a program of job analysis used in the office?

2. What are the advantages and disadvantages of using the questionnaire method of gathering job information?

3. Contrast the interview method and the observation method of gathering job information by examining the advantages and disadvantages of each method.

4. Briefly describe one of the techniques that makes use of all three job analysis methods—questionnaire, interview, and observation.

5. For what reasons should office workers have access to their job descriptions?

6. Distinguish between a *job* specification and an *employee* specification.

7. Explain the procedure to be followed in using the ranking method to evaluate jobs.

8. In what way is the job classification method an outgrowth of the ranking method?

9. Why is the selection of benchmark jobs essential when using the factor-comparison method?

10. What are the main advantages in using the point-factor method of job evaluation?

FOR YOUR DISCUSSION

1. Over the past decade in many offices, the role of secretary has changed as the result of information technology. In fact, some feel that the job title, secretary, is fading from the scene. In what ways do you find the content of the secretary's job changing?

2. Due to a takeover, the Devault Company is downsizing and reducing its workforce by 30 percent. For you, the supervisor of office services, this means that 15 of your people will be laid off. How can the job descriptions of these workers help you and them as you start counseling them about job opportunities in the community?

c
o
n
t

3. Angel Piazza, a technical word processing operator, feels that her job should be ranked higher than it is under her company's ranking method. How would you, as Piazza's supervisor, justify to her your ranking of the job she holds?

4. Darren Howe, a certified medical assistant, supervises five office workers and two laboratory technicians for Marx Medical Services. To be assured that the salaries being paid are equitable, Howe has decided to undertake an evaluation of the jobs. Which job evaluation method do you recommend he implement? Why?

5. Since most office employees have a high school education and, in many instances, some college education, they are qualified to write a satisfactory description of their duties. Discuss the relevance of this statement.

6. When interviewing Rickey Wong, supervisor of accounts payable, to determine the content of his job, you find that he does not remember many of the things that he does daily, weekly, and monthly. What steps should you take to complete your analysis of Wong's job?

7. Indicate what method or combination of methods you would use to obtain information about each of the following jobs in order to prepare job descriptions:

   a. Data-entry operator who spends seven hours each day keyboarding data from copies of shipping orders.

   b. Receptionist and part-time relief in the mailing center.

   c. Supervisor in the records management department.

   d. Payroll clerk who collects and audits time sheets, calculates gross earnings and withholdings, and distributes paychecks.

   e. Chief editor for a large magazine publisher.

8. Jeremy Steele is the administrative office manager of Ban-Ron, a newly formed corporation. The workforce must be recruited and production started within four weeks. Since no job descriptions exist, Steele has decided to use "canned" job descriptions, such as those found in the *Dictionary of Occupational Titles*. What is your reaction to Steele's approach?

CASES FOR CRITICAL THINKING

Case 9–1 Evaluating a Job Description

As an experiment, you, administrative services manager, want to see how well your workers can prepare their own job descriptions. Debra Rosales, your company's receptionist, has given you the following version of her job. What is wrong with her job description? Try your hand at rewriting the job description to reflect the improvements you recommend.

c
o
n
t

Job Description

Debra Rosales   May 23, 19—

Job: Receptionist 1

General duties:

1. Under the direction of Bob Tice, the Asst. Mgr. of H/R, I place, receive, and route phone calls—using the EKS.

2. Also, I do the following:

   • Provide general information to callers or visitors.
   • Greet and direct visitors.
   • Provide telephone directory assistance.
   • Take telephone messages.

3. Sometimes I help out by sorting and opening incoming mail but I don't deliver it.

4. And, often I have to use the FAX machine and the copier. I am being trained to learn electronic mail on the PC and will start doing this work in a few weeks.

5. I do whatever other work Tice assigns me.

Qualifications:

1. I must communicate clearly and accurately.

2. I need to know our company's mailing and shipping procedures.

3. I must use the EKS system to receive and transfer calls.

4. I try to be patient and courteous when working with people.

5. I had to have a high school diploma to get this job.

Case 9–2 Studying the Job Descriptions of Coworkers

In the computer center of Lakeland, Inc., the supervisor of computer operations, Teresa Savage, has become aware of a serious morale problem. She believes that much of the problem stems from her workers who are more concerned with their own individual jobs than the overall well-being of the company. For example, this past week she has sensed a conflict among her data-entry operators who appear to be working in isolation. They try to meet their own individual goals only and are completely unconcerned about the direction in which the firm plans to head. These are the same workers who appear very insensitive to the priorities that were established by the systems analysts and programmers.

Savage believes her people must learn to pull together as a team and become more aware of the firm's perspectives about its future. While she was exploring her concerns with her boss, Bruce York, he broke in to say:

I see where you are coming from, Teresa. What we've got to do is convince these people that they're partners in our company. I've got an idea. Let's give each of your people a copy of all the job descriptions for everyone working in the center—the analysts, programmers, computer operators, data-entry operators, and, yes, my job description and yours. Ask them to study all the job descriptions for the next several days and then let's set up a meeting with them. At that meeting here is what I would like us to do. . . .

c o n t

Prepare a list of the direct questions you would ask your workers to show how their study of the job descriptions can lead to a *team* orientation. What outcomes do you expect the meeting to provide that will enable you to start cultivating a climate in which the workers feel like partners?

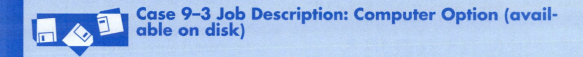

Case 9–3 Job Description: Computer Option (available on disk)

10

ADMINISTERING OFFICE SALARIES

GOALS FOR THIS CHAPTER

After completing this chapter, you should be able to:

1. List the objectives of office salary administration.
2. Describe those factors to be considered when determining office salaries.
3. Summarize the steps taken in setting a price for office jobs.
4. Identify the major features of pay for performance and pay for skill plans.
5. Describe the different kinds of variable pay plans.

The responsibility for administering office salaries depends upon the size and structure of the organization. In most companies, regardless of size, the cost of salaries represents a significant part of the total operating expenses; thus, in companies of all sizes, we often find the responsibility for salary administration assigned to a top-level officer, such as the treasurer, or one or more key executives in the areas of finance and control.

In small and many medium-size firms, the administrative office manager, aided by a committee of other managers and key executives, may assist in establishing the objectives and policies governing the salary program. Line managers and first-line supervisors, although not part of the formal salary administration committee, are often asked to recommend ways of improving the salary program. These managers and supervisors provide most of the guidance and direction received by office employees; therefore, they must thoroughly understand the program so that they can communicate it to their workers.

In large companies, the human resources department, with its responsibility for employee relations, sometimes exercises authority over the company-wide salary program. This department, often staffed with a full-time salary administrator, may be responsible for collecting pertinent salary information, recommending policies and procedures, and answering all questions relating to salary administration. In the human resources field in 1992–93, the median annual salary paid corporate compensation and benefits directors was $67,200; compensation section heads, $51,500; assistant compensation supervisors, $41,705; and compensation specialists, $40,214.[1]

To realize full benefit from the office salary program, those responsible for its administration

---

[1]"For Your Information," *Personnel Journal* (February, 1993), p. 18.

must communicate to all employees the nature and goals of the program. No matter how technically sound, equitable, and competently administered, the program will be effective only if employees perceive it as such. Employee handbooks, with a section devoted to compensation, are perhaps the most common medium for communicating the objectives of the salary administration program. Other communication media that may be used by the salary administrator are described in Chapter 5.

OBJECTIVES OF OFFICE SALARY ADMINISTRATION

Those responsible for any phase of office salary administration must understand its broad objectives. As a rule, you will find that an effective office salary administration program attempts to meet the following objectives:

1. *To attract workers* who will be paid equitable salaries.
2. *To retain workers* by paying them fairly. Employees become dissatisfied and lose confidence in the salary program when they feel that inequities exist. Therefore, the differences in workers' salaries should be supported by objective employee performance appraisals.
3. *To motivate and reward high-level performance,* determined as objectively as possible by periodic employee appraisal. As pointed out in Chapter 8, periodic appraisal helps employees learn how well they are performing and ensures communication between office supervisors and their workers. Employees thus become aware that their extra efforts and achievements will be recognized and rewarded by means of extra compensation.
4. *To maintain a competitive position* with other companies in the same geographic area. At the same time, the company must be able to control its labor costs in order to realize gains in productivity.

To achieve these objectives and to maintain a sound salary program, a company should build its program upon a foundation of job analysis. The importance of job analysis and one of its ele-

ments—job evaluation—is indicated in the establishment of *levels* or *grades* for office positions. For each grade or group of jobs, there must be a maximum and a minimum *salary range,* with provision for salary increases based upon successful job performance. In order to meet future changes in job content and the reassignment of responsibilities, the office salary administrator must recognize that jobs should be periodically reviewed and analyzed in relation to other jobs within and outside the organization.

In designing its office salary program, the company may consider a *variable pay plan,* such as an *incentive system,* to reward workers for increased production and outstanding work. Before installing the incentive system, the work must be measured and standards set, as explained in a later chapter. In order to set standards, the work must be carefully studied and all unnecessary motions and wasted time must be eliminated. Finally, an important aspect of the total compensation package for office employees relates to *employee benefits*—the indirect compensation received by workers. When you read the following chapter, you will see that, on the average, employee benefits amount to about 37 cents of every payroll dollar.

In considering the following factors that determine office salaries, firms must recognize their employees' needs and determine to what extent these needs are being satisfied so that employees are motivated to perform efficiently.

FACTORS TO CONSIDER IN DETERMINING OFFICE SALARIES

Once the office jobs have been evaluated, the next step is to answer the question, "How much should each office worker be paid?" Before we can answer this question, however, we must examine several factors.

Company Philosophy Toward Office Salary Administration

Influenced by the quality of office workers they hope to attract and retain, companies may adopt a policy of paying salaries that are equal to, greater than, or less than the average salaries paid by other firms in the community. Some companies build their salary program around the competition in their area for employees who perform similar types of work. Other companies prefer to relate their salary levels more closely to those of similar firms within the same industry. Firms that provide a wide program of employee benefits may decide to pay a smaller base salary than that paid by other firms not offering such a broad array of benefits.

Some companies have adopted a philosophy toward salary administration that is in keeping with the proposals of behaviorists such as Maslow, McGregor, and Herzberg, whose motivation theories were described earlier. You will recall that according to Maslow and McGregor, workers are not motivated by their lower-order needs, which money can effectively satisfy, because in today's world these needs are largely met. Therefore, managers turn their attention to the higher-order needs and attempt to provide recognition, status, praise, and opportunities for self-actualization. To meet these higher-order needs, you saw that job enrichment and employee participation have been offered as motivational techniques.

Remember Herzberg's two factors—*motivator* and *hygienic*—that strongly influence workers? Herzberg showed that only the *satisfying* factors are able to improve performance by providing more of what he calls *motivators:* achievement, recognition, advancement, growth, responsibility, and the work itself. Company policies, working conditions, interpersonal relationships, quality of supervision, and pay are *hygienic* or *maintenance* factors. Increasing the hygienic factors will not raise performance, but a decrease in the availability of these factors will lower performance. From his research, Herzberg concluded that money is not a motivator. Managers were thus encouraged to adopt job enrichment rather than money as a means of raising productivity and job satisfaction. Thus, workers would benefit by a greater fulfillment of their higher-order needs.

As we know, the debate still goes on as to what extent money actually motivates. Some critics say that most employees always feel that their lower-order needs are never fully satisfied. Also, many people argue that with increases in the cost of living, as well as changes in lifestyles, the amount of money needed to satisfy a person's basic needs has increased greatly. Thus, these critics conclude that not only were the lower-order needs not met in the past, but also they are not being met now; and the amount of money necessary to do so is steadily increasing.

For years, studies and surveys have tried to support or deny the role of salaries in motivating employees. However, today, as in the past, supervisors and managers assume that money is what most people work for. Money is still viewed as the most important motivator that managers and supervisors have at their disposal. They see dollars as a motivating tool that is tangible, objective, and controllable.

Ability to Pay

A basic factor to consider in determining salaries for office workers is that the salaries cannot exceed the firm's ability to pay and still earn a profit. Few companies can afford to keep their employees' paychecks abreast of the inflation rate. Many workers realize that, although their income may be more than twice as many dollars as a decade ago, their *buying power* (real earnings after taxes and inflation) is lower. This factor, ability to pay, is one of several that Peter Pesce of Arthur Andersen & Company cites in the *Dialog from the Workplace,* where he discusses the problems facing him in determining salaries for exempt and nonexempt office employees. (*Exempt* employees are exempt from some, or all, of the Fair Labor Standards Act requirements such as minimum wages, equal pay, and overtime pay. *Nonexempt* employees are paid overtime for all hours worked beyond 40 in a workweek.)

Expectations of Office Employees

Vroom's expectancy theory, presented in Chapter 7, describes the conditions that must be met in order to use pay as a motivator. The key elements of this theory are (1) *effort,* (2) *performance,* and (3) *rewards.* In the case of an office worker, the

DIALOG FROM THE WORKPLACE

PETER PESCE

*Managing Director, Human
Resources Worldwide
Arthur Andersen & Co, SC
Chicago, Illinois*

Peter Pesce, a native Chicagoan, graduated from DePaul University in 1970. Shortly thereafter, he joined the accounting and audit staff of Arthur Andersen & Co. Chicago office. A few years later he transferred to the human resources and administration area, and in 1976 was promoted to manager. In 1989, he was appointed to his present position, managing director, human resources worldwide.

Pete is also a member or consultant of several organizations, including the American Council of International Personnel, Society for Human Resources Management, and Conference Board.

QUESTION: What are the major problems you have encountered in determining the salaries for exempt and nonexempt personnel? How have you solved these problems?

RESPONSE: Some of the problems in salary determination center around the following characteristics of a sound pay program:

- Internal equality
- External competitiveness
- Legality
- Ease of understanding by both employees and managers
- Affordability to the employer
- Efficiency in administration
- Appropriateness of the program for the employer

The points noted above, while not necessarily mutually exclusive, do conflict in some areas. An objective of pay programs is to find the correct balance in order to provide a pay plan that is fair and equitable to the employees while manageable and cost effective for the employer. We attempt to balance these needs by establishing sound market-based pay plans for each group.

For exempt and nonexempt administrative personnel, we use a job evaluation program that aligns positions in one of several salary bands based on a point-factor evaluation system. A number of compensable factors are identified for each job and are weighted to arrive at relative values. The results are reviewed for internal equality and are compared to benchmark positions in the marketplace to establish external competitiveness. Salary bands are used as part of a career-development plan, as well as one of the features in the administration of our merit pay program.

The pay plans are supported by market surveys for exempt and nonexempt administrative personnel in each of our locations, and professional personnel on a national basis. The results of these surveys are used to help ensure the proper application of pay policies after consideration of the compensation objectives appropriate in each market. Guidance is provided from central sources; however, as noted, each business unit develops application compensation philosophies and applies them locally in accordance with individual market conditions.

In summary, we manage the sometimes conflicting objectives of a compensation program by developing plans appropriate for each employee group, obtaining market survey data for each of these groups, and encouraging the application of local initiatives as both appropriate and necessary.

Illustration 10–1 Office employees expect salaries to keep up with the cost of living so they can financially support their dependents and improve their standard of living.

theory might work like this: The office worker decides to expend *effort,* which is expected to result in *performance.* At this performance level, the worker's expectations result in *rewards* in the form of a salary, bonus, pay increase, recognition, and coworkers' friendship.

Like all other employees in the firm, we bring to our jobs our expectations and decisions on how much effort we shall expend to fulfill those expectations. To be reasonably satisfied with our work and motivated to perform, we need a work climate where we can further develop our philosophy of life within which our jobs "make sense." We need a sense of purpose, the will to achieve, and the feeling of being wanted and accepted. As office workers, we expect to get satisfaction from meeting our job challenges successfully and improving our job performance. In turn, we expect our improved performance to result in desired rewards such as equitable salaries, better employee benefits, and improved working conditions.

We expect our salaries to provide us with enough money to support ourselves and any dependents and to be able to continue improving our standard of living. We realize that if our salaries do not increase at least as fast as the cost of living, our standard of living declines. Also, we expect our salaries and pay increases to give us financial security not only during our working careers but also later when we retire.

As office employees, we expect our pay to be fair and reasonable in comparison with that of other workers in the firm. We feel we should make "good" money when we work hard and have the opportunity to earn extra money when we work harder. We want a fair day's pay for a fair day's work; but, in turn, we expect that our fair day's work will be accurately measured. Further, we desire some voice in determining our salaries or at least have an avenue of appeal in the event we are dissatisfied with our earnings.

For work well done, we expect recognition at

the time of employee appraisal when the company takes note of our quality and quantity of work. In companies that use incentive systems, we want assurance that additional rewards will be given for an exceptional amount of top-notch work produced. Finally, we expect promotion from within the business firm not on the basis of seniority alone, but also based on merit and our knowledge and understanding of the requirements of the new position.

Office Salaries Paid by Other Companies

In establishing a salary structure for nonexempt office personnel, the most significant factor is the *local going rate*. In many companies, the salary structures for nonexempt office employees are set after serious consideration of the local community rates. To obtain data on office salaries paid for comparable jobs in similar industries within the community or in surrounding areas, the company may use one or more salary surveys.

The Salary Survey

A **salary survey** is a statistical picture of the salaries for certain jobs in a particular geographic area or for a certain industry at a given time. The survey shows only what the responding firms pay their jobholders; the survey does not state or recommend what AOMs must pay comparable jobholders in their organizations.

As a planning tool, salary surveys enable a company to learn how its salaries for certain jobs compare with those in the labor market. Survey results also aid the company in determining how competitive its starting salaries are in relation to those elsewhere. Often, the need for across-the-board salary adjustment becomes apparent when the survey findings are studied. Salary surveys are also helpful in preparing for wage negotiations with union representatives.

Although salary surveys are a useful tool in planning and adjusting salaries, we should be cautious when using the surveys for the following reasons:

1. The job descriptions in the survey may not match the responsibilities, working conditions,

and employee qualifications for the jobs in the company using the survey results. Therefore, we should not use salary survey data as the *sole* basis for relating the pay of one surveyed job to another job in the organization.

2. The survey may be too broad in scope and thus may not sample the relevant labor market that consists of all the local companies competing for the same labor supply. For example, national surveys may not give an accurate picture of local labor markets.

3. Salary survey data, especially for high-tech positions, become obsolete very quickly.

4. The survey data may not reflect the *total* compensation received by workers if the cost of employee benefits, approaching 40 percent of total compensation costs in some companies, is not included. For example, a company with a 401(k) retirement savings plan may actually be paying an AOM $60,000 a year, although the reported salary range is $48,000 to $52,000 and the actual salary is $50,500.[2] Thus, the salary survey should provide complete information about those benefits that contribute to the total compensation package.

5. Human error exists in salary surveys as in any human endeavor, for it is people who complete the survey questionnaires, who enter the data into the computer, and who make mistakes in interpreting the data. Imagine the effect of a keyboarding error that stated the average weekly salary for a senior general clerk as $382 instead of the correct amount, $328!

Statistical Measures Used in Surveys

To aid the salary administrator in comparing the firm's salaries with those provided by the survey, statistical measures such as those described below are often used. For the purpose of our discussion here, we shall refer to Figures 10–1 and

---

[2]Retirement savings plans that defer part of an employee's income until a later date, with matching company contributions, are discussed in Chapter 11. Such plans, which substantially increase the worker's total compensation, provide that the deferred salaries and earnings thereon are not taxed until the workers begin to withdraw the amounts.

Figure 10–1
Survey Data
for Medical
Assistant

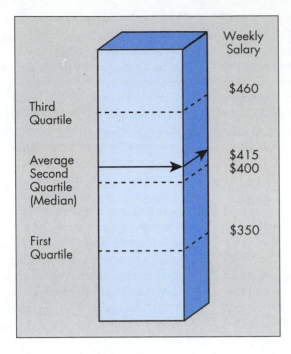

10–2, which show hypothetical survey data for the office job, medical assistant.

Average. The **average** weekly salary (the *arithmetic mean*), $415, is obtained by multiplying the number of employees reported for each salary rate by the rate. These results are totaled and then divided by the number of employees whose salaries are reported for the job.

Quartile. The **quartile** is a measure of position that divides an array, such as the listing of all the salaries paid medical assistants, into four equal parts. In contrast to averages, quartiles are not affected by the high frequency of salaries at either the high or the low end of a distribution. In Figure 10–1, the **first quartile**, $350, represents the actual weekly salary paid the employee whose salary is more than one-fourth and less than three-fourths of all employees reported for the job.

Median. The **median,** or *second quartile,* $400, is the actual weekly salary of the middle employee in the distribution where half of the employees earn more and the other half earn less. The median is the most representative figure in a survey and, like any quartile measure, is not influenced by extreme highs and lows.

Effective Salary Range. The **third quartile,** $460, is the actual weekly salary paid the employee whose salary is more than three-fourths of all the employees reported for the job. The salaries at the first and third quartiles, $350 and $460, are the limits of the middle 50 percent of the employees reported, as shown in Figure 10–2. Some refer to the spread between these salaries as the **effective salary range** for the job because the salaries at the extremes are disregarded.

Continuing with our example, a newly hired employee, with minimum or no related experience, might start at the low or minimum weekly salary of $350. As the worker becomes more proficient on the job, appropriate pay increases should be provided. If the new employee's caliber of performance is average, the beginning pay rate might be $405, which is the midpoint or the midvalue of the range $350 to $460. ($460 – $350 = $110; $110/2 = $55; $350 + 55 = $405.)

Figure 10–2
Effective
Salary Range
for Medical
Assistant

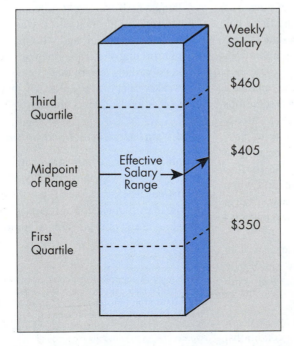

If the performance is above average, the worker should be paid in the upper half of the pay range, $400 to $460, but in no case more than the maximum, $460.

Obtaining Salary Survey Data

The AOM has available the following sources of salary data:

1. Professionally prepared surveys.
2. Consultants.
3. Conducting one's own survey.

A brief description of each of these sources follows.

Professionally Prepared Surveys. Comparative salary data on many benchmark, or key, office positions may be found in the surveys that are conducted regularly by professional organizations, trade associations, and the government. Examples include the surveys conducted by the Bureau of Labor Statistics, which undertakes an annual *National Survey of Professional, Administrative, Technical, and Clerical Pay* in major cities across the country; American Management Association; American Payroll Association; Federal Reserve System; Dartnell; and temporary personnel services such as TempForce, Robert Half, and Accountemps. Many journals, such as *Personnel Journal, Forbes, Training, Fortune, U.S. News & World Report, Business Week, Nation's Business,* and *Monthly Labor Review,* report compensation-related matters. AOMs may also receive helpful information from their local employer associations, state and local government agencies, banks, and consulting firms.

Generally, the surveys described above are professionally conducted and some are free or relatively inexpensive. On the other hand, some surveys may cost $400 or more for nonparticipants versus $200 for those participating in the survey. Usually, large groups participate in such surveys, and thus statistically sound sample sizes are obtained so that valid estimates of salaries may be made for office personnel. On the other hand, when relating the results of a professional survey to the job titles and descriptions found within one's own firm, difficulty may be experienced in interpreting the survey data and tailoring the data to meet the requirements of the firm. Further, the company using the survey has not been able to select the benchmark jobs, to choose the questions asked, to select the time the survey is conducted, or to choose the companies being surveyed.

Consultants. Rather than use professional wage and salary surveys or conduct its own survey, the company may employ the services of a consultant who will professionally conduct, analyze, and interpret the survey. The OM, working with the consultant, is able to help select the benchmark jobs to survey, to choose the questions to ask and the companies to survey, to select the effective date of the salary data, and to determine the time for conducting the survey. The company employing the consultant benefits from the experience gained by the consultant in working with other companies who have undertaken similar surveys. The major disadvantage of using a consultant is the cost of the service, which may amount to several hundred dollars a day. Therefore, the cost of using an outside consultant must be weighed against the benefits to be realized from this source of salary information.

Conducting One's Own Survey. The greatest advantage realized by the firm that conducts its own survey is that the firm obtains salary data stated in terms of its own compensation program. The individual or committee in charge of preparing the survey questionnaire is able to select the benchmark jobs, specify the questions to ask, set the effective date of the data and the time for conducting the survey, and choose the companies to survey. The person in charge of conducting the survey must make sure that information is asked about a satisfactory number of benchmark jobs. A standard job title should be listed on the survey form for each benchmark job. Since the terminology of job content and the level of responsibility may differ from company to company being surveyed, a description of each job should accompany the questionnaire so that all respondents are provided comparable data about each job.

The disadvantages of undertaking one's own survey include the cost of the time-consuming activity itself and the need for competent, experienced persons to conduct the survey. Often it may be difficult to obtain a random sample or statistically sound sample size since companies may fail to respond to the survey or may supply inaccurate or incomplete information. Thus, follow-up time must be spent in contacting each participant to verify the questionnaire contents before computing, summarizing, and interpreting the data, which add considerably to the cost of the survey.

Government Regulations

The most important federal statute for the office salary administrator is the **Fair Labor Standards Act (FLSA),** which is also known as the federal wage and hour law. In addition to this federal law, other federal regulations and state laws must be taken into consideration by the administrative office manager when determining office salaries.

Fair Labor Standards Act of 1938, as Amended

Generally, an office occupation is covered by the FLSA if the firm and the jobholder (1) deal with the movement of goods in interstate commerce involving the interstate transmission of documents or (2) require the use of interstate facilities. For example, employees in the home office of an insurance company are covered if the firm operates in more than one state or if the firm's activities involve regular use of mailing services or other means of interstate commerce. Bank employees are generally covered by the law because bank activities are essential to interstate commerce. Office employees in a real estate business are covered, too, if they regularly prepare documents that are sent out of state or if they use channels of interstate commerce.

Employees covered under the FLSA must be paid a specified minimum wage, equal pay for equal work, and an overtime premium for all hours worked beyond a certain number. The FLSA also places restrictions upon the employment of children, as discussed below.

Minimum Wages. Unless specifically exempted by the FLSA, all employees must be paid at least the minimum wage, whether they are paid a salary by the hour, by piecework, or by any other method. Under certain conditions, wages lower than the minimum may be paid some employees. For example, full-time students may be employed by retail or service establishments and farms at 85 percent of the minimum wage.[3]

Equal Pay for Equal Work. The **Equal Pay Act of 1963** prohibits employers from setting different wages based solely on the sex of workers who are doing equal work. Men and women working in the same establishment under similar working conditions must receive the same pay if their jobs require equal skill, equal effort, and equal responsibility. "Equal" in this sense does not mean "identical." However, jobs to be compared under the Equal Pay Act must involve the same primary job function and must require substantially equal skill, effort, and responsibility.

Wage differences between sexes are allowed when the differences are based on a seniority system, a merit system, a payment plan that measures earnings by quantity or quality of production, or any factor other than sex. If there is an unlawful pay differential between men and women, the employer is required to raise the lower rate to equal the higher rate.

What about the salaries paid men and women who are performing jobs not necessarily "equal," but involving "comparable worth"? It has long been held that traditional female jobs (such as clerk typist) are automatically lower paying than traditional male jobs (such as tree trimmer) of comparable worth. Is this as discriminatory as paying a man and a woman different rates for the same job? Unions and women's groups say "yes" and look upon the concept of comparable worth as a way to close the wage gap that has historically existed between "male" jobs and "female" jobs.

---

[3]For current minimum wage rates, exemption categories, and so on of the FLSA and other legislation affecting office salaries, see Bernard J. Bieg and B. Lewis Keeling, *Payroll Accounting* (Cincinnati: South-Western Publishing Co., current annual edition), or any payroll tax service.

Illustration 10–2 A female mechanic must be paid the same as a male mechanic, according to the Equal Pay Act of 1963.

Under the concept of *equal pay for comparable worth,* the jobs need not meet any criteria of equality or similarity. Instead, the jobs are compensated according to their intrinsic value to the employer, as determined by one or more of the job evaluation methods described in the previous chapter.

Some states and local governments have adopted comparable-worth policies for their employees in the public sector. If, in the public sector, pay for comparable worth were to become an accepted means of narrowing the gap between wages paid males and females, no doubt private employers would be affected also.

Overtime Hours and Overtime Pay. The FLSA states that overtime, or premium, pay is required for all hours worked in excess of 40 in a workweek. The overtime pay required is one and one-half times the employee's regular pay rate. The law does not require extra pay for Saturday, Sun-day, or holiday work, nor does the law require vacation pay, holiday pay, or severance pay. Such types of pay and working conditions may be agreed upon in union contracts, however. Under the FLSA, employers are not required to give rest periods to their employees. If, however, rest periods are given, either voluntarily by the employer or in keeping with the terms of a union contract or a state regulation, the rest periods must be counted as part of the hours worked if they last 20 minutes or less.

Child-Labor Restrictions. The FLSA stipulates that children below certain ages may not be employed in interstate activities. Thus, a business is prohibited from shipping its goods between states if unlawful child labor was used in manufacturing the goods. Generally, the regulations restrict the employment of children under 18 years of age.

Exempt Employees. Certain groups of employees, such as administrators, professionals, and executives, are *fully exempt* from the minimum wage and overtime pay requirements of the FLSA. As an example, let's examine the exempt status of executives.

To be exempted from the FLSA requirements, executives must possess discretionary power (ability to use individual judgment in freely making decisions) and exercise managerial functions. Their primary duty must be to manage the enterprise or at least one of its departments or subdivisions. Generally, *primary duty* is defined to mean that executives must spend the major part or over 50 percent of their time in managerial duties. However, employees who spend less than 50 percent of their time in managerial duties may be classified as exempt if (1) they customarily and regularly direct the work of two or more other employees; (2) they can hire or fire employees or make suggestions and recommendations that are given weight in deciding upon hiring, firing, or promoting; or (3) they customarily and regularly exercise discretionary powers.

Other Federal Regulations

Other federal legislation that affects the salaries and wages paid and the hours worked by employees is summarized in Table 10–1.

Table 10–1
Other Federal
Regulations
Affecting
Salaries and
Wages and
Hours Worked

Federal Law	Employer Coverage	Provisions for Employees' Wages and Hours
Davis-Bacon Act of 1931	Contractors and subcontractors on federal government contracts of more than $2,000 for constructing, altering, or repairing public buildings	
Walsh-Healey Public Contracts Act of 1936	Those who manufacture or furnish materials, supplies, equipment for agencies of the United States in an amount exceeding $10,000	Workers' minimum wages and overtime compensation are determined by the Secretary of Labor
McNamara-O'Hara Service Contract Act of 1965	Those who furnish services (such as transportation of mail by railroad, airlines, and ocean vessels) in the United States or District of Columbia in excess of $2,500	

State Regulations

In most states, minimum wage rates have been established for employees in specific industries. Where both the federal and state regulations cover the same employees, the higher of the two rates prevails. State regulations not only set minimum wages but also contain provisions affecting pay for *call-in time* (compensation-guaranteed workers who report for work and find there is insufficient work for them to do), rest and meal periods, absences, meals and lodging, and tips.

Collective Bargaining Agreements

When office employees are represented by a union, the salary administrator must take into consideration the collective bargaining agreement. **Collective bargaining** is a negotiation process between an employer and labor union representatives on work-related issues such as wages, hours of work, and working conditions. Collective bargaining, which was made an instrument of national policy by passage of the National Labor Relations Act of 1935, includes three duties:

1. The duty of both the employer and the employees' representative to sit down at the same table and work to achieve a mutually acceptable labor contract. The **labor contract** is a private agreement entered into by the employer and the employees for the purpose of regulating certain work-related conditions.
2. The duty of both sides to work sincerely and honestly toward a labor agreement—to bargain in good faith.
3. The duty to limit the bargaining to wages, hours, and other terms and conditions of employment. Over the years, however, the items subject to bargaining have dramatically expanded to include issues such as employee benefits, grievance procedures, no-strike clauses, discipline, seniority, and union security.

Thus, we see that the collective bargaining agreement is a policy guide with provisions that the salary administrator must thoroughly understand not only when determining salaries but also when implementing procedures that affect employee earnings and working conditions. Some of the more important provisions of collective bargaining agreements include the following:

1. Of major importance at the bargaining table is the provision for salary increases during the life of the labor contract. Common in almost all contracts is a **cost-of-living adjustment (COLA) clause,** which is designed to keep the employees' salaries more or less in step with inflation. Such clauses usually provide for salary increases that escalate, or rise, with increases in the cost of living, as measured by an index such as the Consumer Price Index for Urban Wage Earners and Clerical Workers (CPI-W). Thus, we might find that, as a result of a 4.5 percent increase in the CPI-W for the year, the union contract provides a COLA increase of 4.2 percent for the year.

2. The provisions of the collective bargaining agreement are binding on both management and labor for a mutually acceptable period of time and are enforceable through mediation and arbitration, or finally, through state and federal courts. In **mediation,** an impartial third party tries to bring both sides to a point of common agreement. In **arbitration,** labor and management agree to submit the issue in dispute to an individual arbitrator or a board of arbitration that renders a decision binding upon both parties.

3. The National Labor Relations Board is the agency, created by law, that hears testimony, renders decisions, determines the collective bargaining unit or agency, and prosecutes unfair labor practices.

4. Union shop agreements must be in accordance with prevailing state laws and are void where prohibited by state laws. A **union shop agreement** requires that, after workers have been hired, they must join the union or make dues payment within a specified period of time or be fired. (Twenty states have **right-to-work laws,** which ban contracts that make union membership or the payment of fees a condition of employment.)

5. Union dues **check-off** (deducting union dues from paychecks by the employer and remitting collections to the union) requires the written consent of the employee.

6. Individual employees can present grievances directly to their supervisors, but the union representative must be informed and given an opportunity to be present.

7. Supervisors may be unionized, but the employer does not have to recognize or bargain with them since they represent management.

8. Employees may *decertify* (eliminate) the union selected to represent them, but only during the 60- to 90-day period at the end of the contract.

9. Workers who hold religious objections to joining or financially supporting a union cannot be required to do so as a condition of employment. However, such employees can be required, under a collective bargaining provision, to contribute to a nonreligious charity a sum equal to union dues and initiation fees.

PRICING OFFICE JOBS

Having carefully studied and analyzed those factors that influence the determination of office salaries, the AOM is ready to undertake the important task of *pricing* the individual jobs. To illustrate how pay grades and salary ranges are determined and office jobs are priced, we shall use as our example the point-factor method of job evaluation. As you learned in Chapter 9, each factor common to a job is divided into subfactors and degrees, which are assigned values.

Determining Pay Grades and Salary Ranges

The following steps are taken to determine the number of pay grades and salary ranges to establish:

1. *Group the jobs that have the same number of point values.* The number of job groupings is determined by the number of pay grades to be used and how the jobs naturally group themselves according to pay relationships surveyed in the labor market. After the job groupings have been set up, all jobs falling within a particular grouping should have the same basic value.

2. *Establish the pay grades by assigning a constant progression of points to each grade.* The number of pay grades will vary according to the number of jobs in the office and the employee job groupings.
3. *Using the salary survey data, determine the weekly base salary for the benchmark job in each pay grade.* As mentioned earlier, it may be the company's policy to set a weekly base salary that approximates the average salary paid by all firms responding to the survey. Of course, the base salaries must be economically feasible in relation to the anticipated sales revenue.
4. *Establish a pay range for each of the base salaries.* Some firms use the base salary as the midpoint of each range. Here, the theory is that the midpoint represents the "going rate" for each job. Thus, any new employees would be hired at a salary between the minimum and the midpoint of the range. This point would not be exceeded unless the job applicant had unusual qualifications.

Some companies set a flat percentage spread, such as 15 percent, around the midpoint of each range. Other firms may apply a percentage increase that becomes progressively greater, such as 10 percent for the lowest job level up through 40 to 50 percent for the highest level. If the salary ranges have been accurately developed and kept current, the minimum salary at each level should be sufficient to attract new employees. Salary ranges are often set so that the maximums are about 30 to 50 percent above the minimums to provide room for rewarding individual differences in experience and job performance.

Charting the Salary Rates

A *scatter chart,* such as that shown in Figure 10–3, may be used to show the salary rates and salary distribution at a glance. By examining the chart, we can see any discrepancies in the salaries being paid that need to be adjusted in relation to the pay ranges established. Here, briefly stated, are the steps followed in constructing the scatter chart:

1. *Plot each job* on the vertical scale in relation to the current salary being paid each jobholder and on the horizontal scale according to the point value for the job.
2. *Plot the midpoint of the lowest and the highest pay ranges to serve as anchor points for establishing the trend line.*
3. *Draw a straight line through the center of both anchor points.* This line is known as the *basic salary curve* or the *salary trend line.*
4. *Draw two more straight lines to determine the upper and lower limits of each pay range.* These lines are drawn at a fixed percentage distance from the salary trend line. In Figure 10–3, two additional anchor points were established on a perpendicular 15 percent above and 15 percent below the midpoint for the lowest pay range. Similarly, two more anchor points were plotted 15 percent above and 15 percent below the midpoint of the highest pay range. By drawing straight lines through the anchor points above and below the salary trend line, the minimum and maximum salary rates for each pay grade were established.[4]

Adjusting the Salary Rates

After we prepare and study a scatter chart, we often find discrepancies in the amounts currently paid employees. Some workers may be receiving more than, while others are earning less than, the recommended averages. We need to adjust such inequities as soon as practical after the pricing of the jobs has been completed.

Rates of fully qualified workers that fall below the minimum line, such as the person holding Job F in Figure 10–3, are known as **green-circle rates.** These rates should be adjusted upward

[4]Although the anchor-point method is an accepted practice in establishing salary curves, some authorities claim that the method does not produce a perfect curve. From a purely statistical point of view, the claim may be justified because the calculations and plottings established by the method of least squares reflect a somewhat truer curve. For an explanation of the method of least squares, see the accompanying supplementary item, *Practical Experience Assignments* for *Administrative Office Management,* or any basic statistics textbook.

Figure 10–3
Scatter Chart
Showing Relationship Between Weekly
Base Salaries
and Job Evaluation Points

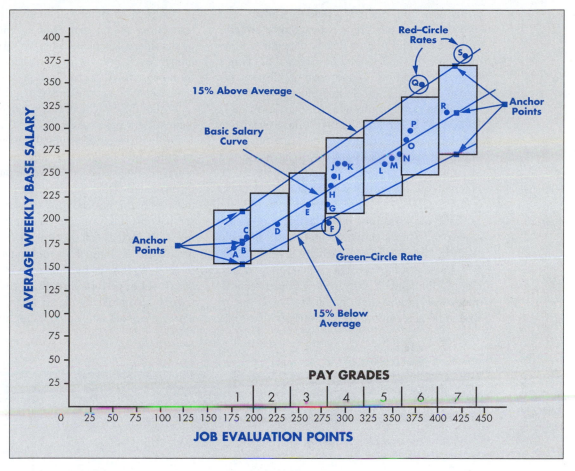

within the pay grade in accordance with the company's salary progression policy. To determine exactly where a worker should fit into the range, each worker should be evaluated individually in relation to the salary progression policy and availability of funds.

Sometimes the plotted salary dots appear above the maximum line, as in the case of jobs Q and S in Figure 10–3. These **red-circle rates** represent overpayments and should be noted for adjustment, such as: (1) training and upgrading the red-circle worker to another job commensurate with the present salary, (2) leaving the employee on the job at the same salary until a promotion opening becomes available, or (3) letting a worker with many years of seniority remain on the job but assign the person additional responsibilities commensurate with the red-circle rate.

Establishing the Salary Structure

In Chapter 2, *broadbanding* is described as a form of organization structure in which jobs are cloistered into wide bands for the purposes of managing employee career growth and administering pay. In some companies, broadbanding is being introduced as an alternative to the traditional pay structure. In this section, we shall examine both structures—the traditional salary progression and the relatively new broadbanding.

Traditional Salary Progression

In a traditional salary progression plan, employees are provided the opportunity to receive periodic salary increases so they may advance from the minimum to the maximum salary level in their pay grade. The system also provides for promotion from one pay grade to another. The spread within a pay grade appears to be an individual company matter that is dependent upon the employees' needs and desires and the firm's financial condition. To motivate employees, the spread of a pay grade should be at least 20 percent. That is, the minimum (or starting) rate is 10 percent below the average salary trend line and the maximum rate is 10 percent above this line. Many companies are likely to have a spread of somewhere between 30 and 40 percent. In Figure 10–3, the spread within each salary range is 30 percent.

Some organizations develop scales of salary grades and ranges similar to that shown in Table 10–2. In this salary scale, each grade consists of a minimum, a midpoint, and a maximum salary. Usually the spread starts at about 30 percent in the lower grades and gradually increases to around 60 percent in the higher grades. The scale

is designed to show that there is progressively less room open for promotion as employees move up the salary schedule. Thus, the salary ranges for higher levels are wider in order to provide room for recognition of meritorious performance on the same job over a considerable length of time.

Within the individual salary ranges, some companies grant base salary increases automatically according to a predetermined time period. Under an **automatic progression plan,** usually found in union contracts, the salary rate is moved in equal interval steps from the minimum of the range to the maximum, based on the employee's length of service only. For example, a company might automatically increase an office worker's salary $50 a month for a limited or unlimited number of months. As long as the worker is attaining a standard level of performance, he or she is entitled to receive automatically the set salary increase over a previously determined period of time.

Table 10–2
Scale of Salary Grades and Ranges

Grade	Minimum	RANGE Midpoint	Maximum
1	$7,150	$8,200	$9,430
2	7,400	8,500	9,800
3	7,650	8,800	10,120
4	7,900	9,100	10,500
5	8,200	9,430	10,850
6	8,500	9,775	11,250
70	118,300	153,600	188,900
71	124,100	161,300	198,500
72	130,300	169,300	208,300
73	136,800	177,800	218,800
74	143,700	186,700	229,700
75	150,900	196,000	241,100
76	158,500	205,800	253,100

As you saw earlier, employees' salaries may be increased periodically as a result of cost-of-living adjustments (COLAs), which link the salary inceases to changes in the Consumer Price Index. In addition to providing base salary increases that keep salaries in line with inflation, companies may provide *pay for performance* or *pay for skill,* as discussed later in this section.

Broadbanding

In companies whose structures have become flatter by eliminating layers of organization as a result of downsizing and reengineering, we find that their traditional rigid salary hierarchies are being altered, too. Broadbanding has enabled the firms to reduce the number of their multiple salary grades with narrowly defined pay ranges into fewer grades with more pay potential. For example, a company that once had 25 or more rungs on its compensation ladder may today place its managers in four or five much wider bands. Thus, a manager might remain in one pay category ranging from, say, $60,000 to $130,000 through an entire career. A survey conducted by Hewitt Associates revealed these main reasons for implementing broadbanding:[5]

1. To facilitate internal transfers/job mobility.
2. To de-emphasize promotions.
3. To support new organizational culture/climate.
4. To foster flatter organizational structure.

Under the usual salary progression plan, employees often are not eligible for promotion until they have passed through each step of the salary grade. This older system, with its narrow salary bands, usually requires companies to promote people to a new salary grade in order to give them a salary increase. With broadbanding, however, workers can move into more challenging and better-paying jobs faster. Thus, companies are provided added mobility and flexibility in transferring workers. When broadbanding is tied in with a skill-based pay system, as explained later, companies can move workers laterally within a band as they receive more pay for newly acquired skills.

Although broadbanding may be labeled "the hottest thing in compensation" in the mid-1990s, the effectiveness of the salary plan is yet to be proved. For example, Johnson & Johnson scrapped its broadbanding experiment after a year when nearly one-third of its affected workers complained. Many workers did not like the lack of a clear path upward, while others were unhappy about being lumped into a job band with people they had surpassed.[6]

Pay for Performance

Under a **pay for performance,** or *merit increase,* plan, the employee's job performance is used as the basis for granting salary increases. According to a Hay Group survey, in 1993, the number one compensation goal of U.S. organizations was to link pay to performance. The study noted this aim was most prevalent in banking, insurance, and utility companies—those organizations that historically have been relatively slow in providing bonus payments.[7]

The pay for performance plan motivates the worker to move from the minimum to the maximum of the pay range based on the employee's performance rather than seniority. Usually a company-wide merit budget is developed each year and divided among the various departments. Individual managers then distribute the monies based on an appraisal of their workers' job performance. Merit increases are judgmental and, as such, must be carefully and objectively determined. Care must be exercised that the merit increases reward merit for improvement in the quality of work and not for some other factor, such as length of service or loyalty to the firm.

Merit increases should also be kept separate from other kinds of raises, such as COLAs, since merit increases lose their significance when lumped together with other considerations. Office

---

[5]"Broadbanding Gains Favor . . . Slowly," *HR Focus* (October, 1992), p. 6.

[6]Fred R. Bleakley, "Many Companies Try Management Fads, Only to See Them Flop," *The Wall Street Journal* (July 6, 1993), p. A1.

[7]"In the Spotlight," *Solutions* (April, 1993), p. 38.

workers must see a definite relationship between their performance and their compensation, or the merit increase becomes forced into a hygienic role, as noted by Herzberg.

The frequency of merit increase reviews varies with the job level. For office workers, the performance reviews are often conducted every six months during the first year of employment and yearly thereafter. In some firms, the review is held on the employee's hiring anniversary date or at a time when all employees are being reviewed. In other firms, the time intervals are varied so the merit increases do not become routine and expected. A complete documentation, including all employee appraisals, should be available to support any merit increase decisions.

Pay for Skill

Under a **skill-based pay system,** compensation is based on the knowledge or skills that the person brings to the job, and salary increases are awarded as the employee acquires additional knowledge and skills. The logic is that workers with a broader knowledge and more skills will be more effective problem-solvers and, in turn, able to make a greater contribution to the company's objectives of improving quality and productivity. Thus, the skill-based pay system runs counter to the traditional job-based system that tends to reward workers for what they are presently doing on the job or for how long they have been doing it.

Skill-based pay systems are growing in popularity as part of the search for better ways of motivating and rewarding workers, especially as companies re-engineer their organizations to respond more rapidly to market changes. In a survey of *Fortune* 1,000 companies, it was found that 51 percent of the respondents used skill-based pay with at least some employees, since in the typical company, less than 20 percent of the employees were covered by the plan.[8] Compared with a similar survey conducted three years ear-

lier, it appears as if skill-based pay has become more popular; however, it still tends to be adopted for only a minority of employees in those companies using it. Plans for paying workers for their skills appear to be well suited to production workers and possibly to administrative and clerical personnel and technical and professional persons such as information systems specialists and engineers. Many of the firms that use skill-based pay plans tend to be large organizations and often the plans are installed in new plants that have a small number of workers in a participative management environment.

Those supporting skill-based pay systems claim that the workers become more competent because they are provided a financial incentive for learning and performing. When employees have many skills, they increase a firm's flexibility because they can cross over into other jobs and fill vacancies when and where they are needed. Further, as the employees acquire more knowledge and skills, they become capable of handling higher-level decision making and problem solving. Thus, an organization can flatten its structure by removing some of the hierarchical layers of middle managers and supervisors. Questioning the potential widespread use of skill-based pay systems, we must consider the huge investment in training that is required and the need for the firm to commit itself to that investment on a continuing basis. For example, a Towers Perrin study of skill-based pay systems found that 75 percent of the respondents reported pay rates that exceeded the market rates and 60 percent said they spent more on training than under their old systems. On the other hand, some reported decreased labor costs as a percentage of goods and services produced and almost three-fourths claimed lower operating costs.[9] Further, some employees may prefer the stability of a traditional job-based compensation plan where they are paid for one job only and are not required to assume additional responsibilities.

---

[8]Edward E. Lawler, III, Gerald E. Ledford, Jr., and Lei Chang, "Who Uses Skill-Based Pay, and Why," *Compensation & Benefits Review* (March–April, 1993), p. 23.

[9]"Skill-Based Pay: A Status Report," *Training* (December, 1992), p. 10.

Illustration 10–3 Companies may decide to reward outstanding employee performance with noncash incentives like airline tickets.

VARIABLE PAY PLANS

Base pay, which we have been discussing up to this point, normally continues to rise higher and higher based on a combination of factors such as merit pay, inflationary pressures, and competitive practice. Thus, the dollars spent for base pay become a fixed cost of doing business.[10] Although base pay is the most common form of compensation, companies are experimenting with *variable* pay plans which will ensure that compensation costs rise and fall to parallel the change in corporate earnings.

Variable pay is any form of direct compensation, not included in the employee's base pay, that varies according to employee or corporate performance. By means of variable pay, companies are better able to provide rewards to teams of involved workers who have the information, knowledge, and power to influence results.[11] Representative of variable pay plans are **incentive systems,** which enable workers to increase their earnings by maintaining or exceeding an established standard of work performance. Some AOMs feel that the reward for increased output and outstanding work should be given in the form of promotions when opportunities arise. For many employees, however, the time of promotion is too far away, especially if they lack some of the necessary qualifications. For these workers, an immediate financial reward, such as a salary incentive payment, is a more effective motivator. Some companies recognize improved employee performance and increased output by offering *noncash incentives* as a way of rewarding and motivating their personnel. Among gifts offered in lieu of cash we find dinner certificates, TVs and VCRs, video cameras, microwave ovens, personal computers, airline tickets, and days off with pay.

Incentive systems may be used in offices where the work has been measured and standards developed. As noted in a later chapter, the measurement of work and the development of standards are not commonly found in the office. It is estimated, however, that two-thirds to three-fourths of all the work done in offices lends itself to measurement. Thus, the AOM should consider the development of standards, if not for the purpose of installing a salary incentive system, at least for more effective quality control and for increasing productivity. Many firms maintain production records that are used when employee performance is evaluated and recommendations for promotions and transfers are made. Thus, these companies achieve partially the effects of an incentive system.

[10]Jay R. Schuster and Patricia K. Zingheim, *The New Pay: Linking Employee and Organizational Practice* (New York: Lexington Books, 1992), pp. 153–155.

[11]Jay R. Schuster and Patricia K. Zingheim, "The New Variable Play: Key Design Issues," *Compensation & Benefits Review* (March–April, 1993), p. 28.

In this closing section, we shall briefly examine several types of incentive plans for office workers—*individual* incentives, such as piecework, and *group* incentives, such as profit sharing, employee stock ownership, and gain-sharing.

Individual Incentives

In an **individual incentive plan,** office workers are paid according to their own production or effort. An example of an individual incentive plan is the **piece-rate** (*piecework*) **system.** Under the piece-rate system, the employee receives a fixed price or wage for each unit produced. For example, an office employee might be paid for each cassette transcribed, the number of data items entered as input to the computer, or the number of keystrokes entered on a keyboard.

The piece-rate system has the advantage of establishing a direct relationship between what a worker produces and what is earned. Underlying the installation of a piece-rate plan is the measurement of the employee's output. The more routine the work and the fewer the number of different kinds of tasks, the easier the job of measuring the output.

A potential problem that may be found in the use of individual incentives is the social pressure that coworkers exert for an individual to reduce output. Since each person is paid for individual performance, competition often develops among people doing the same work. Although a certain level of competition is healthy, it becomes unhealthy when the less productive workers put pressure on the more productive workers to reduce their output. This type of pressure—often subtle in nature—may occur over a period of months or even years. Another disadvantage in the use of the individual incentive plan is that it may not reflect the reality of work. With the exception of certain creative positions, such as systems analyst, designer, editor, and research and development professionals, few people can claim *sole* credit for either the quantity or quality of the product manufactured or the service rendered.

Group Incentives

In a **group incentive plan,** the office worker shares in the achievement of a group of coworkers who are working as a team to produce more than their expected efficiency. Group incentive plans, such as those described below, may cover a small group or an entire department.

Profit-Sharing Plans

Under a **profit-sharing plan,** the payments received by office employees are based on a percentage of the company's profits for the year. Employees can receive cash shares of the profits at regular intervals, or they can defer receiving their shares. In the latter case, their shares are invested by the company and paid to them upon retirement or termination. In the case of death, the value of the employees' shares is paid to their beneficiaries.

To provide a real incentive for workers, the profit-sharing plan must provide a sufficiently large payment to the workers but still permit the company to retain earnings for future growth. The most successful profit-sharing plans provide income to employees that ranges, on the average, from 8 to 15 percent of the employee's annual salary.

Employee Stock Ownership Plans (ESOP)

Today, millions of office employees own stock in their own companies. An **employee stock ownership plan (ESOP)** is designed to increase the long-term interest of employees in the profitability of their companies. Three types of stock ownership plans are: (1) the stock option plan, which at one time was available only to high-level executives; (2) the restricted stock plan, traditionally reserved for top executives; and (3) the stock purchase plan, which is offered to all employees.

Stock Option Plan. Although stock option incentives were originally offered only to top management and key personnel, today we find stock options being made available to junior managers and, in some firms, to nonmanagerial personnel. Under a **stock option plan,** eligible employees are given an opportunity to purchase a specific number of shares by a specific date at a given price, which is normally lower than the market price. In some stock option plans, employee eligibility is related to job performance, job function, and length of service.

Restricted Stock Plan. The **restricted stock plan** provides for giving qualified employees actual shares of stock (equity in the company) as an incentive to foster team spirit, to instill loyalty, and, in a firm faced with a hostile takeover, to put more stock in "friendly hands." Generally, a company restricts or reserves the offering of shares to its top-level officers; however, today we find some firms offering restricted stock to a wider range of employees. Usually those receiving restricted stock cannot sell the shares until three to five years after receiving them.

Stock Purchase Plan. In a **stock purchase plan,** employees who meet certain length-of-service requirements are given the opportunity to purchase shares of the company's stock at a price usually lower than the current market price. Most firms limit stock purchases to a stipulated percentage, such as 10 percent, of the employee's annual salary. In the more popular stock purchase plans, delivery of the shares of stock is deferred until the employee leaves the plan or retires.

Gainsharing Plans

In a **gainsharing plan,** the savings that are realized from improvements in productivity are divided among the workers and their employer. Generally, gainsharing plans require:

1. A management philosophy that stresses the potential of employees and their need to become involved.
2. A highly structured system of teams in which employees are encouraged to participate in

work decisions and contribute ideas on how to improve productivity.
3. A formula that computes and divides the productivity-related savings.

In contrast to most profit-sharing plans that usually pay bonuses once or twice a year, the gainsharing bonuses are paid more frequently, often monthly.

Probably the oldest and best-known gainsharing plan is the **Scanlon plan,**[12] which aims at increasing productivity by stressing the following three elements:

1. *A financial incentive tied to organization-wide productivity.* The incentive or bonus is paid monthly to all workers in the company, from laborer to plant manager, based in most cases on the workers' increased productivity.
2. *A committee system of workers and managers to stimulate increased productivity.* The interlocking system of joint worker-manager committees helps an organization work more efficiently by suggesting ways to increase production.
3. *A philosophy of participative management.* The management philosophy rests upon McGregor's Theory Y assumptions about human motivation, which we examined in earlier chapters. Advocates and successful users of the Scanlon plan believe that all workers are capable of self-directed effort toward organizational goals provided their work gives them the opportunity to take responsibility for their actions and to use their abilities. Further, with workers recognized as a professional resource, the primary task of management is to tap their ideas in order to improve quality and increase production.

---

[12]The plan was developed by Joseph Scanlon, a cost accountant, who in the 1930s led the fight to organize a steel mill into a cohesive body that later became the United Steelworkers of America.

SUMMARY

1. At the heart of effective office salary administration is the firm's ongoing program of job evaluation in which the relative value of each job has been appraised. Only through an intelligently administered program of job evaluation can the firm achieve the objectives of its office salary administration program. These objectives are: to attract and retain qualified personnel, to provide fair and internally equitable salaries, to motivate and reward high-level performance, and to price its goods or services competitively.

2. Among the factors to be analyzed and studied when determining office salaries are the firm's philosophy toward salary administration, the firm's ability to pay those salaries and still realize net earnings, what the office employees expect from their jobs, the salaries paid by other firms in the local labor market, federal and state regulations that specify minimum wages and premium pay for covered employ-ees, and the provisions of a collective bargaining agreement.

3. Because of the significance of the local salary rates paid by other firms, the office salary administrator may find salary surveys useful in pricing office jobs and in adjusting salaries. Salary data may be obtained from professionally prepared surveys; by using an outside consultant to conduct, analyze, and interpret the surveys; or by conducting one's own surveys.

4. After the office jobs have been priced and salary ranges established, a decision must be made on how salary increases will be provided, taking into consideration automatic salary progression, cost-of-living adjustment, pay for performance, and pay for skill. For certain kinds of office work, the AOM should consider the use of variable pay, whereby workers are rewarded for their increased production and outstanding performance.

FOR YOUR REVIEW

1. What are the objectives of an office salary administration program?

2. Explain the interrelationship among office salary administration, job analysis, job evaluation, and employee appraisal.

3. How do the expectations of office employees exert influence upon the kind of salary program developed?

4. What are some of the limitations of salary surveys when used as a tool in planning and adjusting office salaries?

5. a. In a salary survey, which statistical measure is the most representative figure? Why?

   b. Which measures are looked upon as the effective salary range?

6. What drawbacks may be found by the company that uses professionally prepared surveys as a source of salary data?

7. What provisions of the Fair Labor Standards Act are most significant to the office salary administrator?

8. Under the Equal Pay Act, when are wage differentials between sexes allowed?

c o n t

9. What are the three duties prescribed by collective bargaining for employers and employees' representatives?

10. How does the charting of salary rates and salary distributions aid in pricing office jobs?

11. What kinds of adjustments may be made in the case of green-circle and red-circle rates that emerge when salary rates are plotted on a scatter chart?

12. Contrast the granting of salary increases under an automatic progression plan and a skill-based pay system.

13. Why are variable pay plans, such as incentive systems, sometimes built into an office salary program?

14. What problems may face the salary administrator who is considering the use of an individual incentive plan?

15. Explain the operation of a stock purchase plan.

16. Why is participative management a fundamental characteristic of gainsharing plans?

FOR YOUR DISCUSSION

1. Skill-based pay systems have been successfully installed in manufacturing environments, especially when jobs are redesigned to accommodate self-managed work teams. Do you believe that skill-based pay systems, sometimes called pay for knowledge systems, can be effectively set up in an office environment?

2. To remedy several inequities in its salary compensation plan, the Hayes Company has decided to "promote" several long-term office employees into newly created positions that exist "only on paper." What is your reaction to such "phony" promotions? What more effective ways can you offer to deal with the problem of inequitable office salaries?

3. As an office supervisor in the Amity Insurance Company, along with the other exempt supervisors, you receive your annual salary increase "up front." That is, the entire amount of the annual salary increase is given to you in a lump sum on your anniversary date instead of in equal payments throughout the year. As an office supervisor, what advantages do you gain under this plan of providing salary increases? What advantages and disadvantages may your company experience as it grants lump-sum salary increases?

4. Kathy Fuerza, in charge of salary administration for Eden Products, believes that the more her employees know about the design of their company's compensation plan, the better they are likely to perform. In a report to top management, Fuerza outlines her proposed program of attack: to inform all workers how salary grades are determined, to explain how individual salaries are set, and to reveal the company's competitive pay position. What is your reaction to Fuerza's proposal?

c
o
n
t

5. Brett Goulet, one of three computer operators in your firm's computer center, has just left your office after complaining about his present salary. Goulet's main gripe is that although he has been with the firm three years, he sees newly hired employees with similar backgrounds being paid as much as he. How can you explain the salary differentials to him?

6. Many companies grant COLAs in an attempt to keep their workers' salaries in line with living costs and to avoid having to equate economic increases with merit increases. Other companies prefer to recognize economic fluctuations through the use of merit increases, whereby COLAs are part of the merit increase package. What advantages do you see in combining COLAs with merit increases? Do you see any disadvantages in such a practice?

7. The following findings about the equality of sexes and comparative salaries received by men and women are taken from studies conducted in recent years:

   a. The International Labor Organization found that, at the current rate of progress, women will need another 1,000 years to match the economic and political clout of men. Women will hold equal managerial posts with men in 500 years and will reach equal economic and political status 475 years after that.[13]

   b. The Equal Pay Act, passed in June, 1963, was supposed to force equal wages, yet women today are paid 70 cents for every $1 paid to men. For women of color, the gap is greater. In 1991, African-American women were paid about 62 cents and Hispanic women earned 54 cents for every $1 paid to white men. Education does not close the gap either. College-educated women earn $13,000 less each year than college-educated men.[14]

   c. According to a survey by Korn/Ferry International, an executive search firm, and the University of California, Los Angeles, men still outnumber women at the executive vice president level by nearly 3 to 1. Executive women's average compensation still lags behind that of men by more than one-third.[15]

What reasons can you advance to explain the "earnings gap" between women and men?

---

[13]Sandra Sanchez, "Equality of Sexes? Give It 1,000 Years," *USA Today* (February 5–7, 1993), p. 1.
[14]Judith L. Lichtman, "Equal Pay: Women Still Don't Get It," *USA Today* (June 7, 1993), p. 13A.
[15]Sue Shellenbarger, "Executive Women Make Major Gains in Pay and Status," *The Wall Street Journal* (June 30, 1993), p. A3.

CASES FOR CRITICAL THINKING

Case 10–1 Determining a Starting Salary

Danny Costner, purchasing manager for Trout Manufacturing, has been interviewing applicants for the position of purchasing clerk. (See Figure 9–3, page 222, for the job description of this position.) Costner has narrowed down all the applicants to two persons, one of whom, if the starting salary is acceptable, will commence work next Monday morning.

From their interviews and applications, Costner has summarized the following information about the two applicants:

cont

Marilu Slezak: 18 years old, single, no dependents. Graduated last year from North High School; cumulative grade point average, 3.7 out of possible 4.0 (B+); area of concentration: secretarial. Presently unemployed. No prior work experience in field of business.

Anthony Hagman: 20 years old, married, one child. Graduated two years ago from North High School; cumulative grade point average, 3.8 out of possible 4.0 (B+); area of concentration: data processing. Part-time employed as short-order cook. No prior work experience in field of business.

Realizing that Hagman is a "family man" facing the usual dollar crunch, Costner plans to offer him a starting salary of $25 per week more than the midpoint of the salary range established for the purchasing clerk position. Costner plans to offer Slezak a starting salary of $15 per week less than the midpoint since her financial obligations are fewer and she has no dependents to support.

As Costner's superior, what are your reactions to the starting salaries he has recommended? What, if any, additional information about the two applicants do you need before you decide to approve or disapprove Costner's salary offers?

Case 10–2 Evaluating the Effect of Merit Pay upon Productivity

Your boss has just asked you to represent the company in an upcoming seminar dealing with merit pay and its effect upon employee performance and productivity. Since you have been studying your company's merit pay plan for the past several weeks, you quickly agree to the request. After you leave your boss's office, you decide to "touch base" with a few others to get their feedback. Here is what you are told:

Supervisor, Shipping: As you know, my people just got merit pay increases based on the evaluation of last year's work. Most of my workers feel that the difference in dollars between what the outstanding workers and poor performers got is so slim that there's little incentive value at all. Most of them say, "What's the use?"

Manager, Accounting: Most of the gripes I hear are about who gets what. Some workers get a 3.5 percent raise while others get only 1.5 percent. They just don't know why there is this difference in the first place. They can't relate their pay to performance.

Vice President, Marketing: My big problem is that merit pay is a reward for what happened in the past. Workers expect it. They feel they are entitled to it. There is no concern about how well they will do during the following year.

Sensing that these reactions may be typical of others attending the seminar, you start to mull over some questions that may arise: Is merit pay linked to employee performance—past or future? Why do companies such as ours think that workers will continue to produce at the same level this year as last year, upon which the merit pay increase was based? Could our company promise to give workers a merit pay increase in exchange for a promise to perform satisfactory work in the future?

When you make your seminar presentation and participate in the discussion, how will you answer these questions?

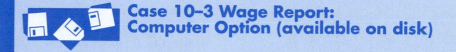

Case 10–3 Wage Report: Computer Option (available on disk)

PROVIDING EMPLOYEE BENEFITS

GOALS FOR THIS CHAPTER

After completing this chapter, you should be able to:

1. Identify the objectives that companies try to achieve in providing benefits for their office workers.
2. Describe the legally required payments that employers must make to provide benefits for employees and their dependents.
3. Summarize the major features of the payments employers make to provide medical and medically related benefits.
4. Describe the types of payments employers make to establish retirement and savings plans.
5. Identify the kinds of life insurance and death benefits usually provided office workers.
6. Give examples of the types of payments made to office workers for time away from their workstations.
7. Describe the role played by the person assigned responsibility for the company's employee benefits program.

Employee benefits (sometimes called *fringe benefits*) include those payments and services that workers receive in addition to their regular wages or salaries. Such benefits may be provided in whole or in part by the employer. Employee benefits, which average about 39 cents of every payroll dollar, form an indispensable part of the office salary compensation package. The cost of employee benefits varies widely from company to company and from industry to industry. The amount of benefits paid annually for each employee ranges from less than $3,500 to more than $13,000. Figure 11–1 shows that, in 1991, the average benefits payment was 39.2 percent of total gross payroll, and $13,126 per year for each employee.

In this chapter we first explain why companies provide such extensive and costly benefits for their office workers. Then, we shall investigate the nature and extent of different types of employee benefits. Finally, we shall examine the role played by the office administrator who develops, implements, and controls the cost of the employee benefits program.

WHY COMPANIES PROVIDE EMPLOYEE BENEFITS

Certain kinds of employee benefits, such as old-age, disability, and hospital insurance benefits; unemployment compensation; workers' compensation; and unpaid family and medical leaves are provided by employers because they are legally required to do so. In addition to legislative requirements, companies provide benefits to office employees to meet the following major objectives:

1. *To attract and retain qualified workers.* A company looks upon the cost of employee benefits as an investment in recruiting and maintaining a stable work force. In a survey

Figure 11-1
Employee
Benefits and
Gross Payroll,
1991

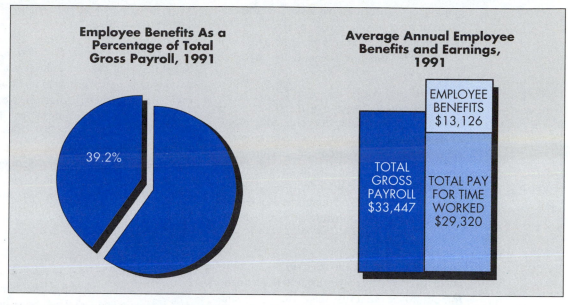

Source: *Employee Benefits, 1992 Edition,* Survey Data from Benefit Year 1991 (Washington, DC: U.S. Chamber of Commerce, 1992), p. 34.

by the Employee Benefit Research Institute and the Gallup Organization, 75 percent of the respondents cited the availability of employer-sponsored benefits as "very important" when they decide to accept or reject job offers.[1] The success of a company's investment in its benefits program depends to a great extent on whether employees need and desire the benefits and whether they understand and appreciate the value of the benefits provided. As pointed out later in this chapter, employees must be given factual information about their benefits in order to understand fully the efforts made by the company on their behalf in providing such benefits.

2. *To motivate workers to become more productive.* The offering of a benefits package that truly meets the needs of employees aids in creating an environment in which workers strive to improve their job performance. However, as we saw in the preceding chapter, not all employee benefits are positive motivators. Adding

a new benefit to the firm's benefits package does not necessarily bring forth a corresponding increase in productivity. It is doubtful that any increase will be apparent for a prolonged period of time. Further, the offering of a new benefit may adversely affect the attitude and, in turn, the output of some workers.

For example, let's say that a company has expanded its benefits package by offering additional retirement protection for married workers with one or more dependents. Such a benefit usually means little to office workers who are unmarried. Thus, benefits, viewed as hygienic factors by Herzberg, may negatively affect performance. Further, if the workers believe that their benefits are inferior to those enjoyed by workers in other firms, productivity may be affected adversely.

3. *To meet the employees' needs for job security and job satisfaction.* The availability of employee benefits helps a company in partially meeting the office workers' primary and secondary needs, as defined in Maslow's hierarchy of needs. By means of the total benefits package, the company is trying to lessen its

---

[1] "Greater Importance Placed on Benefits," *HR Focus* (April, 1993), p. 14.

employees' concerns about loss of salaries because of poor health, layoff, or retirement. In turn, management expects that employees will feel that the company is genuinely interested in their welfare.

4. *To reward employees who improve their performance and increase their productivity.* By means of benefits, the firm can offer incentives, such as profit sharing and stock ownership, in return for outstanding performance, improved productivity, less absenteeism, and decreased turnover. Also, benefits such as vacation time and the accumulation of annual credits toward retirement aid in reducing turnover since these benefits are tied in with the length of company service.

5. *To lessen the company's tax burden.* Employers realize tax advantages from their payments for employee benefits since these amounts represent business operating expenses that are deducted from current income before taxes.

Also, we find companies offer benefits to office workers in an attempt to prevent unionization, to fulfill the obligations contained in a collective bargaining agreement, and to meet the competitive pressures brought about by other firms in the community that may offer more comprehensive benefits packages.

NATURE AND EXTENT OF EMPLOYEE BENEFITS

In the *Dialog from the Workplace,* Andrea Schutz tells us about the nature and extent of the employee benefits program at Educational Testing Service, Inc., in Princeton, New Jersey. She also provides us a glimpse into the future by anticipating several newly emerging benefits. We can analyze the cost of employee benefits, such as those mentioned by Schutz, by classifying them into several broad categories, as shown in Figure 11–2. Therefore, in this section, we shall examine employee benefits under these headings:

1. Legally required payments.
2. Medical and medically related benefits.
3. Retirement and savings plan benefits.
4. Life insurance and death benefits.
5. Payments for time not worked.
6. Paid rest periods, work breaks, and so forth.
7. Miscellaneous benefits.

Working with such a classification, the person in charge of the benefits program can evaluate each benefit as to its appropriateness in meeting the workers' needs, and its cost can be compared with similar benefits offered by other firms.

Figure 11–2
How the Benefit Dollar Is Spent

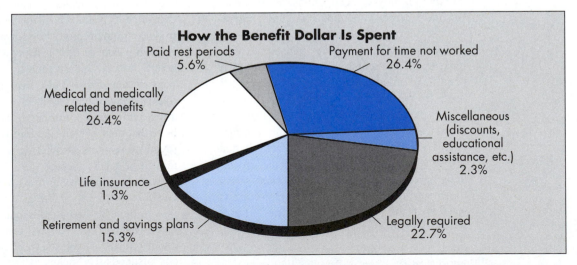

Source: *Employee Benefits, 1992 Edition,* Survey Data from Benefit Year 1991 (Washington, DC: U.S. Chamber of Commerce, 1992), p. 3.

DIALOG FROM THE WORKPLACE

ANDREA L. SCHUTZ

Vice President for Human Resources
Educational Testing Service, Inc.
Princeton, New Jersey

Andrea's background is one of diversified and progressive experience in human resources management, including benefits, employment, affirmative action, compensation, records management, personnel policy development, organizational and staff development, and labor relations. She also has experience in risk management, including property and casualty insurance, loss control, and fire protection.

Previously, Andrea worked at Lenox, Inc., Mathematica, Inc., and Princeton University. She received her B.A. in sociology from Tougaloo College, Tougaloo, Mississippi, and her master of public affairs from the Woodrow Wilson School of Public and International Affairs, Princeton University.

QUESTION: What is the nature of the employee benefits program provided by Educational Testing Service, Inc.? As you look ahead to the year 2000, what new kinds of benefits do you believe will emerge for ETS's employees?

RESPONSE: Educational Testing Service, Inc., is a private, nonprofit corporation devoted to measurement and research, primarily in the field of education. In the provision of a benefits program for its approximately 3,000 employees, ETS is committed to:
• Optimizing the value of each benefit plan to both employees and the organization while maintaining quality in every aspect of benefit administration and communication.
• Designing plans that add to the employees' quality of life and help protect them from financial catastrophe due to illness, injury, death, or loss of income.
• Conferring certain benefits to reward employees for outstanding performance and service.
• Applying sound business judgment to create and modify an employee benefits package that is flexible and responsive to the values and objectives of the corporation.
• Complying fully with all government laws and regulations.

The ETS benefits program is very broad-based and includes insurance programs, wellness programs, dependent care programs, education/training, disability benefits, and time-off benefits.

The Future: The shape of the ETS benefits program in the year 2000 will be heavily influenced by factors internal to the organization such as demographics; the company's academic traditions; the culture and its emphasis on equity, openness, and employee choice; program utilization; and financial considerations. External influences that will affect what ETS chooses to do include our marketplace for obtaining clients and attracting staff; laws and regulations; the shape of government programs; social and political developments; vendor developments; and technological innovation.

So what's likely to be considered?

Health maintenance, i.e., prevention, early diagnosis, and improving medical outcomes, will be the leading influence of our benefit program design.

Communications which emphasize educating the staff about the programs available to them, optimal use of those programs, and overall support for effective decision making will grow.

Finally, work-family concerns will become increasingly important in our programs. The makeup of ETS's staff (which was almost 70 percent female in 1993) contributes heavily to our attention in this direction.

Overall, the direction will be one that facilitates healthy, satisfying, and productive lives.

Legally Required Payments

Included under this heading are those legally required, or mandated, payments to federal and state governmental agencies.

OASDHI Benefits

The largest phase of the federal government's social insurance program is the **old-age, survivors, disability, and health insurance (OASDHI)** program, commonly called the *social security program.* This program was planned by the federal government to provide economic security for workers and their families. Under the social security program, the *Federal Insurance Contributions Act (FICA)* levies a tax on employers and employees in most industries to be paid to the federal government. Amendments to FICA provide for a two-part health insurance program, commonly known as *Medicare,* for the aged and the disabled.

Benefits from the OASDHI program are payable monthly to workers and their survivors who qualify under the provisions of the law. Generally, as the cost of living rises, so does the cost of the benefits—and so do the FICA taxes for workers and their employers.

Unemployment Compensation Benefits

Unemployment compensation insurance is a federal-state program established to provide funds at the state level for compensating unemployed workers in that state during periods of temporary unemployment. Employers are faced with two unemployment taxes: federal and state. Depending upon the state law, employees, too, may be required to contribute to the unemployment compensation fund.

Workers' Compensation Benefits

Workers' compensation insurance is a state insurance program designed to protect employees and their dependents against losses due to injury or death incurred during the worker's employment. The cost of workers' compensation insurance is borne by the employer in all states, except Oregon, where employees also contribute to the program.

State Disability Benefits

Five states (California, Hawaii, New Jersey, New York, and Rhode Island) and Puerto Rico have laws that provide **state disability benefits.** These benefits are paid workers who are absent from their jobs because of illness, accident, or disease *not arising out of their employment.* Although the state laws differ with respect to the amount of employer contributions, each state requires employee contributions.

Medical and Medically Related Benefits

At the time of this writing, President Clinton had presented his health-care plan, which was aimed at providing health-care benefits to all U.S. citizens by 1997. To pay for the plan, businesses would contribute at least 80 percent of the average cost of the basic benefit package, which would include coverage for prescription drugs and mental health. Employees would pay the remaining 20 percent of the cost. Insurance-buying "health alliances" would be created, and all employers with fewer than 5,000 workers would be required to join. Months of debate lie ahead, and surely the health-care plan that finally emerges will significantly alter the following discussion.

In this section, we shall examine several group plans, traditionally financed by insurance premiums and fund contributions, that provide medical and medically related benefits to employees.

Hospital, Surgical, and Medical Insurance

Hospital, surgical, and medical insurance affords office employees protection by covering all or the major part of the hospital, surgical, and medical expenses for employees and their dependents. This type of benefit is very common; and most firms have established group medical insurance plans for their workers, either paying the cost entirely or having the employee contribute part of the cost at a reduced rate.

Employers of 25 or more employees who are subject to the Fair Labor Standards Act and who provide payments for health insurance to their employees are required to offer them the option of membership in a qualified **health mainte-nance organization (HMO)**. The traditional HMO is an organization of providers (physicians, health-care workers, and affiliated hospital) that offer participants medical services prepaid by the employer and the employee. Thus, instead of paying doctors a fee for each service performed, employees enrolled in an HMO pay a fixed premium in advance for all health-care services required during the year.

As an alternative to HMOs, some companies offer their workers the opportunity to participate in a **preferred provider organization (PPO)**. Under a PPO, the employer, care provider, or insurance company develops a list of preferred providers (physicians, hospitals, and other health-care services) that have been selected on the basis of their low cost and high quality. Employees may select from the PPO list that physician or hospital they desire rather than be assigned one by the health-care provider under a traditional HMO plan.

The Consolidated Omnibus Budget Reconciliation Act of 1985 (COBRA) requires companies with 20 or more employees to offer health insurance to *former* workers and their dependents for at least 18 months. Former employees who opt for the health insurance coverage must pay its full cost plus a surcharge to cover administrative expenses. Even with the surcharge, the group plan rates are less expensive than individual coverage. Also, some small companies pay a portion of the continued health-care coverage, even though the law does not require them to do so.

Major Medical Insurance

Many companies expand their group hospital, surgical, and medical insurance coverage by providing **major medical insurance.** This insurance plan protects employees and their dependents from huge medical bills resulting from serious accidents or prolonged illness. In many plans, the company pays the full cost of the employee's own medical expense insurance, while the costs for coverage of dependents may be shared by the company and the employee.

Under many major medical insurance policies, coverage ceases after a lifetime maximum per individual has been reached. Other policies set a maximum benefit for each disability period. Most plans require the workers to absorb a certain dollar amount before they are paid benefits, with annual deductibles of $100 or less for each insured person being common. Many major medical plans pay all covered expenses after a specified level of costs has been incurred during the year. For example, a plan might pay 80 percent of expenses until an employee has paid $1,000 in "out-of-pocket" expenses during the year (in addition to the deductible), and then pay 100 percent thereafter.

Some major medical plans provide coverage for mental or nervous conditions, with a stated lifetime maximum benefit. Also, alcoholic rehabilitation coverage is often provided to cover the costs of room, board, and services.

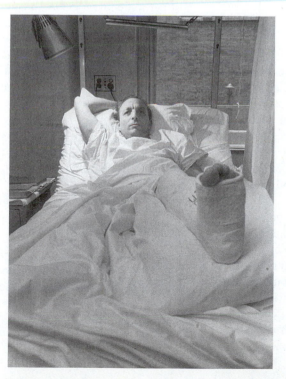

Illustration 11–1 Major medical insurance is designed to protect employees and their dependents from enormous health-care expenses incurred following serious accidents.

Disability Income Insurance

Many office workers receive benefits as a result of their firms' sickness and accident **disability income insurance** plans. The *short-term* plans provide continuing income for workers unable to return to their jobs after they have exhausted their sickness and accident benefits. Generally, the short-term disability protection is provided at no cost to employees. Typically, benefits are not payable to employees who are on vacation or on an unpaid leave of absence.

Long-term disability income insurance, an extension of the short-term program, is often made available to office employees at a group rate. Long-term disability insurance, also known as *wage-continuation insurance,* usually provides a benefit equal to 50 or 60 percent of the base salary for the worker who is found by a physician to be totally disabled. The period of payment may range from a few years to a stipulated age, or for life, depending upon the design of the plan. The benefits paid under the plan are usually reduced, up to a maximum monthly amount, by any social security benefits, workers' compensation benefits, or company-provided pension.

Dental Care

Nearly all dental-care plans cover a wide range of services, including preventive care, such as examinations and X-rays; restorative procedures, such as fillings, inlays, and crowns; dental surgery; and periodontal care (treatment of tissues and bones supporting the teeth). The plans vary considerably by methods of reimbursement, coinsurance provisions, deductibles, and maximum benefits.

In many dental-care plans, the sponsor (employer or union) pays the entire premium for the dental insurance, in which case all members of the group are covered, usually after a brief period of service. In other plans, participation is optional and the participants share the cost with the plan sponsor, usually through payroll deductions. Usually participants may cover their dependents by paying the required premium.

Vision Care

Vision-care benefits are normally available to all participants of the covered employee group, usually after a stated eligibility period. Most plans permit the participants to cover their dependents by paying a premium. Vision-care coverage provides a variety of services that are not usually covered by regular health insurance plans, such as eye examinations, eyeglasses, contact lenses, and orthoptics (eye muscle exercises).

Prescription Drug Plan

Most medical insurance plans cover prescription drugs only when administered as part of hospital care. Therefore, a business may provide a group plan that covers the purchase of prescription drugs. Generally, payment for the purchase of prescription drugs is a "co-pay" arrangement, with the employee paying a deductible, such as $1 to $3, and the insurance carrier paying the remainder of the cost.

In 1992, the cost of prescription drug benefits was $345 per employee, which represented an increase of 37.5 percent over a two-year period; the cost per retiree was $550.[2] To control the cost of prescription drug benefits, employers set up mail-order purchase plans, encourage use of less expensive generic drugs, and use card plans that charge employees a fixed copayment, such as $4 for each generic drug and $7 for a brand-name drug.

Retirement and Savings Plan Benefits

Under this category of employee benefits, we shall examine the major features of retirement and savings plans that provide payments to presently employed, retired, and laid-off workers.

Retirement Income

Most firms modify their retirement plans to supplement the government's social security benefits and thereby attempt to maintain their employees'

---

[2]Michael Clements, "Cost of Drug Benefits Surges 37.5%," *USA Today* (April 1, 1993), p. B1.

interest in long-term employment. Although eligibility rules vary among retirement plans, the coverage is about the same for production workers, office employees, and managers. Most of the plans are financed by employer contributions. When employees contribute toward the cost of their retirement benefits, the contributions are usually expressed as a percentage of their annual earnings.

Retirement plans may provide for early retirement, such as between ages 62–65, with a lifetime monthly allowance based on the worker's accrued benefits. For earlier retirement, such as at ages 55–62, the amount of monthly allowance is reduced. If the office worker is forced to retire early because of a disability, a pension benefit is still provided. If an eligible married employee dies before retirement, the spouse receives a payment based on the worker's length of service with the company.

Individual Retirement Account (IRA). An **individual retirement account (IRA),** created by the Internal Revenue Code, is a pension plan that is established and funded by the *individual* employee. Under certain conditions, employees may put aside each year the lesser of $2,000 or 100 percent of their compensation *without paying federal income taxes on their contributions.* To be eligible for such *deductible* (tax-free) contributions, the worker must not be a participant in a company-funded retirement plan. Further, the employee must report, for federal income tax purposes, an adjusted gross income less than $25,000 if filing a tax return as a single person, or less than $40,000 if filing a joint return.

An employee who is ineligible to make a deductible IRA contribution is permitted to make *nondeductible* contributions to a separate IRA account. The earnings on the nondeductible contributions are not subject to federal income tax until they are withdrawn. The limit on such nondeductible contributions for a taxable year is the lesser of $2,000 or 100 percent of the employee's compensation.

Simplified Employee Pension (SEP) Plan. By means of a **simplified employee pension (SEP) plan,** employers may make contributions to individual retirement accounts on behalf of their employees. In the operation of an SEP plan, the law sets forth strict requirements, such as these:

1. The amount of the employer's annual contribution to the plan is limited.
2. Employers must contribute for all employees who are 21 years of age or older and who have worked for the employer at least three of the past five years.
3. The SEP plan cannot discriminate in favor of employees who are officers, stockholders, or highly compensated employees.
4. The employer contributions must be fully and immediately "vested."

Vesting

Vesting is the process of conveying to employees the right to share in a retirement fund in the event they are terminated before the normal retirement age. The vesting process is linked to the number of years needed for workers to earn an equity in their retirement plans and to become entitled to full or partial benefits at some future date if they leave the company before retirement.

Once vested, a worker has the right to receive a pension at retirement age, based on years of covered service, even though the worker may not be working for the firm at that time. Most retirement plans provide for vesting after the worker has been covered under the plan for a specified number of years. The Tax Reform Act of 1986 provides for full vesting after five years of service, or gradually over seven years (20 percent after three years and 20 percent a year for the next four).

Employee Retirement Income Security Act of 1974 (ERISA). The **Employee Retirement Income Security Act (ERISA)** provides workers with a vested right to their retirement income benefits and assurance of well-managed retirement plans. It is mandatory that all information concerning the operation of the employer's retirement plan, other benefit plans, and the amount of the worker's accrued benefits be fully disclosed and communicated to the workers.

401(k) Retirement Plan. A retirement plan that has gained popularity is the **401(k) retirement plan,** so called because of its authorization under Section 401(k) of the Internal Revenue Code. Under a 401(k) plan, after employees have at least one year of service, they can shelter a certain portion of their salaries from taxes each year and watch the deferred income grow until time of retirement. The deferred salaries and earnings thereon are not taxed until the employees begin to withdraw the amounts. Most employers contribute matching funds, which, with the employees' contributions, are invested in tax-deferred stock funds, bonds, or short-term investments. Employees are totally vested as soon as they commence deferring part of their salaries, and they receive all earnings from their matched-fund investment if they should leave the company.

Illustration 11–2 Contributions to retirement and savings plans during their working years enable retirees to enjoy relaxing activities.

Profit-Sharing and Employee Stock Ownership Plans

As noted in Chapter 10, profit-sharing plans provide employee benefits that are based on a percentage of the company's profits for the year. Also in the discussion of group incentives in Chapter 10, you read about another very popular employee benefit, employee stock ownership.

Employee Savings and Thrift Plans

Savings and thrift plans permit employees to allot a portion of their annual income to an individual retirement account. Usually the employees' contributions are made on a *pretax basis;* that is, the amount of income deferred is not subject to income taxes until the time it is withdrawn. The amount of the employees' contributions is restricted, either by the employer or, in the case of pretax deferrals, by the Internal Revenue Service. A portion of the employees' contributions is matched by the employer, based on a stated formula, and the employer and employees' contributions are then invested.

Supplemental Unemployment Benefits (SUBs)

Many union contracts provide that, in addition to state unemployment compensation benefits, private **supplemental unemployment benefits (SUBs)** may be paid to employees during periods of layoff. Under a common SUB plan, employers contribute to a general fund a certain number of cents for each hour worked by employees. Employees usually have a right to benefits from the fund only upon layoff and after meeting stated eligibility requirements. In another type of plan, the employer's contributions are paid to a separate trust fund for each employee. Workers are entitled to the fund upon layoff and have a right to the fund when their employment is ended. If a worker dies, the beneficiary is paid the amount of the trust.

Life Insurance and Death Benefits

Group life insurance is a type of protection that covers all employees of a single firm and is designed to provide benefits should a worker die or become totally disabled. For office and plant employees, the life insurance benefit may be an amount equal to one year's earnings; for managerial employees, the benefit may be twice the annual earnings. Group life insurance is *term insurance* that expires when the worker leaves the company unless the employee takes steps to convert it to an individual policy. Nearly every large and medium-size firm and many small companies today provide life insurance protection and may pay the entire premium for the office worker's insurance coverage.

The morale-building effect of a group life insurance plan cannot be overestimated, for this benefit relieves employees of much worry and insecurity. Usually the group life insurance plan provides for total and permanent disability benefits, accidental death and dismemberment coverage, as well as modest amounts of life insurance for the employee's survivors. Terminally ill workers can often obtain accelerated benefits to aid in financial planning and to cover their expenses when fully disabled. Many companies also provide life insurance coverage for their retirees.

Office employees may be covered by their firm's **travel accident insurance** plan when they are traveling on company business. Usually at no cost to employees, this coverage provides benefits in the event of death, disability, and dismemberment.

Payments for Time Not Worked

The benefits discussed in this section represent payments that employees receive for time away from work.

Vacations

Vacation time is generally determined by length of service. Most office employees receive two weeks' vacation with pay after one year of employment. Many office employees receive three weeks' vacation after 10 years and four weeks' paid leave after 20 years of service. Few employers allow their workers to carry over vacation time from one year to the next. Also, most employers stipulate that the vacation time must be taken away

from work; in other words, an employee cannot request extra pay instead of time off.

When we compare our vacation time practices with those in other countries, we find that employees in Austria, Denmark, and Sweden are given more than one month's vacation after one year of service.[3] In fact, the government mandates the number of vacation days to be allotted in Sweden (30), France (25), Brazil (22), Japan (19), and Germany (18).[4] In addition to vacation time, some countries provide a cash vacation bonus that may amount to as much as 4 to 12 percent of the worker's annual salary.

Holidays

In its Employee Benefits Survey, the Bureau of Labor Statistics reported that small establishments (fewer than 100 workers) provide 9.5 paid holidays each year. This compares with 9.2 days per year in medium and large establishments and 13.6 per year in state and local governments.[5] In addition to New Year's Day, Independence Day, Veterans Day, Thanksgiving, and Christmas, the following "Monday Holidays" are legal public holidays in most states:

- Martin Luther King, Jr.'s Birthday, third Monday in January.
- Presidents' Day, third Monday in February.
- Memorial Day, last Monday in May.
- Labor Day, first Monday in September.
- Columbus Day, second Monday in October.

Other days such as Good Friday, Christmas Eve, New Year's Eve, and the employee's birthday are often recognized as paid holidays. Many companies have one or more "floating" holidays, which are designated on different days from year to year. Some firms designate the same "floating" holidays for all employees, while other companies allow employee choice. The holidays most often designated as "floating" are July 3 or 5, the

---

[3]Karen Matthes, "In Pursuit of Leisure: Employees Want More Time Off," *HR Focus* (May, 1992), p. 7.

[4]"Where Vacations Are Required," *USA Today* (September 2, 1993), p. D1.

[5]Michael A. Miller, "Time-Off Benefits in Small Establishments," *Monthly Labor Review* (March, 1992), p. 6.

day after Thanksgiving, and the days between Christmas and New Year's.

Sick Leave

Most firms have a company-paid *sick-leave plan* that provides workers with continuing income during short periods of illness. To become eligible for sick-leave coverage, a minimum period of employment is usually specified, with the most common service requirement being three months. Often, this requirement is tied in with the end of a probationary period for new employees. The amount of paid sick leave provided office workers may range from 5 to 15 days after one year of service, with the number of days increasing with the employee's length of service.

Parental Leave

Most firms have adopted formal policies covering *maternity leaves* for office employees. These policies generally have no specific length-of-service requirement for eligibility. Where no policy exists, maternity benefits are often provided under a sick-leave plan, as described above. In these firms, the accumulation of sick-leave days from year to year may be used for maternity reasons. For example, employees with one year of service may receive benefits for two weeks, while five-year employees may be eligible for nine weeks of benefits.

The *Pregnancy Discrimination Act of 1978* bars mandatory leaves for pregnant women that are set at a certain time in their pregnancy, regardless of their ability to work. The law requires employers to treat pregnancy and childbirth the same as other causes of disability under employee benefit plans. Also, the reinstatement rights of women on leave for pregnancy-related reasons are protected. Credit for previous service, accrued retirement benefits, and accumulated seniority are provided the woman on maternity leave.

Many firms offering *paternity leaves* permit their employees to use paid vacation or annual leave for such purposes. Some companies provide male employees with time off work under the heading "unpaid paternity leave." The maximum amount of unpaid paternity leave may range from two days to one year for the office staff.

Several states require employers to grant parental leave to *adopting parents* as well as birth parents and to either male or female employees. Also, a small number of companies provide the adopting parents financial assistance such as reimbursing the parents for legal fees, paying the medical expenses of the birth mother, and reimbursing the adoption agency for its fees.

Jury Duty

When office employees are called to jury duty, some receive full pay from their employers in addition to the payments received from the court. Often, however, if employees are paid jury fees, these amounts are deducted from the pay they receive from their employer.

Time Off to Vote

Over half of the states have laws allowing employees to take time off from work to vote. Most state laws provide that employees entitled to vote in an election may, upon application to their employers, absent themselves from work for a specified period, without penalty or loss of pay. However, in a growing number of states, time off is granted only if there is insufficient time to vote outside the working hours.

Military Training Leave

Employers cannot refuse to grant office employees time off to meet their military training obligations. Many firms treat the required summer training programs as paid leave. Usually in these companies, the employees are paid the difference between their regular pay and what they receive as base pay from the military. In other companies not having a policy regarding military training leave, employees may use their vacation periods for military training and receive accumulated vacation pay in addition to their military pay.

Personal Leave

Paid leave for personal reasons or personal floating holidays are offered fairly commonly to office personnel. Usually, a service requirement, such as three months, is needed before employees become eligible for personal leave, which may be two days each year.

Funeral Leave

Most companies provide office workers paid funeral leaves, usually of three days' duration, when there is a death in the immediate family.

Paid Rest Periods, Work Breaks, Etc.

Rest periods, work breaks, lunch periods, wash-up time, travel time, clothes-change time, get-ready time, and other on-the-job time that is paid for cost the employer an average of $752 for each worker in 1991.[6] The purpose of providing rest periods and refreshment breaks is to increase the productivity and efficiency of workers, a point that should be communicated to the workers.

---

[6]*Employee Benefits, 1992 Edition,* Survey Data from Benefit Year 1991 (Washington, DC: U.S. Chamber of Commerce), p. 20.

Rest Periods and Work Breaks

Underlying the provision for rest periods and work breaks is the principle that certain kinds of repetitive work soon become monotonous. This monotony increases fatigue, which, in turn, slows down production. The work output of employees performing motor-skill tasks, such as data entry, varies at different times throughout the day. Therefore, for this kind of task during an eight-hour workday, it is recommended that work breaks be placed between the second and third hours in the morning and between the sixth and seventh hours in the afternoon.

For office activities that require a high degree of concentration, such as reading information on a computer screen, two work breaks each day may not be sufficient to maintain an acceptable level of performance. Some data-entry operators express complaints such as headaches, tension, eyestrain, and wrist, neck, and shoulder pains,

Illustration 11–3 Well-planned work breaks enable data-entry operators to reduce the stress and monotony that accompany their repetitive activities.

which may be attributed to ergonomic elements such as lighting or the design of the machine, desk, and chair. It has not been conclusively proved that rest periods are the answer to the problems of fatigue and slowdown of production. However, the fact that management provides rest periods shows its concern for the well-being of its employees, which may be the most important aspect of the rest period.

Controlling Work Breaks. Often the amount of control that AOMs exercise over work breaks is related to where the employees get their refreshments. It is much more difficult to control the length of the breaks if employees must leave the premises at break time. In most offices, employees have access to vending machines and cafeteria services. Some firms control work breaks by permitting employees to eat and drink at their desks because it is felt that if food is consumed while the employees are at their desks, the workers will lose less time.

Although most AOMs agree that rest periods are desirable, they object to the abuse of the privilege. Some AOMs excuse their firms' lack of rest periods by stating that the freedom enjoyed by most office workers makes such breaks unnecessary.

The following guidelines should govern the granting of rest periods:

1. *Rest periods are absolutely necessary for some types of work.* For example, to serve effectively during the entire workday as goodwill ambassadors of their firms through contact with the public, receptionists and switchboard operators should be periodically freed from their sedentary, stressful, and repetitive tasks.
2. *Schedule rest periods when they will be most helpful—not too early in the morning and not too late in the afternoon.* The work breaks should be scheduled so that not all employees are absent from their desks at the same time. Such an approach tends to discourage the overly long "talk" sessions that commonly characterize many breaks. Peer pressure by a coworker waiting for a worker to return from a rest period may aid in controlling the length of breaks, too.

3. *Set definite time limits for the length of the breaks and observe these limits.* Habitual offenders should be reprimanded and, if necessary, discharged. The inability of a few to abide by the rules only sets a poor example for others.
4. *If possible, provide facilities for getting refreshments and snacks so the employees do not have to leave the premises.*
5. *Hold supervisors responsible for their workers' abuse of rest period privileges.*

The Cost of Lost Time. Assume that an office employee earns, on the average, $380 each 40-hour week during a 50-week year and spends 20 minutes a day on work breaks. A little over 83 hours—more than 2 workweeks—during the year are spent away from the workstation. The cost of this worker's lost time is about $792. When you add the time employees take for long lunches, leaving work early, being tardy, using sick days when not ill, and extensive socializing, *the costs to business are staggering.*

The cost of lost time becomes clearly evident when the OM makes a few simple calculations, such as those shown in Table 11–1. This table shows for several different hourly rates the annual cost of *only five minutes' lost time* per employee per day. And these costs do not include the average cost of employee benefits provided by the employer, which, as we saw earlier in this chapter, exceed one-third of every payroll dollar!

Miscellaneous Benefits

This final category of benefits includes *unpaid* leaves for family and medical emergencies, childbirth, and adoption; awards, allowances, and other extra payments; and employer-provided programs and services, some of which may represent taxable income to employees. (Overtime or premium pay for time worked and incentive bonuses are excluded since they are an earned portion of the employee's regular compensation, as we saw in the previous chapter.)

Unpaid Family and Medical Leave

The **Family and Medical Leave Act of 1993 (FMLA)** requires employers with 50 or more

Table 11–1
Annual Cost of Lost Time (5 minutes' lost time each day during a 5-day work-week in a 50-week year)

Hourly Rate	NUMBER OF EMPLOYEES				
	10	25	50	100	250
$6.00	$1,250	$3,125	$6,250	$12,500	$31,250
7.50	1,562	3,906	7,813	15,625	39,062
8.00	1,667	4,167	8,333	16,667	41,667
9.75	2,031	5,078	10,156	20,313	50,781
10.50	2,188	5,469	10,938	21,875	54,688
12.00	2,500	6,250	12,500	25,000	62,500

workers within a 75-mile radius to provide up to 12 weeks of *unpaid* leave for family medical emergencies, childbirth, or adoption. Many large and small companies had provisions for such leaves prior to enactment of the law; however, the FMLA is more generous than the policies of all but the largest companies.

Workers who have been employed at least one year and worked at least 1,250 hours during the year before the leave can take their unpaid leave in any 12-month period. If *paid* leave is available, the employer may require the workers to substitute their paid leave for part of the 12 weeks. The reasons for taking a leave include the birth or adoption of a child; the serious illness of a child, spouse, or parent; or a serious illness that prevents the employees from doing their job. Upon returning to work, the employees must be given their old job or an equivalent position. While on leave, the workers cannot collect unemployment or other government compensation.

A company may deny unpaid leave to a salaried employee in the highest-paid 10 percent of the workforce if permitting that worker to take the leave would create "substantial and grievous injury" to the business operation. Employers can require medical certification that establishes the need for a leave. Further, employers must continue to provide health-care benefits during the leave, but they are not required to pay the worker's salary.

The federal law does not supersede any state or local family-leave law that has more stringent provisions. In fact, the federal law specifies that employers are subject to whichever law provides the greater benefit to families. For example, the District of Columbia allows up to 16 weeks of leave over a two-year period. If a worker takes 12 weeks during the first year, under the DC law the employee has only four remaining the following year; however, federal law guarantees the employee 12 weeks each year.

Awards, Allowances, and Other Extra Payments

In this section, we shall examine briefly three benefits: educational assistance, Christmas bonuses, and relocation expense allowances.

Educational Assistance. Many firms provide educational assistance to their employees so that office workers can continue to grow professionally and to prepare themselves for career pursuits and for promotion. Educational assistance may be provided in the form of paid tuition costs or the granting of loans for tuition payments.

Generally, under a tuition-aid plan, the company requires that the courses be taken at certain types of educational agencies, such as colleges and universities, community or junior colleges, technical schools, or private business schools. Another requirement is that the courses be *job related;* that is, the courses must maintain or improve skills required in the employee's present work or be required by the employer so that the employees may keep their current salary or job. Often the courses may be taken on company time, and sometimes they are conducted on company premises by professors from local colleges or universities.

In some tuition-aid plans, employees are reimbursed the entire cost of tuition for the courses completed satisfactorily no matter what grades are received. In other cases, the amount of reimbursement is tied in with the letter grade received. Some firms also make tuition aid or other educational assistance available to employees approaching retirement age so they can develop new interests or activities.

Christmas Bonuses. Many companies give cash Christmas bonuses to their office employees as a gesture of goodwill and to encourage continued employee loyalty and good performance. Other firms base their bonuses on merit, granting them only to workers who have made an extra effort or exceeded predetermined quotas during the year.

Although a bonus is a gift, employees quickly begin to expect it. When business is bad, however, bonuses may decrease or disappear. Giving a worker a cash bonus that is less than the amount received last year tends to cause ill will and can seriously affect morale.

In a union office, the employer may be committing an *unfair labor practice* if a bonus is unilaterally withdrawn. For example, the Christmas bonus may be a gratuity representing a goodwill gesture that has no relationship to the employee's job performance, hours worked, seniority, or position. Thus, the bonus is not a bargainable item. In such cases, the employer can withdraw the bonus for economic reasons without prior notification or bargaining. If, on the other hand, the bonus is part of wages or a condition of employment, good faith bargaining is required preceding the withdrawal of such a benefit.

Relocation Expense Allowances. Many companies offer a relocation expense allowance, often to entice an employee to accept a transfer or a job applicant to accept a position. The relocation expense package may provide loss-on-sale assistance (reimbursement for equity lost in the sale of a house in a depressed market); reimbursement for temporary living expenses; subsidizing a por-

tion of the employee's mortgage interest rate; payment of legal and closing fees and realtors' commissions; and providing job replacement assistance for spouses.

Programs and Services Provided Employees

Included in this category of benefits are those programs and privileges provided by employers to enable employees to avoid or to reduce their personal expenditures.

Food Services. In many on-premise food facilities, catering companies have installed vending machines, with employees obtaining food and refreshments at any time during working hours. Company-provided food services are fairly common in large cities where a deluge of several thousand employees from one building seeking meals in a variety of restaurants is not conducive to the best physical and mental well-being of the workers. Also, in the suburbs, the office building may be located far away from restaurants. Thus, in-house food service becomes a necessity.

Company Medical Facilities. Often companies provide first-aid stations and sick rooms. Also, many firms, especially large organizations, maintain a medical staff that consists of full- or part-time doctors, psychologists, and nurses. Most companies provide preemployment physical examinations, and some firms give periodic examinations to all employees. Some companies provide free eye examinations for employees who frequently use computers or word processors.

Social and Recreational Programs. The social and recreational programs in many firms consist mostly of picnics, employee parties, group tours or trips, and bowling and ball teams. With the additional leisure time resulting from shorter workweeks and flexible work schedules, we find more companies providing additional general-interest programs, sports, and hobbies for the entire family. Some activities that have become a part of company social and recreational programs are chess or checkers, bridge, concerts, golf, fashion shows, dancing, crafts, glee clubs, fishing, theater parties, and sports car rac-

Illustration 11–4 Recreational programs, such as the company's ball team, appeal to those workers who enjoy physical exercise during their leisure hours.

efit to offer employees in 1993.[7] Such fitness programs may include aerobics, jogging, and calisthenics. Often the fitness programs focus attention upon high-risk health problems and offer seminars on smoking cessation, alcohol and drug abuse, weight control, proper nutrition, and stress reduction. Some firms provide in-house athletic facilities with custodial services, or they may offer incentives to their workers to participate in programs elsewhere.

Career Apparel. Providing wearing apparel for office workers is an important employee benefit in some companies. Over a two- or three-year period, wearing apparel may cost a company several hundred dollars for each worker. In some programs, employees pay for the cost of all their wearing apparel. In other plans, the firm may provide the initial wardrobe, with additional or optional items being paid for by employees. In other instances, the cost of apparel is evenly divided between employee and employer.

Parking Space. When parking space is provided by the company, employees are saved the cost of renting their own space and are assured of finding a place in which to park. In large metropolitan areas, such benefits represent a significant savings and peace of mind for the workers. Parking lots or garages are provided by many large firms, often at no charge to the employees.

Counseling and Referral Programs. As you saw in Chapter 7, many companies have employee assistance programs (EAPs) that provide employees with counseling and referral programs for alcoholism, drug abuse, emotional illness, stress, marital problems, and other personal problems.

A company faced with downsizing may assist and counsel its laid-off employees by means of outplacement counseling. An **outplacement counseling** program is designed to assist laid-off workers in applying for unemployment compensation benefits and in obtaining benefits such as medical and life insurance, vacation and holidays, and holdings in the company credit union

ing clubs. Good recreational planning should provide organized activities for those employees who prefer to spend their leisure time in individual or small-group pursuits.

Most firms feel that the improvement in employee morale is worth whatever it costs to achieve. In some companies, employee associations bear some or all of the expenses of the recreational programs. In other firms, the costs of recreation may be partially defrayed by other sources of revenue, such as income from vending machines located throughout the offices and plant.

Physical Wellness Programs. Committed to the premise that successful performance at work is tied to physical health, many companies offer comprehensive physical wellness programs for their workers. In a Robert Half and Accountemps survey, 74 percent of the respondents cited physical wellness programs as the most important ben-

[7]*1993 Robert Half and Accountemps Salary Guide* (Menlo Park, CA: Robert Half International, 1993), p. 20.

or stock purchase plan. Outplacement counseling is often undertaken to give the laid-off workers a much-needed morale boost and to help ease them into the world of unemployment. The terminated workers may be counseled in group sessions where they receive advice on interviewing and preparing resumés. Some company counselors organize job fairs where the firm's laid-off workers can meet prospective employers.

For those workers approaching retirement age, the company may undertake a program of **preretirement counseling.** In these counseling sessions, matters such as the following are commonly discussed: company pensions, earning money after retirement, financial planning, organizations for retirees, recreation and hobbies, social security benefits, wills and inheritances, and health problems.

Financial Services. The most frequently available financial services to office employees are those provided by credit unions. A **credit union** is a financial institution, chartered by the state or federal government, that is organized to assist the employees of a firm in saving money and lending it to one another.

Legal Service Plans. Legal service plans are designed to improve worker satisfaction and performance by handling for the employees such matters as debt difficulties, bankruptcies, and matrimonial disputes.

A common type of legal service plan is the *group legal plan.* In this plan, a group of workers with a common affiliation, such as the members of a union or a company credit union, obtain the services of a lawyer or group of lawyers at a discount. Usually, the members of a group plan must use the services of a designated lawyer who is affiliated with the plan, although some plans may allow the workers a choice. The fees are paid by the company after the legal services have been performed.

Under the *prepaid legal plan,* an advance payment of fees is made by the company, depending upon the type of services to be provided. For example, the *access plan* provides primarily telephone consultation. However, members are also usually allowed additional services such as brief office consultations and the preparation of a simple legal document each year.

In the *comprehensive prepaid legal plan,* a wider range of legal services is provided the employees. Some plans, designed to meet most of the legal service needs of average middle-income families, cover real estate and housing matters, domestic disputes, traffic accidents, consumer debt problems, adoptions, preparation of wills, and estate planning.

Executive Perquisites. Executives are often provided **perquisites,** or *perks,* which are defined as privileges, gains, or profits that are incidental to regular salaries. Some of the most popularly offered perks are use of a personal company car; reserved parking space; periodic free medical examinations; country club memberships; luncheon club memberships; use of company airplane; spouse traveling on company business; stock options; liability insurance for directors and officers; paid memberships in professional, trade, or business associations and civic organizations; financial planning services; and credit cards for business entertainment and travel. The Internal Revenue Service has imposed tax rules on some financial perks, with the effect that they are treated as earned income for income tax purposes.

Other Programs and Services. Other programs and services that companies may provide their employees include:

1. *Childcare service.* The factors that account for an immense potential demand for childcare service include the growing number of women in the workforce and the increased number of mothers with preschool children. However, a relatively small number of companies provide nurseries and daycare services on their premises. The TempForce 1992 Salary and Employment Survey of companies employing almost 2 million workers found that only 6.2 percent of the firms provided childcare services for their employees' children.[8]
2. *Eldercare service.* This service has not yet become a top priority benefit for most firms. The

---

[8]*The TempForce 1992 Salary and Employment Survey* (Westbury, NY: TempForce, 1992), p. 18.

TempForce survey referred to above found that 6.3 percent of the firms made provisions for employees who must attend to eldercare.[9] Some features of eldercare service include consultation with community agencies on problems of the elderly, referrals to medical services, and home-delivered meals.

3. *Company discounts.* Many firms grant their employees a discount on company products or services, with discounts ranging from 10 to 50 percent or more.

4. *Adoption benefit plans.* Another employee service provided by a growing number of companies is coverage of the expenses incurred by employees adopting children. Under most adoption benefit plans, the amount received by the employee is similar to a pregnant worker's benefits provided under the company's medical insurance plan.

5. *Commuter-assistance transportation programs.* These programs are designed to help employees who usually depend on private automobiles or mass transit when commuting to and from work.

   One type of program, *vanpooling,* consists of groups of employees who ride to and from work together in a van that is either company owned or leased. Or the vanpooling services may be obtained from a third party or a van owner-operator. In the latter case, sometimes the employer agrees to subsidize the fares charged by the van driver.

   Carpooling is another popular transportation program that is easy to administer and requires relatively little initial investment by the employer. The main function of the employer is to match up the riders who will commute together in one car. The match-up is often done by accessing a database containing names of interested workers, addresses, phone numbers, and rider/driver preferences.

6. *Domestic partner benefits.* A handful of companies have liberalized their eligibility standards for health insurance coverage and other benefits by extending coverage to unmarried couples of the same sex or opposite sex. Among these pioneering organizations are Ben & Jerry's Homemade, Inc., Apple Computer, Microsoft, Borland International, Lotus Development Corporation, Levi Strauss & Co., MCA, Inc., Warner Bros., Viacom International, *The Village Voice,* Minnesota Communications Group, and the cities of Seattle, East Lansing, West Hollywood, Laguna Beach, and Santa Cruz.

7. *Personal service benefits.* A few companies are experimenting with personal and household service benefits that provide for the little things workers would do if they had the time—make dinner, get the oil changed, pick up the dry-cleaning, make travel reservations, and so on. For example, PepsiCo created a corporate "concierge" service in the New York–New Jersey area in response to an employee survey that showed its workers too pressed for time to handle their own personal errands.[10]

DEVELOPING AND IMPLEMENTING A COST-EFFECTIVE EMPLOYEE BENEFITS PROGRAM

With skillful planning and organizing, a company may develop and implement a cost-effective employee benefits package that represents a major factor in the firm's successful operations. All managers, including the AOM, and supervisors must be aware of the different kinds of benefits offered by their company so they can aid in more efficiently managing these benefits and discussing them intelligently with employees.

Often the number of employee benefits grows without a clear purpose or design. Many times, a specific benefit is added merely because a competitive firm has recently included the same benefit in its package. Rather than investigate the needs of the firm and its employees, often one person or a committee unilaterally adds benefit after benefit, with a resulting mixture of costly and inappropriate forms of coverage.

---

[9]Ibid.

[10]"Companies Try to 'Buy Time' for Employees," *Issues in HR* (July–August, 1993), p. 5.

The person in charge of the benefits program should avoid overreacting to outside competitive pressures, current fads, and presentations of overly zealous salespersons promoting a new or expanded benefit. Instead, the person developing and implementing the benefits program should turn to the fundamental functions and principles of management in order to manage efficiently and effectively an integrated package of employee benefits.

Setting Objectives

You may wish to review on pages 262 through 264 the list of objectives that may be realized by developing a program of employee benefits. A company selects those objectives which, when attained, will meet the needs of the workers and the firm. In making its selection of objectives, the company is guided by many factors such as its size, location, extent of unionization, profitability of operations, patterns previously set by the industry, and management's perception of employee needs. Once the objectives have been selected, they must be clearly stated in keeping with the firm's philosophy and policies. Finally, as discussed later, provisions must be made for communicating the objectives to all persons concerned and for making sure, by appropriate feedback techniques, that the objectives are fully understood.

Assigning Responsibilities

In a small company, we may find that the OM is assigned responsibility and authority for administering the employee benefits program. As indicated in Chapter 1, this person may also be given responsibility for all human resources functions (recruiting, hiring, employee relations, training, employee communications, and wage and salary administration) in addition to information management activities.

Medium-size companies may employ a benefits planning specialist to handle the employee benefits program. Depending upon this person's expertise, he or she may call upon other staff members or outside consultants for help in spe-

cialized areas such as law, accounting, and investments. In the large organization, there is often a benefits director or manager, who, aided by a benefits committee, is responsible for integrating the management of all benefit plans. Some typical position titles and their median total annual compensation are:[11]

Corporate Benefits Director	$58,906
Benefits Manager	49,769
Corporate Benefits Section Head	45,869
Benefits Supervisor	40,201
Benefits Planning Specialist	39,876
Benefits Specialist (Clerical Jobs)	24,202
Benefits Clerk-Typist	19,632

In all firms, however, first-line supervisors have clear-cut communication and advisory responsibilities. As the linking pin between senior management and the employees, supervisors communicate information about the benefits program, such as length-of-service requirements and changes that have been made in the plan. In meeting their downward responsibilities, supervisors should be available to answer employees' questions about applying for certain benefits and to point out the advantages and disadvantages of particular benefits. As part of their upward responsibilities, supervisors advise management of employee reactions to existing plans and their interests in other benefits not currently offered by the company. To fulfill this upward responsibility, supervisors must first determine the employees' needs, as discussed in the following section.

Determining Employee Needs

A firm should seek its employees' opinions before adopting any new benefit plan or making changes in an existing program. Thus, management can determine how employees feel about existing benefit coverage and whether they have particular preferences or priorities with respect to changes in the benefits program. The company might find that the

[11]"For Your Information," *Personnel Journal* (February, 1993), p. 18.

benefits it considers important are not viewed as particularly significant by employees. The reverse may also be true; benefits that have low priority for the company may have high priority among employees. The firm may also find that costly changes in benefits do not necessarily produce the highest level of employee satisfaction. On the other hand, some relatively inexpensive changes may score very high among employees.

Behavioral scientists tell us that employees are better motivated and more satisfied if they take an active role in developing their own benefits packages. Thus, employees can construct a *flexible* benefits package that meets their diverse preferences as dictated by lifestyle, age, family situation, tax bracket, physical condition, and spending needs. A **flexible benefits program,** also called a *cafeteria plan,* is an employer-sponsored benefits package that offers employees a choice between taking cash and certain qualified benefits, such as accident and health coverage or group term life insurance coverage. The selection is made as the employees determine how many dollars to allocate to each type of optional benefit made available by the employer. Usually each employee receives a specified number of credits to "spend" on benefits, depending upon the employee's age, salary level, and length of time on the job.

Communicating the Benefits Program to Employees

The privilege of receiving benefits, those newly emerging as well as those offered in the past, must be communicated to and understood by workers. This means that the benefits must be described in a language and a format employees will remember and understand. Some of the approaches used by companies in communicating their benefits program to employees include the following:

1. Hold annual meetings with employees and their families where the company's benefits program is clearly explained.
2. Conduct small meetings and counseling sessions led by company managers and supervisors to follow up on questions that employees have asked during the year.
3. Distribute up-to-date handbooks and summary plan descriptions to employees, as required by the Employee Retirement Income Security Act.
4. Mail a series of letters, over the signature of the chief executive officer, to employees' homes to involve the entire family. For example, letters may be used to announce an updated benefits program to start on a specified date or to outline the revisions to be made in the present benefits program. Annual statements may be enclosed to show in detail the employees' earnings and their benefits.
5. Develop a slide film or videotape program to tell employees what their benefits are and how they have been designed to meet their needs.
6. Use company publications to answer employees' questions of general interest.
7. Prepare posters and distribute payroll envelope stuffers, pocket calendars, and "gadget" benefit calculators that aid in telling the employee benefits story.
8. Use the employee's PC, linked to the firm's database, to inquire about the current status of the employee's benefit program, to make changes, and to enroll in new benefits offerings.
9. Use voice-response technology to give consistent and confidential answers to commonly asked questions relating to benefit plans and/or the enrollment process. Employees can be given pertinent highlights of a benefit plan and then prompted to make their elections, changes, and so forth.

Controlling the Costs of Employee Benefits

Communications such as those described above aid in making sure that employees are aware of the cost of the benefits provided, especially those for health-care insurance, which is the employer's most expensive benefit. With health-care spending expected to jump between 12 and 15 percent each year, many businesses find that the outlay for employee health insurance outruns their efforts to control the mounting medical costs. Thus, we find companies actively at work trying to *contain,* or reduce within limits, the escalation of their health-care costs while at the same time meeting the health needs of employees and their families.

To contain the costs of health-care benefits, we find that companies take one or more of the following steps:

1. *Investigate the use of health maintenance organizations (HMOs) and preferred provider organizations (PPOs),* discussed earlier in this chapter. Companies that have been using self-insured, self-funded plans, in which they assume a substantial amount of the risk involved, may contract with providers such as HMOs and PPOs to manage their health-care programs.

2. *Place more responsibility on employees to share the costs* by raising deductibles, increasing coinsurance, and increasing the employees' out-of-pocket limits.

3. *Require review programs* to make sure that medical procedures undertaken by employees are necessary. Thus, some firms are redesigning their health plans to include second surgical opinions, to monitor patient admissions to hospitals, and to offer workers an incentive to have minor surgery in outpatient clinics.

4. *Employ third-party specialists* to aid in establishing information systems, overseeing claims processing procedures, and coordinating second opinions.

5. *Apply case-management techniques,* which include monitoring the course of an employee's illness, supervising and authorizing medical services, and using lower-cost outpatient, home, or hospice care instead of hospitalization. Case management is often used in catastrophic illnesses, such as AIDS.

6. *Explore the feasibility of setting up a self-insurance plan,* if the firm is large enough to afford self-insurance. Large companies that provide their own funds to insure employees are exempt from state-mandated benefit laws and from state taxes on health-insurance premiums. (All states have laws that mandate, or require, employers who offer group health plans to include specific benefits, such as al-

coholism treatment, newborn nursery care, orthopedic braces, and breast reconstruction.) Self-insurance also gives the company more control over the plan design. According to the nationwide consulting firm Foster Higgins, in 1992 among companies with more than 1,000 workers, 80 percent were self-insured.[12]

7. *Reduce or eliminate retiree benefits.* Retirees are asked to pay more of their medical-insurance premiums, to pay more of the cost of prescription drugs, or to increase their medical deductibles or copayments.

Investigating Recent Developments in Employee Benefits Programs

Those responsible for the firm's employee benefits program must keep abreast of new developments. The employee benefits administrator must be informed not only of new kinds of benefits that are being offered but also of innovative, cost-effective ways to provide these benefits to the workers. We shall close this chapter by briefly examining three relatively new developments.

Employing Benefits Consultants

To reduce record-keeping costs and deliver better service to its employees, an organization may turn over its key benefits business, such as administering its retirement plans, to a benefits consulting firm. Making use of new communications technology, some consulting firms provide voice-response, automated teller machine-like kiosks and toll-free 800 numbers. Using these media, workers can call to get information about their benefit plans and make changes in their investments.

As an alternative to using outside consultants, IBM set up its own standalone company, Workforce Solutions, to handle its human resources and benefits operations. Workforce Solutions provides support to IBM's business units and customizes its benefits to meet each unit's differing needs rather than rely on "one size fits all." The changeover to

---

[12]Roger Thompson, "Going, Going, . . . Gone?" *Nation's Business* (July, 1993), p. 24.

Workforce Solutions has saved IBM about $45 million each year in the form of reduced staffing, consolidation of offices, and so on.[13]

Modifying Retiree Benefit Plans

Commencing in 1993, companies with 500 or more employees began to make changes in their retiree benefits to comply with a rule issued by the Financial Accounting Standards Board. Under the rule, companies began to accrue the projected cost of their retiree benefits and report their liability for these benefits on their financial statements. (Companies with fewer than 500 employees come under the rule in 1995, when they may deduct the projected expense at one time or amortize it over a longer period.) As a result of this accounting rule, which requires the recognition of large expense amounts, companies have become more aware of the huge cost of retiree benefit plans, such as medical insurance. Therefore, retiree health plans are undergoing changes, with employees shouldering a greater share of health-care costs or retirees' health coverage being phased out. In turn, organized groups of retirees and union members have taken legal action to block any movement to eliminate company-paid retiree benefits.[14]

Creating Portable Pensions

To meet the needs of a changing, more mobile workforce, a growing number of companies are redesigning and simplifying their pension plans by making them *portable*. As a result, when employees leave the company, they can "carry" their retirement income with them and roll it over into the new employer's savings plan or an IRA.

[13]Tim Smart, "IBM Has a New Product: Employee Benefits," *Business Week* (May 10, 1993), p. 58.

[14]Stephenie Overman, "Time to Rethink Retiree Benefits," *HR Magazine* (March, 1993), pp. 52–53.

SUMMARY

1. Companies provide benefits to their office workers in order to attain several objectives: (a) to meet legislative requirements, (b) to attract and retain qualified workers, (c) to motivate workers to become more productive, (d) to meet the employees' needs for job security and job satisfaction, (e) to reward employees who improve their performance and increase their productivity, (f) to lessen the company's tax burden, (g) to prevent unionization, (h) to fulfill the obligations contained in a collective bargaining agreement, and (i) to meet the competitive pressures brought about by other firms in the community.

2. The average cost of employee benefits amounts to about 39 cents of each worker's payroll dollar. The percentage of this dollar spent on benefits is as follows: medical and medically related benefits, 26.4%; payment for time not worked, 26.4%; legally required payments, 22.7%; retirement and savings plans, 15.3%; paid rest periods, work breaks, and so forth, 5.6%; miscellaneous (discounts, educational assistance, etc.), 2.3%; and life insurance, 1.3%.

3. Those responsible for developing and implementing the employee benefits program and containing its costs should be guided by the fundamental functions and principles of management in setting the objectives of the program, assigning responsibilities, determining employee needs, communicating the benefits program to employees, controlling the costs of employee benefits, and investigating recent developments in benefits programs.

cont

FOR YOUR REVIEW

1. What objectives does a company try to achieve by providing benefits for its office workers?

2. Which three categories of employee benefits cost employers the most in 1991?

3. How is the cost of OASDHI benefits financed?

4. What protection do employees receive from major medical insurance coverage?

5. Describe the provisions of a typical group life insurance plan.

6. What is the common practice regarding paid vacations and holidays for office workers?

7. What protection does the Pregnancy Discrimination Act provide for pregnant employees?

8. List the guidelines that an AOM should keep in mind when scheduling rest periods.

9. What are the major provisions of the Family and Medical Leave Act of 1993?

10. What is the nature of educational assistance provided office workers in many firms?

11. Explain how an outplacement counseling program assists laid-off and terminated workers.

12. What kind of help might an office worker expect to receive from a firm's legal service plan?

13. What are the first-line supervisor's responsibilities in the operation of an employee benefits program?

14. Describe five kinds of communication media that may be used to inform office workers of the benefits provided by their firm.

15. What steps should be considered by a company that is trying to contain the costs of its health-care benefits program?

FOR YOUR DISCUSSION

1. As office supervisor in your small company with 150 office employees, you are convinced that something must be done to help solve the problems facing an increasing number of working mothers. However, when you approach your boss with the idea of establishing a childcare center, you are told, "Our company is too small. Besides, we're understaffed." However, you don't give up, and now you are considering how your company might operate a childcare program without a huge cash outlay. Provide some suggestions for ways in which the small firm can economically provide childcare.

2. To reduce their rising health-care costs, companies urge their employees to become more knowledgeable and more aggressive buyers of medical services. Many administrators of employee benefit plans believe that workers should shop around for medical care just as they would for any other service. As a benefit plan administrator, what steps would you recommend your company take to motivate employees to seek lower health-care fees?

3. Eight different employee benefits are listed below:

   a. Long-term disability income insurance.

   b. Retirement plan.

   c. Dental insurance.

   d. Parental leave.

   e. Health insurance.

   f. Group life insurance.

   g. Tuition aid.

   h. After-tax savings/profit-sharing plan.

   Assume, first, that you are an office worker in your early twenties, single, with no dependents. Rank these eight benefits to show how important you personally consider them. Next, assume you are an office worker in your late forties, married, with your two children attending college, and with a spouse who is also employed full time. Now what is your ranking of the eight benefits? How do you account for the differences in your rankings?

4. At a meeting of the Council on Employee Benefits, one of the speakers stated that any future changes in benefits packages should be directed toward providing a more cohesive package that would benefit both the company and its employees. As you look ahead, which benefits of those presently offered do you expect to become more widespread in their availability to office workers? Now, stretch your imagination and list those kinds of benefits that may have emerged by the year 2020.

5. During her two weeks' vacation, Terri Valdez was forced to leave the motel at the seashore and undergo an appendectomy at a nearby hospital. Upon returning to work, Valdez indicated to the office manager that, in view of her hospitalization, the company should reschedule her vacation date and treat her former two weeks' vacation as paid sick leave. As office manager, how would you respond to Valdez?

6. During the hiring process, the office supervisor and the manager of human resources told Clint Plantier that he had his choice of working on an hourly or a salary basis. Neither person happened to tell Plantier that there was a 90-day waiting period before the medical coverage for hourly workers began. However, salaried workers were covered immediately. Plantier indicated he preferred to work on an hourly basis. All went well until 60 days later when Plantier had to admit his daughter to the hospital for emergency surgery. Learning that he had no medical coverage for himself or his dependents, Plantier decided to sue his employer for having given him bad advice about his benefit eligibility. If you were the judge hearing this case, what verdict would you hand down?

CASES FOR CRITICAL THINKING

Case 11-1 Improving the Total Benefits Package

The Dano Software Company, owned by Bryant and Denise Dano, has grown during the past ten years from a "mom and pop" operation into a corporation with 55 office employees and 280 production workers. From the very beginning, the Danos provided their workers only those benefits required by law plus the usual paid vacations; holidays; hospital, surgical, and medical insurance; and group life insurance.

Mrs. Dano has just read an article in *The Wall Street Journal* indicating that some of their competitors are faced with employee benefits that cost, on the average, $190 each week. The Danos' accountant estimates that the weekly cost of the benefits provided a Dano worker is $115. After examining their past operating costs, projecting their future sales volume, and much soul-searching, the Danos realize that they can afford to expand the benefits presently provided their workers. They also feel obligated to do so if they want to retain their workers and ward off unionization. However, neither of the Danos wants to give the employees the impression that the additional benefits are being provided merely to catch up with the competition.

The Danos have come to you, their manager of administrative services, and asked for your help in modifying the present benefits program so an improved package can be presented to the workers at the annual Christmas party in four weeks. In talking with you, the Danos ask the following questions:

1. What are the most meaningful benefits to offer now?

2. How can we be sure that all the workers need, or even want, the benefits you are recommending?

3. What suggestions do you have for announcing the improved benefits package to the workers at the Christmas party?

Case 11-2 Challenging the Vacation Policy

Looking forward to early retirement within one week, Sean Arless has decided to give his employer a claim for unused vacation time. Arless calculates that he has accumulated 20 weeks of unused vacation time, which is the cash equivalent of $15,000.

When he met with Tim Geren, director of human resources, Arless was told, "Look at your employee handbook, Sean. It states very clearly that vacation days must be taken by year end or be forfeited."

Arless argued, "Yeah, Tim, but the company policy also says I am entitled to 15 paid vacation days for every year on the job. As I see it, that's part of my salary. You can't take my vacation days away once I have earned those days even if I don't use them."

1. Assuming Arless decides to press for payment in the court, how would you expect the judge to rule?

2. To protect itself from any future legal actions, how should Geren restate the company's vacation policy?

Case 11-3 Company Benefits: Computer Option (available on disk)

EXAMINING WORKPLACE ISSUES

GOALS FOR THIS CHAPTER

After completing this chapter, you should be able to:

1. Describe how office managers and supervisors respond to workplace issues and problems that affect their office workers' physical and mental well-being.
2. Describe some of the practices that firms follow in solving problems related to job attendance.
3. Identify the advantages and disadvantages that organizations may experience when adopting a modified workweek and work schedule.
4. Describe how a company minimizes the effects of downsizing or a recession by establishing a rotation of layoffs or work-sharing program.
5. Describe the role of the office manager before unionizing activity, while attempts are being made to organize, and after the workers become unionized.

The personal issues and problems of office workers often spill over into the workplace and, as a result, affect job performance and productivity. When we bring problems into the workplace, our *personal* problems become *personnel* problems for AOMs, who must assume responsibility for assisting us in solving our problems. Knowing how other office managers have solved similar problems strengthens the leadership abilities of managers and supervisors, improves the quality and quantity of their employees' work, and aids in creating a better work environment.

In this chapter, we shall examine those workforce issues and problems commonly found in offices of all sizes. First, we shall direct our attention to those issues that affect the physical and mental well-being of office employees. Next, we examine those job-attendance and work-scheduling problems and practices that are concerned mainly with raising the cost consciousness of OMs and their workers. Finally, we shall briefly explore the unionization of office workers.

THE WORKERS' PHYSICAL AND MENTAL WELL-BEING

Each day OMs, supervisors, and department heads are faced with a multitude of issues and problems that affect their employees' physical and mental well-being. Each problem requires a fair and equitable hearing and a decision that will be satisfactory to both the company and the worker. The solutions to some of these problems are often found in the employee handbook or the company's policy manual. Other problems require further study and consultation with employees before decisions can be made.

Alcoholism

It is expected that by 1997 alcohol abuse will cost the U.S. economy nearly $124 billion, with productivity losses comprising the bulk of that cost.[1] **Alcoholism** is a progressive disease characterized by the excessive, repetitive, and uncontrolled consumption of alcohol. The disease cannot be cured, only arrested. Alcoholism is not only a social and physiological problem; it is also considered to be a psychological one. An **alcoholic** is a person who is powerless to stop drinking and whose normal living pattern is seriously altered by drinking.

An employer should develop a straightforward policy regarding alcoholism with the aim of correcting behavior problems in employees before they become unemployable. The company should look upon alcoholism as it would any other disease that affects an employee's output or behavior while at work. In those firms that have instituted some kind of rehabilitation program, the plans usually operate along the lines of the three-step program advocated by the National Council on Alcoholism: (1) education, (2) early detection of the alcoholic, and (3) referral to a treatment center.

Education

The firm must get across to its office workers that alcoholism is a disease and will be treated as such. Many misunderstandings surround the subject of alcoholism and obstruct the development and operation of treatment programs. Thus, the facts must be given to employees through such media as visual aids, group meetings, and company newsletters.

Early Detection

The responsibility for detecting alcoholic problems among office workers usually lies with their supervisor. The supervisor should closely study and understand the employee's behavioral patterns and the visible signs of alcoholism during its several phases, as shown in Figure 12–1. The supervisor must remember, however, that alcoholics strive to hide their problems from others and even deny that they themselves have any problems. Thus, the early detection of alcoholic behavior is often the most difficult phase of the rehabilitation program.

Supervisors should discuss with their workers their declining productivity and carefully document their job performance and behavior. It must be made clear that unless the employees improve their performance or try to solve their problems by treatment, their jobs are in jeopardy. The alcoholic employees should be made to recognize and admit that they have a drinking problem and be motivated to accept rehabilitation or face the consequences of losing their jobs.

Referral

If the company retains a counselor or physician, the supervisor can refer the alcoholic office worker to that person. Sometimes we find that the counselor is a recovered alcoholic who has special empathy for persuading employees to accept suitable treatment, which may be through a lay group such as Alcoholics Anonymous, a residential alcoholism treatment facility, or a detoxification center. The task of the counselor is to impress upon workers that undergoing and responding to treatment are the only ways to avoid endangering their jobs.

Most small and medium-size companies do not retain a full-time doctor or counselor. In these firms, the supervisor can obtain help by consulting the Guide to Human Services in the telephone directory or the yellow pages under a heading such as "Alcoholism Information and Treatment Centers."

As you saw in Chapter 7, many large companies have established *employee assistance programs (EAPs)* that provide specialized aid and counseling. The office supervisor can refer workers with alcohol problems to the EAP, whose staff will confidentially counsel and refer workers to the appropriate agency.

Drug Abuse

Drug abuse, like alcoholism, threatens the work performance and continued employment of some office workers. A **drug abuser** is one who exhibits

---

[1]"Alcoholism Has a High Cost," *HR Focus* (August, 1993), p. 8.

Figure 12–1
Behavioral
Patterns and
Visible Signs
of Alcoholic
Employees

BEHAVIORAL PATTERNS AND VISIBLE SIGNS OF ALCOHOLIC EMPLOYEES

Behavioral Patterns | Visible Signs of Alcoholism

1. *Early Phase—before employee loses control over drinking*

Drinks to relieve tension.
Alcohol tolerance increases.
Blackouts (memory blanks) occur.
Lies about drinking habits.

Attendance
Arrives late for work (especially after lunch).
Leaves job early.
Absent from office.

General Behavior
Overreacts to real or imagined criticism.
Complains of not feeling well.
Lies.

Job Performance
Unable to meet deadlines.
Makes mistakes through inattention or poor judgment.
Efficiency decreases.

2. *Middle Phase—drinking is less controlled*

Guilt about drinking.
Tremors during hangovers.
Loss of interest in work, coworkers, and current events.
Avoids discussion of alcoholism problem.

Attendance
Frequently takes days off for vague ailments or implausible reasons.

General Behavior
Makes statements that are undependable.
Begins to avoid coworkers who were formerly close associates.
Borrows money from coworkers.
Exaggerates work accomplishments.
Sustains repeated minor injuries on and off the job.
Shows unreasonable resentment.

Job Performance
General deterioration.
Work pace is spasmodic.
Attention wanders, lack of concentration.

3. *Late Phase—loss of control over drinking*

Neglects food.
Prefers to drink alone.
Believes that other activities interfere with drinking.

Attendance
Frequently takes time off, sometimes for several days.
Fails to return from lunch.

General Behavior
Grandiose, aggressive, or belligerent.
Domestic problems interfere with work.
Money problems, including garnishment of salary.
Hospitalization increases.
Trouble with the law.
Drinking on the job.
Totally undependable.
Visible physical deterioration.

Job Performance
Uneven and generally incompetent.

strong psychological dependence on drugs, often reinforced by physical dependence on certain drugs. This person has been taking drugs for some time and feels unable to function physically and mentally without them. As a result of drug addiction, office employees are robbed of their motivation to do their jobs. Further, because their salaries are too small to support their increasing drug needs, they may begin stealing and thus become security risks for the company and the community.

In dealing with drug abuse in the office, the OM should follow a three-step program similar to the one for alcoholism.

Education

Cooperative education efforts with the community and its social agencies represent a major means whereby a company can halt the spread of drug abuse in the office. Many firms have undertaken broad educational programs aimed at initially preventing the use of drugs or narcotics. All of these programs support the principle that the only real cure for a **drug addict**—one who is physically dependent upon drugs—is never to start using drugs. Other companies conduct drug-abuse seminars for their supervisors and set up programs for spotting drug-using personnel. Information about drugs and narcotics may be obtained by consulting the Guide to Human Services in the telephone directory or the yellow pages under a heading such as "Drug Abuse and Addiction—Information and Treatment."

Early Detection

Many organizations use preemployment drug-screening testing of urine and blood, and also test their employees when reasonable suspicion of impairment or drug use is detected. However, some state and federal court decisions restrict an employer's right to test for drug and alcohol abuse in the workplace. Thus, it is often difficult for employers to know when they may test and under what circumstances. For this reason, companies should not initiate a testing program without advice from legal counsel.

The Supreme Court has ruled that the federal government may require drug testing of some workers in sensitive or safety-related jobs; however, the court left open any questions about the constitutionality of broad, random testing. Nevertheless, the Supreme Court decision boosted drug and alcohol testing by government employers in some circumstances, and, as a result, has encouraged testing by private employers. In its survey on workplace drug testing, the American Management Association found that three-fourths of major U.S. companies engage in drug testing. Also, as a result of government mandates, periodic or random drug testing increased tenfold from 1987–1991.[2]

Under the *Drug-Free Workplace Act of 1988,* companies that receive federal contracts valued at $25,000 or more must certify that they are taking specific steps to provide a drug-free workplace. In these companies, all employees must be notified that the manufacture, distribution, possession, or use of illegal drugs is forbidden in the workplace. Each company's antidrug plan must also provide for the counseling of employees and their access to rehabilitation.

To detect an on-the-job user and addict is the major responsibility of the office supervisor, who is closest to the worker. However, it is much more difficult to spot the drug abuser than the alcoholic. The addict's symptoms are not always apparent, even to the trained observer. The reaction to a drug, such as cocaine, usually depends on the user's mood and environment and the amount used. To aid in identifying employees addicted to cocaine, office supervisors should know the signs of abuse and dependency, which are listed in Figure 12–2. When dealing with employees who are heavily involved with cocaine, supervisors may obtain information by calling the National Clearinghouse for Alcohol and Drugs: 1-800-729-6686.

Company officials should be very cautious about accusing employees of drug abuse or searching their lockers and personal belongings, for an error in judgment can lead to a costly lawsuit. Those who interview job applicants should be alerted to the telltale signs that may indicate a

[2]"Test-Positive Rates Drop as More Companies Screen Employees," *HR Focus* (June, 1992), p. 7.

Figure 12–2
The Warning Signs of Cocaine Abuse and Dependency

WARNING SIGNS—JOB PERFORMANCE

Absenteeism and Tardiness
- A high rate of absenteeism on Mondays, Fridays, and the day after payday.
- Brief disappearances from workstations.
- Frequent tardiness.
- Often on sick leave.

Erratic Performance
- Temporary burst of energy, followed by fatigue and depression.
- Performance swings between extreme highs and lows without reason.

Errors in Judgment
- Arrogant and grandiose.
- Stops listening to others.
- Loss of good judgment.

Sorry I'm late. Did I miss anything?

WARNING SIGNS—SAFETY

Fitness for Work
- May be unfit for work due to irritability, mood swings, nervousness, hyperactivity, and hallucinations.

Frequent Accidents
- More often sustains accidents because of speed and carelessness.
- Easily distracted because of impaired judgment.

Increased Risk to Coworkers
- Ignores safety rules, uses equipment recklessly, and takes unwise risks.
- Bringing cocaine into workplace increases risk that coworkers will begin using the drug.

drug problem. In the case of a suspicious situation, the interviewer should carefully check the application and ask searching questions about gaps in employment history, frequent job changes, and reasons for leaving former jobs. Previous employers and references should be contacted directly.

Referral

As the law stands, accusing an individual of illegal use of drugs is a cause for libel, and both the super-visor and the employer may be sued. Trying to counsel a drug abuser may cause a supervisor to become involved in the abuser's personal problems and will make it more difficult for the supervisor to reflect accurately the facts in further discussions with the human resources department.

In some companies that have a policy on drug abuse, we find that those who violate the organization's code on drugs are immediately dismissed. In other companies, the firm refers to a rehabilitation agency or an employee assistance program those employees who have problems with drugs. These firms do not dismiss the workers unless rehabilitation efforts fail.

Mental and Emotional Illnesses

The absence of job satisfaction appears to be related to a variety of mental and emotional problems, such as psychosomatic illnesses,[3] low self-esteem, anxiety, worry, tension, and impaired interpersonal relations. Workers with personality disorders (including alcoholism and drug abuse) may find that their mental health problems stem partially from stress, job insecurity, unpleasant working conditions, and hazardous work.

Most companies have policies for dealing with mental and emotional illnesses among their office workers. Firms rely primarily upon employee magazines, reading rack material, and films that describe the various kinds of mental illnesses and identify the sources of help available to troubled workers. In detecting employees with mental health problems, most firms place great emphasis upon observations made by the first-line supervisors, who focus their attention on the workers' job performance and changes in behavioral patterns, such as their mood swings or increased absenteeism.

Because of their pivotal role in identifying workers who may have mental problems, supervisors should be provided with information that will help them recognize mental illness and be able to refer workers to a professional service. The office supervisor may find the names of reputable clinics in the yellow pages of the telephone directory under a heading such as "Mental Health Services." Also, the Department of Labor's Substance Abuse Information Database offers assistance to employers in establishing workplace policies, drug-testing guidelines, supervisory training, and alcohol/drug counseling resources. The information is free and comes on computer disk. To order, call the Department of Labor at 1-800-775-SAID.

AIDS

Acquired immune deficiency syndrome (AIDS) is caused by the human immunodeficiency virus (HIV) that attacks the body's immune system. The virus is transmitted by intimate sexual contact; by infected blood entering the bloodstream through the use of contaminated hypodermic needles; or, in the case of a newborn baby, either while it is developing in the uterus or during birth to a mother infected with the virus. As the immune system becomes weaker, the body becomes more vulnerable to infections and cancers. As AIDS progresses, a person becomes overwhelmed by diseases and eventually dies. The federal Centers for Disease Control estimates that 1 in every 250 Americans has been infected by HIV and that most of those infected are 25 to 44 years old—the core age group of our workforce.[4]

AIDS-based discrimination still exists in the workplace. Unfortunately, this is true, despite all the educational efforts undertaken by governmental agencies, private businesses, the media, and gay and lesbian groups to inform the public that employees with AIDS do not pose a risk of transmitting the virus through ordinary workplace contacts.

The federal and state courts have ruled that AIDS is a handicap and that employees with AIDS are entitled to protection against discrimination. This ruling means that the treatment of employees with AIDS should be the same as that for others with any life-threatening, catastrophic, or terminal illness. Thus, an employee with AIDS should be eligible for the same work privileges and medical benefits as a worker suffering from lung cancer. Further, under the Americans with Disabilities Act, workers with AIDS and HIV infection are part of the group that employers must "reasonably accommodate" on the job. This means that managers and supervisors must understand how the symptoms of HIV and AIDS affect a worker's ability to perform job-related tasks. For example, a worker suffering from extreme fatigue may be unable to sit at the desk for several

---

[3]*Psychosomatic illnesses* are ailments evidenced by bodily symptoms or bodily and mental symptoms as a result of a mental conflict. One of the most common psychosomatic illnesses is the stomach ulcer, which can occur in an employee who is unable to cope with prolonged mental stress.

[4]"Managing AIDS: How One Boss Struggled to Cope," *Business Week* (February 1, 1993), p. 48.

hours, and thus may request part-time work or a flexible work schedule.

For those companies having no formal policy for dealing with AIDS, the AOM needs to develop guidelines for supervisors to ensure that consistent treatment is provided for all HIV-infected employees and those with AIDS. These guidelines should cover topics such as:

1. The need to protect the privacy and confidentiality of infected workers who wish to remain on the job as long as they are able. The workers should be guaranteed that they will not be isolated from others.
2. How to allay the fears and anxieties of employees who believe that the disease can be transmitted by casual social or professional contact.
3. How to prepare employees for working with coworkers who have contracted the HIV virus as well as those with full-blown AIDS.
4. The need for an ongoing education program by means of brochures, pamphlets, newsletters, meetings, and so on, to convey current information.
5. Services provided by the company's employee assistance program (EAP)—professional counseling and support for employees with AIDS, for those being tested for AIDS, and for those groups subject to high risk of HIV infection.
6. Cost-containment measures, such as case management, to deal with AIDS-related medical care. As noted in Chapter 11, case management involves the close monitoring and evaluation of a patient's care.

Stress

Stress is the physical, chemical, or emotional state a person experiences at the time of a crisis or when subjected to irritations and unpleasant situations. Stress brings about bodily or mental tensions and may contribute to serious health problems, such as heart and stomach diseases. Stress is part of every office worker's life. According to a study conducted by Human Synergistics International, the three industries in which employees find it most stressful to work

are telecommunications, financial services, and not-for-profit associations; the two least stressful are educational administration and state and federal government agencies.[5] Some stress may be positive and pleasurable, for it stimulates us to feel more alert, think more clearly and objectively, and function better socially. However, excessive stress becomes *distress,* which robs us of our health and the company of its productivity.

Figure 12–3 lists some of the symptoms of stress identified by office workers and the sources of stress on the job and in the home. Although not all sources of stress can be removed entirely or even reduced, we can learn how to manage stress better.

Some approaches that organizations use to minimize stress include:

1. *Employee wellness programs.* As described in Chapter 11, these programs provide services designed to help employees maintain their mental and physical health and to stay well. Some of the services include testing the employee's physical fitness and designing a tailor-made health-management program and providing facilities for jogging, swimming, relaxing in a sauna, and aerobics.
2. *Stress-management programs.* Conducted either by in-house personnel or by an outside service, stress-management programs include seminars and clinics where office workers learn relaxation techniques such as meditation and yoga. The programs also offer discussion sessions that focus on physical fitness, hypertension control, healthy dietary habits, and control over alcohol and drug abuse.
3. *Employee assistance programs.* As we have seen earlier, EAPs provide specially trained counselors who work with employees in alleviating their symptoms of stress and minimizing their frustrations. Employees are aided in planning three-day weekends, vacations, or sabbaticals for rest, rejuvenation, and mental growth and development.

---

[5]"Study Finds Most Stressful Jobs," Advertising Supplement to *Human Resource Measurements* (April, 1993), p. 3.

Figure 12–3
Stress—Its
Symptoms and
Sources

SYMPTOMS OF STRESS

Physical Symptoms

- Back pains
- Churning stomach
- Exhaustion
- Headaches
- Heavy pounding of the heart
- Hyperactivity
- Inability to sleep
- Nervous tics
- Overeating
- Peptic ulcers
- Skin disorders
- Tight muscles
- Weak or dizzy spells

Behavioral and Psychological Symptoms

- Accidents on the job
- Alcohol and drug abuse
- Being overly emotional
- Depression
- Excessive smoking
- Feelings of great anxiety
- Inability to concentrate
- Job insecurity
- Loss of control over what appear to be overwhelming problems
- Psychological or physical withdrawal from work environment
- Sexual dysfunction

SOURCES OF STRESS

On the Job

- Absence of job description
- Demands of the job
- Fear of, and resistance to, change, especially overnight technological change that may cause displacement
- Having to meet tight deadlines
- Lack of feedback for work well done
- No clear line of command
- Responsibility without authority
- Unpleasant ergonomic conditions such as noise, smoke pollution, and crowding
- Fear of, or distrust of, supervisor and peers
- Layoff brought about by downsizing or economic downturn

In the Home

- Difficulties with children (truancy, drugs, alcohol) and in-laws
- Differences with mate (sex, money)
- Dissatisfaction about role responsibilities
- Emotional needs (caring, love, trust, empathy) not being met

4. *Outplacement counseling service.* Layoffs, brought about by downsizing or economic downturn, are among the most common causes of stress. As mentioned in Chapter 11, outplacement counseling offers laid-off workers a much-needed "shot in the arm" and aids them in adapting to the ranks of the unemployed.
5. *Health incentives.* Some companies offer incentives such as salary increases and "well leave" for employees who do not use their sick leave.

Burnout

Burnout is the depletion of one's physical and mental resources caused by excessive striving to reach unrealistic job-related goals. Burnout affects us at all ages and at all stages of our careers, regardless of our position within the organization. Generally, however, those most affected by burnout are workers with high energy, lofty ideals, and unrealistic expectations.

The symptoms of burnout are similar to those of stress, as listed in Figure 12–3. However, office workers who undergo stress do not necessarily experience burnout. Commonly reported symptoms of burnout include chronic fatigue; emotional exhaustion; job boredom; a negative, cynical attitude toward one's work; unfulfilled need for recognition; moodiness; poor concentration; forgetfulness; and physical ailments such as stomach disorders and backaches. Office employees find that on-the-job stress leads to burnout when they are placed under too many pressures to perform, when they become overly anxious about work problems, or when they seek unattainable goals. Stress in the home, such as family or personal problems, tends to increase the severity of job-related stress and adds fuel to the burnout process.

Figure 12–4 depicts several aspects of office life, each followed by a series of questions that AOMs should examine with the objective of reducing the risks of burnout among office workers. When AOMs can answer most or all of the questions affirmatively, they are assured that their organizations are following an enlightened approach in dealing with burnout. However, even with the best efforts made by organizations to minimize the risks of burnout, the solution to the problem rests with each of us as individual workers. Ultimately, we must (1) remove the cause of the stress, (2) remove ourselves from the stress situation, or (3) manage the situation so that we can take charge of our lives.

Smoking

The problem of smoking in the office and its effect upon productivity must receive the AOM's attention because smoking affects a worker's health, morale, efficiency, and productivity. In addition, sizable costs are associated with smoking in the workplace—excess medical-care costs, increased insurance costs, material and labor losses, and reduced productivity and morale. Today many organizations have an official policy that either restricts or completely bans smoking on the job. A survey by the Bureau of National Affairs and the Society for Human Resource Management revealed that 85 percent of the respondents restrict smoking in the workplace and that 34 percent ban smoking altogether.[6] About one-fifth of this country's employers have recruitment policies that give preference to nonsmoking candidates or simply refuse to hire smokers.[7]

Office workers and supervisors who argue for a smoke-free environment say that smoking is unhealthy and it pollutes the air. Further, it poses an unnecessary health risk to nonsmokers, whose eyes and throats become irritated and whose hearts and lungs may be endangered. Also, some believe that office workers who smoke are impairing their own efficiency. Others point out that the nonsmokers' right to breathe clean air, free from harmful and irritating tobacco smoke, has become recognized by a number of actions. For example, in 1993, the Environmental Protection Agency classified environmental tobacco smoke as a major cancer-causing agent—Group A human carcinogen—just as asbestos, benzene, and radon. In addition, federal regulatory agencies prohibit smoking on domestic airlines and buses and restrict smoking on trains. Further, most states and several hundred cities have im-

Illustration 12–1 More and more companies are adopting a policy that bans smoking in the workplace.

[6]Nancy A. Long, "The Last Gasp: Workplace Smokers Near Extinction," *Management Review* (February, 1992), p. 33.

[7]Larry Reynolds, "Company Policies Could Give Smokers Their Day in Court," *HR Focus* (August, 1992), p. 1.

Figure 12–4
Checklist for
Determining
the Extent of
Burnout
Among Office
Employees

MEASURING OFFICE EMPLOYEE BURNOUT

Evaluate the steps that have been taken by your organization to minimize the risk of burnout among office employees by answering the following questions. Total the number of your "Yes" answers and see the rating scale below for an interpretation of your score.

	Yes	No
Working Conditions		
1. Can office workers do their jobs without excessive red tape and overly rigid regulations that get in the way?		
2. Is stress limited by avoiding states of emergency in which workers are constantly working under deadlines and always trying to catch up?		
3. Is the ergonomic environment free of negative working conditions such as high noise level, overcrowding, an uncomfortable temperature, and drab colors?		
4. Are training programs available where office workers have the opportunity to upgrade their skills?		
5. Is there an employee fitness program aimed at encouraging employees to exercise regularly and become more concerned about their health?		
6. Do groups of employees working together have team spirit so that they can offer support and recognition to each other?		
Treatment of Workers		
7. Are outlets provided for workers to express their feelings and voice their complaints, concerns, and frustrations?		
8. Is there an employee assistance program that helps workers at all levels to cope with their lives on the job and at home? If so, are the burnout victims forced to acknowledge that coping strategies must be developed or else the burnout is unlikely to subside?		
9. Are employees provided work breaks so that they can refresh themselves or take short walks away from the office?		
10. Can employees sit down to a quiet luncheon?		
11. Are employees obligated to take their earned vacations *away from the office*?		
Creativity and Rewards		
12. Are employees aware of the significance of their accomplishments and the linkage between their jobs and the company's end product or service?		
13. Are feedback mechanisms and open communication lines available at all levels so that employees know that their ideas and suggestions for improvement will be properly transmitted and acted upon?		
14. Are office workers receiving equitable salaries under the firm's compensation plan?		
15. Beyond dollar rewards, are employees' creative contributions recognized so that their self-image will be improved and their job satisfaction increased?		

RATING SCALE

No. of Yes Answers	Where Does My Company Stand?
12–15	Your company is operating "on all burners" by effectively minimizing the risks of burnout.
8–11	Your company needs to take steps to improve its working conditions and treatment of workers and recognize the employees' creative efforts in order to reduce the risks of further burnout. In other words, your company needs to "stoke the furnace."
1–7	Your company is doing little to minimize the risks of burnout. If no steps are taken to improve the situation, it's going to be a long, cold winter in your office!

posed smoking restrictions in public places, and nearly half the states have restricted smoking in private-sector workplaces. In one of the country's toughest stands against smoking, Vermont approved a ban on smoking in all restaurants, motels, and hotels, starting in 1995.

The American Civil Liberties Union (ACLU) has been waging a campaign to make it illegal for companies to blackball prospective and current employees because they smoke. It is felt that such discriminatory workplace policies have nothing to do with job qualifications or job performance. The ACLU's stand is that a company must prove there is a direct relationship between smoking and job performance. The ACLU advances the argument that such discriminatory actions are an invasion of the workers' privacy and a violation of their civil rights. More than one-half of the states have passed laws that protect workers from being penalized by employers for smoking or engaging in any other legal activity *outside the workplace.*[8] These laws do not affect office smoking bans or smoke-free zones in the workplace. However, the laws do bar companies from refusing to hire smokers and from firing employees who fail to "kick the habit."

In view of the reports that link active and passive smoking to health hazards, many companies take steps such as the following to encourage workers to quit smoking:

1. Distribute quit-smoking literature.
2. Sponsor wellness programs.
3. Reimburse workers who participate in quit-smoking programs outside the workplace.
4. Sponsor in-house quit-smoking programs either on or off company time.
5. Permit smoking outside the office building only, and only during work breaks.
6. Pay cash awards to workers who quit smoking.
7. Offer lower insurance rates to nonsmokers.
8. Sponsor events such as "Kick the Habit" and the "Great American Smoke-Out."

---

[8]Ibid. Also see Junda Woo, "Employers Fume Over New Legislation Barring Discrimination Against Smokers," *The Wall Street Journal* (June 4, 1993).

Sexual Harassment

The guidelines first issued in 1981 by the Equal Employment Opportunity Commission (EEOC) defined **sexual harassment** as "unwelcome sexual advances, requests for sexual favors, and other verbal or physical conduct of a sexual nature," where such conduct affects an individual's prospects for employment or advancement or unreasonably interferes with work performance. The following 1993 EEOC guidelines reflect court decisions and agency rulings, which have broadened the original definition:

1. Employers have a duty to maintain a working environment free of harassment based on race, color, religion, sex, national origin, age, or disability.
2. Conduct is harassment if it creates a hostile, intimidating, or offensive work environment, unreasonably interferes with the individual's work, or adversely affects the employee's employment opportunities. The conduct includes such things as racist epithets, raunchy jokes, and ethnic slurs.
3. The standard for evaluating harassment is whether a reasonable person in the same or similar circumstances would find the conduct intimidating, hostile, or abusive. The perspective of the victim—his or her race, gender, age, place of origin, and so forth—has an important place in the evaluation.
4. Unwanted sexual conduct is not the only form of sexual harassment. Also classed as harassment is *gender-based animus,* which is the deep-seated dislike or ill will encountered by one gender when entering a profession traditionally held by the other gender.
5. Employers are liable for the acts of those who work for them if they knew or should have known about the conduct and took no immediate, appropriate corrective action. Employers who fail to draw up explicit, detailed antiharassment policies and grievance procedures may put themselves at particular risk.

Traditionally the only legal recourse available to a harassed employee was through civil action against the offending employee. Today, however, all complaints are investigated by the EEOC. If sexual harassment is found, the commission can ask that the victim be given a back-pay award, promotion, reinstatement, or other remedies under the Civil Rights Act. If the conciliation process fails, the commission may sue the employer. The Civil Rights Act of 1991 extended the victim's right to a jury trial and provided for greater damage awards. Therefore, the AOM and all office supervisors must take steps to protect their employees, themselves, and the firm from lawsuits and their costly consequences.

Lawsuits associated with sexual harassment usually involve problems of personal friction, turnover, disruption, and adverse publicity, all of which affect the firm's productivity. Thus, the firm should establish a clearly written policy that prohibits sexual harassment. Most important, the company must ensure that its policy is known and understood by all employees and that the grievance procedure guarantees a fair investigation of any complaints.

Office Romances

Romantic relationships sometimes develop in business offices since people are placed in close proximity to one another and thus their interactions encourage a relationship. The resulting office romance may pose problems for the AOM and the office supervisor since questions may arise about the relationship of the couple during working hours and its effect upon their job performance. In some instances, the couple's actions may result in lower morale and decreased productivity among the office staff; sometimes even jealousy may be exhibited among other workers.

The policies and practices that affect socializing and the development of office romances vary greatly among firms. In some firms, romantic relationships are anticipated and are tolerated until they disrupt work. Other firms discourage socializing by means of explicit rules.

Nepotism

Nepotism is the showing of favoritism in the employment of relatives. Firms that practice nepotism believe that the employment of rela-

tives, compared with nonrelatives, gives them employees who are more loyal and dependable. At the top-management level, especially in a close, family-held corporation, the employment of a relative may assure continuity of the business and its corporate policies. The relative placed in a junior executive position need not be concerned with "making points with the boss" and can thus concentrate on developing his or her potential to the utmost. Some employers feel that relatives working in the same office share a strong sense of responsibility for their work, take more interest in the company operations, and are likely to "fit in" better—all contributing to an improved level of morale.

In other companies, nepotism brings about problems. Often the hiring of relatives creates jealousy and resentment among the employees. Employees ask themselves, "What's the use of trying?" and, as a result, the level of morale sinks. The hiring of relatives may also tend to discourage outsiders from seeking employment in a family-held company. Then, too, some firms have found that if relatives are employed and later prove to be unqualified for the job, they cannot be discharged or demoted as readily as nonrelatives.

Company policy and practice vary greatly with regard to the employment of married couples. In some offices, the employment of husband and wife makes for a close-knit, harmonious working group and the recruitment of couples is encouraged. These firms find that they obtain couples with top-level performance because the husband-and-wife team tends to reinforce each other, share common interests, and understand each other's work problems.

In other offices, the employment of a married couple may bring about personality conflicts, especially when both the husband and wife work in the same department or are in a direct supervisory-subordinate relationship. In these firms, the office supervisors cite potential morale problems (jealousy; forced competition; absenteeism; difficulties in scheduling for holidays, vacations, and deaths in the family; and conflicts of interest) in that the couples may not be able to separate their personal and professional lives.

Some companies do not hire married couples. Other companies will employ them but only in separate offices or departments. In still other firms, husbands and wives may remain on the payroll only if they married after meeting on the job. One restriction that appears fairly widespread prohibits one spouse from having supervisory responsibility over another, a rule that often prevents promotion. Then there are some employers who will hire a couple that lives together but will make one of them quit or transfer to another department if the couple marries.

When considering the employment of relatives and married women, we must keep in mind the provisions of the Civil Rights Act. The EEOC has ruled that it is legal for a company to have a policy against hiring a person whose spouse already is on the company's payroll. However, this rule must apply to male and female workers alike. It is illegal for a company to have a policy against hiring married women unless the same rule is applied to the employment of married men. Also, to discharge women when they get married is illegal unless there is a similar rule for male workers.

Sexual Orientation

By mid-1993, eight states (California, Connecticut, Hawaii, Massachusetts, Minnesota, New Jersey, Vermont, and Wisconsin), the District of Columbia, and more than 100 cities had enacted statutes, executive orders, and ordinances banning discrimination based on **sexual orientation**—a person's preference in sex or affectional partners. The New York City Human Rights Law defines sexual orientation to mean heterosexuality, homosexuality, or bisexuality. A *heterosexual* is a person who is sexually oriented toward a member of the opposite sex; a *homosexual* is a male or a female who has a sexual desire toward a member of that person's own sex; and a *bisexual* is a person who is sexually oriented toward both sexes. Today, depending upon their gender, homosexuals are usually referred to as either *gay* (male) or *lesbian* (female).[9]

It is important for today's AOM and office supervisor to study the trends of gay and lesbian employment in the public sector, for these trends may be tomorrow's law. At the federal government level, lesbians and gays have gained the right to fair and equal employment in the Office of Personnel and Management as long as their homosexuality does not directly interfere with the jobs assigned them. In the District of Columbia, sexual orientation is one of the several bases upon which it is unlawful for any person to practice discrimination in employment.

Millions of gays and lesbians are employed in government, military, and private business offices, although it is probable that most of their superiors and coworkers are unaware of their sexual preferences. Like heterosexuals, not all homosexuals conduct themselves in a businesslike manner. However, most lesbian and gay employees take their work ethics seriously and perform their jobs efficiently. Unlike heterosexuals, however, most of them work daily with the fear of losing their jobs if their sexual orientation is discovered. However, in some companies, such as Apple, AT&T, Boeing, Coors, Digital Equipment, DuPont, Hewlett-Packard, Levi Strauss, Sun Microsystems, and Xerox, we find that gay and lesbian workers have formed employee associations, fully supported by top management. Among the activities sponsored by these support groups are participation in the firm's diversity training program, lobbying for extension of employee benefits to domestic partners, conducting sexual orientation awareness training, networking, planning social events, and publishing newsletters.

Moonlighting

Moonlighting refers to our holding a second job or working at a second profession after our regular "daylight" job has ended. Like many people, we may hold two jobs in order to maintain a desired standard of living, to pay off debts, or to gain experience for entry into another career field. However, many persons in high-income brackets moonlight not for the dollars involved but because they enjoy the second job, which offers them satisfactions not met by their daylight (regular) job.

[9]Alistair D. Williamson, "Is This the Right Time to Come Out?" *Harvard Business Review* (July–August, 1993), pp. 18–28.

Some OMs feel that moonlighting decreases the quality of an office employee's work during the day, depletes the worker's energy, and accounts for less attention being paid to detailed work. Other OMs view moonlighting as evidence of a worker's initiative and desire to succeed and as a safety valve for tensions that have built up during the day on a boring, tedious job.

Moonlighting becomes an issue when the office workers are frequently tardy or absent, sustain accidents on the job as a result of fatigue, become more argumentative and difficult in their work relationships, or are more easily distracted from their work assignments. Taken together, these costly aftereffects of moonlighting exert a major impact on office productivity.

Some companies attempt to deal with moonlighting and its potential problems by banning the practice entirely, which is perhaps as effective as trying to outlaw the grapevine. Such a policy causes the moonlighting employee to engage in secretive activities, especially when the firm makes no effort to curtail the moonlighting activities of its supervisors and managers.

Workaholism

Unlike office workers who moonlight usually in order to supplement their earnings, **workaholics** are *emotionally* dependent upon their work. Work is their drug; they are addicted to it and cannot stop working. Some moonlighters, struggling to make ends meet, run the risk of becoming workaholics, especially if their added work hours reinforce a work-centered lifestyle.

There is little agreement about whether workaholism is a disease or merely a useful label for classifying a behavior pattern and lifestyle. We find research studies that show some workaholics simply prefer labor to leisure. Other psychological reports indicate that workaholics are emotionally disturbed—the product of unresolved conflict, feelings of inadequacy, or defective upbringing. For example, long hours at the office may indicate a family conflict or other crisis.

Office workaholics are easily recognized. They are found working anytime, anywhere,

nights, weekends, and holidays. They report in for work long before anyone else and leave the office long after they have become an obstacle to the night cleaning crew. They eat their lunches at their desks between telephone calls and constantly make efforts to "catch up." However, as far as their coworkers can determine, they have never fallen behind.

In the office, the most frequent problems are not for the workaholics but for those around them. Workaholics tend to create competitive, uncomfortable environments. The perfectionist standards set by workaholics can evoke resentment, which leads to interpersonal conflict or morale problems. For example, the workaholic office supervisor may set unrealistic standards that create more problems than they solve.

The OM should attempt to curb any problems that workaholics may be creating. One approach is to help workaholics recognize their problems by concentrating upon the accomplishment of goals—quantitative and qualitative—during employee appraisals or confidential meetings. The workaholics should be shown how their efforts and styles have created specific problems. For example, the workaholic office supervisor should be shown that, because of his or her ineffectiveness in group situations, talented workers have left the firm. Since the supervisor may respond by commenting about all the hours he or she spends on the job, the OM should concentrate upon the ends to be achieved, not the means.

The key to improving the productivity and performance of office workaholics is to help them gain a balanced perspective on their work and their lives. This requires professional counseling, during which time the workaholics should come to appreciate the benefits of rest and recreation. Office workaholics will probably never change—even if they desire to do so—unless professional guidance is sought.

Theft

The U.S. Chamber of Commerce estimates that employee theft costs U.S. businesses $40 billion each year and that about 20 percent of all businesses fail annually because of internal theft.[10] Office employees steal millions of dollars each year by taking advantage of their companies' indifference to the pens, pencils, stationery, blank diskettes and audiotapes, and typewriter ribbons that find their way into employees' homes and into the classrooms of the employees' children. Other costly examples of theft include time theft (discussed in Chapter 11), unauthorized long-distance telephone calls, and equipment theft. Control over theft and fraud is a problem in human relations, ethics, and value systems, as discussed earlier; moreover, the attitude and policies of management contribute to the problem. If managers and supervisors are indifferent toward the rules that have been established and if the atmosphere is one of "Who cares?" the office can become a school for dishonesty.

Some theories advanced by sociologists and psychologists show that how workers perceive their company is related to whether or not they will steal. Thus, if employees believe that their company is exploiting them in their daily relationships, the employees will tend to steal more. Such workers are searching for an equitable return for the contributions they feel they are making. Sometimes employees who are overlooked or slighted may become frustrated and try to work out a balance between how they behave on the job and what benefits they receive. Often the workers will attempt to remedy the supposed inequity by not working up to their capacity, wasting time in idle talk, and taking prolonged work breaks—all of which are forms of "stealing."

Here are some guidelines the AOM should follow in reducing employee dishonesty:

1. *Assign department heads responsibility for developing and enforcing a program of control over the purchase and issuance of supplies.* In this program of internal control, the person who orders the supplies should not be in charge of their receipt or issue checks to pay for them. Collusion between dishonest purchasers and suppliers is a frequent cause of large losses. The supplies needed by each department should be estimated and planned for in preparing each department's budget. Budgeting a dollar estimate, as explained in a later chapter, impresses upon workers the cost of the supplies and creates greater respect for usage. Supplies should be ordered in bulk only a few times during the year in order to reduce the number of orders and the opportunities for employees to "pad" the orders.

2. *Screen all job applicants by investigating their character references and any gaps in their employment history.* Applicants for positions of trust, such as those handling securities, and those who are promoted to such positions should be covered by a fidelity bond. A **fidelity bond** is a guarantee by the insurer that the insured firm will be compensated, up to an agreed-upon amount and subject to agreement on the terms and conditions, for the loss of money or other property resulting from the dishonest acts of the firm's employees.

3. *Require all terminated employees to report to an executive outside the former employee's department.* Thus, the AOM makes sure that the employee's name is removed from the payroll. Otherwise, an unscrupulous person might continue to issue checks in the name of the former employee and cash them with a forged signature.

4. *Set realistic performance standards.* If standards are not realistic and employees cannot achieve the goals or quotas, they are faced with two alternatives—to fail or to be dishonest. Periodic, unannounced spot checks or audits should be taken upon employee performance at all levels in the office. Employees should be informed that such audits are a normal part of internal control. All critical areas of office operations—cash handling, disbursements, and safeguarding of important records—should be inspected and reviewed periodically.

5. *Enforce policies fairly, firmly, and uniformly at all levels.* Double standards of enforcement by the AOM will break down discipline and morale quickly and lessen the employees' respect for the firm, its managers, and its policies and procedures.

---

[10]Samuel Greengard, "Theft Control Starts with HR Strategies," *Personnel Journal* (April, 1993), pp. 81–82.

Privacy

Workers do not want their employers to invade their personal lives, either on or off the job. Instead, workers want their appraisals, promotions, and terminations based solely upon the most important factor—their performance *while on the job*. On the other hand, employers argue that they are justified in their drive for efficiency, internal control, and productivity improvement. Thus, we find companies monitoring employee behavior, reading the employees' electronic mail, setting standards for on and off the job, and making demands regarding their workers' personal lives.

In this section, we shall briefly examine four areas in which employees question the invasion of their privacy—monitoring, electronic mail, personal and locker searches, and off-job activities.

Monitoring

We find managers listening to their workers' telephone conversations, using closed-circuit television to film employees at their video display terminals, installing electronic surveillance devices to monitor employee performance, and requiring workers to wear computerized clip-on ID cards that signal their location throughout the building.

Legislation was proposed in 1993 that would prohibit employers from monitoring employees by electronic means unless there is a serious reason for suspecting employee misconduct, such as theft and industrial espionage.

Electronic Mail

Electronic mail (E-mail), transmitted by FAX machines, communicating word processors, and computer-based message systems,[11] is not protected by the Electronic Communications Privacy Act. This act holds that nothing on a company computer can be considered private. Therefore, unless employers have promised their employees privacy of their E-mail, employers retain the right to read (and erase) their employees' messages.

Personal and Locker Search

The Fourth Amendment bars the government from unreasonable search, but it does not prohibit private employers from searching the offices used by their workers. To reduce their exposure to workplace problems, companies may establish a policy that gives them this right to search. To prevent possible legal problems, the search policy should be based on legitimate employer interests, such as prevention of theft; drinking on company property; and the use, possession, or sale of illegal narcotic drugs on company premises. Further, to avoid employees' claims of invasion of privacy, the policy must cover all types of searches that may be conducted, such as personal searches and locker searches. For protection against a slander charge, the policy should explain that a request to search a worker does not imply an accusation of theft.[12]

Off-Job Activities

In its survey of workplace privacy and off-job activities, the Society for Human Resource Managers found that most respondents believe that off-job political and recreational activities, such as smoking, should not be considered in employment-related decisions. However, more than 75 percent of those surveyed said that employers are justified in establishing differentials in health-care premiums for smokers. Most respondents approved of coworker dating and dating a competitor, but only slightly more than half would permit employee-supervisor dating.[13]

Although there are exceptions to the rule, generally a company has no right to interfere or suggest that employees conduct their outside social life according to the company's demands. If a company wants to set a rule regarding its employees' off-job activities, such as strictly prohibiting moonlighting, it should have an attorney check the guidelines before announcing them to em-

---

[11]Electronic mail systems are fully discussed in Chapter 18.

[12]Robert J. Nobile, "To Search or Not to Search: What Is The Policy?" *Personnel* (September, 1991), p. 7.

[13]"Managers Agree: Off-Duty Acts Are N.O.Y.B.," *Managing Office Technology* (July, 1993), p. 136.

ployees and placing them in the employee hand-book. As noted earlier, many states have passed laws that protect employees who participate in legal activities when not at work, including "high-risk" recreational activities such as moun-tain climbing and sky diving.

Violence in the Workplace

Since 1980, at least 750 people have been mur-dered each year while at work, making this the third leading cause of occupational death.[14] If you are a supervisor in a company where a laid-off employee walks in and kills several coworkers, your job will be to deal with an emotionally dev-astated workforce. And you may have been the killer's target! Economic conditions have been blamed for the increased number of murders by former employees who return to the workplace seeking revenge against those they feel responsi-ble for their discharge.

The person likely to commit murder in the workplace often gives off signs, but unfortunately these signs go undetected by coworkers and man-agers. The National Trauma Services in San Diego has developed a sociological and psycho-logical profile of the typical workplace murderer, which is shown in Figure 12–5.

When behaviors such as those listed in Figure 12–5 become evident, the person should be re-ferred for counseling. The employer can demand that the employee take a paid leave and get help. To aid laid-off employees, the employer can con-tact an outplacement service to help deal with the worker's trauma of termination. Other steps that may be taken to limit the potential for violence include: establishing a crisis-management team skilled in de-escalating hostile situations; provid-ing safety-awareness training for employees; pro-hibiting former employees from returning to the workplace; and evaluating the need to install a new security system.

JOB ATTENDANCE AND WORK SCHEDULES

In this section, we shall first examine several is-sues pertaining to job attendance. Chronic tardi-ness, absenteeism, and turnover are serious and costly problems for the AOM, particularly during prosperous times when many office jobs are available. Next, we shall see how organizations have modified their work schedules in order to reduce the costs of absenteeism and turnover, raise employee morale, and improve productivity.

Tardiness

The problem of tardiness, which is really a form of absenteeism, is usually handled by a written or an oral reprimand. The reprimand may be fol-lowed by payroll deductions, temporary layoff, and termination if the worker is habitually late.

Tardiness in the office is traceable more often to laxness in discipline than to any other cause. Of course, supervisors themselves must set the proper tone by arriving promptly for work. The practice of many companies in not tolerating tar-diness except under emergency conditions, such as public transportation delays, car trouble, and

[14]"Waging War in the Workplace," *Newsweek* (July 19, 1993), p. 30.

Illustration 12–2 Limiting access and monitoring movements throughout the office building are basic elements in workplace security.

THE POTENTIAL WORKPLACE MURDERER

Sociological Profile
- Middle-age, Caucasian male.
- Uses an exotic weapon, such as an Uzi, an AK–47, or a Samurai sword, legally acquired. May have a fascination with such weapons.

Psychological Profile
- Usually a loner and often angry, paranoid, and guarded.
- May exhibit religious or political proselytizing.
- Experiences a loss of identity because of the shallow nature of his interpersonal relationships.
- Equates layoff with actual loss of existence, and feels that since his life has been lost, why not take a few people with him?
- Has need for revenge and seeks out the perpetrator to pay for the crime.
- May have a history of violent behavior or substance abuse and an unstable work history.

Source: Peggy Stuart, "Murder on the Job," *Personnel Journal* (February, 1992), p. 74. Adapted from "The Potential Workplace Murderer" as described by Tom Harpley of National Trauma Services in San Diego.

driving conditions, proves that it can be controlled. Further, the use of flexible work schedules, discussed later in this section, minimizes the problem of tardiness.

Absenteeism

The absence of employees seriously affects the work of others in most offices unless there are "floating" replacements. Some human resources departments have a database that contains a listing of all employees' capabilities for performing other jobs; thus, these data can be used for transferring employees to take over the jobs of the absentees. But regardless of the firm's size, the problem is one of management and must be studied carefully. The AOM should analyze absenteeism by finding out its *extent, causes, and cost,* and *what action can be taken to control it.*

Extent of Absenteeism

To measure the **absenteeism rate** in an office or a department, the following formula may be used:

$$\text{Absenteeism rate (\%)} = \frac{\text{Worker-days lost during period}}{\text{Average number of workers} \times \text{Number of workdays in period}} \times 100$$

For example, assume that in a bank's computer center an average of 25 workers is employed during a month having 22 workdays. Because of absenteeism, 15 worker-days have been lost. We can calculate the absenteeism rate for that month as follows:

$$\frac{15}{25 \times 22} \times 100 = \frac{15}{550} \times 100$$
$$= 2.73\% \text{ absenteeism rate}$$

After we have calculated the absenteeism rate for each unit, we can compare the extent of absenteeism in the entire firm or among different offices or departments. We can also compare the rate with that of other companies of similar size, in the same industry, and in the same geographic area.[15] The absenteeism rate of 2.73% just calculated means that, for about every 37 workers in the bank (1.00/.0273), the firm is carrying one extra employee to take care of the average absence. Assuming an hourly salary rate of $12 and taking into account the 1991 employee benefits percentage, the one extra worker may be costing the bank about $34,744 each year ($12 × 40 hours × 52 weeks = $24,960) + (39.2% × $24,960 = $9,784 for employee benefits).

[15]Comparative data on absenteeism are available in the *Monthly Labor Review,* published by the Bureau of Labor Statistics, and from private sources such as The Bureau of National Affairs, Prentice-Hall, and Commerce Clearing House.

Data on absenteeism are readily available when the information is stored in a database. When workers have been absent from their jobs for a full day or longer, they should be required to report to the OM, their supervisor, or the human resources department before returning to work. Thus, a record can be kept of the workers' absences and the reasons for the lost time. The absenteeism records should become part of the employees' files so the information may be considered at the time of employee appraisal and when opportunities for promotion and salary increases arise.

The individual absenteeism records can be combined and used to calculate an absenteeism rate. Or a report may be prepared for the entire company or for each department that shows the total days' absence during the year, a classification of the reasons for absences, and the frequency of times absent by each employee. Determining the frequency of times absent for each worker aids in locating and controlling chronic absentees, especially those who exhibit a pattern of being ill on Fridays or Mondays.

Causes of Absenteeism

Illness (defined to include alcoholism and drug abuse) and work-related accidents are the most common causes of absenteeism. Some employees seem to avoid working on the slightest pretext of illness; however, others work when they are so ill that they should stay at home.

A company's sick-leave policy may not necessarily invite absenteeism, but it often seems to condone absences. For example, we find that some firms provide full pay for those ill 5 days or less; other companies may provide full pay for an illness lasting 6 to 10 days. If a company encourages absenteeism by neglecting to control it and if employees feel that management is not concerned, they will not make it a priority to show up for work each day. Instead, they may use their sick leave as vacation days to balance out what they perceive as an unfair working situation. Many employees see the sick days as days "coming to them" for putting up with low pay, poor working conditions, or a disagreeable boss.

Absenteeism varies with the age and gender of the workers. In 1992, the Labor Department reported that the highest average annual absenteeism rate was for workers age 16–19, with 7.3 days; the lowest rate, 4.6 days, was for workers age 25–54.[16] Often the causes of absenteeism among younger workers are not illnesses but, instead, are low morale and a reluctance to accept the workplace discipline. For men, the average annual absenteeism rate was 3.7 days; for women, it was 6.4 days.[17] These figures seem to show that society continues to assign women the traditional responsibility for the home and childcare.

The absenteeism rate is highest among workers who have relatively monotonous, routine jobs. Office workers who find their jobs unchallenging or oppressive, and who derive most of their satisfaction from outside pursuits, have little incentive to maintain a good attendance record.

Newly hired employees are often found among the most chronic absentees. This points to the need for careful selection of new employees by obtaining information from their former employers about their total *days* absent from the job and the total *incidences* of absence (number of times absent). Generally, frequent incidences of absenteeism indicate that leave is being taken for reasons other than illness. Other causes of absenteeism include family responsibilities; transportation problems, which include commuting a long distance from home to work; unreliability of the automobile, van, or bus; and weather conditions.

Cost of Absenteeism

The Absence Survey, conducted by Commerce Clearing House, found that the annual cost associated with unscheduled absences ranged from $247 per employee in small companies to $534 per worker in large firms.[18] The cost of absenteeism can be computed as shown in the following example of a small company having 40 office employees:

---

[16]Maida Odom, "Who Isn't Showing Up for Work?" *The Philadelphia Inquirer* (May 25, 1993).

[17]Ibid.

[18]"Absence Makes the Costs Go Higher," *HR Focus* (August, 1993), p. 24.

Total number of sick days paid
  previous 12 months   200
  (based on 40 employees with an
    average of 5 days' absence each)

Average daily pay multiplied by
  total number of sick days   × ___$64

Annual cost of absenteeism to firm $12,800

The annual cost of absenteeism, $12,800, does not include other costs associated with absenteeism: employee benefits; overtime pay for substitute workers; decrease in employee efficiency; disruption of workflow, leading to missed delivery dates; and costs associated with hiring temporary replacements, all of which could easily double the annual cost.

Controlling Absenteeism

What can we do about the problem of absenteeism? Typically, penalties, fines, and incentive bonuses do not produce the desired effects. Penalties and fines, such as payroll deductions for absences the day before or after a holiday, with their demoralizing effects, create hard feelings and job dissatisfaction. Incentive bonuses are usually only temporary in their effect. However, since only a small number of workers are chronic offenders, each individual case should be studied in solving the problem. In the case of chronic absenteeism, many companies use a three-step disciplinary approach: (1) warning, (2) layoff without pay, and finally, (3) termination.

Supervisors should be held accountable for the attendance records in their departments. Prior to taking disciplinary action when workers are excessively absent, supervisors should talk over job problems with their workers to discover why the workers are so often away from their jobs. Such references to the causes of absenteeism may indicate possible solutions to the problem. Supervisors should make every effort to reduce the absences caused by illness and on-the-job accidents. An educational campaign to maintain the health and safety of employees may be undertaken. For example, providing vitamins and free flu shots has been successful in some offices in reducing substantially the absences caused by

illness during winter and spring months. Providing satisfactory ergonomic conditions, such as good lighting, comfortable levels of heating and air conditioning, and noise control, may also be effective in reducing absenteeism. Further control over absenteeism may be obtained by modifying the work schedule, as noted later in this section.

Before any policy on absenteeism can be established and chronic absenteeism defined, standards must be set by the firm for the amount of absenteeism that will be tolerated. Recognizing that there are no corporate attendance standards for employees, long ago The Bureau of National Affairs recommended the following attendance guidelines for any 12-month period:[19]

Number of Absences	Classification
0–2	Excellent
3–4	Good
5–6	Satisfactory
7–8	Poor
9 or more	Unacceptable

Any absenteeism policy should have as its goal the promotion of regular, consistent attendance. The policy should be fair, enforceable, and agreeable to both management and labor. One form of absenteeism policy that meets most of these criteria is called a **no-fault leave policy,** which eliminates the troublesome sick-leave provision and all forms of unlimited leave. Most no-fault leave policies provide a maximum number of days to be absent for any reason, such as four to six noncumulative leave days with pay per year. Ordinarily, absence due to jury duty, funeral leave, parental leave, military leave, hospitalization, inclement weather, and other company-approved absences are not charged against the no-fault days. Most no-fault policies provide for counseling and disciplining those workers who are absent beyond the number of days allowed.

[19]"Personnel Opinions: How Much Absence Is Acceptable?" *Bulletin to Management* (Washington, DC: The Bureau of National Affairs, September 21, 1978), p. 1.

Turnover

Turnover is the amount of movement of employees, voluntarily and involuntarily, in and out of an organization. Most turnover falls in the *controllable* category, which means that the company could have a major influence over whether the employees leave. The remaining turnover is caused by death, accidents, retirement, sickness, military service, or pregnancy. A degree of turnover must be expected and is healthy for the firm. However, it is also costly. Since firms may experience turnover rates greater than 20 percent among office workers, excessive turnover exerts a strong influence on a firm's profit picture.

Turnover Rate

The **turnover rate,** expressed most often in terms of the number of separations from the payroll (quits and dismissals), is computed as follows:

$$\text{Turnover rate (\%)} = \frac{\text{Total number of separations for the time period}}{\text{Average employment for the time period}} \times 100$$

Assume that a firm had an average employment throughout the year of 750 and that the number of persons who were terminated totaled 120. We calculate a turnover rate of 16 percent, as shown in the following example:

$$\frac{120}{750} \times 100 = .16 \times 100 = 16\% \text{ turnover rate}$$

Reasons for Turnover

The reason given most often by office employees for terminating their jobs is to take another job. Other reasons include: leaving the workforce, dismissal, relocation, retirement, and layoff. When we analyze the major reason for separation—*to take another job*—we find that the main causes are the desire for better salaries and better jobs, which includes the opportunity for advancement. Thus, in a program of turnover reduction, the AOM must evaluate regularly the salary structure, the employee benefits program, and the promotional opportunities in the firm.

Exit Interviews. At the time of terminating an employee's services, an **exit interview** may be conducted to determine the real reasons for termination. During such interviews, there should be a warm, supportive atmosphere in which the interviewer refrains from criticizing or arguing as the employees give their reasons for leaving. A record of the exit interview should be made available to interested supervisors and managers so they may be kept informed of the reasons for separation.

Post–Exit Interviews. Some companies make use of **post–exit interviews** in which questionnaires are sent to former employees asking their opinions of the company and their reasons for selecting work elsewhere. The former employees are asked to be frank in their replies; furthermore, if they wish, they may omit their signatures on the questionnaires.

Reducing the Cost of Turnover

We can break down the cost of turnover into the following three categories:

1. *Separation costs*—the expenses incurred when an employee leaves the company. Included here are the costs of the exit interview and various administrative and record-keeping activities.
2. *Replacement costs*—the expenses incurred in finding qualified applicants for the job opening. Typical costs are those for advertising the job opening, selection interviews, preemployment testing, and meetings held to determine which applicant to employ.
3. *Training costs*—the expenses incurred in helping the new employee learn how to perform the new job. Training costs include the costs for learning materials (booklets, manuals, software, etc.); workshops, seminars, and courses; on-the-job training and coaching; and salary and benefits until the new worker can adequately perform the job.

Let's calculate the turnover cost for a company. In the following example, we assume a 250-employee firm in which the average turnover cost of each employee is $14,500:

Total number of employees
separated in past 12 months
(Based on 250-employee firm
with 14% turnover rate)   35

Average cost of employee turnover $\times$ $ 14,500

Annual cost of turnover $507,500

To reduce excessive turnover cost or to control a satisfactory turnover rate, the OM should make sure that in the selection process the nature and the responsibilities of the job and the expected results are carefully explained to each job applicant. Job applicants should be presented a realistic picture of the job at the time of the interview. That is, the job should not be "oversold," nor should it be "undersold." Thus, any reservations the applicants may have about the work to be done can be investigated prior to employment. Employees must be carefully matched to the job openings, and opportunities must be provided the workers to achieve what they expected when they were hired. Employee creativity and self-improvement should be encouraged, jobs should be kept as challenging as possible, and opportunities for advancement should be pointed out.

Modified Workweeks and Work Schedules

To aid in reducing the costs of absenteeism and turnover, many organizations have established workweeks of less than the standard 40 hours. Also, there are different kinds of work schedules, which resemble only slightly the traditional 9-to-5 workday. In many instances, companies find that by adopting a modified workweek and an alternative work schedule, they are able to raise the office workers' morale, with a resulting improvement in productivity. Then, too, by modifying their work schedules, companies show they are responsive to the needs of workers who want more time away from the job. Alternative work schedules permit jobs to be shared by two employees, work to be completed in the home, and work to be done by employees on a permanent part-time basis. Each of these different kinds of workweeks and work schedules is described in this section.

Compressed Workweek

A **compressed workweek** is a work schedule in which the usual number of full-time hours are worked in fewer than five days (the regular workweek). For example, the *4/40 workweek* is a fixed workweek schedule that consists of 4 workdays, each of which is 10 hours in duration. When it was introduced, the 4/40 workweek represented a radical departure from previous trends since historically labor unions and other groups have tried to reduce both the number of days worked each week and the number of hours worked each day.

The compressed workweek was first introduced mainly in small and medium-size non-union firms as a means of improving employee morale by providing more flexible leisure time and enabling workers to schedule such things as dentist appointments outside of work time. It appears as if, following their rapid beginning in the early 1970s, compressed workweeks have peaked out. A major cause of the decreased rate of growth was the introduction from Europe of a different type of workweek—the flexible work schedule—which is discussed in a later section.

Staggered Work Schedule

Under a **staggered work schedule,** groups of workers arrive at their workplace at different times, according to a master plan. Once set, the hours do not change, and all employees work a predetermined number of hours during the workday. The objective of a staggered work schedule, especially in large metropolitan areas, is to persuade business and government offices to switch from the customary 9-to-5 schedule so a more even distribution of commuting times may be obtained. With staggered work schedules, commuter traffic tie-ups are reduced, waiting times for elevators are reduced, and lobby congestion is lessened in large office buildings.

Flexible Work Schedule

The **flexible work schedule,** also known as *flextime,* replaces the fixed times of worker arrival and departure. Instead, the workday is divided into two different types of time: core time and flexible time. *Core time* is the fixed number of hours during which all employees must be present for work. *Flexible time* is the time employees may choose for their arrival and departure times.

Under a typical plan, shown in Figure 12–6, the span (bandwidth) of the total possible workday, which includes flexible time periods and core time, is 12 hours. Each worker elects to come in at any time from 6 to 9 A.M. and leave at any time from 3 to 6 P.M. The only fixed hours (core time) when all workers must be on the job are the peak workload hours 9 A.M. to 3 P.M. The two requirements of the plan are that all employees be present during core time and that the required number of working hours be accounted for on a daily basis. Beyond this, working hours can be selected to meet the needs and requirements of each firm. The time at which lunch periods and refreshment breaks are taken may vary.

Since the concept of flexible work scheduling made its appearance, there have been many variations of the plan. For example, in some companies flexibility is provided within the working month. Employees must work the number of hours required during the month, but they may work only during core time for several days and make up the required hours during the remainder of the month.

Flexible work scheduling is found most often in insurance, banking, finance, engineering, government, and other service-type establishments rather than in industrial production or retail stores that have set customer hours. Flexible work scheduling does not work well in operations that are continually interdependent, such as the assembly line. Since the beginning of flextime in West Germany in 1967, the concept has been adopted by thousands of firms in the United States.

Flexible work scheduling, in contrast to the fixed 4/40 workweek and the staggered work schedule, permits employees to have a voice in the conditions and processes affecting their work. Thus, workers actively participate in decision making when they decide to work longer hours if there is more work to be done. Flexible working hours also appeal to workers' needs for more responsibility and more autonomy on the job. The main disadvantages cited by firms having flextime include a lack of supervision during working hours, understaffing of personnel at times, unavailability of key people at certain times, difficulty in scheduling meetings and coordinating projects, and difficulty in planning work schedules and keeping track of hours worked.

Job Sharing

Job sharing is an alternative to the traditional 9-to-5 workday that the AOM may wish to evaluate when scheduling office work and recruiting personnel. In **job sharing,** one permanent, full-time job is shared by two people who generally split their working hours, job responsibilities, and employee benefits.

Job sharing appeals especially to working parents with preschool children; to older workers not yet ready to retire; to men and women who want

Figure 12–6
Flexible Times and Core Times in a Typical Flexible Work Schedule

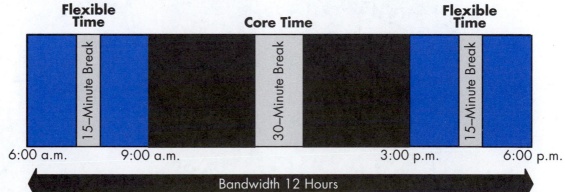

to continue their education; and to full-time employees who want to trade work for more leisure time. Since job sharing involves the whole job with its need for cooperation and commitment, many workers are provided a greater sense of achievement than if they were holding traditional part-time jobs.

Telecommuting

In another type of work scheduling, the AOM schedules work for employees who work away from the traditional office setting, often in homes where telephone lines link home terminals to a company's central computer. This application of telecommunications technology to the processing of information at a location other than the traditional office setting is known as **telecommuting.** LINK Resources, a New York-based research firm, estimates that by the year 2000, about 25 percent of the entire corporate workforce will be telecommuting either full or part time.[20]

One objective of scheduling office work to be completed in the home is to reduce the amount of information processing within the office. Also, in times of chronic shortage of qualified office personnel such as data-entry operators, secretaries, and typists, many qualified workers are available but personal circumstances prevent their working a full schedule in an office. Further, we may find more telecommuting as a result of the federal Clean Air Act. This act requires employers with 100 or more workers to reduce employee commuting by 25 percent by 1996.

---

[20]Barbara J. Farrah and Cheryl D. Dagen, "Telecommuting Policies That Work," *HR Magazine* (July, 1993), p. 64.

Illustration 12–3 Helped by advances in computers and telecommunications, today many Americans work part time or full time in their homes.

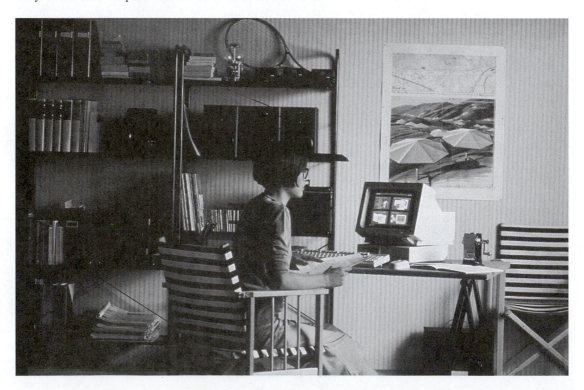

The advantages to the firm that uses telecommuting include a selection of qualified office personnel from a wide range of applicants, including the disabled; productivity improvement; cost savings in reduced office space needed; and the elimination of many employee benefits. Additional cost is incurred, however, for purchasing equipment (portable computer, printer, modem, copier, FAX machine, etc.); a second telephone line, depending upon the volume; and added insurance coverage. Further, the company must ensure data integrity by adopting security measures that permit access to computer files only by authorized telecommuters. For home operators, the major benefit is the freedom of working at their own pace. For example, a home operator may work only part of a day, timing the work to mesh with the firm's rush periods.

The major disadvantages for telecommuters are social isolation—the loss of face-to-face contact with coworkers and supervisors, the limitations upon career development and stifling of promotional opportunity, and burnout because of the tendency to overwork at home. Among the problems cited by managers and supervisors are their inability to manage workers from a distance, the difficulties found in interacting with the telecommuters, and the increased supervisory workload due to the additional time required to monitor the telecommuter's work.

Permanent Part-Time Employment

Another alternative work schedule is **permanent part-time employment,** where regular voluntary employment (not temporary or casual) is carried out during working hours that are shorter than normal. Voluntary part-time employment is more common among women than among men, and more young and older workers are found holding part-time jobs than middle-aged workers. The reasons for working less than a full-time schedule include school attendance, family responsibilities, physical disabilities, and a preference for more leisure time.

Among the advantages gained by firms using permanent part-time employment are the following: reduced labor costs, with savings in overtime payments and employee benefits; improved job performance and increased productivity; reduced fatigue; and reduced absenteeism. Some of the negative effects that face the AOM when considering the use of permanent part-time workers are increased difficulty in communicating internally, increased difficulty in scheduling work, and increased costs of personnel administration and training.

Alternatives to Layoff

In time of recession, a firm may reach the point of having to lay off indefinitely many of its salaried office employees. One result of such an action is that the laid-off persons will find new, permanent jobs, and thus cripple the firm's plans to expand once the recession has ended. To minimize the economic effects of a recession upon the firm's employees and to preserve the company's workforce of qualified employees, alternatives to layoffs, such as rotation of layoffs and work sharing, should be investigated by the AOM.

Rotation of Layoffs. Instead of being laid off indefinitely, under a **rotation of layoffs,** office employees may work for four weeks and then be laid off for one week. During the time of layoffs in some states workers can collect unemployment compensation benefits. Rotation of layoffs is not voluntary and offers only a short-term solution to the problems of recession and mounting unemployment. However, the program provides several advantages for employers and employees. Employees are kept on the payroll and thus retain their benefits, which otherwise they might have lost. Unions generally cooperate with the firm in its rotation plan since the employed persons continue paying their union dues. Although the employees take home less than usual pay, most approve of the rotation plan in preference to being laid off permanently.

Most states require a waiting period, such as one week, before laid-off workers may collect their unemployment compensation benefits. As a result, rotation of layoffs becomes less attractive to workers in these states. Therefore, laid-off employees may be aided by their firms, which pay the employees an equivalent compensation during the waiting period and deduct the amount later from their regular paychecks. Another disadvantage lies in possible increased state unemployment contributions for the employer as a result of the increased number of temporary layoffs during the year. Further, problems may be experienced in scheduling the work among those who are rotating their layoffs and in dealing with the extra paperwork operations in the payroll department.

Work Sharing. Under **work sharing,** a plan of short-time compensation, employees work a shorter week, have their salaries reduced accordingly, and receive partial state unemployment compensation benefits for their lost days' pay. Thus, employees receive partial compensation for their lost wages and retain their jobs and employee benefits. The employer, in turn, enjoys savings by avoiding the costs of rehiring and retraining. On the other hand, the state charges the benefits against the employer's unemployment compensation account.

Fifteen states have adopted legislation that permits the voluntary use of work sharing as an alternative to layoffs. Where these programs have been used, they have generally been well received by both employers and employees. At the same time, the use of short-time compensation has thus far been very limited, especially among larger firms.

UNIONIZATION OF OFFICE WORKERS

As a result of computerized information systems and global company growth, many office workers find that their jobs have become more routine, production oriented, and depersonalized. In the eyes of many office workers, such jobs have become akin to factory production work. Also, there have been changing patterns of values, attitudes, and expectations among office workers, as indicated in Chapter 7. Because of these developments, the unionizing of office workers, especially women and minorities, is regularly in progress in spite of the decline in union membership. In 1992, union membership was 15.8 percent of the employed U.S. workforce, dropping to 11.5 percent among

workers in the private sector.[21] (In the mid-1950s, membership in the private sector had reached 35 percent.)

In this closing section of the chapter, we shall explore the reasons that office personnel join unions and the role of the office manager in office unionism.

Why Office Workers Join Unions

Some of the reasons that office workers offer for joining unions are:

1. Dissatisfaction with earnings, promotion opportunities, working conditions, employee benefits, and the relatively weak position of an individual worker to influence any change in these conditions.
2. Job insecurity in that office workers feel there is no guarantee they will not be laid off arbitrarily, especially in periods of recession or when the company is downsizing.
3. Little involvement in implementing new office technology and redesigning job content.
4. Poor handling of grievances by management, which all too often takes a "don't-care" attitude.
5. Importance of employees' work not recognized by the company, which, instead, takes the employees and their work performance for granted.
6. Inadequate channels of communication between employees and management. For example, office employees object to "overnight" conversions to automated office technology without management's informing in advance those persons who will be using the new equipment and procedures.

The Role of the Office Manager in Office Unionism

Many arguments are given both for and against unionism, none of which seems completely unbiased. However, it is not a question of being for or

[21]"Labor Month in Review," *Monthly Labor Review* (March, 1993), p. 2.

against a union for office workers. Rather, as we shall see below, it is a question of what the OM will do about the formation of office workers' unions or attempts to unionize office workers. What the OM does about office unions involves these time-related factors: (1) before union activity starts, (2) while attempts are being made to organize the workers, and (3) after the workers become unionized.

Before Union Activity

Long before any union activity might start among a group of office workers, the OM should have been listening to employees in order to pinpoint the basic issues that might motivate them to seek unionization. For example, by means of attitude surveys, OMs can learn about employee dissatisfaction and be prepared to answer questions such as the following:

1. Do the working conditions in the office create a desirable level of morale? If not, how can they be improved?
2. How can the work be made more challenging and rewarding by redesigning the jobs?
3. How can the company become more responsive to employee needs for job security in the areas of salaries, promotion opportunities, vacations, suggestion plans, recreational programs, and other employee benefits?
4. How can the human resources management program and its policies be improved to provide impartial supervision?

Efforts should be made to deal with the office employees' concerns about salaries paid, working conditions, job content, employee benefits, and personnel policies in order to compare them with those found in unionized offices. Wherever possible, the salaries paid, working conditions, and benefits should be improved so that they equal or surpass those of unionized offices. But these improvements must be properly explained to workers, using the appropriate communication media described in Chapter 5. In one instance, a firm was paying higher salaries than those of unionized companies in the area, but still the office workers were dissatisfied with their salaries. This dissatisfaction was due not so much to the com-

pany's salary structure as to the employees' lack of reliable information from management about its salary program and exactly how the salaries were determined.

While Attempts Are Being Made to Organize

If a firm does not provide its office workers with salaries, working conditions, and benefits equal to or superior to those offered by unionized offices, it must expect that some dissatisfied workers will seek unionization. Thus, the OM faces the problem of how to deal with a union during an attempt to organize. If the company does not have its own legal staff, the firm should obtain competent legal counsel so the firm will be advised of its statutory rights and obligations and thus avoid possible charges of unfair labor practices. Supplementing such legal help, the OM should be familiar with labor legislation and current labor relations practices.

In many instances when attempts are being made to organize, one or more disgruntled workers contact a union organizer, who is invited to come in to evaluate the situation. Where the opportunity presents itself, the organizer seeks to acquire signed authorization cards from 30 percent of the employees so the union can petition the National Labor Relations Board for an election. The **authorization card** is a formal statement signed by an employee authorizing a named union to represent him or her in collective bargaining. If the union organizer acquires cards from 50 percent plus one of the employees, the union can demand that the employer recognize the union as the bargaining agent and bargain with it. In this case, the National Labor Relations Board certifies the labor organization and the unionization process is complete.

Many employers do not voluntarily accept the signed cards as proof of union interest, however. Such employers feel they should have an opportunity to tell their side of the story to employees. In this case, the regional office of the National Labor Relations Board sends an investigator to the scene to determine if sufficient interest exists among the workers to form a union. If so, the potential bargaining unit is determined, and an election is called so the employees may vote for or against the union.

Prior to the election, free discussion is encouraged. However, many rules surround an election, and any rule violations constitute unfair labor practices. If over 50 percent of the employees voting choose to join a particular union, the labor organization is certified, and the employer must bargain with the organization in good faith. The employees are next classified by salary and job, and a list of specific proposals covering work-related items such as wages, hours, and benefits is prepared. After the proposals have been approved by the workers, management is presented with the suggested changes. At this stage of the unionization process, a bargaining committee made up of the employee representatives and a business agent from the union meet with management to draw up the contract. After the contract has been approved, union members in each department elect shop stewards to serve as their representatives in dealings with management, and a grievance procedure is established.

Any worker or group can request that another election be held at any time 12 months after the first election. If the employees vote against the labor organization, it is decertified, or eliminated. The employer, however, cannot make such a request or even encourage it.

After the Workers Become Unionized

Once the union has been established, management and the employees should work toward achieving the objectives of the firm and those of the union, which will be attained only through harmonious labor relations. New working relationships must be developed between the company and the new union, with a more formal and legal-based system of relationships emerging. To prevent workplace tension and possible litigation, a company may call upon the services of an **ombudsman.** This person, a kind of informal problem-solver, is employed by the company to investigate employees' complaints and to reconcile differences in an impartial way. Companies find ombudsmen especially useful with the increased number of litigations resulting from alleged discrimination, wrongful discharge, or sexual harassment.

The company should make sure that the union contract is uniformly interpreted and applied by all supervisors and managers. Finally, companies should establish rapport and create the best morale-building relationships by working with the union and not against it. At the same time, however, both management and employees must remember that the workers are still employed by the company and that it is the company that hired them, pays them, and expects their support.

SUMMARY

1. AOMs and supervisors easily reach decisions about many workplace issues and problems that arise in their offices simply by referring to their firm's policy manual or employee handbook. However, for other kinds of problems that surface (such as those dealing with sexual and ethical issues), or in those firms where policies have not been established, AOMs must make decisions that are agreeable to both the office employees and their firms.

2. Today's AOM must learn how to deal head on with many topics that traditionally have been avoided but which are significant to both sexes at all levels in the firm. This chapter has described a host of personnel problems, shown how other AOMs have solved these problems, and described the different kinds of policies and practices that may be found in organizations. By acquainting themselves with the information contained in this chapter, AOMs can profit from the successes and mistakes of others.

3. Today's AOMs need to stay abreast of the innovations in traditional work schedules and consider alternatives, such as flextime, as a means of meeting the needs of their firms and employees. AOMs may wish to consider job sharing, telecommuting, permanent part-time employment, rotation of layoffs, and work sharing as means whereby office employees' fears and insecurities, resulting from recession, downsizing, and unemployment, may be lessened.

4. In the event their workers attempt to organize a union, AOMs, aided by legal counsel, should have a clear understanding of the fair labor practices in which their firms may engage. If the workers should become unionized, AOMs must develop new relationships with their company, the workers, and the union and maintain positive, harmonious labor relations in the office.

FOR YOUR REVIEW

1. Describe the three-step program, advocated by the National Council on Alcoholism, that a company should consider in setting up a rehabilitation program for office alcoholics.

2. Why is it generally more difficult for the office supervisor to develop an effective program in handling the drug abuser than the alcoholic?

3. What guidelines should be foremost in the mind of an office supervisor who is confronted by AIDS in the workplace?

4. What approaches may be used by the organization that is trying to minimize stress among its office employees?

5. What steps are companies taking to encourage workers to quit smoking?

6. What are the major features of the current definition of sexual harassment?

7. What arguments can be advanced for and against the practice of nepotism?

8. Under what circumstances does moonlighting become a problem for the office manager?

9. How can the office manager effectively aid the office supervisor who is a workaholic?

10. List the steps that an administrative office manager should take when setting up a system to control employee dishonesty.

11. When establishing a policy regarding the right to search workers and their personal belongings, what precautions should be taken?

12. In what way might a company's policy on sick leave condone absenteeism?

13. Describe the operation of a no-fault leave policy. For what reasons might a firm adopt such a policy?

14. What are the major reasons for employee turnover?

15. Describe the operation of a typical flexible work schedule.

16. What are the advantages and disadvantages of telecommuting?

17. What reasons are advanced by office workers for joining unions?

FOR YOUR DISCUSSION

1. Although grievances will never be eliminated, the office supervisor can take steps, especially in nonunion offices, to reduce and prevent large numbers of complaints. Prepare a list of the steps you would include in your program for reducing grievances in the office.

2. Several months ago one of your employees, Keith Paoli, took you, the office manager, into his confidence and told you that he is gay. Today Paoli tells you how his supervisor has been calling him some very derogatory names and harassing him about his sexual orientation. Although Paoli has informed his supervisor that the remarks are unwelcome and uncalled for, the supervisor has continued his verbal abuse. Paoli wants to remain with the company and he tells you he is thinking about suing his supervisor and the company. How would you advise Paoli?

3. Stuart Duffy and Craig Bunting have worked side by side for the past seven years in the computer center. Over the years the two have shared very intimate details of their personal lives with each other. This morning Duffy comes to see you, the manager of the center, and says:

> Craig told me this morning he just saw his doctor, who diagnosed his illness as AIDS. Although we're very close, I can no longer work alongside Craig. I've my wife and children at home—and myself—to think about. You're going to have to do something—maybe move Craig to an office by himself. What's going to happen when the rest of our group finds out about Craig's problem?

You thank Duffy for talking with you and state that after you meet with Bunting you will follow through. In view of this announcement about AIDS in your company—the first case—what steps should you take at this time?

c
o
n
t

4. Ever since he was hired as office manager, Joe Cirella has been competitive, ambitious, and aggressive. He impressed top management with his devotion to work and his expectations of perfection from himself and his coworkers. Cirella thrived on deadlines, relished risks, and lost patience when he did not reach his goals quickly. Then one day the stress of his job took its toll—a severe heart attack.

   Today Cirella's boss, Angela Miranda, leans back in her chair, reflects, and asks herself: "Why did this have to happen to a young fireball like Joe? Where did the company go wrong by not having anticipated the stresses of his job? What can we do now?" What answers can you supply to the questions raised by Miranda?

5. Marla Young, a secretary in charge of the company's $300 petty cash box, secretly withdraws $100 every Friday to bet on horses. She eventually returns all money borrowed from the petty cash fund. Therefore, she feels no guilt for wrongdoing in that no harm has been done to the company. Do you agree that Young is doing nothing wrong? How can management anticipate and prevent such "borrowing" practices?

6. Matt Erickson has been employed as an accountant in the Maple Leaf Company for more than 20 years. Over the past few years, Erickson has developed a drinking problem to the extent that after his "liquid" lunches, he is often unable to do his job well. Whenever the situation gets out of control, Erickson's supervisor, Laura Epstein, talks frankly with him about his drinking. After each meeting, Erickson seems to work well for about three or four days—but then he goes back to the bottle! He refuses to join Alcoholics Anonymous, and Epstein is reluctant to recommend discharge in view of his long record of service. What approach do you recommend that Epstein use?

7. Both management and organized labor view flextime as part of a broad picture of changing work conditions. Assuming for a moment that flextime were to become the standard form of workweek in the United States by the year 2020, what changes would you expect to see in working conditions?

8. After reading a news release about the introduction of telecommuting by one of his firm's competitors, Vic Borzi, supervisor of the word processing center, stated: "The program will 'never fly.' If people work away from the office, how do you know how well they work or if they work at all?" Do you agree or disagree with Borzi's observations? Explain.

CASES FOR CRITICAL THINKING

Case 12–1 Playing Favorites with Flextime

Shortly after being hired as administrative assistant, Michelle Alpert decided she would give up her lunch hours in order to operate the switchboard. In fact, Alpert made an agreement with Jennifer Fleming, the office manager, whereby she would be allowed to quit work each day at 3:30 in exchange for giving up her lunch hour. Alpert saw this move as an excellent way to solve her problem of having

**c
o
n
t**

someone home with her children when her husband left for night school at 5 P.M. In turn, Fleming was pleased to have someone on hand to receive incoming calls and thus assure customers their calls would be answered during the entire workday.

One afternoon after Alpert had "flexed out" at 3:30, several of her coworkers came into Fleming's office to air their complaints about the favoritism being shown Alpert. One of the executive secretaries, Gail Irwin, remarked, "All of us have agreed to give up our lunch hours, too, so we can leave early every day. You know, Jennifer, more and more firms are allowing their employees to do this sort of thing."

Fleming patiently listened and then made this statement in support of her feeling that the request was out of the question: "This company can't afford to shut down the entire office every day at 3:30. We'd be out of business in six months!"

Fleming went on to say she was surprised by the employees' request, for she felt they all knew about Alpert's problems at home—her husband's attending school and the need for someone to care for their children. The workers said that they understood Alpert's problems and sympathized with her. However, they indicated that they, too, had personal problems—picking up children at the daycare center, avoiding traffic tie-ups during rush hours, being at home when the children got out of school, and so on. Irwin wrapped up the discussion by saying, "What's fair for Michelle should be fair for all of us. Think about it, won't you, Jennifer? It really isn't fair to play favorites."

Assuming the role of the office manager, Fleming:

1. How would you answer the complaints made by the employees who met with you?

2. What alternative courses of action are available to you in order to achieve the company's goals and still satisfy your workers' needs?

Case 12–2 Invading a Worker's Privacy[22]

In a famous case that has vast implications for managers and supervisors regarding invasion of privacy, an employee went back to her company locker on a break only to find that the padlock had been clipped and broken. Inside, her personal belongings and purse were in disarray. Obviously, someone had broken into her locker and gone through her things.

Upon complaining to her supervisor, she found out that he had gone through all the employee lockers because he was searching for some missing property. The employee was miffed, even though none of the property was found in her locker. "You had no right to go through my locker!" she complained. "That was my personal lock that you opened."

"I've got a right to go into any locker at any time," her boss fired back. "I was looking for stolen property. If you had used a company lock like you're supposed to, I wouldn't have had to break your lock."

"You knew I put my own lock on that locker months ago and you said nothing about it."

---

[22]Reprinted with permission from *Manager's Legal Bulletin,* by Alexander Hamilton Institute, Inc., 197 West Spring Valley Avenue, Maywood, NJ 07607. To order, please call (800) 879–2441.

c
o
n
t

"Look, I'm not going to argue with you," the supervisor said. "That locker belongs to the company, and I have every right to go through it at any time."

Did the supervisor illegally search the worker's locker? What are the implications of this case in regard to developing a policy related to employee privacy and searching an employee's personal belongings?

 ## Case 12–3 Absenteeism: Computer Option (available on disk)

MANAGING ADMINISTRATIVE SERVICES

13 • Managing Office Space

14 • Planning an Ergonomically Sound Office Environment

15 • Selecting Office Furniture and Equipment

16 • Automating the Office

17 • Understanding Text/Word Processing Systems

18 • Distributing Information: Telecommunication and Mailing Systems

19 • Managing Records

20 • Managing Microimage and Reprographic Systems

MANAGING OFFICE SPACE

GOALS FOR THIS CHAPTER

After completing this chapter, you should be able to:

1. Identify the objectives to be attained in an efficient space management program.
2. Describe how the space needs of an organization may be analyzed.
3. Point out the characteristics of the principal styles of office layout.
4. Describe the distinguishing features of the individual workcenter, the group workcenter, and the automated workcenter.
5. Apply the space guidelines for efficient work, for personnel, and for furniture and equipment.
6. Describe the methods used in preparing office layout models.
7. Discuss the factors an organization considers when faced with the need for new office space.
8. Outline the details involved in making an office move and the potential personnel problems that may emerge.

When administrative office managers view their offices as a system, they consider the following elements, which are required to attain the objectives of the office:

1. *Space* in which to work.
2. *People* to perform the work.
3. *A comfortable, satisfying environment* in which to work.
4. *Efficient furniture and equipment* to assist in performing the work.
5. *Facilities* for meeting the firm's internal and external communication needs.
6. *An appropriate set of records and related information-cycle activities.*
7. *Adequate controls* to ensure that the office system meets its goals.

In today's offices, these seven systems elements are combined into a network of people, machines, and procedures called administrative services. **Administrative services** are support functions that are responsible for meeting all the information needs of the organization. The model in Figure 13–1 outlines the main administrative services needed to produce information in the office and the environment in which these activities are housed, which constitute Part 3 of this textbook. In addition, the model shows the relationship of each service to the other services. The most basic service involves space and its direct impact on the office employees who must use it. The management of space and the way in which space contributes to the productivity of office employees are discussed in detail in this chapter.

SPACE IN THE ADMINISTRATIVE OFFICE SYSTEM

Space is an economic resource. As such, we know that the availability of space is subject to economic conditions and the changing demands of business

Figure 13–1
Administrative
Services
Model for the
Production of
Information

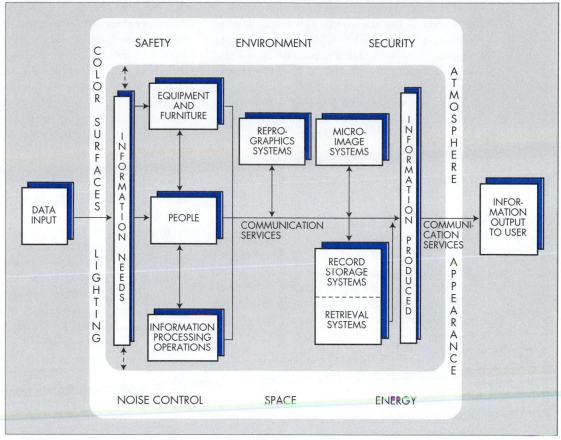

firms. In the central business districts of most large cities in the United States, at certain times the search for more space to house a growing office workforce may increase the demand for space and hence its price. At other times, however, when firms downsize and reduce their workforce, vacancy rates of 30 percent or more may be reported. So that office space is used effectively, several problems require the AOM's attention: (1) the cost of office space, (2) the cost of labor for maintenance and building security, and (3) the need to increase productivity and to improve employee morale through a better working environment.

From a systems point of view as we see by studying Figure 13–1, machines, office workers, and other systems elements function together to create a product—*information*—at the lowest possible cost. All of these elements are combined and arranged in the available space, which must be managed in order to be used effectively. Thus, planning, organizing, and controlling activities are required, under the leadership of the AOM.

In the office, information flows in a manner much like the flow of materials in a factory. In each, we find routes or aisles for the movement of people and materials in the shortest possible time. Further, for the sake of efficiency, a strong need exists to keep the number of *workstations* (desks, chairs, and working space) for the loading and unloading of information (or materials) to a minimum without sacrificing the accessibility of the service or the product. Regardless of the type of product (a factory product, an office paper product, or simply interpersonal communications), how space is planned, organized, and used affects the productivity and morale of workers.

The need to manage space carefully is critical in several situations: when a new office building is being planned, when an old building is being renovated, or whenever a present office is being analyzed with the objective of grouping people, furniture, and equipment more effectively. In such situations, careful planning is required in order to develop and later achieve the objectives of a space management program.

THE SPACE MANAGEMENT PROGRAM

The management of space, like the management of other economic resources, is ongoing and requires periodic attention to ensure that management is getting the most value possible for each "space dollar" spent. For this reason, a formal program of space management needs to be developed and implemented in the organization. The main features of such a program are discussed in this section.

Planning and Organizing a Space Management Program

When purchasing or leasing a new office site or renovating an existing building, management finds it advisable to consult reliable space planners and interior designers. Such specialists make recommendations based on a complete assessment of economic, efficiency, and esthetic or appearance factors. In addition, these experts place special emphasis on the human needs of the space involved.

Within the large firm, space planning is often the responsibility of the facility manager. A **facility manager** is a professional whose responsibilities extend over the following areas: operations and maintenance, real estate, human and environmental factors, planning and project management, facility function, finance, communications, quality assessment, and innovation.[1] Sometimes a

firm uses a project team approach, as found in the matrix organization described in Chapter 2, to help plan and implement the new office design. In such cases, the facility manager heads the project team, which includes the architect, the designer, systems analysts, industrial engineers, department heads, industrial psychologists, and human resources management personnel. The AOM and key office personnel play a significant role in outlining the workflow needs of the administrative services in both large and small offices. However, in the small office, technical advice on office design must be provided by outside specialists.

In planning a *new* office building, generally the essential physical features, such as supporting pillars, stairs, elevators, escalators, employee lounges, and cafeteria, can be located where they are most desirable. More frequently, however, a firm moves into an existing building where the physical features have been planned by former tenants. Therefore, planning the arrangement of working areas and workflows is often carried on around the present location of fixed factors. This approach also describes the firm that is renovating office space in its present location.

One technique of planning long-range projects, such as a new office layout, uses the Gantt project planning chart. The underlying principle of a **Gantt chart** is that the work planned and the work done are shown side by side in their relation to each other and to time.

Henry L. Gantt, along with Frederick W. Taylor (see Chapter 1), was a pioneer in the field of scientific management. In 1877, Gantt joined Taylor in his experiments to raise productivity and decrease costs at the Midvale Steel Works in Philadelphia. Gantt's concerns at first centered on the best and fastest method for completing each piece of work. Later, he became convinced that what really counted were employee morale and motivation.

[1]These competency areas represent those examined by the International Facility Management Association (IFMA) as part of its certification program. Those knowledgeable in all areas are awarded the Certified Facility Manager (CFM) designation.

The Gantt chart is one of the most widely recognized planning methods. In the Gantt chart shown in Figure 13–2, project activities are listed along the left margin from top to bottom in sequence of the planned activity. The numbers to the right of the title represent the number of days required to complete the project. Horizontal bars drawn next to each activity and under the appropriate time period make it easy to visualize the planned starting date, duration, and planned completion date. Across from the first activity, the top bar indicates planned performance time; the second bar shows actual performance time. A vertical date line means that the project has been updated. Also, note that some planning phases (such as phases 3, 4, and 5) may be carried on concurrently, which saves time in completing the layout tasks.

PERT—an acronym for Program Evaluation and Review Technique—is another method for planning long-range projects. PERT is commonly used to determine the time required to complete major projects, such as constructing an office building, after realistic time estimates have been made of the various activities associated with each project. With the aid of computers, PERT has become an important tool in systems-improvement studies. PERT is discussed further in Chapter 21.

Objectives of a Space Management Program

If our goal is to have a space management program that effectively supports the administrative services function, we must understand the two main elements in the office system. The first element includes the *physical features* of the office. Examples of physical features are the design of the building, which includes window and door locations; stairs, elevators, and escalators; and the plumbing, heating, air conditioning, ventilating, and electrical systems. (Firms that are largely automated require high-tech features that are dis-

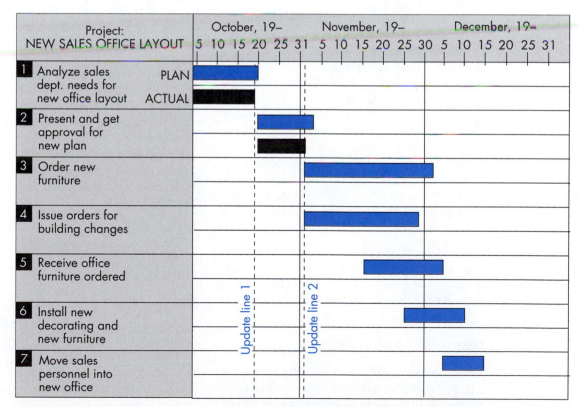

Figure 13–2
Gantt Chart for Planning New Office Layout

cussed later in this chapter.) The second main element involves *functional work requirements*. This category includes the information needs of the organization such as department functions and their necessary locations; open and private work areas; special facilities, such as reference (library) services, computer installations, and executive office requirements; the work being performed; the nature and number of employees presently working as well as the number expected for the future; and the equipment and furniture required to complete the work assigned.

By keeping in mind the important space-related factors just mentioned, the AOM develops these specific objectives for an effective space management program:

1. To provide sufficient space that will be used to the fullest.
2. To develop workflows that are effective and low in cost.
3. To design workstations that permit the use of good working methods which are in keeping with the workflow.
4. To permit flexibility in layout for possible rearrangement of workstations and for expansion or contraction of space needs.
5. To meet the interpersonal needs of the office staff by providing an environment free of communication barriers.
6. To coordinate the use of space with all related factors in the work environment, such as heat, light, color, and noise control.
7. To assure employees, as well as customers and the general public, of comfort and convenience.
8. To review regularly the long-range space needs of the office and to make improvements as necessary.

In the remaining sections of this chapter, we shall use these objectives as a frame of reference to discuss the principles of space management that have been developed through the years.

SPACE NEEDS IN THE OFFICE

The organization of a firm directly affects the layout of the office and plant. In many large manufacturing firms such as automotive, electrical

appliance, and chemical, the production and office facilities are frequently separated. Many of these firms also have branch or warehouse offices that are decentralized geographically. On the other hand, in service organizations such as banks and insurance companies, paperwork is the main product and hence the office is the main facility provided. Probably the most common type of organization for small and medium-size offices is a plan in which the main functions of purchasing, marketing, credit, human resources, and administrative services are arranged by departments.

In this section, the office space now occupied and the space needed are examined first. Next, the workflow—of departments or cost centers—and human space needs are analyzed. Finally, the planning of space by functions is considered in relation to the conventional and open plans as well as the type of facility needed for high-tech offices.

Office Space Inventory

Before many important decisions can be made regarding the best use of office space, much up-to-date, relevant information must be collected. Such information typically includes (1) the organization chart for the office and (2) the operations manual that explains the main functions of the office and the various departments from which the office receives information as well as those departments to which the office transmits information.

To supplement this basic information, AOMs frequently send a *space-use questionnaire* to each department requesting data on the following basic space needs:

1. Department name.
2. Main functions or responsibilities.
3. Amount and type of contact with the public.
4. Relationship of the department with other departments (i.e., which departments are in frequent or regular communication with the department under study and what is the nature of such communication).
5. Number of employees.
6. Functions of personnel in each job category.
7. Type of space each person in the department should occupy.

8. Changes expected in number of personnel and office activities.
9. Equipment presently in use as well as additional equipment expected to be used.
10. Records stored, the volume of records expected in the future, and retention and disposition schedules.
11. Special workcenters, such as private offices, conference rooms, and reception centers, that are needed.

Figure 13–3 shows a form used in surveying the present and expected space needs for an office. The information appearing on the completed form is very useful in analyzing space needs before the design phase of the space management program is begun.

Analyzing Space Needs

From a careful study of the completed form in Figure 13–3, the AOM identifies the following needs for space in the office: (1) *personnel*—working space required by each employee assigned to the department; (2) *support*—space required for administrative services, such as mailrooms, word processing centers, reception areas, and conference rooms; and (3) by implication, *traffic flow*—corridors, aisles, elevators, and lobbies—used by employees, customers, and the general public.

Common sense tells us that it is not difficult to collect information on the present space occupied by a department. However, determining the important work relationships among departments and among employees is complex and requires much consultation and thought before an effective space plan can be created. In this regard, we must remember one basic point—*the space plan must follow workflows or work functions rather than the space or esthetic preferences of personnel.*

In analyzing space needs at regular intervals, the AOM considers personnel space needs, special workcenters, storage areas, and interpersonal communication needs as reported by the department. (See Figure 13–3.) From the square footage estimated, the AOM consults space guidelines, such as those presented later in this chapter, to determine how much space should be allocated to each workstation and employee. To these space allocations is added a fixed percentage of aisle space to determine the total square footage needed for the department or cost center. After the head of each department has undertaken annually such an analysis, possibly as part of preparing the budget, a summary of all analyses can be prepared to guide the firm in estimating its total future space needs.

Workflow Space Needs

Workflow is the movement of information vertically between superiors and subordinates or horizontally among workers on the same level. The best layout for the workflow is not derived simply from a quick overview of an office operation; rather, it emerges slowly from a feasibility study, as discussed in Chapter 4, or from an intensive analysis of the administrative office system, as explained in Chapter 21. Both studies involve an analysis of the division of labor, the nature and frequency of information processing documents, and the flow of documents within and, if needed, outside the firm. Also, the frequency and quantity of documents processed, the number of workstations involved, and the time required to complete each work cycle are analyzed.

As we saw earlier, a common method of analyzing the flow of information and communication is to examine the organization chart. In doing so, we detect the most frequent communications. However, frequent communications also occur in informal channels—those not shown formally on the organization chart. In space-planning programs, interviews are usually conducted by asking the question, "*Who communicates with whom, about what, under what circumstances, and with what effects or results?*" Answers to the various parts of this question provide useful information for analyzing the flow of communication and work among the office staff.

When office workflow is analyzed for efficiency, it will be found that *the flow is most productive when it is continuous*—that is, when intermittent storage stops or work pauses are eliminated. Therefore, the processing time at each workstation must be identified and verified, transport time between workstations eliminated

Figure 13–3
Form Used to
Survey Office
Space Needs

INVENTORY OF OFFICE SPACE NEEDS

Department or Cost Center *Administrative Services*
Date *December 1, 1995*

Office Space:

	Number of Personnel Needed			
	1995	2000	2005	Remarks
Officers, managers, department heads..................................	8	9	9	
Private offices	2	2	2	
Open offices............................	60	75	90	*2000–Add Asst. AOM*
Administrative/executive secretaries	3	3	3	
Other_____......				*2000–Convert to distributive data processing and microcomputers.*

General Offices:

	Square Feet Needed			
Officers, managers, department heads..................................	720	810	810	
Private offices	600	600	600	
Open offices............................	9,000	10,000	10,000	
Administrative/executive secretaries	320	240	240	
Other_____......				

Special Workcenters:

Conference room.......................	250	350	350	*Increased number of conferences on site.*
Training room	150	200	200	
Reference services	135	135	135	
Reception center/switchboard....	225	225	225	
Computer center	300	200	200	
Reprographics...........................	125	225	225	
Mail room	150	200	200	
Work processing center	350	400	400	*Expand WP center.*
Other_____......				

Storage Areas:

Open-shelf filing	—	—	—	*Increased use of micrographics and computer storage.*
5-drawer file cabinets................	600	500	350	
Storerooms (supplies, etc.)	120	200	200	
Vault	80	80	80	
Storage (inactive files)	180	250	250	
Other_____......				

or reduced, and storage time decreased, if not eliminated. However, much of the success of the space management program depends on how well the AOM understands and meets the special human space needs of the workers.

Human Space Needs

In Chapter 5, we noted that nonverbal communication conveys the basic idea that space "communicates" (i.e., affects the feelings of people). Research on this topic shows that, because of the unique cultural and personality features of office workers, we should consider certain human needs in providing working space for the office staff.

Each worker needs a certain amount of personal space. **Personal space** refers to an area of privacy surrounding the worker that is important for keeping out other people. This idea is tested, for example, whenever a stranger comes into our homes or into our offices. Under such circumstances, how comfortable do you feel? The amount of personal space that workers require to maintain psychological comfort differs between

Illustration 13–1 A personal zone of distance ranging from 2 to 4 feet is usually appropriate for a supervisor giving directions to a worker.

introverts and extroverts. *Introverts* often prefer to work alone and hence require more privacy than *extroverts,* who like to be with people. Also, the space requirements for people from different cultures vary widely. For example, people in Middle Eastern countries typically require less personal space than Americans.

Closely related to personal space is the concept of **territoriality,** which refers to the physical area under the control of workers and designed specifically for their use. Hence, no other person can dominate that space. In the office, territoriality is commonly found in the workstation assigned to an office worker. Territoriality is also implied when a secretary is required to knock on the door before entering an executive's private office. Indeed, once within the private office, the secretary realizes the feeling of territoriality and higher status held by the executive. With higher status, as communicated by the private office—or, in some cases by only a greater amount of office space—power and authority are also communicated.

The AOM must understand the concepts of personal space and territoriality in order to meet the human space needs of the office staff. Personal space—and hence the privacy of the worker—will not be violated if, in planning space, the AOM observes the following zones of personal distance:

1. **Intimate:** ranging from skin contact to about 2 feet. This distance is reserved for persons with close emotional attachments, such as very close friends working together on an office assignment.
2. **Personal:** ranging from 2 feet to 4 feet. This distance keeps the other person at "arm's length," although reasonably close, as in the case of an office supervisor giving specific directions to a worker for reorganizing a report.
3. **Social:** ranging from about 4 feet to 12 feet. This distance, especially from 4 feet to 7 feet, is generally maintained in business situations where people work together or salespersons and customers talk. The distance from 7 feet to 12 feet is used for more formal, impersonal situations, such as conferring with one's supervisor across the desk.

Figure 13–4
A Conventional Rectilinear Floor Plan That Accommodates 77 Workers

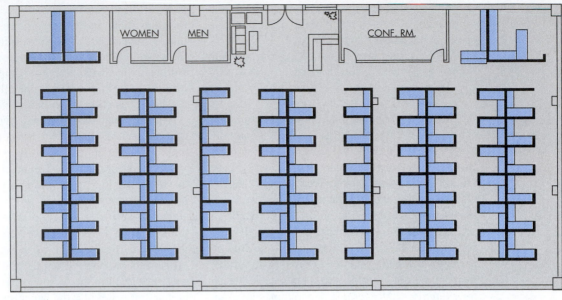

Courtesy of CenterCore

Another human space need concerns disabled office workers. Typical of the space needs of these workers are handrails; door widths that accommodate wheelchairs; ramps; lowered lavatories and water fountains; and elevator controls with Braille symbols next to floor buttons. Further discussion on providing an effective environment for the disabled is included in the next chapter.

Functional Space Needs

In Chapter 2, we saw that the basic organizational unit of specialized functions is the *department*. This fact continues to be true even though computers and other automated systems have caused many significant changes in organizational patterns.

In planning space needs, the AOM considers the main functions to be performed by each department and the space requirements needed to complete those functions. For example, a sales department with its many external contacts has many different types of operational tasks as compared with an accounting department, which performs tasks of an internal nature and almost exclusively related to automated and paper records.

A functionally sound layout should meet three basic goals: (1) It should provide the best workflow within and between departments and people; (2) it should keep to a minimum the movement and noise that are caused by people as they perform their tasks; and (3) it should provide as much visual and auditory privacy as the position requires. We will see an expansion of these points in Chapter 14.

OFFICE DESIGN PLANS

To meet the space needs of all department functions, several design plans are available: (1) the conventional plan, (2) the open plan, and (3) the "high-tech" office plan. In addition, we find various types of workcenters that incorporate elements of both the conventional and the open plans.

The Conventional Plan

The **conventional plan** is a type of office layout characterized by wall barriers that tend to isolate work areas. This design plan, shown in Figure 13–4, provides a specialized work area for a de-

Figure 13–5
An Open Plan
That Accom-
modates 111
Workers

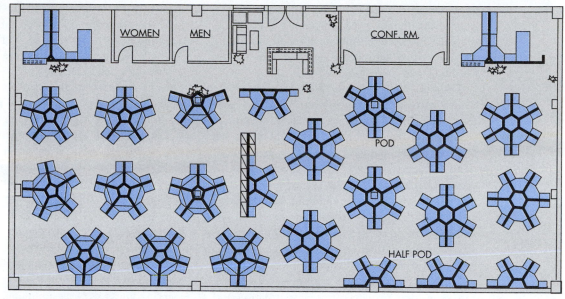

Courtesy of CenterCore

partment that promotes productivity. However, critics of this plan believe that it prevents or reduces human interaction and at the same time hinders interdepartmental workflow. Also, the conventional plan makes for an inflexible arrangement and adds greatly to the cost of redesigning the office.

To be used effectively, the conventional plan should be carefully developed. *Departments should be arranged so that the workflow proceeds in an uninterrupted manner and passes through as few hands as possible.* Such planning can be accomplished only after a careful study of administrative systems and procedures, the arrangement of furniture and equipment, and, of course, the needs and preferences of personnel.

Certain design principles should be followed in preparing a sound layout for departments. For example, *departments with much public contact should be located near the entrance to the plant or office, or, if the layout suggests, they may have direct access to hallways in order to minimize traffic flow through open work areas.* Thus, the human resources department and the purchasing department, which have frequent contact with

outsiders, should be located near the entrance or reception area. Other departments, such as finance and word processing, should be located near the executive and administrative areas, respectively.

The Open Plan

Sometimes called the *office landscape,* the **open plan** originated in Germany after World War II and rapidly became a very popular design plan for office layout. This plan brings together the functional, behavioral, and technical factors needed to design individual workstations, work groups, and departments.

As we see in Figure 13–5, the open plan features open space, free of permanent walls and corridors. Workstations are arranged by using movable elements such as desks, chairs, freestanding screens, bookshelves, files, and live plants without changing the fixed installations (light fixtures, heating and air-conditioning outlets, partitions, or floor coverings). In Figure 13–5, each workstation, called a pod, is designed in a cockpit configuration that accommodates up to six workers. Each grouping of pods is usually arranged, without regard to windows or other traditional design limitations, in a nonuniform fashion dictated by natural lines of information flow and human communication.

In theory, the office landscape is an open-plan model with no private offices. Privacy is provided by using plants and movable, sound-absorbing screens or partitions, usually wired for electricity. The status of workers is determined more by their work assignments than by their locations. High-level executives may have a larger amount of space, a different color desktop, and possibly a different shaped, larger desk; but beyond this, there are few visible signs of rank. In actual practice, however, the open plan is often combined with the conventional plan (called the **American plan**) so that high-level executives can keep their private offices for isolation and confidentiality. Other managers and their staffs are generally located in open work areas close to one another.

Advantages of the Open Plan

Typical of the many advantages of the open plan over the conventional plan are the following:

1. *Lower construction and energy costs.* The open plan permits considerable savings in construction costs, due in large part to the need for building fewer internal walls and hence fewer heating, ventilating, and air-conditioning facilities. In the open plan, a centralized energy system can serve a large, open space with maximum efficiency. Energy costs are lower, too, since fewer light fixtures are needed in a given area because the reduction of walls between offices allows a more efficient placement of the fixtures.

2. *More usable floor space available.* In the open plan, the amount of usable space (expressed as a percentage of the total space available) is greater than in the conventional grid plan of row after row of workstations. The usable space may run as high as 90 percent. Since the open plan requires less floor space, the square footage required by offices may be reduced by as much as 20 to 30 percent, and, in turn,

rental cost per square foot is less than in a traditional fixed-wall office. For example, through the utilization of workstations that make greater use of vertical space for storage, often in open-shelf files or in shelves above desks and tables, the open plan reduces the amount of floor space required for each workstation. At the same time, it provides a more efficient work area for the individual. Note how the conversion from a traditional plan (Figure 13–4 with provision for 77 workers) to an open plan with cluster workstations (Figure 13–5 with its 111 workers) provides up to a 40 percent increase in the number of employees in the same-size layout.

3. *Flexibility of rearrangement.* Office work requirements change periodically, and the open plan provides a flexibility for making changes in layout as work assignments change. Only simple tools are required to rearrange the panels and the component parts that make up each workstation.

4. *Reduced federal income taxes.* The modular workstations, movable panels, and component parts of the open office can be depreciated over a fewer number of years than the structural elements found in a fixed-wall office building. Thus, the organization is able to lower its federal income taxes as a result of a greater amount of depreciation expense over a smaller number of years.

   Most of the tax benefits are available because the panels and components of the open plan are classified as personal property rather than real property. Since personal property can be depreciated for tax purposes, the firm obtains a lower tax base and lower property taxes. Most dry-wall offices are classed as real estate, which can appreciate (grow in value) and thus result in a higher tax base and greater property taxes.

5. *Fewer communication barriers.* When office walls are torn down, the communication barriers between managers and employees tend to diminish and psychological barriers tend to be removed also. Employees in a cluster grouping feel freer to ask questions and to come into a manager's work area to discuss prob-

lems. Managers, too, have more opportunity to supervise employees since the managers are less isolated in open offices and more in touch with their workers.

Disadvantages of the Open Plan

As a result of studies and research on worker job satisfaction, many office designers recommend the American design plan (a mixture of the open plan and the conventional plan) because of the following disadvantages of the "pure" open plan:

1. *Lack of privacy.* Office workers at all levels complain that the open plan strips them of privacy, especially when conducting personal business. Also, because they no longer have private offices, some managers and supervisors sense a loss of status. Some workers say it is difficult to concentrate with so many people located in one large area. Others report that it is difficult to carry out confidential work. Also, workers feel that they are always under someone's observation. As a result of comments such as these, some firms have replaced the low movable panels and screens with partitions extending from the floor to the ceiling, thus creating movable rooms that are completely enclosed.

2. *Too much noise.* Office workers object to the high noise level that results from the conversations of neighboring workers; the din of machines and equipment, especially the computer printers; and the ringing of telephones. Noise-control techniques to handle such problems are discussed in the following chapter.

3. *Poorly designed open-plan systems.* When converting from the traditional fixed-wall office to the open plan, some firms have failed to open up their offices. Instead, they have created many very small cubicles arranged in mazes that cut off communication and necessary conversation among workers. Other companies have learned that the open plan does not work efficiently for some administrative services, such as legal and accounting, where high levels of confidentiality and concentration are required.

Such poorly designed open-plan systems result from the failure of the facility manager, architects, and designers to (1) plan carefully before, during, and after the installation; (2) consult with office workers who will be affected by the change; (3) educate office personnel about the advantages of the open plan over a conventionally planned office; and (4) control unauthorized rearrangements in which office workers abuse the open plan by encroaching on their neighbors' space and disturbing others.

Private Versus Open Offices

In the past, the private office has been widely regarded as an important status symbol of executive success. However, the cost of office space and the popularity of the open plan cause the AOM to study several factors before deciding whether to design private offices, open offices, or a combination of the two.

Management must weigh the relative advantages and disadvantages of using private offices. The reasons usually given for providing private offices are:

1. They create prestige in the eyes of employees and visitors for top management, department heads, and high-level staff people.

2. The confidential nature of the work being done, such as research, planning, and financial report preparation, requires privacy.

3. The work, such as computer programming, requires a high degree of concentration.

On the other hand, the private office makes efficient use of only about 50 percent of the space allocated to it. Thus, the use of private offices is an expensive method of providing utilities, such as heating, lighting, and air conditioning. The private office is relatively inflexible, for its permanent partitions are expensive and difficult to remove; it provides barriers to supervision of employees since the supervisor is separated from the employees; and it sets up arbitrary barriers to oral communications in the office.

The High-Tech Office Plan

Traditionally, office tenants bought space from developers, telephone service and electricity from public utilities, and computers and other equipment from manufacturers. With the increased use of automated systems, we now find that these necessary office services are often provided by landlords in the form of "smart" buildings.

A **smart building** is an office building that has a computer for a brain (control device) and a nervous system of cables and electronic sensors that allow the computer to monitor and interact with building conditions. Tenants are able to access the building's computer for telecommunications and automated office services. The landlord of a smart building may offer the tenant *building management systems* consisting of fire control and security, energy management, environmental and lighting controls, and elevator controls. Also, for an additional square-footage fee, the landlord may provide *shared tenant services.* These services include wiring for local and long-distance voice, video, and data transmission, teleconferencing and electronic mail, as well as word processing, copying, and image transmission.

SPACE PLANNING IN WORKCENTERS

The office, as we know it, is a thinking place for information workers. Personnel must be placed at appropriate locations for thinking—that is, for controlling information through each of the stages of the information cycle. In a related sense, the work of the office revolves around communication, the exchange or distribution of information. Each employee, from custodian to chief executive officer, is assigned a location or workcenter, some simple and some highly complex, for performing the work assigned. The concept of the workcenter and special workcenters found in many offices is discussed in the following paragraphs.

Workcenter Concept

The basic unit of office space planning is the **individual workcenter,** or *workstation,* where each employee performs the bulk of assigned responsi-

bilities. When all the workcenters are combined, whether departmentally or in some other functional sense, the **group workcenter,** or *total workplace,* is the result. Consideration of both the individual and the group workcenter concepts is necessary to achieve the most effective use of office space.

Individual Workcenter

In most offices, certain basic furniture and equipment are assigned to each workstation. Such items as a desk or a table for a work surface; counters, shelves, and files for storage; machines; and seating facilities are normally required for each worker.

The design of a workcenter should be based on an analysis of the work to be performed, communication requirements (telephone, dictation, interviewing, consulting, etc.), and storage needs. A concern for the environment and related tasks is also required.

Group Workcenter

No one workstation exists by or for itself; rather, it serves as part of a larger group working toward a common goal. All workcenters, therefore, must be space-planned and coordinated to fit into the total work environment.

A department is the typical work setting for groups of workers. For example, personnel specializing in hiring, testing, evaluating, and training workers are housed in a human resources department or division. Each of the many tasks and the workcenters at which these tasks are completed in such a department must be planned so they relate to the spatial needs of the total human resources system of the organization.

The responsibilities of the AOM, as a space administrator, include coordinating all workcenters into an arrangement that facilitates the combined teamwork of the individual members. Three special workcenters must be provided for most modern offices.

Special Workcenters

In many large organizations, special workcenters, such as the reception center, the reference services center (sometimes called the library), and the automated workcenter, are commonly found.

Illustration 13–2 Both individual workcenters (right) and group workcenters (below) should be considered in office planning.

Reception Center

The reception center serves to promote efficiency in administrative operations and to enhance public relations for the firm. Thus, this area should be well arranged and kept orderly, for visitors get their first impression of the business when they step into its reception center.

The reception center should be located in an area where visitors cannot interrupt the work of employees who may be distracted by the flow of callers. In planning a reception center, at least 10 square feet should be allocated for each visitor; therefore, its size is determined by the maximum number of visitors expected at any one time.

Reading material should be supplied for visitors, who may have to wait until the people they want to see are ready to receive them. As it may be assumed that many of the callers are interested in some product or service of the company, some literature or a display of these subjects should be provided.

Reference Services Center

To encourage their employees to be well informed on topics relevant to their work, many companies have established libraries or reference services centers. Businesses also maintain special libraries to further the activities of the organization. As such, the special library is really an information bureau, with a limited number of reference books, technical handbooks, and other publications in the special field of the company.

A firm may obtain assistance in setting up its reference services center by contacting a library consultant (unless the company librarian has sufficient background). The consultant will survey the company's existing facilities and offer recommendations on costs, procedures, space and equipment requirements, and staffing needs.

Automated Workcenter

The automated workcenter is designed around the **video display terminal (VDT),** the leading device for entering data into the computer.[2] (Other input hardware is discussed in Chapter 16.) In the design of this modern office workstation, we should consider:

1. *Sufficient space for all types of work.* The VDT is a large device and may crowd a regular-size desktop. Since the use of paper in manual systems will not be eliminated altogether with the addition of a VDT, thought must be given to alternative locations or larger desktops for performing nonautomated tasks. If not, the result will be an inefficient workplace in which materials are stored off the desk or piled high on top of the VDT.

2. *The technical needs of the VDT user.* Motion economy should be incorporated into the design so that items used most frequently, such as manuals and other references, are within easy reach of the operator. The location and height of the VDT keyboard and display screen should be positioned to provide the most comfort for the operator. Other related environmental factors, such as lighting, noise, air-conditioning requirements, and special furniture needed for the automated workstation, are discussed in the next two chapters.

3. *The human-social needs of the worker.* Office workers desire privacy as well as the opportunity to communicate easily with their coworkers. Panels or partitions should be provided to permit worker concentration and to make efficient use of expensive space. In Illustration 13–3, note how the use of modular vertical panels, or tiers, provides privacy and utility. Workers are able to individualize their workstations by using a building-block approach to arrange the clear and the different-color panels.

Illustration 13–3 An open-plan workstation with modular vertical panels.

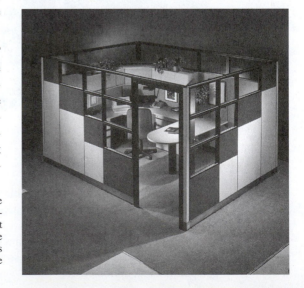

---

[2]As discussed earlier in this chapter, the workstation is the basic unit of office space planning, which includes office furniture and equipment. In the automated workcenter, the most important equipment item is the VDT. Although this is the most common definition of workstation, computer users sometimes restrict the meaning of the term *workstation* to the most powerful desktop computers.

In some firms, the AOM may be asked to help in planning the computer center. In such cases, we note there are organization-wide implications that call for more extensive knowledge and skills than in planning the individual workstation. Thus, company-wide expertise must be sought along with special consulting services in designing the computer center, as noted in the yellow pages of most telephone directories.

PRINCIPLES OF SPACE MANAGEMENT

In this chapter, emphasis is placed upon layout as a major factor in achieving efficiency and worker satisfaction in the office. *Providing sufficient space* and *making the maximum use of that space,* two of the key objectives of space management, are vital to administrative office systems, as discussed earlier. This section presents principles, or guidelines, of space management that apply especially to the following components of administrative office systems: efficient work, personnel, and furniture and equipment.

Space Guidelines for Efficient Work

The following space guidelines, which summarize points we noted earlier in the chapter, will aid the AOM in achieving work efficiency:

1. *Use a straight-line flow of information* (such as forms, records, and reports) *rather than a crisscrossing or backtracking of lines* to reduce communication and transportation lines to a minimum.
2. *Provide large, open spaces,* which are better than small room spaces cut out of one area. In such settings, supervision and control can be more easily maintained; communication with individual employees is more direct; and better lighting, heating, and ventilation arrangements are possible.
3. *Use movable partitions, freestanding screens, and plants as alternatives to private offices with fixed walls.*
4. *Conserve space without cramping individuals in workcenters.* For example, include the space above the surfaces of desks and tables;

replace two- and three-drawer file cabinets with more space-efficient models having four, five, and six drawers; provide a common conference area to eliminate the need for private offices; and store all but the working inventory of office supplies in a central storeroom.

5. *Locate offices such as purchasing, sales, and human resources that require contact with outsiders in areas accessible to the public.* However, those offices requiring confidential work or privacy such as accounting, computer programming, and research and development should be located away from the easy accessibility of the public.
6. *Base space allocation on major workflows,* which function around source documents such as purchase orders, time cards, and sales invoices. Thus, departments having a great deal of cross-communication with other departments should be located near each other. One example of this relationship is the human resources and the payroll departments. Also, common destinations (elevators, copiers, restrooms, etc.) should be close together and accessible by direct routes from workstations.
7. *Forecast future work requirements in relation to the projected sales volume.* One guideline to use in such forecasts is the average rate of increase in volume of office work over several typical growth years.

Space Guidelines for Personnel

The number of employees to be housed in a given area both at present and in the future has an effect on the amount of space to be used. Because there are so many variables in allocating space in an office, it becomes difficult to set standards of space requirements, especially the average amount of space required for each employee. The best that can be achieved in setting space standards is to group employees and set minimum and maximum guidelines for each group as follows:

1. *Private offices* vary from 400 to 600 square feet for senior executives to 200 square feet for senior assistants and from 75 to 100 square feet for cubicles or modules in an open plan.

2. *In fixed-wall plans,* general offices have 80 to 100 square feet per workstation in small departments, in units where there are high-level nonexecutive personnel, or where the visitor traffic is heavy. In large work areas, the space allowance may be reduced to 40 to 80 square feet per workstation.

3. *In open-plan offices* with movable partitions, the average office space for nonmanagerial personnel is: general clerical, 71 square feet; senior clerical, 82 square feet; technical/professional, 92 square feet; and senior professional, 113 square feet.[3] For open-plan offices with undivided areas, the goal is to provide at least 10,000 square feet (100 feet by 100 feet) for 80 to 100 employees.

4. In general, an *automated workstation* requires 10 to 15 percent more space—and in some cases up to 25 percent more when expansion is considered—than the conventional workstation. For example, before automation, the worker needed only a typewriter and writing surface; but after automation, that same worker needs a computer monitor, keyboard, disk drive, disk storage unit, printer, paper storage, and paper.[4] In addition, files should be kept close to those workers who use them.

5. *Aisles and corridors* will probably require about 10 to 15 percent of the total area of private and general offices.

6. *Conference rooms and boardrooms* require 25 square feet per person for rooms housing up to 30 persons and 8 square feet per person for areas housing 30 to 200 persons.

7. *Central files* require about 6 square feet per letter-size ($8\frac{1}{2}$ by 11 inches) cabinet and about 7 square feet for the legal-size ($8\frac{1}{2}$ by 13 or 14 inches) cabinet. *Open-shelf files* occupy approximately 50 percent less floor space than file cabinets.

Space Guidelines for Furniture and Equipment

Before furniture and equipment can be effectively located on a new office layout plan, an inventory of all such items (quantity, description, size, and use of each item) should be taken. In locating each item on the floor plan, the guidelines in Figure 13–6 may be used. Note that the circled numbers appearing in the figure correspond to the guideline numbers at the left of the figure.

Guidelines for Conducting the Office Space Study

The AOM has two options available for conducting the office space study. The first option is based upon a floor plan drawn by hand according to the customary English system (feet and inches). This method can be quickly converted to the metric scale in case the metric system is used.[5] The second option uses the computer in the design process.

Preparing Office Layout Models

Several methods of preparing a model of the office layout are described as follows:

1. The first method makes use of *colored paper cutouts* of all types of equipment, such as desks, chairs, file cabinets, and safes. Each piece of furniture and equipment is drawn to the same scale as the floor plan to maintain proper relationships when the cutouts are pasted into position. The scales $\frac{1}{8}$ inch = 1 foot and $\frac{1}{4}$ inch = 1 foot are commonly used because of their ease in conversion on a standard ruler. This is the simplest and least expensive method of illustrating a proposed layout.

2. The second method makes use of a *template,* illustrated in Figure 13–7, which is available from most book and office furniture and

---

[3]"How's Your Space?" *The Office Professional* (August 15, 1992), p. 7.

[4]Marilyn Joyce and Ulrika Wallersteiner, *Ergonomics: Humanizing the Automated Office* (Cincinnati: South-Western Publishing Co., 1989), p. 108.

[5]Executive Order 12770 required all federal agencies to commence using the metric system by October 1992. By January 1993, all companies doing business with the U.S. government were required to use metric measurements.

Figure 13–6
Space Guidelines for Office Furniture and Equipment

1. a. The width of major traffic aisles may vary from 5 to 8 feet.

   b. Less traveled aisles should be 3½ to 5½ feet wide.

2. Aisle space between desks should not be less than 36 inches.

3. In open planning, the plants should grow to between 3½ and 5 feet, unless they are to be used as visual barriers, when 7-foot plants with more fullness and breadth are recommended.

4. a. Desks should generally face the same direction, unless the employees are clustered together in automated workcenters.

   b. Such workcenters should be provided with visual and acoustical privacy, as discussed in Chapter 14.

5. No more than two desks should be placed side by side so that each desk will be on an aisle, thus permitting easy flow of traffic.

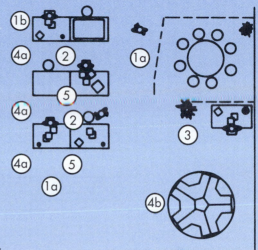

6. Frequently used computer terminals shared by two or more people should be placed as close as possible to the users.

7. Desks should be arranged to give a straight flow of work—that is, so that a person will receive work from the desk beside or in back of him or her.

8. Those whose work requires the most concentration should have the best light. No workers should face the light, and the window light should be at the left of an individual.

9. Space between desks facing in the same direction—that is, the space occupied by chairs—should not be less than 28 inches, preferably 36 inches.

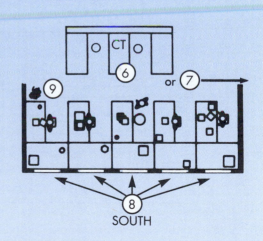

10. If active files open up front to front—that is, to an aisle—the width of the aisle, when the file drawers are open, should not be less than 30 to 40 inches.

11. File cabinets should be placed against walls or railings if possible.

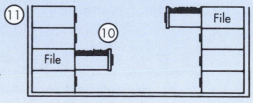

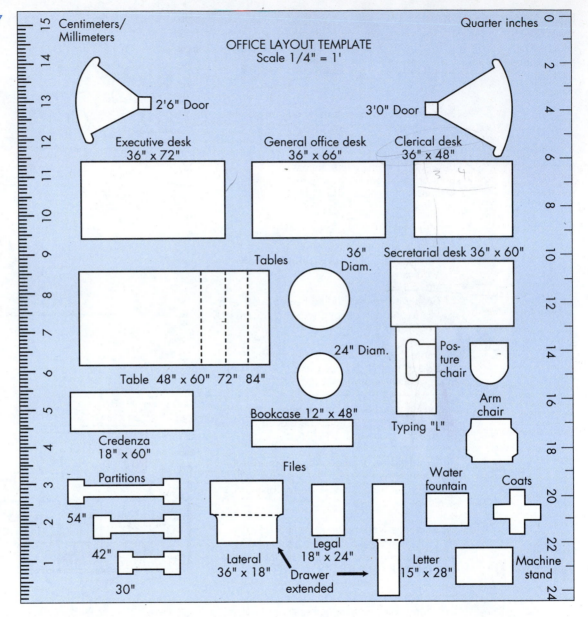

Figure 13–7
A Template

equipment stores. The cutout areas indicate the size and shape of the various types of furniture, equipment, columns, partitions, and so on.

3. A third method uses a *grid board* upon which scale models of furniture, equipment, and so on, are positioned. After the plan has been laid out, it can be used by managers, supervisors, and workers involved in space planning. Pho-

tographs may also be made as a guide for installation.

4. A fourth method—the *simulated office space model*—relies upon the construction of full-size replicas of selected office areas. In such complete mock-up offices, the office personnel can sit in their actual offices and observe beforehand what their workstations will be like. They can examine and test all the various components,

such as the lighting system, chairs, and storage cabinets. Colors and textures can be evaluated and examined together in the same proportions and arrangements in which they will be ultimately used. This method, possibly the costliest of all, is feasible only when large sums of money are available for space management.

Using Computer-Aided Design (CAD) for Office Layouts

The computer is often used to automate the drafting function. In **computer-aided design (CAD),** the programming techniques assign numeric values to graphic information (such as line drawings and various geometric shapes) for processing and printout or display on the VDT screen. In addition to its use in office layout design, CAD is also used for designing parts, as in the automotive field, for plotting and printing out drawings, and for handling design changes.

Various input methods are available for using CAD. One application uses a "mouse," a small plastic device with which the VDT operator controls the movement of the cursor (the small position indicator on a VDT screen) for drawing graphics on the VDT screen. When you use the mouse, the movement of your hand is duplicated by the cursor on the screen through electrical pulses or radio waves sent by the mouse to the computer.[6] Another device, a *light pen,* the size and shape of a pen, is connected to a terminal by wire to permit the operator to draw with the pen on the display screen. This drawing is made possible after the operator calls up a light pen graphics program stored in the computer.

The CAD concept may be used to simulate an office layout. In order to perform this simulation, the operator supplies the computer with information concerning space allocations and workstation dimensions, number of personnel to be distributed over the floor space, and space estimates (in square feet) required for performing the functions of the unit. Given all this basic information, the computer can "create" and display the optimal design on the VDT screen or print out a copy to be used for discussion and decision making.

---

[6]Other input devices related to the mouse are the trackball and the joystick. For more information on these devices as well as a description of off-the-shelf packages used in office space analysis and design, consult an up-to-date computer systems/data processing textbook or a reference on office automation.

Illustration 13–4 Using computer-aided design to simulate an office layout.

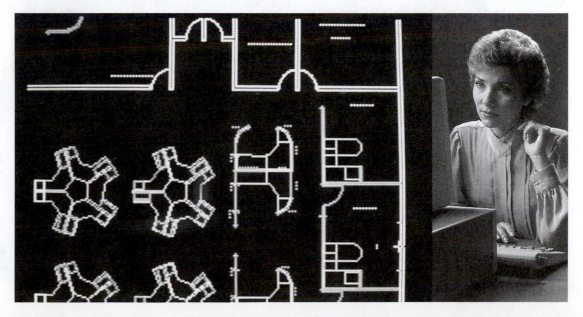

In another CAD application, a software package, Planix™ Visual Office Management, is used to draw office floor plans and generate spreadsheet-style reports. The software creates a very professional-looking office layout, as shown in Figure 13–8, through use of a library of predrawn workplace symbols. The computer operator previews and selects the symbols for modular furniture, office equipment, computer network components, freestanding office furniture, and people. The layout plan is created as the operator "drags and drops" the symbols into the floor plan. As the symbols are placed into the drawing, the software simultaneously creates a database that records everything appearing in the workplace drawing. The database may then be used to print out spreadsheet-style management reports, such as furniture and equipment inventories, telephone and electrical cabling reports, and personnel directories.

Virtual reality, described in Chapter 8, relies upon computer software to create a three-dimensional (3-D) representation of an office layout that "virtually" hurls the viewer into a realistic office setting. In such 3-D simulations, the user experiences the traffic flow of people, a repositioning of furniture and equipment, lights being flicked on and off, wall colors being changed, and so on, without having set foot in the actual office. With graphics workstations becoming less expensive, we can anticipate further technological innovations in office design.

RELOCATING THE OFFICE

Even though an effective layout has been designed and put into action, periodically the long-range needs of the space management program must be reviewed. On the basis of such a review, the space facilities team may recommend that the office be relocated. Factors contributing to such a recommendation include:

1. The rising costs of space (real estate, property taxes, etc.) in the present location.

Figure 13–8
A Sales Department Layout Created by CAD Software

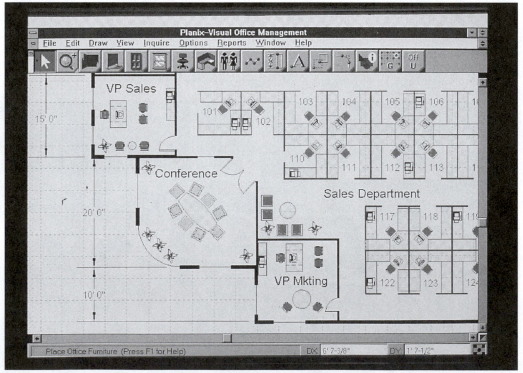

Courtesy of Planix Office for Windows from Foresight Resources Corp.

2. The need to locate nearer the market for the firm's present and future customers.
3. Less space required as a result of downsizing and restructuring or the need for more space as a result of the firm's growth.
4. Traffic congestion and transportation delays facing workers who commute each day.
5. Increased costs of downtown parking.
6. The need to ensure employee safety and reduce security risks.
7. The desire to improve the firm's image by relocating to a more prestigious area.
8. Excessive noise from traffic.
9. Inefficient, as well as insufficient, facilities (elevator service, toilets, building management, and electrical capacity for heating, ventilation, computer usage, and air conditioning).

The problems facing a bank when it decided to relocate its offices are described by the facility manager in the *Dialog from the Workplace.* When an organization, such as this bank, decides to relocate within an existing building, short- and long-term goals must be set that include estimates of the personnel needed to attain those goals. Note the other kinds of problems facing this bank and how they were solved.

In the following discussion, we examine the purchase-or-lease decision, assuming that a firm decided earlier not to construct a new office building. This discussion is followed by some helpful hints on physically moving the office.

The Purchase-or-Lease Decision

The decision to purchase or lease existing office space at a new location should be based upon an analysis of several important factors, as discussed below.

Future Space Requirements

If the space requirements of the organization are going to change rapidly over the next few years, strong consideration should be given to leasing. However, from the viewpoint of reducing income taxes, it may be more economical for the firm to own rather than rent the space. For example, the owner of a small company not needing extensive floor space or a downtown location may reduce the rising costs of office rent and obtain a favorable tax advantage by purchasing a commercial condominium in a suburban location. Income tax deductions may be taken for the mortgage interest and local real estate taxes. Further, the cost of substantial improvements made by the owner may be claimed as reductions in federal income taxes. If the small organization anticipates expanding within the next 5 to 10 years, the firm may consider the purchase of extra space in the condominium, which may be leased until it is needed.

Organizations weighing the decision to purchase or lease office space need to evaluate the net cost of ownership compared with the rental (lease) costs of equivalent space. In calculating the costs of ownership, the following factors should be considered: (1) sales price stated in terms of square footage; (2) interest costs for financing the purchase; (3) maintenance costs (operating and management expenses, association dues, and property taxes); (4) tax bracket of the purchaser; (5) tax benefits from ownership; and (6) the prevailing cost of money (interest rates).

Next, the prospective buyer should compute the rental charges for equivalent space—largely total rent per square foot plus operating expenses—and compare these charges with the cost of ownership in which the owner builds an equity in the business.

Supply of Capital

If the firm is short on capital, it may decide not to tie up its money in the purchase of a building. Rather, it may invest the funds elsewhere and obtain a greater return on the investment. Thus, when the supply of capital is tight, we find that leasing may be preferable to purchasing. When leasing is likely, an understanding of the contents of a lease becomes important for the AOM.

Contents of the Lease

A **lease** is the agreement between the **lessor** (the landlord) and the **lessee** (the tenant) that transfers possession, *but not ownership,* for a period of time. The lease should set forth clearly the rights of the lessor and those of the lessee in order to avoid any misunderstandings. By means of the lease, the landlord grants to the tenant the privilege

DIALOG FROM THE WORKPLACE

JOHN W. HOEKSTRA, JR.
Facility Manager
Fifth Third Bancorp
Cincinnati, Ohio

John W. Hoekstra, who received a B.S. in management from Park College, is responsible for the administration and management of all Bancorp-occupied areas within the headquarters office. His specific responsibilities include maintenance and operations management, long-term facility planning, property and lease management, and coordinating all department relocations.

The Fifth Third Bancorp is headquartered at the Fifth Third Center in Cincinnati. Over a two-and-one-half-year period, the Bancorp completed the renovation of 140,000 square feet of office space within the center. The project involved space planning and renovation of 12 floors and the relocation of 1,000 employees in 40 departments.

QUESTION: In planning the relocation of the offices in Fifth Third's multistory building, what major problems faced you? How did you solve them?

RESPONSE: Over the course of this project, we encountered many different obstacles before reaching our goal. Our main objective was to create a functional, efficient working environment that would accommodate future expansion. Additionally, we wanted to minimize project costs by utilizing internal resources whenever possible. For example, the space design and planning, construction, communication relocations, and move coordination were all performed by Fifth Third personnel.

Space design and planning proved to be a very challenging phase of this project. Each Bancorp division has its own unique needs and requirements based on its operating environment, personnel profile mix, and growth rate.

The workflow, interdepartmental and intradepartmental relationships, and equipment/communication/furniture needs for individual departments were also closely examined versus the physical environment of the building. Determining the optimal placement of each division within the Fifth Third Center was as critical as each individual department layout. The operations division, for example, has many departments with manufacturing-type environments. These departments run 24 hours a day, seven days a week; have special heating, ventilating, air conditioning, and electric needs; require great security; and must be highly accessible to outside transportation. Naturally, only specific areas of the building can satisfy all these requirements.

Move coordination also proved to be challenging. Our goal was to relocate each department without experiencing any disruption in daily business operations. The key to success in this phase was to identify all the departments and support groups involved and establish a primary contact for each group. This person was held responsible for the timely completion of specific work such as coordinating CRT or telephone extension relocations. Distributing all pertinent information and changes to the primary contacts was essential.

Our largest relocation involved moving five departments with 150 employees to 30,000 square feet of newly renovated floors. It was successfully completed over a 60-hour period in one weekend.

One must keep in mind that no matter how thorough a project is planned, the unexpected can happen. Decisions and changes will have to be made while the move is in progress. Staying calm, remaining flexible, and having additional resources available when these hurdles arise will help in finding workable solutions.

of using the property for lawful purposes and without interference providing the terms of the contract are carried out. Although the standard commercial office lease may appear to be a simple business contract, the AOM must understand its contents in order to avoid costly legal problems.

The **work letter** is that portion of a lease which spells out the lessor's and the lessee's obligations for any work to be done to the building and who will pay for it. The work letter should be carefully prepared to consider all possible contingencies so any conflicts about the charges for the completed work may be avoided. The first part of the work letter deals with the plans to be prepared by the lessee and those to be prepared by the lessor. Usually the lessee includes information about the construction and finishing of the office space and the data required (electrical needs, plumbing requirements, weight loads, etc.) for preparing the engineering plans. This section also lists the dates when plans must be submitted by the tenant to the landlord. The second part of the work letter usually deals with the landlord's work and indicates the items to be supplied by the landlord beyond those that are routinely furnished.

The tenant should also consider the effect inflation may have on the type of escalation clause contained in a renewal lease. Although various kinds of formulas are used to determine rent at the time of renewing a lease, the rent is often linked to the Consumer Price Index (CPI) in some way. Thus, as inflation escalates, so does the rental cost to the tenant.

Other important terms of the office lease that should be studied by the AOM include subleasing; options to cancel; options for more space; the hours and seasons for heating, ventilating, and air-conditioning services; and, finally, the rent commencement clause, which states when rent begins. Because a lease is a complex legal document, the AOM should consult the firm's attorney for counsel before completing the lease document.

Resale Value

If the building may be readily resold, its purchase may be a wise move. On the other hand, if there are factors that would limit the resale of the prop-erty (such as little or no land for future expansion or for added parking facilities), leasing may be a better choice.

The Office Move

After the decision has been made to purchase and renovate a building or to rent office space, the day arrives when the office must move into the new quarters. Unlike moving a household, the first priority in moving an office is the immediate restoration of production. With intelligent planning over a sufficient period of time and with careful timing of each phase of the move, we can be sure that the job will be done with minimum disruption in the company's normal business.

Checklist for Planning the Move

Basic to the planning for an office move is a detailed checklist of the tasks to be done, with each job arranged in the order in which it should be accomplished. As we plan the move, the tasks shown on the checklist in Figure 13–9 should be completed, or at least considered, by the AOM and others on the project team responsible for moving the office.

Personnel Problems Related to the Office Move

Whenever we are involved in moving an office, many personnel problems are encountered. Such problems are uncovered when management analyzes its responsibilities to those employees who will be unable to work at the new site and to those who will relocate along with the company.

Employees should be informed of a possible office relocation even before the decision to move is made. After the decision is made, the workers should be told promptly so that those workers the company will not be able to retain have maximum time to seek other employment. Those in the counseling program or the employee assistance program should make every reasonable attempt to aid these employees in finding new local employment, such as canvassing other employers in the area, granting employees time off for interviews, bringing representatives of public and private employment

Figure 13–9
A Checklist
for Planning
the Office
Move

CHECKLIST FOR MOVING THE OFFICE

Organization	Location	Preferred move date: _____
Person in charge of move	Tel. Number	Actual move date: _____

Instructions: Please check off each subitem as it is completed. When all subitems have been completed, check off the main item as being finally completed.

__1. Determine moving date.
  __a. Consider weekend, not overnight move.
  __b. Make sure new site is ready for the move.
  __c. Verify that the terms of lease permit the move.
  __d. Complete Gantt chart (Fig. 13–2) for detailed moves so all personnel know status of move at all times.

__2. Select mover as early as possible.
  __a. Secure recommendations for reliable moving companies from 2–3 firms who have recently moved.
  __b. Obtain written proposals from each moving company.
  __c. Use proposals to notify project team about details of the move.

__3. Appoint project team and manager to carry out all move responsibilities.
  __a. Select team members, as a minimum: project manager, AOM, and assistant with moving experience.
  __b. Expand project team as needed.
  __c. Orient all personnel about site location, expected move date, and location of workstations in the new quarters.
  __d. Brief personnel at special meetings as needed.

__4. Prepare moving instructions.
  __a. Be complete in every detail.
  __b. Be specific about assignments of staff members and employees assisting in move.
  __c. Include instructions for:
    __(1) Scheduled dates and hours.
    __(2) Details of tagging/marking equipment and furniture.
    __(3) Proper handling of desks, chairs, plants, and other items of equipment.
    __(4) Ordering stationery and forms containing new address and telephone number.

__5. Send moving notices.
  __a. Send new address and telephone number to clients, suppliers, banks, etc.
  __b. Change listing in telephone directory and in the directory of new building.

__6. Prepare layout for each department, area, or cost center.
  __a. Draw all items of furniture and equipment to scale.
  __b. Assign number or color code to each area for ease in putting furniture and equipment in place.

__7. Schedule housecleaning and purge records.
  __a. Conduct "throwaway campaign" 2–3 months before moving date.
  __b. Schedule second housecleaning 1–2 days before the move.
  __c. Consult records retention schedule and destroy unneeded records.

__8. Order cartons for packing.
  __a. Provide sufficient quantity of cartons to each department several days before move so bulky materials can be packed in advance.
  __b. Indicate when assistance with packing will be available.

__9. Assign code numbers and tag furniture and equipment.
  __a. Stress importance of accurate coding and tagging to each department.
  __b. Assign a different color of tag for each floor (if moving to multistory building).
  __c. Assign a different color of tag to each department if new building is one story.

__10. Set up directional signs at the new site.
  __a. Indicate locations of elevator lobbies, hallways, doorways, offices, private offices, etc.
  __b. Break down large open areas into small sections with each section identified in the directional marking system.
  __c. Post in each elevator lobby a scale plan of the entire floor.

__11. Provide special maintenance crews.
  __a. Inform present and new landlords of need for service personnel (elevator operators, maintenance personnel, security guards, plumbers, carpenters, and electricians).
  __b. Have standby telephone service persons instructed to remove all telephone equipment from workstations prior to moving.

__12. Assign guides.
  __a. At old office: provide guides to direct movers on proper sequence of moving items out of the office.
  __b. At new office: provide guides to direct the flow of furniture and equipment as indicated by tags and codes.

__13. Establish information centers.
  __a. Establish at each location—old and new—an area with table and telephone to serve as communication headquarters for employees and movers.
  __b. Provide copies of the daily plan to both centers.

__14. Inspect the site prior to moving in.
  __a. Make final check before the move to reduce delay during the move.
  __b. Check that telephone and electrical services have installed proper equipment and that it is working satisfactorily.

__15. Check the new site immediately after the move.
  __a. Have designer, contractor, landlord, tenant, and manager of project team inspect premises to make sure any damage (marred walls and floors, chipped paint, and dented furniture and equipment) is noted.
  __b. Check to be sure all items to be moved are accounted for.
  __c. Be sure that all liabilities for any move-related damages are determined.

services into the company to interview employees, assisting in preparing personal resumés, furnishing statements to employees regarding their rights and equities in the various employee benefit plans, and considering the need for severance pay.

Those employees who relocate along with the company to a distant area should be aided in getting settled with a minimum of inconvenience. The chamber of commerce in the new community can help employees by passing along information on such factors as schools, climate, cultural and sports activities, medical facilities, and the location of apartments, hotels, and motels that can furnish temporary housing.

THE WORKPLACE OF THE FUTURE

Envisioning the workplace of the future, we anticipate that several of the approaches to increasing productivity and creativity, such as problem-solving teams, empowerment, and diversity, will be incorporated into the physical environment of the office. As we shall see in the next chapter, environmental issues should result in an increased use of ergonomically correct office furniture and fixtures. The need to relax will be taken into account in the office layout, the color schemes, and the furniture and equipment. According to an officer of Herman Miller, Inc., an office furniture manufacturer that specializes in research, "There will be a lot less standardization. The changing demographics of the workforce and the changing ideas of work have implications on the physical environment."[7]

Steelcase, Inc., a designer and manufacturer of office furniture, has advanced a concept called *The Steelcase Commons,* which is illustrated in Figure 13–10. Located at the center of this prototype is the

---

[7]Maida Odom, "2001: A Workspace Odyssey," *The Philadelphia Inquirer* (March 30, 1993), pp. F1 and F4.

Figure 13–10
The Steelcase Commons—A Prototype of Tomorrow's Workplace

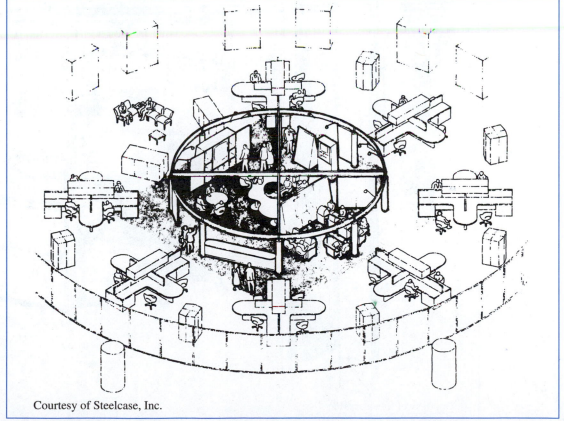

Courtesy of Steelcase, Inc.

common area, where meetings on team projects may be held. Enclosing this common area are overhead tracks that support marker boards and easels, which can serve as space dividers for small meetings. Provision is made for private workstations around the perimeter, where introverted workers may be located near a wall while extroverted workers may be positioned near the common area.

Figure 13–11 illustrates another product designed for tomorrow's workplace—Steelcase's *Personal Harbor, the Thinking Machine.* The Personal Harbor is a 48-square-foot, semi-enclosed individual workstation with a curved door developed to support the visual, acoustical, and territorial privacy needs of knowledge workers. Based on a column-and-beam architecture, the

Figure 13–11
Personal Harbor—The Thinking Machine

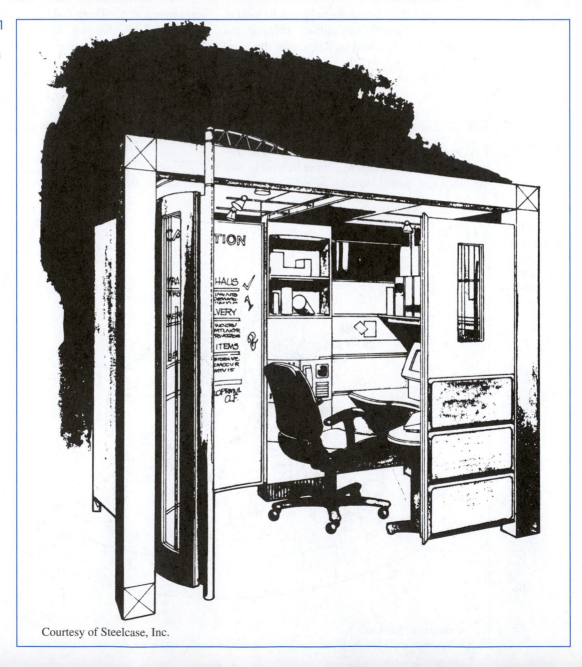

Courtesy of Steelcase, Inc.

workstation provides adjustable work surfaces, marker board, mobile pedestal, personally controlled lighting and ventilation, and an electronic totem pole that provides easy power access for personal CD players, radios, and other devices. Thus, the Thinking Machine is designed to empower the office employee to work more effectively in an environment designed to stimulate psychological comfort and mental focus. Figure 13–12 shows how these workstations may be grouped to meet the needs of work teams, where office workers have access to both the team and their own individual working environment. The option of putting casters on the Thinking Machine and wheeling it to a new location is more efficient than moving a fixed-wall private office.

For those of you who have occasion to use an "office in the sky," the anticipated technological innovations become mind-boggling. For example, airline seats, adjustable to your height and weight, will become interactive and feature video display terminals that let you FAX memos, watch movies, and make restaurant reservations. As the airplane seat becomes an extension of your earth-based office, other possible features include: a touchpad video screen and computer keyboard that unfolds from your armrest, a seat computer that talks to the jet's central computer to relay fax by satellite to a ground link, and a handset that includes a telephone and credit-card reader.

Back down on earth, we anticipate being able to contact our office while on the road—without a telephone or a modem—from anywhere in the country. Thus, our FAXes, voice-mail messages, and computer data will be available with a few commands on our laptop computer. To accomplish this feat, the Federal Communications Commission has set aside a portion of the public airwaves for this new kind of two-way *wireless* communications network. Thus, traveling in our

Figure 13–12
A Grouping of Personal Harbors That Meets the Needs of Office Workers Coming Together as Problem-Solving Teams

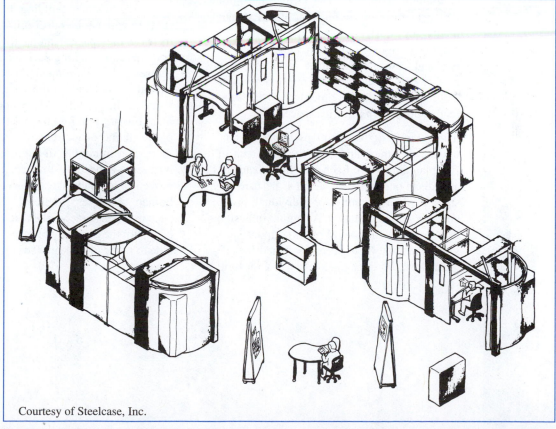

Courtesy of Steelcase, Inc.

"office in the car," we shall be able to stay in contact with our clients or home office without having to use a conventional telephone, cellular telephone, or computer modem. Instead, we shall be using laptop computers or small personal digital assistants outfitted with wireless modems.

For AOMs charged with managing office space—whether in the air, in the car, within thinking machines, or in traditional office settings—the challenge remains the same: to provide a work environment that combines the latest research findings with the most up-to-date technological advances while at the same time keeping space costs to a minimum.

S U M M A R Y

1. In the management of office space, the AOM works toward the goal of creating a well-planned layout that provides a timely, efficient, and economical flow of information to those persons responsible for decision making. In designing such a layout, the AOM is concerned with meeting space needs and personnel needs so that the layout provides for a continuous workflow. The formal and informal relationships among people in departments or cost centers, the number of employees located in each department, the type and flow of information, and the need for private offices are several important factors that must be studied in order to provide for effective utilization of office space.

2. Three kinds of layout plans—conventional, open, and American—plus the high-tech office plan are found. Each plan has advantages and disadvantages, which must be carefully studied when planning for individual, group, and special workcenters. As an aid in designing layouts, the AOM draws upon space guidelines that have been developed for efficient work, for personnel needs, and for furniture and equipment. In developing the layout model, the AOM may use either the English or the metric system and one of several layout techniques—colored paper cutouts, templates, cork board grid with scale models of furniture and equipment, full-size replicas of office areas, or computer-aided design (CAD).

3. Once the decision has been reached to relocate the office in a new building, the organization is faced with another decision—to purchase or to lease the space. Among the factors to be considered in making such a decision are the future space requirements, the availability of capital, the contents of the lease, and the resale value of the property. Many hours of detailed planning are required to make sure that each phase of the office move occurs on time so there is a minimum disruption in the firm's business. Especially important in the office move is a mutually satisfactory solution to any human resources problems that may arise, such as when some workers decide not to relocate with the company or when employees decide to move along with the company to a new location.

FOR YOUR REVIEW

1. a. What essential elements must be considered when the administrative office manager views the office as a system?

   b. How are these elements related to the administrative services provided by an organization?

2. What responsibilities may be assigned the facility manager who is charged with space planning?

3. Describe how the Gantt chart is used in planning an office layout.

4. What kind of information does the AOM seek when undertaking an office space inventory?

5. How does workflow influence the planning of office space?

6. a. Describe the human space needs of office workers.

   b. What types of distance must be observed in meeting these human space needs?

7. What are the main features of the conventional design plan?

8. a. Describe the open-plan concept as it is used in space management.

   b. List the main advantages and disadvantages of the open plan.

9. List the advantages and disadvantages of providing private offices.

10. Describe the workcenter concept.

11. a. Describe the automated workcenter.

    b. What special management principles must be applied in designing this type of workcenter?

12. What kinds of guidelines are available to aid the office manager in managing space?

13. Describe the different methods of preparing a model of the office layout.

14. How is the computer used in designing office space?

15. For what reasons may a company decide to relocate its office?

16. In a leasing arrangement a work letter is often used. Describe its value to the lessor and to the lessee.

17. How may a company aid those workers who decide not to relocate with the firm?

18. What are some features we may anticipate in tomorrow's workplace?

FOR YOUR DISCUSSION

1. In those years when downsizing (or "rightsizing" as some call this approach) was at its height, office workers at all organizational levels lost work space. For example, one office manager who once enjoyed 400 square feet of office space learned to live within a 225-square-foot area. Although downsizing continues, it now takes other forms that do not necessarily mean smaller-size workstations. As an office manager planning a new office on a very tight budget, how can you cut costs without squeezing your workers into smaller work spaces?

2. Sylvia Endo, presently serving as the president of a local management association, has been asked to submit a short article for publication. Endo asks you, her assistant, to compile a list of typical violations of good office layout that she plans to develop in her article. What should your list include?

3. In the law offices of Beale, Horn, and Kidd, there are 32 lawyers, 1 certified public accountant, 10 legal secretaries, and 14 other employees. The firm is now planning its new quarters, which will be ready late next year. The partners realize they have a lot to learn in their planning. What suggestions can you offer them in the area of initial planning to make sure that a satisfactory space plan will be devised for their office?

4. Six workers in your college registrar's office are being retrained as word processing operators using video display terminals (VDTs). Each will be provided with new furniture in an open-plan design that will replace the present bull-pen setting. As office supervisor, you have been asked by the registrar to recommend a layout that will provide the "right amount" of concentration and privacy for these employees. Prepare a clustered as well as a nonclustered layout for the six automated workstations. Assume that 400 square feet (an area 20 feet square) is presently in use by this group. Defend your choice of the more efficient of the two design plans.

5. Currently, six employees are housed in an open-plan portion of the payroll department that occupies 300 square feet (a space that is 12 feet wide and 25 feet long). Because of expansion, two more workers must be added to the space presently occupied, as shown in Figure A. Prepare a revised layout that permits eight workstations using the same desk and chair sizes. No additional furniture and equipment, other than a visitor's chair, should be provided for each workstation.

Figure A
Present Layout for Six Payroll Workstations

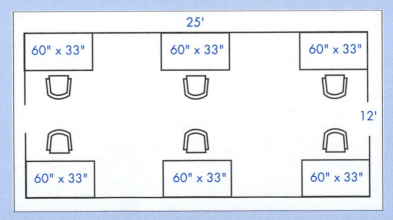

c
o
n
t

6. Doctors Tan and Wong, specialists in psychiatry, have moved to a new second-floor location in a suburban office building. Two of their last unsolved space problems are the layouts for the reception area and the consultation rooms used by each physician. (The present dimensions of the space are shown in Figure B.) The area is an inner section of the building with no outside windows and with permanent wall construction that must be retained.

   As an assistant to the two psychiatrists, you are solely responsible for designing the new quarters. Your experience has told you that no more than three chairs are needed in a small waiting room, since the doctors maintain a very orderly one-hour schedule with each patient; hence, there is no waiting line of patients, there are generally no emergencies, and usually the patients come alone.

Figure B
Layout for
Psychiatric
Office Suite

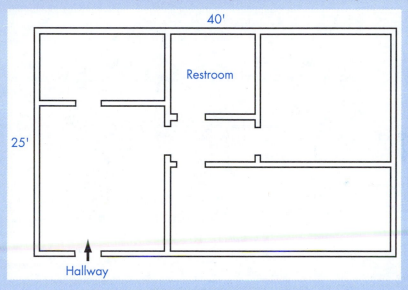

In each physician's office, there is no need for special equipment. However, several comfortable chairs, a small desk, and a reclining couch for the patients' use should be provided.

Sketch a plan that applies the space management principles in this chapter. Assume that only the two physicians and you, as assistant, occupy the office and that a small service area for office supplies and other services should be provided.

CASES FOR CRITICAL THINKING

Case 13–1 Converting to an Open Plan

The Levitt Insurance Agency leases a small office space in an expensive downtown area of a midwestern city. Because of the convenient location, the agency hopes to retain this location even though more space may be needed in the next five years.

Recently, the new owners of the building announced plans for a major renovation of the structure, starting with the removal of all nonweight-bearing walls. (In the case of the Levitt quarters, only the outside walls are considered weight-bearing; thus, all inside walls would be removed.) The reason for this decision is to provide an opportunity to use the open plan for modernizing the office with all the advantages this plan offers.

c
o
n
t

The Levitt office layout in Figure C is reduced in size to a scale of $1/10$ inch = 1 foot. In the office, workstations are provided for four agents (salespersons), one secretary-receptionist, an office manager, a vice president, and president. (The two executives also supervise other business interests of the firm that frequently require small on-site conferences.) Restroom facilities are provided across the hallway from the front entrance to the office suite, which is located on the third floor. Windows occupy the entire west wall (shown vertically at the left on the layout) as well as the short east wall near the secretary-receptionist workstation.

Suzanne and Aaron Levitt, executives of the firm, ask you, the office manager, to redesign the office for an open plan that incorporates movable panels and new workstation furniture and equipment. Prepare a layout of the new office drawn to a scale of $1/4$ inch = 1 foot that provides the same relative amounts of space for each staff member as found in the present layout. Indicate, in a report, the assumptions (on equipment, workflow, etc.) you made in completing this assignment. Also, provide an estimate of the space savings possible by using the open plan.

Figure C
Conventional
Layout for
Small Insur-
ance Office

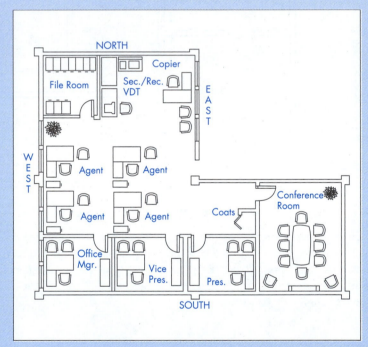

Source: Adapted with permission from Haworth, Inc., One Haworth Center, Holland MI 49423.

Case 13–2 Office Layout

Ellis Ventura, owner of a management consulting service, is moving his service to a new building in which the office area is 40 feet by 20 feet. There are only two windows in the office, both of which are on one 20-foot wall. The office space will be occupied by:

Ellis Ventura, the owner and office manager
Marsha Carr, Ventura's assistant
Lori Alomar, a secretary
Jerry Sprague, a general clerk, who also serves as receptionist
Marina Velasquez, a community college student who works part time

c
o
n
t

Ventura estimates his immediate furniture needs as desks and chairs for all employees, chairs for four visitors, two file cabinets, bookcases, a cabinet and rack for literature, and a coat rack. Ventura believes that he would like to have partitions or screens around his office because he does a great deal of dictating and confidential interviewing.

Ventura has "roughed out" the tentative location of the employees as shown in Figure D. When he showed his sketch to Carr and Alomar, the following conversation took place:

Ventura: Well, here it is—our new home as of three weeks from today. What do you think of it?

Carr: Sure looks roomy compared with where we are now. But I should have known you'd get the windows. Sure must be nice to be No. 1!

Ventura: Well, Marsha, you know that I have a certain image to maintain, especially when I'm talking with our clients. How do you feel about it, Lori?

Alomar: I see your point about the windows, Mr. Ventura. That doesn't bother me too much. I am more concerned about where you have placed my desk. Just look how far I'm going to have to walk every time you call me in for dictation. Why did you put me miles away?

Ventura: I put you there so that you can give a helping hand to Jerry and Marina. They're still pretty new with us and haven't learned the ropes yet. I need someone to watch over them.

Figure D
Ventura's Rough Layout of New Office Area.

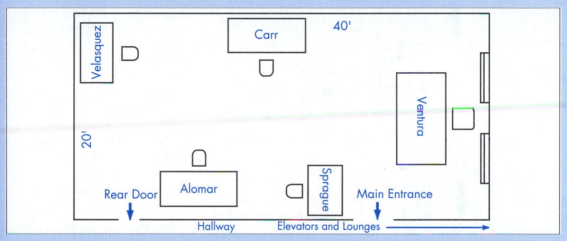

Back in his office, Ventura is mulling over the reactions of Carr and Alomar. He begins to think about his "monopolizing" the two windows and his placement of Alomar's desk. He comes to the conclusion that he does not want it to appear that he is appropriating the only two windows in the office. Yet he feels that he deserves the "two-window" status symbol. Also, he believes that close supervision of Sprague and Velasquez must be provided.

Prepare a report in which you:

1. Offer suggestions to Ventura as he begins to plan the space requirements for his people, the furniture, and the work to be done.
2. React to Ventura's feelings that he is entitled to all window space.
3. Include a layout for the new office area, showing the number of square feet you recommend for each employee's workstation.

Case 13–3 Designing a Home Office: Computer Option (available on disk)

PLANNING AN ERGO-NOMICALLY SOUND OFFICE ENVIRONMENT

GOALS FOR THIS CHAPTER

After completing this chapter, you should be able to:

1. Explain the nature of ergonomics and describe how it affects office productivity.
2. Identify the key factors in the office surface environment and their effects upon productivity.
3. Define these aspects of the seeing environment: the quantity and quality of light, the relative efficiency of daylight and artificial lighting systems, and criteria for evaluating lighting systems.
4. Discuss these features of the hearing environment: the measurement of noise, the effects of noise on employee performance, the methods of controlling office noise, and music in the office.
5. Identify the basic features of the air environment.
6. Explain how a safe and secure environment affects the level of office productivity.
7. Discuss the components of an energy management program designed to conserve energy in the office.

The office environment directly affects the quality and quantity of work produced as well as the morale of all workers. Consider for a moment your own experiences with these common environmental problems:

1. Sitting in an unadjustable chair—one with no padding on the seat or back—for four or more hours while keyboarding.
2. Attending class during the hottest summer days in which the room was not air conditioned, the images shown on a screen from an overhead projector were too small to read, the glare from sunlight invaded your space because of the absence of window shades, and the whispering of students prevented your hearing the instructor's lecture.
3. Operating a video display terminal in a setting in which bright fluorescent ceiling lights as well as reflections from the outdoor sunlight on your terminal screen caused eyestrain.
4. Undergoing long periods of close-concentration work in a noisy location near the front door of an office which hampered the quality of your work, making you irritable and frustrated.

On the job, such environmental problems lower employee morale and productivity and increase operating costs. To address these serious problems, the field of study known as ergonomics has emerged. Ergonomics comes from two Greek words, "ergon" (work) and "nomos" (laws of). As an applied science, **ergonomics,** sometimes called *human engineering,* integrates the use of space, furniture and equipment, and other physiological factors such as light, color, sound, and temperature, to meet the psychological needs of the workers on the job. Thus, ergonomics explains how the performance and morale of workers on the job are dependent on the *physiological* and *psychological factors* in the workers' environment.

Planning an ergonomically sound office environment presents many challenging problems for the administrative office manager. In the *Dialog from the Workplace,* Sharon Glick, a furniture and design administrator for an insurance broker, describes several of the problems that have faced her firm. Note the approaches that she has taken to solve these problems.

In this chapter, we shall discuss ergonomics and analyze its role in the office. Since office automation presents new ergonomic problems to the AOM, methods for ensuring high levels of work in automated workcenters in business and home offices will be discussed. Finally, because most ergonomic factors involve costly economic resources that use energy, the conservation of energy in the office is explored.

ERGONOMIC NEEDS IN THE OFFICE

All office work depends upon the following closely related elements: (1) *human activities* performed in the office, (2) *applications of social psychology* dealing with human behavior on the job, and (3) the *main environmental features* that affect office operations. Thus, it is important for the AOM to understand thoroughly these elements in order to provide for the ergonomic needs of the worker. Each of these elements is discussed briefly in this section so that a foundation can be laid for understanding the ergonomic processes in the office.

Human Activities in the Office

The activities performed by office workers may be classified as:

1. **Cognitive**—activities that are largely mental in nature and revolve around the use of knowledge or judgment. These activities range from simple tasks, such as proofreading, to the complexities included in decision making.
2. **Social**—activities involving the interpersonal tasks of two or more persons. The activities range from simple duties, such as telephoning, to more complex activities, such as conferring.
3. **Procedural**—those activities referring to the predefined work steps followed by office employees, such as filling out forms, which may be performed simultaneously with other activities, such as reading and writing.
4. **Physical**—activities that require the use of human energy. Keyboarding and filing or retrieving office records are common examples.

Research tells us that there is overlap among the four categories. For example, writing and filing, which require physical energy, also entail the use of some cognitive activities; telephoning may also involve the completion of message forms. Regardless, the ability of AOMs to create an ergonomically sound environment depends on identifying the basic tasks in the office and knowing how such tasks can be performed in an efficient manner.

Each of these human activities is performed in both business-office and home-office settings. In the typical business office, we find a greater number of workers and, accordingly, more interpersonal behavior problems than in the home-office setting. In addition, the business office will likely have more rules and greater formality than the home office where typically one worker makes slight modifications in the home setting to provide office space. However, in both locations, ergonomic factors are directly involved in determining how productive and satisfied the workers are.

Human Behavior Problems on the Job

Human behavior problems can cause difficulties for the office manager because these problems are largely intangible and emotional in nature. Many of the problems involve the worker as an individual and deal with status, the need for belonging, and the fulfillment of motivational needs. Problems can also relate to social conditions, such as the degree of satisfaction employees have in working with and for others. Thus, the AOM must take time to study the personalities of workers and attempt to understand their attitudes toward themselves, their work, and their coworkers. All employees—and that includes the

DIALOG FROM THE WORKPLACE

SHARON GLICK

*Furniture and Design
Administrator
Corporate Real Estate and
Facilities Department
Johnson & Higgins, New York,
New York*

Johnson & Higgins, a large insurance broker with over 50 domestic offices and many subsidiaries and international locations, employs over 5,000 people in the United States alone. The corporate headquarters is located in New York City.

Ms. Glick attended Wayne State University in Detroit, where she completed three years of work toward a B.F.A., with a major in painting and art history. She came to work for Johnson & Higgins as a buyer in the purchasing department. Her experience as a furniture buyer, her background in art, and previous business and management skills prepared Ms. Glick for her present position in the facilities department. Here, she is responsible for all furniture, carpeting, and accessory research and acquisition of these for the New York location; contract negotiation; and establishment of furniture and carpeting standards. Involved in company-wide space planning and organization, she serves as a consultant to all other Johnson & Higgins locations.

QUESTION: In planning an ergonomically sound environment, what have been some of the most challenging problems facing your organization? How have you solved these problems?

RESPONSE: Johnson & Higgins, like other companies its size, must balance the important contributions of ergonomics to employee productivity with the economic constraints of our times. Unfortunately, it is impossible to knock down existing office structures in order to make them ergonomically correct.

Our greatest challenge is to correct existing furniture systems to make them ergonomically sound with a minimum capital investment. Often this can be done in a simple manner by repositioning monitors below the sight line, recommending chair height adjustments, and purchasing simple ergonomic aids such as wrist pads and adjustable height keyboard trays.

I deal with this on a one-to-one basis when approached by an employee within our New York location. The question becomes: How do we reach everyone across the nation? Our solution was to publish a general information article in an internal newsletter that answered commonly asked questions on ergonomic issues and invited inquiries for more information. The response to the article was favorable and many employees were given advice on simple and immediate ways to improve their work environment. Another solution would be to establish company-wide standards for facilities planning and furniture purchases which are based on sound ergonomics. This is a project we have been working on for presentation to our upper management.

At the same time, when an office is moving to a new location and a work environment is being created from scratch, our group gives every attention to sound ergonomics. We have national contracts for furniture with companies such as Herman Miller, who are pioneers in ergonomic research and development. Lighting patterns are designed to favor the computer user. In addition, to create a healthy climate, asbestos-free buildings are leased and low-toxin, PVC (polyvinyl chloride) free carpet is selected.

Ergonomics is an important issue for Johnson & Higgins. Our goal, through the course of time, is to provide all of our employees with a healthy, comfortable, and productive work environment.

AOM—must recognize the need for adjusting to other people's diverse personalities and for solving personal job problems. These subjective aspects of management were discussed in Part 2 of this textbook.

Major Ambient Factors in the Office

When we speak of **ambient factors** in the office, we refer to those conditions that *surround and affect* the performance of work and the development of employee satisfaction with the work and workplace. Many of these factors are physical since they involve the human senses, such as sight, hearing, and touch. Other factors, such as the security that comes from working in a safe place and the feelings that arise from visual comfort and working in an attractive setting, are psychological in nature. As such, these factors help to create the communication climate and levels of morale found in the office.

Today's workers want an office setting that is comfortable and efficient. Thus, offices that cling to traditional, "institutional" layouts having row after row of desks and file cabinets are considered impersonal. A manager's office that seems to be "guarded" by a private secretary, too, seems unfriendly. In contrast, today's office staff wants a workplace that is *flexible, comfortable,* and *safe,* with *reliable equipment* and *usable, efficient procedures.* In addition, today's office workers seek an atmosphere, or *ambience,* that fosters a friendly place in which to work.

To provide such an environment, employees should be given an opportunity to assist in planning their work areas and to inject their own personalities into their workstations, such as arranging personal photographs, wall hangings, and plants in their workplaces. When employees are given a voice in designing their own workplaces, they develop a greater feeling of belonging and of participation. A higher level of morale and greater productivity result.

Figure 14–1 shows the complex set of ergonomic factors required to achieve an effective office ambience. All of the factors work "side by side" to affect directly the individual worker's job performance as well as the motivation and enthusiasm that a worker brings to the job. Also, as the information in the four corners of the figure shows, important economic resources must be managed by the AOM when implementing the ergonomic system.

THE SURFACE ENVIRONMENT

The **surface environment** consists of those physical features in the office that are an essential part of the building, its layout, and the work performed. Included in this environment are walls, ceilings, floors, windows, pillars, furniture, and equipment and the coverings placed on them. Another item in this environment is the "plantscaping" integrated within the building. Each of these physical items has a direct effect on the psychological state of the office staff and consequently on productivity and morale.

Effective Use of Color

Color affects our emotions (moods and attitudes) and comfort in the workplace. In addition, color has a direct bearing on the effectiveness of lighting conditions. Therefore, rather than choose colors according to personal preference, AOMs should base their color selections upon a serious study of the following factors: (1) the *work functions* that will be performed in the office area, (2) the *physical location* of the office, and (3) the *type of emotion desired* from employees (to stimulate or to relax). With increased use of the open plan, more attention is required to coordinate the colors used on the office walls with the colors chosen for the individual workstations. Following is a discussion of the emotional effects of color upon the office staff and customers or clients.

Human Reactions to Color

Color sets the mood of an office staff. In this sense, colors can make us feel hot or cold, happy or distressed, and satisfied or dissatisfied with our work space, depending upon the *hue* (the particular shade or tint) of the color, the *lightness* or *darkness* of the color, and the *intensity* (bright-

Figure 14–1
Influence of
Ergonomic
Factors on
Office
Productivity

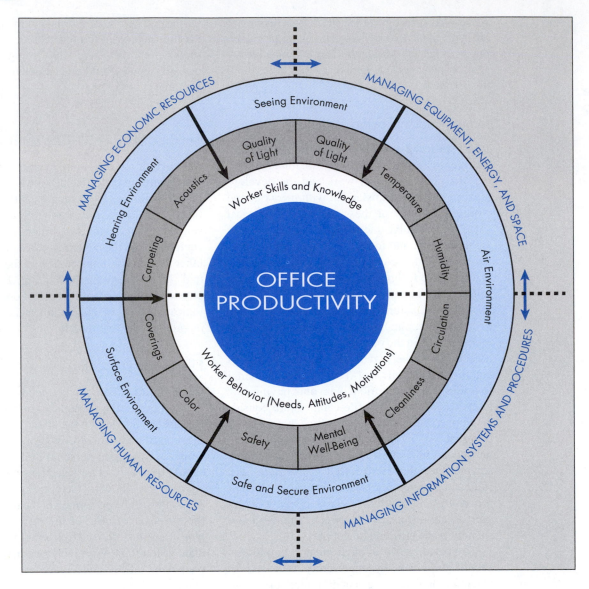

ness or dullness) of the color. Notice the characteristics of color found in your classroom, library, hallways, and cafeteria. What is your reaction to these colors?

Table 14–1 lists various colors and their effects on workers. The *distance effect* tells us how near or far the colored object or area appears to the viewer; the *temperature effect* refers to how warm or cool the color makes the space seem; and the *mood effect* describes how mentally stimulated or relaxed people feel. For example, if you

wish to create a cool and calming effect on people, you might choose a blue color of the proper color intensity. Typically, people perceive lighter colors such as yellow or yellow-green as bright and cheerful and often respond by keeping their work areas clean and tidy. On the other hand, fast-paced offices may create much worker tension, which requires restful colors, such as white or off-white, light gray, and blue.

To create exciting effects, you should choose (but not overuse) orange, red, or yellow colors;

Color	Distance Effect	Temperature Effect	Mood Effect
Red	Close	Warm	Very stimulating; increases blood pressure
Yellow	Close	Very warm	Exciting, cheerful; can cause eyestrain if too bright or overused
Blue	Farther away	Cool	Soothing, pleasant, calm; reduces blood pressure and effects of stress; overuse can cause sluggishness
Green (light)	Farther away	Neutral	Unobtrusive, calming; can be gloomy if too dark a shade is used
Orange	Very close	Very warm	Exciting; overuse can cause eyestrain
Violet	Very close	Cool	Aggressive, dignified, stately; can be tiring
Black, brown, or dark gray	Very close Claustrophobic	Neutral	Gloomy; absorbs light; can create fatigue and drowsiness
Gray (light)	Farther away	Neutral	Calming, soothing; can be boring if not highlighted by other colors
White	Farther away	Neutral	Soothing; can be boring if overused; can cause glare on VDT screens

on the other hand, remember that dark colors, such as black and brown, often depress workers. For eastern or northern exposures, warm colors such as yellow, peach, brown, and tan are recommended; and for the warmer southern or western exposures, cool colors, such as blue, green, and violet are recommended. Because of its neutrality, white produces no strong reactions although it does increase the perception of light and space. Gray colors are usually not recommended, for they produce a numbing effect. On the other hand, the use of bright, cheerful, nonagitating colors provides contrast and vision breaks, and results in a restful feeling that is more likely to boost productivity.

More specific ways in which color affects human behavior are:

1. *Brightly colored offices seem cheerful and ef-ficient looking and tend to inspire feelings of trust;* drab, poorly painted offices, on the other hand, convey a feeling of boredom or in-efficiency.

2. *The color of all office surfaces—walls, furni-ture, equipment, even paper—may cause eye-strain due to improper lighting or reflectance if the colors are not carefully selected.* The result may be eyestrain, headaches, sluggish feelings, and other unhealthy symptoms that cause a staff to perform under par. Under such condi-tions, worker morale is negatively affected, thinking and concentration powers are dimin-ished, and the accuracy of work is reduced.

3. *The perceptions of people can be changed by the use of color.* For example, office dimen-sions appear to be changed by the combina-tion of color and light; long, narrow offices can appear wider by using darker colors on the narrow end walls and lighter colors on the long side walls. Square-room monotony in an

office can be avoided by painting one wall, preferably the window wall or opposite wall, a color different from the others. High ceilings seem much lower when painted a color darker than the walls. Also, light colors make a small office space seem larger.

4. *Color helps people to identify key building locations.* Some high-rise buildings use alternating colors for each floor. Thus, when the elevator door opens, a person looking for the purchasing office immediately recognizes the correct floor when a bright gold color appears (gold being the color code assigned to the purchasing department). A color like red is often used for safety doors because of its attention-getting quality.

Reflection Values of Colors

The colors used in an office reflect light to varying degrees. The **reflection ratio** measures the amount of light reflected from a surface as a percentage of the total amount of light striking that surface. With such a measure, the AOM can restrict the choice of colors to achieve the percentages of reflected light shown in Figure 14–2. Interior designers and representatives of paint manufacturers can provide good advice at little or no cost on the selection of appropriate office colors.

Wall and Ceiling Colors

Since the walls and ceiling constitute the largest surface areas in the office, attractive, psychologically soothing colors should be chosen for these areas. When making such a selection, you should keep this guideline in mind: *Office walls and ceilings should be light enough to reflect light rather than absorb it but not light enough to produce annoying glare.*

Table 14–2 lists a wide selection of colors

Figure 14–2
Recommended Percentages of Light to Be Reflected from Office Surfaces

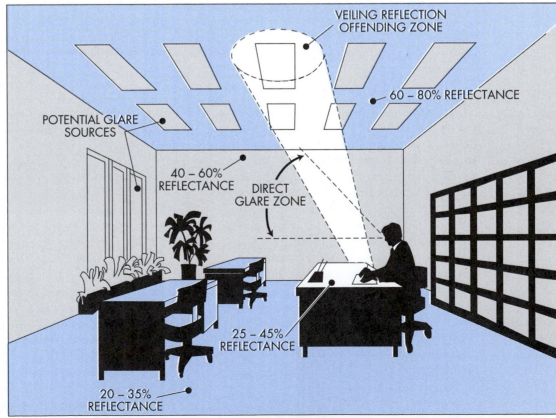

Source: General Electric Company, Lighting Application Bulletin 905-01019, *Office Lighting* (1992), p.8.

Table 14–2
Percentage of Light Reflected by Various Colors

Color	Percentage of Light Reflected	Color	Percentage of Light Reflected
White	82	Golden yellow	51
Gray-white	76	Medium gray	46
Light cream	74	Dark orange	37
Very light green	70	Copper-yellow	27
Lemon-yellow	67	Medium red	21
Medium pink	60	Cadet blue	15
Very light blue	60	Dark red	12
Light gray	56	Dark green	10

and the percentage of light reflected by each color. Generally, a middle reflectance range—from 40 to 60 percent—has been found to be best for office walls. The first four colors in this table are usually recommended for office ceilings and walls because of the high degree of light reflected by these colors. Colors used in an automated workcenter where a computer and documents are being used should have a reflectance value of approximately 50 percent; thus, off-white or white walls should be avoided in computerized offices because of the glare that white creates on the VDT screen. Instead, such office walls should be painted medium-light tones like blue or green for offices exposed to sunlight; or beige or rose, which adds warmth to cooler offices.[1] To complement the wall surfaces, artwork has become an important addition to the office since it can be used to brighten a dark room, widen a narrow corridor, and tie the decor together.

Since annoying glare may be caused by the application of glossy paint, flat paint should be used for ceilings and side walls. The use of window shades will also reduce glare in the office.

Furniture and Equipment Colors

The principles of color selection discussed for walls and ceilings also apply to furniture and equipment selection. In addition, glare must be considered since it is a common hazard caused by the reflection of light from glass tops on desks, other highly polished surfaces, and VDT screens. To prevent this problem, shiny desktops are not recommended; instead, furniture with a nongloss finish should be chosen. Black or white desktops are too harsh for the eyes. Black contrasts too strongly with the surroundings; white is too reflective. Contrasting changes in light- and dark-colored surfaces should also be avoided. The contrast between a white sheet of paper and a dark desktop can cause eyestrain. Therefore, light-colored desktops are recommended. Having a VDT operator look at a dark terminal screen and then quickly glance at white paper unnecessarily strains the operator's eyes. For this reason, manufacturers of VDT equipment select machine surface colors that produce a soft contrast between the light and dark colors in the direct vision of the operators. Also, light characters on a dark background, rather than dark on light, permit easier reading of the characters on the VDT screen.

[1]This recommendation was made by the Color Association of the United States, 343 Lexington Avenue, New York, NY 10016, the source of much reliable information on the human response to color in the office.

Floor Coverings

The color of walls and ceilings should be well coordinated with the color and type of floor coverings to ensure a unified, harmonious environment. Of the several types of floor coverings available—carpeting, wood, solid vinyl tile, vinyl asbestos tile, marble, brick, flagstone, and terrazzo, all of which are durable—carpeting seems the most popular. However, solid vinyl tile lasts twice as long as carpeting.

High-quality carpeting withstands heavy traffic in areas such as reception centers and hallways. Carpeting also creates a quiet, relaxed atmosphere since its surface absorbs sound. Further, it produces a feeling of luxury, which enhances worker satisfaction and adds to the firm's prestige. Since carpeting is the most comfortable floor covering on which to walk, employee fatigue and accidents—especially falls—are reduced when compared with those reported for slippery tile or concrete. Custodial personnel consider carpeting to be easier to maintain than other types of floor coverings.

Carpeting is available in many colors and designs and is easy to coordinate in various decorating plans. Earth colors (beige, brown, and rust) are especially popular choices due to their ease of maintenance; tweed or patterned designs are recommended for heavy-traffic, high-soil areas.

A careful study should be made of the type of office function (e.g., executive or general office) and the traffic volume in each. Once such data are available, carpeting can be assessed regarding (1) *ease of maintenance,* depending on fiber, weight, and resistance to soiling; (2) *sound-absorbing qualities;* (3) *control of static electricity,* which is especially important in areas where automated equipment is used; (4) *flammability,* which is controlled by federal regulations that screen out carpet that is easily ignited; and (5) *resistance to excessive wear.* Reputable carpeting dealers or interior designers can assist AOMs in selecting the best types of carpeting for their offices.[2]

Use of Plants in the Office

To counteract the cold, sterile feeling that automated equipment may bring to the office environment, AOMs make extensive use of plants, or "plantscaping," to personalize work areas. The most popular use of plants on a large scale is in open offices where plants are combined with acoustical partitions and modular furniture. In these locations, the plants provide privacy, brighten and warm the area, and add attractive coloring. Also, some indoor plants, such as philodendrons, golden pothos, and English ivy, effectively absorb many kinds of pollutants and convert them to breathable oxygen.[3] Plants are easy to place and rearrange when compared with fixed partitions and are simpler and less costly to maintain than partition walls.

In some firms, office personnel select the plants for their work areas even though the company furnishes the funds for their purchase. The presence of the living plants, themselves, has a strong positive effect on morale. The plants in effect become the employees' plants. While small offices may use only a few plants, large firms often require hundreds. In this case, the OM must consider whether the plants should be purchased and maintained by the office staff, purchased and placed under a maintenance contract similar to machines, or leased. The cost of leased plants used for decorative purposes in a business office is fully tax deductible.

THE SEEING ENVIRONMENT

The **seeing environment** refers to all the items needed to provide adequate light for performing the work assigned the office. The main goals for the seeing environment are (1) to provide efficient, comfortable lighting and a safe place to work; (2) to help develop a feeling of visual comfort and an esthetically attractive work area,

---

[2] For other reliable information on carpet selection and care, contact the Carpet and Rug Institute, Box 2048, Dalton, GA 30720.

[3] For detailed information about those plants which are powerful air cleaners, see *Interior Landscape Plants for Indoor Air Pollution,* available from the U.S. National Aeronautics and Space Administration, Building 2423, Stennis Space Center, MS 39529.

which includes the effective use of color, as discussed earlier; and (3) to assist in reducing the use of electrical resources, which typically account for approximately 50 percent of the total energy bill. To achieve these goals requires providing the proper quantity and quality of light, factors considered especially necessary to office comfort.

Quantity of Light

To measure the *illuminance,* or quantity of light, the footcandle is used. A **foot candle (FC)** is the amount of light produced by a candle at a distance of one foot from the source of light. It can be compared with a *watt* of light, as one watt per square foot produces about 15 footcandles of light. Lighting levels in many modern buildings are in the 90–150 FC range. Such high quantities of light are preferable for paper-based operations because, generally speaking, more light results in easier reading of paper documents, better health and morale, and greater efficiency of employees.

Ironically, higher quantities of light in the office cause problems for VDT users since it becomes more difficult to read the characters on the screen because of insufficient contrast between the amount of light on the screen and the ambient area in the office. Thus, VDT operations should be carried out in areas with lower quantities of light than in the general office. The best "seeing" location for a VDT operator often involves the proper placement of a luminaire (light fixture) and/or the use of outside light as shown in Figure 14–3. As Figure 14–3B implies, there will be no shadows on the workplace with this arrangement, and the amount of light entering the window can be controlled by the use of blinds.

Inadequate amounts of light, on the other hand, induce eyestrain, which in turn may cause such problems as muscular tension, fatigue, and irritability. Inadequate light may also lead to poor quality, inaccurate work, and lowered production. Most utility companies will measure the amount of light in an office with a light meter and make recommendations for any changes needed. Little or no cost is involved.

Before making decisions on the quantity of light needed in an office, the OM should understand the visual tasks required of the workers. Some tasks, such as drafting, computer pro-

Figure 14–3
VDT Placement in Relation to Window and Overhead Lighting

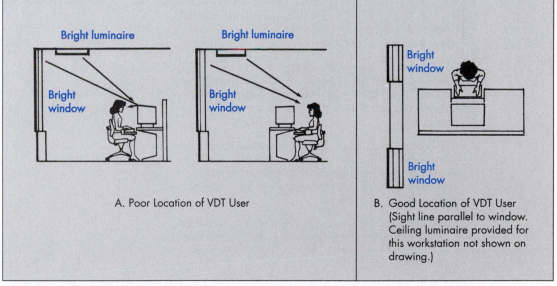

A. Poor Location of VDT User

B. Good Location of VDT User (Sight line parallel to window. Ceiling luminaire provided for this workstation not shown on drawing.)

Source: Marilyn Joyce and Ulrika Wallersteiner, *Ergonomics: Humanizing the Automated Office* (Cincinnati: South–Western Publishing Co., 1989), p. 125.

gramming, and careful reading of dim photocopies or unclear handwriting, require close detail work and high footcandle levels. Other activities, such as conducting meetings and interviews, involve less concentration and thus require much less light. Table 14–3 shows the recommended illuminance levels (footcandles on the work surface) for various types of office work. In using this guide for efficient visual performance, select the type of activity and then decide upon the low, mid, or high value by considering the age of the workers and the importance of speed and accuracy.

Quality of Light

The quality of light refers to those features of a lighting system that provide a visually comfortable work area, free of glare or shadows, and which help to create an attractive office climate. The quality of light cannot be measured as easily as the quantity of light, although several yardsticks for measurement are available.

Since the quality of light is directly affected by the brightness of light, that brightness must be kept under control. One useful yardstick for determining the amount of brightness is the footlambert. The **footlambert** is a unit of measure approximating one footcandle of light emitted or reflected. To find the amount of brightness present, the ratio of footlamberts between two surfaces, such as a desktop and the wall area near the desk, must be computed. For example, assume that the brightness of a visual task is 60 footlamberts and the brightness of a dark desktop against which the task is viewed is five footlamberts. A brightness ratio of 12 to 1 is found, which is much too bright and hence will cause visual discomfort. Usually the brightness ratio, which is, in effect, a measure of contrast in two lighted areas, should not exceed 3 to 1.

The **visual comfort probability (VCP)** is another measure that indicates how much direct glare a luminaire is likely to produce. For example, a VCP of 75 means that at least three-fourths of the people in the worst viewing position in the

Table 14–3 Recommended Illuminance Levels in Footcandles for Office Lighting	Type of Office Activity	Illuminance Range (Footcandles)
	Working spaces where visual tasks are only occasionally performed. Examples: lobbies, reception areas, corridors, stairs, washrooms, circulation areas	10–15–20
	Task lighting involving performance of visual tasks of high contrast or large size. Examples: reading newsprint, typed originals, 8–10-point print, impact printing (good ribbon), ballpoint pen, felt tip pen. Conference rooms, library areas, general filing	20–30–50
	Task lighting involving performance of visual tasks of medium contrast or small size. Examples: mail sorting, reading thermal printing, xerography, 6-point print, drafting with high-contrast media, photographic work (moderate detail), writing (#3 pencil and softer)	50–75–100
	Task lighting involving performance of visual tasks of low contrast or very small size. Examples: drafting (low-contrast media), charting, graphing, reading poor thermal copy, writing (#4 pencil)	100–150–200

Source: General Electric Company, Lighting Application Bulletin 905-01019, *Office Lighting* (1992), p.5.

lighted space find the lighting system comfortable and relatively free from glare. Generally, a VCP of 70 is considered satisfactory for most offices. However, offices in which there are many computer terminals require luminaires with a VCP of 80 or more.

Visual discomfort is caused by overly bright surfaces, such as poorly shaded light fixtures and glossy paint finishes on room surfaces and office equipment. Such problems can be easily corrected by proper light fixtures and color choices. Glare, too, causes visual strain and leads to lowered productivity and muscular and nervous tension. In addition to the problems of glare caused by glossy paint and other shiny surfaces, controlling glare on VDT screens has become a serious problem for the AOM. To reduce glare on such terminals, several control measures are available:

1. Adjust the contrast and brightness knobs on the screen to meet the VCP index of the user.
2. Lower the lighting levels in the areas where VDT equipment is used in order to provide greater contrast and less glare between the surface of the screen and the immediate environment.
3. Tilt the screen, if possible, to the point where viewing is more comfortable.

Illustration 14–1 Adjustable keyboard that splits into halves which rotate up to 30 degrees.

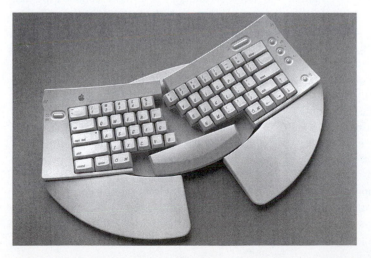

4. Rearrange the VDT equipment so that office windows are at right angles to the operator (see Figure 14–3). Direct or reflected light will thus be channeled away from the eyes of the operator.
5. Use antireflection filters placed over the screen.

VDT users, especially those using the equipment for long periods of time, report many physical and emotional problems after long hours of operation. Included in the list are eyestrain, blurred vision, backache, fatigue, and strained joints. Keyboarding requires long hours of continuous strain on the hands and wrist, sometimes resulting in *carpal tunnel syndrome,* a painful repetitive stress injury involving numbness, tingling, burning sensations, and pain in the palms, fingers, and wrist. The problem, which is thought to stem from too much pressure on the median nerve in the wrist, may require surgery. Another type of repetitive stress injury is *bursa shoulder,* which is caused by continuous work at the VDT or other workstation that requires a great deal of arm movement. Unless treated, bursa shoulder can cause permanent damage. Therefore, AOMs are encouraged to make sure that all VDT operators take frequent work breaks to get away from the VDT.[4] Further, as illustrated in Chapter 15, VDT workstations should be designed around ergonomically sound furniture and equipment, such as adjustable desks and chairs, detachable keyboards, footrests and wrist rests, and antiglare screens. For example, Illustration 14–1 shows a keyboard that breaks into parts, each of which can be angled to help workers keep their wrists in a comfortable, neutral position.

Sources of Light

Two sources of light are available to the office: daylight (natural light) and artificial light.

Daylight

Daylight is a free resource that enters the office through windows or skylights. However, direct

---

[4]In 1992, the Occupational Safety and Health Administration announced plans to create national workplace standards for the prevention of repetitive stress injuries.

sunlight must be controlled since it produces glare, visual discomfort, and eyestrain and increases the temperature in the office. However, on cloudy days, no direct sunlight is available; yet people who favor work settings with windows may become depressed if they are assigned to workstations without access to windows.

Too often, daylight is lost by the use of heavy draperies, venetian blinds, or partitions. To use as much daylight as possible, tinted glass, adjustable (louvered) blinds, and window screens that deflect the direct sunlight and reduce glare while still permitting light to enter are recommended. All windows should be regularly cleaned to admit as much natural light as possible since studies show consistently that workers prefer more daylight rather than more artificial light on the job.

Artificial Light

To supplement natural light, which is not sufficient to meet all the needs of office lighting, three types of artificial lighting systems are used: incandescent light, fluorescent light, and high-intensity discharge lamps (including the relatively new electronic lamp).

Incandescent light, commonly used in the home, is produced in a bulb by heating the tungsten filament to the point of incandescence (glowing with white heat). Such bulbs use much current and give off noticeable heat (only 10 percent of their energy produces light; the balance produces heat). They also produce a steady light that strengthens yellow, orange, and red colors. Incandescent light fixtures and bulbs are less expensive than fluorescent fixtures and bulbs, but they are less efficient because of the difficulty in providing recommended levels of lighting.

Fluorescent light is most commonly produced in long tubelike lamps found in offices and commercial establishments. The lamps operate on a gas-discharge principle, where light is produced by the passage of an electric current through gas. The gas-discharge lamps use a ballast to control the amount of voltage and current supplied to the lamp. The lamps do not give off nearly as much heat as incandescent lamps and consume about

one-third the wattage for an equal amount of light. A 20-watt fluorescent lamp gives the same light output as a 60-watt incandescent bulb but uses much less energy. The chief advantages of fluorescent lighting are low cost of operation, low heat emission, less glare, resemblance to natural daylight, and an even distribution of light. In addition, the tubes last much longer than incandescent bulbs.

High-intensity discharge (HID) lamps represent a still more efficient form of lighting. Most HID lamps (mercury vapor, metal halide, and high-pressure sodium) require several minutes to attain their full light output. The lamps are widely used for street, stadium, and parking lot lighting, and have been adapted to office and hallway lighting systems that allow the intensity of light to be controlled. HID lamps use electrical energy two to three times more efficiently than fluorescent systems and as much as six times more efficiently than incandescent bulbs. However, some forms of HID lamps project a yellow light that has produced health problems for office workers—headaches and dizziness are often mentioned. In addition, lamps such as these require the use of ballasts for starting and operating, which produce an irritating humming sound.

With promise of a life as long as 18 to 20 years and reduced energy usage, the *electronic lamp,* known as the E-lamp, appeared several years ago. Within the bulb is a radio-frequency generator that transmits energy to a surrounding cloud of mercury gas and then to a fluorescent coating that excites electrons which emit visible light. The E-lamp has no fluorescent flicker when turned on and, unlike the fluorescent light, can be dimmed. With its long life, operating in ordinary sockets, and consuming 75 percent less electricity than conventional lights, the E-lamp is hailed as a major advance in electric lighting systems. Counting the cost of the bulb and the electricity to run it, a 25-watt E-lamp should save around 20 cents a week compared with a 100-watt incandescent bulb and give the same amount of light.

The kind of artificial lighting distributed in an office depends on the type of fixture being used. Lighting systems should be designed so the fixtures are spaced (and sometimes ceiling re-cessed) according to the needs of the work area and characteristics of the room. *Direct lighting fixtures* furnish light directly to the work surface, while *indirect lighting fixtures* project the light to the ceiling to be reflected down to the work sur-face. Manufacturers of light fixtures publish in-formation on the various fixture options and other data for making wise selections of fixtures and accessories.

Task/Ambient Lighting

Open-space planning requires that satisfactory lighting be available at the workstations. This practice contrasts sharply with the typical light-ing plan for the conventional office design that provides recommended footcandle levels uni-formly from ceiling fixtures. Traditional ceiling fixtures alone are not efficient for the open work area, which is broken up by screens, panels, and modular furniture that create shadows on the work surfaces. To remedy this situation, **task lighting** was developed in which the light fix-tures are built into the open-plan furniture (desks and cabinets) to light specific work areas. Thus, it is possible to eliminate much overhead lighting and to provide portable lighting that moves with the furniture as it is rearranged.

   Ambient lighting uses indirect fixtures or up-lights that direct light upward to be reflected off the ceiling onto other surfaces that surround the workstation. Usually ambient lighting is com-bined with task lighting (hence, the term *task/am-bient*) to provide a lighting system offering these advantages: (1) *flexibility,* because of the poten-tial for easy, inexpensive rearrangement of office interiors; (2) *ease of installing and maintaining acoustical panels* in the ceiling, because no per-manent ceiling fixtures are required for lighting; (3) *reduced glare and reflection* and a greater uni-formity in lighting; (4) *lower costs,* as less energy is consumed for lighting the work area, and light-ing installation costs are also reduced; (5) *fewer ceiling fixtures and lamps to replace* and easier accessibility to such lamps; and (6) *easier oppor-tunities for office building renovation,* with less wiring for lighting built into the structure.

Evaluation of Lighting Systems

The ideal lighting system in the office should provide light in the *right amount,* of the *right quality,* in the *right work area,* and at the *lowest possible cost.* Questions to be answered in evalu-ating office lighting systems are:

1. How much light does the lighting system pro-duce?
2. How much light is actually needed to perform the required tasks? (The age of the workers must be strongly considered in answering this question since older workers will require more footcandles that the minimum shown in Table 14–3.)
3. What energy-conservation measures are avail-able to keep the wattage used to a minimum? (A list of useful measures is provided in a later section of this chapter.)
4. What appearance does the lighting system cre-ate—free from glare, accenting the surface colors appropriately, and so forth?
5. How much heat does the light produce?
6. How much light is lost as the bulb "ages"? (In-candescent bulbs, for example, are much less efficient, producing less light as they get older.)
7. Is the system easy and inexpensive to maintain?
8. Is the system safe from fires and shocks? Are fixtures, for example, out of reach of the workers to minimize accidents; or, in the case of task/ambient lighting, can the light fixtures be touched without danger of burns?
9. What is the effect of the lighting system on employees? Rather than emphasizing lighting alone, it is wise to emphasize *seeing* and the impact that good visibility has on employee mood and efficiency.

Engineers specializing in lighting systems can assist the AOM in developing an adequate seeing environment for the office. In addition, advice can be obtained at minimal cost from the local power and light company.[5]

---

[5]Many helpful publications, such as *Office Lighting and Pro-ductivity* and *Getting the Most from Your Lighting Dollar,* are available from the National Lighting Bureau, 2101 L Street, NW, Suite 300, Washington, DC 20037.

THE HEARING ENVIRONMENT

The **hearing environment** deals with office sounds, which can be good or bad. When sound, like background music and pleasant conversation, is soothing to workers, it is good and aids office production. However, when sound, like street noises, vibrating office machines, ringing telephones, or squeaky doors, is irritating and distracting, it is bad and hampers production. Unwanted sound is called *noise,* a factor that must be carefully controlled if the office is to be efficient.

To control noise, sound must be measured. The **decibel (db)** is the unit of measure that determines the relative loudness of sounds, equal approximately to the smallest degree of difference of loudness detectable by the human ear. Thus, the faintest sound that the ear can hear is 1 dB; louder sounds have higher decibel values. Table 14–4 shows common sounds in the work environment, their decibel values, and the relative effect of each sound level (from very faint to extremely loud). In addition, recommended maximum levels of noise for efficient office work are included. Permitting office sounds to extend beyond these levels will result in physical and emotional damage to workers, and in turn, production will suffer.

Sources and Effects of Office Noise

Automobiles, motorcycles, sirens, and trucks account for most of the outside noise that is carried into the office. Inside the office, the principal sources of noise are (1) electronic equipment; (2) the reduced square footage for each workstation, which places more workers in a given area; (3) open offices where noise travels freely between work areas; and (4) the use of glass as exterior walls of buildings, which results in more noise being reflected back into the office. Even in the smallest offices, we may find several electric typewriters or VDTs with printers, at least one copier, and several telephones, in addition to air-conditioning and heating equipment. Larger offices have more equipment, such as computers, printers, FAX machines, and telephones, that link all workstations to each other and to the outside world. Many of these machines are in operation at the same time, thus raising the amount of noise to a very high level. The sound from five typewriters alone has been measured at 80 db, only slightly less than the 90 db produced by a pneumatic drill in the street. A person has to shout to be heard at 80 db.

Table 14–4
Common Sounds, Noise Levels, Decibel Ranges, and Recommended Maximum Noise Levels for the Office

Common Sounds	Noise Levels	Decibel Ranges	Recommended Maximum Noise Levels for the Office
Whispers	Very Faint	10–20	
Private office, quiet conversation	Faint	20–40	40 db, for private offices
Average office, typical conversation	Moderate	40–60	60 db, for general offices
Noisy office, average street noise	Loud	60–80	80 db, for data centers
Office machine room, loud street noises	Very Loud	80–100	
Motorcycle and rock band	Extremely Loud	110–130	

Employees also contribute their share to office noise through conferences, telephone calls, and discussions about work assignments and personal matters. Even the movement of workers from one location to another creates unwanted sound, especially where carpeting is not used as a floor covering.

Uncontrolled noise has many undesirable effects on the workers' health. For example, noise interferes with communication and reduces the workers' ability to concentrate. This in turn makes them irritable, tired, and less productive, which leads to discontent, absenteeism, and eventually to high turnover. Hearing may also become impaired from prolonged noise. Over a period of time, excessive noise can cause loss of sleep from the nervous tension created.

Controlling Office Noise

People cannot function well in a "sound vacuum." Rather, a certain level of sound creates a healthy background and helps set a tempo for the work to be accomplished. A properly noise-controlled office keeps sound within comfortable ranges to ensure good hearing and speech privacy.

An effective noise-control program concentrates on two main areas: (1) eliminating the source of the noise and (2) using sound-absorbing (acoustical) materials to reduce the effects of the noise. For this latter approach, a **noise-reduction coefficient (NRC)** has been developed to measure the amount of noise absorbed or removed from an area. An acoustical screen with an NRC rating of 85, for example, as may be used in an open office, absorbs 85 percent of the noise striking it. The highest attainable NRC rating is 95. Illustration 14–2 shows a cabinet with a heavy-duty acrylic cover and a built-in cooling fan designed to eliminate most of the sound caused by the operation of a computer printer, usually measured at 70 to 75 db.

All noise-control programs are based on this important fact: *Hard surfaces reflect sounds while soft surfaces absorb them.* A comprehensive noise-control program applies this concept to each of the noise source problems shown in Figure 14–4. A detailed list of suggestions for curtailing noise relating to layout and location, movement of personnel, inadequate surface coverings, and unprotected equipment is also provided in this figure. One good rule of thumb that you can use for testing the sound levels in any office is this: Can you conduct a normal telephone conversation next to operating machines without shouting? If not, a noise problem exists.

Illustration 14–2 Computer printer within a sound enclosure.

Music in the Office

For most of us in the office, music provides a pleasant background sound that calms the nerves, reduces fatigue due to work strain, and lessens work monotony. Thus, music helps to develop a more efficient climate in which our concentration increases, our errors are reduced, and, as employees, we are better able to enjoy our work setting. However, the benefits received from music in the office depend upon the type of work being performed and the appropriateness of the music for that type of work. The more monotonous or repetitive the work, the greater the soothing effect that music has on relieving mental fatigue.

Common sources that specialize in providing music for the office include vendors, such as Muzak, who have studied what kind of music to use and when to use it; local FM radio stations; and the communication departments of some business firms. Regardless of the source of music, it is important that we keep certain employee needs in mind. For example, the music for offices must be more subdued than music for

Figure 14–4
Main Causes
of Office
Noise and Ef-
fective Princi-
ples and
Practices for
Its Control

Main Causes of Office Noise	General Principles of Office Noise Control	Specific Applications of Noise-Control Principles
1. Poor office layout or location.	1–1 Relocate office to reduce exterior noise. 1–2 Move noisy departments to remote corner locations. 1–3 Locate doors to enhance privacy and stop sound from carrying, especially in open offices.	1–1 Move office from first to, say, tenth or top floor. 1–2 Segregate the printing department from other units requiring work concentration; schedule conferences in private offices. 1–3 Keep doors and windows closed; use acoustical screens for extra privacy; ask that conversations be carried on in low tones.
2. Unnecessary movement of personnel.	2–1 Redesign layout for better workflow and to reduce the amount of walking required of personnel.	2–1 Place workers whose tasks are closely related side by side, thus reducing walking and telephone calls; place machines near the employees who use them.
3. Inadequate surface coverings (where hard walls, floors, and ceilings reflect sounds back and forth).	3–1 Use sound-absorbing coverings on walls, furniture, ceilings, and partitions used in landscaped offices. 3–2 Use "masking" sounds to cover up those sounds that cannot be eliminated but that might be distracting. 3–3 Avoid uncoved floors that reflect rather than absorb sound.	3–1 Use heavy fabrics for draperies, furniture, and inner office partitions. Use carpeting on walls and acoustical tile for ceilings. 3–2 Consider using *background masking*, such as the hum of machines and light fixtures, or music to hide the noise. 3–3 Use sound-absorbing floor coverings such as rubber and asphalt. Carpeting is preferred as the best sound-absorbing floor covering.
4. Unprotected machines and equipment.	4–1 Locate noisy machines in one soundproof location (even though operators' working conditions are not improved). 4–2 Provide acoustical materials at workstations to isolate noise.	4–1 Place work processing and data processing units away from the general office. Hire hearing-impaired persons where noise levels cannot be reduced. 4–2 Use acoustical cabinets (see Illus. 14–2) for muffling machine noise and earplugs for reducing noise; mute telephone bells; keep all equipment oiled.

factories; distracting influences in the music—vocals, loud brasses, or marked changes in tempo—should be avoided; and string and woodwind instruments should be emphasized. Also, all types of music—from classical to popular—should be represented.

The music should be confined to the background so as not to become distracting, and it should be turned off for brief periods. Music should be provided at midmorning and just before lunch and quitting time when fatigue is most likely to be present. While there is a lack of scientific research on the benefits of music for increasing productivity, large firms report highly favorable worker reactions to the use of music.

THE AIR ENVIRONMENT

The **air environment** refers to the total atmosphere created in the office by the principal air factors—*temperature, humidity, circulation (ventilation),* and *cleanliness.* In this sense, we use the term *air-conditioned office* literally; it is an office where the air has been carefully conditioned for human comfort, including the control of temperature, humidity, circulation, and cleanliness. However, the air environment is very subjective since you may feel too warm and open the window while your coworker feels too cold and wants to raise the thermostatic settings.

Workers consider the air environment, especially air circulation and "the right temperature," as very important to their jobs. This is a typical attitude, for a properly maintained air environment improves mental activity, boosts efficiency, increases productivity, and decreases absenteeism. On the other hand, stale, dry, and dusty air dulls the mind and reduces the output of work, which is especially important since many office activities are largely cognitive. Such air may also lower worker vitality, cause headaches, and produce "four o'clock fatigue."

Temperature

Temperature refers to the relative hotness or coolness of the air measured in degrees Fahrenheit or Celsius. Although there is no temperature level

that pleases all of us, the American Society of Heating, Air Conditioning, and Refrigeration Engineers suggests that the most comfortable and healthful temperature *for work* is below 70°F. For energy-conservation purposes, thermostatic settings should be limited to 65°F or lower for heating. Such a temperature level is healthful for work if the proper humidity or moisture level is maintained; for we must not forget that the human body constantly generates heat. With normal office activities, such as keyboarding and walking, the production of heat increases rapidly.

The heating or thermal environment is the result of a proper balance in temperature, humidity, and air motion. This environment can be supplemented by outside temperature, solar heat in combination with lighting fixtures that emit heat, and heat generated by large numbers of workers and machines in the office. Some lighting systems provide enough heat to warm offices without the need for additional heat, depending on the geographical location; in some cases, the excess heat from the air is stored in tanks for later use when the lights are off. Other systems tie into light fixtures that turn on the lights during the night to help heat the offices.

Important considerations in maintaining proper temperatures in an office are the employees' age, sex, and body size. As a rule, people over 40 require a higher **effective temperature** (temperature combined with proper humidity) than young people. Women, it has been found, prefer a higher effective temperature than men; obese people prefer a lower effective temperature than thin people. Thus, we find variation among workers in response to heat for these reasons as well as for the amount of activity involved in their work.[6]

Humidity

Relative humidity refers to the percentage of moisture in the air. Air-conditioning equipment removes moisture from the air (dehumidifies) dur-

---

[6]For a concise discussion of the human needs to be considered in the air environment, see Marilyn Joyce and Ulrika Wallersteiner, *Ergonomics: Humanizing the Automated Office* (Cincinnati: South-Western Publishing Co., 1989), Chapter 8.

ing the summer months and may add moisture to the air (humidify) during the winter months. A high relative humidity makes us feel colder on a cold day and warmer on a hot day. Generally we feel more comfortable with a temperature of 65 to 70°F if the air is reasonably moist than if the air is dry and the temperature several degrees higher. Automated equipment can tolerate a wide range of relative humidity (from 20 to 80 percent), but when the humidity level falls below 20 percent, static electricity builds up. (Static buildup happens when a person walks across a carpeted floor and is "zapped" upon touching a doorknob.) Too little humidity causes magnetic tapes and disks to stick during processing operations and brings about errors. Too much humidity, on the other hand, produces condensation on the electronic parts of the equipment and causes short-circuiting.

The most comfortable range of humidity for most workers is from 30 to 60 percent, which can be maintained by the use of air-conditioning equipment or individual dehumidifiers (in summer) or humidifiers (in winter), depending on geographic location. In addition, static electricity can be partially controlled through the use of antistatic dust covers placed over VDTs during periods of nonuse, floor mats that absorb static generated by shuffling feet, antistatic sprays for carpeting, or table mats placed under VDTs to "drain" the static on contact.

Circulation

Even though a reasonable room temperature is maintained, the air must be circulated to ensure that we do not become surrounded by air that approaches skin temperature and the saturation point. As a rule of thumb, we should be provided 12 to 15 cubic meters of outside air per person per hour, and the flow of air should be slow enough so as not to feel drafty. Even though the temperature is high, this type of circulated air feels cool because it speeds up the evaporation of body moisture. Common methods of keeping air in motion are vent fans and blowers. Electric fans are still used to supplement air-conditioning equipment in smaller offices. However, the drafts from fans and ventilators can be annoying to some people.

Cleanliness

The complete air-conditioning system cleans the air of undesirable pollutants. Health problems associated with indoor air pollution make up what is known as the **sick building syndrome (SBS).** Some of the symptoms of SBS are headaches; eye, nose, or throat irritation; dry or itchy skin; dizziness and nausea; fatigue; sensitivity to odors; memory and cognitive lapses; and Legionnaire's disease. Although there are thousands of possible pollutants in the air which may cause SBS, the following major types are most commonly found in offices:

1. Toxic substances, such as airborne carbon monoxide from vehicle exhaust that filters into the office building and formaldehyde given off by particleboard, wall paneling, and carpeting.[7]
2. Sulfur dioxide from heat and electricity production.
3. Undesirable matter, such as soot, dust, chemicals, and metals. In this category is tobacco smoke, which contains nearly 3,000 polluting compounds. In addition, the presence of the smoke produces carbon monoxide, which interferes with the oxygen-carrying ability of the blood. Dust is especially harmful to the operation of VDTs and other hardware in the computer system. Also, the building materials and equipment in new offices give off fumes containing formaldehyde, and copiers use chemicals that can pollute the air. Over the course of the day, these pollutants are drawn into the ventilation system which may only partially replace the air that is recirculated back into the office.[8]

[7]As a result of the 1990 Clean Air Act, as amended, states with high air-pollution ratings require their employers (generally with 100 or more workers in a single location) to develop transportation management plans that limit automobile use by their employees.

[8]Further information on means of combatting sick building syndrome may be obtained from the International Facility Management Association (IFMA), 1E Greenway Plaza, Suite 1100, Houston, TX 77046–0194.

In one air-filtration system, unfiltered air is drawn through intake louvers located above the surface of each workstation. After this air is filtered, it cascades over the workstation and beyond, thus covering the area with an umbrella of safe, clean, breathable air. According to the manufacturer, this type of system, used in tandem with a firm's heating, ventilating, and air-conditioning system, eliminates more than 99 percent of harmful air contaminants such as bacteria, viruses, and molds.

A cleansed environment is more healthful for workers and at the same time permits complex equipment to function more satisfactorily. A clean, sparkling office suggests a feeling of efficiency and a regard for both customers and employees. As pointed out in Chapter 12, to reduce office pollution, many firms ban smoking within the building, a practice found in many public establishments, or restrict smoking to areas with separate ventilation. This ensures cleaner air, as does the use of mechanical air filters that strain foreign particles out of the air. In addition, the air environment can be further upgraded by a regular office maintenance program that includes sweeping, mopping, scrubbing, waxing, and buffing the floors; vacuuming the carpeting; cleaning the draperies and upholstered furniture; and washing and repainting the walls and ceilings as needed.

THE SAFE AND SECURE ENVIRONMENT

Our safety and security are important to our mental well-being both on and off the job. The **safe and secure environment** protects our physical needs as workers, and, in so doing, it gives us a sense of well-being that soothes our emotions and improves the total working environment. Thus, the two factors—*safety* and *security*—work together in achieving a comfortable ergonomic level for the office.

Facility managers in large companies and OMs in smaller firms are commonly assigned responsibility for maintaining the firm's safety-security environment. Such responsibilities include (1) protecting the firm's assets, especially its physical plant; (2) ensuring that all relevant laws on safety are observed; (3) maintaining the well-being of employees, especially their physical comfort and convenience; and (4) helping to sustain public confidence in the firm, its products, and services, including customer safety while on the company premises.

An office is usually not as hazardous a place in which to work as an industrial plant; nonetheless potential dangers lurk everywhere for which safety measures must be provided. Some of the main safety-security problems in the office and systems for ensuring their control are discussed in this section. (Computer security is discussed in Chapter 16, and protecting records is treated in detail in Chapter 19.)

Safety Problems

Office personnel are typically not exposed to serious industrial hazards, such as power hand tools, highly poisonous chemicals, and moving machine parts. However, many potential safety problems do exist in the office amid the desks, file cabinets, conveyor belts, and VDTs. Accidents within the office that frequently occur include:

1. *Trips and falls* caused by thick or loose and torn carpeting; highly waxed floors; tracked-in rain or snow, spilled coffee, and other slippery liquids; dropped pencils, paper clips, rubber bands, and paper; dangling electrical and telephone cords; and broken or loose stairs.
2. *Back problems* caused by improperly fitted chairs (discussed in detail in Chapter 15); leaning back and "flipping" over in a chair with casters; improper lifting; and general poor physical condition.
3. *Electrical problems* caused by improper or lack of grounding of machines, exposed wires, or plugging too many appliances or machines into the same outlet.
4. *Miscellaneous problems,* such as collisions with other persons or with obstructions improperly marked, or unmarked, within the building; falling objects, especially tipping file cabinets; colliding with open file drawers in the aisle; freak accidents with dangling

jewelry and neckties near office machines; and horseplay.

As an administrative services manager, the OM may be assigned responsibility for controlling safety problems that occur in areas external to the office. Examples are:

1. Falls and physical assaults that occur in unlighted or poorly lighted exits, aisles, halls, stairways, and parking lots.
2. Fires that occur because of lack of proper control or prevention measures including training programs.
3. Unlawful entrance to the premises caused by unlocked doors or poorly patrolled areas.

Most of these problems can be eliminated or at least reduced in number by the careful application of the control methods presented later in this chapter.

Security Problems

The basic security problem for all office employees is being assured of a job. Beyond this problem, office employees are exposed to many other security risks that relate directly to the work environment. These problems arise in the day-to-day operation of the office and cause stress and general apprehension. Both of these types of mental insecurity can have serious and long-lasting effects upon the person and the job if left unchecked.

Following is a list of typical security problems, some of which are related directly to office safety:

1. *Lack of fire protection.* Employees may become anxious about the lack of fire protection when smoke alarms and automatic sprinkler systems are not provided, or if provided, are not checked regularly. Employees may not be instructed in the procedures to follow in case of fire. With a lack of effective first-aid training, employees may feel unprepared in case of accident or sudden onset of a medical emergency (heart attack, stroke, or epileptic seizure).

2. *No contingency plan in the event of violence and disaster.* In Chapter 12 when discussing violence in the workplace, we presented several steps that may be taken to limit the potential for murder on the job. Foremost among these measures is the need to establish a crisis management team that is skilled in de-escalating any possible hostile situation. There is also need to set up a contingency plan that can be put into action should a disaster strike your city or town. Although the risk of terrorist attack may be very slim in your community, natural disasters such as fire, earthquakes, floods, hurricanes, and tornadoes may strike and inflict considerable damage to your organization. Thus, there is need for a readiness program for any type of emergency situation.

3. *Basic production and comfort needs of employees being ignored by employers.* As indicated earlier, employees are concerned about the importance of comfortable heating, air conditioning, and ventilation to their productivity. Further, employees expect protection from dangers inherent in the workplace, especially those relating to the use of VDTs. For example, although the radiation danger posed by VDTs has not been established, some companies regularly monitor the distance between the VDT operator and the terminal screen and install grounded VDT filters that block some radiation. Users of cellular telephones await a clear answer about a possible link between long-term exposure to electromagnetic fields (EMFs) and leukemia, brain tumors, and birth defects.

4. *Special problems facing disabled workers.* Such problems include working in an unstable environment with unannounced changes, such as the rearrangement of furniture; being unable to read colored warning lights in case of fire (for the visually impaired employee); or being unable to hear sirens, signals, or warning alarms (for the hearing-impaired person).

A reduction in security problems such as those listed above can be expected if the control methods discussed next are followed.

Safety and Security Control Methods

Measures to provide a safe and secure environment should be a cooperative venture between management and employees, usually on a company-wide scale. With such participation from all workers in the firm, safety problems ranging from the simplest to the most complex can be understood and adequate measures for their control put into practice. Some of the most common measures for ensuring safety and security are discussed in the following paragraphs.

Safety related to space planning includes providing a well-lighted, dry work space free of debris. Stair treads should be provided, damaged floors repaired, and slip-resistant finishes applied to floors; carpets should be kept in good condition. Desks and cabinets should be arranged so as not to open into walkways, and file cabinets should be bolted together to prevent tipping. Electrical cords and telephone cords should be shortened or taped to the desks. Heavy materials should not be stored on top of cabinets. Equipment should be properly maintained and inspected regularly for health and safety standards. Many OMs conduct a monthly safety check by means of a safety checklist that covers the above items and others, such as policing the general office area, housekeeping, condition of tools and equipment, first-aid supplies, and storage of other materials.

In addition, management must conform to the provisions of federal legislation such as OSHA (mentioned earlier) and the Americans with Disabilities Act (ADA). Under OSHA, employers must furnish workplaces free from recognized hazards that are likely to cause death or serious physical harm. Further, employers are required to keep records of work-related deaths, illnesses, injuries, and exposure to potentially toxic materials. Organizations that employ 11 workers or more must post summaries that detail the number and type of work-related injuries and illnesses that occurred at the work site. Finally, employers must notify any employees who have been exposed to such materials that exceed the set standards. The rights of employees are protected in that they cannot be discharged or discriminated against because they have filed a complaint. OSHA inspectors enforce these standards by visits to the work sites.[9]

The Americans with Disabilities Act of 1990, discussed earlier in Chapter 6, requires an employer of 15 or more workers to make "reasonable accommodations" for disabled workers who are qualified to handle the essential job functions but only if the employer does not suffer undue hardship. A few examples of the steps to take in creating a barrier-free office environment for disabled persons include the following:

1. Provide access ramps wherever the floor level changes more than one-half inch.
2. Install elevators in buildings of three stories or more and in those having more than 3,000 square feet of floor space per story.
3. On floors of accessible routes, install carpets no higher than one-half inch in pile. Floors of accessible routes must be slip resistant.
4. Provide accessibility to toilet facilities, water fountains, and telephones, if provided, in both new construction and alterations. If alterations do not permit access to all toilets, one unisex toilet for the disabled is allowed instead. Mirrors, urinals, and dispensers must conform to certain height standards.
5. Make sure that public phones on any floor are accessible to people in wheelchairs. Volume controls must be provided for 25 percent of other public phones. When public phones are in clusters of six or more, at least one must have a telecommunicating device for the deaf.

The modern, smart office building is designed to meet the safety and security needs of all personnel. A typical smart office building is commonly equipped with an **integrated security system (ISS),** which, under computer control, brings together intercommunication systems,

---

[9]OSHA's voluntary ergonomic guidelines are available from the U.S. Department of Labor, Room N3653, Office of Ergonomic Support, 200 Constitution Avenue, Washington, DC 20210.

burglar systems, and building-wide monitors. Typical features of the ISS are closed-circuit television that monitors the interior and exterior of the building; a burglar alarm control system that protects exterior doors, vaults, and safes; a control system for automated locking and unlocking of exterior and certain interior doors; walkie-talkie and related intercom systems for speedy communication throughout the building; turnkey stations for guards who patrol the building after office hours; fire protection devices that constantly monitor the water supply of the sprinkler system; ionization detectors that scan the air for traces of combustible gases or smoke; air rescue nets for emergency escapes from high-rise areas; electronically controlled locks on stairwell fire doors to prevent illegal entry into office areas; computer terminals showing the type and location of alarms; and, finally, an identification card containing employee photograph, name, number, and other related information encoded for insertion into an access control device to regulate after-hours entrance and exit. With such a comprehensive program for protecting employees, such a firm assures the workers peace of mind and protects its investment in facilities.

THE ERGONOMIC ENVIRONMENT IN TOMORROW'S WORKPLACE

The several environments discussed in the preceding pages will continue to be the major focus in providing an ergonomically sound workplace for tomorrow's office workers. We can anticipate an increased use of ergonomically correct office furniture and fixtures as companies become more concerned about employee health issues, worker disabilities, and an aging workforce. Greater attention will be paid to the employees' need for relaxation when planning the layout, color schemes, and office furniture for their workstations.

Considerations such as these played a major role in the design of the *Office of the Moment,* by Herman Miller, Inc., a firm specializing in systems and furniture for office and health-care environments. The Office of the Moment is *temporal* since at one moment it is a place to participate, while at the next moment it is space where

the person can engage in quiet work. Or, the next moment the office becomes unnecessary since the worker may now be found in a home office, in a car, or aboard an airplane. Thus, office workers have space available at the moment it is needed on a first-come, first-serve basis. For example, part-time workers and those assigned to special projects can store their belongings in maneuverable units that are transported from department to department.

Illustration 14–3 depicts a work area in the Office of the Moment. Note at the bottom left the modular design of the work table, which can be broken apart and moved into different work arrangements. The workstations are equipped with adjustable-height desks and chairs, task lighting, and generous provision for L-return flow space, and shelf storage. Noisy equipment, such as a computer printer, may be housed in a sound-absorbing cove, as shown along the right side. Note also how the colors, in conjunction with the lighting system, present a vibrant—yet subtle and lush—statement that this office area is a colorful, playful place for creativity and problem solving.

Illustration 14–3 The Office of the Moment.

MANAGING ENERGY IN THE OFFICE

Cutting energy usage and reducing energy costs are ongoing, high-priority problems for all managers. Thus, the AOM shares with other managers the responsibility for studying overall energy needs and for developing energy-conservation programs within their firms. Governmental agencies and private industrial and professional associations are assisting in meeting this goal. Further, with enactment of the National Energy Policy Act in 1992, light bulb manufacturers will be required to label incandescent lamps to show how much energy they consume. After 1995, lighting manufacturers are required to stop making energy-inefficient fluorescent light fixtures and to start producing substitutes that use less power.[10]

The Energy Management Program

Managing energy within a firm entails the same management techniques that are required for man-

aging other functions, such as finance, marketing, and production. Successful approaches to energy management typically include these three steps:

1. *Top management appoints an energy manager or coordinator* who heads a company-wide energy control committee usually assisted by a representative from each department.
2. *An energy audit is conducted* to determine how much energy is presently used in each department and how much is actually needed for efficient operation.
3. *Energy conservation goals are set* and methods for achieving them are made available. Employees should regularly be made aware of the need to save energy and to reduce energy costs and should know the impact that such savings will have on their jobs.

Energy Conservation Methods

To reduce energy costs, well-operated conservation programs employ methods such as those outlined in Figure 14–5. Most of these cost-savings methods can be achieved with little additional cost or training of personnel and the use of a well-constructed, fully insulated office building.

---

[10]Information on energy management is available from the Office of Energy Programs, U.S. Department of Commerce, Washington, DC 20230. Also, local power and light companies will furnish practical suggestions for saving energy in the office.

Figure 14–5
Methods of
Conserving
Light, Cool
Temperatures,
and Heat

Conserving Light

1. Design the lighting system for the tasks to be performed, with less lighting in surrounding nonwork areas. The task/ambient system reduces energy consumption up to 50 percent. Individual switches and dimmers for each fixture can often be provided to allow workers at each station to select desired lighting levels.
2. Provide regular maintenance procedures by keeping lighting equipment clean and in good working order. Old bulbs should be replaced regularly since their output of light is reduced by age. Since incandescent lamps are only about 30 percent as efficient as flourescent lamps, greater use of flourescent lamps and high-intensity discharge lamps should be considered.
3. Turn off lights when not needed for work tasks but keep in mind the firm's safety and security requirements. In some locations, such as inactive storage areas, lobbies and hallways, every other light can be turned off without harm.
4. Use daylight if possible through control of window draperies. Some modern buildings use skylights and atriums to bring in additional daylight.
5. Choose light colors on wall surfaces to increase the amount of light available (as much as 30 FC in some cases), which decreases the amount of artificial lighting required.

Conserving Cool Temperatures

1. Maintain an efficient cooling system.
2. Keep a careful watch on thermostatic settings.
3. Do not cool unused rooms.
4. Provide shades, draperies, and awnings to keep out the heat in summer months.
5. Wear lightweight clothing. Temperatures approaching 80°F and 60 percent relative humidity may then be acceptable, with much savings in energy, if proper air circulation is provided.

Conserving Heat

1. Maintain an efficient heating system. Air filters should be cleaned or changed, and vents, flues, and burners kept clean.
2. Make effective use of heat generated by the human body and VDTs. Set thermostats lower in the winter. Settings should be lowered to 65°F during the workday, and office personnel should be encouraged to wear warm clothing. Generally for each degree above 65°F of a thermostatic setting, it will cost an additional 3 percent for heating. Overnight and weekend settings should be lowered to 60°F.
3. Reduce temperatures in public spaces, corridors, hallways, lobbies, and other nonwork areas. In these spaces, people are usually moving rather than sitting for hours at a time; hence a lower temperature can be tolerated. Heat should be turned off in rooms not in use.
4. Program the computer to keep track of thermostat temperatures in every room and to decide whether more or less heat is needed and then to activate the necessary equipment.
5. Reduce to a minimum the openings to the office. Windows and doors should be checked for air leakage; and where constant streams of people enter and leave a building, double sets of doors should be used.
6. Use solar energy for heating as much as possible. With sunlight entering the office, less heat is required for the heating plant; but shades and draperies should be drawn at night to confine the heat.
7. Recycle the heat generated by other sources. One firm collects heat through ceiling vents and transmits it by fan in order to heat water. In turn, the hot water surrenders heat to the air from the outside as it is mixed with recycled air.

SUMMARY

1. To be productive, office employees must be housed in a physical setting that is well planned and that possesses the best conditions for meeting their ergonomic needs. Such a setting includes a surface environment made attractive through effective use of color and plantscaping; a seeing environment that provides adequate amounts of light and high levels of visual comfort; a hearing environment that controls noise yet provides music or other pleasant background sounds to stimulate employees to a high level of work; an air environment with controls maintained through proper air conditioning; and a safe and secure environment that provides for the physical safety and mental well-being of employees on the job.

2. Many aspects of the ergonomic environment can be monitored by computer; but the maintenance of a high level of morale, security, and confidence on the job must be the main, personal responsibility of the OM. Understanding how all these environments contribute to office productivity has become a major concern for all office administrators.

3. All features of the physical environment require the expenditure and conservation of energy. Thus, a well-planned energy management program becomes a necessary function of office management, especially in times of inflation and energy consciousness.

FOR YOUR REVIEW

1. Explain what ergonomics is and how it affects the work produced in the office.
2. a. Identify the four categories of human activities performed in the office.
   b. What are some common examples of each human activity?
3. What ambient factors do today's office workers desire in their workplace?
4. List the main ways that color influences a firm's image and the health, morale, and efficiency of its employees.
5. a. What is the reflection ratio?
   b. How does this ratio relate to the effective use of color?
6. What factors should be considered in selecting floor coverings in the office?
7. a. Define footcandle.
   b. How does the AOM make decisions regarding the number of footcandles required for adequate office lighting?
8. What yardsticks are available for measuring the quality of lighting?
9. a. Compare the relative advantages of incandescent light, fluorescent light, and high-intensity discharge lamps.
   b. Which type of lighting is recommended for general office use?
10. a. How is task/ambient lighting integrated into an office layout?
    b. What are the main strengths of this form of lighting system?
11. What questions should be answered when evaluating an office lighting system?
12. In what ways can sound in the office be measured?
13. a. What physical and emotional effects does noise have upon office employees?
    b. How can these effects be eliminated or reduced in severity?
14. What factors make up the air environment in the office?
15. What measures are available for ensuring a safe and secure environment for office workers?
16. Cite three effective methods for conserving light, cool temperatures, and heat in the office.

FOR YOUR DISCUSSION

1. After you visited the tax collection office in your community, you recorded the following observations:

   a. Data-entry operators are housed in two large rooms, one for smokers and one for nonsmokers.

   b. The operators sit at tables, each about 36 inches wide, with white formica tops.

   c. The chairs can be adjusted for height and to rock, but nothing else. A few operators use their own pillows.

   d. The VDTs are about 15 years old and take up about one-half the size of today's desktop computers. Neither the keyboards nor screens can be tilted, turned, raised, or lowered. Instead, you note that the operators have to adjust their bodies.

   e. In your conversation with one operator, you learn that her required keystroke rate is 10,000 an hour. However, her actual rate is 18,000 to 21,000. She tells you that, in spite of the aches and pains, she likes to push herself to earn more dollars.

   What are your recommendations for improving the ergonomic conditions in this office?

2. A recent issue of an office technology magazine carried this theme: "Plants are a metaphor of life and can have a positive effect on the nature of people." Discuss the meaning and implications of this theme for office productivity.

3. Because of low office salaries in your area, many large offices are staffed mainly with two types of workers: older workers in their late 50s or early 60s nearing retirement, who complain of feeling cold during much of the winter season; and young workers just out of high school and on their first full-time job, who have the opposite problem—feeling warm much of the time. Can these conflicting reactions to the temperature be resolved? If so, how?

4. The office manager of your firm, Sherry Bauer, has asked you, her assistant, to evaluate the lighting system in the office. This request stems, in large part, from a company-wide effort to increase productivity and improve the firm's position in the market. Bauer mentions that the present lighting system (100 percent recessed fluorescent fixtures in the ceiling) is adequate, but she likes the task/ambient lighting concept. However, she feels there may not be enough money available to purchase new equipment to accommodate this new concept, but perhaps the present workstations can be modified to incorporate the task/ambient idea. Discuss how you would evaluate the present lighting system in this office having 34 workstations. On the basis of this information, decide whether you would accept or reject Bauer's preference for office lighting.

5. You and the other 20 members of your office staff have become accustomed to the inexpensive energy supplies required to operate your office headquarters. As a result, heating, lighting, and cooling costs have never been questioned. Suddenly, however, you have been given an ultimatum by your office manager to reduce by 15 percent the costs of all forms of energy used in your office. Discuss how you would plan, organize, and implement an energy management program, indicating from whom you would seek advice and how you would handle the principal human reactions to energy reductions.

cont

6. Anxiety has permeated your 23-person office staff since the recent murder of a veteran night-shift accountant in your firm's parking lot. Also, reports have circulated around the office that personal property has been missing from the workstations and coatrooms. The general manager, Vito Payton, has become concerned, since the mental state of the employees has deteriorated rapidly during the past three weeks, causing a marked decrease in efficiency and accuracy of the work. What was formerly an easygoing group of employees who enjoyed their work and their workplace has changed into a frightened staff. Payton has discussed his concerns with you, the office supervisor, and has asked that you conduct an audit of present safety-security methods and then recommend whether additional precautions are needed. How will you proceed?

CASES FOR CRITICAL THINKING

Case 14–1 Designing an Effective VDT Environment

Over the past three years, the Reliance Insurance Company has installed new automated equipment in its open office for handling the claims work. Most electronic typewriters have been replaced by word-processor terminals for correspondence personnel. Supervisors and managers as well as claims specialists now have VDTs that are linked to the firm's mainframe computer. However, since obtaining the automated equipment was a top priority, the ergonomic environment within which the equipment is used was put "on hold" until adequate funds were available.

Yesterday, the vice president of administration, Alex Butler, called you, the AOM, into his office and made this announcement:

I've got good news. The president tells me to go ahead with planning the necessary equipment, layout, plants—you know what I mean—to make our claims department a model workplace of comfort and convenience. Within the month I'd like your specific ideas in a report that can be circulated throughout the department and later discussed at a meeting of all employees.

Comply with Butler's request, by considering the different workstation needs of executives and support personnel, such as administrative assistants, secretaries, word processing staff, and files workers. Assume that the department manager and various supervisors will not be assigned private offices (your open-office layout does not provide for these) but require privacy. Also, keep in mind that the support personnel need efficient workstations that combine the ergonomic principles discussed in this chapter with the space guidelines in Chapter 13. Figure 13–6 should be especially helpful in preparing your report to Butler.

Case 14–2 Planning the Ergonomic Environment for a Home Office

Bob Williams plans to design a home office where he can write and illustrate books for preschool children. Williams now turns to you for advice on the basic ergonomic needs in his home office and asks for your thoughts about a desk and chair, lighting, floor covering, paint colors, and decor. To help him out, prepare a list of requirements in terms of "essential," "useful," and "nice-to-have" categories.

Case 14–3 Office Environmental Study: Computer Option (available on disk)

15

SELECTING OFFICE FURNITURE AND EQUIPMENT

GOALS FOR THIS CHAPTER

After completing this chapter, you should be able to:

1. Enumerate the guidelines that the administrative office manager considers when selecting office equipment.
2. Identify the main differences between conventional and modular office furniture.
3. Explain the nature and purpose of the four types of VDT workstations.
4. List the guidelines the administrative office manager considers when selecting office equipment.
5. Describe the five categories of lease agreements used in procuring office furniture and equipment.
6. Contrast the advantages of leasing to the disadvantages of purchasing office equipment.
7. Explain the valuation methods used by the administrative office manager to compare the relative net cost of purchasing with the net cost of leasing office equipment and explore the various factors involved in this decision.
8. Identify the main features of the three principal methods for providing service and maintenance of office equipment.
9. Discuss the need for a well-planned replacement program for office furniture and equipment.
10. List the activities commonly found in the centralized control of office furniture and equipment.

To ensure that the ergonomic environment discussed in Chapter 14 is properly maintained, we must give special attention to the selection and use of furniture and equipment, the key physical factors in the office. This is important to remember since the use of suitable tools and the provision for reasonable worker comfort help to create an effective psychological condition in the workers that is essential in achieving high levels of productivity.

Traditionally, office furniture and equipment have been designed and used with the efficiency of space planning and cost consciousness in mind. While these factors are important in "living within the budget," they overlook a more critical consideration—the ergonomic needs of the modern office worker. Thus, in order to manage the furniture and equipment needs of the office, the AOM must understand (1) the nature of the work being performed, (2) the ergonomic needs of the workers, and (3) the increasingly complex physical environment of the modern office, particularly in light of the "reengineering of business tasks" occurring in all types of offices. *Reengineering* means looking at better ways to perform all tasks and functions in the office. This suggests multiple changes to furniture and equipment requirements at workstations. For these reasons, the AOM has important responsibilities for selecting, procuring, maintaining, replacing, and centralizing the control of office furniture and equipment. Each of these responsibilities is discussed in this chapter.

SELECTING OFFICE FURNITURE AND EQUIPMENT

As the firm's chief specialist in administrative services, the AOM must be knowledgeable about office furniture and equipment. Thus, we expect the AOM to have on hand, or know where to obtain, up-to-date information about each of the following:

1. Principal types of furniture and equipment and reputable suppliers of each.
2. Reliable statistics for comparing the effectiveness of competing brands of furniture and equipment.
3. Current prices on all items and, preferably, catalogs representing each major supplier's merchandise.
4. Criteria for deciding on the need for such furniture and equipment.
5. Knowledge about the impact of the equipment on the information system, particularly the training or retraining needed, the availability of suppliers, and operating costs.
6. Possibilities for standardizing furniture and equipment throughout the firm.
7. Procurement alternatives (such as renting, leasing, or purchasing) and quantity purchasing options.
8. Maintenance, repair, and replacement considerations.

In today's world, we find a seemingly endless number of new furniture and equipment items for the office. For this reason, office managers must take special care to have the best equipped physical environment possible—one that matches the work requirements with the individual needs of each worker. This match can best be ensured with a detailed **workstation analysis** that arranges in an orderly fashion information about each employee's work and workstation needs. This analysis helps the AOM develop a basic understanding of the principal uses of the various types of office furniture and equipment and assists in making sound decisions regarding the selection of furniture and equipment.

Office Furniture

Generally, manufacturers provide furniture that includes filing cabinets, desks, tables, chairs, storage units, panels and screens as well as other related items for executive, managerial, and employee workstations. The most common types of furniture (with the exception of filing equipment) will be described in this chapter. Specific guidelines for selecting office furniture are outlined in Figure 15–1.

The cost of office furniture is a significant part of the overall expense incurred to accomplish office work. As a rule, furniture is purchased rather than leased or rented, for it is intended to last for a long period of time. Thus, the OM should give serious attention to the selection and use of office furniture. If properly selected, office furniture can assist the OM to increase productivity, to lower production costs, and to retain satisfied personnel. Both types of general office furniture—conventional and modular—are discussed briefly in the following paragraphs.

Conventional Furniture

Conventional furniture is a collection of independent furniture components, such as freestanding desks and credenzas, filing cabinets, and bookshelves. The arrangement of conventional furniture in traditional offices typically consists of rows of desks in large, open areas; conventional furniture is also found in private offices and in conference rooms of traditional offices. With the exception of chairs, conventional furniture is typically not adjustable. Until the early 1980s, conventional furniture was found almost universally in offices and is still commonly used today; for this reason, conventional furniture remains an important factor for the AOM to understand.

Office Desks. The desk is considered to be the central unit of the workstation. We use it as a working surface for handling information as well as a place to store supplies and collect data. Desks may be broadly classified according to their (1) *physical characteristics* (size and shape or style) and (2) *use* or *function*. Figure 15–2 shows examples of desks classified by function. These types of desks are available in standard sizes and as a rule are not adjustable.

Cost is an important factor in the selection of office desks. In most cases, even when a company owns its office building, we make estimates of the space rentals that should be charged against each department and division. For example, assume that the annual cost of floor space in large city offices ranges from $20 to $45 per square foot. Then we must consider that a standard size desk 60 inches

Figure 15–1
Guidelines for
Selecting Of-
fice Furniture

Guidelines for Selecting Office Furniture	Assistance in Using the Guidelines
1. The furniture should contribute to safe and comfortable working conditions.	1. The AOM must understand the nature of the work to be performed and the economy of physical effort as well as the speed of various operations. The edges of furniture should be smooth or rounded to prevent injury to persons or damage to clothing.
2. The furniture should be attractive and harmonize with the office decor.	2. The manner in which productivity is affected by these factors is discussed at length in Chapter 14. This material should be reviewed for a better understanding of esthetic considerations.
3. The furniture should be of good quality, solid construction, and suitable design to facilitate the work to be done.	3. High-quality furniture is usually attractive and economical to maintain. The main alternatives—wood or metal—should be weighed. Metal furniture provides great durability under hard wear and is usually more flexible since it is constructed with interchangeable parts. It is widely used in general office areas. Wood furniture is also long lasting but has the added values of warm tone, rich appearance, and prestige, which improve the attitudes of office workers toward their jobs. Wood furniture is usually recommended for executive offices, however, and with lowering costs, it is becoming more widely used in general office areas.
4. The quantity of furniture should be sufficient for the number of employees and suitable for the types of tasks performed.	4. Systems studies within each department, along with input from the office staff, will help determine the quantity of furniture needed.
5. The furniture should be adaptable to multipurpose use wherever possible.	5. Office machine stands should be able to serve as VDT tables. Executive desks may be used as conference tables. Tops of counter-high file cabinets can serve as working areas.
6. Specialized furniture should be purchased only if justified by cost savings, greater efficiency, improved productivity, and convenience.	6. Furniture such as sorting racks, credenzas, and folding chairs may be desirable, but unnecessary. Existing desks may serve part-time VDT operations.
7. The furniture should meet the preferences of the workers.	7. The workers should assist the AOM in new purchases of furniture. When workers' suggestions cannot be followed, reasons for the decision made should be communicated to them.

Figure 15–2

Types of Desks According to Functions Performed

A. Specialized Desk for Word Processing Personnel

Specialized VDT desks provide built-in features, such as this model that houses a compartment for activating the media (tapes or diskettes) and a storage compartment for tapes, diskettes, or paper files.

B. Modular Desk System for Data Processing/Word Processing Personnel

Electronic workstations are engineered to use modules that provide maximum flexibility for changing surface heights, depths, and equipment storage/support facilities.

C. Executive Desk

General-purpose, double-pedestal desks are commonly used by executives and managers, either individually or incorporated into a larger multipurpose executive workstation.

by 34 inches occupies a space of over 14 square feet, which, at $30 a square foot, would rent for more than $420 per year. Also, the rental for the chair space, which would approximate 60 inches by 30 inches, or 12½ square feet, would be $375, making a total of $795 for the desk and chair space. However, a desk 48 inches by 30 inches would be satisfactory for many office workers. Such a desk and a smaller chair occupy only 20 square feet of space with a space rental cost of $600 per year, or $195 less than that charged for the larger desk and chair.

388

Part 3 • Managing Administrative Services

Tables. Tables serve as desks or desk substitutes, as a place for sorting when considerable flat work surface is necessary, as a work surface for conferences and meetings, and as a place for storage. For many office jobs, the use of a table is preferred to a desk of any kind and may be more economical. Such a table should contain one or two small drawers, which will be sufficient for most purposes for the person using it.

In many firms where executives and others meet and work together in groups, a large conference table is usually provided. The conference tables found in boardrooms of many large corporations are custom designed to harmonize with the office decor. A wide variety of styles is available—from the traditional rectangular shapes to the more modern boat-shaped, oval, curved, and round styles.

Modular Furniture

Because of the widespread acceptance of automation and the need for office furniture to meet ergonomic requirements as well as the trend toward open-space planning, AOMs recognize the value of using furniture that is adjustable, easy to move, and multipurpose. For these reasons, we see a trend toward the use of modular rather than conventional furniture.

Modular furniture (sometimes called *systems furniture*) is a collection of integrated, interdependent furniture components that can be quickly and easily assembled, disassembled, and rearranged to meet employee and department needs. A **module** is one unit or component of office furniture that has a specific function, such as a desk, an acoustical partition, or a work surface with a pedestal containing several drawers. Each of the separate furniture units is designed according to the modular construction principle. This principle is based upon an approach to building office workstations composed of modules. Functionally designed modular furniture has a panel-dependent workstation with detachable components that can be adjusted to fit a worker's individual needs.

A modular workstation typically occupies less space than that required for conventional layouts. (For example, in Figures 13–4 and 13–5, pages 330 and 331, note how the use of clustered workstations

accommodates 40 percent more workers in the same place as the conventional layout.) Vertical panels are used for hanging shelving and storage units in modular layouts while conventional layouts require floor space for shelving and storage cabinets. Modular furniture permits many furniture arrangements, which are subject to both the imagination of the AOM and the limitations of space.

Modular furniture can also provide tremendous cost savings. By comparing the traditional method of remodeling with construction of walls, doors, and so forth, to the cost of simply reconfiguring modular furniture, large organizations realize significant savings from use of modular furniture. Some organizations report savings of as little as $100,000 and as much as $500,000 a year when they modify their furniture structures annually or more frequently. The AOM needs to project comparative cost savings when considering modifying workstations and procuring furniture.

Chairs. Today, 75 percent of the workforce sits while working. Hence, it is obvious why today's office furniture designers emphasize the importance of providing *ergonomic chairs* in the office. We know that physical comfort—good lighting and a comfortable chair—is closely related to the worker's mental condition upon which performance ultimately rests. It is important that office workers be comfortable to prevent strained posture when sitting for hours while performing their work. It is clear that worker comfort is a real concern in the workplace. The Communications Workers of America's *1992 Repetitive Motion Illness Survey* reports 86 percent of the operators of VDTs complained of neck and back pain; 73 percent claimed early symptoms of hand and wrist pain.[1] The OM can detect signs of fatigue by taking a close look at the workers' postures. When workers sit humped over their work with their feet entwined around the chair legs, the chair or the desk or both are not the right height. Such incorrect sitting positions may not be due to careless posture, but rather to defective seating. The workstation analysis should study the functions

[1]Patricia M. Fernberg, "Laying Down the Law on Ergonomics," *Modern Office Technology* (October, 1992), p. 74.

performed by a worker, the worker's posture, the degree of arm reach required by the worker to the computer keyboard and mouse, the worker's feet position on the floor, as well as other ergonomic considerations discussed in Chapter 14.

The main types of office chairs are classified as:

1. *Executive chairs,* adjustable to the physical characteristics of the person, in swivel and tilt-back styles, and often constructed of wood to match the wooden executive desks.
2. *Administrative support posture chairs,* with or without a swivel base, with or without arms, and adjustable to the physical needs of the person. These chairs are used by secretaries; keyboard specialists; and word processing, data-entry, and computer operator personnel.
3. *Side chairs,* often straight back with four legs, designed for use by visitors.

All office chairs, other than side or visitor chairs, should be adjustable for height and should swivel. The back support should be vertically and horizontally adjustable. If the back support is provided with a spring tension, the tension should be adjustable. Whenever workers have to bring the work to their eyes, they need armrests on their chairs. If workers have to bring their eyes and arms to the work, they do not need armrests on the chairs. Studies of VDT operators have found that proper posture while working in the office not only reduces fatigue and backaches but also improves the health of workers by making them less susceptible to colds and headaches. Healthier employees benefit the firm by reason of less absenteeism, fewer errors, a larger volume of production, and, finally, lower costs.

Most office chairs are designed to fit as closely as possible the contours of the body. Saddle seats are one example of the contour designs often used in the construction of office chairs. Correctly contoured seats, especially those covered with foam latex, add to the workers' comfort.

Furniture for Automated Workstations

Furniture for the automated office environment is the fastest growing segment of the business furniture industry. This growth is due in large part to the rapid influx of VDTs and other computer equipment into every size of office including the home. Many workers are full-time VDT operators, and for this group especially, personal comfort and office productivity depend on the choice of ergonomically sound furniture and equipment.

Four types of VDT workstations exist: (1) the full-time operator's workstation used in computer and word processing systems; (2) the multifunction workstation in which several persons periodically share the use of a VDT; (3) the executive workstation at which, to an increasing degree, a VDT and related equipment are used by managers; and (4) the technical specialist/professional workstation for workers using high-level technical software. The furniture needed for each type of VDT workstation is briefly discussed in the following paragraphs. The equipment needed to operate workstations such as these is discussed in later chapters.

Furniture for the Full-Time VDT Operator. Working for long hours at a VDT screen "freezes" an operator into one fixed position. The keyboarding and viewing tasks restrict the movement of operators so that much discomfort and many postural problems result. To eliminate such problems, the National Institute of Occupational Safety and Health (NIOSH) recommends that VDT workstations and devices be made as adjustable as possible to allow for the unique physical characteristics of the operator. (See Figure 15–3.) Thus, the workstation for the full-time VDT operator should have the following features:

1. *Detachable keyboards* that permit the adjustment of keyboard height.
2. *Adjustable screen height and tilt* to improve viewing and reduce glare.
3. *Sufficient leg room* to permit freedom of movement.
4. *Adjustable chair features* (seat height, backrest height, and armrests) as well as the capability of swiveling and movement using casters. Studies show that a seated person changes positions on the average of at least once every six minutes.
5. Preferably *an L-shaped workstation arrangement* that enhances the efficiency of motion between the two sections of the workstation.

6. A variety of *hanging components* to accommodate the normal reach of an operator (22 to 24 inches). Included are storage shelving, task lighting, space for a printer (if needed), and space for performing other nonautomated administrative duties.

7. A variety of other accessories such as a *footrest* to raise knees to proper position and enhance blood circulation.

Furniture for the Multifunction Shared Workstation. In many cases, a community workstation is provided in which a group of office workers

shares an automated workcenter. Each may use the computer for short periods of time for data processing, word processing, and communication tasks. In such cases, adjustable furniture features should be provided in the furniture, although this aspect is not so important as it is for the full-time operator's workstation. Many furniture arrangements are available for this type of workstation.

Furniture for an Executive Workstation. More and more, automated workstations are being installed in the private offices of executives to provide them with immediate access to the firm's computerized facilities. In such workstations, ex-

Figure 15–3
Adjustable Furniture for Full-Time VDT Operator

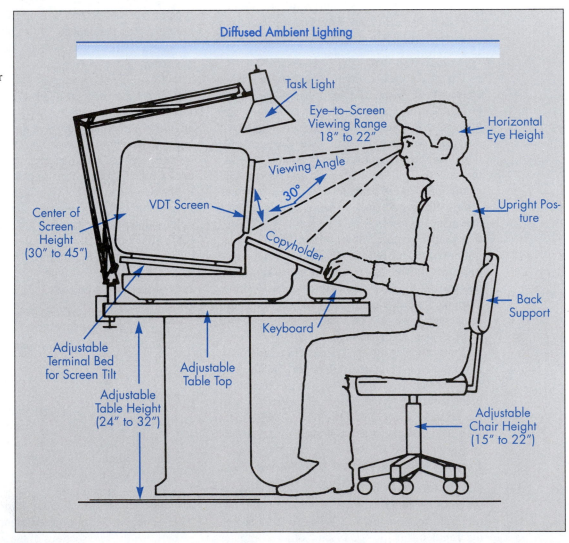

Illustration 15–1 Adjustable furniture for a VDT operator.

ecutives can compose letters, make computations, store and retrieve information, and send and receive messages using their VDTs. In the executive workstation, the VDT is used on an irregular basis, as a rule, and thus occupies a more secondary location in the workstation than is required for full-time operators.

Furniture for a Technical Specialist/Professional Workstation. With the restructuring of offices, more individual contributors or technical specialists are emerging. This type of worker performs tasks on a daily basis requiring extended work surfaces and related equipment. In addition to the VDT and automated equipment, layout tables for high-level technical software (such as CAD, CAM, and desktop publishing discussed in later chapters) are required.

Other Furniture and Accessories

The preceding discussion has indicated that desks, tables, and chairs are the key furniture items in any office. While this continues to be true, the forward-looking AOM will modify the working environment as the conditions (particularly in the layout), the financial resources, and the tastes of management dictate. It has become common to

find extra furnishings such as sofas, end tables with harmonizing table lamps, coffee tables, art objects, credenzas, bookcases, planters, privacy screens, office valets or wall and coat racks, and magazine racks in the office. Other accessories commonly found include clocks, safes, bars, office refrigerators, movable carts, and stools. These accessories provide an environment that is more conducive to relaxed work, concentration, and enjoyment of the hours spent on the job.

Office Equipment

In addition to the furniture required for the office, a great array of office equipment is available. The term *office equipment,* as used here, refers primarily to office machines and devices found in the office.[2]

The principal office machines are information machines, such as typewriters, electronic calculators, copiers, telephones, facsimile (FAX) machines, and computers. As such, office equipment is the intermediary between people and their work. It enables employees to accomplish more work in less time with greater accuracy and with better quality. Furthermore, telecommunication equipment helps employees to transmit the results of their work to others over long distances and to receive rapid feedback. The types and brands of equipment and the number of their possible uses continue to grow at an increasingly rapid rate.

The selection of office equipment starts with a feasibility study—introduced in Chapter 4—that seeks to answer these questions: (1) *Is the equipment necessary?* (2) *If so, which equipment is the best?* and (3) *Is the equipment cost effective as well as ergonomically sound?* To answer these questions, the entire information system is identified and the role of equipment in such a system is clarified. Such a study requires concentrated and extended thought with well-documented an-

[2]For discussions concerning specific types of office equipment, see Chapter 16 (Automating the Office), Chapter 17 (Understanding Text/Word Processing Systems), Chapter 18 (Distributing Information: Telecommunication and Mailing Systems), Chapter 19 (Managing Records), and Chapter 20 (Managing Microimage and Reprographic Systems).

swers to the three key questions involved. To assist the AOM in undertaking an office equipment feasibility study, the guidelines for selecting office equipment outlined in Figure 15–4 should prove helpful.

PROCURING OFFICE EQUIPMENT

The procuring of office furniture and equipment is an important and complex responsibility of the OM. Office *furniture,* which is intended to last for a long time, is usually purchased rather than leased or rented. However, the same is not necessarily true of office *equipment,* which is subject to much wear and tear as well as to technological obsolescence.

Purchasing Office Equipment

When a company purchases its office equipment, it owns an asset that it can later sell. Also, the company can reduce its income taxes by claiming as an operating expense the depreciation occurring during the estimated useful life of the equipment.

When buying office equipment, the company may obtain financial aid from the equipment manufacturer. By means of lending programs, some leading manufacturers of office machines and equipment finance a significant portion of their U.S. sales. Customers see such loans as bargains since the interest rate offered by the manufacturer is usually lower than the rates charged by banks. Of course, purchasing office equipment also has disadvantages, which are explained in a later section when the advantages of leasing are explored.

Leasing Office Equipment

Although office equipment may be purchased outright, estimates indicate that almost one-third of all newly acquired equipment is leased. The figure tends to be higher for firms that have large investments in material-handling systems, word processing and office equipment, and energy-related equipment, all of which are subject to rapid obsolescence.

An **equipment lease** (similar to the office space lease discussed in Chapter 13) is a contract that enables an equipment user (lessee) to secure use of a tangible asset by making periodic payments to the owner (lessor) of the asset over a specified time period. Under a lease, which usually extends over a longer period of time than a rental, there is no intent—stated or implied—for the user to obtain equity or to purchase the equipment. *During the life of the lease, the lessor retains ownership of the asset and the claim to any remaining value in the equipment at the end of the lease period.*

Almost all types of office machines and equipment including computers and computer software can be leased. Equipment can be leased from a variety of sources: directly from the manufacturer's distributor, from a local office equipment dealer, from an independent leasing company that leases various brands of office machines and equipment, and from many other organizations that provide some form of equipment-leasing service.

Kinds of Lease Agreements

Since leases can be designed to meet the special needs of the parties involved, we find an almost limitless variety of actual lease contracts. For this discussion, the various kinds of lease agreements will be grouped into five categories: (1) short-term, (2) long-term with renewal option, (3) long-term with purchase option, (4) conditional sales contract, and (5) sale-leaseback.

The **short-term lease,** which is really a rental contract, is used to obtain extra equipment, such as typewriters and calculators, for peak workload jobs for a relatively short time period. For example, at the time of year-end inventory, a firm may rent several electronic calculators for three or four weeks. The major advantage of this leasing plan is that the needed equipment is made available immediately for a short period of time with the need for little cash outlay. In the computer and computer-driven office equipment field, the short-term lease is referred to as an *operating lease* when client firms want to lease the equipment for a short period of time (two to two-and-one-half years) because they are unsure as to the type of equipment they will need in the future.

Figure 15–4
Guidelines for
Selecting Of-
fice Equip-
ment

Guidelines for Selecting Office Equipment	Considerations in Using the Guidelines
1. Equipment should be chosen for any job or task when it helps workers to be more efficient.	1. Where job monotony due to repetitive work tasks is found, a machine should be considered to enrich the job as well as increase production.
2. High-volume (rather than low-frequency or one-time only) applications point to the need for machines.	2. From high-volume applications come better service, more prompt preparation of financial reports, and other good results.
3. Where equipment can provide higher quality of output, it should be used.	3. Compare typewritten with handwritten reports for neatness and legibility.
4. The need for accuracy should be determined; and where internal machine checks and controls can provide such accuracy, a machine should be selected.	4. This guideline relates to numeric data (financial and accounting reports) as well as textual matter. Accuracy of text can be verified through word processing software.
5. Equipment should be installed whenever it will reduce the actual cost of performing office work.	5. The costs of service contracts, of operation and supplies, and of layout alterations required must be considered in calculating the total cost of an equipment installation.
6. To handle urgent work, high-speed requirements, or peak loads in the office work schedule, appropriate equipment should be considered.	6. Some equipment may be shared by several departments if the work schedule permits.
7. Both the capabilities and the limitations of equipment must be carefully considered.	7. Capabilities include ease of use, durability, accuracy, and high operating speeds. Limitations may involve the maximum number of digits that can be handled, size of forms and records to be used, cycling speeds, number of copies required, complexity of mathematical processes, number and capacity of internal storage media, longevity of expected performance, and trade-in value.
8. Both operative and supervisory personnel involved with the equipment should be consulted for their machine preferences.	8. The ease of use and amount of retraining required for proper machine operation should be considered.
9. The availability of ready, reliable maintenance service should receive top priority in equipment selection.	9. The cost of office operations and customer inconvenience increases if equipment is not functioning properly or not at all.
10. If its usage allows, equipment should be selected that has these features: a. Simplicity b. Flexibility c. Portability d. Adaptability	10. Simplicity is suggested for ease of operation, of learning, and of maintenance; flexibility, for use of the equipment in many situations; portability, for easy movement of machines to be used in several departments; and adaptability, for immediate integration into an existing office system.

Figure 15–4
Continued.

Guidelines for Selecting Office Equipment	Considerations in Using the Guidelines
11. Before purchase, lease, or rental, equipment should be "test run" in the office situation where it is being considered for installation.	11. For small machines, a one- or two-week trial period is recommended; for the larger, more expensive machines in the computer family, a longer period of time is needed.
12. Standardization of office equipment is desirable, including sizes, styles, and brands.	12. With standardized office equipment it is possible: a. To obtain lower prices through larger purchases. b. To lower the maintenance costs by having fewer brands of machines to service. c. To develop, if necessary, the company's own service department more easily and economically. d. To economize by having one group of employees who can operate any of the machines. e. To train operators more quickly and easily. f. To purchase and use office forms to fit the brands of machines. g. To simplify the computation of depreciation and trade-in value of the equipment.
13. Ensure that software as well as hardware is ergonomically sound.	13. The software/human interface should be a part of the needs analysis: a. Determine user friendliness for learning. b. Reduce number of keystrokes to ease hand and wrist fatigue. c. Ensure screen quality to reduce eyestrain. d. Ensure other factors as discussed in Chapter 14.

The **long-term lease with renewal option** usually runs between 75 and 80 percent of the useful life of the equipment. On the average, such leases run from three to five years. At the end of the initial lease period, the lease can be renewed. The lease payments during the renewal period should be lower than those in the initial term of the lease since at this point the lessor should be recovering only the residual value (estimated market value) of the leased property.

The **long-term lease with purchase option** is similar to the long-term lease discussed previ-

ously except that during the lease period the lessee is building up equity to take ownership of the equipment at the end of the period. The user gains the flexibility of being able to upgrade the equipment, without any penalty, during the lease period. Since the equipment has a tangible value that can be used as a trade-in on new equipment when a new lease is signed, the threat of obsolescence is lessened. Under income tax regulations, however, this form of lease may be interpreted as a conditional sales contract. Therefore, the lessee may be denied tax deductions for the lease payments for federal income tax purposes.

A **conditional sales contract** is a contract in which the user of the equipment, for federal income tax purposes, is treated as the owner of the equipment at the time of signing the lease. Thus, the company may be denied tax deductions for the lease payments. To enable both the lessee and the lessor to arrange terms that result in favorable tax treatment, advice from tax experts, legal counsel, and/or the Internal Revenue Service (IRS) should be sought.

Under the **sale-leaseback plan,** the company purchases its office equipment, sells it to a lessor, and then leases it back under a long-term lease. Thus, the company has use of almost the entire value of its plant assets in the form of usable cash. This plan may prove very economical to the firm in need of working capital for other more productive purposes.

Advantages of Leasing

The advantages of leasing office equipment point up some of the drawbacks of an outright purchase. These advantages include:

1. *Working capital is freed for day-to-day cash flow and thus can be used for more productive ventures.* In some leases, no down payment is required. In other leases, a down payment equal to the first-year's leasing cost may be needed to acquire the equipment. Such minimum stipulations free a firm's capital for other revenue-producing investments or for expansion.

2. *Budgetary control is facilitated and accounting procedures are simplified since the amount of regular lease payments is easily determined.* A hedge against inflation is also provided since the same dollar lease payments are spread over a period of years. Thus, in times of increasing inflation, a constant sum of money paid out five years into the future on a five-year lease will be paid in inflated dollars, which have less purchasing power than the same amount spent in the current year.

3. *Some leases offer the lessee an opportunity to contract out specialized services such as*

maintenance and record keeping which are associated with the use of certain kinds of equipment. For example, under some leases, the lessor services and maintains the equipment for the user, keeps plant asset records, and provides insurance coverage. The lease also relieves the lessee of the necessity of disposing of the equipment when it is no longer needed.

4. *Flexibility, unavailable in other methods of financing, is provided the lessee.* New firms often need equipment immediately but are initially unable to budget substantial funds for lease payments. Under long-term leases, payment schedules can easily be worked out to mesh with the lessee's seasonal pattern of cash flow. For example, a deferred-payment lease offers flexibility in payment methods. By deferring its payments, a company is able to generate income before the first lease payment comes due.

5. *Leasing offers the equipment user an additional source of financing.* Lease financing may be available to companies when other sources of financing cannot be obtained on reasonable terms. For example, leasing offers one of the few ways that small companies without access to credit can obtain new equipment.

6. *For companies that use highly specialized equipment, protection may be obtained against the risks of obsolescence.* In many cases the equipment can be replaced during the life of the lease; thus, throughout the lease period, the company can take advantage of the latest advances in technology. Moreover, updating or altering equipment and furniture for any reason is easier under leasing arrangements.

7. *Tax benefits may be realized since the lease payments may be treated as business expenses which are fully deductible for income tax purposes.* As noted earlier, however, under some lease contracts an option to buy during or at the end of the lease period may be looked upon by the Internal Revenue Service as an installment purchase or a conditional sales contract. Thus, the lease payments may not be tax deductible.

Generally, if a lessee anticipates sufficient taxable income, borrowing to purchase equipment offers greater tax benefits and is less expensive than leasing, especially *when methods of accelerating depreciation are used.* (See the following discussion of accelerating depreciation in the section *Replacing Office Equipment.*) Even so, deductible lease payments under short-term leases or leases with variable payment schedules may be attractive to lessees under certain circumstances.

8. *Rapidly expanding companies and those opening branch offices are aided by the package plans of some lessors, under which equipment can be added as the needs of the company grow.*

9. *Leasing enables the firm to bypass the approval for capital expenditures by top management.* In many firms, the process for obtaining capital appropriations is very complex and time consuming. Thus, by means of leasing, managers can obtain the needed equipment without going through corporate management or obtaining the board of directors' approval.

The Lease-or-Buy Decision

If, after we perform a feasibility study, a need for equipment is determined, the relative net cost of purchasing and leasing should be carefully analyzed before making the decision to lease or to buy. In addition, several other important factors, discussed later in this section, should be considered.

Relative Net Cost of Leasing or Buying

If we wish to use the equipment for more than one shift a day, it may, in terms of direct cost, be more economical for many firms to purchase than to lease the equipment. However, each firm should conduct its own capital budgeting study, as in the case of any other capital investment, by using valuation methods such as payback period, break-even analysis, and the average rate of return on the investment. Each of these methods is briefly described below.

Payback Period. The **payback period** is the period of time over which a capital expenditure, such as the purchase of six computer terminals, will generate cash equal to the cost of the proposal. With this technique, we can estimate how long a company will have to wait in order to recover sufficient cash from the proposed purchase to equal the cash invested in the proposed items to be bought.

When several proposals or projects are under consideration and a payback period is calculated for each one, a selection can be made of the project that is the most economically feasible. Generally, a firm's capital budgeting policy states that any proposal must pay for itself within a specified number of years—*the cutoff point.* A short payback period is usually desired since over a relatively short period of time the company is exposed to less risk of recovering its capital. Further, for the firm that greatly needs cash, a short payback period improves the financial position by creating additional cash inflow.

Cash inflow includes (1) the cash savings that the company anticipates as a result of undertaking the purchase and (2) depreciation expense, since depreciation is an expense for which no cash is spent by the firm. Thus, the company has available an amount of cash that consists of the net income after taxes plus depreciation.

As an example, let us assume that the cash inflow from a proposed equipment purchase is in equal amounts of $8,000 each year. The cost of the equipment is $24,000, which is divided by the amount of the cash inflow to obtain the payback period, three years. When this three-year period is compared with the firm's cutoff point, the proposal may be rejected, revised before acceptance, or ranked in priority order with other proposals being considered.

Break-Even Analysis. Another method that may be used by the AOM in making the decision to expand operations by purchasing or leasing additional equipment is break-even analysis. In this kind of analysis, the **break-even point** is that level of operations at which the company neither realizes income nor incurs loss. Thus, *it is that point at which revenues and costs (or expenses)* *are equal*. When the break-even point is charted, as shown in Figure 15–5, the relationship among sales volume, costs, and profits (or income) can be seen graphically. However, before undertaking break-even analysis and charting such a relationship, the AOM needs to understand costs and their behavior as affected by changes in the firm's volume of business activity. Also, there is a need to be familiar with the fixed and the variable costs involved in the firm's operation.

Fixed costs tend to remain fairly stable (unchanging) over a stated time period even when the volume of business changes. Examples of fixed costs are office space and equipment rent, real estate taxes, property insurance, and the salaries of administrative and supervisory personnel.

Variable costs change in response to changes in the volume of work activity. Examples of variable office costs are direct labor costs, such as the wages and salaries paid office workers; direct materials, such as stationery and supplies; equipment repair and maintenance expenses; and mailing expenses.

The cost-volume-profit relationships that are inherent in break-even analysis may be shown graphically as in Figure 15–5. In this break-even chart, the sales volume (units produced × unit selling price) is plotted on the horizontal axis,

and the expense items (fixed and variable costs) are plotted on the vertical axis. In this example, for a sales volume of $1 million (50,000 units at $20 each), the fixed costs are $300,000 as shown by the straight line parallel to the horizontal sales volume axis. The area below this line is called the *fixed expense area*. At this sales volume, the variable costs are $600,000. The total cost line shows that for a sales volume of $1 million, the total costs are $900,000. The income line, representing the total income to the company, is plotted against the vertical expense and income axis to show that expenses are paid out of income and that the difference remaining is profit. *The break-even point is found at the intersection of the total cost line and the income line.* At this point, a total sales volume of $750,000 equals the total expenses.

The AOM may use break-even analysis in estimating the effects of future actions. For example, if the office lease payments were to increase by $15,000 for each of the next five years, how much must sales increase to cover this growth in fixed costs and still produce a profit of $300,000? If additional part-time office workers were employed, with the variable costs increasing by $45,000, how much must sales expand to cover such an increase? What amount of sales would be needed to break even if variable costs (such as mailing expenses) were reduced by 5 percent but at the same time fixed costs (such as real estate taxes and property insurance) increased by $20,000? Break-even analysis may also be used when evaluating proposed capital expenditures, such as the purchase or lease of new office space. By charting the cost-volume-profit relationship, the effect of the proposed expenditure on the overall financial structure of the firm can be determined.

Average Rate of Return. Another approach the AOM may use to analyze proposed capital expenditures is the average rate of return. This method measures the anticipated profitability of a proposed investment *by dividing the average savings to be obtained from the investment by the average amount of the investment.* The rate of return on the proposed expenditure is then related

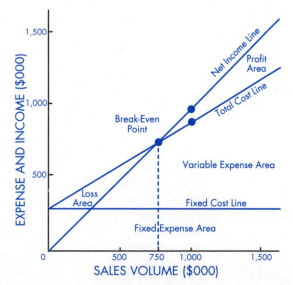

Figure 15–5
Break-Even Chart

to certain conditions that have been established by the company. For example, a company may decide that the cost of acquiring the funds that will be tied up in the investment shall be less than, say, 11 percent, which is the amount of interest currently being charged the company by its lenders.

Other Factors to Consider in the Lease-or-Buy Decision

Several other factors that must be carefully studied before a decision is made to lease or to buy office equipment are listed below.

1. *Threat of obsolescence.* Companies that are concerned about their office equipment becoming obsolete as the result of technological advances often decide to lease even though it may be less expensive to buy.
2. *Useful life of the equipment.* Although an analysis of useful life is very difficult to do, a realistic appraisal must be made of how long the equipment will serve the company's needs. For example, in some firms, long-range planners are at work designing changes for the future that may radically affect the role of the present computer and word processing installations. To forecast the future, the computer and word processing staffs must analyze the firm's plans and trends for sales, production, and purchases in order to determine the need for new or expanded automated processes.
3. *Amount of base fee.* Often a firm pays a base fee that entitles it to operate the equipment, such as a computer, a certain number of hours each month. Regular overtime usage requires the payment of additional rent, which can be directly determined with the installation of time recorders on the equipment. All terms governing the basic rental period should be spelled out in advance. For example, if the equipment breaks down for a few hours, is the company charged for these hours or does the vendor assume the loss?
4. *Maintenance services.* The contract to buy or to lease should clearly indicate the type of maintenance services—preventive and re-

pair—that will be provided by the manufacturer or the vendor. The availability of skilled help, when needed, should be determined.
5. *Trade-in value of equipment.* In making cost comparisons between leasing and buying, the trade-in or residual value of equipment at the end of its useful life is often overlooked. With a growing market for used equipment, the firm may realize a substantial trade-in value for equipment that has a systems life shorter than its productive life.
6. *Interest costs.* When comparing the costs of leasing and buying, the firm should consider the rate of interest it pays for borrowed money and the rate it expects to earn on an investment of the funds.

In making a wise decision on whether to lease or buy equipment, the AOM may obtain assistance from the firm's own financial specialists and auditors and from independent consultants. Also, many lessors, such as equipment manufacturers, will prepare a detailed analysis of the purchase and lease factors.

MAINTAINING OFFICE EQUIPMENT

As we have seen in the previous discussion, maintenance is an important factor to be considered by the AOM when purchasing or leasing equipment. When any piece of office equipment is purchased, there is generally a warranty period during which time equipment repairs are made by the manufacturer at no cost to the firm. Once the warranty period has passed, however, and unless the equipment is covered by a service contract, any future repairs are charged against the user on a time and materials basis.

Many office machines are operated almost continuously each workday. With automated machines and equipment handling the bulk of information processing, the servicing of these machines becomes a major consideration. When machines and equipment break down, office workers are unable to perform their work until repairs have been made unless backup equipment is available.

Depending upon the complexity of the equipment and the number of machines used, the maintenance of office equipment may be provided by internal or external service personnel.

Internal Service

To operate its own service department, a company must be fairly large. Involved in the installation of such a department are the following important costs:

1. The relatively high salaries paid to trained service personnel.
2. The hidden costs of their employee benefits.
3. The cost of retraining the personnel as new machine models appear on the market.
4. The cost of the space and repair equipment allotted to the service department.

External Service

External service may be provided by the manufacturer of the equipment or by an independent service firm under a service contract or on a per-call basis.

Service Contract

A **service contract** (also known as a *maintenance agreement* or *maintenance guarantee*) provides for periodic cleaning and lubrication, inspection, and replacement of worn-out or defective machine parts. Preventive maintenance, which forms a part of the manufacturer's service contract, usually reduces or eliminates the number of breakdowns.

In the servicing of standard office machines and equipment, such as typewriters and copiers, some companies, especially those in small outlying communities, enter into an agreement with a local service firm. For a fixed fee, the service firm inspects, cleans, and repairs each machine in the office at regular intervals.

Per-Call Basis

Some companies find it is more economical to pay for each individual service call as the service is needed. In the case of complex and highly automated equipment, however, repeat service calls are often necessary. When a fixed-fee service contract

Illustration 15–2 Computer repairs and preventive maintenance are commonly provided by outside firms under service contracts.

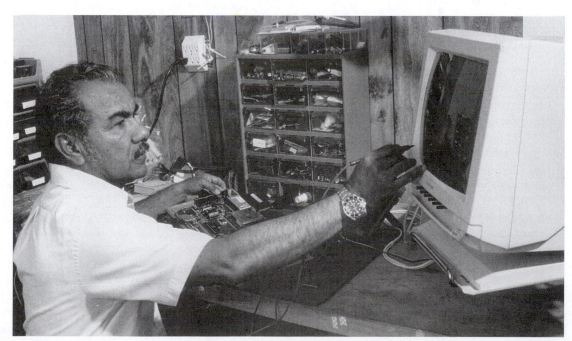

DIALOG FROM THE WORKPLACE

CRAIG S. MACK (SEATED)

Building and Facilities Engineer
Bachelor of Architecture Degree,
University of Nebraska
Deere & Company
Moline, Illinois

Mr. Mack is responsible for all maintenance, security, safety, fire protection, janitorial services, and preparation of the design for the reconfiguration of the corporate headquarters at Deere & Company in Moline, Illinois. Mr. Mack has been with Deere & Company for 14 years and has held his current position for the past six years. Previously, he was one of the corporate architects in the facility engineering department.

WARREN W. POWER (STANDING)

Manager, Office Administration
B.S. Mechanical Engineering, Iowa State University
M.B.A., University of Iowa
Deere & Company, Moline, Illinois

In his position at Deere & Company, Mr. Power is responsible for providing the services, equipment, and furniture employees need to perform their daily jobs. Mr. Power has been with John Deere for 26 years and has held positions in manufacturing, engineering, corporate standards, and engineering systems and for the past 12 years has been in general office personnel and administration.

QUESTION: How does the accelerating rate of change in the office environment influence you in selecting, procuring, and maintaining office furniture and equipment?

RESPONSE: Since we've been in our current jobs, the rate at which new technologies are being introduced into the office has increased dramatically. Office equipment, such as typewriters and telephones, were previously pur-

chased with the expectation of a useful life of 10 to 15 years. The advent of the microchip changed all of this. Today the primary office equipment consists of computers, printers, and facsimile machines, which are rapidly becoming smaller and less expensive. As a result, firms today are able to give their employees more tools to do their job than they ever have in the past. While this additional equipment improves efficiency and productivity, it also creates additional problems for the office manager.

The rapid changes that are occurring in the office environment significantly impact the design of our facilities, both old and new. All aspects of new facilities, including wiring, lighting, walls, windows, environmental requirements, and furniture are designed or selected to enhance today's office technology and to ensure the ability to adapt to foreseeable changes. While this changing environment makes the facility designer's job more difficult for new construction, the real challenge lies in changing our existing facilities.

Large firms, such as Deere, have millions of dollars invested in office facilities and furniture. Most of these facilities were built and furnished prior to the microchip revolution. As a result, many of our existing buildings and furniture do not meet the needs of today's office environment. Our firm, like most firms, can't afford to replace all of our buildings and furniture to accommodate these emerging technologies, so it's up to the office manager to find alternatives. Fortunately, our problem is not unique and businesses throughout the world have developed products and accessories to make existing furniture and facilities more compatible with new technologies. The facility manager's challenge is to select a set of products that provides employees with an ergonomically acceptable workstation that still provides an aesthetically acceptable office environment.

is used, such calls become the responsibility of the manufacturer or the local service firm.

REPLACING OFFICE EQUIPMENT

With the continuing advances that we see in the information technology field, office equipment becomes obsolete quickly because of newer and better models placed on the market. Therefore, it is necessary for the AOM to select the best machine available at the time of purchase and to use this machine until its efficiency lessens. In the *Dialog from the Workplace,* Craig Mack, building and facilities engineer for a large corporation, and Warren Power, manager of office administration for the same company, describe the challenge of replacing and updating equipment to meet the needs of technology in a rapidly changing office environment. Note their emphasis on making efficient use of existing resources.

When the efficiency of existing machines lessens, the old machine may be replaced with a newer model without too great a loss. This loss can be absorbed by the business if a sound trade-in policy has been established at the time of purchase. Also, at the time of purchasing the office equipment, plans must be made for calculating the depreciation of the property, as described next.

Office equipment may be *depreciated* (written off as an operating expense) over the useful life of the equipment. The Tax Reform Act (TRA) of 1986 established property class lives for various kinds of assets to indicate the length of time over which the cost of different kinds of assets might be recovered. For example, the five-year property class includes assets such as computers and peripheral equipment and office machinery (typewriters, calculators, copiers, etc.). In the seven-year property class, we find office furniture and fixtures (desks, files, etc.).

Under one method of calculating depreciation called *straight line,* the cost of the equipment is spread rather evenly over the estimated life (property class life) of the asset. However, since office equipment usually declines in value more rapidly during the first years of its useful life than in the later years, an *accelerated* depreciation method is often more appropriate to use. When using such a

method, firms "write off" (or record among the firm's operating expenses) a larger depreciation expense in the earlier years of the asset's life and a smaller depreciation expense during the later years. Thus, the amount recorded as depreciation expense each year more correctly matches the decline in value of the asset during that year.[3]

Whether office machines and equipment are replaced at the end of their estimated useful life or earlier, we still find a need for a well-planned replacement program. Such a program enables a firm to predict accurately each year the exact cost of its equipment. The cutoff point (of operating efficiency and economy) can then be established for each piece of equipment; the number of new items to be purchased can be forecast; and the amount for maintenance during the coming year can be budgeted. A planned replacement program also enables the firm to establish better control over its maintenance costs, especially those that tend to rise during the latter years of machine usage. By closely controlling the replacement schedule of office machines, the firm can avoid those additional expenses that arise during the period when the equipment is old and requires extensive reconditioning, replacement of parts, and special cleanings. An intangible advantage of prestige and morale is also found in the company that has a planned replacement program. By using such a program, the company presents a businesslike, well-equipped, up-to-date image to its customers, visitors, and employees.

CENTRALIZING THE CONTROL OF OFFICE EQUIPMENT

For purposes of effectively controlling the selection, procurement, maintenance, and replacement of equipment, the office equipment function should be organized on a centralized basis. This is particularly true in large offices where specialized functions are found and where large sums of

---

[3]For a complete discussion of depreciation accounting, see Harold Q. Langenderfer, Willis C. Stevenson, and Herbert C. Sieg, *Federal Income Taxation* (Cincinnati: South-Western Publishing Co., current edition). Also very helpful is the annually updated *Tax Guide for Small Business,* available free from the Internal Revenue Service.

money are invested in machines and related equipment. Usually, the function of centralized control is the responsibility of the AOM and consists of the following activities:

1. Maintaining a current file of information on office equipment and developments in information technology.
2. Setting up a system of centralized control over plant assets that covers the following kinds of information:
   a. Equipment owned, leased, or rented by the firm.
   b. Description of equipment.
   c. Company asset number and manufacturer's model and serial numbers.
   d. Department or cost center assigned responsibility for the equipment.
   e. Date of purchase, lease agreement, or rental contract.
   f. Purchase price plus installation costs or amount of lease or rental payments.
   g. History of maintenance and repair services and costs.
   h. Depreciation expense, accumulated depreciation, and book value (purchase price less accumulated depreciation).
3. Controlling the selection and purchasing or leasing of machines in line with the use to be made of machines.
4. Developing effective procedures for maintenance and replacement of machines.
5. Reviewing periodically all equipment and machine installations to make sure all items remain on company premises.
6. Functioning as a clearinghouse for all equipment needs within the firm and as the contact point for all vendors.

Small offices, too, have need for similar controls over their machines and equipment. Although little specialization of function is found in small offices, the control of such assets should be assigned to one individual.

SUMMARY

1. In selecting office furniture, the AOM must understand that costs and employee satisfaction are affected by the proper choice of desks, chairs, tables, and other accessories. A study of modular furniture layouts will indicate how employees may work more comfortably and expend less physical energy. Prior to selecting office equipment, a feasibility study should be undertaken to assure the AOM and others on the project team that the equipment is actually needed. If the equipment is needed, the AOM must examine which equipment will do the job most economically, efficiently, and accurately with the goal of fulfilling ergonomic considerations. Special care should be given to the selection of furniture for automated workstations, keeping in mind the unique features of VDTs and their effect upon various kinds of operators in the workplace.

2. When office furniture and equipment are procured, the AOM should carefully study the advantages and disadvantages of purchasing, leasing, and renting. One factor of great importance in making the lease-or-buy decision is the relative net cost of purchasing and of leasing. The payback period, the break-even point, and the rate of return on the investment are commonly determined in calculating the net cost. Other factors to be investigated as part of the lease-or-buy decision include the potential technological obsolescence of the equipment, the useful life of the equipment, the cost of the base fee, the maintenance service, and the trade-in value of the equipment. Also, a comparison should be made of the interest costs involved in borrowing money to buy the equipment with the rate of return the firm might obtain by investing the funds in some other business transaction.

c
o
n
t

3. Other important phases of equipping the physical office environment include (1) selecting the most practical approach to maintaining and servicing the equipment, (2) planning a sound program for replacing the office equipment, and (3) providing for effective centralized control over the plant assets whether they are purchased, leased, or rented.

FOR YOUR REVIEW

1. What is the meaning of reengineering?

2. What types and sources of information should administrative office managers have available to meet the office furniture and equipment needs of their office?

3. Assume you have been asked to provide a comprehensive set of guidelines for selecting office furniture. What would you include in your set?

4. What is a workstation analysis?

5. In the selection of office furniture, how important is the cost of square footage occupied by desks and chairs?

6. What is the modular construction principle, and what are its advantages?

7. Discuss the characteristics of a good office chair. What can the posture of workers reveal about their office chair? Why is the selection of a chair just as important as the selection of a desk?

8. What are the various categories of office furniture in automated workstations?

9. Why should a feasibility study be undertaken prior to the selection of office equipment? What basic questions are to be answered in the office feasibility study?

10. From the standpoint of equipment usage, what guidelines must be taken into consideration before making the decision to select an office machine?

11. List the advantages of standardizing the sizes, styles, and brands of office equipment.

12. What are the characteristics of an equipment lease?

13. What is a long-term lease with purchase option? What are the advantages and disadvantages of a long-term lease with purchase option?

14. What are the advantages that a firm may realize by leasing rather than buying its office equipment?

15. How may a break-even analysis be of value to the AOM when making the lease-or-buy decision?

16. What factors other than a comparison of cost should be carefully studied by the AOM before making the decision to lease or buy the needed equipment?

17. What are the various cost considerations for an internal service department?

18. Contrast a service contract with a per-call basis for servicing.

19. Office managers should develop a definite replacement program for their office machines and equipment. Indicate the advantages of such a replacement program.

20. Describe the activities involved in a program of centralized control over the selection, procurement, maintenance, and replacement of equipment.

FOR YOUR DISCUSSION

1. The Hampton Company, an investment consulting firm, is totally remodeling its office. Heated discussions are occurring between executives and administrative support staff about whether the new office furniture should be conventional or modular. You are an expert in the field of office furniture. Explain the advantages and disadvantages of conventional and modular furniture and then make a specific recommendation based on your preference.

2. At a recent national business conference, a well-known office management consultant stated that "office managers today focus too much on economic and tax considerations and too little on the human needs of the office." Discuss.

3. The Tunalaki Company is considering the purchase of automated information processing equipment with an installed cost of $26,000. However, the firm estimates that this investment will be offset by a savings of $7,000 in its first full year of use. Discuss the kinds of additional information, including the human element, needed before a decision is made to invest capital in this new equipment.

4. To understand the importance of good seating and related student learning needs, analyze the workstation provided for each student in your administrative office management class. As a basis for your discussion, use the furniture selection guidelines provided in this chapter as well as other commonsense principles that might apply.

5. Skog Communication Services (SCS) has long had an active program for standardizing office furniture and equipment. Presently, SCS is replacing 400 secretarial and clerical posture chairs at a cost of $45,000. Beth Warning, office manager of SCS, is finding the selection of office furniture and equipment increasingly difficult. Seven competing firms have offered her chairs that not only look alike and operate the same and seem to have the same degree of seating comfort, but also cost nearly the same. Warning wants her selection of a supplier to be a wise one that reflects both economic and human concerns. Discuss the procedure you would follow if you were Warning.

6. A leading management consulting firm, with 65 branch offices in the United States, has recently centralized the purchasing of all office equipment through its headquarters office in Chicago. Each branch office selects its equipment from a manual published by the company. If, for example, one office wishes to purchase a copier, the branch manager investigates the equipment available in the company's manual and requisitions the purchase of the copier through the central purchasing unit in Chicago. What advantages can you cite for this type of centralized procurement of equipment? What disadvantages can be anticipated?

7. For three years your firm has had a service contract on all its office machines but has not taken the time to develop any records to document the service activities on the machines. Recently, your supervisor assigned you the responsibility of setting up a record system that would serve as a history of activities on all office machines in the company. What type of information should such a record file include? How should such a set of records be created and maintained?

CASES FOR CRITICAL THINKING

Case 15–1 Setting Up an Automated Workstation in the Home

Linda Lyons has had seven years' experience with automated processing equipment in the Minneapolis area. After the birth of her son two months ago, she decided to resign her previous position and begin a home-based processing service specializing in word processing and customer billing operations. Lyons has taken a "giant step" by purchasing a personal computer and the software necessary to commence operations. The remaining tasks of laying out the office and procuring the necessary furniture and equipment for her new service business must still be faced.

Lyons has given you the following sketch of the room in her home that will be dedicated to her business:

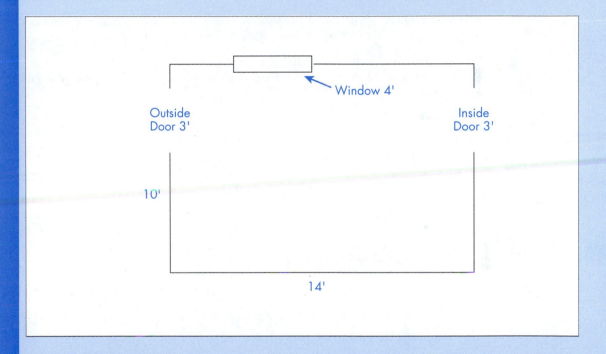

Lyons is not aware of what constitutes an ergonomically sound workplace or an efficient use of office space. Accordingly, she asks you, a student of office ergonomics, to make recommendations to her in a very practical way, for she would like to start her business operations within the next month.

Prepare a brief report in which you discuss an ideal office for Lyons from the standpoint of (1) ergonomics and (2) furniture and equipment. In addition, develop an easy-to-use checklist of furniture and equipment needed for the room to be operational. Include the physical dimensions and typical costs, which may be found in office furniture and equipment catalogs. No office layout is required, although the furniture and equipment recommended must effectively "fit" the area that Lyons has chosen for her office.

c
o
n
t

Case 15–2 Determining Whether to Buy or Lease Office Equipment and Furniture

Wyatt Law Firm recently added five new lawyers in commercial litigation, raising its total size to 22 lawyers practicing in all fields of law. With the recent addition of professionals and staff, Laura Downing, the office manager, realizes that the firm needs to upgrade its microcomputers, adding two word processing production centers (complete with equipment, furniture, and whatever else may be required) and overhaul the workstations for five of the long-term support staff who are using outdated furniture and equipment.

To investigate the problem, Downing has completed a feasibility study that reveals the following information:

1. If purchased, the required microcomputers and word processing equipment would cost $43,375. The annual insurance cost would be $400; the estimated annual maintenance cost would be $1,500.

2. If leased, the lease payments for the equipment over a five-year period would total $48,500, which includes insurance and all maintenance costs.

3. Downing has been assured by a reliable investment consultant that the purchase price of the computers could be invested in another endeavor where the interest on the investment would earn $38,750 over the five-year period.

4. Research needs to be completed on furniture options.

5. Each of the two word processing production centers will support one full-time word processing and data processing operator. For one of the positions, the firm has selected a person who has a preexisting back problem. A general search will be undertaken to fill the second position.

As Downing's assistant, you are asked to (1) determine what additional information, if any, is required to make the decision on what furniture to buy or lease and the advisability of buying or leasing the equipment; (2) recommend whether the equipment should be purchased or leased; and (3) indicate what unique considerations might have to be examined regarding the installation of equipment and purchase of furniture within the law firm setting. Comply with Downing's request in memo report form directed to her.

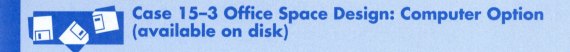 ## Case 15–3 Office Space Design: Computer Option (available on disk)

16

AUTOMATING THE OFFICE

GOALS FOR THIS CHAPTER

After completing this chapter, you should be able to:

1. Identify the basic characteristics of computers and classify them according to purpose and size.
2. Describe the fundamental phases of computer systems technology and the role of each in the flow of data through the system.
3. Compare the traditional office with the modern office in terms of how the main information functions are integrated.
4. Enumerate the most common applications of information technology in the automated office.
5. Explain the role of feasibility studies in planning and organizing automated office systems.
6. Describe the basic methods used to maintain the security of automated office systems as well as important considerations in evaluating such systems.

From their earliest years in elementary school, today's students have become acquainted with computer operations and the many advantages that computers offer. No doubt you have also been using a computer to help you with your class assignments. Away from school, computers affect our lives, too. For example, in many homes we find personal computers used to keep business records, to prepare correspondence, and to file address lists, telephone numbers, recipes, and tax records. When you check out at the supermarket, you may find that a scanner, as an input device to the computer, "reads" the price of each item you buy and a printer prepares a slip that itemizes all the items. At any time of day or night when you find you are short of cash, possibly you drive up to an automatic teller machine (ATM), which dispenses money from your account when you insert your card. Or perhaps you use your touch-tone telephone at home to complete your school registration each semester, or you take classes through a computer hook-up at home. Either directly or indirectly, all of us, in and out of offices, use computer services to process information; in order to use these services effectively, we must become computer literate.

Computer literacy is a broad concept that describes (1) the ability to use or operate a computer or (2) the ability to understand the capabilities of a computer without being able to operate one. Of these two abilities, the second represents the more basic and more widely acknowledged sign of computer literacy. Four areas in which an understanding of computers should be achieved are illustrated in Figure 16–1. The figure suggests that if we understand what a computer *can do* (its capabilities) and *cannot do* (its limitations), *how it can be used* (its applications), and *the effects of its use* (its implications for information systems and office workers), we are computer literate. This figure does not imply, however, that we must be able to program the

Figure 16–1
The Concept
of Computer
Literacy

computer or handle many of the highly technical aspects of managing a computer system.

The purpose of this chapter is to provide sufficient background on computer fundamentals so that you may develop computer literacy, which in turn will provide you with the knowledge to understand office automation and broader information systems. We place special emphasis on office automation because of the vital role that computers play in the office.

THE NATURE AND PURPOSE OF COMPUTERS

The computer is the central information-processing tool in the modern organization. As an information-systems machine, the computer provides incredible power in the office where information is the principal product. Because of this power, work processes have changed, new work skills and new management challenges have appeared, and tighter systems controls are made available to office managers.

When the computer processes words or numbers, some of its operations are automated. Others, however, are not since the computer operates under the direction of people. Thus, *people are still the dominant force in any computer system.*

A *computer system* typically is composed of the following elements:

1. *Equipment* to convert human-readable data (handwritten or keyboarded) into a form that the computer can process. Equipment is also needed for entering and storing data and for later converting the processed data into human language, the output of VDT screens and printers. Usually, the equipment in a computer system is called *hardware.*
2. *Programs,* the instructions or *software,* necessary to operate the computer system.
3. *Personnel* who operate, program, and manage the system.
4. *Procedures and training* that define the proper uses of the system and ensure that the personnel understand the applicable procedures and know how to use the system.
5. *Environmental considerations* and *ergonomics* as discussed in Chapter 14.

Computer technology is the basis for the automated office systems that move information through the organization. Your ability to use the technology available in today's office begins with an understanding of the basic characteristics of computers.

Basic Characteristics of Computers

In general, all computers receive and process information, retain information as needed in the future, and communicate that information to users. In order to do so, all computers share the following basic characteristics:

1. *Electronic circuitry* (switches) through which the computer routes data to be processed. Present-generation computers use *integrated circuits (ICs)* called **microprocessors** built on very small silicon *chips*. These chips can hold more than one million electronic transistors that perform the many types of electronic switching functions necessary to computing operations. A digital watch, for example, holds about 5,000 ICs and a small computer, about 50,000. The number of ICs can be expanded in many computers which, in turn, increases their processing and storage powers. With such expansion, remarkable increases in operating speeds become possible. For example, many computers operate at the *nanosecond* level (one billionth of a second); and even faster speeds, such as *picoseconds* (trillionths of a second) and *femtoseconds* (quadrillionths of a second), are reported.

2. An *internal memory* that receives and stores the data to be processed and the *program* that contains the detailed instructions necessary to process the data. The computer's internal memory is divided into many small sections called *storage locations,* each of which has a specific numeric address much like the address given to a residence in a city. When the address is known, we can easily access the data item "residing" in that storage location.

   The capacity of a computer is measured by the number of bytes that can be stored in internal memory. A **byte** is a computer term for a basic data character, such as a letter, number, or symbol. One common byte format consists of eight bits plus a ninth bit that checks the accuracy of the data represented. (**Bit** is an abbreviation of the term *binary digit,* the basic

value in a numeric system that uses two digits—0 and 1—to represent alphabetic, numeric, and related data within the computer.)

Usually, memory is expressed in terms of thousands of bytes. For example, a computer with 640K has approximately 640,000 storage locations, since the letter *K*—an abbreviation of the word *kilo*—represents 1,000. However, in computer circles, K equals 1,024 bytes. A broader measure of computer memory is the *megabyte (MB)*—1,024K or 1,048,576 bytes. For convenience, this measure is frequently rounded to and expressed as one million; thus, a computer with 40MB actually stores 41,943,040 or about 40 million characters.

3. The *ability to perform mathematical operations and machine logic.* For example, the computer can (a) perform arithmetic operations (addition, subtraction, multiplication, and division); (b) determine if a number is positive, negative, or equal to zero; and (c) "decide" whether one of two numbers, when compared, is equal to, higher than, or lower than the other. (Alphabetic characters are converted to numeric codes and thus can be compared in the same way as numeric data.) Thus, the computer is said to have a "logical" ability when it compares numbers and on the basis of such comparisons moves or advances from one set of instructions to another.

4. The *automated control of input, process, and output activities.* The computer is automated in that it self-regulates the flow of program instructions and data to be processed from the various input devices. It can also perform many processing steps and store or print out the processed information as the program directs without the need for human operators. As a result, labor costs are lowered and productivity in the administrative office system is enhanced.

There is a common perception that all computers are the same. However, some computers, called **analog computers,** measure continuously changing conditions, such as temperature and atmospheric pressure, and convert them into quantities. Analog computer applications are commonly found in refineries, chemical plants, and utilities.

The computers used in business offices are typically **digital computers,** which count numbers or digits while processing numeric and alphabetic data that have been converted to a numeric code. Since most data processed in business are either numeric or alphabetic, only the digital computer is discussed in this textbook.

Sizes of Computers

The most common way of classifying business computers is by *size,* which refers to their capacity for processing volumes of data. Usually computer size is described in terms of the number of storage locations in internal memory (64K, 128K, 256K, 640K, and so on). The largest computers are called *mainframes;* smaller computers, represented by *minicomputers* and *microcomputers,* have less internal memory, fewer input-output (I/O) units, and more limited storage capacity. These different-sized computers also perform at different levels

and speeds for different costs. For example, a $5 million mainframe computer can perform about 50 million instructions per second, or 50 MIPs. This is about $100,000 per MIP. An $800 personal computer (microcomputer) can perform 2.5 million instructions per second. That's about $320 per MIP.[1] Let's examine each of the three kinds of computers specified above in greater detail.

Mainframes

A large computer is referred to as a **mainframe** since it serves as the principal source of power and direction for complex company-wide data processing and telecommunication networks. Mainframes, such as the type shown in Illustration 16–1, provide millions of units of internal memory and can process information at very high

---

[1]John Schneidawind, "Explosive Growth Ahead for Industry," *USA Today* (January 22, 1993), pp. B1 and B2.

Illustration 16–1 Mainframe system.

speeds with millions—and, as indicated earlier, billions—of operations per second. In addition, we find that mainframes often serve as **host computers,** which direct the input, processing, output, and distribution of information to, from, and among a group of small computers. Mainframes are typically located in central data processing departments that are managed by specialists in computer science and data processing systems.

Minicomputers

A small computer equipped with integrated circuits and housed in a compact desk-size or desktop cabinet is called a **minicomputer.** A minicomputer is a direct "descendant" of the mainframe, and, with the addition of integrated circuits, is able to take over many mainframe responsibilities. Minicomputers are capable of supporting a large number of terminals that perform a variety of operations simultaneously. Typical of these operations are the following: accounts payable, sales systems reporting, interest com-putations, and word processing. In addition, minicomputers serve as standalone systems in departments and in small firms or as I/O systems attached to mainframes.

Microcomputers

The smallest and least expensive class of computers is the **microcomputer.** Today, as a result of microprocessor technology and the availability of peripheral devices for entering, storing, and printing data, microcomputers have become more powerful and fully operational. For these reasons, the lines of distinction separating minicomputers and microcomputers are fuzzy.

A microcomputer is designed for use by one person; hence, we often use the term *personal computer* or *PC.* A typical PC, such as the one shown in Illustration 16–2, is placed on a desk and takes up about as much space as a typewriter and a portable television set. Portable PCs are also available. According to most computer hardware tracking services, more than 50 percent of all PCs sold by 1995 will be portable machines.[2] For example, small PCs, called *laptop, notebook, subnotebook,* or *briefcase*

Illustration 16–2 Microcomputer.

computers, weigh from two to ten pounds, have a flat display screen, and can operate up to ten hours on rechargeable batteries. *Hand-held computers* usually refer to pocket computers used for calculations and remote data collection—such as performing inventories, reading meters, and collecting information—which is then sent to the mainframe computer at a headquarters location. For example, Federal Express, with corporate offices in Memphis, Tennessee, has a bin in each of its worldwide locations for its employees' hand-held computers. At the end of each day, the computer is placed into its bin, where it transmits the data to Memphis from all over the world and recharges for the next day's activities.[3] A newer technology that allows users to record on-screen notes is the powerful *Personal Digital Assistant (PDA).* (See Illustration 16–3.) Instead of recording data on a tiny keyboard, PDA users employ a special pen to write commands on the screen for carrying out tasks such as sending FAXes and for interpreting their handwriting to create printed memos.[4]

---

[2]Richard M. Sherwin, "Portables Go Mainstream," *The Spring 1993 Review of Computers,* 1993, p. 12RC.

[3]Discussion on hand-held computers from Kathleen P. Wagoner and Mary M. Ruprecht, *End-User Computing* (Cincinnati: South-Western Publishing Co., 1993), p. 68.

[4]"Power in the Palm of Your Hand," *Business Week* (March 15, 1993), pp. 128–130; Walter Mossberg, "Personal Assistants Lend Users a Hand at the Stroke of a Pen," *The Wall Street Journal* (February 15, 1993), p. B1.

Illustration 16–3 Personal digital assistant.

Portable computers are used by people whose jobs require them to travel extensively and to make computations, prepare reports, and store records en route, as well as communicate to a home office. Most hotels, trains, and airline clubs are equipped with computer modem connections for business travelers with portable computers. Most portable computers are compatible with the larger machines maintained in the home office. Laptops are also used by students who take notes in class and at the library and then write their reports in their dorm rooms.

The PC has revolutionized the computer industry; because of its small size, ease of use, and relatively low cost (usually under $3,000), it has been successfully introduced into all types of offices and into millions of homes throughout the world. In the late 1980s, over 50 percent of small businesses (those with fewer than 100 employees) used PCs.[5] It is estimated that in the early 1990s 40 to 50 million office workers use VDTs daily.[6]

In 1993, 3 out of 10 U.S. homes had a PC.[7] BIS Strategic Decisions (a consulting and marketing research firm) predicts that annual shipments of PCs will have grown from 11 million units in 1990 to 16 million units in 1995.[8] Most of today's managers spend about 75 percent of their working time communicating business information, often using PCs to accomplish this task.[9] *Since its use in the office is the primary reason for the tremendous growth of automated office activities, the PC is the main point of emphasis in the discussion of office automation in this chapter.*

Figure 16–2 provides a visual comparison of the PC with the minicomputer discussed earlier. Note the same types of components found in both systems. Also, observe that the basic PC is limited to one of each component and thus has less processing, storage, and printing power. The five components of the PC system illustrated in Figure 16–2 are:

1. A *central processing unit (CPU),* the heart of the computer system in which computing operations are performed. In the PC, the size of the CPU (measured by the amount of memory provided) ranges from 2MB to 8MB or more as needed. Microcomputers with 2MB hold about 2 million characters, or about 400,000 words of text.
2. A *keyboard* for entering instructions and data into the system and a *display screen (monitor)* for viewing the data. Some screens are capable of displaying 120 characters across and 256 colors.
3. One, two, or three *disk drive* units in which are placed the media (floppy disks 3½ inch and/or 5¼ inch) used to send information to, and store information produced by, the system. One drive unit may hold a hard disk, as described later.
4. A *printer* that produces reports, charts, letters, and memorandums.

5"Small Firm Big on PCs," *The Office* (June, 1989), p. 89.

6Carla J. Springer, "Ergonomics in Computerized Offices: The Time to Act Is Now," *Managing Office Technology* (November, 1993), p. 21.

7Thomas Stewart, "Welcome to the Revolution," *Fortune* (December 13, 1993), p. 70.

8John B. Dykeman, Foreword, *End-User Computing* (Cincinnati: South-Western Publishing Co., 1993), p. iii.

9Kathleen P. Wagoner and Mary M. Ruprecht, *End-User Computing* (Cincinnati: South-Western Publishing Co., 1993), p. 13.

Figure 16–2
A Comparison
of the Micro-
computer and
the Minicom-
puter

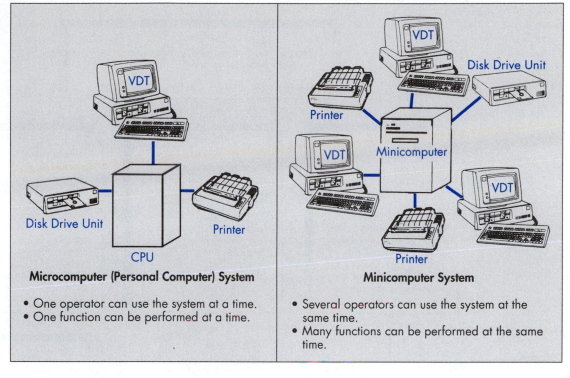

Microcomputer (Personal Computer) System

- One operator can use the system at a time.
- One function can be performed at a time.

Minicomputer System

- Several operators can use the system at the same time.
- Many functions can be performed at the same time.

The desktop PC has become more sophisticated, and its power greatly expanded through more powerful microprocessors, networking capabilities, and operating systems designed to handle many tasks. Computer experts refer to these powerful PCs as *workstations*. At one time, these very expensive workstations were reserved for specific applications such as engineering and design, which involve much work in graphics. Today, however, computer manufacturers are promoting a broader range of uses for these high-powered machines. As a result, the PC and the computer workstation are becoming more and more similar in their features and capabilities. (Remember, from our Chapter 13 discussion, that in our textbook we follow the widespread practice in management and use the term *workstation* to describe a unit of office space planning, which includes the furniture and equipment—computer and noncomputer—used by each employee in performing work assignments.)

Personal computers are **user friendly;** that is, they are easy to operate since they require no technical knowledge. Application programs, which include accounting, payroll, financial planning, graphics, inventory control, production control, word processing, desktop publishing (DTP), personal information management (PIM), and many other applications, are readily available. Also, advances in telecommunications technology provide for the connection of PCs to telephone lines for transmitting data among networks of PCs or to minicomputers or mainframes. In addition, the use of PCs in homes and other nonoffice locations has ushered in *telecommuting,* which was discussed in Chapter 12.

COMPUTER SYSTEMS TECHNOLOGY

In administrative office systems, we find that many technologies are combined to provide an automated environment. Even though they perform a variety of functions, these technologies may be classified according to the various phases of the systems model explained in Chapter 4.

Figure 16–3 outlines the basic systems functions and the means by which they are performed in each

Figure 16–3
Computer
Systems
Phases and
Related Func-
tions

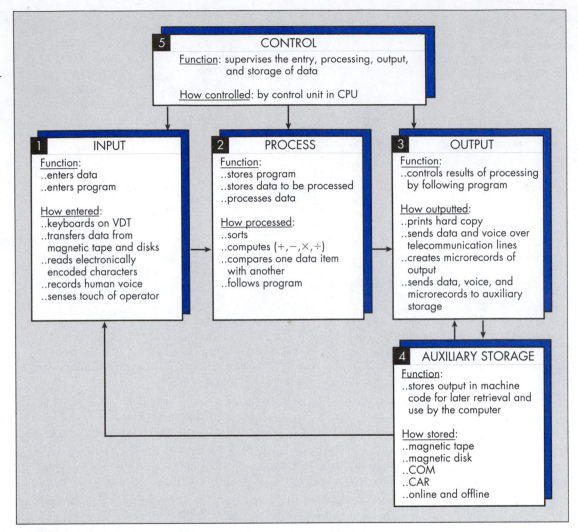

Source: Adapted from Mina M. Johnson and Norman F. Kallaus, *Records Management*, 4th ed. (Cincinnati: South-Western Publishing Co., 1987), p. 335.

of the phases of a computer system. To understand the main concepts shown in this figure, let's examine briefly the most common technologies found in automated offices. (More complex systems are explained in detail in advanced references on computer science and data processing systems.)

Input Technology

Technology must be provided to enter into the computer (input) the data to be processed as well as the program that instructs the computer what operations to perform and in what order. Highly skilled technical personnel, known as **programmers,** write computer programs and plan the conversion of unprocessed data onto one or more media. The most common forms of input to the computer are achieved by using one or more of the following media:

1. *VDTs (video display terminals)* on which the data and the program are keyboarded.
2. *Magnetic tape,* upon which data are coded, as

Figure 16–4
Data Storage
on a Magnetic
Tape Code

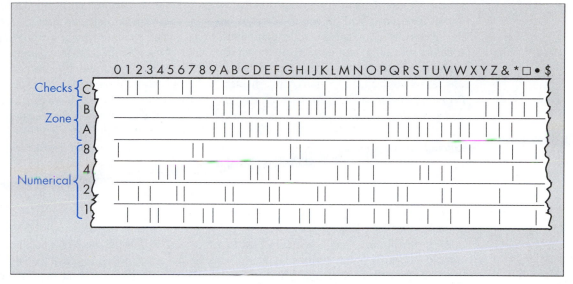

shown in Figure 16–4, and stored as magnetized spots. A typical reel of tape ½ inch by 2,400 feet is mounted on a device called a *tape drive* for use in a large computer system. From this device the contents of the tape are sent as input to the internal memory of the computer.

3. *Magnetic disks,* which provide storage locations on both sides of the round magnetic medium. Data are recorded on a disk in the form of magnetized spots arranged in concentric (parallel) tracks on each recording surface. Figure 16–5 shows the storage of one data record on a magnetic disk. In large computer

Figure 16–5
Data Storage
on a Magnetic
Disk

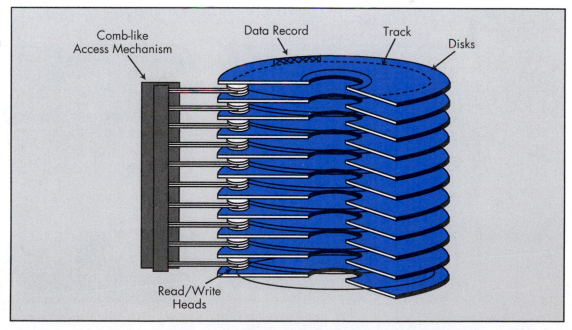

systems, disks are usually arranged in stacks called *disk packs* and placed in a disk drive unit that is used to transfer to the computer's memory the data maintained on the disks. Small computer systems use diskettes, which are discussed in a later section of this chapter.

4. *Scanning devices* that read electronically encoded characters on printed or handwritten documents and thus provide *source data automation (SDA)* whereby data are converted to machine-readable form. SDA bypasses the need for data entry by human operators. Optical-character recognition and magnetic-character recognition readers, discussed in Chapter 19, are examples of this type of device.

5. *Speech* (the human voice), which is used to a limited extent as input to the computer. Two types of speech-recognition, or voice-recognition, input systems have been developed: (a) isolated speech recognition in which the sender is restricted to a limited vocabulary with short pauses between words and (b) continuous speech recognition in which words are spoken in a natural, connected speech pattern. Early voice-recognition systems had tiny vocabularies but the newer systems can recognize up to 50,000 words, or ten times the range needed for routine business correspondence. Further, the new systems do not require a user to spend many hours reading test words into the mike to "train" the machine in the user's voice.[10] Voice-recognition and audio- response systems are discussed more fully in Chapter 18.

6. *Graphics and image devices,* such as:

   a. The *mouse,* a device used to move the cursor (the blinking box symbol or blinking underscore) around on the display screen. As the VDT operator moves the mouse, the cursor moves correspondingly, with great precision and speed, on the screen. The mouse is shown in Illustration 16–4. Another device used to manipulate the cursor is the *trackball.* Here, the user spins the ball, housed in a mounting, to move the cursor at the speed and direction of the ball's motion.

   b. The *light pen,* an electrical device resembling a pen, used for writing or sketching on the display screen to provide input to the computer. As the pen reacts to the light from the screen, the image written or sketched is

---

[10]Gene Bylinsky, "At Last! Computers You Can Talk To," *Fortune* (May 3, 1993), p. 89.

Illustration 16–4 (a) Mouse (b) Touch-sensitive screen.

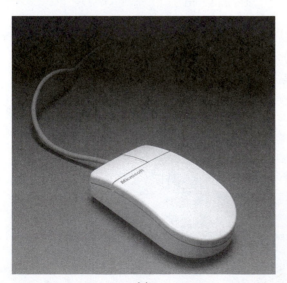

(a)

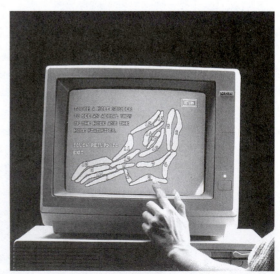

(b)

digitized (converted to a numeric code) by the computer for processing, storing, and printing in the system.

   c. The *touch-sensitive screen* whereby the operator enters commands by pressing designated areas with a finger. For example, by touching a file name listed on the screen, the operator can retrieve a desired file from computer storage. See Illustration 16–4b.

Other input media, such as punched cards and punched paper tape, are generally obsolete and for this reason are not included in this textbook.

Processing Technology

The processing phase in the computer system involves the tasks of receiving input and performing arithmetic, logical, and output operations under program control. The computer unit responsible for this processing is called the *central processing unit (CPU)*, which, as the "brain" of the system, contains the circuits that control and execute the instructions. The equipment and devices that are directly connected to the computer are said to be *online*. This is in contrast with *offline*, which refers to the equipment and devices not directly connected to the computer.

In the CPU, we find three main components as shown in Figure 16–6: (1) the *memory*, (2) the *arithmetic-logic unit*, and (3) the *control unit*, which regulates all processing operations through built-in monitoring capabilities that are beyond the "reach" of the user. The memory unit and the arithmetic-logic unit are explained in this section

Figure 16–6
Sequential Flow of Data in the Central Processing Unit (CPU) of the Computer

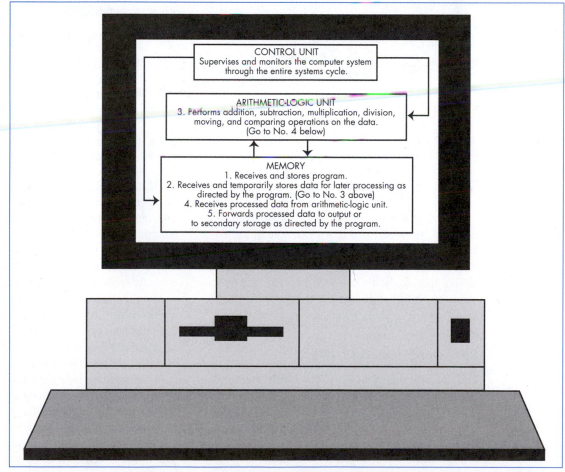

CONTROL UNIT
Supervises and monitors the computer system through the entire systems cycle.

ARITHMETIC-LOGIC UNIT
3. Performs addition, subtraction, multiplication, division, moving, and comparing operations on the data.
(Go to No. 4 below)

MEMORY
1. Receives and stores program.
2. Receives and temporarily stores data for later processing as directed by the program. (Go to No. 3 above)
4. Receives processed data from arithmetic-logic unit.
5. Forwards processed data to output or to secondary storage as directed by the program.

along with a brief description of the process of programming a computer. The control unit is discussed in a later section.

Memory

Memory, or *primary storage,* is an area where data and programs are temporarily stored before, during, and after processing. Whenever a program is entered into the computer, it is either stored in memory where it remains until processing is completed or it is retained in memory until needed for further computing operations. In a similar way, data entered from input devices are placed in memory to be available for processing. However, *no actual processing takes place* in memory; this function is reserved for the arithmetic-logic unit. As we shall see below, there are two major types of primary storage.

Random Access Memory (RAM)

In the **random access memory (RAM),** the array of memory locations on one or more microchips is activated when electrical power reaches the unit. At this time, data can be entered into a memory location without regard to any other memory location. *When the power is turned off, all data in RAM are lost.* For this reason, it is important that we store all processed data in the diskette file before turning off the power.

Some application programs called *memory resident* or *TSR (terminate-stay resident)* are loaded into the RAM when the machine is turned on and continue to operate while other applications are being performed. An example of such a program is a *screen blanker* program which blanks the screen after a preset time period, such as five minutes. This program prevents the permanent burning of an image onto the VDT when the PC is unattended or unused for extended periods of time.

Read-Only Memory (ROM)

The special type of memory, **read-only memory (ROM),** is permanently programmed with one group of frequently used instructions. No additional data or instructions may be stored in the ROM memory. Thus, the program residing in ROM cannot be changed by the user; only its

contents can be read. In contrast to RAM, ROM does not lose its program when the computer's power is turned off.

Both RAM and ROM are *random access,* which means that the computer can go directly (at random) to any set of data without first "reading" each of the sets that have been stored in sequential order.

Arithmetic-Logic Unit

In microcomputers, the **arithmetic-logic unit** is often referred to as a microprocessor, a microchip on which reside the control and arithmetic-logic functions shown in Figure 16–6. In such computers, the data and the programs are brought into the microprocessor and executed one step at a time, after which the results are returned to memory. The processing cycle is repeated until all program steps have been completed. This sequence is shown in consecutive-number order in Figure 16–6.

Programming the Computer

No computer can perform its processing tasks unless it is properly programmed. In order to write an effective program of *instructions,* the programmer must follow the steps in the problem-solving process identified in Chapter 3 and the steps in the systems study cycle discussed in Chapter 4. In particular, these steps are followed:

1. *Analyze the problem and chart the strategy for solving the problem.* Often a *general systems flowchart* using the standardized program charting symbols shown in Figure 16–7 is prepared. In this figure, a general solution to the valuation of an inventory is charted. More specific steps must be created for charting and writing the actual detailed program.
2. *Write and test the program.* In computer systems, the most common programming languages are:
   a. *Business programming languages:*
      (1) *COBOL* (**C**ommon **B**usiness **O**riented **L**anguage)—a high-level language developed for business applications, especially where large volumes of alphanumeric files are handled. (*High-level languages* allow users to write their programs using terms with which

Figure 16–7
A General
Systems Flow-
chart Using
Standardized
Program
Charting
Symbols

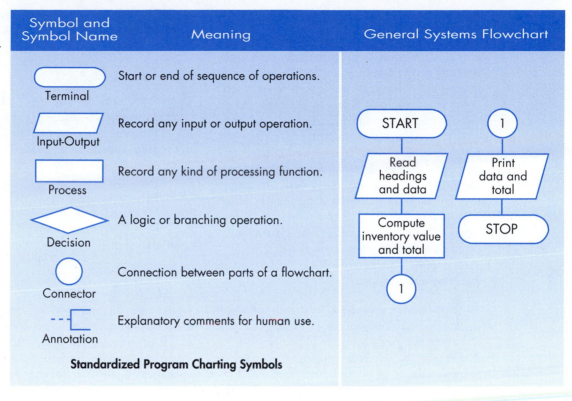

Symbol and Symbol Name	Meaning	General Systems Flowchart
Terminal	Start or end of sequence of operations.	
Input-Output	Record any input or output operation.	
Process	Record any kind of processing function.	
Decision	A logic or branching operation.	
Connector	Connection between parts of a flowchart.	
Annotation	Explanatory comments for human use.	

Standardized Program Charting Symbols

they are familiar rather than using the computer's machine code.)

(2) *RPG* (**R**eport **P**rogram **G**enerator)—a business-oriented language that is highly structured and relatively easy to learn. The language allows users to program many business operations as well as create reports.

b. *Scientific programming languages:*

(1) *BASIC* (**B**eginner's **A**ll-Purpose **Sy**mbolic **I**nstruction **C**ode)—an easy-to-learn, easy-to-use algebraic language with a small number of commands and simple statement formats. Even though the commands are written in a mathematical-equation format for reasons of simplicity, BASIC is widely used in programming instruction, in personal computing, and in business and industry.

(2) *Pascal*—a high-level language, named for the French mathematician, Blaise Pascal, which is easy to use and is taught widely in schools and colleges.[11]

An *application program,* or application software, refers to a computer program written to perform a specialized computer task. Application programs are available from vendors or software firms for many common applications, such as word processing, payroll, and inventory control. Software purchased from vendors is usually copyrighted and thus should not be reproduced without the vendor's permission.

-----

[11]For detailed explanations of the nature and purpose of these programming languages, see James F. Clark and Judith J. Lambrecht, *Information Processing: Concepts, Principles and Procedures* (Cincinnati: South-Western Publishing Co., 1985), Chapters 13–15.

Output Technology

The output, or the results of the computer processing operations, is prepared according to the program instructions residing in the computer. If the end use of the processed data is a report (text copy) or a completed business document, the results will be printed in planned report form or on a business form, such as a customer invoice or a paycheck. If the output is to be used in later computer processing, as in the case of preparing a payroll or updating inventory data, the output may be placed in secondary storage as discussed later. In this case, the data contained in secondary storage are fed back as input to the system for executing another information-processing cycle.

The most common output devices used in computer systems are:

1. *VDTs (video display terminals),* many of which have the capability for displaying copy in color to enhance the presentation of graphics.
2. *Printers* that produce in plain (decoded) language single or multiple copies of the information processed by the computer. We find two types of printers, as explained below.
   a. *Impact printers* that create the printed output by means of movable print heads that strike the paper through a ribbon, thus transferring the impression onto the paper.
   b. *Nonimpact printers* that have no movable print heads; instead, these printers create characters on paper by means of a process (laser, heat, or chemicals) similar to that used by office copying equipment. One example of a nonimpact printer is the new colored laser printer that produces colored pie charts and graphs for attractive presentations.
3. *Voice (audio) response units* that create the human voice in two ways: (a) from a prerecorded set of words stored in memory or (b) from sounds that the computer receives as input and converts to digitized (numeric) form.
4. *Special-purpose output devices,* such as computer output microfilm (COM) and computer-assisted retrieval (CAR) discussed in Chapter 20. Another specialized output device is the *graph plotter,* which is used to make engineering drawings and graphs and charts that are to be reproduced in printed reports.

Storage Technology

Technology provides two types of data storage within the computer system: (1) primary storage in which the data and the program reside temporarily in the CPU's memory unit and (2) secondary or auxiliary storage in which the processed data are stored outside the computer on an online or offline basis. New developments in both types of data storage lowered the cost of storing one million characters of data from \$27 in 1985 to less than \$6 in 1990.[12]

Primary Storage

In addition to the internal storage provided by integrated circuits, another form of primary storage—**bubble memory**—has been developed as a type of miniaturized computer storage. When viewed under a microscope, each unit of storage appears as a small circle, or bubble. In order to represent binary data in bubble storage, the presence of a bubble represents the value of "1," and the absence of a bubble represents a binary value of "0." A one-inch-square bubble package stores 92,000 bits of data in the form of magnetic bubbles that move in thin films of magnetic material. This type of storage provides an economical medium for data storage and, unlike microchip storage, has the advantage of retaining the data in storage when the power is turned off.

Secondary Storage

Secondary, or auxiliary, storage is external storage provided in a computer system because the amount of data that can be stored in internal memory is limited. Secondary storage takes several forms, as explained below.

Magnetic Tape. *Magnetic tape* (see Figure 16–4) is commonly used in large computer systems to store serial (or sequential) information, such as

[12]"Small Disks Can Save a Lot More Than Data," *Business Week* (December 24, 1990), p. 43.

the payroll data, by employee number, for all persons in a firm. Magnetic tape must be placed on a tape drive before the data can be read onto, or read from, the tape. As is true of most magnetic media, magnetic tape may be erased and reused.

Magnetic Disk. By means of a *magnetic disk* (see Figure 16–5), users have direct access to any portion of the tracks on the recording surface. For many operations, this feature is useful as compared with other media, such as magnetic tape, in which unwanted portions of the tape must be sorted through in order to locate the desired data. For example, a disk file provides more efficient storage and retrieval in a college registrar's office since students usually come to the office in random order to get information from their records rather than in alphabetic order.

The **floppy disk** is a flexible diskette made of Mylar™ that is encased in a paper or plastic jacket. The floppy disk resembles a small phonograph record. The data, stored in sectors much like storage on magnetic disks, can be retrieved randomly. Used widely with microcomputers and minicomputers, floppy disks provide storage at relatively low cost. The durable 3½-inch floppy disk is permanently housed within a plastic casing and holds more data than a 5¼-inch disk.

The **hard disk,** made of rigid aluminum, is usually encased within the computer. Since data are stored more closely together on hard disks than on floppy disks, more data can be stored in less space. Because hard disks rotate at a much faster speed than floppy disks, faster retrieval and storage capabilities are possible. Retrieval time is about 10 times faster from a hard disk as compared with the floppy disk.

Optical Disk. Another type of secondary storage uses the **optical disk** (sometimes called the *videodisc*), which is discussed in more detail in Chapter 20. Optical disk storage is created when a laser-beam recorder scans a document, film, or slide and then copies it and transfers the image onto a metal disk. Between 50 and 100 times more data can be stored on optical disks than on magnetic disks, and the cost of storing information on optical disks is only a fraction of the cost of storing data on magnetic disks.

The **compact disc read-only memory (CD-ROM)** is an optical disk used to store large quantities of data. For example, a 5-inch CD has the storage capacity of about 1,500 floppy disks, or nearly 250,000 typed pages. A 20-volume encyclopedia or the entire parts list for all Honda cars can be stored on a compact disc similar to the CDs you buy at a record store. After you have inserted the CD-ROM into a special peripheral on your PC, you can access the information, read it, save it on a floppy disk, or print it. Many CD-ROM applications are found in systems designed to manage the data for libraries, medical centers, and financial institutions.

A powerful application of secondary storage, such as the CD-ROM, is the *database*. As we learned earlier, a database is a central master file that contains company-wide (or, in the case of a large department, department-wide) information from the major systems of the firm. The database concept originated with large computer systems in which data were collected, organized, and stored centrally in a computerized library to be accessed by telecommunication lines throughout the firm. Such an arrangement eliminates duplicate files and the related manual storage and retrieval tasks and provides a single information source that furnishes complete, accurate data storage and retrieval. On the other hand, a database has certain weaknesses that in-

Illustration 16–5 Inserting a 3½-inch disk into a disk drive unit.

clude: problems of security (protecting the confidentiality of stored data), expensive technology and file maintenance procedures, the difficulty of sharing department information for integration into a centralized data file, and the company-wide problems that are created when unreliable equipment causes work stoppages and a drop in office productivity.

With the use of a software package called a **database management system (DBMS),** databases can be distributed, or decentralized, throughout the firm, which allows each user to keep track of an organized collection of files. Thus, any department with a microcomputer can define, create, and process its own set of files on, say, customer records.

On a broader scale, specialized databases are constructed by professional, governmental, and research agencies to provide a huge reservoir of centrally held information for the benefit of subscribers or association members. For example, with a VDT and a communication link, municipal police departments may access state and national databases in search of security and crime-control information. Many of these networks are also connected to the state and federal judicial systems for quick response to inquiries about crime history.

Control Technology

Two types of controls are required to ensure an effective computer system. The first and most important is the set of *human controls* that regulate the performance of managers, supervisors, and workers. (This aspect of control is discussed in a later section.) The second type of control relates to the *technological controls* that must be functioning properly in the system.

An effectively written and properly tested program is a major type of control, for without it the goal of the computer system cannot be achieved. In addition, control resides in the control unit of the CPU, which operates in the following manner:

1. *The control unit processes the instructions recorded in the program.* It directs the various processing operations spelled out in the pro-

gram and checks to see that the instructions are properly carried out.
2. *The control unit also "authorizes" the receipt of information from secondary storage units.* It stores the intermediate results of the operations in *buffer storage,* a temporary storage location, until such results are finally stored in auxiliary storage or are printed out.
3. *The control unit then instructs the computer to prepare the results on the appropriate output devices* (printing, plotting, COM, etc.).

The hardware and software discussed in the chapter up to this point apply generally to all computer systems, unless otherwise indicated. However, in the next section, we shall discuss those major applications in information technology that center on the automated office.

THE AUTOMATED OFFICE

Since the office is the organizational function responsible for all phases of the information system, logically the office should be a prime target for automation. However, many offices continue to use traditional systems and procedures despite the availability of computers. In this section, we examine the nature of the traditional office and its gradual conversion to automated systems. Also, we shall discuss briefly the benefits of office automation.

The Traditional Office: Separate, Manual Functions

The traditional office relies entirely on manual labor that is supplemented by the use of simple hand-operated equipment, such as typewriters, telephones, copiers, calculators, and filing cabinets. In such a setting, letters are dictated and transcribed; incoming and outgoing telephone calls are handled; reprographic equipment is used for copy making; ten-key calculators prove the accuracy of invoices for customer billing; and copies of the records made in all these operations are filed and later retrieved for use.

Each of these common office tasks exists as a separate, somewhat unrelated operation performed by support personnel. Also, each of these tasks is usually carried out in a separate location—in a private secretary's office or in a mailroom, typing pool, reprographics center, microfilm reading room, or data processing department. For office operations, this system results in low productivity, high costs, and an inability to provide the best type and level of services to information users inside and outside the firm.

Despite the tremendous inroads made by computers and other information technology, many of the inefficient practices of the traditional office remain. However, as the costs of technology decrease and the demands of office managers for greater productivity increase, gradually more and more phases of the traditional office are being replaced by automated systems, as discussed in the next section.

The Modern Office: Integrated, Automated Functions

Early in this century, technology focused on the mechanization of information processing with the development of punched-card data processing systems. In these systems, an integrated family of machine functions was developed for recording, storing, processing, and printing information, which was largely numeric. Later, this type of system evolved into a computer-based operation that further integrated the activities found in the information cycle. As time passed, word processing systems were developed as separate systems for storing, processing, and printing alphabetic information (text). Once it was accepted in business, the word processing system began to use the computer and its peripheral equipment for performing a growing number of functions, including communications. (We shall examine word processing systems in detail in the following chapter.) This *integration,* or *merging,* of the two principal information subsystems in the office, in turn, sparked a growing trend toward further linkage of information functions. Thus, the term *office automation (OA)* was coined to describe the integration of computer, communications, and related information technologies to support the administrative service re-

sponsibilities and to improve the productivity of office personnel.

Ideally, OA seeks to create a *paperless* information system, although, from a practical standpoint, creating a *less-paper* office is a more realistic goal. In an OA system, the key steps in the information cycle are handled in the following manner with most, if not all, the steps controlled from one multifunction workstation:

1. *An idea is created and captured* on some type of magnetic medium through the entry of data on a VDT or by using one or more of the input devices described earlier.
2. *The information is processed* in various ways within the integrated system (typically by computer or word processor.)
3. *The processed information is reproduced* by an automated microprocessor-based device.
4. *The processed information is retained* in an automated file for use as needed.
5. *The processed information is distributed electronically* to the user. Hard copies can be made available if desired.

Major Information Functions and Systems

In OA, the five operations listed above are integrated into one joint computer-communications system. To understand such a system, let's review the main information functions and the media, equipment, and systems that are discussed throughout this textbook. These factors, identified within five circles in Figure 16–8, are:

Circle 1. Here, we see the four main forms in which information appears in the office: data, voice, image, and text (words).
Circle 2. This circle shows the basic information-cycle activities that are performed for each of the four forms of information.
Circle 3. In this circle, we identify the formal systems that are responsible for carrying out the information-cycle activities.
Circle 4. To link these four systems functions, we find that the organization requires a local-area network (LAN), similar to that illustrated in Figure 18–4. As we shall see in Chapter 18, a **local-area network (LAN)**

consists of a telecommunication facility that links together the various types of information-processing equipment for transmitting and receiving data.

Circle 5. Finally, this circle shows us the processing power that is available from electronic workstations within the automated office. In such an environment, the computer serves as the major source of automated power and control but is subject to the final decisions of the individuals who have access to the system through terminals.

Automated Workcenters

When discussing the workcenter concept in Chapter 13, we pointed out that in the automated office we find workcenters with VDTs for both the office support (clerical) staff as well as the executives they serve. Let's examine briefly these important facilities of the automated office.

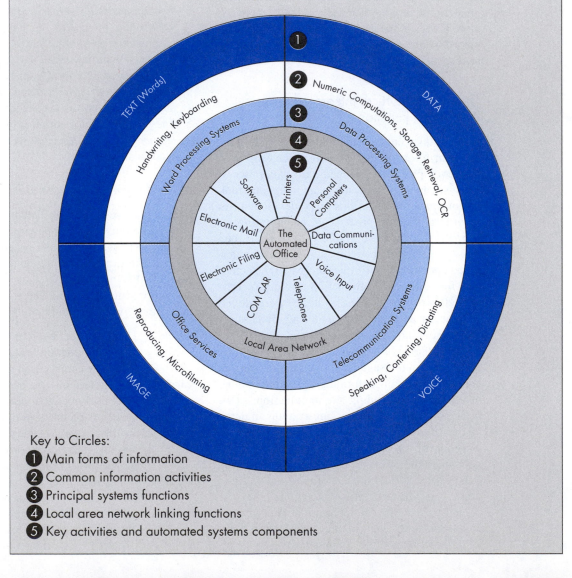

Figure 16–8
Principal Information Functions and Systems in the Automated Office

Key to Circles:
1. Main forms of information
2. Common information activities
3. Principal systems functions
4. Local area network linking functions
5. Key activities and automated systems components

Clerical Workcenters. In the automated office, a *clerical workcenter,* or *clerical workstation,* which includes a VDT, performs many computer-based functions. This workstation links the support personnel (data-entry operators, records clerks, secretaries, and administrative assistants) to the total operating power of the firm's computer system. Through the use of a LAN, a VDT user in the automated office possesses great information-handling power. Depending on the hardware and software available, some or all of the following clerical-support activities may be carried out at the clerical workstation:

1. *Running data processing programs* for making computations.
2. *Performing word processing tasks,* such as preparing letters and reports.
3. *Storing and retrieving information* from the computer and microrecord files and transferring documents from one file to another using database management systems.
4. *Printing out information* processed by the computer or information retrieved from the computer files.
5. *Setting up and maintaining electronic calendars* that schedule meetings, appointments, and teleconferences.
6. *Receiving and responding to messages* stored in electronic mailboxes and other electronic mail systems.

In addition, through the use of a switchboard system (discussed in Chapter 18), the VDT operator can use the telephone for interactive voice and computer functions. Thus, each department with clerical workstations has full access to word processing, data processing, and other technologies provided by the firm for use inside and outside the firm.

Executive Workcenters. Early efforts to automate the office included only the clerical support staff. However, experience has shown that managers and other professionals can improve their productivity if they, too, have direct access to automated systems from their offices. Thus, *executive workcenters,* or *executive workstations,* provide managers with immediate electronic access to the firm's database as well as to outside information sources. This type of workstation offers to the executive information-handling capabilities that include:

1. *Preparing text, graphics, and spreadsheets.* *Spreadsheet* programs display a gridlike formation of rows and columns on the display screen. Each grid box, called a *cell,* is defined by its column-and-row position. As the data stored in any cell are changed, all data and summary totals linked to that cell's content are automatically updated. A spreadsheet program, such as the one shown in Figure 16–9, is often prepared for income statement analysis, budgetary control, forecasting, and other financial analyses.
2. *Receiving and sending electronic mail and voice mail.*
3. *Retrieving data from computer files.*
4. *Checking the electronic calendar* to make sure that all scheduled appointments are met and that no meetings are missed.
5. *Using inside and outside databases.*
6. *Maintaining "To Do" lists* for scheduling tasks in an organized manner.

Corporate officers, such as controllers, planners, and information managers like the AOM, need "push-button" access to information that an executive workstation provides. Being linked to a LAN allows executives to communicate with one another within the firm as well as with support personnel located at the clerical workstations.

Benefits of Office Automation

The office automation concepts and plans for their implementation described in this section are technologically feasible. They exist, however, in varying degrees of completeness. Where OA is properly planned, organized, and introduced to the workers, productivity can be enhanced in the following ways:

1. *Increased efficiency* (tasks are performed in less time with more output from each worker). Thus, we can make better use of human resources, either by reducing the number of employees or having the same number of employees perform more work.

Figure 16–9
A Spreadsheet
Program

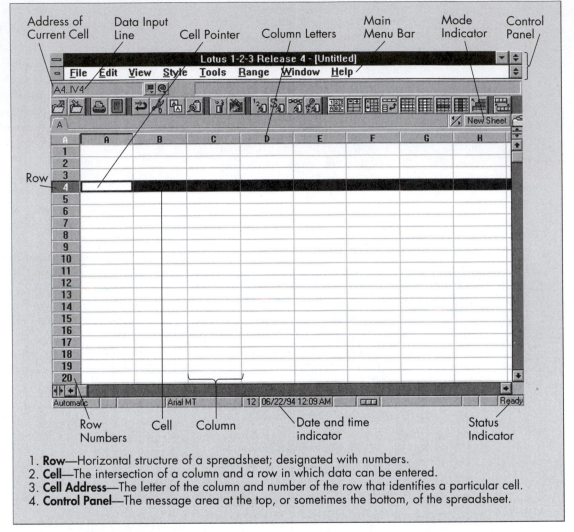

1. **Row**—Horizontal structure of a spreadsheet; designated with numbers.
2. **Cell**—The intersection of a column and a row in which data can be entered.
3. **Cell Address**—The letter of the column and number of the row that identifies a particular cell.
4. **Control Panel**—The message area at the top, or sometimes the bottom, of the spreadsheet.

2. *Greater effectiveness in organizational communication,* including a decreased need for meetings because of electronic mail and teleconferencing, which also decreases the need for travel, and a decreased number of telephone calls since internal communication is carried out via the LAN.
3. *Fewer transfers of control over the work.* For example, word processing operators type and edit their own copy rather than have other persons perform the editing.
4. *Better control over the work.* This includes

fewer interruptions from telephone calls; a reduced need to depend on workcenters in the firm (data processing and word processing centers especially); higher quality of work because of the ease with which revisions can be made with document-creation hardware; and better, more timely, and more accessible information.

Ideally, the benefits of OA may have many positive effects on people. Workers "in tune" with OA experience an improvement in morale,

Illustration 16–6 Scanning a bar code as input to a store's computer.

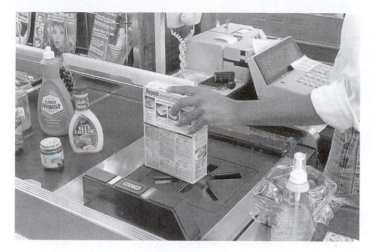

which leads to increased job satisfaction. Faster service leads to increased goodwill and customer satisfaction, and as a result, AOMs and other department managers can better meet the objectives of their individual units.

APPLICATIONS OF AUTOMATED SYSTEMS

Each year we read reports of newly emerging applications of automation. The following discussion briefly examines several applications of automated systems at two levels: (1) mainframe and minicomputer systems and (2) microcomputer systems.

Figure 16–10
The Two-Dimensional Bar Code

A two-dimensional bar code allows greater storage of information in a smaller space. For example, an entire speech the length of Lincoln's Gettysburg Address can be coded onto a space the approximate size of a one-inch square.

Mainframe and Minicomputer Applications

In addition to the computer applications discussed elsewhere in this textbook, several other examples of successful mainframe and minicomputer operations are described below:

1. *Point-of-sale (POS) terminals,* commonly found in retail stores, use the *universal product code (UPC)* on the label of a product. (See Illustration 16–6.) The UPC is sensed by a laser scanner that is built into the checkout counter terminal. The scanner reads the UPC symbol and transmits this code number to a computer that stores price and other information on all items carried in the store. The computer transmits back to the checkstand the item's price and description, which are instantly displayed and printed on the customer's receipt tape. The POS system speeds checkout operations and allows the collection of complete and accurate information for sales analysis and inventory control. The newest development on the bar-code scene is the *two-dimensional bar code (2-D bar code)* (see Figure 16–10). Unlike one-dimensional bar codes which hold 20–30 characters, the two-dimensional bar code stores about 100 times more information—the equivalent of two pages of text—in the same space.[13]

   In some retail stores, we are able to use another computer-based record, the *debit card.* We give our debit card to the checkstand attendant, who inserts it into a device that checks our credit standing. (The retail store has a communication link to our bank's computer where our credit is checked.) If it is approved, the bank charges (debits) our bank account for the amount of the purchase and credits the store's account for the same amount. This paperless transaction eliminates the need for checkwriting.

[13]Mark Alpert, "Building a Better Bar Code," *Fortune* (June 15, 1992), p. 101.

2. *Automated teller machines (ATMs)* are terminals found at scattered locations throughout the country that enable us to deposit and withdraw funds, transfer funds from one account to another, and verify account balances. ATMs are part of the *electronic-funds transfer system (EFTS)* used nationally by banks.

3. A *decision-support system (DSS),* sometimes called an *executive information system (EIS),* integrates data from sources inside and outside the firm into the computer files for use in decision making. Managers use a DSS to project future operating results based on historical and current data, and, by looking at the consequences of a number of alternatives, select a specific course of action.

4. A wide variety of other emerging applications. The technology of *computer-aided software engineering (CASE)* is being used to automate the job of writing computer programs in the same way that computer-aided design and computer-aided engineering have sped up the work and improved quality in product development.

Computers are widely used to *monitor the work of employees* second by second throughout the business day. For example, the computer may be programmed to record the volume of keystrokes per hour, the length of work breaks, the number of errors, and the amount of time airline agents spend with each caller.

Robots, or automated machines for standardizing repetitive tasks, are programmed to perform an increasing number of tasks in the factory, and plans are in place to extend their use to mechanical-type tasks in the office.

The field of computer science known as *artificial intelligence (AI)* uses the computer to perform functions normally associated with human intelligence, such as reasoning, learning, and self-improvement. AI requires the development of mammoth, highly complicated programs and rules that simulate the logical qualities of the human brain. However, certain human qualities, such as creativity, intuition, and empathy present great problems to the specialists working on the advancement of this highly complex computer application.

Personal Computer Applications

Businesses of all sizes use software for specific PC applications such as word processing, spreadsheets, data management, financial accounting, and desktop publishing (discussed in the next chapter). Further, we expect that companies' will realize more savings in these applications through *networking,* as they interconnect their computer systems and terminals. For example, networking enables sales data, entered as part of billing operations, to flow smoothly as the data are fed to the sales department for analysis, to the accounting department for record keeping, to the marketing department for tracking, and to production management for inventory control. The corporate president, when preparing a speech for the stockholders' meeting, can call up from an executive workstation the same sales data for use in the presentation. Thus, networking enhances the efficiency of each application and improves communications within the organization.

MANAGING AUTOMATED OFFICE SYSTEMS

As an information manager, the OM must know what conditions in the office justify the purchase or lease of a computer system and what services managers and supervisors typically expect of such a system. If planning studies show that a computer system is feasible, other managerial problems, such as organizing and operating the system, providing security for the systems operation, and evaluating the system, must be resolved. On the other hand, if an in-house computer system is not feasible or if additional computing power is required from time to time, the advantages of using a data services center should be explored. Each of these aspects of managing automated office systems is discussed in this section. In the *Dialog from the Workplace,* Brother David Nagle, director of development at a residential child services facility, describes several of the challenges that have faced his organization. Note his emphasis on an accurate evaluation of the needs of the organization in establishing a management approach to an automated office system.

DIALOG FROM THE WORKPLACE

BROTHER DAVID NAGLE, SCJ

Director of Development
St. Joseph's Indian School
Chamberlain, South Dakota

Brother David Nagle, SCJ, is a member of the Congregation of the Priests of the Sacred Heart. Brother David received his associate of arts degree in foods and nutrition and bachelor of science degree in business administration from Cardinal Stritch College. After receiving his masters of theology studies at Catholic Theological Union in 1990, he assumed the position of director of development at St. Joseph's Indian School.

St. Joseph's employs 245 people in a variety of ministries, with its primary program being a residential child services facility. All funding for the school and its outreach programs comes from private donations. The development office provides a full line of services from its own printing shop and computer department to a mailing department.

QUESTION: Take a look back, Brother David, and think about your success in managing the various technologies within St. Joseph's Indian School. What skills and competencies have helped the most? What advice do you offer to those who are managing in an automated environment?

RESPONSE: First, you need to understand your business and how you meet the needs of your customers, both in house and outside of the organization. Define the natural divisions of labor for your endeavor and choose managers for each of these divisions.

The team model works best for management. Set aside two days a week for team meetings; one day for policies, procedures, and learning, and the other day for production schedules and labor-related issues. Invite all the managers to share the issues of their operation. Educate all the managers about the other departments so everyone can see how their roles relate and interconnect.

Since managers are learning about other areas of the operations, see where employees can share related jobs. Cross-train employees within a department and between departments. This promotes an understanding of the job functions for all departments.

Periodically update managers in the progress they are making in their positions. Give them feedback on how the entire operation is doing. In a more general, less detailed way, explain the current situation to the entire staff. Let them know what is going on and how they can and do influence the final outcome.

The most important aspect of the operation is computer services, or information management. Let the organization direct the selection of the hardware and software. Bigger hardware is not always better in the area of information services. It is easy for an MIS manager to try to answer the organization's needs by putting in a larger computer or more hardware. If the software and skill levels of the staff are not there, the software and hardware are useless.

Be critical of proposed hardware and software changes. Let your MIS department demonstrate the value and ease of using all products. The user of the hardware and software should decide what is best for your organization. Involve managers and staff in the final selection and then pick the final product to purchase.

The key is team involvement. Ask questions of managers and staff to keep communications going. Praise good work; challenge when needed; give constructive feedback constantly. Together, as a team, the organization can fill its mission if everyone has a chance to be a part of the process through both the difficulties and rewards.

Planning and Organizing Automated Office Systems

Office managers must understand the computer's capabilities in order to make intelligent decisions about which administrative office systems to computerize and which operations to perform using more traditional methods. Such information is usually obtained from a *feasibility study,* which, as we saw in Chapter 4, is conducted to determine whether a system can be improved and, if so, whether a computer can be economically justified for the system under study.

Conducting Feasibility Studies.

A feasibility study group analyzes the information needs of the firm, the proposals of the computer manufacturers for meeting the firm's needs, and the attitudes and opinions of the staff concerning the improvements needed in the administrative office system. Although the study may point to the need for computerizing the system, on occasion the OM finds that the investment in the feasibility study returns a dividend whether or not it is decided to install a computer. For example, such a study often identifies tasks that no longer need to be performed or that can be performed more effectively with the present equipment. In addition, undertaking a feasibility study often increases communications across department boundaries, provides greater insight and understanding of the human and information interrelationships within the firm, and improves morale on the part of those who participate in the study. Finally, a feasibility study helps to justify the purchase or lease of a computer and its related equipment.

Generally, a computer is feasible when the following conditions exist in the office information system:

1. *Large volumes of data input, many reusable data files, and frequent references to these files.*
2. *Speedy processing and accurate reporting requirements.*
3. *Regularly scheduled information processing,* such as the weekly payroll or a daily inventory update.

4. *Continuous need for current management information.*
5. *A high probability of reducing the unit costs of processing the data.*
6. *The possibility of providing better service to customers* as a result of more quickly and accurately processing their orders.
7. *The ability to expand the system* if conditions warrant.
8. *High volume of organizational memorandums.*

Top managers are interested in studying answers to all the questions asked in the feasibility study. The overall costs of installation and operation and the quality and speed of maintenance are also important considerations. Figure 16–11 provides a set of guidelines that will assist the managers of small offices in selecting PCs.

In addition, managers are interested in the possibilities for the "coordinated office of the future"—an office software system that would connect computers, phones, copiers, FAX machines, and printers into a seamless digital web, thus permitting office staff to exchange information and circulate documents electronically.[14] For example, a person writing a document on a PC could instantly order 100 copies with just a click of the computer mouse—instead of printing the document on a printer, taking the document to the copier, and making the copies.[15] Many organizations are actively working to develop and implement such a "coordinated office" approach, as described in Figure 16–12.

Establishing Automated Office Systems

Various plans for establishing an automated office system are possible, depending on the size of the computer and the goals set for the system. In a small firm, the responsibility for all phases of the minicomputer system might be assigned to the OM; the system itself might be located in a small computer center. The department in charge

---

[14]Thomas McCarroll, "Ending the Paper Chase," *Time* (June 14, 1993), p. 60.

[15]Evan Ramstad, "Microsoft Will Unveil Its Version of Coordinated Office of the Future," *The Philadelphia Inquirer* (June 9, 1993), p. C8B.

Figure 16–11
Checklist for
Use in Micro-
computer
Selection

Selection Factor	Points to Consider
1. Systems capabilities	Word processing and spelling check, database management, financial spreadsheeting, graphics, desktop publishing, personal information management (PIM) and other software applications needed.
2. Hardware	Computer, a monitor (display), at least one disk drive, and a printer. To display graphics, a graphics monitor and an adapter are needed.
3. Memory capacity	At least 2–4MB, but for a few hundred dollars more, investigate RAM up to 16MB; try to get the most memory for the money.
4. Hard disk storage	A minimum of 60MB, unless there are many applications with extensive data files, for which more storage is needed. Check access time, since some hard disks are faster than others. An access time of 80 milliseconds (thousandths of a second) is not exceptional.
5. Expansion slots	By inserting expansion cards into the PC slots, graphics, extra memory, a modem, multimedia, or a hard disk can be added. A few vacant slots provide flexibility for expansion.
6. Training	Little need to learn to write programs but need to learn how the machine operates and how to run programs.
7. Maintenance and repair	Investigate community and other users to determine sources of reliable service at reasonable rates.
8. Best computer to purchase	Depends on the needs of the user, the tests made on competitive brands, and the reputation of various computers for providing reliable service.
9. Amount of money to spend	Depends on the funds available for purchase or lease, the amount of processing power required, and the amount of RAM needed to store and run the application software.

of the computer may be organized with a basic staff consisting of a programmer-analyst, a full-time programmer, a computer operator, and a small data-preparation group—all reporting to the computer center manager. A larger computer system requires the same type of organization, which, in turn, would merit a larger and more specialized staff, perhaps reporting to the director of information systems or to a vice president or director of administrative services.

The widespread adoption of microcomputers in offices of all sizes expands the organizational possibilities for managing computers. In the small office with, say, ten or fewer workers, several PCs may be managed by the OM on a day-to-day basis. A large firm having a mainframe as well as microcomputers may centralize the control of all computers under the person in charge of the computer center even though the machines may be physically located in all departments.

The personnel using the computer systems hardware and software must be carefully chosen, properly trained, and regularly supervised. The Institute for Certification of Computer Profes-

Figure 16–12
An Office Au-
tomation
Scheme for
the Coordi-
nated Office
of the Future

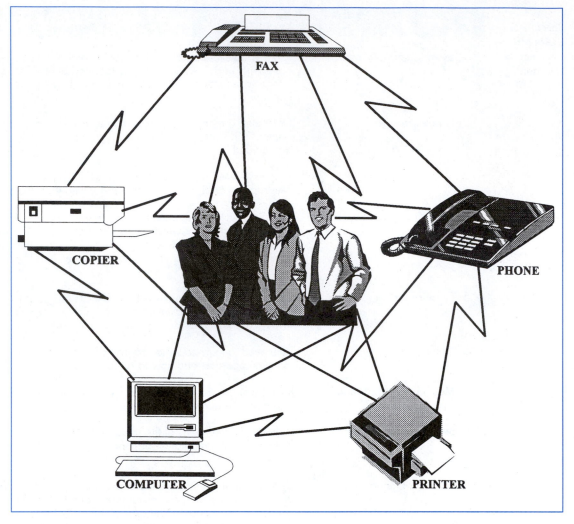

Figure 16–12
An Office Automation Scheme for the Coordinated Office of the Future

sionals (ICCP) maintains a program for certifying data processing personnel. Individuals who pass the certification requirements earn the designation Certified Computing Professional.

The OM should be acutely aware of the effects on noncomputer personnel when additional hardware is brought into the firm. Fear of layoff, transfer to another job or department, and mandatory early retirement are typical personnel problems that must be given equal attention along with the efficient use of the equipment in the system. By using all available human resource media—company newsletters, bulletin boards, and department meetings—to inform the workers of planned changes several months before the installation date, some of the employees' fears can be averted. But perhaps the best method of allaying fears is for the office workers to spend several hours of hands-on time just "getting to know" the PC. Its simplicity, ease of use, and unusually great operational capabilities alone will "sell" the users on its many advantages. Many organizations involve their staff in evaluating and selecting equipment to allay fears and establish "ownership" among the users of the equipment.

Maintaining the Security of Automated Office Systems

To maintain the security of automated office systems and to preserve automated records, here are some steps that can be taken:

1. *Protect magnetic media* from improper handling and storage. Just as magnetic tape and floppy disks are sensitive to abuse, hard disks are sensitive to dust and physical shock.

2. *Provide a backup copy of magnetic media* for control purposes. Usually two magnetic tapes—the original and a copy—are made. The accuracy of such records is maintained in several ways: (a) by internal computer checks, (b) by means of carefully tested computer programs, and (c) by verifying the accuracy and completeness of the data before the data enter the computer system.

3. *Establish safeguards that prevent unauthorized entry into the automated system.* The availability of VDTs throughout an organization makes it possible for many employees to access automated files. To guard against the unauthorized entry into an automated system, the OM should consider the use of: (a) *passwords,* which are special words, codes, or symbols that must be presented to the system in order to gain access; (b) *encryption systems,* which scramble data in a predetermined manner at the sending point and decode the data at their destination in order to protect confidential records; (c) *call-back systems,* which require the computer to verify that the person requesting data is authorized to enter the system, after which the computer calls back such approval to the requesting party, (d) *keys and cards,* which give access to physical locations and computers by way of a special key or magnetically striped card similar in appearance to a credit card; and (e) *personal attributes,* such as voice or fingerprints, which determine whether an individual is to be granted access.

4. *Use security measures to protect the information in internal memory.* Fluctuations in electrical power, called *power surges,* can alter or even destroy the data within the machine. By installing an inexpensive *power surge protector* in the electrical outlet, you can eliminate this problem. However, if the power surge is strong enough, the power may be shut off to equipment, causing data loss.[16]

Another form of security is the *uninterruptible power supply (UPS).* The UPS is a box-like electronic device that is connected to the computer through a cable. If the electrical power source should fail, the UPS provides a few minutes up to an hour of reserve power for the major units, such as the CPU. This reserve power allows enough time to safely shut down the system before the data are lost. In addition, there are *standby power supplies* that switch on power supplied by a built-in, backup battery when the normal electrical level falls below the specified limits.

Worldwide publicity was given in the late 1980s to another computer systems risk, the *computer "virus,"* which is a contamination of a computer program. The security problem is created when a programmer buries within the software a "virus"—lines of hidden code that cause "out-of-memory" messages, printing problems, and application malfunctions. Running the infected program damages or destroys the software or database files, which results in inaccurate, incomplete, or distorted output, or no output at all! Further, modems and LANs can pass the virus on to other programs and thus infect an entire group of computers that share the same files.

To fight a potential virus invasion, systems analysts recommend: buying a virus detector and/or virus treatment software package to check for the presence of viruses on any existing software; making backup copies of each software package as soon as the package is opened; and, from that moment on, making copies once a month along with the data entered into the system during that month; reviewing carefully all

---

[16]Kathy Yakal, "Surge Protectors and UPS Can Save Time and Money," *Office Systems92* (February, 1992), pp. 38–41.

software before installation; and checking regularly for changes in the size of software programs, for such changes may indicate human tampering with the programs.

Along with the above dangers to security, earthquakes, fires, tornadoes, and other disasters pose threats that can damage or destroy a computer system. Contingency planning for such catastrophes should be part of any security plan. For example, the *disaster recovery plan* should provide for off-site storage of backup computer data, along with a procedures manual that spells out the steps to be taken to recover the data on another computer in a remote location.

Evaluating Automated Office Systems

OMs evaluate automated office systems for the same reason that other systems are evaluated—*to determine how well they are meeting their objectives.* Thus, the computer center or the PC in an individual workstation must maintain a high level of work performance in order to meet user needs. The following objectives of computer systems are useful in the evaluation process:

1. *To provide reasonable assistance in solving the data and word processing problems of users.* For example, users may be advised to assign preprinted numbers to basic documents, such as bank checks, purchase orders, and invoices, to facilitate accounting for all such records.
2. *To provide effective control over data preparation.* For example, controls should be designed so that there is checking at each step of data preparation (recording and verifying). These steps eliminate the chance of transcription errors and ensure accurate input.
3. *To identify and count all source documents brought to the computer for processing.* This may entail issuing a document receipt that shows document count; first and last document number, if consecutive; and the total number of documents in the batch to be processed.
4. *To use standard procedures for returning doc-*

uments to the originators for correction before processing.
5. *To use only properly tested programs to be sure that all output meets the goals of the system.*
6. *To maintain reasonable turnaround time schedules with little variation from one processing period to another.* These adjustments can cause employee morale problems and delay the completion of work.
7. *To reduce the costs of processing data.* Today, a small business (or a department in a large firm) can purchase a desktop computer system for less than $3,000 and obtain more computational power than provided by the minicomputers of the 1970s and the mainframes of the 1960s. Around 1996, the desktop computer will be roughly equivalent in power to the largest mainframe in existence in 1988.[17]
8. *To maintain tight control over the information stored in computer files.* For individuals, protecting the confidentiality of social security numbers is one prime example of information controls, for this information is widely used by credit bureaus, retail stores, banks, major oil companies, check validation services, utilities, hospitals, motor vehicle departments, employers, and schools and universities. The risk to maintaining security will only grow greater as the number of people having access to computers increases. Currently, some 50 million people have direct access to computers. Over the next few years, the spread of microcomputers will dwarf that number. By the year 2000, the worldwide PC population will reach into the billions and the ways in which we employ computers will have expanded.[18] As a result, maintaining tight control over stored information will become a greater challenge. Occasionally, managers turn to a data service center for assistance in processing their firms' data. A **data service center,** or *service bureau,* is an

---

[17]Dr. James Martin, *The Consultant's Forum,* International Edition, Volume 3, Number 4, Digital Equipment Corporation, 1988.

[18]Kathleen P. Wagoner and Mary M. Ruprecht, *End-User Computing* (Cincinnati: South-Western Publishing Co. 1993), p. 270.

independent, profit-making organization that specializes in processing data for customer firms. Such centers may be used during peak-load periods when a firm's equipment is not adequate to handle all its needs. OMs find that such an arrangement has many advantages that include: no large investment in computer hardware and software; accurate work; a pre-arranged turnaround time; savings in the unit cost of processing data because of the service center's skilled personnel, efficient programs, and up-to-date equipment; savings in payroll taxes and employee benefit costs because the user's staff is not increased; and maximum convenience provided the user, such as on-site pickup of data and delivery of processed information. We also find organizations making use of **outsourcing**—using external computing centers to handle their internal data processing needs. With outsourcing, a company pays only for that share of the computer storage and processing time it uses. Advantages of outsourcing include the ability to reduce overhead, forego expensive equipment maintenance, and avoid buying larger computers each time a company's data processing demands grow.

SUMMARY

1. This chapter discusses in detail computers and their basic characteristics, which include: electronic circuitry; internal memory; ability to perform mathematical operations and machine logic; and the automated control of input, process, and output activities.

2. Business computers are digital computers and are classified by size. Large computers or mainframes control the data processing needs of entire firms; small computers (minicomputers and microcomputers) operate within departments or in small firms.

3. Input technology in computer systems includes the following: VDTs (video display terminals), magnetic tape and magnetic disk drive units, scanning devices, speech, and various graphics and image devices.

4. Processing occurs in the central processing unit (CPU) where the arithmetic and logic operations are performed. Primary storage in the computer system is provided in the integrated circuits and, to a lesser extent, in bubble memory. Secondary storage is provided on magnetic tape, magnetic disk (floppy disk and hard disk), and optical disk such as the CD-ROM used in database management systems. All of these operations are regulated by the CPU's control unit.

5. The major kinds of output are the hard copy produced by printers, data displayed on the VDT screen after processing, voice (audio) response units, and special-purpose output devices such as COM, CAR, and graph plotters.

6. The automated office integrates its principal operations into one unified system. Integration is made possible by the use of a communication link (the local-area network) capable of transmitting data, voice, image, and text. Two sites for such information transmission are clerical workstations (for support personnel) and executive workstations (for professional and managerial personnel). Ideally, each workstation, or workcenter, interacts with other workstations and thereby increases the effectiveness of communications and systems operations.

7. Before a computer system is installed, a feasibility study should be conducted to justify the acquisition of a computer and its related equipment. If such a system is justified, it should be set up and competent personnel selected to keep a watchful eye on operating costs and to maintain security over the information in the files. Whenever a firm's computer facilities are not adequate to handle its needs, a data service center in the community should be consulted.

FOR YOUR REVIEW

1. Explain the concept of *computer literacy,* indicate its importance in the modern office, and list the elements of a computer system.

2. List the basic characteristics that computers have in common.

3. Describe the interrelationships among the three types of computers—mainframe, minicomputer, and microcomputer—in a business firm.

4. What is the relationship between personal computers and microcomputers?

5. What kinds of portable PCs do we find in use today?

6. What are the five components of a PC system?

7. What are the common forms of input in computer systems?

8. Define the differences between the two major types of primary storage—RAM and ROM.

9. What is the purpose of the arithmetic-logic unit in the computer's central processing unit?

10. Describe the most common forms of output technology used in computer systems.

11. What are the major differences between the primary and the secondary, or auxiliary, storage of data in a computer system?

12. Explain how human controls and technological controls operate in a computer system.

13. Compare traditional offices with modern offices in terms of the organization and operation of basic information functions. Include office automation and the role of the computer in automating the office.

14. Explain the capabilities and various activities that can be performed at clerical and executive workstations.

15. Discuss the principal benefits of office automation.

16. Discuss four common computer applications of mainframe and minicomputer operations.

17. Explain how companies may realize additional savings through the use of networking in their PC applications, such as data management and financial accounting.

18. Why is a feasibility study undertaken? What happens after the study is completed?

19. What is the "coordinated office of the future"?

20. Describe the measures that may be taken to maintain the security of automated records.

21. What are the objectives that an office manager uses to evaluate a computer system?

22. What advantages does an effective data service center hold for a small business firm?

23. What is outsourcing? What are its advantages?

FOR YOUR DISCUSSION

1. An experienced programmer told your class last week that "ATMs operate, in principle, just like the bar-code readers in supermarkets or the scanners that are used to check out library books." Do you agree with this statement? Discuss.

2. Knowing that you plan a college major in business, your parents have offered to buy you a personal computer for use in many of your classes. But first they need some information and have asked your advice with this statement, "We need to know what type of computer you'd like and some estimate of its cost." You are happy to comply! Outline for them what type, size, and model of computer and peripheral equipment you prefer and what other equipment and supplies are needed. Also, provide them with an estimate of the costs for this purchase and a brief list of the advantages your preferred model will give you as a student.

3. As you walk around your campus, what additional uses of computers do you find that are not discussed in this chapter? Also, what types of work are being performed manually that you think should be computerized?

4. Before making a decision to obtain a computer for a firm, the benefits and costs of such a system must be determined. Identify the major costs and benefits of such a system. Which factor—costs or benefits—is more objective and easier to determine? Why?

5. A year ago, Darren Morgenstern, your neighbor, purchased a personal computer for use in his rapidly growing stamp business. He has used the computer for inventory and billing applications but is not convinced he is getting enough "mileage," as he calls it, out of his machine. Morgenstern knows of your background in systems and personal computers and asks you to help in evaluating how well he is using his system. Discuss how you would comply with his request.

6. The manager of the accounting department in which you are employed as supervisor of accounts receivable has just told you that all accounting operations will be fully computerized within three years. The manager justifies the decision to computerize by making statements such as: "Having a PC on each desk will help us reduce staff. The computers will prevent workers from forgetting to enter their transactions. Getting a computer will help eliminate our rapid personnel turnover in the accounting department." Evaluate your manager's reasons for having decided to computerize the accounting operations.

7. Assume you are a senior manager in a large investment firm. You have just received the company's monthly newsletter which discusses a possible plan to automate your office at the management level by giving a PC to every senior manager (there are 18 senior managers). After reading the newsletter, you discuss the proposed expansion with other senior managers and discover three very different reactions: (a) some of them are uncomfortable with using computers and are fearful of the change and how their work production may be evaluated once the computers are operational; (b) some have no particular interest in computers and don't see the advantages of implementation at the senior management level; and (c) a few have innovative ideas for implementation strategies and possible new programs that might be used for research and reference purposes in the firm. What is YOUR reaction to the proposed idea? If asked to serve on a committee to develop an implementation plan for this proposal, what kinds of criteria would you recommend be used in the selection and implementation of the proposed system?

8. Your friend, who is studying for a Ph.D., knows you are taking computer courses and seeks your help in acquiring a computer for her immediate needs of writing her dissertation and for her future career as an educator. She asks you to provide a plan for purchasing a computer system that will satisfy both of her needs. She has indicated she would like to be able to make charts and graphs as well as use graphics to complement her text. What type of PC would you recommend and what further questions would you ask to determine the user's needs?

CASES FOR CRITICAL THINKING

Case 16–1 Determining the Feasibility of an Automated Office System

The television station where you work is having more and more difficulty in scheduling and controlling its commercial advertisements. All too often, advertisements purchased by clients are not aired at the appropriate time. The reason for this problem appears to be that the paperwork is not processed in time for the production department to produce the commercials. As a result, the programming department is unable to prepare an accurate schedule of the commercials on the daily programming log.

With advertisements not being aired at the clients' requested times, sales have fallen off and profits have been drastically reduced. As a result, there has been a sense of frustration and hostility among the personnel in the sales, production, and programming departments.

Currently, when a commercial advertisement is sold to a client, the salesperson writes an order request, which states the content of the ad, the dates and times the ad is to air, the price of the ad, and other billing information. The order request is given to the sales department secretary, who types the information from the order request on three different forms: (1) a billing form that is sent to the accounting department to initiate the process of billing the client, (2) a production request that is sent to the production department to request production of the ad, and (3) a start order form that is sent to the programming department to authorize the entry of the commercial on the daily programming log.

When the requests are received by the various departments, personnel in those departments must enter the information into their record-keeping systems. Currently, only the accounting and the programming departments use computers to keep such records. However, their computer systems are not compatible.

Julie Burns, the new general manager, has decided that something must be done to curb the loss in revenue. She believes that some type of computerized system is needed to overcome these problems and has asked you to suggest ways to improve the present system of processing information—the sales orders in particular. You know that Burns is interested in automating the process; however, you also realize that she is not "sold" on office automation because of the costs associated with it.

To complete this assignment, provide answers to the following questions:

1. What is the problem that exists at the television station?
2. What approach do you recommend be taken to alleviate the problem?
3. In your opinion, what are some major considerations that will help determine whether it is feasible for the station to computerize its information-processing activities? Discuss.
4. Assuming it is feasible to automate, discuss the type of computer system you recommend be installed.

cont

Case 16–2 Responding to Computer Security Threats on Campus

You are employed by the University of Nanicoke, a large 40,000-student research university located in a major metropolitan area, as the head of the computer labs around campus (approximately 15 different lab locations in all kinds of departments and divisions). Recently, a number of students have been breaking into the college computer network as "hackers" and changing their test scores for various courses. In addition, campus police confiscated a poster prepared by an unknown person threatening to introduce a computer "virus" into the campus computer network that would effectively erase existing data and cause all VDT screens around campus to show a graphic of a nuclear bomb exploding. It is clear that existing procedures to maintain security of the computer network are inadequate, and central administration has asked you to prepare a memorandum addressing possible solutions to the threats posed to the university computer network. Specifically, you are to make recommendations in memo form to establish a security system that will protect the campus from intrusion from outsiders and prevent destruction of data. Be sure to specify all the alternatives available to the university to combat these threats and then specify which options you favor for this situation and why.

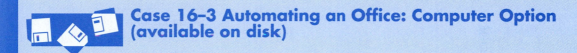

Case 16–3 Automating an Office: Computer Option (available on disk)

17

UNDERSTAND-ING TEXT/ WORD PROCESSING SYSTEMS

GOALS FOR THIS CHAPTER

After completing this chapter, you should be able to:

1. Define the role of text/word processing in the preparation of verbal messages.
2. Describe the responsibility of senders/receivers in the written communication process and why written communications are important in the office.
3. Understand the key written communication media and their purposes.
4. Explain the role of text/word processing in the communication process in manual and automated systems.
5. Recognize the need for networked text/word processing in the office.
6. Understand the main features of text/word processing in the management of text.
7. Explore the various organizational structures of text/word processing.

In Chapter 5, we highlight the vital role that communication plays in the office and describe the various forms of verbal and nonverbal communication. Nonverbal communication, especially that dealing with human gestures, actions, and related behavior patterns, occurs more frequently than verbal communication. However, verbal communication, which deals with *words* (both oral and written), receives more attention. This is true because the most important activities in the office are based on verbal communication. For example, meetings are held (oral communication) to discuss important changes in company products, services, and policies. During such meetings, minutes (notes) are taken and ultimately converted into written documents needed for the operation of the firm. In our research we find that these documents—and the many related records that "flow" from them—receive continued use in the office rather than the oral discussions that take place during conferences and meetings. Further, we see that, on the average, *nine out of ten pages created by business are strictly alphanumeric;* the remaining one out of ten pages requires some type of illustration, from simple ruled outlines or boxes to statistical graphs to the reproduction of photographs.[1]

To handle this vital function of producing written communications—now popularly known as **text**—organizations apply the latest information technology. Under the "umbrella" term **text management (TM),** we find systems that electronically and/or mechanically capture or enter, process, output, and store words and sometimes graphic images. Thus, *TM is to words what a data or computer system is to numbers.* But text means more than words; it means words used to create meaning in messages, usually in sentence form.

---

[1]David Barcomb, *Office Automation: A Survey of Tools and Technology,* 2nd ed. (Bedford, MA: Digital Press, 1989), p. 135.

This chapter discusses the role of written communications in office administration. From this discussion, you should understand that (1) the written communication process is a subdivision of the total communication system in the office, and (2) we now have many different methods of producing written communications. (In the next chapter, we discuss how these messages are sent to their ultimate destinations.) Thus, the contents of this chapter focus on the modern administrative services concept for producing written communications—word processing and a related tool, desktop publishing.

Shortsighted managers often make the mistake of believing that the production of text is solely a secretarial or an administrative support responsibility and hence give little or no thought to its management. Farsighted managers, on the other hand, realize that *the production of effective written communications is one of their foremost administrative responsibilities* and thus take the necessary steps to ensure that effective TM systems are operating in their firms.

WRITTEN COMMUNICATIONS IN THE OFFICE

For decades, bulletin boards in offices have promoted this conservative message-sending practice:

PUT IT IN WRITING!

Such a suggestion clearly implies that written messages offer tangible evidence (that is, a record) of business transactions. Written messages provide security to message senders, since such messages can be reviewed whenever necessary; oral messages, on the other hand, are easy to forget and misinterpret.

As we saw in Chapter 5, the preparation, analysis, and transmission of written communications constitute a major portion of the work performed in all offices. Such text messages are usually recommended when the following conditions exist:

1. The message is long (and hence difficult for a listener to recall precisely).
2. The message is complex and detailed, requiring much study.

3. The message must serve as a record for reference from time to time.
4. The speed of transmission and feedback is not of primary importance. If these factors are important, oral communications are recommended.

Written communications are recorded messages, such as letters, memorandums, and reports, by which we transmit information from senders to receivers. As such, written communications represent an application of the communication process model illustrated in Figure 5–1, page 106. In the case of written communications, the sender is a writer and the receiver a reader, both of whom have responsibilities to ensure the effectiveness of the messages sent. In this section, we discuss the responsibilities of senders and receivers and the most common written communication used in the office.

The Written Communication Process

As background for understanding how the written communication process works, we should be able to answer these questions:

1. Where does the message-creation process start?
2. What role does information technology play in this process?
3. To what extent is the process of creating written messages dependent upon human skills, perceptions, and the motivation to fulfill human needs?

The answers to these questions are rooted in each person—the AOM, the office supervisor, and the office employees themselves.

Usually, we create a written communication in the office as a response to a stimulus received. For example, we receive telephone calls or letters from customers that stimulate us to respond. Most office communications are based on this stimulus-response pattern. When the response to a stimulus requires a written communication, a highly complex process is required to prepare, send, receive, and understand written messages, using a wide variety of information-processing hardware and software. Figure 17–1 shows this

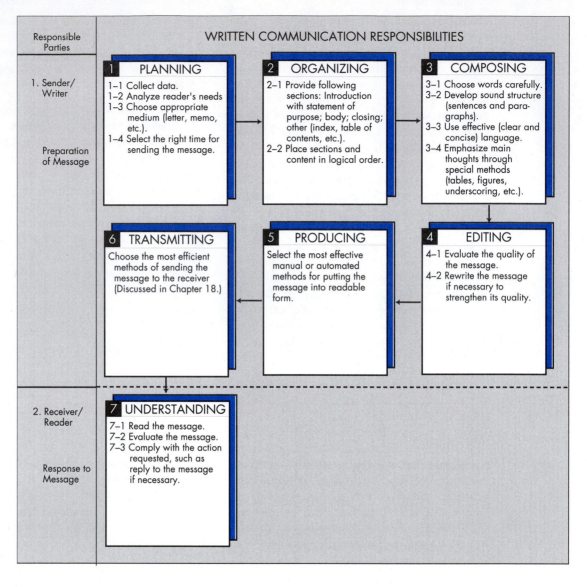

Figure 17–1
A Model of
the Written
Communica-
tion Process

process which, in essence, is a *management process,* for it involves the following management-level responsibilities of the writer:

1. *Planning* the message (Phase 1).
2. *Organizing* the message (Phase 2).
3. *Composing* the message (Phase 3).
4. *Editing* or *controlling* the message (Phase 4).
5. *Producing* the message, using either manual or automated systems (Phase 5). During this phase, the writer has a basic management responsibility of motivating—getting the re-

ceiver to take the desired action in Phases 3, 4, and 7.

6. *Transmitting* or *sending* the message to the receiver (Phase 6), discussed in the next chapter.

Once we receive a message, as readers, we have the important responsibility of *understanding* the message (Phase 7), which is enhanced if the message is well planned, organized, and composed. When we reply to messages received, our roles are reversed. We now become sender/writers and the original senders become receiver/readers.

Such a response is known as *feedback,* as shown in Figure 5–1.

Written Communication Media

In today's computer age, we produce vast numbers of written communications using both manual and automated systems. Statistics have long shown that we retain 90 percent of written and illustrated communications, thus, the continued emphasis on written communications both internal and external.[2] In this section, we review the most common written communication media produced in manual systems. In a later section, *Automated T/WP Systems,* we discuss automated means of producing written messages.

Internal Written Communications

Internal written communications are created and used solely within the firm. Usually these communications fall into four categories: (1) interoffice or interdepartmental memorandums; (2) reports and related working papers; (3) written procedures, sometimes called standard practice instructions; and (4) manuals.

Interoffice Memorandums. We use *interoffice memorandums,* or *memos,* within or among departments of a company to record short messages, often in handwritten form, and to speed them to their destinations with a minimum of time and clerical effort. Interoffice memos are informal, brief, and are produced at very low cost. Usually we destroy memos once their use has been realized. A typical memo is shown in Figure 17–2A. This type of memo is often replaced by *E-mail,* the electronic transmission of messages from one workstation to another through connected cables. (E-mail is discussed in the following chapter.)

Reports. As a rule, reports are longer and more formal than memorandums. We find that many large organizations have established reports management programs designed to: (1) eliminate unnecessary reports, (2) reduce the number and cost of report copies, and (3) standardize (if possible, automate) the report formats for ease of reading. The principles of report writing are discussed and illustrated in Chapter 5.

Written Procedures. *Written procedures* are formal instructions that explain step by step how to complete a task or solve a problem. Such communications, when properly prepared and understood, ensure uniform, efficient work at a lower cost. Procedures manuals or handbooks are developed in large organizations where considerable detail and many people must be combined in order to accomplish the work. A portion of a written procedure is shown in Figure 17–2B; a more detailed discussion of procedures is found in Chapter 21.

Office Manuals. *Office manuals* are formal communications of management control developed to acquaint employees with the policies and regulations of the company. In addition, manuals are used to assign responsibility for performing certain duties and to establish procedures for performing those duties. With such information readily accessible in printed form, the worker's time is saved and the need for constant repetition of instructions is eliminated.

Manuals should be written in a simple, direct, readable style, prepared as economically as possible, and distributed to all employees requiring the information. Such manuals should be evaluated and revised regularly to ensure that they are both *usable* and *used.*

Typically we find four types of manuals in large firms: (1) *policy manuals,* for communicating top-level decisions, resolutions, and pronouncements of the board of directors who establish company policies; (2) *organization manuals,* for explaining the organization and the duties and responsibilities of the various departments; (3) *administrative practice manuals,* which contain the standard procedures and methods for performing the company's work; and (4) *departmental practice manuals,* such as the two closely related manuals on communications described next.

The *correspondence manual* is designed to standardize the policies, procedures, and methods

2"Words on the Wall," *ALDUS Magazine* (September–October, 1992), p. 39.

Figure 17–2
Portions of
Four Key Internal Written
Communications

MANNIX CORPORATION

Interoffice
Memorandum

TO: Managers, All Departments
FROM: George Gobel, Manager, Facilities Planning **GG**
DATE: November 12, 19--
SUBJECT: Resurfacing of the Parking Lot

Please remind all members of your department that our parking lot will be resurfaced during the week of December 20-27. During this time, parking spaces will not be available; thus, employees must find parking elsewhere and use the shuttle bus that will be available to bring employees from the main gate to the front entrance of the main office.

If there are any questions, please call me at Extension 286.

INTEROFFICE MEMORANDUM

A

Scholastica University
Registrar's Office
140 Old Myrtle Street
Duluth, MN 55811-5018

PROCEDURE: APPLICATION FOR GRADUATION

In order to be included on the graduation list and to receive your degree at the next graduation ceremony, you must follow the steps listed below:
1. Obtain an Application for Degree form at the Registrar's Office, 140 Old Myrtle Street.
2. Take the form to your adviser's office for approval and signature.
3. Indicate your height (to determine gown size) and hat size.
4. Return the approved form to the Registrar's Office <u>one month</u> prior to graduation.
5. Watch campus bulletin boards for reminders.

Mary Donatelli, Registrar

WRITTEN PROCEDURE

B

ARRANGING PARTS OF THE REPORT

The report may consist of all the 13 parts enumerated below. These, in turn, may be divided into three main divisions: preliminaries (1-7), text (8-10), reference matter (11-13). (Parts 8-10 are the main divisions of the report, such as chapters, sections, parts, or topics; subdivisions, if desirable; and footnotes.) These should be arranged in the following order, even though in a particular circumstance, one or more parts may be omitted.

1. Cover
2. Title Page
3. Preface or letter of transmittal, including acknowledgements
4. Table of Contents
5. List of Tables
6. List of Illustrations
7. Summary
8. Introduction
9. Main body or text
10. Conclusions and recommendations
11. Appendix
12. Bibliography
13. Index

Source: Erwin M. Keithley and Philip J. Schreiner, <u>A</u> <u>Manual</u> <u>of</u> <u>Style</u> <u>for</u> <u>the</u> <u>Preparation</u> <u>of</u> <u>Papers</u> <u>and</u> <u>Reports</u> (Cincinnati: South-Western Publishing Co., 1980), p. 22.

CORRESPONDENCE MANUAL

C

RIGHT OF CONSULTATION

It is the desire of the Company management that employees' questions be answered and problems solved to the satisfaction of all parties. To this end, a problem-solving procedure has been established so that all employees might exercise their right of consultation. The procedure consists of a series of steps as follows:

First, the employee discusses the issue with the immediate supervisor. The supervisor will answer the issue within three working days.

If the employee is not satisfied with the supervisor's answer, the issue may be presented to the Department administration in writing. The administratrion will answer the issue within five working days.

If the employee is not satisfied with the administration's answer, the issue may be presented to the President in writing. The President will answer within five days; this decision is final.

An employee who follows this procedure may proceed alone or may select another employee from the Department for assistance. This other employee may attend all meetings to discuss the issue. Assistance is also available from the Human Resources Department in following this procedure.

The Company gives its assurance that no retaliation will be made against any employee exercising the right of consultation and that no permanent record will be made of the process.

COMMUNICATION MANUAL

D

of creating correspondence in a company. Typical contents of such a manual include the organization and composition of letters to create goodwill, quality and cost control of company correspondence, word selection, sentence and paragraph constructions, formatting guidelines, and supervision of correspondence (see Figure 17–2C).

The *communication manual* guides employees in selecting suitable communication and telecommunication services at the least cost to the company. The advantages and disadvantages of the various media are presented and their relative costs are compared. This information helps the office manager, for example, in deciding whether to use the telephone, send a letter, FAX the message, or arrange a computer conference.

Some companies include in their communication manuals a section that explains to employees those company policies and procedures that directly influence interpersonal relationships. Here, employees are instructed on their responsibilities and rights as well as what steps to take when personal problems, such as grievances, arise. Figure 17–2D shows a portion of a communication manual in which the grievance-handling procedure is outlined.

External Written Communications

In addition to the internal communications produced within business firms, we note a large amount of **external written communications** that are sent to receivers outside the firm. External communications may be sent by telecommunication media, which is explained in the next chapter, and by traditional written media (such as business letters and forms).

The business letter remains in widespread use because of its value to management. Even though it cannot interrupt an important conference with a loud ring, the business letter continues to be one of the best devices for getting management's attention. Even in the age of automation when telephone and computer communications receive increasing attention, the popularity of the business letter remains. Estimates show that in the United States, several million letters are written every hour of the day, resulting in millions of dollars being spent daily on letter production alone. Communication by mail is a multibillion dollar operation. Note the modern formats for the two business letters shown in Figure 17–3.

TEXT/WORD PROCESSING (T/WP) SYSTEMS

To manage *text,* as mentioned earlier, we must manage *words and related symbols.* Thus, to provide written communications in the right form and at the least possible cost, we must develop an effective text-management system. We now recognize **text/word processing (T/WP) systems** as the most widely used form of text management. Such systems combine *people, equipment,* and *procedures* for converting words into a final product and forwarding it to the user.

Figure 17–4 outlines the basic steps and operating methods we find in all complete T/WP systems (input, processing, output, feedback, control for approving the communications, and delivery or transmission to the user). The specific mix of people, equipment, and procedures varies from office to office, depending upon needs and available resources.

The T/WP concept has been closely linked to automated systems since it originated in the 1960s with office automation pioneers who developed far more efficient means of recording typewritten text on magnetic tape. This innovation made it possible for typists to erase and rerecord, change, and reproduce text stored on tape, which revolutionized the processing of text. What has emerged since that time, however, is the realization that *all levels of systems for creating and producing text are indeed word processing systems.* For this reason, in this textbook, we assume that text management (a new term) and word processing systems are essentially the same. Hence, we will use the letters T/WP as an abbreviation of the merged terms, text/word processing. Also, in this textbook, we emphasize the fact that T/WP systems range from simple, manual systems to the most automated systems, as discussed in the following sections of this chapter.

Figure 17–3
Modern For-
mats for Busi-
ness Letters

DESTINATION TOURS
World Wide Travel Services
5981 Miller Street
Duluth, MN 55811-5018

December 25, 19--

Mr. Charles E. Ellsworth
91 Waukenabo Road
St. Louis, MN 56469-1234

PLANNING YOUR EUROPEAN TRIP

Mr. Ellsworth, we appreciate your interest in a European trip this coming summer and will be pleased to
send you economy-tour information as it becomes available. As you requested, we will be on the alert for
interesting tours of France, the land of your birth.

Enclosed is a set of suggestions for preparing for
such travel, including forms for visa and passport applications. Other brochures will be sent as soon as
they are received from the printer.

Thank you for considering Destination Tours in preparing your travel plans.

Gregory E. McCarthy

GREGORY E. MCCARTHY, MANAGER

mmr

Enclosures

B—SIMPLIFIED LETTER STYLE

DESTINATION TOURS
World Wide Travel Services
5981 Miller Street
Duluth, MN 55811-5018

December 25, 19--

Mr. Charles E. Ellsworth
91 Waukenabo Road
St. Louis, MN 56469-1234

Dear Mr. Ellsworth

We appreciate your interest in a European trip this
coming summer and will be pleased to send you economy-
tour information as it becomes available. As you requested, we will be on the alert for interesting tours
of France, the land of your birth.

Enclosed is a set of suggestions for preparing for
such travel, including forms for visa and passport applications. Other brochures will be sent as soon as
they are received from the printer.

Thank you for considering Destication Tours in
preparing your travel plans.

Sincerely

Gregory E. McCarthy

Gregory E. McCarthy
Manager

mmr

Enclosures

A—BLOCK LETTER STYLE

Figure 17–4
Basic Steps and Operating Methods in a T/WP System

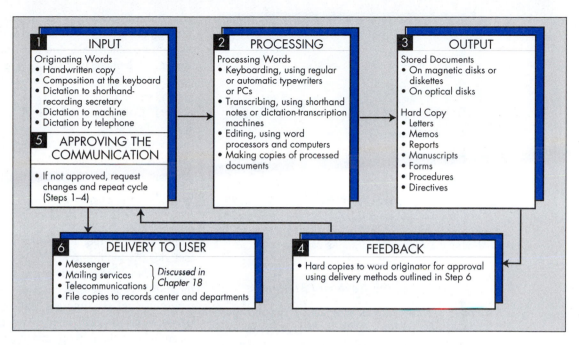

MANUAL T/WP SYSTEMS

In traditional offices, many of which will continue to operate for a long time, written communications are created by manual methods. (T/WP specialists call this message-creation process **word origination.**) Next, the words must be converted into a *medium* (letter, report, memorandum, graphic) that is usable and that reflects well upon the originator's employer. This section discusses the most common message-creation and production methods used in manual T/WP systems.

Message-Creation Methods

In manual T/WP systems, we usually create messages in one of several ways. A brief discussion of each method follows.

Handwritten Method

Many business executives favor handwritten messages, because they can organize, compose, and edit the messages in one complete operation. Such a method ensures privacy and time for concentration; it can be used in many locations—both inside

and outside the office. However, the handwritten method is very slow, when compared to other methods. The handwriting may be illegible, which slows the completion of the next step in the message-creation process—the transcription of the message into final form. Despite its significant weaknesses, the handwritten or "yellow-tablet" method continues to be widespread even in an age when office automation seeks to reduce the amount of human effort needed in performing administrative work. For example, Table 17–1 shows the results of a survey undertaken to determine the popularity of several techniques used to create written communications. The 220 respondents to the survey represented more than 200 companies in 32 states. Of the four major message-creation methods, nearly half of the executives used the handwritten technique. The executives were also asked which technique they preferred. As you see, their first preference was the handwritten, followed by dictation to a machine.[3]

---

[3]Frank Andera, "Written Communication: What Business Executives Are Using," *Business Education Forum* (February, 1991), pp. 17–19.

Technique	Used	Preferred
Handwritten	48%	34%
Dictation to machine	22	29
Dictation to secretary	10	18
Typed personally	19	17
Other	1	2

Source: Frank Andera, "Written Communication: What Business Executives Are Using," *Business Education Forum* (February, 1991), p. 17, by permission of the National Business Education Association.

Composing-at-the-Keyboard Method

Some executives and other administrative personnel possess unusual skills of organizing their ideas in their heads and converting these ideas to words at the keyboard, thus bypassing handwriting the message on paper. Similarly, some managers can take a brief outline of a message (words written in the margin of a letter to be answered, for example) and "fill in the gaps" with connected sentences as they compose at the keyboard. This method works well for some workers, since it saves time in handwriting the complete message. However, for most workers with organizing and writing problems, this method is not recommended unless sufficient time is spent, say at the VDT keyboard, to effectively edit each message. At the same time, the National Research Council says there is a demand for workers to fill technology-based positions. It predicts that, by the year 2000, these jobs will be more than 75 percent of the total workforce.[4]

Shorthand-Recording Method

The shorthand-recording method is considerably faster than the handwritten method used to create messages. However, this method requires the presence of both the manager who dictates the mes-

sage and the secretary who records the message. During this time, both persons are prevented from performing other tasks and are frequently interrupted by telephone calls, office visitors, and other unexpected problems. The use of the shorthand method in the modern office has declined. A 1993 Dartnell Corporation survey of corporate managers indicated that less than 7 percent of newspaper want ads from 17 major cities throughout the United States and Canada for administrative support staff required shorthand skills.[5]

Machine-Recording Method

Dictation to a voice-recording machine overcomes most of the disadvantages of the other methods. As input to the T/WP system (Step 1 in Figure 17–4), machine dictation is estimated to be three times as fast as face-to-face shorthand recording and six times as fast as handwriting. Dictation can be performed at any time or in any location since the portable machines discussed in the next section can be easily carried on the executive's person (shirt pocket or purse). From the standpoint of processing (producing) the written message (Step 2 in Figure 17–4), the secretary can transcribe the machine-dictated material more than twice as fast as handwritten copy and faster, too, than poorly recorded shorthand notes. When the machine-dictation method is used, only one person—the word originator—is required; thus, any distractions disrupt only one person's work.

Despite these advantages, machine dictation is not as widely used as might be expected. Many managers refuse to leave the "comfortable habit" of handwriting their messages, where they can easily see and control the results of their work. Others lack the training necessary to dictate in a clear, organized fashion; as a result, they produce garbled, wordy, rambling messages. To overcome these problems, many firms provide training in dictation as discussed later in this chapter. Figure 17–5 summarizes the main characteristics of documents appropriate for each method of word origination.

[4]Lura Romei, "Will We Never Learn?" *Modern Office Technology* (September, 1993), p. 9.

[5]"1993 Secretarial Want Ad Survey," *From Nine to Five* (August, 1993), p. 2.

Figure 17–5
Characteristics
of Messages
Appropriate
for Each
Method of
Message
Creation

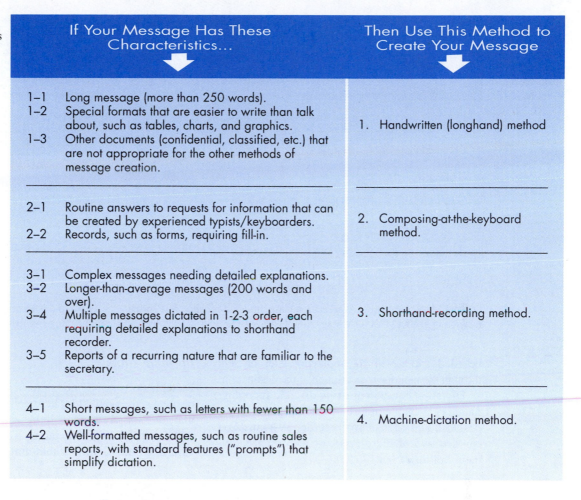

If Your Message Has These Characteristics...	Then Use This Method to Create Your Message
1–1 Long message (more than 250 words). 1–2 Special formats that are easier to write than talk about, such as tables, charts, and graphics. 1–3 Other documents (confidential, classified, etc.) that are not appropriate for the other methods of message creation.	1. Handwritten (longhand) method
2–1 Routine answers to requests for information that can be created by experienced typists/keyboarders. 2–2 Records, such as forms, requiring fill-in.	2. Composing-at-the-keyboard method.
3–1 Complex messages needing detailed explanations. 3–2 Longer-than-average messages (200 words and over). 3–4 Multiple messages dictated in 1-2-3 order, each requiring detailed explanations to shorthand recorder. 3–5 Reports of a recurring nature that are familiar to the secretary.	3. Shorthand-recording method.
4–1 Short messages, such as letters with fewer than 150 words. 4–2 Well-formatted messages, such as routine sales reports, with standard features ("prompts") that simplify dictation.	4. Machine-dictation method.

The research reported in Table 17–2 shows that managers equipped with VDT workstations generally use their terminals to key in or create documents. Those without such hardware are likely to use the handwritten method. Also, note in the table that the two most common document-creation methods of managers with VDTs were (1) composing at the keyboard and (2) handwriting. Since only 5.2 percent of all managers without VDTs and no managers with VDTs reported using machine dictation, we see that machine dictation with voice-recording and transcription equipment was not widely used by the managers included in this research.[6] How machine dictation works at the manual level is discussed in the next section.

Dictation-Transcription System

As a rule, with a **dictation-transcription system,** messages are recorded on paper or on magnetic media through the process of dictation. These recorded messages must then be converted to final form as needed for use in management information systems. To store the dictated messages, a large number of machine models and brands are available. Each may be used at individual workstations or in centralized locations.

Most manual systems for recording messages use a **discrete** (separate) **recording medium** that is removed from the machine for transcription after the dictation has been completed. Discrete media on which the dictation is recorded in electronic, magnetic form include belts, disks, cassettes, minicassettes, and cartridges. The discrete medium can

[6]Mary Sumner, "A Workstation Case Study," *Datamation* (February 15, 1986), p. 71.

Table 17–2
Document
Creation Prac-
tices of Man-
agers With and
Without VDTs

| DOCUMENT CREATION PRACTICES OF MANAGERS (in percent) | | | | | |
| | Managers with VDT's | | | | |
Method Used	Supervisors	Mid Management	Top Management	Average	Managers Without VDTs
Handwriting	35.3	20.5	28.8	28.2	80.0
Composing at the keyboard	59.6	57.0	51.3	56.0	7.8
Shorthand recording	0.0	22.5	2.5	8.3	7.0
Machine dictation	0.0	0.0	0.0	0.0	5.2
Other	5.1	0.0	17.4	7.5	0.0

Source: Mary Sumner, "A Workstation Case Study," *Datamation* (February 15, 1986), p. 71. Reprinted with permission of **DATAMATION magazine**, February 15, 1986 © 1986 by Cahners Publishing Company.

be filed and saved for replaying later or sent through the mail for transcription at the destination.

Dictation equipment using discrete recording media is available in three types: (1) portable, (2) desktop, and (3) central recorder systems. You can see two of these types of recording equipment in Illustration 17–1.

Portable Units

Portable units small enough to fit in shirt pockets or purses are available. These units are very popular, due largely to their light weight, low cost, and compatibility with larger transcribing machines. In addition, portable units permit dicta-

Illustration 17–1 Discrete recording media are available on various types of dictation equipment.

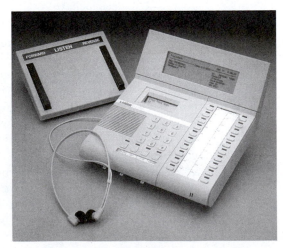

(a) Portable Unit

(b) Desktop Unit

tion away from the office and thus are valuable time-savers for busy executives and salespersons who are required to make regular reports. The minicassettes used in portable machines can easily be mailed to the office, which speeds the preparation of written communications.

Desktop Units

As the name implies, desktop units are larger, heavier, and therefore more stationary than portable units. One type is a dictation-only machine, while a second type combines the dictation and transcription functions. Desktop machines are primarily used by decentralized groups of *transcriptionists* (personnel who convert voice-recorded messages into hard copy), with primary responsibilities for preparing written communications. Thus, the desktop system is especially suitable for word originators who have a secretary and whose work requires considerable correspondence. Such a system is also suitable for those who want to keep communications within their department for security or privacy reasons. With the desktop system, the word originator or secretary has immediate access to the communications.

In small offices, a decentralized dictation-transcription plan is often found, with each department retaining a staff that specializes in T/WP duties. Often one transcriptionist is assigned to serve one or more word originators. In larger firms, greater efficiency is obtained by centralizing this function as discussed in the following section.

Central Recorder Systems

A **central recorder system** is a dictation system where the telephone may be used as a dictation instrument to access a recording device located in the T/WP center. By using the telephone in this manner, we gain wide access to the system, which, in turn, permits us to dictate at any hour of the day or night through an outside line that ties into the system. Central systems are most effectively used where there are large numbers of managers who occasionally need to dictate and can share the services of a transcriptionist. This arrangement is more cost effective than placing a desktop unit on every manager's desk. If a manager travels extensively and has a secretary whose work supports, say, 10 people, all of whom create considerable correspondence, a central system with long recording time is necessary.

Typewriters: Message-Producing Machines

A history of the office tells us that, for more than a century, typewriters have served as the principal means of producing communications in a manual T/WP system; further, we know that their widespread use continues. However, some office equipment manufacturers predict the demise of this universally used machine because of the more powerful features possessed by the increasingly less expensive automated T/WP hardware described in the following section.

Even though this prediction seems credible, experienced OMs maintain that the typewriter will remain for many years to come. They cite the many small typing jobs, such as preparing envelopes, labels, file folders, index cards, and the like, that cannot be processed conveniently and quickly with existing T/WP hardware. In addition, there are many small offices in which the present durable typewriter is the only equipment needed to process words.

The two main categories of typewriters are described next.

Standard Electric

The **standard electric typewriter** is intended for small-volume typewriting. This machine is capable of increased output and higher-quality copy and requires less human energy than manual machines. On most electric machines, operations such as erasing are mechanized.

Electronic

The **electronic typewriter (ET)** evolved by adding to the standard electric typewriter many automated features made possible by the use of microprocessors. Compared with standard electric typewriters, ETs have fewer moving parts and can perform many additional functions. With the passage of time, we find more and more optional automated features available on ETs. One category of ET is shown in Illustration 17–2, along with specific features of the machine. Other intermediate levels are also available.

Illustration 17–2 Electronic typewriters are popular in several sizes and styles. Shown here are a simple entry-level model (left) and an advanced text-editing model with monitor (right).

ETs have several advantages over electromechanical typewriters and PCs. Secretaries prefer ETs for their simplicity and ease of handling many routine tasks—typing labels, envelopes, and filling in forms—quickly and simply. These office workers are comfortable with the technology since it is simple and does not require a long training period. ETs can be built for less money than standard electrics and are much more reliable since they have fewer moving parts.

Generally, we should use ETs rather than word processors or PCs if the applications are: (1) labels or envelopes for infrequently used addresses or (2) filling in infrequently used or single copies of preprinted forms. In 1992, ETs accounted for 20 percent of the typewriter marketplace, with T/WP accounting for 80 percent.[7]

AUTOMATED T/WP SYSTEMS

Even with the advent of the electronic typewriter, the copier, and other forms of information technology, the output or productivity of office workers

[7]Lura K. Romei, "Processing Words: Weighing Your Options," *Modern Office Technology* (Cleveland: Penton Publishing Company, August, 1992), p. 29.

responsible for written communications has remained, at best, constant. At the same time, we observe that the cost of producing written communications continues to increase. To combat this serious problem, automated systems for producing text have been developed to bring the efficiency and economy of computer systems to the office. As Judy Norberg notes in the *Dialog from the Workplace,* phrases such as "ease of document preparation," "better and quicker communication," and "greater efficiencies" are common descriptions of the benefits of enhancements in text/word processing systems. She also notes the challenges for employees and administrators in today's office and the need for adaptability.

In this section, we discuss in detail the basic T/WP hardware and software used in such systems, along with a powerful application—desktop publishing—that creates many new benefits and challenges for the AOM. In a later section, we examine the management of T/WP systems.

T/WP Hardware

In the automation marketplace we find many brands and types of T/WP hardware that offer dozens of features, functions, and options. However, the role of hardware is basically the same: to create, modify, merge with other applications, duplicate, file, retrieve, delete, and store text. The hardware used in automated T/WP systems shares these basic components, which are shown in Figure 17–6.

1. A *keyboard* (the input unit) on which the layout of the alphanumeric keys is identical to the standard typewriter keyboard. (In some automated systems, the Dvorak keyboard is used. It represents a more efficient design based on the frequency of alphabetic characters used in the English language. However, it has never achieved the usage of the standard keyboard. In addition, there are extra command and function keys.)

2. A *video* (or *visual*) *display terminal (VDT)* that enables the operator to see the text. The screen may show a portion or an entire page of text on which revisions to the text (additions, deletions, movement of blocks of copy, merging, correc-

DIALOG FROM THE WORKPLACE

JUDY NORBERG

Firm Administrator
Messerli & Kramer, P.A.
Attorneys at Law
Minneapolis, Minnesota

As firm administrator of a 32-attorney law firm located in Minneapolis, Judy Norberg is responsible for managing the business activities of the firm. Her responsibilities include: general administration, human resources management, financial management, and facilities management. In addition, Judy is responsible for managing and coordinating all nonattorney personnel, space lease negotiations, and expansion design. She has five staff reporting directly to her as well as all non-lawyer personnel. Judy has been in legal administration for over 10 years. She also has over 10 years of corporate management experience. Judy received her B.S. in business administration from the University of Minnesota.

QUESTION: How have enhancements in text/word processing changed the role of administrative personnel in the last three years; and how have efficiencies been increased by the networking of microcomputers with text/word processing software?

RESPONSE: When I think of how the computer has changed the role of administrative personnel over the last few years, thoughts come to mind like: "ease of document preparation," "better and quicker communication," and "greater efficiencies."

Having been in the legal administration profession for over 10 years, I can reflect on how things were when I began. Secretaries had mag-card typewriters; word processing centers existed equipped with standalone word processors with screens. That equipment had a fraction of the flexibility and capability that microcomputers have today. There was no E-mail; there was no voice mail. Lengthy turnaround time for document production and seemingly endless telephone tag were ways of life. Today, many of our documents can be produced by calling up a short program (macro) and completing it with variable information. Documents that used to take hours, now take minutes.

Today an administrative assistant or secretary needs to be a top-notch technician and administrative liaison. As a technician, he or she must be able to learn new software and hardware quickly and identify ways to streamline workload by its use. The role of administrative liaison is so important because as executives continue to move at a faster pace, the administrative assistant who can learn to think like they think and be willing to do more than is expected is truly invaluable. Employees with those traits are not easy to find, and when they are found, they must be valued!

The truly valuable administrative person is also adaptable. His or her natural way of thinking focuses on what *can* be done, rather than what *cannot* be done. Administrative personnel who exhibit this attitude energize themselves by constantly looking for a way to "build a better mousetrap." It is a win-win deal. The employee wins by growing; the employer wins because that individual is helping create a better organization.

Figure 17–6
Hardware
Components
in an Auto-
mated T/WP
System

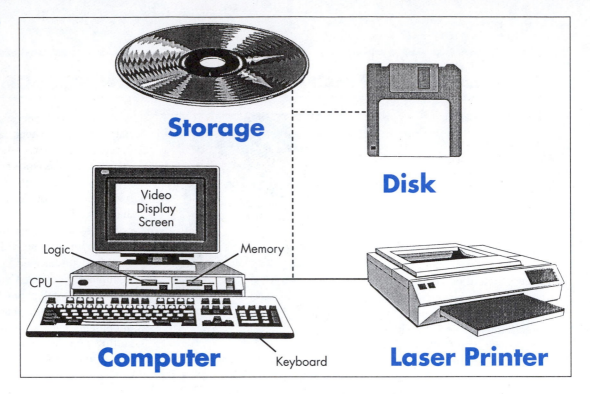

tion of spelling errors, etc.) may be made. Additional information about the use of visual display terminals is found in Chapters 16 and 18.

3. A *central processing unit (CPU)* that provides *internal memory* for storing text and the programs to process the text in line with the *logic* of the system that is built into the circuitry of the machine for directing the execution of the programs.

4. *Text-storing media,* such as magnetic cards, floppy disks or diskettes, and hard disks, all of which are examples of storage media.

5. A *printer* that is used to produce hard-copy output of letters, memos, reports, and filled-in forms. Typically, the text that is stored in internal memory is moved to a printer and printed as directed by the program.

The power of automated T/WP equipment lies in its ability to (1) store rough-draft copy, (2) edit the copy so that it reaches the author's high standards of excellence, (3) store the final copy for immediate playback, (4) print out error-free copy,

and (5) send copy through electronic transmission processors described in Chapter 18. Automated T/WP equipment for preparing and editing text is commonly divided into two classes: (1) standalone word processors, often called personal computers (PCs), and (2) computer-connected word processors, often called networked computers. We discuss both of these classes of hardware in nontechnical terms in the following paragraphs.

Standalone Word Processors

A **standalone word processor** is a self-contained system with a video display terminal. As shown in Illustration 17–3, this type of system is composed of a keyboard for the input of the message, a screen for displaying the text, a CPU for editing and processing the text, a printer for producing the hard copy, and a diskette for the external storage of the text or the program for operating the system.

Sometimes a standalone word processor or PC may be dedicated. That is, its use, based on the installed hardware, is restricted to a stated list of T/WP functions of the installed word processing software. In effect, such word processors are computers built to perform one type of job only. When multiple standalone systems are interconnected to share one or more common devices, such as a disk drive or a printer, they are called *integrated or networked systems.* Standalone systems are placed on desktops where they can operate independently of other automated equipment. Thus, if one unit fails, the others can still function.

Computer-Connected Word Processors

A **computer-connected word processor,** as the name suggests, is a word processing machine that is linked to, and dependent upon, a computer for its operation. In such an arrangement, the computer (often called a file server) provides the power for processing the text and for activating the printer to produce hard-copy output. Although we find many different combinations of word processors that edit text, only the two most common arrangements of equipment are discussed in this section.

Shared-Logic Word Processors. In contrast to the standalone system, the **shared-logic word processor** is only one unit in a system of multiple processors and printers that operate simultaneously under the direction of a small computer, hence, the term "shared." As shown in Figure 17–7, this type of word processor may also share the services of a printer and diskette files, as well as the larger memory capacity of the host computer.

The shared-logic system is less expensive when many stations are attached to one computer and many word processors can access the same document simultaneously. A major weakness that we see in the shared-logic system is its total reliance on the computer. When the computer is not operating, all shared-logic word processors are "dead." The shared logic system is rapidly being replaced by **networked personal computers** (PCs linked together through a network or file server).

Microcomputers in T/WP. Because it is low in cost and easy to operate, the microcomputer has been widely adopted for use as a word processor in

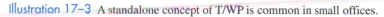

Illustration 17–3 A standalone concept of T/WP is common in small offices.

Figure 17–7
The Shared-
Logic Concept
of T/WP Sys-
tems, Using
Microcomput-
ers, Through a
Network
Server

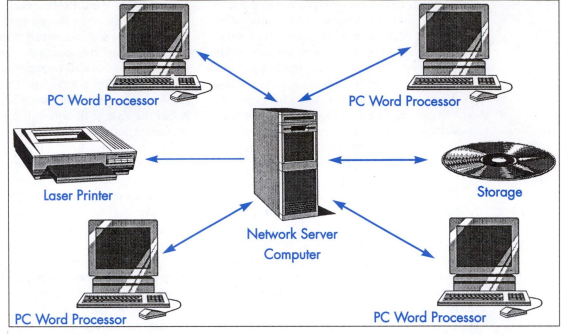

offices and in homes. By simply loading the personal computer with appropriate T/WP software, an effective system is created for the preparation of written communications. A fast-growing segment of the computer marketplace includes the laptop computer and the palmtop, lightweight portable devices discussed in the previous chapter. These types of computers are used for creating messages "on the road" or in **floating offices,** a management system that allows employees to set up mobile offices wherever convenient: at home, corporate headquarters, or branch facilities using laptops and computer capabilities for written communications.[8]

T/WP Software

As we know from our earlier study of computer systems, efficient software must be available to make the hardware perform its "duties." Today we can list dozens of T/WP software packages offering a wide variety of capabilities using natural-language commands. Powerful T/WP software, such as WordPerfect™, Microsoft Word®, and MultiMate™, are periodically updated as new developments in technology occur. What these software packages share in common are the capabilities for performing the basic T/WP functions (editing and indexing documents, creating graphics, and analyzing message composition). Thus, if you want to erase a report file, you can simply key in the word ERASE with the name of the file; or, if you want to move a section of a report, you can define the section and touch the MOVE function key. Such software is simple to use and quick to learn and generates little fear of learning in the user. The value of these systems can be increased by the use of "add-ons," which are software subprograms that offer extra processing power, for example, software programs such as SpellCheck and GrammarCheck.

Desktop Publishing (DTP)

What began as a software novelty in 1985 has mushroomed into a powerful new application of microcomputers to business. The **desktop pub-**

[8]"Floating Offices Complement Portable Technology," *Modern Office Technology* (Cleveland: Penton Publishing Company, November, 1993), p. 49.

lishing (DTP) application is a T/WP software application that enables the user to design, edit, assemble, and produce documents with a professional look that includes typeset text and graphics, business reports, newsletters, brochures, sales flyers, price lists, manuals, and resumés. In its simplest form, we find that DTP uses a computer as the basic workstation for preparing and distributing documents, including text, with a variety of typefaces, graphics, and illustrations. Commonly, DTP uses a microcomputer with page layout software and a laser printer to produce a master copy that, to most readers, seems to be very close in quality to that produced by commercial typesetters. This copy is camera ready since DTP software allows the user to combine at one time T/WP input, graphics input, charts and drawings—everything needed for producing a document. In this system, users function at their microcomputers as writers, editors, and page layout designers; as a result, users are given control over not only the content of what is written but also over the way it is presented on a page.

Users note considerable savings when they compare the costs of composition and printing of DTP with commercial publishing costs. To publish a 250-page handbook by commercial printers, for example, we might incur a total cost of about $10,000. Using DTP, on the other hand, *two* editions of the handbook, plus another 750 to 1,000 pages of documentation, can be printed for less than $5,000, assuming that well-trained operators are available within the firm.[9]

The hardware needs of DTP systems vary according to the needs of the firm. Typical hardware includes a microcomputer with 8 to 16MB of internal memory, an internal hard drive of 200 to 400MB storage, one or two floppy disk drives, a mouse, a monitor with graphics capability, and a laser printer. Such a printer is not vital to a DTP system; however, it does ensure more professional-looking copy at one-tenth the noise and much faster speeds (in one case, one page per second) than impact printers. Also, laser printers offer the use of many **fonts** (typefaces in specific sizes and styles). Scanners often serve as input devices to bring logos, line art, and photographs onto the screen. Scanners are also used to input and interpret typeset text in various sizes, and optical disks store the completed documents.

The complete DTP process includes these steps:[10]

1. *Designing the document,* which includes developing a "blueprint" as to where to place headlines, text, and graphics on the final product.
2. *Creating the text,* which involves using T/WP or DTP software for inputting text and headlines.
3. *Selecting or creating graphics to enhance the document,* in line with the capabilities of the DTP software.
4. *Laying out the page,* which includes making decisions on the placement of title, text, and graphics. Other decisions are needed regarding the number of columns, page size, margin widths, and the setting of "frames" or boxes for holding text and graphics. During document preparation, illustrations can be enlarged or reduced in size, cropped (trimmed electronically), and positioned on a page.
5. *Creating the page,* in which the operator inputs the text and graphics created during the previous steps. To do so requires deciding on typeface size and style and "sizing" graphics until they fit comfortably in the space allotted. In addition, you may edit and adjust the copy to produce a neat, professional-looking document.
6. *Printing the document,* which starts with a rough draft for proofing and, after getting approval of the proofed copy, producing final hard copy on the laser printer.

[9]William M. Cowan, "Get in the Picture with Desktop Publishing," *Office Systems '89* (March, 1989), p. 52.

[10]Janice Schoen Henry and Heidi R. Perreault, "Guidelines for Helping Business Education Teachers Choose a Desktop Publishing System: Part II," *Delta Pi Epsilon Tips* (Winter, 1989), pp. 3–4.

Typically, firms use DTP for producing catalogs, price lists, sales literature, invitations, business reports, newsletters, notices of employee and corporate activities, and interim and quarterly meeting notices. More and more organizations are using DTP and colored laser printers to enhance office communications. As with T/WP packages, there are many add-on packages, such as **clip art,** to enhance DTP. Clip art is a software package with digitized pictures for use with DTP and T/WP software systems.

Emerging Developments in Automated T/WP Systems

The field of information technology continues to affect all phases of the office, including systems for producing text. Two of the latest developments to emerge are (1) digital dictation and (2) voice-to-print systems.

Digital Dictation

From the earliest days of recorded dictation to the present time, we have recorded the voice in a mechanical, analog form; that is, there has been a one-to-one relationship between the voice and signal stored on the tape. Stated simply, loud sounds made big "scratches" or impressions and soft sounds created little impressions on the recorded medium. In **digital dictation,** vocal sounds are recorded and stored on magnetic media after being automatically converted to digits (the binary numbers, 0 and 1, used in computer systems). When words are stored in numeric form on disk, they can be processed and retrieved in a rapid, random manner in the same way that computers store, process, and retrieve data. Thus, changes in dictated copy (corrections, additions, deletions) can be made quickly since it is a relatively simple matter to locate the digital dictation copy that is stored by a record number. (In contrast, messages in traditional dictation systems are recorded as vocal sounds in sequential order and can be retrieved only by scanning the tape and listening for the desired words.) With digital dictation, messages dictated earlier in the day can easily be reviewed and changed and instant access can be given to high-priority documents without searching all of the material recorded earlier.

Voice-to-Print Systems

One of the longtime dreams of AOMs has been the development of a "talk-writer," a machine that converts spoken dictation directly to written words and thus eliminates the need for a typewriter. In such a **voice-to-print system,** the word originator speaks directly into a recorder, after which a computer-connected word processing terminal converts the spoken words into visual words on the display screen. Areas requiring editing and other text revision can be identified visually, and the dictation is corrected and stored like any other text. One voice-to-print system has a stored vocabulary of 5,000 words, which can be doubled in size through the addition of more software. Some automation specialists predict that voice-to-print systems will be widely used in the late 1990s.

MANAGEMENT OF T/WP SYSTEMS

Historically we could accurately describe the management of T/WP systems for producing written communications as lacking in planning, organizing, operating, and controlling. Written communications were produced using the skills, attitudes, and experiences that the writers brought to the job. A general attitude prevailed that "everyone can write." However, poor writing habits, failure to consider the important impact that written communications have on the firm's future, bottlenecks in work processes, and a host of other problems related to written communications have prevented managers from achieving effective administration in the office.

To prevent the recurrence of such problems, we must carefully manage the T/WP system as we do any other administrative office system. A company-wide communication program must be well planned, carefully organized, and capably staffed. Further, we must place appropriate controls on all phases of the system, as discussed in this section.

Planning T/WP Systems

When an AOM senses the need for greater productivity in written communications, several planning operations are necessary. As a first step, the AOM conducts a feasibility study to determine the need for, and the practicality of, designing a new or revised system. If the results of such a study indicate the need for a T/WP system, then further planning, including the development of program objectives, must be implemented. We present each of these planning steps in the following discussion.

Feasibility Study

In the feasibility study, the practicality of developing a T/WP system must be assessed. Usually a special committee is appointed to conduct such a study, with representation from each of the key departments and from various levels of employees. Outside consultants and equipment vendors can provide useful assistance to such a committee. The same general approach is recommended for studying the T/WP needs within a department.

Completing the feasibility study requires collecting information about the present methods and problems of originating and typing/keyboarding information. Questions such as the following should be answered by all departments in the firm:

1. How is secretarial work distributed?
2. What administrative support tasks (typing and nontyping) are performed in each department?
3. How much time is required and taken for each task, and how important is each in relation to the time being consumed?
4. Are duties being performed at the most appropriate level of competency?
5. What word-origination activities occur in each department, in what volume, and requiring what amount of time?
6. What methods are employed by word originators to initiate written communications?
7. To what extent do word originators revise their communications from time to time, and to what extent are standardized communications, such as form letters and paragraphs, used or desired?
8. What is the estimated **turnaround time** (the time that elapses from word origination until the finished document is returned for approval)?
9. How much of the work of producing written communications can be measured adequately?
10. How much does the production of written communications cost each department on an annual basis?
11. Should hardware and/or T/WP software be purchased?

The feasibility study often reveals many unrelated, unnecessary, time-consuming tasks, wasted motions, and duplications of work, all resulting in poor work quality and low productivity. Further, when reasonable estimates are computed for the cost of producing written communications, too often such costs are clearly excessive, compared with other necessary processes in the firm. These excessive costs point to a need for new efforts in managing the T/WP function.

Objectives of T/WP Systems

The cost-conscious administrator expects topnotch efficiency and high quality in the production and distribution of written communications. This includes a faster turnaround time and an increasingly lower unit cost of producing letters and reports than is normally possible with traditional methods.

Advocates of automated T/WP systems point to the following benefits that should be expected—and hence may be considered as objectives—of such systems:

1. *Increased production* of text by executives who use machines for originating communications. Many word originators are able to increase their dictation speed from a range of 10 to 15 words per minute using the handwritten method to a range of 60 to 80 words per minute using dictating machines. With the growing use of executive workstations, more and more top-level managers create first-draft copy of written communications on their own VDT keyboards. T/WP software packages are all very much alike and have reached a com-

mon ground, with easy-to-use software enabling all levels of management and staff access to simple methods of T/WP. "Everything looks the same and works the same, and more managers are using T/WP."[11]

2. *Higher productivity* since the work is performed by expert operators. The results include a reduction in retyping of copy and an increase in error-free hard copy. The amount of proofreading and revision time is reduced.

3. *Better supervision* of the work. In the T/WP center (sometimes referred to as the centralized text-production department or work group), operators are supervised by a specialist in the production of written communications rather than by an executive with more general management responsibilities.

4. *More opportunities for measurement* of the amount and quality of the output. Simple tallies of documents completed to line counts or keystrokes per day, week, or month permit quantity measurement. Thus, an incentive system based upon work quantity and quality can be set up.

5. *Better use of equipment and personnel.* Providing a system that keeps both the personnel and the equipment busy reduces the typical peak-and-valley periods in the work.

6. *Closer ties between the company's T/WP center and the data processing system.* In today's administrative office systems, the same hardware can be utilized for both types of systems.

7. *Greater career opportunities.* In both the T/WP and the administrative-support areas, more management positions open up for the secretarial personnel. As we learned earlier, by the end of the 1990s, 75 percent of the workers will be using computer technology. Companies are looking for connectivity, and they want T/WP that addresses their business needs and brings workers closer together.[12]

---

[11]Kevin Richard, "The Paper Chase," *Computer User: Office Technology of the 90's* (September, 1993), p. 1.

[12]Jim Manzi, "Software Support," *Fortune* (December, 1993), p. 95.

Organizing T/WP Systems

Since T/WP systems are organized according to the special needs of each firm, their organizational plans will vary. This section discusses typical organizational plans for T/WP as well as the personnel needs of this type of system. The selection of equipment, another organizing responsibility of a T/WP manager, is discussed in Chapter 15.

Organizational Plans

Several basic organizational plans exist, ranging from highly centralized to totally decentralized arrangements. Generally, the more centralized, routinized, and highly specialized the T/WP function becomes to handle large-volume keyboarding operations, the more the personal (human) touch is sacrificed. In the same way, the less centralized and less specialized the word processing function, the more difficult it is to control the work assigned. Typically we find the following basic organizational structures.

Centralized Text Production. A production operation as pictured in Illustration 17–4 brings all of the written communication responsibilities together in a central location under a company-wide supervisor. This organizational plan, usually found in large firms, requires large volumes of work, major investments in equipment, considerable training of staff and supervisors, and qualitative and quantitative controls over the work. In effect, it represents automating the production of written communications. Nonkeyboarding duties are directed by an administrative-support supervisor who may report to the T/WP manager. However, even in such a centralized structure, top managers usually retain executive secretaries who continue to perform both keyboarding and general administrative duties.

Decentralized Text Production. In decentralized text-production systems, small, scaled-down versions of the centralized plan, such as mini- or branch-office centers commonly referred to as work groups, are located in major functional areas of the firm. Under this plan, the operators

Illustration 17–4　A T/WP center work group.

are closer to the word originators and can function more efficiently as a result. Also, with more personal contact possible, operators report greater job satisfaction.

Other Organizational Plans. Other plans for operating T/WP systems include retaining the traditional secretaries equipped with automated word processors for written communications but using word processing units to handle overflow keyboarding. A modification of this plan has secretaries performing light keyboarding tasks, while extensive keyboarding projects are assigned to a word processing unit equipped with more powerful data-entry capabilities. With this arrangement, the personal contact between the managers and the secretarial staff is maintained while retaining several advantages of centralization (especially work measurement, quality control, and data-entry competence).

T/WP Personnel

In traditional offices, secretaries, typists, and other types of transcriptionists are responsible for the message-producing tasks. However, firms using more complex, automated systems to produce written communications are interested in obtaining more specialization (and, it is hoped, more productivity) by dividing the office tasks between two types of staff members: (1) correspondence secretaries and (2) administrative secretaries.

Correspondence secretaries (sometimes called *text/word processing operators*) are keyboard specialists capable of far greater keyboarding output per hour than traditional general secretaries, whose keyboarding is continually interrupted by other required tasks. (The average worker has 36 hours of work stacked on a desk in an average day and only 90 minutes to spend on it.[13]) Correspondence secretaries usually perform the heavy-volume keyboarding work in a centralized department under production supervisors, or they may be located in several decentralized areas. In either case, the correspondence secretaries are not assigned tasks such as filing, running errands, and answering the telephone.

In contrast, **administrative secretaries** are freed from large-volume keyboarding responsibilities and thus are better able to handle the remaining office services—answering the telephone, filing correspondence, scheduling travel, arranging meetings, and performing various mailing tasks. Some of these tasks are performed on networked PCs using personal information management (PIM) software. PIM software provides the user with the ability to schedule, organize, sort, file, and remember associated, work-related information, such as maintaining schedules, making travel arrangements, filing, and other administrative secretarial functions. In the small firm, secretaries perform both correspondence and general administrative duties since separating such specialized functions is not feasible.

In a T/WP center, the T/WP manager and the administrative-support manager each direct a staff of specialists responsible for written communications and general office services, respectively. The T/WP manager must be familiar with the organization's communication needs and be able to direct the supervisors and the staff in the implementation of the system. Administrative requirements of such a position include managing the budget, developing production controls, and coordinating the services of the center with the administrative-support group. In some firms, the position may also be expanded to include responsibilities for photocopying, photocomposition, printing, mailing, FAX, and graphics services.

A **departmental work group system** describes both a centralized structure of T/WP and administrative-support secretaries, as well as the software that links them together. Reporting to the T/WP manager are staff members that include the supervisor who schedules and assigns work; T/WP specialists who, in addition to some keyboarding, may be assigned the tasks of designing complicated documents; proofreaders; and the typists (the T/WP operators and trainees). The T/WP staff members are frequently divided into work groups by department and receive cross-training in proofreading, keyboarding, and designing DTP applications. The reporting relationships are charted as shown in Figure 17–8. This chart also reflects responsibilities in systems that are not fully centralized. The staff must possess high levels of language skills. Operators must enjoy production keyboarding, possess at least 60 words per minute as a keyboarding skill, and be able to prepare a realistic document on automated keyboard equipment. A 1993 Dartnell Corporation survey indicated that managers are most interested in hiring operators with general computer abilities, word processing skills on the most common programs, organization skills, and communication abilities.[14]

Organizing the transcription of written communications in the small and medium-size office starts with the selection of an experienced, well-trained person who can coordinate the work of the word originators and the transcribing personnel. As a full-time supervisor, this person may be responsible for training transcriptionists, setting work standards, measuring the output of each employee, and analyzing the quality of communications produced. In a small office, this person may function as a supervisor on a part-time basis and devote the remaining time to more complex transcribing duties.

Operating T/WP Systems

The operation of a T/WP system requires the development and installation of procedures, standards, and other controls to ensure effective performance. For this task, many T/WP managers initially borrow ideas from other firms and adapt them to their own situations. Professional

[13]Fred V. Diers, "2001: An Information Odyssey," *Office Systems Management* (December, 1993), p. 11.

[14]"1993 Secretarial Want Ad Survey," *From Nine to Five* (Chicago: Dartnell Corporation, August, 1993), p. 34.

Figure 17–8
T/WP and Administrative Support in a Work Group Structure

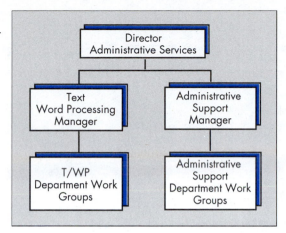

The most difficult phase of machine dictation revolves around the mental planning and organizing of the message prior to, and during, the dictation period. Many large firms—especially insurance companies and banks where much correspondence originates—use a step-by-step method to train their correspondents in giving dictation. First, the word originator is asked to write and then read the material to a secretary and then to a machine to avoid dictating too quickly and to ensure clarity of pronunciation and adequate instructions to the transcriptionists. Next, the originator is taught to dictate from an extensive written outline of key thoughts in each paragraph, which is later followed by dictation from a more concise outline. Gradually, as each step is mastered, the word originator becomes able to dictate from a mental outline alone.

Besides this dictation training, such firms periodically review the quality of the letters written through (1) conferences with supervisors, originators, and transcriptionists and (2) the use of a correspondence manual that the firm has developed to guide the originators in improving their work and standardizing their output. Frequently an evaluation report, as shown in Figure 17–9, is used to analyze the work of each word originator. Dictation machine manufacturers also provide instructional materials (films, tapes, and workbooks). In addition, independent communication consultants are available to assist word originators in learning good dictation techniques and effective letter-writing skills.

consultants and word processing user groups, too, are excellent sources of information regarding the development of effective operating procedures. However, with more experience, firms develop their own production and time standards based upon counts of work produced. Time studies and other work measurement techniques are used as a basis for setting standards, as discussed in Chapter 22. Cost data, such as per-page or per-report costs for keyboarding and proofreading, are prepared for use in analyzing the efficiency of each operator. Further, maintaining cost records for equipment, maintenance, and supplies facilitates charging each department its proportionate share of the communications produced by the T/WP system.

The T/WP manager may also be required to facilitate training of business executives in the use of dictating machines. The following procedures for effective dictation may be helpful and are recommended:

1. Collect all relevant information necessary to organize, compose, and dictate the message.
2. Plan and organize the information in a form that facilitates the dictation process.
3. Control the dictation by providing proper sequence of the thoughts to be communicated, by eliminating distracting mannerisms, and by effectively using the voice.
4. Maintain quiet physical surroundings.

Controlling T/WP Systems

Like other administrative office systems, T/WP systems must be carefully controlled if the system is to meet its goals. As Figure 17–1 on page 442 suggests, effective writing is a very complex process that requires considerable planning and organizing as well as the use of important human skills. Particularly important to the management of the written communication process is the control of the quality of the messages produced and the costs of preparing and transmitting the messages.

Figure 17–9
A Transcriptionist's Report Evaluating the Quality of Dictation

Evaluation of Dictation

| Name of Word Originator | *M. Thomas* | Department *Customer Service* | Date *4/14/--* |

As a help to you in planning and organizing your future dictation, I am sending you the following list of difficulties that I encountered recently while transcribing your dictation:

✓ Dictation was started before the recording medium was in motion.
___ Dictation continued beyond the end of the recording medium.
Dictation was, as a rule,
___ too fast   ___ too slow   ✓ too loud   ___ too faint
___ Enunciation was not clear.
___ Proper names or unusual words were not spelled out. Examples are:

_____

✓ The location of corrections in dictated material was not given.
✓ Length of letter or memo was not given.
___ No indication was given that paragraphs or tabulations were to be inserted.
___ No instructions were given on how to set up the transcript.
___ No instructions were given at the beginning on the need for extra copies.
___ The extra number of copies needed appeared in the middle of the memo or letter, or at the end of the dictation, instead of at the beginning.
___ No indication was given as to beginning or end of quotation, indentation, or tabulation.
___ No mention was made of the number of the recording medium when dictation was continued on two or more tapes or disks.
Additional comments:_____

_____

If you have any questions or comments on this report, please call the correspondence supervisor at Extension 5981.

                                        S. Presson
                                        _____
                                        Transcriptionist's Name/Number

Distribution: White Copy – to word originator with correspondence folder
                Pink Copy – to correspondence supervisor
                Buff Copy – to transcriptionist's file

Quality Controls

The quality of written communications involves the originator's writing skills and concern for the needs of the receivers (clients, customers, etc.). The following problems should receive top priority in controlling the quality of written communications:

1. *Poor writing quality.* While most people can write well enough to be understood, one source suggests that "the real art in writing is to be able to write so that one cannot be misunderstood."[15] Writing weaknesses abound, especially those relating to sentence and paragraph structure, organization of the message, and a knowledge of sound writing psychology. However, these problems can be overcome through intensive self-study and the use of communication clinics. Some useful guidelines for creating effective written communications are outlined in Figure 17–10.

2. *Use of gobbledygook.* Excessive use of technical terms or gobbledygook often causes the reader to misunderstand the message the sender meant to convey. It is preferable for management to emphasize sending clear, straightforward messages, omitting all gobbledygook.

3. *Excessively long response time.* Responses to written communications received in the office

[15]*Correspondence Management* (Washington, DC: General Services Administration, National Archives and Records Service, Office of Records Management, 1973), p. 1.

Figure 17–10
Guidelines for
Creating Ef-
fective Written
Communica-
tions

1. Write for your reader, keeping in mind the purpose of the message and the background of the reader.

2. Organize facts in a logical order, appropriate for the situation and anticipated reader attitude.

3. Use simple, familiar words.

4. Use action verbs.

5. Keep sentences as brief as possible but vary length to maintain interest.

6. Maintain good transition and flow within paragraphs.

7. Create a friendly, positive, sincere tone.

8. Give careful attention to appearance (neatness, placement, and appropriate form).

9. Proofread carefully to avoid mechanical errors (spelling, punctuation, capitalization, and incomplete sentences).

10. Read carefully before signing. Remember that the message represents you and your organization or company.

should be prompt. Delays can lose customers and slow down operating effectiveness. By using faster production methods—such as machine dictation of letters and standardized, preprinted (form) letters—most messages can be answered within hours rather than days or weeks. The use of automated T/WP equipment also speeds up the production and distribution of letters.

4. *Lack of effective communication controls.* Without controls over the communication function, the problems outlined in this section occur repeatedly. However, with a realistic management program that includes setting policies and standards for all communication media, the company can effectively meet its objectives of conveying information between the firm and its customers or, internally, between management and employees or departments. To achieve these goals means identifying and maintaining the quality of written communications, improving the systems for producing documents, and reducing correspondence costs.

Cost Controls

While the actual costs of business correspondence vary from office to office depending upon local circumstances, all offices share a common set of factors that must be controlled if costs are to be held in line. Unfortunately, too many executives either do not understand what these factors are or do not consider the cost of correspondence to be significant enough for concern. Such persons fail to recognize the tremendous volume of such correspondence and the time required to produce it, which quickly accumulate to a very high office cost.

The basic time-related factors that must be considered when analyzing correspondence costs are:

1. *Preparing and giving dictation,* which cover the time required for jotting down notes, consulting records, conferring with others, and actually giving dictation. For the average-length letter of 175 to 185 words, 10 minutes are required for preparation, and from 5 to 10 minutes for actual dictation.

2. *Transcribing,* which covers the work of the secretary or the transcriptionist. For the average-length letter, the actual keyboarding takes 15 to 20 minutes.

3. *Reviewing and signing* the average-length letter takes 2 more minutes of originator time (see Table 17–3).

In addition to these basic costs, we find the costs of stationery, supplies, mailing, filing, and general office overhead (such as depreciation and utilities expenses).

The Dartnell Corporation estimates the costs of dictating, typing, mailing, and filing an average business letter in the United States to be $14.95, which represents an increase of more

Table 17–3
Time Factors
in Creating a
Typical 175-
Word Aver-
age-Length
Letter

| Message-Creation Action | TIME ESTIMATES (in minutes) REQUIRED BY USING: | | |
	Dictation to a Shorthand-Recording Secretary	Dictation to a Machine	Form Letters
Planning what to say	10	10	0
Dictating	10	5	0
Looking up a letter	0	0	1
Transcribing—keyboarding	20	15	1.5
Reviewing—signing	2	2	0.5
Total minutes	42	32	3

than 100 percent in 10 years. This letter cost is based upon face-to-face dictation involving an executive word originator, with a weekly salary of $1,098, and a secretary/transcriptionist, with a weekly salary of $508. These two salaries represent the largest cost factors ($6.10 for the 10 minutes of dictation time and $5.88 for the estimated 21 minutes of secretarial transcription time). Thus, labor cost is the factor where the greatest savings can be made.[16] Note, for example, in Table 17–3, the savings in time that are realized as the method of originating words moves from dictation to a shorthand-recording secretary to the use of form letters where no executive dictation time is involved. For an executive earning $50,000 a year (or about 40 cents a minute), such dictation costs alone would range from $2 to $4 for each average-length letter.

The major objective of a program to control correspondence costs is to reduce the critical labor time necessary to produce each letter or memorandum without impairing its effectiveness.

To achieve this objective, consider carefully the following suggestions:

1. *Learn to write short letters and interoffice memorandums.* They are more effective and save time for both the dictator and the transcriber, as well as the reader.
2. *Teach word originators how to prepare for efficient dictation.* All dictation should be done at one time, as early in the day as possible. Have all necessary information available to complete uninterrupted dictation. Also, schedule letter writing in accordance with its urgency and importance. A good rule to follow is to answer all mail the same day it is received, if possible. However, this should not be done if it results in unnecessary overtime costs.
3. *Eliminate unnecessary dictation* by training transcriptionists to compose replies to routine correspondence.
4. *Use form letters and automated keyboarding equipment where applicable.* Form letters play an important part in reducing the cost of correspondence, if they are carefully prepared and intelligently used (see Table 17–3). For example, use preprinted postal cards or form letters to acknowledge incoming letters when no special answer is required.

---

[16]"1993 Cost of Business Letter," *Dartnell Target Survey* (Chicago: The Dartnell Corporation, 1993), pp. 1–4. Reprinted with the permission of "From Nine to Five," Dartnell, 4660 N. Ravenwoods Avenue, Chicago, IL 60640, (800) 621-5461.

5. *Conduct correspondence-improvement clinics.* Having a communication consultant in the organization examine all copies of letters and make suggestions for reducing their length and improving their quality will help to improve the correspondence function. The application of the guidelines shown in Figure 17–10 will also assist in preparing more effective written communications.

6. *Use simplified letter styles to reduce keyboarding time.* One such letter style developed by the Administrative Management Society is characterized by (a) use of block form (all letter parts begin at the left margin), (b) omission of salutation and complimentary close, (c) keyboarding subject line in uppercase letters, and (d) leaving three or more blank lines for the originator's signature (see Figure 17–3B, page 446.) Advocates of this letter style have found that about 10 percent of keyboarding time can be saved on a 96-word letter.

7. *Answer letters by telephone whenever possible,* especially when no written record of the conversation is essential.

8. *Record handwritten answers to incoming queries in the side or bottom margins of the incoming documents and make copies of these documents to send out as answers.* The originals can then be filed, which requires less space and thus less cost.

9. *Limit the number of copies of correspondence prepared* since many copies are later thrown away. Thus, filing time as well as supplies costs are saved.

S U M M A R Y

1. Many methods are available for communicating information within and outside the firm. Where a record of these messages is needed, written communications, which include internal communications (memorandums, reports, procedures, and manuals) and external messages (principally letters), are used.

2. Written communications may be produced in both manual and automated T/WP systems. In manual systems, dictation-transcription systems are used for originating the messages, and both standard electric and electronic typewriters are used for transcribing the messages. In automated systems, messages are transcribed, stored, and, in some cases, transmitted on electronic machines with keyboards, display screens, and logic components. Later, the messages can be printed or stored on magnetic media.

3. In the modern T/WP system, we use hardware (standalone word processors, computer-connected processors, and microcomputers); software for editing and indexing documents, creating graphics, analyzing composition, and desktop publishing; and personnel with appropriate training and experience.

4. Benefits must be documented: improved productivity, increased quality, better use of equipment and personnel, closer ties among users of T/WP.

5. T/WP systems must be managed properly. To do so requires planning and organizing, developing a highly trained staff, procuring efficient equipment, and preparing appropriate control procedures.

6. Controlling correspondence costs is a major objective. Properly structured organizations and training of management and staff are critical.

FOR YOUR REVIEW

1. Define the two types of communication in the office (verbal and nonverbal). Which receives more attention and why?

2. What is text management, and what role does it serve in the communication process?

3. List four conditions under which written communications, rather than oral, are recommended for use in the office.

4. What are the management responsibilities of the writer in a communication process?

5. Define written procedures and explain the benefits of such communications.

6. What purpose is served in using office manuals as tools of managerial control?

7. Name and define four types of manuals in large firms.

8. What methods are commonly used in creating messages in a manual T/WP system? Which method is fastest and why?

9. Why would you use ETs?

10. What are the main components of automated T/WP equipment?

11. Compare traditional standalone word processors and computer-connected word processors.

12. List the six steps involved in desktop publishing (DTP) and name the types of documents produced using DTP software.

13. Name two important developments that are emerging in automated T/WP systems.

14. Outline the various organizational plans for operating a T/WP system.

15. Identify the typical responsibilities assigned to correspondence secretaries and administrative secretaries.

16. Describe measures available for reducing correspondence costs.

FOR YOUR DISCUSSION

1. Text management systems have been identified as a necessity in today's office. Yet many managers often make the mistake of believing that this function is strictly secretarial. Discuss why this statement is not true and identify at least one other user of T/WP.

2. In this chapter, written communication was defined as a management process, and yet you know that a management process involves high-level responsibilities. Is this definition correct? If so, discuss the management responsibilities in the process.

c
o
n
t

3. As office administrator, you have interviewed and hired a new secretary who will begin work in two weeks. During the interview, the job candidate asked one question: "Why do you organize your secretarial staff as T/WP and administrative secretaries?" The question continues to bother you, since you had no good response prepared. What answer should you be prepared to give—and defend—when the question is asked again—as it will be?

4. Last week a new four-part supplies requisition form was distributed to all 30 departments in the King Company. Attached to each package of forms was this note: "This new form must be filled out completely before requisitions for office supplies will be approved. Call Extension 2847 if there are questions." Discuss the communication effectiveness of such a procedure that must be followed by 400 office employees in the firm. What improvements in communications would you suggest?

5. On your computer network, Sally Stark, your new supervisor, sent you the following draft of a short letter—in very rough form. Your VDT screen shows this message:

Dear Ms. Avery I am pleased and excited to be able to inform you that are latest T/WP sofware updates are off and running. I know you will be as happy to learn of this hapning as I am to write you about it? So, why not let me explain all it's advantages to you! I just happen to be in your city Teus all day and can stop into your office at your convience. A discription of what I have to show you is inclosed for your information to accomodate your needs. Yours truly,——

Edit this message—on a VDT if available—so that it is grammatically and mechanically correct, reads well, and gets the desired response—an appointment to explain your firm's new T/WP software packages to an unhappy client. The return of her goodwill is very important to your firm.

6. As a new AOM hired by a local firm, you have been asked to help organize a communication manual for the 20-person office staff. Discuss the skills and nonskills content needed in such a manual.

7. As administrative office manager for Bethel Engineering Consultants, you sense that the cost of the keyboarding and transcription work in your firm is excessively high—perhaps as much as 30 to 40 percent above the costs of doing similar work in nearby firms. From your analysis of keyboarding/typing work patterns and costs during the past six months, you have concluded that most of the problems can be attributed to (a) improper employee selection due to the shortage of qualified clerical help; (b) the absence of any valid preemployment tests for measuring the skills, aptitudes, and interests of job applicants; (c) the fact that beginning keyboarders/typists are poorly trained and have little knowledge of business systems, work costs, English fundamentals, and spelling; (d) inadequate supervision, including a certain amount of laxness in discipline; and (e) no records of the production rates of the clerical staff. How can each of the problems cited above be resolved, given your goals of improving the quality and quantity of the work and at the same time reducing the costs?

CASES FOR CRITICAL THINKING

Case 17–1 Identifying the Basic DTP Skills

As office manager, your management has informed you that the organization is bringing its DTP in house. You have been asked to identify the DTP process, software, and hardware necessary to prepare company newsletters and brochures.

You know the necessity of this new policy (to reduce costs) and set out to complete your assignment as soon as possible.

1. List the steps involved in DTP.
2. Identify the minimum configuration of hardware.
3. Determine the software options.

Case 17–2 Designing a Collegiate T/WP System for Students

As you complete your study of T/WP systems, your instructor writes on the chalkboard: "The proof of the pudding is in the eating." The instructor elaborates by saying that you can demonstrate your overall understanding of T/WP systems by designing a prototype system for the preparation of written assignments in your class, as well as in every other class in your school. The assignment, as discussed, has these two main objectives: (1) designing a basic system that combines the main concepts found in all T/WP systems (manual or automated) and (2) offering practical suggestions for other students who must regularly apply the concepts in the preparation of reports and other written communications required for their classes.

Several sources of T/WP equipment were identified in the discussion about this case: (1) equipment available at a student's place of employment; (2) word processors, personal computers, or standard electric typewriters at home; or (3) equipment available at the college for student use in preparing written assignments.

Based upon this discussion, prepare a report in which you:

1. Provide a drawing of the basic T/WP functions required by students to produce written assignments in your college. A review of the elements making up the model of the written communication process will assist you in completing this first task (see Figure 17–1, page 442.)
2. Develop a list of practical suggestions for using the T/WP facilities available to you personally. In your list include (a) "dos and don'ts" in composing, producing, and sending written messages and (b) ideas to ensure the effective use of the T/WP facilities available to you. A review of this chapter, as well as Chapter 5, especially the sections *Barriers to Effective Communication,* page 116, and *Report-Writing Principles,* page 123, will be helpful in solving the second part of this case problem.

 ## Case 17–3 Organizational Chart/Hardware Linking: Computer Option (available on disk)

18

DISTRIBUTING INFORMATION: TELECOMMU- NICATION AND MAILING SYSTEMS

GOALS FOR THIS CHAPTER

After completing this chapter, you should be able to:

1. Define the basic components of telecommunication systems and describe how they are used in business.
2. Identify the tools of telecommunication systems that relate to the transmission of voice, data, text, and image messages.
3. Describe the most important telecommunication services that the administrative office manager must be familiar with, giving reasons for the important role each plays in administration.
4. Discuss the key phases in managing a telecommunication system, giving special attention to the problem of reducing telecommunication costs.
5. Indicate how the basic principles of management can be applied to the mailing function and differentiate between electronic mail and other mail processes.
6. Contrast the techniques for handling external mail with those available for handling internal mail in the modern firm.
7. Identify the main components in an efficient mailroom.
8. List five practices used to control mailing costs in the office.

Telecommunications can be defined, in simplified terms, as the electronic transfer of data from one point in an information system to another. In today's business environment, telecommunications is the tool for linking computers and other devices to exchange information.

As a phase in the information cycle shown in Figure 1–4, page 7, **information distribution** transmits or moves information from the place in which it is processed to the point where it will be used. In the office, much information continues to be transmitted by telephone, a term that comes from two Greek words—*tele,* far, and *phon,* sound—which explains the basic purpose of this universal "information-movement" device. The telephone instantly transmits sounds over distances too far for the human voice to carry. The ease of use, expanded features, and general availability of the telephone have made it a necessary tool in modern telecommunications.

If we are to believe the futurists, telecommunications will interconnect the world. As business continues to move to international marketplaces, telecommunications will become increasingly important in today's competitive environment.[1]

Telecommunication systems, along with emerging technologies, as a basic tool of administrative office management, are discussed in this chapter. In addition, we shall examine effective mailing systems as a vital method for transmitting messages over long distances. Special emphasis is given to ensuring the proper use and control of operating costs in both of these information-distribution systems.

---

[1]Kathleen P. Wagoner and Mary M. Ruprecht, *End-User Computing* (Cincinnati: South-Western Publishing Co., 1993), p. 240.

TELECOMMUNICATION SYSTEMS

To maintain a competitive edge, both small and large firms recognize the need for effective communications. Successful large businesses expand from local to national and multinational concerns, because we as consumers accept their products and services and because of the firms' abilities to compete. Much of this growth depends upon communication facilities that enable firms to respond quickly to the demands of markets and suppliers of raw materials wherever they are located.

Smaller companies use voice communications to an increasing degree for speeding up the flow of information. With such simple devices as the telephone and some of its services described later in this chapter, orders can be received and processed, raw materials and supplies purchased, personnel recruited, and financial transactions processed. With the advent of microcomputers that are within the price range of the small office,

the telephone is commonly linked to the computer, which opens up many new opportunities for improving communications.

In this section, you will see that all telecommunication systems revolve around the same basic concepts found in the communication model shown in Figure 5–1, page 106—a sender-receiver relationship built around a message. However, in the case of telecommunications, the media may differ in certain cases. Elements in a telecommunication system may be classified as (1) *voice communication,* (2) *data communication,* (3) *text communication,* and (4) *image,* or *graphics communication.* Messages sent in telecommunication systems require a certain **bandwidth**—the amount of space needed to transmit messages on telecommunication channels similar to the number of lanes on a freeway system. Voice systems require a narrower—hence, less expensive—bandwidth than nonvoice systems.

Figure 18–1

The Principal Elements in a Telecommunication System

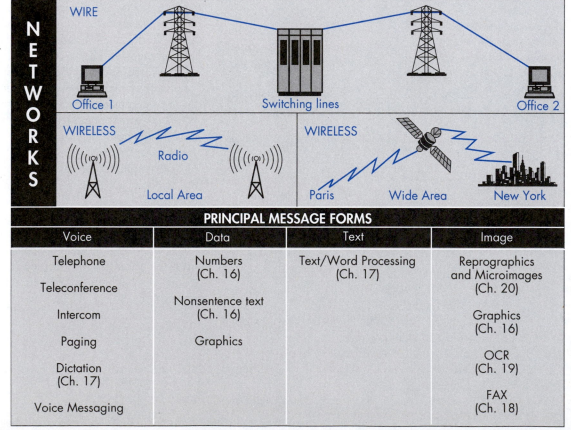

Voice	Data	Text	Image
Telephone	Numbers (Ch. 16)	Text/Word Processing (Ch. 17)	Reprographics and Microimages (Ch. 20)
Teleconference	Nonsentence text (Ch. 16)		
Intercom			Graphics (Ch. 16)
Paging	Graphics		
Dictation (Ch. 17)			OCR (Ch. 19)
Voice Messaging			FAX (Ch. 18)

PRINCIPAL MESSAGE FORMS

Both wire and wireless methods of telecommunication are used in and between organizations, as shown in Figure 18–1.[2] Also, both methods are used in *local-area, metropolitan-area,* and *wide-area* (long-distance) *networks,* which are discussed later in this chapter.

Figure 18–1 outlines the principal types of messages sent through telecommunication channels and the networks available for sending these messages. Each type of message—voice and non-voice—is discussed in detail in this chapter. Other related uses of telecommunication systems in the office (word processing, reprographics, and microimages) are also shown in this figure. A discussion of these uses can be found in the textbook chapters shown in parentheses.

THE TOOLS OF TELECOMMUNICATION SYSTEMS

Specialists in telecommunications classify the tools or technology used in their systems according to the basic nature of the message transmitted. The technological "tools" used in each of these message-sending systems are discussed in this section.

Voice Communication Tools

In a **voice communication system,** messages are originated by speakers and sent by wire or wireless methods to listeners who receive and respond to the messages. Generally, we should use voice communications rather than written messages when the following conditions exist:

1. The message to be sent is short and simple.
2. The speed of transmission is important.
3. There is no need for lengthy study or for later reference to the message. However, by using

recording equipment, voice messages can be retained for later reference.
4. The personal touch found in face-to-face communication is needed.

Other circumstances may suggest the need for voice communications, such as when the channels we use for sending written messages are overloaded. A telephone call, for example, gets more immediate attention from an executive than a special-delivery letter on the executive's desk. In some cases, a voice message is more easily received, as in a dim or dark hallway, or when workers have to move around frequently in their work environment.

Each of these criteria should be evaluated carefully by the AOM in considering the communication needs of the office. When most of these conditions are present, a voice communication system should be considered.

Telephone Systems

As we see in Figure 18–1, the basic telephone has been incorporated into telecommunication systems that handle images or graphics and text, as well as voice. However, the basic nature and common purpose of the telephone remain the same—to transmit voice messages between two persons.

The volume of telephone calls determines the kind and size of system needed. Two basic types of telephone systems—key and switching—are discussed below.

Key Telephone Systems. A small business, at the outset, may have only one telephone with one local line. As the company grows, however, it needs more telephones and a greater number of lines, which require the use of a larger system. A **key telephone system (KTS)** has two or more telephones connected to several telephone lines, each of which can be reached by each telephone set. For typically fewer than 50 to 60 users, the KTS is the main form of telecommunication in the small office.[3] A typical example is the KTS set with caller identification (ID) shown in Illustration 18–1. With this equipment controlled by efficient switchboard operators, each telephone

---

[2]Wire communications have greatly expanded because of the introduction of fiber optics as replacements for copper wires. **Fiber optics** are fiberglass threads along which units of information are translated into light waves by a laser beam and then "pumped" through the glass fiber. With fiber optics, message transmission is much faster and less expensive since more messages can be sent over networks in a given period of time and in a more reliable fashion. This is true since fiberglass threads are not as subject to atmospheric conditions as copper wires.

[3]G. Gordon Long, "Technology Is Enhancing Telephone and Fax Systems," *Office Systems'89* (January, 1989), p. 16.

Illustration 18–1 Modern telephone equipment with caller ID.

provides access to all central office lines for both incoming and outgoing calls; one of the buttons permits placing a call "on hold"; another may be assigned to an intercom system. In today's modern office, an increasing number of telephones transmit more than voice messages, as we shall see later in this chapter. When the number of telephones in use becomes too large (more than 50 as a rule), a switching system must be installed.

Switching Systems. A **switching system** receives and distributes internal and external calls without the need for a switchboard operator. The earliest switching system—the **private branch exchange (PBX)**—was operated manually by a switchboard operator where the number of extension telephones was not great and the volume of calls was not heavy. Gradually, electronic functions were built into the PBX, and the **private automatic branch exchange (PABX)** was created. When operating under computer control, PABX switching systems perform many time-saving calling tasks, such as the following:

1. *Executive override,* which enables an operator to cut in on another extension that is in use.
2. *Automatic call distribution (ACD),* which allows the sharing of calls among a number of answering locations so that calls are served in order of arrival; and *call-waiting display,* which provides the worker with an indication of the number of calls waiting to be answered. Another feature, called *camp-on,* extends an additional call to a busy station.
3. *Conference calls* in which three or more persons are connected for local or long-distance conversation.
4. *Automatic call-back,* which alerts a user when a desired number is no longer busy and then redials the desired number.
5. *Automatic least-cost route selection,* which completes outgoing calls automatically over the least-expensive route available.
6. *Call forwarding,* which automatically transfers calls to another internal or external telephone number. A related feature, *hunting,* routes calls automatically to an alternate station when the called station is busy.
7. *Automatic dialing of frequently called numbers* in which some devices can store up to 60 numbers in their memory for local and long-distance calling and "remember" the last number dialed manually. Programming to add new numbers or to change numbers already stored takes only a few seconds. Another dialing aid is *speed dialing,* which allows calls to be completed internally and externally by dialing an abbreviated number. Many of the most automated telephones are equipped with boards or screens on the telephone console for displaying the number called or other pertinent information.
8. *Hands-free operation,* which allows two-way communication without lifting the telephone handset.
9. *Night service,* which routes calls normally directed to one station to an alternate destination. This is a useful service during lunch breaks and after normal business hours.
10. *Voice mail,* which allows for a recorded message to respond to the caller, and can be stored indefinitely and transported to many persons. In addition, voice mail has two-way voice messaging capability which allows an individual to send, receive, redirect, and reply to voice messages using a touch-tone telephone.

The advances in telephone technology provide options to business and home users, as never before seen. A variety of helpful features such as programmable memory keys for automatically dialing frequently called numbers and a convenient display window are available. The number of telephone features continues to grow and, if properly applied, will help to improve productivity in the offices of the future.

Intercommunication Systems. For many employees making internal calls, an outside line is not necessary. When many internal calls are made, an **intercommunication** (or **intercom**) **system** should be considered. This system is a privately owned, small-scale telephone system that ties together all departments. Typically, two types of intercommunication systems are found: telephone-based systems and dedicated systems. Both types of systems transmit information rapidly and enable personnel to remain at their desks. Thus, productivity is enhanced.

In *telephone-based systems,* such as the one shown in Illustraion 18–2, the intercom functions are built into the telephone unit as an added capability of the PBX or PABX systems. Such an intercom system requires low installation charges and offers privacy as well as excellent sound quality. Its main drawback is the potential danger that internal calls may block incoming or outgoing telephone calls.

A *dedicated system* uses a unit that is separate from the telephone. In this case, the problems of blocking telephone calls and tying up a switchboard are eliminated. However, a dedicated system must be leased or purchased, which adds to overhead costs.

Manufacturers of intercom equipment provide many options, including the following:

1. *Hands-free operation,* which lets users talk into a speaker without the need for a handset. Thus, users are free to work with their hands, search through files, or move about.
2. *Handset systems that give privacy to workers.* These units can be installed on desks, walls, or in drawers to avoid distractions or being overheard by a caller from another workstation. With a "silent," dedicated intercom system, a

quiet audio "beep" announces incoming messages on the display dial. Each workstation is assigned its own one or two-digit number to use in identifying the sender. Messages up to 64 characters in length are repeated automatically on the dial until a response is received.

3. *Priority features* that allow a designated station to cancel or interrupt ongoing conversations in order to transmit urgent messages.
4. *One- or two-conversation arrangements* between managers and their staffs, or simultaneous conference calls to a number of stations.
5. *Tie-in between the intercom system and centralized support centers,* such as the text/word processing center, enabling all word originators to dial a number on the intercom set, dictate their correspondence, and have it keyboarded without leaving their desks.

Since intercommunication machines connect two or more departments within a firm, an interdepartmental systems study must be conducted to determine the most effective equipment installation required. For example, after one large insurance firm installed a new central filing system, it became clear that new communication services would be required since telephone requests for files were being delayed due to other uses of the

Illustration 18–2 Intercom system.

telephone system. As a result, a private intercom system was installed, making it possible to request files without disturbing regular telephone conversations.

Voice-Recognition and Audio-Response Systems

A **voice-recognition system**—sometimes called *speech recognition*—is a computer-based system in which the computer "understands" and records the human voice as input and performs operations based upon this input. In order to recognize a voice, the computer system stores patterns of words that must be matched to words that we speak; and only when the spoken word is in the computer "library" does recognition occur. Small systems provide 1,500 or fewer word vocabularies, and the largest systems, 20,000 and higher word vocabularies.

Voice-recognition applications include data entry, instructions for controlling various systems, dictation, and a wide range of specialized functions. Such systems bypass the need to convert the message to written form. Thus, we no longer must learn to operate a terminal but only to speak in a manner that a computer can understand. With this system, data-entry errors, such as the transposing of digits or the misspelling of words, almost disappear, and processing responses by the computer to the messages are immediate.

A typical example of a voice-recognition system involves an incoming telephone call from a customer. The call is transmitted to the voice-recognition device of the person called, at which point the voice message is translated into the digital (numeric) code required for computer processing. Because of certain peculiarities of human speech (dialects, slurring of words, speaking too fast or too slowly, and speaking indistinctly), we notice limitations to this type of system; but these restrictions can be overcome. Currently, customer ordering, internal ordering of parts from stockrooms, and hotel and airline reservation systems accept voice entry rather than requiring speaking in person to an order clerk.

In an **audio-response system,** a computer-activated voice answers questions using a vocabulary stored in the system. Such systems have been in widespread use for years in the time-of-day and temperature-reporting systems arranged through local telephone companies. Also, in account-inquiry systems in banks, customers can simply request their current account balance or transfer funds, and a mechanical voice responds. A larger system is illustrated in the freight-carrying industry where shipment status reports must be furnished 24 hours a day. In one such system, with an 800-word vocabulary, a customer dials a toll-free number to receive quick, concise shipment status reports (route data, trailer numbers, times of arrival and departure, etc.) delivered by a computer-generated voice. Responses by voice alert people more rapidly than visual messages, and labor costs are reduced by eliminating the need for human operators.

Wireless (Radio) Communication Systems

Just as voice mail did a few years ago, wireless data networks will change the way you communicate on the job. As distances increase between senders and receivers of messages and as the channels of communication by wire become overloaded, managers turn to *wireless* (or *radio*) *communication systems* for transmitting messages of all kinds. It is estimated that eventually 90 percent of our workers will be "wireless"—freed from their desks, telephones, and computers. Thus, as the workforce becomes more mobile, the ability to move information without wires becomes crucial.[4] Traditional wireless systems, such as paging, as well as modern systems (cellular telephones and microwave and satellite systems) are discussed briefly in this section.

Paging Systems. We use **paging systems** to locate persons—often executives, doctors, and emergency personnel—who are away from their desks or workstations. Typically, paging systems are available as one-way radio receivers (pocket-size equipment such as "beepers") that receive short-duration messages in the form of voice, a digital readout, or a "beep" up to several miles from a paging transmission center. After you, the

---

[4]Andrew Kupper, "Look, Ma! No Wires!" *Fortune* (December, 1993), p. 147.

paged party, receive a message, you may access the caller over regular telephone lines. Currently, doctors, sales representatives, and others who must maintain close contact with their firms represent the largest users.

Some paging systems are telephone based. In such a system, each executive is given a number that must be dialed for paging. When the number is dialed, a signal corresponding to that number will sound. As soon as the executive hears the sound, he or she goes to the nearest telephone, calls the switchboard, and receives the message. Two-way contact is thereby provided.

Cellular Telephone Systems. The **cellular telephone,** or *mobile telephone,* is a radio-based wireless communication system for receiving and transmitting voice messages within a limited geographic area, such as a large city or an overall area of approximately 50 to 150 miles. The cellular telephone system uses individual phone units that pick up signals being transmitted from multiple radio towers provided in each of the areas covered. The system is tied together by a computer system that switches signals from one "cell" or geographic area to another as the user moves, usually in an automobile. Typical local users—sales and field service representatives of firms operating within a few miles of the main office, real estate agents, and doctors and medical

Figure 18–2
A Cellular Telephone System

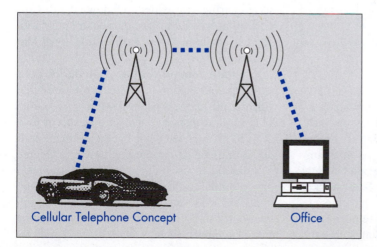

Cellular Telephone Concept   Office

Illustration 18–3 A typical cellular telephone in operation.

technicians who need to maintain contact with their offices or with hospitals—spend a significant part of their working day in their automobiles. Advances in communication technology permit cellular phones to be used nationwide. While the cellular telephone permits such persons to keep in touch with their "bases" of operation, it has several disadvantages. Such disadvantages include high costs of equipment and relatively high costs for service.[5] Figure 18–2 shows the cellular telephone concept.

Microwave and Satellite Communication Systems. Microwave and satellite communication systems represent further extension of the cellular telephone concept. In a **microwave communication system,** a radio-relay system sends signals between towers located many miles apart (see Figure 18–3A). The signals are amplified and retransmitted until the message reaches its destination.

A **communication satellite (Comsat)** consists of two or more ground transmitter-receiver stations and a satellite "parked" in space above

[5]Thomas J. Housel and William E. Darden III, *Introduction to Telecommunications: The Business Perspective* (Cincinnati: South-Western Publishing Co., 1988), p. 174. This publication offers, in nontechnical language, a comprehensive discussion of telecommunications from a managerial point of view.

Figure 18–3
Common
Wireless Com-
munication
Media

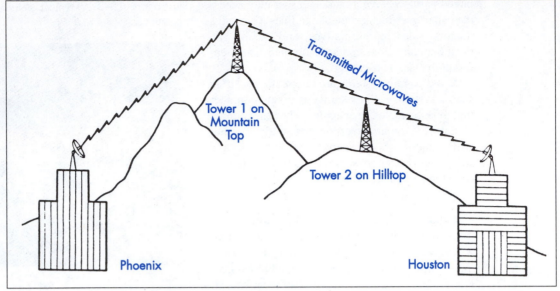

A—A Microwave System

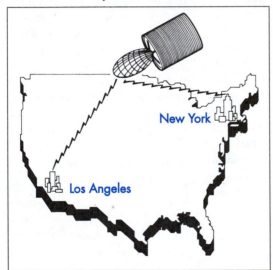

B—A Communication Satellite

the earth. Information is beamed from the transmitter on earth to the satellite, where the message is directed to a receiving point at another earth location (see Figure 18–3B). As an example of the use of Comsat, *Time* magazine in New York City prepares the copy for its latest weekly edition and transmits the copy (text and color) in under one minute by Comsat to its remote printing facilities all over the United States near the points of distribution. Thus, the magazine is ready for local distribution, and the typical problems of length of time, distance, and cost are greatly reduced.

Data Communication Tools

As information systems become more complex, management relies on high-speed interstate communication systems that send and receive information of all kinds at high rates of speed in several forms—voice, and, to an increasing extent, nonvoice (data, text, and image). The limitations of voice communication systems, discussed earlier, are widely acknowledged. Consequently, we find that data communication systems are used when transmitting over long distances.

In a **data communication system,** the computer or other electronic systems are combined with the telephone system to send prerecorded data over long distances at electronic speeds to be received by a related device at the destination. In this setting, the *data* represent, to a large degree, (1) numeric records and words in *nonsentence form* essential to the operation of business functions, such as accounting, finance, banking, order-entry statistics, and remote data processing; and (2) symbols, such as @, #, $, %, &, and the

Greek letter symbols commonly used in business statistics.[6]

Basic Data Communication Concepts

Data communication has rapidly evolved into a highly complex profession that includes computers, engineering communications such as the telephone system, and electronics. To understand it thoroughly, we must have a technical background beyond that necessary for managing the modern office. However, if you are holding a position as an AOM, you will be responsible for office communications; hence, you must understand the following basic nontechnical concepts that underlie the data communication process:

---

[6]Early data communication systems were limited to the transmission of nonvoice information. With the passage of time and the integration of many communication forms, modern data communication systems have been developed for sending and receiving both voice and nonvoice information. However, their main thrust remains the same—to transmit nonvoice information to remote locations.

1. *Data communication systems specialize in the movement of information through networks of interconnected machines.* In telecommunications, a *network* is simply a series of points connected by one or more communication channels.

In the automated office discussed in Chapter 16, you are likely to find local-area networks. *A local-area network (LAN) is a telecommunication facility that links together various types of information-processing equipment (by coaxial cable or fiber optics) for transmitting and receiving data.* A LAN permits departments to (a) share resources, such as all PC operators using one departmental printer; (b) exchange interoffice mail with other computer users in the office building; (c) keep track of how often software is used, by whom, and for how long; and (d) provide an efficient method of handling interoffice communications. Figure 18–4 shows a typical LAN.

Figure 18–4
A Local-Area Network (LAN)

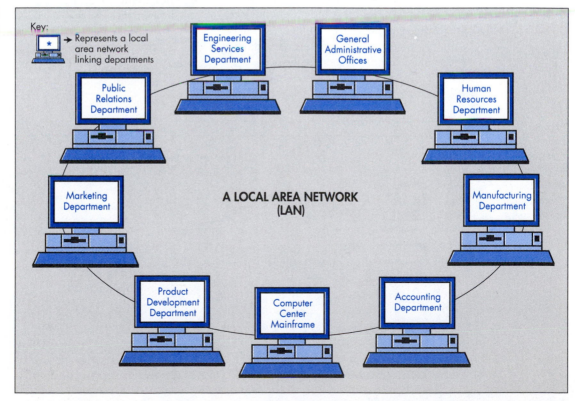

Key:
→ Represents a local area network linking departments

Engineering Services Department

General Administrative Offices

Public Relations Department

Human Resources Department

Marketing Department

A LOCAL AREA NETWORK (LAN)

Manufacturing Department

Product Development Department

Computer Center Mainframe

Accounting Department

A **wide-area,** or *long-distance,* **network (WAN),** discussed later in this chapter, covers a large geographic area and consists of dedicated and private or public channels for transmitting and receiving messages.

An intermediate-distance network, the **metropolitan-area network (MAN),** has been in use for several years. MANs are networks covering a geographic area of up to 30 miles (50 kilometers) that are capable of transmitting voice, data, text, and image signals at the same time. We expect MANs to be used to connect common-carrier long-distance service to local lines, as well as to serve companies needing a local network of great capacity.

2. *The simplest form of data communications involves data transmission only.* This process requires the use of sending and receiving equipment linked to a communication medium, such as a telephone line or a microwave system.

3. *The computer-based communication process is more complex than a transmission-only system.* The computer-based process involves *capturing* or *entering* data, frequently using the VDT, processing such data by computer or related word processor, and transmitting the data over one or more communication facilities.

The computer-based data communication system in its most simplified form is shown in Figure 18–5.

Note that the data must first be entered into the system, typically through one or many VDT keyboards. Within the terminal, the data are encoded automatically in digital (numeric) form, as a series of discrete binary electrical impulses (1's and 0's) for processing in the local computer or for transmission in unprocessed form to a destination computer. Next, the electronic digital codes representing the computer output must be converted to an *analog code*—that is, a continuous electronic signal "analogous" to the sound being transmitted—by a device called a *modem,* in order to be acceptable to the telephone system.[7] With this code conversion accomplished, the data are transmitted by telephone line to a modem at the destination. This time the coded signals are converted back to digital code

---

[7]**Modem** is an abbreviation for *modulator-demodulator.* This device converts the digital code of the computer into an analog code used by the telephone system. Modems are also used to convert an analog code back to digital code for use within the computer-based data communication system, as shown in Figure 18–5.

Figure 18–5
Basic Components of a Computer-Based Data Communication System

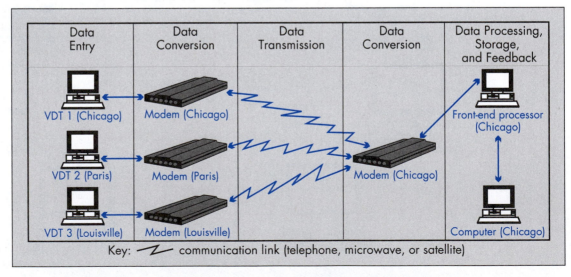

Data Entry	Data Conversion	Data Transmission	Data Conversion	Data Processing, Storage, and Feedback
VDT 1 (Chicago)	Modem (Chicago)			Front-end processor (Chicago)
VDT 2 (Paris)	Modem (Paris)		Modem (Chicago)	
VDT 3 (Louisville)	Modem (Louisville)			Computer (Chicago)

Key: ⟿ communication link (telephone, microwave, or satellite)

form so that the computer—a digital machine—can process, store, or route the data. The controls for handling the automated phases of this system reside in a *front-end processor,* which takes some of the burden off the computer. The results of computer processing can be returned to any terminal located in any part of the world.

Organizations with complex information-processing requirements and with widely dispersed office locations make great use of data communication systems. For example, a multinational firm with a main office in Chicago receives and transmits information to and from its Paris branch office with the same efficiency as to its Louisville branch office (see Figure 18–5). With these capabilities, management can expect such administrative improvements as:

• Reduced time in preparing payrolls and delivery of orders.
• Added operational efficiencies because all distant branches are tied together and more current information is available to all.
• Reduced costs from more efficient order handling, inventory control, accounting, and data processing.
• Improved customer service stemming from better stock availability, better work scheduling, and prompt delivery of orders.

Data Communication Equipment

Two types of equipment are basic to the operation of a data communication system: (1) telephone or related wireless equipment and (2) computer systems equipment and software. The first category is highly technical in nature and is typically outside the direct responsibility of the AOM. The second category, on the other hand, is an AOM's responsibility. Computer systems equipment includes computers, principally mainframes and microcomputers, and terminals. Each of these equipment items, as components of a telecommunication system, is briefly discussed below.

As we saw earlier, a *mainframe* is a large computer that processes large amounts of data at very fast speeds, and a *microcomputer,* or personal

computer, is a small computer that can be adapted with software packages to operate in a data communication system. We may think of these two types of computers as terminal equipment when they are connected to an internal (LAN) or external (WAN) network. Modems are required for conversion of the computer data, which is in digital form, to the analog form required by the telephone system. Both mainframes and microcomputers can be equipped with built-in jacks for a telephone plug in order to link the computer hardware to the telephone system for transmitting electronic messages. At one time, networks contained only a single type of computer hardware and/or software. However, with the development of *gateways* (connection devices), virtually any kind of hardware and software can communicate.

The most common application of data communications is a mainframe, minicomputer, or a file server (referred to as the host computer) with a network of computer terminals connected to it.[8] Typically, we find three categories of terminals, which are described below in increasing degrees of automation:

1. A **dumb terminal** is a data-entry terminal with an alphanumeric keyboard and printer (the teletypewriter) or a video display terminal (VDT), which is connected to a mainframe via a communication link. A dumb terminal has no capability for processing data on its own (that is, no capability of being programmed); rather, it can only receive, display, and send information through its communication link to the mainframe. Specialized applications of dumb terminals include banking terminals that accept coded identification cards and/or keyed input to permit banking transactions to be carried out automatically; point-of-sale terminals for automating retail sales transactions; and industrial data collection terminals operated by factory workers to collect production control, inventory, and timekeeping information.

---

[8]Robert Moskowitz, "Building Server-Based LANs," *Modern Office Technology* (May, 1992), pp. 50–54.

2. A **smart terminal** is a dumb terminal to which have been added more powerful features capable of processing operations independent of the mainframe. It may have a limited amount of memory with a built-in program, which cannot be altered by the user. Typical uses of smart terminals involve composing electronic mail, editing messages, and controlling attached printers and other input devices. By performing these operations, a smart terminal reduces connect time to the mainframe and thus overall telecommunication costs. Most such terminals are being replaced with intelligent terminals.

3. An **intelligent terminal** is programmable by a user and can operate independently of the computer system to which it is attached. Since an intelligent terminal can store internally its own operating instructions, it can operate as a computer as well as a terminal. For example, the operator of an intelligent terminal can direct the device not only to display a business invoice on the screen but also to compute the extensions and totals on the displayed document. As such, this intelligent terminal removes many of the routine storage and processing tasks from the mainframe, which then has added time for larger-volume jobs.

Text Communication Tools

The preparation of text, commonly called word processing, is treated in detail in Chapter 17, along with the hardware, software, and systems needed to manage the *text-producing* function. In this section, we shall examine the tools for *transmitting* text messages.

Electronic Mail

As the name implies, **electronic mail** is the process of delivering mail by electronic signals over telecommunication lines, thus eliminating the need for the physical delivery of paper documents. However, it is more a concept than a technology, for the "umbrella" term "electronic mail" includes a broad range of devices that substitute the transmission of electronic codes over wire or wireless for the physical delivery of paper documents through the mails.

Electronic mail (E-mail) transmits information in many forms from terminals within organizations or via public service networks, such as MCI Mail, Sprint, Western Union's Easy-Link, or Tymnet, Uninet, and Telenet. Historically, its use has been in firms with three or more locations, 50 or more employees, and a large volume of communications that must be delivered under the pressure of time. The basic process of sending and receiving electronic mail, as well as the major types of equipment for doing so, are charted in Figure 18–6. Each type is covered in this section.

Facsimile. The **facsimile,** or *FAX,* **process** permits exact copies of written, printed, or graphic information to be sent and received over regular telephone lines as well as by satellite. Thus, handwritten notes, signatures, forms, drawings, and other graphics may be sent over long distances in a kind of "remote photocopy" process. In addition, with software provided by communication carriers, such as Western Union, we can send FAX messages directly from computer terminals or our PC. At the sending end, a *transceiver* (equipment that both *transmits* and *receives*) scans or "reads" a document and converts the data to electronic signals to be sent by wire or wireless. At the receiving end, a second transceiver accepts the message and decodes it to produce an exact error-free copy (a facsimile) of the original document. (Only black, white, and gray characters can be transmitted.) In a few seconds, the receiver has an exact copy of an original document at less than a dollar per page. Any offices that are linked by telephone can be connected by facsimile equipment, as shown on Figure 18–6. FAX modems are a step in the right direction to a paperless office.[9] In addition, PCs can be equipped with internal FAX boards, which allow an individual to send a FAX directly from a PC to a receiver.

Over the last few years, facsimile has achieved major acceptance in business firms. Users are

---

[9]Steve Deyo, "Are We Paperless Yet?" *ComputerUser* (August, 1993), p. 4.

Figure 18–6
The Electronic
Mail Process

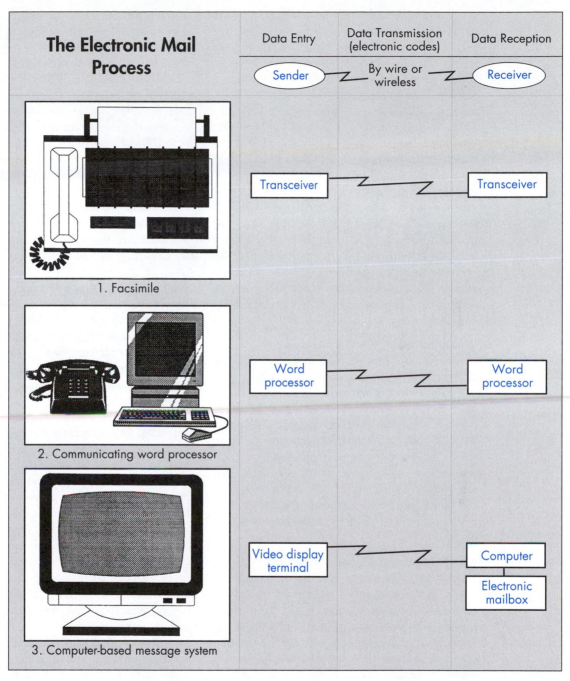

The Electronic Mail Process

	Data Entry	Data Transmission (electronic codes)	Data Reception
	Sender	By wire or wireless	Receiver
1. Facsimile	Transceiver		Transceiver
2. Communicating word processor	Word processor		Word processor
3. Computer-based message system	Video display terminal		Computer / Electronic mailbox

now "FAXing" documents as common practice. Even company letterheads and business cards display an alternate FAX number beneath the company telephone number. FAX users can make quick copies of documents, let callers leave voice messages on the FAX machine, or use the telephone built into the machine to make calls.

FAX is especially valuable for international communications since, in effect, it eliminates time differences because the message can be stored until the receiver is able to retrieve it. At the same time, FAX has destroyed an important period of communications "float." While writing a letter takes time to compose, type, seal in an envelope, stamp and post, FAX does not give an executive time for second thoughts. The FAX market, which was approximately $2.5 billion in 1985, is expected to top $12 billion by 1995; Dataquest, a San Jose, California, market research firm, projected 3.2 million units would have been installed by 1993.[10] By sending FAX messages, we give the receiver a suggestion of urgency, when, in fact, the message may be routine. In addition, since many FAX machines are installed in the mail room or some other central location, information-security problems arise. To prevent this type of problem, the most advanced machines store communications that receivers may retrieve only by punching in a code or using a passkey.

Communicating Word Processor. Some of the advanced word processors discussed in Chapter 17 have communicating capabilities. Thus, on a **communicating word processor,** after a document is keyed, edited, and recorded, the entire message is transmitted over telephone lines at the push of a button. At the destination, the message can be displayed on the word processor screen or printed out. As a result, at the receiving end, rekeying is eliminated, as is the need to proofread and make corrections a second time. Most major word processing software systems have these capabilities.

Computer-Based Message System. A sophisticated type of electronic mail is the computer-based message system, sometimes called an *electronic message system (EMS).* In a **computer-based message system,** specialized instructions or programs are added to an existing computer system in order to send and receive written messages electronically almost anywhere in the world. Each system user is assigned a computer storage area called an **electronic mailbox,**

which is identified by a location code or a special user-name code. At the sending site, a user keyboards a message on the VDT keyboard and directs the message to the receiver's electronic mailbox at the destination. Here the message is received by an audible "beep" and filed until the receiver makes an inquiry of the system. At a convenient time, the receiver sits down at a similar VDT and keys in his or her name and authorization code. On command, the system instantly *identifies a list* of senders and their incoming messages (by subject only). The reader then decides which messages to view on the terminal screen and has them *printed out* if desired. Other messages are left in the computerized file for later reading. In this system, the sender and the receiver are not required to be in simultaneous communication, which eliminates the expensive time "game" called *telephone tag* in which an office worker keeps calling back until the called party is available to talk. Studies show that about 75 percent of all telephone calls do not reach the intended receiver on the first try, which costs, at the vice-presidential level, an average of *$10 per completed call.*[11]

This computer-based system enables office personnel to handle from 25 to 30 mail items an hour, which is comparable in time to placing 5 or 6 telephone calls. Problems can be handled in their order of importance, and multiple copies of messages can be sent to persons on a distribution list. Not counting the cost of the terminals, such messages can be sent for less than $1 each.

The benefits of E-mail are ongoing and quickly identifiable. In the *Dialog from the Workplace,* Roger Courts, director of a not-for-profit organization with over 100 employees, describes several steps to achieve the benefits of electronic mail.

A slight variation of the electronic mailbox is a computer-based system called **voice mail,** or *voice store and forward system.* In this system, the telephone, the computer, and a special recording device are used for immediate or later delivery of one-way voice messages. The person

---

[10]Kathleen P. Wagoner and Mary M. Ruprecht, *End-User Computing* (Cincinnati: South-Western Publishing Co., 1993), p. 258.

[11]David Barcomb, *Office Automation, A Survey of Tools and Technology,* 2nd ed. (Bedford, MA: Digital Press, 1989), p. 174.

DIALOG FROM THE WORKPLACE

ROGER COURTS

Director and CEO
Sacred Heart League
Walls, Mississippi

Mr. Roger Courts, a native Mississippian, is in his thirty-fifth year of service for the League. The Sacred Heart League is a not-for-profit Catholic communications and direct-mail, fund-raising organization with member-donors in all 50 states and Puerto Rico. In his position as director and CEO, he is responsible for directing the entire operation of the Sacred Heart League, a 120-employee organization. All funding for the programs in education, social services, housing, and transportation is provided through the efforts of the League, which has a full line of services from information systems and printing to a fully equipped mail department. In recent years, Mr. Courts has served as either chairman or board member for a number of local and national organizations including: chairman and board member of the National Federation of Nonprofits, a Washington-based, grass roots organization overseeing the concerns of the charitable sector in legislative, regulatory, and postal issues; and committee member of the United States Postmaster General's Work-Share Task Force, 1988. Mr. Courts received his B.A. in psychology and English from Memphis State University.

QUESTION: How has electronic mail and networked microcomputers changed the way you communicate within the office?

RESPONSE: When I came to work at the Sacred Heart League 35 years ago, most of us were located in a large, open, cinderblock building. Our desks were in close proximity, and it was easy to physically pass documents to one another, along with a spoken message. As the organization grew, our work space grew commensurately. Soon, we had to resort to an intercom system (at that time intercoms were separate from the telephone system) and an interoffice mail system to prevent a significant waste of time, as employees at all pay levels trotted about the office, dropping off materials and, of course, visiting and "catching up on the latest" along the way. Then came the day when our office facility had expanded to a plant of over 50,000 square feet. A more efficient means of communication was a necessity. Our office automation consultant, Mary Ruprecht, provided the answer: electronic mail.

At first, we were reluctant to explore the possibilities, feeling that virtually every information system need deserved a higher priority than this one. In time, we did install a mainframe electronic mail system for communicating and scheduling meetings. In no time, this E-mail system became as much a part of everyone's routine as a stapler and a coffee mug. Now, we are using a greatly enhanced electronic mail and scheduling system on our LAN which serves some 60 PCs throughout the organization. One out of every two employees has a PC.

The tremendous advantage afforded by an E-mail system was dramatically illustrated to me recently, when I returned to work after a two-week vacation. There were 65 E-mail messages awaiting me, along with a foot-high stack of interoffice envelopes (over 50 in number). The E-mail messages required 29 minutes to read, answer, or otherwise dispose of. It was midmorning of my second day back before I was able to process the accumulation of interoffice envelopes.

Our goal is to decrease the volume of interoffice mail by transferring as much of it as possible to the E-mail system. A paperless office is not yet possible in our applications, but without a doubt, we are moving on an uninterrupted course in that direction. In today's climate of competitiveness, an organization simply cannot tolerate the inefficiencies of yesterday's technologies and processes.

placing the call enters the code number (i.e., the voice-mail address) of the person being called and dictates the message into the telephone. This message is automatically converted into digital, or numeric, form for immediate delivery. If the person called is not in the office, the message is stored in the computer's mailbox. Later, when the recipient dials the code number of his or her mailbox to obtain messages, the computer reconverts the messages of the callers into their own voices. Such voice mail can be stored indefinitely and transported to many persons. The advances in technology have made it very easy for those in "floating offices" to do business. One of the most beneficial features for people "on the road" is voice mail's two-way voice messaging capability. Two-way voice messaging allows an employee to send, receive, redirect, and reply to voice messages using a touch-tone telephone, rather than simply receive messages (as with an answering machine). Messages are recorded in the employee's own voice, which allows the employee to convey emotion or urgency.

Typically, a voice mailbox can store more than 50 five-minute messages at any one time, and messages can be saved for approximately two weeks. When a message is deposited into someone's mailbox, that person hears a stutter dial tone or sees a "message waiting" light displayed on the phone, depending on the PBX. With 24-hour availability, two-way voice messaging eliminates the problems of telephone tag and time zone differences.[12]

Videotext

Videotext is a telecommunication process in which textual data—and sometimes graphics—are transmitted to specially adapted television sets. Videotext allows users to interact with each other and various databases through computer systems. Systems are able to use a telephone network or cable television network. Information is provided through a special editing terminal that permits the user to construct pages for sending

copy to a computer for storage in a central computer file. To retrieve information, the user must have a special television set or a special adaptor to a regular television set. Access to the computer system is gained by dialing the computer's telephone number. If the call is answered, the user must supply an approved password or passnumber, after which a link is established and communication can begin. A related process, **videofax**, enables users of video equipment to send still images, such as photographs, over public or dedicated telephone lines in the same manner that documents are sent via conventional FAX devices. Photographs in color may be printed on the color unit at the destination. The merging of several major companies, such as Sony and Columbia Broadcasting System in 1993, has ensured acceleration of this technology by bringing together a major electronics company and a major television broadcasting company. This merger provides the opportunity to bring to market new and improved videotext options.

Image Communication Tools

Image communication involves communication symbols that are mainly transmitted in nonword, nonvoice, and nonnumber form. Three categories of image communication are available: facsimile, video, and graphics. However, with the many advances made in information technology, including the integration of functions originally performed by one-function machines, we find that the distinctions among the methods of transmitting messages become more blurred with the passage of time. For example, FAX was originally designed for transmitting drawings, signatures, and charts that earlier methods of sending messages could not handle; now, however, FAX machines transmit all forms of nonvoice communication, as we noted earlier.

Video, or television, *transmission* provides audiovisual communication on an interactive basis. *Graphics,* as output from the computer, are most frequently used by engineers in the design of cars, airplanes, bridges, water systems, electronic equipment, and houses, because it is much less expensive to build a computer system to create

---

[12]Lura K. Romei, "Telecommuting: A Workstyle Revolution?" *Modern Office Technology* (May, 1992), p. 40.

models than to build and test the physical models themselves. The transmission of video and graphics communication requires broad bandwidths (1,000 times the bandwidth of voice transmission) and hence considerable cost.[13] AOMs must continue to analyze the rapidly emerging multimedia capabilities. Multimedia is the integration of a few or many computing capabilities, including numbers, text, image, sound, animation, full-motion video, and graphics.

TELECOMMUNICATION SERVICES

With the onward march of telecommunication technology, the entire world becomes accessible through the standard office telephone. Business firms grow larger as they merge with national and international companies, and their offices, scattered around the globe, develop an enormous "thirst" for useful information. Thus, many complex business operations require "by-the-hour" global communication services to compete in the international world of commerce. The need for maintaining worldwide military security and facilitating global financial services has also increased the demand for greater telecommunication efficiency. To meet these needs, the telecommunication industry has responded with an impressive array of services that continues to expand with the passage of time. In this section, we shall discuss briefly the services most widely used in office administration. They are (1) leased lines, (2) voice communication services, (3) data communication services, and (4) integrated telecommunication services.

Leased Lines

A **leased line** is a telegraph or telephone line between specific points that is made available to subscribers on a full-time basis. Such a line is useful for large-volume, point-to-point transmission of voice, data, text, and image messages for a flat

---

[13]Thomas J. Housel and William E. Darden III, *Introduction to Telecommunications: The Business Perspective* (Cincinnati: South-Western Publishing Co., 1988), p. 45.

rate. Leased-line rates, which are based on the message-sending capacity of the communication line and distance spanned, as well as terminal charges, are substantially lower than those for an equivalent number of single telephone channels.

Other leasing arrangements are available to business subscribers. From common carriers, such as U.S. West, Inc., users may lease private lines that provide dial-up lines in which users can call, or be called by, any interconnected telephone in a distant area.

Voice Communication Services

We noted earlier that voice messages have several advantages over other message forms, and, for this reason, voice communication services remain a very popular means of transmitting messages. This situation is expected to continue, using the services we discuss in this section.

Centrex

Centrex, or *central exchange,* provides direct inward dialing in which all local and long-distance calls go directly to the number dialed. Thus, a call into a company is made without first having to go through an operator. In turn, employees make all internal and outgoing calls by dialing direct. (Usually the caller dials a "9" to get a local telephone line.) Centrex is considered worthwhile when at least 90 percent of all users desire to reach an individual extension rather than a department. However, a central operator is not available in the typical Centrex system, shown in Figure 18–7. Thus, the called telephone often goes unanswered when left unattended (except when the telephones are programmed with the call-forward feature). Also, nearby workers are often committed to answering extension telephones that continue to ring when unattended, which interrupts their concentration. Answering devices are effective remedies for this problem, as well as for recording calls after regular hours when the office is not open for business. An alternative is to have incoming calls channeled to a central answering center after a predetermined number of rings using call-forward and/or voice mail at the individual extension number.

Figure 18–7
Centrex Sys-
tem

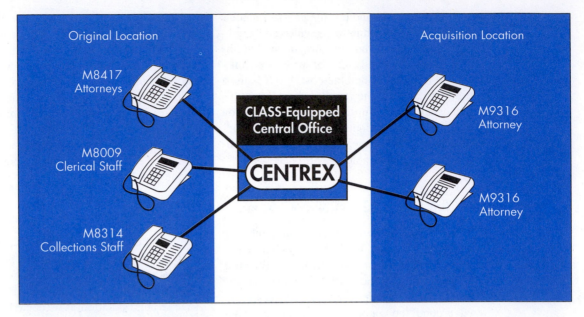

Courtesy of Northern Telecom, Research Triangle Park, NC.

WATS, 800-, and 900-Number Services

Wide-area telecommunications service (WATS) is a long-distance telephone service for sending voice, data, text, and image messages at discounted rates. WATS charges are based on two components: (1) a fixed-access charge for each subscriber and (2) a usage charge that varies with the length and number of calls made.

Two forms of long-distance service are available: outward and inward. *Outward* WATS is designed for only outgoing calls in which the user dials a number in the same way as an ordinary long-distance call. Inward dialing is available under an *800 number,* a service created and still maintained by AT&T for placing toll-free calls. With the *900 number* service, callers pay a small fee (typically 50 cents) for voice information, such as voting in public opinion polls and receiving financial information.

WATS has become an efficient communication tool in many organizations. It facilitates placing sales calls to customers and suppliers and enhances fund-raising and maintaining good investor relations. The 800 service is widely used in media advertising and sales literature. Allow-

ing customers to communicate toll-free helps to increase sales and gives greater customer satisfaction. When properly used, these long-distance services can reduce toll costs by as much as 70 percent, depending upon the volume and length of conversations.

Users can obtain assistance in the proper use of long-distance services from their local long-distance carriers. The computers of some firms also provide assistance by monitoring long-distance calls, which is helpful in detecting improper telephone usage.

With the deregulation of the telecommunication industry (discussed later), alternatives to the Bell System's WATS service are now offered by other common carriers, such as General Telephone Electric Corporation (GTE), Sprint Corporation, AT&T, and MCI Telecommunications Corporation. AOMs in large organizations with many distant customers should compare the costs of these highly competitive services before deciding which WATS service to acquire.

Other carriers, such as Tymnet and Telenet, lease communications channels from the common carriers and provide services beyond those offered by the common carriers. Carriers such as

CompuServe and Prodigy offer electronic mail, bulletin boards, conferencing, and other services, such as online information databases.

Foreign Exchange (FX)

Foreign exchange (FX) is a long-distance service that permits a telephone in a distant location (within or outside the United States) to be connected to a local telephone. For example, by using FX, a customer in Des Moines may be immediately connected to the London or New York office of the ABC Corporation by dialing a local number instead of ABC's long-distance number. For businesses making frequent calls between distant locations, FX is more economical than regular long-distance calls. The ABC Corporation, in this case, would subscribe to this service between the two cities.

Data Communication Services

In addition to the voice communication services discussed earlier, we typically find three data communication services: (1) Telex and Teletex, (2) electronic banking services, and (3) database access.

Telex and Teletex

With **Telex,** an international telegraph network operated by Western Union, small and medium-size firms lease existing public utility lines and rent teletype equipment to transmit long-distance messages. A main drawback of Telex compared with facsimile is the need for an operator to type all outgoing messages. This results in the possibilities of data-entry errors and slower processing speeds. Also, there is no provision for transmitting graphics. To overcome these problems, Teletex was created.

Teletex is a high-speed, desk-to-desk message service that allows users to type, edit, and transmit nonvoice messages over the telephone lines to their destinations. In addition, Teletex permits the automatic sending and receiving of calls with facilities for storing incoming and outgoing messages. The speed of Teletex is estimated to be 30 times faster than Telex. For this reason as well as the greater number of other capabilities provided, Teletex is expected to cause the phaseout of Telex systems.

Electronic Banking Services

Electronic banking services allow bank transactions to be carried on without making direct personal contacts with tellers. In addition to the use of automatic teller machines (ATMs) discussed in Chapter 16, another electronic banking service allows customers with personal computers and modems to perform most of their banking functions from home. Often this home service is offered to customers at a low cost or free (for a short time or trial period). Not only does this service provide added convenience for customers, but it also helps the bank to automate most of its labor-intensive functions, particularly the work of tellers. Customers can also use their ATM cards to purchase necessities, such as utilities and groceries. Most banks offer customers the ability to pay routine bills by automatic transfer or telephone transfer.

Database Access Service

Database access is an information-retrieval service in which the user, usually through the use of a modem, calls up a database and secures the information needed. Such dial-up services are available for most professional fields and for general users. For example, physicians access medical databases provided by organizations, such as the National Institute of Health, to help diagnose patients' conditions. As previously stated, business executives may subscribe to databases, such as CompuServe or Prodigy, that carry a variety of information, allow computer conferencing, and provide electronic mail functions. Users subscribe to these services for a monthly fee. Students in a growing number of colleges and universities have free access to databases maintained by their central libraries. Thus, students can be linked to computer-cataloged library references from their dormitory or apartment telephones, or they can access various commercial databases from their college libraries.

Teleconferencing

One useful alternative to the business conference is the **teleconference** in which telephone lines or satellites tie together three or more people at two or more separate locations. Teleconferences have proven very successful, especially since several forms of teleconferences have been made available.

Audio Teleconference. An **audio teleconference** is the simplest, least expensive, and most commonly scheduled kind of teleconference, since it requires no more than a telephone or speakerphone and operator assistance to be connected to the other participants. Audio teleconferences are designed to replace regularly scheduled "fly-in," on-site meetings of key people who already know one another and can conduct business using this medium. The audio teleconference, however, is not a replacement for the once-a-year gatherings that are held for the purpose of meeting new people, sharing a key event (unveiling a new computer system, for example), or attending a meeting at which face-to-face negotiation is needed.

Experience has shown that audio teleconferences are more democratic and objective than other forms, far shorter in length, and hence, less expensive. Audio teleconferences work best for exchanging information, giving directives, brainstorming and other forms of creative thinking, resolving minor conflicts, presenting proposals, conducting cooperative problem solving, and making decisions.

Video Teleconference. The **video teleconference,** or *videoconference,* which is more personalized and costlier than its audio counterpart, combines the audio dimension of voice with color television. The use of a video teleconference helps to humanize a telecommunication event in the same way that any face-to-face communication helps to develop personal rapport. As an example, U.S. West, Inc., offers Desktop Video Services, which use a digital, intrastate/interstate, dedicated private-line service that gives its customers flexibility in satisfying their videoconferencing needs. Illustration 18–4 shows equipment that may be used in a video teleconference.

A related video teleconference system—**the electronic blackboard**—permits handwriting or graphics on a chalkboard to be photographed and sent over telephone lines to widely scattered locations. At the receiving end, the message is displayed on television screens. At the same time, telephone connections carry two-way voice messages to discuss the visual messages with the audience. Frequently, we find the electronic blackboard used in centrally located classes taught by an instructor some distance away.

Computer Conference. The use of electronic mail, voice mail, and other types of telecommunication has changed the ways in which office workers communicate. Because of our overwhelming acceptance of the VDT, it is natural that we find conferences being conducted using such computer facilities.

A **computer conference** allows people who are geographically separated to exchange information in a convenient fashion through the use of computers. Today's business executives conduct computer conferences on PCs or portable display terminals while traveling or at home. Instead of meeting face to face in one place at the same time, the participants "meet" via their VDTs, which are arranged in an interconnected network.

In a computer conference, users dial up (check into) their computer communication files to determine all the messages waiting for them to be displayed on the screen. In turn, the user com-

Illustration 18–4 Using video teleconference equipment.

Illustration 18–5 VISIT Video application screen.

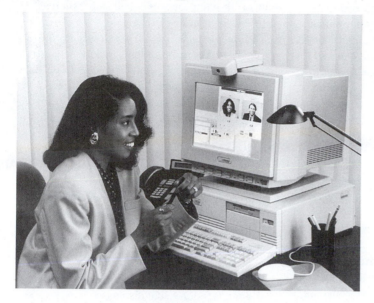

poses, edits, and sends messages to the other participants in the conference and thus may take part in many different conferences that are being recorded in the computer conference network. Usually, the messages range from one to five lines, and often only short phrases are used. Since these messages are short, they require little file storage. The user may read the messages on the VDT screen or print them out as hard copy similar to electronic mail. However, electronic mail is usually sent from one person to another; in contrast, a computer conference involves a "many-to-many" type of communication where groups of individuals "converse" with one another when each feels inclined.

Integrated Telecommunication Services

Traditionally, all machines used in the office performed single functions. Telephones and radio networks carried only sound, and facsimiles carried only visual messages. With each successful breakthrough in information technology, more and more functions were combined, or integrated, into one multifunction service. Several of the most important services that have been integrated in telecommunications are as follows:

1. *Integrating voice and data communications.* In the Displayphone Plus, two telephone line inputs provide concurrent voice and data communication. Also, this device provides hands-free options, a tickler file with audible alarm signaling, and small computer capabilities, including memory, processing, and data storage.

2. *Integrating voice and video communications.* Illustration 18–5 shows VISIT Video, which can be used by workers who require face-to-face communications with their colleagues, especially when undertaking joint projects. This service, which provides the following features, offers a complete, collaborative working environment for the personal computer:
   - *Personal videoconferencing* for desk-to-desk, face-to-face communications—across town or around the world.
   - *Shared-screen workspace* to collaborate on documents, drawings, and more.
   - *High-speed file transfer* to exchange information quickly—20 times faster than a standard modem.
   - *Call management features* to control telephone and voice messaging services from the computer.

3. *Integrated Services Digital Network.* Most telephone service is based upon analog codes for transmission in which separate lines are required for transmitting voice, computer data, video, and image. With transmission technology, known as the **Integrated Services Digital Network (ISDN),** data are carried in telephone channels using *digital* (0 and 1) signals. Thus, all four forms of communication mentioned above can be transmitted along the same line simultaneously. ISDN enables otherwise incompatible computer systems to communicate with one another, and greater amounts of information can be transmitted much more rapidly through ISDN than with analog equipment.[14]

The U.S. House of Representatives passed the National Information and Infrastructure Act in

---

[14]Janice Castro, *Time* (March 30, 1987), pp. 50–51.

1993 which provides $1.36 billion in research funds for the development of new telecommunications networking technologies and applications. The telecommunications marketplace will change dramatically in the years ahead, and every AOM should continue to study these technologies. Before decisions are made on new telecommunication services, the AOM should carefully study the information needs of the firm, as discussed in the next section.

MANAGING TELECOMMUNICATION SYSTEMS

The modern organization could not exist without telecommunications, for this administrative service has become essential to large-firm and inter-firm operations alike. However, even though they are widely used, telecommunication systems are often badly abused. As we discussed earlier, communication systems must be carefully planned and organized, and controls must be established over their costly operations. We must exercise the same care in the operation of telecommunication systems, as we see in the following discussion.

Planning and Organizing Telecommunication Systems

"Planning First—Hardware Last" is a slogan long advocated by systems consultants. Since modern telecommunication systems normally involve all departments, we find that a total-systems approach is necessary in order to study the communication needs of the entire firm. One effective way to plan such a study is to appoint an ongoing committee of personnel who represent all departments and who know firsthand the communication needs of their units. Most manufacturers of communication equipment will provide, without obligation, consultants to survey the needs of the company. In fact, the willingness of a sales representative-analyst to perform this service may be used as a guide to the dependability and reliability of the company represented.

A telecommunication system must be organized using the objective approach to problem solving discussed in Chapter 3. This approach requires following certain logical steps, such as:

1. *Define the information problems facing the business.* Typical problems include late arrival of information, obsolete and inaccurate data, and mutilation of records.
2. *Gather and analyze the facts relating to the problem.* Special attention should be given to these features of information systems:
   - Type of information distribution (one source to one receiver or one source to many receivers).
   - Information volume, such as the average daily volume of messages currently in the system, the average number of characters in each message, and the average daily total transmission time.
   - Form of the information (hard copy, magnetic tape, or visual display).
   - Accuracy of the information. For example, greater accuracy is required of numeric information when sending a communication satellite into space than is required of alphabetic information when sending a business letter. Typically, the most common human errors are made in data entry and in telephone dialing.
3. *Consider the urgency of the information.* Considerable ranges in urgency exist in firms. For instance, there is less urgency in sending out accounting statements than that required for making air reservations for an imminent flight.
4. *Determine the cost of the system.* Cost should not be evaluated in terms of dollars alone, but rather in light of the benefits accruing to the organization for the dollars invested. Also, improved customer service and the effect of good communications on competition should be considered.

Some firms recruit telecommunication personnel from their computer departments as well as from the common carriers, such as GTE, AT&T, and MCI Telecommunications Corporation. Usually, we find that a firm's employees are familiar with the organization, its communication needs, and the existing hardware. Smaller firms obtain the services of consultants through professional associations such as the Association of Systems Managers (ASM), Data Processing Management Association (DPMA), Office Automation Society International (OASI), and the Institute of Management Consultants (IMC). In addition, vendors of communication equipment are valuable sources of personnel and training. Other sources of personnel are discussed in Chapter 6.

Because of the technical nature of telecommunications, the AOM is not likely to be in charge of staffing such a function, nor will the AOM be responsible for procuring the equipment. Rather, he or she may serve on a committee for planning and organizing such a function, for office communications constitute a major portion of the total communications workload. However, all members of such a committee should understand the history of telecommunication equipment.

Prior to 1969, telecommunication equipment and services were purchased or leased from common carriers. However, with the landmark Carterfone decision of 1968, it became legal for other firms to provide equipment to telecommunication users. These firms—called **interconnect companies**—offer a variety of voice, data, text, and image communication equipment that can be connected to the lines of the common carriers. In 1980, the Federal Communications Commission ruled that data processing and telecommunication firms may freely compete in the telecommunication equipment market. Further, in January 1984, under court mandate, the Bell System divested itself of its operating companies, making them independent firms competing in the telecommunication market. The result of these decisions has allowed equipment production and prices to be ruled by competition, rather than by monopoly. The market has, to use a common term, become "deregulated."

Business executives now face a complex array of options in the procurement of telecommunication equipment. In long-distance calling, there are dozens of carriers, such as AT&T, MCI Telecommunications Corporation, and Sprint Corporation; telephones and telephone equipment of varying prices and models may be obtained from local retail outlets as well as from carriers. Also, there is wide variation in the availability and quality of service. For these reasons, the office manager should take special pains to study carefully the needs and message traffic patterns of the firm, as discussed earlier.

Establishing Telecommunication Controls

Basically, control involves defining the information requirements of each department—*who sends what type(s) and number(s) of message(s) to what destination(s) under what circumstances?*

An appropriate means of consolidating information on the use and control of all telecommunication media is the communication manual, discussed in Chapter 17. Such a manual provides company guidelines on all phases of telecommunication equipment and services within the firm and helps employees to make wise choices in the use of alternate telecommunication methods. Thus, the manual serves as a yardstick by which the effectiveness of the telecommunication system can be measured. A firm may simplify the collection of such information regarding its telephone requirements by using a form, such as that shown in Figure 18–8, for both inside and outside calls. By compiling data from each of the extension telephones, the analyst is able to determine which features of the telephone system are needed and which are largely provided for personal convenience.

Some companies periodically monitor their telecommunication usage by the hour to determine which departments send the most outside messages. As a result of such studies, the communication patterns of departments can be determined, and the type of equipment needed to serve such departments can be justified. More economical use of the telecommunication equipment results. Often, equipment vendors as well as the local telephone company will conduct a free traffic study, showing both the amount and type of messages sent, for guidance in determining how much equipment and how many operators are required at each hour of the day. Further,

Figure 18–8
A Telephone
Usage Report
Form

TELEPHONE USAGE		Department *Human Resources*				Ext. No. *806*

Figure 18–8
A Telephone
Usage Report
Form

TELEPHONE USAGE

Department: *Human Resources*　　Ext. No. *806*

Employee Name: *Jane Marner*　　Position Title: *Administrative Assistant*

INSTRUCTIONS
In the space below (1) record the number of calls placed and received during the day and (2) record the average call length (in minutes using the code provided). Reasonable estimates of calling information are satisfactory.

No. of Calls/Day
Small (S) = 1–3
Average (A) = 4–7
High (H) = 8+

Calls Placed: CP
Calls Received: CR

Call Length (in Min.)
Average (A) = 1–3
Above Aver. (AAv) = 4–7
Long = 8+

Number of Calls/Day						Comments	Length of Call (in minutes)		
Internal		Local		Long Dist.			A	AAv	Long
CP	CR	CP	CR	CP	CR				
A	H					*I call the boss's office every hour with routine messages to the department secretary.*	✓		
		S	S			*Occasionally I talk with the employment service agencies to find new employees.*		✓	
				A	S	*Talks to HR offices in branch plants about recruiting and training problems.*			✓

they can offer assistance in using the telecommunication system and in selecting and training personnel.

Reducing Telecommunication Costs

Telecommunication costs continue to spiral to the point where they rank third on the list of corporate expenditures, exceeded only by labor and rental costs. And when we examine the total telephone expenses, we find that from 70 to 90 percent of all such expenses relate to local and long-distance calls.[15] To control these costs, large firms use telephone management systems that often are linked to an automatic switching system. One such system, called the *station message*

detail recording, makes records of all outgoing calls. As we see in Figure 18–9, typical information that is collected and reported by this system is the station number or extension making the call, the number dialed, and the duration and cost of the call. With such information, an AOM can determine the type of usage of each station and the source of unauthorized calls. Thus, a system of this type gives some measure of the effectiveness of telephone usage.

Whether a telephone management system is available or not, both small and large firms should consider these cost-reduction suggestions regarding the use of their telephones:

1. *Compare the costs of mail, telephone, and other communication media* and provide instructions in their proper use.
2. *Request from the telephone company an itemized list of its service and equipment charges.* Also, request the telephone company to con-

[15]Janet A. Tufford, "Planning and Controlling Telephone Costs" *Office Systems'89* (February, 1989), p. 34.

Figure 18–9
A Telephone
Extension De-
tail Report

TELEPHONE EXTENSION REPORT					Ext. No. 806
Date of Call	Time of Call	Called Number	Call Length	Cost of Call	Account Charged
03/01	09:25	515-555-7821	00:10	04.85	0604-2000
03/01	15:30	214-555-0091	00:05	03.75	0604-2000
03/02	08:45	319-555-5782	00:25	12.90	0604-2000
03/31	14:40	405-555-8543	00:12	05.75	0604-2000
Total			02:15	42.25	

duct a survey to determine how intensively the equipment is being used. With such information, alternatives to the telephone company, such as interconnect companies and other common carriers, can be considered and the most economical equipment and services chosen.

3. *Keep records of all toll calls.* Department managers should stress that each user keep a daily log of all toll calls made, including the purpose of the call. If calls are placed by switchboard operators, a similar log should be kept by the operators so all toll calls may be charged back to the calling departments. These records may be compared against the monthly invoices to ensure accuracy of the call record. (Only authorized personnel should be permitted to place toll calls using telephone credit cards.) If many toll calls are being made to one area—the rule of thumb is 300—the installation of a WATS line or an equivalent long-distance service may be justified. Whenever there is heavy telephone traffic between two widely separated cities, foreign exchange service should be considered.

4. *Provide monthly summaries to each department concerning the equipment cost, the volume of toll calls, and other communication charges or credits assigned to that department.* With this information, department managers can better meet their responsibilities for staying within their operating budgets.

5. *Publicize economical calling practices.* For example, unusually long calls should be dis-

couraged, even though rates for time beyond the first minute are given a discount. Thus, the shorter the call, the lower the cost. Savings of as much as one-third can be realized by direct dialing, as well as by calling after 5 P.M., which is reasonable for calls to West Coast offices from the eastern half of the United States. Greater discounts (up to 60 percent) are available for night and weekend calls.

6. *Periodically remind employees to keep personal calls at an absolute minimum.* A survey of personnel directors in *Fortune* 1,000 companies found that the average employee makes and receives 3.14 personal phone calls daily and spends almost 5 minutes on each call. On a yearly basis, this employee spends 62 hours—over one and one-half weeks—in personal on-the-job phone calls.[16] Some firms use their computers to check on this type of expensive problem.

7. *Provide experienced, well-trained telephone operators who can give undivided attention to placing and receiving special calls.* All personnel should be instructed to answer and place their routine telephone calls rather than through third parties—usually secretaries—which saves time. The proper use of company and city directories also expedites incoming and outgoing calls.

---

[16]"Personal Phone Calls," *Small Business Report* (February, 1985), p. 16.

MANAGING MAILING SYSTEMS

Even in the age of telecommunications, the mails continue to be the lifeline of business. More than 190 billion pieces of mail are handled annually by the U.S. Postal Service (USPS), a number that continues to climb each year. A USPS study revealed that 17 percent of third-class advertising mail is never opened, and that, in 1991, 4.5 billion pieces of third-class mail were undeliverable due to incorrect addresses.[17] Furthermore, over 1.9 million shipments per day are processed by alternate mail services, such as Federal Express. Many large firms receive more than 100,000 pieces of mail daily and frequently send an equal number of items. The rise in the cost of energy, including transportation costs, and the continuing increase in postage rates create the need for effective management of a firm's mailing system.

Business mail may be classified as *internal mail* (interdepartmental or intradepartmental mail, which is distributed by messengers, conveyors, and delivery vehicles) and *external mail* (incoming and outgoing). Since mailing services exist for all departments of a business, the mailing center is a key part of the company's communication system. Good mailing service ensures the quickest, most economical, and most direct flow of mail from the sender to the receiver, reduces delays in completing work, and creates a positive image with customers. The mailing center, therefore, enhances all business relationships and presents a true service posture to customers.

Historically, we find that the mailroom has been one of the most neglected departments in the company. It has been characterized by low pay for its staff, high operating costs due in part to wasted postage, lack of work standards, poorly utilized space or too little space provided, and lack of supervision. Many of the related functions, such as copying, folding, stuffing, and bulk-mail sorting, have been performed in a haphazard fashion outside the mailing center. Too often, the result has been, at best, a "get-by" operation. To overcome these problems, the mailing

system should be organized and operated according to sound management principles.

Planning and Organizing Mailing Systems

Before setting up a new or revised service function, management typically considers whether to centralize or to decentralize the function. While there are strengths and weaknesses in each of these organizational patterns, the general trend continues to be a centralized organizational plan for mailing services. Such a plan may take two forms. In some offices, both internal and external mail are handled through a centralized mailing department. In other offices, incoming mail is handled centrally by one person or department, and outgoing mail is processed by the department in which it originates. In a small office, one person may handle both incoming and outgoing mail.

Proper planning and organizing are needed to bring about savings in time and costs, not only in the mailing center, but in other departments as well. Such economy is achieved when higher-paid office workers are released from the time-consuming necessity of interrupting their regular duties to attend to matters that can be handled more efficiently by the mailing department. The mailing center personnel can also bring increased specialization to their work, a fact that becomes increasingly essential as more and more mailing services become mechanized. With the centralization of mailing services, operations for handling both incoming and outgoing mail are more easily systematized and supervised, and labor-saving devices can be applied where feasible. The fact that the mailing service is centralized makes it more accessible and usually more valuable to the departments it serves. Overall improvements in control then tend to follow.

The key steps in planning and organizing a mail system include (1) providing a trained staff; (2) developing an effective internal mailing system; (3) designing an efficient mailing center, as shown in Figure 18–10, (4) procuring efficient mailing equipment; (5) developing efficient operating procedures; and (6) using automated mailing equipment when feasible. Each of these steps is discussed briefly in this section.

---

[17]Mary E. Skelly, "Let the Mailroom Deliver Savings," *Modern Office Technology* (October, 1992), p. 44.

Figure 18–10
Main Components and Workflows in a Modern Mailing System

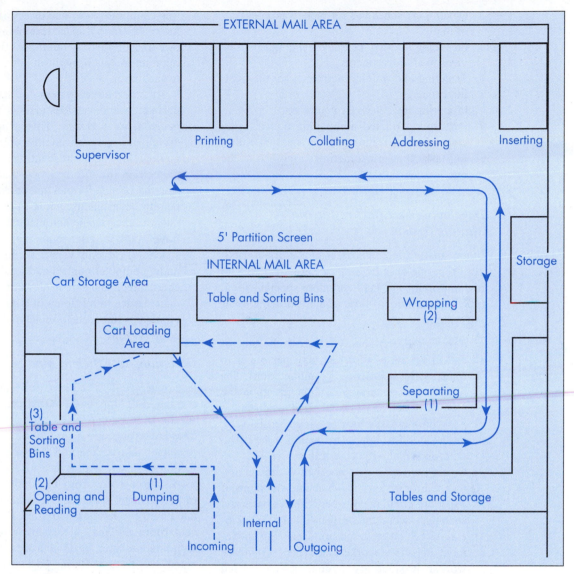

Providing a Trained Staff

In the small organization, a part-time office employee may combine the duties of mail clerk with those of messenger, file clerk, or another related job. On the other hand, the large organization appoints one person as full-time mailing center supervisor and provides this person with sufficient workers to handle the operation satisfactorily.

The supervision of the mailing function requires an experienced person who understands the company organization, the mailing routines, the regulations of the USPS, and alternate methods of sending mail. Such a person must also be able to recruit, train, and command the respect of the staff, which usually includes one or more clerks in addition to delivery personnel. The following duties are usually assigned to the mailing center supervisor and staff:

1. Designing an efficient mailing center. See Figure 18–10.
2. Handling incoming and outgoing mail.

3. Developing schedules for pickup and delivery of mail.
4. Providing internal messenger and mailing services to all departments.
5. Selecting and training personnel for the mailing center.
6. Procuring the necessary equipment.
7. Performing related nonmailing duties, especially those pertaining to copying and collating tasks that are sometimes assigned to the mailing center staff.

Developing an Effective Internal Mailing System

In the small office, internal mail is carried manually from one desk to another. Larger firms, with higher volumes of mail and more specialization, typically use one or more of the following mailing systems:

1. *Personal messengers,* which save the time of executives and other high-pay personnel in transporting interoffice communications. The retention of such service depends upon the number of delivery locations and the distances between them, the time provided for delivery, the bulk and weight of the papers to be delivered, and finally the cost of the service.
2. *Office conveyor systems,* which are recommended for systems in which large amounts of paper are circulated on a continuing basis and such paperwork can be distributed to fixed locations. Such systems minimize the movement of office workers and hence increase worker productivity by decreasing wasted hours spent away from the workstation. *Horizontal conveyors* transport papers between workstations in an upright position between two stationary guides that are moved by a motor-driven belt beneath them. Such conveyors are fast (several hundred feet per minute), quiet, clean, and safe, but they cannot climb vertically from one floor to another.

   For sending internal mail from one floor to another, *vertical conveyors* are used. This equipment consists of a series of trays spaced along a vertical chain for moving documents.

The chain moves in one direction only and is motor driven in a space resembling a small elevator shaft, thereby linking all floors. Incoming mail is thus brought in consecutive order to each floor.

An alternative system for handling both horizontal and vertical mail is the *self-propelled delivery vehicle*. This vehicle is battery driven and follows an invisible, horizontal guidepath—a fluorescent chemical line painted on the office floor—that is coded to stop the vehicle for pickup and delivery of papers to departments. After a preset stop-time interval, the vehicle automatically resumes its travel route in order to maintain its published schedule. Several vehicles can be operated under computer control and used to summon, enter, direct, and exit an elevator for providing mail service to all floors of a building. Its use eliminates the need for costly vertical distribution systems.

Designing an Efficient Mailing Center

Adequate space is required for handling all incoming, outgoing, and internal mail procedures. As shown in Figure 18–10, all three of these routines are arranged in a straight-line sequence that reduces backtracking and delays in processing. Additional space is provided for the supervisor's workstation away from the main mail routine traffic. Nearby space has been allocated for related mail-preparation activities. From this adjacent room the mail items are returned to the outgoing mail area for final processing, which includes sealing and affixing postage.

Modular furniture is recommended for the mailing center, for it permits many arrangements of tables, sorting units, and shelving. Furniture that is selected should be durable to withstand the heavy usage common to this function. Making such decisions is facilitated by an analysis of the volume of mail and how it must be distributed.

Procuring Efficient Mailing Equipment

When considering which equipment to use in the mailing center, a systems point of view is needed; that is, the center must be viewed as a smoothly

Illustration 18–6 Modern mailroom furniture.

running, unified combination of various mailing functions upon which the entire organization must depend. Thus, the equipment must be selected in relation to its contribution to overall efficiency of the operation and to the time it saves employees. *A good measure of the need for or worth of a machine is whether the value of the employee's time saved is greater than the depreciation and cost of the machine used.* If so, the purchase of the machine is worthwhile.

Today, we find a wide variety of furniture and machines for handling *incoming and outgoing mail.* The most common types of furniture and equipment used in the mailing center include:

1. *Sorting bins and tables.* Sorting bins attached to tables speed up the sorting and disposition of the mails. A wide variety of types of bins is available to provide the greatest number of bins per square foot of floor space.

2. *Postage meters.* Postage meters are leased from the manufacturer and licensed for use by the USPS. The meter prints the amount of postage and accounts for government revenue under official "lock and key." The postage is paid in advance just as when buying ordinary stamps. Or, through a toll-free number, a postage-by-phone system may be used to reset the meter in 90 seconds.

Postage meter equipment offers several advantages: speed in sealing, stamping, and stacking the mail; elimination of waste and misuse of postage; and better control over postage costs. Also, by means of the postage meter, the firm's trademark, slogan, or advertising message can be imprinted on the mailing piece at the same time the postage impression is made.

3. *Addressing machines.* These machines range from hand-operated portable models to large, automated models which imprint a complete name and address on a label or envelope faster than a typist can keyboard a single line. Some models imprint account numbers, district or territory codes, and sales representatives' code numbers. Automated versions of addressing machines are described later. In selecting addressing machines, the size of the mailing list, the frequency of mailing, and the size and variety of labels used should be considered.

4. *Folding and inserting machines.* For volume mailings, such as promotional mail, routine billings, or bulletins, folding and inserting machines are necessary. Some of these machines fold, insert, and seal units of three or more mail items at one time at a rate of more than 5,000 units per hour.

5. *Mailing scale.* Probably the simplest but most essential item of equipment is the mailing scale. Studies have shown widespread problems with overpayment of postage because of an inaccurate scale or the underestimating or overestimating of postage required when no scale is available. The accurate weighing of mail eliminates these problems as well as the delays of mail returned because of insufficient postage. Electronic scales described below are especially valuable in the precise computation of postage for all types of mailed items.

Developing Efficient Operating Procedures

The mailing center staff is responsible for developing effective operating procedures that cover all phases of the mailing function. Whenever feasible, these procedures should substitute machines for manual operations in the center in order to reduce the high costs of labor.

Particularly important are the following procedures that help to assure sound operations:

For incoming mail:

1. *Ensure early delivery of mail from the post office* by the use of company or private delivery service vehicles that pick up the mail at the post office.
2. *Sort personal and company mail and then time-stamp the first-class mail for prompt delivery to addressees.* A register or log should be used for recording the receipt of important mail.
3. *Establish and maintain efficient schedules for the delivery of mail to all departments.* If possible, mail should be processed and delivered within one hour after it is received or one hour after the beginning of the workday.

For outgoing mail:

1. *Understand and apply the postal regulations* and observe carefully the dispatch time schedule of the post office, airlines, Federal Express, UPS, and other private carriers.
2. *Maintain a prompt, regularly scheduled pickup service so mail received in the mailing center during working hours is dispatched the same day.*
3. *Develop an efficient routine for processing the outgoing mail.* In some firms, the outgoing mail is handled departmentally, in which case each department seals, stamps, and mails its own correspondence. Firms having a centralized mailing unit may deliver mail to the mailing center with the letters folded and inserted in envelopes, leaving only the sealing and stamping to be done by the center personnel; others deliver the addressed envelopes with enclosures, giving the mailing center the additional duties of folding and inserting.

For general mailing center operations:

1. *In small offices, combine the activities of the mailing unit* with other services, such as filing and copying. Some employees in the filing and reprographics units may, in turn, be assigned to the mailing unit during rush periods.
2. *Periodically check the postal scales* against

USPS scales to ensure accuracy and dependability.
3. *Ensure proper conformance to the center's standard operating procedures by periodic evaluation of the center's operations.* Standards for routine mail handling tasks, such as folding, inserting, addressing, and opening mail should be developed.
4. *Discourage the handling of personal mail except under unusual conditions.*

Using Automated Mailing Systems

New equipment frequently emerges to automate further the mailing function. For example, *electronic scales* have digital panels powered by a solid-state circuit to compute and display the most economical rate for letters or parcels. When rates change, a new programmable memory unit is inserted. One unit computes two mailing fees, with one meter used to determine USPS fees, and another meter for computing fees for UPS parcels. In this system, a printer records (on invoices or other documents) the date, dollar amount, and parcel identification number.

More advanced systems integrate the feeding, sealing, postage imprinting and postmarking, stacking of envelopes, and bar coding to take advantage of USPS discounts. Even more advanced systems include (1) a computer process for billings, statements, and letters; (2) a weigh-in motion device that eliminates hand sorting and ensures accurate weighing; and (3) word processing software that automates the printing of addresses on labels that can be affixed to envelopes by machine.

Controlling Mailing Costs

Improvement of office productivity demands that AOMs find more effective methods of controlling mailing costs. Basic to the achievement of such controls are a thorough knowledge of the postal regulations and a company-wide education program that stresses the impact of needless communications on mailing costs. AOMs should take advantage of the frequent seminars sponsored in their cities by the USPS. Some cost-cutting practices used by the mailing center in a large firm are outlined in Figure 18–11.

Figure 18–11

Practices for Controlling Mailing Costs in a Large Business Firm

Help Us Cut Mail Costs

Let's follow these cost-cutting practices	Then the result will be . . .
1. Update your mailing lists at least once a year.	1. A decrease in the materials and handling costs (of material being mailed).
2. Combine mailings whenever possible. Enclose all branch mail in one envelope at the close of the day.	2. Sending two letters in one envelope—cuts first-class mail costs in half.
3. Reduce the weight of mailed items. Condense letter length; reduce enclosures; use both sides of letter paper except official letterhead; reduce weight and size of stationery.	3. Places mailing in lower weight class.
4. Use first-class postage (not airmail) for all letters within the continental United States (except bulk mailings).	4. Delivery as speedy as with airmail except for overseas mail where airmail postage is recommended.
5. For rush items, consider overnight delivery service, such as Express Mail, for delivery of domestic letters and parcels. Other alternatives: See below.	5. Speedy delivery at reduced costs.
6. Use special delivery service only if necessary.	6. Prompter delivery to the addressee.
7. Insure mail items accurately.	7. Insures items according to their actual, not their declared, value.
8. Use registered mail only when the item has insurable value. Otherwise, use the less expensive certified mail.	8. Provides a receipt for the sender. Certified mail does not insure the value of the mailed item.

9. Use:
  a. Bulk mail when there are 200 or more items to be mailed at one time.
  b. Business-reply envelopes instead of enclosing stamped return envelopes.
  c. Two-day priority mail for packages and heavier envelopes.
	9. a. Large decrease in mailing costs; actual costs of items mailed available.
	  b. Our post office collects the regular postage plus a small fee for the reply privilege.
	  c. Two-day delivery likely at reduced cost.

10. Print in advance the envelopes for branch mail. Computer-printed labels should be used if possible.	10. Saves cost of keyboarding addresses each day.
11. Use window envelopes to eliminate the keyboarding of the recipient's name and address.	11. Eliminates keyboarding name and address on the envelopes and the problem of matching the addressed envelope with the appropriate letter.
12. Substitute postal cards for first-class letters in sending short messages (making announcements to customers, for changes in addresses, etc.).	12. Reduces first-class mail costs by 40 percent.
13. Use presorted mail privileges available upon application to the post office. Check with the mailing center supervisor (Ext. 124). Use ZIP + 4 code for identifying more specific address locations.	13. Saves several cents per item by presorting by ZIP codes and delivering bundles to the post office. ZIP + 4 code provides further discount.

OTHER MESSAGE-DELIVERY METHODS FOR CUTTING COSTS

A. The Telephone: Use for two-way communication unless a hard copy is needed.

B. The Mailgram: Use for delivery by USPS and Western Union to any U.S. address the next business day.

C. Private Delivery Service: Use for fast delivery of all mail (other than first-class). Compare costs of UPS, Federal Express; see the yellow pages.

D. Electronic Delivery Methods: Call the Computer Center, Ext. 214.

S
U
M
M
A
R
Y

1. To handle the growing number of messages that must be transmitted over long distances, a wide range of telecommunication services has been placed at the disposal of management. Voice communications that incorporate expanded telephone, intercommunication, voice recognition, and audio-response systems are being increasingly used by office administrators.

2. Wireless communication is achieving greater acceptance by business firms. In addition, firms use paging systems for in-plant and local-area messages and cellular telephones for communication from moving vehicles.

3. Many messages require more than the transmission of the voice. For this reason, large firms, particularly those with many widely scattered branches, develop data communication systems that frequently merge the computer and the telecommunication network to send all forms of communication, such as electronic mail, and to transmit nonsentence words, numbers, and graphic information.

Used in this electronic delivery method are facsimile, communicating word processors, and computer-based message systems.

4. In telecommunication systems, many services are required, depending upon the size of the system and the volume of messages sent. Some firms place special importance on these services: leased lines, Centrex, long-distance calling using WATS lines, 800- and 900-number lines, foreign exchange, and teleconferencing.

5. Within the firm, messages are sent via personal messengers, conveyor systems, and self-propelled vehicles. To send and receive mail at the lowest cost and in the shortest time, a centralized mail center is usually set up with appropriate staff, equipment (including an increased number of automated machines), and procedures. The center manager is committed to the most efficient use of mailing services and must be aware of alternate methods of delivery.

FOR YOUR REVIEW

1. Define telecommunications and describe its purpose.

2. Name at least six conditions that should be considered before designing a voice communication system.

3. What are the nature and common purpose of the basic telephone?

4. List at least four options of intercom systems that improve internal communications and define each.

5. Define audio response and voice recognition as used in telecommunication systems. What are the purposes of each?

6. Name several systems in wireless communication. What significant savings can be realized by using wireless rather than wire communication systems?

7. Explain how cellular telephones and microwave and satellite communication systems operate in a similar fashion.

8. What is meant by the term *data communication system?* Explain the basic concepts underlying the data communication process.

9. What types of equipment and processes make up the collective term *electronic mail?* Identify the comparative advantages of each type of equipment.

10. List several benefits of electronic mail.

11. Discuss the benefits of voice mail for those in "floating offices."

12. Define database access and explain, through an example, how this service works.

13. Identify three types of teleconferences and the typical uses of each.

14. What factors should be analyzed and studied before developing a telecommunication system?

15. Cite six steps to plan and organize a mail system.

16. What are the duties of a mailing center supervisor and staff?

17. What are some of the principal methods available for reducing the costs of mailing services?

FOR YOUR DISCUSSION

1. In your new capacity as office administrator, you have discovered that customers are getting busy signals, waiting on the line, and complaining that they are being ignored. How would you approach the solution of this problem and still retain the goodwill of your customers?

2. You have been hired as the AOM of a large benefits consulting organization. The manager has indicated that he is frustrated because his consultants can never be reached by phone, and he often has highly confidential client issues to discuss with them. He also states he cannot reach the designated consultant's secretary. What considerations will you give to the problem, and how can the problem be resolved?

3. On Monday morning, you checked into your electronic mailbox and found the interoffice memos listed below. Each memo should be answered, in memo form as shown in Chapter 3, and sent to the electronic mailboxes of your correspondents (or use an equivalent method to be determined by your instructor). Indicate at the beginning of each message whether the message should be classified as urgent, regular (routine), or confidential.

   a. From Betty Simonson, Accounting Department

   Message: I'm still planning on having lunch with you on Tuesday. Is 12:15 still OK with you?

   b. From Ned Samanski, Stockroom Supervisor

   Message: The inventory supply of your department letterhead stationery is quite low. Have you any changes to make in the present design? If not, should I reorder the usual quantity—10 reams—for delivery in four weeks?

   c. From Brad Stevens, Director of Human Resources

   Message: Effective this date, office employees are required to report their absences from department meetings to their supervisors unless specific permission for missing a meeting is given by the supervisor. Notify all employees in writing. Let me hear from you at the end of this month regarding the effectiveness of this policy.

4. During the past six months you have surveyed all your office personnel and uncovered these communication "situations" that may become potential problems in your office:

   a. Workers are writing many memos because the memo seems to be the only way they can reach groups of people.

   b. Workers are frequently busy on the phone, away from their offices, or tied up in meetings.

   c. Your customers have difficulty contacting specific personnel in your office.

   d. Many people on your staff handle the thankless chores of call coverage or message taking.

   e. Your customers have a continuing need to communicate after local business hours.

   f. Branch offices in your firm are scattered across all four time zones in the continental United States.

   g. Your executives, who are frequently away on business, have difficulty calling for their messages.

   Explore the nature of each "situation" and how it could result in a communication problem for your firm. What recommendations do you have for improving or preventing such problems?

5. As AOM, it is your responsibility to develop a checklist for evaluating new key telephone system (KTS) phone sets. Define what you would include in this list.

6. The following statements represent your employees' attitudes toward the usage of their telephones:

   a. *Clerical worker:* I have the right to use my desk phone as much as I want so long as the boss doesn't say anything.

   b. *Staff member:* Without that phone on my desk, I'm nobody in this company.

   c. *Middle manager:* What I use the phone for is *my* business.

   d. *Top management:* I'd give anything to get the blasted thing disconnected so I can get some work done.

   What are the implications of these attitudes for you, the person responsible for getting the most value from your telephone system? Discuss.

CASES FOR CRITICAL THINKING

Case 18–1 Analyzing Small-Business Telecommunication Problems

Marten's Country Crafts (MCC) handles consignments of quilt and other sewing patterns and do-it-yourself kits of small country furniture and accessories for a national market. After a meteoric rise in sales with only five years' business experience, Marta Kimball, the owner-manager, has organized a nationwide mail-order business built around a country theme depicting her base of operation in rural Iowa. Her office and sales staff are small, consisting of:

1. One office supervisor, Debra Roberg, who handles all correspondence.
2. One sales-order clerk, Lynne Sims, who is responsible for processing all sales orders.
3. Two stock clerks, Meg Mitchell and Ben Williams, who receive shipments of merchandise to be sold from contact persons. (There is a contact person in each of seven midwestern states who "scouts" the territory in search of items to be offered on consignment through the MCC catalog.) The stock clerks also fill orders.
4. Two part-time workers who are hired during busy holiday seasons.

As business increases, so do the telecommunication problems. The contact persons call "collect" into Kimball's office three or four times a day. Typically, they place long-distance calls, which are growing more expensive. Often, too, they are forced to play "telephone tag," hoping to find Kimball, who makes all management decisions, in her office. With a growing number of mail orders also come collect calls from customers who register complaints about the merchandise received. In the rush to fill orders, no one has given serious thought to the importance of a well-organized telecommunication system.

Kimball turns to you, a new part-time worker with much office experience, to help resolve the problems identified. Specifically, she asks you to find out (1) what problems exist, (2) what can be done about them, and (3) how to prevent such problems from recurring.

How would you proceed with such an assignment? On whom would you rely for assistance? What types of forms are needed to report communication problems? Consolidate your suggestions in a brief written report to Kimball.

Case 18–2 Planning an Electronic Mail System

The United Charity of America, a not-for-profit organization, has hired you as a consultant to assist in identifying the needs and benefits of an electronic mail system. The director has assigned you an office working directly with the information systems manager. The 100+ employees at all pay levels are spending many hours per month writing memos, delivering messages, and tying up the telephone system. No prior planning was performed regarding the internal messaging function. You believe this function has been placed at the bottom of the list of management activities. The director has seen the benefits of E-mail in other organizations and has asked you to assume that this function is now "top priority" for the firm. The information systems manager has informed you that he is in full accord with the new priority and that there is ample computer and networking equipment available to implement such a system.

You are to identify the feasibility of an electronic mail system and list the benefits of implementing such a system.

Case 18–3 Mailroom Workflow Pattern: Computer Option (available on disk)

MANAGING RECORDS

GOALS FOR THIS CHAPTER

After completing this chapter, you should be able to:

1. Describe the records management function and the objectives of records management programs.
2. Identify each of the key phases in the records life cycle and explain the importance of each as it applies to both physical and electronic systems.
3. Discuss the principles of forms management and the role that each plays in a records management program.
4. List the various levels in the data hierarchy and the importance of this concept to records managers.
5. Explain the basic methods of organizing and operating records management programs.
6. Discuss the most common methods used to evaluate the effectiveness of a records management program.

You will recall from Chapter 1 that sound decision-making depends upon the accuracy and timeliness of the relevant information upon which decisions are based. Having the right information in the right format at the right time is "all" you need to make a sound decision. Building and maintaining a records system that meets these crucial performance criteria, however, is not an easy task because information can be stored in a variety of locations, formats, and media.

Before the Information Revolution, paper documents were the primary medium of information, and they were usually stored on site in filing cabinets. Today, information resides not only on paper but also on diskettes and tapes, on network databases, on CD-ROM and optical disks, and on any number of microforms. Further, these media may be physically located far from the office's workstations, interconnected by elaborate telecommunication systems. For an office worker to successfully access needed information from such a complex array of sources requires that records be carefully managed.

With the growth of both the number of records and the formats and media in which they are stored comes a host of problems that seriously affect office operations and administrative costs. Typical problems include the creation of unneeded records, overloaded file drawers and folders, poorly labeled files, misfiles, and incompatible equipment and software. These weaknesses are a result of a lack of understanding of the role of records and their overall costs and a serious lack of training in the management of records—often called the "anyone can file" syndrome.

To prevent or solve such problems, records management programs have been developed as a vital responsibility of administrative office management. All such programs are organized around the life cycle of records—from their creation through their destruction or permanent storage. In this chapter, we examine (1) the basic principles of records management including the management of forms, (2) the records life cycle in both manual and electronic systems, and (3) the programs for managing records.

THE RECORDS MANAGEMENT FUNCTION IN THE ORGANIZATION

A **record** is written or oral evidence that information has been collected and kept for use in making decisions. The most common records such as forms, correspondence, reports, and books are written on paper. Other records, however, are much less tangible. Oral records capture the human voice on either magnetic or electronic media; film, such as movies, photographs, and microfilm, store visual images; and computers store data, images, and sound on tapes, disks, and other storage media.

Each of the major business functions—finance, production, marketing, and human resources—creates and uses its own set of records. *External* records are sent to customers, creditors, and others outside the organization. Such records include purchase orders, sales invoices, billing statements, checks, and form letters. Also, departments create *internal* records for use solely by employees within the firm. Examples of internal records are memorandums, requisitions, time cards and time sheets, journals and ledgers, and reports used in presenting data gathered from other records. Without proper management, the number of records (especially the internal ones) becomes excessively costly and, finally, goes out of control.

About two-thirds of all records involve correspondence, reports, and operating papers used in administration. The remaining one-third are forms. **Forms** are specially designed records upon which constant information is preprinted, with space for the entry of variable information. Forms are used to store information of a recurring nature that may be used inside or outside the firm.[1] Inservice firms or service departments, the ratio of forms to total records may be much higher. For example, in an insurance company or in a typical purchasing department, two out of three paper records may be forms.

The Records Management Program

Records management *is an organization-wide administrative service responsible for creating and maintaining systematic procedures and controls over all phases of the records life cycle.* Figure 19–1 shows these phases as responsibilities of the records manager. As such, records management is an important function upon which all departments of the organization depend. By means of both manual and automated procedures, the modern records function has developed into a vital administrative service. In turn, this service has added new responsibilities to the AOM or an equivalent position, the director of administrative services, as shown in Figure 19–1. This field also offers many new opportunities to qualified persons desiring challenging positions in management.

The leading professional organization specializing in the management of business records is the Association of Records Managers and Administrators (ARMA). This organization publishes the *Records Management Quarterly;* sponsors a professional certification program called the Certified Records Manager (C.R.M.); and conducts local, regional, and national conferences. The General Services Administration of the federal government has also developed a continuing education program that emphasizes the management of correspondence, reports, forms, directives, and mail as well as records maintenance, disposition, and program evaluation.

Objectives of Records Management

Like any other administrative function, records management should be goal oriented and service minded. By this we mean that objectives, or goals, for the program must be set up as standards against which the performance of the program can be measured. In addition, the program must provide

---

[1]Lura K. Romei, "Electronic Forms: Winning Against High Costs and Obsolescence," *Modern Office Technology* (April, 1989), p. 42.

Figure 19–1
Placement and
Responsibili-
ties of Records
Management
in the Admin-
istrative
Services
Organization

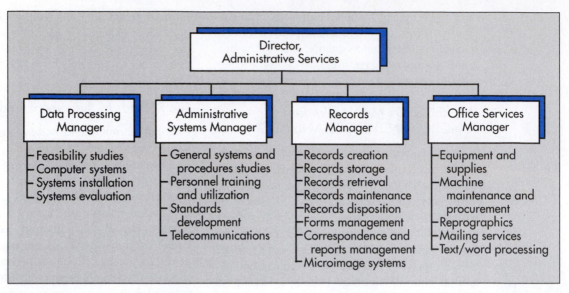

useful services to all departments. In order to do so, the program objectives must include:

1. *Providing accurate, timely information* as economically as possible whenever and wherever it is needed in the firm.
2. *Developing and maintaining an efficient system for the records life cycle*—creating, storing, retrieving, maintaining, and disposing of the firm's records. Figure 19–2 outlines each of the specific phases in the records life cycle and the most important objectives of each phase. Each of these phases is discussed at length in later sections of this chapter.
3. *Designing and using effective standards and evaluation methods* relating to the management of the records, equipment, and procedures.
4. *Assisting in educating personnel* in the most effective methods of controlling and processing the company's records.

THE RECORDS LIFE CYCLE

A record, like the information system of which it is a part, follows a set of steps during the time it is used in the office. These steps, or sequential phases in the life of the record, are called the

records life cycle and are outlined in Figure 19–2. They include creation, storage, retrieval, maintenance, and disposition.

Records Creation

Everyone in the firm, from a file clerk to the chief executive officer, creates and uses records. Managers write letters and directives; support staff fill in forms, compose and circulate memorandums, and generate reports. Because creating a record necessitates the additional need to store, retrieve, maintain, and eventually dispose of it, all personnel should understand the importance of controlling records creation. For example, if a telephone call or a face-to-face conversation can substitute for a memo or a letter, the need for a document is eliminated. Without such control measures, records continue to multiply and soon clog the firm's communication channels. Many organizations are finding that the amount of information they are storing is *doubling* every 10 years. For this reason, the records management program begins with records creation.

Records creation is a preventive maintenance program that seeks (1) to determine who creates records and why and (2) to ensure that only supervisors can authorize the creation of records in their departments and approve revising old forms or designing new ones.

Records Storage

The procedures and equipment used to house physical and electronic documents are known as **records storage.** Where and how a record is stored obviously depends upon the media in which it resides. We can divide storage media into two general categories: physical and electronic. *Physical storage* encompasses the various types of cabinets and shelves designed to store paper documents, as well as those cabinets designed to house microfiche film and other nonelectronic media. In small and large offices alike, physical filing systems continue to provide the majority of storage service, and experience shows that these systems clearly cannot manage themselves, regardless of how well they are organized. On the contrary, AOMs must carefully consider many important administrative factors such as the following: (1) setting up effective filing systems, (2) organizing the files, and (3) procuring filing equipment and supplies. Subsequently, the effectiveness of the filing equipment must be evaluated, as discussed later in this chapter.

Electronic storage involves the special environment that contains computer disks and tapes. This environment must meet a double set of standards criteria. First, it must meet the physical re-

Figure 19–2
Objectives of a Records Management Program

RECORDS CREATION Objectives	RECORDS STORAGE Objectives	RECORDS RETRIEVAL Objectives	RECORDS MAINTENANCE Objectives	RECORDS DISPOSITION Objectives
1. Eliminating needless records from present files.	1. Providing classification and coding systems for records storage.	1. Providing immediate access to the information requested.	1. Developing a classification system for retaining records.	1. Setting up an inactive records center (or storing records in a commercial center).
2. Controlling the creation of records.	2. Selecting proper storage equipment and supplies.	2. Developing efficient procedures for charging out records.	2. Surveying departments to determine type and amount of records kept.	2. Reducing records to microform wherever possible.
3. Designing records for efficient use.	3. Developing and maintaining well-controlled file storage and protection procedures.	3. Controlling the return of records to the files.	3. Setting up a retention schedule.	3. Transferring outdated records from active to inactive storage.
4. Applying cost standards and controls to records creation.	4. Selecting and training files personnel.		4. Protecting and preserving active and inactive records.	4. Developing control procedures for inactive storage and for destruction of records.

quirements of the media: accessibility, organizational flexibility, easy retrieval, and protection from unauthorized intrusion. Additionally, it must protect the records from any magnetic fields that may adversely alter the data in the records. Some of the specific criteria for electronic storage facilities will be discussed later in this chapter.

Records Retrieval

A record that has been efficiently created and stored is of little value unless it can be retrieved when needed. **Records retrieval,** the process of locating stored information, is a critically important phase of records management. Precisely what is an acceptable retrieval time depends upon the situation in which the information is required. Retrieving a record while an irate customer waits, for example, requires a considerably shorter access time than a request to compile some historic information for an annual report. An effective records administrator must design the records system to align with the various retrieval speeds necessary to support the decision-making needs of the organization.

Retrieval appears to be an easy operation: simply "go get it." However, retrieval is becoming decidedly more complex because organizations are not only storing greater quantities of records but are also storing them in increasingly diverse formats. Retrieving physical documents requires locating the area where the documents reside. The area may be near the workstation, in a general records department several floors away, or in an off-site warehouse. (Sometimes it is a combination of all three.) Retrieving electronically stored documents requires the availability of technology that is compatible with the records. As storage diskettes and tapes continue to evolve into different sizes, densities, and formats, records stored by either a previous version of software or on a now-obsolete generation of hardware can be left without a means of convenient retrieval.

Records Maintenance

Records maintenance refers to the set of service activities needed to operate the storage and retrieval systems. These activities include classify-

ing records; developing efficient procedures for operating the records system; updating, purging, and retaining records; and preserving or protecting the records. Only the retention and protection activities are addressed in this section, for these are management-level responsibilities as opposed to the other records maintenance tasks that are usually delegated to clerical support personnel.

Records Retention

Deciding how long each record should be kept in the files is a decision based upon a survey of all existing records. From such a survey of the records' needs and uses of all departments, a **records retention schedule** is prepared. This is a document describing how long each key record is to be kept in the files.

The records retention schedule is based upon policies of the firm that relate to (1) microfilming or electronic-imaging records, (2) transferring materials to inactive storage, (3) protecting the records, and (4) destroying the records. Such internal policies must also observe federal and state laws and regulations, including the statutes of limitations in the various states, regarding the retention of records. Based upon these record-keeping requirements and the specific needs of the firm, most companies classify their records in four ways: *vital, important, useful,* or *unnecessary.* Records considered vital or important are retained indefinitely; those considered useful may be retained for several years; and unnecessary records are destroyed. Figure 19–3 outlines typical retention periods for common office records, as extracted from one firm's records retention schedule.

Protection of Vital Records

When accurate operating information about a firm's customers, creditors, inventory, and employees is lost through theft or some disaster, the business may be forced to close. To protect against such an occurrence, business executives insure their property, including business records, against risk of loss. However, information is a unique asset and difficult, if not impossible, to replace, and no insurance protection is available for the loss of information contained in records.

Figure 19–3
Portion of a
Records
Retention
Schedule

Record	Retain (Years)	Record	Retain (Years)
Accounts Payable Invoices	7	Production Records	1
Attendance Records	7	Purchase Orders	3 AE
Bank Statements	3	Sales Commission Reports	3
Check Registers	P	Sales Correspondence	7
Checks, Canceled	7	Stock Certificates, Canceled	7
Correspondence, General	2	Time Cards	7
Depreciation Schedules	P	Work Orders: Cost $1,000 or Less	3
Employee Withholding Statements	4	Work Orders: Cost More than $1,000	6
Expense Reports (Employee)	7		
General Journal	P		
Income Statements	P		
Inventories	7		
Job Descriptions	3 or SUP		
Licenses (federal, state, etc.)	UT		
Mailing Lists	SUP		
Office Equipment Records	6		
Payroll Records	7		
Price Lists	OBS		

Legend	
AE:	After Expiration
OBS:	Until Obsolete
P:	Permanently
SUP:	Until Superseded
UT:	Until Termination

Should there be a major disruption of services caused by an earthquake, fire, flood, or extended power outage, firms must be prepared to implement plans that restore the vital documents segment of the records system as quickly as possible. To accomplish this important task, astute administrators often compile a carefully detailed document called a **disaster recovery plan.** This plan includes information on activating prearranged sites for temporarily relocating the records department, establishing alternative power and communications links, acquiring compatible equipment, and implementing other contingency arrangements such as staffing to expedite access to vital records.

Records Disposition

The last phase in the records life cycle, **records disposition,** or *disposal,* involves two types of records: inactive records that are transferred to less accessible, lower-cost storage and inactive records that must be destroyed. The decision to transfer records to inactive storage should involve records personnel and the members of each functional department responsible for the records. Several transfer practices are available, depending upon the nature of the records operation, but the following two approaches are most common.

Periodic Method

One transfer practice, called the *periodic method,* requires filed materials to be examined at fixed intervals, often every six months or one year. Physical materials considered inactive are placed in inexpensive record boxes and sent to storage. Electronically stored records are transferred, or *downloaded,* onto less accessible media.

Continuous Method

Under the *continuous* or *perpetual method,* records are transferred to inactive files as they reach a certain age or when it seems likely they will no longer be used. Such a method works well with client files in law offices, customer files in real estate offices, or job files in construction firm offices where the completion of a job usually means very infrequent, if any, reference to the files. For other types of offices, the continuous method may be considered rather inefficient because there are no clear-cut completion points in the chronology of a project.

PAPER FORMS AND RECORDS SYSTEMS

As you study business activity and its global use of computers and other electronic devices that send records around the world, it is easy to mistakenly assume that there is no longer a need for paper records. However, you need only to count the number of times you hear office workers either ask that a copy be made or refer to "a hard copy" to arrive at a basic conclusion: *Even in an increasingly automated world, people need, demand, and use paper records or electronic records converted to paper form in order to perform their responsibilities.* Thus, paper records continue to serve as the most basic medium for storing information, making up 90 to 95 percent of all recorded information.[2]

To verify this point, look about you. As you visit the offices of your physician, your dentist, your attorney, your banker, or your academic adviser, in what form do you find most of the records? In what form do you receive monthly statements for paying your utility bills, your cable television charges, your annual automobile license, and insurance premiums? The answer has been, is, and will be, for the foreseeable future, paper records.

Because organizations still rely mainly upon information that resides on hard-copy records, the increasing size of the paperwork load staggers the imagination of even the most experienced office manager. One systems authority estimates its size in this way:

1. Over one *trillion* pages of paper were generated, processed, stored, and retrieved last year.
2. There are approximately 318 billion paper documents on file in the United States.
3. In 1990, 3.1 million tons of paper were used in offices in the United States (twice the amount used in 1985).
4. The average physical file grows by 25 percent per year.[3]

[2]Mark Langemo, "Ten Steps for Improving Your Filing System," *Office Systems'92* (April, 1992), p. 18.

[3]In a telephone conversation with Robert N. Allerding, CRM, FAI, of Delaware, OH, on November 8, 1993, as a follow-up to his speech at the ARMA Conference, Seattle, October 17, 1993.

The Relationship of Records Management and Forms Management

Traditionally, the management of office forms has been considered to be an area of responsibility separate from the management and control of records. However, records and forms are closely related administrative tools. In many service industries, such as insurance and banking, forms often comprise as much as 75 percent of the total number of records in use. Thus, *completed (filled-in) forms represent a common illustration of business records.* For this reason, a study of records management must involve a study of forms as well as other business records (see Figure 19–4). Therefore, in this textbook we include forms management in a discussion of managing physical documents. We also acknowledge that forms are a major component of many organizations' electronic information systems, and that some of the fundamentals presented in this section can be applied to electronically generated forms.

A form has *constant* information preprinted on it and space provided for *variable* information. For example, on a bank check, the words "Pay to the order of" (the constant information) are preprinted on the form. The name of the payee entered on the blank line represents variable information. Forms are used in administrative systems to simplify and standardize the recording and use of information in order to facilitate decision making. In addition, filled-in forms become records that assist in the accumulation and transmission of information for historical or reference purposes.

Types of Paper Forms Used in Records Systems

In addition to the "destination" classification of records—external or internal—discussed earlier, AOMs also classify physical records according to the number of copies made. *Single-copy,* or *single-ply, records* refer to records commonly used within a department solely for its own needs; *multiple-copy records* are composed of an original and one or more copies. Multiple-copy records are used to transmit information outside

Figure 19–4
Relationship
of Records
Management
and the
Management
of Forms, Cor-
respondence,
and Other
Operating
Records

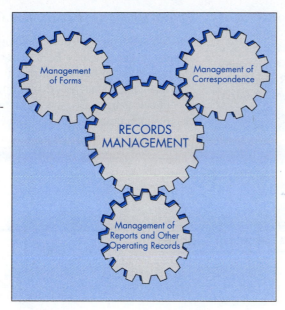

sales tickets and billing forms. Because of its simplicity, the flat form is the easiest of all forms to design and reproduce on reprographic equipment. Flat forms that cannot be produced internally may be purchased from an office supply dealer or a forms manufacturer.

Specialty Forms

A much broader category of forms in manual systems is the **specialty form,** so called because special equipment is required for its manufacture or use. Figure 19–5 shows common specialty forms that have the following features:

1. **Unit-set forms**—multiple-sheet forms that are preassembled with either carbon or carbonless paper. Carbonless paper, sometimes called NCR ("no carbon required"), transfers an image from one sheet to another by using a special coating on the back.
2. **Spot-carbon unit-set forms**—forms in which only certain areas of each copy in the unit set have carbon coating. Thus, confidential or unneeded information will not be readable on each subsequent copy of the form. Such a design withholds or conveys information to users as the needs of the information system dictate.
3. **Continuous forms,** or *fanfold forms*—a series of connected forms folded in a prearranged manner and perforated for easy separation of each form. Printed forms, such as invoices and special accounting forms, are designed in continuous single- or multiple-copy sets with preassembled carbonless sheets or carbon sheets arranged in proper numeric order.

the creating department or to provide additional information for other departments or for persons outside the firm. Both types of records are used in manual and automated systems. The forms needed in each type of records system are discussed briefly in the following sections.

Flat Forms

The **flat form**—a single sheet of paper often used as a single-copy record—is the most common type of record in manual systems. Examples are

Machine-Readable Records Forms

With the steady progress made by computer technology, many automated systems use machine-readable printing on specialty forms, as shown in the examples in Figure 19–6.

Magnetic Ink Character Recognition (MICR)

This is a system used by banks to interpret and process numeric data that have been recorded in special magnetic ink characters on checks and

Figure 19–5
Specialty
Forms

Unit set with no carbon required

Unit set with carbon pack

Unit set with spot carbon

Continuous forms

other business papers. Automatic equipment is used to read, sort, and transmit to a computer the data printed on the business forms for further processing, such as the preparation of customer bank statements. Examples of such MICR characters in Figure 19–6 are the bank's Federal Reserve routing number and the customer's account number recorded in machine-readable form.

Optical Character Recognition (OCR)

This is a scanning system for reading numeric and alphabetic data that have been printed in a distinctive type style on business forms and records. As each character on the business document is read by an optical character reader, it is translated into electrical impulses that are transmitted to the computer for processing. On the OCR form in Figure

Figure 19–6
Forms for
Machine-
Readable
Records
Systems

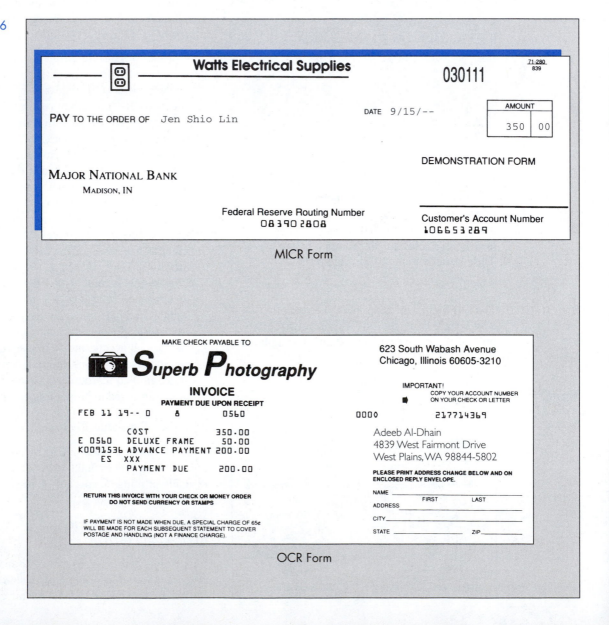

MICR Form

OCR Form

19–6, the customer's name, address, and invoice amount are printed in OCR type.

Principles of Paper Forms Management

In Part 1 of this textbook, basic principles needed to manage the office were specified: principles of management, principles of organization, principles of problem solving, and principles of communication. The records manager, to be an effective administrator, must also apply certain basic principles to address the wide variety of information needs and the equally wide variety and complexity of forms and records. Thus, a sound records management program is built upon four basic principles that pertain to forms: (1) the principle of use, (2) the principle of standardization, (3) the principle of effective forms design, and (4) the principle of centralized control. Although each of these principles, which will be presented in the following section, is intended primarily for paper forms, you should be aware that they often have relevance to electronic forms.

PRINCIPLE OF USE

Forms should be approved and made available only when their use is justified.

This principle is basic. A form should be created for use only when these conditions are met:

1. When certain information, such as orders, requests, and instructions, must be collected for use in the administrative system.
2. When the same type of information must be recorded repeatedly. With the constant information preprinted on each copy of the form, time is saved in information processing.
3. When it is necessary to have all information recorded in the same place on each copy of the form, as in the case of duplicate copies. This arrangement serves as a check on the completeness of the record and ensures identical information on all copies.
4. When it is desirable to fix responsibility for work done by providing spaces for signatures of those responsible for the work.

PRINCIPLE OF STANDARDIZATION

The physical characteristics of the paper and printing styles used in all forms should be standardized to improve operating efficiency and reduce costs.

Standardization of forms affects primarily their physical characteristics—size, quality of paper stock, color, and printing styles.

Size of Forms. The number of approved form sizes should be kept to a minimum. Forms are printed on standard-size sheets of paper stock, such as 17″ × 22″. Odd-size forms, which cannot be cut from standard-size sheets without waste, increase printing costs. Odd-size forms also contribute to increased office costs by making the filing and handling tasks more difficult, often requiring the purchase of odd-size envelopes or containers for transmittal through the mail. Before the size of any form is selected, a study should be made of the envelopes, file cabinets, and mechanical equipment to be used with each form. Table 19–1 shows the size of common forms that can be cut without waste from standard-size sheets of paper stock.

Quality of Paper Stock. A second factor affecting the standardization of office forms is the *quality of paper stock*. The durability and ease of handling the forms, as well as the length of time that the forms may be kept, are determined by the quality of stock. Paper stock is sold by the ream (usually 500 sheets) and in multiple packages of reams by the carton. The weight is figured by the ream in 17″ × 22″ size. For example, a ream of 17″ × 22″ paper that weighs approximately 20 pounds is called *substance 20, or 20 lb. stock.*

For multiple-copy forms, weight is particularly important because it determines the number of copies that can be made in one writing. The weight of the stock used also affects mailing costs.

The physical handling that a form receives must also be considered in deciding upon the quality of stock to be used. Normal treatment, such as that given an invoice form, can be provided for by using a relatively inexpensive sulfite

Table 19–1

Standard Form Sizes

(1) Size of Form (in Inches*)	(2) Standard Sheet That Permits Form in Column 1 to Be Cut Without Waste (in inches)	(3) Number of Forms Obtained from Single Standard Sheet	(4) Number of Single Forms Obtained from One Ream of Paper
$2\frac{3}{4} \times 4\frac{1}{4}$	$8\frac{1}{2} \times 11$	8	4,000
$2\frac{3}{4} \times 8\frac{1}{2}$	17×22	16	8,000
$5\frac{1}{2} \times 8\frac{1}{2}$	$8\frac{1}{2} \times 11$	2	1,000
$5\frac{1}{2} \times 8\frac{1}{2}$	17×22	8	4,000
$8\frac{1}{2} \times 11$	17×22	4	2,000
$8\frac{1}{2} \times 14$	17×28	4	2,000
11×17	17×22	2	1,000

*The equivalent metric sizes are available from the American Paper Institute and from forms manufacturers.

(wood-pulp) paper. On the other hand, company stationery, such as letterhead sheets and matching envelopes, is usually printed on more expensive cotton-content bond paper, which is a hallmark of quality and prestige for the firm. Extremely hard treatment received by some factory orders requires a tough sheet with great tensile strength so that the paper will not crack after many foldings. Some forms, such as shipping tags, are printed on cloth. Sometimes we find it advisable to use a celluloid facing to protect such forms.

The manner in which the form is filled in determines the finish of the paper to be used. Forms completed in ink must be printed on nonabsorbent paper that withstands erasures and that prevents the ink from "bleeding." Forms created on some types of duplicating equipment must be sufficiently absorbent so the inks will dry quickly and not offset on each succeeding sheet being duplicated. Continuous multiple-copy forms are usually printed on a lighter weight of paper with a medium finish to ensure copying legibility.

Most business forms are printed on the **commercial writing class** of papers, a group of writing papers commonly used in ordinary business transactions and for advertising purposes. The types of paper falling under this heading are

bond, copy or onionskin, ledger, index, and recycled, each of which is described in Figure 19–7.

Color. Colors used on office forms should be standardized. The use of carefully selected colors expedites the routing, sorting, and filing of forms. Forms may be color coded to indicate departments, branches, or other divisions to which copies are to be sent or in which they are to be used.

Printing Styles. Printing styles should be standardized since a uniform typography improves the appearance and readability of forms, thus reducing the possibility of error.

PRINCIPLE OF EFFECTIVE FORMS DESIGN

Sound forms design should be based upon the use of the form in the system and should ensure the effective recording and flow of information in the firm.

The designer of forms must know what information is needed, by whom, and in what order as well as the physical requirements of each form. Such physical factors as the form's size, quality, and color must be combined with the functional needs of the form.

Figure 19–7

Types of Paper and Recommended Uses in Records Systems

Type of Paper	Characteristics of Each Type of Paper	Recommended Uses
1. Bond	Fine appearance and durability; good erasing quality and uniformity of finish and color; more expensive than other commonly used papers.	Use sulfite (wood-based) bonds for standard office papers. For legal forms, insurance policies, and letterhead stationery, use cotton fiber bonds.
2. Copy	Lightweight paper, such as onionskin.	Use 9–11 lb. stock for carbon copies and for permanent records where little bulk is desired. If the number of copies needed exceeds 5, use 7 lb. stock.
3. Ledger	Heavier card-like stock with a good writing surface that withstands abuse (erasing and creasing).	Use 20–40 lb. ledger paper for accounting and other systems records. Also use for looseleaf records.
4. Index	Heaviest paper stock with smooth finish that withstands more rugged wear than ledger paper. Common weights are 43, 53, 67, and 82 lbs.	Use for machine-posted records, punched cards, and index and library files.
5. Recycled	Paper stock produced by adding new fibers to waste paper. Cost is lower than paper manufactured entirely from original wood pulp. Appearance is not as refined as bond paper.	Use for most internal records but avoid using for external records.

Designing Efficient Forms in the Records System. The forms designer must have access to information compiled in systems studies in order to find answers to the *who, what, when, how, where,* and *why* questions concerning a form's use. Thus, a designer must understand the needs of (1) the person preparing the form, (2) the printer or reprographic department producing the form, and (3) the personnel and equipment involved in mailing and filing the form.

A well-designed form is easy to fill in and easy to read and use. Moreover, it clearly defines what information is needed in its preparation and simplifies the task of data handling. In turn, such a form creates a better attitude on the part of the users, which results in increased efficiency and decreased costs.

Guidelines for Efficient Paper Forms Design. Figure 19–8 outlines efficient guidelines for design-

ing forms. By following these recommendations, you will avoid poor design problems and, at the same time, ensure the creation of a more efficient, usable form. To analyze the design of a form, note that Figure 19–9A shows a poorly designed form in which the guidelines are not observed. Figure 19–9B, on the other hand, demonstrates the use of most of the effective design guidelines. The circled numbers in this figure correspond to the five design guidelines outlined in Figure 19–8.

PRINCIPLE OF CENTRALIZED CONTROL

The entire life cycle of the form, including its approval, design, use, distribution, and replacement should be centrally controlled.

Too many offices create new forms and perpetuate all the old forms without seriously question-

Figure 19–8
Guidelines for
Designing Ef-
ficient Forms

GUIDELINES FOR DESIGNING FORMS

1. *Identify and sequence the data to be entered on the form.*

   a. Make a list of all data items needed by the forms user.

   b. Arrange the items in the order of fill-in or the order in which they are extracted from the form. For example, if a purchase order is prepared from the information on a purchase requisition, the sequence of data on the two forms should be identical. For automated systems, efficient keyboarding of input data requires the same sequence for the computer system form as that appearing on the source document.

   c. Keep related information together. Place personal data (name, address, sex, date of birth) in the same section of the form.

2. *Provide a simple, efficient design.*

   a. Eliminate unnecessary information. For example, do not request age on a form that requests date of birth.

   b. Eliminate any request for information that is discriminatory. A request for data on religious or ethnic background may be discriminatory and should be avoided.

   c. Avoid using horizontal ruled lines for typewritten fill-in. Use horizontal and vertical ruled lines to subdivide the form into sections, each of which is composed of related data items. An employment application form typically has a personal data section, a work experience section, and a references section. Rule or "box-in" each section to enhance fill-in and readability.

   d. If possible, use a box design that requires a check mark rather than writing for fill-in and that uses upper left captions (box names) to identify each box. (See Figure 19-9.)

   e. Specify sizes and weights of paper stock needed on the form in line with requirements of the machines, such as typewriters, and equipment, especially file cabinets. Use standard-size paper stock, standard typefaces, and standard (familiar) terms on the form.

   f. Adapt spacing on the form to the method of fill-in (machine or handwriting). For handwriting, ¼″ vertical space is adequate; for typewriting, double spacing (½″ vertical space) is satisfactory.

3. *Provide proper identification for the form.*

   a. Assign a form name (located at the top of the form) that reflects its function and a number (usually placed at the bottom of the form) that indicates its age. The form number also serves as a cross check in referring to the form in a requisition for forms or in a written procedure in which the form is used.

   b. Label each copy of a multicopy form at the bottom with the name of the main user (Sales Copy, Customer Copy, Human Resources Department Copy).

4. *Include clear instructions for using the form.*

   a. Locate short fill-in instructions (such as "Prepare in triplicate") at the top of the form.

   b. Place lengthy instructions (such as legal requirements accompanying many purchase orders) on the reverse side of the form.

5. *Choose the best available source for printing the forms.*

   a. External sources: printing firms with capabilities for producing complex, multicopy forms.

   b. Internal source: the firm's printing, reprographics, or word processing departments including desktop publishing equipment.

ing their need. A procedure for approving requests for new or revised forms should include (1) a formal written request with documentation regarding the need for the form, (2) a central control log showing the date and nature of the request and the decision made regarding the request, and (3) preparation of the approved design of the form.

MANAGING THE RECORDS LIFE CYCLE WITH MANUAL SYSTEMS

Now that we have investigated the fundamentals of good forms management, let us examine how paper forms and other physical documents progress through the five steps of the records life cycle in a manual system.

Creating Physical Records

As pointed out earlier, physical records are created by just about every office worker; as technology such as computers, facsimile machines, and high-speed copiers proliferates, the number of ways physical documents can enter records systems continues to grow. There are two possible avenues for controlling physical document creation: (1) increasing worker awareness of the costs of managing physical documents through the records life cycle and (2) designing and using automated information systems that minimize the generation of physical documents. Because totally paperless information systems continue to be a realistic impossibility, AOMs must continue to manage the mountain of physical documents created by organizations.

Storing Physical Records

Physical documents create a communications link between originator and recipient; therefore, it is important that these documents be readily accessible whenever they might be needed. How well this important function is accomplished depends upon how well records are stored.

Storage Filing Systems

Quick access to all types of stored physical records is assured with an effective filing system. The term **filing system** refers to the procedures and methods used to classify, sort, and store records for fast retrieval. We use two systems, *alphabetic* and *numeric,* which we subdivide in this manner:

1. Alphabetic systems
   a. Correspondence filing (by name)
   b. Geographic filing
   c. Subject filing
2. Numeric systems
   a. Numeric filing
   b. Chronologic filing

Most firms use both of these systems. For example, the credit office may maintain accounts receivable files in alphabetic order by customer name; the purchasing department, its purchase orders in numeric order; the human resources department, its personnel requisitions in files by type of position (subject); or the traffic department, the incoming receipt of goods in files by delivery dates or by a time-of-day scheduling chart (chronologic). Numeric filing may be used to protect the privacy of clients, such as in a law office.

Organization of the Files

The requirements for records systems differ from office to office, depending upon the size of the office staff, the nature of the business operations, the type of equipment being used, and such factors as competition and government regulation and control. Two plans of files organization are commonly found in offices: *decentralized filing* and *centralized filing*. A variation of the centralized filing plan, called *network filing,* may also be found. The advantages and disadvantages of each form of files organization are given in Figure 19–10. The AOM must weigh carefully the strengths and weaknesses of each plan and arrive at a suitable compromise. Frequently, both decentralized and centralized filing plans are used by large organizations, as their needs dictate.

Figure 19–9
An Internal Form Showing Poor and Efficient Design

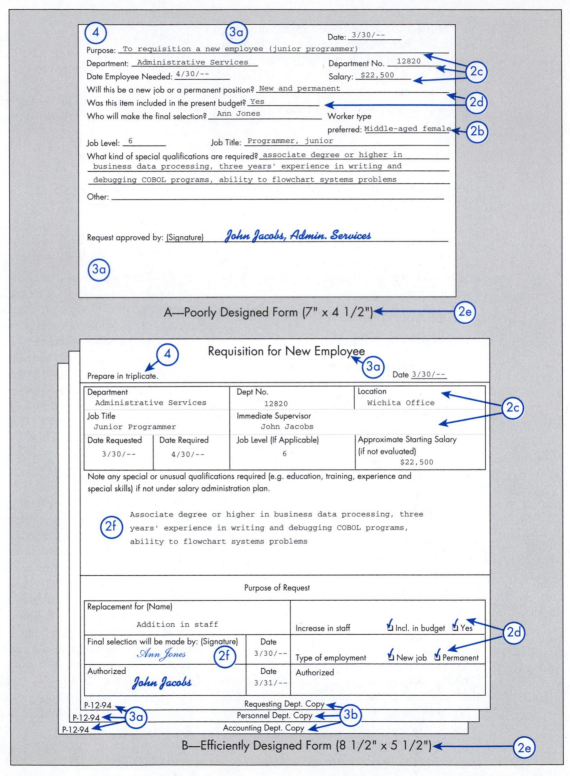

Figure 19–10
Advantages and Disadvantages of Three Files Organization Plans

Types of Files Organization	Advantages of the Plan	Disadvantages of the Plan
Decentralized filing—each office maintains its own filing system; the work is performed by employees who have other work to do.	Privacy of confidential records is maintained; delays in obtaining records from the centralized department are avoided; and records filed are not required by other departments.	This plan results in needless duplication of equipment; less efficient personnel to do the filing work as they have other tasks to perform; and sometimes a confusing filing system since one department's filing methods may be different from others.
Centralized filing—records of general value throughout the firm are stored in one location and controlled by one centralized records department.	Control over creation, retention, and disposition of all records is more easily achieved; more personnel efficiency is possible since the files are placed in the hands of specialists; needless duplication of equipment, supplies, and records is avoided; related records are kept together; and more uniform filing methods are followed, which results in greater accuracy and quicker retrieval.	Workers have access to confidential information; delays occur in obtaining records—forms to be filled in, charge-out procedures, messenger delivery problems; much stored information is never requested by other departments.
Network filing—department files are located within each department, but centralized control resides in a central records management department. A *locator index* is maintained centrally for records that are filed in each department for quickly tracing the location of all records.	In general, this plan has the advantages of the centralized and decentralized plans.	In general, this plan has the disadvantages of the centralized and decentralized plans.

Filing Equipment and Supplies

In the selection of filing equipment, the AOM should first consider the intended use of the equipment and then the savings possible through standardization of equipment and supplies. Other factors the AOM should study before an investment is made in filing equipment are (1) the types and sizes of records; (2) managerial preferences for requesting information; (3) the appearance, design, space-saving features, and durability of the equipment; (4) its capability for saving worker time; (5) the type of security required for the records; and (6) the cost of the equipment.

Physical records vary widely in size from small cards to large drawings and blueprints. As a result, many different kinds and sizes of files are required. Filing equipment may be classified as (1) vertical, (2) horizontal, (3) rotary, and (4) mobile and motorized (power-driven) files. See Illustration 19–1 for examples of some kinds of filing equipment. The storage of computer-generated and microform records is discussed in Chapters 16 and 20, respectively.

(a) Lateral Files

(b) Vertical Files

(c) Mobile Files

(d) Motorized Files

Illustration 19–1 Filing equipment can be obtained in many sizes and styles.

Vertical Files. The **vertical file,** as shown in Illustration 19-1b, with one to six drawers is the most common filing cabinet. In it, we store cards as well as larger documents, such as letters and reports, *on their edge* for easy accessibility. The dimensions of file cabinets involve important space considerations, because each cabinet requires approximately 6 square feet of floor space. Figure 19–11 illustrates how we can achieve better use of floor space by increasing the number of file drawers and, at the same time, decreasing the amount of floor space needed for a given number of files.

A **lateral** (or *side*) **file** is a vertical file in which the long side of the cabinet opens out. (See Illustration 19–1a.) This arrangement requires less depth and results in savings in floor space. Also, because we can view the entire contents of the drawer when it is opened, we gain quicker access to the records.

To eliminate dust and fire hazards, manufacturers provide models with doors or retractable roll-out shelves that can be opened to provide additional working space. Lateral files are also available without doors (the open-shelf concept), which allows an unlimited view of the folders. Open-shelf filing is far more compact and generally less expensive than cabinet filing. As a rule, open-shelf files cost about one-half as much as cabinet files and require about 20 percent less space. On the other hand, the costs of open-shelf supplies are usually higher, although this factor is minor when compared with the costs of equipment and space.

Horizontal Files. A **horizontal file** is used for storing papers or records, such as maps and drawings, in a flat position. Often horizontal filing equipment of counter-high design is purchased so that, at no extra expense, the files may also serve as a counter-high working area.

Rotary Files. In a **rotary file,** the records rotate in a circular fashion around a common hub, and documents may be removed or added by rotating the file to the desired location for access. Larger rotary files are motorized, permitting an operator to have push-button control over a cabinet of record trays to bring the desired work to desk or counter height.

Mobile Files. As shown in Figure 19–1c, a **mobile file** uses sliding shelves placed on tracks in order that the shelves can be moved together when not in use. Such shelves can also be moved apart as needed to create double-access aisles or moved to other locations on the track as needed. Mobile files permit a file clerk to work on both sides of a shelf and reduce by up to 50 percent the amount of floor space required for the files. However, such an arrangement may increase the amount of time needed to access most files since it eliminates the possibility of several clerks concurrently using various shelves in the same system. This is because when one shelf is accessible, the shelves behind it are not. Another type of mobile file, *motorized* or *power-driven equipment,* provides trays on movable shelves for the storage of records. Such shelves are pow-

Figure 19–11
Space Savings Achieved by Using Vertical Filing Equipment

	Space Savings* Number of Drawers	Approx. Percent Saved
	6 vs. 5	20
	6 vs. 4	50
	6 vs. 3	100
	5 vs. 4	25
	5 vs. 3	67
	4 vs. 3	33

Counter Height

Varying sizes of file cabinets.

*Each cabinet occupies approximately 6 square feet of floor space.

ered by an electric motor and mounted on a frame inside the cabinet using a revolving motion. Any shelf can be brought to the front of the machine (and to the operator) by pressing one of a series of buttons mounted on a control panel. (See Illustration 19–1d.)

Retrieving Physical Records

Retrieving a physical record from the files appears to be an exceedingly easy process: A worker goes to the file and extracts the record desired. Such a system is simple in theory but is often difficult to put into practice. For example, when an AOM asks a secretary to "Get that report on our plans for reducing labor costs for next year from the files," the search may be unsuccessful because the files may not divulge any report with the key words "reducing labor costs for next year." More than anything else, the difficulty in this case involves a problem in communication. The secretary must search for the record using the words given by the requester; if unsuccessful, the secretary must find synonyms (cutting, worker pay, etc., for the key words listed above) and use them in the search until the record is found.

Frequently, an index of manual files is set up to help locate filed information when users ask for a record on a basis different from that by which the record is filed. In a human resources department, for example, records might be filed under the employees' social security account numbers. When employees' records are requested by name, however, there is need for an index file of employees' names cross-referenced to their social security numbers. Sometimes the index and cross references are stored in a computer, and to locate a document, an operator accesses the computer index to find the location of the stored document in the file.

Maintaining Physical Records

The following special measures are frequently provided to protect all vital physical records:

1. *Special heat- and fire-resistant files, vaults, and safes* both on and off the premises. Adequate smoke alarms, proper sprinkler systems, and fire extinguishers should be installed.

2. *Dispersion of records* to locations away from the business site. Small firms may combine their resources with those of other firms and establish cooperative storage centers or use commercial centers. Large firms can exchange records among their branch offices to ensure adequate protection.

3. *Duplication* of vital documents so copies may be stored in locations away from the original records.

4. *Restricting access to the files,* which includes controlling keys to file cabinets, using locks that require magnetically encoded cards or codes to be entered before access, providing internal alarm systems and motion detectors that spot movement in the files area during certain time periods, and employing around-the-clock guard service.

Disposing of Physical Records

Once documents are no longer considered active, they must be systematically removed from the active files. Depending upon the guidelines of the retention schedule, discussed earlier, these documents are either transferred to inactive files or are destroyed.

Storing Inactive Records

In the small firm, transferred physical materials should be kept in that part of the general office area that is least used. (Examples are storerooms or unattractive, inaccessible portions of a main office.) Housing for inactive files should be of inexpensive but durable construction, usually fiberboard, and kept in an orderly manner so desired information may be located without undue delay.

In larger offices, a *records center,* or *archives,* is often set up for storing the inactive physical records of all departments. With these facilities available, records personnel periodically transfer the contents of the file cabinets to cardboard storage cases on steel racks that extend to the ceiling of the records center. With less-expensive storage containers arranged compactly, the costs are about one-fourth the price of active storage, and annual savings can be sizable.

DIALOG FROM THE WORKPLACE

ELIZABETH A. REGAN, PH.D.

Systems Consultant
Information Systems
Development Division
MassMutual Life Insurance
Company
Springfield, Massachusetts

As a consultant at MassMutual Life Insurance Company, Elizabeth A. Regan currently has responsibility for implementing a major strategic effort for the company's insurance and financial management line of business. This multiyear project involves significant business and cultural changes in the company's insurance agency distribution system as well as re-engineering in the home office. Dr. Regan has served as president of the Office Systems Research Association (OSRA).

QUESTION: A classic problem of records management is helping people "put their finger on the right information at the right time." How are information systems helping the insurance industry address this problem, and what effect are these efforts having on records management?

RESPONSE: In a world where change has become a constant, employees are continually barraged with communications, but often have trouble finding the information they need to get the job done. Existing procedures for documenting, learning, and managing business information are no longer meeting the demand.

The emphasis today is on integrated solutions that support business processes rather than isolated functional solutions. I think we'll see more of a trend in that direction. The emphasis on systems support is on active records rather than archival records; however, steps taken to put information online will eventually have an impact on all records management. Just the fact that the information is available online, whether or not it is also available on paper, has many implications.

To a large extent, paper files have become a major bottleneck in restructuring business processes. Dependency on paper forces many tasks to be done in a linear, step-by-step sequence as the paper file is passed from one workstation to another. If all the information were online, many steps in the process could be handled simultaneously. Two new tools for addressing these issues are image systems and workflow processing software. Although image systems have not won wide acceptance as a records management tool in the past, I think the opportunities they offer, when coupled with workflow software, to restructure business processes will win widespread application.

Getting rid of paper is an issue of getting users to accept electronic media as a delivery platform for information. In order to induce people to give up their paper, online systems must be flexible, accessible, and easy to use. They must deliver real benefits that are immediately apparent to the user. If they do, little arm twisting will be necessary.

Rather than set up their own archives, some firms prefer to use commercial records centers, which offer a wide range of services at a low per-record storage cost. In addition to providing centralized storage, commercial records centers offer specialized services such as regular records destruction, inventory control, reference activity reports, file purges, copying and microfilm services, and access to records by telephone. Experience shows that over 95 percent of all references to records in commercial centers are handled over the telephone.

Destroying Obsolete Records

An important way to control the mountain of physical documentation accumulating in most organizations is to destroy stored records that are no longer required or useful. Effective records administrators implement logical procedures, based upon clear communications between the records personnel and the department managers, to assure that only obsolete documents are destroyed. Often an authorization form signed by the department manager is used and retained in the records center (or in the files of the small office) as evidence of the final disposition of the records.

Within the office, *paper shredders* are often used to destroy records containing confidential information. Documents may also be sent to local paper companies to be recycled if the information on the records is not confidential in nature.

MANAGING THE RECORDS LIFE CYCLE WITH AUTOMATED SYSTEMS

The five steps of the records life cycle, although constant in concept, must be addressed from a different perspective when records exist in electronic form, instead of as words, numbers, symbols, and graphics on sheets of paper. In this section, we shall review the records life cycle as it applies to most automated systems with one exception: The electronic applications to micrographics will be discussed in Chapter 20.

Creating Electronic Records

Creating a record in an automated system requires an important bridge between the system and the office workers. People must use an input device that converts physical-world information to digital data that are meaningful to the electronic system. We can place the data-entry devices that perform this important function into three general categories: keyboards, scanners, and voice-recognition units.

A keyboard can be very similar to the one on an office computer, or it can be a device specially designed for a particular application, such as a hand-held unit for taking physical inventory. Whatever the device, the **keyboard** enables the office worker to enter data and commands to electronic equipment to create new records or to command the system to manipulate data previously stored in the system.

A **scanner** converts printed or handwritten words, numbers, symbols, and graphics into electronic impulses. Paper forms that utilize MICR and OCR fields, discussed earlier, are often used in conjunction with scanning devices. Some scanners, often shaped to be held in the hand, are designed to read the vertical bars of the universal product code (UPC), which can be used to identify inventory items, file folders, and employee badges (to name just a few applications). Other scanners, called flat-bed scanners, look much like office copiers. They are designed to support *imaging,* a process in which entire documents, including graphics, are digitalized for storage on optical disks. Electronic notepads, another form of scanner, digitalize material that has been handwritten on a tablet-like device.

A **voice-recognition unit,** still being refined but presently capable of various applications, enables workers to speak directly into the unit which decodes and converts the human voice into electronic impulses.

Electronic Forms

Just as forms constitute a major share of the paper documents being created, they constitute an equally large share of the documents created in electronically supported systems. With the increased popularity of microcomputers, we find the creation of more "soft-copy" forms (in contrast to "hard-copy" forms that appear on paper). **Soft-copy forms** are created by using a forms design computer program and are stored in a computer file for later use. To use the form, the office worker retrieves it from the file and displays it on the VDT screen. At that time, the operator fills in the form by using either a keyboard, scanner, or voice-recognition unit. The operator may then store this information in the computer file for later use or for printing a hard copy of the filled-in form for use in the physical information system. Figure 19–12 shows a computer-designed form.

Smart Forms. An even more automated method for designing forms makes use of a smart form. A **smart form** is an electronic form that is created

with a special set of forms design and fill-in instructions stored in a computer file. With this software, the computer is able to combine two separate automated files—a file containing the blank form, called a *template;* and a file of data to be entered in a form's blanks, called *fields*. When an operator enters data into the form's fields, the software assesses this input and enters data in subsequent fields based upon the logic of the previous fields.

To tell the smart form what to do with the data entered in each blank, you create a "form map" of software instructions. When you create such a map, you must tell each field (1) what to do with the data to be filled in (such as perform an automatic calculation); (2) in what other locations these data should go on the form and on other forms; (3) what other forms to include (in the case of collecting a set of related forms); and (4) what

Figure 19–12
A Computer-Designed Form

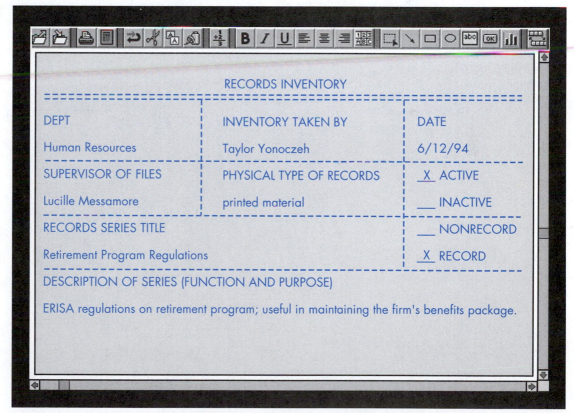

criteria to use for validating data (i.e., for determining whether the data should be letters, numbers, dollars, how many digits, how many decimal places, etc.). For example, by accessing an existing database, a smart form can compute and add the sales tax to an invoice form as well as fill in the address, telephone and customer account numbers, and billing instructions on an order form. With this highly automated form, you can fill in, approve, revise, and file forms as well as distribute copies on a local- or wide-area network without ever creating a hard-copy document.

Electronic Performance Support Systems. In some organizations, smart forms are evolving into an **electronic performance support system (EPSS).** These forms not only fill in routine fields based upon the logic of what has been entered but also supply *functional* decision-making support for completing certain fields. For example, suppose an office worker in an insurance company is processing a claim for a broken collarbone. Before an accurate amount can be au-

thorized, this worker needs to access information about the typical treatment, the cost for this type of fracture, and the list of physicians authorized to perform the procedure. Using an EPSS, as illustrated in Figure 19–13, the operator enters "Collarbone" in the field labeled "Type of Fracture." The system immediately provides a window of information relating to broken collarbones: a sketch of the injured area, types of treatment, recommended recovery times, and any other appropriate information to help the worker understand the fracture. When the operator moves the cursor to the field on the form labeled "Authorized Payment," the system indicates the costs usually associated with this type of claim and provides a list of doctors authorized to provide the treatment.

Office workers who have EPSS's are more efficient because functional information is available quite literally at the touch of a keystroke or the click of a mouse. Perhaps more important, EPSS's enable office workers to be more effective because the workers make decisions based

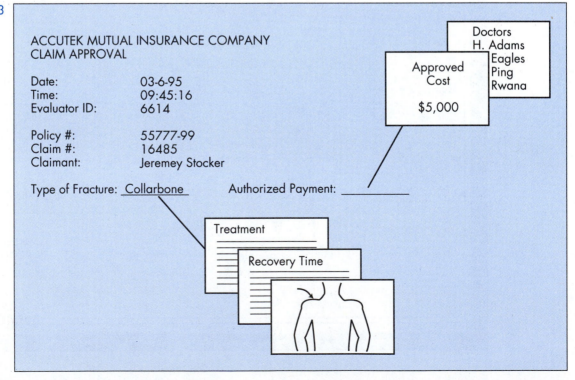

Figure 19–13
An Example of an EPSS Screen

upon the availability of more current information. It is far faster for an organization to upgrade the information in an EPSS database than to print and distribute paper or microfilm reference materials.

The Data Hierarchy

From our investigation of smart forms and EPSS's, you have seen that the computer directly affects how AOMs and records managers view the creation of records in the firm. As a result of using the computer on an organization-wide basis, AOMs and records managers have developed a much broader view of the organization and how its parts work together. (This point of view represents the central focus of the systems school of management discussed in Chapter 1.) From their need to consider the entire firm as one production unit, administrators look at records on a company-wide basis, studying their common purposes and features and noting particularly how these features are interrelated.

Figure 19–14 shows how a portion of a common human resources record—the employment application—fits into the overall structure of information in the firm. The **data hierarchy,** sometimes called the *file structure* or *file organization,* is a five-level organization structure of information that ranges from the most basic level—the *character*—to the broadest level—the *database* or *library.* As you build from lower to higher levels, observe how each successive level represents a group of related data units found at the previous level. Thus, a *data field* (level 2) represents a *group* of related characters (level 1); a *record* (level 3) a *group* of related data fields (level 2); a *file* (level 4) a *group* of related records (level 3); and a *database* or *library* (level 5) a *group* of related files (level 4).

Note the strong emphasis on the *group concept* and how this concept helps us to understand the data relationships in the files. Through grouping, the basic concept underlying a data hierarchy, the entire set of data can be accessed (retrieved for use) at one time, which eliminates the need for an item-by-item reference to each individual element. For example, all students taking the same class can be treated as a group for examination and grading purposes. For scheduling examinations, only the

time and place for a specific course examination need be posted. This grouping has the same effect as posting a notice that lists the name of each person enrolled in the course.

Understanding the data hierarchy assists the records manager in many ways, such as:

1. In designing forms and files since the data hierarchy shows how many characters and spaces are required to provide the needed data in each field.
2. In classifying, coding, and sequencing related information.
3. In detecting duplicate data on records.
4. In building a logical, operational structure for all related records in the firm's database.
5. In converting paper records to electronic records in which precise record size and other operating data must be provided.

Thus, the data hierarchy provides many benefits to records managers since it gives a comprehensive "view" of the firm's information system and the interrelationships of all its parts. The effectiveness of information storage and retrieval operations is thereby enhanced.

Storing Electronic Records

When records are initially created in an electronic environment, they are considered *volatile.* This means that unless they are stored on some medium, they will become nonexistent the moment they leave the screen of a VDT. Records can be stored either in separate files or in a database. Separate files generated on a microcomputer can be stored on diskettes and kept close to the workstations. The files can also be stored on the hard disk of the network file server if the microcomputer is connected to a local-area network. A database management system, discussed earlier in Chapter 16, is designed to store, change or update, sort, and retrieve related information about entities such as documents, customers accounts, and employees. Determining the best storage medium and format depends upon an understanding of the necessary accessibility, speed, portability, security, and any other considerations normally associated with accessing records from an information system.

Figure 19–14
Data
Hierarchy
in a Human
Resources
System

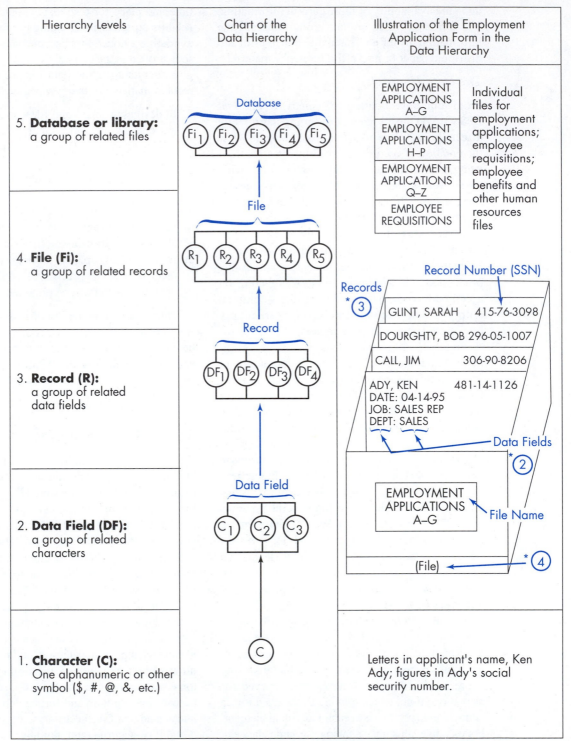

Hierarchy Levels	Chart of the Data Hierarchy	Illustration of the Employment Application Form in the Data Hierarchy

5. **Database or library:** a group of related files

4. **File (Fi):** a group of related records

3. **Record (R):** a group of related data fields

2. **Data Field (DF):** a group of related characters

1. **Character (C):** One alphanumeric or other symbol ($, #, @, &, etc.)

Letters in applicant's name, Ken Ady; figures in Ady's social security number.

*Circled numbers refer to the corresponding hierarchy levels in the left column of this figure.

Retrieving Electronic Records

To understand the automated retrieval of information, we must first remember that such systems store information in various locations and on a variety of media: tapes, disks, and optical disks. Such information is stored in invisible, coded form and must be accessed by the computer for use by the office staff. To access electronically stored information, the office workers usually follow this procedure:

1. A record is requested by entering the file label information into a VDT.
2. The computer compares the label information in Step 1 with the label information in its files.
3. When the file is located, the computer either prints or displays the information in the file as instructed.
4. No controls are required other than those built into the hardware and the program. The original records remain on tape, disk, or in the database after being printed or displayed. Thus, there is no need to return the retrieved record to the file, as is required in a physical storage system.

This four-step process is relatively simple, *provided that the office worker knows the file label information required in Step 1*. Problems arise, however, when office workers, working independently at their VDTs, routinely make decisions about where and under what label a record is initially stored. When you consider the personal computer directory of files illustrated in Figure 19–15, it is easy to understand why the "anyone can file" syndrome is a serious records management problem. The creator of these labels, let alone someone else, would have a difficult time identifying and retrieving a particular file. To prevent such retrieval nightmares, effective AOMs or records administrators train all office workers in the basics of records management, so that information can be accessed efficiently by all authorized personnel.

Maintaining Electronic Records

Specialized procedures must be implemented to preserve electronic records commonly used in the office:

1. Diskettes must be protected from improper handling and filing, especially from the danger of fingerprints, dust, and scratches.
2. The temperature of diskette and tape storage areas must be between 50 and 125 degrees Fahrenheit.
3. Diskette and tape storage areas must be free from all devices that may generate magnetic fields which can cause data to be fully or partially erased.
4. Original and backup copies must be made and filed in separate locations.
5. Security safeguards must be in place, which may include: (a) a **password** or code that employees must use to protect records and retrieve data; (b) an **encryption system** that

Figure 19–15
An Example of Poorly Labeled Files

```
10-02-94  01:17p                      Directory C:\BURNHAM\*.*
Free: 270,196,736

        Current <Dir>              . .     Parent    <DIR>
        AMAX                       MEMO.XX
        APOLLO                     MEMO.YY
        BID                        MEMO.ZZ
        BUDGET                     MISC
        LETTER1                    PERSNL
        LETTER2                    REF
        LETTER3                    REPLY
                                   REPORT.DFT
                                   REPORT.FIN
```

scrambles data in a predetermined manner at the sending point and decodes data at the receiving point; and/or (c) a **call-back system,** in which the computer sends requested information only to a party authorized to use it.

Disposing of Electronic Records

One of the greatest areas of efficiency of electronically stored records lies in managing the last step of the records life cycle—disposition. The retention schedules and procedures governing the transfer of inactive or obsolete electronically stored records follow the same logic as physical records, discussed previously. However, electronically stored records can be downloaded onto less accessible media quickly, accurately, and usually without concern for storage space.

Sometimes the transfer process can be automated. Using a technique called *data migration,* records that follow a particularly predictable use-life can be automatically moved from one storage area to another. As illustrated in Figure 19–16, routine records, such as orders, reservations, and bills, will most likely be accessed close to the occurrence of the transaction. It is logical to have these records readily accessible, perhaps in primary storage, during the time that office workers need these records to answer inquiries, to make adjustments, or to cancel transactions. When the transactions are completed and there is less probability that this information will need to be accessed immediately, these records can be automatically downloaded to a secondary storage medium, such as tape. When there is little or no probability that the records will need to be accessed quickly, they can again be moved to a lesser accessible medium, providing space for newer information to be stored online.

Destroying obsolete electronic records can be accomplished by commanding the system to search for and delete records identified by a given date, key word, file number, or other meaningful descriptor. However, the ease of destroying records is obviously a two-edged sword because it is all but impossible to restore records that have been inadvertently erased. Therefore, records administrators must be particularly diligent in demanding that office workers follow carefully prescribed procedures when eliminating electronically stored documents from the system.

ADMINISTRATION OF THE RECORDS MANAGEMENT PROGRAM

To achieve the objectives of a full-scale records management program as outlined in Figure 19–2, page 509, the required management functions must be planned and put into action. These functions are explained in this section.

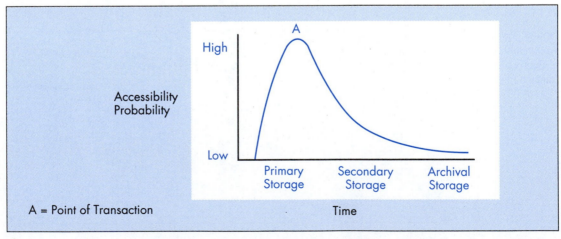

Figure 19–16
A Typical Data Migration Accessibility Curve

Organization and Personnel of the Records Management Program

Because records management is one of several information service functions in administration, we place records management on the organization chart alongside other related services. Figure 19–1, page 508, shows a typical setting for records management in the large organization. In such a setting, the director of administrative services, often a vice president, is responsible for such major information functions as data processing, administrative systems, records management, and office services. In such cases, the records manager is responsible for meeting the records management program objectives specified earlier as well as administering other technical services, such as microfilming, which is discussed in the next chapter. Also, such a manager may coordinate forms management activities and word processing systems with the appropriate department managers.

In the small firm, this degree of specialization will not be found, but the same general administrative functions remain. For example, a human resources manager may be able to handle administrative services, such as systems analysis and data processing. In another firm, the office services manager may handle personnel selection, placement, training, and general office management functions including records and forms control, while the systems and data processing services may be the responsibility of another person. Most important is that related work be grouped together and assigned to those individuals who by aptitude, interest, and training are most highly qualified for such assignments.

Because the records management program involves the entire organization, an executive familiar with the information needs of the total firm, its objectives, and its structure should be chosen as records manager. This position requires a generalist who can manage people and promote and coordinate the program among all units of the firm. Such a person should also be familiar with accounting, finance, and other business administration areas as well as be a specialist in information storage, retrieval, and files management. Although records managers need not be computer experts, they should understand the basic concepts and applications of computerized files, databases, networking, and telecommunication equipment.

Two levels of records specialists typically report to the records manager, as we see in Figure 19–17. At the *supervisory level,* the records supervisor selects, trains, and evaluates the staff and advises departments on records policies and procedures. At the same level, microfilm and forms supervisors design and install new systems. At the *operating level,* records clerks assist in sorting, storing, retrieving, and performing other operating duties. Larger firms also employ clerks with special assignments in the microfilming of records; forms and records analysts also assist in the design of new records. In more highly automated systems, such positions as documentation clerk, tape librarian, and program record clerk may be found.

Operation of the Records Management Program

As we have seen, a variety of operating responsibilities is found in the records management program. Two of these responsibilities are considered basic: (1) the responsibility for developing efficient procedures for performing the work and (2) the responsibility for identifying and controlling costs. Each is discussed briefly in this section.

Developing Efficient Procedures

In cooperation with supervisory personnel, the records manager must develop efficient procedures for operating the program. To do so requires making decisions on:

1. The specific responsibilities of the program.
2. The assignment of duties to each member of the records management staff.
3. The necessary priorities that must be established for the completion of the work.
4. Instructions on how to accomplish the assigned work.
5. Deadlines for the completion of the work.
6. Methods for evaluating the work and the personnel in the program.

Figure 19–17
Position
Levels and
Titles in
Records
Management

Position Level	Position Title
Managerial	Records Manager or Records Administrator
Supervisory	Records Supervisor Micrographics Supervisor Forms Supervisor
Operating	Records Clerk Micrographics Clerk Forms Analyst Records Analyst Documentation Clerk

For example, operating procedures must be developed for indexing, storing, and filing correspondence; for retrieving and controlling outgoing records; for designing and purchasing forms, equipment, and supplies; and for hiring, training, and appraising employees. In the development of these procedures, both operating efficiency and cost consciousness must be given major consideration.

Controlling Records Costs

With costs continually rising and with administrative work taking more and more of the profit dollar, AOMs are stepping up their efforts to isolate and control records costs. As indicated in Figure 19–18, the AOM identifies and assigns costs to four specific areas—personnel, supplies, space, and furniture and equipment. The two greatest cost factors—personnel and supplies—are the most variable, so we will examine them more fully than the more fixed costs associated with space and furniture and equipment.

The Cost of Personnel. While each of the other cost factors offers good opportunities for saving paperwork dollars, the records manager must give primary attention to reducing the costs of personnel, which typically represent from 70 to 80 percent of total records costs. Salaries, for example, may be controlled through better selection and training of workers and through improved work methods and performance standards for the processing, storage, and retrieval of records. In addition, the records manager must regularly

Figure 19–18
Records
Costs in
Administrative
Operations

Cost Factors	Specific Records Costs	Percent of Total Records Cost
1 Personnel	Clerical and supervisory salaries Employee benefits	70–80
2 Supplies	Forms and stationery Folders, cartons, and labels Printing Postage	10–15
3 Space for active and inactive records	Owned space Rented or leased space Taxes Utility expenses (telephone, light and heat) Janitor service	5–10
4 Furniture and equipment	Cost recovery of assets Rental and lease charges Maintenance expenses	3–7

stress the important effect that better use of staff time, equipment, and supplies has on profit.

AOMs of firms that have centralized records operations can relatively easily ascertain personnel costs by accumulating the salaries and employee benefits of those individuals assigned to the records management function. However, it is considerably more difficult for an AOM to identify and assign personnel costs in an organization that has decentralized the records management function. In some firms, office workers perform most of the records management function as a routine part of their job descriptions. It becomes a judgment assessment of how much of their job is involved with the records life cycle. For example, suppose a sales representative receives an E-mail message from a customer who is requesting that a delivery date on an order be changed. The representative accesses the database, determines the status, changes the delivery instructions, composes and sends an E-mail response, and stores a copy of the response in the customer's file. How much of this transaction was the individual functioning as a sales representative, and how much as a records management person? Clearly it is a judgment call. Once made, however, the AOM can assign a percentage of the representative's salary and benefits to records management.

The Cost of Supplies. Manual records systems utilize the bulk of the supplies needed to operate a records system: stationery, forms, and other filing materials. While the axiom, "Paper is cheap," may be relatively true, the functional costs of filling in, using, distributing, and filing forms are extremely expensive since they require the use of human effort. Many systems experts estimate that the functional costs are 25 to 50 times higher than the physical costs of the paper and print used for the form. For this reason, records management programs set up functional files in which all forms having identical or similar functions (recording, listing, ordering, and requesting) are grouped together. With such forms groupings, it becomes easier to spot duplicate forms and opportunities to eliminate, consolidate, or standardize forms.

The following suggestions for reducing the cost of supplies should be considered:

1. *Provide close supervision of department copiers* to reduce the number of unauthorized forms.
2. *Establish standard procedures for all phases of the paper forms management program* so the physical costs of paper and ink used in printing the form and the more important functional costs involved with the form's use are brought under control.
3. *Take advantage of the savings resulting from large-quantity purchases of forms.* Usually such quantities can be developed through grouping forms by categories, such as unit-set forms and continuous forms.
4. *Compare the cost of printing flat forms internally* on the firm's reprographic equipment to utilizing the services of an outside printer.
5. *Reduce in number the different paper items (forms, letterhead sheets, and envelope sizes and types) to the minimum.* This practice in turn simplifies quantity buying, warehousing problems, and inventory control.
6. *Design forms so printing costs can be controlled.* For example, by avoiding the use of a department name, employee name, or similar information, the form neither becomes obsolete so quickly nor is its use restricted to a specific department or office.
7. *Reduce the number of copies of a form to the minimum required,* as extra copies add to the cost of printing, stocking, filing, and distribution.
8. *Consider postage costs* when specifying the weight of forms and stationery. Through the course of a year, the use of 20 lb. rather than 36 lb. paper stock will result in considerably lower postage costs.
9. *Use less expensive recycled paper* for internal forms.

Other Costs of Administering the Records Management Program. In addition to the cost-reduction suggestions already discussed, the following suggestions should help the AOM increase efficiency and reduce costs in administering the records management program:

1. *Centralize and share those files used by all departments.* A database connected to a local-area network can provide this service.
2. *Provide an efficient layout* for the manual records center that will speed up the flow of records to and from the files.
3. *Purchase durable equipment* that speeds the completion of the work. It is estimated that the typical file drawer is opened and closed 100,000 times during its useful life. Thus, cheap cabinets would be wasteful under such heavy usage. Special equipment, such as map files and blueprint files, should be procured for records that do not fit into regular letter-size or legal-size file drawers.
4. *Develop efficient operating procedures,* such as regular schedules for the collection and distribution of materials to be filed or to be delivered from the files. Also, efficient methods for transferring inactive records to the archives should be used.
5. *Consider either microfilming or imaging* in lieu of storing records in transfer cases, as discussed in Chapter 20.
6. *Obtain the expert services of specialists in records management* for analyzing the files and for making the best selection and installation of equipment.
7. *Develop a records management manual that contains all program policies and operating procedures.* Such a manual helps to fix responsibilities for carrying out all phases of the program and assists in the training of employees and in the systematizing of records control practices throughout the company. The small office may incorporate these control techniques in an operations notebook for use by the files personnel and the AOM.

Evaluation of the Records Management Program

The administrator of any business function, including the records manager, must determine how well a program is meeting its objectives. Although the concept is simple, the evaluation of records management programs is complex because of the company-wide scope of such programs. Evaluation involves assessing the performance of personnel (which was included in an earlier discussion) and, as explained in this section, the efficiency of the files, filing procedures, and filing equipment to be sure each is functioning properly in the system.

One rule of thumb recommends that an evaluation or audit be conducted at least every two years to answer the types of questions shown in Figure 19–19. As soon as weaknesses in the records management program have been identified by the audit, corrective measures, such as improved records controls, can be instituted.

Using Efficiency Ratios

Through the years, records managers have created guidelines for evaluating the efficiency of the records program. Expressed as **efficiency ratios,** the most useful of these guidelines are:

1. The **files activity ratio:**

$$\frac{\text{Number of files requested}}{\text{Number of records filed}}$$

To illustrate, a records management audit shows 600 documents requested out of a total file of 12,000. The files activity ratio is .05, or 5 percent. A reference ratio of 5 percent or less is normally considered low and points to the need for transferring records from active storage to archives or possibly even destroying them. On the other hand, if the ratio is 20 percent or greater, the files are considered active and should be retained.

2. The **files accuracy ratio:**

$$\frac{\text{Number of records found}}{\text{Number of records requested}}$$

For example, 9,250 records out of a possible 9,500 requested are located. This means that there is 97.37 percent accuracy for the filing system and that the files are in excellent operating condition. If this ratio falls below 97 percent, the files should be studied carefully, especially for these problems: (a) too many private files (as in executives' desks), (b) improper indexing and coding, (c) poor charge-out procedures, and (d) insufficient cross-indexing and cross-referencing.

Figure 19–19
A Records
Audit
Checklist

Audit Factor	Specific Questions
1. Scope of the records management program	a. How is the program organized? b. How many files are in use?
2. Type of filing system and retrieval methods	a. What filing systems are used? b. What types of controls are used (charge-outs, cross-references, etc.)? c. How are records retrieved and what is the average wait-time for retrieval?
3. Records personnel	a. Who does the filing and finding? b. How are records clerks supervised? c. What kind of performance standards are in effect?
4. Records users	a. Who uses the files? b. What access do users have to the files?
5. Records control procedures	a. What filing policies and procedures are set up? b. Is a records manual available and in use? c. Are records retention and disposition programs in effect? d. How are private, confidential, and department files protected? e. What special provisions are in effect for protecting automated records?

3. The **retrieval efficiency ratio:**

$$\frac{\text{Time (in seconds) to locate records}}{\text{Number of records requested}}$$

The retrieval efficiency ratio measures the speed with which physical records are found and verifies how files personnel spend their time. A ratio of .75 (retrieving 80 records in 60 seconds) suggests an efficient records system and a productive files operator. Files efficiency standards are typically developed in a firm's work measurement program, as discussed later in the textbook, and should be included in the records manual.

With these common measures of efficiency as evaluation tools, we can obtain objective data on the operating effectiveness of the records program. Such data can then be used for further improvement of the total records management program.

Evaluating Filing Equipment

Because manual records personnel depend heavily upon tools and equipment in the performance of their work, an objective appraisal of such equipment should be made as one measure of the efficiency of the filing system. In such a study, all of the following components of the filing system that interact with the equipment should be included:

1. *The time required to use the equipment,* including the relative merits of using such equipment as open-shelf versus drawer file cabinets.
2. *The methods used by the workers,* such as whether the use of certain equipment decreases the transportation time of records.
3. *The flexibility of the equipment* to meet changing needs.
4. *The reliability of the equipment* to function and the *availability of service* to ensure minimal machine downtime.

5. *The costs of purchasing and operating the equipment.*

6. *The materials,* such as guides and folders, required in using the equipment.

7. *Miscellaneous factors,* such as the training required for personnel to use the equipment and the space required to use it.

SUMMARY

1. To control the growing number of records, many of which are office forms, companies have developed records management programs. In large firms, these programs are a part of the administrative services function; in small firms, records management is an added responsibility of the AOM.

2. Records management programs cover the life cycle of a record: (a) the creation phase, which seeks to prevent the origination of unneeded records but which requires the effective design of all forms initiated; (b) the storage phase, which includes the supervision of all filing procedures, equipment, and supplies; (c) the retrieval phase, which aims for speedy access to paper as well as to electronic records; (d) the maintenance phase, which includes the development of a retention schedule and provision for adequate protection of the records; and (e) the disposition phase, which is concerned with transferring and storing inactive records and destroying unneeded records.

3. Records management programs must be properly organized and operated. During such operations, evaluation of the program is carried out using special techniques, such as the records audit, efficiency ratios, and appraisals of the effectiveness of personnel and the filing equipment.

FOR YOUR REVIEW

1. Define *record* and *form* and show how the two terms are related.

2. List the five phases or steps in the records life cycle.

3. What is the purpose of a records retention schedule?

4. Distinguish between the periodic and the continuous methods of records transfer.

5. Identify the four principles of forms management with which the records manager should be familiar.

6. List five characteristics that should be present to conclude that a form is "well designed."

7. a. Identify the most common types of filing systems.

   b. When is each most likely to be used?

8. Compare the advantages and disadvantages of records systems that are decentralized, centralized, and networked.

9. Explain the difference between a smart form and an electronic performance support system.

c
o
n
t

10. a. What is the data hierarchy?

    b. Of what value to the records manager is an understanding of this concept?

11. Explain how the "anyone can file" syndrome can hamper records retrieval in an automated system.

12. How does the manual retrieval of physical records differ from the automated retrieval of records?

13. What determines how quickly records should migrate through a records system?

14. a. Describe the organizational setting for records management in a large firm.

    b. How does it differ from a small firm?

15. Define the various levels and types of positions typically found in a records management program.

16. a. List the main records costs in administrative operations, from the highest to the lowest percentage of total records costs.

    b. Why is it difficult to assign precise amounts of personnel cost to each area?

17. In what ways is the cost-effective records manager able to cut the costs of operating the records management program?

18. What evaluation measures are used to assess the efficiency of records management programs?

FOR YOUR DISCUSSION

1. The records manager in your company, a 200-employee real estate firm, has resigned, and you have been asked to write a list of qualifications that the replacement should possess. Make a list of at least eight attributes. Then place them in order of importance, beginning with the most important qualification.

2. Construct a list of at least five major reasons for the constantly increasing number of records that are produced in offices.

3. The records manager asks you, an administrative assistant, to prepare a "model" of an efficiently designed form. Discuss what features such a model should possess.

4. As the office manager of Copies Now, a copy-making service located across the street from your school's campus, you must frequently hire part-time workers to handle copying, assembling, binding, and other related tasks. Usually such workers are students. To collect job-application information, you need a simple form that will be used in making hiring decisions. The form will be filled in either on the office typewriter or by hand. Your assistant suggests the following information arranged in a 6″ × 4″ format. Evaluate the proposed design by listing at least four areas that may need improvement.

6"

Name _____	Days available _____
Address _____	Hours available _____
Telephone number _____	Hours desired _____

4"

Additional information:

5. The three efficiency ratios (files activity, files accuracy, and retrieval efficiency) appeal to you as simple, useful techniques for evaluating your filing system. What organizing and operating procedures must be set up in order to use these ratios in your records center?

6. To a few department managers in your firm, records management sounds like a fancy name for filing. Yet you know from your experience as an office supervisor that this area of work is much more comprehensive in scope. What specific steps could you take to change this stereotype of records management in order that a management orientation to the subject might be developed in your firm?

7. In a large hospital, Juan Gutierrez, the hospital administrator, is searching for better methods of handling the expanding volume of records. Reporting to the hospital administrator is the director of the medical records department, who supervises 40 word processing personnel, file clerks, and general office workers. The director has compiled the following list of urgent problems and discussed the priorities for solving these problems with Gutierrez:

a. On the average, 600 X rays are developed and processed daily (none of which is destroyed).

b. Records for 300 outpatients and 2,500 inpatients must be handled daily, with Medicare forms adding to the problem by 15 percent each year.

c. Approximately 15,400 health insurance forms were processed during the past six months.

d. No central depository of records is available.

e. Physicians are growing more impatient with the slow retrieval of medical records from the files but are resisting the use of microfilmed records.

Assuming the accuracy of these facts and the existence of other equally pressing problems, you, as assistant to the director, are asked to recommend to Gutierrez a comprehensive plan for improving the records management practices of the hospital, including records retention and protection programs. The plan must first be discussed with the director before it is forwarded to the office of the hospital administrator.

8. You have been assigned responsibility for helping to design an invoice form from the draft shown in Figure B. This draft was prepared in handwritten form by the user department, accounts receivable, and when completed will be stored electronically on the local-area network. The actual size of the form is $7\frac{1}{2}" \times 9"$. Evaluate the design of this form using the principles of forms design presented in this chapter.

Figure B
Draft of
Invoice Form

7½"

INTEGRATED PAPER PRODUCTS

PAGE #_____

DATE_____

SHIP TO _____

REMIT TO _____

CUSTOMER NAME _____

INVOICE # _____

SALES PERSON'S NAME _____

CUSTOMER # _____

SALESPERSON NUMBER _____

SHIP VIA _____

TERMS _____

9"

| STOCK# | QTY. | DESCRIPTION | PRICE | AMOUNT |

TYPICAL ORDERS AVERAGE 5 ITEMS SOLD

SAMPLE ENTRY:

| 0024615 | 0060 | WHITE 20# SULPHITE BOND | 5.75 | 345.50 |

AMT. DUE _____
AMT. REMITTED _____
BALANCE DUE _____

CASES FOR CRITICAL THINKING

Case 19–1 Building an Understanding of Systems Thinking in Records Personnel

Early in your administrative office management class, your instructor emphasized the importance of systems thinking. At the same time your class was assigned the responsibility of visiting, in small groups, records centers in medium-size and large offices in your city. Each of the eight groups was to visit one office, observe the procedures in use, and report their findings to the class.

When the groups reported to the class, these general conclusions were drawn:

1. All the records personnel were friendly and answered all questions asked. In all cases reported, such persons seemed to be most concerned about the neatness of their files and their work areas and having all their filing work "caught up."

2. These personnel seemed to work in their "own little worlds," in that filers only placed records into and took records out of the files, coding clerks only coded records, and supervisors seemed to oversee their workers from a "safe" distance.

3. Generally each records supervisor appointed a liaison person in each department to coordinate the department's records work with the records center. As a rule, little personal communication existed with these liaison persons; they seemed "to do their own thing" within their departments.

4. Computers were used throughout the firms, but only paper records—including hard copies of computer records—were responsibilities of the records supervisors. Several supervisors mentioned that "one of these days we'll have to think about automated records systems."

On the basis of class discussion, your instructor assigns a report in which you are to do the following:

1. Recommend ways of building an understanding of systems concepts in the records personnel, specifically addressing the conclusions noted above.

2. Discuss what objections records personnel would likely have to your recommendations and suggest how these objections could be overcome.

Case 19–2 Building a Records Retention Schedule

The general manager of Gateway Security, a 20-person insurance agency, has concluded that it is time the firm did a better job of managing its records. No one has been officially assigned to manage the records system, and, until that position is created and filled, each department manager has been asked to contribute to improving the records function. You, the commercial sales manager, have been asked to investigate how the firm should build a retention schedule. The first step in this process (after you clarify what a retention schedule is and how it works) is to identify which individuals or positions *both inside and outside the organization* should be involved in creating the schedule.

Create an executive summary that will be sent to the general manager. The summary should (1) explain the purpose of a retention schedule, (2) identify the positions of those people who should help establish retention times, (3) explain why getting recommendations from these positions is necessary, and (4) supply a sample of a typical retention schedule format.

Case 19–3 Designing a Smart/EPSS Form: Computer Option (available on disk)

MANAGING MICROIMAGE AND REPRO-GRAPHIC SYSTEMS

GOALS FOR THIS CHAPTER

After completing this chapter, you should be able to:

1. Identify the various types of microrecords and the principal uses of each.
2. List the criteria for deciding when to use microrecords.
3. Discuss the various stages involved in managing microimage systems.
4. Discuss the role of the computer and optical disks in automating microimage systems.
5. Discuss the technology of reprographic systems.
6. Discuss the main components of a program for managing reprographic systems.

It is a generally accepted axiom that paper records continue to be the common medium for storing and using information in most offices. However, an increasing number of firms are utilizing photographic and electronic systems that convert paper records to smaller, more easily accessible media. In the first section of this chapter, we shall investigate the technologies used in these nonpaper systems and their managerial implications.

Despite the progress that these systems are making toward reducing the amount of paper being used, we acknowledge that offices are still copying huge amounts of paper records. In the second section of this chapter, we examine copying systems, called reprographic systems.

MICROIMAGE TECHNOLOGY

Business records have been photographed and reduced in size on microfilm for more than half a century. During this time, the microimages of records have generally been called *microfilm* and the process for converting paper records to reduced size, *microfilming*. Thus, the process of microfilming results in the creation of a **microrecord,** the name for a paper document that has been converted to microfilm. *(Note, however, that it is still a common business practice to consider microfilm as the generic classification for all types of microrecords stored on film.)*

Later, to reflect the expansion of services available in the microfilm field as well as the integration of microfilm with other technologies, the term *micrographics* was created. Most recently, to reflect a growing emphasis on the form and size of the record, the total system for creating, using, and storing microrecords has been called a **microimage system.** We shall be using this term in this textbook. However, you should be aware that many professionals use a similar term, *imaging,* to refer to any technology that captures, reduces, and stores images of documents through either photographic or electronic processes. As evidence of this evolution in terms, a leading professional association in this field—the National Micrographics Association—has changed its name to the Association for Information and Image Management.

Figure 20–1 outlines in greater detail the full set of procedural steps involved in creating, using, and storing a microrecord. There are two key, basic aspects of a microimage system: (1) the storage, retrieval, and use of the most common types of microrecords (steps 6 to 9 in Figure 20–1); and (2) the management of microrecords in manual and automated systems. The remaining aspects of microimage systems (steps 1 to 5 in Figure 20–1) are more highly specialized and require the attention of personnel with technical training in the field.

Types of Microforms

The film used in microimage systems comes in a variety of sizes, types, and formats; any film that carries a microrecord is a **microform.** Microforms, in turn, can be divided into two broad classes: unitized and nonunitized. The **unitized microform** is prepared as one complete set or unit of data, such as a payroll file, and does not include any unrelated material. The **nonunitized microform,** on the other hand, frequently contains random or unrelated items of information from many departments of a firm on the same continuous length of film. This type of microform is illustrated by microfiche, aperture cards, and filmstrip in jackets.

Because of its simplicity and widespread usage, roll film—the principal nonunitized microform—is discussed first. The microforms commonly included in the nonunitized category (microfiche, aperture cards, and microfilm strips inserted into plastic jackets) are described later in this section.

Roll Film   *inexp. can't update*

Roll film is a continuous length of microfilm 16mm, 35mm, or 105mm in width and 100 feet in length on which original documents are photographed and reduced in size for storage. Note the drawings of the three sizes of roll film shown on the following pages. It is the most frequently used—and usually is considered the most economical type of microrecord.

The width of film selected depends upon the size of the original material to be photographed, the desired reduction ratio for the microimage, and the intended use of the microrecords. The **reduction ratio** expresses the number of times the

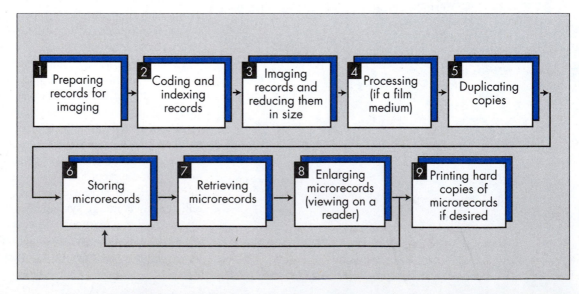

Figure 20–1
Procedural Steps in Operating a Microimage System

size of a record is reduced photographically. For example, a page from this book measures 7¾″ × 9⅛″. If a typical reduction is used, the book is reduced at the ratio of 24 to 1 (expressed as 24×). This means that the microimage is 1/24th the width of the original page, or about 0.32 inch wide and would look similar to this drawing:

Thus, a 16mm roll of film that is 100 feet in length would hold more than 4,000 textbook pages.

16mm Roll Film

Roll film is most commonly used for filing large volumes of records stored in sequence, such as employee time sheets, correspondence, checks, and sales records in a very small space at a very low cost. Generally, 16mm film is used for storing alphabetic and numeric data, such as correspondence, checks, and invoices. The wider 35mm film (and less frequently, 105mm film) is used for storing microimages of larger documents, such as X-rays, newspapers, and maps. Microrecords produced by the computer output microfilm process discussed later are stored on 105mm film.

35mm Roll Film

105mm Roll Film

When the film is in negative form, we can use it to reproduce a positive film roll. The negative may then be sent out to an off-site facility for vital records protection. Unlike other types of microforms, roll film makes browsing and updating difficult. To add related documents requires splicing, which is a slow and costly process.

Storage of Roll Film. Roll film is easily stored on reels, similar to the storage of movie films or the magnetic tapes used in computer systems. Other methods of packaging roll film are cartridges and cassettes, which ease the handling of microfilm rolls. In these containers, the film is protected from fingerprint smudges and other possible damage. The use of a cassette also eliminates the need for rewinding since each cassette provides both "advance" and "reverse" features. Similarly, cartridges are self-threading.

Retrieval of Roll Film. Microrecords are indexed and coded so that they may be quickly retrieved. Before being photographed, the paper records are sorted in the same order as for paper-based files. Later as the sorted records are photographed, code marks are recorded on the film adjacent to each microimage or frame. One common coding system uses a type of identifier or "flash" (similar to a flash card) between regular sections of the filmed material (usually every 20 feet of film) to assist the user in determining the section of the film being scanned. Sequential numbers may also be placed on the film to identify each frame.

Once the documents have been coded and photographed, an index of the coded frames is created manually to assist in their retrieval. This index contains information about the microrecord file, such as the subject or invoice number of each stored document, the roll film number, and the code number of each frame. The original documents may then be retained or discarded.

To retrieve a record from a roll film file, the user consults the index to determine the appropriate reel of tape, cassette, or cartridge. This container is then located and placed in a **reader,** a device that enlarges or magnifies the microrecord to its original legible size and projects the image onto a viewing screen. (See Illustration 20–1.) Generally microrecords are stored sequentially along the length of the film, like magnetic tape recordings, so that the user can advance a film or move it backward as the retrieval needs require. With motorized units, the user obtains the index location of the desired microrecord from a separate index. This information is then entered into the keyboard of the unit, which searches for and locates the desired record.

Microfiche

Microfiche (pronounced mī′ krə fēsh′) means small index card and refers to a microform that appears in a grid pattern on a transparent sheet of film. (See the drawing shown on the next page.) The most common size of microfiche is 6″ × 4″

(a) Desktop Microfiche Reader

(b) Hand-held Microfiche Reader

Illustration 20–1 Microrecord readers.

(or 108mm by 105mm). Because of their light weight, eight 6″ × 4″ microfiche can be sent by first-class mail at the one-ounce rate.

A special type of microfiche, **ultrafiche,** per-mits very high (ultra) reduction ratios, commonly from 150 to 400×, and sometimes as great as 2,400×. (In one notable example of an ultra-fiche record, the entire contents of the *King James Bible*—approximately 800,000 words stored on almost 800 pages—were microfilmed onto a fiche measuring less than two inches square.) Banks use ultrafiche to record customer transactions. Other large organizations, such as General Motors Corporation, use ultrafiche for storing inventory and parts data. Copies of fiche records may be duplicated easily and inexpensively for mailing throughout the world. Updating is accomplished in two ways: (1) by replacing an obsolete fiche with a current one or (2) by using **updatable microfiche** in which a special camera erases an obsolete record and places a new image over the erased record. Another version of updatable microfiche affixes the word "Void" or "Superseded" over an obsolete microrecord and adds a current or updated record to the same microfiche.

Storage of Microfiche. A microfiche record is as easy to store as any other 6″ × 4″ card and hence

makes use of standard vertical card filing equipment. As the microfiche drawing shows, the format of the microfiche permits the placement of an eye-readable index along the top margin of the record. Since microfiche has become increasingly popular for storing active records, we find that such records are stored in a convenient location near their point of use. A typical means of housing small numbers of microfiche is a desktop tray or a looseleaf ring binder. Larger numbers of microfiche are stored in cabinets.

Retrieval of Microfiche. Microfiche records that are stored in small quantities at or near the workstation are retrieved like regular file cards. The user manually scans the top margin of each fiche,

Illustration 20–2 Tray for storing microfiche records.

which bears the indexed information by which the record is stored. As soon as we locate the desired fiche, we can physically remove it from the file and place it in a reader in order to locate the appropriate frame for viewing.

When large files of microfiche are maintained, automated storage and retrieval systems are used. One microfiche storage and retrieval system uses up to 100 positions of code along the top edge of the fiche for storage in standard or electro-mechanical files. When the proper cartridge of fiche is selected after consulting a separate file index, the cartridge is placed in an automatic desk retrieval unit. This unit locates the desired fiche, extracts it from the cartridge, and presents it to the operator for manual insertion in a reader. A more advanced system uses codes in the form of notches that are punched in the top or bottom edges of the fiche. When the operator presses the appropriate buttons or turns the correct dials on the retrieval unit, the unit searches the fiche file for the notch codes that refer to the page and frame numbers of the desired fiche. As soon as the requested frame is located, its image is displayed on the reader screen. The most automated systems for retrieving microfiche operate under the direction of a computer, a topic that is discussed later in this chapter.

Aperture Cards

The **punched aperture card** shown at the left is a standard-size 80-column punched card with a pre-cut hole over which a portion of 35mm microfilm 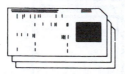 is mounted. Aperture cards have traditionally used punched-card codes for storage and retrieval. Today, however, a **data aperture card** with the same dimensions and weight as the punched aperture card is often used. These cards contain computer-readable OCR indexing text at the top of the cards for retrieval and display on the VDT screen.

The punched aperture card still represents the best, smallest, handiest, and most economic storage medium for blueprints, other technical drawings, and charts. Also, since these records are likely to be used and updated frequently, they are readily accessible as "individual" copies as a unitized record. One card may contain a single microrecord or up to eight images on a single 35mm frame. Besides its space-saving qualities, the punched aperture card has the advantage of permitting the keypunching of information into the card, which aids in the speedy storage and retrieval of the microrecord. Typically, the punched aperture card bears identifying information that is printed in the upper margin as well as punched in the body of the card. It is this information that determines the location of the card in the file.

Storage of Aperture Cards. Trays and boxes designed for desktop locations are available to store small quantities of cards. If large quantities of cards are required and retrieval time is critical, motorized bin-type storage systems can be obtained.

Retrieval of Aperture Cards. Like microfiche, aperture cards are separate units (rather than sequential records on roll film) that can be scanned by hand and taken from the file like regular index cards. Mechanical sorting equipment can also be used to retrieve aperture cards using the identifying information keypunched into the upper margin of the card. These cards can be returned to the files using either the manual or mechanical storage systems.

Microfilm Jackets

Sections of roll film containing blocks of related microrecords may be cut into strips, which are then inserted into plastic jackets to serve as unitized microrecords. *Microfilm jackets,* shown at the left, are suitable for records that must be retrieved together (such as personnel files) and for 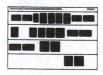 convenient distribution of film records through the mail. Filmstrips in jackets may be duplicated directly from the jacket, which eliminates the need for removing the film. In addition, obsolete records may be easily removed from the jacket and new microrecords inserted, which speeds storage operations. The storage and retrieval of filmstrips housed in jackets are similar to the storage and retrieval of microfiche discussed earlier.

Automated Microimage Systems

Thus far, our discussion of microimage technology has been based on two ageless principles of learning: (1) *Proceed from the known to the unknown,* and (2) *Move from the simple to the complex.* The typical microfilm operations described early in this chapter are based upon the separate, distinct activities of a manual system similar to those we recognize. One person creates a document; another files it. A third person microfilms the record while a fourth person files the microrecord. Such separate activities depend upon the availability and smooth coordination of a group of office personnel in order to have a continuous flow of work from the beginning to the end of the microrecord cycle. When such an efficient workflow is not found, the time used for preparing microrecords is extended unnecessarily, and the cost of such operations is increased. (At this point we move from the simplicity of the manual system to the relative complexity of the computer system.)

As a partial solution to such problems, the computer has been successfully applied to various phases of microimaging. As a result, many of the microimaging functions have been automated, with greater volumes of microrecords stored and more rapidly retrieved and the administrative expenses budget more effectively controlled.

Two of the most significant developments for automating micrographic services are (1) computer output microfilm (COM) and (2) computer-assisted retrieval (CAR). Each is discussed briefly below.

Computer Output Microfilm (COM)

One of the first successful efforts to automate microimage systems produced **computer output microfilm (COM).** In the COM process, the computer's output (machine-readable, digital data) is automatically photographed and converted to human-readable images on microfilm or microfiche without creating an intervening paper copy. (When the final record is on microfiche, COM refers to *computer output microfiche.*) This process is made possible through the use of a special device called a **recorder** that uses either photographic or laser technology to transfer the computer output to microimage size on film. As Figure 20–2 shows, two types of COM applications are used: (1) *online,* in which the computer

Figure 20–2
The Computer Output Microfilm Process

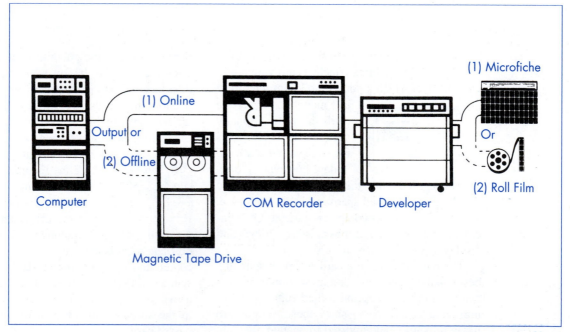

output is sent directly to the recorder similar to the way data are transferred from a computer to a printer; or (2) *offline,* in which the computer output is sent to a magnetic tape drive to be read into the recorder for microfilming independent of the computer. COM recorders produce records, usually on microfiche and sometimes on roll film, for use in the microimage system described earlier.

The COM process eliminates the earlier steps of preparing a hard-copy printout by the computer and then taking the printout to a microfilm camera for filming and reduction to microimage. Great savings may be realized from COM-produced microrecords: (1) savings in the weight of records (40 pounds of computerized paper records can be stored on seven ounces of microfilm), (2) savings in postage from mailing much lighter records, and (3) savings in materials and space for storing the microrecords as compared with storing cartons of computerized paper records. A closely related process—**computer input microfilm (CIM)**—has been developed. Using special equipment, CIM translates uncoded data on microrecords into computer language code for storage on magnetic tape as input to a computer. With COM and CIM available, the computer's role in microimage systems is expected to grow.

Computer-Assisted Retrieval (CAR)

In addition to its use in COM and CIM, we find the computer has become a powerful tool for retrieving records. **Computer-assisted retrieval (CAR)** is the process of merging the computer (with its fast data storage and data search capabilities) and the microrecording process to access data on microfilm. In CAR, an index of all records in the microimage system is stored in the computer while the records themselves are stored on roll film, microfiche, or aperture cards. The index is created from the codes affixed to each record during the filming process described earlier. Commonly, we find two CAR systems whose main features are discussed in this section.

Basic CAR System. *Basic CAR* is an indirect-access system in which the various types of microrecords are stored manually according to the index code developed at the time of filming.

When a microrecord is desired, the operator consults an index register for the identification (ID) code number of the desired record. This number is then entered into the VDT, after which the computer searches its index file for the code number. Once the number is found, the computer displays (or prints out) the location number of the document (the page and frame numbers of the microfiche, for example, or the frame number and cartridge or roll number of the record on roll film, which is often stored in cassettes). After we locate this microrecord file, we can insert it manually into the reader and scan the file for the desired frame for viewing on the reader screen.

Advanced CAR System. In an *advanced CAR system,* the computer performs greater portions of the work required to find and display the desired microrecord. The microrecords used in an advanced retrieval system may be stored in an offline or in an online file. Both file processes require the development of an index of microrecords that is stored in the computer.

In the offline retrieval process, the operator enters the code number of the desired microrecord into the terminal. The computer searches its index file and displays the location number of the desired record on the VDT screen. The user then manually finds the proper microfiche or roll film file and places it in an automatic retrieval device. The desired microimage, with its specially coded ID number, is automatically found in seconds and displayed on the screen once the location/ID number has been keyboarded into the retrieval unit.

The online retrieval process operates in the most automated fashion. As soon as the operator enters into the VDT the index code number of the desired record, the computer searches its index file and then directs the online microimage terminal to locate and display the proper microimage on the terminal screen. (The retrieval of microrecords from a COM-generated file may follow this same automated retrieval procedure.) Depending upon the power of the computerized index file, the system can retrieve the desired document from a variety of approaches.

To illustrate the power of an advanced CAR system, consider Figure 20–3. In addition to assigning code numbers to the incoming records, the indexing system also captures key fields of data from each document as it is being scanned. In Figure 20–3, the database contains the client's name, the invoice number, and the date of the transaction. Should it be necessary to retrieve the document without knowing the index code number, the database searches for a match of whatever key descriptors are available. For example, if a client named Creative Software has lost a bill (so has no invoice number) but knows that the transaction occurred on December 7, an office worker enters the two known key descriptors into the system: Creative Software and December 7. The database searches all transactions for Creative Software that occurred on December 7, finds the match (or matches), and displays the image of each invoice.

Firms having advanced CAR systems like these are greatly improving their operating efficiency and effectiveness. However, many firms must store greater numbers of records and desire even faster retrieval times. To meet these needs, many records systems managers are implementing an alternate technology to film-based systems: optical disks.

Optical Disks: Totally Electronic Microimage Storage

The most powerful microimage storage technology is the optical disk (sometimes known as "laser optical disk," "videodisk," or "optical digital disk"). The optical disk is a mass memory device that captures, stores, and retrieves document images by using laser technology. Because the images are digitized (converted to numeric code) and stored as data, many microimage professionals refer to optical disk storage as *imaging.*

An optical disk looks like a phonograph record and is available in many sizes (with diameters of 3″, 5″, 8″, 12″, and 14″). Technically these disks are called *optical digital data disks (ODDD)* and abbreviated as OD³.

Figure 20–3
An Advanced CAR System

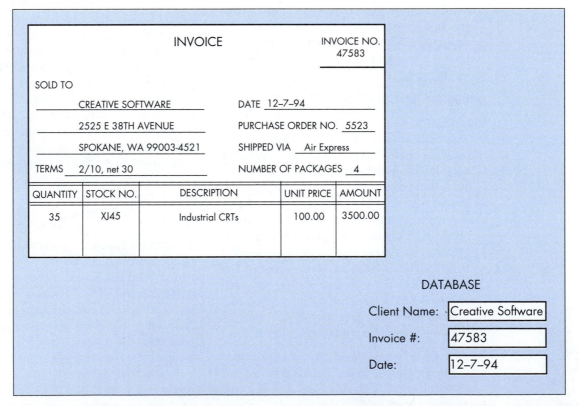

How Optical Disks Work

We can summarize the principal characteristics of optical disks and the systems in which they operate in this way:

1. *An OD³ is usually configured to store images on a format called* **WORM** *(write-once, read-many) storage,* which limits the user to writing to the disk just once. However, the user is provided many opportunities for "reading out" the contents of the disk.

2. *Data are entered on, and read from, OD³s using lasers.* During the data-entry operation, the laser forms a tiny hole—less than one micron in diameter, or 1/100 the width of a human hair—in a thin metal layer inside the disk to represent binary data. Both sides of the disk can be used for data storage. This hole-burning operation gives write-once disks their permanence. Read operations use the same laser at a lower intensity to recover the data from the disk. The laser reader reflects back to a sensor if a hole is, or is not, present (the presence or absence of stored information) at an incredible speed—several million bits of data per second.

3. *Each optical disk can store vast amounts of data.* One 14″ disk can store 6.8 million bytes of information, comparable to the storage capacity of 15,000 floppy disks.[1] Typically disks are stored online in a "jukebox" cartridge containing hundreds of disks. A user requests a file from a disk in the same way as requested in a CAR system, and a hard copy of the file, if needed, can be made on a laser printer.

4. *The disk cartridges can be easily removed from the drive,* which allows transportability to other computers. Like other disks, random access is provided to the hundreds of files or large databases stored on a single cartridge.

5. *Operation of the disk drive is identical to that of any other disk drive.* The drive is attached to the computer via cables.

6. *Records stored on OD³s are subject to the same retention, legality, and control procedures as other records.*

The Advantages of Using Optical Disks

Organizations are installing optical disk information systems in far greater number than any other microimage technology for several reasons:

1. *Faster retrieval times.* As pointed out so many times in this textbook, an organization's efficiency and effectiveness are directly correlated to the quick retrieval of necessary information. Most optical disk systems can retrieve and display on the VDT any online document in less than four seconds.

2. *Shared access.* Since the images are stored entirely electronically, they can be transmitted just like any other data through the organization's local-area networks (LANs), allowing many workstations to share the images simultaneously. As a result, a document is never unavailable because it is "out of the files."

3. *Enhanced image integrity.* Electronic images, once properly captured and stored, retain their fidelity. There is no reduction of quality over time, and it is estimated that the

Illustration 20–3 Optical disk storage.

[1]Michael J. Berkery, "Optical Disk Storage Is an Alternative to Paper," *The Office* (June, 1992), p. 64. Reprinted from the June issue of *The Office,* and copyrighted 1992 by Office Publications, Inc.

disks will store data accurately and clearly for 100 years.

4. *Integrated records retrieval.* Electronic images can be retrieved and displayed in a multi-window screen presentation alongside other retrieved files. An office worker, for example, could retrieve and simultaneously display the image of the source document that originated an order, the database record that tracked the handling of the order, and the image of the canceled check that completed the transaction.

5. *Lower records costs.* Optical disk systems are admittedly expensive primarily because they are relatively new and are technologically sophisticated. However, because of their high-storage capability, image integrity, and speed of accessing and communicating information, the cost *per unit* of optical disk storage is lower than any other disk system.

MANAGEMENT OF MICROIMAGE SYSTEMS

In a typical organization, microimaging services were not always planned. Rather, they just "grew" as the need to save the space occupied by the volume of common paper records, such as canceled checks and accounts payable files, became critical. When new microforms like microfiche appeared on the market, too often they were added without the necessary coordination among the departments. The result was a set of fragmented, nonstandardized, inefficient, and poorly directed programs. Under such conditions, duplication of equipment occurred and a lack of standardization in storage equipment, indexing, and retrieval prevailed. As a result, operating costs became much higher than necessary.

Before undertaking a carefully developed program to avoid these problems, we must obtain answers to two fundamental questions: (1) When should we microimage records? and (2) Are microimage records legal? Answers to these questions as well as considerations for ensuring the effective management of microrecords are included in this section.

Why Use Microrecords?

"Why microimage?" managers ask. From research studies completed since the 1920s when microfilmed records were first used in business, administrators have recommended converting paper documents to microrecords to meet the following office needs:

1. *The need to conserve space and to reduce the costs of storing records.* Great savings can be achieved by converting paper documents to microrecords, depending upon the reduction ratio used. For example, at a 24× reduction, the contents of a four-drawer vertical file cabinet—from 8,000 to 14,000 documents—can be reduced to four or six rolls of 16mm microfilm (assuming that there are 2,000 letter-size documents per 100 feet of roll film). This same four-drawer vertical file cabinet can store 1,000 rolls of 16mm microfilm—the equivalent of 750 to 1,750 drawers of paper documents.[2]

2. *The need for a more efficient records system.* A high number of file searches can be conducted easily, quickly, and inexpensively by an automated retrieval system discussed earlier. Microrecords have uniform dimensions since their sizes are reduced to fit standard microfilm dimensions regardless of their original size or shape. The handling of aperture card microrecords, rather than bulky engineering drawings, also simplifies the records work of the office staff. Also, books, periodicals, catalogs, and other library references are often available on a microform at a fraction of the paper-copy costs.

3. *The need for maintaining file integrity,* that is, the assurance that none of the documents filmed in sequence is lost or misfiled. The records on microfilm are usually arranged in a fixed sequence, which protects against misfiling, mislaying, alteration, or record loss. Also, AOMs want to be sure that there are no documents charged out so that the file is always

---

[2]William Saffady, *Microfilm in Records Management* (Silver Spring, MD: National Micrographics Association, 1982), pp. 10–11.

complete. Microrecord files ensure such completeness.

4. *The need for periodic duplication of a regularly updated file and for maintaining duplicate records stored in several locations.* An off-site duplicate microfilm file protects against loss of information due to fire or theft. The small size of microrecord packages, the low cost of duplication (one microfiche or jacket holding 50 to 100 pages can be duplicated for little more than the cost of one paper page on an office copier), and the ease with which such records can be mailed make microrecords a valuable information-storage service in the office.

5. *The need for long-term preservation of records.* Under carefully controlled conditions, microrecords can be preserved for well over a hundred years.

With all their advantages, however, microrecords have several limitations. Since they are very small, microrecords require the use of reader equipment to enlarge the photographed records for the user. Such equipment adds to the cost of administrative operations. Further, since the reader equipment is often bulky, it typically lacks portability. However, the availability of portable readers has partially overcome this limitation. Usually records that are subject to constant change are not filmed except on microfiche, for the updating of filmed records is a costly process and is more easily carried out on the original paper documents.

Other costs attached to microrecords include the costs of imaging the original records or similar costs of having records imaged by an outside agency; costs of processors, duplicators, and related supplies; special storing and retrieving equipment; and unique climate controls needed for microrecord files. AOMs must weigh these cost factors against the benefits of satisfying the other needs discussed in this section.

Determining the Legality of Microrecords

If we are to ensure the legality of microrecords in a firm, we must answer two "legality" questions: (1) Is a records retention requirement met by retaining the document image in microform and discarding the paper document? and (2) Are microimages acceptable in courts of law as substitutes for paper documents?

To ascertain the legality of microrecords, AOMs should be familiar with both state and federal legislation on the subject. In 1951, Congress passed the Uniform Photographic Copies of Business Records in Evidence Act. This act established that microfilmed copies of business records (as replacements for the original documents) could be admitted as evidence in courts of law if these conditions were met: (1) the filming occurred in the normal course of business, (2) the original records were accurately photographed in their entirety, and (3) they were legible. Thus, the provisions of this Act, which are still in effect, permit records that meet these conditions to be used as evidence in court.

Most federal and state agencies have their own microimage regulations concerning the substitution of microfilmed or optical disk records for hard copies. The Securities and Exchange Commission, for example, allows filming, provided a duplicate of each microrecord is stored separately from the original microrecord. A good guideline to follow is to file a certificate of authenticity as the last document on every roll of film. This certificate is an official record of the firm's routine microfilming policy and provides information about the dates and ranges of the records filmed, the date photographed, and the signature of the photographer. The firm's legal department should prepare this certificate.

Planning Microimage Systems

Even though we assume that a program of microimage services is warranted, we should conduct a feasibility study in order to compile unbiased information on the real need for microrecords. To assist in collecting and organizing the large volume of data needed for such a study, microimage management specialists recommend the use of a systems grid form as shown in Figure 20–4. For the input phase of such a study, answers should be requested for questions such as the following:

Figure 20–4
A Systems Grid Form for Collecting Feasibility Data for a Microimage System

		People	Equipment	Materials	Facilities
I N P U T		1. Document preparation clerks 2. Systems supervisor 3. Delivery and mail service	1. Cameras 2. Worktables 3. Floodlights 4. Meters 5. Duplicators 6. Storage equipment	1. Source documents 2. Film, disks 3. Microimage service record forms	1. Preparation area 2. Imaging area 3. Temporary storage area
P R O C E S S		1. Supervising work 2. Microimaging records 3. Processing film 4. Delivering film or disks to users	1. Tables 2. Cameras and equipment 3. Processing equipment 4. Delivery cart	1. Record forms 2. Film, optical disks 3. Source documents 4. Processed film	1. Preparation and imaging areas 2. Processing area
O U T P U T		Records of worker performance	Same equipment as used for input	1. Microrecords created 2. Records of microrecords created and delivered 3. Source documents retained	Newer storage area in user system

1. What are the objectives of a proposed microimage system?
2. What are the characteristics of the files to be microfilmed? (How many items to be filed, how often are additions or modifications made to the records, how frequently is the file consulted, and how long must the file be retained?)
3. What are the characteristics of the documents to be microimaged? (Are all documents the same size, what are their sizes and condition, are they clear and readable, and are they paper or computerized?)
4. What are the anticipated retrieval needs for the files? (What is the average number of retrievals per day/week, by how many people, in what departments, and in what proximity to each other; and must the entire file be accessed or just single documents within the file?)
5. What kinds of materials and supplies will be needed?
6. What facilities are necessary to start and maintain such a system?

In a similar way, questions must be asked about the paper-based records system: the volume of paper used, the space required, the format of each record, the way information flows from its origin to its destination, the turnaround time needed to obtain the stored information, and the security of the documents. From this wealth of information and a discussion of its implications with departmental managers, the AOM can compare *anticipated benefits* and *expected costs*. If such benefits exceed costs, a decision should be made to convert paper-based records to microrecords.

During the process of conversion, the AOM or the records manager should continue to maintain hard-copy files until the records retention committee decides that the original documents are no longer needed. In a manual information system, many active records will still be maintained in their original form. If, on the other hand, the information system is highly automated and the active records can be easily retrieved from the microfile itself, the paper records may be destroyed. However, a duplicate (backup) file of microrecords should be created for security purposes.

Organizing Microimage Systems

Microimage systems should be considered as an important subsystem of the total information system. As such, microimage systems are a complex mix of the equipment, environmental conditions for records storage, human resources, and procedures necessary to provide efficient microrecord operations for the company. In large firms, these responsibilities are assigned to a specialized unit under the supervision of the records manager. In smaller firms, commercial microimaging agencies are used to photograph the records for storage in the firm under the direct supervision of the AOM.

Microimage Equipment

Although highly specialized equipment (cameras and scanners to capture images, processors to convert film into negatives, duplicators to reproduce copies of microrecords, and readers to display images) is necessary in a full-scale microimage program, the office staff usually operates only two types of equipment. Such equipment, which can be operated with little or no training, includes storage equipment for each of the microforms discussed earlier, and readers. (See Illustration 20–1.) There are readers of various sizes and for each type of microrecord. *Reader-printers* combine the reading function and the production of hard-copy printouts of microrecords. To obtain such a printout, the user simply presses a button and a paper copy of the image appearing on the screen is generated.

Optical disk microimage systems operate just like any other peripheral device connected to the computer system. Office staff who have been trained to use VDTs, therefore, need little more than knowledge of the software commands that govern the optical disk system.

Storage Environment

Records on film are highly sensitive to temperature and humidity conditions. Generally the average air-conditioned office is well suited to preserving microrecords. Where controlled atmospheric conditions are not found—as in some company *archives* (inactive records center)—over long periods of time the microrecords may crack, mold, or attract dust or dirt that can scratch the surface of the image. If this occurs, all or a portion of the stored information may be destroyed. Other hazards, such as fire, theft, and unauthorized access to microrecords, require the same environmental and security controls as given to paper records.

Optical disks generally require storage environments that are well within normal office conditions: temperatures between 40 and 120 degrees Fahrenheit, and relative humidity between 8 and 80 percent. The major handling precaution is training users not to touch the surface of the disks.

Personnel

A microimage system is typically an administrative service that is delegated to the records manager. Such a program requires certain managerial, technical, and user skills for effective operation. Figure 20–5 outlines these three personnel needs. Due to the simple nature of the reader-printer equipment, most users can be taught the fundamentals of machine operation in a few minutes. As mentioned earlier, office workers who have been trained to operate a VDT for routine office applications will have little trouble utilizing the workstation to retrieve and display disk-supported microimages. The managerial and technical skills, on the other hand, require considerably longer training and extensive administrative experience.

Establishing Operating Procedures

To operate a full-fledged microimage system, a set of effective procedures, as shown in Figure 20–1, must be established. These procedures include instructions for indexing, photographing or scanning, and processing records as well as control procedures for ensuring that all records are properly protected. Some of these procedures are entirely manual in nature while others, such as those required for computerizing the microimage

Figure 20–5
Personnel
Needs of the
Microimage
Systems Pro-
gram

Managerial Needs	Technical Needs	User Needs
Understanding the microimaging needs of the firm.	Imaging, processing film and disks. Duplicating film and disks.	Understanding procedures for storing, retrieving, maintaining, preserving, and destroying records.
Designing an effective system of microimage services. Coordinating the use of microrecords throughout the firm.	Procuring, maintaining, and updating equipment.	Using basic equipment (readers, printers, and retrieval or display units) to retrieve information and produce hard copies.
Preserving and controlling all microrecords.	Providing continuous service to users.	Keeping the records manager informed on the effectiveness of the microimage system.

process, operate according to computer program instructions.

The AOM or the records manager should conduct orientation sessions for each department, explaining in detail the nature and purpose of each of the new procedures, how such procedures are to be carried out, and where assistance can be found if needed.

The principal procedures for operating microimage systems include:

1. *Describing the records to be microimaged.* Defining paper documents includes specifying the names and sizes of the records as well as the type and color of paper stock on which they are printed; the volume of records to be filed; whether the records are one- or two-sided; and a general statement about the condition of the records. Defining COM-generated records requires specifying file names and the length of the fields within the files.
2. *Preparing the records to be microimaged.* The person who submits paper records for microimaging is responsible for putting them in correct filing sequence, for mending torn pages and crumpled sheets, and for removing staples and other fasteners. If the data on the records are not legible, the records should not be captured.

3. *Determining the requirements for personnel and equipment.* Information should be obtained regarding (a) the total number of records to be captured; (b) the estimated number of records to be captured per day; (c) the number of cameras, scanners, or COM units required; (d) the total working days required to complete the jobs; (e) the average number of persons regularly assigned; and (f) the number of readers required after the microimaging has been completed.
4. *Imaging and processing records.* Departments should provide information regarding (a) the desired microform; (b) the number and type of duplicate microforms to be made; (c) the coding system to be used; (d) the desired reduction ratio; and (e) any tests needed to evaluate the quality of the microimaged record.
5. *Packaging and indexing the microimaged records.* The completed microimaged package, either as processed film or as loaded optical disk, should be indexed and a log maintained to reflect when and where the records were delivered.
6. *Storing and retrieving the microforms.* Effective procedures for storing the records should specify (a) the current retention period for each microrecord; (b) how the records are to be filed (alphabetically, numerically, or

chronologically); and (c) how to request and retrieve microrecords from the file. Also, logs should be maintained that show how often each of the microrecord files is requested.

7. *Disposing of original records.* The location of the original records for all microrecord files should be noted. In addition, the decisions on disposing of original records (when, how, and by whom) should be recorded.

Evaluating Microimage Systems

We should evaluate any system periodically to determine how effectively its objectives are being met. The major points in the evaluation of a microimage system include:

1. How well users accept and actively use the microrecord files.
2. The adequacy of the equipment (sufficient number, properly scheduled and allocated among departments, properly maintained and serviced, and easy to use).
3. The quality of environmental controls and protective measures for safeguarding the microrecords.
4. The effectiveness of operating procedures, such as making available to all departments information on microimage applications; contacts with vendors of equipment and supplies; and effective methods of capturing, storing, and retrieving documents.

5. Provision for follow-up studies to improve the service to all users.
6. Careful monitoring and control of operating costs and benefits, as discussed in the following paragraphs.

The AOM or the records manager responsible for a microimage system must understand fully the entire range of costs and benefits involved in its operation. While the same general costs apply to a microimage system as to other administrative operations as shown in Figure 19–18, several additional factors must be considered. Figure 20–6 outlines the major *direct* costs required in the use of space, personnel time, equipment, materials, and supplies associated with microimage systems. However, Figure 20–6 does not address either the *indirect* costs or benefits that must also be considered. To overcome this limitation, competent AOMs gather information that indicates how effectively the microimage system supports the organization's need for high-quality, readily accessible documents. An example of an indirect cost is the estimated loss to the organization because a document cannot be located when it is needed; an example of an indirect benefit is the impact that an excellent microimage system has on employee morale and on public relations. Although data in these indirect areas are sometimes difficult to gather, they often are the best indicators of the worth of the system.

Figure 20–6
Major Types of Costs in Microimage Systems

Types of Space Costs	Types of Personnel Time Costs	
Storage area	Indexing	Duplicating
Records preparation area	Sorting	Filming
Transportation areas	Filing	Distributing
Related service areas	Retrieving	Supervising

Types of Equipment Costs	Types of Materials & Supplies Costs
Storage cabinets and shelving	Microfilm, disks
Readers or reader-printers	Storage supplies
Cameras, processors, and duplicators	Paper and carbon paper
Maintenance charges and replacement parts	General administrative supplies

REPROGRAPHIC TECHNOLOGY

Can you imagine any office today as well as in the future that does not require making copies of forms and records on a daily, or even an hourly, basis? In fact, one of the most basic systems maintained in the office is copy making. For decades, multiple copies of records were made using either carbon paper or machine duplicating processes. Later, a new phase of copying emerged with the application of photographic and telecommunication processes. Since all these processes share one key function—the *reproduction* of information and records for management—they are called **reprographic systems.** A full knowledge of such topics is essential in order that the AOM be able to provide copy-making information to all areas of the organization.

Reprographic Processes

The earliest form of reproducing copies in an office involved a clerk making a handwritten copy of a record. This slow, painstaking process was later replaced by carbon paper, which continues to offer many economies to the office even in this age of automated copy making. The major use of carbon paper (or carbonless paper, as discussed in Chapter 19) is in the preparation of multiple copies of forms. Because office copiers have largely replaced duplicating machines and the use of carbon paper, in this section we give major emphasis to copying processes and the growing role of copiers in integrated systems.

Copiers are used in every size and type of office and come with features as diverse as the offices they serve. Copying machines can be relatively inexpensive and easy to operate or they can be extremely sophisticated and require highly trained operators. Three broad classes of copiers, based on the volume of copies that can be made, are available. Figure 20–7 lists the main features of each copier class.

Advances in electronics and machine design have resulted in a growing number of convenience features in office copiers. The most common features include: (1) the ability to reduce the size of documents, such as computer printouts, to smaller-size copy paper, or to enlarge the original document to a more readable size; (2) automatic

Figure 20–7
Copiers Classified by Volume of Copies Made

Copiers Classified by Volume of Copies Made	Main Features of Each Copier Class
1. Low–volume or convenience copier	Compact units, sometimes portable, produce up to 25 copies per minute; recommended for copy volume levels not exceeding 15,000 copies per month; used as sole copiers in small offices or as satellite units in a decentralized reprographics program.
2. Mid–volume copier	Desk-top units larger than the convenience copier; produce copies at speeds ranging from 21 to 50 copies per minute for firms requiring 20,000 copies per month; or, as floor-console units, for firms requiring up to 100,000 copies per month; used in centralized copy centers.
3. High–volume copier	Floor units that produce copies at speeds ranging from 51 to 90 copies per minute for firms needing 50,000 to more than 200,000 copies per month; includes in this class *copier/duplicators,* which combine the convenience of high-speed copiers with the low per-copy cost of duplicators; used in centralized reprographics departments or in decentralized locations within large firms.

feeding of documents; (3) collating of copies produced; (4) **duplexing,** or copying on both sizes of a sheet of copy paper in one operation; (5) the use of color toners in throwaway packages for copying documents in color; (6) edge erase [eliminating the edge and "gully" (center) in copying from thick, bound volumes]; (7) blue erase (ignoring the blue-pencil editing on the original); (8) margin/image shift, which shifts the image to either the right or left for duplexing or binding; and (9) electronic editing (the operator uses an electronic writing instrument to delete or relocate on the copy a portion of the original's image displayed on the screen). This last feature effectively replaces old cut-and-paste methods of editing copy. Other more automated features of the new reprographic technology are discussed below.

Usually we classify the copying process in two ways: (1) the *wet process,* which uses coated paper; and (2) the *dry process,* which may use special paper or plain paper depending upon the type of copier used. Plain-paper copiers, the most popular copying machines, are used for preparing file copies of correspondence, records to be distributed to other departments, business forms and form letters, transparencies, and drawings. The copies made from such machines can be produced at low per-copy cost and stored and preserved permanently. Wet-process copiers using *diffusion transfer* and *stabilization* copying methods have more specialized applications, such as producing copies of photographs and engineering drawings.

Generally office copying processes involve chemical and mechanical operations of a highly complex, technical nature that must be understood by the personnel who sell and service the equipment. However, office personnel can learn quickly the relatively simple methods of dry-process machine operation; therefore, technical information is not necessary.

Xerography, which is an electrostatic dry process, exposes a positively charged drum surface to light reflected through lenses from the original document. When light from white areas of the original copy strikes the drum, the charge disappears and a negatively charged black powder (toner) clings only to that portion of the surface still charged—the image area. The image is transferred from the drum to copy paper where it is permanently set by heat. The advantages of xerography include: (1) its ability to copy in full color, (2) no requirement for chemicals other than toner or powder, (3) the use of plain paper, and (4) easy machine operation. Its disadvantages are: (1) the per-copy cost (2 cents and above), which is higher than the costs of duplicating for a large number of copies; and (2) for the low-volume user, expensive equipment that requires special maintenance. Figure 20–7 discusses a typical small-office low-volume copier.

Copiers can also be classified as *analog* or *digital. Analog copiers* are most commonly used in offices, and with the exception of being able to enlarge or reduce the size of an image, these machines are capable of reproducing only the image that lies on the original paper document. *Digital copiers,* on the other hand, convert scanned images into binary code, which can then be manipulated much like the binary data in a computer file. Because these digitized images can be edited, colored, and reconfigured, digital copiers have reproduction capabilities that were once available only through sophisticated graphics departments. Many offices create and reproduce advertising layouts, brochures, and presentation transparencies on digital copiers, sometimes called intelligent copier/printers, which will be discussed in greater detail later.

Automated Reprographic Processes

Many of the technical advances in information technology have also included improvements in copying processes. In some cases, we see that these improvements have been brought about by integrating copying equipment with other types of information-processing and communication hardware. Examples of the continuing developments in copying processes include the following:

1. *The copier is integrated with the telephone to transmit facsimile and xerographic copies of information over regular telephone lines.*
2. *Copiers use fiber optics* (discussed in Chapter 18) *to simplify the complex lens-and-mirror*

systems required in the photographic process. As a result, copying costs are lowered and the quality of the copies is improved. The printing quality has also been improved through the use of a laser beam, which is a very intense light. Such a beam forms character or type patterns in the copier's printing mechanism under the control of a microcomputer.

3. **Phototypesetters** *are used to create print on a special VDT screen from data obtained from word processing or computer systems or from direct keyboard entry.* The characters on the screen are photographed by an attached photocomposition unit that also directly sets the type for the production of paper records or, commonly, newspapers. The main purpose of phototypesetting is to produce a professional-looking original copy that will be printed on an offset press or photocopied using a compatible copying process.

4. *New computer technologies are making possible the integration of many information functions.* By merging a microprocessor, a small computer, with the copying function, an operator can monitor numerous copier functions on the VDT screen as well as messages of the copier's operational status. **Intelligent copier/printers,** which are a cross between a photocopier and a mini- or microcomputer, combine the capabilities of a copier with those of a computer and phototypesetter. With an intelligent copier/printer, you can create hard-copy images directly from the magnetic files of a computer or word processor. Their "intelligence" or programmability lets you merge logos, signatures, and form-ruling lines into the text as printing occurs. The machine's computer-like capabilities permit receiving, storing, and communicating information in electronic, rather than paper, form from computers or word processing systems or from other intelligent copier/printers linked by telecommunication lines. This type of copier can store up to 1,000 pages of incoming documents in electronic mailboxes until hard copy is needed. Graphics and forms can also be designed using a wide variety of typefaces and stored for later use. In fact, the designing of forms and the printing of variable information can be done simultaneously on this equipment. Such a multifunction machine becomes a valuable item of equipment for all text and graphics production in the office. An intelligent copier/printer is shown in Illustration 20–4.

MANAGEMENT OF REPROGRAPHIC SYSTEMS

Like other administrative functions, reprographic systems must be managed carefully in order to meet the responsibilities assigned them. These managerial responsibilities include planning and organizing the necessary resources, establishing operating procedures and controls, and controlling costs. Each of these topics is discussed briefly in this section.

Planning Reprographic Systems

Before installing a reprographic services system, the AOM should carefully consider the following: (1) the copy requirements of each of the departments in the company; (2) the resources (especially the personnel, equipment, and space) needed to meet the copy requirements; (3) procedures necessary to control the total reprographic operation; (4) ideas from users whose support of

Illustration 20–4 An intelligent copier/printer.

the reprographic program is vital to its success; and (5) reliable methods for measuring the effectiveness of the program.[3] This information may in turn help to determine what portion of the reprographic work should be done internally or by an outside firm.

To obtain such information, the manager should ask each department to furnish answers to these questions:

1. How many copies of each form, report, and other documents are required?
2. To whom is each copy sent?
3. How is each copy used and stored?
4. For how long is each copy filed?
5. How frequently are copies reproduced?
6. What size copy is desired for reduction and enlargement purposes?

Much, if not all, of this information may be available from the company-wide survey of records required in the operation of a records management program, as discussed in Chapter 19.

Organizing Reprographic Systems

The size of the firm affects directly the manner in which the reprographic services function is organized. In small firms, for example, one low-volume copier may be sufficient to handle the needs of the entire firm with no special operator required. Large companies, on the other hand, frequently organize centralized reprographic services departments that utilize many machines and highly trained operators. In some cases, copiers are placed within individual departments (physical decentralization of machines) even though central control is maintained by reprographic services. Other firms leave both the equipment and its control to the individual departments.

Centralized control of reprographic services is preferred for the following reasons:

1. It makes available specialized personnel who can provide high-quality copy work and take better care of the equipment.
2. It permits a greater variety of equipment and more flexibility in its use.
3. It requires a minimum investment in equipment by reducing the number of duplicate machines.
4. It provides better scheduling of work.
5. Ideally, it increases productivity.

On the other hand, physical decentralization, which is usually self-service, offers each department more flexibility as to what is copied and also reduces travel and turnaround time. Under a decentralized plan, however, it may be more difficult to maintain company-wide operating standards and controls over the use and maintenance of the equipment. A greater amount of supervision would doubtless be required.

Personnel

The responsibilities for operating the reprographic systems normally fall on the AOM or the supervisor who is in charge of communication services. In a small firm, such a supervisor may be assigned many duties including the responsibilities for the copying function. The day-to-day reprographic tasks may, in such a setting, be handled by secretaries and other office workers. For more complex copy-making needs, the firm may contact commercial printers.

In the large firm, on the other hand, a full-time, specialized supervisor with knowledge of such equipment should be appointed. This type of supervisor has responsibility for selecting and training the staff, for developing sound procedures for scheduling and operating the reprographic equipment, and for establishing the necessary operating controls to conduct a credible program. In addition, the supervisor should plan and conduct a continuing education program among the various departments to ensure that the staff realizes two important legal implications of copied materials:

1. *Legal acceptability.* Because exact reproductions can be made with copiers, copies are acceptable in courts of law and by government agencies.

---

[3]For highly useful information on the strengths and weaknesses of copiers as well as the copier features that users like and dislike, consult the latest annual copier survey of Datapro Research Corporation, Feature Reports Department, 1805 Underwood Boulevard, Delran, NJ 08075.

2. *Copyrights.* Copyrights, which legally recognize the ownership of original recorded work, apply to printed materials such as books and periodicals, recorded lectures, drawings, and photographs that are officially registered with the Registry of Copyright of the United States Library of Congress. Since copying machines are widely used to reproduce materials from copyrighted sources, the AOM or reprographic manager should be sure to secure the permission of the copyright holder—usually the publisher of the material—before permitting such material to be reproduced. If such permission is not obtained, the copyright owner may sue the violator in a civil court. In 1988, Congress strengthened copyright laws by ratifying the Berne Convention for the Protection of Literacy and Artistic Works. This treaty, which was ratified by 78 countries, calls for reciprocal protection over the copying of software or films and is designed to eliminate the "softlifting" or illegal copying of copyrighted computer programs.[4]

"'The Battle Raging Over 'Intellectual Property,'" *Time* (May 22, 1989), pp. 78–79, 82.

Reprographic Equipment

With the increasing use of the computer to reproduce and transmit information, most large firms can produce internally the major portion of their copy needs. In fact, with the use of computers and desktop-publishing software, camera-ready copy can be produced error free in a matter of minutes. Even so, such firms as well as a large majority of small firms must select, maintain, and use equipment to meet their copying needs. Figure 20–8 provides a checklist that may be used by AOMs in the selection of copying machines. Several models of competing brands of such machines should be evaluated according to the degree of effectiveness of each machine for handling the reprographic tasks required in the office.

Considerable advantage is found in the local purchase of equipment and supplies, especially where service is concerned. Environmental requirements, particularly temperature and humidity, should also be studied for their effects upon machine operation.

Information on equipment selection is readily available from equipment manufacturers and from professional groups like the Association for

Figure 20–8
Checklist for Selecting Reprographic Equipment

Brand _____ Model _____ Date _____

Type of Work to be Reproduced

___ Black and white originals
___ Colored originals
___ Reduction of copy
___ Enlargement of copy
___ Duplexing of copy
___ Other: _____

Quality of Work
___ Print quality for external records
___ Regular quality—uniformly clear— for internal records

Quantity of Work
___ Rate per minute: _____
___ Rate per hour: _____
___ Turnaround time needed: _____

Preferences of Personnel
___ Workers
___ Supervisors and Managers

Operation of Equipment

___ Ease of use
___ Ease of maintenance
___ Need for trained operators

Reliability of Equipment
___ Typical machine problems
___ Likelihood of downtime
___ Other firm's experience with machine

Service
___ Location of nearest vendor
___ Reputation of vendor

Costs
___ Initial cost of equipment purchase/lease
___ Per-copy cost of operating equipment
___ Cost of materials, supplies, and labor
___ Cost of service

Information and Image Management and the National Office Machine Dealers Association. Managers may also obtain assistance in the careful selection of equipment from such useful periodicals as *Managing Office Technology* and *Office Systems,* which highlight equipment for information systems.

Space

Along with maintaining standards for good work layout, the reprographic center should provide adequate storage space for the large quantities of copy paper and supplies required. Other needs include a sink for cleaning up after operating the machines, darkroom facilities if photographic equipment is used, and acoustical materials and cabinets to reduce the noise of equipment, which can be annoying to office workers in adjacent areas.

Establishing Operating Procedures and Controls

When we hear the comment that "paper is cheap," we usually suspect a lack of understanding of administrative operations and their costs, which in turn causes the AOM many problems. To prevent these problems from occurring, the AOM should assign the highest priority to setting up efficient operating procedures and appropriate controls for regulating the personnel in the reprographic unit. Since costs are involved in all phases of operations and are of great importance, they are covered later in this chapter.

Personnel Controls

The most effective use of equipment and supplies can be achieved by training one or more individuals in machine operation, machine maintenance, and control of copy quality. This training should emphasize not only the benefits accruing to the entire firm from providing an effective reprographic center, but also the costs of such services and how each employee can help to keep such costs in line.

Reprographic policies should be developed to ensure that only authorized personnel from each department be permitted to use the equipment. Violations of this requirement result in misuse of the equipment, which in turn causes downtime

and delays in the completion of work. Also, many unauthorized copies may be made. With such problems, office operating costs increase.

Procedure Controls

Orderly, efficient procedures for operating the reprographic services function must be developed in order to meet the information needs of all departments. The following practices will assist the supervisor of reprographic systems in achieving control over the procedures:

1. *All departments should be informed about the copyright laws and their effect on copying practices in the firm.* Copying practices must observe the provisions of the copyright laws which cover what can be copied, how many copies may be made, and the purposes for which authorized copies may be reproduced. Note that "copy" extends beyond hard copy to include other types of media, such as sound (music and lecture), graphics (drawings), and any computer software that is copyrighted. Other materials, such as securities of the U.S. government (e.g., U.S. bonds, certificates of deposit, and paper money), may not be copied.

2. *A policy should be developed that clearly identifies how each type and quantity of job will be reproduced.* For example, multicolor advertising brochures may require technical design skills as well as special color reproduction available only from commercial printers. Also, the types of copying to be assigned to copiers and other reprographic equipment should be publicized throughout the firm and such regulations consistently enforced.

3. *Some type of record should be created and used to ensure that data on copies made are available to management.* In the small office, the "honor system" may be used by requiring that each user note how many copies of what type of original were made on what date and by whom (the user). A form similar to that shown in Figure 20–9 is commonly used in a firm with many departments for each copy request from a department. The form has space for important control information (code number for the type of run, account number of the department to be charged, time received and

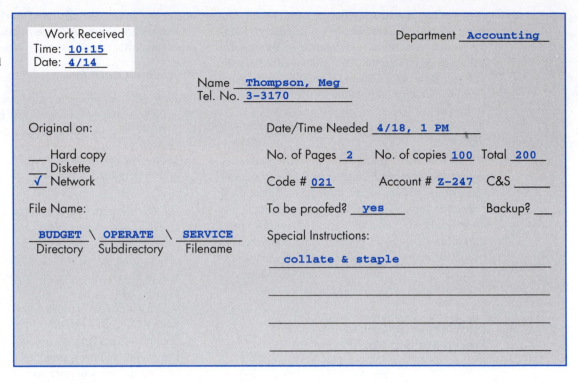

Figure 20–9
A Combined Form for Requesting Word Processing and Reprographic Services

needed, and proofreading requirements) needed in a reprographic center. Special instructions may be needed for collating, reducing of copy size, punching, and binding of copies. Unless permission of the publisher of copyrighted materials is obtained, as discussed earlier, some copying requests cannot be approved.

4. *Access guidelines must be established.* The AOM must weigh the costs and benefits of who should actually operate the equipment. At one end of the spectrum is assigning a full-time trained operator; at the other end is allowing total access by all staff. Whatever guideline is adopted, the machine should be locked when it is not being used by authorized personnel.

5. *Shredders should be placed alongside office copiers to destroy unneeded copies of important documents.* Reprographic managers are then able to reduce the risk of corporate information falling into the wrong hands.

6. *Records of equipment usage should be kept.* Some firms keep a log at the machine site and

require that entries be made for all copying done. However, this practice lacks accuracy, requires considerable supervision and accounting, and does not provide security over the machine.

A more effective method of copier control makes use of a plastic access card that must be inserted into the machine before it can be used. Such a card contains information that identifies the department or user number. In addition to activating the machine for making copies, this control device accumulates data regarding the number of copies made so that the appropriate department users may be charged for copies made. (Other standalone alternatives to cards are keys, keyboards, or plug-in cartridges that are issued to users who connect the cartridge to the copier, thus "authorizing" the machine to operate and to record and display the number of copies made.)

Centralized systems use a terminal with a keyboard connected to the copier. Through identification codes, such a system "gives permission" for the machine's use and records operating data, such as user's name and department, copier used, the date and time of access, and the number of copies made. At the end of the accounting period, the computer generates copier usage reports from this information.

7. *To maximize the use of the copier, similar types of copying work should be grouped together to speed the completion of the work.* Job priorities should be established and publicized among the departments—computers can be instructed to monitor and control such priorities—and feedback from department users should be collected regarding the quality of the copying work.

Controlling Reprographic Costs

The number of office copies made annually continues to grow to the point where it staggers the imagination. It is estimated that businesses in the United States make some 350 billion photocopies a year and throw away some 130 billion copies.[5] Thus, the cost of reprographic services represents a large portion of the office budget. Good management of the copying function dictates that a program be set up to identify and control reprographic costs. These topics are discussed briefly in this section.

Identifying Reprographic Costs

If we are to calculate the total costs of providing reprographic services, we must first identify each of the administrative costs. Administrative costs are outlined in Figure 19–18 (page 534), and each must be included in the computation of per-copy costs in a reprographic systems operation.

A large number of *hidden* costs that creep into the reprographic operation are often overlooked because they are not directly a part of the copy-making process but which, on the average, account for 60 to 70 percent of the copier's total cost.[6] These include the costs of:

1. Ordering reprographic supplies and equipment (e.g., getting quotations from suppliers).
2. Storage space and shelving for storing reprographic supplies.
3. Labor involved in keeping stock and handling invoices and other records.
4. Mailing, since a large portion of the output is mailed.
5. Messenger service for work that must be delivered.
6. Overordering and underordering.
7. Charging back all work produced to the user department.
8. Overtime and borrowed help.
9. Furniture and equipment used by supervisory personnel.
10. Supervisor's time.
11. Wasted paper caused by overruns, defective work, and excessive use of paper in preparatory operations.

When these hidden costs—sometimes adding as much as 100 percent to reprographic costs—are brought to light, a much more accurate determination of total reprographic costs is obtained.

Reducing Reprographic Costs

The availability of good controls over reprographic services as well as the constant vigilance of personnel to enforce such controls can help to keep the costs of reproducing documents within reasonable limits. To achieve such controls, we suggest you consider the following points:

1. *Select the most suitable process for the job to be done.* If a choice of equipment is available, match the number of copies needed to the volume capabilities of the copier. One of the most frequently cited reasons for breakdowns of low-volume machines, for example, is lengthy production runs that should have been handled by a larger-volume unit.
2. *Standardize equipment, methods, and supplies to eliminate an unnecessary variety of machine models from many manufacturers.* Following this guideline permits using uniform supplies bought in large volume from one vendor under quantity purchase discounts. The systems and procedures department, if

[5]Erik Mortensen, "Today's Office: Automated, Partially Paperless," *The Office* (June, 1993), p. 16. Reprinted from the June issue of *The Office*, and copyrighted 1993 by Office Publications, Inc.

[6]Patricia M. Fernberg, "Copiers: What You Need Is What You'll Get," *Modern Office Technology* (July, 1987), p. 50.

one exists, should be consulted for advice in increasing the efficiency of reprographic methods, materials, equipment, and personnel. Sometimes self-service, departmental copiers can be replaced by satellite reprographic centers staffed with full- or part-time operators, messengers, and an office supplies center.

3. *From the current copy-production records, compute per-copy costs and make semiannual surveys of anticipated needs of departments.* Some firms provide usage and cost figures by departments on a monthly cumulative basis compared with the past year's figures. This in-formation helps in planning future equipment needs as well as in developing guidelines for selecting the most cost-effective copying method.

4. *Do not overlook the highly competitive nature of the equipment market and the free services offered by vendors.* Manufacturers' sales representatives can assist AOMs in controlling their reprographic costs and can make suggestions for work improvement. Sales representatives can also provide data on maintenance costs, leasing metered copying equipment, equipment reliability, and free equipment trial plans.

SUMMARY

1. Two types of information systems assist the AOM in providing the information needed in the modern firm. Microimage systems, which use very small records, represent a continually expanding form of compact records storage that started with the photographing of records onto microfilm. Presently there are two types of microrecords (unitized, such as microfiche, aperture cards, and microfilm jackets; and nonunitized, such as roll film) that may be packaged in various ways to facilitate the storage and retrieval of filmed records. To automate these processes, the output of a computer is linked to a device that photographs the records for storage on film. More recently, computer-assisted retrieval, which provides techniques for automating the retrieval of information stored in microform, has been developed, and optical disks have emerged as a highly effective, space-efficient, computerized storage and retrieval medium.

2. A reprographic system is a related area that refers to the wide range of hardware and procedures for reproducing information, primarily through copiers. Xerography, because of its ease of operation and convenience, has become the most popular copying process. Although all copying processes photograph or scan the records to be reproduced, some copiers are capable of performing multiple functions. Copier-duplicators not only make copies of an original document, but also duplicate the original in large quantities. The intelligent copier/printer is capable of storing data in its memory, making copies of the data in the format prescribed, printing out the requested number of copies, and distributing them by wire to various locations.

3. Most large firms have organized central microimaging and reprographic departments and provide a specialized staff, proper equipment, and adequate space. Small firms, on the other hand, usually purchase microimage services and some printing services from commercial agencies. All firms, however, should place strong emphasis upon controlling the costs of these operations.

FOR YOUR REVIEW

1. What procedural steps are involved in the creation and use of microrecords?

2. Identify the various kinds of microforms and compare the relative advantages of each.

3. How are microrecords retrieved from (a) roll film, (b) microfiche, and (c) aperture cards?

4. Define the computer output microfilm (COM) process and trace the flow of information from the computer to the point of storage.

5. Explain how data are stored and retrieved in an advanced computer-assisted retrieval (CAR) system.

6. Explain what an optical disk is and how it differs from typical media used for microrecord storage.

7. What types of conditions must be present in an office before the use of microrecords can be seriously considered?

8. What are the typical personnel needs to be provided in a microimage systems program?

9. What are the principal procedures needed to operate an effective microimage system?

10. In what direct and indirect ways should an office manager evaluate the microimage program?

11. How are copying processes frequently classified?

12. Explain why a digital copier can be more useful than an analog copier.

13. What is an intelligent copier/printer? How does it function in the production and transmission of information?

14. What factors should be considered in the process of selecting copiers for an office?

15. What good arguments can be given for the physical decentralization but organizational centralization of reprographic systems?

16. List some of the most common hidden costs that creep into a reprographic systems operation.

17. Outline some of the principal methods for reducing reprographic costs.

FOR YOUR DISCUSSION

1. A long-time friend of yours, Chris Burnham, mentions that the number of records maintained in his small insurance office has gotten "out of hand." Burnham asks you for suggestions about handling this common problem. What key issues and questions need to be answered before Burnham can begin solving his problem?

2. In most of the small offices you have visited, a single copying machine is located in an area that is accessible to everyone. What advantages and disadvantages does such a layout have as far as reprographic cost controls are concerned?

cont

3. "Most office workers consider the costs of copy making to be insignificant compared with other costs in the office." Is this an accurate assessment? If not, how can this common point of view be changed?

4. The department heads in the Public Safety Bureau remain opposed to the idea of converting their inactive records to microfilm for one reason—they believe it would be very inconvenient and time consuming to go to a reader to use the records. What arguments can you advance to refute their reasoning?

5. The offices of Fullerton Products, Inc., require the documents listed below for the month of February. Indicate which of these items might be reproduced most economically and efficiently (a) on each department's convenience copier, (b) on the large-volume copiers maintained in the firm's reprographics center, or (c) on more highly specialized equipment provided by commercial printers.

   a. 500 copies of time cards for the office employees. The employee's name, clock number, and date are to be inserted on each card.

   b. 30 copies of a two-page bulletin to be sent to each department head.

   c. 5 copies of the minutes of the directors' meeting held on February 10, to be sent to board members.

   d. 5,000 copies of a two-page form letter to be sent to prospective customers.

   e. 550 copies of the eight-page company newsletter. This newsletter, issued monthly to all employees, contains snapshots, illustrations, and reading material.

   f. 250 copies of notices to stockholders announcing the annual meeting on March 15.

   g. 20 copies of a sales analysis report, eight pages in length, for distribution to each of the 20 district sales managers.

   h. 25 copies of bulletins to keyboarders listing suggestions for improving their work. Similar bulletins are issued weekly to the keyboarders, who keep them in binders for future reference.

6. Representatives of a local microimaging services firm have recently discussed the advantages of converting your paper records system to microrecords. Regardless of the representatives' efforts, the officers of your company remain vehemently opposed to the idea and cite the following objections:

   a. Microrecords are "out of sight" and thus "out of mind."

   b. Microrecords are difficult to retrieve.

   c. Microrecords are more costly to maintain than paper records.

   d. Microrecords are useful only for inactive records.

   What is your reaction to these objections?

7. After studying Chapters 19 and 20, you have become much more conscious of the importance of records. As a result, you make an extra copy of your automobile license, your driver's license, and your automobile certificate of title. Can you legally do so? Discuss.

CASES FOR CRITICAL THINKING

Case 20–1 Determining Where to Begin Microimaging

You are the newly hired administrative assistant to Elthea Case, records manager of city government for a Midwestern city. Ms. Case is considering implementing a microimaging system, but the exact type of technology has yet to be determined. Her problem is this: She needs to determine which hard-copy documents should be captured onto a microform first—those from the active files or those from the inactive files.

Ms. Case has asked you to "find out what the experts recommend" by reading some appropriate articles from such publications as *Managing Office Technology, Office Systems,* and *Records Management Quarterly* and to submit a two- to three-page report that examines the possible advantages and disadvantages of beginning the microimaging in either area. She realizes that you do not have good data on the amount of records involved, so she wants you to "brainstorm" the advantages based on a variety of possible amounts of records that each area might contain.

Your paper should follow the format that Ms. Case most likely is expecting: a brief discussion of whatever advantages and disadvantages you might think would exist if there were "many" or "few" records to be imaged in each area. After discussing the implications of either approach, make a general recommendation to Ms. Case, based on your readings.

Case 20–2 Deciding Whether to Microimage Paper Records

Chin Kuo, office manager of Winterhaven Wholesale Plumbers Supply, recently returned from an administrative cost reduction conference. During the conference, Kuo was impressed by the speakers' persuasive appeals for cutting costs by converting paper records to microfilm. As a result, Kuo has given you, the assistant office manager, this challenging assignment: "Find out for me whether our 'small-time' office should consider microfilming our active records (inventory, billing, and correspondence). I think this is 'big-time stuff' for large offices only, but give me your ideas in a short report."

The small office to which Kuo refers has seven full-time employees who spend much of their time creating new files and updating existing paper records related to the more than 4,700 plumbing and heating supplies maintained by the firm. Other common record tasks involve buying from 45 supplies manufacturers and selling to 275 retail hardware stores.

From your study of administrative office management, it seems clear that your assignment requires the study of basic information storage and retrieval systems and procedures in your firm.

1. What steps would you follow in completing this assignment?
2. What types of information—about microfilm as well as your office operations—would be needed? From whom would you obtain such information?
3. What personnel problems should you anticipate? (Note Kuo's "attitude" toward big-office ideas; also, keep in mind that the average tenure of the seven office employees is 17 years.)
4. How would you suggest the findings of your study be presented in order to receive a fair hearing by Kuo?

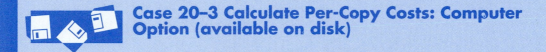

Case 20–3 Calculate Per-Copy Costs: Computer Option (available on disk)

CONTROLLING ADMINISTRATIVE SERVICES

21 • *Improving Administrative Office Systems*

22 • *Improving Office Productivity*

23 • *Budgeting Administrative Expenses*

IMPROVING ADMINISTRATIVE OFFICE SYSTEMS

GOALS FOR THIS CHAPTER

After completing this chapter, you should be able to:

1. Describe the major elements typically examined in the systems development life cycle and the goals set for its successful completion.
2. List several influences within and outside the organization that can cause systems to be changed.
3. Differentiate between an effective system and an efficient system.
4. Compare and contrast the work simplification model with the input-output model.
5. List the principal systems communication tools and their typical uses.
6. Discuss the various means used to communicate systems improvements, giving reasons for the use of each type of communication.
7. Explain the steps involved in designing, installing, and evaluating administrative office systems.

A *system,* as you recall from your study of Chapter 4, is a *set* of *related elements* that are *linked together* according to a *plan* for achieving a specific *objective.* In the **systems development life cycle (SDLC),** office workers—always the most important systems element—perform six activities in the following order:

1. Define the objectives of the project.
2. Survey the present system.
3. Propose changes to achieve the objectives.
4. Design and test an improved system.
5. Install the improved system.
6. Evaluate the system and correct any operating flaws.

In this chapter, you will be introduced to methods of improving all types of administrative office systems (AOS) by exploring these six steps in greater detail. In so doing, we shall examine some of the models and tools used to achieve the common goal of the systems development life cycle: higher productivity.

WHY SYSTEMS MUST CHANGE

The preceding 20 chapters of this text should have convinced you that quality systems result only when committed and competent people recognize and address the complexities of managing information. This chapter is based on the premise that all administrative office systems must continually evolve, beginning almost from the moment that they are initially brought online. Why, you might ask, must systems be modified? Quite simply, systems must constantly react to the dynamic environments that exist both inside and outside the organization. Consider how any of the following areas might trigger a need to adjust an organization's information systems:

1. *Changes in client needs.* All organizations, both profit and not for profit, have one com-

mon mission: to serve their clients. Since clients' needs constantly change, so must every organization's product or service. Consequently, the information systems that support these endeavors must also be adjusted.

2. *Changes in objectives.* In private enterprises, management is constantly exploring alternatives to improve product lines, markets, or image. In the public sector, government may instruct its institutions to add, modify, or delete responsibilities. In either case, any shift in management direction may necessitate a comparable shift in the information systems.

3. *Changes in laws and regulations.* All organizations must operate within the legal requirements and accepted practices of their industry or profession. Forms, data, and procedures—all integral components of information systems—must be constantly evaluated and refined so that they comply with these constraints.

4. *Changes in procedures.* Organizations are constantly looking for ways to increase productivity and to reduce costs. To accomplish these desired goals, the organization often must change how it accomplishes its work. When there is a change in how an organization functions, so might there be a change in its information systems.

5. *Changes in technology.* Office equipment manufacturers introduce improved products approximately every six months. Whenever there is a technological breakthrough, enterprises often discover that what was cost effective yesterday is not the case today, or what was formerly financially prohibitive is now feasible. When an organization introduces new technology, it must examine and update its procedures, office layouts, job descriptions, and other aspects of the system.

6. *Changes in human resources.* People are constantly being hired, reassigned, retired, or terminated. Each personnel change alters the unique complement of skills, handicaps, attitudes, abilities, and cultural backgrounds. The information systems must accommodate the changing individual needs of the organization's most important resource—people.

7. *Changes in organizational structure.* Often, as product lines, objectives, laws, and other factors change, so must an organization's lines of communication. A revised organization chart can cause departments to be created, eliminated, reorganized, merged, relocated, or realigned according to whatever logic appears to facilitate internal communications. Because information systems are designed to facilitate good communications, they must be changed to reflect a revised organizational structure.

8. *Changes in unforeseen circumstances.* Every organization is subject to both natural and manmade conditions that may affect operations. A severe storm, an outbreak of influenza, a protracted labor dispute, a rise in the rate of inflation, to name just a few possibilities, can in some way impact the enterprise's operations. When operations must be changed to react to unforeseen circumstances, so, too, must the information systems.

When you consider that each of these eight areas influences an organization in an infinite number of ways, you will arrive at this important conclusion: *Even the best designed office systems need to be constantly adjusted so that they reflect and support the information needs of the organization they serve.*

Generally the improvement of sophisticated automated systems that involve vast amounts of information requires highly technical skills and broad backgrounds of a specialization called *systems analysis and design,* the study of which is beyond the scope of this textbook. However, it is important that office workers understand the nature of this discipline for two important reasons:

1. Office workers know the day-to-day operations of the office better than anyone. Therefore, *they are the primary source of information for systems analysts and other specialists.*

2. Since office workers must ultimately *use* the product that systems designers create, it is in the workers' best interest to validate any change to ensure that it indeed enhances productivity.

THE SYSTEMS IMPROVEMENT PROCESS

On the bulletin boards in their departments, many systems managers post this simple, meaningful description of systems improvement studies: *Systems improvement studies help us decide whether we are doing the right thing rather than doing the thing right.* The thinking behind this systems philosophy is based on two important terms used to describe the general requirements for a properly operating system. Such a system should be *effective* and at the same time *efficient*. You may hear people using these terms interchangeably, but in systems circles these words have different but closely related meanings.

A system is **effective** when it is actually *doing the right thing*—that is, producing the desired quantity and quality of goods or services (the output). To be effective, the value of its output must exceed the costs involved in the input and transforming/processing steps of the systems cycle. On the other hand, a system is **efficient** when it is judged to be operating in an economical manner, or, as mentioned earlier, *doing the thing right.* Usually three factors are considered in evaluating the efficiency of a system:

1. *Time,* which refers to the number of minutes, hours, days, weeks, months, or years needed to complete the output requirements of the system.
2. *Reliability,* an efficiency measure used to determine the accuracy of the system (its freedom from errors).
3. *Cost,* which refers to the dollars spent for all the components required to design and operate the system. (The cost factor usually receives the most attention in systems studies since department managers wage a continuing battle to "live" within their operating budgets. The control of administrative costs is discussed in detail in Chapter 23.)

You will find that analysts and office managers use both *effectiveness* and *efficiency* measures in evaluating the productivity of AOS. However, of the two measures, *effectiveness is considered the more basic,* for it directly relates to the attainment of systems objectives, as discussed in the next section.

The scope of activities involved in studies of simple manual systems, such as payroll and inventory control, is still relatively comprehensive because of the complex nature of most organizations. In such studies, the office manager first identifies all the basic elements in the system—*human resources; physical resources, including equipment, machines, and supplies; forms and related records required for operating an AOS; data to be processed; and various types of controls.* Next, the office manager determines how these elements interact in the work environment in order to improve the system under study.

DEFINING OBJECTIVES, SURVEYING THE PRESENT SYSTEM, AND PROPOSING CHANGES FOR SYSTEMS IMPROVEMENT

We study systems in order to meet one general objective: *to improve the performance of the systems;* that is, to solve present problems and to prevent the occurrence of anticipated problems. Analysts find that problems occur in any of the basic systems phases illustrated in Figure 4–5, page 90. However, most problems occur during two phases of a system: (1) *at the input phase,* when problems are reported to the systems personnel from other systems in the organization; and (2) *at the feedback phase,* when the quantitative and qualitative levels of output fail to meet the standards of performance expected. In both situations, the same general administrative problem is recognized: *Personnel performance or the operational levels of the other elements in the system do not meet the system's objectives. The gap between actual performance and expected performance thus represents the extent or severity of the problem.*

A Prototype of Systems Improvement

In order to understand how the systems approach is applied to the improvement of systems, a prototype of the improvement process may be used. The **prototype,** or basic model, shown in Figure 21–1, simplifies our view of the complex relationships found in systems operations and serves as a foundation for most of the work involved in systems studies. Most systems studies emphasize an intensive analysis of the present systems; Figure 21–1A outlines this set of activities. On occasion, however, a department in a firm senses the need for creating an entirely new system. When this condition exists, the prototype is modified slightly, as shown in Figure 21–1B. However, in both cases, the same systems study cycle is followed.

The Ideal System

To use the prototype for systems improvement in an effective manner, we must previously have developed a clear idea of an **ideal system.** In such a utopian system, all systems elements function at their most effective and efficient levels at all times. Personnel perform at their peak; machines function properly and, with proper maintenance, are not subject to downtime; forms and reports are well designed and function as planned; data are available as needed; controls effectively regulate the system according to the plan; and operating costs are minimized. *Such a perfect system does not—and will never—exist.* However, from a conceptual standpoint, a systems staff benefits by having this idealistic system as a model. Such an ideal "target" provides a sense of direction and motivation to an administrative staff to analyze, design, and install a higher-quality system than if such a model did not exist.

The Effective Real-World System

In the real world, we must be practical minded and recognize that an ideal system cannot be attained. What can be developed, however, is an *effective* **real-world system** that provides the best possible service to the departments concerned but subject to certain limitations. As the main element in the system, the human being is prone to fatigue and dissatisfaction on the job. Machines, unlike people, do not become fatigued or dissatisfied; however, machines are subject to downtime through lack of or careless service. Through human error, inaccuracy, or indifference, forms and reports are often used in an ineffective way. Data may be received late or transmitted to the wrong parties, which results in failure to meet reporting deadlines, thereby delaying business decision making. Controls, even though properly designed, may not be understood or, worse yet, may not be enforced. Thus, standards of worker performance, quotas, budgets, computer programs, and other AOS controls fail to function properly. Under such conditions, operating costs in AOS skyrocket.

Figure 21–1
Prototypes for Improving Administrative Office Systems

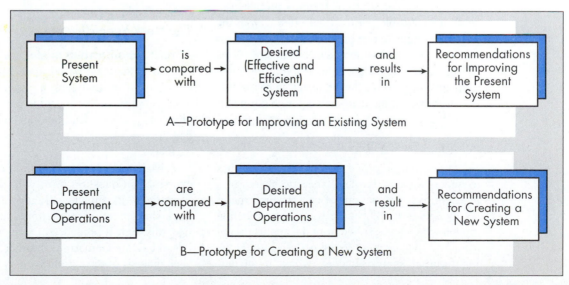

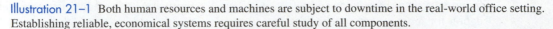

Illustration 21–1 Both human resources and machines are subject to downtime in the real-world office setting. Establishing reliable, economical systems requires careful study of all components.

Studying all of these elements is complicated by the need for an in-depth study of each element if a more reliable, more economical system is to result from the study. Realistically, systems analysts "attack" the study of systems problems in small, manageable portions and often restrict the scope of a study to one of the elements mentioned earlier. Specialized systems analysts in large firms use this same approach by identifying the main segments, or parts, of the organization of the system under study, and then studying each segment.

Systems Improvement Models

When the analyst, office worker, or AOM wishes to undertake a study of the specific phases of a problem, we find that one of two systems analysis models is used: (1) the work simplification model, which has resulted from the application of scientific management to the office; and (2) the input-output analysis model, which is an out-growth of computer systems studies. Whenever complex systems need improvement and highly specialized analysts are available, several mathematics-based models are used, two of which are discussed later.

The Work Simplification Model

A **work simplification model** describes a set of general guidelines, based upon logic and common sense, for analyzing a system. Behind the work simplification concept is the basic philosophy that all work operations can be improved and that there must always be a better way to perform each task.

A basic model of work simplification may be expressed in question form with the key words capitalized, as shown in Figure 21–2. When a work simplification program is started in the office, this logical sequence of steps is followed in Phase 1 (Data Gathering) in order to facilitate a later analysis of the system:

1. The analyst gathers information about WHAT work is being done.
2. The analyst questions WHERE and WHEN the work is done, WHO does the work, and HOW it is being done.
3. Each step in the sequence is followed by a request for an explicit reason WHY the work is performed in a certain way as well as how it SHOULD be done. These questions are intended to uncover the facts that have the most bearing on the system under study.

This type of verbal model can be applied to all phases of systems improvement studies, for it structures the systems study into identifiable, orderly steps, which make the problem-solving, or systems improvement, tasks easier to complete.

When the data have been gathered in Phase 1 of the work simplification model, the analyst is prepared to undertake Phase 2 (Data Analysis). In this phase the analyst probes for answers to questions such as the following:

1. *What can be ELIMINATED?* Areas in systems that no longer align with the functions and needs of the organization can often be identified by asking these types of questions:
   - Are paper copies still being sent to departments even though departments primarily access information through local-area networks?
   - Is software being carried online that supports functions or activities no longer performed by the organization?
   - Are there duplicate copies of documents being stored within departments even though these records are stored elsewhere on electronic or micrographic media?

2. *What can be COMBINED?* As individual tasks at workstations and workflows within and among departments change, these types of questions will identify opportunities for consolidating activities and forms:
   - Are there two or more forms that can be combined into one?
   - Could logically related tasks be assigned to one worker rather than to several people making marginal contributions?
   - Could a single high-speed printer replace all the individual printers connected to the network?

3. *What can be RESEQUENCED, REARRANGED, or AUTOMATED?* Efficiency often results after an examination of when and how activities are performed. Analysts ask these types of questions to identify areas for improvement:
   - Can the fields on a form be resequenced to more logically align with the order in which the information is used?
   - Can handwritten reports be scanned into the system rather than keyboarded?
   - Can the data stored in the database be reordered so that they can be more readily accessed by more users?

Figure 21–2
The Work Simplification Model Used in AOS Improvement Studies

Phase 1—Data Gathering	Phase 2—Data Analysis
1. WHAT work is being done? WHY? What work SHOULD be done? 2. WHERE is the work being done? WHY? Where SHOULD the work be done? 3. WHEN is the work being done? WHY? When SHOULD the work be done? 4. WHO does the work? WHY? Who SHOULD do the work? 5. HOW is the work being done? WHY? How SHOULD the work be done?	1. What can be ELIMINATED? 2. What can be COMBINED? 3. What can be RESEQUENCED, REARRANGED, or AUTOMATED? 4. What can be SIMPLIFIED?

4. *What can be SIMPLIFIED?* Processing speed, accuracy rates, and user satisfaction are enhanced when unnecessary complexity is eliminated from documents and processes. Here are some examples of the types of questions analysts ask:

- Are instructions on forms clear and easy to understand?
- Are there HELP screens available on computerized processes?
- Has computer software been selected for its compatibility with other software presently being used in the organization?

With sufficient time, patience, and attention to detail, the analyst can identify basic questions that require answers if the system is to be improved. Such improvement results in better, faster, more convenient, more simplified, and less costly methods of performing the work. A discussion of the techniques used in work simplification is provided in a later section of this chapter.

The Input-Output (I/O) Model for Systems Improvement

If properly done, input-output analysis generally can be applied to the improvement of all types of systems operations. Thus, an **input-output (I/O) systems improvement model** furnishes a generalized method for analyzing each of the phases in an AOS. Such a model is shown in Figure 21–3, which represents a modification of the basic systems model discussed in Chapter 4.

As you can see in Figure 21–3, the topmost priority in studying a system is to determine the objectives of the users. To illustrate the use of the input-output model for improving systems, assume that, in the design of an accounting system, all hourly employees are paid by noon on Friday of each week. In studying the effectiveness of such a system, the analyst must determine the requirements for satisfying the needs of each phase in the system (represented by blocks in Figure 21–3). These requirements include:

1. *User's objectives:* Paychecks available by noon each Friday; all checks and related records accurately prepared; and sufficient security and privacy maintained over the payroll records.
2. *Output requirements:* Same as user's objectives; in addition, copies of payroll records are fed back into the payroll system for use in computing the next cycle of paychecks and the related payroll and tax records.

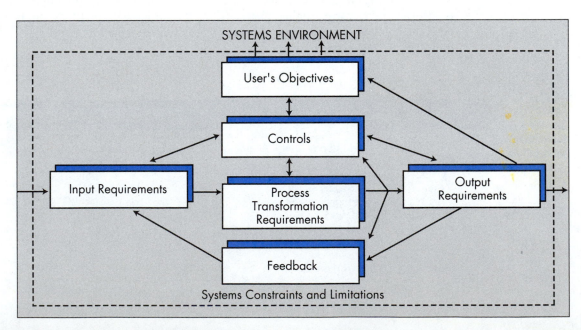

Figure 21–3
An Input-Output (I/O) Model for Systems Improvement

3. *Input requirements:* Relevant data (hours worked—regular and overtime, rate of pay, deductions, and other payroll information); and appropriate equipment, procedures, and work schedules. Each must be provided early enough in the workweek to complete the required output on time.

4. *Process requirements:* Manual procedures or computer programs that transform the payroll system's data into the output required.

5. *Feedback:* A record of the output—a correctly processed paycheck and related records, such as an earnings statement—as fed back into the system to be used in computing the paychecks for the following pay period.

6. *Controls:* Ensuring that the system operates properly by: (a) checking on the accuracy of the input data, (b) pretesting the computer program or manual procedures, (c) monitoring the arrival time of the payroll data, (d) providing security over the paychecks until delivered to workers, and (e) maintaining a complete set of all records produced in each cycle of the payroll system's operations.

If each of these requirements is met, the output will be accurate and reliable; thus, the user will have faith in a system that has demonstrated its effectiveness and efficiency.

While the input-output model revolves around the various phases in the system, such an analysis is performed by systems personnel who use whatever techniques are available for problem solving. Thus, analysts ask meaningful questions (illustrated in the work simplification model) in order to gain insight into the operation of each phase of the system (as indicated in the input-output analysis model). In reality, therefore, both models discussed in this section can be used—one as a supplement to the other—in order that the analysis of the system be as thorough as possible.

Other Models

When managers require great precision and predictability as to the likely outcomes of installing a certain type of system, they turn to analysts highly trained in mathematics, logic, and the scientific method of problem solving. For example, *sampling models* are used to learn the characteristics of a group of people without examining each individual member in the group. In addition, analysts use **operations research (OR)** to determine the best possible solutions to decision-making problems in complex systems. An OR model represents a simplified conceptual picture of the system—usually set up in a mathematical equation—that contains all the factors of primary importance to the problem. Once the model is developed, we can test it to see how well it answers many of the questions asked of a real-world system.

Simulation is a basic OR technique for creating a mathematical model of a real-world system. Simulation involves the identification of alternate courses of action to consider for maximizing profits and minimizing costs after studying the various resources available. Less complex simulation methods use simple logic—or plain common sense—to model the same conditions an AOM would find in a real-world problem. Figure 21–4 simulates, in outline form, a typical set of conditions routinely faced by the manager of a travel agency. By addressing each of these situations, the AOM can begin the systems development life cycle using the work simplification model, the I/O model, or both. Another OR technique, **linear programming (LP),** is used to determine the best mixture of components in a system, such as the best complement of operators and equipment to handle an anticipated word processing workload in an office.

Systems Communication Tools

Because of the great amount of detail involved in improving an AOS, analysts search for concise, understandable methods of organizing and communicating the detailed operations of the system being studied. One of the most effective methods of communicating these operations is the systems chart. Such a chart tells a pictorial, sequential story of the system with few or no words required.

A second type of systems communication is the decision table, which emerged in the computer age as a useful device in documenting the makeup of a system. Each of the commonly used systems charts is defined in this section along with a discussion of the use of decision tables.

Figure 21–4
Simulating the
Operations of
a Small Travel
Agency

Typical Operations

1. Customer wants to change reservation to later flight.
2. Telephone customer checks on flight reservations to Hawaii.
3. Airline calls informing travel agency of changed departure times for passengers who made reservations through agency.
4. AMTRAK calls to confirm reservation for waiting customer.
5. Group wants to arrange tour to Washington, DC.
6. Three customers want to be waited on at once.
7. Customer complains about accommodations on his last trip to NYC.
8. Foreigner (with very poor English skills) calls to ask information about one-way ticket to Pakistan.
9. Customer calls for quotation on fare; and upon learning quotation, begins to argue because friend went same route at less cost.
10. Customer calls because she lost her ticket and needs a new one.
11. Equipment (telephone, computer, copier, etc.) breaks down.
12. Personnel problems arise: one clerk 30 minutes late; another, ill on the same day.

Resources Needed to Conduct Operations

1. Personnel
2. Space
3. Furniture, equipment, and supplies
4. Procedures including needed references
5. Operating budget

Other systems communication tools, including written procedures and manuals, are explained in a later section of this chapter.

Systems Charts

A **systems chart** is a graphic device used to portray an existing or a proposed system, including the flow of information and the various elements required to operate the system. Charts help the analyst to display information clearly so that the users can validate the problems in the present system as well as the solutions recommended.

Analysts begin systems studies by familiarizing themselves with the entire organization and examining in detail the specific parts of the organization to be studied. If there is no organization chart, the analyst must prepare one that shows the present plan of organization and the role of the departments to be studied.[1]

Many types of systems charts are available, depending upon the information needs of the analyst. For example, a **flowchart** is used to show the logical sequence of steps involved in the flow of work, usually in a manual system. A **forms distribution chart** traces the flow of forms and related paperwork through the departments under study. Layout charts, illustrated in Chapter 13, are useful in understanding the problems involved with the management of office space. Information regarding the scheduling of work is often presented on a Gantt chart, also discussed in Chapter 13, or on a PERT chart, which is discussed later. For analyzing work assignments among a department staff, a **work distribution chart,** which identifies and compares the principal tasks of all workers in the system, is a useful tool.

Systems charts are also useful in studying automated systems. However, two charts in particular—the systems flowchart and the program flowchart—are most often identified with computer systems. Both of these charts are discussed in Chapter 16.

---

[1]The purpose of organization charts is discussed in Chapter 2, along with suggestions for constructing such charts.

Decision Tables

A **decision table** is a tool for presenting the logic and the sequential operations in a system by showing what action must be taken to satisfy each information-related condition. The decision table was originally designed to illustrate the logic found in computer programs; however, this type of systems tool is used in situations where the logic and the sequential flow of data cannot be clearly represented on a chart.

A decision table may be very simple and describe only a few conditions, or it may involve dozens or even hundreds of steps. The basic decision table is divided into four sections:

1. *A conditions section* sets forth in an explicit or implied question form the conditions that may exist in the system.
2. The *action section* lists the action to be taken for satisfying each condition.
3. The *condition-entry section,* or set of rules, provides answers ("yes," "no," or "not applicable") to the questions in the conditions section.

4. The *action-entry section* indicates by an X the appropriate action resulting from the answers entered in the condition-entry section.

Figure 21–5 illustrates a decision table for determining the vacation time and amount of bonus for the workers in a major corporation. Each of the four possible conditions and the actions that may be taken for satisfying each condition can be easily understood by using this simple device.

MAJOR STUDIES IN ADMINISTRATIVE OFFICE SYSTEMS

Analyzing and improving AOS may involve all or only a portion of the elements making up these systems. Depending upon the availability of staff and the necessary time and funds, one or more of the following major studies in AOS may be undertaken:

1. Flow of work.
2. Flow of data.
3. Use of space.

Figure 21–5
A Decision Table Showing the Rules for Granting Employee Vacations and Bonuses

CONDITIONS / ACTIONS	Employee Vacation and Bonus	Rule 1	Rule 2	Rule 3	Rule 4
CONDITIONS	Worker employed for less than 1 year?	Y	N	N	N
	Worker employed from 1–2 years?	—	Y	N	N
	Worker employed from 2–5 years?	—	—	Y	N
	Worker employed 5 or more years?	—	—	—	Y
ACTIONS	No vacation	X			
	One-week vacation and $50 bonus		X		
	Two-week vacation and $100 bonus			X	
	Three-week vacation and $500 bonus				X

CONDITION ENTRY — ACTION ENTRY

Legend: Y = Yes X = Completion of action statement
N = No — or blank = Not applicable

4. Forms and related documents.
5. Performance of human resources.
6. Use of equipment.
7. Scheduling of work.
8. Costs of operating the AOS.

We discuss each of these areas of study in this section. However, before such studies can be started, it is important that the analyst or the OM has followed the guidelines contained in the systems models discussed earlier and that relevant, accurate, and complete information about the system is on hand.

Workflow Studies

In **workflow analysis,** we study the origination and distribution of documents and the clerical operations required to process the information. To document the workflow involved in a typical system, the analyst prepares a flow process chart that records each of the steps in the system. The symbols and definitions used in flow process charting are illustrated in Figure 21–6.

Figure 21–7 illustrates a flow process chart of the steps involved in keyboarding data on a purchase order. By studying each of the steps in the flow of work—the operation, transportation, inspection, delay, and storage activities—the analyst is able to compute the time and delay problems detected and from such information develop improvements in the system.[2] Typical problems that can be disclosed by a study of the flow process chart include undue delays in transferring work between workstations, too much duplication of effort at workstations, duplicate forms and work sheets, too much travel or transportation time from one workstation to the next, and unfair work assignments that cause an overworked clerk to delay the processing of information.

Flow of Data

As information systems become increasingly automated, it is often useful to chart what data flow to, through, and from the systems. A tool called a **data flow diagram (DFD)** facilitates this study.

---

[2]Note that only the present method of entering purchase orders is shown in Figure 21–7. A similar chart would be prepared for an improved (proposed) method as well as for keyboarding such information on "soft-copy" forms in the VDT. At the top of the chart, numeric data are shown for a proposed method, along with the savings in number of steps and in minutes required to complete the two versions of the system. Thus, the proposed method of operating the system saves three steps and 121 minutes, on the average.

Figure 21–6
Standardized Flow Process Chart Symbols

Symbol	Key	Example of Systems Activities
○	Operation	A productive activity (computing, filling in a form, interviewing an employee).
⇨	Transportation	The physical movement of workers, information, or materials.
▢	Inspection	Proofreading, checking, or verifying data.
⬠	Delay	A pause (momentary or longer) in the processing or flow of work.
▽	Storage	Temporary or permanent filing of information or materials.

Figure 21–7
Flow Process
Chart of
Present
Method of
Entering Data
on Purchase
Orders

FLOW PROCESS CHART OF _Entering data on purchase orders_

Department _Purchasing_

☐ Worker ☑ Form Material _#124_

Chart begins _Step 1_

Chart ends _Step 13_

Chart _____ Page _1_ of _2_

Charted by _Jason Carroll_

Date _9/8/--_

Dept. approved _B.J. Falk_

Date _10/17/--_

SUMMARY

		Present		Proposed		Savings	
		No.	Time	No.	Time	No.	Time
◯	Operations	5	5.95	4	5.1	1	0.85
⇨	Transportations	2	0.8	2	.8	0	—
☐	Inspections	2	0.7	1	.5	1	0.2
◻	Delays	2	180	1	60.0	1	120
▽	Storages	1	—	1	—	0	—
	Totals	12	187.45	9	66.40	3	121.05
Distance traveled _(ft.)_		10		6		4	

SYMBOLS

Step No.	Description of Present Method ~~Proposed~~	Operation	Transportation	Inspection	Delay	Storage	Quantity	Time in minutes	Distance in feet	Notes
1	Retrieve PO shell from electronic file	◯	⇨	☐	◻	▽	1	.25	—	Consider scanner
2	Keyboard PO from requisition	◯	⇨	☐	◻	▽	1	3	—	
3	Proofread	◯	⇨	☐	◻	▽	1	.5	—	
4	Print form	◯	⇨	☐	◻	▽	1	.25	—	
5	Remove form from printer; burst	◯	⇨	☐	◻	▽	1	.5	3	
6	Place in "PO complete" basket	◯	⇨	☐	◻	▽	1	.5	3	
7	Wait until 25 PO's accumulate	◯	⇨	☐	◻	▽	—	100	—	Average wait time
8	Pick up batch of PO's	◯	⇨	☐	◻	▽	25	2	—	
9	Count number in batch	◯	⇨	☐	◻	▽	25	.2	—	
10	Place rubber band around batch	◯	⇨	☐	◻	▽	25	2	—	
11	Place in Out Basket	◯	⇨	☐	◻	▽	25	.3	—	
12	Wait for pickup	◯	⇨	☐	◻	▽	—	80	4	Daily wait, on the average
13	PO entry completed	◯	⇨	☐	◻	▽				
		◯	⇨	☐	◻	▽				
		◯	⇨	☐	◻	▽				
		◯	⇨	☐	◻	▽				See page 2 for chart of proposed system.

Figure 21–8
Standard DFD
Symbols

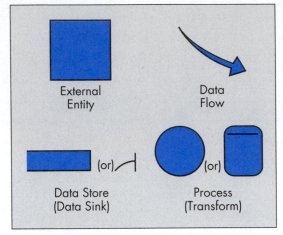

Figure 21–8
Standard DFD
Symbols

To prepare a DFD, we use the following four symbols, which are illustrated in Figure 21–8:

1. **External entity:** People, processes, or departments that lie outside the area being examined, but yet either communicate to or receive communications from the area.
2. **Data flow:** The path of the data being carried by either a physical or an electronic document.
3. **Data store** (sometimes called a *data sink*): A point in the process where data are at rest, often a file cabinet for physical records or a database for electronic records.
4. **Process** (sometimes called a *transform*): An activity in which data are being manipulated. For example, lists are alphabetized, columns are totaled, and/or reports are printed.

A simple example of how these four symbols are used to trace the flow of data through a system is given in Figure 21–9. The upper area of the figure illustrates the **contextual data flow diagram,** which gives the most general overview of the system. The figure indicates that data, in the form of a purchase order, flow to the system from an external entity named "Client." The system processes the order and responds to the client with a different data flow, the sales order.

The lower area of Figure 21–9, called the **leveled data flow diagram,** examines the same process in greater detail. Level 0 indicates that the general process called "Process Order" in the contextual diagram is really a series of subprocesses—

"Log-in order," "Generate shipping instructions," and "Print sales order." Each subprocess, in turn, can be analyzed in greater and greater detail, or levels, until it is precisely clear what data are transformed, moved, and stored. For example, one of the subprocesses, "Print sales order," is examined in greater detail at Level 1. We see that this subprocess really consists of two activities—"Verify sales order" and "Print form."

From the data flow diagram, the analyst can construct a **data dictionary (DD)** that contains a precise description of each data flow, transform, store, and external entity. This information is invaluable when automated office systems that are supported by databases are upgraded. In this case, an analyst uses a DFD to determine which data are already in the database, which need to be added, and which can be deleted.

Space-Use Studies

The effective use of space is an important responsibility of the OM and a topic that is closely related to workflow analysis. In fact, the physical layout of the efficient office is built around the major flows of work, with the workstations arranged to minimize backtracking and wasted motion. Also, the combined ergonomic aspects of the environment must be studied, for these environmental factors directly affect the manner in which the space is used.

In addition to ergonomic studies of office space, we should give attention to **workplace analysis,** which seeks to improve the arrangement of all resources needed to function efficiently at a workstation. Also, we should study the flow and frequency of movement of each of the forms and of the workers who transport the records throughout the office. This may be accomplished by studying the office layout, preparing separate before-and-after layout charts for each important system, and drawing lines to indicate the movement of the various papers throughout the organization.

Office layout charts should be prepared for the transactions that occur most frequently. Studying the direction and distance of movement in the office will point out wasted motion and needless

Figure 21–9
A Contextual and Leveled DFD of an Order Processing System

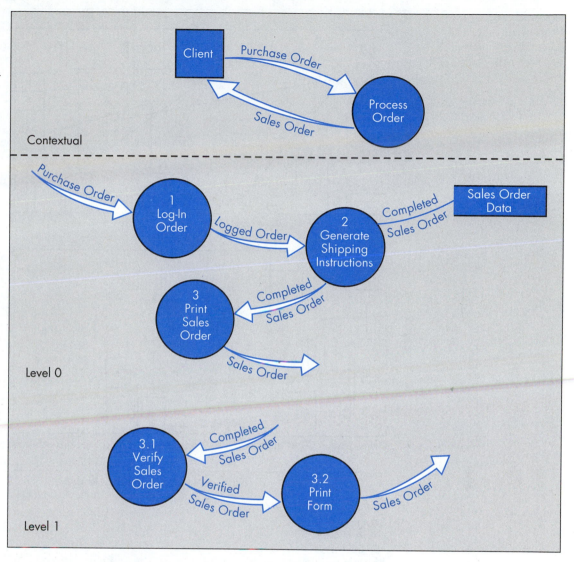

backtracking. Measuring the distance traveled *before* and *after* changes in the system are made will indicate the distance and time saved in performing the office activities.

Figure 21–10 shows an example of the effective rearranging of office space in order to minimize the movement of workers and the paperwork for which they are responsible. A study of the before-and-after illustrations in this figure shows the waste in steps, time, energy, and money that was eliminated in this space study. The "after" example shows a reduction of approximately 40 percent in distance traveled for the combined flows of mail and other work. In addition, other important savings result from the fact that two data scanner operators and their workstation equipment replaced five keyboard operators and their workstations in the office under study.

Forms Studies

The systems analyst approaches the study of the forms used by collecting copies of all the key forms in the system. With this information, the

Figure 21–10
Before-and-
After Office
Layout Charts

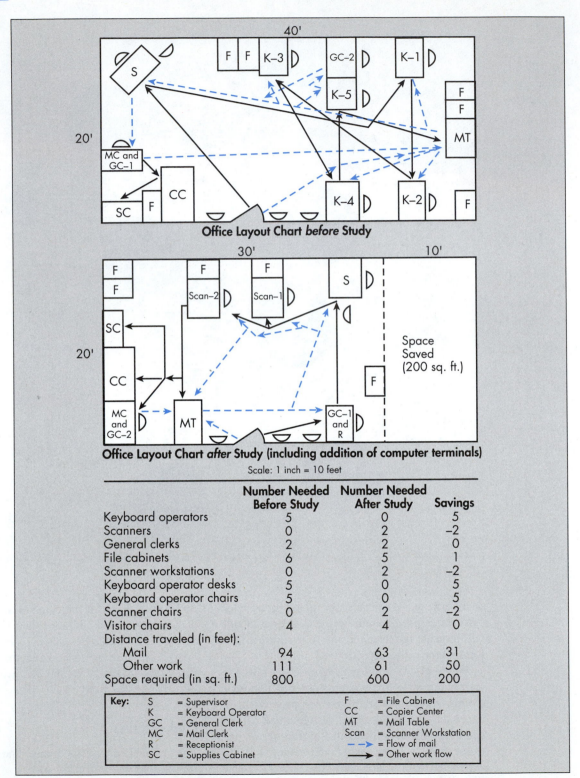

Office Layout Chart *before* Study

Office Layout Chart *after* Study (including addition of computer terminals)

Scale: 1 inch = 10 feet

	Number Needed Before Study	Number Needed After Study	Savings
Keyboard operators	5	0	5
Scanners	0	2	–2
General clerks	2	2	0
File cabinets	6	5	1
Scanner workstations	0	2	–2
Keyboard operator desks	5	0	5
Keyboard operator chairs	5	0	5
Scanner chairs	0	2	–2
Visitor chairs	4	4	0
Distance traveled (in feet):			
Mail	94	63	31
Other work	111	61	50
Space required (in sq. ft.)	800	600	200

Key:	S	= Supervisor	F	= File Cabinet
	K	= Keyboard Operator	CC	= Copier Center
	GC	= General Clerk	MT	= Mail Table
	MC	= Mail Clerk	Scan	= Scanner Workstation
	R	= Receptionist	- - - -	= Flow of mail
	SC	= Supplies Cabinet	——▶	= Other work flow

analyst studies the need for each copy of each form. Generally, the users of forms in all the related departments are asked to justify the use of all forms. Guidelines for studying this aspect of forms analysis are included in Chapter 19, pages 515–519.

An analyst may approach a study of the workflow from many vantage points. In addition to the narrow scope (within a department), an organization-wide or multidepartment analysis of such a system may be undertaken, as pictured in the forms distribution chart, Figure 21–11. This chart illustrates the multidepartment routing of a form—the purchase order—and its relationship to the purchase requisition and receiving report forms. In this simplified type of systems chart (sometimes called a *block diagram*), no special symbols are used. Instead, the blocks are provided to identify the various copies of forms and their respective destinations. Scaled-down drawings of file cabinets also help the reader to understand the storage of forms without the need for committing additional charting symbols to memory. Before-and-after versions of this type of chart, similar to the flow process and layout charts discussed earlier, may be prepared.

Human Resources Performance Studies

People are the most important element in an AOS; hence, we should give the highest priority to the study of human resources performance in the office. Regardless of how well the other elements in the system are planned—machines, furniture, forms, and space—a system will not perform well if the people assigned to do the work are incapable of performing satisfactorily or are undermotivated or simply refuse to do a fair day's work.

Three of the most important aspects of the human element in the system are (1) *the needs and skills of the individual workers,* (2) *the nature and distribution of tasks performed by the workers,* and (3) *the quality of their supervision.* You read about the first and third aspects of personnel performance in Part 2 of this textbook. In the following discussion, we present the remain-

ing aspect of the human element—the tasks performed by workers and the distribution of such tasks among the office staff.

Task Analysis

Task analysis is a systems technique used by analysts to determine who does what work. Generally the contribution of the human element to the total performance of the system is determined by the tasks people perform in the system.

A **task** is a definable unit (or piece) of work, as illustrated by the work activities shown in Figure 21–12. We can divide the tasks in most AOS into five *productive* operations: (1) *input tasks* that relate to the receiving and recording of data; (2) *transforming (processing) tasks* in which the data are converted into the form required for the output; (3) *data storage and retrieval tasks;* (4) *control tasks,* such as verifying or proofreading; and (5) *transmitting tasks,* designed to prepare in-

Illustration 21–2 A system will perform well only if the people assigned to it are capable and motivated.

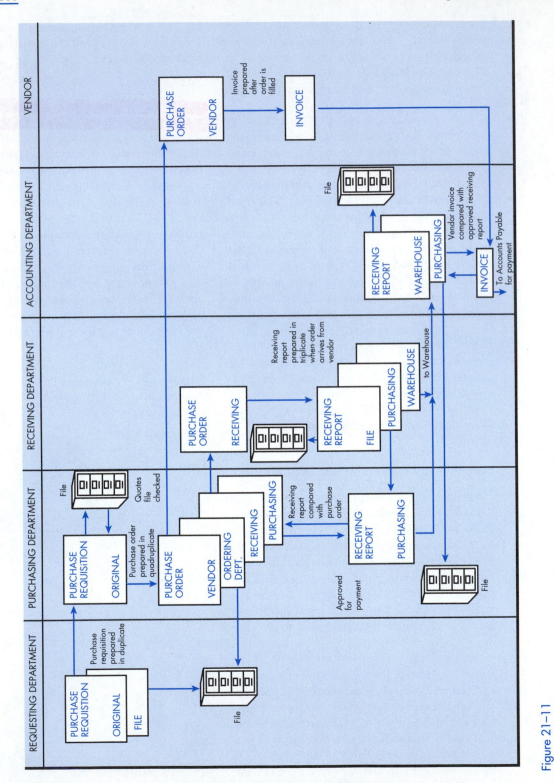

Figure 21–11
A Forms Distribution Chart of a Purchase Order Procedure

WEEKLY TASK CHART

Employee Name: Carl Snell Date: 10/17/--

Title: Jr. Clerk

Principal Tasks: Completing a purchase order

System: Purchase Order Processing Department: Purchasing

		PRODUCTIVE OPERATIONS										NONPRODUCTIVE OPERATIONS	
Receiving Inputs	*Hrs.	Recording	Hrs.	Processing	Hrs.	Storage and Retrieval	Hrs.	Control	Hrs.	Transmitting Outputs	Hrs.	Miscellaneous	Hrs.
Purchase requisition	1.25	Key order data	13.5	Compute totals for each item to be purchased	4.0	Retrieve vendors' catalogs and price lists	.4	Check purchase order data against purchase requisition	1.5	Purchase order (6 copies)	1.25	Carry purchase requisitions from purchase requisition section head to desk	.6
Vendors' catalogs and price lists	1.0	Key terms data	2.5	Compute sales tax	.5	File purchase department copies	.6	Confirm major purchases with secretary of purchase agent	1.0	Distribute copies			
Telephone calls to expedite processing of orders	3.0	Write order information on dept. order schedule	2.4	Compute grand total for each purchase	1.5							Carry purchase orders to supervisor	.6
		Address envelopes to transmit copies of purchase orders	1.6	Update schedule of outstanding orders	.5							Carry file copies to file	.8
												Separate copies of completed purchase orders	1.5
	5.25		20.0		6.5		1.0		2.5		1.25		3.5

* Figures in Hrs. column represent the approximate number of hours required weekly for completing each task.

Figure 21–12
Weekly Task Chart for a Purchase Order Clerk

formation for transmission to those who must use it. In addition, there are *nonproductive* operations, such as excessively long transportation routes; time spent in creating, processing, and filing unneeded records; and excessive numbers of supervisors monitoring the process.

By completing a task chart listing the duties performed by each worker, an analyst can confirm the *productive* tasks (those adding value to the system) as well as the *nonproductive tasks* (those not contributing value to the system). By carefully challenging the necessity of each task on the chart, the analyst can reduce *the amount of nonproductive tasks as a percentage of the total systems tasks to a minimum.*

Work Distribution

If we complete the task chart in Figure 21–12 for each of the three clerks assigned to a purchasing department, we have laid the groundwork for studying the distribution of the workload among this office staff. We prepare the *work distribution chart* in order to identify and classify the principal tasks of all the clerks in the office. From the information shown on the work distribution chart in Figure 21–13, the analyst can tell how many work units are produced and how much time is spent on each type of activity for all three clerks. With this type of information, the analyst can obtain answers to such questions as:

1. How much time is *each* clerk (as well as all clerks) spending on each type of task?
2. Is the group spending too much time on unimportant tasks or on relatively unproductive work? If so, what are they?
3. Is the distribution of tasks fairly assigned, or are more rewarding tasks needed by certain workers?
4. In what ways can the workers' assignments be rearranged so that the overall performance can be raised and operating costs lowered?
5. How much time is unaccounted for?

Next, the analyst compares the times observed or reported for each clerk performing related work. With this information, the analyst evaluates the assignments, notes the ratio of time used for productive to nonproductive operations, and de-

termines the rates at which the work is performed (as calculated from the work-count figure). For each task reported on the work distribution chart, the analyst can classify the operation as input, transformation (processing), output, or some other systems category by referring to the appropriate task chart. With this information, the analyst determines what category of operation is occupying the most time and then concentrates on reducing the time.

Equipment-Use Studies

Because of the continuing increase in the cost of labor, AOMs place much emphasis upon the effective use of labor-saving equipment. An analysis of the use of equipment may be part of a broader systems study, such as total workflow, or the use of equipment may be studied separately.

Most studies of equipment usage start with an identification of the various tasks performed. Once this has been accomplished, the analyst attempts to find out which of the main administrative operations (recording, computing, sorting, filing, retrieving, summarizing, and communicating) are performed by human means and which are performed partially or wholly by machine. The use of machines in performing administrative operations may afford cost savings—usually in labor costs—and thus help to increase profits. In addition, the output produced by machines is usually more legible, neater, and more accurate than that produced by human means. For many applications, such as calculating, machines are much faster than workers, and therefore larger volumes of information can be handled in shorter periods of time.

A feasibility study provides criteria for the selection of machines as well as operating information about the system in which the machines are used. Regardless of what type or level of machine is used in the system, the AOM or the systems analyst in charge of studying the use of machines should try to match the benefits of available hardware with the tasks to be performed. If that goal can be accomplished, machines can help to provide an efficient means of performing office work.

Figure 21–13
A Work Distribution Chart Comparing the Work Performed and Time Spent by Three Clerks in the Purchasing Department

WORK DISTRIBUTION CHART

Department Purchasing	System Purchase Order		Analyst Betty Binelli		Date 10/17/–	
Productive Operations	Title: Jr. Clerk Name: Carl Snell		Title: Jr. Clerk Name: Sandi Heinz		Title: Jr. Clerk Name: Kim Lee	
	Hrs./ Wk.	Work Count	Hrs./ Wk.	Work Count	Hrs./ Wk.	Work Count
1. Receiving inputs (vendors' lists, purchase requisitions, telephone calls, etc.)	5.25	27	7.0	43	12.0	38
2. Keying order data	13.5	50	15.5	35	20.0	60
3. Keying terms data	2.5	50	2.0	40	1.5	30
4. Writing order information on order schedule	2.4	50	2.0	45	1.0	22
5. Addressing envelopes	1.6	85	1.4	70	1.0	64
6. Computing totals for each item to be purchased	4.0					
Productive time spent	36.5		30.0		36.0	
Nonproductive Operations						
1. Carrying purchase requisitions from purchase requisition section head to desk	.6	50	1.0	50		
2. Carrying purchase orders to supervisor	.6	50				
3. Carrying file copies to file	.8	50				
4. Separating copies of completed purchase orders	1.5	50	2.0	50	2.0	20
Nonproductive time spent	3.5		3.0		2.0	
Summary of Time Spent (in hrs./wk.)						
Productive operations	36.5		30.0		36.0	
Nonproductive operations	3.5		3.0		2.0	
Time not reported	.0		7.0		2.0	
Total time	40.0		40.0		40.0	

Work-Scheduling Studies

One of the most critical elements to control in a system is time, because, as the business axiom maintains, "Time is money." All of the labor hours devoted to administrative work are very costly since studies show that labor time is consistently the most expensive factor in producing administrative services. Thus, we must carefully manage the time used in the operation of an AOS.

Of special importance to the success of an AOS are (1) scheduling techniques that help to reduce the time required for completing work and (2) the concept of time management, which seeks to reduce the amount of time required by individuals in performing their assigned jobs. Time management is discussed in Chapter 22 as one phase of a work measurement and control program;

scheduling techniques are discussed briefly in this section.

A major problem in most systems operations is coordinating the flow of materials, energy, and information over a period of time in order to achieve the desired output as soon as possible. The flow of these factors must be orderly, logical, and uninterrupted. One technique to handle such logistics problems is called PERT, mentioned earlier in this chapter. The main function of PERT, an acronym for Program Evaluation and Review Technique, is to answer the question: "How much time is required to complete a project?" PERT charts are built by following the five-step sequence outlined in Figure 21–14. A PERT chart for scheduling the time required to design and install an improved local-area network (LAN) is illustrated in Figure 21–15. The chart consists of two components:

Figure 21–14
Steps to Follow in Developing a PERT Chart

Steps	Comments
1. Determine the activities to be performed, such as digging a basement, writing a computer program, or conducting an employee attitude survey.	An **activity** is an action that takes time to perform. On a PERT chart, the activity is shown as a line with an arrow pointing in the general direction to the right. Usually a time measure (in days, weeks, or months) is indicated on the line.
2. List the events that will occur in the completion of the project.	An **event** is a point in time when an activity starts or when it ends. An event does not consume time or cost money. It is represented by a small circle on a PERT chart. All PERT networks begin and end with an event.
3. Determine the sequence of activities and events from all parties to the transaction or contract. In a building project, for example, the various contractors and suppliers would be able to furnish such information along with estimates of expected arrival times.	Note in Figure 21-15 that some activities can be performed concurrently rather than sequentially, which reduces the time and cost of the project.
4. Assign a reasonable time for completing each of the activities.	A common method is to request three time estimates from knowledgeable persons and to calculate an average figure from these estimates.
5. Construct the PERT network as shown in Figure 21-15. The path through the network requiring the greatest time (20 weeks) is called the **critical path**.	If the job is to be speeded up or completed on time, the critical path must be most closely controlled.

Figure 21–15
A PERT Chart
for Scheduling
the Time Re-
quired to
Install an Im-
proved LAN

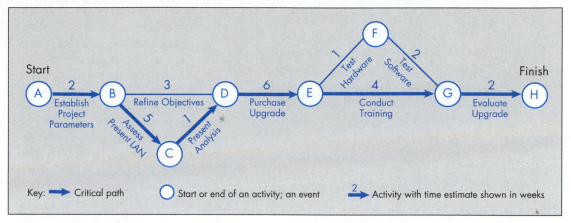

Key: → Critical path   ◯ Start or end of an activity; an event   →2 Activity with time estimate shown in weeks

1. *Activities:* Actions that take time.
2. *Events:* Points in time when an activity starts or ends.

Notice that some activities must be sequential ("Present Analysis" must follow "Assess Present LAN"); on the other hand, other activities may occur concurrently ("Test Hardware" can be completed at the same time as "Conduct Training"). After laying out a PERT chart, the analyst can determine the **critical path,** the sequence or path of activities that require the greatest amount of time to complete if the project is to meet its deadline.

Simple PERT charts can be constructed by hand from the mental computations of the systems analyst or the OM when relatively few activities are involved. However, when more complicated projects are to be charted, application software is used to generate such charts. Whether developing PERT charts by hand or with computer support, the most difficult tasks for the analyst are identifying the activities involved in the project, developing their logical sequence, and assigning realistic completion times.

Administrative Cost Studies

The importance of controlling costs is well recognized by most OMs. However, at times some managers become so preoccupied with cutting costs

(the efficiency goal discussed earlier in this chapter) that they fail to understand the real purpose of AOS (the effectiveness goal). Such systems can meet their broad goal of service to the organization only if they are delivering the required level of service to the users. Thus, a manager should not fall into the trap of achieving lower costs that, unfortunately, result in substandard service. Rather, *the most basic cost goal should be to reduce costs without impairing service.*

The need to control costs is a continuing theme throughout this textbook. Periodically, this emphasis takes the form of concrete examples showing the OM how administrative costs can be controlled after the various elements of costs have been pointed out. Such cost emphasis is intended to develop a strong cost "conscience" in each worker, which is the basis for all effective cost-control programs. For example, many managers are concerned about "time theft" or lost time (long lunch periods, personal business during work hours, tardiness, and early departure from work), which studies show averages four hours and five minutes weekly. Table 11–1, page 275, shows the tremendous costs incurred when an office staff loses five minutes of time each day during a five-day workweek in a 50-week year. Time lost has great significance to office productivity as well as to budgetary and cost controls, the main focus of the two final chapters in this textbook, respectively.

Other Studies in Administrative Office Systems

We find several other types of systems improvement studies conducted by analysts depending upon the nature of the systems problems and the skills and resources available to the firm. Examples are:

1. *Broad studies of company organization,* which concentrate on the structure of the firm and the comprehensive responsibilities assigned to each division.
2. *Limited-scope studies,* such as motion economy, in which the various motions of the right hand and the left hand are analyzed in order that the fewest and the least fatiguing motions are adopted by workers.
3. *Quality-control programs,* which are installed in some administrative centers that seek to eliminate the following problems: (a) incorrect or inaccurate work, (b) unattractive work, (c) wasted materials and time, and (d) costly reprocessing of work required because of errors. The major thrust in such programs is to provide adequate training of the workers so that errors are prevented and thus do not have to be corrected.
4. *Complex studies to maximize the use of expensive resources.* By using simulation or some other appropriate OR technique, an analyst can solve systems problems on paper much more economically than if the real-world system were designed and put into operation before its problems were resolved. The applications of OR continue to expand as administrators increase their knowledge of advanced mathematics, statistics, and other areas of study that relate to the improvement of AOS.

DESIGNING, INSTALLING, AND EVALUATING THE IMPROVED SYSTEM

The goal of systems improvement is a highly productive system—one that is as free of problems as possible. After an analyst has completed a study of the present system, an improved version of that system is designed. When the basic func-

tions of a system are valid, its performance can often be enhanced by integrating improved hardware, software, procedures, and personnel training. However, sometimes the fundamental functions of the system are so antiquated and irrelevant that no amount of improved technical and personnel support will achieve the performance objectives sought. In these cases, the designer sometimes conducts a process of **reengineering,** in which a system is completely rebuilt from its most fundamental components.

To reengineer the entire system, we begin by redefining the processes that need to be accomplished and then integrate the best complement of technology and human resources to support these processes. For example, say we plan to reengineer an existing accounting system that concentrates a majority of its resources on generating bills. By means of **outsourcing,** the billing function, which was formerly performed within the organization, is contracted to an outside agent. Without the billing function, the reengineered accounting system now operates completely differently from the former model.

However the upgrade is approached, the finished design must be presented to the users for approval. Users need systems that meet these standards:

1. *Quality standards:* Systems that result in a better product or service or require less work than the previous system.
2. *Quantity standards:* Systems that have shorter processing or response time, lower costs of production and maintenance, the capability of handling peak workloads and increased levels of productivity, and fewer errors and a reduced number of breakdowns.
3. *Acceptability standards:* Systems that satisfy the needs of those employees who must use them and those managers who are responsible for employee productivity and morale.

Designing the Improved System

As many of these criteria as possible must be met by the improved systems design. In the design, the OM or the systems analyst plans the proposed

DIALOG FROM THE WORKPLACE

RODNEY W. SCHEYER

Director of Finance
Boeing Computer Services
Seattle, Washington

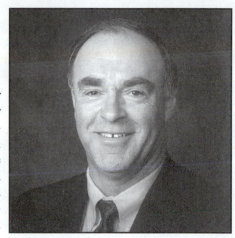

Mr. Scheyer has been director of finance for Boeing Computer Services since 1988, having previously been a systems analyst in Boeing's Aerospace division. He holds a B.A. in accounting from the University of Washington and an M.B.A. from Seattle University. He has also participated in the Program for Management Development at Harvard University.

QUESTION: In your experience, what is usually the most difficult aspect of upgrading the system within your organization?

RESPONSE: System upgrades can be a source of considerable aggravation. Change happens! Customers' needs change. Technology provides more alternatives. Environments change. New employees require changes in training and preparation. Cost pressures require management to seek the most effective and efficient means of process and product management. Since our administrative systems must constantly be evaluated and changed because of these factors, a critical requirement for the manager today is to transition to a more effective and efficient system with a minimum amount of disruption and cost.

The most effective management technique we have found is *planning*. We start with a careful understanding of customer requirements, followed by a detailed understanding of the "as is" condition. Next, we work with our systems and technology people to bring the most current technology and products to bear on the problem. The result of these activities is a detailed plan.

In many cases, the management of a system application can be illustrated by an old sports analogy. When you throw the forward pass in football, three things can happen, and two of them are bad! In managing a system upgrade, three things can happen, and *all* of them can be bad, including the functionality and expectation of the system design, the schedule, and the cost. The secret to making sure that all three don't turn out badly is the creation of and the attention to a carefully constructed milestone plan.

system and selects and organizes the elements (people, equipment, furniture, procedures, space, and workflow) in line with realistic objectives set for the system. On occasion, there may be situations in which the proposed design must be returned to the systems department for further revision and then resubmitted to the users for final approval.

Before the new system can be formally installed, however, it is put into final form. The main consideration at this stage is good, accurate communication—presenting to the users a system that is clearly defined with understandable, measurable goals and in a form that the user department can implement. For this purpose, two types of systems communications are usually recommended: (1) a documented account of each of the phases of the system, which includes both charted and narrative forms; and (2) a systems manual that integrates the new or improved design into the presently operating system. Both of these types of communications are discussed in this section.

Documenting the Improved System

To illustrate the manner in which a new or improved system is formally presented to a department, we have selected the purchasing system discussed earlier. By referring to Figure 4–2, page 85, we see that the purchasing system is one of the major systems in an organization and that such a system is typically divided into smaller interrelated segments called subsystems, such as ordering, buying, and expediting. How the details of operating these subsystems are communicated to workers is discussed next.

Charting the Improved System. Earlier in this chapter we pointed out the variety and purpose of systems charts. From the various charts available, two in particular lend themselves to charting the present system and the proposed improved system. For example, Figure 21–7, page 583, illustrates the processing of information on a purchase order in one department; Figure 21–11, page 588, shows a broader, multidepartment flow of information on three key forms involved in the purchasing system. Each of these charts can be used to present graphically both the present and pro-

posed systems in their final forms. Through an analysis of the system, the main resources used and the sequence and flow of information through the system can be documented, that is, made a matter of written record on the chart. Also, such charts are invaluable tools to the systems analyst and the OM for educating the user's staff about the improved system.

Writing a Narrative for the Improved System. While charts are useful in documenting an improved system, generally they do not provide the specific, step-by-step details needed to operate the system. For this purpose, a written narrative is required.

One of the most effective forms of narrative is the **playscript procedure,** so named because it follows the format (*who* says *what?*) used by a playwright (see Figure 21–16). This type of systems communication lists, in sequential order, the detailed steps necessary to operate a system and also shows who is responsible for performing each step. Such a simple format is easy to construct and understand; only a few rules must be observed in order to develop this type of narrative. These rules are:

1. *Clearly identify the system* (the purchasing system in Figure 21–16).
2. *Indicate the responsible departments or workers in a separate column.* (See the Responsibility column in the figure.)
3. *List in sequentially numbered order the steps to be followed by the workers to put the system into operation.* (This rule is illustrated in the Procedural Steps column in the figure.)
4. *Start each step or action with a verb* (an action word), thereby shortening and simplifying the language used. This eases the reading load of the user. (See the first word in each of the procedural steps in Figure 21–16.)
5. *Refer to related forms and other paperwork at the earliest reference point.* (Note Steps 1 and 6 in the figure as well as the related chart reference.)

Although only a portion of the system's steps are shown in Figure 21–16, all five of the rules for constructing an effective narrative are illustrated. It is important that the forms distribution

Figure 21–16
The Playscript
Procedure

SYSTEM: Purchasing	DEPARTMENTS INVOLVED:
FORMS: Purchase Requisition #124 Purchase Order #507 Receiving Report #632	Ordering (or Requesting) Purchasing Receiving Accounting (and Vendor)
RELATED CHARTS: Purchase Order Forms Distribution Chart	

RESPONSIBILITY	PROCEDURAL STEPS

Ordering (Requesting) Department	1. Prepares Purchase Requisition #124 in duplicate.
	  a. Sends original to purchasing department.
	  b. Retains file copy in pending file.

Purchasing Department Requisition Section	2. Receives Purchase Requisition #124 from ordering (requesting) department. 3. Verifies approval of #124. (If ordering department head has not approved form, returns for approval.) 4. Verifies prices from quotes file. 5. Forwards batches of approved requisition forms to purchase order section twice daily.
Purchase Order Section	6. Keyboards Purchase Order #507 in quadruplicate. 7. Staples original copy of #124 to purchasing department copy of #507. 8. Files in order pending file by department number.

chart (Figure 21–11) and the supporting narrative (Figure 21–16) be presented as one communication package when the improved system is explained to all members of the user department. Later changes in the system should be reflected in the charts and the narrative that document the system.

Creating Systems and Procedures Manuals

Many organizations assemble all their systems communications, including the narratives and the charts correlated with the procedures, in various types of manuals. Such communication media can be useful to managers throughout the firm, for they provide a paper "picture" of the main information systems and workflows in the organization. To be useful, these manuals should be distributed to all user departments and regularly updated as changes occur in the systems. For a more complete discussion of manuals, see Chapter 17.

Installing the Improved System

After the proposed systems design has been approved (usually by the department manager), we are ready to install the improved system. But such an installation process is highly complex, for it means essentially that workers, supervisors, and managers must change their work patterns and their attitudes toward work procedures. A department manager must convince the workers of the values of the improved system, summarizing how users will benefit from the improved system and communicating this information *before* the system is put into operation.

Additionally, the systems designer, in conjunction with the AOM's recommendations, must decide how to best bring the improved system online. There are three possible implementation strategies:

1. *Direct:* The former system is entirely discontinued when the new system is installed.
2. *Parallel:* The former system continues to run alongside the new system until the new system's integrity is verified.
3. *Phase:* Segments of the former system are gradually taken offline as the comparable segments of the new system are validated.

Whichever implementation strategy is used, the analyst and designer must be on hand to explain the operations of the newly installed system, answer questions from workers, and adjust its operations until it is working smoothly.

Evaluating the Functioning System

A system should complete several cycles before it is evaluated. A system whose operations are repeated several times daily can be evaluated after a few days; one that has a monthly cycle will not show reliable results until after several months (i.e., several cycles) have elapsed. Systems operating on a once-a-year basis will require two or three years for an accurate evaluation.

To evaluate a functioning system, we use many performance measures, with the measure(s) chosen depending upon the type of system to be assessed. Some of the most common criteria for judging the performance of systems are:

1. *Time,* which measures the number of clock units (hours, minutes, etc.) required for a particular action to be performed, such as the speed at which data move through a workstation. However, time does *not* measure quality. Two important time measures are (a) *lead time,* or response time, which is the time that elapses before a system responds to a demand placed upon it; and (b) *turnaround time,* which is the length of time required before results are returned. A slow turnaround means a relatively long period of time is required for processing; a fast turnaround means a short period of time is needed.
2. *Costs,* which are used to measure profit, return on investment, errors in production, and shipping. The principal cost factors encountered in the office are described in detail in Chapter 23. Certainly a cost-effective system requires fewer dollars to operate than a poor system.
3. *Performance of the hardware,* especially its speed, reliability, service, maintenance, power requirements, and operating costs.
4. *Performance of the procedures and software,* which includes computer programs, office procedures, manuals, and other documentation related to operating a system.
5. *Productivity,* which states the relationship of input and processing costs to output level. Thus, to arrive at a productivity measure, we divide the level of output produced by the system by the input and processing costs. High productivity levels are obvious when we find relatively low input costs and high output levels. In this category, the performance of people plays a major part.
6. *Accuracy,* which, as stated earlier in this chapter, is a measure of the freedom from errors obtained by a system. Rates of accuracy, such as the number of misfiled orders or misshipped goods, may be measured by comparing the results of processing from one system to the results from another. Also, the frequency of errors during a time period gives another measure of systems performance.
7. *Systems integrity,* which measures the degree of security and control that can be maintained over the documents and records in the system. High document integrity means that records are safe, confidential, and under systems control at all times.
8. *Morale,* which reflects the satisfaction and acceptance that employees feel toward the system (and their jobs). The higher the morale, the greater the expected work performance level. Although morale is difficult to measure, we can take a fair "reading" of morale by comparing absences and late arrivals that occurred before and after installation of an improved system.
9. *User and customer reactions,* in which responses of persons who use or are affected by the system can be evaluated. Large numbers of complaints from customers concerning errors in monthly statements indicate poor performance at one or more points in the system. Fewer complaints might indicate that the new billing procedure is more adequate than the old one.

SUMMARY

1. All of the phases of the systems development life cycle are directed toward systems improvement. All of the elements in a system are identified and, time and resources permitting, studied in their entirety. Realistically, however, smaller-scale studies are usually conducted to improve on manageable portions of the system. Two types of systems improvement models are employed in such studies: (a) the work simplification model, which is built upon the same logic that characterizes the problem-solving process; and (b) the input-output model, which furnishes a general approach for examining each of the phases in the system. The available resources and time constraints, as well as the analytical skills of the administrative staff, dictate whether one or both of these approaches are followed. In more complex systems, mathematics-based models are used by operations research specialists.

2. Typically major systems studies focus on the following areas: work and data flows, which are organized around the origination and distribution of key documents in a system; the use of space; the use and distribution of forms; the performance of human resources; the use of equipment; the scheduling of work; and the control of administrative costs. Often other types of studies are conducted, such as motion economy, quality control, and operations research studies that help the OM predict the outcomes of using various mixes of resources in the office.

3. To design and implement the improved system, various types of communications are used. The most common are charts that show the sequence, logic, and overall framework of the system, and written narratives that provide the specific details for operating a system. The playscript procedure is one of the most useful formats for narrating such operating steps. After the system has been implemented by either the direct, parallel, or phase strategy, it is evaluated to determine how effectively and efficiently it is performing and to correct any deficiencies found in the system.

FOR YOUR REVIEW

1. List the six steps of the systems development life cycle and give one example for each step in which office employees might offer input.

2. List five influences that could cause an organization's office system to be changed.

3. Explain why office employees must understand the basics of systems analysis and design if they are to make a contribution to improving administrative office systems.

4. Compare and contrast the terms *effective* and *efficient* as they are used to describe desirable qualities of systems.

5. If there can never be a truly ideal system, of what value is the concept of such a system to a systems analyst or office manager?

6. Define what a work simplification model is and explain how it functions in the systems improvement process.

7. List the major types of communication tools used in systems improvement and state the principal purposes of each.

8. a. What is the main purpose of workflow analysis?

   b. What type of communication device is commonly used to record the flow of work in a system?

9. Are workflow analysis and space-use studies closely related? If so, how and why?

10. What factors should be studied in an analysis of the use of equipment in a system?

11. What three elements of data are necessary before a PERT chart can be constructed?

12. Describe the types of documentation that are often used to communicate the details of an improved system to the user department.

13. Describe the procedures recommended for effectively installing an improved system.

14. List seven of the most common criteria for evaluating the performance of a system.

FOR YOUR DISCUSSION

1. A nationally prominent systems expert once called systems improvement "a war against habit." Why is such a statement made?

2. The office management class in which you are enrolled is the one organization in which all your classmates are "employed." Using the input-output systems improvement model, analyze the operations of your class from a systems standpoint. Include as many systems elements in your analysis as possible. Before proceeding with this task, develop a class consensus on the objectives of your exercise.

3. From the standpoint of administrative costs, how can the attainment of cost reduction result in an efficient but ineffective system?

4. Assume that your AOM has asked you to consider the six-step SDLC for improving a system in your office. Which of these steps do you believe will be the most difficult to accomplish? Why?

5. As the office manager for Output Support Services, a distributor of computer printers and other peripherals, you are responsible for the work of four general clerks, five accountants, three secretaries, and four data-entry operators. In this small office, no one has been assigned the responsibility for maintaining effective systems, for this function is assumed to be an implied duty of the office manager. However, you recognize that you do not have the time to devote to this work. Considering the size of the office staff, how would you proceed to ensure that the major administrative office systems in the firm are designed and operated in an effective manner?

6. Recently a new set of rules has been proposed to update the system for granting credit in the New Zealand Jade Mart. In an effort to communicate these proposals to all the department managers and to the 20 members of the credit department staff for consideration, Janece Connor, the credit manager, has asked you, her assistant, for help. In particular, Connor asks that you develop an effective communication that will clearly and logically present the following credit-granting rules that have been suggested:

c
o
n
t

Application Conditions	To Be Approved By
Applications for credit, $0 to $100	Credit supervisor
Applications for credit, $101 to $500	Assistant credit manager
Applications for credit, $501 to $1,000	Credit manager
Applications for credit, $1,001 to $10,000	Credit committee
Applications for credit above $10,000	Store president

Using this information, develop a decision table that clearly shows the various possible conditions in the new procedure and what action must be taken to satisfy each condition. Present your table with an attached explanation for its use, as directed by your instructor.

7. Assume that you, as AOM, are discussing the three conversion strategies—direct, parallel, and phase—for bringing an improved system online.

   a. Assess each strategy by generating the major advantage and disadvantage for each.

   b. Determine which strategy would be more appropriate if the systems improvement were a massive versus a minor change.

8. Typically, the analyst develops a proposal for improving the system and presents it to the department for approval. Unfortunately, too often, a department considers such a proposal to be a personal affront to its competence. Since the user is the boss and the analyst is only an adviser, such an attitude sometimes causes more problems than the systems study eliminates. Discuss the psychological problems created in such a situation. What types of strategies must be put into practice by the analyst in order to guarantee that a proposal will be objectively evaluated by a department manager?

CASES FOR CRITICAL THINKING

Case 21–1 Brainstorming an Improved System

WWRX-TV has historically been the least popular television station in its market. A new program director was hired six months ago, and her innovative programming decisions have caused the number of viewers watching the station to skyrocket. As a result, local and national advertisers have tremendously increased their use of WWRX-TV to air their commercial messages.

While everyone at the station is delighted with the increased business, the station's success has created a real headache for its administrative office manager because the present system for scheduling commercials cannot keep up with the increased business.

The problem centers on the way that the commercials are placed on the schedule. Each Monday morning the sales staff is given a printout of the times that are available for commercial messages that week. The sales staff uses this printout to sell announcements to clients. The problem with this system is that the salespeople never know which times may have been sold until they compare orders at the end of each workday. Invariably, two or three salespeople have sold the same time slot and tempers flare. Clearly, an improved system is needed, and the AOM has directed you to develop one.

c
o
n
t

1. Suggest three possible ways that a new system might be designed to solve the problem.
2. Rank the three models according to their degree of sophistication (least sophisticated first).
3. Be prepared to discuss each model's positive attributes and any possible disadvantages.

Case 21–2 Charting a System in a Small Business

In a discussion of systems charting in your office management class, your instructor has emphasized the ease with which charts can be understood. In addition, the instructor mentions that all systems, even those in the least complicated small businesses, are full of complex and partially hidden details that may be overlooked when data about the systems are collected. To prove this point, the instructor has directed the class to go to restaurants in the local community and, with the approval of the respective managers, to observe the main workflows involved in completing one cycle of a common system in the firm selected.

To complete this assignment, your specific instructions are as follows:

1. Two students are to observe and record the steps involved in ordering, preparing, delivering, and receiving payment for a hamburger in a small restaurant near your school. Each of the two students must observe and chart the system independently so the differences in perception of the events and the relative effectiveness of the recording methods can be discussed in class.
2. For charting the system described in the preceding instruction, use the techniques of flow process charting discussed in this chapter.
3. Prepare a narrative of the charted process using the playscript procedure.

Present this material to your instructor along with a cover letter (sometimes called a letter of transmittal), as directed.

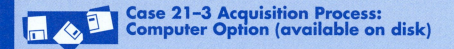

Case 21–3 Acquisition Process: Computer Option (available on disk)

IMPROVING OFFICE PRODUCTIVITY

GOALS FOR THIS CHAPTER

After completing this chapter, you should be able to:

1. Cite the benefits that an organization gains by establishing a program of work standards.
2. Describe the kinds of office operations that can be measured in order to prepare work standards.
3. Indicate the preliminary steps involved in preparing for a work measurement program.
4. Evaluate the pros and cons of the different methods for measuring routine office work and for setting standards.
5. Relate how performance standards may be developed for nonroutine office jobs.
6. Describe how office productivity may be improved through quality management.

Office productivity is a major factor in the economic struggle to control the mounting costs of administrative operations. In Chapter 3, *productivity* was viewed as the relationship between the output of goods or services and the input of basic resources—labor, capital, energy, and materials. Thus, increased productivity depends upon a more effective use of resources, or more output per unit of input. Faced with rising office salaries and increased employee benefits, organizations must closely examine the means available for controlling administrative costs, obtaining more output per employee, and thus improving productivity.

Major improvements in productivity are often made through a systems approach to the study of office activities. As we saw in earlier chapters, all systems studies emphasize the role of office personnel, whose skills, knowledge, and attitudes must be used more effectively in order to increase productivity and improve performance. The pressing need for establishing cost-control programs becomes evident when we see that, in offices having no cost-reduction programs, many workers are being utilized effectively only *one-fourth* to *one-half* of each workday.

To use their workdays and their employees more efficiently, managers should closely study Leffingwell's principles of effective work—*plan, schedule, execute,* and *measure* the work, and *reward* the worker. These principles, discussed earlier in Chapter 1, can be applied in today's offices to improve productivity, for AOMs have the tools, the know-how, and the human resources. Managers must learn how to release the energies of their human resources, for these workers know where savings and productivity improvements can be made. However, to apply Leffingwell's principles in productivity-improvement programs, AOMs must make sure that they themselves do not become an obstacle to productivity improvement by accepting the myth that nothing much can be done to reduce administrative costs.

In this chapter, we first highlight the importance of reducing administrative costs by investigating the measurement of office work and the development of work standards. Then we shall examine several methods used by office workers and their administrators to improve their productivity.

WORK MEASUREMENT AND WORK STANDARDS

Work measurement is a tool of cost control used to determine how much work is completed and how effectively it is completed. Usually this suggests a measurement of the volume of work and the amount of time required (*quantitative measurements*) as well as the accuracy and appearance of the work (*qualitative measurements*). A **work standard** is a yardstick of performance, or par, which indicates what is expected of workers and how their output can be evaluated. Work standards are tools of managerial control that are best applied to routine and repetitive operations such as keyboarding, transcribing, calculating, filing, billing, and posting. Although we usually exclude nonroutine, semicreative jobs from a formal work measurement program, we can measure some types of nonroutine work to provide useful standards.

By means of work standards, AOMs can determine what quantity and quality of work should be produced. They can then compare this output with the quantity and quality of work actually produced and thus have a basis for managerial control. All work standards are aimed at obtaining *100 percent efficiency,* which is defined as the rate of production at which an average, well-trained employee can work all day without undue fatigue. Or, we can say, simply, 100 percent efficiency means "a fair day's work."

To work at this level of efficiency, we need standards that are *reliable, realistic,* and *attainable* under normal, reasonable working conditions. The standards should not be changed too often or confusion will result. They must be understood both by employees and by management. Also, standards must be flexible in order to meet

variations in working conditions. For example, the standard for keyboarding a one-page, 100-word letter of straight copy is not the same as the standard for keyboarding a one-page, 100-word report involving columns of statistical data. Similarly, the standards set for the number of invoices to be filed under an alphabetic filing system and those under a numeric filing system are not the same.

Benefits of a Work Standards Program

By providing data on *quantity* (volume and time) and *quality* (accuracy and appearance), a program of work standards offers the AOM many benefits. Standards aid in:

1. *Determining the cost of the work performed,* an unknown element in many offices. Thus, management is aided in establishing realistic work targets, planning human resources needs, preparing budgets, and measuring the effectiveness of forecasts.
2. *Exercising better control over the scheduling and routing of administrative work,* which results in improved service to customers by reducing the elapsed time for processing the work.
3. *Evaluating employee performance.* Employees know the performance goals expected of them in terms of volume, time, and quality. Further, they know that these are objective figures based upon reasonable working conditions. The superior worker receives recognition for a job well done, and the poorer worker is appraised accordingly.
4. *Installing incentive systems* in which employees' earnings are based upon their productivity.
5. *Evaluating the need for improving administrative office systems and determining the feasibility of installing new machines and equipment.* The OM knows what volume of production can be maintained and the labor cost of maintaining that volume. Thus, the manager is able to study and to lower the costs of systems operations. The OM can realistically compare proposed costs and output with present costs and volume of production and learn whether a gain or a loss will be realized. Thus, the manager is better

able to answer questions pertaining to the installation of new equipment and the use of facilities.

6. *Measuring the effectiveness of department operations* by comparing department achievements with the standards. Consistently lower performance by a department or a wide variation in performance levels among several departments indicates that something is wrong. Thus, supervisors are prompted to study the causes and to correct them.

7. *Enabling the supervisor to measure the effectiveness of a new employee and the rate of learning that has taken place.* At what point should a trainee be able to handle a normal workload? This is the type of question that supervisors must be able to answer so that they may follow up on employees and determine if the necessary training has been provided to ensure a high level of work performance.

In spite of the benefits to be realized from work standards, formal programs of work measurement are not commonly found in many offices, as noted in the following section.

Difficulties in Applying Work Measurement in Offices

In view of the rapid rate of growth in the size and cost of office staffs, we would expect that administrative work would be measured to a much greater extent. However, the measurement concept is not universally accepted. Thus, a top priority of the AOM is to convince both management and workers of the need for a work measurement program.

Several reasons are frequently cited to explain the low incidence of work measurement in offices. The major reason is that the work is either impossible to measure or that measurement is too difficult and costly to be practicable. People holding this point of view feel that administrative work is so varied and complex that it does not lend itself to measurement. For example, repetitive information-processing operations do not exist in many phases of office work to the same extent as assembly-line operations in manufacturing. Often an office employee processes several

kinds of work units—orders, invoices, checks—in a single day. Even though the work may be repetitive, some phases of the job, such as answering and placing telephone calls and looking up information, prove difficult, if not impossible, to measure.

Some people feel that measurement is not needed in those offices where the number of employees is small. In other instances, top management lacks the desire to engage in any work measurement program. It is felt that administrative work is going along well enough, and there is no need to disturb the workers' peace of mind by attempting to measure their productivity. Also, managers and supervisors are often suspicious of and have misconceptions about the nature and intent of work measurement.

Many management consultants contend that most of the reasons offered for the failure to establish a work measurement program in the office are more imaginary than real. They claim, as we shall see below, that most routine and many semi-routine office activities can be effectively measured.

Office Operations That Can Be Measured

Estimates of the amount of administrative work lending itself to measurement range from two-thirds to three-fourths of all work done in the office. If this major portion of work were measured and work standards prepared, OMs would have a tool of cost control that could improve their office operations and enable them to gain a competitive edge. For measurement and the setting of standards, office tasks should meet three criteria:

1. *Repetitive*—the tasks should repeat themselves, be highly routine, and be done in a consistently uniform manner. Examples: opening the incoming mail, verifying the quantity shipped and the selling prices on sales invoices, posting to customers' and creditors' ledger accounts, preparing customers' statements, and filling in insurance claim forms.
2. *Countable*—the work units can be counted in precise quantitative terms. Examples: 12 cassettes transcribed, 394 forms filled in, or 1,408 letters filed.

Illustration 22–1 Keyboarding is a fine example of an office task that meets all of the criteria for measurement and the setting of standards.

3. *Sufficient*—the volume of work must be sufficiently great to justify the cost of its measurement. Examples: filing 600 copies of sales invoices each day or calculating the regular and overtime hours worked on several thousand time cards each week.

Office tasks that meet these criteria are commonly found in those cost centers or departments that have the largest number of employees performing routine, repetitive tasks. For jobs such as drafting, editing, proofreading, programming, and writing specifications, where the work is semicreative, the task of measurement becomes more difficult, as explained later in this chapter.

PREPARING FOR THE WORK MEASUREMENT PROGRAM

For a work measurement program to be effective, top management must fully support the program and its objectives and actively use the information obtained. The nature of the program and its aims must be communicated to employees so that they fully understand the program. A supervisor must administer the program at each level of office operations. Analysts who have some college training or equivalent work experience and a "feel" for paperwork should be properly selected. Finally, all personnel must realize and accept the fact that the work standards developed are feasible and accurate.

Gaining Top Management's Support

Work measurement must receive complete and unqualified endorsement by those for whom the tool has been designed; otherwise, there is little point in installing the program. Therefore, top management must (1) understand the objectives of the program and how it will work, (2) take an active interest in the program, (3) be willing to make the decisions needed to put the program into operation, and (4) demonstrate in a tangible way that all managers stand behind the program. To do so, top-level managers must impress upon all other managers and supervisors that work measurement is a permanent, ongoing program that must be accepted at all levels in the organization.

Communicating the Program to Employees

Before the work measurement program is installed, the AOM must provide workers with an honest and satisfactory answer to the question: "How is this program going to affect me?" What is important is that the workers understand the work measurement techniques to be used and how the results of the program will apply to them. Thus, employee fears and natural resistance to change will be lessened. Employees must be convinced that they will not lose their jobs as a result of work measurement.

When informing workers of the program, the timing and the nature of the communication are very important. Rather than have knowledge about the program circulate via the grapevine, we suggest that a letter announcing and fully explaining the program be sent to all employees at the same time and from the same source. Thus, any suspicions and questions on the part of employees may be anticipated before the first phase of the program gets underway.

Administering the Program

The backbone of a work measurement program is the first-line supervisor, for ultimately this person determines the success of the program. If the workers are given adequate supervision and leadership, most of them can meet the performance standards and will do so willingly.

Supervisors must be able and willing to review their operations and to weed out inefficiencies that can cause the failure of their departments to meet the standards. They must plan and schedule the workload of their units in order to maintain a balance of work among employees. To coordinate the workflow and keep peak loads at tolerable minimums, a supervisor has to plan and consult with other supervisors. Adequate records must be kept to provide a sound basis for performance reports. Importantly, supervisors must evaluate individual productivity and use the results of the program to determine training needs, to prepare people for promotion, and to justify salary increases. Thus, the program takes on meaning in the eyes of the workers, and management is able to identify and to reward outstanding workers.

In training sessions, first-line supervisors are introduced to the program and to the roles they will play. Here, it must be made clear that the results of the program will not dictate how the supervisors' departments are to be operated, nor will their ability to operate the departments be restricted. The program should be introduced to supervisors as a managerial tool that will aid them in doing a better job.

Selection of Analysts

As a means of reducing employee fears about the work measurement program and to prevent any undue resentment, employees from within the firm may be selected and trained as work analysts. Acceptance of the program is better assured when the analysts are known to their fellow employees. An important qualification needed by employees selected from within the firm is the ability to sell their ideas to others. In addition, analysts who have been recruited from within the ranks, such as from the administrative office systems division, are familiar with company routines, methods, and procedures. This knowledge is a valuable contribution when defining methods and setting standards. Although an analyst selected from within the firm must be trained in work measurement, an outside analyst must spend time in getting acquainted with the firm's systems and the individual jobs performed—an orientation that costs the company several hundred dollars each day.

Feasibility and Accuracy of the Standards

Regardless of the office task, some mental and physical effort is required to complete a unit of work, and the amount of productive activity used to accomplish the job can be measured. As noted earlier, there is a natural reluctance by many firms to establish administrative work standards, a fact that must be accepted at the outset when installing a work measurement program. Thus, the OM should be resigned to obtaining something less than perfection in the program. When the development of a work measurement program is approached from this point of view, the OM will be pleasantly surprised at how much can actually be accomplished through work measurement.

To encourage employee confidence in the standards, the workers must understand how the standards have been developed, what is included in each standard, and how they are to proceed if unforeseen conditions, such as machine breakdowns, occur. Standards must be accurate and consistent, as explained later; approximate standards do not provide accurate, reliable yardsticks, nor do they gain the confidence of employees.

METHODS OF MEASURING ROUTINE OFFICE WORK AND SETTING STANDARDS

Many of the first attempts to measure office work were clumsy since the techniques used had been designed to measure the output of workers in machine shops and foundries. Because managers applied work measurement techniques that paid little attention to the feelings of the individuals being measured, many of the programs failed. In some cases, the discontent among office workers paved the way for unionization activities. Today, however, measurement techniques center around a consideration for human values.

In this section, we first describe several methods used to measure routine, repetitive office work and to set performance standards. Then, in the following section, we briefly present a few methods for establishing standards for nonrepetitive, semicreative office jobs.

Historical Data

Under the **historical data,** or *past performance,* **method,** we study the past production records of various office activities such as transcribing, keyboarding, filing, and billing to measure what was produced in the past. For example, we may measure the output of workers in a text/word processing center by using one or more of the following bases:

1. *Page, letter, disk, or cassette.* Measurement according to this base is probably the simplest method to use. However, simply counting the number of pages, letters, disks, cassettes, etc., is too inaccurate to be of much value; letters vary in length, and disks and cassettes hold varying amounts of dictated matter.
2. *Standard lines.* Some companies count the number of standard lines of copy. A *standard line* is usually 60 spaces—15.24 centimeters (6 inches) for pica type and 12.7 centimeters

(5 inches) for elite type. The number of lines may be counted either by hand or by use of a line counter, which is a cardboard or plastic scale graduated for pica and elite type. Such a base cannot easily be used for tabulated or statistical matter. The standard-line basis is particularly useful, however, where workers are paid on a piece-rate basis.

3. *Weighted lines.* Many word processing centers use the weighted-line count as a means of measuring production. A *line* is defined as 72 characters of typed material on a single-space line, 6 inches long. The supervisor of the center assigns various *weights* to the work according to the difficulty of the material. Some factors considered in determining the weighting include the degree of difficulty in reading, the amount of unusual terminology, and the complexity of format.
4. *Square centimeters (cm²) or square inches.* Some companies use the square-centimeter or square-inch base in place of the standard-line base. In these firms, the production of typists is measured by using transparent celluloid sheets blocked off in square centimeters or inches. When a sheet is placed over a letter or a report, the number of square centimeters or inches of typewritten material may be read at a glance. This base is especially satisfactory in the measurement of tabulated material.
5. *Keystrokes.* A commonly used base is the number of keystrokes made at the keyboard. By means of an electronic counter, attached to the equipment, the number of keystrokes can be accurately and automatically recorded by a computer.

The past production of the group of workers, measured by one or more of the bases described above, is used as a means of measuring what employees can do in the future. The *best performance* may be selected as a standard on the theory that "we did it before; we should be able to do it again." Or the average output of the *best* worker and of the *poorest* worker may be used as a standard. The average output may be more reasonable than the best performance; however, the historical data method is little better than having no standards at all. By means of historical data, we learn how long a certain job took *in the past* rather than the amount of time the job should take *at the present* or *in the future*. Built into the performance reporting system are all the inefficiencies present during the period from which the data are drawn. On the other hand, the historical data method can be easily installed at a very low cost, and there is no need for highly trained personnel to administer the method.

Time Log

Another simple method of measuring office work and establishing work standards is the **time log,** or *time ladder,* **method.** To use this method, it is first necessary to identify the work activities performed during the day. For each of the various activities, a simple code number is established. On a time analysis recording sheet, such as the activity log shown in Figure 22–1, employees measure their output by recording the actual time spent and the units of work produced for a period of a week to a month. At the end of the time period, the employees' forms are summarized, reviewed, and edited to isolate any unusual patterns. A time log for the entire department is prepared, upon which each activity is summarized by code number. This report provides the total time spent on each activity in a particular department. Dividing the total hours into the quantity produced converts the data into a rate-per-hour figure and places all the performances on a comparable basis. From these figures, we can establish a standard time for each item being processed.

The major advantage of the time log method is that it can be used with little additional cost. Permanent control over activities can be maintained by continuing to record work assignments on the activity log. The time log method becomes unreliable, however, when, intentionally or not, employees do not accurately record the personal time allowances and absences from their workstations.

Work Sampling

Work sampling is a method of measuring work based upon the statistical law of probability. According to this law, observing a smaller number of chance (random) occurrences tends to reveal the same patterns that the observation of a larger number of random occurrences would produce. Thus, by means of work sampling, we take a sufficient number of valid random samples to supply information that would be impractical to obtain by continuous observation because of the time and cost involved.

Using Work Sampling

To understand how the work sampling method is used, we shall examine the steps taken by a trained observer to find out how much time a team of office workers spends on the various tasks that make up their workday. In our example, the observer takes the following steps:

1. *Randomly observes the work being performed.* (The time of each observation and the person to be observed were statistically predeter-

Figure 22–1
Time Log
Recording
Sheet

ACTIVITY LOG					
Date: July 23, 19—				Employee: Marian Mackensen	
Activity Code	Units Produced	Time			Remarks
		Start	Finish	Elapsed	
43	10	8:20	9:10	50 min.	
38	176	9:15	12:30	3 hrs.	15 min. break
33	52	1:30	2:45	1 hr. 15 min.	
38	91	2:50	4:30	1 hr. 25 min.	15 min. break

mined for the observer.) After each observation, the observer immediately records what the worker was doing when observed, along with a production volume count for each activity. When the sampling is completed, the observer determines what percentage of the total observations is represented by each activity, as shown below.

2. *Calculates the total time that employees were available for work during the study.*
3. *Multiplies the time, expressed in employee minutes, by each of the observation percentages developed in Step 1.* The product of each

multiplication equals the time spent on each activity observed.

4. *Divides each activity time by the corresponding volume count (obtained in Step 1) to obtain the unit time, or standard.*

The unit times calculated above are based on the premise that the percentage distribution of the various activities as they occurred during the random observation period tends to equal the same percentage distribution that would be found by continuous observation. The accuracy and validity of the study depend upon the care with which the observer performs each step.

Activity	Observations	Ratio	Percentage of Total
Filing	100	100/1,000	10
Keyboarding	300	300/1,000	30
Sorting	150	150/1,000	15
Assembling	200	200/1,000	20
Personal	<u>250</u>	250/1,000	<u>25</u>
Total observations	1,000		100

Name	Minutes
Lucas	429
McTovish	429
Van Horn	324 (part-time employee, 9:30–3:30)
Doerr	Absent
West	<u>254</u> (training session, 8:45–11:55)
Total available minutes	1,436

Activity	Percentage of Total Observations	×	Minutes Available for Work	=	Minutes Spent on Each Activity
Filing	10		1,436		143.6
Keyboarding	30		1,436		430.8
Sorting	15		1,436		215.4
Assembling	20		1,436		287.2
Personal	25		1,436		359.0
Total	100				1,436.0

Activity	Minutes Spent	÷	Work Counts	=	Unit Time or Standard
Filing	143.6		450 cards		0.32 min.
Keyboarding	430.8		110 policies		3.92 min.
Sorting	215.4		600 pieces of mail		0.36 min.
Assembling	287.2		150 applications		1.91 min.
Personal	359.0				
Total	1,436.0				

Determining Proper Sample Size

The number of observations to be made in any work sampling study depends upon three factors: (1) how much tolerance will be accepted, (2) what portion of time is expected to be consumed by the smallest activity to be measured, and (3) how reliable the results have to be.

Tolerance refers to the degree of accuracy desired. Suppose it is specified that a tolerance of 10 percent will be acceptable. If our study results show that an activity consumed 5 percent of the available time, we are assured that the actual time consumed was within 10 percent of that 5 percent; that is, it was not less than 4.5 percent or more than 5.5 percent. *The larger the tolerance one is willing to accept, the smaller the number of observations that must be made.*

Besides providing an acceptable tolerance in the sampling study, we must estimate the percentage of time consumed by the least time-consuming activity for which reliable results are required. This is an educated guess made after we have become familiar with the operations of the unit to be studied. The smaller this estimated critical percentage becomes, the larger the sample must be. For this reason, we often set up observation codes so that the smallest activity will account for at least 5 percent of the total number of observations. Whenever possible, we eliminate separate observation codes for those activities that are estimated to consume less than 5 percent of the available time. We can combine these activities with related work codes or group them under a miscellaneous observation code.

As the size of a sample is increased, the reliability of the results also increases. However, nearly every sampling application reaches a point of diminishing returns—the increased reliability achieved does not justify the additional time, effort, and expense required. A sample size that produces a reliability of 80 percent is generally considered to be sufficient for work sampling purposes.

Suppose we are planning a work sampling study with the following requirements:

1. An acceptable tolerance of 10 percent is specified.
2. The critical percentage is estimated to be 5 percent.
3. A reliability of 80 percent has been determined to be adequate.

Given these conditions, the sample sizes shown in Table 22–1 indicate that 3,210 observations must be made.[1]

Further, suppose we decide that greater reliability, say 90 percent, was needed. In that case, the number of observations for 80 percent reliability shown in Table 22–1 would be multiplied by the appropriate factor given in Table 22–2.

To find the net number of observations (N) required for $P = .05$, $T = .10$, with a reliability of 90 percent, we first identify the correct value for N from Table 22–1:

When $P = .05$ and $T = .10$, $N = 3,210$

Then, using Table 22–2, we find the reliability factor for 90 percent and multiply:

$$N = 3,210 \times 1.601$$
$$= 5,139$$

Pros and Cons of Work Sampling

If we take enough random samples over a long enough period of time to make the samples representative and valid, the data obtained under work sampling are much more reliable than those we secure from the time analysis method. The major disadvantage of work sampling is the need for trained analysts to set up the study and to perform the required observations. In some cases, the sampling method may prove to be uneconomical if the sample size required to produce valid results is too great. Also, some employees may not fully understand the sampling technique employed and may be skeptical of statistical evidence. Some office employees feel that the analysts are spying on them, while other workers state that they cannot perform naturally while their work is being observed. Some may alter their performance, such as slowing down, so that the sample taken produces a performance standard on the low side.

Using Probability Sampling in Quality Control

Joseph M. Juran, introduced in Chapter 1, has been a leading proponent of quality for almost 50 years. Author of several books on quality, including *Quality Control Handbook,* Juran looks upon the 20th century as one of productivity and the 21st, as the century of quality.[2] **Quality control** is a regulatory process in which the quality of performance is measured and compared with standards so that any difference between performance and standards may be acted upon. Under a quality-control program, we attempt to recognize and remove the identifiable causes of the defects and the variations from the standards developed for the particular process or operation.

---

[1]For those interested in learning how the sample size is derived by statistical formula, consult any textbook in basic statistics.

[2]"Juran on Quality," *Management Review* (January, 1994), p. 12.

Table 22–1

Sample Sizes Computed for 80 Percent Reliability

P is	Net Number of Observations When:			
	T is ± 5% (of P)	T is ± 10% (of P)	T is ± 15% (of P)	T is ± 20% (of P)
1%	66,920	16,730	7,440	4,180
2	33,120	8,280	3,680	2,070
3	21,860	5,460	2,430	1,370
4	16,220	4,060	1,800	1,010
5	12,840	3,210	1,430	800
6	10,590	2,650	1,180	660
7	8,980	2,250	1,000	560
8	7,770	1,940	860	490
9	6,840	1,710	760	430
10	6,080	1,520	680	380
15	3,830	960	430	240
20	2,700	680	300	170
25	2,030	510	230	130
30	1,580	390	180	100
35	1,260	315	140	80
40	1,020	260	110	60
45	830	210	90	50
50	680	170	80	40

P = Estimated critical percentage.

T = Tolerance factor.

Through the use of probability sampling, we can reduce the costs of some types of quality control. For example, rather than check the output of all billing clerks and record all errors made, we can take a random sample of the work produced by each clerk. The sample size required to give valid and reliable findings can be statistically determined so that the costly checking of all records can be avoided. However, many companies continue to use "old-line" methods of quality control, such as 100 percent inspection and reinspection.

Motion Study and Time Study

In most administrative office systems, there is usually one best way in which to perform each operation. By observing and timing workers at their jobs, we can eliminate much wasted motion and effort. However, the purposes of motion study and time study are not synonymous. *Motion* study is used primarily to improve work methods, while *time* study is used to determine time standards. Nevertheless, in relation to measuring work performance and setting standards,

Table 22–2
Reliability
Factors

Reliability	Factor*	Reliability	Factor
50%	0.269	85%	1.227
55	0.337	90	1.601
60	0.420	95	2.273
65	0.517	96	2.496
70	0.637	97	2.786
75	0.783	98	3.204
80	1.000	99	3.926

* Factors to be applied to sample sizes in Table 22–1 provide indicated degrees of reliability.

motion study and time study are inseparable. To improve an old work method or to introduce a new job, it would be difficult to determine the most desirable procedure without utilizing motion economy. Similarly, the gains realized from the new method could not be measured without time values for comparison.

Motion Study

Detailed motion studies were originated by Frank and Lillian Gilbreth, whose contributions to management thought were discussed in Chapter 1. Motion study is a recognized fundamental of obtaining "the one best way to do work," a phrase used by the Gilbreths, who considered motion study a scientific method of waste elimination. According to their definition, "**Motion study consists of dividing work into the most fundamental elements possible; studying these elements separately and in relation to one another; and from these studied elements, when timed, building methods of least waste.**"[3]

In a simple motion study, we visually examine a single operation or a series of operations by means of a stopwatch. However, if management can justify the cost of implementing a motion

study and the time required for analysis, the precise micromotion study is preferred. The Gilbreths originated the term **micromotion study** when they began to use motion pictures for studying the component parts of an operation. In a micromotion study, we observe and analyze human and mechanical movements in order to reduce a given operation to the fewest component parts in their logical sequence. Instead of relying upon our uncertain eye as an observer, we use a motion picture camera. On each picture frame appears the face of a specially prepared clock called a *microchronometer,* which is divided into 100 sections. Since the clock revolves 20 times each minute, it is possible to obtain 2,000 pictures per minute. The 1/2,000 of the minute time division, shown on each picture frame, is the unit of measurement in a micromotion study.

Micromotion studies are especially useful in studying office work of a repetitive nature and of long-range duration. Although the micromotion technique involves time-consuming methods, expensive motion pictures, and detailed records, the study is worth the expenditure since the entire office operation is being analyzed and recorded simultaneously. As a result, ineffective work motions are eliminated or reduced, and thus overall efficiency is increased.

Following either a motion study or a micromotion study, *standard time data* are determined, which in turn become the basis for determining a

---

[3] Frank B. Gilbreth and Lillian M. Gilbreth, *Applied Motion Study* (New York: Sturgis & Walton Company, now Macmillan Company, 1917), p. 43.

fair day's work for a fair day's pay. The standard time data form the basis for determining the most efficient method of doing a particular type of office work. However, as explained below, we must adjust the data to allow for the worker's fatigue and personal needs as well as for delays due to machine difficulties.

Time Study

The main purpose of **time study** in measuring job performance is to establish a *time standard*—the time required to perform an operation at an average pace. Another aim of time study is to develop standard time data that can be used for the performance rating of similar operations without making further time studies. (The development of predetermined times is explained later in this chapter.) Time studies are also helpful in comparing relative wage rates as well as aiding in the control of production.

Generally, workers accept time standards if they are assured that the time studies have been made under the best standardized conditions. Management in turn expects the operator to perform the job in the established time. Of course,

Illustration 22–2 A clock is commonly used in simple motion studies when examining a series of operations performed by a worker.

adherence to a time standard requires that all working conditions and job specifications be described in detail.

Unless the time study analyst has gained the confidence of the office personnel, the efforts expended in the study will be ineffective and morale problems will follow. The analyst must be capable of dealing with people honestly, tactfully, and sympathetically. Also, the analyst must build a reputation for making fair and accurate studies by using a systematic and exacting procedure when analyzing operations.

One limitation of the time study method is that a degree of subjectivity is involved in the initial selection of people who will be studied to determine time standards. The employees selected to be observed should be average and fully qualified because such persons are respected by their coworkers. The workers should be chosen for their consistency in using the most efficient movements in working at a normal work pace.

On a time study sheet, the analyst describes each element in the operation according to the sequence in which it occurs. Extreme care must be exercised to see that all operations are included. The analyst must also decide on the number of work cycles to be studied. Generally, the more observations made and the more accurate the basic time, the greater the assurance that unnecessary delays and inconsistencies will be eliminated.

The stopwatch studies cover only the actual time that it takes the observed employees to perform the operational elements. Thus, we must adjust the actual time required in order to determine a realistic time standard for all employees. The technique of adjusting individual differences is called **performance rating** or *leveling*. The goal of performance rating is to obtain a theoretical normal time—neither slow nor fast—that average workers require to complete their jobs under standardized conditions.

Since workers cannot produce steadily throughout the day with no interruptions, we must make allowances for the extra time that is not consumed in actual job performance. Therefore, in addition to the normal working time, we determine proper time allowances for delays, fatigue, and personal needs such as walking to the drinking fountain or washing the face and hands. For most office situations, the time allowances are expressed as percentages, which may vary from 10 to 20 percent of the normal workday. Thus, if the elemental times of a particular work cycle add up to a total standard time of 2 minutes, a minimum allowance of 10 percent for delays would increase the standard time to 2 minutes and 12 seconds.

After we have determined all the allowances, our time study is complete. We can then make the necessary entries on a time study observation sheet for a permanent record and prepare a list of the time standards.

Predetermined Times

The development of **predetermined times** is based upon the assumption that if the same motions are used in all work activities and under the same conditions, the time values are constant. Therefore, we can reduce subjective judgment by combining the time values as necessary to synthesize a time standard. In using predetermined times methods, we describe the elements of an operation according to various physical or mental factors. Then, as we analyze a job and divide its elements into basic motions, we assign each motion a time value that is obtained from a table. The total time for all motions involved in performing the element plus the addition of a time allowance for conditions such as delay, fatigue, and personal needs become the time standard for the job. The time values are usually developed from engineered stopwatch studies, micromotion studies, or laboratory studies of work motions. Many of the tables of time values, developed and copyrighted by management consulting firms and professional associations, may be obtained for a fee.

Advantages and Disadvantages of Using Predetermined Times

The advantages of using predetermined times include:

1. *Micromotion or stopwatch time study can be eliminated on many job studies,* thus conserv-

ing time in establishing time values and wage rates.
2. *The time standards are more precise, consistent, and objective than those obtained under time study* because the standards do not vary as does the daily efficiency of time study analysts.
3. *Use of predetermined time values may settle labor disputes more effectively.* Predetermined time values are more realistic in settling grievances since the data have been established after much experience and many observations rather than having been based upon a small sample or a possibly faulty time study.
4. *Workers are usually convinced that wage rates based upon the use of time standards are equitable.*

On the other hand, there are several disadvantages in establishing time standards through the use of predetermined times:

1. *There is less personal contact with employees.* Standards set from observation, where the workers who have to live with the standards can actually see the measurement of their work, tend to create greater confidence.
2. *Only those tasks that are highly routine and repetitive lend themselves to measurement by predetermined times.* Thus, the method is unacceptable for studying many office activities.
3. *A higher caliber of staff, requiring fairly high initial training costs, is usually needed* more when synthetic time standards are being determined than under other methods where the staff can be quickly taught the measurement techniques.

Methods for Determining Predetermined Times

There are more than a dozen methods available for determining standard time data, but the basic techniques of each method are essentially the same. Among these methods are Motion Time Analysis (MTA), Universal Maintenance Standards (UMS), Work-Factor (W-F), Methods Time Measurement (MTM), and Master Clerical Data (MCD). We shall describe and illustrate the latter method in the following discussion to indicate the basic techniques common to all methods.[4]

Master Clerical Data (MCD)

The *Master Clerical Data (MCD)* method of determining standard time data consists of various categories of elements tailored for measuring work performed in the office.[5] As a result of the need for more economical methods of measuring office tasks and to provide for new tasks emerging as a result of technological changes in text/word processing, data entry, and photocopying, the basic MCD method was modified. The modified plan, known as MCD-MOD-I, provides for measuring a wide variety of tasks completed on word processing and data-entry equipment.

The basic categories of MCD-MOD-I elements used in measuring office work are shown in Figure 22–2; some of the typical elements are presented in Figure 22–3. Initial use of the method requires training under the guidance of a consultant who has experience in using the basic element categories and the correct techniques for gathering information. Once the person who will be responsible for measuring work has gained confidence from this practical guidance and has applied the method, the work measurement program can be expanded and handled by the firm's own personnel.

The MCD-MOD-I method uses the word *task* to describe an activity performed in the office. For example, in the task, "Prepare Advertising Material," an advertising clerk collates six pages, aligns the six pages in two directions, staples the pages in the corner, places the collated material in a manila envelope, and puts the envelope aside. MCD-MOD-I is used to measure this task as shown in Table 22–3. For each element listed

in Table 22–3, the appropriate MCD Code and standard time are obtained from Figure 22–3. For example, the first element, "Collate six pages of," is identified as MCD Code ACT. In Figure 22–3, we see in Box A, Arrange Papers, that the standard time for ACT is 42. This element occurs once in the task, so "1" is entered in the Frequency column of Table 22–3. The total number of units for each element is obtained by multiplying the standard time by the frequency. The total number of units, 550, in Table 22–3 represents the total time for doing the task. This number of units is equivalent to .33 minutes since each unit is equal to .00001 hours, .0006 minutes, or .036 seconds.

To use this total time as a standard, we must add an allowance for break periods, personal time, and unavoidable delays. The average allowance used is about 15 percent. Adding 15 percent results in a standard time of .38 minutes. This is equivalent to .00633 hours per item, or about 1,263 items in an eight-hour day. If the advertising clerk produced 1,200 items in an eight-hour day, the performance is 95 percent [(1,200 ÷ 1,263) × 100].

PERFORMANCE STANDARDS FOR NONROUTINE OFFICE JOBS

Most measurement of administrative work focuses upon routine and repetitive jobs. However, we should also consider developing standards for those activities classified as nonroutine, varied, or creative. Some examples of such jobs are drafting, designing, editing, proofreading, and processing investment trust portfolios. Many nonroutine office jobs are complex and consist of ever-changing mental activities that affect job performance. Since such jobs are accomplished in a variety of ways, it is extremely difficult, if not impracticable, to measure the work and to develop sound performance standards. However, certain kinds of nonroutine work may be measured in the *aggregate*, or as a whole, in order to provide useful standards.

As an example, in the word processing center of one large insurance company, no one operator

---

[4]The background information on the Master Clerical Data (MCD) method is reprinted with the permission of H. W. Nance, President, Serge A. Birn Company, 5328 Wooster Road, Cincinnati, OH 45226.

[5]The time values for each of the elements in the MCD method were developed from the most widely used predetermined time system, Methods Time Measurement (MTM). MTM and its application data are copyrighted by the MTM Association for Standards and Research, Fair Lawn, NJ 07410.

Figure 22–2
MCD-MOD-I
Elements
Used for Mea-
suring Office
Work

Arrange Papers	This contains the elements needed to collate or sort papers by various methods.
Body Elements	This contains the elements needed for moving from one location to another.
Calculate	This contains elements for measuring machine or mental calculations.
Duplicate	This contains the basic elements needed for measuring photocopying.
Eye Times	This contains the elements needed for reading, looking up information, and making simple decisions.
Fasten/Unfasten	The elements for various fastening and unfastening of papers are in this category, such as rubber bands, paper clips, staples, etc.
Get and Aside	These elements are used for getting and putting aside papers, files, books, etc.; they are the most used category.
Handle Paper	This category contains elements for folding, tearing, aligning, etc., of paper.
Insert	These elements cover placing and removing of material, folders, or cards in files or binders.
Keystrokes	This category provides times for keystrokes located on the various keyboard configurations found on office equipment.
Locate	The basic elements needed for locating folders, cards, pages, etc., are in this category.
Mailing	The elements in this category cover folding letters, inserting them in envelopes, closing the envelope as well as opening envelopes, removing contents, etc.
Open and Close	Covers the elements needed for opening and closing binders, drawers, boxes, etc.
Post	Provides elements for reading information and writing it down.
Read	Provides elements for reading addresses, lines, names, numbers, etc.
Type	Provides elements for all forms of typing.
Write	Provides elements for writing names, numbers, or printing them.

Source: Serge A. Birn Company, © Training Techniques Company, Inc.

is assigned to any particular keyboarding task on a daily basis. The workload of the center is cyclically repetitive in that each day the same keyboarding tasks—from preparing the initial application form to filling in the completed policy—occur over and over again. The workload of the center is probably measurable in terms of *total production* for the cycle. Such a type of measurement can be used to determine optimum staffing needs or to compare the production of one cycle against another.

When measuring the productivity of managers and supervisors, we may find that an analysis of *goal achievement* may be used. First, the mission

Figure 22–3

Typical
MCD-MOD-I
Elements

A	ARRANGE PAPERS		
Collate			
Two Sheets		ACT	42
Additional Sheets		ACA	27
Sort			
Groups		ASG	47
Pigeonholes		ASP	69
Alphabetically			
0 Thru 19		ASA01	72
20 Thru 29		ASA02	79
Over 30		ASA03	85

G	GET AND PUT ASIDE		
Get Only			
Batch of Papers (Loose)		GGB	31
Jumbled Object		GGJ	27
Medium Object		GGM	18
Sheet of Paper		GGS	21
Aside Only			
To Fixture		GAF	23
To Other Hand		GAH	20
To Pile		GAP	32
To Table		GAT	15
Combined Get and Aside			
Batch to Fixture		GBF	54
Batch to Pile		GBP	63
Batch to Table		GBT	46
Jumbled to Fixture		GJF	50
Jumbled to Other Hand		GJH	47
Jumbled to Table		GJT	42
Medium to Fixture		GMF	41
Medium to Other Hand		GMH	38
Medium to Table		GMT	33
Sheet to Fixture		GSF	44
Sheet to Other Hand		GSH	41
Sheet to Pile		GSP	53
Sheet to Table		GST	36

B	BODY ELEMENTS		
Arise and Sit		BAS	208
Seated Turn		BST	122
Bend and Arise		BBA	61
Walk Per Step		BWS	17

M	MAILING		
Fold			
Insert			
No-Seal			
Regular Envelope		MFIN01	195
Manila Envelope		MFIN02	240
Stringed Envelope		MFIN03	226
Seal			
Regular Envelope		MFIS01	275
Manila Envelope		MFIS02	340
Identify			
Label / Sticker			
Dry		MIL01	49
Wet		MIL02	85
Stamp			
Normal per Time		MIS01	13
Self-Inking		MIS02	56
Date Set		MIS03	49
Open			
Sealed			
Folded			
Regular Envelope		MOSF01	192
Manila Envelope		MOSF02	199
Unfolded			
Regular Envelope		MOSU01	132
Manila Envelope		MOSU02	169
Unsealed			
Folded			
Regular Envelope		MOUF01	101
Manila Envelope		MOUF02	110
Stringed Envelope		MOUF03	148
Unfolded			
Regular Envelope		MOUU01	41
Manila Envelope		MOUU02	80
Stringed Envelope		MOUU03	118
Unfolded			
Insert			
Seal			
Regular Envelope		MUIS01	130
Manila Envelope		MUIS02	258
No-Seal			
Regular Envelope		MUIN01	50
Manila Envelope		MUIN02	158
Stringed Envelope		MUIN03	145

F	FASTEN / UNFASTEN		
Binder			
Duo-Tang			
Fasten		FBDF	125
Unfasten		FBDU	77
Three Ring			
Open		FBTO	31
Close		FBTC	31
Clip			
Paper			
Place		FCPP	75
Remove		FCPR	43
Rubber Band			
Place		FRP	129
Remove		FRR	16
Staple			
Hand			
First		FSHF	77
Additional		FSHA	35
Table			
First		FSTF	37
Additional		FSTA	20
Remove			
First		FSRF	84
Additional		FSRA	52

H	HANDLE PAPER		
Jog			
Cards			
Up to 1" Thick		HJC01	5
Over 1" Thick		HJC02	9
Sheets			
Up to 1" Thick		HJS01	8
Over 1" Thick		HJS02	12
Punch			
Three Hole		HPT	30
Shift			
Flip or Turn		HSF	23
General		HSG	27
Tear			
Care		HTC	32
No-Care		HTN	23

O	OPEN AND CLOSE		
Binder			
Cover			
8 1/2" x 11"		OBC01	48
Drawers and Doors			
Desk Drawer		ODD	62
File Drawer		ODF	78
Tops			
Flaps		OTF	95
Hinged Lid		OTH	35
Loose Lid		OTL	71

Source: Serge A. Birn Company, © Training Techniques Company, Inc.

Table 22–3
Measuring the Task, "Prepare Advertising Material," by Use of MCD-MOD-I

Description	MCD Code	Standard Time	Frequency	Total Units
Collate six pages of	ACT	42	1	42
advertising material	ACA	27	4	108
Move material up	GAT	15	1	15
Align end of material	HJS01	8	3	24
Turn material to side	HSG	27	1	27
Align side of material	HJS01	8	3	24
Staple corner of material	FSTF	37	1	37
Place material in manila envelope	MUIS02	258	1	258
Seal and put aside	GAT	15	1	15
				550

Source: Serge A. Birn Company, © Training Techniques Company, Inc.

of a department or a division is defined in terms of measurable goals that support the overall objectives of the organization. Next, the contributions of the managers and supervisors are measured in terms of how successful they were in achieving the goals. For example, assume that a departmental goal is to reduce overhead expenses by 12 percent during the next six months. The productivity of that department's manager can be clearly evaluated in terms of the overhead-reduction goal.

In establishing performance standards for administrative personnel, a company may utilize the Program Evaluation and Review Technique (PERT), which was described in an earlier chapter. You may recall that the PERT network is divided into the three aspects of time, cost, and performance to show the sequence, interrelationships, and dependencies of individual tasks in the project. PERT lends itself to use in computerized projects, and most software manufacturers offer PERT programs.

At about the same time the PERT technique was being devised, a similar network control system, the **Critical Path Method (CPM),** was being developed. In this method, we arrange all the activities of a project in sequence, estimate the time allowance (standard) to complete each activity, and plot all factors on a network diagram. Our objective is to determine the minimum elapsed time for completing the entire project. Fi-

Illustration 22–3 Although creative work such as this designer is performing is difficult to measure, it is important to establish standards for such activities.

nally, we relate the time required to complete each activity to its cost and determine whether the time can be shortened by spending additional funds. Thus, with both CPM and PERT, our aim is to strengthen the cost effectiveness of programs or projects as part of the goal of office productivity improvement, which we discuss in the following section.

IMPROVING OFFICE PRODUCTIVITY THROUGH QUALITY MANAGEMENT

To manage an ever-expanding workload without a corresponding increase in costs is the goal of programs designed to improve office productivity. What we are seeking is "to have all our information workers deliver the desired results of their particular job description, preferably without waste, that is, error free, or at the very least with the highest degree of accuracy possible."[6] At the heart of any productivity improvement program is the organization's acceptance of increased productivity as a philosophy, a basic "value" of the firm. Productivity improvement must be woven into the fabric of the organization so that it becomes an essential element in the quality management of the enterprise. Any productivity improvement program requires the involvement of *every* employee—from top managers to those at the operative level—in identifying and pursuing opportunities for improving productivity.

In the closing sections of this chapter, we describe several facets of office productivity improvement, each of which is designed to improve the productivity of office employees, their managers and supervisors, and, ultimately, their entire organization.

Total Quality Management (TQM)

Defined simply, **quality management,** or *total quality management,* is the systematic and continuous improvement of the quality of products,

services, and life using all available human and capital resources.[7] In Chapter 1, you read briefly about the contributions of Deming and Juran to the quality management school of thought, which emphasizes a philosophy and set of principles that guide the *entire* organization in *continuous improvement.* Deming, who died in 1993, developed a philosophy which stresses that *bad systems*—not workers' mistakes—are responsible for most defects and errors made by an organization. From his teachings come many of today's managerial buzzwords—statistical process control, worker empowerment, and continuous improvement. Juran, a leading proponent of quality management, sees top-level managers and their failure to become personally involved as a common reason for the failure of quality programs. To guard against senior managers' trying to delegate nondelegable matters, Juran stressed that CEOs should sit in on, and possibly chair, their quality councils; senior managers should themselves become trained in order to train their subordinates; and CEOs should follow and review the progress of their TQM programs and recognize and reward those responsible for quality performance.[8]

Throughout the preceding chapters, we have described several strategies of total quality management programs, which are recapped below. Following this listing, we present in more detail two other aspects of quality management—quality circles and time management.

Continuous Improvement

As indicated earlier, the ongoing quest of quality management is *continuous improvement,* where companies use tools and techniques such as statistical process control, brainstorming, feedback from employees and suppliers, and customer surveys. All of these aid the firms in measuring their current operating performance and help identify where corrective actions are needed. By securing

[6]M. Glynn Shumake, *Increasing Productivity and Profit in the Workplace: A Guide to Office Planning and Design* (New York: John Wiley & Sons, Inc., 1992), p. 10.

[7]Bruce Brocka and M. Suzanne Brocka, *Quality Management: Implementing the Best Ideas of the Masters* (Homewood, IL: Business One Irwin, 1992), p. 4.

[8]"Report Card on TQM," *Management Review* (January, 1994), p. 23.

information from these sources, the firms can correct their problems and set higher-quality management goals.[9] Some firms set their sights on obtaining the prestigious Malcolm Baldrige National Quality Award, which is given to American firms whose quality efforts are judged the best in the nation.[10]

Benchmarking

The International Benchmarking Clearinghouse defines **benchmarking** as "the process of identifying, understanding, and adapting outstanding practices and processes from organizations anywhere in the world to help your organization improve its performance."[11] Some of the practices and processes include customer service, human resources, and warehousing and distribution.

By learning from other firms with similar practices and processes and comparing performance, an organization that is behind tries to achieve breakthrough performance by catching up and then staying ahead by continually improving its performance. As a result, the organization can avoid reinventing existing solutions that other firms have already discovered and tested. As Ms. Carla O'Dell, director of the International Benchmarking Clearinghouse, states, "Benchmarking is the practice of being humble enough to admit that someone else is better at something and wise enough to try and learn how to match and even surpass them at it."[12]

Downsizing

To achieve their goals of cutting costs to obtain higher productivity, improve customer service, and, as a result, improve their competitive position and increase earnings, many American firms have *downsized,* or *restructured,* by slashing their payrolls. For example, by late 1993, more than three million middle-management jobs had disappeared over the past five years. Furthermore, some experts predicted that 30 to 40 percent of the seven million management positions remaining in the workforce would disappear during the next decade.[13]

Leonard R. Sayles, senior research scientist at the Center for Creative Leadership, stresses that middle managers play a critical role in boosting an organization's productivity, quality, and service. Instead of reducing the number of managers who are in the best position to get critical work done, they should be trained to serve as "working leaders" who can combine their business knowledge with their ability to negotiate with senior managers and across department lines.[14] A word of caution was also sounded by Secretary of Labor Reich, in quoting these findings of a 1993 Wyatt Company study of 531 mostly large companies: Of 58 percent expecting higher productivity, only 34 percent experienced it; earnings increased for only 46 percent of the firms; and while 61 percent sought to improve customer service, only 33 percent achieved the goal. And, within a year after making the payroll cuts, more than one-half of the companies had refilled some of their positions.[15]

In 1992, the American Management Association conducted its annual downsizing survey in 836 companies and found the following key effects of downsizing:

1. Companies that had downsized since January 1987 are nearly as likely to report a decline in productivity as an increase.

[9]Richard M. Hodgetts, "Blueprints for Continuous Improvement: Lessons from the Baldrige Winners" (New York: American Management Association, 1993), p. 99.

[10]The Malcolm Baldrige Award, named for a former secretary of commerce (1981–1987), is a joint effort of government and private enterprise managed by the National Institute of Standards and Technology, the Department of Commerce, and the American Society for Quality Control. Past winners include Motorola, Inc.; Milliken & Company; Xerox Business Products and Systems; Federal Express Corporation; IBM Rochester; Zytec Corp.; AT&T Network Systems Group/Transmission Systems Business Unit; Texas Instruments, Inc., Defense Systems and Electronics Group; and The Ritz-Carlton Hotel Co.

[11]Carla O'Dell, "Out-of-the-Box Benchmarking," *Management Review* (January, 1994), p. 63. The International Benchmarking Clearinghouse is a service of the American Productivity & Quality Center.

[12]*Ibid.*

[13]Julia Lawlor, "Cuts Don't Spare Middle Managers," *USA Today* (October 21, 1993), p. B1.

[14]Ceel Pasternak, "Keep Middle Managers," *HR Magazine* (September, 1993), p. 28.

[15]Robert B. Reich, "Companies Are Cutting Their Hearts Out," *The New York Times Magazine* (December 19, 1993), p. 54.

2. Fewer than half the downsized firms said profits increased after the cuts were made, and a quarter said they went down.
3. Most companies paid a heavy price in worker morale.
4. The more often a company downsized, the worse the aftereffects.
5. Community relations suffered, though customer relations and product quality tended to improve.[16]

With white-collar layoffs having become a way of life for corporate America, some view the concept of *rightsizing* as a remedy to the downsizing dilemma. Here, recognizing that the employment relationship between workers and their employers is changing *fundamentally*, managers and employees alike are called upon to take a more holistic, intuitive, and humanistic approach to the management of human resources.[17] This approach includes: eliminating "by the numbers" cost cutting; rebuilding employee loyalty; producing superior products and services; shaping employment strategies to coincide with workplace trends; and approaching problems from the employees' perspective and building a more flexible, human-centered workforce.

Re-engineering

In the preceding chapter, we saw how business processes are analyzed and studied to redesign the processes and then implement new processes—an approach known as *re-engineering*. For example, at IBM Credit, management cut the credit approval process from six days to 90 minutes—simply by having one employee handle each financing request from beginning to end, rather than handing off a segment of the work from department to department.[18] It is presumed that, by using tools such as flowcharting and work process mapping to streamline the processes, the firm can

produce a lower-cost product or service and increase its quality. As a result, the firm will be able to gain a competitive advantage. However, to assure competitive advantage over the long term, re-engineering should be done on a repeated basis. That is, the company should position itself to change its processes quickly whenever there is an advantage in doing so.[19]

Employee Participation on Work Teams

Total quality management involves employee participation and empowerment on different kinds of teams. For example, a *total quality* team may include a cross section of members representing some part of the information-gathering process under study: those who work within the process, the suppliers of services and materials brought into the process, and the beneficiaries of the process—the customers. Or, an *interdisciplinary* team may be set up to tackle specific tasks as part of the firm's re-engineering. Still another form is the *cross-functional* team formed along functional lines such as marketing, finance, and engineering. Here, the team's objective may be to develop ideas for new products across all of the company's product lines. Then there is the *self-managed*, or *self-directed*, team, which, to a greater or lesser extent, performs roles and makes decisions traditionally reserved for management. Functions commonly performed by self-managed teams include: setting work schedules, dealing directly with external customers, setting production quotas and performance targets, training, purchasing equipment or services, dealing with vendors and suppliers, conducting performance appraisals, and budgeting.

As indicated in Chapter 2, employers should use caution when forming teams intended to deal with workplace issues, such as productivity improvement and competitiveness. There, it was noted that the National Labor Relations Board ruled that work teams in a nonunion company constituted an attempt to negotiate wages and working conditions with workers, which made the teams illegal. However, the overall effect of

[16]"Trends," *Compensation & Benefits Review* (March–April, 1993), p. 13.

[17]Charles F. Hendricks, *The Rightsizing Remedy: How Managers Can Respond to the Downsizing Dilemma* (Homewood, IL: Business One Irwin, 1992), p. 6.

[18]"The Future of Middle Managers," *Management Review* (September, 1993), p. 51.

[19]Daniel Morris and Joel Brandon, *Re-Engineering Your Business* (New York: McGraw-Hill, Inc., 1993), p. 5.

DIALOG FROM THE WORKPLACE

LYNN ANN LEW

Vice President, Payroll, and principal of ACE Services and California Comprehensive Employees' Services, West Coast employee leasing companies

Lynn's payroll career began as a payroll technician for Beaver Insurance Company. From that beginning she held payroll management positions with Pacific Stock Exchange, Tropicana Products, Inc., Action Staffing, Inc., and served as client liaison for ODIN, Inc., and Systems Tax Services, Inc. Lynn is a lecturer and guest speaker for the American Payroll Association (APA) and has served as a director for that association. She is an enthused teacher and prolific writer, having contributed many articles to the APA's monthly magazine, *PaytecH,* and Commerce Clearing House.

Lynn is the APA's first woman recipient of the Special Recognition Award for her exemplary contribution toward promoting the importance of the payroll professional to the business world. Lynn was further honored by her peers as the 1994 Payroll Woman of the Year.

QUESTION: What are the advantages and disadvantages to a company that outsources its payroll tax filing to a service bureau?

RESPONSE: The advantages include:
- The service bureau keeps up to date and abreast of the ever-changing tax rules and regulations.
- The service deposits and files all payroll tax-related returns. Some bureaus prepare the returns and send them to their clients for review, signature, and mailing. Other bureaus provide clients with a statement and copies of the filed returns.
- The client-company is assigned a customer service representative (CSR) who handles the account daily.
- Amended returns may be prepared by the service bureau, if required.
- Some bureaus allow clients to review their accounts online.
- Some service bureaus have the capability of receiving and processing clients' payroll data via modem.
- Most services will provide clients with magnetic tape specifications for their computer mainframe. Clients download their quarterly/annual tax data directly to the bureau, which generates wage lists and tax returns.
- If the bureau provides payroll tax services, they will prepare, balance, and reconcile annually filed forms such as federal Forms W-2 and 940 and state annual reconciliation forms.
- If any mistakes or missed deadlines are the fault of the tax service bureau, penalties are paid by the bureau, not by the client-company.

Some disadvantages are:
- Service bureaus process the tax filings and deposits by the most effective means available (magnetic tape). In order to meet the magnetic tape specifications, the ID number formats may be changed, which can generate agency inquiries for mismatched numbers.
- Change in pay periods (e.g., weekly to biweekly) may change the tax filing frequency, which may generate inquiries.
- If the client uses a standalone tax filing service, two wage lists must be provided—one for the completed return and one for the files.
- Using a tax service bureau may not be the right choice for all companies. Some firms wish to maintain complete confidentiality and control *all* payroll data.
- The client-company may have to compromise its "float" dollars. However, current tax laws have shortened the lag periods, thus reducing the float available.

Illustration 22–4 Many organizations look upon their self-directed teams as crucial to becoming more flexible, quality conscious, and competitive.

the National Labor Relations Board's ruling appears to be minimal for companies having quality circles, work process teams, and other employee involvement programs. To provide a "safe" method of employee participation, the employee group should fall within one of the following areas:

1. An employer/employee communications program that is compatible with the National Labor Relations Act.
2. Employee groups that set their own goals and regulate themselves.
3. Teams implemented as part of a job enrichment program.
4. Groups in which managerial functions, such as grievance resolutions, are delegated.[20]

---

[20]Bob Smith, "Employee Committee or Labor Union?" *Management Review* (April, 1993), p. 57.

Outsourcing

To cut costs in their competitive struggle and to conduct business with smaller staffs as a result of downsizing, many firms turn to *outsourcing*—using an outside vendor to handle in-house tasks or services such as mailroom management, payroll accounting, benefits administration, data processing, legal services, computer operations, telecommunications, and temporary staffing. In the *Dialog from the Workplace,* Lynn Ann Lew, a Certified Payroll Professional, discusses the pros and cons of outsourcing the task of payroll tax filing. Additional examples of outsourcing are given in the next chapter.

Quality Circles

Another example of employee involvement on work teams is the **quality circle**—a group of workers who voluntarily meet together to identify, analyze, and solve job-related quality problems and to develop employee potential.[21] The proposed solutions, designed to lead to cost reduction and increased productivity, are submitted to management for adoption or rejection. Quality circles were first introduced into manufacturing operations, but the concept grew to include other areas such as engineering, research and development, and clerical support.

The number of members in a quality circle varies from 3 to 15, with an ideal size being 7 or 8. The members of a circle should be from the same work area or do similar work so that the problems they select will be familiar to all of them. The quality circle teams must be allowed to meet regularly on company-paid time. To help focus the activity of the quality circle, each group has a leader, who may be a supervisor or a person selected by the group. The leader, a key person in each circle, helps keep the team "on course" and acts as spokesperson for the group. Quality circle members should be trained in statistical methods, group dynamics, and problem-solving techniques. The members should be permitted to choose the problems they will tackle and, where possible, become involved by implementing the solutions and monitoring the results. To do so, of course, management must share with the circle members all the information they need.

Working with each group is a *facilitator,* or *coordinator,* a company employee who serves as a consultant to a number of circles. When a solution to a problem has been developed by the circle, the facilitator arranges to have the solution considered by the appropriate managers and takes part in installing acceptable improvements. The facilitator may report to a steering committee or a senior manager with top-level responsibility for company programs.

---

[21]Quality circles were conceived in Japan in 1961, where they are known as *quality control circles.* Under the leadership of Dr. Kaoru Ishikawa, the theories of behavioral scientists such as Maslow, Herzberg, and McGregor were tied together with the statistical quality control practices advanced by Deming, Juran, and other practitioners of productivity improvement. Quality circles are sometimes called *quality-of-worklife programs, self-managed work teams, problem-solving committees,* or *labor-management steering committees.*

In Chapter 3 we described the *nominal group technique,* which is a variation of the quality circle and brainstorming techniques. The nominal group technique is distinguished from the quality circle in that the participants work alone in small *noninteraction* groups, where they silently generate ideas. Next, the ideas are presented and discussed, priorities are established, and a decision is made.

Time Management

As we have seen, the productivity of managers and supervisors cannot be measured by traditional methods such as motion and time study and the setting of production standards. Many managerial functions require weeks or months to complete, with the full effect of the work not being felt for years, if at all. Thus, measurements that are limited by the element of time do not apply well to the work of managers and supervisors. However, the element of time and how that time is spent are very important considerations in developing yardsticks to measure managerial productivity. As discussed in the following paragraphs, there is need for all office employees, but especially managers and supervisors, to develop effective time management programs.

The need for an effective time management program becomes clear when AOMs and supervisors answer the following questions:

1. Do I never seem to get everything done that I had hoped to accomplish? As a result, am I being placed under too much stress?
2. Is my desk cluttered with papers that I constantly reshuffle but never take care of?
3. When making a decision, do I usually have incomplete information?
4. Do the meetings that I schedule to last an hour go on for two hours or more?
5. Do I often work overtime at the office?
6. Do I frequently take work home over the weekend?
7. Am I continually being interrupted by telephone calls, visitors, employees who monopolize my time, and coworkers who want to socialize?
8. By failing to delegate, do I spend most of my time on trivial items, with not enough time left over to tackle the big jobs?

Managers who answer "Yes" to all or most of the questions above probably spend the bulk of their time on projects that produce only minimal benefits. In order to obtain the most out of their working hours, these managers must realize that they may be the chief cause of their own time problems.

The aim of time management is to provide for efficient use of all resources, including time, so that individuals become productive in achieving their important professional and personal goals. Therefore, managers must break their old, inefficient habits and establish new routines to overcome the stumbling blocks to time management.

Using a Time Log[22]

A common technique for determining how much time is used on various tasks throughout the workday is to keep a time log, such as that shown in Figure 22–1, page 609. In the log we record what we have done during stated time intervals, such as every 15 to 20 minutes. After we have listed the activities for several days, we should have a sufficient number of typical observations for analysis. Next, we analyze the time log to determine what could have been done to make better use of our available time. In analyzing the time log, we should answer questions such as these:

1. What are the major activities or events that cause me to use my time ineffectively?
2. Which of these tasks can be performed by me only?
3. What activities can be delegated, better controlled, or eliminated?

Analyzing Time Wasters

After we have developed a list of the time wasters, we can pinpoint those activities that require change or elimination. Some of the most common time wasters appear in the eight questions raised at the beginning of this section.

As a result of analyzing time wasters, we may find that we are spending 80 percent of our time on items that produce only 20 percent of the real benefit. Getting bogged down on low-value activities could be the reason for our inability to do important tasks. Low-value items are generally easy to do and give a sense of accomplishment, but they are often time consuming.

Time wasters may be *internally* generated by ourselves or *externally* created by events or other people. Internally generated time wasters (procrastination, failure to delegate, failure to set priorities, and failure to plan) are the easier ones to resolve because they stem from our own actions or inactions. Thus, we, who are part of the problem, can become part of the solution. Time problems that are externally generated (telephone and FAX interruptions, meetings, visitors, and socializing), however, require more imagination and creativity because they are not totally within our control.

Office managers may find that they are grossly overpaid for some of the tasks they perform. Some people become so involved in work that they lose sight of why they are doing it and how much it really costs. The cost of performing each of the tasks listed in the manager's log should be determined. Thus, managers will find that doing certain tasks themselves simply is not worth the cost. For example, sitting in front of a PC to input one's own correspondence may not be a very efficient use of a manager's time. This does not mean that the task is not important, but rather, that some tasks are worth doing only if done by lower-paid individuals.

Setting Goals and Listing Priorities

Having analyzed time wasters, we may find we have failed to make the best use of our time because we lack specific goals. We may become easily sidetracked and waste time due to a lack of direction and focus. To determine what we really want to accomplish, we must set short- and long-range goals and allocate specific blocks of time to each. We should put the goals in writing and review them frequently by ourselves as well as with our immediate supervisors.

To make these goals operational, we can use a daily "to-do" list. We should begin each workday

---

[22]The remaining parts of this section are adapted from H. Kent Baker, *Techniques of Time Management,* Management Aid 239, U.S. Small Business Administration.

with a plan of the tasks to be performed and the priority of each task. In budgeting our time, we should allocate part of each day to those tasks that will lead to the accomplishment of our goals. Thus, by blocking out part of the day or week for major projects, we are assured of having time to do the important tasks.

Using Time Productively

Ten useful tips on effective time management follow.

1. *Consolidate similar tasks.* This step aids in minimizing interruptions and economizes on the use of resources and efforts. For example, instead of placing calls sporadically throughout the day, combine and make outgoing calls at specific times each day. Also, inform frequent callers of the best time to reach us directly rather than leave messages in our E-mailbox. Thus, callers can be helped to develop a habit of calling when we prefer, not when the callers prefer.

2. *Tackle tough jobs first.* We have a tendency to work on the less difficult tasks first with the idea of working up to bigger projects. What often happens, however, is that the tough jobs simply do not get done because we spend too much time doing the less important tasks. By the time the tough jobs are ready to be tackled, we are too tired to work on them. The solution is to reverse the process. Start the day with the important work when the energy level is high; then work down the list of priorities. If time is available at the end of the day, the "low-value" items can be completed.

3. *Delegate work and develop others.* Try to break the "do-it-yourself" habit. Delegate work whenever possible. Delegation does not mean "dumping" a task on someone else. Rather, delegating carries with it the responsibility of making sure that the individual has the requisite skills and knowledge to do the job. The time we devote to training and motivating people to do tasks that customarily we perform will reduce our own time burdens in the future and enrich the jobs of others.

    For example, we can give more work to our secretary or executive assistant, if we have one. A secretary can perform many tasks that are great time savers, such as screening visitors and telephone calls, composing letters, and anticipating problems before they arise.

4. *Learn to use idle time.* Always try to maintain a list of tasks to do during idle periods. Instead of doing nothing while waiting for an appointment, we can read an article, review a report, or catch up on correspondence. Travel time can also be converted into useful time. For instance, if we have always wanted to take a management improvement course but could not find time during our workday, we can listen to tapes on the way to and from work.

5. *Get control of the paper flow.* To help stem the flood of paperwork, decide what can be streamlined or eliminated. Throw out junk mail, cancel unused subscriptions, and have mail routed directly to subordinates. If possible, handle each piece of paper once and do not pick up a piece of paper unless there is a plan to do something with it. For example, a complaint does not go away simply because the letter has been put aside; so, move the paperwork along to the appropriate person instead of letting it stack up on the desk. Being a paper shuffler wastes time and leads to inefficiencies.

6. *Avoid the cluttered-desk syndrome.* If our desk is piled with paper and we waste time looking for buried items, we should clear the desk of everything except the work to be done during the day.

7. *Get started immediately on important tasks.* Putting things off until tomorrow is easy. Like most people, we generally do the things we enjoy first and procrastinate on the tasks we dislike. Here is where we need self-discipline to overcome that procrastination. First, rather than put off doing a job because it seems overwhelming, poke holes in the task by breaking it down into bite-sized pieces that are more palatable to digest. By following this "Swiss cheese" technique, we will soon find that poking holes in the project makes it less overwhelming. Second, unfinished work is more of a motivator than un-

started work. By having started a job, we have made an investment of our time and are more likely to complete the task.

8. *Reduce meeting time.* No doubt, many meetings should not take place. Sometimes the only reason for a weekly staff meeting is because a week has passed since the last one. Such meetings disrupt work. Reduce the number and improve the quality of meetings by following an agenda; it saves time and money. If needed meetings are too long, schedule them to precede immediately the lunch hour or quitting time. Thus, most people will be motivated to end the meeting promptly. Also, a stand-up meeting helps to guarantee a short meeting.

9. *Take time to plan.* Sometimes we may be heard saying, "I just don't have the time to plan." No doubt we are very busy but not very effective. Although it appears to be a contradiction, by taking time to plan, we end up saving time. Instead of spending the day "fighting fires," we should develop a schedule for doing the things that must be done in the available time.

10. *Learn to say "no."* Someone is always asking us for a piece of our time. Instead of being honest and saying "no" to requests, we often tend to hedge and end up accepting responsibilities that are neither wanted nor for which we have time to perform. Saying "no" requires some courage and tact, but it is necessary for effective time management.

By applying the 10 tips listed above, we can use our time far more productively. This in turn will help us cope with overly stressful situations that place undue physical or psychological demands on us. Along with interpersonal problems, either at home or at work, time management problems have been identified as a major source of stress. By adopting time management strategies, we can learn to control the sources of stress more effectively. Also, for our own increased effectiveness and personal well-being, we should work toward identifying those personal and organizational goals that will provide balance in our daily lives.

SUMMARY

1. The organization that designs an effective program of measuring work and setting standards can determine more precisely the true cost of performing many kinds of administrative services and thus budget more realistically the firm's needs for resources.

2. An ongoing program of work measurement contributes directly toward improving office productivity by effectively controlling the scheduling of work, providing realistic performance goals for employee appraisal, compensating employees according to their productivity, developing cost and volume information for use in feasibility studies, providing interdepartment cost comparisons to use in diagnosing wasteful practices, and indicating when employees are sufficiently trained for entry onto their jobs or for assignment to new positions.

3. Work whose content is repetitive, consistent, countable, and sufficient in volume can be measured, and standards for such work can be set. The methods to measure this kind of work include historical data, time log, work sampling, motion and time study, and predetermined times. Techniques are also available for measuring some types of nonroutine office work in the aggregate.

4. For the organization that accepts the improvement of office productivity as part of its philosophy, many strategies are followed for improving the quality of its products, services, and life using all available human and capital resources. Some aspects of total quality management include continuous improvement, benchmarking, downsizing, re-engineering, employee participation on work teams such as quality circles, and outsourcing.

c
o
n
t

5. Regardless of the strategy employed by an organization in managing its productivity improvement program, there is need for all personnel, and in particular supervisors and managers, to use more effectively all of their resources, including time. Only through the effective use of their resources can all office employees attain their important professional and personal goals and thereby maximize office productivity.

FOR YOUR REVIEW

1. Describe the kinds of office activities for which work standards are most commonly established.

2. What benefits are available to an organization that establishes a program of work standards?

3. Why are formal programs of work measurement not commonly undertaken in many of today's offices?

4. What criteria are used to determine if office tasks are capable of being measured?

5. What role do supervisors play in administering a work measurement program?

6. What are the limitations of the historical data method when used to measure work?

7. How do office employees use the time log method when measuring their work?

8. What is the underlying premise upon which work sampling is based? In determining the proper sample size to be used in work sampling, what factors should be considered?

9. A work sampling study is planned with the following specifications: 15 percent tolerance, 9 percent critical percentage, and 95 percent reliability. To meet the requirements of this study, how many observations must be made?

10. What are the disadvantages of using work sampling to set standards?

11. How does motion study differ from time study?

12. Why must the actual time required by a worker to complete operational elements be leveled?

13. Compare the advantages and disadvantages of using predetermined times in setting standards for office work.

14. What role does benchmarking play in a firm's total quality management program?

15. What is the relationship between downsizing and re-engineering to the improvement of office productivity?

16. What is the objective of a time management program?

FOR YOUR DISCUSSION

1. Some large organizations are becoming concerned about how much time computer games are costing them in lost productivity. A director of information services remarked, "The PC is for productivity. If you let people play games on them, you may as well let them insert a TV-reception board so they can watch *The Beverly Hillbillies*.[23] How can the AOM control the hours wasted by office workers who play computer games? Is there any rationale for the AOM to promote game-playing?

2. Explain how the 72-stroke par for an 18-hole golf course serves as an excellent example of a standard.

3. Assuming that you accept the premise that creative work *does* occur in the office, can there be any measurements for creative work?

4. During the past decade, companies spent $860 billion on information technology and got only half a point of productivity growth each year. "This is a horrible result for all the money spent," commented one economist. Yet, this person sees a reversal of complacency and finds that managers are finally getting their long overdue payback from computing.[24] How do you explain that computers are finally improving productivity?

5. After having set up four quality circles at the Top-Line Paper Company, the manager of office services, Pierre Morneau, has been able to document a savings of 9 percent in administrative costs. At the last weekly meeting of Quality Circle 4, the following questions were raised by several of the members:

   a. How will the 9 percent financial gain that resulted from our greater productivity be shared?

   b. Since we have been in operation for three years, we feel that our group has dealt with at least 95 percent of the obvious problems. What do we do now at our weekly meetings?

   As the facilitator for the company's quality circles, how would you answer these two questions?

6. Harriette Blackfoot, accounting manager for the Tempe Company, was recently asked how many errors she accepts from the accountants she supervises. Right to the point, Blackfoot stated, "We don't permit any errors." Do you conclude from her reply that the performance standard for the error rate of accounts is zero? Explain.

7. The time study analyst at Garzuela, Inc., measured the posting work in the accounts receivable department and arrived at a standard of 100 postings per hour. This standard was announced to the supervisor of the accounts receivable department and then in a separate memo to the posting clerks. Shortly thereafter, a confusing and panicky situation arose, which resulted in more errors, morale problems, and less work done than before.
   Assuming that the output of 100 postings per hour is feasible and accurate, discuss the use of this standard and the analyst's method of presenting it to the supervisor and employees.

---

[23]"The Games People Play in the Office," *Time* (October 11, 1993), p. 40.
[24]William M. Bulkeley, "Computers Start to Lift U.S. Productivity," *The Wall Street Journal* (March 1, 1993), p. B8.

CASES FOR CRITICAL THINKING

Case 22–1 Surviving Downsizing

This week the Piedmont Insurance Company has just undertaken phase 2 of its quality improvement program and passed out 113 pink slips notifying workers of their layoff. Toni Espinosa, a middle manager in the actuary department, is talking with three of his workers, who offer these bleak comments:

"Well, my day is coming. After last month's cutback of 80 and this month's 113, I know my days are limited. I'll be glad to get out of this hell-hole—I can't stand any more of this waiting around to get the bad news."

"I'm still here—at least until the next load is carted out. But I've lost all confidence in this company and its top brass. Talk about insecurity—I am its No. 1 candidate! But I guess I should be fortunate just to have a job."

"I've been trying to adjust after last month's cutback. But working with these new faces and trying to do the work of three are giving me bleeding ulcers. No wonder I'm popping all of these pills! I never knew stress like this!"

Typical comments of downsizing survivors? Mild, to say the least. But let's back up in time prior to Piedmont's decision to inaugurate its quality improvement program. What steps should the company have taken to ward off the employees' feelings of insecurity and lack of confidence and to alleviate undue stress? Now, in the midst of downsizing, what can the firm do to recommit its employees?

Case 22–2 Overcoming Resistance to Time and Motion Study

Barry d'Arcy, director of administrative services for Steiger Controls, has just examined the results of the company's semiannual employee attitude survey. The survey results confirm many of the comments that d'Arcy has heard via the grapevine—too many inequities in the salaries paid newly employed workers and those with years of seniority, and very little relationship between output and salaries earned.

d'Arcy firmly believes that if a time and motion study were undertaken, meaningful standards could be set for many of the office tasks. However, before drafting his recommendations for a time and motion study, he has decided "to kick it around" with several employees. Here is a little of his conversation with Ruth Olsen, supervisor of the computer center:

d'Arcy: Your data-entry people are "naturals" for a time and motion study. And you know, Ruth, they yell the loudest about their salaries.

Olsen: That's true, Barry; they do gripe a lot—I'll grant you that. But just look at the kind of work they do—you can't measure it! They jump around during the day from purchase orders to sales invoices to purchase invoices to time cards. There's just too much variety in their daily work to think about setting standards that will make sense. I'm sorry, Barry, but this time I just can't "buy" your thinking.

Then d'Arcy talks with Rose Juarez and Harry Epstein, two of the data-entry personnel:

d'Arcy: Well, there you have the gist of how a time and motion study will help you in ironing out the salary problems you have described.

Juarez: All of that sounds good in theory. But I don't want anyone standing over me, breathing down my neck while I work. Besides, all those analysts do is try to speed us up so we can grind out more strokes.

Epstein: That's right, Barry. I heard that after they did a study at Sterling's down the street, seven of their workers were let go. You know very well that's what's going to happen here, and I don't want to be one of them out pounding the pavement. Isn't there some other way you can "clean up" this lousy salary structure so we'll be paid for what we produce? You know, I've been with the company for 19 years, and never before have I heard anyone talk about needing a time study.

Prepare a report in which you:

1. Outline the approach you would follow in working with Olsen, the supervisor of the computer center.
2. Include all possible points and factors that will convince Olsen and her workers that the time and motion study will bring favorable results not only to the company but also to them.

Case 22–3 Unit Time: Computer Option (available on disk)

BUDGETING ADMINISTRATIVE EXPENSES

GOALS FOR THIS CHAPTER

After completing this chapter, you should be able to:

1. List the objectives that management seeks to attain through the use of budgets and budget performance reports.
2. Identify the principles that guide administrative office managers in preparing budgets of administrative expenses.
3. Discuss the different kinds of costs to be considered when formulating a budget of administrative expenses.
4. Distinguish between incremental budgeting, zero-base budgeting, and compromise budgeting.
5. Describe the role of budget performance reporting in a program of budgetary control.
6. Discuss the contribution made by a work standards program to the analysis of administrative expenses.
7. Describe alternate methods for controlling fluctuations in the volume of office work.

To conduct business operations efficiently, managers must *plan* how the resources of their organization will be acquired and used. Also, they must *control* the acquisition and use of these resources. To obtain financial information quickly about these two very important activities—*planning and controlling*—management relies upon budgeting.

Budgeting is the process of planning future business activities and expressing those plans in a formal manner. The carefully prepared formal statement of plans for the future, expressed in financial terms, is called a **budget.**

We may develop budgets for a short period of time such as a month, a quarter, or a year. In most companies, however, the budget period is one year in length. We often divide the annual budget into quarterly or monthly budgets so that managers and supervisors are able to evaluate performance and take corrective actions promptly over a relatively short period of time. On the other hand, we may find that other budgets are developed for a long time period such as three to five or ten years. Long-range budgets are important in planning major expenditures such as the purchase of buildings, machinery, and equipment. Both short-term and long-range budgets are vital to the organization's program of budgetary control.

Budgetary control, the theme of this chapter, refers to the use of a budget in regulating and guiding those business activities concerned with acquiring and using resources. These activities may relate to developing new products, expanding or contracting product lines, increasing revenues, or decreasing operating expenses. In the *Dialog from the Workplace,* William P. Englesbe, a vice president in charge of corporate purchasing and environmental affairs, describes the role he plays in his firm's program of budgetary control.

Of great importance in budgetary control is the preparation of periodic **budget performance reports** that compare the actual operating data with the budgeted data. For example, we can compare

DIALOG FROM THE WORKPLACE

WILLIAM P. ENGLESBE

Vice President
Corporate Purchasing and
Environmental Affairs
Wheaton Industries, Inc.
Millville, New Jersey

Wheaton Industries is a $500 million worldwide manufacturer of glass, plastic, rubber, and aluminum seal packaging. It has 4,000 employees and is a privately owned company.

William P. Englesbe received his B.S. in finance from the Wharton School, University of Pennsylvania. Prior to assuming his post with Wheaton, Mr. Englesbe served as the director of corporate purchasing for The West Company, Phoenixville, Pennsylvania, and as senior purchasing agent for Rohm & Haas Company, Philadelphia.

QUESTION: What role do you, as vice president of corporate purchasing and environmental affairs, play in your company's program of budgetary control?

RESPONSE: Purchasing has three business areas of responsibility where budgets are useful tools in the decision-making process. These areas are (1) raw materials and components, (2) capital expenditures, and (3) manufacturing, repairs, and operational (MRO) supplies. The nature of the enterprise (manufacturing, distribution, service, etc.) influences the degree of sophistication required in each budget area. For our purposes here, we shall examine the latter two areas—capital expenditures and MRO supplies.

Capital Expenditures. The decision to spend capital funds is made by senior management after input from various groups within the organization. Sales, marketing, engineering, research and development, accounting, finance, and purchasing should all contribute to capital expansion decisions.

Purchasing is the primary source for creating estimated expenditures for any capital project. Once the project is begun, the actual costs will be compared to the estimated costs because management wants to know how well, or how poorly, the project compares to its stated goals. The accounting department is responsible for providing these comparative data; however, it is in purchasing's best interest to provide accurate data during the early budget process. The true test of these data will come when a capital project is approved and purchasing must then provide the labor, equipment, machinery, and materials at prices comparable to their estimates.

MRO Supplies. Budgeting for MRO and supply items can be as simple or sophisticated as a company wants. Many organizations, especially manufacturing or assembly-type operations, budget these costs as a factor of labor hours, machine hours, or some other easily reportable component of the level of business activity.

Organizations that operate centralized storerooms produce annual budgets for the items they inventory and for items that might not warrant inventorying, but which are purchased through the storeroom's purchasing programs.

Annually, purchasing publishes a storeroom components budgeted costs list for distribution to the departments drawing from the storeroom. Each operating department draws on this information to create its annual operating budget.

Purchasing must routinely compare its actual costs to its budgeted costs to identify changes as they occur. These data are distributed regularly to the storeroom's customers.

COMMENT: Budgets are snapshots of estimates of the future. They should be used for comparisons to actual events and should evoke legitimate questions and answers when significant differences occur.

the $15,000 revenue earned from the sales of Product A during April with the $20,000 sales volume budgeted for April. As a result of this comparison, we can identify and explain the causes of any significant **variance,** or difference, between actual operating data and budgeted data. In our example of Product A sales, we might conclude that the $5,000 variance between actual sales and budgeted sales seemed to be caused by a lack of sales promotion in April. As a result, we may plan to advertise Product A more intensively in May.

By means of budgets and budget performance reports, management tries to attain the following objectives:

1. *To establish procedures for planning and studying future revenues and expenses* so the organization's budget may be reviewed and modified when needed.
2. *To coordinate the activities of the various departments of the organization* so that individual department heads become more aware of the financial problems of others on the management team.
3. *To build a basis for administrative control* by providing managers with factual measures of performance that they helped to develop and for which they are held responsible.
4. *To communicate formally the plans that have been approved by management* and the actions that management wishes the organization to take during the budget period.
5. *To motivate all individuals by creating a climate of cost consciousness* in which they are stimulated to reach desired performance levels.

In the following section, we describe the role of the administrative office manager in achieving these objectives of budgetary control. As you will see, the responsibilities of AOMs vary among business organizations.

THE AOM'S ROLE IN BUDGETARY CONTROL

In Chapter 1, we pointed out that the differences in responsibilities assigned to AOMs are due to several factors, the most important of which is

the size of the organization. In small and medium-size firms, the AOM may be an accountant who, in addition to regularly assigned duties, has responsibility for all administrative services. In large companies, the person responsible for administrative services may be a top-level executive such as a controller or a vice president. As the head of administrative services in an organization, the AOM has responsibility for the support services described earlier in this textbook.

The reports prepared by (or for) the AOM typically include the following:

1. *Budgeted expense reports for the various administrative services.* The estimated expense reports are usually supported by detailed schedules of costs, which in large organizations may be prepared by first-line supervisors.
2. *Budget performance reports.* These department reports show in detail the actual costs incurred compared with the budgeted figures, the amount or percentage of variance, and explanations of significant variances.
3. *Analytical reports.* These reports show an analysis of the total costs in each department. For example, the supervisor of text/word processing services may prepare reports showing unit costs such as the cost per page or the cost per line of each letter produced.
4. *Special reports.* Most special reports document studies that are prepared at the request of a company officer or initiated by the AOM to improve some phase of the information management function. For example, a report may be prepared to compare the costs of a desktop dictation-transcription system versus a central recorder system.

The accountant in the small or medium-size firm, assisted by department heads or supervisors, may prepare the operating budget for general and administrative expenses. In a like fashion, those in charge of the selling and purchasing functions prepare operating budgets. The individual budgets are then submitted to the people whose job is to study and consolidate all the budgets into one master budget of operating expenses for the entire company.

In large organizations, the executive in charge of administrative services receives reports of budgeted expenses from department heads, such as those in charge of records management, word processing, mailing, and accounting. The administrator analyzes these reports, consolidates and condenses them into one budget covering all the information management expenses, and submits the final budget to the budget committee.

The Budget Committee

The *budget committee* may consist of the budget director and other executives such as the controller, treasurer, production manager, sales manager, and possibly the AOM. After receiving all the various estimates of income and expenses, the budget committee reviews and revises, if necessary, the dollar amounts. If a department head submits estimates that do not accurately relate to the goals of the company, the budget committee usually returns the estimates to the department head with recommendations for change. The originating department then either alters or justifies the amounts first submitted. After agreement has been reached, the figures are finally assembled and consolidated to form the master budget.

The Master Budget

The **master budget** consists of a number of budgets that collectively express the planned activities of the organization. The number and arrangement of the individual budgets included in the master budget depend upon the size and complexity of the organization. The individual budgets typically found in a master budget are listed in Figure 23–1.

Some of the budgets listed in this figure cannot be prepared until other budgets have first been completed. For example, in a retail merchandising company, the buyers and other retail personnel cannot prepare the merchandise purchases budget until the sales budget has been completed. The number of units to be sold must be forecast before the buyers can estimate the number of units to be purchased. Thus, the sales department prepares its budget first since the remaining budgets depend upon the information contained in the sales budget.

In preparing the sales budget for a manufacturing company, the sales department or division estimates the quantity of goods to be sold and the revenue to be derived from those sales. After the sales division has prepared the company's sales budget, the other divisions prepare their operating budgets. The production division prepares its budget before the manufacturing budget is developed since the number of units to be manufactured is affected by the amount of material, labor, and overhead to be budgeted. Generally, after the production budget has been prepared, we find that the budgets for manufacturing costs or merchandise costs, selling expenses, and general and administrative expenses may be prepared in any sequence.

The Flexible Budget

The master budget is based upon *the one most likely level of activity that will take place*. Also, the master budget is prepared *before* any activity occurs. However, we often find that many companies prepare one or more **flexible budgets,** which are a prediction of costs at *various levels of activity*. We may prepare a flexible budget *before* the time period begins and indicate what the predicted costs will be for different levels of future activity. In this way, the flexible budgeting process aids managers in their planning for that time period. Having developed flexible budgets shows that managers have done some contingency planning and know what steps should be taken when performance begins to fall short of expectations. On the other hand, we may prepare a flexible budget *after* the period has ended and the actual activity is known. In this case, the flexible budget shows the costs that we might have expected for the actual production.

Let us say that the King Company's master budget shows an estimated output of 20,000 units for April. However, a flexible budget showing the *estimated* costs for output above and below 20,000 units might be useful. For example, the company may wish to know how an output of 15,000 or 25,000 units would affect the items listed on its budgeted income statement and balance sheet.

Figure 23–1
Contents of a
Typical Mas-
ter Budget

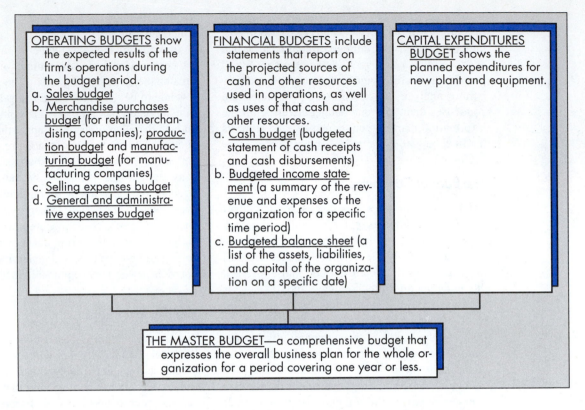

OPERATING BUDGETS show the expected results of the firm's operations during the budget period.
a. Sales budget
b. Merchandise purchases budget (for retail merchandising companies); production budget and manufacturing budget (for manufacturing companies)
c. Selling expenses budget
d. General and administrative expenses budget

FINANCIAL BUDGETS include statements that report on the projected sources of cash and other resources used in operations, as well as uses of that cash and other resources.
a. Cash budget (budgeted statement of cash receipts and cash disbursements)
b. Budgeted income statement (a summary of the revenue and expenses of the organization for a specific time period)
c. Budgeted balance sheet (a list of the assets, liabilities, and capital of the organization on a specific date)

CAPITAL EXPENDITURES BUDGET shows the planned expenditures for new plant and equipment.

THE MASTER BUDGET—a comprehensive budget that expresses the overall business plan for the whole organization for a period covering one year or less.

After April has ended and the *actual* output and costs are known, we can prepare another flexible budget to be used for the budget performance report. This flexible budget is based upon the actual output, say 21,500 units. In the budget performance report, we show the variance between the actual costs and the flexible budget amounts and thus indicate whether the output was produced efficiently.

Spreadsheets, discussed in Chapter 16, have taken much of the drudgery out of the budget development process, such as the preparation of flexible budgets. As we modify one set of numbers on the spreadsheet screen, other numbers that share a relationship with that set are automatically recalculated and displayed. Thus, with the ability of spreadsheets, we can create "what if" models to forecast how something will turn out in the future. For example, what if there is a 5 percent increase in sales revenue next year? How will that affect the amount of each operating expense appearing on the income statement?

PRINCIPLES OF PREPARING ADMINISTRATIVE EXPENSES BUDGETS

Of the budgets listed in Figure 23–1, the most important ones to the AOM are the operating budgets and more particularly the general and administrative expenses budget. **Administrative expenses** (or *general expenses*)[1] are those expenses incurred in the general operations of the organization. Examples of administrative expenses are office salaries and wages, depreciation of office furniture and equipment, and office supplies used. In medium-size and large firms, some expenses such as rent, insurance, and taxes are partly related to revenue-producing activities and partly related to administrative operations. Such *mixed expenses* may be divided between the two categories—selling expenses and administrative expenses. In small

---

[1]On income statements, the heading "General and Administrative Expenses" is often used to identify those expenses incurred in general operations.

businesses, however, mixed expenses are commonly reported as administrative expenses.

Well-prepared budgets of administrative expenses help AOMs and others plan and control operations and give them the financial information needed for decision making. Budgets aid in heading off emergencies; they also direct attention to unprofitable office services and provide a yardstick for measuring progress in all areas for which AOMs have responsibility. We should remember, however, that administrative expenses budgets are effective only in relation to the skill, understanding, and effort that have gone into their preparation. In preparing budgets of administrative expenses, AOMs should pay close attention to each of the following principles.

PRINCIPLE OF RESPONSIBILITY

Assign initial responsibility for preparing budgets to key employees at the operative level so that budgets flow upward from department heads to the AOM.

Beginning the budget-making process at the operative level (see Figure 2–6, page 36) develops cost consciousness among workers and a common understanding about the budgeting process. Having those who are close to the work participate in the budgeting process also aids in gaining acceptance of the plan, improves morale among employees, and assists in increasing productivity. Participating in the preparation of a budget becomes a form of job enrichment for workers and may serve as a motivator to improve job performance. If, on the other hand, the budget originates at the top-management level and is imposed on the departments from that level, the budget may have a negative impact on the attitudes of employees.

PRINCIPLE OF OBJECTIVITY

Be realistic when stating budgeted amounts and show as objectively as possible what each service department is capable of producing.

A sound budget is neither unduly optimistic nor pessimistic about future revenues and costs. Instead, the budget sets forth in an objective fashion

what each department is capable of producing along with a realistic statement of the costs to be incurred in producing that volume. We can use records from previous accounting periods as guides, but we should not be bound to the past, for cost factors and their interrelationships do not remain static. To ensure the development of objective, realistic budgets, some organizations use zero-base budgeting, which is discussed later in this chapter.

PRINCIPLE OF TARGET SETTING

Make sure that each budget shows specific targets.

In its long-range planning, an organization sets goals such as a 5 percent increase in the share of the market. After the goal has been set, it must be translated into projected sales dollars and the number of units to be produced to generate the anticipated volume of sales. Specific targets are then set for each department or for the entire office in order to achieve the company's goal. At the operative level, employee performance standards of the past should be reviewed and necessary adjustments made so that the performance of each department is geared to the newly established company goal. For example, a projected growth in sales volume may require that the supervisor of the order processing department modify the department budget to provide for the purchase of two computer terminals, the employment of two data-entry operators, and the additional allocation of 125 square feet of office space.

PRINCIPLE OF FLEXIBILITY

Provide sufficient flexibility in the budget so that in the event of emergencies, action may be taken quickly to adjust the estimates.

A flexible budget provides *safety valves*—measures that can be taken in case the company experiences emergencies such as a sharp reduction in revenue, a strike, or a sudden price-slashing move by competitors. The budget must not be so rigid that it stifles progress and prevents timely decision making. Although budget figures serve as standards, they should never become straitjackets. If, after a budget has been prepared, it is

Illustration 23–1 Workers at the operative level play a pivotal role in the initial stage of the budgetary process.

discovered that some targets cannot be realized or that they are impractical, the conflicts must be resolved. For example, the budget amounts will have to be changed to agree with the reality of a prolonged strike that has decreased by 20 percent the estimated annual production.

A common approach to budgeting, known as *tight but attainable,* is based upon better than average performance. Any unfavorable variances are critically reviewed since this approach usually includes allowances for less than ideal performance. The *ideal performance* approach to budgeting, on the other hand, presumes that nothing will go wrong in the company's operations; it allows for no alterations in schedules and contains no provisions for contingencies. Following another budgeting method, termed the *suicide approach,* top-level managers set a budget that is practically impossible to meet and push hard enough so that unfavorable variances are kept to a minimum. Often the impossible is accomplished, and the budget is met. However, when the suicide approach is followed, many department managers soon learn that the budget is an impossible goal and stop trying to achieve it.

PRINCIPLE OF ADHERENCE

Department managers, supervisors, and their workers must accept and adhere to the completed administrative expenses budget, as adjusted by the master budget.

How the budget is accepted and adhered to at each level depends upon the tone set by top management. If top-level managers are neutral or passive about budget making and "budget following," they cannot expect that department managers, supervisors, and their workers will be much concerned about attaining the planned goals.

PRINCIPLE OF REVIEW

Review the budget frequently in order to determine variances that can be corrected before the budget has lost its effectiveness.

Delay in comparing actual expenses with estimated expenses can be extremely costly. To overcome such delay, a program of reliable measurement and reporting of actual performance must be established. Computers are often used in budget performance reporting to spot favorable and unfavorable variances from the budget. Depending upon the individual company, variances of plus or minus 1 to 3 percent are normal. At the department level, managers should require written reports to explain significant deviations from the budget; at the operating level, employees may give oral explanations to their supervisors.

THE ADMINISTRATIVE EXPENSES BUDGET

The administrative expenses budget must be coordinated with the estimates of those who prepare budgets for other departments or cost centers. For example, the administrative expenses budget is directly related to the sales volume estimated by the sales department. Also, we find that management policies and economic ups and downs affect the estimates appearing on the administrative expenses budget. As indicated in the following discussion, we can control some of the costs that are incurred to earn revenue; on the other hand, we know that certain costs lie outside our control.

Some administrative expenses are directly traceable to the operations of a particular department. Other administrative expenses are incurred in order to meet the needs of several user-departments or the entire organization and are charged to the users on some basis. Therefore, we must analyze the nature and behavior of costs when preparing an administrative expenses budget.

Nature and Behavior of Costs

In planning and controlling administrative expenses, one of the most important considerations is an *analysis* of costs. This analysis is especially useful in setting production levels, in budgeting costs, in estimating costs for special projects, and in determining break-even points.

If we have properly planned administrative costs and they are being controlled, each person responsible for carrying on certain activities of the business is identified, and the controllable costs of those activities can be assigned to that person. Generally, responsibility assignments are made at the lowest supervisory level since the supervisor or department head nearest the action is in the best position to control costs at that level. For example, the supervisor or department head in charge of receiving and issuing office supplies

is assigned the responsibility for safeguarding this asset and monitoring its usage.

Through the design of the firm's accounting systems, internal control procedures aid the supervisor in protecting the firm's assets from theft, waste, and fraud. **Responsibility accounting**—one of these accounting systems—provides means for establishing control over costs and expenses. The accounting system is designed to record and accumulate costs so that timely reports can be made to managers and supervisors of those costs for which they are responsible. The ability to control costs and keep them within the budgeted range is then used as a basis for judging performance. In modern budgeting practice, it is widely held that managers should not be charged with those costs over which they have no control. Thus, an analysis of costs and their behavioral patterns must be undertaken. In such an analysis, costs are usually classified as fixed, variable, and semivariable.

Fixed Costs

Fixed costs, described in Chapter 15, are usually related to a time period and tend to remain unchanged when the volume of activity changes. As shown on the cost-volume graph in Figure 23–2, fixed costs do not respond to changes in the volume level. Therefore, fixed costs are represented

Figure 23–2
Graphic Representation of Variations in Cost Behavior

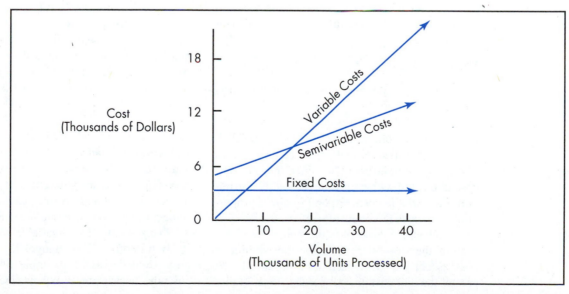

Illustration 23–2 Examples of the most controllable kind of costs—variable costs—includes the various supplies used in most offices.

by a horizontal line. Examples of fixed costs are the rent expense for office space and equipment, real estate taxes, property insurance, depreciation expense on buildings and equipment, and administrative and supervisory salaries. Over a period of time, the AOM has little or no control over fixed costs.

Variable Costs

The most important and most controllable costs are known as *variable costs.* As explained in Chapter 15, variable costs change in response to changes in the volume of activity. In Figure 23–2, you see that the variable cost pattern passes through the origin point "0" since there is zero cost associated with zero volume. In this illustration, the variable costs respond in direct proportion to changes in volume; therefore, the variable costs line slopes upward to the right. The steepness of the slope depends upon the amount of cost associated with each unit produced; the greater the unit cost, the steeper the slope. In Fig-

ure 23–2, where volume is measured in thousands of units processed, the total variable dollar cost is twice as great for 20,000 units as for 10,000 units.

Examples of variable office costs include direct materials such as stationery and supplies, equipment repair and maintenance expenses, and mailing expenses. To control variable costs, AOMs are continually striving to improve their administrative office systems and procedures.

Semivariable Costs

Another important group of controllable costs, the *semivariable,* or *mixed, costs,* contains both fixed and variable components. A semivariable cost increases or decreases with changes in activity. At the zero level of activity, the semivariable cost is some positive amount, as shown in Figure 23–2.

Changes in total semivariable costs are not directly proportional to changes in operating volume. Consider as an example of semivariable costs the electric power expense incurred in operating the computer center. If the center were closed for a period of time, the company would still be required to pay a minimum base fee for power. Then, when the center reopened, the cost of the electric power would increase as the processing of data increased. Another example of mixed costs is the *total* payment for office wages and salaries. Earlier we saw that the salaries paid administrators and supervisors are fixed costs since these salaries are paid regardless of the level of activity. However, the wages and salaries paid part-time workers and temporary service personnel tend to vary according to the volume of work to be completed.

Allocating Administrative Expenses

To analyze administrative expenses from a budgetary viewpoint, managers prepare department budgets of operating expenses. Some expenses, called **direct expenses,** originate in and are chargeable directly to one department. For example, the direct expenses of the reprographics department include the salaries of the workers and the depreciation expense of the machines and equipment used in that department. Other admin-

istrative expenses, known as **indirect expenses,** are general in nature and may benefit several departments or the entire company. Such indirect costs are not directly traceable to any one department and probably could not be eliminated if the operations of a specific department were terminated. Indirect expenses are often allocated or prorated among various user-departments. Several indirect expenses and their common bases of allocation are listed in Figure 23–3. When selecting an appropriate basis for allocating indirect expenses, the AOM must verify that a reasonable relationship exists between the expense and the selected basis.

To control the rapidly rising costs of administrative services, some companies use chargeback accounting systems as a means of directly allocating the costs of office services. In a **chargeback accounting system,** each department or cost center is charged for its actual usage of support services such as text/word processing, reprographics, graphic arts, office supplies, and computing. Included in the amount charged back to the user departments are salaries, supplies, machine expenses, and training costs.

To illustrate the operation of a chargeback accounting system, take a look at the offices of a util-

Figure 23–3
Indirect Expenses and Bases of Allocation

Indirect Expense	Basis of Allocation
1. Long-distance (toll) telephone services	1. Itemized charges for each user telephone as listed on the telephone bill.
2. Text/word processing	2. Cost-per-page or cost-per-line produced for each user department.
3. Rent or property taxes	3. Square feet of space used by department.
4. Office supplies	4. Items listed on requisitions filled for user department.
5. Filing	5. Number of documents, microforms, etc., filed and retrieved for each user.
6. Data processing in computer center	6. Terminal hours used.
7. Postage	7. Volume of outgoing mail for each user department.
8. Utilities	8. Number of kilowatt-hours of electricity or cubic feet of gas consumed by user department.

ity company. Here we find that every month each department manager receives a monthly accounting statement showing how much was spent by the department on office services. The charge for each work order, as determined by the office services division, depends upon the amount of time required to perform the service and the complexity of the work. The total amount charged each month is subtracted from the department's budget for office expenses, thus reminding each department head of the cost of such services.

Another example of cost allocation, which also provides effective cost control, is the *call accounting system.* This system provides managers and supervisors with information on *which* extension is calling *what* number *when,* thus making it easy to identify any telephone misuse. In a typical call accounting system, each user's handset is linked directly into the firm's telephone system. Here, a record is kept of every call made, including its length, cost, and destination. A computer collects and processes the call records from the telephone system, and a printer outputs daily, weekly, or monthly telephone reports. By means of exception reports, management is alerted to calls placed at odd times of day, to unusual area codes, or a large quantity of calls to the same number, which may highlight likely abuse.

Methods of Budgeting

After we have assigned responsibilities for planning and controlling administrative costs and identified their behavioral patterns, we must determine which method of budgeting will provide the best opportunities for control. In the following discussion, two of the many methods of budgeting are briefly described.[2] Because neither of these methods completely meets the needs of managers as they establish their programs of budgetary control, we shall also discuss a form of compromise budgeting.

_____
[2]Other budgeting methods, which are modifications of those presented in this section, are described in accounting principles and financial management textbooks.

Incremental Budgeting

The traditional or conventional approach to budgeting is called **incremental budgeting.** This method involves the addition of a given percentage of increase (the *increment*) to the budgeted amounts of the preceding period to arrive at new figures. Cost data from the prior period are revised upward under the assumption that a given percentage of increase in business activities will bring about a like increase in department expenditures. In many cases, the base to which the increment is added is treated as though it were already authorized and requires little additional review or evaluation. In a similar fashion, if it becomes necessary to reduce the budgeted amounts, all budget items are reduced by a stipulated percentage. Thus, under incremental budgeting, all departments, regardless of their cost effectiveness, share equally in increases or decreases.

Table 23–1 illustrates the use of incremental budgeting in establishing the estimated administrative expenses for 1996. To obtain these estimates, the actual figures for 1995 were simply increased by 20 percent and rounded to cover the company's projected growth in sales and the anticipated inflation increase.

Incremental budgeting carries forward into each new budgeting period the inefficiencies and wastes of the prior period. Thus, the cost of such waste becomes part of an ever-growing budgeting base. With this type of budgeting, there is little opportunity for managers and supervisors to assess which projects or programs are deserving of special attention and additional funds, and managers have no incentive to control the cost of resource allocations. Also, since requests often exceed the availability of funds, managers and supervisors are obligated to rethink and redo their budgets. Anticipating a lack of funds to cover their budget requests and realizing that their requests will be slashed, managers often inflate the amounts requested. Even cost-conscious managers who have prepared realistic, cost-effective budgets soon learn that their budgeted amounts will be cut very much the same as those managers who initially inflated their budget requests. Thus, the budgeting

Table 23–1
Croushorn,
Inc.
Administrative
Expenses—
Actual and
Budget (Thousands of Dollars)

Expense	Actual 1995	Budget 1996
Salaries	$ 500	$ 600
Rent	80	100
Supplies	35	40
Telephone	120	140
Travel and meetings	70	80
Maintenance and repairs	15	20
Postage and mailing	50	60
Utilities	60	70
Miscellaneous	25	30
Totals	$ 955	$1,140

process becomes routine. Managers tend to be very complacent about budgetary control, and motivation declines in those departments that are operating profitably.

Zero-Base Budgeting (ZBB)

The objective of any budgeting method is to allocate resources to those operations that contribute most to the goals of the organization. **Zero-base budgeting (ZBB)** is a resource–allocation method that requires budget makers to examine every expenditure anew each budget period and to justify the expenditure in light of current needs and developments. Thus, unlike incremental budgeting, the budget figures are not based upon a percentage of increase or decrease related to the previous budgetary period. Instead, each year the budget is reduced to zero. The budget maker starts from the base line (zero) each time an expenditure is examined and justifies the first as well as the last dollar to be spent.

In using ZBB, we assume that each of the current operations and functions is of no value. Next, we review the cost of every budget program or project (old and new), as well as the output of each program. Then, we rank each program according to its cost effectiveness. Finally, we pre-

pare the master budget to reflect the highest cost-effective programs.

Most of the data collected about a program are presented in a document called a *decision package*. This document describes the program broken down into the smallest decision units that can be defended. A *decision unit* represents the lowest operating level where meaningful cost data can be compiled. Each decision unit is summarized in terms of the reasons for its existence, the benefits the organization gains from the unit, and the consequences for the company if the unit were to be terminated. Also included in the decision package is the manager's evaluation of alternative ways of getting the job done.

As an example of the procedure for preparing a decision package, consider Mark Gunning, a records manager who is responsible for both micrographic and reprographic services. In describing the micrographic services, Gunning lists each activity, or decision unit, that can be evaluated for budgetary purposes. Once he has identified the decision units, he develops a decision package for each unit. In the decision package, he summarizes the benefits that the company realizes by retaining each activity. Also, Gunning evaluates the cost effectiveness of other approaches for getting the job done: microfiche versus aperture cards versus computer output microfilm versus outsourcing the work to an outside micrographic service. In a similar fashion, he breaks down the reprographic services into decision units and evaluates each of them. After Gunning has described all the decision packages, he ranks them in their order of importance. As a result of listing all the packages in rank order, he has converted the budget process from primarily a clerical task into a managerial function where he must declare and defend his administrative priorities. In turn, when the budget committee ranks the decision packages of all departments prior to preparing the master budget, the committee learns what each manager considers important and thus is aided in adjusting the differences in priorities.

The benefits realized from the use of ZBB include:

1. Alternative ways of performing the same job are evaluated so that cost savings may be compared.
2. Managers focus their attention upon analysis and decision making, thus improving the planning process.
3. Each budget request must be justified in relation to the costs and benefits of each program.
4. Top-level managers are enabled to follow up and exercise control over costs and performance.

On the other hand, users of ZBB experience problems such as these:

1. There is difficulty in evaluating and comparing different decision packages because departments differ in both structure and purpose and may use different performance measures.
2. The method requires more time and effort of operating managers who may have had little training in ZBB.
3. There is difficulty in ranking a large number of decision packages.
4. The required cost-performance information may not be available or may be difficult to obtain.

However, some of the problems associated with ZBB are minimized or eliminated by using computers to process information, to rank the decision packages, and to consolidate the packages and assign priorities at the higher level as the master budget is prepared.

Compromise Budgeting

The incremental budgeting and ZBB methods are often modified in order to overcome the disadvantages described earlier and to realize the benefits to be gained from each method. Under a *compromise budgeting approach,* the budget maker does not start from zero but instead accepts the realities of business conditions as they exist and makes the needed adjustments or compromises. That is, the budget maker reduces the amount of funds allocated to those programs or activities that have been evaluated as less beneficial; however, the funds are reduced only to a realistic base. For example, under a compromise budgeting approach known as *modified ZBB,* the budget committee may undertake the preparation of the current budget by accepting 90 percent of last year's budget. Thus, operating managers are asked to submit ZBB decision packages only for the least essential 10 percent of their costs. As a result, operating managers prepare detailed justifications for only those parts of the budget where real decisions are likely to be made.

Budget Performance Reporting

As you read earlier, budgetary control provides a means of comparing estimated expenses with actual expenses and of analyzing variances so that the controllable causes of the variances may be eliminated. Figure 23–4 shows one type of budget performance report prepared monthly by each department of the company for this purpose. Variances that have been defined as significant (such as 5 percent over or under the budgeted amounts) should be investigated immediately to determine their causes and to seek means of preventing their recurrence. Possibly, corrective action cannot be taken because of a change in economic conditions that occurred after the budget was prepared. In such a case, future budget amounts should be revised accordingly.

Figure 23–4
An Example
of a Monthly
Budget Perfor-
mance Report

MONTHLY BUDGET PERFORMANCE REPORT

Sales department   For the month ended May 31, 19 - -

Expenses	Budget	Actual	Variance Over	Variance Under
Salaries............................	$ 8,000	$ 8,500	$500	
Rent	200	200		
Property taxes	90	90		
Insurance..........................	60	60		
Depreciation	300	300		
Office supplies	210	200		$10
Word processing	600	750	150	
Data processing	900	940	40	
Filing...............................	140	120		20
Telephone	330	345	15	
Postage and mailing	500	570	70	
Totals	$11,330	$12,075	$775	$30

Variances of 5% Over (+) or Under (−) Budget

Line Item and Percentage of Variance

Salaries	+ 6.3
Word processing	+25.0
Filing	−14.3
Postage and mailing	+14.0

Reasons for Variance

__x__ Change in volume of work (specify): Part-time sales correspondent employed; not anticipated in budget.

____ Work postponed or eliminated:

__x__ Procedural changes affecting work: Form letters and form paragraphs now held in storage on diskettes rather than filed hard copies; brochures keyboarded in May rather than June.

__x__ Special assignments received, not anticipated in budget: End-of-season brochures mailed in May rather than in planned month of June.

____ Other reasons:

June 2, 19 - -
Date

Debra Ling
Department Head

The amounts in the Budget column are obtained from the sales department's schedule of estimated operating expenses that accompanied the master budget. The amounts in the Actual column, supplied by the accounting department, represent costs actually incurred during the month. The last two columns show the variances—the amounts by which actual costs were over or under the budgeted figures. At the bottom of the report, the department head has indicated for each line item the reason for the variance if it is more than or less than 5 percent of the amount budgeted.

Year-to-date cumulative figures may be more significant than monthly figures when comparing budgeted and actual expenses. The use of cumulative figures also aids in more effective budgetary control than monthly figures alone. For example, the year-to-date actual expenses tend to smooth out some of the variances caused by events not in existence at the time of preparing the original budget figures. Year-to-date figures also diminish the significance of month-to-month figures, such as when it is unexpectedly decided that an expense planned for one particular month will be carried forward into the following month. A partially completed year-to-date budget performance report is illustrated in Figure 23–5.

COST-ANALYSIS PROBLEMS RELATED TO BUDGETARY CONTROL

Among the various problems arising in cost analysis through the use of budgets, two stand out: (1) the need for developing a work standards program and (2) controlling fluctuations in the volume of administrative services as a result of periodic or seasonal factors.

Using Work Standards in Analyzing Costs

In Chapter 22, we described the benefits to be gained from installing a work standards program. One of these benefits relates to the establishment of work targets and the planning of human resources. As a result of a work standards program, the AOM is able to prepare realistic budgets, to plan the number of workers needed to provide administrative services, and to measure the effectiveness of the budgeted amounts.

In the following example, you will see how work standards may be used to calculate the unit cost of administrative support services and to determine the need for additional workers. Consider a firm that has divided its text/word processing function among several cost centers, each of

Figure 23–5
A Partially Completed Year-to-Date Budget Performance Report

YEAR-TO-DATE BUDGET PERFORMANCE REPORT								
Sales department					For the month ended May 31, 19--			
Expenses	Budget Month	Actual Month	Monthly Variance		Budget Year to Date	Actual Year to Date	Year-to-Date Variance	
			Over	Under			Over	Under
Salaries..............	$ 8,000	$ 8,500	$500		$40,000	$40,500	$ 500	
Rent.................	200	200			1,000	1,000		
Property taxes........	90	90			450	450		
Insurance	60	60			300	300		
Depreciation.........	300	300			1,500	1,500		
Office supplies	210	200		$10	1,050	1,180	130	
Word processing	600	750	150		3,000	3,220	220	
Data processing	900	940	40		4,500	4,800	300	
Filing...............	140	120		20	700	690		$ 10
Telephone	330	345	15		1,650	1,600		50
Postage and mailing ..	500	570	70		2,500	2,390		110
Totals........	$11,330	$12,075	$775	$ 30	$56,650	$57,630	$1,150	$170

Full-Time Senior Word Processing Operator		
Salary and benefits	$31,000	
Materials and supplies	2,300	
Telephone	450	
Depreciation expense	2,600	$36,350

Part-Time Word Processing Operator		
Salary and benefits	$13,000	
Materials and supplies	1,200	
Telephone (shared with full-time operator)	—	
Depreciation expense (new processing unit)	3,000	17,200
Total costs		$53,550

which serves a group of technical writers. Through the use of a daily time log completed by the senior word processing operator, the supervisor of one cost center has determined the standard production rate to lie within the range of 115 to 134 lines of copy per hour. The midpoint of this range, 125, has been adopted as the standard number of lines to be produced per hour. For the past 52 weeks of 37½ hours each, the standard output was 243,750 lines. The costs allocated to word processing in this center total $33,100 for the year, as shown below:

Salary and benefits	$28,000
Materials and stationery	2,100
Telephone	400
Depreciation expense	2,600
Total costs	$33,100

The standard unit cost for each line produced during the past year is calculated as follows:

$$\frac{\$33,100 \text{ (total costs)}}{243,750 \text{ (standard lines of output)}}$$
$$= \$ .1358 \text{ standard unit cost per line}$$

Assume that for next year, the sales department projects a sales volume that converts into a 50 percent increase in the number of lines to be produced in the cost center. Thus, the estimated standard output for the following year would be 365,625 lines (243,750 × 150 percent). The estimated output is then translated into personnel needs as follows:

$$\frac{365,625 \text{ estimated lines to be produced}}{243,750 \text{ standard lines per year}}$$
$$= 1.5 \text{ operators}$$

To meet the need for an additional part-time operator in the center, the supervisor has studied several options such as overtime work, part-time help, and temporary office help. Assume that the supervisor has decided to employ a part-time worker next year to meet the increased needs. The total costs of operating the center, taking into consideration the effects of inflation and the purchase of additional equipment, are estimated by the supervisor as shown above.

As a result of employing a part-time operator, the standard unit cost per line produced during the following year will increase by a little more than one cent, as calculated on the next page:

$$\frac{\$53,550 \text{ (total costs)}}{365,625 \text{ (standard lines of output)}}$$
$$= \$.1465 \text{ standard unit cost per line}$$

Unit cost for new year	−	Unit cost for last year	=	Increase in unit cost for new year
\$.1465	−	\$.1358	=	\$.0107

During the new year, the AOM should strive to increase the output of each operator while at the same time searching for means of reducing the variable costs. The present system and its supporting procedures should be analyzed in order to eliminate poor work habits, wasted motions, and unnecessary physical effort. Also, close control should be exercised over the issuance and usage of materials and supplies. If the output of each of the two operators could be increased by about 9.8 lines per hour during the new year, the standard unit cost of production would be reduced to its former level, \$.1358.

Controlling the Cost of Peak-Load Fluctuations

In many organizations, there are periods of time during which peak-load needs must be considered when preparing and using an administrative expenses budget. For example, during certain periods of each month, the payroll must be prepared. Statements must be completed and sent to customers. Quarterly or annual financial reports and statements must be compiled; inventories must be taken periodically. Although occurring with a certain amount of regularity, these activities complicate the planning, scheduling, and estimating of administrative costs, especially when the tasks must be completed by a definite date.

Management must recognize the problem of peak-load fluctuations and develop efficient means of controlling the costs. Office managers have used some or all of the following means to control the costs of peak-load fluctuations in office work.

Cycle Billing

Firms use cycle billing to overcome peak workloads at the end of the month. A **cycle billing sys-**tem distributes evenly throughout the month the work related to preparing and mailing monthly statements of customers' accounts (accounts receivable). Cycle billing is an effective accounting technique used by most utilities, retail stores, banks, stock brokerage houses, and industrial firms.

In firms that use cycle billing, the customers' accounts are divided into groups. There may be as many as 16 to 20 groups, each of which is approximately equal in size in order to balance the workload among the billing department personnel. Each group of customers' accounts covers certain letters of the alphabet and certain days of the month. For example, statements to customers in the alphabetic group A–B may be sent out on the first day of each month; on the fifth day, statements are mailed for the C–D group. The system is continued during the entire month until the last cycle group—W–Z—is completed.

Following the closing day for each cycle group, a single billing operation is performed. Thus, the statements for all active accounts may be printed out in one run on the computer printer. By dividing the accounts receivable ledger into alphabetic groups and closing each of these groups at a different time during the month, we spread the daily workload more evenly throughout the month. In turn, this procedure reduces the need for overtime and part-time workers. As a result, collection schedules, cash intake, and all supporting operations flow more evenly.

Split-Payroll Dates

We find that some payroll accounting systems are designed similarly to a cycle billing plan. By having different payroll dates for different departments, peak-load fluctuations in preparing the payroll may be minimized. For example, for many years in one firm, all personnel were paid on the 15th and the last day of the month. As part of a study to reduce peak-load activities in the payroll department, the firm decided to pay the office workers and workers in the shipping and packing departments every two weeks; administrative and executive personnel continued to be paid twice a month on the 15th and the last day. Thus, the company was able to smooth out the peak load that formerly occurred at the time of every semimonthly pay period, and the firm more effectively used the services of the personnel in the payroll department.

Using Current Personnel on an Overtime Basis

Overtime work is best scheduled where the overload is unexpected or of short duration and is not expected to recur with any degree of regularity. Scheduling work beyond the firm's standard workweek is an expensive method that may increase costs 50 percent or more. In addition to increased labor costs, a firm may find that during the overtime hours, employee productivity continues to decline while the probability of error rises. The major advantage of using current personnel on an overtime basis is that the people doing the work come from the regular skilled staff who are already familiar with the organization's operations and procedures.

Hiring Part-Time Workers

Part-time workers (nonpermanent employees) make up a significant portion of the working population and represent a growth that has stemmed partly from the rising number of women, retired persons, and young people who want to work only a part of each day. Hiring part-time employees may initially represent an economical move for the organization since the hourly labor costs would be relatively low. However, since all new part-time employees start from a zero-base salary, most, if not all, of their annual salaries would cause the employer's payroll taxes to increase substantially. In addition, the employer may be faced with added costs such as an increased premium for group life insurance coverage. Other factors to consider include the costs facing the human resources department in recruiting, orienting, and training the part-time people and the payroll department's costs of processing additional payroll records.

Using Temporary Office Workers

As indicated in Chapter 6, a company that uses the services of temporary office personnel for varying periods of time realizes significant savings. The only cost to the employer is the fee paid to the temporary help service. The employer is not faced with payroll taxes and costly employee benefits, and the human resources department incurs very little, if any, recruitment and orientation expense.

Often, during a recession, a company will lower its variable expenses by reducing the size of its full-time office workforce. Shortly thereafter, the firm may find that there is more work than the reduced workforce can handle. The company may then turn to the use of temporary office help until the return of a stable economy—and the need for hiring additional full-time workers—is indicated. Thus, the firm can fill in with temporary workers as needed without adding to its overhead costs.

Floating Workers

Office workers often "float" from one peak-load area to another as the firm's needs require. Some organizations hire workers whose major function is to float from one department to another during peak-workload hours. In other companies, workers leave their regularly assigned workstations and "lend a helping hand" in peak-load areas during rush periods. For example, during the peak hours when the mailing center receives the incoming mail or when it is processing the outgoing mail, the center may temporarily use the services of "floaters" who regularly work in other departments such as order processing, billing, and filing.

Service Bureaus

The increase in the number of service bureaus, or data service centers, indicates that many companies find these sources to be an answer to the periodic overloads of office work. To illustrate how a service bureau is used to reduce peak loads, let's look at a typical payroll department. The peak loads in payroll operations occur right before and after a payroll is processed. Depending upon how often employees are paid, we find additional resources required during these peak periods, but not every day. The need for additional resources may be met by using floating workers from other departments, by hiring part-time workers, or by paying overtime to present payroll personnel. However, by taking advantage of the service bureau's services, we can reduce some of the added

Illustration 23–3 Hiring temporary office workers is an effective approach in controlling the cost of peak-load fluctuations.

costs associated with the peak loads. For example, most service bureaus will sign, burst, stuff, and

distribute checks according to our instructions. The bureau will also print out reports, such as labor cost analyses, and tax forms. Thus, these services reduce the resources required in the mailing center and the payroll department.

As we saw in Chapter 16, the high degree of skill, the confidential nature of their work, and their comparatively low cost have much to recommend service bureaus as a means for establishing cost control over peak-load fluctuations. Also, as pointed out in the previous chapter, many organizations turn to outsourcing and use service bureaus to handle their former in-house activities such as payroll, tax accounting, and data processing. For example, each pay period 15 million workers get paychecks that do not come from their own firm's accounting department. Instead, their checks come from Automatic Data Processing, Inc., a data services company, which pays one-eighth of the workforce in the United States.[3]

[3]"They Make Money Paying Us," *Forbes* (January 4, 1993), p. 99.

SUMMARY

1. Budgets are used by AOMs in acquiring and using resources for the information-processing activities under their supervision and control. By means of periodic budget performance reports, the AOM compares actual operating expenses with budgeted expenses and determines the variances. Thus, the AOM can take steps to improve productivity by reducing or eliminating significant variances.

2. Depending upon the size of the organization, the AOM may prepare budgets; receive budgets from subordinates; or analyze, consolidate, and condense budgets into a final report for the budget committee, which is responsible for preparing the firm's master budget.

3. When preparing an administrative expenses budget, the AOM is guided by the following principles: (a) assign initial responsibility to key employees for budget preparation, (b) ob-jectively develop budget figures, (c) set realistic targets for each department, (d) provide flexibility in the budget so that timely decision making is not impeded, (e) ensure that the budget is accepted and adhered to, and (f) plan for frequent review of the budget in order to detect and correct variances.

4. The AOM evaluates various methods of budgeting, such as incremental budgeting and zero-base budgeting. From these methods, the AOM selects one method or a combination of methods that provides the best opportunities for analyzing and controlling costs. With an effective budgeting method, the AOM is also aided in solving cost-related problems, such as relating work standards to budget preparation, estimating future needs for additional employees, and reducing the fluctuating output of office work during peak-load periods.

FOR YOUR REVIEW

1. How are budget performance reports used in a program of budgetary control?

2. What objectives is management trying to attain when using budgets and budget performance reports?

3. What is the function of a budget committee?

4. How does a master budget differ from a flexible budget?

5. How do well-prepared administrative expenses budgets aid the AOM in planning and controlling office operations?

6. Why should the budget-making process begin at the operative level?

7. Why should a budget contain safety valves?

8. Explain how the establishment of a responsibility accounting system provides control over costs and expenses.

9. Why are variable costs and semivariable costs more controllable than fixed costs?

10. Distinguish between direct expenses and indirect expenses and give examples of each kind.

11. What is a commonly used basis for allocating each of the following indirect expenses: (a) text/word processing, (b) filing, and (c) data processing in the computer center?

12. What disadvantages are associated with incremental budgeting?

13. Describe zero-base budgeting and list the major benefits to be realized from its use.

14. How is a monthly budget performance report prepared?

15. Briefly describe how the use of work standards contributes to the preparation of realistic budgets and planning the number of workers needed for a future time period.

16. Describe how a cycle billing system aids in minimizing peak-load fluctuations.

FOR YOUR DISCUSSION

1. When discussing his ideas of expense budgeting, Jerry Hunt, manager of office services, remarked, "There's really no reason for preparing a sloppy expense budget. The salaries in my department remain the same regardless of the sales figures. And my general office expenses, including my share of depreciation, taxes, rent, etc., don't change. Of course, some expenses, like office supplies, do vary. But if you're any kind of manager, you can estimate them pretty close. Really, these expenses are no more than a fixed expense. Keeping this in mind, I don't have to change my budget every year. I've got to remember that our company president doesn't like surprises. So I don't give him any." What is your reaction to Hunt's approach to budgeting his fixed and variable expenses?

c
o
n
t

2. "An organization must use a budget for a long period of time before it becomes an effective tool of management." Explain the meaning of this statement.

3. The effectiveness of a budgetary control program is measured by making department heads responsible for their department budget figures. Explain.

4. An axiom widely circulated in the business world by management gurus, garden-variety consultants, and even trainers themselves is that, in tough times, training is the first budget allocation to be cut.[4] Do you look upon this statement as a myth or "the gospel truth?"

5. In discussing her budgetary needs for the forthcoming year, Anna Samaroo remarked to her supervisor of accounting operations, "I really need only eight workers, but those up above always cut my budget by 20 percent. So this year I'll ask for ten." How do you explain this type of attitude on the part of Samaroo? What is your reaction to her philosophy of budgeting?

6. Tim Hernandez, a supervisor in the computer center, offers these comments to you: "Since I don't work directly with our company's financial managers, I don't feel as if I need to get involved with all this budgeting jargon, numbers crunching, and priority-setting." Explain to Hernandez why he should try to understand budgeting and become involved.

7. Carla Attardi, a word processing manager, has been laying out plans to automate some of the procedures that will link all branch offices together with the headquarters office. In discussing her proposed pilot test with Daniel Radison, head of the budgeting committee, she is told: "Take a look around and see what you can get for $50,000." Evaluate Radison's statement as the first step to be taken in the budgetary process.

CASES FOR CRITICAL THINKING

Case 23–1 Evaluating a Budgeting Procedure

About the middle of August, Harrison Arless, president of Raines Manufacturing, told Janice Tylo, the controller, that it was time to commence thinking about next year's budget. As her first step, Tylo gathered all the data about this year's performance and then prepared comparative statements in which she compared this year's results with the budget the company adopted a year ago. Tylo's inspection of the statements convinced her that what the company was doing was "right on the button."

In the meantime, Arless passed along to Tylo his thinking about current economic conditions and indicated the direction he thought the firm should head the next year. Armed with her statements and Arless's thinking, Tylo called a meeting of the top-level executives. During the meeting, Tylo pooled all their ideas on topics such as raw material costs, price changes, global economic trends, and downsizing prospects. The group then agreed on the percentages that would be used to adjust this year's volume in accordance with next year's plans. With this forecast for the next year, Tylo prepared the firm's operating budget.

Evaluate the procedure followed by Tylo in formulating next year's budget.

---

[4]Chris Lee, "The Budget Blahs," *Training* (October, 1992), p. 31.

Case 23–2 Spending to Budget

c
o
n
t

At the first meeting of the budget committee of Beale Products, the newly appointed budget director, Fred DePeza, was reviewing the year-to-date performance figures of each department. After he read the budget figures for the office services department, headed by Donna Masur, the following conversation took place:

DePeza: Donna, I know some people in this company feel that it's common practice to "spend to budget." I sense that you, like some others, feel that if you don't spend all that was budgeted this year, you're going to be cut in next year's allocations.

Masur: That's true, Fred. Along with most of the others, I know that if we're to prosper next year, each of us must get more. So, we spend all of our allocated funds each year, knowing very well that next year the amount will be reduced if we don't spend this year's funds.

DePeza: Well, I think it's time we changed that attitude on the part of all of you who prepare department budgets. I don't believe any of you should be penalized for holding the line on costs. Rather, you should be rewarded for not spending needlessly.

Masur: That sounds good in theory, Fred, but in all my years with Beale, this hasn't been the case. How are you going to overcome the practice of spending to budget?

DePeza: Let me think about that question. I'm sure there are some steps we can take.

A few days later, DePeza calls a department meeting to discuss the problems related to budgeting and spending. He indicates he is seeking specific steps that can be taken to halt the practice of spending to budget. Masur now approaches you, her assistant, for your recommendations.

What specific steps do you recommend that the firm take to reduce the common practice of spending to budget?

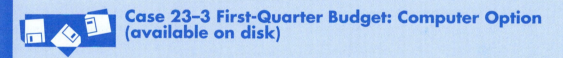

Case 23–3 First-Quarter Budget: Computer Option (available on disk)

GLOSSARY

401(k) retirement plan—a plan, authorized by the Internal Revenue Code, in which each year employees shelter from federal income taxes a certain portion of their salaries and the earnings thereon until time of retirement or withdrawal of the funds.

Absenteeism rate—the extent of unscheduled days absent.

Achievement test—an employment test designed to measure the degree of proficiency in a given type of work.

Acquired immune deficiency syndrome (AIDS)—a disease caused by the human immunodeficiency virus (HIV) that attacks the body's immune system.

Activity—an action in a PERT chart that takes time to perform.

Administrative expenses—those expenses incurred in the general operations of the organization.

Administrative office management—the process of planning, organizing, and controlling all of the information-related activities and of leading people to attain the objectives of the organization.

Administrative office manager (AOM)—the person responsible for planning, organizing, and controlling the information-processing activities and for leading people in attaining the objectives of the organization.

Administrative office systems (AOS)—specialized systems responsible for managing all phases of the information cycle.

Administrative secretaries—office workers who are freed from large-volume keyboarding responsibilities in order to handle the remaining office services in a T/WP center.

Administrative services—support functions responsible for meeting all the information needs of the organization.

Affirmative action plan—a program designed to eliminate, limit, or prevent discriminatory treatment on the basis of race, ethnic group, and sex.

Age Discrimination in Employment Act of 1967—a federal law that prohibits age discrimination against persons over the age of 40.

Air environment—the total atmosphere created in the office by the principal air factors—temperature, humidity, circulation (ventilation), and cleanliness.

Alcoholic—one who is powerless to stop drinking and whose normal living pattern is seriously altered by drinking.

Alcoholism—a progressive disease characterized by excessive, repetitive, and uncontrolled consumption of alcohol.

Ambient factors—those conditions that surround and affect the performance of work and the development of worker satisfaction with the work and the workplace.

Ambient lighting—the use of indirect fixtures or uplights that direct light upward to be reflected off the ceiling onto other surfaces that surround the workstation.

American plan—an office layout design that combines features of the open plan and the conventional plan.

Americans with Disabilities Act of 1990—a federal law that protects from discrimination those persons who suffer any physical or mental disability that substantially limits their major life activities.

Analog computer—a type of computer that measures continuously changing conditions, such as temperature and atmospheric pressure, and converts them into quantities.

Application form—a personnel form on which the job applicant provides personal information, educational background, business experience, and references.

Aptitude test—an employment test designed to measure the ability to perform a particular kind of task and to predict future performance on the job or in training.

Arbitration—the process in which labor and management agree to submit any issue in dispute to an individual arbitrator (or an arbitration board) that renders a decision binding upon both parties.

Arithmetic-logic unit—the portion of the central processing unit (CPU) that performs computational and logical operations.

Assessment center—a training center that uses simulation exercises to provide the same kind of work situation that trainees will find on higher-level jobs.

Assistant-to—a personal assistant with staff authority whose administrative duties vary, depending upon the responsibilities assigned; also called *administrative assistant*.

Attitude survey—a polling of workers to determine their moods and feelings toward supervisory treatment, salaries and employee benefits, their jobs, and the firm.

Audio-response system—a system in which a computer-activated voice answers questions using a vocabulary stored in the system.

Audio teleconference—the simplest, least expensive, and most commonly scheduled teleconference.

Authoritarian organization—an organization that subscribes to the traditional view of supervising workers—Theory X—and thus is very dependent upon authority.

Authority—the right to command and to give orders and the power to make decisions.

Authorization card—a formal statement signed by an employee authorizing a named union to represent him or her in collective bargaining.

Autocratic leader—one who rules with unlimited authority; an authoritarian.

Automatic progression plan—a type of salary increase in which the salary rate is moved in equal interval steps from the minimum of the range to the maximum, based upon the employee's length of service.

Average—the quotient obtained by dividing the sum of a set of figures by the number of figures in that set; also known as the *arithmetic mean*.

Average rate of return—the average savings to be obtained from an investment divided by the average amount of the investment.

Bandwidth—the amount of space needed to transmit messages on telecommunication channels.

Behavioral school—a group of theorists who emphasize the social, psychological, and physiological needs of people within the organization.

Behavioral science approach—an approach followed in the management process that emphasizes interpersonal relations and democratic actions on the part of workers.

Benchmark job—a job whose present rate is not subject to controversy and is considered to be neither underpaid nor overpaid.

Benchmarking—the process of identifying, understanding, and adapting outstanding practices and processes from organizations anywhere in the world to help an organization improve its performance.

Bias—the highly personal judgment or opinion formed by an individual before the facts are known.

Bit—an abbreviation of the term *binary digit;* that is, one encoded character in the binary coding system.

Body language—a person's gestures, expressions, and body positions.

Bona fide occupational qualification (BFOQ)—a job qualification, such as race, sex, or religion, that in good faith is a job-related requirement necessary to the normal operations of the business.

Bond paper—a type of paper used for letterheads, office forms, and certificates where fine appearance and durability are essential.

Brainstorming—a group technique for creating a large quantity of ideas by freewheeling contributions made without criticism.

Break-even point—that level of operations at which a company neither realizes income nor incurs loss; that point at which revenues and costs are equal.

Broadbanding—an organization structure in which the employees are loosely organized into a few broad job categories.

Bubble memory—a type of computer storage in which large amounts of data are stored in the form of magnetic bubbles that move in thin films of magnetic material.

Budget—a formal statement of plans for the future, expressed in financial terms.

Budget performance report—the periodic comparison of actual operating data with budgeted data.

Budgetary control—the use of a budget in regulating and guiding those business activities concerned with acquiring and using resources.

Budgeting—the process of planning future business activities and expressing those plans in a formal manner.

Bureaucracy—a model of organizational design that is formal, impersonal, and governed by rules.

Bureaucratic leader—one who sets and follows fixed rules; a hierarchy of authority; and narrow, rigid, formal routines.

Burnout—the depletion of one's physical and mental resources caused by excessive striving to reach unrealistic job-related goals.

Byte—a computer term for a basic data character, such as a letter, number, or symbol.

Call-back system—a records protection measure in which the computer verifies that the party requesting a record is authorized to use it.

Career goal planning—the process of working with employees to assess their personal strengths, weaknesses, preferences, and values; to select and formulate career goals; to develop action plans so the workers can carry out their goals; and to put their action plans to work.

Case study—a written history of a business problem or situation that trainees study for problem solving and class evaluation.

Cash inflow—a source of funds provided by savings (net income after taxes) and depreciation expense.

Cellular telephone—a radio-based wireless communication system for receiving and transmitting voice messages within a limited geographic area.

Central recorder system—a dictation system where the telephone may be used as a dictation instrument to access a recording device located in the T/WP center.

Centralized authority—similar functions are carried out in one place.

Centralized filing—an organizational plan in which records of general value throughout the firm are stored in one location and controlled by one centralized records department.

Centrex—(or **central exchange**) provides direct inward dialing in which all local and long-distance calls go directly to the number dialed.

Certified Administrative Manager (C.A.M.)—a person holding professional certification from the Academy of Administrative Management.

Chain of command—the means of transmitting authority from the top level (the chief executive officer) through successive levels of management to the workers at the lowest operative level.

Chargeback accounting system—a plan for directly allocating the costs of support services by charging each department or cost center for its actual usage of the services.

Check-off—the process of deducting union dues from paychecks by the employer and remitting the collections to the union.

Choice making—the process of evaluating and selecting among alternatives available for solving a problem.

Civil Rights Act of 1964—the federal law containing Title VII, "Equal Employment Opportunity," which, as amended, defines certain actions or inactions as unlawful employment practices.

Classical school—an early group of theorists who emphasized the essential nature of management and its relationship to the production process.

Climate survey—a two-way feedback process in which supervisors and subordinates provide for interpersonal exchange of opinions.

Clip art—software packages with digitized images for use with DTP and T/WP.

Closed system—a type of system that operates as a self-regulating unit and thus does not interact with its environment.

Cognitive activities—those human activities that are largely mental in nature and that revolve around the use of knowledge or judgment.

Collective bargaining—a negotiation process between an employer and labor union representatives on work-related issues.

Commercial writing class—a group of writing papers commonly used in ordinary business transactions and for advertising purposes.

Committee organization—an organization structure where authority and responsibility are jointly held by a group of individuals rather than by a single manager.

Communicating word processor—a word processing machine that has the capability of transmitting and receiving messages over telephone lines.

Communication—the process by which information and human attitudes are exchanged with others.

Communication audit—an evaluation of the communication system to determine how effectively and efficiently it is working.

Communication network—the pattern of channels used to communicate messages to and from, or among, a group of people.

Communication process—the transmission of a message from one person (the sender) to another person (the receiver).

Communication satellite (Comsat)—a communication system that consists of two or more ground transmitter-receiver stations and a satellite "parked" in space above the earth.

Compact disc read-only memory (CD-ROM)—an optical disk used to store large quantities of data.

Compressed workweek—a work schedule in which the usual number of full-time hours are worked in fewer than five days.

Computer-aided design (CAD)—a designing technique in which the computer automates the drafting function.

Computer-assisted retrieval (CAR)—the process of merging the computer and the microrecording process to access data on microfilm.

Computer-based message system—a form of electronic mail in which a computer directs the received messages to be filed in electronic mailboxes later to be accessed by persons as their needs require.

Computer-based training (CBT)—a training method in which trainees operate terminal input-output units to learn materials that have been programmed on the computer.

Computer conference—a form of teleconferencing in which geographically separate persons communicate with each other through the use of computers.

Computer-connected word processor—a word processing machine that is linked to, and dependent upon, a computer (file server) for its operations.

Computer input microfilm (CIM)—the process of translating uncoded data on microrecords into computer language code for storage on magnetic tape as input to a computer.

Computer literacy—a broad concept that describes the ability to use or operate a computer or to understand the computer's capabilities without being able to operate one.

Computer output microfilm (COM)—the process in which a computer's output is automatically photographed and converted to human-readable images on microfilm without creating an intervening paper copy.

Computer system—a group of interconnected machines, including the computer, that process data at the speed of light and in which the data and the instructions for processing the data are stored within the computer.

Conceptual skill—the ability to use existing knowledge in order to acquire additional knowledge.

Conditional sales contract—an agreement under which the user of equipment is considered, for federal income tax purposes, to be the owner of the equipment at the time of signing the lease.

Contextual data flow diagram—a graphic representation of a system from the most general perspective.

Contingency theory of leadership effectiveness—the situation confronting the leader and the workers determines the style of leadership that will be successful in the firm.

Continuous forms—a series of connected forms folded in a prearranged manner and perforated for easy separation of each form.

Control—the systems phase that dictates what can and cannot be performed in each of the other phases.

Controlling—a function of management which ensures that operating results conform as closely as possible to the plans made for the organization.

Conventional furniture—a collection of independent furniture components, such as free-standing desks and credenzas, filing cabinets, and bookshelves.

Conventional plan—an office layout design characterized by wall barriers that tend to isolate work areas.

Copy paper—a lightweight writing paper used for making carbon copies; an example is onionskin.

Correspondence secretaries—keyboard specialists who are employed to convert words into a finished communication.

Cost-of-living adjustment (COLA) clause—a provision in the labor contract that indicates how salaries are to be kept in alignment with inflation.

Creativity—the ability to apply imagination and ingenuity in developing a novel approach or unique solution to a problem.

Credit union—a financial institution, chartered by the state or federal government, that is organized to assist the employees of a firm in saving money and lending it to one another.

Critical path—the sequence or path of activities in a PERT network that require the greatest amount of time to complete if the project is to meet its deadline.

Critical path method (CPM)—a network control system that shows the sequence of activities in a project and the time allowance (standard) for completing each activity, with the objective of determining the minimum elapsed time for completing the project.

Cross-training—training to develop multiskilled workers who can adapt to changes in job requirements and advancing technology and thus become ready to assume more responsible or more demanding positions.

Cycle billing system—a plan for evenly distributing throughout the month the work related to preparing and mailing monthly statements of customers' accounts.

Data aperture card—a microform that is identical to the punched aperture card except that it uses one or more lines of computer-readable OCR indexing text at the top of the card for display on the VDT screen.

Data communication system—a powerful information-transmitting system that merges the computer, the telephone, and other electronic systems to send prerecorded data over long distances.

Data dictionary—a description of each data flow, transform, store, and external entity in a data flow diagram.

Data flow—the path of the data being carried by either a physical or electronic document.

Data flow diagram (DFD)—a chart that shows what data move to, through, and from a system.

Data hierarchy—a five-level organization structure of information that ranges from the most basic level—the character—to the broadest level—the database or library; also known as the *file structure* or *file organization*.

Data service center—an independent, profit-making organization that specializes in the processing of data for customer firms; also known as a *service bureau*.

Data store—a point in a data flow diagram that indicates where data are at rest.

Database—a central master file containing company-wide information about a firm or department-wide information within a department.

Database access—an information-retrieval service in which the user calls up a database and secures the information needed.

Database management system (DBMS)—a computer software package that allows a user to keep track of an organized collection of files.

Decentralized authority—the delegation of much authority to the lower levels in the organization.

Decentralized filing—an organizational plan in which each office division maintains its own filing system.

Decibel (dB)—the unit of measure that determines the relative loudness of sounds.

Decision making—the making of a conscious choice between two or more alternative courses of action.

Decision simulation—a training method based upon a model that simulates an actual business or one of its functions, in which competing groups of trainees assume managerial roles, perform tasks, and make decisions.

Decision table—a tool for presenting the logic and the sequential operations in a system by showing what action must be taken to satisfy each information-related condition.

Decision tree—a chart used to show the alternate courses of action for solving a problem and some of the probable consequences stemming from each course of action.

Delegation—the process of entrusting work to employees who are qualified to accept responsibility for doing the work.

Departmental work group system—describes both the organization structure for centralized groups of secretaries and the software that links them together.

Departmentation—the process of organizing work into distinct areas based upon some common characteristic.

Desktop publishing (DTP)—a T/WP software application that enables the user to design, edit, assemble, and produce documents with a professional look that includes typeset text, graphics, business reports, newsletters, brochures, sales flyers, price lists, manuals, and resumés.

Diagonal communication—the transmission of messages to workers at higher or lower levels in the organization using communication networks other than those formally shown on the organization chart.

Dictation-transcription system—the equipment and procedures used to record messages on paper or on magnetic media through the process of dictation.

Digital computer—a type of computer that counts numbers or digits while processing numeric and alphabetic data that have been converted to a numeric code.

Digital dictation—vocal sounds that are recorded and stored on magnetic media after being automatically converted to binary digits.

Diplomatic leader—one who is skillful in helping people solve their problems.

Direct expenses—expenses originating in and chargeable directly to one department.

Direct interview—an interviewing technique in which job applicants are asked direct questions related to their qualifications and ability to fill the job.

Disability income insurance—an insurance plan that provides continuing income for workers unable to return to their jobs after they have exhausted their sickness and accident benefits.

Disaster recovery plan—a document that contains contingency arrangements for relocating, equipping, and staffing the records system during a major disruption of its regular operations.

Discipline—the teaching or molding of employees in a constructive and consistent manner so that they may learn to change their behavior and performance in the future.

Discrete recording medium—a separate magnetic record for storing dictation that can be removed from the dictation machine for transcription after the dictation has been completed.

Diverse workforce—employees who differ in gender, age, race, culture, religion, education, lifestyle, sexual orientation, and so on.

Diversity training—sharing information about the changing demographics of the workforce, new approaches to managing the workforce, the dynamics of stereotyping and its effects upon teamwork, and the workers' changing cultural and ethical values.

Downsizing—reducing the size of a workforce by layoffs, attrition, or other means; also known as *rightsizing*.

Downward communication—the transmission of messages that flow vertically from the top of the organization to one or more levels below.

Drug abuser—one who exhibits strong psychological dependence upon drugs, often reinforced by physical dependence on certain drugs.

Drug addict—one who is physically dependent upon drugs.

Dumb terminal—a data-entry device with an alphanumeric keyboard and printer (the teletypewriter), or a video display terminal that is connected to a mainframe via a communication link.

Duplexing—copying on both sides of a sheet of copy paper in one operation.

Effective salary range—the spread between the salaries found at the first and the third quartiles of a distribution.

Effective system—a system that is actually producing the desired quantity and quality of output.

Effective temperature—the temperature combined with the proper humidity.

Efficiency ratios—the guidelines used by records managers to evaluate the efficiency of their records programs.

Efficient system—a system that is operating in an economical manner, that is, one that is highly reliable and minimizes the time and costs involved in its operation.

Electronic banking services—a service that allows bank transactions to be carried on without direct personal contact with a teller.

Electronic blackboard—a telecommunication service in which a chalkboard message is photographed and transmitted over telephone lines to distant television receivers.

Electronic mail—the process of delivering mail by electronic signals over telecommunication lines, thus eliminating the need for the physical delivery of paper documents.

Electronic mailbox—a computer storage area identified by a location code or a special username code for the storage of an individual's electronic mail.

Electronic performance support system (EPSS)—software that supplies functional decision-making information for completing fields on an electronic form.

Electronic typewriter (ET)—an electric typewriter to which automatic functions have been added by the use of microprocessors.

Employee assistance program (EAP)—a plan that provides specially trained persons who diagnose and offer help in solving personal problems that affect employees' performance and attendance.

Employee benefits—the payments and services that workers receive in addition to their regular wages or salaries; also called *fringe benefits.*

Employee handbook—a communication medium that provides employees with essential employment information.

Employee leasing service—an organization that assigns workers to client firms under contract to provide on-the-job services, usually on a permanent basis.

Employee performance appraisal—the study of an employee's traits, personal qualifications, attitudes, and behavior.

Employee Polygraph Protection Act of 1988—a federal law that bars *private* employers from requiring that most job applicants and current employees be given polygraph (lie detector) tests.

Employee Retirement Income Security Act (ERISA)—legislation that provides workers with a vested right to their retirement income benefits and assurance of well-managed retirement plans.

Employee specifications—the minimum qualifications a person must possess to be considered for employment.

Employee stock ownership plan (ESOP)—a group incentive plan designed to increase the long-term interest of employees in the profitability of their company by permitting employees to acquire shares of stock in their own company.

Employee suggestion system—a channel of upward communication in which employees offer ideas that result in cost reduction and the elimination of inefficiency and waste.

Employment at will—the doctrine which states that the employee and the employer have the right to enter freely into the employment relationship and to sever this relationship at any time for any reason.

Empowerment—a technique of increasing employee participation by delegating to them the authority to act and to make decisions on their own.

Encryption system—a computer system safeguard that scrambles data in a predetermined manner at the sending point in order to protect confidential records.

Entry-level training—training designed to qualify employees for entry-job assignments; also called *initial training.*

Equal Employment Opportunity—Title VII of the Civil Rights Act that affects the hiring practices of business firms, unions, and employment agencies and defines certain actions (or inactions) as unlawful employment practices.

Equal Employment Opportunity Act of 1972—a federal law that subjects state and local governments to provisions against employment discrimination contained in the Civil Rights Act.

Equal Employment Opportunity Commission (EEOC)—the regulatory body created by the Civil Rights Act to enforce the law.

Equal Pay Act of 1963—a federal law that prohibits employers from setting different wages based solely upon the sex of workers who are doing equal work.

Equipment lease—a contract that enables an equipment user (lessee) to secure use of a tangible asset by making periodic payments to the owner (lessor) of the asset over a specified period of time.

Ergonomics—an applied science that integrates the use of space, furniture and equipment, and other physiological factors such as light, color, sound, and temperature to meet the psychological needs of workers; also called *human engineering*.

Ethics—the systematic study of that part of science and philosophy dealing with moral conduct, duty, and judgment.

Event—a point in time on a PERT chart when an activity starts or ends.

Executive orders—the presidential directives that strive to require equal employment opportunities in firms doing business with the government.

Exit interview—an interview conducted at the time of terminating an employee's services to determine the real reasons for termination.

Expectancy theory—the view that a person's motivational force to perform depends upon the individual's expectations concerning future outcomes and the value placed on these outcomes.

External entity—people, processes, or departments that lie outside the area being examined in a data flow diagram but communicate to or receive communications from the area.

External written communications—messages that are sent to receivers outside the firm.

Facility manager—the person responsible for areas such as operations and maintenance, real estate, human and environmental factors, planning and project management, facility function, finance, communications, quality assessment, and innovation.

Facsimile process—a form of electronic mail that permits exact copies of written, printed, or graphic information to be sent and received over regular telephone lines as well as by satellite; also known as *FAX*.

Factor-comparison method—a method of evaluating jobs in which each job is evaluated in terms of money according to five critical factors: mental requirements, skill requirements, physical requirements, responsibility, and working conditions.

Fair Credit Reporting Act of 1968—a federal law that governs the use of credit and investigative agencies that supply information about a person's character, general reputation, and lifestyle.

Fair Labor Standards Act (FLSA)—the federal law that sets minimum wages and overtime pay, provides equal pay for equal work, and regulates the employment of children.

Family and Medical Leave Act of 1993 (FMLA)—legislation that requires employers with 50 or more workers within a 75-mile radius to provide up to 12 weeks of unpaid leave for family medical emergencies, childbirth, or adoption.

Feasibility study—a systems planning method that seeks to find out whether systems operations can be improved and if the addition of new resources is economically justified for making such improvements.

Feedback—the systems phase that compares the system's output with standards of performance.

Fiber optics—fiberglass threads along which units of information are translated into light waves by a laser beam and then "pumped" through the glass fiber for transmitting information in a telecommunication system.

Fidelity bond—the guarantee by an insurer that the insured firm will be compensated, up to an agreed-upon amount and subject to agreement on the terms and conditions, for the loss of money or other property resulting from dishonest acts of the firm's employees.

Files accuracy ratio—a measure used to evaluate a records system in which the number of records found is compared with the number of records requested.

Files activity ratio—a measure used to evaluate a records system in which the number of records requested is compared with the number of records filed.

Filing system—the procedures and methods used to classify, sort, and store records for fast retrieval.

First quartile—that position in a distribution of values which is more than one-fourth and less than three-fourths of all the values listed.

Fixed costs—those costs tending to remain fairly stable (unchanging) over a stated time period even when the volume of business changes.

Flat form—a single sheet of paper often used as a single-copy record.

Flexible benefits program—an employer-sponsored benefits package that offers employees a choice between taking cash and certain qualified benefits; also known as the *cafeteria plan*.

Flexible budget—a prediction of costs at various levels of activity.

Flexible work schedule—a work plan under which the workday is divided into *core time* (those hours during which all employees must be at work) and *flexible time* (the time employees may choose for their arrival and departure times); also known as *flextime*.

Floating offices—a management system that allows employees to set up mobile offices wherever convenient: at home, corporate headquarters, or branch facilities using laptops and computer capabilities for written communications.

Floppy disk—a flexible diskette on which the data can be retrieved randomly.

Flowchart—a type of systems chart used to show the logical sequence of steps involved in the flow of work, usually in a manual system.

Fonts—typefaces in specific sizes and styles.

Footcandle (FC)—a measure of the amount of light produced by a candle at a distance of one foot from the source of the light.

Footlambert—a unit of measure approximating one footcandle of light emitted or reflected.

Forced relationship—a technique for developing creativity that requires problem solvers to consider in a new way something that is already known.

Foreign exchange (FX)—a long-distance telephone service that permits a telephone in a distant location (within or outside the United States) to be connected to a local telephone.

Form—a specially designed record having constant information preprinted on it with space provided for the entry of variable information.

Formal organization—the plan of organization graphically depicted in an organization chart.

Forms distribution chart—a systems chart that traces the flow of forms and related paperwork through the departments under study.

Free-rein leader—one who sets goals and develops clear guidelines for the workers, who then operate freely with no further direction unless they ask for help.

Functional organization—an organization structure that provides specialists at the supervisory level who are in charge of the work related to their specialties in departments other than their own.

Gainsharing plan—a group incentive plan in which the savings realized from improvements in productivity are divided among workers and their employer.

Gantt chart—a technique of planning long-range projects in which the work planned and the work done are shown side by side in their relation to each other and to time.

General problem-solving model—a framework for solving problems that has general use in the solution of all types of problems.

General Schedule—a job classification method used by the federal government for evaluating professional, scientific, clerical, administrative, and custodial jobs.

General systems model—a broad explanation of a system in which more concrete details may be added as needed.

Grapevine—an informal oral communication network within an organization.

Green-circle rate—a wage or salary that lies below the minimum of a particular pay range.

Group incentive plan—a compensation plan in which each worker shares in the achievement of a group of coworkers working as a team to produce more than their expected efficiency.

Group life insurance—the protection that covers all employees of a firm and is designed to provide benefits should a worker die or become totally disabled.

Group workcenter—a combination of all workstations, either departmentally or in some other functional sense.

Groupthink—a situation that occurs when a group's desire for consensus and cohesiveness overcomes its desire to reach the best possible decisions.

Habit—the product of learning in which changes occur in the trainee's previous behavioral patterns and attitudes.

Hard disk—a rigid storage medium, usually encased within the computer, that provides faster retrieval and greater storage capabilities than a floppy disk.

Health maintenance organization (HMO)—an organization of providers (physicians, health-care workers, and affiliated hospital) that offer participants medical services prepaid by the employer and the employee.

Hearing environment—that area of the ergonomic environment dealing with sound.

Historical data—a work measurement method in which past production records of various office activities are studied to measure what was produced in the past.

Horizontal file—equipment for storing papers or records, such as maps and drawings, in a flat position.

Horizontal promotion—the transfer of an employee to another department where promotional opportunities are greater than in the present department.

Hospital, surgical, and medical insurance—the protection covering all or the major part of hospital, surgical, and medical expenses for employees and their dependents.

Host computer—a mainframe that directs the input, processing, output, and distribution of information to, from, and among a group of small computers.

Human relations approach—a behavioral approach followed in the management process that calls attention to the importance of the individual within the organization.

Human skill—the ability to use knowledge and understanding of people as they interact with others.

Hygienic factor—a component (such as pay or working conditions) related to productivity on the job but external to the job itself.

Hypotheses—alternate solutions to a problem.

Idea quota—a technique for stimulating the creation of ideas in which a fixed number of new ideas is required in a stated period of time, thus forcing extreme concentration by participants.

Ideal system—a utopian system in which all systems elements function at their most effective and efficient levels at all times.

Image communication—messages that involve communication symbols transmitted in nonword, nonvoice, and nonnumber form.

Immigration Reform and Control Act of 1986—a federal law that requires employers to verify the employment eligibility of newly hired persons.

In-basket training—a training technique in which trainees assume higher-ranking positions and solve a representative sample of problems under the pressure of time.

Incentive system—a means of increasing the earnings of workers who maintain or exceed an established standard of work performance.

Incident process—a training method in which, after trainees are given a series of incidents occurring in a mythical company and only a minimum of related information, they must obtain all additional data and make decisions.

Incremental budgeting—a budgeting method in which a given percentage of increase (or decrease) is added to (or subtracted from) the budgeted amounts of the preceding period to arrive at new figures.

Index paper—a heavy, durable paper used for machine posting of manual records, punched cards, index files, and library files.

Indirect expenses—general expenses that benefit several departments or the entire company but are not directly traceable to any one department.

Indirect interview—an interviewing technique in which job applicants are stimulated to talk about themselves through the use of open-ended questions.

Individual incentive plan—a compensation plan in which workers are paid according to their own individual production or effort.

Individual retirement account (IRA)—a pension plan, created by the Internal Revenue Code, that is established and funded by an individual employee.

Individual workcenter—the basic unit of office space where each employee performs the bulk of assigned responsibilities; also known as a *workstation*.

Informal organization—those interpersonal relationships that do not appear on the formal organization chart.

Information cycle—the collecting, processing, storing, retrieving, and distributing of information for internal and external use.

Information distribution—that phase of the information cycle in which information is transmitted or moved from the place of processing to the point where it will be used.

Information manager—the person responsible for all information-handling activities in the organization.

Information overload—the communication of an excessive amount of details about company operations and personnel activities.

Information system—the major system for collecting, processing, storing, retrieving, and distributing information within a firm.

Input—the first phase of any system in which data, labor, and other energy, materials, equipment, money, or information are received from another system.

Input-output (I/O) systems improvement model—a general model for analyzing each of the phases in an administrative office system.

Integrated security system (ISS)—safety and security control system made up of intercommunication systems, burglar systems, and building-wide monitors under the control of a building's computer system.

Integrated Services Digital Network (ISDN)—an information-transmission technology in which data are carried in telephone channels using digital (0 and 1) signals.

Intelligence test—an employment test designed to measure mental and reasoning ability.

Intelligent copier/printer—a machine that combines the capabilities of a photocopier with that of a computer and a phototypesetter.

Intelligent terminal—a device that is programmable by a user and that can be operated independently of the computer system to which it is attached.

Intercommunication (intercom) system—a privately owned, small-scale telephone system used to tie together all departments within a firm.

Interconnect companies—those firms that offer a variety of voice, data, text, and image communication equipment that can be connected to the lines of common carriers.

Interest test—an employment test designed to identify a person's likes and dislikes to aid in career counseling.

Internal written communications—communications created and used solely within the firm.

Interview method—a method of obtaining job information in which the job analyst interviews employees and their supervisors to determine the job duties performed and the minimum requirements for holding the job.

Intimate zone—a personal space ranging from skin contact to about two feet that is reserved for persons with close emotional attachments.

Intrapreneurs—those managers who create innovation of any kind *within their organizations.*

Investigative consumer report—information supplied by a credit or investigative agency used to verify data provided by job applicants.

Jargon—those technical terms and idioms that are peculiar to a specific group or activity.

Job analysis—the gathering of information about a specific job and determining the principal elements involved in performing it.

Job classification method—a method of evaluating jobs in which jobs are analyzed and grouped into predetermined classes or family groupings before the jobs are classified.

Job description—an outline of the information obtained from job analysis, which describes the content and essential requirements of a specific job.

Job enrichment—the redesigning of jobs by building in higher-order responsibilities and authorities and more challenging content.

Job evaluation—the process of appraising the value of each job in relation to other jobs in order to set a monetary value for each specific job.

Job rotation—a training method that exposes trainees to a number of functions in a relatively short period of time by rotating them through the various departments of the company or sections of a department.

Job sharing—a work plan in which one permanent, full-time job is shared by two people who generally split their working hours, job responsibilities, and employee benefits.

Job specification—a detailed record of the minimum job requirements explained in relation to the job factors (skill, effort, responsibility, and working conditions).

Key telephone system (KTS)—a voice communication system having two or more telephones.

Keyboard—an input device for entering data and commands to electronic equipment.

Kinesics—the study of the relationship between body motions and communication.

Labor contract—a private agreement entered into by the employer and the employees for the purpose of regulating certain work-related conditions.

Lateral communication—the transmission of messages among personnel at the same level in the organization.

Lateral file—a vertical file in which the long side of the cabinet opens out; also called *side file.*

Leadership—the human process of influencing people to work willingly and enthusiastically to attain organizational objectives.

Leadership style—the consistent pattern of behavior found in a leader.

Leading—a function of management in which workers are motivated and directed so that the objectives of the organization will be successfully achieved.

Learning—the changes that occur in trainees' behavioral patterns and attitudes as a result of training.

Lease—an agreement between the landlord and the tenant that transfers possession of property for a period of time.

Leased line—a telegraph or telephone line between specific points made available to subscribers on a full-time basis.

Lecture—a nonparticipative, one-way communication technique in which an instructor imparts factual information to a group in a relatively short period of time.

Ledger paper—a type of paper that has a good writing surface for use with pencil or ink and that will withstand heavy use because of its cardlike strength.

Legal service plan—a program under which employees obtain company-paid legal advice.

Lessee—a tenant.

Lessor—a landlord.

Leveled data flow diagram—a segment of a data flow diagram in which the flow of data is presented in great detail.

Line organization—an organization structure where authority is passed down in an unbroken chain of command from top management through middle managers and supervisors to workers at the operative level; also known as the *scalar* or *military* type.

Line-and-staff organization—an organization structure that combines features of the line and the functional organization forms; line personnel have the power to act and to command, and specialized staff personnel serve as advisers.

Linear programming (LP)—an operations research technique for determining the best mixture of components in a system.

Local-area network (LAN)—a telecommunication facility that links together various types of information-processing equipment for transmitting and receiving data.

Long-term lease with purchase option—a contract in which the lessee has use of equipment for a stated time period, with the choice of purchasing the equipment at the end of the time period.

Long-term lease with renewal option—a contract in which the lessee has use of equipment for a stated time period, with the choice of renewing the lease at the end of the time period.

Magnetic ink character recognition (MICR)—a system used by banks to interpret and process numeric data recorded in special magnetic ink characters on business forms.

Mainframe—another name for a large computer that serves as the principal source of power and direction for complex company-wide data processing and telecommunication networks.

Major medical insurance—an insurance plan that protects employees and their dependents from huge medical bills resulting from serious accidents or prolonged illness.

Management—the process of planning, organizing, and controlling all the resources and of leading or directing people to attain the goals of a productive, unified organization.

Management by objectives (MBO)—the concept in which objectives are set forth for every area where performance and results directly and vitally affect the survival and prosperity of the organization.

Management development (MD)—training, education, and development provided for employees who aspire to—or are already functioning in—the management ranks.

Management information system (MIS)—an organizational process designed to supply timely information to managers.

Management science—a discipline that uses engineering and mathematical skills to solve complex decision-making problems.

Management theory—a set of principles that are classified and grouped into a managerial framework to predict accurately the outcomes of management operations.

Manager—the person who performs the functions of management: planning, organizing, leading, and controlling.

Manual system—the earliest and most prevalent type of system in which the human being functions as the data processor.

Master budget—a number of budgets that collectively express the planned activities of the organization.

Matrix organization—an organization structure that combines both vertical authority relationships and horizontal or diagonal work relationships in order to deal with complex work projects.

Mechanical system—the system in which many of the data are processed by electromechanical machines.

Median—the middle position in a distribution of values; also known as the *second quartile*.

Mediation—the process in which an impartial third party tries to bring labor and management to a point of common agreement.

Memory—the area in the central processing unit (CPU) where data and programs are temporarily stored before, during, and after processing.

Mentoring—a training arrangement whereby senior managers (*mentors*) impart their expertise to younger managers and supervisors (*protégés*) in the company.

Method—the manual, mechanical, or automated means by which each procedural step is performed.

Metropolitan-area network (MAN)—an intermediate-distance network, covering a geographic area of up to 30 miles, that is capable of transmitting voice, data, text, and image signals at the same time.

Microcomputer—the smallest and least expensive class of computers; also known as a *personal computer* (PC).

Microfiche—a microform that appears in a grid pattern on a transparent sheet of film.

Microform—a microrecord captured on any size or type of film.

Microimage system—the total system for creating, using, and storing microrecords.

Micromotion study—the use of motion pictures to study and analyze parts of a given operation with the objective of eliminating wasteful movements.

Microprocessor—an integrated circuit built on a very small silicon chip.

Microrecord—a paper document converted to microfilm.

Microwave communication system—a radio-relay system that sends signals between towers for ultimate delivery of messages to distant locations.

Minicomputer—a small computer with integrated circuits that is housed in a compact desk-size or desktop cabinet.

Mobile file—equipment in which files move on a track in order that the shelves can be moved together when not in use, or on motorized Ferris-wheel type arrangements in which the records are brought directly to an operator seated at a console.

Model—a simplified, general explanation of the complex interrelationships and activities of an organization or its parts.

Modem—an abbreviation for the term *modulator-demodulator*. This device converts the digital code of the computer into analog code used by the telephone system and also converts the analog code back to digital code for use within the system.

Modular furniture—a collection of integrated, independent furniture components that can be quickly and easily assembled, disassembled, and rearranged to meet employee and department needs.

Module—a unit or component of office furniture that has a specific function.

Moonlighting—the practice of a person holding a second job or working at a second profession after the regular "daylight" job has ended.

Morale—the mental and emotional attitudes of persons toward the tasks expected of them by their group and their loyalty to that group.

Motion study—a work measurement method in which work is divided into its most fundamental elements, which are studied and timed in order to eliminate wasteful movement and effort.

Motivate—to create the kind of environment in which workers are enthusiastic and have a desire to work.

Motivation-hygiene theory—a theory of motivation that examines the effects of hygienic and motivator factors upon people in a work environment.

Motivator—a factor (such as the feeling of self-improvement or recognition) that creates positive attitudes toward work.

Multimedia—the combining of audio, video, text, graphics, still images, and animation to present learning materials in a computer-based setting.

Nepotism—the showing of favoritism in the employment of relatives.

Network analysis—a communication research technique used to find out where people go to get their needed information.

Network filing—an organizational plan in which records are retained in each department but controlled centrally.

Networked personal computers—PCs linked together through a network or file server.

No-fault leave policy—a plan for reducing absenteeism by providing a maximum number of days to be absent for any reason.

Noise-reduction coefficient (NRC)—a measure of the amount of noise absorbed or removed from an area.

Nominal group technique (NGT)—a technique for developing creativity in which participants work alone, silently, in small noninteraction groups to solve problems.

Nonunitized microform—a microrecord that contains random or unrelated items of information on the same continuous length of film.

Nonverbal communication—any information not spoken or written that is perceived by one's senses.

Objective—a desired goal, sometimes considered a target or an aim.

Observation method—a method of obtaining job information in which the analyst observes employees performing their duties and learns about working conditions, equipment used, and requirements for special skills.

Office automation (OA)—an MIS process that aims to maximize the productivity of managing information.

Old-age, survivors, disability, and health insurance (OASDHI) program—the program planned to provide economic security for workers and their families.

Ombudsman—an informal problem-solver employed by a company to investigate employees' complaints and to reconcile differences in an impartial way.

On-the-job training (OJT)—training in which the trainees are provided the knowledge and skills needed to perform their jobs while using the actual equipment and materials required on the jobs.

Open plan—an office layout design characterized by open space, free of conventional walls and corridors, which brings together all the functional, behavioral, and technical factors needed to design individual workstations, work groups, and departments.

Open system—a type of system that interacts with its environment in order to attain its goals.

Operational decisions—those decisions that concern the day-to-day operations of the office.

Operations research (OR)—a method of analysis to obtain the best possible solutions to decision-making problems in complex systems.

Optical character recognition (OCR)—a scanning system used for reading numeric and alphabetic data that have been printed in a distinctive type style on business forms.

Optical disk—a form of computer storage in which a laser-beam recorder scans a document, a film, or a slide and then copies it and transfers the image onto a metal disk.

Oral communication—that form of verbal communication which is spoken.

Organization—any form of group endeavor.

Organization chart—a graphic picture of the functional units in a firm showing the principal lines of authority.

Organization manual—a book that describes the organization, duties, and responsibilities of the firm's departments and all other functional areas.

Organization structure—the arrangement of functions—the framework—that must be constructed to achieve the organization's goals.

Organizing—a function of management that brings together all economic resources (the work, workplace, information, and workers) to form a controllable (manageable) unit—the organization—to accomplish specific objectives.

Orientation—a carefully planned, systematic, and effective program that introduces new workers to their jobs.

Orientation checklist—a tool of orientation containing items to be covered by the person who is introducing new employees to their firm and their jobs.

Outplacement counseling—an employer-sponsored program designed to assist laid-off workers in applying for unemployment compensation benefits and in obtaining company benefits.

Output—the ultimate objective of a system that results after the input has been transformed into the desired form.

Outsourcing—a technique in which functions formerly performed within the organization are contracted to be performed by an outside agent.

Paging system—a system used to locate persons who are away from their workstations.

Paralanguage—those aspects of oral communication such as voice qualities and vocalizations that are free of words.

Parkinson's law—a concept which explains that work expands to fill the time available for its completion, that work expands to fit the organization designed to perform that work, and that each unit tends to build up its importance by expanding the number of its personnel.

Participative leader—one who openly invites workers to join in and take part in decision making, setting policy, and analyzing methods of operation.

Participative management—a technique in which workers are given a voice in determining what they are to do, how they are to do it, and how they are to be appraised.

Participative organization—an organization that adheres to the democratic relations found in Theory Y, where all workers have the opportunity to achieve their full potential.

Password—a code used to protect records and retrieve data in an automated records system.

Patterned interview—an interviewing technique in which a standard printed form or questionnaire containing specific key questions is used by an interviewer to record the job applicants' responses.

Pay for performance—a compensation plan in which salary increases are determined by the employee's job performance; also called *merit increase.*

Payback period—the time period over which a capital expenditure will generate cash equal to the cost of the proposal.

Perception—a way of interpreting situations based upon the individual's personal experiences.

Performance appraisal—the evaluation and constructive criticism of an employee's work.

Performance rating—the adjustment of individual differences obtained in stopwatch studies in order to obtain a theoretical normal time required by average workers to complete their jobs under standardized conditions.

Permanent part-time employment—the employment of persons on a regular voluntary basis (not temporary or casual) during working hours shorter than normal.

Perquisites—the privileges, gains, or profits provided executives in addition to their regular salaries; also called *perks.*

Personal space—an area of privacy surrounding the worker that is important for keeping out other people.

Personal zone—a personal space ranging from two feet to four feet.

Personality and psychological tests—employment tests designed to measure abstract concepts, such as aggressiveness, honesty, integrity, independence, conformity, and passivity.

Personnel requisition—a personnel form, originating in the department needing workers, that specifies the number of persons required and the kind of work to be done.

PERT (Program Evaluation and Review Technique)—a long-range planning technique that is used to determine the time required to complete major projects after realistic time estimates have been made of the various activities associated with each project.

Phototypesetter—a machine capable of creating print on a special VDT screen from data obtained from word processing or computer systems or from direct keyboard entry.

Physical activities—those human activities requiring the use of human energy.

Physical decentralization—the geographic separation of home-office managers from the division or branch managers; also known as *geographic dispersion.*

Piece-rate system—a compensation plan in which workers receive a fixed price or wage for each unit produced.

Planning—a function of management that analyzes relevant information from the past and the present and assesses probable developments of the future so that a course of action—the plan—may be determined that will enable the firm to meet its stated goals.

Plateau—a period of time or a level of learning where no observable improvement occurs or where the rate of increase in learning levels off.

Playscript procedure—a systems communication that lists, in sequential order, the details necessary to operate a system and who is responsible for performing each step.

Point-factor method—a method of evaluating jobs in which the factors of skill, effort, responsibility, and job conditions are divided into subfactors, with degrees and points assigned to each subfactor.

Policy—a broad guideline for operating the organization.

Post-exit interview—an interview conducted after the terminated employees have left the firm, usually by means of questionnaires sent to the former employees.

Predetermined times—the constant time values applied to basic motions of each job element so that the time value for performing the entire job may be read from a table in order to set time standards.

Preferred provider organization (PPO)—an employer, care provider, or insurance company that develops a list of preferred providers (physicians, hospitals, and other health-care services) that have been selected on the basis of their low cost and high quality from which employees select that physician or hospital they desire.

Pregnancy Discrimination Act of 1978—an amendment to the Civil Rights Act that states it is unlawful for employers to fire or refuse to hire a woman because she is pregnant.

Preretirement counseling—an employer-sponsored program that provides assistance to workers approaching retirement age.

Principle—a broad, general statement considered to be true and that accurately reflects real-world conditions in all walks of life.

Privacy Act of 1974—a federal law regulating the collection and use of personal data by the government.

Private automatic branch exchange (PABX)—a switching system that performs many time-saving calling tasks under computer control.

Private branch exchange (PBX)—a switching system for manually handling telephone calls where the number of extension telephones is not great and the volume of calls is not heavy.

Private employment agency—a source of labor supply that charges a fee to either the job applicant or the employer.

Problem—a question to be answered; the difference between a state or condition that exists and the state or condition that is desired.

Problem solving—the process of recognizing or identifying a discrepancy (or gap) between an actual and a desired state of affairs and then taking action to resolve the discrepancy (i.e., to close the gap).

Problem-solving environment—the conditions surrounding the problem and the specific factors directly involved in its solution.

Procedural activities—those human activities that refer to predefined work steps followed by office employees.

Procedure—a planned sequence of operations for handling recurring transactions uniformly and consistently.

Process—an activity in a data flow diagram in which data are being manipulated.

Productivity—the ratio between the resources used by a business firm and what the firm realizes from using those resources.

Profit-sharing plan—a group incentive plan in which employees receive payments based upon a percentage of the company's profits for the year.

Program—a set of instructions for processing data in a computer system.

Programmer—a highly skilled technician who specializes in writing computer programs and plans the conversion of unprocessed data onto one or more media.

Promotion trials—promotions made with the consent of the persons being transferred and with the promoted employees given the option of returning to their previous jobs if they are unsuccessful or unhappy on their new jobs.

Prototype—a basic model.

Proxemics—the study of how individuals use physical space in their interactions with others and how physical space influences behavior.

Public employment service—a source of labor supply at the state level affiliated with the Department of Labor.

Punched aperture card—a standard-size 80-column punched card with a precut hole over which a portion of 35-mm microfilm is mounted.

Quality circle—a group of workers who voluntarily meet together on a regular basis to identify, analyze, and solve job-related quality problems and to develop employee potential.

Quality control—a regulatory process in which the quality of performance is measured and compared with standards so that any difference between performance and standards may be acted upon.

Quality management—a philosophy and a set of principles used to guide the entire organization in continuous improvement.

Quartile—a measure of position that divides an array into four equal parts.

Questionnaire method—a method of obtaining job information in which employees, often aided by their supervisors and the job analyst, describe their job duties and indicate minimum requirements for holding the job.

Random-access memory (RAM)—the array of memory locations or addresses available on one or more microchips for the storage of data or programs.

Ranking method—a method of evaluating jobs in which jobs are analyzed and ranked according to the difficulty and overall responsibility of each job.

Read-only memory (ROM)—a special type of memory that is permanently programmed with one group of frequently used instructions.

Reader—a device that enlarges or magnifies the microrecord to its original legible size and projects the image onto a viewing screen.

Real-world system—a system that provides the best possible service to departments, subject to certain limitations.

Record—written or oral evidence that information has been collected and kept for use in making decisions.

Record of employment—the personal resumé and history of an applicant's employment with the firm.

Record of interview—a personnel form containing all the information acquired during the interview.

Recorder—a device that uses either photographic or laser technology to transfer the computer's output to microimage size on film.

Records creation—a preventive maintenance program that determines who creates records and why, and ensures that supervisors approve the creation or redesign of forms.

Records disposition—a phase of a records management program that is responsible for transferring and storing inactive records and for destroying unneeded records.

Records life cycle—the steps or sequential phases in the life of records that include creation, storage, retrieval, maintenance, and disposition.

Records maintenance—a set of service activities in a records management program needed to operate the storage and retrieval systems.

Records management—an organization-wide administrative service responsible for creating and maintaining systematic procedures and controls over all phases of the records life cycle.

Records retention schedule—a document describing how long each key record is to be kept in the files.

Records retrieval—the process of locating stored information.

Records storage—the procedures and equipment used to house physical and electronic documents efficiently and securely.

Recycled paper—the waste paper that is reduced to a pulp state by paper manufacturers before new fibers are added for the production of economical second-use papers.

Red-circle rate—a wage or salary that lies above the maximum of a particular pay range.

Reduction ratio—an expression of the number of times the size of a record is reduced photographically.

Re-engineering—the process of completely rebuilding a system from its most fundamental components.

Referrals—a source of labor supply originating with present employees, company officers, or customers who recommend a person for employment.

Reflection ratio—a measure of the amount of light reflected from a surface as a percentage of the total amount of light striking that surface.

Reinforcement—a condition following a response that results in an increase in the strength of that response.

Relative humidity—the percentage of moisture in the air.

Reliability—the extent to which a test measures consistently whatever it is designed to measure.

Remedial training—training to remedy or correct deficiencies in work habits, attitudes, knowledge, skills, or job performance.

Reprographic system—a system related to the reproduction of information and records for management.

Responsibility—the obligation and accountability for properly performing work that is assigned.

Responsibility accounting—the system that provides means for establishing control over costs and expenses so that timely reports are made to managers and supervisors of those costs for which they are responsible.

Restricted stock plan—an employee stock ownership plan in which qualified employees are given the actual shares of their company's stock as an incentive to foster team spirit and to instill loyalty.

Retraining—training provided for workers whose jobs have changed, have become obsolete, or are no longer required.

Retrieval efficiency ratio—a measure used to evaluate a records system in which the time (in seconds) to locate a record is compared with the number of records requested.

Right-to-work laws—the state laws that ban contracts which make union membership or the payment of fees a condition of employment.

Role playing—a training technique in which trainees act out their own parts or those of others under simulated conditions.

Roll film—a continuous length of microfilm, 16 mm, 35 mm, or 105 mm in width, and 100 feet in length, on which original documents have been photographed and reduced in size for storage.

Rotary file—equipment for storing records in which the records rotate in a circular fashion around a common hub.

Rotation of layoffs—a program whereby employees may work for four weeks and then be laid off for one week, with the possibility of collecting unemployment compensation benefits.

Safe and secure environment—all the factors that protect the physical needs of the workers and give them a sense of well-being.

Salary survey—a statistical picture of the salaries for certain jobs in a particular geographic area or for a particular industry at a given time.

Sale-leaseback plan—a contract in which a user

purchases equipment, sells it to a lessor, and then leases it back under a long-term lease.

Satellite administrative services center—a compact workstation that handles information processing and general office activities for users of the office services.

Savings and thrift plans—employer-sponsored plans that permit employees to allot a portion of their income to an individual retirement account.

Scanlon plan—the oldest and best-known gain-sharing system.

Scanner—an input device that converts printed or handwritten words, numbers, symbols, and graphics into electronic impulses.

Scientific management—the approach toward the management of work and of organizations that uses the scientific method of problem solving.

Scientific method of problem solving—a tool of scientific management that uses logical, systematic steps to develop effective solutions to problems.

Seeing environment—all the items needed to provide adequate light for performing the work assigned the office.

Semantics—the study of word meanings and their effect upon human behavior.

Service contract—an agreement between the user of equipment and the manufacturer or other service organization that provides for periodic cleaning and lubrication, inspection, and replacement of worn-out and defective machine parts.

Sexual harassment—first defined by the EEOC as unwelcome sexual advances, requests for sexual favors, and other verbal or physical conduct of a sexual nature, where such conduct affects an individual's prospects for employment or advancement or unreasonably interferes with work performance.

Sexual orientation—a person's preference in sex or affectional partners.

Shared-logic word processor—one unit in a system of multiple processors and printers that can operate simultaneously under the direction of a small computer.

Short-term lease—a rental contract in which a user obtains equipment for peak workload jobs for a relatively short time period.

Simplified employee pension (SEP) plan—a plan in which employers make contributions to the individual retirement accounts (IRAs) on behalf of their employees.

Simulation—a basic operations research (OR) technique for creating a mathematical model of a real-world system.

Skill-based pay system—a compensation plan in which remuneration is based upon the knowledge or skills that the person brings to the job, with salary increases awarded as the employee acquires additional knowledge and skills.

Slanting—the conscious manipulation of facts in order to distort events.

Smart building—an office building that has a computer for a brain and a nervous system of cables and electronic sensors that allow the computer to monitor and interact with building conditions and which tenants can access for telecommunications and automated office services.

Smart form—an automated form that is created with a special set of forms design and fill-in instructions stored in a computer file.

Smart terminal—a dumb terminal to which have been added more powerful features capable of processing operations independent of the mainframe.

Social activities—those human activities that involve the interpersonal tasks of two or more persons and that range from simple duties, such as telephoning, to more complex activities, such as conferring.

Social zone—a personal space ranging from about 4 feet to 12 feet; generally maintained in business situations where people work together.

Soft-copy form—a VDT-designed form that appears on the terminal screen for the entry of data into the computer system.

Span of control—the number of employees who are directly supervised by one person.

Specialist—a person who masters or becomes expert at doing a certain type of work.

Specialty form—a form that requires special equipment for its manufacture or use. Types of specialty forms include carbonless forms, continuous forms, unit-set forms, and a wide variety of miscellaneous forms requiring special printing processes.

Sponsor system—an orientation technique in which a new employee is assigned to a worker (the sponsor) who takes care of the new employee, acquaints him or her with the duties of the job, and answers questions.

Spot-carbon unit-set form—a form on which a carbon coating has been applied only to certain areas in order to convey or withhold information from users as the needs of the information system dictate.

Staggered work schedule—a plan under which groups of workers arrive at their workplace at different times, according to a master plan.

Standalone word processor—a self-contained T/WP system with a video display terminal.

Standard electric typewriter—typewriter for small-volume typewriting.

State disability benefits—payments from a state insurance plan to workers who are absent from their jobs because of illness, accident, or disease not arising out of their employment.

Status—the level of individuals in the organization structure.

Stereotyping—the formation of a commonly held mental picture of how people or a particular sex, religion, or race appear, think, feel, and act.

Stock option plan—an employee stock ownership plan in which eligible employees are given an opportunity to purchase a specific number of shares of their company's stock by a specific date at a specific price that is often lower than the market price.

Stock purchase plan—an employee stock ownership plan in which qualified employees are given the opportunity to purchase shares of their company's stock at a price usually lower than the current market price.

Stress—the physical, chemical, or emotional state a person experiences at the time of a crisis or when subjected to irritations and unpleasant situations.

Structured questionnaire—a form that requests information on whether specific tasks are part of the worker's job in order to learn the importance the jobholder attaches to each task.

Subsystem—a subdivision of a system that is responsible for accomplishing specialized functions of the total system.

Supervising diversity—the process of accepting, understanding, and appreciating differences among employees and creating an environment that allows *all* kinds of people to reach their full potential in pursuit of company and personal objectives.

Supervisory training (ST)—training that provides experiences, education, and development that helps promising employees qualify for supervision.

Supervisory training and management development (STMD)—the training program designed to qualify workers for the added responsibilities and challenges of higher positions.

Supplemental unemployment benefits (SUBs)—the benefits provided by an employer's private plan to supplement the state unemployment compensation benefits received by employees during periods of layoff.

Surface environment—those physical features in the office (walls, ceilings, furniture, equipment, and floor coverings) that are an essential part of the building, its layout, and the work performed.

Switching system—an exchange for receiving and distributing internal and external telephone calls without the need for a switchboard operator.

Symptoms—the signs or conditions that indicate the existence of a problem.

Synergism—the overall effect created in a system whereby interrelated parts produce a total effect greater than the sum of each of the parts working independently.

System—a group of parts that are interrelated in such a manner that they form a unified whole and work together to attain a definite objective.

Systems approach—a method of problem solving used by the systems analyst in which interrelationships in the work system are emphasized.

Systems boundary—that element of a system which defines its scope or limits and which separates a system from its environment.

Systems chart—a graphic device used to portray an existing or a proposed system, including the flow of information and the various elements required to operate a system.

Systems development life cycle (SDLC)—a logical six-step sequence of activities used to create a new system.

Systems study—the process of improving systems.

Systems study cycle—a set of sequential problem-solving steps required to improve the systems function.

Task—a definable unit (or piece) of work.

Task analysis—a systems technique used to determine who does what work.

Task lighting—a type of lighting system in which the light fixtures are built into open-plan office furniture to light specific work areas.

Technical skill—the ability to understand a specific function, with its specialized knowledges, and to use efficiently the tools and techniques related to that function or activity.

Telecommunications—the electronic transfer of data from one point in an information system to another.

Telecommuting—the application of telecommunications technology to the processing of information at a location other than the traditional office setting.

Teleconference—a telephone service that ties together three or more people at two or more separate locations.

Teleconferencing—a telephone service (audio only) that ties together three or more people at two or more separate locations.

Teletex—a high-speed, desk-to-desk message service that allows users to type, edit, and transmit nonvoice messages over telephone lines to their destinations.

Telex—an international telegraph network operated by Western Union.

Temporary office help service—a source of labor supply that provides temporary workers for varying time periods, with a flat fee being charged the employer.

Territoriality—the physical area under the control of a worker and designed specifically for that worker's use.

Text—the written communications composed and produced in the office.

Text management (TM)— a system that electronically and/or mechanically captures or enters, processes, outputs, and stores words and sometimes graphic images.

Text/word processing (T/WP) system—a combination of people, equipment, and procedures for converting words into a final product and forwarding it to the user.

Theory—a set of principles grouped into a general framework that explains the basic relationships among the principles.

Theory X—the view of worker behavior in which workers are characterized as disliking work and avoiding it if they can, preferring to be led rather than lead, lacking ambition, and being irresponsible.

Theory Y—the view of worker behavior in which workers are viewed as willing to work and accept responsibility, capable of self-direction and self-control, and able to use their imagination and originality.

Theory Z organization—an organization, modeled after the Japanese style of management, that relies greatly upon such factors as long-range planning; strong, mutual worker-employer loyalty and trust; stable, long-term employment; slow evaluation and promotion; and decision making by consensus.

Third quartile—that position in a distribution of values which is more than three-fourths of all the values listed.

Time log method—a work measurement method in which workers measure their output by recording the time spent and units of work produced for a stipulated time period.

Time management—a program in which all resources, including time, are efficiently used to achieve one's important professional and personal goals.

Time study—a work measurement method in which the time required to perform each operation at an average pace is determined.

Tolerance—the degree of accuracy that will be accepted when determining sample size.

Total entity management—an approach toward the management of work and of organizations characterized by the search for effective means of directing the business firm as a whole, or as an entity.

Total system—a company-wide information network composed of a large number of major systems.

Training—the process of providing individuals with an organized series of experiences and materials that comprise opportunities to learn.

Transactional leadership—an approach in which the leader sees job performance as a series of task-oriented and/or people-oriented transactions with the workers.

Transformation process—the phase of a system that changes inputs into outputs.

Transformational leadership—an approach in which the leader inspires workers to achieve outstanding performance by influencing their beliefs, values, and goals.

Travel accident insurance—a plan of protection that provides benefits to covered employees in the event of their death, disability, or dismemberment while traveling on company business.

Turnaround time—the time that elapses from word origination until the finished document is returned for approval.

Turnover—the amount of movement of employees, voluntarily and involuntarily, in and out of an organization.

Turnover rate—the extent of movement of employees, expressed most often in terms of the number of separations from the payroll.

Ultrafiche—a special type of microfiche that permits very high (ultra) reduction ratios.

Unemployment compensation insurance—a federal-state program established to provide funds at the state level for compensating unemployed workers in that state during periods of temporary unemployment.

Union shop agreement—the requirement that after workers have been hired, they must join the union or make dues payment within a specified time period or be fired.

Unit-set form—a preassembled multisheet form of either carbon or carbonless paper.

Unitized microform—a microrecord that is prepared as one complete set of data, such as a payroll file.

Unity of command—a management principle which states that each employee should receive orders from, and be responsible to, only one supervisor.

Updatable microfiche—a type of microfiche in which a special camera erases an obsolete record and places a new image over the erased record.

Upward communication—the transmission of messages that flow vertically from one level in the organization to one or more levels above.

User friendly—a computer systems term meaning "easy to operate."

Validity—the extent to which a test serves the purpose for which it was intended.

Value system—the sum of one's moral and social perception of those things that are intrinsically desirable or valuable.

Variable costs—those costs that change in response to changes in the volume of business activity.

Variable pay—any form of direct compensation, not included in the employee's base pay, that varies according to employee or corporate performance.

Variance—the difference between actual operating data and budgeted data.

Verbal communication—the most basic form of communication, which consists of words—spoken or written.

Vertical file—a filing cabinet that contains one to six drawers in which records are stored on edge.

Vestibule training—training that takes place in an area away from the site where the job is usually performed, with the workstation simulated and the necessary equipment provided.

Vesting—the process of conveying to employees the right to share in a retirement fund in the event they are terminated before the normal retirement age.

Video display terminal (VDT)—the leading device for entering data into the computer.

Video teleconference—a type of teleconference that combines the audio dimension of voice with color television.

Videoconferencing—a communication method that uses a combination of audio and video equipment to join two or more distant groups.

Videofax—a telecommunication process that enables users of video equipment to send a still image, such as a photograph, over public or dedicated telephone lines in the same manner that documents are sent via conventional FAX devices.

Videotext—a telecommunication process in which textual data—and sometimes graphics—are transmitted to specially adapted television sets.

Vietnam Era Veterans' Readjustment Assistance Act of 1974—a federal law requiring employers with government contracts of $10,000 or more to take affirmative action to employ and to advance in employment qualified veterans.

Virtual reality—a computer-created sensory experience that immerses the participant in an artificial setting of virtual realism.

Visual comfort probability (VCP)—a measure that indicates how much direct glare a luminaire is likely to produce.

Vocational Rehabilitation Act of 1973—a federal law designed to provide employment opportunities for qualified physically and mentally handicapped individuals and to eliminate employment discrimination based upon such handicaps.

Voice communication system—a telecommunication system in which messages originated by speakers are sent by wire or wireless methods to listeners who receive and respond to the messages.

Voice mail—a system in which messages are stored in digital form in the computer and later delivered in the caller's voice when the called person requests such messages from the computer's mailbox.

Voice-recognition system—a computer-based system in which the computer "understands" and records the human voice as input and performs operations based upon these inputs.

Voice-recognition unit—an input device that decodes and converts the human voice into electronic impulses.

Voice-to-print system—the process in which a word originator speaks directly into a recorder, after which a computer-connected word processing terminal converts the spoken words into visual words on the display screen.

Wide-area network (WAN)—a telecommunication facility that covers a large geographic area and provides public and private channels for transmitting and receiving messages.

Wide-area telecommunications service (WATS)—a long-distance telephone service for sending voice, data, text, and image messages at discounted rates.

Word origination—the process of creating messages.

Work distribution chart—a systems chart for identifying and comparing the principal tasks of all workers in the system under study.

Work letter—the portion of a lease that spells out the lessor's and the lessee's obligations for any work to be done to the building and who will pay for it.

Work measurement—a tool of cost control used to determine how much work is completed (a quantitative measure) and how effectively it is completed (a qualitative measure).

Work measurement and setting work standards—the procedure for determining the time required to accomplish each job or task and for setting up criteria by which the degree of work performance may be measured.

Work sampling—a work measurement method based upon the statistical law of probability in which findings representative of the universe are obtained by taking valid random samples of work done.

Work sharing—a short-time compensation plan in which employees work a shorter week, have their salaries reduced accordingly, and receive partial state unemployment compensation benefits for their lost days' pay.

Work simplification model—a set of general guidelines, based upon logic and common sense, for analyzing a system.

Work standard—a yardstick of performance, or par, which indicates what is expected of workers and how their output can be evaluated.

Work team—an organization structure, either permanent or temporary, that is created to improve lateral relations and to solve problems throughout the organization.

Workaholic—one who is emotionally dependent upon work.

Workers' compensation insurance—a state insurance program designed to protect employees and their dependents against losses due to injury or death incurred during the worker's employment.

Workflow—the movement of information vertically between supervisors and subordinates or horizontally among workers on the same level.

Workflow analysis—a type of systems study that concentrates on the origination and distribution of documents and the clerical operations required to process information in an administrative office system.

Workplace analysis—a systems space study that seeks to improve the arrangement of all resources needed to function efficiently at a workstation.

Workstation analysis—a detailed study that arranges in an orderly fashion information about each employee's work and workstation needs.

WORM (write-once, read-many) storage—a type of data storage that limits the user to writing to the disk just once but that provides many opportunities for reading out the disk contents.

Written communication—that form of verbal communication which consists of nonspoken words.

Xerography—an electrostatic dry process that exposes a positively charged drum surface to light reflected through lenses from the original document.

Zero-base budgeting (ZBB)—a budgeting method in which budget makers examine anew and justify each expenditure each budget period.

Index

Absenteeism, 304–306
  causes of, 305
  controlling, 306
  cost of, 305–306
  extent of, 304–305
Absenteeism rate, definition of, 304
Abuse
  alcohol, screening for, 144
  drug. *See* Drug abuse
Access legal plan, 278
Accountemps, 245
Acquired immune deficiency syn-
    drome (AIDS), 292–293
Activities in office, 357
Adherence, principle of, 640
Administration, definition of, 2
Administrative assistant. *See* As-
    sistant-to
Administrative cost studies, 593
Administrative decisions, defini-
    tion of, 3
Administrative expenses
  allocating, 643f, 643–644
  definition of, 638
Administrative expenses budget,
    640–648
  principles of preparing,
    638–640
Administrative office manage-
    ment
  careers in, 9–11
  definition of, 2
  functions of, 3
Administrative office manager
  definition of, 4

leadership styles of, 46–50
as problem solvers, 56–59
responsibilities of, 4–8, 6f–7f
skills of, 8–9
Administrative office systems
  (AOS)
  definition of, 82
  functions of, 83f, 83–86
  objectives of, 84–86
  organization of, 84, 85f
  problems with, 86, 88f
  space in, 322–324
  studies in, 581–594
Administrative practice manuals,
    443
Administrative secretaries, defini-
    tion of, 462
Administrative services, defini-
    tion of, 322
Adoption benefit plans, 279
Advertising, help-wanted, 134
Affirmative action, 151
Age Discrimination in Employ-
    ment Act of 1967, 153f
Air environment, 373–375
  circulation in, 374
  cleanliness in, 374–375
  definition of, 373
Alcohol abuse, screening for, 144
Alcoholic, definition of, 288
Alcoholism
  behavioral patterns and visible
    signs of, 289f
  definition of, 288
  early detection of, 288

education about, 288
referral for, 288
Ambient factors
  definition of, 359
  in office, 359
Ambient lighting, 369
American Management Associa-
    tion (AMA), 11, 221, 245
American Payroll Association,
    221, 245
American Psychological Associa-
    tion (APA), and honesty test-
    ing, 145
Americans with Disabilities Act
    of 1990 (ADA), 153f, 377
Analog computers, definition of,
    409
Analysis
  job. *See* Job analysis
  network, 110
  systems, 95–98
  task, 587–590
AOM. *See* Administrative office
    manager
Aperture cards
  retrieval of, 547
  storage of, 547
Application form, 136–137
Application program, 419
Applications, and recruiting office
    workers, 135
Appraisal, employee performance.
    See Performance appraisal
Arbitration, definition of, 249
Archives, 555

Note: The letter *f* following a page number indicates that the item is found in a figure.
The letter *t* following a page number indicates that the item is found in a table.

Arithmetic-logic unit, 418
Artificial light, 368–369
Artificial reality, 195
Assessment centers, 199–200
    definition of, 199
Assistant-to, 38
Association for Information and
    Image Management (AIIM),
    11, 562–563
Association for Systems Manage-
    ment (ASM), 11, 98
Association of Information Man-
    agers (AIM), 11
Association of Records Managers
    and Administrators (ARMA),
    11, 99
Attitudes, 61
Attitude surveys, 178–179
    definition of, 178
Audio-response system, definition
    of, 476
Audio teleconference, definition
    of, 490
Authoritarian leader. *See* Auto-
    cratic leader
Authoritarian organization, defini-
    tion of, 172
Authority
    centralized, 33
    decentralized, 33
    definition of, 29
    delegation of, 31
Authorization card, 313
Autocratic leader, 48
Automated mailing systems, 500
Automated office, 422–428
Automated office systems
    establishing, 430–432
    evaluating, 434–435
    managing, 428–435
    planning and organizing,
        430–432
    security of, 433–434
Automated teller machines
    (ATMs), 428
Automated text/word processing
    systems, 452–458
    components of, 452–454, 454f
    emerging developments in, 458
Automated workcenters, 336,
    424–425
    furniture for, 389–391

Automatic progression plan, defi-
    nition of, 252
Automation, of office, 7–8
Average, definition of, 244
Average rate of return, definition
    of, 397–398

Bandwidth, definition of, 472
Base pay, 255
BASIC (Beginner's all-purpose
    symbolic instruction code), 419
Beginner's all-purpose symbolic
    instruction code (BASIC), 419
Behavioral school of management,
    16–19
Behavioral science approach
    definition of, 17
    to worker behavior, 17–19
Behavior problems, on job,
    357–359
Benchmarking, definition of, 622
Benchmark jobs
    definition of, 228
    factor-comparison ranking of,
        229t
Benefit dollar, division of, 264f
Benefits
    dental care, 268
    legally required, 266
    life insurance, 270–271
    medical and medically related,
        266–268
    miscellaneous, 274–279
    payments for time not worked,
        271–273
    prescription drug plan, 268
    retirement and savings plan,
        268–270
    state disability, 266
    supplemental unemployment
        (SUBs), 270
    vacation, 271
    vision care, 268
Bias, as barrier to communication,
    119–120
Bisexual, 299
Bit, definition of, 409
Block letter style, 446f
Body language, 121–122
Bona fide occupational qualifica-
    tions (BFOQ), 150
Brainstorming, 63–64

Break-even analysis, definition of,
    396–397
Break-even chart, 397f
Brevity, in report-writing, 124
Briefcase computer, 411
Broadbanding, 44, 251, 253
Bubble memory, definition of, 420
Budget, 645t
    administrative expenses. *See*
        Administrative expenses bud-
        get
    definition of, 634
    flexible, 637–638
    master, 637, 638f
Budgetary control
    AOM's role in, 636–638
    cost-analysis problems related
        to, 648–652
    definition of, 634
Budget committee, 637
Budgeting
    approaches to, 640
    compromise, 646
    definition of, 634
    incremental, 644–645
    methods of, 644–646
    zero-base (ZBB), 645–646
Budget performance reporting,
    646, 647f–648f
Budget performance reports, defi-
    nition of, 634–636
Building management systems,
    334
Bulletin boards, 112
Bureaucracy, definition of, 14
Bureaucratic leader, 48–49
Bureau of Labor Statistics, 221, 245
Burnout, 294–295
    checklist for measuring, 296
Business Week, 245
Buying, relative net cost of,
    396–398
Buying power, 240
Byte, definition of, 409

Cafeteria plan, 281
Call-back system, definition of,
    532
Capital, supply of, 343
Card-ranking method, 225–226
Career apparel, provision for em-
    ployees, 277

Career conferences, for recruiting office workers, 135
Career goal planning
definition of, 165
guidelines for, 165*f*
Careers, in administrative office management, 9–11
Carney, John M., 69
Carpooling, 279
Case study, definition of, 199
Cash inflow, definition of, 396
CD-ROM, 421
Cellular telephone, definition of, 477
Cellular telephone system, 477, 477*f*
Central exchange, 487
Centralization
advantages of, 45
of office operations, 45–46
Centralized authority, 33
Centralized control, principle of, 517–519
Centralized filing, 519, 521*f*
Central processing unit (CPU), 417–418, 454
data flow in, 417*f*
Central recorder system, definition of, 451
Centrex, 487, 488*f*
Certified Administrative Manager (C.A.M.), 12
Chairs
administrative support posture, 389
ergonomic, 388
executive, 389
side, 389
Charge-back accounting system, definition of, 643–644
Chart
forms distribution, 580, 588*f*
Gantt, 324–325, 325*f*
systems, 580
work distribution, 580, 591*f*
Check-off, definition of, 249
Chief Information Officer (CIO), 6
Childcare service, 278
Child labor restrictions, 247
Choice making, 56*f*
definition of, 55
Christmas bonuses, 276

Circulation, air, 374
Civil Rights Act of 1964, 146–151
Civil Rights Act of 1991, 298
Clarity, in report-writing, 124
Classical school of management, 13–16
Clean Air Act, 311
Cleanliness, air, 374–375
Clerical workcenters, 425
Climate surveys, definition of, 179
Clip art, definition of, 458
Closed system, 87–89
COBOL (Common business oriented language), 418–419
Cocaine, warning signs of abuse and dependency, 291*f*
Codetermination, as type of committee organization, 41
Cognitive activities, definition of, 357
Cognitive resource theory, 47
Collective bargaining
definition of, 248
and office salaries, 248–249
Color(s)
distance effect of, 360
effective use of, 359–363
furniture and equipment, 363
human reactions to, 359–362, 361*f*
mood effect of, 360
reflection values of, 362, 363*t*
temperature effect of, 360
wall and ceiling, 362–363
Commercial writing class, of papers, 516
Commitment, principle of, 187
Committee organization
advantages of, 41
disadvantages of, 41
types of, 39–41
Common business oriented language (COBOL), 418–419
Communicating word processor, definition of, 484
Communication
barriers to, 116–121
definition of, 105
flow of, 110*f*, 110–116
nonverbal, 121–125
purposes of, 107, 108*f*
verbal, 107

written. *See* Written communications
Communication audit, 110
Communication manual, 444*f*, 445
Communication networks
formal, 107, 109*f*
informal, 107–109
Communication process model, 105–107, 106*f*
Communication satellite (Comsat), 477–478, 478*f*
Community agencies, for recruiting office workers, 134
Commuter-assistance transportation programs, 279
Compact disk read-only memory. *See* CD-ROM
Company courses of study, 193–194
Company discounts, 279
Company medical facilities, 276
Composing-at-keyboard method, of message creation, 448
Comprehensive Occupational Data Analysis Programs (CODAP), definition of, 216
Comprehensive prepaid legal plan, 278
Compressed workweek, definition of, 308
Compromise budgeting, 646
Computer, programming, 418–419
Computer-aided design (CAD), for office layouts, 341–342, 342*f*
Computer-aided software engineering (CASE), 428
Computer-assisted retrieval (CAR), 549–550
advanced system, 549–550, 550*f*
basic system, 549
Computer-based message system, 484–486
definition of, 484
Computer-based training, definition of, 194
Computer-connected word processor, 455–456
definition of, 455
Computer-input microfilm (CIR), 549
Computer literacy

concept of, 408*f*
definition of, 407
Computer output microfilm
(COM), 548*f*, 548–549
Computers
analog, 409
characteristics of, 409–410
digital, 410
host, 411
mainframe. *See* Mainframe
nature and purpose of, 408–413
sizes of, 410–413
Computer system(s), 93
elements of, 408
phases and related functions of,
414*f*
Computer systems technology,
413–422
control, 422
input, 414–417
output, 420
processing, 417–419
storage, 420–422
Conceptual skill, definition of, 8
Conditional sales contract, definition of, 395
Consolidated Omnibus Budget
Reconciliation Act (1985), 267
Consultants, for systems analysis,
97–98
Contextual data flow diagram,
584, 585*f*
Contingency theory of leadership,
46–47
Contingency theory of leadership
effectiveness, 47
Continuous forms, 513
Continuous improvement, 621–622
Control, 90*f*, 90–91
Control technology, 422
Conventional furniture, 385–388
definition of, 385
Conventional plan, 330*f*, 330–331
Cool temperatures, conservation
of, 379*f*
Coordination, 161*f*
Copier/printer, intelligent, 560
Copiers
analog, 559
digital, 559
by volume of copies, 558*f*
Core time, 308–309, 309*f*

Correspondence manual, 443–445,
444*f*
Correspondence secretaries, definition of, 461–462
Cost-effectiveness, of report-writing, 125
Cost-of-living adjustment (COLA)
clause, definition of, 249
Costs
facilities, 188
instruction, 187
nature and behavior of, 641
time, 187
transportation, 188
work standards in analysis of,
648–650
Counseling, 164–165
Counseling and referral programs,
277–278
Courts, Roger, 485
Creative ability, 63–64
Credit reports, of potential em-
ployees, 145
Credit union, definition of, 278
Criminal records, of potential em-
ployees, 144
Critical incident technique (CIT),
220
Critical path, definition of, 593
Critical Path Method (CPM),
620–621
Cross-training, definition of, 185
Customer satisfaction, 41, 42*f*
Cyberspace, 195
Cycle billing system, definition of,
650

Darkness, of color, 359
Dartnell, 221, 245
Data aperture cards, definition of,
547
Database, 91–92
Database access, definition of, 489
Database access service, 489
Database management system
(DBMS), definition of, 422
Data communication, concepts of,
479–481
Data communication services,
489–491
Data communication system
computer-based, 480*f*

definition of, 478
equipment for, 481–482
Data communication tools,
478–482
Data dictionary (DD), definition
of, 584
Data flow, definition of, 584
Data flow diagram (DFD), 582–584
symbols for, 584*f*
Data hierarchy, 529–530*f*
definition of, 529
Data migration, 532, 532*f*
Data Processing Management As-
sociation (DPMA), 11
Data service center, definition of,
434–435
Data store, definition of, 584
Daylight, 367–368
Decentralization, advantages of,
45
Decentralized authority, 33
Decentralized filing, 519, 521*f*
Decertification, 249
Decibel (dB), 370
Decision making, 56*f*
definition of, 19, 55
Decision simulation, definition of,
199
Decision-support system (DSS),
428
Decision table, definition of, 581,
581*f*
Decision tree, 67, 68*f*
Delegating, 171–172
Delegation, definition of, 31
Deming, W. Edwards, 20
Dental care, 268
Departmental practice manuals,
443
Departmental work group, 462,
463*f*
Departmentation, 34
Desks, 385–387
types of, 387*f*
Desktop publishing (DTP),
456–458
definition of, 456–457
Diagonal communication,
115–116, 116*f*
Dictation
digital, 458
evaluation of, 464*f*

Dictation-transcription system, 449–451
central recorder systems, 451
desktop units, 451
portable units, 450–451
Dictionary of Occupational Titles, 221
Digital computers, definition of, 410
Digital dictation, definition of, 458
Diplomatic leader, 49
Direct expenses, definition of, 643
Direct interview, 140*f*
Disability income insurance, definition of, 268
Disaster recovery plan, definition of, 511
Discipline, 161–164
definition of, 161
developing system for, 164
need for, 163
Discrete recording media, definition of, 449
Disk packs, 416
Displayphone, 491
Dispute-resolution systems, alternative, 208
Dissatisfier, 170
Distance effect, of color, 360
Diverse workforce, 159, 162*f*, 197*t*
supervising, 159–167
Diversity training, 196
definition of, 185
Document creation practices, of managers with and without VDTs, 450*t*
Domestic partner benefits, 279
Downsizing, definition of, 32, 622–623
Downward communication, 110*f*, 110–112, 111*f*
Dress codes, 137–139
Drucker, Peter F., 19, 47–48
Drug abuse, 288–292
early detection of, 290–292
education about, 290
referral for, 291–292
screening for, 144
Drug abuser, definition of, 288–290

Drug addict, definition of, 290
Drug-Free Workplace Act of 1988, 290
Dumb terminal, definition of, 481
Duplexing, definition of, 559

Economic problems, 72
Educational assistance, 275–276
Educational institutions, and recruiting office workers, 135
Effective, definition of, 574
Effective forms design, principle of, 516–517
Effective salary range, definition of, 244
Effective temperature, definition of, 373
Efficiency ratios, 536
Efficient, definition of, 574
800-Number services, 488
Eldercare service, 278–279
Electronic banking services, definition of, 489
Electronic blackboard, definition of, 490
Electronic-funds transfer system (EFTS), 428
Electronic lamp, 368
Electronic mail, 443
definition of, 482
privacy of, 302
process, 483*f*
Electronic message system, 484
Electronic performance support system (EPSS), 528*f*, 528–529
Electronic records
creating, 526
disposing of, 532
maintaining, 531–532
retrieving, 531
storing, 529
Electronic typewriter, 451–452
E-mail. *See* Electronic mail
Emotional illness, 292
Employee, identifying promotion potential of, 206
Employee assistance programs (EAPs), 288
definition of, 164
for stress, 293
Employee benefit plans, modifying for retirees, 283

Employee benefits
controlling costs of, 281–282
definition of, 262
nature and extent of, 264–279
percentage of gross payroll, 263*f*
recent developments in, 282–283
why companies provide, 262–264
Employee benefits consultants, 282–283
Employee benefits program
assigning responsibilities for, 280
communicating to employees, 281
determining employee needs for, 280–281
developing and implementing, 279–283
setting objectives for, 280
Employee handbook, 146, 147*f*
Employee leasing services, 134
Employee performance appraisal, definition of, 200
Employee Polygraph Protection Act of 1988, 145
Employee Retirement Income Security Act (ERISA), definition of, 269
Employees
floating, 651
part-time workers, 651
physical and mental well-being of, 287–303
salary expectations of, 240–243
temporary, 651
using on overtime basis, 651
Employee savings and thrift plans, 270
Employee specifications, definition of, 221
Employee stock ownership plan (ESOP), 256–257, 270
definition of, 256
Employee suggestion system, 115
Employee wellness programs, for stress, 293
Employment-at-will doctrine, definition of, 208
Empowerment, definition of, 173
Energy
conservation methods, 380
management program, 380

Englesbe, William P., 635
Entry-level training, 191–195
    definition of, 185
    instructional staff for, 191
    methods and techniques for,
        192
    program for, 191–192
Equal employment opportunity,
    146
Equal Employment Opportunity
    Act of 1972, 146
Equal Employment Opportunity
    Commission, (EEOC),
    150–151
    regulations on criminal records,
        144
Equal Pay Act (1963), 246
Equal pay for equal work,
    246–247
Equipment lease, definition of,
    392
Equipment-use studies, 590
Equity, sharing, 168
Ergonomic environment, in tomor-
    row's workplace, 378
Ergonomic factors, influence on
    office productivity, 360f
Ergonomic needs, in office,
    357–359
Ergonomics, definition of, 355
Essay, 201f
Esteem, need for, 169
Ethics, 175–176
    definition of, 175–176
Evaluation, principle of, 188
Executive information system
    (EIS), 428
Executive orders, 151
Executive perquisites, 278
Executive workcenters, 425
Executive workstation, furniture
    for, 391
Exempt employees, 240, 247
Exit interview, 208, 307
Expectancy theory, definition of,
    175
External entity, definition of, 584
External service, of office equip-
    ment, 399–401
External written communications,
    definition of, 445
Extroverts, 329

Facilities costs, 188
Facility manager, definition of, 324
Facsimile process, definition of, 482
Factor comparison, 201f
Factor-comparison method,
    228–230, 229t, 231t
    advantages and disadvantages
        of, 230
    definition of, 228
Fair Credit Reporting Act of 1968,
    145
Fair Labor Standards Act (FLSA),
    246
Family and Medical Leave Act
    (1993), definition of, 274–275
Fanfold forms, 513
FAX. See Facsimile process
Fayol, Henri, 16
Feasibility studies
    for automated office systems,
        430
    for text/word processing sys-
        tems, 459
Feasibility study, 85–86, 87f
Federal Insurance Contributions
    Act, 266
Federal Reserve System, 245
Feedback, 90, 90f
    principle of, 188–189
Fiber optics, definition of, 473
Fidelity bond, 301
Fiedler, Fred E., 47
Files
    horizontal, 523
    lateral, 522f, 523
    mobile, 522f, 523–524
    motorized, 522f
    organization of, 519
    poorly labeled, 531f
    rotary, 523
    vertical, 522f, 523
Files accuracy ratio, 536
Files activity ratio, 536
Filing
    centralized, 519, 521f
    decentralized, 519, 521f
    equipment and supplies for,
        521, 537–538
    network, 519, 521f
Filing system
    definition of, 519
    storage, 519

Films, training with, 194
Financial services, 278
First quartile, definition of, 244
Five Principles of Effective Work,
    15–16
Fixed costs, 642
    definition of, 397
Flat forms, 513
Flexibility, principle of, 639–640
Flexible benefits program, defini-
    tion of, 281
Flexible budget, 637–638
    definition of, 637
Flexible time, 309, 309f
Flexible work schedule, 308–309,
    309f
Flextime, 308–309
Floating offices, definition of, 456
Floating workers, 651
Floor coverings, 364
Floppy disk, definition of, 421
Flowchart, definition of, 580
Flow process chart, 583f
    symbols for, 582f
Fluorescent light, 368
Follett, Mary Parker, 16
Food services, 276
Footcandle (FC), definition of,
    365
Footlambert, definition of, 366
Forbes, 245
Forced distribution, 201f
Forced relationship, 64
Forecasting, definition of, 19
Form, internal, 520f
Formal organization, 34–44
    charting of, 34–35
    types of, 36–41
Forms. See also Physical records
    color of, 516
    computer-designed, 527f
    continuous, 513
    definition of, 507
    designing efficient, 517, 518f
    electronic, 526–529
    fanfold, 513
    flat, 513
    machine-readable records, 513,
        514f
    principles of management,
        515–519
    printing styles of, 516

quality of paper stock for, 515–516, 517*f*
and records systems, 512–519
size of, 515, 516*t*
smart, 527–528
soft-copy, 527
specialty, 513
spot-carbon unit-set, 513
studies of, 585–587
types of, 512–515
unit-set, 513
Forms distribution chart, 588*f*
definition of, 580
Forms management, and records management, 512
Fortune, 245
401(k) retirement plan, definition of, 270
4/40 Workweek, 308
Free-rein leader, 50
Fringe benefits, 262
Functional job analysis, 220
Functional organization, 36–37, 37*f*
Functional space needs, 330
Functional work requirements, 326
Functions, unification of, 29–30
Funeral leave, 273
Furniture
for automated workstations, 389–391
conventional, 385–388
for executive workstation, 391
for full-time VDT operator, 389–391, 390*f*
modular, 388–389
for multifunction shared workstation, 391
selecting, 385–392, 386*f*
for technical specialist/professional workstation, 391

Gainsharing plan, definition of, 257
Gantt, Henry L., 324
Gantt chart, 324–325, 325*f*
Gay, 299
General and Industrial Management, 16
General problem-solving model, 70

General Schedule, 227–228
definition of, 227
General systems model, 87–91, 88*f*
Geographic centralization, 45
Geographic decentralization, 45
Gilbreth, Frank and Lillian, 14, 614
Glick, Sharon, 358
Goal setting, 201*f*
Government regulations, of office salaries, 246–248, 248*f*
Grading, 201*f*
Grapevine, 44, 108–109
Graph plotter, 420
Green, Lisbeth K., 10
Green-circle rates, definition of, 250, 251*f*
Grid board, 340
Grievance-handling procedure, 115
Griggs v. Duke Power, 141–142
Group incentive plan, definition of, 256
Group legal plan, 278
Group life insurance, definition of, 270–271
Groupthink, 68
Group workcenter, 334, 335*f*

Habit, definition of, 189
Hand-held computer, 411
Handwritten method, of message creation, 447
Hard disk, definition of, 421
Hawthorne experiments, 17
Health incentives, for stress, 294
Health maintenance organization (HMO), definition of, 266–267
Hearing environment, 370–373
definition of, 370
Heat, conservation of, 379*f*
Herzberg, Frederick, 18–19, 170, 240
Heterosexual, 299
High-intensity discharge (HID) lamps, 368
High-level languages, 418–419
High-tech office plan, 334
Historical data method, 608–609
Hoekstra, John W., Jr., 344
Holidays, 271–272

Homosexual, 299
Honesty, of potential employees, 144–145
Horizontal files, 523
Horizontal promotion, definition of, 207
Hospital, surgical and medical insurance, definition of, 266
Host computers, definition of, 411
Hours regulations, 152
Hue, of color, 359
Human attitudes, and problem solving, 61
Human engineering, 355
Human problems, 70–72
Human relations approach
definition of, 17
to worker behavior, 17
Human resources
case example from, 69
case example of, 40
Human resources performance, studies of, 587–590
Human Rights Law of the District of Columbia, 151
Human skill, definition of, 8
Human space needs, 329–330
Human system, 99
Humidity, 373–374
Hygienic factors, 170, 240
definition of, 18

Ideal performance approach, to budgeting, 640
Ideal system, definition of, 575
Idea quota, 64
Illiteracy, as barrier to communication, 121
Illuminance
definition of, 365
recommended levels for office lighting, 366*t*
Image communication, definition of, 486
Image communication tools, 486–487
Immigration Reform and Control Act of 1986, 153*f*
Impact printer, 420
Implementation, principle of planning and, 187–188

Improved system. *See also* Systems improvement
  charting, 596
  designing, 594–597
  documenting, 596–597
  evaluating, 598
  installing, 297–598
  writing narrative for, 596–597
In-basket training, definition of, 199
Incandescent light, 368
Incentive systems, definition of, 255
Incident process, definition of, 199
Income, retirement, 268–279
Incremental budgeting, definition of, 644
Indirect expenses
  allocation of, 643f
  definition of, 643
Indirect interview, 140f
Individual differences, 190
Individual incentive plan, definition of, 256
Individual retirement account (IRA), definition of, 269
Individual workcenter, 334, 335f
Informal organization, 44–45
Information, administrative services model for production of, 323f
Information cycle, 5, 7f
Information distribution, definition of, 471
Information manager, 6
Information overload, as barrier to communication, 119
Information services, case example of, 10
Information systems, 91
In-house seminars and workshops, 197
Input, 89, 90f
Input-output (I/O) systems improvement model, 578–579
Input technology, 414–417
Institute for Certification of Computer Professionals (ICCP), 431–432
Instructional staff
  for entry-level training, 191
  for supervisory training and man-

agement development, 196
Instruction costs, 187
Insurance
  disability income, 268
  group life, 270–271
  hospital, surgical and medical, 266–267
  major medical, 267
  term, 271
  travel accident, 271
  unemployment compensation, 266
  workers' compensation, 266
Integrated security system (ISS), definition of, 377
Integrated Services Digital Network (ISDN), 491
Integrated systems, 455
Integrated telecommunication services, 491–492
Intelligent copier/printers, definition of, 560
Intelligent terminal, definition of, 482
Intensity, of color, 359–360
Intercommunication (intercom) system, 475–476
  definition of, 475
Interconnect companies, definition of, 493
Internal service, of office equipment, 399
Internal written communications, definition of, 443
International Office Management Association (IOMA), 11–12
Interoffice memorandums, 443, 444f
Interview, 137–139, 140f
  record of, 139
  types of, 140f
Interview method, definition of, 219
Intimate zone, definition of, 329
Intrapreneurs, definition of, 13
Introverts, 329
Intuitive ability, 65
Investigative consumer reports, 145

Jargon, as barrier to communication, 120–121

Jennings, Madelyn P., 198
Job analysis, 213f
  combined approach to, 220
  definition of, 212
  functional, 220
  purpose of, 212
  uses of, 213–215
Job attendance, 303–308
Job classification method, 226–228
  advantages and disadvantages of, 228
  definition of, 226
Job classifications, 227t
Job description
  definition of, 212
  typical, 221, 222f
Job descriptions, 220–221
  writing, 221
Job element method (JEM), 220
Job enrichment, 170–171
Job evaluation, 223–233
  definition of, 212
  implementing method of, 233
  nonquantitative methods of, 223–228
  quantitative methods of, 228–233
Job fairs, for recruiting office workers, 135
Job information, gathering and analyzing, 215–220
Job information sheet, 217f–218f
Job inventory, 215
Job rankings, in factor-comparison method, 231t
Job rotation, definition of, 194
Jobs
  benchmark, 228
  key, 228
  pricing, 249–255
Job security, 167–168
Job Service, 131–132
Job sharing, 309–310
Job specification
  definition of, 212
  sample, 223f
Job specifications, 221
Job-to-money method, 228
Job vacancies, publicizing, 205–206
Juran, Joseph M., 20

Jury duty, payment for time spent in, 272
Just-cause standard, 208

Keyboard, 452
  definition of, 526
Key job, 228
Key-job system, 228
Key telephone system (KTS), 473–474
  definition of, 473
Kinesics, 122
Knowledge of results, 189
Kreicker, Noel A., 166

Labor contract, definition of, 248
Labor Department, predictions of, 11
Labor-management committee, 41
Laptop computer, 411
Lateral communication, 115, 116*f*
Lateral files, 522*f*, 523
Layoff, alternatives to, 311–312
Leadership
  contingency theory of, 46–47
  definition of, 46
  transactional, 47
  transformational, 47–48
Leadership styles, 48, 49*f*
Leading, definition of, 159
Learning
  part, 190
  psychological factors in, 189–190
  whole, 190
Lease
  contents of, 343–345
  definition of, 343
Lease agreements, kinds of, 392–395
Leased line, definition of, 487
Lease-or-buy decision, 396–398
Leasing
  advantages of, 395–396
  relative net cost of, 396–398
Lecture, definition of, 192–193
Leffingwell, William H., 15–16
Legal service plans, definition of, 278
Lesbian, 299
Lessee, definition of, 343
Lessor, definition of, 343

Letter, time factors in creating, 466*t*
Letters
  block style, 446*f*
  simplified style, 446*f*
Letters of recommendation, 139
Leveled data flow diagram, 584, 585*f*
Lew, Lynn Ann, 624
Light
  conservation of, 379*f*
  quality of, 366–367
  quantity of, 365–366
  reflection of, 362*f*
  sources of, 367–369
Lighting, recommended levels for office, 366*t*
Lighting systems, evaluation of, 369
Lightness, of color, 359
Light pen, 341, 416–417
Line-and-staff organization, 37–39, 38*f*
Linear programming (LP), definition of, 579
Line organization, 36, 36*f*
Local-area network (LAN), 479, 479*f*
Local going rate, 243
Locker searches, 302
Logical ability, 65
Long-term lease
  with purchase option, 394–395
  with renewal option, 394
Love, need for, 169

Machine-readable records forms, 513, 514*f*
Machine-recording method, of message creation, 448
Mack, Craig S., 401
Magnetic disk, 415*f*, 415–416, 421
Magnetic ink character recognition (MICR), 513–514
Magnetic tape, 414–415, 415*f*, 420–421
Mail
  external, 496
  internal, 496
Mailing center, efficient, 498
Mailing costs, controlling, 500, 501*f*

Mailing equipment, efficient, 498–499
Mailing systems
  automated, 500
  components and workflows in, 497*f*
  effective internal, 498
  efficient procedures, 499–500
  managing, 496–500
  planning and organizing, 496
  staff for, 497–498
Mainframe, 410–411
  applications for, 427–428
  definition of, 410
Major medical insurance, definition of, 267
Malcolm Baldrige National Quality Award, 622
Management
  definition of, 3
  functions of, 3
  global, 166
  levels of, 3, 4*f*
  participative, 172–173
  principles of, 26–33, 27*f*
  schools of thought of, 12–21
Management by objectives (MBO), 19, 201*f*
  and goal setting, 174–175
Management development (MD), definition of, 195–196
Management information system (MIS), 5–6
Management science, 19
Management science school of management, 19
Management theory, definition of, 26
Manager, definition of, 3
Managerial authority, 33
Managing for the Future: The 1990s and Beyond, 19, 47
Manuals
  administrative practice, 443
  communication, 444*f*, 445
  correspondence, 443–445, 444*f*
  creating systems and procedures, 297
  departmental practice, 443
  office, 443–445
  organization, 35, 443
  policy, 443
Manual systems, 92*f*, 92–93

Married couples, hiring of, 298–299

Maslow, Abraham, 18

Maslow's hierarchy of needs, 168*f*, 169

Massed training, 190

Master budget, 637–638, 638*f*
  definition of, 637

Master Clerical Data (MCD) method, 617

Maternity leave, 272

Matrix organization, 43*f*, 43–44

Mayo, Elton, 17

MCD-MOD-I, 617, 618*f*–620*f*

McGregor, Douglas, 18

Mechanical systems, 93

Median, definition of, 244

Mediation, definition of, 249

Medicare, 266

Meetings, 112

Memory, definition of, 418

Memos, 443, 444*f*

Mental illness, 292

Mentor, 197

Mentoring, 197–199
  definition of, 197

Message-creation methods, 447–449, 448*f*
  appropriate messages for, 449*f*

Metropolitan-area network (MAN), definition of, 480

Microcomputer, 413*f*
  definition of, 411
  selection of, 431*f*

Microcomputer(s), in text/word processing systems, 455–456

Microcomputers, 411–413

Microfiche
  definition of, 545–547
  retrieval, 546–547
  storage of, 546
  updatable, 546

Microfilm jackets, 547

Microforms
  definition of, 544
  types of, 544–545

Microimage system
  definition of, 543
  operating, 544*f*

Microimage systems
  automated, 548–550
  costs of, 557*f*

equipment for, 555
evaluating, 557
management of, 552–557
operating procedures for, 555–557
organizing, 555
personnel for, 555, 556*f*
planning, 553–555, 554*f*
storage environment for, 555

Microimage technology, 543–552

Micromotion study, definition of, 614

Microprocessor, definition of, 409

Microrecord, definition of, 543

Microrecords
  determining legality of, 553
  reasons for using, 552–553

Microwave communication system, 477*f*
  definition of, 477

Military organization. *See* Line organization

Military training leave, 272

Minicomputer, 413*f*
  applications for, 427–428
  definition of, 411

Minimum wage, 246

Mixed costs, 642–643

Mobile files, 522*f*, 523–524

Mobile telephone, 477

Model, definition of, 87

Modem, definition of, 480

Modular furniture, 388–389
  definition of, 388

Module, definition of, 388

Monitoring, 302

Monthly Labor Review, 245

Mood effect, of color, 360

Moonlighting, 299–300

Morale
  building and maintaining, 167–170
  definition of, 167

Motion study, 613–615
  definition of, 614

Motivation, 167–175, 189
  definition of, 167
  expectancy theory of, 175

Motivation-hygiene theory, 18

Motivation-maintenance theory, 170

Motivator, 170

Motivators, 240
  definition of, 18

Motorized files, 522*f*

Mouse, 416

Multicultural backgrounds, and problem solving, 60–61

Multifunction shared workstation, furniture for, 391

Multimedia, definition of, 195, 487

Murderer, profile of potential of, 304*f*

Music, in office, 371–373

Nagle, Brother David, 429

Narrative, 201*f*

National Clearinghouse for Alcohol and Drugs, 290

National Energy Policy Act (1992), 380

National Labor Relations Board, 313–314

National Office Machine Dealers Association, 563

National Survey of Professional, Administrative, Technical and Clerical Pay, 245

Nation's Business, 245

Needs
  Maslow's hierarchy of, 168*f*
  primary, 167–169
  secondary, 169–170

Nepotism, 298–299

Network analysis, 110

Networked personal computers, definition of, 455

Networked systems, 455

Network filing, 519, 521*f*

Network operations, case example from, 114

Nielson, Charles F., 40

900-number services, 488

No-fault leave policy, definition of, 306

Noise, as barrier to communication, 121

Noise levels, 370*t*
  recommended maximums for, 370*t*

Noise-reduction coefficient (NRC), definition of, 371

Nominal group technique (NGT), 64

Noncash incentives, 255
Nonexempt employees, 240
Nonimpact printer, 420
Nonunitized microform, definition
 of, 544
Nonverbal communication,
 121–125
Norberg, Judy, 453
Norris, Tony, 138
Notebook computer, 411

Objectives
 defining and explaining of,
  27–28
 definition of, 27
Objectivity, principle of, 639
Observation method, definition of,
 219–220
Occupational Outlook Handbook,
 221
Office
 automated, 422–428
 definition of, 3
 ergonomic needs in, 357–359
 human activities in, 357
 modern, 423–425
 physical features of, 325–326
 relocating. *See* Office move
 space needs in, 326–330
 traditional, 422–423
 use of plants in, 364
 written communications in,
  441–445
Office automation (OA), 7–8
 benefits of, 425–427
 definition of, 423
 information functions and systems in, 424f
 for office of future, 432f
Office design plans, 330–334
Office environment
 air, 373–375
 hearing, 370–373
 safe and secure, 375–378
 seeing, 364–369
 surface, 359–364
Office equipment
 centralizing control of, 401–402
 definition of, 391
 leasing, 392–396
 maintaining, 398–401
 procuring, 392–398

 purchasing, 392
 replacing, 401
 selecting, 385–386, 391–392,
  393f–394f
Office Ethics Quotient, 177f
Office landscape, 31
Office layout
 before-and-after charts, 586
 preparing models of, 338–341
Office manager. *See* Administrative office manager
Office manuals. *See* Manuals
Office move, 342–347
 personnel problems related to,
  345–347
 planning checklist, 345, 346f
Office noise
 controlling, 371, 372f
 sources and effects of, 370f,
  370–371
Office of the Moment, 378
Office operations
 centralization of, 45–46
 decentralization of, 46
 measurable, 605–606
Office productivity improvement
 quality circles for, 625–626
 through quality management,
  621–629
 time management for, 626–629
Office romances, 298
Offices, private versus open, 333
Office salaries
 ability to pay, 240
 and collective bargaining agreements, 248–249
 expectations of employees,
  240–243
 factors in determining,
  239–249
 government regulations on,
  246–248, 248f
 paid by other companies,
  243–246
Office salary administration
 company philosophy toward,
  239–240
 objectives of, 239
Office space inventory, 326–327,
 328f
Office space study, guidelines for
 conducting, 338–342

Office supervision process,
 158–167
Office supervisors, responsibilities
 of, 159
Office training program, 186f
 effectiveness of, 188f
Office workers
 selection of, 136–141
 sources of, 131–136
Off-job activities, privacy of,
 302–303
Offline, definition of, 417
Old-age, survivors, disability, and
 health insurance (OASDHI)
 program
 definition of, 266
Ombudsman, definition of, 314
Online, definition of, 417
On-the-job training (OJT), definition of, 192
Open offices, versus private, 333
Open plan, 331f, 331–333
 advantages of, 332–333
 disadvantages of, 333
Open system, 87
Operational decisions, definition
 of, 3
Operations research (OR), defini-
 tion of, 579
Optical character recognition
 (OCR), 514–515
Optical disk, definition of, 421
Optical disks, 550–552
 advantages of, 551–552
 definition of, 550
 working of, 551
Organization
 authoritarian, 172
 forms of, 33–46
 nontraditional types of, 41–44,
  42f
 participative, 172
 in report-writing, 124
Organizational plans, for
 text/word processing systems,
  460–461
Organization chart, 34–35, 35f
Organization manual, 35
Organization manuals, 443
Organizations, Theory Z, 173–174
Organization structure, definition
 of, 33

Orientation, of office staff, 145–146

Orientation checklist, 146, 148f–149f

Ouchi, William, 20

Outplacement counseling, definition of, 277

Outplacement counseling service, for stress, 294

Output, 89–90, 90f

Output technology, 420

Outsourcing, 625
  definition of, 435, 594

Overtime, 651

Overtime hours/pay, 247

Paging system, definition of, 476–477

Paired comparison, 201f

Paired-comparison method, 226
  form for, 226f

Paper shredders, 526

Paralanguage, 123

Parental leave, 272

Parking space, provision for employees, 277

Parkinson, C. Northcote, 33–34

Parkinson's Law, 33–34

Participative leader, 49–50

Participative management, 172–173
  definition of, 172

Participative organization, definition of, 172

Part learning, versus whole learning, 190

Part-time, 651

Pascal, 419

Paternity leave, 272

Patterned interview, 140f

Payback period, definition of, 396

Pay for performance, 253–254
  definition of, 253

Pay for skill, 254

Pay grades, determining, 249–250, 252t

Payments for time not worked, 271–273

PC specialist, case example of, 138

Peak-load fluctuations, controlling cost of, 650–652

Pensions, portable, 283

Per-call basis, 399–401

Perception, as barrier to communication, 117–118

Performance appraisal, 165–167
  frequency of, 202
  methods of, 200, 200f
  responsibility for, 205

Performance appraisal form
  sample, 202, 203f–204f
  weakness of, 202

Performance rating, definition of, 615

Performance standards, for nonroutine office jobs, 617–621

Permanent part-time employment, definition of, 311

Perquisites, definition of, 278

Personal computer (PC), 411
  applications for, 428

Personal computer system, elements of, 412, 413f

Personal Digital Assistant (PDA), 411

Personal Harbor, 348f, 348–349, 349f

Personal leave, 272

Personal searches, 302

Personal security, 169

Personal service benefits, 279

Personal space, definition of, 329

Personal zone, definition of, 329

Personnel, 97
  space needs for, 327

Personnel Journal, 245

Personnel requisition form, 136

PERT, definition of, 325, 592

PERT chart, 592f–593f

Pesce, Peter, 241

Phototypesetters, definition of, 560

Physical activities, definition of, 357

Physical decentralization, of office operations, 46

Physical distance, as barrier to communication, 121

Physical records
  creating, 521
  disposing of, 524–526
  maintaining, 524
  retrieving, 524
  storing, 519

Physical space, 122–123

Physical wellness programs, 277

Physiological needs, 167

Piece-rate system, definition of, 256

Piecework system, 256

Placement firms. *See* Private employment agencies

Planning and implementation, principle of, 187–188

Plants, use in office, 364

Plateau, definition of, 189

Playscript procedure, 597f
  definition of, 596

Point-factor method, 231–233, 232f
  advantages of, 232
  definition of, 231
  disadvantages of, 232–233

Point-of-sale (POS) terminals, 427

Policy, definition of, 28

Policy manuals, 443

Polygraph tests, 145

Portable pensions, 283

Position Analysis Questionnaire (PAQ), definition of, 216

Post-exit interview, 307

Power, Warren W., 401

Practical leadership, 47–48

Practice, 190

Predetermined times
  advantages and disadvantages of using, 616
  definition of, 616
  methods for determining, 616–617

Preemployment testing, 141–142
  types of, 142–145, 143f

Preemployment tests
  reliability of, 143
  validity of, 143–144

Preferred provider organization (PPO), definition of, 267

Pregnancy Discrimination Act of 1978, 150, 272

Prejudice. *See* Bias

Prepaid legal plan, 278

Preretirement counseling, definition of, 278

Prescription drug plan, 268

Primary duty, definition of, 247

Primary needs, 167–169

Primary storage, 418, 420
Principle of adherence, 640
Principle of centralized control,
    517–519
Principle of commitment, 187
Principle of effective forms de-
    sign, 516–517
Principle of evaluation, 188
Principle of feedback, 188–189
Principle of flexibility, 639–640
Principle of objectivity, 639
Principle of planning and imple-
    mentation, 187–188
Principle of responsibility, 187,
    639
Principle of review, 640
Principle of standardization,
    515–516
Principle of target setting, 639
Principle of use, 515
Principles, definition of, 26
Printer, 454
    impact, 420
    nonimpact, 420
Privacy, 302–303
    of electronic mail, 302
    monitoring and, 302
    of off-job activities, 302–303
Privacy Act of 1974, 141
Private automatic branch ex-
    change (PABX), definition of,
    474
Private branch exchange (PBX),
    definition of, 474
Private employment agencies,
    132–133
Private offices, versus open, 333
Probability sampling, in quality
    control, 612–613
Probationary periods, 206
Problem, definitions of, 56–57,
    57f
Problems
    elements causing, 61–63
    types of, 70–72
Problem solving, 56f, 56–59
    barriers to, 70–72, 71f
    case example of, 72–77, 76f
    definition of, 55
    environment, 60–61
    and multicultural backgrounds,
        60–61

process, 59–70
    steps in, 65–70, 66f
    worksheet for, 75f
Problem solving abilities
    creative, 63–64
    intuitive, 65
    logical, 65
Procedural activities, definition of,
    357
Procedure, definition of, 84
Procedures manuals, creating, 297
Process, definition of, 584
Productivity, 58–59, 59f
    improvement of office. See Of-
        fice productivity improve-
        ment
    white-collar, 59, 59f
Professional workstation, furniture
    for, 391
Profit-sharing plan, definition of,
    256
Profit-sharing plans, 270
Programmers, definition of, 414
Programming
    computer, 418–419
    linear (LP), 579
Project organization. See Matrix
    organization
Promoting, 205–207
    factors in, 206
    identifying employee potential
        for, 206
Promotion, horizontal, 207
Promotion trials, definition of,
    206
Protégé, 197
Prototype, definition of, 574
Proxemics, 122–123
Psychosomatic illness, 292
Publications, 112
Public employment services,
    131–132
Punched aperture cards, definition
    of, 547
Purchase-or-lease decision,
    343–345
Purpose, in report-writing, 123

Qualifications, for employment,
    150
Quality circle, definition of,
    625–626

Quality control
    definition of, 612
    using probability sampling in,
        612–613
Quality management, definition
    of, 621
Quality management school,
    19–20
Quantitative business methods.
    See Management science
    school of management
Quartile, definition of, 244
Questionnaire
    designing, 215–216
    on office space needs, 326–327,
        328f
    structured, 215–216
Questionnaire method
    advantages and disadvantages
        of, 216–217
    definition of, 215
Queuing theory, definition of, 19

Radio communication systems,
    476–478
RAM, 418
Random access memory (RAM),
    definition of, 418
Ranking, 201f
Ranking method, 223–224, 225t
    advantages and disadvantages
        of, 226
    definition of, 223
Rank order, 201f
Rating scales, 201f
Reader, definition of, 545
Read only memory (ROM), defi-
    nition of, 418
Real-world system, 575–576
    definition of, 575
Reception center, 335–336
Recommendation, letters of, 139
Record(s)
    definition of, 507
    destroying obsolete, 526
    electronic. See Electronic
        records
    external, 507
    internal, 507
    physical. See Physical records
    protection of vital, 510–511
    storing inactive, 524–526

Records maintenance, 510
Record of employment, 139
Record of interview, 139
Records retention schedule, 511f
  definition of, 510
Records audit, checklist, 537f
Records creation, 508–509
Records disposition
  continuous method of, 511
  definition of, 511
  periodic method of, 511
Records life cycle, 508–511
  definition of, 508
  managing with automated sys-
    tems, 526–532
  managing with manual systems,
    519–526
Records management
  definition of, 507
  and forms management, 512
  function in organization,
    507–508, 508f
  objectives of, 507–508
  position levels and titles in,
    534f
Records management program,
  507
  administration of, 532–538
  controlling costs of, 534–536
  cost of personnel for, 534–535
  cost of supplies for, 535
  efficient procedures for,
    533–534
  evaluation of, 536–538
  objectives of, 509f
  operation of, 533–536
  organization and personnel of,
    533
Records retrieval, 510
Records storage, 509–510
Records systems, and paper forms,
  512–519
Recruitment, of office workers,
  131, 132f
Red-circle rates, definition of,
  251, 251f
Reduction ratio, definition of,
  544–545
Reengineering, 623
  definition of, 385, 594
Reference checks, 139
References services center, 336

Referrals, 134–135
Regan, Elizabeth A., 525
Reinforcement, 189–190
  definition of, 189
Relative humidity, definition of,
  373
Relocation expense allowance, 276
Remedial training, definition of,
  185
Replacement costs, 307
Report program generator (RPG),
  419
Reports, 443
Report writing, principles of,
  123–125
Reprographic costs
  controlling, 565–566
  identifying, 565
  reducing, 565–566
Reprographic processes, 558–560
  automated, 559–560
Reprographic systems
  definition of, 558
  equipment for, 562f, 562–563
  establishing personnel controls
    for, 563
  establishing procedure controls
    for, 563–565
  management of, 560–566
  organizing, 561–563
  personnel for, 561–562
  planning, 560–561
  space for, 563
Reprographic technology,
  558–560
Resale value, 345
Responsibility
  acceptance of, 28–29, 29f
  definition of, 28
  principle of, 187, 639
Responsibility accounting, definition of, 641
Rest periods, 273–274
Restricted stock plan, definition
  of, 257
Results, knowledge of, 189
Résumé databases, for recruiting
  office workers, 135
Résumé-search services, for recruiting office workers, 135
Retirees, and recruiting office
  workers, 136

Retirement and savings plan bene-
  fits, 268–270
Retirement income, 268–279
Retraining, definition of, 185
Retrieval efficiency ratio, 537
Review, principle of, 640
Rightsizing. See Downsizing
Right-to-work laws, definition of,
  249
Robert Half, 245
Role playing, definition of, 199
Roll film
  definition of, 544–545
  retrieval of, 545
  storage of, 545
ROM, 418
Rotary files, 523
Rotation of layoffs, definition of,
  311–312
RPG (Report program generator),
  419

Safe and secure environment,
  375–378
  definition of, 375
Safety
  control methods, 377–378
  problems with, 375–376
Safety needs, 167
Sahl, Robert J., 224
Salaries, 168
  of administrative office man-
    agers, 11
Salary progression, traditional,
  251–253
Salary ranges, determining,
  249–250, 252t
Salary rates
  adjusting, 250–251
  charting, 250, 251f
  factor-comparison ranking of,
    231t
Salary structure, establishing,
  251–253
Salary surveys
  conducting one's own, 245–246
  consultants on, 245
  definition of, 243
  obtaining data, 245–246
  professionally prepared, 245
  statistical measures used in,
    243–245

Sale-leaseback plan, definition of, 395

Satellite administrative services center, 45–46

Savings and thrift plans, definition of, 270

Scalar organization. *See* Line organization

Scanlon plan, definition of, 257

Scanner, definition of, 526

Scanning devices, 416

Scatter chart, 250, 251*f*

Scheduling, in report-writing, 124–125

Scheyer, Rodney W., 595

Schutz, Andrea L., 265

Scientific management, 14–16

Scientific method of problem solving, 14

Scientific Office Management, 15

Searches, 302

Secondary needs, 169–170

Secondary storage, 420

Second quartile, definition of, 244

Security. *See also* Safe and secure environment
control methods, 377–378
problems with, 376

Seeing environment, 364–369
definition of, 364

Self-actualization, need for, 169–170

Self-development, 161*f*

Semantics, as barrier to communication, 119

Seminars, in-house, 197

Semivariable costs, 642–643

Separation costs, 307

Service bureaus, 434–435, 652

Service contract, definition of, 399

Sessa, Josephine Soviero, 100

Sexual harassment, 297–298
definition of, 297

Sexual orientation, 299
definition of, 299

Shared-logic word processors, 455, 456*f*

Shared tenant services, 334

Shorthand-recording method, of message creation, 448

Short-term lease, definition of, 392

Sick building syndrome (SBS), definition of, 374

Sick leave, 272

Simplified employee pension (SEP) plan, definition of, 269

Simplified letter style, 446*f*

Simulated office space model, 340–341

Simulation
definition of, 579
of operations, 580*f*

Skill-based pay system, definition of, 254

Smart building, definition of, 334

Smart forms, 527–528

Smart terminal, definition of, 482

Smoking, 295–297

Social activities, definition of, 357

Social and recreational programs, 276–277

Social security program, definition of, 266

Social zone, definition of, 329

Society for Advancement of Management (SAM), 11

Society for Human Resources Management (SHRM), 11

Soft-copy forms, 527

Software, text/word processing, 456

Sounds, common, 370*t*

Source data automation (SDA), 416

Space
in administrative office system, 322–324
studies of, 584–585

Spaced training, 190

Space guidelines
for efficient work, 337
for furniture and equipment, 338, 339*f*
for personnel, 337–338

Space management, principles of, 337–342

Space management program, 324–326
objectives of, 325–326
planning and organizing, 324–325

Space needs
analyzing, 327
functional, 330
human, 329–330
in office, 326–330
workflow, 327–329

Space planning, in workcenters, 334–337

Space requirements, future, 343

Span of control
definition of, 32, 32*f*
limiting of, 32–33

Span of management. *See* Span of control

Specialist, definition of, 30

Specialization, 30–31

Specialty forms, 513

Speech, in input technology, 416

Split-payroll dates, 650–651

Sponsor system, for office orientation, 146

Spot-carbon unit-set forms, 513

Spreadsheet, 426*f*

Spreadsheets, 638

Staff group, as type of committee organization, 39

Staggered work schedule, definition of, 308

Standalone word processor, 454–455
definition of, 454

Standard electric typewriter, definition of, 451

Standardization, principle of, 515–516

State disability benefits, definition of, 266

State laws, governing employment procedures, 151

Station message detail recording, 494, 495*f*

Status, as barrier to communication, 119

Steelcase Commons, 347*f*, 347–348

Stereotyping, as barrier to communication, 120

Stock option plan, definition of, 256–257

Stock purchase plan, definition of, 257

Storage technology, 420–422

Stress, 293–294
 symptoms and sources of, 294*f*
Stress-management programs, 293
Structured questionnaire
 definition of, 215–216
 techniques of using, 216
Study
 case, 199
 company courses of, 193–194
Subnotebook computer, 411
Substance Abuse Information
 Database, 292
Substation. *See* Satellite administrative services center
Subsystems, 84
Suicide approach, to budgeting, 640
Supervising diversity, 159–161
Supervisor
 definition of, 158
 reporting to, 31–32
 responsibilities of, 160*f*–161*f*
Supervisors, successful, characteristics of, 163*f*
Supervisory training and management development (STMD), 195–200
 definition of, 185
 instructional staff for, 196
 methods and techniques for, 197
Supervisory training (ST), definition of, 195
Supplemental unemployment benefits (SUBs), definition of, 270
Support, space needs for, 327
Surface environment, 359–364
 definition of, 359
Surveys
 attitude, 178–179
 climate, 179
 salary, 243
 statistical measures used in, 243–245
Switching system, definition of, 474
Symptoms, definition of, 65
System, definition of, 20–21
Systems analysis, 95–96
 consultants for, 97–98
Systems approach, to problem solving, 94–95
Systems boundary, 90

Systems chart, definition of, 580
Systems communication tools, 579–581
Systems concepts, basic, 86–93
Systems cost, 97
Systems design, 96
Systems development life cycle (SDLC), definition of, 572
Systems environment, 90
Systems evaluation, 96
Systems function
 in large firms, 98
 organization of, 97–99
 in small firms, 98–99
Systems furniture, 388
Systems improvement. *See also* Improved system
 input-output model of, 578–579
 process of, 574
 prototype of, 574–575, 575*f*
 reasons for, 572–573
 work simplification model of, 576–578, 577*f*
Systems installation, 96
Systems levels, 92–93
Systems manuals, creating, 297
Systems operation, 96
Systems problems, 72
Systems school of management, 20–21
 components of, 21
Systems structure, 91–92
Systems studies, 94–97
 typical areas of, 96–97
Systems study cycle, 95*f*, 95–96
Systems survey, 95

Tables, 388
Tape drive, 415
Tardiness, 303
Target setting, principle of, 639
Task, definition of, 587, 617
Task analysis, 587–590
 definition of, 587
Task chart, 589*f*
Task force, as type of committee organization, 39
Task inventory, definition of, 216
Task lighting, 369
Task statements, 220
Taylor, Frederick W., 14, 36
Technical skill, definition of, 8–9

Technical specialist workstation, furniture for, 391
Telecommunications, definition of, 471
Telecommunication services, 487–492
 integrated, 491–492
Telecommunications systems
 data communication tools, 478–482
 text communication tools, 482–486
Telecommunication systems, 472–473
 elements in, 472*f*
 establishing control over, 493–494
 image communication tools, 486–487
 managing, 492–495
 planning and organizing, 492–493
 reducing costs of, 494–495
 tools of, 473–487
Telecommuting, 310–311
Teleconferencing, 489–491
 audio, 490
 computer, 490–491
 definition of, 194–195, 489–490
 video, 490
Telephone, usage report form, 494*f*
Telephone systems, 473–476
Teletex, definition of, 489
Telex, definition of, 489
Temperature, 373
Temperature effect, of color, 360
Temp Force, 221, 245
Template, 338, 340*f*
Temporary office help services, 133–134
Temporary workers, 651
Terminating, 207–208
 developing procedure for, 207–208
 at will, 208
Term insurance, 271
Territoriality, definition of, 329
Testing, before employment, 141–145
Text, definition of, 440
Text communication, tools of, 482–486

Text management (TM), definition of, 440
Text production
  centralized, 460
  decentralized, 460–461
Text-storing media, 454
Text/word processing operators, 461
Text/word processing software, 456
Text/word processing (T/WP) systems
  automated, 452–458
  controlling, 463–467
  cost controls on, 465–467
  definition of, 445
  management of, 458–467
  manual, 447–452
  objectives of, 459–460
  operating, 462–463
  organizing, 460–462
  personnel for, 461–462
  planning, 459–460
  quality controls on, 464–465
  steps and operating methods in, 447f
The Career Television Network (TCTN), for recruiting office workers, 135
Theft, 300–301
Theory, definition of, 26
Theory X, definition of, 172
Theory Y, definition of, 172
Theory Z management, 20
Theory Z organizations, 173–174
  characteristics of, 174f
  definition of, 173
Third quartile, definition of, 244
Tight but attainable approach, to budgeting, 640
Time
  as barrier to communication, 121
  using productively, 628–629
Time costs, 187
Time log, 215, 609f
Time log method, definition of, 609
Time management, 159, 626–629
  definition of, 627
  and listing priorities, 627–628
  and setting goals, 627–628

Time study, 613–616
  definition of, 615
Time wasters, analyzing, 627
Tolerance, definition of, 611
Total Entity Management, 16
Total quality management (TQM), 621–625. *See* Quality management school
  definition of, 621
Total system, 91
Total workplace, 334
Touch-sensitive screen, 417
Traffic flow, space needs for, 327
Training, 245
Training
  computer-based, 194
  definition of, 184–191
  effectiveness of, 188f
  entry-level. *See* Entry-level training
  in-basket, 199
  massed, 190
  objectives of programs for, 185, 186f
  outcomes of, 190–191
  principles of, 185–189
  spaced, 190
  vestibule, 194
Training costs, 307
Transactional leadership, 47
Transfers, 207
Transformational leadership, 47–48
Transformation process, 89, 90f
Transportation costs, 188
Travel accident insurance, definition of, 271
Troy, Leonard D., 114
Turnaround time, definition of, 459
Turnover, 307–308
  reasons for, 307
  reducing cost of, 307–308
Turnover rate, definition of, 307
Two-dimensional bar code, 427, 427f
Typewriters
  electronic, 451–452
  standard electric, 451
Ultrafiche, definition of, 546
Unemployment compensation insurance, definition of, 266

Uniform Guidelines on Employee Selection Procedures, 142
Uninterrupted power supply (UPS), 433
Unionization
  of office workers, 312–314
  role of office manager in, 312–314
Unions, why office workers join, 312
Union shop agreement, definition of, 249
United States Employment Service (USES), 131
Unitized microform, definition of, 544
Unit-set forms, 513
Unity of command, definition of, 31
Updatable microfiche, definition of, 546
Upward communication, 113–115
U.S. News & World Report, 245
Use, principle of, 515
User friendly, definition of, 413

Vacation benefits, 271
Value systems, 176–178
  definition of, 176
Vanpooling, 279
Variable costs, 641f, 642
  definition of, 397
Variable pay, definition of, 255
Variable pay plans, 255–256
Variance, definition of, 636
VDT. *See* Video display terminal (VDT)
Verbal communication, 107
Vertical files, 522f, 523
  space savings with, 523f
Vestibule training, definition of, 194
Vesting, 269–270
  definition of, 269
Videoconference, 490
Videoconferencing, definition of, 195
Videodisk, definition of, 421
Video display terminal (VDT), 414, 420, 452–454
  definition of, 336

furniture for, 389–391, 390*f*
placement in relation to light sources, 365*f*
Videofax, definition of, 486
Videotapes, training with, 194
Video teleconference, definition of, 490
Videotext, definition of, 486
Vietnam Era Veteran's Readjustment Assistance Act of 1974, 153*f*
Violence, in workplace, 303
Virtual reality, 342
definition of, 195
Vision care, 268
VISIT Video, 491
Visual comfort probability (VCP), definition of, 366–367
Vocational Rehabilitation Act of 1973, 153*f*
Voice (audio) response units, 420
Voice communication services, 487–489
Voice communication system, definition of, 473
Voice communication tools, 473–478
Voice mail, definition of, 484–486
Voice-recognition system, definition of, 476
Voice-recognition unit, definition of, 526
Voice-to-print system, definition of, 458
Voting, time off for, 272

Wage regulations, 152
Wages, 168
Waiting-line theory, definition of, 19
Walk-ins, and recruiting office workers, 135
Weber, Max, 14–15
Well-being, of employees, 287–303
Whole learning, versus part learning, 190

Wide-area network (WAN), definition of, 480
Wide-area telecommunication service (WATS), definition of, 488
Wireless communication systems, 476–478
Word origination, definition of, 447
Word processors
computer-connected, 455–456
shared-logic, 455, 456*f*
standalone, 454
Workaholic, definition of, 300
Workaholism, 300
Work breaks, 273–274
controlling, 274
cost of lost time from, 274, 275*t*
Workcenters
concept of, 334
space planning in, 334–337
special, 334–337
Work diary, 215
Work distribution, 590
Work distribution chart, 591*f*
definition of, 580
Workers' compensation insurance, definition of, 266
Workflow, 96
space needs for, 327–329
Workflow analysis, definition of, 582
Workforce, diverse, 159, 162*f*, 197*t*
Work letter, definition of, 345
Work log, 215
Work measurement
definition of, 212, 604
difficulties in applying, 605
methods for, 608–617
Work measurement program
administering, 607
communicating to employees, 606–607
feasibility and accuracy of standards for, 607–608
gaining management support for, 606

preparing for, 606–608
selection of analysts for, 607
Workplace
of future, 347–350
violence in, 303
Workplace analysis, definition of, 584
Work sampling, 609–610
definition of, 19
determining sample size for, 611–612
pros and cons of, 612
using, 609–610
Work schedules, 308–312
Work-scheduling studies, 592–593
Work sharing, definition of, 312
Workshops, in-house, 197
Work simplification model, 576–578, 577*f*
Work standards
in analyzing costs, 648–650
definition of, 604
methods for setting, 608–617
setting, 212
Work standards program, benefits of, 604–605
Workstation analysis, definition of, 385
Workstations, 323, 334, 413
Work teams, 42–43
employee participation on, 623–625
Workweek, modified, 308–312
Written communications
definition of, 441
effective, 465*f*
external, 445
internal, 443–445
media, 443–445
in office, 441–445
process, 441–443, 442*f*
Written procedures, 443, 444*f*

Xerography, definition of, 559

Zero-base budgeting (ZBB), 645–646

PHOTO CREDITS

For permission to reproduce the photographs on the pages indicated, acknowledgment is made to the following:

Contents   p. iv: Photo Courtesy of International Business Machines Corporation; p. v: Photo Courtesy of International Business Machines Corporation; p. vi: Photo Courtesy of International Business Machines Corporation; p. vii: Photo Courtesy of International Business Machines Corporation

Part 1   p. xii: Photo Courtesy of International Business Machines Corporation

Chapter 1   p. 5: Photo by Alan Brown/Photonics; p. 10: Intel Corporation; p. 15: Courtesy of Apple Computer, Inc./Photo by John Greenleigh

Chapter 2   p. 28: Location Courtesy of Discovery, Hyde Park Square, Cincinnati; p. 40: Texas Instruments Incorporated

Chapter 4   p. 100: International School of Naples

Chapter 5   p. 117: Photo by Richard Younker

Part 2   p. 128: Courtesy of International Business Machines Corporation

Chapter 8   p. 198: Gannett Co., Inc.

Chapter 10   p. 241: Arthur Andersen & Co., SC

Chapter 11   p. 265: Courtesy Andrea Schutz/Educational Testing Service; p. 267: © Stan Levy/Photo Researchers, Inc.; p. 270: Stock, Boston

Chapter 12   p. 295: © Mark Richards/PhotoEdit; p. 303: © John Coletti/Uniphoto Picture Agency; p. 310: Courtesy of International Business Machines Corporation

Part 3   p. 320: Photo Courtesy of International Business Machines Corporation

Chapter 13   p. 329: Courtesy of International Business Machines Corporation; p. 335: (top) Photo Courtesy of Marvel; (bottom) Photo Courtesy of Marvel; p. 336: Photo Courtesy of Center Core; p. 341: (left) TAB Products Co.; (right) TAB Products Co.; p. 344: Courtesy John W. Hoekstra/Fifth Third Bancorp

Chapter 14   p. 358: Courtesy Sharon Glick/Johnson & Higgins; p. 367: Courtesy of Apple Computer, Inc./John Greenleigh, Photographer; p. 371: Ring King Visibles, Inc.; p. 378: Photo Courtesy of Herman Miller, Inc.

Chapter 15   p. 387: A. Adaptive Information Systems, a U.S. Subsidiary of Hitachi; B. Haworth, Inc.; C. Kimball International, Office Furniture Division; p. 391: Haworth, Inc.; p. 399: © Elena Rooraid/PhotoEdit; p. 400: Courtesy of Craig Mack and Warren Power/Deere & Company

Chapter 16   p. 410: Photo Courtesy of Amdahl Corporation; p. 411: Guennadi Maslou/Photonics Graphics; p. 412: Apple Computers, Inc.; p. 416: NCR Corporation; p. 429: Courtesy Brother David Nagle

Chapter 17   p. 450: (a) Photo Courtesy of Lanier Voice Products; p. 452: Brother International Corporation; p. 453: Courtesy Judy Norberg; p. 461: Bull HN Information Systems, Inc.

Chapter 18   p. 474: Photo Courtesy of Northern Telecom, Inc.; p. 475: Photo Courtesy of Northern Telecom, Inc.; p. 485: Courtesy Roger Courts/Sacred Heart League; p. 490: Courtesy of Sprint; p. 491: Photo Courtesy of Northern Telecom, Inc.; p. 499: Courtesy of Pitney Bowes

Chapter 19   p. 522: (a) HON Industries, Inc.; (d) White Power Files, Inc., Union, New Jersey; p. 524: Courtesy Elizabeth Regan/Massachusetts Mutual Life Insurance Company

Chapter 20   p. 546: (a) Photography Courtesy of Eastman Kodak Company; (b) Bell & Howell; p. 551: Photography by Erik Von Fischer/Photonics; p. 560: Photogaphy Courtesy of Eastman Kodak Company

Part 4   p. 570: Photo Courtesy of International Business Machines Corporation

Chapter 21   p. 576: Photo Courtesy of International Business Machines Corporation; p. 595: Courtesy Rodney Scheyer/Boeing Computer Services

Chapter 22   p. 606: Comstock, Inc.; p. 615: H. Armstrong Roberts; p. 620: Photo Researchers, Inc.; p. 624: Courtesy Lynn Ann Lew/Hazar, Inc.

Chapter 23   p. 635: Courtesy William Englesbe/Wheaton, Inc.; p. 652: Courtesy of Kelly Services, Inc.

701

Mary Shelley

Twayne's English Authors Series

Herbert Sussman, Editor

Northwestern University

TEAS 526

MARY WOLLSTONECRAFT SHELLEY. MINIATURE BY REGINALD EASTON.
Courtesy of the Bodelian Library, Oxford.

Mary Shelley

Johanna M. Smith

University of Texas—Arlington

Twayne Publishers
An Imprint of Simon & Schuster Macmillan
New York

Prentice Hall International
London • Mexico City • New Delhi • Singapore • Sydney • Toronto

Twayne's English Authors Series No. 526
Mary Shelley
Johanna M. Smith

Copyright © 1996 by Twayne Publishers

Twayne Publishers
An Imprint of Simon & Schuster Macmillan
1633 Broadway
New York, New York 10019

Library of Congress Cataloging-in-Publication Data
Smith, Johanna M.
    Mary Shelley / Johanna M. Smith.
      p.   cm. — (Twayne's English authors series ; 526)
    Includes bibliographical references and index.
    ISBN 0-8057-7045-3 (alk. paper)
    1. Shelley, Mary Wollstonecraft, 1797–1851—Criticism and
interpretation. 2. Women and literature—England—History—19th
century. I. Title. II. Series: Twayne's English author series ;
TEAS 526.
PR5398.S55   1996
823'.7—dc20   96-10575
                                                       CIP

10 9

Printed in the United States of America

For Kathryn Harmon Smith
1907–1975

Contents

Preface   *ix*
Acknowledgments   *xi*
Chronology   *xiii*

Chapter One
Mary Wollstonecraft Shelley: Biography   *1*

Chapter Two
Plays and Poems   *19*

Chapter Three
Science Fiction:
Short Stories, *Frankenstein,* and *The Last Man*   *33*

Chapter Four
Historical Fiction: Short Stories,
Valperga, Oriental Tales, and *Perkin Warbeck*   *55*

Chapter Five
Domestic-Sentimental Fiction:
Mathilda, Short Stories, *Lodore,* and *Falkner*   *92*

Chapter Six
Literary Biography and Criticism   *119*

Chapter Seven
Travel Narratives   *155*

Notes and References   *171*
Selected Bibliography   *186*
Index   *193*

Preface

Until quite recently, a book on Mary Shelley would have justified itself by reference to her husband, Percy Shelley, and to her novel *Frankenstein,* the only one of her works to be regularly reissued since its publication in 1818. In his 1972 book, William A. Walling extended this focus by removing Shelley from the shadow of her husband and by claiming recognition for the merits of her novels *Valperga* and *The Last Man.* Within the last few years, a collection of essays on *The Other Mary Shelley* as well as the eight-volume Pickering edition of her works attest to a heightened recognition of the extent of her literary production.

With this book I hope to increase that recognition of Mary Shelley as more than a one-book Romantic writer. The book is organized by genre in order to emphasize the breadth of her writing. I have placed her works in the literary history of the several genres in which she wrote, and I have discussed each work exhaustively so as not to perpetuate what seem to me invidious distinctions between "major" and "minor" works. In a similar spirit, while I refer throughout to autobiographical elements of her works, for the most part I subordinate those elements to other concerns. I do so to combat a long-standing critical tendency to reduce Shelley's writing to a coda on her life. Certainly she drew on her own experience for her writing; indeed, despite her disclaimers about putting herself forward, many of her works make direct references to her life. But of more than merely autobiographical interest, it seems to me, are her *reflections* on the experience that she puts in her fiction, her characteristic rethinking and reshaping of such episodes. Furthermore, an exclusive focus on autobiography occludes the commentary on contemporary questions and issues in Mary Shelley's writings, the continuing interest in political questions and gender issues that salts her work. To emphasize that interest, throughout the book I have located her work in political and cultural, as well as literary, history. Although my critical methodologies are consistently feminist and Marxist, then, I also see this book as a work of cultural studies.

More generally, I have tried to suggest the artificiality of the categories of genre and period fixed by literary history. The variety of genres in which Shelley wrote—and her cross-pollination of ideas commonly

regarded as exclusively "Romantic" or "Victorian"—should call into question such categorizations. A figure like Mary Shelley, much of whose work bridges the Romantic and Victorian periods as currently conceived, has much to tell us not only about those years but about the limits of periodicity.

Johanna M. Smith

Acknowledgments

It is a pleasure to acknowledge the debts I have accumulated in the writing of this book. All students of Mary Shelley are indebted to Betty T. Bennett for her edition of the letters, to Paula R. Feldman and Diana Scott-Kilvert for their edition of the journals, and to Charles E. Robinson for his editions of the short stories and of the *Frankenstein* manuscripts. The painstaking recovery and editorial work of these scholars makes it possible for others such as myself to continue to flesh out Mary Shelley's personal and professional life. To Charles Robinson, Jane Blumberg, and Emily Sunstein I owe an additional debt for generously sharing their knowledge of Mary Shelley's early writings with me. I am grateful for gracious aid from the librarians and staff members of the research, newspaper, and rare-book divisions of the British Library, Oxford's Bodleian Library, the Boston Public Library, and the University of Michigan Library. Without a leave from the University of Texas and the use of interlibrary loan and other facilities at the Bowdoin College Library, I doubt that I could have finished the manuscript on deadline. I am grateful to Herbert Sussman and to the Twayne editors for their patient and helpful comments on the manuscript. Permission to reproduce the Reginald Easton miniature of Mary Shelley was kindly granted by the Bodleian Library.

On a personal note, I would like to thank Ross C. Murfin, who initiated my involvement with Mary Shelley's work by inviting me to edit *Mary Shelley: "Frankenstein."* I am grateful to Mary Loeffelholz for recommending me to Twayne, to Celeste Goodridge for encouraging me to undertake this project, to Tim Morris for *Frankenstein* sightings, and to C. Jan Swearingen for general collegiality. Members of the Brain Trust were an inspiriting resource for Italian translations, critical theory, Romantic texts, and much more; they and Leslie Spelman helped stiffen my spine for what sometimes seemed an overwhelming task. First and last, I am grateful for the support and friendship of Carolyn A. Barros.

Chronology

1789   French Revolution begins.

1793   England declares war on France; war continues until 1815.

1797   On 30 August Mary Wollstonecraft Godwin is born in London to William Godwin and Mary Wollstonecraft. On 10 September Mary Wollstonecraft dies.

1801   On 21 December William Godwin marries Mary Jane Clairmont, whose daughter, Jane (later Claire), becomes Mary's stepsister.

1805   The Godwins begin publishing firm of M. J. Godwin & Co.

1808   Mary Wollstonecraft Godwin writes initial version of "Mounseer Nongtongpaw."

1811   Boards at a girls' school in Ramsgate.

1812   From June through following ten months, stays with Baxter family in Dundee, Scotland. On 11 November, during brief visit to London, first meets her father's disciple, Percy Bysshe Shelley. "Mounseer Nongtongpaw," completed by others, published by M. J. Godwin & Co.

1813   From June through following nine months, stays again with Baxter family. On 5 May again meets Percy Bysshe Shelley. On 28 July elopes with him to France, accompanied by Claire.

1815   On 22 January, first child is born; the baby, a daughter, dies on 6 March.

1816   On 24 January, son William is born.

From May to August, the Shelleys and Claire live in Italy, in close contact with Lord Byron; in July, begins *Frankenstein*. On 11 October, her half-sister Fanny commits suicide. On 10 December, Percy Shelley's wife, Harriet, pregnant with her lover's child, drowns herself. On 30 December, Percy Shelley and Mary Wollstonecraft Godwin marry.

1817   On 27 March, Percy Bysshe Shelley denied custody of his and Harriet's two children. In June, *History of a Six Weeks' Tour* is published anonymously. On 2 September, Mary's and Percy's daughter Clara born.

1818   In March, *Frankenstein* is published; the Shelleys and Claire leave England for a four-year residence in Italy. On 24 September, daughter Clara dies in Venice.

1819   On 7 June, son William dies in Rome. Early November, completes her novella *Mathilda*. On 12 November, son Percy Florence is born.

1820   In May, sends *Mathilda* to Godwin; writes *Proserpine* and *Midas*.

1821   On 1 December, completes *Valperga*.

1822   On 8 July, Percy Bysshe Shelley and Edward Williams are drowned. Later this month, Mary writes "The Choice."

1823   In March, *Valperga* is published. On 25 August, returns to England. A story and an article are published.

1824   In June, moves to Kentish Town to be near Jane Williams; develops friendships with Vincent Novello and John Howard Payne. Her edition of Percy Bysshe Shelley's *Posthumous Poems* is published in June but suppressed in August; a story, three articles, and a translation are also published.

1826   In February, *The Last Man* is published; three articles also appear.

1827   During the summer, helps Isabel Robinson and Mary Diana Dods "elope" to the Continent. An article is published.

1828   In April, contracts smallpox while in Paris; later meets Prosper Mérimée. Two stories and two translations are published.

1829   Three stories, three articles, and three translations are published.

1830   In May, *Perkin Warbeck* is published; two stories, two articles, and two poems also appear.

1831   Edits Trelawny's *Adventures of a Younger Son* and negotiates for its publication; publishes a story and three articles of her own.

1832   First Reform Bill. Two stories, an article, a poem, and *Proserpine* are published.

1833   Two stories are published; possible romance with Aubrey Beauclerk.

1834   Two stories are published.

1835   *Lodore* and two volumes of *Lives of the Most Eminent Literary and Scientific Men of Italy* are published.

1836   In April, her father dies. A story is published.

1837   *Falkner* and *Lives of the Most Eminent Literary and Scientific Men of Spain and Portugal* are published.

1838   A story and two poems are published.

1839   Volume 2 of *Lives of the Most Eminent Literary and Scientific Men of France* and four-volume edition of *The Poetical Works of Percy Bysshe Shelley* are published; revised one-volume edition appears later this year.

1840   Her two-volume edition of Percy Bysshe Shelley's *Essays, Letters from Abroad, Translations and Fragments* is published. Begins extensive travels in Europe with her son Percy.

1842   Canzonet is published. Again travels with Percy in Europe

1844   *Rambles in Germany and Italy* and an article are published. In April, Sir Timothy Shelley dies and Percy inherits the Shelley baronetcy and estate; Mary Shelley much involved in managing estate.

1845   In September, blackmail attempts by Ferdinando Gatteschi and "G. Byron."

1846   In May, possible extortion attempt by Thomas Medwin.

1848   In April, distraught over Chartist demonstration. On June 22, Percy marries Jane St. John, who is devoted to Mary Shelley and nurses her in her final illness.

1851   On 1 February, dies in London of meningioma.

Chapter One
Mary Wollstonecraft Shelley: Biography

Until Muriel Spark's *Child of Light* in 1951, most biographies of Mary Shelley paid far more attention to her as Percy Shelley's wife than as the woman and writer who survived him by almost thirty years. Following the lead of the more inclusive studies of the last twenty years, this chapter's biography of Mary Wollstonecraft Godwin Shelley emphasizes her politics and her "fundamental consciousness of herself as author."[1] The chapter concludes with a discussion of the political and gender ideologies that interested and affected her throughout her life.

Mary Shelley was born on 30 August 1797, the daughter of feminist radical Mary Wollstonecraft and of philosopher radical William Godwin. Both her parents were prominent in revolutionary movements that peaked in the late eighteenth century. Among these was a long tradition of feminism that demanded education for women and saw women's oppression in political terms. In 1696 Mary Astell had called for institutions where upper-class women could educate themselves beyond the "accomplishments"—needlework, drawing, music—to which they were commonly restricted. And in *Some Reflections on Marriage* (1700), Astell joined a feminist critique of women's position in marriage with a political critique of absolutism; "if absolute Sovereignty be not necessary in a State," she wrote, "how comes it to be so in a Family?"[2] Such novels as Sarah Scott's *Millenium Hall* (1762) and Mary Hamilton's *Munster Village* (1778) explored the possibilities of independence for educated women, while eighteenth-century writers and scholars like Lady Mary Wortley Montagu, Elizabeth Elstob, Elizabeth Carter, and Helen Maria Williams began to live out these possibilities. By the 1770s and 1780s, women such as Mary Hays and Catherine Macaulay Graham were making feminist claims more strongly, in part because political actions—the American Revolution of 1775 and the French Revolution of 1789—seemed to promise new liberty for women.

Among those who welcomed this liberty was Mary Shelley's mother, Mary Wollstonecraft. Now best known for *A Vindication of the Rights of*

Woman (1792), Wollstonecraft was also known to her contemporaries for her revolutionary writings. Her *Vindication of the Rights of Men* (1790) was the first full-length response to Edmund Burke's conservative *Reflections on the Revolution in France* (1790). In her 1795 *Historical and Moral View of the Origin and Progress of the French Revolution*, Wollstonecraft again countered Burkean attacks on the Revolution and its British sympathizers (known as Jacobins) in part by enumerating the "continual miseries" that impelled the working poor toward revolution.[3]

Wollstonecraft knew the grievances of the working poor from experience. Although her father rose from master weaver to gentleman farmer, his drunkenness and general fecklessness impoverished his family, and, before she turned to writing, Wollstonecraft had worked variously as lady's companion, seamstress, director of a girls' school, and governess. As a working woman, she also recognized that workers and women were equally underrepresented in Parliament. Prior to the 1832 Reform Bill, the suffrage was restricted to men with substantial property; out of a population of 8.5 million, only 11,000 men of the propertied classes were eligible to vote in parliamentary elections.[4] This supposedly representative government was to Wollstonecraft "only a convenient handle for despotism";[5] under such a system, she says ironically, women are "as well represented as a numerous class of hard-working mechanics, who pay for the support of royalty when they can scarcely stop their children's mouths with bread." The main focus of the *Vindication*, however, is women's social rather than political position. Wollstonecraft's own hand-to-mouth existence doubtless influenced her view that more professions should be open to "honest, independent women" (148). More generally, she argues that women are "human creatures, who, in common with men, are placed on this earth to unfold their faculties" (8). Hence they should be "prepared by education to become the companion of man" (4), rather than to develop the "gentleness, docility, and spaniel-like affection" (34) commonly regarded as women's given or natural "sexual characteristics" (9).

But the *Vindication* supports this position with contradictory arguments that suggest some difficulties of conceiving a revolutionary feminism. On the one hand, Wollstonecraft criticizes "tyrants" who "force all women, by denying them civil and political rights, to remain immured in their families" (5), and she argues that women should be educated to foster the "strength, both of body and mind" (9), that will make them "respectable members of society" (10). On the other hand, she concludes that women so educated will become "more observant daughters, more

affectionate sisters, more faithful wives, more reasonable mothers—in a word, better citizens" (150). Thus, while she is clearly concerned to improve women's position as "members of society" and "citizens," she represents that larger social position as rooted in domestic roles. Granted, in 1792 educating a woman to be her husband's companion and friend rather than "play-thing" (24), "humble dependent" (29), or "upper servant" (40) was a fairly revolutionary aim; Wollstonecraft's argument nonetheless tends to define women not as "human creatures" but according to their domestic relationships with men.

Similar contradictions appear in Wollstonecraft's life as a feminist. Although she warned her readers that "love, from its very nature, must be transitory" (30), she had an obsessive affair with the American adventurer Gilbert Imlay and twice attempted suicide over his affairs with other women. After she married William Godwin they maintained separate households, but despite this independence, she sometimes felt that she "was not treated with respect, owing to [Godwin's] desire not to be disturbed."[6] In a note asking him to settle a business matter, for instance, she remarks that "I am perhaps as unfit as yourself to do it, and my time appears to me as valuable as that of other persons accustomed to employ themselves" (319). Her sharp tone here suggests the contradictions facing a woman who attempted to live out an ideal of shared responsibility in marriage. It is thus a poignant but fitting coda to this marriage that Godwin's *Memoirs of the Author of A Vindication of the Rights of Woman* (1798), which he intended as a tribute to his wife, instead adversely affected her early reputation. Because he gave full details of Wollstonecraft's unconventional sexual life, many of his shocked contemporaries considered both the book and its subject "'shameless'," "'lascivious'," and "'disgusting'."[7] Within forty years, however, Wollstonecraft's feminism was receiving recognition from working women. In 1834 Francis Morrison, coeditor of the radical union journal *The Pioneer*, used an extract from the *Vindication of the Rights of Woman* to "beautify" the Woman's Page of her newspaper.

Wollstonecraft's radical politics and feminism profoundly influenced her daughter. Mary Shelley greatly admired her mother's "sound understanding, her intrepidity, her sensibility and eager sympathy";[8] she read Wollstonecraft's works over and over, and to be told that she resembled her mother was "the most flattering thing" one could say to her.[9] Although she too believed in what she called "the 'good Cause'" of "the advancement of freedom & knowledge,"[10] she felt herself unable to "support it openly in writing" as her mother had done (*MWSJ*, 2:554). Her

feminism was similarly displayed in private rather than public; "[i]f I
have never written to vindicate the Rights of women," she said of herself, "I have ever befriended women when oppressed" (*MWSJ*, 2:557).
The conclusion of this chapter will return to the ways in which the prob-
lematics of Wollstonecraft's life and books reappear in Mary Shelley's
history.

Mary's legacy from her father was perhaps less fraught, but it too
suggests some of the dangers and contradictions in living out a political
ideal. The son of a Sandemanian minister, Godwin was himself a minister of this dissenting sect until 1783, but he later became an atheist
and turned his attention to ethics and politics. He was one of many
radicals in England who initially welcomed the French Revolution of
1789 (Wollstonecraft's was only the first of some thirty enthusiastic
defenses of the Revolution). These Jacobins formed "corresponding
societies" in order to discuss how best to extend the French example
into England; the phenomenal sale of Paine's *Rights of Man, Part Two*
(1792)—200,000 copies by 1793, or approximately one for every 50
Britons[11]—further testifies to the revolutionary fervor of these years.
With his *Enquiry concerning Political Justice* (1793) and his novel *Caleb
Williams; or, Things as They Are* (1794), Godwin surpassed even Tom
Paine as a spokesperson for radical ideals; in the fifteen years after the
publication of *Political Justice*, 758 books and articles discussed Godwin
or his writings (St. Clair, 87).

But the year of *Political Justice* also began a period of repression that
made it more dangerous for Godwin and other Jacobins publicly to support the French Republic. In December 1792 Paine had been outlawed
from England and his *Rights of Man* banned as seditious libel; in February 1793 England declared war on France and moved no less harshly
against the French Republic's English adherents. Booksellers were prosecuted for selling Paine's book; leaders of corresponding societies were
arrested; *habeas corpus* was suspended in 1794, large public meetings
without permits were banned in 1795, secret organizations were outlawed in 1797, and Combination Laws against workers' associations
were passed in 1799. It is not surprising that in May 1793 the government considered prosecuting Godwin for *Political Justice*. Eventually
they decided not to proceed, apparently agreeing with the *Critical
Review* that a book "which of its very nature and bulk can never circulate
among the inferior classes of society" could do little damage.[12] Yet *Political Justice*, while by no means a best-seller, sold 4,000 copies in three licit
and two pirated editions; the "inferior classes" often pooled their money

to buy one copy which was then read aloud, so Godwin's revolutionary ideas "circulated" further than the sales figures might suggest.

But in some ways *Political Justice* is antirevolutionary, and a brief consideration of its contradictory political philosophy will prepare for the contradictions of Mary Shelley's politics. Godwin later recalled that in 1789 "[m]y heart beat high with sentiments of liberty," but he added that he "never for a moment ceased to disapprove of mob government and violence" (quoted in Locke, 40). *Political Justice* displays this same ambivalence toward political change. As a radical, Godwin regards all governments as pernicious. Coming into existence via "the errors and perverseness of a few," governments are perpetuated "by the infantine and uninstructed confidence of the many,"[13] for the lower orders confuse the reverence due a superior in *wisdom* with the obedience enforced by a superior in *rank*. Because the upper ranks have "no equitable claim" (*PJ*, 123) to the many advantages they have "usurped," revolutionaries who are "angry with corruption, and impatient at injustice," are motivated by "the excess of a virtuous feeling" (*PJ*, 139). The key word here is "excess," for it signals the conservative element of Godwin's politics. Revolutionary disruption forces "the many" toward changes for which they are unprepared, because it suspends the "patient speculations" that will gradually produce "salutary and uninterrupted progress" toward "political truth and social improvement" (*PJ*, 137–38). Yet revolution and violence are not simply destructive; often they have led to "important changes" (*PJ*, 139). Godwin *is* a revolutionary in his belief that the gradual decay of government is a "euthanasia" devoutly to be wished (*PJ*, 125) and in his view that revolutionary violence may be useful. Yet he is also antirevolutionary in his belief in *gradual* progress toward a point at which government is unnecessary because, "the plain dictates of justice" having become evident to all, "the whole species [has] become reasonable and virtuous" (*PJ*, 221).

Unavoidably such a summary oversimplifies Godwin's arguments, and he underestimated neither the length of time required for progress toward political justice nor the difficulties in educating people toward this goal. Yet *Political Justice* has moments of sunny optimism that Mary Shelley, despite her agreement with some of her father's ideas, did not share. She respected his "passion for reforming the world," but her response to his views was complicated by her tendency to "feel the counter arguments too strongly" (*MWSJ*, 2:553, 554). Examining her life and her conflicted view of her dual heritage may thus aid in understanding both her revolutionary and her reformist impulses.

The first decade of Mary Shelley's life was eventful. Her mother died of a puerperal infection on 10 September 1797, ten days after Mary's birth. Godwin's proposals of marriage to Harriet Lee in 1798 and Maria Reveley in 1799 were rejected, and for four years he raised Mary and her half-sister, Fanny (Wollstonecraft's daughter by Imlay), with the help of friends and extended family. Although he regarded the girls as "favourite companions and most chosen friends,"[14] he felt "incompeten[t] for the education of daughters," and this was "one among [his] motives"[15] for marrying Mary Jane Clairmont on 21 December 1801. The marriage added to his household Mrs. Godwin's two illegitimate children, Charles—who was seven years old in 1801—and Jane (later Claire), who was eight months younger than Mary; Mary's half-brother, William Jr., was born on 28 March 1803. The older children were expected to perform such household duties as waiting at table, and although Mary later called herself "an Ignorama" at giving elaborate dinners (*MWSL*, 2:334), as a girl she learned simple cooking and needlework from her stepmother and her governess Maria Smith. Godwin taught the children mythology as well as ancient and English history, and they also learned more informally from the poet Samuel Taylor Coleridge, the painter Sir Thomas Lawrence, the novelist Maria Edgeworth, the scientist Sir Humphry Davy, former Vice President of the United States Aaron Burr, and the many other writers, artists, scientists, and inventors who visited Godwin. In 1805 Mrs. Godwin persuaded her husband to open M. J. Godwin and Co., a publishing and bookselling firm. By 1807 Godwin had moved his family and business to a commercial area of London, and he and his wife devoted themselves to running the firm and writing its Juvenile Library series.

In the following years, Mary's relations with her father and stepmother were sometimes strained. She took to "wander[ing]" near her mother's grave and reading Wollstonecraft's works there (*MWSJ*, 2:543). Yet she also contributed to the family business; her satiric poem "Mounseer Nongtongpaw," which became a Godwin & Co. "staple" (Sunstein, 42), was published in January 1812.[16] By this time she had masters for French, Italian, and drawing, and Godwin was teaching her Latin and the sciences as well as training her in such research skills as making chronologies. But he had "faults as a teacher," Mary recalled; with too much "temper" and too little "sympathy" toward his pupils, he was "too grave and severe" in general as well as "too minute in his censures" (quoted in Paul, 1:37). And while Mary later remembered many instances of her "excessive & romantic attachment" to the father she

regarded as "my God" (*MWSL,* 2:215, 1:296), she also felt that he inadvertently "chill[ed] and stifle[d]" his children's expressions of affection (quoted in Sunstein, 37). Godwin himself admitted that, as a busy father, he was apt to be "somewhat sententious and authoritative" toward his children (quoted in Spark, 16). For example, while Mary was boarding at a girls' school in order to recover from a severe skin rash, Godwin transmitted through her stepmother his hope that, "in spite of unfavourable appearances," she would grow up to be "wise" and "good" (quoted in Sunstein, 55). Small wonder that Mary remembered with pleasure her next absence from the Godwin home. In June 1812 she began a visit to the family of Godwin's admirer, William Baxter, in Scotland; during these ten months and a subsequent visit from June 1813 to March 1814, she not only enjoyed an "eyry of freedom" on the Scottish shore but developed the "flights of [her] imagination."[17]

Soon after her return from Scotland in 1814, the seventeen-year-old Mary first met her father's newest disciple, Percy Bysshe Shelley. Long an admirer of Godwin's principles, Shelley had introduced himself to Mary's father in 1812 and was soon dining regularly at the Godwins' with his wife Harriet. With his usual quixotism, in 1811 Shelley had eloped with Harriet, to rescue her from her father's "most horrible" persecutions but also to "cultivat[e]" her latent talents.[18] Despite a sudden recognition after meeting Mary that his "rash & heartless" marriage had become "loathsome & horrible" (*PBSL,* 1:402), in March 1814 he married Harriet a second time "in order to legitimate the earlier ceremony" (St. Clair, 322). He "speedily conceived an ardent passion" for Mary, however, and on June 27 she confessed her love to him; treated with "cruelty & injustice" (*PBSL,* 1:403) during a flurry of meetings with Mary's parents and Shelley's wife, the lovers determined to flee. After assuring his pregnant wife of his "unimpaired" affection for her and their daughter Ianthe (*PBSL,* 1:389), Shelley eloped with Mary to France on 18 July 1814. Her stepsister, Jane/Claire, accompanied them on the journey; although Shelley wrote to Harriet inviting her to join them in Switzerland, she declined. During these six weeks Mary wrote a story, "Hate" (since lost), and she later commemorated the trip itself in her *History of a Six Weeks' Tour* (1817).

The trio returned to England in September 1814. Both sets of parents were unforgiving to the lovers, and so long as Sir Timothy Shelley withheld his son's allowance, Percy Shelley was often in danger of arrest for debt. Until May 1815 he and Mary frequently changed their lodgings; to mislead bailiffs, they lived apart for one three-week period. As

Shelley's mistress, Mary Godwin was the subject of scandal and social ostracism; it was rumored, for example, that her father had sold her to Shelley (*MWSL*, 1:4). Her first baby was born on 22 February 1815 but lived only eleven days. Although Mary felt a sense of "regeneration" (*MWSJ*, 1:79) when Claire left their ménage in May, her life with Percy remained unsettled until they moved to Windsor in August 1815; her son William was born there on 24 January 1816. Some four months later the family left for Geneva at the instigation of Claire, who was having an affair with Lord Byron and wished to follow him. She and the Shelleys settled in Italy near Byron for the summer of 1816; in July, as the result of a ghost-story competition with Percy, Byron, and Byron's friend Polidori, Mary Godwin began *Frankenstein*.

The Shelleys returned to England with Claire in September, and while Shelley searched for a house, Mary accompanied Claire to Bath, where Claire's illegitimate daughter, Allegra, was born on 12 January 1817. These four months in Bath were full of trouble for Mary. Her half-sister, Fanny Imlay, committed suicide on 9 October 1816; three months later Shelley's wife Harriet, pregnant and apparently abandoned by her lover, drowned herself. Years later Mary Shelley regarded her own "heavy sorrows" (*MWSJ*, 2:560) as "the atonement claimed by fate" for Harriet's tragic death; she may well have felt something of this guilt at the time, for she was "much agitated" (*MWSL*, 1:24) after Harriet's suicide, and she married Shelley a scant three weeks later. Certainly she regretted that her marriage came too late for her to provide a home for "[p]oor dear Fanny," and the marriage failed to resolve the other problems that it was intended to address. Although Shelley believed that his marriage would help prevent Harriet's family from winning legal custody of his and Harriet's two children, the Court of Chancery gave judgment against him. And although Mary's marriage to Shelley on 30 December 1816 pleased her father, reconciliation came at a cost: for the remainder of their marriage Godwin would hound them for money—over the years he wheedled £4700 from his son-in-law—without forgiving them for the "accumulated horror" of the elopement (quoted in *PBSL*, 1:391n).

The year 1817 was relatively calm. Established in March at a house in Marlow, the Shelleys were "very political as well as poetical" (*MWSL*, 1:29). Mary took "extreme pleasure" (*MWSL*, 1:32) in the "boldness" of their friend Leigh Hunt's radical politics, and she closely followed the year's controversy over taxation reform. A second child, Clara, was born on 2 September. Mary completed *Frankenstein* during this year, and it

was published in March of 1818. That same month the Shelleys sailed with Claire and her daughter for what was to be a four-year residence in Italy.

Mary recalled her life with Percy as "happy, though chequered" (*MWSJ*, 2:430), and "checkered" well describes their Italian years. In many ways this was a productive and happy period for her. The Shelleys frequently traveled in Italy, and another source of interest was Italian politics; Mary's letters attest her delight in the revolts against Austria by Naples (July 1820) and Piedmont (April 1821). Excepting these periods of travel, her journal generally records only her everyday reading and writing, but this "very ordinariness" indicates her "desire to conserve textually the record of a shared life" with Shelley.[19] He often read aloud to her from English Renaissance poetry and drama, and they studied Italian and Spanish together. He taught her Latin, and by 1817 she was translating Apuleius with him; by 1818 she was reading Livy with "thorough mastery,"[20] and by 1820 she was collaborating with Shelley on his translation of Spinoza. She also studied Greek with the exiled Prince Alexander Mavrocordato, and she shared his excitement when Greece "declared its freedom!" from Turkish rule (*MWSL*, 1:186); the Shelleys translated the proclamation of freedom and wrote an account of the rebellion, which was published in Leigh Hunt's *Examiner*. The birth of their son Percy on 12 November 1819 and his continuing good health were further sources of pleasure. Furthermore, Mary Shelley was writing: in 1819 she completed her novella *Mathilda*, and between 1818 and 1821 she researched and wrote her Italian historical novel *Valperga*.

Other elements of her years in Italy were less pleasant. In addition to persistent rumors that she, Percy, Claire, and Byron had formed a League of Incest (Sunstein, 119), there were intermittent domestic disturbances. Godwin's persistent demands for money were troubling in themselves and twice affected his daughter's writing career. In May of 1820 she sent *Mathilda* to him for his comments, and he retained it during subsequent estrangements; that she "want[ed] it very much" (*MWSL*, 1:224) suggests that she would have revised the manuscript for publication had his intransigence not kept it from her. In late 1821 Godwin was again in financial difficulties and she authorized him to sell *Valperga*, but he delayed publication in hopes of getting a higher price for the copyright. With "an authors [sic] vanity" (*MWSL*, 1:218) Mary "long[ed]" to see the book in print, but with a daughter's devotion she not only subordinated that desire to her father's financial needs but later allowed him to rename and trim the novel. Claire was another recurring

irritant during these years. Although she had ceded Allegra to Byron in
April 1818, she entangled both Mary and Percy Shelley in her consequent quarrels with him; when Byron placed the child in a convent, for
instance, in April 1822 Claire proposed to Mary that they kidnap the
child.

Finally, Mary Shelley's relations with her husband during their Italian
years were sometimes troubled. In August 1821 she was "[s]hocked
beyond all measure" (*MWSL*, 1:204) to learn of the rumor that Claire
had had a child by Percy, and although her refutation states her "perfect
trust" in her husband (*MWSL*, 1:207), Claire remained a source of
estrangement. Percy's letters to Claire, for instance, sometimes contain
plans not to be "mention[ed]" to his wife (*PBSL*, 2:243). Attempting to
mediate Claire's quarrels with Byron, Percy twice "packed [Mary] off"
(*MWSL*, 1:236) on hasty and uncomfortable journeys; during—and
perhaps due to—one of these, their daughter, Clara, died on 24 September 1818. Further estrangement resulted from his efforts to conceal
"thoughts that would pain her" (*PBSL*, 2:435), and these concealments
were not always so well-meaning: he warned Byron not to tell Mary
"the whole truth" about his own infatuation with Emilia Viviani, since
she "might be very much annoyed at it" (*PBSL*, 2:347). In the last
month of his life he complained to a friend that Mary did not "understand" him (*PBSL*, 2:435), and she did sometimes withdraw from her
husband. She was so deeply depressed by the death of their son William
in June 1819 that she felt she "ought to have died" too (*MWSL*, 1:108),
and her mid-1822 miscarriage caused another depression and estrangement from Percy. When he drowned with their friend Edward Williams
on 8 July 1822, Mary's mourning was heightened by distress over their
recent differences.

Mary Shelley's journal and letters for the following months show her
grief but also the stamina with which she would meet the subsequent
years' "stock of sorrow" (*MWSL*, 1:254). During this period she wrote
her mourning poem, "The Choice," and her journals and letters further
attest her "hatred of life" without Shelley (*MWSJ*, 2:433) and her
"agony" (*MWSL*, 1:253) at the loss of her "guide, protector & companion." Much has been made of Mary's guilt over her withdrawal from her
husband during his last months, and years later she recorded her
"unspeakable regret and gnawing remorse" over her failure to be "atten-
tive" to his "discontent and sadness."[21] But Percy himself half recognized
that his concealments had reduced the "sympathy" between them
(*PBSL*, 2:435), and even in her first grief Mary acquitted herself of

charges that her heart was "cold to thee" (*MWSJ*, 2:430). She believed that "in spirit" (*MWSJ*, 2:436) her husband would "visit & encourage" her, and she consistently struggled against what she knew to be a "morbid" self-pity (*MWSL*, 1:512). Within three months of Shelley's death she determined to collect and reissue his manuscripts (*MWSL*, 1:261), and within four months she could joke that Byron's poem *Don Juan* would "cause Milman to hang himself" (*MWSL*, 1:284).

Along with mental stamina, material necessity prompted Mary Shelley's determination to pursue "[l]iterary labors, the improvement of [her] mind, & the enlargement of [her] ideas" (*MWSJ*, 2:431). Percy's allowance from his father ended with his death, and, as a widow of 25 with a two-and-a-half-year-old son, Mary planned to support herself by her writings and by publishing her husband's manuscripts (*MWSL*, 1:260). For the first year after Percy's death she remained in Italy, economizing by sharing a house with Leigh and Marianne Hunt. Byron paid her to fair copy *Don Juan*, and manuscript evidence[22] indicates that she also edited the poem and "omitted all that hurt [her] taste" (*MWSL*, 2:120). There were calls on her earnings from Godwin and her own needy friends, and the necessity of supporting herself became even clearer during the protracted negotiations for an allowance from her father-in-law. In February 1823 Sir Timothy refused to aid her or her son unless she brought the child to England and placed him with a person meeting Sir Timothy's approval; initially she rejected these conditions, but by April she had decided that her son's "interests" as his grandfather's heir required her return to England (*MWSL*, 1:337). Soon after Mary's arrival, her father arranged for a new edition of *Frankenstein* in order to capitalize on the success of Richard Brinsley Peake's 1823 stage adaptation of the novel. The profits of this reissue, she wrote, "seemed all I had to look to" (*MWSL*, 1:379) until November, when Sir Timothy agreed to give her an annual allowance of £200. After she published Percy Shelley's *Posthumous Poems* in 1824, an angry Sir Timothy made her allowance conditional on her promise not to bring the family name before the public during his lifetime.

After ten months in central London, in June 1824 Mary Shelley moved to suburban Kentish Town, where she remained until August 1827. During these years she wrote several articles and stories, as well as her novel *The Last Man* (1826), and she "beg[a]n to live again" (*MWSL*, 1:476). She drew particular consolation from her close friendship with her neighbor Jane Williams, the common-law widow of the Edward Williams who had drowned with Shelley. Jane was "bound up with the

reality of [Mary's] lost life," and they spent many of their first evenings together "living over & over again in memory [their] happy months" (*MWSL*, 1:395, 404). Later Mary enjoyed musical evenings with friends and attending the theater with her admirer John Howard Payne, but Jane remained her "saving Angel"; "I live to all good & pleasure only thro' her" (*MWSL*, 1:514, 528).

Mary was thus appalled when she discovered that Jane had "proved false & treacherous!" (*MWSJ*, 2:502). Not only did Jane betray Mary's confidences about "not having been all [she] shd have been" to Percy (*MWSL*, 1:366), she also hinted to several mutual friends that the poet had turned to her for comfort. Soon after this revelation Mary left Kentish Town, feeling her years with Jane had been "a disturbed and unreal dream" (*MWSL*, 1:572). But "feelings are my events," Mary had written soon after Percy's death (*MWSL*, 1:312), and her love for Jane is perhaps the most significant event of this period. Ten years later Mary referred dismissively to that love: "I was so ready to give myself away—& being afraid of men, I was apt to get *tousy-mousy* for women" (*MWSL*, 2:256). The nature of this "tousy-mousy" feeling is suggested by the letters Mary wrote to Jane during a trip to the Continent. To help her friends Isabel Robinson Douglas and Mary Diana Dods ("Doddy"), Mary accompanied them to Paris, where Doddy dressed as a man and masqueraded as Isabel's husband to enable Isabel to live openly with her illegitimate child.[23] The letters to Jane during this escapade have homoerotic undertones and one overt sexual reference[24] which suggest that, at least on paper, Mary followed the lead of Doddy's impersonation and experimented with her own sexual role vis-à-vis Jane.

The late 1820s and the 1830s were years of almost frenetic literary activity for Mary Shelley. In September 1827 she returned from the Continent, and in the following months she arranged with Sir Timothy's lawyer an addition of £50 to her annual maintenance. In April 1828 she visited Paris; although she contracted smallpox there, she recovered sufficiently to enjoy Parisian society and the friendship of the poet Prosper Mérimée. By September 1828 she was negotiating with Sir Timothy's lawyers for another increase in her maintenance, to cover the expenses of her son's schooling; in September of the following year her allowance was raised to £300. From 1828 to 1830 she wrote eight short stories and five articles in addition to the novel *Perkin Warbeck*. In February 1832 Sir Timothy increased her allowance to £400 per annum. While this sum was considerably more than a working-class family's annual income, it was not princely, and after Mary entered her son at the Har-

row prep school in September 1832 she economized by moving from London to Harrow in May 1833.

Mary's letters during the following years attest to both her loneliness at Harrow (she may have had an abortive romance with Aubrey Beauclerk at this time [Sunstein, 321–22]) and her continuing efforts to obtain paid literary work for her father as well as herself. Along with eight short stories for the high-paying annuals, by 1835 she had written three reviews, revised and reissued *Frankenstein* (1831), written her novel *Lodore* (1835), published several original and translated poems, and completed the first of four volumes of literary biography for Lardner's Cabinet Cyclopedia. Her father's death in 1836 removed one source of financial anxiety, and although she did not finish the biography and edition of his works that she had planned for his widow's benefit, she obtained a charitable grant for Mrs. Godwin. By 1839 she had written *Falkner*, her final novel, and completed the Cabinet Cyclopedia biographies as well as two editions of Percy Shelley's complete poetry; the following year she published a two-volume edition of his prose and letters. Although she attributed her ill-health in 1839 to being "torn to pieces by Memory" (*MWSJ*, 2:559) as she edited the poems, her illness was probably the onset of meningioma, the brain disease that would eventually kill her. After 1840, Mary Shelley's literary production slowed. Her son Percy was now old enough to be a companion, and in 1840 she took him on a summer tour of the Continent, during which he and a friend studied for their degree exams. When Percy graduated from Cambridge in early 1841, Sir Timothy settled an annual allowance of £400 on him, and for the first time in twenty years Mary "began to feel a little above water" (*MWSL*, 3:19).

For the next two years, however, she was anxious about her son's future, an anxiety exacerbated by her sense of her own shaky social position. As early as 1824, she had felt "under a cloud" (*MWSL*, 1:438) of the elopement with Shelley and the League of Incest rumors, and she continued to fear that old scandals would injure her son's prospects by "rouzing the slumbering voice of the public" (*MWSL*, 2:72). Worried because her son Percy had "no aim" (*MWSL*, 3:83) and "no ambition," by 1842 she was "trying to form a society in which he might improve himself" by contact with "his own rank" (*MWSL*, 3:22), but her efforts were painfully unsuccessful. Under the "ban" (*MWSL*, 3:83) imposed by ancient scandal, Mary could do little more than introduce him to "a few distinguished people," and Percy, who took no "pleasure in good society" (*MWSL*, 3:25), "refuse[d] to cultivate" them. Feeling it thus "very

necessary to get him out of England" (*MWSL*, 3:74), from June 1842 to August 1843 she took him and two of his friends on a second continental tour. This too was "all in vain" (*MWSL*, 3:83); the young man lacked his mother's interest in "pictures & antiquities" (*MWSL*, 3:57), and the "impertinence" (*MWSL*, 3:68) she suffered from other British travelers again brought home to her how "entirely exiled" (*MWSL*, 3:92) she was from "good society." After their return to England, Mary continued to worry that her "detestable want of means" (*MWSL*, 3:99) kept her from introducing Percy to the improving "society of women." In 1844 she wrote her final book, *Rambles in Germany and Italy*, in part to earn enough money to "*settle* somewhere" with her son (*MWSL*, 3:73).

Another event of 1844 was instrumental in shaping Mary Shelley's final years. Sir Timothy Shelley died on April 24, and Percy succeeded to the baronetcy; from this time on, Mary was much occupied in managing the estate jointly with her son. Although she initially hoped for an annual £3,000 with which to fulfill her "dreams of being a good landlord & taking care of [the] tenants" (*MWSL*, 3:157), the income from rents was far less than she expected, and the property was encumbered with debts. Like many early Victorians, she turned to speculating in railroad stock; in addition, she conducted a long correspondence with Claire about investing in an opera box. Reading of these speculations, it is difficult to sympathize with Mary's complaints about the "great evil" of "a burthened estate." Still, she consistently aided Claire, several impecunious old friends, and the poor suffering from the "general destitution & scarcity" (*MWSL*, 3:305) of 1847 and 1848.

These charities were curtailed by a second important element of Mary Shelley's final years, the importunities of blackmailers. In 1843 Claire had introduced Mary to a group of Italians exiled for their involvement in the revolutionary Carbonari movement; taking a particular interest in Ferdinando Gatteschi, Mary often aided "this poor devoted Struggler" (*MWSL*, 3:104) and also wrote him several "open heart[ed]" letters (*MWSL*, 3:206). By September 1845 Gatteschi was using the letters to blackmail her; convinced that the details of her "past history" in the letters would "destroy [her] for ever" if made public, Mary spent £250 on a complicated but successful plan to retrieve them. In addition to the shame of being Gatteschi's "easy dupe" (*MWSL*, 3:210), she felt guilty about concealing the transaction from her son and "wast[ing] so disgracefully" money that might have been spent "to benefit the deserving" (*MWSL*, 3:241, 235). Being "so imposed upon & pillaged" by Gatteschi (*MWSL*, 3:280), however, helped her to dispose

briskly of two later extortion attempts. When a man representing himself as Lord Byron's illegitimate son attempted in 1845 to sell her several of her own and Percy Shelley's letters that she had believed were lost, she bought the letters but flatly refused to pay more than £5 for them. In 1846 she asked Thomas Medwin to omit details about her and Claire from his proposed biography of Percy Shelley; when Medwin offered to suppress the book if she would "make [him] some indemnity" for his consequent losses (quoted in *MWSL*, 3:287n), she simply stopped answering his letters.

Like her early years with Percy Shelley, Mary's final years were "chequered." She was delighted when, in 1848, her son married Jane St. John, "the sweetest creature I ever knew" (*MWSL*, 3:339), and she lived comfortably with them. Although Mary was worried by Lady Shelley's months of illness, her own lingering illness was eased by the care of this "beloved daughter" (*MWSL*, 3:370). Yet she was harassed by continuing requests for money and by a contretemps with her stepsister Claire that ended a decade of affectionate relations between them. It is hard not to feel that death, on 1 February 1851 after a week of unconsciousness, released Mary from the "ill health—& extreme depression" which oppressed her last years (*MWSJ*, 2:565).

Mary Shelley lived during a period of turbulent change in England, and these changes can be tracked in her ideologies of gender and of politics. Her elopement with a married man at the age of seventeen suggests that she was indifferent to cultural prescriptions of chaste and dependent femininity, and although in later life she often reiterated her "love of that privacy which no woman can emerge from without regret" (*MWSL*, 2:72), her writings consistently violated that privacy with their overtly autobiographical references. During their marriage, Percy Shelley clearly depended on her "young wisdom,"[25] and she often "interfered in the legislative . . . part of our little government" (*MWSL*, 1:316). But his was "the executive part," and Mary's comments on femininity often echo this conservative gender ideology. She felt that the "desire to find a manly spirit where on to lean" (*MWSL*, 2:17) was "inherent" in women; she believed that women lacked "the higher grades of intellect" (*MWSL*, 2:246) which men possessed, and that women were "better though weaker" than men. While Mary admired the feminist and abolitionist Fanny Wright as "a bright specimen of our sex" (*MWSL*, 2:123), she also felt that women's "purer, & more sensitive feelings render them so much less [capable] than men" of overcoming opposition (*MWSL*, 2:4).

Her own literary ambitions, she often said, depended on her husband's support; in her introduction to the 1831 *Frankenstein*, the sentence that begins assertively—"I certainly did not owe the suggestion of one incident, nor scarcely of one train of feeling, to my husband" (23)—concludes meekly that she would not have developed her tale "but for his incitement." And despite an impressive body of literary work, by 1835 Mary Shelley still craved "fosterage & support"; "always a dependant [sic] thing," she felt she was "nothing" when "left to [her]self"(*MWSL*, 2:246).

Such signs of dependent femininity suggest that Mary failed to live up to her parents' radicalism. One critic feels she tried to "conform to conventional expectations of what a woman should be,"[26] while another sees a "gravitation" away from her politically "radical heritage" as early as the 1818 *Frankenstein*.[27] There is some truth to these claims. Unlike such feminist contemporaries as her friends Caroline Norton and Fanny Wright or the French socialist Flora Tristan, Mary Shelley did not publicly campaign for women's rights. Nor was she long a Jacobin; the young girl who in 1814 enjoyed "frighten[ing]" away a bore by "talking of cutting off kings [sic] heads" (*MWSJ*, 1:23) was by 1817 decrying revolutionary sentiments that encouraged "the worst possible human passion *revenge*" (*MWSL*, 1:49). In 1830 Mary rejoiced that France's July Revolution, a bloodless coup dethroning the Bourbon Charles X and instituting a bourgeois republic under Louis-Philippe, had "wash[ed] off the stains" of the 1789 revolution (*MWSL*, 2:118). An 1832 letter criticizes her friend Edward Trelawny as "too violent in his politics" (*MWSL*, 2:170), and in 1838 she records her "repulsion" from radicals of his stripe who are "violent without any sense of Justice" (*MWSJ*, 2:555). In March of 1848 she shares a prevalent fear of Chartism, the sometimes revolutionary political movement; "the Chartists are full of menace," she writes, for their movement threatens "tyranny & lawlessness" (*MWSL*, 3:336). Equally conservative and classist remarks appear in letters written after her son inherited the Shelley title and estate. One hears neither Wollstonecraft nor Godwin in Mary Shelley's plaint about "the number of Maids one must keep in the country," or in the self-satisfied statement that "giving work to the industrious" is "one of the best ways in the world of doing good" (*MWSL*, 3:347).

Against all this evidence for Mary Shelley's betrayal of her parents' and her own early principles, however, it is important to remember the contradictions in both Wollstonecraft's and Godwin's politics. Their daughter's late assumption of the Lady Bountiful role should not

obscure her early radicalism or her lifelong sympathy for the poor. Her contradictory views are better seen as symptomatic of England's troubled industrial development.

During Mary Shelley's lifetime England moved from a predominantly agricultural to an increasingly industrial economy, a process that enlarged an underclass of the poor. Already in the mid-eighteenth century, hitherto "common land" which had been cultivated collectively by small farmers was being bought up by great landowners. This enclosure accelerated during the early nineteenth century—from 1809 on, Parliament passed over 100 Acts of Enclosure annually[28]—with the result that many small landowners, tenant farmers, and laborers who were squeezed out of agriculture began to migrate to the new industrial centers. Conditions in these areas, however, were little better. The boom-slump cycle of early capitalism caused intermittent but chronic unemployment, further exacerbated in such industries as cotton by competition from the more efficient mechanized Continental producers.[29] In addition, displaced agricultural laborers competed for work with the 300,000 soldiers discharged at the end of the Napoleonic Wars in 1815; as it doubled and sometimes trebled local work forces, this influx of potential workers kept wages depressed. Lacking the vote, many workers sought improvement of their economic conditions through extra-Parliamentary agitation. Between 1790 and 1810, there were 500 riots protesting the high cost of bread; in the Luddite risings of 1811 to 1813, unemployed textile workers smashed knitting frames.

Mary Shelley was familiar with, and critical of, these economics of industrialism. Although she decried revolution in 1817, another letter of the same year calls Leigh Hunt's attack on economic conditions "hardly *strong* enough" (*MWSL*, 1:54). In other early letters, her "radicalism" appears in criticism of England's "enslaved state" and its rulers' "despotism" (*MWSL*, 1:131, 137, 124). Similarly, during the first stages of debate over the Reform Bill in 1830, she hoped "the Autocrats" would "make the necessary sacrifices to a starving people" (*MWSL*, 2:120). Recalling in 1839 the "very poor population" of lacemakers in 1817 Buckinghamshire, she criticized the poor-laws which had ground these workers "to the dust."[30] Later letters record similar concerns. An 1845 letter shows her disgust with Lord Norfolk's suggestion that starving Irish laborers drink hot water and curry—"very warm and comfortable to the stomachs of the people," he explained, "if it could be got cheap" (*MWSL*, 3:267n)—and in 1847 she and her son are spending large sums to relieve the "bitter want" of the poor (*MWSL*, 3:305).

It is possible to fault Mary Shelley's sympathy for the poor as the sort of Dickensian sentimentality that gives liberals a bad name, but the example of Lord Norfolk is a salutary reminder that there are worse attitudes than compassion. The fluctuation in her views—between fear of the revolutionary working class and sympathy for the laboring poor—illuminates the contradictory politics of midcentury English liberalism. Mary Shelley's long and much-revised 1838 journal entry of self-blame for "not being more of a reformer" (*MWSJ*, 2:555) documents this oscillation.[31] She respects her parents' and Percy Shelley's "passion for reforming the world" (*MWSJ*, 2:553), but not her contemporaries' "violent extremes which only bring on an injurious reaction" (*MWSJ*, 2:554). If she has "never written a word in disfavour of liberalism"," neither has she "supported it openly in writing"; if she has "never written to vindicate the Rights of women," she has ever "defended & supported victims to the social system" (*MWSJ*, 2:557). Finally, this journal entry documents the link between the timidity of Mary Shelley's reformist politics and her conservative gender ideology. After her husband's death she might have "raved & ranted about what [she] did not understand" and thereby "gathered" the radical party around her; or she might have been "a good partizan" for the radicals, with her "woman's love of looking up & being guided" and her "willing[ness] to do any thing if any one supported & brought [her] forward" (*MWSJ*, 2:255). In fact, however, this dependent femininity *kept* her from politics, because it rendered her "unable to put [her]self forward unless led, cherished & supported." Such contradictions of liberalism recur throughout Mary Shelley's writings.

Chapter Two
Plays and Poems

Best known for her fiction, Mary Shelley also wrote and published verse drama and poetry. Her two blank-verse mythological dramas, *Proserpine* and *Midas*, were written in 1820 as she was studying Latin and Greek; they are redactions of classical myth that reveal some of her interests in gender and politics. The poems and translations she wrote between 1823 and 1839 are driven by a more personal interest in the forms and duration of grief. After a discussion of the two verse plays, this chapter will analyze the poems in two groups, those which speak directly to Mary's feelings of loss and those which transmute those feelings into new poetic situations.[1]

Proserpine and *Midas*

These verse dramas were both written in Italy during the winter of 1820; although *Midas* remained unpublished until 1922, *Proserpine* appeared in the annual *Winter's Wreath* for 1832. While writing these plays, Mary was also studying Greek, reading Virgil and Ovid's *Metamorphoses*, and transcribing her husband's "lyric & classical drama" *Prometheus Unbound* (*PBSL*, 2:43). Thus she was steeped in classical mythology, and the somber *Proserpine*, as well as the comic *Midas*, show her rewriting of her sources. Because Percy Shelley contributed songs to both plays, the finished products are "unusual collaborative ventures" that suggest some gendered differences in early-nineteenth-century modes of poetic invention.[2]

The story of Proserpine, her mother Ceres, and her abductor Pluto may be interpreted as an etiological myth of the rotation of the seasons. More specifically, the myth explains how seeds buried in the winter earth can return from the dead to produce new life in the spring. According to the myth, a bargain between Ceres, the goddess of fertility, and her brother Pluto, the god of the underworld who had kidnapped and raped her daughter Proserpine, stipulates that Proserpine will reside underground with Pluto for six months of every year—fall and winter—and then return to her mother for spring and summer. Hence the

19

months of her absence, during which the earth appears to die, are only half of the seasonal cycle, the other half of which is the rebirth begun with her return. Furthermore, the rape of Proserpine both dramatizes "the male usurpation of the female agricultural mysteries"[3] and represents that usurpation as necessary and ultimately beneficial as it results in new life. Mary Shelley rewrites this myth into a vehicle for exploring the two-fold mortal/immortal composition of humans and, crucially, the workings of gendered power relations.

The first of the play's two acts opens on a scene of both pastoral tranquility and submerged danger. Although the setting is "a beautiful plain," the first line is Proserpine's plea to Ceres, "dear Mother, leave me not!"[4] And although Proserpine then sketches a pastoral idyll of gathering flowers while listening to her mother's stories, the tales she wishes to hear—of the combat between the Titans and the gods, the battle between the Python and Apollo, and the attempted rape of Daphne by Apollo—foreshadow the coming violence and struggles for power. Further omens are Proserpine's sense that "blossoms fade" (6) and "grasses droop" when her mother is absent, and Ceres's warning against "wandering alone" (7). She then commands Proserpine to remain with the attendant nymphs Ino and Eunoe, for "no earth-born Power/Would tempt my wrath" by "steal[ing]" her from "that fair guard." But the limits of Ceres's power are suggested when she leaves in obedience to "high Jove's command" (6), and after her departure Ino tells an ominous tale of sexual power relations. In this song written by Percy Shelley, "The Earth's white daughter" (12) Arethusa is pursued by the river god Alpheus; the ocean opens to receive her, but Alpheus follows her like "an eagle pursueing [sic]/A dove to its ruin" (13). The poet passes over the subsequent rape "without transition or comment" (Richardson, 126), and he ends the song without explaining how Arethusa and Alpheus come to be reconciled and "single hearted" (14). But his song of love is revealed as a tale of subjection by Mary's earlier allusions to Apollo's rape of Daphne and Jove's dominance of Ceres. In this context, "Earth's daughter" Arethusa prefigures another daughter's fate: Proserpine's abduction by a male divinity from the feminine care of mother and attendants. In addition to the binary of "earth-born" and immortal, then, the beginning of act 1 sets up oppositions between masculine and feminine power.

The act continues with an emphasis on maternal feeling. Proserpine and her nymphs separate to gather flowers, and she fails to return. As Eunoe and Ino search for Proserpine, their references to her as Ceres's

child (20, 22, 24) keep the focus on maternal loss, as does Ceres's long speech mourning "My only loved one, my lost Proserpine" (25). Even as she recollects that Proserpine is "immortal" (24), she fears that her "child of heaven" (25) was "seized" by "Earth-born Typheus," a monster sometimes associated with earthquakes and volcanic eruptions.[5] The act ends with its antagonists poised: the immortal child endangered by the "earth-born" monster, maternal "high power" (24) stymied by that masculine force.

Act 2 pursues the contest between these forces. Ceres "forever weeps" (26) but also acts in "rage," striking the earth with "blight" so that the "withered" fields "seem to share [her] grief" (28). Shelley departed from her source in Ovid's *Metamorphoses* by keeping the abduction offstage; in a second departure, she now has Arethusa rather than Alpheus bring the news to Ceres (Rose, 100). While watching the "mixed waters" (30) of Alpheus and herself, Arethusa saw "the King of Hell" abducting Proserpine; when she heard the girl cry "My Mother!" (21) and rushed to her aid, however, Pluto caused the earth to open and dragged his captive into Tartarus. Arethusa's new prominence serves two contradictory functions in the play. On the one hand, her attempt to aid Proserpine suggests a feminine alliance that may reverse the failure of Proserpine's women attendants. On the other hand, Arethusa's heterosexual alliance with and subjection to Alpheus is recalled by her pleasure in their "mixed waters."

Ceres precipitates the final struggle between the play's antithetical forces. Against her brother Pluto, Ceres calls on her brother Jove; unless he retrieves her daughter, she warns, "all your wide dominion" will become Pluto's "prey" (31). It is significant that Jove, like Pluto, remains offstage; although both have undoubted power, their absence dilutes the effect of that power by shifting attention to the play's "community of women" (Richardson, 128). When Jove's messenger Iris says that his "will" (32) is "fixed by fate," the comment serves as another diminution of his power. Jove's decision, that Proserpine may return unless she has "polluted by Tartarian food/Her heavenly essence" (33), returns to the first act's opposition between mortal and immortal. Ceres is joyously certain that her "child of heaven disdains Tartarian food," and the play lingers on this maternal triumph as she is reunited with her daughter. After Pluto's minion Ascalaphus reveals that Proserpine ate a few pomegranate seeds, Shelley again departs from her sources. In Ovid's *Metamorphoses*, mother and daughter take vengeance on the tattling Ascalaphus; in Virgil's *Georgics*, Proserpine willingly accepts Jove's decision and

returns to Pluto's domain (Rose, 100). In Shelley's *Proserpine*, however, mother and daughter do not bother to punish Ascalaphus, and it is he rather than Proserpine who accepts Jove's "high will" (40); although she knows she cannot resist what "fate decrees" (38), her grief is shown when she asks "can immortals weep?" Finally, in Shelley's version the women join to oppose fate; as Ino and Arethusa league with Ceres in threats to withdraw from the earth, the forces of "a Mother's prayer" (40) are allied against the "tyrant" Jove (38).

The resolution of this struggle, however, is not clear-cut. Proserpine's "fate" (41) is "sealed by Jove," and each year, after six months with her mother, she must return for six months to Pluto. But in a sense she evades that fate, when she promises Ceres that during the winter "in dreams we shall companions be" (42); thus "Jove's doom is void," for "we are forever joined." Ceres then vows that while Proserpine is underground, the earth too "shall lie beneath in hateful night" (43), and the play's final lines further suggest that Jove's will has redounded on him. Pluto has "changed the reign of Jove" (44), says Ceres, for when he takes Proserpine he "seizes half the Earth" and thus half of Jove's domain; in this sense, Ceres's maternal loss is also a diminution of Jove's power. If mother and daughter must accept the law of the father, still they maneuver within it, and in this way Shelley rewrites a myth of male usurpation to affirm a mother-daughter bond. If Percy's song in act 1 celebrated heterosexual "mixing," Mary's play as a whole stresses alliances among women. And if *Proserpine* is collaborative, Mary Shelley as author remains, like the early Arethusa, "unblended" (13).

When Mary Shelley was trying to interest the editors of annuals in publishing her plays, she suggested that *Midas* would be suitable for the *Juvenile Forget-Me-Not* or the *New Year's Gift and Juvenile Souvenir* (*MWSL*, 2:122, 161). Certainly this play is more lighthearted than *Proserpine* and less focused on philosophical issues, and it ends with a fairly simple and straightforward moral. Nevertheless, Shelley uses this myth of the golden touch to explore the issues of class privilege and tyranny that were of perennial interest to her.

As king of Phrygia, from the outset Midas embodies the arrogance of power. As act 1 opens, Midas and his prime-minister Zopyrion come upon a "solemn conclave"[6] of the satyr Pan with his fauns, the god Apollo with the Muses, and the hill-god Tmolus. When Zopyrion suggests that their presence "may offend" the gods, Midas scorns his "base thought" and "coward blood"; admitting that his own lineage is not

"noble," he nevertheless intrudes on the conclave. Moreover, when he learns that Tmolus is to adjudicate between the music of Pan's pipe and Apollo's lyre, in an aside he arrogates this power to himself by judging Pan the winner before hearing the contest. Following the two songs—both written by Percy Shelley—Tmolus awards the palm to Apollo, since the "wisdom, beauty, & the power divine/Of highest poesy" (55) in his song outdo Pan's "merry" pipings. Appealed to by Pan, Midas again shows his arrogance by calling Apollo's song "drowsy" (56) and disputing Tmolus's decision. Angry that Midas "dar'st among the Gods/Mingle [his] mortal voice," Apollo punishes his "impious soul" and "blunted sense" by giving him asses' ears.

The remainder of act 1 ridicules other excesses of power. After threatening Zopyrion with death if he reveals his secret, Midas departs to create a crown that will hide his ears and, more importantly, that "all other kings shall imitate" (57). When the courtier Asphalion divines that Zopyrion is concealing "some great state secret" (61) and offers to be his "counsellor," Zopyrion responds "with great importance" (62) that he cannot betray the trust of the "great master" who treated him as "a fit friend" by confiding the "weighty secrets of his royal heart." This exaggerated courtly language satirizes the "*Cant*" (*MWSL*, 1:137) and intrigues of such politicians as Britain's Foreign Secretary Lord Castlereagh, whom Mary criticized at length in a letter she wrote while working on the play. Midas is further satirized as, clutching his new crown, he attempts to maintain his dignity while Zopyrion "tries to smother his laughter" (66), and the reeds to which Midas has told the secret whisper it aloud. To a suggestion that he remove his crown, Midas responds with the language of tyranny: "[S]hall a vile calumnious slave/Dictate the actions of a crowned king?" (67). The height of royal arrogance comes when, offered a reward by the god Bacchus, Midas requests that all he touches become "glorious gold" (69). As Zopyrion points out, Midas would have done better to make "one God undo the other's work"; his arrogant folly is contrasted with Zopyrion's wisdom. In the tradition of Lady Folly in Erasmus's *In Praise of Folly*, which Shelley may have known, and the fool in Shakespeare's *King Lear*, which she certainly knew, the comic remark of the seeming fool reveals him to be wiser than his supposed better.

The opening of act 2 extends the satire of royal prerogatives. Midas rejoices that "Now I am great!" (72), for his gold collects armies to conquer "Asia's utmost Citadels" in his name; and, he claims, if war "grows wearisome,/I can buy Empires." His boast, "India shall be mine," again

connects vainglory with the foreign policy of Britain's Lord Castlereagh; such rulers, it is suggested, consider themselves "akin to Gods" (73). "[W]hat a slave I was," Midas then muses, when fields and flocks "were all my wealth." His erroneous valorization of gold over agricultural wealth alludes to the physiocratic doctrine, which recurs in *Valperga*, that agriculture is the only nonsterile form of economic production.[7] Another politico-economic issue emerges when Midas's courtiers "petition" (74) for "relief" from the "huge weight" of their now-golden cloaks, for the term *relief* suggests the contemporary controversy over forms of relief for the poor. Shelley considered anti-poor-relief arguments as "excuses and palliations" by the rich for their "luxury and hard-heartedness" (*MWSL*, 1:75); this view appears in her play when Midas dismisses his courtiers with the suggestion that they "clothe [their] wretched limbs in ragged skins" (74).

The remainder of the act traces Midas's education in humility and proper political economy. Thinking himself "not remote in power/From the immortal gods" (77), he considers his need for food no more than a "remnant of mortality"; even when his "life-killing lips" change fruit into gold, he believes he can "coin some remedy" (78). Gradually he realizes that, without food and drink, he is in fact "Poorer than meanest slaves" (81); he recognizes the fatuity of his class privilege when he prays Bacchus, "Make me a hind, clothe me in ragged skins" like his courtiers. After Bacchus rescinds Midas's golden touch, one courtier rejoices in the physiocratic prospect of the Phrygians again "tend[ing] our flocks and reap[ing] our corn" (82). With new humility, Midas then rejects the signs of power and wealth, vowing to replace his golden palace with "a little bower of freshest green" (86) and his courtiers with "poor men." Only "the meanest peasants shall have gold" (87), for Midas now values true wealth; he has learned that "Nature displays the treasures that she loves," the grass and flowers that adorn the earth.

Midas concludes with an antigreed moral that is also a political statement: the king and his subjects will be "Rich, happy, free & great, [now] that we have lost/Man's curse, heart-bartering, soul-enchaining gold" (89). Rich and happy in nature's treasures, free of greed for gold and the class privilege it connotes, Phrygia—and by extension Britain—will be truly great. Yet signs of class still exist in Midas's kingdom, albeit inverted—"the meanest peasants" (87) are now known by their use of "sordid, base" gold, and "poor men" now serve at court. In this play, then, a radical politics remains tinged with class distinctions.

Poems

Of the several grieving verses Mary Shelley wrote about her husband's death, "The Choice" is the first; containing more than 140 lines of rhymed heroic couplets, it is also the longest and most technically sophisticated of her poems. "The Choice" exists in two versions, which I have called "the journal text" and "the Hunt text." The journal text was written into Shelley's journal in 1823 while she was living in Italy with Leigh and Marianne Hunt; it was then torn out and apparently left with them when she returned to England. The Hunt text, including fourteen additional lines and a more standard punctuation, was found among Leigh Hunt's papers and published in 1876. My discussion focuses on the Hunt text, with attention to its variants from the earlier journal text.

"The Choice" is an extended meditation on memory and loss. It opens with the speaker's lament: "My Choice, my life, my hope together fled." She is now a "wanderer" and Italy is a "tomb."[8] Sometimes, however, she feels herself a "pilgrim" (297), with a "faith" that her "suffering" and "patience" will "earn" the return of lost "companionship and love." She is also "linked to [her] orphan child," in the Hunt text by "strong love's chain," in the journal text by "duty's chain." Shelley's journals and letters show a similar oscillation, between love for her son and the feeling that, but for her boy, she should soon be free of life (*MWSL*, 1:327). "Since I must live," the poem's speaker continues, how can she "find delights/As fireflies gleam through interlunar nights?"

The speaker's first step in this search is to call on her lost lover, that "gentle Spirit" (298). But doing so raises "fierce remorse," for although her moments of anger were "atoned" during his life, still unatoned are the "cold neglect, averted eyes,/That blindly crushed thy soul's fond sacrifice." The next lines are a new twist on the hackneyed notion of a broken heart.

> My heart was all thine own,—but yet a shell
> Closed in its core, which seemed impenetrable,
> Till sharp-toothed misery tore the husk in twain,
> Which gaping lies, nor may unite again.

The speaker then asks that the Spirit's love descend on her as "soft repentance." Thus strengthened by "remorse and love" and "all our best

companionship," she "dare[s]" to call his "sacred name." The speaker now prays—to him, then to the star "ascendant at my birth," and finally to the "Inscrutable"—that she be allowed to "live and die" (299) in Italy.

As the next stanza shifts to the speaker's dead children, it refines the earlier image of Italy as a tomb. The first lines celebrate Italy as a place of young life, where the speaker was a "happy mother," her baby daughter (Clara) slept "near Venetian seas," and her first-born and "dearest" son (William) was "Rocked by the waves" as they sailed with his father. These calm water images are of course an ironic foreshadowing of Percy Shelley's death by drowning. The subsequent lines, which link William to the Italian towns he explored with the speaker, conclude with the equally ironic memory that "there were no taints/Of ruin on his cheek." The boy died at Rome and is buried there, but "[h]is spirit beats within his mother's heart," and he "shin'st the evening star among the dead" (300). Despite these gleams of life among death, the stanza ends with the speaker's grief for her daughter, another "victim" to "the black death that rules this sunny shore."

The speaker then returns in the next two stanzas to memories of her husband. Although his recurrent ill health at first produced "forebodings dark," gradually his "very weakness" became her "tower of strength": "Methought thou wert a spirit from the sky,/Which struggled with its chains, but could not die." She then asks Rome's "ancient walls" if his spirit visits his tomb, but breaks off these thoughts of death with "No more! no more!" The stanza ends with dual affirmations: "Thou liv'st in Nature, Love, my Memory" and "The wife of Time no more, I wed Eternity." If Italy remains a tomb, it is now a loved sepulchre, for "the Past—on which my spirit leans,/Makes dearest to my soul Italian scenes." Because these scenes "all breathe his spirit which can never die" (301), by the end of the stanza they become "the haven of [her] rest."

The journal text of "The Choice" concludes with eight lines in this mood of tranquil rest. "Here will I live," in the "lovely wood" the speaker pictured in a recent dream; she and "My dearest, widowed friend" (Jane Williams) will pass their days in Italy as "we before have done." The journal text stops here; the final line has no period, suggesting either a rough but completed draft or Shelley's intention to continue the poem. The Hunt text recurs to the idea of what "we before have done" but turns it to the speaker's memory of watching with Jane for their husbands' boat, which "ne'er appeared." The earlier calm of the

stanza disappears as the speaker realizes that "The sad revolving year has not allayed/The poison of these bleeding wounds"; and her earlier belief in the comfort of repentance gives way to the continuing "anguish" of "corroding thought" and "grief." The final lines bring Jane's husband Edward Williams into the "heaven-resum'd past," and conclude that "Thy spirit waits with his in our far home." Thus, the Hunt text ends not with a tranquil memory of the past but with the speaker's desire for "our far home." As these twists and turns indicate, "The Choice" in both its versions is tightly organized conceptually and imagistically. Furthermore, the poem is more than an autobiographical effusion; rather Shelley turns her own mourning into a sustained exploration of mourning itself.

Immediately following "The Choice" in Mary Shelley's journal are a fragment from 1826 and a completed poem written in December 1825. The fragment is addressed to Jane Williams and was apparently intended to accompany a gift copy of Shelley's novel *The Last Man*. The few lines characterize the novel as a "tale of woe" but also as a "tribute" for Jane, whom she refers to as "dear solace of my life" (*MWSJ*, 2:495). Mary's completed poem, "On Reading Wordsworth's Lines on Peel Castle," explores similarly contradictory feelings at greater length. The speaker begins by comparing her widowed state with Wordsworth's emotions; for her, too, the "summer seas" are changed and "storm sits brooding every where" (*MWSJ*, 2:494). The next stanzas develop sea and storm images: the waves' "gentlest rustling" is a "dirge" for Percy Shelley, and in the stormy sea's "furious billows" the speaker hears a voice calling her to "a kindred bier." When the sea is again "smooth," she imagines she sees the poet sailing and she rushes "wildly" (*MWSJ*, 2:495) to the shore for a boat to take her toward him. The next stanza slightly misquotes the lines of Wordsworth's poem in which he recognizes his inability to "e'er again behold/The sea, and be as I have been"; but where Wordsworth could regard this loss "with mind serene," Mary Shelley cannot. Her poem concludes with a return to its initial "brooding": "on past joys I vainly brood,/And shrink in fear from coming years." Since the verb "brood" meant "to hatch" as well as "to ponder," its use here is an ironic reflection on the speaker's inability to "hatch" or create comfort out of "past joys."

In 1831 Shelley revised *Frankenstein*; perhaps memories of her early years with her husband prompted the four poems of this year, all of which continue to explore her grief for him. Two four-line poems, written in the August 1831 journal, attest that, nine years after Percy's

death, Mary continued her mourning yet realized its debilitating effects. The poem of August 14 begins, "Alas I weep my life away/And spend my heart in useless sorrow" and concludes by reflecting on "a yet more hopeless morrow" (*MWSJ*, 2:522). Although "alas" and "useless" suggest that the speaker is tiring of melancholy, the poem written two days later gives in to it; the speaker counsels her soul, "Struggle no more" and "Yield thy lost life" (*MWSJ*, 2:523).

The published poems of this year, "Absence" and "A Dirge," both appeared in *The Keepsake* as "by the author of Frankenstein." Their publication in an annual under this attribution shows the marketability of both Mary Shelley's name and her grief; despite her desire to remain in "my proper sphere of private obscurity" (*MWSL*, 2:22), then, she was on occasion able and willing to violate that obscurity. And the fact that both poems were revised indicates that, like "The Choice," they are not only personal expressions but also crafted explorations of grief. In the following discussion, I will note differences between each poem's manuscript text and its *Keepsake* text.

The twelve lines of "Absence" are particularly sophisticated in their use of dark/light imagery, and *The Keepsake* revisions of the manuscript text show Mary rethinking this imagery. As *The Keepsake* poem begins, all seems "dark and dreary" because "he is gone—and I alone!"[9] The speaker then compares her mood to the moment when "Night rushes o'er the Indian clime." The next stanza first asks if no "soothing twilight" or cheering star exists, then answers that memory provides such a light. Where the manuscript text describes memory's light as "[b]eaming at sunset's golden west" (Grylls, 302), *The Keepsake* line reads "[p]leasing as sunset's golden west." This slight change shifts the emphasis from the light itself to its effect on the speaker and thus leads more smoothly into the "hope of dawn" in the first line of the last stanza. That hope is "brighter" than the "Orient" clouds alluded to in the first stanza and "more welcome than the morning sun"; here the sun completes the imagistic cycle that began with twilight. In the final line, the speaker's "hope of dawn" turns into the "dear thought" that the absent one will return.

"A Dirge" is less sanguine. Shelley believed that, to "speak to the many," poetry must appeal to "emotions common to us all,"[10] and she felt able to write verse only "under the influence of a strong sentiment" (*MWSL*, 2:246). "A Dirge" is specific to her own "strong sentiment" of grief over Percy Shelley's drowning, but grief is also "common to us all";

perhaps for that reason, in 1835 she called this poem "the best thing [she] ever wrote." In 1839, however, she revised it for inclusion in her edition of her husband's poems, and the reader who prefers a poetry of restraint will applaud her decision. Even without a full analysis of the two texts, a comparison of their final stanzas will indicate how the 1839 text throttles back the emotions of the 1831 poem.

Keepsake (1831)	*Poetical Works* (1839)
From far across the sea, love,	From far across the sea
I hear a wild lament,	I hear a loud lament,
By Echo's voice, for thee, love,	By echo's voice for thee,
From Ocean's caverns sent:—	From ocean's caverns sent.
O list! O list! O list!	O list! O list,
The spirits of the deep—	The spirits of the deep;
Loud sounds their wail of sorrow,	They raise a wail of sorrow,
While I for ever weep!	While I for ever weep.

In the 1831 poem, the repetitions and the four exclamation points, combined with the poetic diction of the word *list* and the syntactic reversal of *loud sounds,* are meant to indicate the depth of the speaker's sorrow. And because the poem was written for music (*MWSL*, 2:246), it might successfully convey this grief to a hearer. To a reader who favors subtlety, however, the emotion is so insistent as to verge on the bathetic, and such a reader may find the 1839 poem's restraint more moving.

Two of the three poems Shelley wrote in 1833 show her reworking the images and themes of earlier poems and experimenting with new verse forms, while the third begins her move into more distanced poetic situations. The unpublished poem entitled "La Vida es sueño" ("Life is a dream") returns to the sea images and the despair of "On Reading Wordsworth's Lines on Peel Castle" of 1825. As long as "The tide of Time was at my feet,"[11] the speaker says, she was "gladdened" to see "the sunlit ocean." But Time's tide ebbs after a "fatal storm," and in the next two stanzas the sea image is linked to memory as the speaker follows the ebbing tide backward in time. As she pursues Time's "inconstant fleeting surge," however, her hopes "grew cold," for the "blank and desart [sic]" sands (234) suggest her own "vacant prospect" (233). At this point

comes "a dream of joy" (234), and the speaker "thought no more of
Ocean's frown." But the final stanza begins "Where is my Dream?" and
the speaker again hears "Time's vast flood"; thus returned from memory
to "the waste sands," she is "lonely as before" and hope has vanished "as
if it ne'er had been!" In this poem, as in "Reading Wordsworth's Lines,"
Shelley has "vainly brood[ed]" on the past.

The second unpublished poem of 1833—"Tempo è più di Morire/Io
ho tardato più ch'i' non vorrei" ("It is full time to die/I have lingered
longer than I wish")—uses familiar sea images but in a new stanzaic
form. As it begins, the speaker hears "Sadly borne across the waves" a
"voice from many graves"[12] calling the living to hasten "To our home"
(232). The next stanza specifies a single voice, that of "my life's Lord"
calling to his "gentle Bride," and the remainder of the poem details his
efforts to persuade "Mary dear" to join him. The sea and storm images
continue; the voice states that "Storm & Ocean bore me here" and calls
his wife to "cross the turbid stream," and the final stanza calls her to
"Onc[e] again in storm tossed bark/Speed across the Ocean dark" (233).
The dark ocean and "Dark" world (232) recur to the imagery of dark
and light found in "Absence" but without its movement toward hope;
the mood of this poem is closer to the despair of "La Vida es sueño" and
"Reading Wordsworth's Lines." An echo of the Hunt text of "The
Choice" appears in the poem's emphasis on home, but where that idea
merely concluded the earlier poem, here it takes on a new prominence
with Shelley's new stanzaic form. The unique rhyme scheme emphasizes
the prospect of home; the stanzas rhyme a-a-b-c-c-b, d-d-b-e-e-b and so
on, with the b eye-rhyme of "come" and "home" repeated throughout
the poem. The hypnotic effect of the rhyme thus reinforces the poem's
content, the dead man's desire that his bride come "To his Home" (233).
The technical experimentation of this poem suggests that Shelley has
distanced herself from sorrow sufficiently to seek new forms in which to
embody it.

The third poem of this year, "Stanzas," is the first of Mary's poems to
extend her experience of loss from her husband's death into a different situation. The first line, "I must forget thy dark eyes' love-fraught gaze,"[13]
indicates that the blue-eyed Percy Shelley is not the poem's subject. The
stanza then lists the aspects of lost love—his voice, his "vows," and especially the "interchange of thought"—which the speaker must forget, and
in the next stanza she realizes that she must also forget to show her love,
"to deck myself with flowers" and "count the day-bright hours." The second
half of the poem begins with the realization "I must forget thy love!" In

her desire for the insensibility to grief "[w]hich corpses find," the speaker turns to classical models: the sorrowing nymph transformed into a weeping willow; the weeping mother, Niobe, turned to stone; the "Lethean wave" of forgetfulness. Not even these aids would save her, she concludes: "Love, hope, and thee, I never can forget!" While this line doubtless draws on Shelley's unwillingness or inability to forget her own lost love, overall the speaker and her situation are imagined rather than remembered.

Like "Stanzas," the three poems written in 1838 move away from Mary's focus in her earlier poems on mourning. One of the 1838 poems, "O listen while I sing to thee," was later slightly revised and set to music by Henry Hugh Pearson, a composer whom Mary Shelley had met in Europe; the canzonet was published in 1842. The poem describes a speaker's song of love for "thee." The "melody"[14] of the speaker's song derives from thoughts of the beloved listener, and the song both inspires and feeds their love; if the beloved were "far" or "false," the singer's "voice would die." The poem concludes with lines—"And now that thou art near to me/I pour a full impassioned tone" (235)—which keep this focus on the singer's love. In no other of Shelley's poems is the emotion of the speaker so unambiguously joyous.

Two other love poems written in 1838, both entitled "Stanzas," appeared in the *Keepsake* of 1839. They were never republished. Both "Stanzas," which follow, display a gentle melancholy perhaps traceable to her loss of Aubrey Beauclerk; certainly the mildness of the emotion strikingly differentiates these last poems from her earlier verse.

Stanzas[15]

By the Author of Frankenstein

How like a star you rose upon my life,
    Shedding fair radiance o'er my darkened hour!
At your uprise swift fled the turbid strife
    Of grief and fear,—so mighty was your power!
And I must weep that you now disappear,
    Casting eclipse upon my cheerless night—
My heaven deserting for another sphere,
    Shedding elsewhere your aye-regretted light.

An Hesperus no more to gild my eve,
    You glad the morning of another heart;
And my fond soul must mutely learn to grieve,
    While thus from every joy it dwells apart.
Yet I may worship still those gentle beams,
    Though not on me they shed their silver rain;
And thought of you may linger in my dreams,
    And Memory pour balm upon my pain.

Stanzas[16]

By the Author of Frankenstein

O, come to me in dreams, my love!
    I will not ask a dearer bliss;
Come with the starry beams, my love,
    And press mine eyelids with thy kiss.

'Twas thus, as ancient fables tell,
    Love visited a Grecian maid,
Till she disturbed the sacred spell,
    And woke to find her hopes betrayed.

But gentle sleep shall veil my sight,
    And Psyche's lamp shall darkling be,
When in the visions of the night,
    Thou dost renew thy vows to me.

Then come to me in dreams, my love,
    I will not ask a dearer bliss;
Come with the starry beams, my love,
    And press mine eyelids with thy kiss.

Chapter Three
Science Fiction: Short Stories, *Frankenstein*, and *The Last Man*

Frankenstein (1818) has been called "the first science fiction novel," and *The Last Man* (1826) has also been claimed for science fiction.[1] Of course, if the term connotes a predominant focus on science and/or technology, then neither these novels nor the four stories discussed in this chapter are science fiction. More broadly defined, however, the term *science fiction* does identify the elements common to these novels and stories.

Darko Suvin defines science fiction as "the literature of cognitive estrangement."[2] He uses *cognitive* to mean "not only a reflecting *of* but also *on* reality" (6), and *estrangement* to mean confronting an accepted set of norms with another point of view that implies a new set of norms (10). The "main formal device" of science fiction so defined is "an imaginative framework alternative to the author's empirical environment" (Suvin, 8). These terms are useful less for locating a work within a genre, however, than for pointing to a "tendency" operating within a text which is itself "conceptualized as a complexly structured whole."[3] Thus this chapter uses Suvin's two concepts—cognitive estrangement and an imaginative framework contrary to empirical reality—to analyze the science fiction *tendency* of the Mary Shelley texts that speculate on the unprecedented. In four short stories— "Valerius: The Reanimated Roman" (1819), "Roger Dodsworth: The Reanimated Englishman" (1826), "Transformation" (1830), and "The Mortal Immortal" (1833)—and the two novels noted above, Shelley places a protagonist in an imagined framework and analyzes his responses to those unfamiliar circumstances. These texts then work by cognitive estrangement to critique contemporary culture and to explore the possibilities for change, for rejecting past norms and creating a future based on new ones.

Short Stories

"Valerius: The Reanimated Roman" (1819)

Probably written in 1819, "Valerius: The Reanimated Roman" was not published in Mary Shelley's lifetime; left untitled and unfinished in manuscript, it may have been intended as a novel or novella. The surviving two fragments by two different narrators suggest how a longer text might have developed the relations between them, and the narrators' differing perspectives on Valerius's experiences suggest Shelley's views on possible connections between past and future.

The story's first fragment is narrated by Valerius, who lived and died in ancient republican Rome. The circumstances of his reanimation are left unexplained; instead this section details his bitter disappointment with a "fallen Italy."[4] In place of ancient Rome's "holy religion" (337), he finds "Catholic superstition"; instead of men "full of virtue and wisdom" (333), he finds "wretched Italians" who have "lost all the characteristics of Romans" (337); and instead of a Roman republic approaching "perfection" (336), he finds an Italy in "servitude and degradation" (333). Only three elements relieve his gloom. One is the river Tiber, because it is "ever the same" (334); another is the Coliseum, for it is a "noble relict of imperial greatness" (335); the third is his friendship with Isabell Harley, "the only hope and comfort of my life" (339).

The second fragment of the story shifts from Valerius's point of view to Isabell's, and to her efforts to make him feel "linked to the world" (342). As this section brings together the three redeeming elements noted above—nature, the Coliseum, and human affection—it presents an alternative to Valerius's narrative of an Italy degenerated from Roman greatness. To Isabell, one ancient ruin overlooking the Tiber joins "the beauty and fragrance of Nature to the sublimest idea of human power" (341); similarly, the Pantheon is irradiated by "the glory [which] came from nature" (342), and there she feels "that Pantheic Love with which Nature is penetrated." If nature can redeem the ruins of human effort, the Coliseum shows how those ruins can encourage humanity to further effort. For Valerius, the Coliseum "awaken[s] in the imaginations of men all that can purify and ennoble the mind" (335); and even though it was built by the "most wicked" tyrants of imperial Rome (340), in Isabell too it awakens "awe and reverence" for the ancient Romans' "republican virtue and power." Finally, Isabell herself comes to embody that virtue through her affection for Valerius. As often in Shelley's work, here affection is contrasted with passion. Where "the

fierce strife of contending passions" destroyed Rome (337), says Valerius, Isabell "nursed with angelic affection every wound of my heart" (339). She becomes "Country, Friends—all, all that I had lost," and she creates "links" (340) between him and the unfamiliar modern world.

Through its dual narratives, "Valerius" is a reflection of and on reality that confronts the accepted norms of modern Italy with those of its past. If Valerius, instead of simply mourning the past, could issue a "last awakening call to Romans and to Liberty" (336), he and Isabell might then awaken Italian imaginations to create the republican future once promised by Rome's virtues. Against this utopian vision, however, is the refrain of history, for the tale persistently reminds readers that republican virtue was succeeded by imperial tyranny and modern degeneration. Tantalizingly unfinished, this early story both records the hopeful revolutionary Mary Shelley of 1819 and hints at the pessimist who again took up the theme of the last man in 1826.

"Roger Dodsworth: The Reanimated Englishman" (1826)

Although less a story than an essay, "Roger Dodsworth: The Reanimated Englishman" is included here to indicate Mary Shelley's continuing interest in the idea of reanimation. In 1826 an actual newspaper report claimed that Roger Dodsworth, supposedly preserved in suspended animation after a 1654 avalanche, had been resuscitated and brought to London. The report was soon known to be a hoax and called forth a series of comic responses;[5] Shelley's essay was intended to catch the crest of this wave, but it was rejected by the *New Monthly Magazine* and remained unpublished until 1863. With a wit seldom evident in her fiction, the piece gives a lighter yet more pessimistic view of human perfectibility than did "Valerius."

The first section of the essay compares old and new political norms. After discoursing learnedly on the scientific possibility of suspended animation, the speaker turns to speculation: since Dodsworth died during Cromwell's Commonwealth and was himself probably a republican, how has he adapted to the monarchy of 1826? Where "Valerius" took a dour view of such a change, "Dodsworth" uses it to mock the past as well as the present. This reanimated republican is neither a "zealous" commonwealthman[6] nor a "violent" monarchist; he cautiously avoids both extremes until he must propitiate a "high Tory" (46), at which point his monarchism "late a tiny bud suddenly expands into full flower." Having learned this "first lesson in politics" (47), says the speaker ironically,

Dodsworth will adapt to the "temporising . . . now so much in vogue" (48) and "become whig or tory as his inclinations lead." And where Dodsworth initially considered modern Englishmen to be "much deteriorated from his contemporaries" (47), now he admires "this enlightened nineteenth century." As the last Roman republican, Valerius was both a tragic and a hopeful figure; as the last English republican, Dodsworth is neither. Instead he demonstrates that new circumstances cannot create "intellect, noble aspiration, and energetic constancy" (48) from "dulness, wavering of purpose, and grovelling desires."

The next section of the essay performs the cognitive estrangement lacking in the first section, where old and new political norms were identical. The speaker imagines another set of norms by wondering how "heroes of antiquity would act, if they were reborn in these times" (48). If the reborn compared their present acts with those of their past selves, "nothing but benevolent actions and real goodness would come pure out of the ordeal" (49). Neither the reanimated nor the modern English, the essay finally suggests, would measure up to this norm of benevolence and goodness. The imaginative framework of reanimation lacks the hopeful tendency of "Valerius"; "Dodsworth" is not optimistic about human perfectibility.

"Transformation" (1830)

Because "Transformation" is one of the many stories Mary Shelley wrote for an annual, it is important to know something about this form of nineteenth-century serial publishing. The first British annual, *The Forget-me-not*, appeared in 1822; by 1831 there were sixty-two annuals, and although the fashion had run its course by 1840, a few series, such as *The Keepsake*, lasted into the 1850s.[7] An annual was a collection of poems, stories, and engravings intended as a gift book; they were published once a year, usually in November or early December for the Christmas trade. Annuals were intended for a wealthy and leisured bourgeois audience; at one guinea, they were fairly high-priced, and because they were designed to be seen as well as read they were richly bound in silk, embossed leather, or engraved and embossed paper.[8] The "new and fashionable" process of steel engraving was particularly important to the annuals,[9] for this new technology could both "signify the privileges of art and art ownership . . . and circulate these privileges more widely than ever before" through the medium of the annual.[10] In its first issue *The Keepsake* stated its "principal object" was "the union of literary merit

with all the beauty and elegance of art,"[11] and the second issue boasted that "the enormous sum of *11,000 guineas*" had been spent on engravings that would make *The Keepsake* a "standard work in every well-selected library."[12] Indeed, in many annuals the stories were secondary to the engravings; most of Mary Shelley's stories, for example, were commissioned to accompany a particular engraving. But the annuals were also an important stage in the nineteenth-century "transformation of reading from an elite to a majority practice."[13] This is not to say that they sought a working-class readership; "the best annuals," according to one editor of *The Keepsake*, "were always written for the educated and cultivated reader" (quoted in Adburgham, 262). As "recognized signs of education, taste, [and] luxury" (Hofkosh, 206), however, the annuals contributed to the consolidation of the bourgeois press, a consolidation which eventually encompassed lower-middle- and working-class print culture.

Most importantly, the annuals industry was dominated by women. Many annuals were edited by titled women, and they provided an "elegant prestige outlet" for women writers like Mary Shelley (Adburgham, 235). In the nineteenth century, women became "the major consumers of magazines" (Ballister, 77), and annuals in particular were designed to be bought and read by bourgeois women. *The Keepsake* is an especially good example of this feminization. Recognized by contemporaries as "the annual of the Aristocracy,"[14] it was edited by the Honorable Caroline Norton (1836), Lady Emmeline Stuart Wortley (1837–40), and the Countess of Blessington (1841–47); it consistently published women writers; and its stories were "directed toward women."[15]

"Transformation" was published in *The Keepsake* for 1831. It uses a framework familiar to its intended audience, the love story with a Byronic hero,[16] and it also incorporates three equally familiar Christian frameworks—the fall of Lucifer, the Faust legend, and the parable of the prodigal son. But "Transformation" also works as an "impure" fantasy, to cause "a grotesque tension between arbitrary supernatural phenomena and the empirical norms they infiltrate" (Suvin, 8). Thus the story teaches the moral lesson of the first two Christian frames, the downfall of pride; but a grotesque tension complicates the lesson of the third frame, the sinner's reform.

Initially, the protagonist Guido is a Byronic sinner-hero. With an "imperious, haughty, tameless spirit" and a "rebel heart," Guido throws off "all control,"[17] leaves his native Genoa, and squanders his inheritance in Paris. "Ashamed at the part of the prodigal returned," Guido

nonetheless goes back to Genoa and is initially welcomed as "a favourite son" (124) by his "second father," the Marchese Torella. When the Marchese opposes Guido's marriage to his daughter Juliet, however, Guido becomes "a fiend" (125) and "a slave" to "the violent tyranny of [his] temper." Clearly Guido has only been playing the part of the returned prodigal, and his story now turns to the Satan/Faust frame. Banished from Genoa for twice attempting to abduct Juliet, Guido meets a dwarf with supernatural powers who greets him as "cousin of Lucifer" (128). "Fascinat[ed]" with the dwarf's "power" and needing his fortune, Guido agrees to exchange bodies with him for three days.

As in the Faust story, the irony of this bargain is that Guido does not achieve the power he desired. The dwarf is the external sign of Guido's "fiendly pride," which is not the instrument of his will but its "despot" (121, 125). When the dwarf returns to Genoa in Guido's body and woos Juliet, another irony appears. It is this false "penitent" (*Tales*, 132) who is "welcomed even as the prodigal son," this false Guido who wins Juliet by playing the role of a "penitent, reformed" prodigal (131). A tension is thus created between the conventional Christian parable and the devilish parody of its norms, and a third version of the prodigal son parable becomes necessary. In this version, repentance is sealed by self-sacrifice; Guido must not only repudiate his "demoniac violence" (131) but risk himself to rescue Juliet from the fiend. Determined to save her or "die in the attempt" (132), Guido does in a sense die: when he kills the dwarf, he kills his own "accursed pride" (131). Although this third parable ends happily, Guido does not fully recover from "the wound I had given myself" (135). Like Rochester in Charlotte Brontë's *Jane Eyre* (Cantor, 103), or Romney Leigh in Elizabeth Barrett Browning's *Aurora Leigh*, the hero who thought that "to be a man" (*Tales*, 122) was to be "insolent and domineering" does reform but bears the mark of his earlier error.

Nor does "Transformation" fully resolve its other "grotesque tensions," for Guido's happy ending does not extend to the society he represents. The story is set in fifteenth-century Paris during the reign of the mad Charles VI, who like Guido is sometimes master of his demons and sometimes their "abject slave" (122). In his early carousing, Guido is also a figure for the irresponsible ruling class, who, "blind to the miserable state of their country" (123), indulge in "dissolute enjoyment or savage strife." And just as Guido injures himself when he battles the dwarf, so does France wound itself: during Guido's stay in Paris, the Duke of Burgundy assassinates the Duke of Orleans. The tension within Guido is resolved by supernatural intervention; the tension in France

cannot be so resolved. This story was published in 1830, soon after the July revolution in France. Shelley believed the "moderation and hero-ism" of that bloodless coup had "wash[ed] off the stains" of the 1789 revolution (*MWSL*, 2:118), but her story does not offer this happy end-ing. Unlike Guido, the France of "Transformation" continues to embody "the folly and misery of pride" (*Tales*, 135).

"The Mortal Immortal" (1833)

In the Greek myth of Tithonus, a mortal who was granted immortality was miserable without the equally necessary quality of eternal youth. "The Mortal Immortal" gives this myth a twist that creates a tension between "supernatural phenomena and the empirical norms they infil-trate" (Suvin, 8). In Shelley's story, the supernatural immortality of a man's good looks is played off against the empirical norm that it is women's beauty which should be ageless. Published in *The Keepsake*, the story would surely have struck a chord in its women readers.

The story's plot is simple. Winzy becomes an apprentice to the alchemist Cornelius Agrippa, despite "feeling as if Satan himself had tempted [him]" to the work.[18] In a fit of pique with his beloved but haughty Bertha, Winzy drinks one of Agrippa's potions, believing it to be a cure for love. But the mixture was "the Elixir of Immortality" (224), and it inspires him with the "courage and resolution" to woo and win Bertha. The remainder of the story details the quotidian problems of a handsome, immortal youth married to an aging, querulous wife. Yet when Bertha dies, Winzy loses all that bound him to humanity (229); like Valerius, he perceives himself as the last man. At the story's end, Winzy realizes that his immortality violates "the established laws of [human] nature" (229), and he decides to embark on an expedition, hoping that either its rigors will kill him or he will return "the wonder and benefactor of the human species" (230).

The story uses Winzy's capacity for self-knowledge to differentiate him morally from Bertha. Initially, both are peevish and infantile; Bertha torments Winzy by her "inconstancy" (221), and Winzy tor-ments himself with "jealous[y]." As Winzy remains youthful and Bertha ages, however, it is she who becomes consumed with jealousy; in addi-tion, she makes herself ridiculous by using "a thousand feminine arts" (228) in a vain attempt to disguise her fading charms. While the tension between Winzy's resignation to eternal youth and Bertha's resistance to advancing age is meant to be critical of Bertha, another reading is possi-ble. The woman's pathetic effort to conceal her physical decay in fact

reveals "both the power and the tenuousness" of the ideal of ageless beauty that the man "has apparently accomplished, risk-free" (Hofkosh, 212). And where the immortal Winzy can release himself from that ideal by escaping to the pole, the mortal Bertha is released only by death. If this story intends the reader to commend Winzy's self-knowledge and compassionate his imprisonment in immortality, it may also arouse the woman reader's sympathy for Bertha's imprisonment in the cultural prescription that feminine beauty be immortal.

Frankenstein; or, the Modern Prometheus

The best known of Mary Shelley's science fictions, *Frankenstein* was first published in 1818; she revised the text and added an introduction for the edition which appeared in 1831. While the central story of Victor Frankenstein and his creature is familiar to most readers, the narratives of Robert Walton and the creature are less so. For that reason, this section focuses on the themes of those narratives as well as on the more familiar creation story. Through its central imaginative framework of creation, *Frankenstein* reflects on contemporary science; in its other narratives too, the novel works toward a cognitive estrangement from contemporary norms of family relations, education, and science.

The novel's framing narrative, Robert Walton's letters and journals addressed to his sister Margaret Saville, introduces several of the novel's significant themes. The first is the curative powers of affection. Walton "greatly need[s] a friend" whose "affection" will "regulate" his mind, "approve or amend" his plans, and "repair" his faults.[19] But this friend must be a "cultivated" (28) person, so the "wholly uneducated" ship's master does not qualify (30); and despite Margaret's "gentle and feminine fosterage" (29), a sister apparently cannot be a friend. Thus Walton's ideal of masculine friendship introduces exclusion as well as inclusion to the novel's concept of curative affection; in particular, the exclusion of his sister from this ideal introduces the strict gender distinctions within the family that the novel will interrogate. A second theme of Walton's narrative is partial or ill-regulated education. He regrets that he is "self-educated," that he has read only poetry and travel narratives and is thus "illiterate" in many areas. This problematic of education is more fully developed in Victor's and the creature's narratives.[20] The final theme introduced in Walton's letters is the aims and dangers of scientific discovery. By learning "the secret of the magnet" (26) and finding a passage to the north pole, Walton hopes both to "satiate [his]

ardent curiosity" and to confer an "inestimable benefit" on "all mankind." In pursuing this "great purpose" (27), however, Walton also desires "glory" as well as "dominion" (37) over an "untamed yet obedient" (32) nature. He sounds this note of the overreacher when he exults, "What can stop the determined heart and resolved will of man?" Walton's voyage thus presages both the humanitarian possibilities of scientific discovery and the reckless scientific ambition which Victor himself will characterize as "madness" (37).

Victor's narrative of his childhood picks up the themes of affection and education in its representation of ideal family relations. While the dominant domestic ideology of the nineteenth century characterized the public sphere of business and politics as masculine and the private sphere of home and family as feminine,[21] *Frankenstein* suggests that men, too, have an important role in the family. Victor's father, Alphonse, once inhabited the masculine realm of "public business" (38), but he prepares for his marriage to Caroline Beaufort by "relinquish[ing] all his public functions" (40) and withdrawing into the domestic sphere. As a husband, he takes the masculine role of protector by rescuing Caroline from poverty "like a protecting spirit" (39) and then by "shelter[ing] her" within his home. As a father, however, Alphonse is less a masculine protector than a maternal nurturer. His relation to his children is consistently associated with Caroline's; both embody "the very spirit of kindness and indulgence" (43) toward their children, and through the "active spirit of tenderness that animated both" (40) they are joint "agents and creators" of Victor's childhood joys. Alphonse is thus a feminized patriarch, the ideal husband and father of an ideal domestic sphere.

The parental affection that suffuses this home also informs Victor's education. "Guid[ing him] by a silken cord" (40), Alphonse and Caroline teach their son the "lesson of patience, of charity, and of self-control." In Mary Shelley's ideology of the domestic sphere, affection and education should create a Victor in Alphonse's feminized image. But there are two contradictions in this apparently ideal family that ideology fails to resolve.

The first is the constraining effects of domestic affection. Victor "long[s] to enter the world" (49) precisely because he feels "cooped up" by his "remarkably secluded and domestic" upbringing (48). Although he insists on his "gratitude" for his parents' care (43), this very gratitude becomes suffocating. Gratitude implies an obligation, which in turn implies a debt to the person to whom one is grateful or obligated. This

insistence on gratitude and obligation, on an emotional *quid pro quo*, permeates the novel's familial relations. The parental care and affection that seem freely given in fact require something in exchange; the Frankenstein family is thus "a paradigm of the social contract based on economic terms," and its parent-child relation is one of "unpayable debt."[22] Victor owes his parents gratitude for the life they have "given" him (40) and for their care, and that unpayable debt confines and encloses him within the family. Rather than Victor's picture of Alphonse as a gentle patriarch guiding by "silken cord," then, what emerges is a pattern of constricting domestic relations, of an endlessly repeated gratitude/obligation economy in contradiction with domestic affection.

The second contradiction in the Frankenstein family emerges in its complicated relations of inclusion and exclusion. Initially this family seems inclusive: Alphonse brought Caroline into his sheltering home; Caroline took Elizabeth into the Frankenstein family, giving her to Victor as a "more than sister" (41) to "protect, love, and cherish"; Caroline also rescued Justine from a lunatic mother and brought her into the Frankenstein home. But such benevolence extends only to beautiful and/or useful women; thus it teaches Victor not inclusive affection but rather an "aristocratic protectionism" that "erects an aesthetics of exclusion to perpetuate its ascendancy."[23] Furthermore, this familial seclusion confines women within their separate sphere. Where the young Victor and his friend Henry Clerval actively prepare to enter the sphere of public life, Elizabeth simply exists as a "living spirit of love" (43) in "our peaceful home." Granted, the novel tries to represent the separate spheres as *complementary*, by showing how Elizabeth functions to "soften" Henry and Victor. Henry aims to be one of the "benefactors of our species"; Elizabeth tempers his "soaring ambition" and his "passion for adventurous exploit" by teaching him "the real loveliness of beneficence." As Victor pursues his scientific studies, he is kept from becoming "sullen" or "rough" because Elizabeth "subdue[s him] to a semblance of her own gentleness." Such complementarity gives Elizabeth the important function of preparing Henry and Victor to enter the public sphere, but it also limits her to that function, and it requires her seclusion within the family. Furthermore, since women's sole function is the domestication of men, and since they can perform this function only within the home, that feminine sphere must be strictly separated from the masculine realm.

There is thus a contradiction in the domestic ideology, between the domestic woman's seclusion in her sphere and her quasi-public function

of preparing men to enter the public sphere. In *Frankenstein* this contradiction remains invisible as long as Victor lives at home; it is revealed when he enters the public sphere of science, for women's "subduing" function of affection and education is no match for modern science's imperative of domination. Before turning to Shelley's gendered critique of science, it is important to establish her focus on *modern* science.[24] Certainly she uses older models of presumptive quests for creative power through science, but she also revises them. As the novel's subtitle makes clear, Victor is a "modern Prometheus" who updates his mythical predecessor's creation of a new species; his desire for scientific knowledge also modernizes the dabbling in forbidden lore of Marlowe's Dr. Faustus. But Shelley reworks these models into a critique specific to modern science, to "the experiments of Dr. [Erasmus] Darwin" (22), of the chemist Humphry Davy (whose *Elements of Chemical Philosophy* she read while writing *Frankenstein*), and of other early-nineteenth-century scientists who were attempting not only to "re-animate" corpses but to create new life.

The most significant element of Shelley's critique is her analysis of the "alignment" between scientific discourse and gender discourse.[25] The language of her novel emphasizes the masculinity of Victor's callous experimentation on feminine nature.[26] In his desire to "pursue nature to her hiding-places" (56) and to divine the "mystery" of "her immortal lineaments" (45), Victor turns to the "almost unlimited powers" of modern chemistry (51), for this science promises to "penetrate into the recesses of nature, and show how she works in her hiding places." Most significantly, when Victor assembles and animates a human being in an act of solitary science, he appears to violate the norm of human reproduction that requires a woman's body. According to contemporary science, however, Victor is in fact *following* this norm. For Ludwig Holbach, whose *System of Nature* (1770) Shelley may have read, nature is a female principle which creates by parthenogenesis; thus "inanimate matter can pass into life,"[27] and the scientist who helps it to do so is acting in accord with a principle of nature. In this sense, Victor's assembly of the creature is the action of science on *and* with the female principle of nature. Where Victor errs is in taking sole credit, in ignoring the role of nature when he deems himself the "creator and source" (55) of "a new species." He further errs when he rejects the creature in "horror and disgust" (58) at its appearance. By thus disowning "his technological son,"[28] Victor violates a cultural norm—that parental care is owed to an offspring.

This violation displays the contradictions of the domestic ideology, between its affective relations and its debt economy, and between the seclusion of the family and its public functions. Within his ideal home, Victor learned lessons of feminized paternal care and was subdued by Elizabeth's feminine gentleness. But he also learned a bookkeeping mentality of gratitude and obligation, and it is this domestic pattern that motivates his scientific creation. A new species "would *owe* their being to me," he gloats; hence "no father could *claim* the *gratitude* of his child so completely as I should deserve theirs" (55; emphasis added). This claim to paternal dominance parallels modern science's imperative to the dominance of nature. Domestic affection operates only in the domestic sphere; once Victor leaves that sphere, the oppressive debt structure of domesticity operates in conjunction with the aims of masculine science.

Victor's rejection of his creature again reveals this latent contradiction of domestic ideology, and the consequences of that act show the principles of the masculine and feminine spheres to be not only separate but fatally opposed. No longer subdued by Elizabeth's gentleness, Victor's science turns deadly; the creature of his scientific sphere destroys all the inhabitants of his domestic sphere. The "hapless victims to [Victor's] unhallowed arts" (82) are his younger brother William, the family servant Justine, Henry Clerval, Elizabeth, Alphonse, Victor, and finally the experiment himself: at the novel's end, the creature vows to immolate himself so that his carcass cannot serve as a model for the creation of "such another as I" (184). If the creature is a product of science, he is also Victor's "spirit, let loose . . . to destroy all that was dear" to him (73); and that "spirit," no longer "cooped up" by feminine domesticity, is "the male principle in its extreme, monstrous form."[29] Outside the home, femininity and masculinity exist not in complementarity but in destructive opposition. Thus the creature, produced by science and by the Frankenstein family's oppressive economy of obligation, destroys the feminine sphere of domestic affection.

The three themes introduced in Walton's narrative and developed by Victor's story—domestic affection, education, and science—recur in the creature's narrative. And like Victor's, the creature's domestic education fails because of contradictions within its ideology. That ideology is apparent in two of Percy Shelley's comments on *Frankenstein*. His "Preface" to the novel describes its "moral tendencies" as "the amiableness of domestic affection, and the excellence of universal virtue" (25). His unpublished review of the novel links that virtue with social affection as

well: the novel's "direct moral" is "treat a person ill, and he will become wicked," for dividing "a social being from society" produces "malevolence and selfishness."[30] The creature's contradictory education teaches these moral lessons, but it also shows their limitations; hence he is caught "between the ideology his education teaches and his own experience" (McWhir, 73).

The De Lacey family is the creature's first "school" of "human nature" (112). From it he learns that a father "doat[s]" on his children (106), that a mother is "wrapped up" in them, and that family relations "bind one human being to another in mutual bonds." When Safie arrives to join Felix De Lacey and the family extends those "mutual bonds" to her, the creature learns about "benevolence and generosity" (111). But this family circle also shows the creature his own anomalous position without parents, friends, or relations (107).

From his reading the creature then learns of ideal social affections. Goethe's *Sorrows of Young Werther* teaches him "lofty sentiments and feelings" (112) for objects beyond "self," and Plutarch's *Lives* teaches him "to admire peaceable lawgivers." But his books also show the failure of such social bonds. From Plutarch he learns of men "massacring their species"; from Volney's *Ruins of Empire* he learns "the strange system of human society" (106) whereby the "division of property" creates "immense wealth and squalid poverty." From Milton's *Paradise Lost*[31] he learns that, like Adam, he has "no link to any other being in existence" (113), and from Victor's scientific journal he learns that he is "solitary and abhorred" (113). This lesson of social isolation is reinforced when Felix De Lacey drives him from human "society and sympathy" (117). Among the De Laceys as among the Frankensteins, domestic affection is not all-inclusive; although the De Lacey family circle opened to admit the beautiful Safie, it excludes the ugly creature. Because he is "unsympathised with" (118)—by his creator, the De Laceys, and society at large—the creature begins his murders. Like Victor's scientific career, the creature's murderous career results from his contradictory education, from the irreconcilability between the lessons of domestic affection and "the lessons of Felix and the sanguinary laws of man" (124).

Circling back to the narrative frame of Walton's journal, the novel concludes with its protagonists' final lessons in science and the domestic and social affections. Yet in both areas the conclusion does not offer a single lesson but rather puts a dialectic in play (Suvin, 136). At one moment Victor warns against Walton's ambition of "distinguishing [himself] in science and discoveries" (181); at another he exhorts the crew to pursue

Walton's polar expedition "for honour, and the benefit of mankind"
(178). When the crew refuses and Walton turns back, it seems he has
taken to heart Victor's "precepts" on "how dangerous is the acquirement
of knowledge" (54–55); in fact, however, Walton rails that his "hopes of
utility and glory" (179) have been "blasted by [the] cowardice and inde-
cision" of his crew. The creature's education similarly concludes in dual-
ity. On the one hand, he insists that "all human kind sinned against me"
and reiterates his anger at this "injustice"; on the other, he plans to "sacrifice" himself in "remorse" for his misdeeds (184–85).

Because the creature has been read as a figure for the emergent working classes,[32] the contradictions of his final speech raise the oft-debated
question of *Frankenstein*'s politics. When the novel was first published in
1818, voting eligibility in England was restricted to men of the propertied classes, but the working class's right to vote had been claimed and
debated since the revolutionary 1790s. By 1831 the issue was bitterly
disputed, and it is significant that Mary Shelley's novel was reissued
during this year, when "[t]he burnings—the alarms—the absorbing
politics of the day render book-sellers almost averse to publishing at all"
(*MWSL*, 2:120). The "politics" to which Shelley refers was the increasing, and increasingly violent, public debates over a Reform Bill which
might enfranchise the working as well as the middle classes. The propertied classes feared to lose their exclusive legislative power to the prop-
ertyless rabble, a fear exacerbated when supporters of the Reform Bill
rioted after the House of Lords rejected it in September 1831.

Shelley's characteristically double view of the Reform Bill appears in
her letters. To her friend Fanny Wright she wrote that "[t]he people *will*
be redressed" (*MWSL*, 2:124), and that England would be "revolutionized" unless "the Aristocrats sacrifice enough to tranquillize them." To
the social reformer Robert Dale Owen, she described the controversy in
phrenological terms:

> *Progressiveness* is certainly finely developed just now in Europe—together
> with a degree of *tyrant quellingtiveness* which is highly laudable—it is a
> pity that in our country this should be mingled with *sick destructiveness*;
> yet the last gives action to the former—and without [it], would our
> Landholders be brought to reason? Yet it is very sad—the punishment of
> the poor men being not the least disaster attendant on it. (*MWSL*,
> 2:122)

One might view this passage as waffling, but it might more usefully be
seen as an effort, like her father's in *Political Justice*, to come to terms

with a period of complicated political change. Similarly, her delight that the Whigs "triumphed gloriously" in passing a Reform Bill which excluded the working classes from the vote (*MWSL*, 2:133) demonstrates both her reformist enthusiasm for an extended franchise and her conservative relief that the more revolutionary bill was defeated.

Like this letter, the novel's judgments of the creature are conflicted. When the creature asks nicely for a mate, Victor recognizes the justice of his claims, just as the more benevolent liberals of the middle and upper classes recognized those of the respectable working classes. But when Victor imagines the consequences of ceding his power to create life to a "monster" and his mate, he fears the "sick destructiveness" they might engender. Victor then destroys the monsterette and justifies himself by arguing the creature's "malignity and selfishness" (180), just as opponents of enfranchising the working classes justified themselves by arguing that the lower orders were "helots."[33] In Victor's self-justification, as in Mary Shelley's delight with the Whigs' triumph, is relief that revolutionary "monsters" are disempowered.

But the creature can also be read as a justification of rebellion against class oppression. By dedicating the novel to her radical father William Godwin, Shelley proclaims the political allegiances evident in her "extreme pleasure" (*MWSL*, 1:32) with the "boldness" of Leigh Hunt's revolutionary newspaper the *Examiner.* Moreover, as one contemporary review noted, the creature's "code of ethics" is formed in part by the "atheistical jacobinism"[34] of Volney's *Ruins of Empire* (1791), an extremely influential text in radical circles. The fact that Shelley revised only a few words of the creature's narrative for the 1831 edition indicates that she continued to agree with Volney's critique of a privileged class parasitic on the laboring class. Furthermore, the creature's argument that he is the product of his culture incorporates both elements of the author's radical heritage: Wollstonecraft's view that women's capacities have been stunted by a masculine culture that treats them as "alluring objects for a moment,"[35] and Godwin's view that human character and behavior "flow entirely from the operation of circumstances and events" rather than from "innate principles or instincts."[36] If Victor and his culture have created a monster, then there are clear grounds for two claims: that a society and not its outcasts creates revolutionary violence, and that the creature's rage is the revolutionary's "excess of a virtuous feeling" (*PJ*, 1:284). This tension embodied in the creature, between fear of revolution and sympathy with the revolutionary, reveals Mary Shelley's personal ambivalence; but it does more than that.

By making both the conservative and the revolutionary arguments, *Frankenstein* dramatizes the tension between the two that characterized England between 1789 and 1832. In this sense, the trope of monstrosity marks Mary Shelley's novel as a "late product" of the British debate over the French Revolution.[37]

The Last Man (1826)

The Last Man has often been read as a record of Mary Shelley's years in Italy.[38] The author herself wrote that the character of Adrian was meant to "give some idea" of Percy Shelley (*MWSL*, 1:512), that Lord Raymond was a "faint portrait" of Lord Byron (*MWSL*, 1:566), and that she could "well describe" Lionel Verney, the last man, because she felt herself to be "the last relic of a beloved race" (*MWSJ*, 2:476–77). One contemporary reviewer noted this *roman à clef* element of the novel,[39] and another rather unkindly suggested that Shelley should have named her book *The Last Woman* to better indicate her "distress at having nobody left to talk to."[40] But there is more to the novel than "authorial therapy."[41] Although Shelley had vowed "never to make money of [her] acquaintance with Lord Byron" (*MWSL*, 2:89), putting the notorious Byron in her novel may in fact signal "business acumen,"[42] and this acumen might also have led her to tap the contemporary interest in "last man" texts.[43] Furthermore, Shelley's vision of a plague destroying humanity drew on the contemporary scientific controversy about theories of geological change,[44] and it had particular resonance after the cholera epidemics of 1817 and 1826.[45] Most importantly, the novel analyzes issues of love and power that were of perennial interest to Shelley. With its imaginative framework of the decline and fall of human civilization, *The Last Man* performs a cognitive estrangement on contemporary norms in political and domestic relations.

The Last Man is a first-person narrative by Lionel Verney, but prior to the novel proper is an "Author's Introduction." Here an unnamed and ungendered speaker recounts a visit to the cave of the Cumaean Sibyl, a mythological figure punished for rejecting Apollo's sexual advances by being given eternal life without eternal youth and by being forced to prophecy. The speaker claims that the novel is a redaction of the Sibyl's prophecies. *The Last Man*, then, is to be read as "prophetic" or "futuristic" history;[46] like that of Volney's *Ruins of Empire* and Percy Shelley's *Queen Mab* (1814), its imaginative framework is a vision of the future

that reflects on the present. Volume I interweaves political with personal relations to explore the transformative power of love and the destructive tyranny of passion.

The imaginative framework of the novel's politics is England's peaceful transition from a monarchy to a republic; in 2073 the last king abdicated, "in compliance with the gentle force" of his subjects' wishes (13). Future discord, however, is foreshadowed in the personal-political relation between the ex-king's widow, the Countess of Windsor, and her son Adrian: the Countess is educating Adrian toward her "ambitious end" of regaining the throne, but he is developing "republican principles." A second important personal-political relation is Adrian's friendship with Lionel Verney, shepherd and poacher. Initially they represent opposed political principles. Lionel exemplifies unregulated working-class passion, the Hobbesian rather than the Rousseauian natural man. Even as he criticizes the "neglect," "unkindness [and] injustice" (12) of the ruling class, his own "wild" dreams of greatness are "unchecked by moral considerations"; his "lawless career" of poaching is marked by "acts of tyranny," and his "savage" life is a "war against civilization." In contrast is Adrian's republicanism, which functions not by lawless savagery or the tyranny of force but by the "power" (18) of "love and wisdom." With these principles Adrian opens to Lionel both the "demesne of civilization" and "a new career in innocence and love" (19). Crucially, he teaches Lionel that power lies not in being "hard of heart, ferocious, and daring; but kind, compassionate and soft."

The novel further develops this thematic of power by gendering it. To be "kind, compassionate and soft" was generally coded in the nineteenth century as feminine; indeed, Lionel learns these traits of republican power from Adrian like "a child lisping its devotions after its mother" (19–20). In contrast, the Countess's desire for power is represented as masculine. Adrian's mother lacks "the virtues of domestic life" (20); instead she has "courage and daring," "determined ambition" (22), and a "love of rule." These qualities link her with Lord Raymond, Adrian's "opposite" (31) and the novel's figure of martial masculinity. Like the Countess, Raymond exhibits "reckless courage" (27) and "open ambition"; he aims "to attain the first station in his own country" so that it will feel his "power" as "an iron yoke." Raymond and the Countess are further allied when she abets his plan to "rebuild the throne" (39) by marrying her daughter Idris; in contrast to Adrian's maternal care for Lionel, the Countess here sacrifices her daughter to her own "ambitious schemes" (35).

Volume I's several "political love tales" (*Panoramic*, 380) play out
these gendered thematics of love and ambition, power and tyranny.
When Adrian falls in love with the Greek princess Evadne, his unhappy
passion becomes a "tyranny" (*Last Man*, 32). Lionel is "mad with an
excess of passionate devotion" (55) for Adrian's sister Idris, and Evadne
is "overpowered" (31) by an equally "tyrannical" passion for Raymond.
Raymond's sexuality and politics are particularly rich in significance. He
"tyranniz[es]" over women (33) like a "despot," and he courts Idris to
achieve his monarchical ambitions. But he loves Lionel's sister, Perdita,
and this love is both "the tyrant and the tyrant-queller," for Raymond is
the "slave" (45) of a love that "rebel[s]" against his ambition. The interrelation of the political and the personal in these love stories is dramatized when "civil war" (34) impends in both England and the royal family. As Raymond schemes to marry Idris and restore the monarchy, he is
opposed by Ryland, the leader of the popular party; and when Idris
resists her mother's plan to marry her to Raymond, the Countess longs
to take her to imperial Austria, "where obedience can be enforced" (63).
As in *Valperga* and many of her Italian stories, Mary Shelley uses Austria
to exemplify the tyrannical state, but here she also connects political
with domestic tyranny.

After these love triangles are sorted out, a period of domestic and
political peace ensues. Adrian recovers from his passion for Idris, Raymond marries Perdita, Lionel marries Idris, and the five form a "happy
circle" of domestic "tranquillity" (64, 66). But this "pleasant dream" is
evanescent; as in *Frankenstein*, the separate sphere of domestic affection
is a "false security" against masculine ambition (Blumberg, 133). Sated
with the domesticity of "amusing our wives, and dancing our children"
(*Last Man*, 67), Lord Raymond enters the political sphere and is elected
Protector of England. This resurgence of Raymond's ambition reactivates his other passions, and they have "acquired fresh strength, from
the long sleep in which love had cradled them" (91). Even as he plans
"entire dominion" in politics (84), then, he cannot command himself
when he again encounters Evadne. She is similarly mastered by "the too
great energy of her passions" (83), and they conduct a secret intrigue
until he abandons her and she leaves England for Greece. When his
wife, Perdita, confronts him with her suspicions about his goings-on,
Raymond lies to her and thereby destroys the hitherto "entire sympathy" of their once "indivisible" love (87, 93).

To this nexus of illicit passion and unregulated ambition, Shelley now
adds the language of disease that comes to dominate the novel. Ray-

mond's lie to Perdita is a "contagion" (91) that spreads from his personal life to his political role. Angry over her coldness, Raymond turns to carousing; thus ruled by the "tyrant" (109) of his "passions," he first neglects and then renounces the Protectorate. When he joins the Greeks' war against Turkey, the contagion extends further; just as the 1817 cholera epidemic spread via "English trade and troops" (Clemit, 193), so Raymond's contagion travels with the troops securing England's "extensive commercial relations" with Greece (*Last Man,* 115). War, passion, ambition—all these forms of disease join as the scene shifts to Greece. The earth is "cor[p]se-strewn" (131) because of the war; Evadne curses Raymond with "fire, and war, and plague" and then dies, a "monument to human passion" (132); Raymond storms plague-ridden Constantinople and dies there, "the victim of ambition" (141); Perdita, who had reconciled with him, then throws herself into the sea, "the victim of too much loving" (156).

In the "political love tale" of Raymond, Perdita, and Evadne, the betrayal of love by ambition creates a contagion that joins with the plague which will destroy humanity. This connection raises the question of how to interpret the plague. Certainly it seems associated with the destructive effects of men's "rapacious desire for power" (Clemit, 195), and especially with the "critique of male egoism" (Mellor, 151) enacted in the story of Raymond's ambition. Although the novel carefully distances Evadne's excessive passion for Raymond from Perdita's proper feminine love for and service to him, Raymond's "contagion" kills them both, Evadne because he abandoned her and Perdita because "her whole existence was one sacrifice to him" (*Last Man,* 84). But since the plague is gendered throughout the novel as feminine, it can also be read as "the eruption of pent-up female discontents."[47] Specifically, if the plague represents Evadne's "over-abundant desire," then the spread of her passion is "subversive to the novel's cultural order."[48] In personal terms, the novel's cultural order works to domesticate passion into love; in political terms, cultural order is the efforts of European "civilization" (*Last Man,* 127) not only to liberate Greece but also to "eradicate" Turkey's "antique barbarism." Raymond's death by plague heralds the failure of both elements of cultural order. He can neither escape the curse of Evadne's passion nor conquer Constantinople, and this double "reversal of [his] domination" (Goldsmith, 293–94) signals the cultural *disorder* that will spread with the plague.

Volume II traces the progress of the plague and the accompanying disruption of political order. As the plague approaches England, it cre-

ates political disorder there. The legislators cannot agree on quarantine laws, and the republic is further undermined when Ryland, the new Protector, in order to tax the aristocracy for the "starving multitudes" (*Last Man*, 170), must abandon his plans to abolish hereditary rank. When the plague reaches London and Ryland succumbs to "debility of purpose and dastard fear" (175), the republic ends. Adrian becomes Protector, but to do so he claims "the rights of his ancestors" (184); despite his republican principles, then, his "noblesse oblige" is royal in effect if not in name (Blumberg, 142–43). As the plague spreads, it creates more disorder: "deeds of heroism" (193) but also of "wickedness," closer "ties of kindred and friendship" (197) but also more evils of "an advanced state of civilization." Adrian institutes procedures that reduce "vice and folly" (195), and at one point his pleas create "a gush of love and deepest amity" (219) which halts a battle between the English and an invading force of North Americans and Irish. Eventually, however, the fact that "Adrian had preserved order" (220) means only that "property continued sacred," and this seems "a wretched mockery" as the death count rises.

Volume III plays out the dialectic between cultural order and disorder. Without "the rules of order and pressure of laws" (230), many people "transgress the accustomed uses of society." Absent "the boundaries of private possession," the poor have luxuries while the rich lose their "powers of command" (235). Ex-Protector Ryland is discovered dead among piles of hoarded food; his death represents the futility of republican principles, for although "we were all equal now" (231), the plague creates "an equality still more levelling." Thus plague and disease, which earlier radical writers had used as "hopeful symbols of the revolutionary process,"[49] now signal the end of that process. Although the members of Adrian's council are elected for their "benevolence" rather than their "station" (*Last Man*, 240), the meetings of this last vestige of republicanism degenerate into "passion, and the spirit of angry contest" (271).

Perhaps the most striking instance of disorder is the religious group calling itself the Elect. Its leader is a "merciless cannibal of souls" driven by "ambition" (282, 273), and its members are "fanatical" adherents of his "unrelenting tyranny" (274, 281). The Juliet subplot demonstrates the infectious power of this religious disorder. In the plague's early stages, Juliet's marriage was the final example of "the spirit of love . . . which once had been the life of the world" (207); after her husband's death she is "easy prey" for the Elect (283), and although she rescues Lionel from their clutches, she remains with them because they have her

child. That this last embodiment of maternal love ends her days in the "pestilential atmosphere" (286) of the Elect signals the coming victory of the plague.

In nature as in culture, "disorder" (166) disturbs a once "benignant influence." Although nature seems still "the kind mother of the human race" (239), her "fertility" becomes "a mockery" when summer, once a time of growth, now spreads the plague. The sudden appearance of meteors shows that the earth is no longer ruled by its "ancient laws" (270); such evidence of "the savage enmity of nature" (271) then infects human nature, as "diseased imagination" (288) creates "almighty fear." The final inversion of nature's benignancy is the storm at sea that kills Adrian and his daughter, leaving Lionel, the last man, in a "savage, ungrateful nature" (333).

Like *Frankenstein*'s conclusion, that of *The Last Man* is open to more than one interpretation. Early in the novel Adrian claims that "the Spirit of Good" infuses both the laws of nature and the human imagination; hence, "let us will it, and our habitation becomes a paradise. For the will of man is omnipotent" (53–54). While the coming of the plague contradicts this rosy view, the novel's final volume again posits the power of the will. When Lionel and three other survivors take consolation from hearing Haydn's "New-Created World," the moment seems not a savage parody but a resurgence of the will that can find "wonders of nature" (305) amid the desolation. Similarly, Lionel is able to sympathize in the joys of the animals who live on as "nature's selected darlings" (334), and to take comfort in the sight of the Coliseum's ruins "robed by nature" in verdure (336). At other moments, however, Lionel believes in neither nature nor the human will; rather he turns to the philosophy of necessity. This philosophy, drawn from David Hume and popularized by Mary Shelley's father, William Godwin, remained influential well into the nineteenth century; it posited Necessity as the force governing nature and human actions. Shelley terms this force "the visible laws of the invisible God" (337). Lionel's earlier "sickness of the soul" (290) was cured when he recognized "eternal, changeless Necessity" as "mother of the world" and submitted to her "unchangeable laws"; near the end of the novel he again "admitted her authority, and bowed to her decrees" (338). Submitting to the authority of necessity restores order to Lionel's universe, yet in the novel's final paragraph he rejects that order. "Wild dreams" (342) now "ruled [his] imagination," and he takes to the sea; with "restless despair and fierce desire of change" as his "pilots," he seeks a companion or death. Unlike the crea-

ture's journey which concludes *Frankenstein* or Winzy's purposive quest which ends "The Mortal Immortal," however, Lionel's expedition is wholly "delusive" (340) in its aim.

Is Lionel's delusive quest a sign of heroic fortitude or of Romantic fatuity? Is the plague susceptible to interpretation, or "a limit-phenomenon" (Snyder, 445) whose meaning is "precisely its absence of meaning"? The reader is left, like Lionel, to "read fair augury" (342) or "menace," "some lesson" or no lesson in the novel. If love and Adrian's compassionate power are meant as moral guides, even in the pre-plague world they are not always effectual, and by the end of the novel they are irrelevant. *The Last Man*'s extreme cognitive estrangement seems finally to offer not new norms but no norms, making this the bleakest of Mary Shelley's science fictions.

Chapter Four

Historical Fiction: Short Stories, *Valperga,* Oriental Tales, and *Perkin Warbeck*

It might seem simple enough to define historical fiction, but in the late eighteenth and early nineteenth centuries the definitions of fiction itself were in flux. By choosing to write historical fiction, Mary Shelley involved herself in the complex literary and political issues surrounding the definitions and uses of fiction and of history. This chapter begins with those issues and their relevance for Mary's historical novels and stories.

Any literary field is mapped and remapped, structured and restructured, by "struggles for literary legitimacy."[1] From the 1780s through the 1830s, the field of fiction became a site of such struggles for legitimacy. The instability of this field was due in part to the spread of literacy during the eighteenth century, and the consequent fragmentation of a once "consensual public sphere" (Ferris, 21) into two reading publics. One of these publics continued to be the "articulate classes," mainly university-educated men occupying "sites of social power"; the other, newer reading public included women and was much larger and more varied in class and occupation (Ferris, 22). The older public often perceived the fiction read by the newly literate as dangerously inflammatory; women readers might be erotically aroused by tales of love written by women, and working-class readers might be politically aroused by tales of class struggle written by Jacobin revolutionaries. Hence the older reading public attempted to discipline and control these new readers. Education itself could be an "agency of bourgeois moral imperialism," as Sunday schools for the working classes taught respect for existing institutions and also preempted time that might otherwise go to political action.[2] Another means of control, exercised by the many critical reviews founded in the early nineteenth century, was to divide the literary field of fiction into respectable and suspect genres. Thus the struggle for legitimacy in fiction was conducted in part by the defining of genres.

This struggle was particularly acute for historical fiction because it crossed so many genre lines. The genres of most relevance for Mary Shelley's historical fiction are the realistic novel, the romance, the Gothic, and Jacobin fiction.

The realistic novel was expected to be mimetic, to represent faithfully "the ordinary train of human events, and the modern state of society."[3] This genre could be respectable if it was properly didactic, if a novel about courtship and marriage, for example, warned women readers against seduction and urged the control of passion. The realistic novel thus offered legitimacy to women writers if they were "scrupulous about fulfilling the office of educator."[4] Jane Austen was such an educator, and Maria Edgeworth's novels were particularly admired for their "education and disciplining of the newly literate" (Ferris, 61).

The realistic novel was often defined in opposition to the romance, a term meaning not a love story but a nonrealistic fiction; in 1822 Walter Scott defined the romance as "a fictitious narrative" that "turns upon marvellous and uncommon incidents."[5] But these two genres were not easily differentiated, for a realistic novel set "in modern times" and recording "every-day life" might also incorporate the "mysterious and terrible" incidents or "powerful passion" which characterized "the sphere of the romance" (Moir, 42). Two 1823 reviews of *Valperga* show the slippage between the realistic novel and the romance: while the *Examiner* considered *Valperga* a "historical novel"[6] and *Blackwood's* termed it a "historical-romance," both reviews compared it to Mary Shelley's prior "romance fiction,"[7] *Frankenstein*.

A further slippage between genres appears in another contemporary definition of romance, which linked it to history as well as other forms of fiction. By the late eighteenth century, romance could mean "the fiction of pre-modern cultures" (Duncan, 10); in Britain from roughly 1750 to 1830, antiquarian scholars and poets redefined romance as the record of a national culture which was "disintegrating under the pressures of modernization" (Duncan, 4). The subject of Walter Scott's *Waverly* (1814), for example, is the "ancient traditions" of the Highland Scots; although the book is often called the first historical novel, Scott considered it a "romance."[8] Of course, a romance was still fiction and its history might be criticized on those grounds. Reviewing *Perkin Warbeck*, the *Athenaeum* complained that historical fiction abandoned the "truth" of history for the "falsehood" of romance and that history was thereby "degrade[d]" into "a mere vehicle of romance."[9] Such complaints indicate that fiction was struggling for political as well as generic legitimacy.

If a figure whom history had consigned to "everlasting infamy" (*Athenaeum*, 323) was given "romantic virtue" by fiction, for example, such judgments on the past might lead to equally revolutionary judgments on the present.

This potential for critique connects the romance with a third genre, Gothic fiction. The Gothic was often set in a secluded and mysterious medieval castle; the heroine was generally an inexperienced young woman mistreated by tyrannical parents and/or pursued by an aristocratic would-be seducer. Like the romance, the Gothic was "a mode of history"[10] which reflected a late-eighteenth-century "upsurge in antiquarian interest in the national past."[11] But because the Gothic recorded a "period of sensed overlap" between the end of medieval culture and the beginnings of modern society (Miles, 32), it was also concerned with the present. Writers and readers of the emerging middle classes used this genre "to come to grips with their changing relations to a myth of aristocracy" (Punter, 116). Thus the Gothic was a way of interpreting the past for the present, of exploring "what the violence and crudity of past economic and social relations can reveal about those relations in the present" (Punter, 107). Moreover, Gothic novels gendered this economic and social violence, especially when they were written by women. Ann Radcliffe's Gothics reveal the "public domain," both of history and of "patriarchal coercion," as a sphere of "power and terror" endangering the heroine (Duncan, 13). But they also define "a feminine principle of private subjectivity" which transforms that masculine public world; even though such fictional transformation is imaginary, it serves to critique "the antagonistic realm of patriarchal history." Through the Gothic elements of Mary Shelley's historical fiction, women's subjectivity takes on this critical function.

Critique in Shelley's historical fiction also draws on the Jacobin novel, one of whose major practitioners was her father, William Godwin. Jacobinism was a political philosophy of the 1780s and 1790s sympathetic to the French Revolution. It opposed the rule of "statecraft" (monarchy and aristocracy) and "priestcraft" (the allied power of the established church), and it sought an end to the unreason and superstition that perpetuated the tyranny of class and religion. Jacobin novelists rejected the romance genre for its association with prerevolutionary "feudal and chivalric culture."[12] Instead, such novels as Godwin's *Caleb Williams; or, Things As They Are* (1794) and Robert Bage's *Hermsprong* (1796) addressed the present, to reveal the tyranny of a feudal past and the failure of its chivalric ideals. Jacobin novelists also rejected the

romance's episodic structure of "detached and independent adventures,"
aiming rather for a plot with "unity of design" (quoted in Kelly, 14).
Such a plot dramatized the doctrine of necessity, which held that "the
characters of men originate in their external circumstances";[13] unity of
design showed how circumstances form character and thus how a
change of circumstances could create a change of character. Finally,
Jacobin novelists challenged a conservative view of history as stasis, as a
"natural, 'organic' growth . . . which alters nothing in the time-hon-
oured, legitimate institutions of society."[14] Rather, Jacobins saw history
as a series of struggles to defeat "error and prejudice" and "establish the
rule of reason" (Kelly, 7), and Jacobin novels intended to begin a similar
"moral revolution" in the reader (Kelly, 19). Believing in human perfectibility, these novelists hoped to initiate the process of discussion and
reasoning which would have the same effect on the reader that the
French Revolution had on "legitimate institutions of society." Where
Shelley's historical fiction critiques the tyranny of those institutions, it
follows the Jacobin novel's impulse; this is especially true of the Italian
fictions, which are animated by her support of Italy's "quiet revolutions"
in 1820 and her delight in the "glorious" prospect of Italy's liberty from
Austria (*MWSL*, 1:158, 156).

Like the four genres I have reviewed, the historical novel crosses the
boundary between fiction and history. It is a "hybrid" genre (Ferris, 5)
that blurs the distinction between the factuality of history and the fic-
tionality of the novel. And rather than privilege one over the other, the
historical novel often sets up a dialectic between history and fiction. The
ground of that dialectic is experience, as both the stuff of history and the
realistic novel's claim to authenticity. The French Revolution and the
Napoleonic wars "for the first time made history a *mass experience*"; people came to see that history "deeply affect[ed] their daily lives and
immediately concern[ed] them" (Lukács, 23–24). The historical novel
similarly juxtaposes the big picture of history with the small stories of
historical actors. As it does so, it creates a dialectic that calls into question "the official, inscribed plot of history" (Ferris, 205).

Frequently in Mary Shelley's historical fiction, this dialectic is gendered as she juxtaposes a public masculine realm of history with a private
feminine realm of domestic life. She embeds a love plot in an "explicitly
historical revolutionary setting," such as the Italian wars of independence
or the French Revolution.[15] The love plot then "mutates under the pressure" of that setting, to produce sometimes a critique of reactionary
tyranny, sometimes a "disciplining [of] revolutionary energy." In this way,

Shelley's historical fiction brings "the historical formation of the modern imperial nation-state" into conjunction with "the sentimental formation of the private individual." But that conjunction is also a site of disjunction, of "dialectical contest" (Duncan, 15) which is often represented in gender terms.

Short Stories

"A Tale of the Passions" (1823)

"A Tale of the Passions" was published in the second issue of *The Liberal*, a short-lived journal produced by Lord Byron and Leigh Hunt. The tale analyzes the effects of partisan political passions, and like much of Shelley's historical fiction, it embeds these political reflections in a domestic plot.

"A Tale of the Passions" explores the public and private consequences of the "violent party spirit"[16] displayed by both Guelphs and Ghibellines in thirteenth-century Italy. The story begins on 1 May 1268, the date on which the Guelphs recaptured Florence from the Ghibellines. This public history then impinges on private life; as the Guelphs celebrate their triumph, their partisan Gegia quarrels with her Ghibelline husband, Cincolo, and reminds him that her "mother's heart" (4) mourns their son's death in Italy's civil wars. The arrival of the young stranger Ricciardo halts the domestic quarrel, and he later averts a political quarrel when he "calm[s] his passion" (9) after accusing Gegia's friend Bosticchi of assassinating the Ghibelline leader Arrigo dei Elisei. Ricciardo is then revealed to be Despina dei Elisei, daughter of the murdered Arrigo.

The reader is told Despina's history, which shows the interpenetration of political and romantic passions. While an attendant to the Queen of Sicily, Despina "worshipped" (12) the Ghibelline king Manfred; she was unaware of this love until Manfred's counselor Lostendardo declared a passion for her that "reflected in too faithful a mirror my own emotions." Lostendardo's romantic passion for Despina causes his political treachery to Manfred; in contrast, Despina was "saved" from a possible illicit passion for Manfred by the "purity of [her] affections." She "consecrate[d]" herself (13) to his "most righteous" political cause, and after his death she transferred her allegiance to his nephew Corradino. The story then returns to the present, as Despina tries to

persuade Lostendardo to help Corradino succeed to his uncle's throne. But "the fury of [his] passions" (14) has consumed all Lostendardo's "human sympathies" (16) and turned him into a "devil." Momentarily swayed by Despina's "angelic . . . belief in good" (15), he returns to Gothic villainy and imprisons her in his castle. At this point the political and domestic plots again meet: because Gegia had been "a mother" (21) to Despina despite their political differences, her husband seeks Corradino's help for their "foster-child" (20). But Corradino is defeated and captured by Lostendardo's forces, and the story ends with the events of 26 October 1268; historically the date of Corradino's execution, in Shelley's political/romantic plot it is also the date of Despina's death.

Embedded in historical events, Despina's story works like a realistic fiction to show that political and romantic passions must be "purified" (14) from "baser feelings." Despina channels her sexual passion for Manfred into devotion to his "sacred" cause (10) and finally into "an aspiration to another life" (13) in which his spirit "is a part of all things." Lostendardo's love for her is so riddled with "baser" passions as to be "dishuman" (12), until he tames them with "self-inflicted torture" in a religious order (23). The story's taming mechanisms seem severe, but they are almost warranted by the damage that "dishuman passion" does in private and public histories.

"The Heir of Mondolfo"

Although it was not published until 1877, manuscript evidence suggests that "The Heir of Mondolfo" was written in the early 1820s.[17] Like the "Tale of the Passions," it is a story of tyrannical passions set in late-thirteenth-century Italy; this story, however, has a happy ending in instructive contrast to the warfare which concludes "Tale of the Passions."

"The Heir of Mondolfo" turns on conflicting notions of heirship. It takes place in a period of warfare over the inheritance of Italian kingdoms, with Naples having been conquered by the house of Anjou. In this context of political tyranny, Shelley places a masculine and domestic tyranny reminiscent of the Gothic novel. In the Gothic setting of Mondolfo castle, Prince Fernando Mondolfo makes his wife "the slave of his unbridled temper."[18] He "hate[s]" his son Ludovico (309); indeed, their father-son relation is that of "lord and vassal, oppressor and oppressed." The story then introduces the problematic of heirship through a contrast between maternal and paternal training. Ludovico's mother "tempered" his Mondolfo "blood" and nurtured his "virtue and affectionate feeling." After her death, however, the son's virtues "slept" under the

father's "tyranny," until Ludovico is saved by a feminine influence that reactivates his maternal training. He helps Viola, a young peasant girl in distress, and "for the first time since his mother's death" (313) he feels "tender sympathy." When he marries Viola he comes into his maternal inheritance of "virtue and affectionate feeling," as Fernando's "haughty, resentful" (318) son becomes Viola's "benign and gentle husband."

Two events reactivate the problematic of heirship: the death of his elder brother leaves Ludovico the heir of Mondolfo, and his own "heir" is born (320). Fernando objects to his son's "unworthy alliance" (319) and to a grandson "contaminated" by peasant blood (318); here as throughout, the story discredits this paternal obsession with class-based inheritance. Ludovico again shows his inheritance of maternal virtue by insisting that, "in all but birth" (320), Viola is worthy of her station. To force his heir to make "a suitable marriage" (323), Fernando then abducts Viola and her child and imprisons them in a tower. She escapes from this Gothic tyranny, she and Ludovico are reunited, and a fear of being left "heirless" (331) reforms Fernando. He brings his son's family into his castle, and the story concludes with him accepting the peasant Viola as "the mother of the Heir of Mondolfo."

In this story the virtues of women—Ludovico's mother and then his wife—defeat the tyranny of the aristocratic father, thereby creating a virtuous heir. Granted, the story's critique of aristocracy is limited; Viola's peasant cottage may be the "humble" (321) abode of nature, for example, but it is floored in marble and filled with priceless vases, and in any case she leaves it for the castle. As in Radcliffe's Gothic novels, however, a feminine principle creates imaginary transformations, first of Ludovico and then of Fernando, that critique a class-based system of patrilineage.

"The False Rhyme" (1830)

This is the first of several historical stories Mary Shelley wrote for the annual *The Keepsake*. Much shorter and crisper than her usual style, "The False Rhyme" is closely focused on a theme of treason that connects the historical and the romantic realms.

"The False Rhyme" centers on two historical personages, King Francis I of France and his sister, Margaret, queen of Navarre; the story is set in the 1520s, during Francis's war in Italy against Charles V of Spain. References to "troubadour and minstrel"[19] further locate the tale in the courtly-love tradition of poems and ballads which exalted ladies' virtue. The historical Margaret both wrote and patronized poems in this tradi-

tion, and when the fictional Margaret finds her brother etching onto a window a verse about women's inconstancy, she playfully accuses him of "*lèse majesté*" (117). Francis admits the "treason" but defends the sentiment by adducing Emilie de Lagny, who is thought to have abandoned her husband Enguerrand after Francis imprisoned him for treason; he then bets Margaret that she cannot prove Emilie's constancy in one month. At the month's end, Francis is jubilant at his army's victory over Charles's forces, and he allows Enguerrand to be brought from prison with evidence relating to the wager. The prisoner who appears is a woman, and Francis suspects "treason" (120) until the woman is revealed to be Emilie. Constant to her husband, she had taken his place in prison so he could prove his loyalty to Francis; the day's victory over Charles is in large part due to him. Proved wrong in all his charges of inconstancy and treason, Francis pardons Enguerrand, rewards Emilie, and breaks the offending window.

While this tale may seem little more than a *divertissement* in romance form, it is also a Jacobin antiromance in its critique of chivalric culture's state and sexual politics. Francis violates the chivalric ethic that enjoins a king's loyalty to his faithful knights, and a further critique is suggested by his subsequent history: in 1530 he lost the Italian war to Charles. Francis also violates the courtly love ethic that exalts a lady over a king, and for this too he is punished. Yet the story hints that an ideal of feminine constancy ultimately enforces the "authority of the sire."[20] Signs of that authority are etched on Emilie's "faded cheek" and "emaciated form" (*Tales,* 120); these proofs of her constancy are also proofs of the sacrifices demanded of women by a masculine chivalric culture.

"The Swiss Peasant" (1831)

"The Swiss Peasant" was published in the annual *The Keepsake*. The story uses the conventions of romance familiar to an annual's readers and apparent in the story's engraving. But Shelley also critiques those conventions; "The Swiss Peasant" is another of her Jacobin antiromances that shows the interrelation of sexual and political tyranny.

The opening frame narrative introduces several romance conventions. When the narrator's friend Ashburn posits a "tragic variety and wondrous incredible change" in life,[21] the narrator scoffs that "this is pure romance"; Ashburn then wagers there is a "romantic tale" in the peasant mother pictured in the story's engraving. An upper-class woman reader would be drawn into the story by this engraving, for it shows a mother

"beautiful and refined" (138) despite her peasant origins. This readies the reader to accept a peasant woman as "a fitting heroine for romance." The story also meets another contemporary definition of romance as it memorializes the "pre-modern culture" (Duncan, 10) of historically republican Switzerland, by references to William Tell and other fourteenth-century "Swiss patriots [who] swore to die for freedom" (*Tales,* 136).

The romance of the peasant heroine Fanny Chaumont brings this premodern Switzerland into the more recent history of the French Revolution. Orphaned at ten, Fanny was taken in by the district Governor Monsieur de Marville and given "a bourgeois education" (140) to "raise her above the hardships of a peasant's life" without "elevat[ing] her above her natural position in society." Young Henry de Marville falls in love with Fanny, but she loves the peasant Louis Chaumont, and this romantic triangle is embedded in a political plot. Fanny "look[s] up to" (141) and "depend[s]" on Louis; as a peasant he "understands" her as Henry cannot, and unlike the "gay thoughtless" Henry, he can "direct" her. Although the sober manly peasant is here contrasted with the flighty young aristocrat, the two men are alike in being mastered by their passions. Henry's passions are romantic; his desire for Fanny becomes his "tyrant" (142). Louis is mastered by political passions; inheriting his father's hatred of a social system ruled by "tyrants" (141), Louis is "too full of passion" and the revolutionary "spirit of resistance and revenge." Learning that Louis aspires to marry his ward, Governor de Marville sees the "spirit of the French Revolution" (142) in the peasant's "presumption." He responds with "tyranny," banishing Louis and ordering Fanny to give him up; with similar "intemperate passion" (143), Louis commands Fanny to "quit the roof of his oppressors." These demands place her in an "irreconcilable double bind" between "family and lover, the state and the revolution."[22]

The story's politics are equally conflicted. At some points the reader is clearly intended to side with the Jacobins. Governor de Marville acts as a "bigoted" aristocrat (144) when his forces attack a group of peasants; because his "violence" creates "resistance to his authority," the reader is meant to sympathize with that resistance and its leader, Louis, "the champion of liberty." But when the peasants besiege the Marville chateau, Shelley discourages the reader's sympathy with them by shifting the story's politics into a domestic register. The revolutionaries' assault on "the feudal halls of their tyrants" (144) becomes "the destruction of [a] home" (145); when their "sanguinary designs" (148) light on Madame de Marville and Henry, "mother and son were torn asunder."

As Louis then menaces "his rival [and] his oppressor," Fanny saves Henry by crying that he is "no aristocrat" but her husband (149). This deception is the culmination of her double bind, for by saving Henry she loses Louis. Like "A Tale of the Passions" and "False Rhyme," this story shows how political tyranny infiltrates women's domestic histories.

Fanny's story has a happy ending, but it hints at the continuing "tensions and conflicts that structure women's lives" (Langbauer, 194). Her appeal on Henry's behalf defeats Louis's "tyrants" (151), his revolutionary "rage and hate"; at her "shrine" (152) he sacrifices "every evil passion," and he joins the French army "to prove himself worthy" of her. Louis thus expiates his "guilt" by "repentance and reform," and the nation too seems to have expiated its revolutionary guilt as the Napoleonic wars end and peace is restored. When Louis and Fanny are reunited, they achieve the gender complementarity that is Shelley's ideal: his faults are "tempered by her angel disposition" (138), and her "too melancholy" spirit is enlivened by his "energy and activity." But "rather than blending disparities into harmony" (Langbauer, 194), such complementarity testifies to continuing disparity. If overt sexual and political tyranny has been defeated in the masculine realm of politics, gender difference in the domestic realm continues in uneasy truce and potential conflict.

"The Dream" (1832)

Another story published in *The Keepsake*, "The Dream" takes up several themes of Shelley's earlier historical fiction. As in "Tale of the Passions" and "Heir of Mondolfo," political passion creates family feuds; as in "Swiss Peasant," a woman is caught between conflicting masculine demands; and as in "False Rhyme," a historical monarch is convicted of *lèse majesté*.

The story is set early in the reign of Henry IV of France, after his adjuration of Protestantism in 1593 and his coronation in 1594 had ended France's civil-religious war. But "deep wounds" and "inimical parties" still fissure this "apparently united" nation and its families.[23] Constance, Countess de Villeneuve, had hoped to bring "peace to our houses" (158) by marrying Gaspar, son of her father's enemy; now in mourning for her father and brothers, "victims of the civil wars," she believes Gaspar was responsible for their deaths and feels she must renounce him. To Gaspar their love is sanctified by "the God of peace" (157); to Constance it is "impiety toward the unreposing dead." Bound by her grief to a fatal national history of civil war and family feuds, Con-

stance is also subject to the living Henry IV. "I know woman" (158), says he, and Constance will be won over by his own "earthly power" (159) and Gaspar's "earthly kindness." Like Francis's view of women's inconstancy in "False Rhyme," Henry's view of "woman's waywardness" (160) is proved wrong. Resolving to be commanded not by "earthly" forces but by "the dictates of Heaven" (158), Constance decides to sleep on the rocky ledge known as St. Catherine's bed; according to Catholic legend, the saint will send her votary a dream to guide her conduct. Believing that Gaspar has departed for the religious wars in Palestine, Constance dreams that he has been captured by "infidels" (164) in "Paynim land" and rises to rescue him; she is saved from falling off the ledge by Gaspar. Her salvation thus comes from a combination of "the dictates of Heaven" and Gaspar's "earthly kindness."

From her dream Constance draws two morals, that "to make the living happy was not to injure the dead" (165), and that it is wrong to locate "virtue and good in hatred and unkindness." Gaspar embodies the latter, personal/political moral. The dissension between Catholics and Calvinists within France put Constance in a double bind, like Emilie's in "False Rhyme" and Fanny's in "Swiss Peasant"; unlike Enguerrand and Louis, however, Gaspar eschews public conflicts to watch over his beloved. The happy ending of this story, although as hard-won as those of the earlier tales, seems less temporary, for Constance and Gaspar are the last of their families and thus free of family and national feuds.

"The Brother and Sister: An Italian Story" (1833)

The last of Mary Shelley's medieval tales, "The Brother and Sister: An Italian Story" returns to the political-domestic feuds of "Swiss Peasant." The title of this story indicates its domestic focus, and the first sentence introduces the related thematics of "the hatred borne by one family against another, and the strife of parties" in medieval Italy.[24] Unlike the earlier story of an irreconcilable double bind between family and lover, this tale suggests that family love is the problem and that romantic love is the solution.

The story takes place during the "warfare" (167) of fourteenth-century Siena, when families were driven from "the endearing associations of home" (166) until some "lucky accident" made these "sufferers" again the "tyrants." Among the exiles are Ugo Mancini and his children, Lorenzo and Flora. As in "Swiss Peasant," politics are a paternal inheritance: Ugo instills in his son a "violent hatred" (168) for the Tolomei

family that now rules Siena. After Ugo's death, Lorenzo returns to Siena with Flora and begins her domestic education. As "[f]ather, brother, tutor, guardian" (170), he "carefully" guards her; he also educates her in "the virtues becoming her sex," to prepare her for the seclusion proper to women in general and to a Mancini woman in particular. In return, Flora adores her brother's "unequalled kindness" and "regard[s] his virtues as superhuman."

Subsequent events confine Flora to this role as sister. When young Fabian de' Tolomei, "with all the bitterness engendered by family feuds" (171), banishes Lorenzo from Siena, Lorenzo entrusts Flora to him; Fabian accepts this "honour" (174) and promises to restore her "as spotless as she is now." In this chivalric exchange between the two men, Flora is defined as Lorenzo's sister; she is doubly locked into this role by her vow not to marry until his return. Furthermore, "her ambition, her pride, her aspiring thoughts were spent upon her brother" (176); she hates Fabian both as "Lorenzo's destroyer" and as his "opposite," for Fabian's "wit" and "good-humour" cannot measure up to "serious, ardent, noble-hearted" Lorenzo, "the crown and glory of manhood." In paragraph after paragraph Flora exalts her brother, and the manuscript contains additional encomia which were cut from the published version (*Tales,* 386–88). But sisterly devotion has a darker side: Flora's "quiet stock of family hate" (180) for the Tolomei.

If at this point sisterly love entails family hate, the remainder of the story works to reconcile those two emotions. When Fabian falls in love with Flora, he reverses Lorenzo's banishment, restores his fortune, and rebuilds his palace. Initially, Flora holds to her "sacred" vow (183) not to marry until Lorenzo's return, for her brother is "part of her religion"; more importantly, her dawning affection for Fabian is as a "ripple" to the "mighty tide" of her obsession with "Lorenzo's return—Lorenzo's existence—obedience to Lorenzo." When Flora sets out to locate her brother, Fabian follows her, finds Lorenzo ill at an inn, and nurses him "like a twin brother" (188). More familial language confirms the final political-domestic reconciliation, as Flora recognizes that Fabian fulfilled the chivalric contract by taking her brother's place as "protector and guardian" (189). In the story's final sentence, Fabian envisions himself, Lorenzo, and Flora together in Siena, "foes no longer."

In "Dream," Constance and Gaspar escaped the tyranny of the domestic past by being the last of their families. In contrast, "The Brother and Sister" solves the problem of family hate by extending sibling love outside the original family and then turning this broader love

into a new family. Fabian wakes Flora from the trance of sisterly devotion, yet he also reunites her with her brother and himself functions as a brother in this newly constituted family. Where the story began with a cycle of families exiled from and returning to Siena, it concludes with a joining of families that promises an end to cyclic political warfare.

"The Invisible Girl" (1833)

Although it was published in the same *Keepsake* as "Brother and Sister," "The Invisible Girl" is very different in setting and tone. It is a romance of the wondrous that parodies romance conventions, and its fairy-tale elements burlesque the themes of class and paternal tyranny which also appear in "The Heir of Mondolfo" and "The Swiss Peasant."

Writing at the beginning of the eighteenth century, the narrator, Henry Vernon, finds himself in the Gothic setting of a "ruined tower" in Wales.[25] He is intrigued by a painting of a girl who, reading a "folio romance" and surrounded by such romance trappings as a mandolin, herself seems a romance heroine. Henry's role is less clear. When he is introduced rapt in "unutterable thought" (193), the seasoned reader recognizes his mourning attire, deep melancholy, and brooding as signs of either a Gothic villain or a romance hero. The story parodies such signs by making them unreadable, and by mocking both Henry's "romantic fit[s]" and his insensitivity to the "romantic adventure" (194) of the invisible girl.

The story then turns to the "horrors" (195) of Henry's "fate" and "unspeakable wretchedness," but Shelley again parodies these Gothic markers by telling his history in four paragraphs rather than the "good-sized volume" it deserves. The only child of the "violent and tyrannical" Sir Peter Vernon, Henry was raised with the orphan Rosina and grew to love her. Rosina believed herself to be Henry's "destined bride," until she was rudely awakened from this romance fiction by Sir Peter's sister, Mrs. Bainbridge. This Gothic villainess, "having succeeded in killing her husband and children" (196) with her "vile temper," first confined Rosina in the Vernon house and then imprisoned her in the Wales tower. Cowed by "the howling of Sir Peter and the snarling of his sister" (197), Rosina ran away and was presumed dead; Henry commenced his wanderings, "haunted" (198) by the belief that his father "was guilty of so dark a crime."

At this promising Gothic point, the story shifts into a fairy-tale register. Henry finds the tiniest slipper "[s]ince Cinderella" (199); "as plain as shoe could speak," it tells the reader that the invisible girl in the tower is Rosina. Henry, however, is not a good reader, and it is some time before

he recognizes Rosina. The story's final paragraphs alternate between Gothic and fairy-tale; although the conclusion recurs to the "cruel persecutions" (201) Rosina suffered from Sir Peter and Mrs. Bainbridge, it also magically disposes of the latter by stating that she was never seen again. In its alternating appeal to and satire of fictional conventions, this story resembles Jane Austen's anti-Gothic novel *Northanger Abbey* (1818), which parodied Gothic conventions but also presented a realistically tyrannical father. Insofar as "The Invisible Girl" takes seriously Sir Peter's similar tyranny to Rosina, it belongs with Shelley's Jacobin historical stories; insofar as it mocks Gothic and romance conventions, it stands with "The Bride of Modern Italy" as one of her few comic stories.

Valperga (1823)

Mary Shelley researched and wrote *Valperga,* her first historical novel, from March 1817 to August 1821. In September Percy Shelley tried to interest his own publisher in the novel, but without success. To ease her father's financial difficulties, Mary Shelley gave him the novel's copyright to sell "to [his] best advantage" (*MWSL,* 1:237). Godwin held the novel for a year, and by the time it was published in February 1823, he had changed the original title and "taken serious liberties" with the rest of the book (quoted in *MWSL,* 1:323), mainly by cutting the "long detail of battles & campaigning" in Volume III.

The publication history of *Valperga* suggests how economics affected Mary Shelley's writing and the marketing of her work. Ceding the novel's profits to Godwin was only one instance of her lifelong need to be writing "any thing that was a certain gain" (*MWSL,* 2:125). In order to capitalize on *Frankenstein*'s popularity, *Valperga* and much of her subsequent fiction were advertised as "by the author of *Frankenstein,*" but this strategy had drawbacks. Worried that some readers might be "prejudiced" if *Valperga* were marketed as "by the author of Frankenstein," Percy Shelley assured his publisher that this novel contained no "peculiar theories in politics or religion" (*PBSL,* 2:312, 355). Contemporary reviews of *Valperga* suggest that these fears were well founded; *Blackwood's,* for instance, objected to the author's "very mischievous" politics (284). Another difficulty was the status of historical fiction. Mary Shelley agreed with a friend's opinion that, while the novel's original title, *Castruccio, Prince of Lucca,* was a "dignified" indication of the historical "nature of the work," its new subtitle, *Life and Adventures,* suggested such popular tales as "Jack the Giants Killer or Mother Hubbard"

(quoted in *MWSL*, 2:332). In fact, however, the full title—*Valperga; or, the Life and Adventures of Castruccio, Prince of Lucca*—appeals to the two reading publics for historical fiction: to "the articulate classes" (Ferris, 22) as a sober work of history, to the newer and more various readership as a wondrous romance.

Valperga's several relations to history first appear in its Preface. Here Shelley acknowledges her debts to such historical sources as Machiavelli's "romance" of Castruccio's life and the record of his "real adventures"[26] in Sismondi's *History of the Italian Republics* (1809–18). But *romance* and *adventures* suggest a fictional admixture to history, and in another departure from fact, Shelley changes the dates of Castruccio's life. Furthermore, the novel as a whole uses history to explore a thematic of recurring interest in Shelley's fiction, the ways that public history infiltrates private life. That infiltration also reveals conflicts between masculine history and feminine domesticity, and her novel uses thematics of education and imagination to examine those conflicts.

The first pages of the novel foreground the theme of public history infiltrating private life. Late-thirteenth-century Tuscany has been "almost destroyed" (1:2) by "domestic faction" and civil war between Guelphs and Ghibellines. Castruccio's parents Ruggiero and Danora were among the Ghibellines expelled from the Tuscan town of Lucca in 1301, and Shelley emphasizes the father's fears for his family. But when Ruggiero complains that these fears make him "a very woman" (1:7), this feminizing of domestic affection signals the coming conflicts between it and masculine public history.

Further signals appear when the novel takes up the thematics of education and imagination. Debarred from an "active life" (1:13) in politics, Ruggiero turns to educating his son; despite "the fears of his anxious wife," he encourages the boy's adventurous spirit. Through the sufferings of his parents and their fellow exiles, Castruccio also learns the "rage and desire of vengeance" (1:11) that generate adult "party spirit." The second site of Castruccio's education is Valperga, the castle of the Adimaris; here he learns "chivalric accomplishments" (1:30), so that his "imagination" (1:42) pictures a future of love, "glory and success." This masculine training is contrasted with the education of his fellow pupil, Euthanasia Adimari. Her education is inflected by the fact that neither of her parents is conventionally gendered: the aged and blind Antonio dei Adimari has retired from military and civil service to a life of scholarship; his wife takes the active public role and is immersed in party politics. Educated by her father, Euthanasia learns not to be like her mother

and instead to eschew "the spirit of party" (1:29); he also teaches her to share his hopes of "freedom for Italy," "revived learning," and "peace for all the world." These principles are later favorably contrasted with Castruccio's, but they also foster Euthanasia's "ardent imagination" and "wild dreams" (1:30); this problematic of imagination will recur in Castruccio and become acute in the character of Beatrice.

After he and Euthanasia vow eternal friendship, Castruccio leaves Valperga to stay with his father's exiled friend Francesco de Guinigi. This stage of his education exposes him to a "simple but sublime morality" (1:47) reminiscent of physiocracy, the French Enlightenment philosophy whose "leading assumption" was the moral and political superiority of agriculture to other occupations.[27] Guinigi values "the harmless peasants who cultivate the earth" (1:48), for his "taste and imagination" (1:48) dignify occupations that "the vulgar would term ignoble." In his view, kings are merely "the privileged murderers of the earth" (1:49); their knights "deluge the fields with blood" (1:48); local rulers are "full of party spirit" (1:65) and a desire to enrich themselves and their city "in opposition to the rest of the world." But Castruccio rejects Guinigi's education in "love of peace" (1:51) and "rural pleasures," and he continues to hanker for "fame" (1:53) in "a more glorious world" (1:57).

Castruccio then meets three men whose teachings draw him further away from the principles of Guinigi and Euthanasia. The first is Alberto Scoto, a historical Guelph leader who sows in Castruccio the "seeds of craft" and "hypocrisy" (1:101, 95); he also counters Guinigi's lessons and Euthanasia's example by characterizing the common people as "more fickle and deceitful than the famed faithlessness of woman" (1:96). Even more cynical is Benedetto Pepi; his maxims—for example, that "there . . . must be weakness in the people to create power in the prince" (1:117)—seem adapted from Machiavelli's *The Prince* (1513). In contrast to Guinigi's physiocracy, Pepi hopes to see "the rich rule, and the vulgar sink to their right station as slaves of the soil" (1:124); and in contrast to Euthanasia's hopes for freedom, Pepi prefers the "healthy tree" (1:127) of tyranny. From his third tutor, the historical Duke of Milan Galeazzo Visconti, Castruccio learns "artful policy and unprincipled motives" (1:161). Through his early education, as through Victor Frankenstein's, Shelley shows the importance of exposing children to lofty principles, but she also shows that those principles may not take. By 1314 Castruccio's "ruling feeling" is an "ambition for power, conquest, and renown" that makes treachery and cruelty seem "venial faults"; on this principle he betrays his native town of Lucca to the Pisan

tyrant Ugoccione. Less sanguine about education than Rousseau's *Emile* (1762) or the first edition of Godwin's *Political Justice* (1793), Mary Shelley's history instead suggests the limits of human perfectibility.

At this point the chapter of "Euthanasia's Narrative" details her personal and political education during the previous decade. Her father taught her "to fathom [her] sensations, and discipline [her] mind" (1:194); where she had believed that she could "follow [the] dictates" (1:198) of the heart, she learned to "constrain" her will and to be ruled by judgment rather than passion. By reading Dante she developed an enthusiasm for the freedom that produced his genius and that may awaken "the fallen hopes of the world" (1:197–98). Her political ideal is a republic in which citizens do not obey "the mere word of command" (1:188) but rather acquire "energy and virtue" as they "discuss and regulate their own interests." Left "independent and powerful" (1:169) after her parents' death, as Countess of Valperga she devotes herself to "doing good" (1:170). Euthanasia thus seems to have tempered the example of her mother—a "violent" Guelph (1:199) immersed in "all the pygmy acts of a petty state" (1:201)—with her father's domestic scholarship. But the efficacy of such an education is called into question when Castruccio returns, for Euthanasia not only falls in love but "made a god of him" (1:188). She is not represented as a dupe of his craft; rather her love story again suggests that an education in principles does not guarantee successful deployment of them.

Because "sexuality and politics are fused" in the Euthanasia-Castruccio plot, her attraction to him also dramatizes the "magnetism of despotism."[28] When Castruccio leads the tyrannical Ugoccione's army against the Florentine republic, Euthanasia's love for him struggles with her "duty" to resist an "enemy of Florence" (1:213–14). Later Castruccio repudiates Ugoccione, becomes consul of Lucca, and promises Euthanasia: "You shall direct me" (1:239). Seduced into believing that he will ally and protect Lucca and Florence, she hopes to join her territory with those republics so as to liberate her people from the "power to which [she] ought not to have a pretension" (1:247). But Euthanasia occasionally recognizes Castruccio's "craft" (1:244) and "cruelty," and the personal-political dissonance between them is highlighted by the arrival of Benedetto Pepi at the end of Volume I.

Volume II traces the advance of Castruccio's political and sexual tyranny. Rejoining Galeazzo Visconti, he heeds this mentor's advice to give up the "old-fashioned name of consul" (2:12) and "make yourself a prince," and he opens a campaign to "master" Florence (2:13) for the

Ghibellines. Plotting toward this end with the Ghibelline Bishop of Ferrara, he meets the Bishop's ward Beatrice. Like Euthanasia, Beatrice is more than a love interest; she too represents a political alternative to Castruccio, and she becomes a second victim to his "magnetism of despotism."

Beatrice is the daughter of Wilhelmina of Bohemia, who believed herself to be the Holy Ghost incarnated "for the salvation of the female sex" (2:26). Shelley added this phrase to her source for the historical Wilhelmina,[29] and her description of Beatrice as a *donna estatica* includes a footnote that such "inspired women" still exist in modern Italy (2:43). By placing Beatrice in this tradition of inspired women, the author creates a feminine history, an alternative to the novel's masculine history of tyranny and warfare. When Beatrice preaches against the Ferrarans' "want of fervour in the just cause" (2:45), her politics of spirituality critiques the craft and tyranny of such as Castruccio. Beatrice further serves as a "critique of religious orthodoxies";[30] for her preaching she is arrested by Inquisitors, who represent tyrannical priestcraft. In all these ways Shelley uses a feminine sensibility as Radcliffe did in her Gothics, to critique an "antagonistic realm of patriarchal history" (Duncan, 13).

Yet the belief in divine inspiration that is the source of Beatrice's power is also her downfall. At her arrest she demands to prove her innocence by the Judgment of God (walking barefoot over hot ploughshares); surviving this trial confirms her belief in her powers, and she prophecies a Ghibelline victory. But her success in the Judgment of God resulted from a Ghibelline plot endorsed by Castruccio's co-conspirator, the Bishop of Ferrara; thus Beatrice becomes "a pawn in the great game" (Lew, 172) of masculine Italian politics. Moreover, when she has an affair with Castruccio in the belief that her sexual desire is divinely "inspired" (*Valperga*, 2:86), she becomes "the dupe of her undisciplined thoughts" (2:88). Having inherited her mother's "ardent imagination" (2:86), she indulges it in passion when she ought rather to have "bound [it] with fetters" and "curbed and crushed [it] by every effort of reason" (2:87).

This highly colored denunciation may seem surprising, since Mary too surrendered herself to passion when she eloped with Percy Shelley. Through Beatrice's story, Mary may be "review[ing] her own past" and recognizing her complicity in Percy's abandonment of his wife (Lew, 173). Her deep distrust of Beatrice's imagination is also consistent with the didactic concern to control the passions that recurs throughout her fiction. But her critique is not limited to feminine sexual imagination.

For many male Romantics, the poetic imagination was a mode of "masculine empowerment" through "aggressive desire and conquest."[31] Castruccio's "imagination" of love, "glory and success" (*Valperga*, 1:42) is a case in point; his political conquest of Florence is parallel to his sexual conquest of Beatrice, and like Raymond in *The Last Man,* he carelessly abandons a woman to pursue other ambitions. Like Raymond's victim Evadne, Beatrice then goes mad; Castruccio's perfidy "tore away the veil" from "all nature" (2:88) and revealed "life as it was—naked and appalling." Of course this view of the world is no less distorted than her earlier visions, but it is much more destructive. Thus if Beatrice is damaged by her own too-creative imagination, also at fault is Castruccio's conquering imagination.

Castruccio's subsequent depredations against the Tuscan republics create a similar disillusion in Euthanasia, but unlike Beatrice she is able to recover. For Beatrice, Castruccio had "torn the veil" from "all nature"; for Euthanasia, however, he has merely "unveiled" his own "falseness" (2:154), and because she remains "a child of nature" (2:181), she is consoled by its beauties. "The power of virtue in a well formed human heart" (2:157) also helps "arouse" her "pride" against her love. Despite the drawbacks of Euthanasia's education, then, it gives her resources for a struggle against passion. Beatrice lacks these resources, and she also lacks the advantages of Euthanasia's class position—power, independence, and a base for her alternative politics.

That base is the castle of Valperga, and Shelley now adapts the castle, Gothic symbol of women's victimization, into a symbol of the feminine sensibility that the Gothic opposes to masculine power. Where the enclosure of the Gothic castle enabled violence against women, Valperga "performs the opposite function":[32] it is a maternal legacy of political liberty and public virtue. When Euthanasia inherited the castle "and the power annexed to it" (*Valperga*, 2:244) from her mother, she determined to "exercise and preserve" that power for the good of her people, and this sense of "duty [and] benevolence" (2:193) now strengthens her political opposition to Castruccio. After having himself declared prince of Lucca, he attempts to strip Euthanasia of Valperga's "independence" within his territory (2:218); vowing not to abandon her people to "a usurper and a tyrant" (2:224), Euthanasia barricades herself within the castle.

But when Castruccio declares war on her, the feminine inheritance and principles represented by Valperga are undermined by masculine admixtures. Arriving at the castle with troops, Euthanasia's guardian

Bondelmonti informs her that battle is "not fitting work for you" (2:256). When he recognizes in Euthanasia her father's "courage" and "admirable fortitude," this paternal legacy begins to displace the maternal inheritance of Valperga. First quailing at the sight of her wounded defenders, she cries "spirit of my father, aid me" and nurses them "like an angel" (2:265). Where she earlier asserted her power to protect her people, now her soldiers die "voluntary sacrifices" to protect her (2:278). Most significantly, Valperga becomes a conventional Gothic castle when Castruccio's forces invade it—adding insult to injury, he enters Valperga by a "secret path" (2:230) he recalls from their courtship. This act of personal-political betrayal condemns the masculine will to conquest, but it also suggests a flaw in Euthanasia's politics. By retaining the power over Valperga's people to which she admits she had no right, as a ruler Euthanasia is Castruccio's double; the power represented by her castle is thus vulnerable to a similar but stronger power.

Volume III details the consequences of her defeat. To punish Castruccio for the ruin of Valperga, Euthanasia's servant Bindo seeks out the witch Mandragola, whose "evil nature" (3:8) and "love of power" make her a feminine version of Castruccio; she assures Bindo that she "rule[s] the spirits" and can help them destroy Castruccio (3:3). Beatrice reappears, a "fallen prophetess" (3:27); imprisoned for heresy, she asks Euthanasia to intercede for her with Castruccio. He arranges her release and, admitting that he "destroyed" her (3:37), asks Euthanasia to "repair [his] work" (3:37). The need for "repair" is evident in Beatrice's ravings about "the eternal and victorious influence of evil . . . eating into us and destroying us" (3:44). Shelley worried that this "Anathema" would shock the "Literary Gazettes" (*MWSL*, 1:336), and one reviewer did regret that "any English Lady should be capable" of speeches that he "dare not transcribe" (*Blackwood's*, 290–91). To a twentieth-century reader, Beatrice's anathema is shocking not as heresy but as a sign of Castruccio's destructive effect on her. The narrative of her recent history further evidences her victimization by the masculine world he represents. Learning from the Bishop that her Judgment of God was fraudulent, Beatrice became "possessed by a spirit of martyrdom" and "a desire to mortify and punish" herself (*Valperga*, 3:73). Again a victim of priestcraft, she embarked on a penitential pilgrimage. Held captive for three years in what the novel hints was a brothel, she was tortured and went mad. After escaping Beatrice met a gentle old man who converted her to the Paterin heresy, which holds that a Good God created and rules the invisible universe while an Evil God created and rules the visible world. When this man was mar-

tyred, the "half-maddened" Beatrice (3:96), further convinced of the truth of his creed, "cursed the creation and its cruel laws." This Gothic narrative functions to reveal the masculine world as "an alien dimension of power and terror" for the heroine (Duncan, 13).

Beatrice's story then returns to the thematic of imagination. Euthanasia exercises her imagination by creating an allegory to educate Beatrice in "the lessons of true religion" (3:54) and to teach her how to "regulate" the "powers" of her mind (3:101), including her imagination. Euthanasia's allegory locates imagination in the same "inner cave" as poetry and heroism; because this "dangerous" cave also houses "the madman," imagination can be an "evil pilot" (3:135), but only to those who have no "command" over themselves (3:118). The remainder of Beatrice's story reinforces this lesson. Her willingness to "risk her soul" (3:135) for "a moment's power over Castruccio" makes her easy prey for Mandragola's offer of that power. Although she seeks Euthanasia's help against the "dreadful and maniac thoughts" (3:146) instilled by Mandragola, Euthanasia dismisses them as merely "heated imagination" (3:146); given henbane by the witch, Beatrice goes mad and dies. Euthanasia's mistake suggests a failure of the sympathy or fellow feeling that was a prime moral function of the Romantic imagination. But because the destruction of Euthanasia's imaginative sympathy is due to Castruccio, Beatrice's death becomes another item in the account against him. Although Mandragola is executed for witchcraft, her powers seem rather the external sign of Castruccio's evil.

The novel then turns to the relationship between Castruccio's evil and Euthanasia's enthusiasm. Deprived of her base of opposition at Valperga, Euthanasia now attempts to "heal the wounds" that Castruccio inflicts (3:178). When his army pillages the peasants, for instance, she "follow[s], like an angel, in his track" so as "to atone for [his] crimes" (3:179). When Bondelmonti proposes a plot against Castruccio, she initially resists but eventually joins it, partly because she agrees that Castruccio uses his power "like a fiend" (3:192), but also because she wants "to restore her affections to him" (3:196) once adversity makes him "gentle and humane." Thus Euthanasia "cheat[s] herself" by believing in "the purity of her intentions" and daydreaming about saving Castruccio from himself (3:206, 203). Trusting to "the sense of right which nature has implanted in [her] own heart" (3:201), she forgets her father's lesson against "following [the] dictates" of her heart (1:196).

But the remainder of Euthanasia's story complicates any simple judgment of her actions and motives. The reader inclined to condemn

Euthanasia is warned off by the extremely harsh judgment passed on her by Castruccio's aide, Vanni Mordecastelli. Because Vanni had idealized Euthanasia as "too wise and too holy" (3:222) for "midnight plots," the "angel face" (3:227) which had seemed the sign of "a meek and forbearing woman's love" now marks her as "like the rest of them, well looking outside, but worms and corruption within." Shelley then contrasts this "infallibility men assume" with Castruccio's continued faith in Euthanasia as "the saint of my life" (3:229, 234). And her own verdict on Euthanasia is typically double-voiced. On the one hand, Euthanasia's error "was one of judgment" only (3:236); on the other hand, she says, "why should I call it error" to unseat "a cruel tyrant" and to "wish to preserve him" from the "misery" his crimes would cause him?

Castruccio's faith in Euthanasia and its effect on her further complicate the novel's final judgments of both characters. When Castruccio tries to persuade her to accept a pardon, she replies that she will do so only if he also releases her co-conspirators. He then weeps, and because a man's tears express a "depth of passion" (3:250) that cannot be feigned, the reader is invited to believe that even the evil Castruccio retains a spark of goodness. But manly tears also create an answering "excess of tenderness" in the woman who causes them, and Euthanasia accepts a pardon for herself alone. This yielding is excused as not only womanly but almost unconscious, and Euthanasia is later apotheosized when the ship carrying her from Italy sinks and she is drowned; it is as if "the eternal spirit of the universe" (3:255) rescues her from an "earthly dross" (3:184) that would otherwise contaminate her.

The novel partially recuperates Castruccio as well. In addition to hinting his grief over Euthanasia's death, the novel reminds us that it was Galeazzo's "lessons" (3:267) which deprived Castruccio of "peace, sympathy and happiness." And he has *Valperga*'s last words; the concluding "moral" (3:269) is the inscription on his tomb. Beginning with Castruccio's belief that "I live and will live in the fame of the splendid deeds of the Italian militia," the inscription continues "I suffered, I sinned, I wept." Thus, Castruccio insists on his military exploits, yet he acknowledges the accompanying faults and offers an apology of sorts for them. As a Jacobin novel with Gothic elements, *Valperga* condemns a political tyranny that damages women as well as the state; as a realistic novel, it teaches control of the passions. Finally, as a historical fiction, it offers a judgment of Castruccio that brings together all those elements by suggesting that he suffered for his ambitious passions and his sins against the domestic affections.

Oriental Tales

Mary Shelley's two Oriental tales, "The Evil Eye" (1830) and "Euphrasia: A Tale of Greece" (1839), form a subset of her historical fiction. Both stories evince her interest in Greece, especially in the Greek revolution of 1821–32. To understand her views of Greece and its history, it is important to place them in the context of the literary-political ideology of Orientalism.

Orientalism is a system of representations that constructs "the Orient" or "the East" as an "imaginary geography," an Other in binary opposition to a European "West."[33] In eighteenth- and nineteenth-century Britain, the literary construction of that Other was accomplished by the Oriental tale; this genre was thus a crucial component of the imperial politics that transformed Asiatic cultures into European colonies. The fad for translations of Persian poetry in England during the 1780s, for example, is "clearly linked" to the India Act of 1784,[24] which established a policy of governing India "through Indian languages and Indian institutions"[35] and required administrators to have a knowledge of Persian, the official language of correspondence with the Mughal empire. By the 1820s, British imperial policy had shifted from an economic plundering of colonies to a concern with developing them as sources of raw materials and markets for domestic goods. Corollary to this economic shift was an ideology of Britain's civilizing mission to an Orient subjected to despots and corrupted by superstition. In imperial and literary texts, "the Orient" was constructed as Albania, Greece, and Turkey—areas of the collapsing Ottoman Turkish empire that seemed in particular need of civilizing.

Much of this civilizing impulse focused on Greece, as both the "'lost source' of European civilization" (Leask, 23) and the site of a revolution in the 1820s against Turkish despotism. Mary Shelley's friend Byron embodied both aspects of this impulse, by writing a series of *Eastern Tales* (1813–16) and by joining the Greek revolution in 1823. Shelley was also friendly with Edward Trelawny, who accompanied Byron to Greece, and with Prince Alexander Mavrocordato, one of a community of exiled Greek aristocrats in Pisa. At the outbreak of the revolution in 1821 she shared his joy that "Greece has declared its freedom!" (*MWSL*, 1:186), and with heavy irony she characterized England as "so moral & religious . . . that we help Turks & Tyrants against Xtians & the Would-be-free" (*MWSL*, 1:189). This sincere yet Orientalist excitement over revolutionary Greece inspired both of Shelley's Oriental tales, and "Euphrasia" also explores the civilizing function of Englishwomen.

"The Evil Eye" (1830)

Published in *The Keepsake,* "The Evil Eye" makes literary capital of Mary Shelley's known friendship with Byron and of her own expertise in Greek customs and politics. She also tailored her story to the *Keepsake*'s women readers by placing its exotic elements in a framework of wifely and maternal devotion.

The story's opening paragraphs alternate between Orientalist exotica and familiar domestic frameworks. The epigraph is from Byron's *Childe Harold's Pilgrimage,* and the story twice references Byron; these allusions connect Shelley's story with his tales in the Orientalist tradition. Her first paragraph includes such exotic words as *pashalik* and *pobratimo;*[36] as in other Oriental tales (Leask, 20), these details testify to the writer's knowledge of Eastern customs. Set in a romantic and picturesque Greece of "savage mountaineers and despotic Turk[s]," the story presents its protagonist Dmitri as savage yet civilizable. The young Dmitri had "a gentler disposition and more refined taste" than his fellow Albanians. These traits were fostered by his learning in "European arts" (*Tales,* 101) and by his years on Scio, the "most civilized" Greek island; while most Albanians are "despisers of women," Dmitri learned a "more chivalrous rule" and "better creed" on Scio. In a familiar domesticating scenario, marriage to his Sciote wife Helena rendered Dmitri a "tamed barbarian." When Helena was murdered and their daughter abducted by a tribe of Mainotes, however, Dmitri reverted to a "savage" state; now "ferocious and hard-hearted," he delights in casting spells with his Evil Eye.

Dmitri is enlisted by a friend, Katusthius Ziani, to help Ziani reclaim his paternal inheritance from his brother Cyril. The exotic Dmitri—with his "savage eyes" (103), "barbaric grace," "ferocity and bandit pride"— invades Cyril's "rural abode" and uses the Evil Eye to terrify Cyril's "lovely wife" (104), Zella, and later to abduct his "blooming" son, Constans. With characteristic irony Shelley shows Cyril and Zella "congratulat[ing] themselves on their tranquil life and peaceful happiness" (105) at the very moment that Dmitri is abducting their son.

The remainder of the tale demonstrates the civilizing effect of the domestic affections by shifting Dmitri between a savage and a parental register. The engraving and description of Zella create sympathy for the "bereft mother" (106) victimized by the savage Dmitri. Yet Dmitri develops maternal virtues as he guards the kidnapped Constans "with woman's care" (111). When Cyril and his father-in-law Camaraz appear and Camaraz demands his grandson, however, Dmitri abandons maternal care for paternal revenge. Because Camaraz is a Mainote and Main-

otes killed his wife, Dmitri vows to kill Constans: "the son of the accursed race shall be the victim of my just revenge" (114). Camaraz then cries that Zella is not his blood-daughter but rather a child he abducted from the island of Scio; she is, of course, Dmitri's lost daughter, and the tale concludes by reuniting Zella with her father, her husband, and her son. Saved by paternal affection from savage superstition, Dmitri now "cradle[s]" Constans (116) instead of threatening him with the Evil Eye. As this domestic reconciliation shows Dmitri conquering his savage passions and in effect civilizing himself, it also functions as a fantasy of imperialist ideology. Such a "fantasy of oriental peoples *colonizing themselves*" (Leask, 78) mystifies the imperial violence that imposes "European arts" on "savage mountaineers."

"Euphrasia: A Tale of Greece" (1839)

Like "The Evil Eye," "Euphrasia" was published in *The Keepsake,* and it too appeals to a feminine readership by juxtaposing exotic Oriental scenes with familiar domestic emotions. To dramatize the superiority of Western over Eastern mores, the story focuses on women's civilizing mission and plays on Orientalist representations of the Turkish harem.

"Euphrasia" begins with details familiar to British readers. "[A]ny one who was in Sussex" at Christmas "[t]wo years ago"[37] must remember the heavy snowfall that has marooned the story's travelers in their carriage. The setting then shifts to the Greek revolution, as the traveler Harry Valency tells a father and daughter about his experiences in Greece. The beginning of his narrative is both exotic and domestic; allusions to "the cause of Greece" (296) and "the usurping Turk" are juxtaposed with the familiar figure of a "restless" young man led by "a desire for adventure" to leave his widowed mother. Another appeal to maternal readers appears in his narrative when the wounded Harry weeps for his "poor mother" (299). A similar appeal informs the description of the Greek chief Constantine. Despite his Byronic brooding, Constantine is "gentle and kindly as a woman" (279); he takes a bullet meant for Harry and then nurses the wounded "English boy" (300) like "a mother tending her sick first-born." Almost Anglicized in this devotion to Harry, Constantine is further familiarized by a flashback to his education. He learned to revere Greece's "classic lore" (301) and heroic "martyrs," but also to look to "civilized" Europe and America for a politics that would bring "liberation" to Greece (302).

The flashback to Constantine's early life also introduces his sister, Euphrasia. Educated in classical Greek literature, Euphrasia uses it as an

ideal European sister would: to "cheer and watch over her brother, to
regulate his wilder and more untaught soul," and to inspire him "to dare
and do greatly for Greece." When he joined the revolution, her "angelic"
letters "teach him patience" (303) and "hope." Euphrasia also indicates
women's social mission as "fosterers" of "civilization and knowledge":

> [When she realized] the honor and happiness that a woman must derive
> from being held the friend of man, not his slave, she thanked God that
> she was a Greek and a Christian; . . . she looked forward eagerly to the
> day when Mahometanism should no longer contaminate her native land,
> and when her countrywomen should be awakened from ignorance and
> sloth . . . and learn that their proper vocation . . . was that of mothers of
> heros [sic] and teachers of sages. (303)

The "Oriental" Euphrasia is here assimilated to a European ideology of
women's civilizing mission.

The importance of this mission is further elaborated in the remainder
of Euphrasia's story. Her imprisonment in a Turkish harem, "the prey of
the oppressor" (303), is a standard of the Oriental tale; while such a
trope might titillate masculine readers, for *The Keepsake*'s woman audience it is meant to emphasize the opposition between Oriental despotism and feminine civilization. Constantine and his companions stormed
the Pasha's palace and found his sister among the "poor victims" (304)
of "the tyrant." Unlike those "frightened deer," Euphrasia stood "majes-
tic and fearless"; when she recognized her brother, however, she dropped
her dagger and clung to him. The accompanying engraving shows Constantine carrying her from the harem, "fearless" heroine turned damsel
in distress. In this posture she is hit by a Turkish bullet and fulfills her
mission by dying in "pious resignation" (306). At the end of his narrative Constantine too dies, but his sister's image "shed peace over the last
moment of life" (307).

This conclusion Europeanizes Euphrasia's feminine mission. Her
death might seem to show that Greek women's civilizing mission cannot succeed until Greece is, like Euphrasia, rescued from "the oppressor"; since Greece had been liberated by the date of Mary Shelley's story,
however, Euphrasia becomes a model for European women. Within the
story, Harry, moved by her fate, returns to his widowed mother; also
within the story, the young woman listener is taught her feminine functions by his narrative. Outside the story, *The Keepsake*'s women readers
are intended to learn their own civilizing mission toward the men who
will spread that mission throughout the British empire.

Perkin Warbeck (1830)

The Fortunes of Perkin Warbeck: A Romance was published by Colburn & Bentley in 1830. Like *Valperga's* title, this one is addressed to two audiences: the historical Perkin Warbeck would appeal to readers of history, while the "romance" would appeal to readers of fiction. Furthermore, where many contemporary historians rejected the fifteenth-century Perkin Warbeck's claim to be the true heir to the British throne, Shelley wrote her novel to support that claim. Thus *Perkin Warbeck* reveals an author sufficiently sure of her literary reputation and powers to challenge the genre of history.

Shelley's research for, and marketing of, the novel show the confidence of that challenge. She began work on *Perkin Warbeck* in 1828, with extensive reading in British history as well as the topography and manners of fifteenth-century Spain, Ireland, and Scotland. Against David Hume and other historians who considered Perkin an impostor and pretender, the novel's Preface adduces several fifteenth-century historical chronicles to support its contention that he was in fact King Edward IV's son, the Duke of York, and hence a legitimate claimant to the throne.[38] Although one of her letters termed the novel not "sober useful history" but her "usual trifling" (*MWSL*, 2:65), Shelley took her "trifling" seriously enough to poach on Walter Scott's fictional preserve of Scotland and to consult him about Scottish "antiquities" (*MWSL*, 2:78). She also marketed the novel seriously. She was careful to preempt objections to her politics, assuring one publisher that historical writing "affords no scope for *opinions*" (*MWSL*, 2:27) and that he would find nothing to object to "on that score." When her publisher proposed to distinguish *Perkin Warbeck* from a new history of Perkin by changing the novel's title, Shelley convinced him instead to market her fame as " 'The Author of Frankenstein' " (*MWSL*, 2:108).

Crucial to her novel's challenge to history is her use of the romance genre. Admitting her initial view that Perkin was "a subject for historical detail" (*Warbeck*, 1:v), the Preface then argues that no narrative "confined" to historical fact could do justice to the "romance" of his life. Her novel thus counters an "official, inscribed plot of history" (Ferris, 205) with the genre of romance. More significant than the element of marvellous events, however, is the romance's historical record of "ancestral culture" (Duncan, 4). *Perkin Warbeck* interrogates the official history of a "United Kingdom"—of an emerging nation-state peacefully assimilating Irish and Scottish clan cultures—by recording the incessant civil

wars and "micro-colonizations" of fifteenth-century Britain (Leask, 86). Furthermore, like the Jacobin novel, this romance calls into question the chivalric ideals which underpin that official history. In the 1820s chivalry was being represented as "a living code, still relevant to modern life."[39] During these years when the middle classes were gaining commercial and political prominence, a chivalric code of honor and *noblesse oblige* served to claim "continuing privilege and power" for the aristocracy.[40] In 1812, for instance, when Lord Ellenborough sentenced two tradesmen for dueling, he criticized their "spurious chivalry of the compting house and the counter" (quoted in Simpson, 104). While such a statement reserves true chivalry for the ruling classes, it is precisely that ideology of aristocratic chivalry that Mary Shelley's romance interrogates.

Perkin Warbeck begins in 1485, but understanding how the novel problematizes history requires some knowledge of events prior to that year. Edward IV, king of England from 1461 to 1483, may have contracted a secret marriage and certainly had numerous affairs; these irregularities fueled contemporary charges that his acknowledged marriage was bigamous and his children illegitimate. These children, whose fates are central to the novel, were Edward V; Richard, Duke of York; and Princess Elizabeth of York. After the death of Edward IV, his brother Richard III became king; to legitimate his claim to the throne, Richard declared two of his brothers—including Edward IV—and those brothers' children illegitimate. Because his own surviving son, Edmund Plantagenet, was in fact illegitimate, Richard then named a nephew, the earl of Warwick, as his successor; later fearing that Warwick might claim precedence, the king imprisoned him in the Tower of London. Many historians believe that Richard III also murdered his nephews, Edward V and the young Richard, Duke of York—the "princes in the tower." Shelley's novel constructs an alternative history: Edward V died of natural causes, Prince Richard is alive in protected seclusion, and King Richard spread the rumor of his death to keep his own enemies from uniting behind the boy's legitimate claim to the throne.

Perkin Warbeck opens in 1485 after the battle of Bosworth, which ended the War of the Roses between the houses of York and Lancaster. With the death of the Yorkist King Richard III and the accession of the Lancastrian Henry VII, peace seems restored. But "civil dissension" (*Warbeck*, 1:1) reappears as Edmund Plantagenet, the dead Richard's illegitimate son, joins the Yorkists, who are planning an "insurrection"

(1:43) to "discrown the usurping Henry" (1:18) and enthrone Prince Richard, duke of York.

Mary Shelley figures the Yorkist claim as a familial problematic both of legitimate dynastic succession and of children trapped in the struggle for succession. The issue of dynastic succession hinges on paternity, on the king's lawful marriage and legitimate offspring; Edward IV's sexual escapades thus resulted in the civil wars devastating Britain. Also victimized by these struggles for succession are the Queen Dowager Elizabeth's two surviving children, Elizabeth of York and Richard, Duke of York. Early in the novel, Shelley accuses the dowager of trying to restore her own "lost station" (1:34) by marrying Princess Elizabeth to King Henry VII. The dowager is thus responsible for Elizabeth's subsequent misery; Henry marries her only to secure his throne, and he treats her with "systematized and cold-hearted tyranny" (1:118).

Richard represents a more complicated set of familial issues, which is worked out in several stages. The first stage, establishing Richard's royal lineage, hinges on the Queen Dowager. Initially, Shelley represents the dowager as careless of her son. By marrying Elizabeth to King Henry, she legitimated his claim to the throne; "giving away [Richard's] inheritance" (1:34) in this way, she "deprived her son of his rights, and afterwards of his life." Richard is represented as the good son to an unworthy parent when he vows to claim his rights and thus "restore [his] mother's honour" (1:47) from the imputation that her marriage to his father was bigamous. The dowager is then made worthy of him when she succumbs to "[m]aternal tenderness" (1:80) and acknowledges Richard as her son. Here, Shelley proves Richard's parentage not by paternal succession but by maternal acknowledgment, and the dowager's change of heart in turn shows her to be a good mother.

To further legitimate Richard, Shelley rewrites David Hume's history of Perkin Warbeck. She first disposes of Hume's claim that Perkin was perhaps an illegitimate son of Edward IV but certainly not the rightful duke of York.[41] To protect Richard, she explains, his supporters disguised his paternal lineage, by arranging for him to take the identity of a dead child, Perkin Warbeck, and to be raised by the boy's aunt, Madeline de Faro. Shelley then adds to Hume a meeting between the Queen Dowager and Richard which continues their mutual legitimation. The dowager proves both her motherly care and Richard's maternal lineage by committing "her beloved child" to Madeline's protection (*Warbeck*, 1:106); she also endorses Richard's pursuit of the throne by telling him, "[n]ever forget that you are a King's son" (1:105). Another addition to

Hume is a scene at the Queen Dowager's deathbed, in which the mother's final thoughts are of her son (1:324). In all these ways, Shelley creates a motherly queen whose care for her son stands in sharp contrast to kings and fathers who produce and then neglect bastard children.

Shelley will later interrogate the ideals of chivalry; initially, however, she uses them to further legitimate Richard's claim to the throne. Even though the first assertion of that claim creates civil war—an insurrection in Ireland which ends in "slaughter and captivity" (1:137)—the reader is encouraged to admire one fallen Yorkist's chivalry, because he feels "responsible for the lives of all" (1:136) and is "sickened at the idea of battle and bloodshed." Shelley admits that such knights' "chief happiness" (1:140) lay in a glory "acquired by inflicting misery on others"; yet such chivalric combat created their "high virtues and exalted deeds." Most importantly, an "unselfish" (1:141) braving of danger and death marks chivalry as specifically masculine; facing death not only hones "the spirit of manhood," it is a "school" (1:142) in the "heroic friendship" with which men defend each other. Finally, "in those times" man was "closer linked to nature," which "exalted his imagination, and elevated his enthusiasm." The imagination and enthusiasm that were so dangerous for *Valperga*'s women here ennoble the manly creed of chivalry.

Richard is early associated with this manly chivalry. He longs for the "danger and glory" absent from his life as Perkin Warbeck (1:159); if he remains "[m]ewed up here with women," he frets, "I shall play the girl at the sight of blood." But an incident then suggests that chivalry may feminize its adherents. King Henry's spy, Frion, recognizes Richard and tricks the boy into accompanying him to the castle where he is then imprisoned like a Gothic heroine. Feminized vulnerability is also evident in his rescue; the handsome young Sir Robert Clifford smuggles him out of the castle disguised as a girl, and a loutish stable-boy leers at the "gentle dame" (1:192). Richard is most like a Gothic heroine in being endangered by his own feelings, the "benevolence and sweetness" (1:180) that put him at risk from his enemies. But these qualities also show his fitness to be king: benevolence is chivalric. At this point, then, the novel's view of chivalry remains ambivalent.

In the chapters about the war in Spain between Christians and Moors, chivalry is again both lauded and critiqued. One exemplar of chivalry is Hernán De Faro, Madeline's husband. He has a "fiery spirit" (1:205) but also a "manly heart" (1:209); he is "a tower of a man" (1:196) but also a "refuge" for "the timid and endangered." He is often

compared to Columbus in his desire to be among the "pioneers who opened new paths across the unexplored West" (2:178). As this language suggests, the voyages of Columbus "inaugurated the age of European imperialism" (Leask, 27), and in *Frankenstein* Shelley noted the consequent "hapless fate of [America's] original inhabitants" (Smith, 105); here, however, the explorer De Faro is meant to be admired. He takes to the sea, "where man destroys not his brother" (*Warbeck*, 1:210), because as both a Moor and a Catholic he abhors the Christian "ravages" against the Moors in Spain. In contrast are Edmund Plantagenet and Richard, who are both fighting on the Christian side. Edmund welcomes the war as a "knightly exercise in the land of chivalry"; like the other Christian knights, he and Richard "adorned [war] by their virtues" (1:211). When Edmund is wounded, however, Richard abandons "glorious" combat (1:214) to nurse "his best and dearest friend." In this complicated analysis of chivalry, war can be slaughter and/or a "knightly exercise," and Richard can be a warrior and/or an embodiment of the "heroic friendship" that exalts chivalry.

At this point, Shelley expands and then contracts an ideal of chivalry through the several functions of Richard's childhood companion, Monina de Faro. After Richard is wounded in a secret chivalric duel, Monina nurses him as he had nursed Edmund; thus she represents a feminine version of heroic friendship. When he characterizes her as "destined" to "save" him and his partisans, this ideal becomes "the master-impulse of her fervent and devoted spirit" (1:238–39). Devotion to Richard's cause makes Monina an exemplar of feminine chivalry.

During the Spanish war, however, she and her mother Madeline function as feminine victims. Madeline dies attempting to save her daughter from "impending slavery" (1:220) in, one assumes, a Moorish harem; Richard then frees the "fainting" Monina (1:219) from two "fierce" Moors, and all the "Christian hero[es]" (1:217) proceed to "avenge their desolated hearths" (1:218) with "rage" and "fury." As helpless victims, women here require, and thus excuse, the excesses of manly chivalric war; in the words of the novel, "where women looked on the near face of war, even the timid [knights] were inspired to bear arms" (1:223). From an expanded ideal that included a heroic Monina, chivalry is now contracted to a homosocial bond between men. In this male-dominant European culture, chivalric protection of women becomes one of the "structures for maintaining and transmitting patriarchal power."[42] It is also a structure for maintaining Christian power over the Moors described in Orientalist terms as ravagers of women. Again, chivalry is

an ambiguous ideal: a manly rescue of Christian women from dastardly
Moors, and a "heroic frenzy" (*Warbeck*, 1:224) of "death and misery"
(1:220).

The next section of Volume I returns to the familial problematic of
civil war. Driven to "madness" (1:249) by the deaths of three sons in
the War of the Roses, Meilar Trangmar becomes a "scarcely human
tool" (1:250) in King Henry's plot against Richard's life. Meilar invei-
gles Richard onto his ship but is won over by the Prince's "paternal
love" (1:261) for the crew, his "natural subjects;" here the contrast
with Henry's exploitation of Meilar marks Richard as the fitter sover-
eign. But this royal paternalism then creates two small-scale civil
wars. In his belief that "I reign here" (1:262), Richard inadvertently
insults Meilar; the man retaliates, and Richard must kill him. When
he then reveals that he is Edward IV's son, the "reckless and ignorant"
crew (1:271) offer to mutiny against the ship's Lancastrian captain.
Richard again shows his paternal care and his fitness for rule by refusing to "make lawless acts the stepping-stones to my throne" (1:272).
By this point, however, simply asserting his right to the throne seems
to cause civil war.

As Richard begins an Irish campaign against King Henry, the introduction of Ireland shifts the civil war thematic into a different register.
The 1800 Act of Union had incorporated Ireland into the United Kingdom, and the 1829 Catholic Emancipation Act had given Irish, as well
as English, Catholics some civil rights long denied them. This section of
the novel, however, is set in 1492, when Ireland was far from subdued
to England; thus it reflects on the nineteenth-century ideology of a
peacefully assimilated United Kingdom. When Richard inserts the
question of his right into an Ireland of "warlike" Irish chiefs (1:274),
"degenerate" English lords (1:279), and "internal struggles for power"
(1:275), his cause simply inflames the chiefs' "natural hatred" of the
English (1:291). Eventually Richard abandons his plan to invade England with his Irish partisans, lest he "make a Granada of [his] native
land" (1:307). If Shelley's repeated descriptions of the Irish as "savage"
and "uncivilized" (1:274) function as domestic Orientalism, they also
undermine any easy notion of a United Kingdom.

Volume II opens with the personal/political triangle of Richard, Monina de Faro, and Sir Robert Clifford, which complicates the thematics of
civil war and chivalry. As Monina plans a conspiracy against King Henry
in favor of her "beloved friend" Richard (2:2), she is stirring up civil war
but also demonstrating a feminine heroic friendship. When she urges

Clifford to similar "deeds of chivalry" (2:6), however, she rouses instead his passion. Earlier Richard's rescuer and ally, Clifford is now a spy for King Henry, and his internal battle between his "desperate passion" (1:334) and his "better feelings" embodies the nation's civil war. As his "better nature" (1:338) gradually spurs him on to "folly and crime," this divided knight also comes to figure the contradictions of chivalry. In contrast is Richard's love for Monina, a romantic passion he subdues to chivalric protection as he becomes "her friend, her brother" (2:40–41). In this triangle, Clifford's sexual desire becomes a corruption of chivalry, a "distorted reflection" (2:14) of Monina's personal-political devotion to Richard and of Richard's chivalric friendship for her.

A complicated dialectic then ensues between Clifford's distorted chivalry and the true chivalry of Monina and Richard. At first Clifford's villainy serves to call their chivalry into question. His attempt to abduct Monina turns her into a feminine victim who, as in the Spanish war, requires a manly rescuer (her father appears to save her). Richard too is victimized by Clifford's false chivalry; like a Gothic heroine, he is "allur[ed]" (2:68) by Clifford's "discourse of honour," and when he chivalrously forgives this false knight for betraying Monina's conspiracy, he becomes vulnerable to Clifford's later acts of treachery. In fact, Clifford's "shame, despair, and rage" (2:75) over Richard's goodness drive him deeper into villainy; it is as if Richard's masculine chivalry, like Monina's feminine version, creates its own "distorted reflection." The subsequent dialectic creates an ever more heroic chivalry. Monina goes to England to rescue the betrayed conspirators from the Tower; obeying "the laws of chivalry," Richard follows to "protect" her (2:87–88). Although he must be rescued from this escapade, his "generous rashness" on Monina's behalf (2:115) embodies masculine chivalry.

The novel now introduces Jane Shore, who brings the problematic of dynastic succession into sharp relief. Jane Shore was seduced by Edward IV and later became the Marquis of Dorset's mistress; although the historical Jane had great political influence, Shelley represents her as a "miserable outcast" (2:133). Abandoned by Edward, she is "a living lesson of the woes of love" (2:135), of women's victimization by masculine struggles over dynastic succession.

The question of Richard's claim to the throne is further complicated as the novel analyzes that claim in terms of honor and right. Richard first publicly asserts his right to the throne as a "call of honour" (2:147); honor further requires that he "maintain his claims" (2:149). When the Earl of Surrey objects that chivalric "honour" (2:146) includes avoiding

"unholy civil war" (2:147), Richard scoffs that Surrey is "turn[ing] spinster." Two codes of chivalric honor are in conflict here; Surrey's code mandates protection of the "sacred ties of humanity" (2:147), while Richard's requires that he "waste life" (2:148) to defeat "the usurper of [his] right." Even though Shelley characterizes Richard's form of honor as "a magic word with the good and brave" (2:149), by pitting it against Surrey's she calls into question the legitimacy of an abstract right maintained through chivalric honor.

Richard's year at the court of Scotland's James IV continues Shelley's analysis of sexual-political chivalry and honor. James displays heroic friendship by welcoming the outcast Richard, and "[w]oman's sway" (2:188) at his court seems to further attest his chivalry. But the court is in fact a site of sexual contention—between James's former mistress and his current favorite, Lady Jane Kennedy—and the king's heroic friendship cools when Richard counsels him not to seduce Lady Jane. Richard's honorable counsel convinces the king that Richard is worthy to marry his own royal cousin, Lady Katherine Gordon, but relations between James and Richard remain strained.

Shelley uses this strain to explore the fraught relations between England and Scotland. Like the novel's earlier Irish section, the Scotland chapters constitute a romance-history that interrogates the ideology of a British nation-state smoothly incorporating an alien culture. Scotland is represented as the opposite of "gentle" (2:197) England: the Highlanders are "wild and warlike" (2:183), the Lowlanders "hardly more cultivated or less savage." When James and Richard invade England, their uneasy alliance further signals the dissension within a "united kingdom." Once their combined troops cross into England, Richard feels the "rage and hate" (2:296) of an English "king and father of this realm" against its Scots invaders. The following pages detail the "waste" (2:304) and "atrocities" of civil war, of "national rivalship" (2:306) and hence "natural war" between English and Scots. As James's troops pillage Richard's "native home" (2:300), "all the Englishman" (2:298) revives in Richard, and he begs James to stop the slaughter. Here, Shelley departs from Hume's view that Perkin Warbeck merely "feigned great compassion" for his "plundered subjects" so as to "support his pretensions to royal birth" (*History,* 4:144). Her reader is intended to admire Richard's paternal care for "[his] countrymen, [his] children" (*Warbeck,* 2:312), especially in contrast with James's royal contempt for "cottagers and villains." Despite his compassion for the "victims of his right" (2:307), however, Richard still defends that right (2:299), and Shelley

explicitly terms "narrow and selfish" his belief that one man's right can excuse "the misery of thousands." As Volume II ends, paternal Richard has become "the parent of evil" (2:316).

Volume III begins the shift to Richard's wife, Lady Katherine, as the true sign of his right to the throne. After King James repudiates Richard, Katherine insists on "perform[ing] a wife's part" (3:3) by accompanying him into exile in Ireland. She is repeatedly referred to as "the White Rose" (3:4), the emblem of the house of York, and gradually Richard invests his right in her: "*thy* husband" must not be "less than King," he says (2:317). Once Richard's Irish adherents declare him "the true Lord of Ireland" (3:30), however, they also begin a civil war within Ireland that again complicates the issue of Richard's right. As his forces besiege Waterford to force the city to acknowledge his right, he fights with an "excess of chivalrous ardour" (3:39) that seems legitimated by the aid of the heroic Hernán de Faro. But both chivalry and right are undermined, by Katherine's recognition that the siege has "small chance" of success (3:34) and by Shelley's statement that "honour, magnanimity, devotion" (3:45) have turned the "seeming paradise" of Waterford into "a hell."

Several contrasts between Monina and Katherine underscore the complexities surrounding chivalry, right, and honor. To Monina, Richard's "honour" (3:59) is at stake in his claim to the throne; to Katherine, his cause is a "futil[e]" (3:58) struggle for "vain power" (3:59). When Richard's partisans hesitate to mount an insurrection in Cornwall, Monina urges him to "dare all, and triumph" (3:67); Katherine foresees "fruitless danger for a mistaken aim" (3:94). The question of right then becomes moot when Richard initiates the Cornish campaign not to "conquer a kingdom" (3:84) but to "redeem his honour." When Katherine contests his and Monina's chivalric notion of honor, Richard replies that without it he would not be "worthy" of her (3:90). But Shelley calls honor "a mere word here" (3:92), and one that will destroy Katherine's "life and happiness." As long as Richard's honor and chivalry served his right, all three had some legitimacy; but when he abandons even an ambiguous right, honor is no more than a destructive abstraction. Even Monina's feminine chivalry now seems tainted, although it is hard to interpret Shelley's statement "there was no evil in Monina; if . . . too passionate an attachment to one dear idea, too enthusiastic an adoration of one exalted being, could be called aught but virtue" (3:93).

At this point in the novel, honor seems completely devalued. Under King Henry, "[the] spirit of chivalry, which isolates man" (3:99), has given

way to the unifying "commercial spirit" of trade; few are willing to go to war to "benefit one man alone" (3:100), and Richard's faith in honor and chivalry is now represented as a cultural throwback. Shelley also casts Richard's chivalry in the all-too-modern form of class unrest. His only partisans are "the discontented" working classes (3:106), who can hardly be kept "within the boundaries of law" (3:98) even "in modern days."

As Richard clings to his honor, however, this devalued concept is gradually recuperated. When the Cornish insurrection falters, Richard sends King Henry a chivalric challenge to single combat, in order both to "spare the people's blood" (3:111) and to defend his "honour." Moreover, his distaste for his unchivalric forces—"unwashed artificers; ragged and rude peasants; vulgar-tongued traders" (3:121–22)—detaches his honor from their low-bred discontent; he is also linked to such noble outlaw leaders as Robin Hood (3:148). Finally, he leads his remaining supporters to an abbey, claims sanctuary for them, and chivalrously offers Henry his own life in exchange for the partisans Henry has imprisoned; "duped" (3:191) by his own "generous proud spirit," Richard is captured. If his honor is "a more valued treasure" (3:184) than his right, "dearer still" are his "poor fellows," and the reader is meant to share the onlookers' "compassion and respect" (3:185) for him.

It is a truism that history is written by the victors. The final pages of Shelley's romance depart significantly from Hume's *History,* in order to vindicate the vanquished. According to Hume's narrative, after King Henry imprisoned Katherine he treated her "with many marks of regard" and a "generosity" that "does him honor" (*History,* 4:156). Shelley represents Henry's "regard" as a base passion, thereby constructing Katherine as a double victim of his tyranny. As the "White Rose" (*Warbeck,* 3:194) she is a prisoner of Henry's "state policy" (3:203); as Richard's wife, she suffers from Henry's schemes against "her woman's fears, tenderness and weakness" (3:213).

Three additions to Hume complete the novel's contrast between womanly devotion and masculine chivalry. Where Hume makes no mention of Jane Shore, Shelley again brings her into the novel when Richard escapes from his captors and finds himself at Jane's cottage. As he reflects that women have been his "resource and support," and that even the outcast Jane exceeds his "doughty partizans" in "fidelity and affection," men's heroic friendship pales in comparison to women's "energies," "devotion," and "enthusiasm" (3:223–24). When Jane tells Richard of her continuing love for his father, this second addition to Hume's history again shows women's fidelity. "[T]hrough hunger, and cold, and shame"

(3:239), she says, "I love." If Jane's obsession is "a living lesson of the woes of love" (2:135), still this dishonored woman's devotion seems nobler than Richard's equally obsessive pursuit of his right and his honor. Shelley's third addition to Hume, the final contest between Clifford and Richard, further devalues Richard's quest. As Hernán de Faro attempts to ferry Richard to his ship, Clifford attacks Richard and both fall overboard; Richard kills Clifford but can free himself from his enemy's grip only by cutting off a portion of his own hair. This incident indicates the extent of Clifford's malignity, but it also tropes the destructive homosocial bonds of masculine struggles over chivalric honor.

The most significant difference between Shelley's romance and Hume's history is their final representations of Katherine. Shelley adds to Hume a scene in which Katherine visits Richard's cell after he has been tried and sentenced to death; the dangers of this secret expedition and the language of Katherine's loving farewell attest her wifely virtues. Shelley concludes with another incident not found in Hume, explicitly intended to clear Katherine from charges that her "devotion and fidelity" to Richard declined after his death (3:339). Edmund Plantagenet, who considers King Henry's court "stained" by Richard's blood (3:345), blames Katherine for remaining with her husband's "murderer" (3:347). Her response is in part Shelley's justification of her own recovery from grief over her husband's death (O'Sullivan, 153), but it is also a more general meditation on women's cultural roles. Katherine was given "a woman's education" (*Warbeck,* 3:348), which is "of the heart—alas! for us—" (3:349) and which teaches women that "to love is to exist" (3:350); after Richard's death, then, "I felt that I must die." Instead, she redirected her love for him to his sister, Elizabeth, and to Elizabeth's children, and she connected herself to others through "mutual good offices and sympathy" (3:352). While she admires disinterested benevolence, she can serve only where she loves, and if needing to feel that her "chosen friends are happier through [her]" (3:353) is a weakness, it is also "a part of [her] strength" (3:252). She concludes with a plea that she not be blamed for finding "what joy [she] can" (3:354) in her need "to be sympathized with—to love."

Certainly this is a limited ideal, but that very limitation continues the novel's critique of lofty chivalric ideals which result in the slaughter of civil war. If this is a purely individual philanthropy rather than the feminine politics represented in *Valperga* by Euthanasia, still Katherine's speech offers an alternative to the abstract masculine honor which *Perkin Warbeck* has shown to be so destructive.

Domestic-Sentimental Fiction: *Mathilda,* Short Stories, *Lodore,* and *Falkner*

The novella *Mathilda* and the eight stories analyzed in this chapter have in common a domestic/sentimental focus on the affections; they also exhibit the range of Mary Shelley's concerns with contemporary issues. Many of these issues recur in the final novels, *Lodore* (1835) and *Falkner* (1837), in which she again turned to this genre of domestic/sentimental fiction as well as to the related genre of fashionable fiction. As with all of her "generically mixed work," however, it is important to keep in mind the "impossibility of coherence, and the price we pay [by] striving for it."[1] While I begin with definitions of domestic/sentimental and fashionable fiction, then, my discussions of the stories and novels will also point to the elements from other genres that disrupt the predominant emphasis on domesticity.

The domestic/sentimental novel is a subset of the realistic novel discussed in chapter 4. Its subjects are "the daily life and work of ordinary people," and it focuses on "human relationships within small social communities," the familial and romantic relations of contemporary life.[2] Thus the "real" of the domestic/sentimental novel is that of domestic and private life, the separate sphere which the dominant Victorian ideology assigned to women. But the genre's realism is not a simple reflection of the private sphere; rather it is implicated in the cultural construction of that sphere.

To read domestic/sentimental fiction in this way, "both as the document and as the agency of cultural history,"[3] is to see how it functions as political and gender ideology. An eighteenth-century tradition of sentimentalism had been "politicized" by women writers who were inspired by the French Revolution to interrogate "existing social, economic, legal, and cultural practices" in their fiction.[4] In the reaction against the French Revolution, this fiction was in turn "reconstructed" by the new domestic/sentimental novel,[5] to tame the emotions that might otherwise issue

in political rather than romantic desire. The "new-style" male dominance of "noncoercive" authority in gender relations was legitimated by domestic/sentimental fiction, as it tamed transgressive feminine desire into "female selflessness" by focusing on the pleasures of "domestic fulfillment."[6] For women readers, these pleasures functioned as "compensatory gratifications, ideal rewards"[7] for giving up other desires. But domestic/sentimental fiction also offered the pleasure of fantasized power; by investing "common forms of social behavior with the emotional values of women" (Armstrong, 29), it made women the authorities on those forms of behavior. Women writers thus "inserted into the novel" the authority of "the woman as moralist."[8] In the plots of domestic/sentimental fiction, women are often "the legitimate agents for socializing men" (Poovey, 169), and as such they may "retaliate" against or punish men who do not submit to their domestic instruction. One reason that this new paradigm of feminine propriety "consolidated its power so quickly" (Poovey, 170)—and that the genre which valorized that paradigm achieved such popularity among women writers and readers—was this prospect of compensatory power. Within the genre's domestic framework, of course, as within the bourgeois home, feminine power was *only* compensatory; in the sexual politics of monogamy, women remain subordinate to men. Perhaps the most significant ideological function of domestic/sentimental fiction is thus its capacity to "represent an alternative form of political power without appearing to contest the distribution of power that it represented as historically given" (Armstrong, 29).

The fashionable novel was realistic fiction on a higher social scale than the domestic/sentimental novel. Fashionable novels aimed at "verisimilitude to the day-to-day detail of fashionable living."[9] Often called silver-fork novels because of their obsession with such trappings of the *beau monde,* they catered to middle-class fascination with the high life and indeed served as handbooks to that life for *nouveaux riches* readers (Adburgham, 1). Catherine Gore, however, one of the most successful practitioners of the genre, insisted that fashionable novels also exposed the "vices and follies . . . generated by the corruptions of society" (quoted in Colby, 57). Like domestic/sentimental novels, then, fashionable novels had a moral function; if they served middle-class "voyeurism" (Adburgham, 2), they also served middle-class morality by representing the triumph of "domestic virtues" over fashionable society (Colby, 74). In Mary Shelley's domestic/sentimental and fashionable stories, a contemporary and realistic setting gives particular urgency to her thematics— Romantic passion, fate, education, and the construction of gender.

Mathilda

Shelley wrote the novella *Mathilda* in 1819, and in May 1820 sent the manuscript to her father for his comments. He found its subject of incest "detestable";[10] perhaps for that reason, he held onto the manuscript and it remained unpublished until 1959. Shelley may have been drawing on her own childhood "excessive & romantic attachment" to her father (*MWSL,* 2:215), but *Mathilda* is predominantly an analysis of the cultural roles of daughters. It is unrevised but complete, and it examines the thematics of untamed passion, domestic affection, and curative sympathy that appear throughout Shelley's domestic/sentimental fiction.

Mathilda both exemplifies and interrogates a family romance plot in which a daughter is constructed to the "specifications of an omnipresent and unvoiced paternal desire."[11] In such a plot, the father's secret desire must be discovered by the daughter; thus she is positioned as the origin of the narrative, the one who *"makes* the unspoken story happen" (Zwinger, 3). The point of that story is to construct her as "the daughter of sentiment" rather than of incestuous sexuality (Zwinger, 5), for such a daughter protects her father from his incestuous desire and thereby "ground[s] the system of cultural constraints and perceptions" that constitutes sanctioned heterosexual desire. *Mathilda* tells this story, but from a daughter's point of view that calls into question the cultural construction of the "daughter of sentiment."

The novella is narrated by Mathilda, who is "about to die"[12] and is writing her story for the poet Woodville. She first describes her father's education, his marriage to her mother Diana, and his grief at Diana's death. Leaving Mathilda to the care of an aunt, her father left England for sixteen years; when he returns, Mathilda enjoys several months of blissful reunion until she forces from him the secret of his incestuous desire for her. He flees and dies; Mathilda at first desires death, but instead she retreats to a "death-like solitude" (216). Gradually she develops a friendship with the young poet Woodville, and tries to convince him to join her in a suicide pact. His explanation of the meaning of life dissuades her; soon thereafter, however, she develops consumption, and the novella ends with her projected death.

In her later novel *Falkner,* Shelley gently chides a man who engrosses his adopted daughter's affections; in contrast, Mathilda's father is represented as guilty of untamed passions of every sort. If "the intensity of his passion" (178) for his wife Diana renders him properly susceptible to the "lessons" of her "superior wisdom" (180), it also plunges him into "the

deepest melancholy" after her death. Living "for himself only" (181), he abandons his daughter, indulges his grief in "lonely wanderings" (188) through India, and develops an "independant [sic]" moral creed that does nothing to restrain his passions. When he returns to his daughter, "all his affections" remain focused on his dead wife, and he convinces himself that Diana's spirit was "transferred" (210) into Mathilda and that Mathilda, therefore, "ought to be as Diana" to him. The father's incestuous desire is thus due to a lifelong indulgence of his passions.

Mathilda is represented as the victim of both her father's and her own passions. As "the offspring of the deepest love" (183), she was born with "the greatest sensibility"; later she centered "all [her] affections" (185) on her absent father and "nursed" them until he became her "idol." When he returns, it is the "frantic heedlessness" (201) of her own "passion" that draws from him the secret of his incestuous desire for her. Like her father's, Mathilda's passions are nurtured and distorted by solitude; because of her "lonely life" (239) after his death, she comes to believe that she is "polluted by the unnatural love [she] had inspired." As the daughter thus takes on the father's guilt, she falls "in love with death" (244) and desires to join her dead father in "an eternal mental union." Mathilda is the apotheosis of the "daughter of sentiment," and the costs of this cultural construction are dramatized by her projected death and even more by her excess of daughterly melancholy. Because such sadness signals "a resistance to 'normality' that is both dysfunctional and profoundly legitimate," Mathilda's "incurable melancholy"[13] is an obsessive but legitimate response to being positioned solely as daughter.

What complicates this critique of the "daughter of sentiment" in *Mathilda* is the question of curative sympathy. Realizing her father's "sorrow" (200) but ignorant of its cause, she insists "with the freedom of a friend and equal" (199) that her "deep sympathy" will soothe his despair; instead, of course, her "presumptuous" sympathy forces the revelation of "unlawful and monstrous passion" (207) that destroys them both. The flaw in Mathilda's approach becomes clear later in the novella when it is contrasted with Woodville's "tender sympathy" (223). Unlike Mathilda, he does not insist on revelations; indeed, he repeatedly assures her that he will not "intrude" (231) on her sorrow, and he specifically enjoins her not to tell him why she grieves. Instead of claiming a friend's "freedom," he asks her for "the name of friend" (231) and promises to "fulfill its duties." Finally, in his long speech dissuading her from suicide, he outlines a more comprehensive form of sympathy. Each person's

"earthly task" (237) is "to smooth the way for our posterity"; by influencing others "from ill to good" or by "bestow[ing] happiness" on others
(238), this form of sympathy helps lessen present pain and leads toward
a better future.

Woodville's ideal suggests a move away from a domestic affection
which may become incestuous into a larger sympathy which may make
earth's "future inhabitants" happier. But as it reflects back on Mathilda's
flawed form of sympathy, in effect it shifts the blame for her tragedy
away from her father's incestuous desire and onto her. Nor does
Woodville's eloquence convince Mathilda to follow his ideal; imprisoned
by a misery that "hardens and dulls the feelings" (246), she remains a
daughterly mourner. Since her narrative is addressed to Woodville, his
speech about sympathy extends only to him; in effect, he is talking to
himself. Finally, although Shelley attempted to put her novella into "circulation,"[14] it remained with her father. Despite its ideal of an extended
sympathy, then, *Mathilda* remains a circular narrative of the domestic
affections that critiques but remains bound by them.

Short Stories

"The Bride of Modern Italy" (1824)

This early story exhibits Mary Shelley's little-known talent for satire.
Humor was not her forte, but she had a strong sense of irony—of the
gap between desire or expectation and its fulfillment. While this sense
most often appears in her work as tragic irony, in "The Bride of Modern
Italy" the irony is comic; she satirizes modern Italian marriage customs
by writing a parody of Gothic and domestic/sentimental tales.

Clorinda Saviani, who has been placed in a convent by her father
until he can find her a husband, falls in love, first with the young Italian
Giacomo de' Tolomei and then with his English friend Marcott Alleyn;
after much hand-wringing, she finally marries her father's choice, the
wealthy Romani. The innocent young girl imprisoned in a convent by
her evil parents was a staple plot of the Gothic novel, but it was also a
feature of modern Italian life. Mary became familiar with the reality of
such "domestic tyranny" (*MWSL,* 1:166) through the tribulations of
Emilia Viviani, and the Horatio-Clorinda subplot of *Lodore* is her serious
domestic/sentimental treatment of this theme; here, however, she parodies the conventions of the form. During her imprisonment Clorinda is
fed not a "dainty feast of convent-like confectionaries" but "eggs fried

with garlic" and "vegetables swimming in oil";[15] her "boudoir" (35) is no delicate chamber but a "miserably furnished" room (34) containing a glass of holy water "rather the worse for long standing" (35); her jailer is not a wicked nun but a Mother Superior with a fondness for rum; and so on. Most important, Clorinda is not a martyr of love but an inconstant young girl. Instead of devoting herself to piety, she "change[s her] saint as [her] lover changes name" (33), and when she and Giacomo share stolen moments in the convent, they speak not the ideal language of love but the practical language of contracts and settlements.

Although Shelley invites the reader to laugh at Clorinda, she also delimits such laughter. An early passage tells the reader that Clorinda's plight is an actual feature of modern Italy and gives a tripartite excuse for her inconstancy: "the Catholic religion, which crushes the innate conscience"; the systematic "artifice and heartlessness" of Catholic convents; and a notion of dishonor peculiar to Italy. While this passage does not fully exonerate Clorinda, it places her conduct in context, and, appearing thus early in the story, it requires the reader to judge the context as well as Clorinda. Without overlooking or excusing Shelley's dislike of Catholicism, it is worth noting that—unlike, for example, Nathaniel Hawthorne in *The Marble Faun*—she does not regard it as a peculiarly Latin phenomenon; as her treatment of English Catholics in *Falkner* shows, she considered Catholicism benighted wherever she found it. While she is certainly intolerant of some traits of what she and her contemporaries would have called the Italian race, her story qualifies its criticism of Italian mores by similar criticism of English customs. Shelley cautions "the fastidious English" (*Tales,* 34) against being "disgusted" with Italian customs, for a similar form of courtship "takes place at every ball-room with us." In addition, the story satirizes not only Clorinda but also her British admirer Marcott Alleyn. When he visits the convent expecting "the impenetrable grate" (36), or when he moons over Clorinda's "unaffected manners" (41), Marcott stands in for the British reader with similar delusions derived from Gothic fiction. When he encourages her transfer of interest from Giacomo to him, his disloyalty to his friend parallels her inconstancy to her lover; and by "heedlessly foster[ing]" (38) her belief that he will help her escape from the convent, he is at least irresponsible. The story ends with his decision to turn from romantic entanglements to his painting of "The Profession of Eloisa"; the allusion to the tragic romance of Eloisa and Abelard reflects badly on Marcott as well as Clorinda. If the story satirizes the bride of modern Italy, then, it also mocks the reader of modern England.

"The Sisters of Albano" (1829)

"The Sisters of Albano" shows Shelley's admiration for the love of liberty that she regarded as basic to the Italian character. She was an enthusiastic partisan of the 1820 "quiet revolutions" (*MWSL*, 1:158) in Italy against Austrian rule, and she sets this story in those times. The tale combines a romance with the exotic element of Italian banditti in order to teach a domestic/sentimental moral, but it also incorporates a political commentary which calls that fairly simple moral into question.

Published in the annual *The Keepsake*, "The Sisters of Albano," like many annual stories, was designed to accompany an engraving. Shelley almost jokingly builds the engraving—of Lake Albano and two figures on the shore bartering with a pedlar—into her tale, as a member of a boating party muses that "one might easily make out a story" from the scene.[16] The Countess Atanasia then tells a story intended to show that the "combination" of love with banditry causes "dreadful tragedies." Maria, one of the sisters of the title, is a nun; the other, Anina, is in love with the outlaw Domenico but forbidden by her father to see him. The story is set during the French occupation of Rome and Naples, and Anina is arrested by the French but escapes with the aid of her sister Maria, who disguises Anina in her own nun's habit. Domenico leads the banditti to rescue Maria from the French; learning that they have murdered her, he and his band storm the prison and are killed. Anina becomes a nun, and the story ends as the Countess reflects with horror on Anina's "passion" (64).

This conclusion reiterates the domestic/sentimental morals with which the story began, that such "lawless pursuits" (53) as Domenico's bring "ineffable misery" to all concerned and that such "unhappy passion" as Anina's similarly "spread[s] destruction and sorrow." But this censure of outlawry and passion is complicated by the story's politics. Domenico is admittedly a robber and bandit, but the French definition of such outlawry is political: French troops pursue the banditti not to punish them but to "awe-strik[e] the peasantry" (63) with "merciless" (57) persecution. In addition, the French execute Maria even though it was Anina who broke their law, for "one peasant girl to them was the same as another" (63) and "any victim suited their purpose" of terrorizing the Italians. If "ineffable misery" is abroad in the land, then, it seems due less to the bandits than to the French. And if Anina flouts her father's ban on contact with Domenico, Maria characterizes her sister's "sole crime" as "disobeying an arbitrary command" of the French (60). Finally, if Anina finds "calm and resignation" as a nun, she also desires

"repose in the grave" (64); there is at least a suggestion that, while passion may have its pains, the convent can have no pleasures. Such elements of the story undercut its ostensible domestic/sentimental moral.

"The Smuggler and His Family" (1833)

Another moral tale centering on crime, "The Smuggler and His Family" appeared in *Original Compositions in Prose and Verse,* a volume published "for the benefit of a family in reduced circumstances" (*Tales,* 389). The story places Shelley's familiar theme of maternal love in a setting of "reduced circumstances" and criminality, so as to appeal to the benevolent emotions of the volume's readers and to teach several lessons in domestic morality.

The story opens with a sympathetic representation of Jane Harding. Married for love to Jem, a man morally "unworthy of her" who has become a smuggler, she devotes herself to keeping her son, Charles, from being led into crime by his father's evil influence.[17] Because Charles "stored up her moral and religious lessons" (206), he is untainted by his one criminal experience with Jem's crew of smugglers. He refuses to rejoin the crew but goes to his father when Jem is captured by revenue officers. After his father's death in jail, Charles sails home during a storm; the story's final line reassures the reader of his safe reunion with his mother.

The story teaches its moral lessons by filtering them through Jane's maternal consciousness. While smuggling may seem a "venial" (205) and even "heroic" crime, as seen by "the anxious mother" it causes passions "utterly at war" with "a virtuous character." Here, as in *Lodore* and *Falkner,* the problem of "untamed passions" (204) is given a domestic/sentimental slant; Jane's unceasing maternal vigilance is necessary because Jem's paternal "good intentions" (209), based on neither "principle nor truth" (210), are overwhelmed by his "bad passions" (213). The need for maternal care is heightened by the story's final scenes. When Charles is saved from moral danger by his determination to "earn an honest livelihood" but then endangered by the storm, the reader is positioned to join in Jane's maternal fears, share her relief at her son's safety, and learn the importance of instilling and/or practicing the virtues that prevent moral as well as financial "reduced circumstances."

"Ferdinando Eboli: A Tale" (1829)

Published in the same *Keepsake* as "The Sisters of Albano," "Ferdinando Eboli" is also set in Italy during a time of political unrest. The focus here

is less on politics than on those "more romantic days,"[18] and, while the tale has domestic/sentimental elements, it also raises some disturbing questions about romantic love.

As the tale opens, Count Ferdinando Eboli seems the favorite son of fortune: "young and gallant" (65), favored by the king of Naples, possessing a sizable patrimony, betrothed to the high-born and beauteous Adalinda. After a love scene in which they anticipate communing "through the medium of divine nature" (67) while apart, Ferdinando leaves on a secret mission for the king; he returns to court to find a counterfeit count in his place. Unable to convince the king or Adalinda of his identity, Ferdinando is then imprisoned on a trumped-up charge of theft. Eventually Adalinda confronts the counterfeit and learns that he is Ferdinando's illegitimate older brother, Ludovico; to avoid marrying him, she runs away dressed as a page. Meanwhile, Ferdinando has escaped from prison with a bandit chief; the lovers are reunited when Adalinda takes refuge in the banditti cave, and later the bandit chief captures Ludovico as he pursues Adalinda. Ferdinando is restored to fortune and favor, and he persuades the king to allow Ludovico to enter the army. Ludovico not only distinguishes himself in battle but on one occasion saves his brother's life and later dies in Ferdinando's arms. It is worth noting that Ludovico not only goes unpunished for his imposture but is readily forgiven and, in effect, rewarded; the question of guilt and expiation elided here will be fully explored in *Falkner.*

A significant element of the story is its ambivalent attitude toward nature. For many Romantics, nature was not only a locus of beauty, healing, and nurture but a guarantor of truth. In *Frankenstein,* however, the representation of nature is deeply ironic, and in *The Last Man* the fatal plague is a force of nature. A similar resistance to Romantic views of nature is evident in "Ferdinando Eboli." Ferdinando and Adalinda are secure in their belief that "their hearts, through the medium of divine nature, might hold commune during absence" (67); neither the reader nor Adalinda suspects that these lofty sentiments are uttered not by Ferdinando but by Ludovico. His deception here is reminiscent of the Shakespearean bed trick, but in his plays the audience is privy to the deception, and the trick is a virtuous character's stratagem to teach a faulty character a lesson in true love. Perhaps the reader of "Ferdinando Eboli" is intended to overlook this unlikely misrecognition, or to accept it as possible in "those romantic days"; perhaps, however, the reader is meant to ponder the fragility of true love and the unreadability of its guarantor, nature.

"The Elder Son" (1835)

Like "Ferdinando Eboli," "The Elder Son" is concerned with imposture, but unlike the earlier story, it focuses on the consequences of that act for the deceived woman. One of Shelley's few stories with a woman as first-person narrator, and published in the annual *Heath's Book of Beauty,* the story is clearly addressed to an upper-class feminine audience. As the story explores parent-child and romantic relationships, its domestic/sentimental focus is designed to educate women readers in moral issues especially significant for women.

The story begins with the narrator, Ellen, recalling the legacies of her dead father: a fortune that renders her independent; a ban on marrying until she is twenty-one, which guarantees her "freedom of choice, and time for deliberation";[19] and the "sublime morality" he taught her (245). Yet the story goes on to show the inadequacy of even such paternal preparation. Brought by her uncle and guardian, Sir Richard Gray, to his estate, Ellen is soon engaged to her handsome, sweet-talking cousin Vernon but then develops a true love for his brother Clinton's virtues. The lesson here is the folly of haste in what a contemporary would see as a woman's most important decision, the choice of a husband. Although Ellen is represented not as a passive martyr to her own "irreparable mistake" (253) but as a clear-headed woman bent on doing her duty with "courage" (258), she is released from this duty when Vernon breaks their engagement. Clinton, the supposed elder son, is now revealed to be illegitimate; Sir Richard then confesses that he married Clinton's mother only after the boy's birth and that he hoped to atone for this wrong by marrying Ellen to Clinton. Distressed at this "system of dissimulation and guilt" (262), Ellen nonetheless forgives her uncle and marries Clinton. Vernon is not punished but disappears from their lives; Sir Richard denies himself luxuries to create a patrimony for Clinton, and after their marriage Ellen and Clinton devote themselves to "calming his remorse" (264).

Like several of her other stories, this one shows how carefully Shelley differentiates among criminal acts. In "The Sisters," banditry is criminal but excusable under the provocation of political oppression; in "The Smuggler," on the other hand, smuggling is truly criminal because it creates and fosters criminal passions. In "Ferdinando Eboli," Ludovico's later heroic and self-sacrificing acts are meant to make amends for his earlier faults. In "The Elder Son," too, the agent of imposture is readily forgiven because he both repents and atones; Vernon neither repents nor

atones for his malevolence yet is not punished because he has been victimized by his father's faults. As these stories—and *Falkner*—show, Shelley is interested less in meting out guilt than in exploring the constructions, motivations, and consequences of criminality.

"The Trial of Love" (1835)

Published in *The Keepsake,* "The Trial of Love" is another story which assumes a feminine audience. Like "The Elder Son," this tale explores the consequences of a woman's mistaken passion, but, like "The Smuggler," it is concerned less with romantic love than with domestic/sentimental forms of feminine devotion.

Daughter of the steward to Count Montcenigo, the heroine Angeline loves the count's daughter, Faustina, "like an elder sister" and with "maternal" feeling.[20] Angeline also feels a "passionate" love for her betrothed Ippolito (233), but she accepts his father's condition that the lovers not communicate for one year; in contrast, the "fiery and impetuous" lover chafes at this restriction and at what he perceives as her coldness. When Ippolito is wounded rescuing Angeline and Faustina from a runaway buffalo, he recuperates in Faustina's home; falling in love with her, he repudiates his betrothal with Angeline. Although Angeline grieves, she freely forgives Ippolito for marrying Faustina and becomes a nun. As the story concludes, Faustina is disappointed in her "light, inconstant" husband (243) and longs for Angeline's "friendship" and "kind sympathy"; in contrast, Angeline is supported by "her piety, her resignation, her noble, generous nature" (242) and so lives "cheerful, if not happy" (243).

In this story the reader is invited to commiserate with Angeline but also to admire her domestic/sentimental qualities. She erred in loving Ippolito but did not compound that error with fruitless regret; her romantic love was "sacred and immutable," but she subdued it to a higher sisterly/motherly love for Faustina; and throughout she practices that greatest of virtues for Shelley, the ability to "nurse" feelings into passions (232) yet "regulate their effects" (233). Unlike many of Shelley's stories, this one represents the convent as a reward; "dedicated to heaven" (243), Angeline escapes a world unworthy of her virtues.

"The Mourner" (1830)

In sharp contrast to "The Trial of Love," the disturbing story "The Mourner" brings unwavering feminine devotion to a tragic end. Here,

the love of father for daughter—a subject of continuing interest to Shelley—is not incestuous, as in *Mathilda,* but neither is it protective, as in "The Elder Son"; instead it seems to draw "the daughter of sentiment" (Zwinger, 5) toward self-destruction.

The tale was published in *The Keepsake* to accompany two engravings of Virginia Water, and Shelley uses this tranquil lake to counterpoint a tale of storm and despair. The narrator, Horace Neville, tells of his childhood acquaintance with Ellen Burnet, the mourner of the title; she was despairing and at times suicidal, but the cause of her grief remained a mystery. Years later Horace meets Lewis Elmore and hears the story of Lewis's lost fiancée, the Honorable Clarice Eversham. Trapped with her father, Lord Eversham, on a burning ship, Clarice was saved when he tossed her into a lifeboat; Lord Eversham then attempted to save himself but was drowned, and Clarice disappeared from society in the belief that she was responsible for her father's death. After Horace and Lewis realize that "Ellen Burnet" is Clarice, they hurry to her cottage but arrive too late; she is dead and, the reader assumes, by her own hand. The story closes with her letter to Horace, stating her love for Lewis and her guilt as a "parrici——."[21]

The story connects Horace's relation to Ellen with Clarice's relation to her father by presenting both as ideal forms of education. While at Eton, Horace fagged for an older student whom he thrice calls a "tyrant" (86–87), and he laments that "the tender years of aristocratic childhood" are thus subject to a "bondage, far beyond the measured despotism of Jamaica" (86). The topical parallels between Eton—"distorted miniature of a bad world" (89)—and "West Indian slavery" (86) indicate the need for a countereducation of the aristocracy which Ellen provides: as her "pupil" (90), Horace has learned "a sense of the just, the good, the beautiful." The pupil-teacher relation of Clarice and her father seems equally laudable. Lord Eversham "devoted himself" to her education (92) both of "intellect and heart"; in turn Clarice regards him as a "gift of Providence, a guardian angel." Thus they are "a matchless example of happiness in the dearest connexion in life," for "when a father is all that a father may be," a daughter's love is "one of the deepest and strongest, as it is the purest passion of which our natures are capable."

The domestic/sentimental tone could hardly be clearer, but here, as in *Mathilda,* there is something suffocating about such daughterly devotion. Clarice seems unable to live without her father, and her guilt over his death is not only obsessive but unwarranted; the story carefully shows that Clarice could not have saved him. If "The Mourner" intends to rep-

resent Ellen/Clarice as an admirable example of feminine devotion, still it hints that such total devotion can be fatal. Thus the story displays, but simultaneously critiques, a cultural "ideal of perfect daughterhood."[22]

"The Parvenue" (1837)

"The Parvenue" is another story of daughterly devotion, but here a daughter's love for her mother illuminates the larger issue of women's contending responsibilities. The story was published in *The Keepsake,* and while Shelley is perhaps drawing on her own "divided loyalties" to both her husband and her father,[23] she is certainly addressing women readers subject to conflicting demands in their several roles as daughters, wives, and social caretakers. But the story also critiques the class society of such readers as it traces the difficulties of a parvenue, a woman lifted out of her class and uncomfortable with her new station.

Fanny, the story's narrator and heroine, recounts her childhood of working-class poverty but also "enjoyment" in a family "linked by strong affection" and presided over by an "earthly angel" of a mother.[24] After Lord Reginald Desborough saves Fanny from a fire, he woos her and they are married; he then helps her father financially and gives his patronage to Lawrence Cooper, enabling him to marry Fanny's sister, Susan. But Fanny's marriage soon sours. When she heeds the "senti-ment of justice" (269) instilled by her mother's "enlightened piety" and spends her allowance on feeding the hungry, Sir Reginald reproves her "sordid" ideas, and he later refuses her family's secret and "exorbitant" demands for money (270). Fanny accepts his decision as just, but when her mother has convulsions after attempting to shield her from further such demands by her father, Fanny asks her husband for money. Sir Reginald insists that she choose between him and her family, and her devotion to her mother supersedes her love for her husband. After her mother's death she offers to return to her husband, but he will not relent; as the story ends, Fanny plans to join her sister in America but also "desire[s] to die" (274).

In *Falkner,* a daughter is able to reconcile the conflicting demands of filial and romantic love; Fanny cannot do so. The story's title seems to attribute her failure to marrying above her station, and the subplots appear to bear out this interpretation: Fanny's father is ruined by specu-lating beyond his means, Lawrence Cooper is "rendered absolutely insane by the idea of having a lord for a brother-in-law" (273), and Susan laments that she and her husband did not "remain in virtuous poverty." But Fanny denies that her story is intended to "prevent any

other from wishing to rise [in] rank" (266), and the tale in fact hints that the upper classes could only be improved by an infusion of Fanny's "sense of justice," her belief that what they call charity is in fact "the payment of [her] debts to [her] fellow-creatures." Perhaps the lesson is not for parvenues but for titled husbands who cannot overcome "the prejudices and habits of rank and wealth" (268), and for a ruling class which regards a wife's "first duty" (269) as not to help her fellow creatures but "to please [her] husband and do honour to his rank."

Lodore (1835)

Although Shelley's last two novels fall into the domestic/sentimental category, they are also "generically mixed" (Langbauer, 187). Certainly the first reviews stressed the novels' domestic/sentimental elements: one praised "the romance of sentiment" in *Lodore;*[25] another admired *Falkner's* "appeal to our more generous sympathies" and "display of the finer affections."[26] But Shelley regarded both *Lodore* and *Falkner* as tales "of the present times" (*MWSL,* 2:267), so their focus on domestic relations and emotions is firmly placed in the context of contemporary British class and gender relations.

Lodore's generic mix includes the wealth of economic and social detail reminiscent of Jane Austen's novels of manners and characteristic of the fashionable novel. But it also plays off fashionable society against the exotic settings of America's wilds and London's prisons, and it works throughout with the thematics characteristic of the domestic/sentimental novel. As it explores the effects of destructive passion, *Lodore* also analyzes the interrelated issues of femininity and education.

From the outset Lord Lodore is represented as ruled by his passions. Chapters 2 and 3 hint at a past of Romantic guilt, of "ungoverned" passions,[27] which issued in "unspeakable wretchedness" (1:18) and "abstracted melancholy" (1:46). Subsequent chapters relate his history. After a period of "unlawful pursuits" (1:95) and travel shrouded in "mystery and obscurity" (1:83), at the age of 34 Lodore returned to England and married 16-year-old Cornelia. This ill-assorted union was disrupted by Lady Lodore's continued dependence on her mother, Lady Santerre, and by the "proud and imperious" Lodore's ill-advised efforts to mold Cornelia into his "ideal of a wife" (1:108). Husband and wife eventually separated, due to Lodore's unregulated passions but also to "the eternal law which links ill to ill" (1:161). The initial "ill" arose from Lodore's passion, his earlier affair with Countess Lyzinski, and it resur-

faced when his ex-mistress and their son, Count Casimir, appeared in London. Casimir then became excessively friendly with Lady Lodore; out of a jealousy "that bordered on insanity" (1:166), Lodore then insulted his son. To avoid the consequent challenge to a duel, the "impetuous" Lodore (1:168) left his wife and took their daughter Ethel with him to the wilds of Illinois.

The domestic/sentimental focus on the emotions which destroy the Lodore marriage warns against a passion "extreme in all things" (1:197). That lesson then leads into a larger theme of perennial interest to Shelley: the fact that "the consequences of our actions *never die*" (1:250). Even his solitary life in America cannot protect Lodore from the linked ills of his past. Accused of cowardice for failing to duel with Casimir twelve years earlier, he accepts his accuser's challenge and is killed. Edward Villiers, Lodore's second in the duel, turns out to be another link to his past. Edward's cousin, Horatio Saville, is in love with Lady Lodore, and the two men are in America trying to locate and recover her daughter. The conclusion of the first volume prepares for further links between past and present; the grieving Ethel returns to England to live with her paternal aunt, Elizabeth Fitzhenry, and Edward returns to England and visits Lady Lodore.

In London, Edward again encounters Ethel, and they soon fall in love and marry. As Volume II relates the development of this relationship, it contrasts Edward's and Ethel's wedded bliss with three mishandled marriages. The first is Lodore's; as husbands, he and Edward are "totally dissimilar" (2:2). Where Lodore was impetuous from "pride" and "the violence of passion," Edward is "imprudent from his belief in the goodness of his fellow creatures" and because he "had not yet learned to be a man" (2:3). He requires seasoning, and, unlike Lodore, he acquires it from his wife. Lodore's marriage was a series of misunderstandings and battles with his wife, and although the novel clearly locates part of the blame in Lady Lodore, still her husband's behavior justifies her criticism of "the tyranny and dark jealousy of [his] vindictive nature" (1:192). In contrast, Edward's admittedly lesser faults—his "thoughtless profusion" with money (2:95), his submission to the "tyranny" of fashionable society (2:140), his "aristocratic pride" (3:142)—are reformed by marriage to Ethel, and he comes to see and accept the duties "assigned him in this world" (3:147).

As Edward's flexibility is contrasted with Lodore's tyranny, it is also contrasted with the excessive supineness of another husband, his cousin Horatio. After Horatio's proposal is rejected by the widowed Lady

Lodore, he marries the volatile Neapolitan Clorinda, who (unlike the carefree Clorinda of "The Bride of Modern Italy") loves with an "Italian fervour" (2:175) that often becomes "uncontrollable violence" (2:193). Like the Lodore marriage, this is one of "mutual torments" (3:201). The novel heaps blame on Clorinda for behaving "like a maniac" (3:206), but it also hints that Horatio is culpable for marrying without love, for ignoring Clorinda's justified complaints, and for remaining "the slave of a violent woman's caprice" (2:207). Edward's and Ethel's calm happiness, then, is contrasted with the recurrent eruptions of Horatio's and Clorinda's marriage. It is also briefly contrasted with the alliances of fashionable London, through the subplot of Edward's widowed father, Colonel Villiers, maneuvering to marry a young heiress. The failure of the Colonel's schemes impoverishes Edward and Ethel, and Shelley then draws on her own "early adventures" with Percy to describe their poverty (*MWSL,* 2:261).

More significant than this autobiographical element, however, is Shelley's rationale for dwelling on such adversity, for that rationale foregrounds the novel's thematic of ideal femininity. Shelley realizes the risk of "being censured for bringing the reader into contact with degrading and sordid miseries" (*Lodore,* 2:282) or, at the other extreme, for treating as miseries what for "those in a lower sphere of life" would "scarcely deserv[e] the name of misfortune." But if she did not use "vulgar" terms for "common-place and degrading" scenes, she would "fail utterly" in her aim, for Ethel's "youth and feminine tenderness" would not "shed light and holiness around her."

Now, the realistic prison scenes which Shelley defends were themselves a fictional convention of the "Newgate" or prison novel in vogue during the 1830s. Incorporating its "vulgar" realism into a fashionable and domestic/sentimental novel, then, is a strategy for representing Ethel's ideal femininity. A useful comparison is George Eliot's *The Mill on the Floss* (1860): to preempt possible reader resistance to her focus on "sordid life," Eliot argues that she must represent "our own vulgar era" to show how her heroine has "risen above [its] mental level."[28] Similarly, Shelley uses a "degrading" realistic background in order to emphasize the domestic/sentimental "simplicity" and "beauty" of "the *devotion* of a young wife" (*MWSL,* 2:185). The author caps this ideal femininity at the end of Volume II, when Ethel "resign[s] her being and destiny to a Power superior to any earthly authority" (*Lodore,* 2:297).

Ethel's resignation appears to approve a conventionally passive femininity, but Volume III complicates such a reading by validating other

and contrasting forms of feminine conduct. When Ethel joins Edward in prison, her passivity is represented as a "fortitude and patience" (3:139) that encourage Edward to "more manly endurance" (3:147). But Ethel is "perfectly fearless" only "under the shelter of another's care" (3:23), and in this she is contrasted with her friend and "opposite," Fanny Derham. Fanny's "first principle" is to do "what she ought to do" without "hesitation or regard for obstacles." Where Ethel can be useful only to Edward, Fanny seeks help for them both from Ethel's mother (3:21–23). Lady Lodore is the novel's third version of femininity. Initially she represents a "mere personal pride" (1:202) that conduces to an "aimless, unprofitable, blank" life (3:95) and also conflicts with "a distant and faint, yet genuine sense of duty" toward her daughter (2:64). After visiting Ethel in prison, however, Lady Lodore "find[s] all to be Vanity, except the genuine affections of the heart" (*MWSL*, 2:185), and she decides to "sacrifice every thing to her daughter" (*Lodore*, 3:127). With this change from fashionable frivolity to maternal self-sacrifice, Lady Lodore becomes another model of admirable femininity. Unlike Caroline Beaufort in *Frankenstein*, Lady Lodore is not destroyed by motherly devotion; after she sells her jointure to pay Edward's debts and absents herself from felicity awhile in Wales, her "heroism" (3:283) is rewarded by communion with nature, reunion with Ethel, and marriage to the now-widowed Horatio. An instructive contrast is the fate of Horatio's first wife. Clorinda died of a fit, the "victim" (3:128) of her own "uncontrolled passion," of the "violence of passion and ill-regulated feelings" (3:196) that the domestic/sentimental novel works to control or expel. As with Evadne in *The Last Man* or Beatrice in *Valperga*, women readers are here reminded that passion can be fatal.

To such passion, *Lodore* opposes the domestic affections. "A Mother & Daughter are the heroines" of the novel (*MWSL*, 2:185), and Lady Lodore's admission to her new husband—that the "better part" of her heart is devoted to "maternal love"—is approvingly contrasted with Clorinda's "violence of passion" for her husband (*Lodore*, 3:306). Yet the novel occasionally seems uneasy with an exclusive domestic love, for it verges on uncontrolled passion. By "mingling every hope and wish," Edward and Ethel "confirmed the marriage of their hearts" (3:35); still, such a "singleness" of devotion is, and ought to be, diminished by the "duties" to others that afford humans "a greater scope for utility" (3:36–37).

While Shelley values the total unity of such a domestic love, she also hints at the limits of this emotion-centered mode of femininity by con-

cluding the novel with Fanny Derham. Shelley may have intended this character as a tribute to her friend Fanny Wright, the feminist social reformer who established a number of experimental communities in the United States during the 1820s;[29] she admired Wright's "noble mind" and "heroic spirit" and loved her "as a bright specimen of our sex" (*MWSL,* 2:123–24). Like Fanny Wright, Fanny Derham "aspire[s] to be useful" (3:7) in a sphere larger than that bounded by the domestic emotions. The "web of human passion" may "occasion her many sorrows" (3:309), but Fanny's life will be "a useful lesson" in how our "passions" can be "purified and ennobled" by "a love of truth" and "a sincere sympathy with our fellow-creatures" (3:310–11). Fanny is the harbinger of a non-domestic/sentimental heroine: not a wife or a mother, but a single woman "palliating the woes of life" (3:310).

That such a heroine cannot be produced by the "sexual education" (3:21) Ethel received is perhaps the novel's final lesson. *Lodore* focuses throughout on forms and consequences of education—defined less as a learning of data than as a training in conduct—and on class- as well as gender-specific dangers of miseducation. Edward's financial difficulties are due in part to "his education and [class] position" (2:96), which together "fostered habits of expense and prodigality." In her description of Lodore's education, Shelley directly counters the theories of Jean-Jacques Rousseau's *Emile.* Rousseau advised a "purely negative" moral training for a boy, to consist "not at all in teaching virtue or truth, but in shielding the heart from vice, and the mind from error."[30] Lodore's "moral nurture" (*Lodore,* 1:73) on such Rousseauian lines was "perniciously indulgent." It was also excessively masculine, for it lacked "those habits of effeminacy" that might prevent "our young self-indulged aristocracy from rebelling against the restraints of society." At Eton, Lodore develops a praiseworthy hatred of injustice but cannot distinguish between rebelling against authority and "pardonable resistance" to it (1:76). With this mingled praise and criticism, Shelley may be commenting on her husband's tempestuous conduct at Eton.[31] And although she believed that the "bustle" of a public school would develop her own son's "character" (*MWSL,* 2:134), certainly Lodore emerges from Eton "wholly unconscious" (*Lodore,* 1:77) that he is ruled by his own "passions and pride."

Upper-class women seem more at risk from a faulty training than men of their class. Clorinda suffers from the "convent education" (2:176) given Italian girls of her station. Ethel's aunt Elizabeth, who appears to have received no education at all, lives in "dreamy" (1:10)

devotion to the memory of that "celestial luminary" (3:248), her dead brother. Lady Lodore received a "bad education" (1:202) which so "narrowed" her that "her loftiest ideas were centered in worldly advantage," and her years of fashionable *ennui* were due in part to having "never occupied herself by intellectual exertion" (3:101). When Lodore tries to "educate her mind," she regards his "manly guidance" as "tyrannous and cruel" (1:117–18). The novel suggests that she is right, for Lodore's educational principles are at odds with his practice; hoping to educate his wife in "an ideal of what he thought a woman ought to be," in fact he has "no lofty opinion of women" (1:119).

Against these clearly inadequate educations, Shelley places those of Ethel and Fanny. As a daughter educated only by a father, Ethel develops the "portions of mind, which are folded up, and often destroyed, by mere feminine tuition" (1:28). Lodore trains her to be "fearless" but "ductile and dependent," to "scorn pain" but maintain "womanly reserve," to understand "honour" but act with "sweetest gentleness." With his daughter's education as with his wife's, however, Lodore "drew his chief ideas" from Milton (1:38), and in criticizing those ideas Shelley echoes her mother's view of Milton's Eve as designed, "in the true Mahometan strain," to "gratify the senses of man."[32] Furthermore, Lodore's system is "lamentably deficient" in inculcating independence (*Lodore*, 1:40). Ethel "seldom thought, and never acted, for herself" (1:41), difficulties "annoyed and dismayed her," and she believes that obedience to her father fulfills "all her duties." Such a woman is what Sarah Ellis called approvingly a "relative creature," one whose existence is dedicated to "promoting the happiness of others."[33] But Ethel is "so caressingly affectionate" (*Lodore*, 1:41) to her father, and Lodore so "bind[s] up his life" in his daughter (1:197), that there is a hint of incest in the "more than a father's fondness" she inspires in him. While Ethel eventually learns to cope with difficulties—indeed, in prison her education renders her "greatly [Edward's] superior" (3:139) in this respect—"morally" (3:23) she continues to require guidance.

"[N]othing could be more opposite" (3:21) than Fanny Derham's education. Where Lodore created in Ethel "his ideal of what a woman ought to be" and formed her to be a wife, Fanny's father educated her in "the duties and objects befitting an immortal soul" so as to "make her complete in herself." He also gave her the "abstract learning" (1:223) which girls "seldom" receive; hence she is guided by her "understanding" (3:22) rather than, as Ethel is, by her heart, and "the landmarks of her life" are "religion, reason, and justice." Although her future is left

uncertain, Fanny is clearly intended as an example of how to educate women for "what goodness and genius can achieve" (3:310).

Fanny's education, then, is superior to Ethel's. Several specifically American elements of Ethel's education, however, are represented as making her less committed to class society and more open to republican ideas. When Ethel suggests that justice "orders" the rich man to give "his superfluity to the poor," and Edward replies that a "community of goods" is "philosophy for the back-woods only" (3:55–56), he is speaking for the ruling class; certainly Shelley is no proponent of "community of goods," but she endorses Ethel's "back-woods" view of social justice. She also endorses Ethel's belief that poverty cannot be "shameful" (3:140) since it so often afflicts "the most worthy and industrious"—a "practical philosophy" Ethel acquired in the "school" of the Illinois "wilderness." Finally, that school taught her a sympathy that has political consequences. Because "all that bore the human form was sanctified to her by the spirit of sympathy," Ethel recognizes that the American Indians are "subject to the same necessities" and moved by "the same impulses" as she. Granted, there is a whiff of condescension in this speech; still, Shelley here departs from her friend Fanny Wright's view of Native Americans as "savage hordes,"[34] and in this sense there is something to be said for Ethel's "spirit of sympathy." Moreover, that sympathy functions to critique the "high notions of aristocratic exclusiveness" (*Lodore,* 3:140) bred into Edward and especially evident in Lord Lodore's politics. He was too averse to "familiar community with the rude and unlettered" (1:19) to adapt to the "republican equality" of America, and his "disdain of most of his associates" (1:127) made for a short political career in England. Even the otherwise admirable Horatio Saville does not seek Parliamentary office because he is "too delicate, too finely strung, to sound in accord with the many" (2:221). Fanny Derham's education in "sincere sympathy with our fellow-creatures" (3:311) foreshadowed a role for single women; Ethel's politics of sympathy suggests a future "accord with the many" that is partly feminine but also partly American/republican.

Falkner (1837)

Mary Shelley's last novel, *Falkner* is in some ways a return to the Romantic themes that pervaded her early fiction. The character of Falkner recalls the guilty *isolato* popularized by Byron and familiar from *Frankenstein,* and his trial and redemption look even further back, to

Godwin's *Caleb Williams*. The Romantic theme of what Keats called "the holiness of the Heart's affections"[35] is contrasted in this novel with "the hardness of heart" that "too often subsists in aristocratic English families."[36] Still, the affections are a domestic/sentimental thematic as well, and *Falkner* fits even more completely than *Lodore* into the domestic/sentimental frame. Falkner's crime is not the Romantic stand-by of incest explored in *Mathilda,* but the more domestic/sentimental one of wife-abduction, and the Romantic "heart's affections" thematic is firmly grounded in a contrast between fashionable society and domestic/sentimental familial relations. Shelley is also much concerned with contemporary laws and norms, and she does not valorize Romantic outlawry as, for example, Byron's *Manfred* (1817) does; her subject is closer to that of Coleridge's *Ancient Mariner,* "the man hath penance done/And penance more will do."[37] As *Falkner* examines the motivation and expiation of "criminal" acts, it also explores social constructions of criminality and the gendering of those constructions.

If Wordsworth captured a nineteenth-century fascination with the innocent child "trailing clouds of glory" from its heavenly origins,[38] Mary Shelley captured the Victorian interest in mistreated children found in such novels as Dickens's *Oliver Twist* (1837) and Emily Brontë's *Wuthering Heights* (1848). *Falkner* opens with the tribulations of six-year-old Elizabeth Raby, "a friendless orphan" cast "pennyless [sic] on a thorny, stony-hearted world" (1:7). From a letter Elizabeth's mother wrote to her friend Alithea, the reader learns that Edwin Raby's "bigoted family" (1:20) had disowned him for repudiating their Catholicism and for marrying beneath his station. After his death, Edwin's family offered to raise Elizabeth on condition of her total separation from her mother; the young Mrs. Raby's rejection of this "barbarous offer" (1:22) echoes Mary Shelley's indignation when Sir Timothy made a similar offer after Percy Shelley's death (*MWSL,* 1:314–29; *MWSJ,* 1:453–59]. Following her mother's death, the orphaned Elizabeth lives with a "sordid" caretaker, Mrs. Baker (1:27); like the teenage Mary Godwin who often read and wrote by her mother's tomb (*MWSJ,* 2:543), Elizabeth spends much of her time at her mother's grave. To this graveyard comes a mysterious Romantic stranger, whose face hints a life of "singular, perhaps tragical, incidents" (1:38) and who rails at himself as a murderer. Attempting to shoot himself, he is saved when Elizabeth pulls his arm; because the woman he accuses himself of murdering was Mrs. Raby's friend Alithea, he determines "to expiate and to atone" for that misdeed (1:61) by raising Elizabeth as his child.

With this introduction of the title character, the novel begins its exploration of Romantic and domestic/sentimental ideals. Falkner's "proud and reserved" disposition (1:88) and "wild and fierce passions" (1:90) betoken the Romantic *isolato.* His belief that he can be "called out of himself" (1:89) by the "force" of Elizabeth's affection is Romantic too, but the form in which he implements this belief receives a domestic/sentimental criticism. Falkner is not "strictly just" (1:78) when he "mould[s]" and "model[s]" (1:90) Elizabeth into a "cure" (1:89) for his own misery. Moreover, if their quasi-familial relationship is "a perpetual interchange of benefit" (1:97), there are incestuous undertones in the "boundless excess" (1:102) of Elizabeth's "rapturous, thrilling adoration" of Falkner. Finally, his "fearful experiment" (1:93) displays a Frankenstein-like Romantic hubris about the workings of fate. Although he believes that in raising Elizabeth he is yielding to "the fatal net" (1:69) of his past with Alithea, in fact his effort to replace "the vain love of his youth" (1:90) with love for Elizabeth is an attempt to reshape that "fatal" past. By creating and encouraging Elizabeth's adoration, then, Falkner has irresponsibly tied her fate to his, for the past "never dies" (1:126) and his past sins are "unatoned" (1:120).

Fate's "net" further extends when Alithea's son Gerard Neville appears in Falkner's life. Falkner blames himself for the motherless boy's sullen ferocity, and decides to die in the "good cause" of Greek independence. In her descriptions of this war (as in *The Last Man* and "Euphrasia"), Shelley makes literary capital of her friendships with Lord Byron and the Greek prince Alexander Mavrocordato. Elizabeth accompanies Falkner to Greece, nurses his wounds, and devotes herself to reconciling him to life. While returning to England they again meet Gerard, whose temper has improved but who is still melancholy because of a mysterious "sacred purpose" (1:229) to which he has devoted himself. In the following years Elizabeth often wishes for a "link" (1:238) between Gerard and her father; "little did she think of the real link that existed" or "that to pray for the success of one, was to solicit destruction for the other." With such foreshadowings, Shelley of course intends to create reader suspense; but this suspense is thematic as well as narrative, for it dramatizes the "secret agency" (1:68) of an unknowable but inescapable fate.

After her return to England, Elizabeth is reunited with Gerard at the house of her friend Lady Cecil, who turns out to be Gerard's half-sister. He tells Elizabeth that his sacred mission is to clear his dead mother's name, and Lady Cecil then details the history of this mission. When Gerard was nine, his mother Alithea was abducted by a mysterious

Rupert; at this point the reader, way ahead of Elizabeth, recognizes the "real link" between Gerard and Falkner. Alithea's husband, the "dissipated" (1:286) and "selfish" (1:291) Sir Boyvill Neville, then initiated divorce proceedings and forced his son to testify before the House of Lords to his mother's supposed immorality. To avoid publicly defaming his mother, Gerard ran away, and when he was brought home his father treated him "like a criminal" (2:50). That treatment persisted until Sir Boyvill's marriage to Lady Cecil's mother, at which point Lady Cecil's softening influence and Gerard's growing determination to prove his mother's innocence together "reform[ed]" him (2:57). Lady Cecil concludes her tale with the "worldly" judgment that Gerard's mission is "madness" (2:63, 61), but Elizabeth feels he is "obeying the most sacred law of our nature" (2:93) and enthusiastically writes of his purpose to Falkner. From this letter Falkner first learns of the slur on Alithea's "sacred name" (2:127); reawakened to remorse, he determines to "meet the consequences of his actions" (2:110). To protect Elizabeth from his fate he tries to return her to her relatives, but her grandfather Oswald Raby, acting on "the vulgar, sordid prejudices of [a] narrow-minded bigot" (2:122), refuses to acknowledge her.

Falkner then reveals his history to Elizabeth. Raised by his uncle after his parents' death, he received kindness only from his mother's friend Mrs. Rivers, and he fell in love with her daughter, Alithea. Her father forbade them to marry, and Alithea's timidity—her "one fault" (2:210)—kept her from defying him. After a ten-year absence, Falkner returned to find Alithea married; "erecting [him]self into a providence" (2:233) to "put that right which God had let go wrong" (2:232), he first led Alithea to admit that she did not love her husband and then abducted her. He soon decided to release her, but Alithea, ignorant of this decision, attempted to flee and was drowned. Falkner and his henchman, Osborne, buried the body; the following day Falkner attempted to shoot himself but was saved by Elizabeth.

With these delayed revelations of Gerard's mission and its connection to Falkner's past, Shelley returns to two techniques she first used in *Frankenstein:* flashback narratives and multiple points of view. Like her use of foreshadowing, these techniques create reader suspense; in *Falkner* as in *Frankenstein,* however, Shelley's primary intent is educative and moral. She draws the reader to evaluate a character's past in terms of her or his present acts, and then to reevaluate both past and present acts from various points of view. Thus, as Elizabeth tries to reconcile her filial devotion to Falkner with her romantic love for Gerard, the reader

must similarly work to reconcile Falkner's and Gerard's versions of their tangled history. Then, using Lady Cecil's and Elizabeth's perspectives on Gerard's quest, as well as others' opinions of Falkner, the reader must weigh all these views to judge Falkner's crime and its consequences. That process commences in Volume III, as Sir Boyvill initiates a prosecution against Falkner for willful murder of Alithea.

This volume focuses on the definitions and judgments of Falkner's criminality. In Elizabeth's view, "the chief principle of religion" (2:290) is that "repentance washes away sin"; thus Falkner "is pardoned, and the crime forgotten." For Sir Boyvill, Falkner's "unparalleled guilt" (3:21) and his own "wounded vanity" (3:42) require legal action, the "cruel triumph" (3:45) of a public revenge against his enemy. Between these two positions stands Gerard. For him, Falkner is "sacred" (3:48) for having been loved by his mother but also guilty for dooming Elizabeth to "a partnership in guilt and misery" (3:30); and while Gerard disapproves of Sir Boyvill's "fierce and vulgar revenge" against Falkner (3:47), he feels he must join in that revenge in order to prove that his mother did not desert her "first and most sacred duty" (3:57), her child. To find this proof, he tracks down Falkner's accomplice Osborne, who testifies at the trial not only that Alithea's death was an accident but that she died trying to return to her son. Falkner is acquitted on the basis less of this evidence, however, than of his character. Supported by a combination of "Christian resignation" (3:165), "belief in fatality," and "philosophical fortitude" (3:166), he overwhelms the jury with "the power of a clear conscience and a just cause" (3:275).

Did Falkner commit a crime? He is certainly not guilty of willful murder, the crime with which he is charged. He *is* guilty of abducting a married woman, but Shelley represents that act as a moral rather than a legal issue, and even in this light it resists straightforward condemnation: Falkner's initial love for Alithea was honorable and she would have married him if she had been allowed to. Falkner's narrative of his history also amply demonstrates his recognition of his misconduct and his efforts to atone for it. Finally, as a "result of his suffering" Falkner develops an "elevated tone of moral feeling" (3:318). He also achieves a tranquillity which is both "the reward of much suffering" (3:288) and the sign of "a noble disposition throwing off former evil as alien to its nature" (3:289) and "embracing good as its indefeasible right." What is at issue, then, is less a crime than its expiation, and in these terms the reader is invited to forgive Falkner as he "was forgiven, we may believe, in heaven" (3:317).

With this representation of Falkner, Mary Shelley is working to reconcile two concepts of fate. To a classical notion of fate—the "secret
agency of a thousand foregone, disregarded, and trivial events" (1:68)
that enmeshes even "a noble disposition"—she joins a Christian notion
of a divine Providence, which allows those events to occur but also
allows a sinner to expiate misdeeds by repentance and suffering. One
contemporary review of *Falkner* used precisely these Christian terms to
claim that a novel showing "the action of a never-dying remorse upon
the soul of one naturally noble" has "the most important moral uses."[39]
But another, unfriendly review saw Falkner as a criminal and the novel
as a tissue of sophistries. After abducting Alithea, this reviewer sniffed,
Falkner "becomes as penitent as men usually are when they fail in a villainous enterprise"; because "there will be no use, and some inconvenience to himself, in returning a dead wife," Falkner ensures, "for selfish
reasons, that the woman he has destroyed shall be supposed infamous";
finally, Sir Boyvill is "perfectly warranted" in considering Falkner a murderer.[40]

At issue here is the social construction of criminality. To this reviewer,
Falkner is simply a miscreant who "cause[d] the loss of an innocent life"
and defamed "the reputation of a virtuous woman." The reviewer resists
the novel's careful representation of Falkner's penitence; for him, the
"head and front" of this defense is Gerard's several references to Falkner's
status as a gentleman. The review is on solid ground here; the novel often
suggests that Sir Boyvill, whose title is recent, is not quite a gentleman
and that Falkner, a true gentleman despite his flaws, is demeaned by
being brought to court among "vulgar rogues or hardened ruffians"
(3:258). But the novel also suggests that guilt, even criminal guilt,
should receive "the indulgence of a correcting father" rather than "the
cruel vengeance of the law" (3:108–09). Thus Sir Boyvill, who treated his
own son "like a criminal instead of an unfortunate erring child" (2:53),
can hardly be trusted to treat his enemy with paternal "indulgence."

The problematic of class relations suggested by Sir Boyvill is related
to the novel's constructions of gender, and thence to its gendering of
criminality. Unlike some of Shelley's earlier fiction, *Falkner* is not critical
of class society *per se*. The reader is invited to share Gerard's oft-
expressed horror of being "in the mouths of the vulgar" (2:80), Falkner's
disgust that his own defense rests on "so abject a poltroon" as Osborne
(3:157), Elizabeth's assumption that her visit to the prison will draw
"the hootings of the mob" (3:111), and so on. The novel's critique of
class relations, then, is reformist rather than revolutionary, and it is

made in part through Elizabeth's unorthodox but proper femininity. As her conduct exposes the artificialities and constraints of fashionable society's notions of propriety, she becomes the standard against which even the novel's admirable upper-class women are judged. In an important episode, Elizabeth argues that "gratitude, duty, every human obligation" (3:91) require her to visit Falkner in prison; Lady Cecil counters with arguments from "worldly wisdom" (3:98) and "feminine delicacy," and Mrs. Raby insists that Elizabeth must obey her relatives. Elizabeth's response is notable:

> [W]as she to adopt a new system of conduct, become a timid, home-bred lady, tied by the most frivolous rules, impeded by fictitious notions of propriety and false delicacy . . . [W]hether indeed such submission to society—such useless, degrading dereliction of nobler duties, was adapted for feminine conduct, and whether she, despising such bonds, sought a bold and dangerous freedom, she could not tell; she only knew and felt, that for her, educated as she had been, beyond the narrow paling of boarding school ideas, or the refinements of a lady's boudoir, . . . to preserve her faithful attachment to [Falkner] amidst dire adversity was her sacred duty—a virtue, before which every minor moral faded and disappeared. (3:99)

This argument excuses offenses against feminine propriety in the name of higher claims and duties; although it is clearly limited only to women who recognize those claims and duties, still it recuperates conduct that was deemed improper by fashionable society.

A similar recuperation is suggested by the parallels between Shelley's novel and the highly publicized legal difficulties of her friend Lady Caroline Norton. In 1836 Lady Caroline's husband, George Norton, began legal proceedings for divorce by suing Lord Melbourne for "criminal conversation," or adultery, with his wife. Although the jury dismissed his suit without leaving the jury box, once Lady Caroline had separated informally from her husband, she found that she had no legal right to custody of her children. Her reputation was "badly damaged" by the court case,[41] and during this period of social ostracism, Mary Shelley remained her friend, supporter, and confidante (*MWSL,* 2:244n). Furthermore, Lady Caroline acknowledged Shelley's help in the writing of her 1837 pamphlet *Observations on the Natural Claim of a Mother to the Custody of her Children* (*MWSL,* 2:283n).

Although Lady Caroline's troubles are in some respects widely different from Alithea's, there are three areas of resemblance. One is the

importance of a lady's reputation for wifely chastity; like Lady Caroline's, Alithea's good name was seriously tainted by the mere suspicion of sexual misconduct. Another resemblance is the extreme fragility of that reputation; as Lady Caroline's was damaged by an unfounded scandal initiated by her husband, so Alithea was assumed to be an adulteress as soon as her husband "first uttered the fatal word" (1:316). The novel specifically addresses this easy imputation of criminality to women who deviate from feminine propriety. Because "we are apt to consider every deviation from stony apathy as tending at last to the indulgence of passions against which society has declared a ban" (1:318), Alithea's "goodness" (1:317), "purity," and "devoted attachment to her children" count for nothing once she is suspected of adultery.

The third and most important resemblance between the cases of Lady Caroline and Alithea is the emphasis in both on the sacred claims of motherhood. Lady Caroline's pamphlet is based on this claim; similarly, throughout *Falkner* Alithea's maternal devotion is presented as evidence that she is innocent of adultery. In his history, Falkner records that Alithea spurned his advances by saying that "mother" is "a more sacred name than wife," and that caring for her children is "a higher purpose than even conducing to [his] happiness" (2:251, 249). Elizabeth too feels that in Alithea's "finely-formed nature" (2:63) maternal love must have been "paramount to every other feeling." But it is worth noting that Sir Boyvill believes his wife is an adulteress precisely because "even maternal duties and affections [were] sacrificed to irresistible passion" (2:9). Although he is hardly a reliable narrator, his intolerance of the slightest impropriety in women is not unique in the novel. Gerard says of Falkner that "the noble penitent is more welcome [in heaven] than the dull follower of a narrow code of morals, who never erred, because he never felt" (3:302); it is inconceivable that he would make such a remark about his mother, and indeed the novel's plot would fall to the ground if he could imagine her a "noble penitent" rather than a spotless innocent. *Falkner's* focus on the "angel mother" (1:271) may cloy, but it also shows how Mary Shelley uses such conventions of domestic/sentimental fiction to address contemporary issues of significance to women.

Chapter Six
Literary Biography and Criticism

Since Mary Shelley is now known primarily for *Frankenstein,* it is often forgotten that she also wrote a great deal of literary biography and criticism. Between 1823 and 1844, she wrote the short pieces—biographies, book reviews, and essays on various subjects—that I classify as literary journalism. In 1834 she was commissioned to write biographies of European literary figures for Dionysius Lardner's Cabinet Cyclopedia; by 1839 she had written four volumes of *Lives* for this series. In 1824 she produced an edition of Percy Shelley's posthumous poems, and in 1839 and 1840 she published the first critical editions of his poetry and prose. This chapter discusses Mary Shelley's literary journalism in terms of its contribution to the relatively new profession of literary criticism. The sections on the *Lives* focus on her methods of literary biography and criticism, while the section on her editions of Percy's works emphasizes her role in the construction of a "Shelley legend."[1]

Literary Journalism

From her first piece for *The Liberal* in 1823 to her last review for *The Athenaeum* in 1844, Mary Shelley contributed four short literary biographies, eleven book reviews, and essays on assorted subjects to various literary periodicals. With these short pieces of literary biography and criticism, she participated in the professionalization of literary criticism begun during the eighteenth century and consolidated in the 1820s and 1830s.

British literary criticism of the eighteenth century had national, political, and economic bases. The older concept of "learning" as an "international body of knowledge founded upon the classics" was being succeeded by a new concept of "literature" that was "nationalistic."[2] Editions of Shakespeare's plays and British poets included critical apparatus that helped to "magnify the aura and authority of English works, to make them appear as classics."[3] With these critical editions and in essays defining literary taste, eighteenth-century writers began to formalize the genre of literary criticism. Another important innovation was the lit-

erary review or journal; the *Gentleman's Magazine,* the *Monthly Review,* and the *Critical Review* were all founded in the eighteenth century. Reading such journals became "a sign of cultivation,"[4] but it was also a sign of party allegiance, because many reviews were founded for political purposes. Like the controversies over the nature of fiction and its reading public discussed in chapter 4, then, eighteenth-century literary criticism was often politicized. Into the 1810s, for example, the conservative *Quarterly Review* "hunted down 'infidel,' irreligious, or sexually explicit" matter in such novels as *Frankenstein* (Butler, 141). Finally, criticism became a paid profession in the eighteenth century, and the canon of national literature critics constructed had economic, as well as literary and political, force. An example is Samuel Johnson's *Lives of the English Poets;* in 1777 a consortium of London booksellers commissioned him to write biographical prefaces for an edition of British poets "deliberately designed" to displace the only other edition affordable for common readers (Ross, 20). Similar economic factors inflected the literary reviews, many of which were founded, run, and distributed by booksellers.

In the early nineteenth century, literary criticism was increasingly informed by economics. An economic language of "value" came to dominate criticism as reviewers and critics became "advisers" for "literary consumers anxious to know the worth of their purchases."[5] One form this advising took was the public lectures begun in 1802 under the sponsorship of London's Royal Institution. Although these lectures drew the already cultivated (Mary Shelley attended several with her father[6]), they were tailored to an audience "earnest" for "useful" literary instruction (Parrinder, 57). They also produced consumers; lecturers, such as the poet Samuel Taylor Coleridge and the critic William Hazlitt, created buyers for their own works and for such journals as the *London Magazine,* which printed Hazlitt's essays. A second form of advising was the "explosion" of reviewing in literary journals which themselves proliferated in the 1810s and 1820s (Parrinder, 55). These periodicals began to represent literature and criticism as "a sphere separated from money-making, social conflict, and heterodox politics" (Butler, 143). But literary journals—often closely affiliated with other publishing ventures—were "conscious of a mass readership waiting to be recruited" (Butler, 146), and reviewers accomplished that recruiting. In the 1830s, for instance, Mary Shelley's publisher Henry Colburn achieved a virtual monopoly on novel publishing by creating a demand for his product with reviews and advertising in the several journals of which he was full or part owner.[7]

Designed for readers eager to tap the cultural capital afforded by literature, literary reviews created an audience for a literary knowledge both arcane and accessible: arcane because this "discrete, autonomous literary sphere" (Butler, 145) was the province of highly-educated literary critics, accessible because those experts were offering their knowledge to the uninitiated. Mary Shelley's literary journalism indicates both the range of that knowledge and some functions of such criticism.

Shelley's journalism about travel and tourism is discussed in chapter 7; although her essay "On Ghosts" is not, strictly speaking, literary criticism, I include it here to introduce her view of the imagination. The essay begins by characterizing explorers' narratives as distinctly inferior to the "strange tales" created by "men's imaginations" of an unknown world.[8] Included in this "empire of the imagination" (335) are ghosts. Here Shelley distinguishes between "phantoms unreal" (336), which only "appal the senses" (337), and apparitions, which are "impalpable to the coarser faculties" (336) but nonetheless convince "the feeling heart" that "influences do exist to watch and guard us." She then tells three ghost stories of the latter sort and concludes with a more comic tale that makes her main point: "[t]here is something beyond us of which we are ignorant" but to which the imagination gives us access. This early view of the imagination will undergo review in her later essays.

Biographies

The first of Shelley's four short literary biographies, "Madame d'Houtetôt," was written in 1823 for the journal *The Liberal*. Established by her friends Leigh Hunt and Lord Byron to "publish all their original compositions, and share the profits" (*PBSL*, 2:344), this commercial venture was almost universally condemned by other literary journals for its radical politics.[9] In "Madame d'Houtetôt," elements of that radicalism appear in Mary Shelley's comments on gender and social customs. Sophie d'Houtetôt is initially interesting as the friend of Rousseau because genius "gift[s] with immortality" everything it touches; but she is also worth studying "on her own account" as "a woman of talent."[10] Although the essay mentions Houtetôt's "great poetical talent" (73), it focuses on such conventional feminine traits as her "natural modesty" and the "sweetness" of disposition (81) that made her a "sympathizing companion" (77) and "an angel of consolation." Yet this femininity is not merely conventional, for Shelley uses it to critique the social custom of arranged marriages, which takes advantage of such

feminine gentleness. Houtetôt "permitted herself to be disposed of according to the customs of her country" (69), and such "disposal of the person of woman, however legalized," is "disgraceful." Although Houtetôt then took a lover, Shelley points out that such affairs were "not considered criminal" (75), that her "mistake" (81) was due to "the tenderness of her heart," and that her nature remained "unblemished" (72). She further exonerates Houtetôt by criticizing her "cold" husband (75), her "estranged" father, and the "heartlessness" of French marriage customs (72). As often in Mary Shelley's biographies, the life of a "woman of talent" becomes a vehicle for criticizing cultural systems injurious to women.

In a later essay, Shelley combined literary criticism with reflections on the gendered and other trials of authorship. This 1831 essay, a biography of Lady Caroline Norton, was published anonymously in the *New Monthly Magazine and Literary Journal* series on "Living Literary Characters." Norton's poetry has "an energy of thought and power of imagination" unequaled by other women writers, and she excels them in "having a *meaning* for her words."[11] Shelley attributes the latter ability to Norton's having received "masculine teaching" (181) rather than the "daily doses" of "accomplishments" that constitute most women's education. She then uses Norton's difficulties in publishing her early work to decry the "obstructions" (182), "anxious toils," and "defeated hopes" whereby "every new candidate for literary fame" is "pertinaciously discouraged." It is worth noting, however, that as an author Shelley is hardly disinterested here. Moreover, the *New Monthly Magazine* was owned by her publishers, Colburn & Bentley, and the Living Literary Characters seem designed to advertise as well as inform.

Mary Shelley's second literary biography for this series makes even clearer the link between critical and economic judgments. Her essay on the American novelist James Fenimore Cooper discusses both his novels and their reception in Britain. Cooper tends to be prolix, she writes; "[i]f a man pulls a rope, he tells you first how it was manufactured."[12] But his characters show his "deep knowledge of our nature" (359), his women characters display "an almost Shaksperian [sic] subtlety of perception," and his novels "encourage" human nature and "inculcate a better and brighter philosophy." In addition, Cooper's emergence forced even "the most prejudiced" (357) of British readers to admit that the usual "ridicule" of America's political "laws and institutions" could not be extended to its literature. Although Shelley gently mocks Cooper's bumptious "republicanism" (361) and his "national notion of equality" (362), a concluding footnote predicts that his books will become "even

more extensively" known via Colburn & Bentley's "cheap but clear and beautifully printed" editions. This particularly egregious piece of advertising, for the same Standard Novels series in which Mary Shelley's *Frankenstein* was reprinted later that year, dramatizes how such critical judgments as "most valuable" (362) can be inflected by economics.

The last of Shelley's short biographies is the "Memoirs of William Godwin," which she wrote in 1831 for the Colburn & Bentley reissue of his novel *Caleb Williams*. To round out her view of her father, I include here the biographical notes, unpublished in her lifetime, which she made after Godwin's death in 1836. The "Memoirs" show her high regard for his books. The *Enquiry concerning Political Justice* achieved immediate "eminence" for its "daring" and "eloquence" and also for Godwin's "heartfelt sincerity and love of truth."[13] *Caleb Williams* raised his reputation even higher through the character of Falkland, which Shelley considers "the most real" and "grand" since Hamlet (xiii). She praises Godwin's novel *St. Leon* for the "dignity and grandeur" (ix) of its heroine, whom she reads as a tribute to her mother Mary Wollstonecraft. The "Memoirs" and notes also record Shelley's admiration for Godwin's politics. His "lofty, independent, and elevating" (xi) rebuttal to Malthus's *Essay on Population* failed to convince only because Malthus's book appealed to "the vices of the great, and all that is rotten in our institutions." Her 1836 notes are equally critical of the "vindictive" sedition trials of 1795 which turned "the whole force of the law" against radicals, and she takes pride in her father's "enthusiastic and intrepid" support of the defendants.[14] Still, Shelley is careful to dissociate Godwin from "agitators" (vii); his writings were "[b]oldly speculative," she writes, but his practical politics were "moderate." In the 1836 notes she distinguishes between his "inner and more private feelings" and "the supposed gist of his doctrines" (quoted in Paul, 1:238); she points out that he married Wollstonecraft despite *Political Justice*'s criticism of marriage. The "Memoirs" concludes that if Godwin is "the mighty parent" (xiii) of what contemporary reformers advocate, he is also "the monument" of a "more contemplative" generation's "profounder and loftier views." This eloquent but careful tribute encapsulates not only Godwin but the conflicted politics that are everywhere apparent in Shelley's own writings.

Book Reviews

Mary Shelley's book reviews cover numerous literary and historical subjects. Literary reviews show the range of her knowledge and opinions

about the practice of literature, and, like the reviews on historical subjects, they also show how criticism is inflected by cultural concerns.

Her 1827 review of Thomas Roscoe's *The Italian Novelists* begins with political and literary reflections on the history of British literature. "Our northern imaginations" have been influenced by the "sun-inspired literature of the East," she writes, so that England's "imaginative writers" join the "common-place reality" of their "cold, damp, unfruitful country" with "the ideality of the golden fields of eastern culture."[15] Such Orientalism performs various ideological functions in Shelley's stories; here it is used to suggest the superiority of hybrid British literature to a one-sided Italian literature. While some Italian novels excel at portraying the "external surface of human proceedings" (118), "the highest place in the intellectual world" (117) is reserved for works that show the "distinction and individualization" of human character. Although Shelley defends the Italian novelists against charges of "licentiousness" (118), she approves Roscoe's "judgment" (121) in altering passages "not admissable [sic] by the English reader." Despite this deference to English taste, she faults Roscoe's translations; while "an elegant English style is desirable," a translator should "keep as near the words of his original" as possible. Shelley's confidence in her own "right reading" (122) of Italian literature will recur in several of her *Lives* for Lardner's Cabinet Cyclopedia.

Her 1829 review of several works by Prosper Mérimée takes up both political and literary issues. The plays in Mérimée's *Comédies de Clara Gazul* show an admirable "spirit of freedom from political and religious servitude,"[16] and his poem *La Jacquerie* gives a "frightful and true" (80) picture of the "crimes and misfortunes" suffered by the French peasantry under "the iron heel of feudal tyranny" (78). Shelley then defends the literary imagination in her discussion of Mérimée's tragedy *The Family of Carvajal*. The play is about incest, and there is at least "a question" (80) whether literature should address such subjects. But a writer who yearns to "trace the boundaries of the unknown intellectual world" will find it difficult to obey rules imposed by those confined within "the narrow bounds of their personal experience." She then uses Columbus as a figure for "the imaginative writer" who "courageously" seeks "fresh and untried ground." Such literary explorers can treat an unpleasant subject—which they know only through "the innate force of the imagination"—in ways that excite "interest" without shocking "tastes." If this essay does not celebrate the "empire of the imagination" as "On Ghosts" did, still it differentiates the literary imagination from the "tamer

thoughts" that govern the morality of personal experience. For Mary Shelley, as for Percy, then, incest may be "like many other *incorrect* things a very poetical circumstance" (*PBSL,* 2:154).

Perhaps Mary Shelley's fullest definition of the "poetical" appears in her 1829 review of Anna Jameson's *The Loves of the Poets.* She begins by stating the insufficiency of all pleasures but love: only the affections "take the sting from life,"[17] and love is "the best form of affection" due to "the excess of its sympathy." Citing the authority of Plato and her husband, Mary Shelley then defines the poet as "an incarnation of the very essence of Love," because he is inspired by "the desire for sympathy." This equation of the poet with love appears again in a comment on Jameson's contrast between the admirable constancy of women poets, who mourn their lost loves, and the inconstancy of male poets, who leap from elegiac verses on a first love to "epithalamiums on a marriage with a second" (369). Shelley agrees that women's "tenderness" *may* extend to the dead and men's "passion" *must* "expend itself on the living," but she adds that feminine constancy is one of the cultural "superstitions" that "rather injure than exalt" women by relegating them to "perpetual widowhood." Moreover, what seems inconstancy in men is in fact poetical. The "fervency and truth" of a man's passion is attested by "the force of the imagination" which creates a new love-object; a solitary man, then, lacks "every poetical attribute." During her husband's life Mary Shelley was sometimes impatient with his poetical tendency to invest an unworthy object with celestial traits; in this essay, however, that tendency becomes the sign of the poet.

Many of Shelley's reviews contain strictures about proper novelistic practice. The review of Jameson's *Loves of the Poets* comments in passing that the same author's novel, *The Diary of an Ennuyée,* married reality and fiction—"who are brother and sister, and who may not therefore too closely unite"—to produce "an offspring which is neither true nor false" (367). In an 1830 review Shelley calls the novel "the very frame" for "a picture of manners"; hence Mérimée's novel better represents social customs than did his plays, for drama lacks a "canvas wide enough for the painting of manners."[18] In this review Shelley also comments on the educational function of novels. Discussing the absence of overt moralizing in Mérimée's novel, she suggests both that truth carries "its own moral" (502) and that toleration is "the best lesson a novelist can give." This concern with literature's moral effect shows Shelley's shift away from an earlier belief in the primacy of the imagination; at the same time, she trusts a reader's ability to discern a novel's implicit lesson.

Shelley's 1830 review of William Godwin's novel *Cloudesley* includes an extended analysis of the lessons of art. Noting that her father ranked the novelist's art "very high" above that of the historian and the dramatist, she goes on to explain why Godwin's novels surpass even this high point.[19] Where other writers represent "manners rather than passions," or only "vague and incomplete" passions, Godwin gives an event "in its entireness." Novelists like Bulwer, who are "merely copying from [their] own hearts" (712), or Walter Scott, whose scenes and characters are "unsurpassed" but lack "connexion," fail to mold their materials into "a new form" (711). In contrast, Godwin reaches "the highest species of perfection" (712) possible to novels, for "all is blended into one whole" as events "naturally flow one from the other" (712–13). In her analysis of Mérimée's tragedy about incest, Shelley had valued imaginative exploration over the rules imposed by "tamer thoughts"; here she states that "the completion and elevation of our nature and its productions" requires a "degree of obedience to rule and law." Shelley reserves her highest praise for *Cloudesley*'s didactic elements. Its episodes of a child's upbringing contain "many a lesson" for parents and teachers (713), and every page has "some lesson to teach us confidence, love, and hope" (716). A reader leaves the book with "elevating" emotions of "compassion for the criminal" and "admiration for the innocent," because the author teaches that "'the true key of the universe is love'." Through Godwin as through Mérimée, Shelley's reviews teach her audience the moral benefits of proper reading.

In the last of her reviews of novels, Shelley returns to James Fenimore Cooper but takes a slightly different approach from her earlier literary biography. There, she had read Cooper as a distinctively American writer, and in this 1832 review of *The Bravo* she is dismayed that the novel is set in a Renaissance Venice where society is "sophisticated and enervated,"[20] "man is a creature of forms" (182), and woman is "veil[ed]." Yet the novel is a success, she believes, because it is "based upon passions, not manners" (183). For Shelley, representing manners requires specialized knowledge; in contrast, the passions are "eternal feelings" that do not change with "the modifications of society," so *The Bravo* succeeds despite its departures from Cooper's usual locales and themes. Like her "Living Literary Character" of him, however, this review subtly denigrates his politics. One suspects, for instance, that she praises one character's "simple feelings" (185) in part because they show his "deference and submission towards his superiors in rank" (186). Shelley's ambivalent response to Cooper again indicates how political

and other cultural elements inflect the evaluative language of literary criticism. Such inflections are especially evident in her reviews of books on historical subjects.

In her 1823 review of historian Giovanni Villani's *Chroniche Fiorentine* for *The Liberal,* Shelley presents a view of genius at once more political and more sanguine than that of her later *Lives.* A "Man of Genius" is "the sublimest work of God,"[21] and it is "both presumptuous and sacrilegious" (281) to "give the law to genius." Thus the "most reasonable" way to evaluate the art of different eras is "to admire the beauties of all," using a "standard of excellence" which is not reducible to "narrow systems and arbitrary rules." In the Cyclopedia *Lives,* Shelley will critique literary conventions as well as the excesses of unfettered genius. Here, however, rules are "the leading-strings and go-carts of mediocrity" (282), not of "those superior minds that are themselves the law" of "intellectual creation"; hence, if a genius "appear[s] to err, the failure is in our understanding," not his practice. When "men of genius" (283) engage in "self-analysation and display," their works inspire readers "of imagination and sensibility" to pursue "the science of self-knowledge." With this dual confidence in the genius of the writer and the imagination of the reader, Shelley states perhaps her most Romantic and revolutionary view of the primacy of the individual.

Two later reviews of books on historical figures take a more restrained view. Written for the reformist *Westminster Review* in the aftermath of popular agitation over the Reform Bill of 1832, Shelley's review of Thomas Moore's book on the Irish radical Lord Edward Fitzgerald shows her shift away from a purely individual politics. Fitzgerald was a leading spirit in the Society of United Irishmen and in Ireland's rebellion against English rule in 1798; Shelley begins her review by noting that, until recently, such views as his would have been met with "affected horror and disgust, if not with rancorous persecution."[22] "Happily," however, due to the "recent tenor" of social progress, "the absurd doctrine of passive obedience is exploded." She goes on to praise Fitzgerald's adherence to "classical republican heroism" (111), his "undaunted courage and correct intentions" (111–12), and the "domestic affections" (114) often found with "the purest and most disinterested" patriotism. She notes too that he was rightly influenced by the "intoxicating excitement" of the French Revolution (115) and by the distaste for "the shackles and restraints of crowded society and corrupt government" that he imbibed during his time in the New World. Like many "high-spirited individuals" (111), however, he valued "abstract principles" over "practi-

cal" action, and he lacked the "prudence [and] caution" (112) that are "essential" in the leader of "a grand social movement." Moreover, in Shelley's view, resistance to a government is "lawful" (118) and indeed "a social duty" only when there is no other redress. She prefers the strategy of "moral combination" which resulted in the Catholic Emancipation bill of 1829; "[o]ther benefits will follow from similar unity." In its critique of "high-spirited" individualist politics and armed rebellion, Shelley's review points to the political functions of literary criticism.

Her criticism of Moore's "excess of panegyric" (113) also demonstrates Shelley's own more restrained critical method. Where her 1823 *Liberal* article tended toward sweeping judgments, the 1831 review of Moore maintains a delicate balance between praise and fault-finding. In her 1844 review of Caroline Halsted's book on Richard III, Shelley again displays this characteristic method of calm advocacy; of the many efforts to prove or disprove Richard's crimes, she remarks that "disputation" is no substitute for the "patient care" of research.[23] Drawing on her own research for *Perkin Warbeck* (1830), she carefully analyzes Halsted's evidence and concludes that Richard was neither "quite so blameless" as Halsted believes (#876, 731) nor as villainous as "tradition and Tudor history" insist. Although Mary Shelley's own opinion of Richard is quite clear, still the measured tone of this final review is in telling contrast with her earlier journalism's almost joyous confidence.

Lives of the most Eminent Literary and Scientific Men of Italy, Spain, and Portugal (1835–37)

The three volumes of *Lives of the most Eminent Literary and Scientific Men of Italy, Spain, and Portugal* were commissioned for Dionysius Lardner's Cabinet Cyclopedia; Shelley wrote most of the first two volumes and all of the third. She took on the project to earn the money "so very needful" to support herself and her son, but she also felt she was "*much* better" at this work than at "romancing" (*MWSL*, 2:293, 3:93). Before turning to her methods of literary biography and criticism in the *Lives*, it is important to identify the intended audience for texts like Lardner's Cyclopedia.

The creation of that audience during the early nineteenth century depended on increased literacy, class-specific education, availability of reading matter, and the profession of literary criticism. With regional variations, by 1800 the literacy rate for the English middle classes was approximately 75 percent, for the working classes roughly 50 percent; following a drop after 1800, both rates rose steadily from 1830 on.[24]

The literacy measured in the working-class rates might have been merely functional, since children were increasingly employed in factories and would perforce receive only sketchy and intermittent schooling; indeed, initially literate laborers with limited access to reading matter sometimes forgot how to read (Smith, 156). Still, many readers who were adults in the 1830s benefited from an increase in educational facilities during their childhoods. The Sunday schools begun for working-class children in 1780 taught reading, writing, and basic arithmetic (although by the 1790s many had ceased to teach writing because of Sabbatarian doubts about the propriety of writing on Sunday).[25] Also serving laboring-class children were the church schools established and run by the British and Foreign School Society (founded 1810) and the Anglican National Society (founded 1811), with the assistance after 1830 of government funding; in addition to the fundamentals, these schools taught religion and bible study. Because such schooling implied not only charity but church-state control, many working-class parents preferred to pay small, privately-run day and dame schools to educate their children. The educational institutions available to middle-class children were similarly diverse. In the early 1800s, many parents in the newly prosperous urban commercial classes became dissatisfied with grammar schools, the free charitable institutions that taught elementary and classical subjects to girls as well as boys of all classes. Thus many grammar schools began to teach commercial subjects for business use, in addition to or instead of the classics required for university entrance; some became single-sex boarding schools, and others began to charge fees (Sanderson, 34). By the 1830s, then, schools and their curricula were increasingly class-specific, so that many school-leavers were literate but lacked the literary and classical education that signaled true cultivation.

A new availability of reading matter helped make up for that lack. After 1774, the breaking of perpetual copyright enabled the printing of cheap editions of copyrighted works (Smith, 157). The development of more efficient paper-making technology in the 1810s facilitated book production (Sanderson, 23), and the introduction of steam printing and cheap cloth bindings in the 1830s, along with the reduction of the tax on paper in 1836, further lowered book prices. A greater variety of texts thus became available to the newly literate working classes. In addition to the cheap religious tracts produced by such early groups as the Society for the Promotion of Christian Knowledge (founded 1698), popularized treatises on secular subjects were issued by the Society for the

Diffusion of Useful Knowledge (founded in 1826) and available in the
libraries of Mechanics Institutes. For the middle classes, encyclopedias
and other "knowledge texts" offered information in an organized form
that "emphasized the tractability . . . of knowledge."[26] In the 1830s novels became more accessible to middle-class readers as circulating
libraries began to extend from London into the provinces. Such literary
reviews as the *London Magazine* (1820–29) aimed at introducing this
newly available fiction to readers "with little or no prior knowledge" of
literature (Butler, 127). Like fiction publishers—for example, Henry
Colburn—the publishers of "knowledge texts" were often closely affiliated with such journals. Dionysius Lardner was general editor of the
Cabinet Cyclopedia when he founded the *Monthly Chronicle* with novelist
Edward Bulwer in 1838; the following year Robert Bell, who was writing the Cyclopedia's *Lives of the English Poets,* became the *Chronicle*'s editor (Cross, 119).

Issued from 1829 to 1846 in 133 volumes, Lardner's Cabinet Cyclopedia made accessible an even broader range of knowledge. Eschewing
the relatively new alphabetical arrangement of contents, the Cyclopedia
followed the older organization by subject,[27] so the volumes were organized into six subject "cabinets": arts and useful arts, biography, geography, history, natural history, and natural philosophy (proposed cabinets
of philosophy, literature, and dictionaries did not appear).[28] The Cyclopedia was written by recognized experts. J. C. L. de Sismondi, who had
written a sixteen-volume history of Italy (1808–18), contributed a volume on Italian republicanism; the Scottish antiquarian and novelist
Walter Scott wrote on Scotland, and the Irish poet Thomas Moore wrote
on Ireland; the treatise on optics was written by Sir David Brewster,
who had made important discoveries in the polarization of light; and
Lardner himself, first holder of the chair of natural philosophy and
astronomy at London University, was well known for his many treatises
on useful arts from mechanics to railway transport. Although one critic
classes Mary Shelley with the Cyclopedia writers that he considers "literary hacks" (Peckham, 46), in fact she was in excellent company and was
held to adorn it: reprints of the *Lives* list the authors as "Mrs. Shelley
and others."

The marketing of Shelley's reputation as a popular writer suggests
that the Cabinet Cyclopedia was intended for a wide audience. Bound in
cloth rather than leather and priced at six shillings each, the volumes
were affordable for middle-class readers with both the leisure and the
desire to extend their knowledge. Lardner intended to "stimulate the

diffusion of knowledge" to the "general reader" by making the arts and sciences "attractive" and "universally intelligible," but he also intended to "inculcate sound principles" and "raise the tone of the public mind" (quoted in Peckham, 42). Some critics were skeptical. *Fraser's Magazine* considered the volumes so tedious as to be "still-born,"[29] and other commentators criticized the Cyclopedia's accessibility. In an 1838 satire by Thackeray, a drunken Lardner promotes his volumes on the ground that they are "cheap as durrt," and an ill-educated footman boasts of being commissioned to write "'The Lives of Eminent Brittish and Foring Wosherwomen.'"[30] But more sympathetic critics welcomed the Cyclopedia as "a rich library of universal knowledge" for "ordinary readers," and such reviewers clearly had designs on the newly literate "common reader."[31] The *Monthly Review* hoped one volume's "popular and accessible" historical "lessons" would reach "the hands of every man," in order to teach "gratitude" for the "blessings" of civil government and "cautio[n]" in reforming that government.[32] With similar didactic intent, Sismondi wrote the *History of the Italian Republics* to prove "ill-fated Italy['s]" claims to the "freedom" crushed the previous year by French invaders.[33] While Shelley's educative intent is seldom so overt, increasingly her *Lives* draw the reader's attention to moral and political lessons as well as literary issues.

The first volume of *Lives of the Most Eminent Literary and Scientific Men of Italy, Spain, and Portugal* (1835) covers the life and work of several four-teenth- and fifteenth-century Italian authors. Sir James Montgomery wrote the lives of Dante and Ariosto, and Mary Shelley wrote the remaining essays on Francesco Petrarch, Giovanni Boccaccio, Lorenzo de' Medici and his circle, Matteo Bojardo, Francesco Berni, and Niccolo Machiavelli. The *Monthly Review* praised these lives as a corrective both to the "general ignorance of Italian literature" in Britain (#138, 317) and to "the authority of the French critics" who had pronounced Italian works "unworthy of attention" (#136, 298). The fact that twentieth-century critics no longer regard some of these poets as "eminent" points to the role of literary criticism in constructing, maintaining, and altering the rosters of canonical writers. In the first volume, Shelley is primarily concerned with establishing the lesser-known writers' claims to attention and extending the better-known writers' claims to eminence. Hence her commentary displays not the objectivity that literary criticism sometimes claims for itself but the advocacy that has marked criticism from its inception.

This advocacy is most apparent when Shelley defends her subjects; indeed, for her "there is no more delightful literary task" than justifying a writer who has been "misrepresented and reviled."[34] She dismisses charges of impiety against passages of Luigi Pulci's poem *Morgante Maggiore* by noting that "in those times men were on a much more familiar footing than now" with their gods (1:171). Machiavelli had been accused of plagiarism on the grounds that he was a mere clerk, and she criticizes such efforts to "degrade celebrated men, by impeaching their station in society" (1:258). Against charges that passion in Petrarch's poetry is "defaced by conceits," she insists that only "hard and dry critics, who neither feel themselves nor sympathize in the feelings of others," are unaware that conceits "spring naturally" from passion (1:80–81). These defenses are based on cultural or social rather than textual arguments; in contrast, when Shelley analyzes the critical controversy over whether Machiavelli's *The Prince* is pro-republican, she uses his writings and letters to "adduce all the evidence, and, after summing it up impartially, leave[s] the jury of readers to decide" (1:256). While she is not finally impartial—one suspects that her own republicanism leads her to conclude that Machiavelli's "heart was with the republicans" (1:312)—she does recognize that his book is "enigmatic" (1:299), and she presents sufficient data to enable a reader to question her conclusions.

Her view of what constitutes true poetry is clear throughout this volume, but she does not judge all poetry by a single standard. When she compares Petrarch's poetry with Dante's, she treats the poets as "essentially different" and gives due weight to the merits of each (1:106); her comparisons of their poetry with Lorenzo de Medici's, and of Berni's poetry with Ariosto's, are similarly even-handed (1:154, 191–93). Nor is she dismissive. Although she judges Petrarch's epic a failure in "cold dull Latin hexameters," she notes his belief that only by writing an epic in Latin could he win "a high place among poets" (1:83), and she praises both him and Boccaccio for copying and thereby preserving many classical Latin texts (1:73, 135). While she finds Boccaccio "essentially not a poet" (1:124), she praises the "delicacy and tenderness of feeling" in his *Decameron* (1:129). Thus her critical standards are firm, but they are also sufficiently flexible to accommodate poets' varying aims and achievements.

When she addresses the moral "lessons" to be derived from "the feelings and actions of celebrated men" (1:293), however, Shelley is somewhat more overt in leading the reader toward her own views. Her essay

on Petrarch is designed to "impress the reader" (1:115) not only with his literary "genius" but with his "honest worth" and "many virtues," and when she notes that Boccaccio learned from Petrarch the "small avail" (1:138) of knowledge without "moral principle and virtuous habits," the reader is clearly intended to learn the same lesson. Despite occasional jokes—Bojardo wrote love poems to more than one lady because "unfortunately, men, whether poets or not, are apt to change" (1:182)—this volume's moral tone is generally serious.

The second volume of *Lives* (1835) covers Italian literary and scientific figures from the sixteenth through the nineteenth centuries. Sir David Brewster wrote the life of Galileo, Sir James Montgomery that of Tasso; Shelley contributed the essays on Francesco Guicciardini, Vittoria Colonna, Battista Guarini, Gabriello Chiabrera, Alessandro Tassoni, Giambattista Marini, Vincenzo da Filicaja, Pietro Metastasio, Carlo Goldoni, Vittorio Alfieri, Vincenzo Monti, and Ugo Foscolo. Her extensive knowledge of contemporary Italy lends a note of authority absent from the first volume. Her literary criticism is equally authoritative, extending to definitions of genres and analyses of the relation between literary conventions and genius. Citing Samuel Johnson's authority for her method, she uses "minute, yet characteristic details" (2:206) of writers' lives to examine the morality and politics of their poetry. Her life of a woman poet and her discussion of the *cavalier servente* system analyze the politics of cultural constructions of gender.

At several points in this volume Shelley uses her familiarity with modern Italy to buttress her arguments. That Alfieri's father sometimes walked to visit him was "a strong mark of affection," she states, because the Italian nobility's "greatest pride is never to go on foot" (2:250). In her view, "a person who has never visited Italy" lacks the knowledge of Italian language and manners needed "to enter into the spirit" of Goldoni's plays and appreciate their merits (2:239, 246). She comments knowledgeably on both the "attractive art" of the Italian *improvvisatore* and its "pernicious" effect on "the strength and critical delicacy of poetry" (2:186, 307). She suggests her own expertise in Italian dialects when she judges a translation's "accuracy and force of diction" (2:166), or explains the controversies over whether thirteenth-century Tuscany's "classical language" or modern Italy's "living language" is more suitable for poetry (2:334, 340).

At other points, Shelley displays her knowledge of literature in general. The "chief pleasure" of the pastoral is its language rather than its

"ideal" situations (2:90–91); mock-heroic poems are "adapted" to their place of origin (2:170–71); "the essence of the tragic art" is "the development of feeling and motive" (2:277). Shelley's analyses of literary conventions are similarly authoritative. The weakness of Foscolo's tragedies and the monotony of Monti's plays are due to the "unfortunate" Aristotelian unities (2:388). She criticizes the "obedience to arbitrary laws" of style that "limited and chilled the poetic fervour" of seventeenth-century Italian poets, as well as the "rules and precedent" that a century later had again "shackled" the "free course of genius" (2:165, 181–82).

These comments indicate an opposition between genius and literary conventions, but the issue is more complex than it first appears because of Shelley's emphases on education and morality. If "fervour and exalted spirit" are the signs of genius, its "chief attribute" is that it "spontaneously form[s] and manifest[s] itself, despite every obstacle or adverse circumstance" (2:195–96, 302). It would seem to follow from this spontaneity that genius is antithetical to literary conventions, but Shelley notes that genius "can never surpass what is already written" (2:282) without "study[ing]" those earlier writings. And while she admits the difficulty of "making rules for the education of genius" without "fetter[ing]" it (2:309–10), she often suggests that genius requires moral education. Although she calls Guicciardini's history of Italy a "monument of his genius and industry" (2:72), she faults his lack of "political integrity" (2:65) and his "oppress[ion] of his fellow citizens" (2:69). She repeatedly cites the "impiety and thoughtlessness" (2:185) of "men of genius," and the "mistakes" they make when guided by "the pettier passions" (2:298). Moreover, a writer's moral life may inflect his art, and an art that makes vice attractive may be morally dangerous to readers. In one of Foscolo's novels, for example, the hero's "morbid shrinking from the woes of existence" and "total want of fortitude" became a pernicious "model" for "the youth of Europe" (2:367).

Moral conduct for Mary Shelley includes politics, and a politico-literary criticism, as it were, informs this volume's last four lives. Writing in the wake of the 1831 Carbonari uprisings against French occupation of Italy, Shelley states her "hope" of further political change (2:213). That hope leads to analyses of Goldoni, Alfieri, Monti, and Foscolo in terms of an earlier period of change in Italy, the years before and after the French Revolution. Goldoni's life (1707–1792) spanned both the years of "demoralization" before Italians recognized their oppression, and the post-Revolution years of "noble and impatient disdain of servitude." The essay on Alfieri then extends this history back to the fourteenth-century

Italian poets who were "distinguished for their patriotism" (2:247), and to the subsequent decline of this "national spirit" in the sixteenth-century poets due to the "depressing influence of courtly servitude." In contrast, Alfieri (1749–1803) "dedicated all the powers of his mind" (2:249) during the French Revolution to "awakening his countrymen from their lethargy"; because of his efforts, "the day must come" when "the oppressors will be unable to oppose" the Italians' "moral courage." The poet Monti (1754–1828), however, considered the French Revolution "a series of crimes" (2:315) and had no "ardour for liberty"; hence his poetry praising Napoleon has "a slavish spirit" that "jars with our notions of real independence and patriotism" (2:326, 321). Such politico-literary criticism also inflects the final Italian life, that of Ugo Foscolo (1778–1827). Shelley approves one of his novels for its "ardent patriotism" and "compassion for the physical evils of the poor, which are too often disregarded" (2:368). The political lesson is brought home to English readers when she discusses Foscolo's retreat to England, "the refuge of exiles," and when she praises the "liberal" Englishmen who made up to Foscolo for England's "cruel" foreign policy during the Napoleonic wars (2:386).

Shelley's literary criticism also includes gender politics, which are most apparent in her life of the woman poet Vittoria Colonna and her comments on the Italian custom of the *cavalier servente*. Of the many Italian women who "distinguished themselves in literature" during the sixteenth century, Vittoria Colonna conferred the greatest "honour on her sex" (2:77), by her "virtues, talents, and beauty" and especially by the "fidelity and unblemished honour" (2:78) of her politics and her relations with her husband. It is difficult to believe, however, that Colonna was "almost divine," or that "none can criticize, while all are touched" by the "intense and fond sorrows" recorded in her poetry (2:81, 79).

Shelley's valuation of feminine virtue takes a more complex form in her discussions of the *cavalier servente* system. In this system a wife, who had married for status or property rather than love, openly took a lover; he was "constantly in attendance" (2:273), and the affair was "rendered respectable by constancy" (2:198). Discussing one such relationship, Shelley censures "a system which blights the affections [and] degrades the moral feelings," but she adds that the woman's "virtues, we may presume to say, redeemed an error, the very existence of which is, after all, uncertain." Her ambivalence here evinces her reluctance to blame one woman for following "a system belonging to a whole country" and

of long standing; furthermore, a woman's "error" might be redeemed by "disinterested affection" and, as in this case, by generosity to and encouragement of her poet-lover. In contrast, Shelley is sharply critical when the *cavalier servente* system serves masculine lust rather than feminine devotion. She calls Alfieri's first term as a *cavalier* a "degradation," for his "phrensy" of passion is "difficult to understand, and impossible to sympathize with" (2:273). Her final words on the custom show the political importance she attached to seemingly private relations: until this system is abolished, "there can be no hope of moral regeneration, or for the happiness of [Italy's] inhabitants" (2:289). Thus the "delicacy and refinement" (2:393) of her contemporary Foscolo's relations with women signal both his personal morality and his patriotism.

Volume III of the *Lives* (1837) constitutes a literary history of Spain through the seventeenth century and of Portugal through the sixteenth century. Written entirely by Shelley, the volume contains brief discussions of numerous poets and dramatists as well as complete lives of Mosen Boscán, Garcilaso de la Vega, Diego de Mendoza, Luis de León, Alonso de Ercilla, Miguel de Cervantes, Lope de Vega, Vicente Espinel, Esteban de Villegas, Luis de Góngora, Francisco de Quevedo, Pedro Calderón, and Luis Camoëns. Shelley's perseverance in researching these subjects is particularly striking in view of her initial "ignorance" about them and her "difficulty [in] getting books & information" (*MWSL*, 2:257). Spanish texts were "very rare in London" (*MWSL*, 2:255) and difficult of access; she could not afford to buy them, and her reluctance to "voluntarily go among strange men in a character [like] their own" kept her from researching with male scholars in the British Museum's reading room (*MWSL*, 2:160). The obstacles posed by poverty and gendered timidity, which recur throughout Shelley's writing career, make doubly impressive the range of writers and material covered in these *Lives*. Of primary interest in this volume are her biographical method, her politico-literary history of Spanish and Portuguese national literature, and her representation of the effect of politics on the reputation and rewards of genius.

Because little was known of many Spanish and Portuguese writers, Shelley often quarries their works for biographical information; in fact, "[t]here is nothing so attractive to a biographer" (3:301) as piecing together a subject's life. She recognizes the dangers of this "patchwork" method (3:200) and the importance of an "accurate" (3:301) and "careful" investigation, for "[t]ruth is all in all in matters of history." Still, Shelley criticizes the current "fashion" (3:200) of "ransack[ing] every

hidden corner" of a writer's life for "errors and follies," and she tends instead to emphasize positive parallels between life and art. From "the pleasures of home" depicted in Boscán's poetry, for instance, she imagines "the perfect home-felt, heart-reaching happiness of his married life" (3:25, 70).

In addition to individual biography, Shelley's literary criticism also focuses on national traits. Like other critics who were constructing a national literature for England, she sees the literature of Spain as determined by its national characteristics. These are "originality," "independence," "enthusiasm," and "earnestness" (3:1–2), and this "genuine Spanish spirit" (3:2) appears in their literature as early as Lucan (A.D. 39–65). The originality that is "distinctive of the Spanish character" (3:101) also marks Spanish writers. Shelley sometimes faults such originality, for example when she describes the *culto* style, a Spanish invention, as "so metaphoric and obscure" that it is not only almost unreadable but finally a convention in its own right (3:245); on the other hand, she also praises the dramatist de Vega for "wholly disregard[ing]" (3:236) the conventional dramatic unities.

More even than national traits, national politics pervades this volume. Shelley organizes her literary history of Spain so as to demonstrate that "[d]espotism and the Inquisition" failed to "level the noble altitude of [Spanish] souls" (3:2). A truly national Spanish literature, however, arose only with the liberties initiated by Charles V (1518–58). Before Charles, Spain's court poetry had treated of "false learning" (3:16) and "obsolete knowledge" (3:11) rather than the feelings; other writers were "too circumvented by the inquisition to dare say much" (3:101), so the nation had yet to find a form "to embody [its] characteristics." Under Charles V, however, the national originality reemerged in the "strikingly novel" themes of such poets as Ercilla (3:103). Most importantly, "authorship became general" (3:102) as it extended from the court to men of "genius" but "inferior rank." As Shelley associates noncoterie authorship with a national literature, she also identifies drama, the most public of literary genres, as "the most truly national" form of Spanish literature (3:16). Lope de Vega's plays represented "to the life the manners and feelings of his day" (3:218) and "made visible to an audience the ideal of their prejudices and passions" (3:233). Shelley also notes drama's political effect on its audiences. Cervantes wrote his tragedy *Life in Algiers* to create "sympathy" for Christian captives in Algeria, and a performance of his play *Numantia* during the Peninsular War gave the Spanish "fresh inducements to resist" Napoleon's forces (3:178).

Shelley's discussion of later Spanish writing continues this linking of politics to literature. The work of the sixteenth-century poet Espinel is "pretty and graceful" (3:238) but has "few ideas," because "[d]espotism" discourages "boldness." The "false style" (3:278) and "false taste" of seventeenth-century Spanish literature are evidence of "[m]isrule and oppression." Other moments in Spain's literary history give Shelley hope for contemporary Spanish politics. Because Ercilla's epic *Araucana* chronicled a South American tribe's rebellion against Spain's "thirst of plunder" (3:106) and "religious zeal," his poetry shows the dislike of royal absolutism that came to fruition in Spain's rebellion against Napoleon. Similarly, the poems of Garcilaso de la Vega foreshadow the "new poetry" (3:57) of "heroism" and "genius" that would appear if Spain "regain[ed] her ancient freedom."

Like her literary history of Spain, Mary Shelley's history of Portuguese literature amalgamates national traits, language, and politics. When Portugal separated from Spain in the twelfth century, this "poetic people" (3:289) developed a language "adapted to poetry." Early Portuguese poetry's "poverty of ideas" (3:290) and lack of "classical correctness," however, show its "infancy," and a national poetry was further retarded by many poets' "unpatriotic" decision (3:291) to write in Spanish. In contrast, Ferreira wrote in his native language and of patriotic themes, "[t]he glory, the advancement and the civilization of Portugal" (3:293). Portuguese poetry evinced the "valour," "spirit and enthusiasm" of a nation of navigators and explorers until the sixteenth century, when Portugal's "glory days" (3:311) of exploration declined into "mere commercial or piratical speculations" and "court favour" (3:331) ruled its political system. The effects of court politics on literature are most evident in Shelley's lives of the Spanish novelist Cervantes and the Portuguese poet Camoëns, both of which show moral merit and literary genius going unrewarded.

Shelley addresses her life of Cervantes to "those capable of feeling a generous interest in the fate of genius" (3:120). To persuade readers to "commiserate his misfortunes, and sympathize in his sorrows," she concentrates on his moral qualities: his "sagacity, resolution, and honour," as well as "dauntless courage" (3:131, 135) when captured by Algerian pirates; his "bearing all with courage and equanimity" (3:182); his feeling "no querulousness, no causticity, no bitterness" (3:174). "For the honour of human nature" (3:120), then, the author of *Don Quixote* should have enjoyed "prosperity" and "triumph"; instead he suffered poverty and neglect by a court and nobility which retained all political

and literary patronage "within their magic circle" (3:167). *Don Quixote's* popularity injured Cervantes with this ruling class, as did the fact that the "natural elevation" (3:141) of his "soul" defeated their insistence on "difference of rank"; the nobles' refusal to reward him thus "inspires infinite contempt for the arbitrary distinctions of society." Like Shelley's discussion of Spanish drama, this statement shows that she values public or popular literature over coterie art; it also critiques a system of literary value determined by class.

Although Camoëns's destiny was "similar" (3:295) to that of Cervantes, Shelley's biography of him focuses less on merit than on the workings of fate. Camoëns's life seems destined to miscarry. A balked romance with a woman of a higher class had a lifelong "disastrous" influence (3:303); ten years of military service, during which he lost an eye, brought him "neither reward nor preferment" (3:310); he "hoped much" from his patriotic epic *The Lusiad* (3:308) but was "doomed to solitude and misfortune" (3:319); he was shipwrecked and later imprisoned for official malfeasance. In short, the star that "ruled [his] fate" (3:320) was "full of storm and wreck"; fortune "conquered at last," and he died in want (3:330). The lesson Mary Shelley intends is twofold. Like Cervantes's life, Camoëns' fate conveys a social critique: he was "a martyr to [the] political system" (3:331) of primogeniture that forced younger sons to rely on a "court favour" which was "never bestowed on the worthiest." But Shelley's life of Camoëns also sounds a moral note which is less critical than resigned. "Heaven has established a law, that the best men are to suffer most"; hence a poet's reward is an eventual "claim on universal sympathy" when "[t]he future, glorious and calm, brightens over the grave." From this law the reader should learn "to revere those cast in adversity" and to "glory" in "the frowns of fortune." Like the conclusion to *The Last Man*, the last life in this volume presents a bleak picture of human existence and its rewards.

Lives of the Most Eminent Literary and Scientific Men of France (1839)

The first volume of *Lives of the Most Eminent Literary and Scientific Men of France* appeared in July 1838, the second in August 1839. While most Mary Shelley scholars have assumed that she wrote the whole of both volumes, the attribution is questionable. The participation of other writers is suggested by the title page of the 1840 edition, which names "Mrs. Shelley and others" as authors. Furthermore, in July 1837 she was

still working on the Spanish and Portuguese *Lives* (*MWSL*, 2:288–90), and in March 1838 she was in the early stages of Volume II of the French *Lives;* since Volume I was published four months later, it seems unlikely that she could have written it while engaged on two other projects. She may have contributed to Volume I, but none of the lives in that volume can be positively attributed to her, and her letters provide evidence of authorship only for lives in Volume II (*MWSL*, 2:296, 317). Accordingly, this section will consider only the second volume.

Published in 1839, Volume II of the French *Lives* covers the life and work of Voltaire, Jean-Jacques Rousseau, the Marquis de Condorcet, Honoré-Gabriele Mirabeau, Mme. Manon Roland, and Mme. Germaine de Staël. While the volume contains literary criticism and some strictures on its uses, Shelley focuses more on the writers' lives than their works. She also reflects on Christianity, natural and social morality, the politics of pre- and postrevolutionary France, education, and the role of women in politics.

Shelley's literary criticism in Volume II of the French *Lives* frequently focuses on the moral elevation of literature. She praises Voltaire's writings for their "spirit and life and genius,"[35] but she also notes the "reigning blemishes" (93) of "grossness" and "impiety"; one work contains so much "indecency and ridicule of sacred things" (56) that "we cannot understand the state of manners when such a poem could be read aloud to women." This comment suggests that literature reflects the moral standards of its audience but should also raise those standards. Mme. de Staël receives particular censure, for her novel *Delphine* "displays too eager a desire for happiness," and "worse than this, it inculcates no spirit of courage under disaster"; none of her novels teaches "the most needful lesson—moral courage" (342). Some of Shelley's critique is gender specific; to raise "the dignity of womanhood" (332), for example, de Staël's novel *Corinne* should have taught its heroine "resignation or fortitude." In general, however, it "ought to be the aim of every writer" (328) to teach the "lesson" that adversity brings "higher wisdom," for "we fly to the pages of the sage to learn to bear."

Literary criticism, too, should raise readers' moral standards, by praising and encouraging the right kind of writer. Especially in England, critics "are so afraid of compromising their reputation" (108), and readers are so afraid of judging for themselves, that writers "very seldom" (306) find the "real sympathy or admiration" needed to "sustain" them (108). They may achieve "popular favour", but it signals only their

"servile fosterage of prejudices." In the Spanish *Lives*, "popular favour" was a reliable indicator of genius; here it indicates only that public taste must be raised to the critic's level if readers are to recognize true merit. Not the general reader but the literary critic thus becomes the arbiter of literary value and, given Shelley's view of literature's moral aims, of moral value as well. These ideas—of literature as "a sphere separated from money-making" (Butler, 143), and of literary criticism's social functions—prefigure the more "conscious and deliberate" views of the later critic Matthew Arnold (Baldick, 10).

Many of the French *Lives* develop Shelley's view that "Catholicism is not Christianity" (26). French Catholicism in particular "entangl[ed] the absurd and the true" (187), causing many to cast off the true with the absurd as Condorcet did, or to fail as Voltaire did to distinguish "the truths of the Gospel" (27) from the "impostures of papacy." Thus the French Catholic church, being "utterly devoid of the principles of Christianity" (124), must take "much of the blame" for Voltaire's "bitter hostility to Christianity." Still, Voltaire "went too far" (27) when, "not content with warring against superstition," he assaulted "rational piety." Shelley then locates the bases of such an "enlightened" piety (26) in Christianity's "divine origin," "sublime tenets," and "excellen[t]" morality, and she also addresses the reader directly: "[l]et Christians be real disciples of the Gospel, and men like Voltaire will neither have the power nor the will to injure the religion they profess" (124).

As this appeal suggests, Shelley judges her subjects' moral lives less on theological than on practical grounds. Voltaire's writings were impious, but his work in "the noblest cause" (96) of helping the poor was "almost superhuman" (115); Condorcet's philosophical works tended to "subvert Christianity" (187), but he supported "[e]very useful and liberal cause" (189). She excuses the "anti-Christian" element (165) of Rousseau's *Emile* for the sake of its "sincerity" and "love of truth," but she faults Rousseau for a lack of "moral courage" (136) and "fixed principles" and for sins against the domestic affections. He treated his mistress Thérèse "as a sort of convenience" (144), and he "failed in the plainest dictates of nature and conscience" (145) by depositing their illegitimate children in a Foundling Hospital. From this "extreme instance of paternal neglect"[36] she draws the general conclusion that "[n]othing can be more unnatural than [the] natural man" of Rousseau's writings (148), for "[t]he most characteristic part of man's nature is his affections," and these issue as "protection" of women and "care" for children.

Although she distrusts a Rousseauian natural morality, Shelley agrees with Rousseau about the corrupting effects of social morality. Like the Italian *cavalier servente* system, the "old customs of France" (221) sanctioned arranged marriages and extramarital affairs; the result was "the most depraved state of society ever known" (224). Children were "sacrificed" (146) in a system that winks at sexual liaisons but not illegitimacy, and women too were "sacrificed" (221) to a "social law" (224) both "nefarious and unnatural." Against that social and legal morality, Shelley defines a woman's "true distinctive virtue" (140) as "self-sacrifice," and adds that "personal fidelity is the purifier and preserver of the affections." Although such statements are certainly prescriptive of feminine virtue, they also function to critique a masculine culture of "heartless gallantry" (162).

Because these customs were the product of France's *ancien régime*, Shelley's views on social morality cannot be separated from her views on French politics. Her life of Mme. Roland contrasts "a virtuous simple state of society" (269), such as that of the ancient republics, with "the corrupt state of society" in prerevolutionary France. Rousseau was persecuted by "the intolerance and tyranny of the old régime" (174), in which "all worth was trampled on by rank and wealth" (142). Under the "bigotry, hypocrisy, and dullness" (30) of Louis XIV, Parisian society was given over to "pleasure and license"; despite his attacks on "revealed religion," then, Voltaire performed a "noble" and "useful" function in freeing France from "political and priestly thraldom" (27).

For similar reasons Shelley presents with some sympathy, if not complete agreement, the views of the early French revolutionaries. Condorcet's belief that human nature is degraded by "the frauds of priests and the oppression of political institutions" (188) led logically to his belief that, with the "improvement" of those institutions, humans would become "wise, just, and equal." His "great but regulated enthusiasm," founded on "abstract principles" and "severe reason," becomes a symbol of the Girondist revolutionaries who acted from "a sense of right." But Condorcet also typifies the early revolutionaries' excessive trust in reason, which blinded them both to "the influence of passion" and to the ease with which "the interested few" can lead the many into "error and crime." Thus an initially "noble and heroic" spirit (193) was turned by "base and sanguinary men" into the Terror. In contrast, Mirabeau attempted to lead the revolutionary multitude toward his own desire for a limited monarchy based on "the image of the English constitution" (241).

Shelley's analysis of prerevolutionary France shows the importance of political as well as moral education. She praises Voltaire for learning from his years in England that knowledge was not "for the few" (41) but "a blessing for the many" and that "the duty of the enlightened" was therefore to ensure a "general diffusion of knowledge" (47). Justice is essential in educating children, lest they regard their elders as "treacherous enemies." Nor should education be enforced by punishment; the "[b]eaten, maltreated" (129) Rousseau became "idle, timid, and lying." Shelley's distrust of a Rousseauian natural morality leads her to emphasize a moral education. "Nature seems to point out the way" to educate children, "but who in society as it is formed, takes nature for a director?" (129); hence "every teacher of morality" (148) ought to focus on cultivating the affections.

Because it centers on the political and moral education of women, Shelley's life of Manon Roland repays extended study. This essay shares with Mme. Roland's own *Memoirs* "an active principle of instruction" (266). By showing men "an example of female excellence" and by "teaching women how to be great" without foregoing "the duties or charms of their sex," Mme. Roland's *Memoirs* and Mary Shelley's *Life* dramatize that women who "dedicate themselves to useful and heroic tasks" will "find helpmates in the other sex."

Shelley's discussion of Mme. Roland's childhood focuses on both gender- and class-specific uses of education. The young Manon was educated by her mother, who guided her by appeals to "her reason or her feelings" (268). By studying philosophy, Manon not only "enlarged the sphere of her ideas" (269) but developed "rules of morality" for her own conduct. Along with a "bourgeois" (268) distaste for both aristocratic "debauchery" and the lower orders' "brutal ignorance and licentiousness," she "drank in republicanism." Manon "rejected distinctions of rank" (270) because, as an artisan's daughter whose education had "refined" her mind, she resented the "condescension" of aristocrats. From these feelings Shelley draws a general lesson about upward mobility through education. Since "there must be difference of position" due to a differential distribution of property, it is "mean" of the poor to envy the rich. But as Manon's case shows,

> the disdain that springs from knowing that others assume superiority from mere adventitious circumstances—[that] the ignobly born must remain, vainly desiring a career in which to distinguish themselves—is a noble feeling, and is implanted in the human heart as the source of the highest virtues. (270–71)

If this statement is a warrant to ignore "adventitious circumstances," it is also carefully hedged around with distinctions between "mean" envy and "noble" disdain, which indicate that it is applicable only to the educated and the exceptional.

Shelley then turns to the married and political life made possible by Mme. Roland's education. Under her mother's tutelage, Manon's "early development of feeling" (268) led to "sympath[y] with the emotions of others" rather than "an untimely awakening of passion." Still without passion, she married M. Roland and became "absolutely necessary" to him (276); her marriage was thus a "servitude," but her early education in self-denial enabled her to "devote herself to a life of self-control" (275). When the French Revolution gave "scope for practice" of her republican principles, here too her education bore fruit: from her early enthusiasm for the classical republics grew her adherence to the moderate Girondists who desired constitutional change "without anarchy or public convulsion" (278).

As she had hedged on the "noble" aspirations of the educated, however, so Shelley treads warily over Mme. Roland's politics. Long before Madame Defarge in Dickens's *A Tale of Two Cities* (1859), British conservatives represented revolutionary Frenchwomen as harpies and viragos.[37] Shelley's life of Mme. de Staël leaned in this direction with its representations of a woman "passionately loving glory" (321) and seeking "her own elevation" through politics. In contrast, the life of Mme. Roland carefully stresses the feminine propriety of her political activity. She used her influence over the Girondists "covert[ly]"; instead of speaking at public meetings, for instance, she buttonholed individuals "in privacy, and without ostentation" (279). Although she later supported the more radical Jacobins, Shelley excuses this defection with the xenophobic argument that Mme. Roland trusted "the many" without realizing how "difficult it is to restrain . . . the French." But she also stresses that Mme. Roland "desired to be great" (281) only to "exercise [her] virtues" through "activity and usefulness on a grand scale" (281–82). Shelley admits that "to put herself forward" was "presumptuous" in a woman, and that Mme. Roland was sometimes guilty of "the vehemence with which women too usually follow up their ideas" (283). But she ends the biography by admiring her subject's "grandeur, courage, and sincerity" (297) and by criticizing the "ridicule" that "low-minded men" direct at "superior" women. On balance, then, Mme. Roland's life remains a model for "teaching women how to be great."

Editions of Percy Shelley's Works

In 1824 Mary Shelley edited her husband's *Posthumous Poems*; in 1839 she produced a four-volume edition of his *Poetical Works* and a corrected one-volume edition, and in the following year she edited his *Essays, Letters from Abroad, Translations and Fragments*. These editions have been important but controversial sources for Percy Shelley scholars, with controversy centering on Mary's construction of both his texts and his reputation. This section will address those controversies in the context of her editorial tasks and methods.

Three months after her husband's death in July 1822, Mary Shelley determined to publish his posthumous poems so as to "commemorate the virtues of the only creature on earth worth loving or living for" (*MWSJ*, 2:434). If she wanted to memorialize her husband, however, she also wanted to catch the tide of interest in him; to a suggestion that she postpone the volume, she replied that "Shelley has celebrity even popularity now" (*MWSL*, 1:411). She also hoped to increase that popularity, by introducing readers to "a specimen of how he could write without shocking any one" (*MWSL*, 1:397). With the poems first published in 1824, then, she intended to invest Percy Shelley with a particular set of poetic virtues; in the preface to the *Poetical Works* of 1839, these virtues are spelled out more explicitly.

The *Posthumous Poems of Percy Bysshe Shelley* (1824) consists of seventy-one poems, two unfinished plays, and six translations—three of poems, one of a Greek drama, and two of scenes from Calderón's play *Magico Prodigioso* and Goethe's *Faust*. Sixty of the poems, the unfinished plays, and four of the translations were previously unpublished; along with this truly posthumous material, Mary Shelley included the out-of-print *Alastor* as well as poems and translations that had been "scattered in periodical works."[38] Her preface distinguishes between the poems that have Percy Shelley's "ultimate corrections" and those he had "never retouched." The latter she has "carefully copied" from his notebooks; his final poem, *The Triumph of Life*, was left "so unfinished" that she "arranged" it only with "great difficulty." The critical controversies over Mary Shelley's copying and arranging are too numerous to discuss in detail here; generally, modern critics have disagreed over whether or to what extent she "emended, altered, misdated, and suppressed while at the same time proclaiming her fidelity to" her manuscript sources.[39] While some critics argue that she misrepresented her husband's politics

by her "uncertain and not always honest transmission" of his poems,[40] others consider her editorial procedures "fairly scrupulous"[41] by the standards of the time, especially in light of the "incoherent jumble" of the poet's notebooks (Massey, 9). In either case, this controversy is a useful reminder that the published version of a text is not an infallible guide to its author's intentions.

In addition to the poems, Mary Shelley's edition presents the public with a specific version of Percy. During his life, both his poetry and his behavior had been attacked; reviewing *Queen Mab* in 1821, for example, the *Literary Gazette* had hinted that "the damned sophistry of the seducer" Shelley had morally "ruined" Mary and her stepsister, Claire (quoted in *PBSL*, 2:320). Like "other illustrious reformers" (*WPBS*, 327), Mary Shelley writes, her husband suffered such "hatred and calumny" because of "fearless enthusiasm" for "the improvement of the moral and physical state of mankind." Furthermore, his life was spent in "the contemplation of Nature", "arduous study," and "acts of kindness and affection." "Before the critics contradict me," she writes, they should consult "any one who had ever known him," for those friends feel his loss to be "irremediable." Here, as throughout her construction of Percy Shelley, she is also constructing her own editorial credentials. As she repeatedly stresses "the solitude in which [they] lived" and the fact that Shelley was "known to few," she and not his critics becomes the true authority on his character. Perhaps because some of his friends felt her "cold heart" had made his last months unhappy (*MWSJ*, 2:444), she stresses her "anguish" (*WPBS*, 328) over his death. She also insists that her husband's last months were his "happiest"; in her idyllic picture, he enjoyed "the companionship of a few selected friends" and "our entire sequestration from the rest of the world." The preface closes with an appeal to the reader. Aware that "the critics" might fault her inclusion of "the most imperfect" of Percy Shelley's poems, she states "frankly" that she was more concerned to preserve every "monument of his genius" than to present only complete poems to "the fastidious reader." Her audience is not fastidious critics but "the lovers of Shelley's poetry," who know that "every line and word he wrote is instinct with peculiar beauty," and she "consecrate[s]" the book to them.

Contemporary reviews of *Posthumous Poems* indicate that Mary Shelley's construction of herself and Percy met with mixed success. The *Ladies' Monthly Museum* noted her desire to "honour" Shelley's memory but felt that the poems would "hardly add to [his] literary reputation."[42] While Hazlitt found her preface "imperfect but touching" (quoted in

Reiman, C.1.402), his long piece in the *Edinburgh Review* was markedly hostile to Shelley's poetry and character. The *Literary Gazette* grudgingly admitted that the book contained "some fine poetry," albeit "embedded in sand, mud, slime, and filth"; Mary Shelley's preface "may perhaps be excused" as a widow's "panegyric" but is "too hyperbolical" (quoted in Reiman, C.2.533–34). In contrast, sympathy with "the yet bleeding heart of an affected and devoted widow" led the *Belle Assemblée* to soft-pedal its criticism of the poet's "moral aberrations" (quoted in Reiman, C.1.46), and the *Edinburgh Magazine* seems to have been persuaded that he had no aberrations. This reviewer did fault Mary Shelley for publishing fragments of her husband's poetry, because doing so "dissolves entirely the illusion" of a poet's "intuitive inspiration" (quoted in Reiman, C.2.834). Overall, however, the *Edinburgh Magazine* review typifies the tolerant and sympathetic reception of Mary's first public representation of herself and her husband.

Between the *Posthumous Poems* of 1824 and *Poetical Works of Percy Bysshe Shelley* of 1839, Mary Shelley had little direct influence on the growing "Shelley myth."[43] As a condition of her annual allowance from her father-in-law, Sir Timothy Shelley, she was forced to withdraw the *Posthumous Poems* from circulation and to promise not to bring the Shelley name "before the public" during his lifetime (*MWSL*, 1:444). Sir Timothy was doubtless responding to his son's notoriety as a political reformer, a notoriety that inflected his poetic reputation. Shelley's poem *Queen Mab* became one of the "standard pieces of radical literature," through its twenty "enthusiastically circulated" pirated editions and the 140 items about him and the poem that appeared in working-class and radical periodicals between 1823 and 1841.[44] "Reproduced by low publishers primarily for 'vulgar' readers," Shelley's poetry was initially "a signifier of culturally prohibited knowledge and behavior."[45] Already in the 1820s, however, some critics were "recuperating Shelley for legitimate high culture" (Fraistat, 416); the entry in the *Encyclopaedia Londinensis* of 1828, for example, termed him "'a poet of considerable eminence'" and thereby recommended him to readers of "superior sensitivity and perception."[46] This is the Shelley that Mary Shelley wanted to memorialize. Debarred from reissuing the *Posthumous Poems*, she quietly aided in preparing the 1828 Galignani edition and even considered secretly writing a brief biography for it (*MWSL*, 2:86). Following the "commercial success" of an unauthorized edition of 1834,[47] the respectable publisher Edward Moxon offered her £600 to prepare a

complete edition of Percy Shelley's works with a life and notes. In 1838 she persuaded Sir Timothy to permit her to publish her husband's works, on condition that she not include a life. With her 1839 edition of the poems, she reentered the discourse of the Shelley myth with her own, authorized version of Shelley and his politics.

That version was partly dependent on texts, and it is worth noting the magnitude of Mary Shelley's task in compiling the complete poems. The four-volume *Poetical Works* of 1839 included Shelley's published and posthumous poems, dramas, translations, and fragments as well as six poems first reprinted by Thomas Medwin in 1832; the second, one-volume edition added *Peter Bell the Third*, which was previously unpublished, and *Swellfoot the Tyrant*, which was published in 1820 but immediately suppressed. One of Mary Shelley's major difficulties was obtaining copies of these works, and she was still searching for a copy of *Queen Mab* while the first volume of *Poetical Works* was in proof. Editorial decisions about *Queen Mab* posed additional problems. Although the initial edition of 1814 included Shelley's dedicatory poem to his first wife, he had "rejoiced" that it was omitted from the 1821 pirated edition (*MWSL*, 2:309); on these grounds Mary Shelley too omitted it but was "insult[ed]" by several of his friends for doing so (*MWSJ*, 2:560). Moxon asked her to omit *Queen Mab*'s sixth and seventh cantos, fearing that he would lose the copyright if he were prosecuted for publishing these "too shocking and atheistical" sections (*MWSL*, 2:301). Although she disliked "irreligion" and believed that Percy Shelley "would never have [re]printed" several of the poem's opinions (*MWSL*, 2:305), she was averse to publishing a "mutilated" edition; she agreed to the omissions only reluctantly, and after a firestorm of criticism she restored them in the second edition. As well as being "torn to pieces by Memory" (*MWSJ*, 2:559), then, Mary Shelley felt the lack of "encouragement & kindness" as she struggled to gather her husband's poems and thereby preserve her version of him.

She outlines this version in her preface to the edition. The *Poetical Works* fulfills the "important duty" (v) of "giving the productions of a sublime genius to the world" and of "detailing the history of those productions." She makes the best of Sir Timothy's ban on a biography by stating that "this is not the time to relate the truth" of her Percy Shelley's life. As in the 1824 preface, however, she turns her privileged knowledge of Shelley to account. She reminds her readers of his youth and "inexperience" (vii), and of the physical pain that "wound up his nerves" to a "susceptibility" that affected "his views of life." She identi-

fies the "ruling passion of his soul" as the cause of "human happiness
and improvement"; because he believed "political freedom" would
ensure those ends, he rejoiced in any "new-sprung hope of liberty."
Without her knowledge of his devotion to "general and unselfish subjects," and of the "scorn and hatred" directed at his politics, the
"younger generation" (vi) of radicals cannot understand Percy Shelley.
Thus she undercuts the Shelley whom these 1830s radicals were constructing; rather it is her Shelley, the persecuted reformer, whose influence is "fast augmenting" (viii) the political changes signaled by the
Reform Bill of 1832.

The preface then makes two influential statements about Percy Shelley as a poet. The first is that his politics "breathe throughout his
poetry" (vi). The second, and more controversial, is her distinction
between Shelley's ideal, or "purely imaginative," poetry and the "more
popular" poems, which "sprung from the emotions of his heart." Some
recent critics have faulted her preference for the second category, and it
is true that she valued the ideal poems but preferred those of the heart.
Nonetheless, critics who dismiss the popular "heart" poetry risk simply
replicating such mid-nineteenth-century cultural arbiters as Thomas
Macaulay, who defined a popular style as one "which boys and women
could comprehend."[48] Given the dislike of coterie poetry evident in
Mary Shelley's *Lives*, it is not surprising that she would resist her contemporaries' efforts to restrict Percy Shelley's poetry to readers with "the
cultural competence necessary to decode it" (Fraistat, 416). Instead she
constructs a "contradictory poetics of audience"[49] for the ideal poetry *and*
the popular poetry. She admits that in his "purely imaginative" poems
Shelley indulged a desire to "idealise reality" (*WPBS*, vii) that is "shared
by few," and she often uses "exclusionary signs" (Wolfson, 45) and a relatively "inaccessible mode of representation" that appeal to this "select
readership." But she also presents a popular poet for a broader readership: Percy Shelley's "more popular" poetry (*WPBS*, vii) treats of "emotions common to us all" (vi) and thus "speaks to the many" (vii).

Mary Shelley consolidates these political and poetical representations
of her husband by her arrangement of his poems. The preface promised
a "history" (v) of the poems as they emerged from his "heart and brain";
thus they are arranged and discussed in order of composition. Substitut-
ing a textual history for a biography enabled Mary Shelley both to "cir-
cumvent" Sir Timothy's ban on a life[50] and to "slip silently by" incidents
she preferred to ignore (Norman, 143). But her historical method has a
more important function: her notes preempt criticism of Percy Shelley

by demonstrating "the alterations his opinions underwent" (37), specifically his movement away from what she considered the erroneous dogmas of his early years.

This strategy is particularly evident in her notes to *Queen Mab*. Written in 1813, *Queen Mab* was "the production of a boy of eighteen" (37),
with a boy's "unworldliness" (38). Because his youthful reading was "not
always well chosen," he "temporarily" converted to the irreligion evident in the poem. Moreover, "youth is rash," and *Queen Mab* embodies
that youthful impatience with "gradual" human and social improvement. "A very few years" (47), however, checked this excessive "ardour,"
and thus the tone of *Alastor* (1816) is "very different" from that of *Queen
Mab*. Similarly, if *Prometheus Unbound* (1820) retains *Queen Mab*'s faith
that humans can be "perfectionized" (126), it also shows a new "calm
and holy spirit of love." Mary Shelley's strategy was later used by
Moxon's solicitor, when the publisher was prosecuted in 1841 for printing the unexpurgated *Queen Mab;* the defense argued that publishing
Queen Mab with the whole of Percy Shelley's works demonstrated that it
was only one "feature" in the "development" of his "entire intellectual
history."[51]

Another element of Shelley's history that the notes use to defend his
politics is his lifelong concern for human suffering. In 1813, Shelley's
"compassion for his fellow-creatures" (*WPBS*, 38) and "sympathy" for
their misery produced *Queen Mab*'s political vision of "a brotherhood of
property and service." His belief that he could "excite his countrymen"
(251) to revolution "faded with early youth," but the poems of 1819
show that "his warmest sympathies" were still "for the people." The parodic *Swellfoot the Tyrant* (1820) again demonstrates Shelley's "deep sympathy for the sorrows of humanity, and indignation against its oppressors" (191). He felt "sympathy" (180) for the Spanish and Italian
revolutions begun in 1821; during the same year he wrote *Hellas*, to
record not only his "enthusiasm" for the Greek revolution and the
"regeneration of man" it heralded but also his "grieving" over the suffering entailed by revolution.

Mary Shelley also uses Percy's sympathy with misery to bridge the
gap between his ideal and his popular poetry. The preface explains that
he was so "keenly alive" (vi) to the "pain" produced by "human sympathies" that he "sheltered himself" in the poems that "idealised reality";
but these poems also aimed to join a love of "abstract beauty" and of
"abstract good" with "our sympathies" for others. The notes continue
this history of Shelley's ideal poems as both a shelter from his own emo

tions and a sign of "sympathies." In 1817 he had lost the "eager spirit" (205) with which he earlier pursued "immediate" social change, and he "sheltered himself" from the "disappointments" of this year in "ideal" poems. *The Revolt of Islam* (1818) seems to be ideal "forms" (96) emptied of "all the weakness and evil which cling to real life," but Shelley's practical aid to the poor of Marlow attests his "active sympathy" (97) and "stamps with reality" (97) the poem's "pleadings for the human race." He wrote *Prometheus Unbound* (1820) hoping not only to "induce some one or two" (128) to share his belief in perfectibility but also to "shelter himself" from illness and the "persecution," "injustice," and "aversion" of his countrymen.

In a further turn on this connection between ideal poetry and sympathy, Mary Shelley uses Percy's poetic history to elicit the reader's "commiseration" with him.[52] She stresses his physical and nervous debility, using "a class-coded language of sensibility to stress his refinement" (Fraistat, 411) but also to disarm criticism. Shelley was "too delicately organized for the rough treatment" (*WPBS*, 37) he received at Eton, and he wrote the revolutionary *Queen Mab* while "fragile in health" (38) and hence "trembling" with sensitivity to this "oppression." *The Revolt of Islam* again displays his nervous "anguish" (96) over the "persecutions" he endured (for, Mary omits to say, leaving his wife Harriet to elope with her). Solitude is another trope used to create sympathy for Shelley's fragility and the ideality of his poetry. His "lonely musings" (47) over illnesses and misfortunes in 1815 are embodied in the "ideal hues" of *Alastor*; his "solitary hours" (204) of illness inflected the "ideal" poetry (205) of 1817. Perhaps the most striking appeal to reader compassion is Mary Shelley's revelation of her own lapses in sympathy. In 1818 the poet's physical suffering drove him to "solitude" (230) and to poems of "discontent and sadness" which he hid from his wife; her notes to those poems record her "unspeakable regret and gnawing remorse" over her failure to recognize his melancholy. In the preface, Mary used their "utter solitude" to signal her privileged access and editorial authority; here she uses it to lament the "wall of prejudice" (230) that divided his contemporaries from him. The effect is to draw readers toward a sympathy for and appreciation of his misunderstood genius.

Sympathetic appreciation, Mary Shelley's strategy for winning recognition of her husband's ideal poetry, was also her strategy for convincing him to write popular poetry. Believing that his play *The Cenci* (1819) demonstrated his "sympathy with human passion" in a "style that commanded popular favour" (160), Mary urged him to "increase his popularity" (278)

by writing about subjects that "suit[ed] the popular taste." This would not require "truckl[ing] in opinion" (279) or lowering his "lofty aspirations for the human race to the low ambition and pride of the many," she argued; rather, poetry that addressed "the common feelings of men" would achieve true "popularity." If "the chord of sympathy" were thus touched, Percy Shelley's "proper rank" as a poet would be acknowledged, and "his countrymen" would "do justice to his character and virtues." For Mary Shelley, popularity and sympathy become reciprocal formations: popular poetry embodies the poet's sympathy for his potential readers, which then calls forth the readers' sympathetic appreciation, which is expressed in the form of popularity. But her husband did not follow her advice; instead he "shelter[ed] himself" in "the airiest flights of fancy," and in 1820 he "discard[ed] human interest and passion" to write the "abstract and dreamy" *Witch of Atlas.*

If Mary Shelley sometimes works to create reader sympathy for the poet, she criticizes his failure to write the popular poetry which would have created that sympathy. There is an "implicit irony" even in her "sympathetic method,"[53] for her very effort to draw Shelley and his poetry "within the circle of our sympathies" in fact implies that "both poet and poetry are innately unsympathetic" (Favret, 21). Perhaps this explains why, in the final note to the poems of 1822, the focus of sympathy shifts from Percy Shelley to herself. As this long note relates the drowning of her husband and his friend Edward Williams, it emphasizes less those deaths than the "harrowing" fate (*WPBS*, 325) of the survivors. Indeed, as she details the "weakness and languor" (322) resulting from her "years of painful and solitary struggle," she seems to take on the young Shelley's illness and nervous susceptibility. While her intention is doubtless to celebrate the poet by mourning the loss of her "source of happiness, peace, and good" (325), the effect is to turn reader sympathy from him to his editor.

If *Poetical Works* was "the first stone of a monument" (viii) to her husband's "genius," "sufferings," and "virtues," Mary Shelley completed this "most sacred duty" in 1840, with the two-volume *Essays, Letters from Abroad, Translations and Fragments by Percy Bysshe Shelley.* The book prints the *Journal of a Six Weeks' Tour* (first published in 1817), sixty-seven of Shelley's letters, and "the most interesting portion" of his unpublished essays and fragments;[54] these included his translation of Plato's *Symposium,* several fragments of translation, *A Defense of Poetry,* "Speculations on Metaphysics," and "Speculations on Morals." Even more than the

Posthumous Poems, this edition is carefully selected to present readers with a particular version of Shelley.

Several concerns dictated Mary Shelley's selections. In publishing her husband's letters, she "shr[a]nk from all *private* detail for the public" (*MWSL*, 2:221). She wanted to restore material deleted from several letters already published by Leigh Hunt; if the omissions were not "wholly private," then she wanted "to shew [Shelley] not ourselves—& each word of *his* is *him*" (*MWSL*, 2:330, 331). When privacy was not at issue, she aimed to "preserve as many of Shelley's *own words* as possible" (*MWSL*, 2:327). When Hunt wanted to correct Shelley's translation of "On Love" from Plato's *Phaedrus*, she retained Shelley's "uncouth" expressions because he considered them "more Greek" and also, she explained, because "I like to leave it as he left it" (*MWSL*, 2:328). "On Love" also raised a more delicate issue of translation in its description of love between men. Mary Shelley was "puzzled" (*MWSL*, 2:327) by Hunt's contradictory translations of the Greek word for "love," and her own expression "our civilized love" is unclear; what is clear is her felt editorial duty to "phrase it so that the common reader will think common love is meant" and "the learned alone will know what is meant." Percy Shelley's radical prose also required difficult editorial decisions. Like *Queen Mab*, his essay "On the Devil and Devils" raised the problem of mutilation. Initially she omitted "a few lines which might be too shocking," for "so many of the religious particularly like Shelley," and she "want[ed] these two volumes to be popular"; on the other hand, she "hate[d] to *mutilate*" and considered it her "duty to publish every thing" (*MWSL*, 2:326). "On the Devil" was in proof stage when she finally withdrew it for fear it would "excite a violent party spirit against the volumes" (*MWSL*, 2:327). Her anxiety about political "party spirit" may also explain why she reversed her original intention of publishing the controversial "A Philosophical View of Reform." With his prose as with his poems, she was careful to construct a broadly popular Shelley.

Since her notes to the prose are factual rather than evaluative, Mary Shelley's preface is her only public statement of her editorial aims. She hopes the *Essays* will increase her husband's popularity and lead "those who did not know him" to "a juster estimate of his virtues and his genius" (5). She also hopes that "lovers" (6) of his poetry will discover in the prose the "sincerity" of his "gentle sympathies and lofty aspirations." To that end, she instructs her audience in the correct reading of the essays. A neglected poet, for instance, should "learn" (6) from *A Defence of Poetry* that his "best claim" to praise is belonging to "the holy brother-

hood" whose "vocation" is "to divest life of its material grossness" and to
animate it with the "power of turning all things to the beautiful and
good." More practical is her advice to the reader of Shelley's "Essay on
the Punishment of Death"; since "our legislators" (9) are already nearing
his views of justice, this fragment may suggest additional "motives for
carrying his beneficent views into practice." She also guides the reader to
see not "puerile vanity" (16) but "honest pride" and "helpful and generous benevolence and friendship" in Shelley's letters about his steamship
project. Drawing on her special knowledge of Shelley's admittedly
"vague" views (10), she interprets his "Essay on a Future State" for the
reader. She notes the "[t]races" (11) of her own belief that "spiritual
improvement in this life prepares the way to a higher existence," and she
focuses on her own "faith" (12) that becoming "worthy of him" will
ensure her "the bliss of a reunion." Like Tennyson's immensely popular
poem *In Memoriam* (1850), her preface thus moves from an ostensible
tribute to the dead toward consolation for the living.

The preface's final paragraph demonstrates again how literary criticism is imbricated in a culture's other evaluative discourses. Mary Shelley is "far from satisfied" (18) with others' literary criticism of her husband, for even those who praise his poetry with "enthusiasm" and
"discrimination" do not "understand the man." *A Defence of Poetry*
demonstrates his "faith in good"; his letters reveal the qualities that
"form the perfection of man" (18–19); his writings on morals show his
"keen insight into human motive" (19). The pain of his loss can "never
pass away," she concludes, but "I gain resignation" by believing that
"those to whom he was united on earth . . . may hope to join him." This
final paragraph, which moves from literary criticism through political
comment to spiritual consolation, well illustrates how Mary Shelley's
methods of biography and criticism come to literature with personal and
aesthetic but also political and moral expectations.

Chapter Seven
Travel Narratives

Both Mary Shelley and her husband were "passionately fond of travelling."[1] They began their life together with the Continental trip recorded in the *History of a Six Weeks' Tour* (1817), and they later traveled extensively in Italy. Long after Shelley's death, Mary and their son Percy took the journeys that comprise her *Rambles in Germany and Italy* (1844). This chapter covers those two books as well as the reviews and essays in which she focused on travel.[2] After a short account of British tourism, the chapter introduces concepts—the differentiation between traveler and tourist, and the consequent forms of taste and distinction—which her travel writings exemplify.

From the sixteenth through the eighteenth century, travel on the Continent was generally considered educational rather than recreational. In the Renaissance, England's young male aristocrats went abroad "for *discourse* rather than for picturesque views or scenes."[3] The gentleman traveled to complete his education by learning European languages, conversing in those languages at European courts and with learned men, and "assimilating classical texts appropriate to particular sites." (Adler 9) In the late sixteenth and early seventeenth centuries, however, there was a shift away from this emphasis on discourse, classical learning, and the "traditional authority" associated with them.[4] Travel remained educational but came to focus on empirical experience. Such texts as *Profitable Instruction* (1613) set out checklists of "routine topics" for the traveler, who was now expected to return home with hands-on knowledge of Continental topography, history, and culture.[5]

This "investigative" form of travel, "governed by an ideal of objectively accurate vision" (Frow, 143), continued into the eighteenth century. Investigative travel literature had an "overwhelming popularity" (Curley, 53); eight encyclopedic collections of travel lore, forty-five smaller compilations, and over a thousand individual accounts and travel miscellanies were published between 1660 and 1800. Men involved in trade who began to travel to the Continent were interested not in "courtly contacts and a cosmopolitan sensibility" but in investigating "investment opportunities, commercial competition, and labor

utilization."[6] The similar "drive for empirical enquiry" (Curley, 49) that motivated the eighteenth century's physical sciences also inflected individual travel. From her Turkish travels in the 1720s, for example, Lady Mary Wortley Montagu brought back to England the first information on inoculation against smallpox. In his 1742 essay "On Travel," Samuel Johnson recommends the older ideal of a moral and ethical study of men and manners, but he also encourages the traveler to study topography and geography according to modern "principles of scientific enquiry" (Curley, 73). Young aristocratic men still took the Continental journey now known as the Grand Tour, but for wider educational purposes. The earlier focus on "intellectual networks" between learned men remained (Frow, 143), but the Grand Tourist was now more apt to exchange scientific information than classical learning with his Continental network. Crucially, his studies in European knowledge and manners were to teach a heightened "patriotic appreciation" of English customs.[7] As it completed the education of young aristocrats, then, increasingly the Grand Tour "performed the forthright ideological work" (Buzard, 120) of maintaining ruling-class hegemony. An experience of travel shared by the privileged, the Grand Tour gave "pseudohistorical legitimation" to such privilege by helping Britain's future rulers to imagine their nation as "heir to the great but fallen Roman imperial tradition" (Buzard, 121).

If the Grand Tour was intended as educational travel, however, it could also be condemned as frivolous tourism. As early as 1676, Etherege's play *The Man of Mode* mocks Sir Fopling Flutter for returning from his Grand Tour with an extensive knowledge of French dancing. In 1742 Pope's *The Dunciad* ridicules callow youth who are too ignorant to learn from a Grand Tour and whose vanity and pretensions make the English gentleman a laughingstock. As the failure of an educational function became a standard criticism of the Grand Tour, it also heightened the perceived difference between the traveler and the tourist. Instead of exchanging knowledge with learned scientists, the frivolous Grand Tourist gathered specimens for his curio collection; instead of becoming cultivated by studying other nations' manners, he picked up "superficial social polish" (Buzard, 99); instead of fitting himself to govern, he indulged in sexual adventures and wasted his time sightseeing.

In the early nineteenth century, the distinction between traveler and tourist took a new, Romantic form. The Continent was virtually closed to England's would-be Grand Tourists during the Napoleonic Wars, and by the time of England's victory over France in 1815 the Grand Tour

itself had lost status for a new generation. The class privilege it connoted had been challenged by radicals such as William Godwin and his daughter Mary, and its "tired classical associations" (Buzard, 109) and "hierarchy of attractions" became signs of tourism rather than travel. To young Romantics, the Grand Tourist relied on "a preplanned narrative of space" and on "itineraries that organized experience."[8] In contrast, such novels as Mme. de Staël's *Corinne* (1807) presented the would-be traveler with an immediate, sensitive, and above all enthusiastic experience of the Continent. The Romantic traveler might see the same sights as the Grand Tourist and experience them with *Corinne*-like enthusiasm, but unlike the tourist, the traveler obeyed "unique inner dictates" (Buzard, 111), enthused in his or her own way. This personal response to the Continent attested to the traveler's "distinction"—to the "privileged position in social space" that displayed difference from and superiority to the tourist.[9] Romantic distinction centered on "the cultivation and display of 'taste'" (Frow, 143). Where Grand Tourists accumulated the objects appropriate to their class and wealth, Romantic travelers cultivated and displayed taste by simply responding to the experience of travel. Furthermore, while such travelers might lack the economic capital of tourists, they achieved "cultural capital." If capital is understood as "actually usable resources and powers" (Bourdieu, 114), then cultural capital is the resources and powers arising from one's "acquisition of legitimate culture" (Bourdieu, 70); one such acquisition is the "aesthetic competencies" of taste (Frow, 148). Mary Shelley's *History of a Six Weeks' Tour* and her travel essays of the 1820s exemplify the Romantic traveler's enthusiasm, distinction, and taste.

The *History of a Six Weeks' Tour* was published anonymously in 1817. The first section consists of the journal Mary Shelley kept during her 1814 trip through France, Switzerland, Germany, and Holland with Percy Shelley and her stepsister Claire Clairmont; she cobbled together the second section from her and Percy's journals and letters written during a second trip in 1816. According to its preface, this "unpresuming" *History* was written with "the enthusiasm of youth."[10] One reviewer approvingly contrasted this "vivacity" with the "stateliness of intellect" assumed by the "modern imbecil [sic] tourist"—"really one is quite out of breath at the end" of the *History*.[11] As this reviewer recognizes, enthusiasm distinguishes the *History*'s traveler from the standard tourist.

One sign of travelers' enthusiastic openness to experience is their unconventional vehicles. Mary and Percy Shelley and Claire travel in a

weather-beaten cabriolet that would appear "ludicrous" (15) to tourists. Riding by turns on an ass (later a mule) is another "eccentric" (17) procedure; they have several misadventures with a mule-drawn *voiture* (wagon). Another mark of enthusiasm is their frequently changing itinerary. After a week in Paris, dwindling funds force them into two unfurnished rooms in Switzerland; again in financial difficulties, they abandon their planned journey to Italy and return to England. Despite these vicissitudes, Mary Shelley reports feeling "as happy as a new-fledged bird" (45), and this joyous sense of novelty is a third sign of the true traveler's enthusiasm. At Calais she is immediately struck with the "different language" (15) and the clothes "very unlike" English dress. In Germany she marvels at the "entirely new" colors of a sunset (34); in Geneva she relishes sunshine of a "splendour and heat unknown in England" (46), forests "to which England affords no parallel" (53), and "such flowers as [she] never saw in England" (55).

Another, more substantive form of enthusiasm is Mary Shelley's radicalism. France's "discontent and sullenness" (41) toward the English occupying army is "encouraging" (42) to those who support the "cause of liberty" and have a "fellow feeling with the oppressed." She fears that the gate of St. Denis in Paris, which she saw before Napoleon's defeat, may since have been "disfigured" by France's British "conquerors" (17). At a monument to Rousseau in Geneva, she reflects that the French Revolution, despite its "temporary bloodshed and injustice" (47), produced "enduring benefits to mankind." As Shelley thus separates herself from conservative English politics, her enthusiastic radicalism becomes a form of distinction.

A negative manifestation of distinction in the *History* is Mary Shelley's moments of disgust. Such moments dramatize that taste both "unites and separates" (Bourdieu, 56), that it "unites all those who are the product of similar conditions" while at the same time "distinguishing them from all others" who do not share the correct tastes. Tastes, or preferences, are thus "the practical affirmation of an inevitable difference" between those with taste and those who lack it. Another such affirmation is the distaste for another's difference that Shelley's *History* often manifests. The French town of Troyes is "dirty and uninviting" (22) and the people of another French village are "squalid with dirt" (21) and correspondingly "disgusting and brutal." Although she notes approvingly that the German town of Mannheim is "strikingly neat and clean" (35), the German working class inspires distaste. Shelley is appalled by the "vulgarity and rudeness" (34) of Germans "of the mean-

est class" (32); "nothing could be more horribly disgusting," and even the "paradise" of the Rhine and its "picturesque ruins" are polluted by "disgusting Germans" (36–37). She is more ambivalent about the servant class of various nations. One "consequence of republican institutions" (47) and "equality of classes" in Switzerland is that the Genevan "lower orders" have a "greater freedom and refinement of manners" than British servants. Swiss peasants, however, lack the "vivacity and grace" of France's peasants, and despite her revulsion from French dirt, Shelley praises the manners of French servants. When British servants become "familiar" (16), they are "impudent", but when French servants "treat you unaffectedly as their equal," they "have the easiness and politeness of the most well-bred English."

This complicated mixture of revulsion and appreciation mirrors Mary Shelley's equally complicated politics, in which a theoretical adherence to revolutionary principles of liberty, equality, and fraternity extends to French servants but not to British servants or the German working class. Her political tastes and aesthetic distaste reinforce each other. In this "system of aesthetic positions" (Bourdieu, 57), the disgusting working class serves as a foil or "negative reference point" for her own version of radicalism. Her political distinction from conservative England is thereby consolidated.

In the essays written during the 1820s, Shelley develops sharper differentiations between tourist and traveler as well as new standards of distinction and taste. The semi-fictional essay entitled "Recollections of Italy," published in 1824 in the *London Magazine*, defines the traveler by his ability to appreciate Italy as well as England. Edmund Malville values the English "Mother Earth"[12] as "a domestic wife, keeping house" with "earnest care"; but he also values the Italian earth, "a young affectionate wife" (29) who "dresses [her] home in smiles." A visitor with "false notions" (27) of Italy might be "disappointed with the reality," Malville adds, but only if he behaves like a tourist: journeying too fast, staying in hotels with other Englishmen, expecting to find "gorgeous temples" on every corner, lounging in coffee-houses, sampling high society, art, and opera. In contrast, Malville experienced Italy as a traveler rather than a tourist. He explored the country with the "ardent curiosity and delight" of a "lover of nature"; unlike English tourists who were "much shocked" (29) by "the manners of the common people and servants" (28), he recognized their "charm." And instead of following the "tedious routine" (27) that governs "most men's lives," he separated

himself from the crowd to "live to myself and to my affections." In his solitary sensitivity and unique openness to Italy, Malville is a true Romantic traveler.

He is also a forerunner of the figure Mary Shelley later calls "the Anglo-Italian." She first introduces this term in 1826 in a review of three novels—Lord Normanby's *The English in Italy*, Charlotte Eaton's *Continental Adventures*, and Anna Jameson's *The Diary of an Ennuyée*—which begins with an account of Continental travel after the Napoleonic Wars.[13] When the peace of 1815 opened England's "island prison," she writes, every Briton "addicted to vagabondizing" hurried to the Continent "to imitate [their] forefathers in their almost forgotten custom, of spending the greater part of their lives and fortunes in their carriages." She follows this gentle ridicule of the Grand Tour with a mocking comparison between the "vast stream" of 1815 tourists and the Norwegian rats who cross water on the backs of their dead comrades (such tropes of "deluge, invasion, or infestation" [Buzard, 83] were common denigrations of tourists during the 1820s). In contrast, the tourist of the 1820s is "almost cloyed with foreign travel" (342), yet even he feels an "enthusiastic transport" at the prospect of visiting Italy.

Shelley then distinguishes between the tourist and the Anglo-Italian. Because the tourist cannot speak Italian, he believes he is being "'starved here, upset there, and robbed every where'" (343); the Anglo-Italian's wishes are met because he can communicate them. The tourist either remains within the "narrow experience" of his "stayathomeativeness" or tries to "adopt the customs of the natives"; the Anglo-Italian seeks out "the most refined" Italians and "appreciates their native talent and simple manners" without losing his Englishness. The tourist visits sights "anxious, not to see, but to say that he has seen"; the Anglo-Italian develops "a real taste for the beautiful" in art. In this construction of the truly cultivated Anglo-Italian, "real taste" becomes an exclusive and exclusionary "aesthetic competency" (Frow, 148).

Shelley's literary criticism in this review is similarly predicated on an exclusionary standard of Anglo-Italian taste. She praises Lord Normanby's *The English in Italy* as a specimen of Anglo-Italian "taste and knowledge" that faithfully depicts "the complicated form of Italian society" (344). Charlotte Eaton's *Continental Adventures* lacks the "perfect Italian stamp" (353) of Lord Normanby's book, because it is grounded not in the true Italian character and manners but in the "all English" situations of "a common novel." Yet Shelley asserts her own Anglo-Italianness by distinguishing her experience of Italy from that of the authorita-

tive Lord Normanby. Even when she "assent[s] to the truth of his facts" (344), that assent marks *her* experience as the standard to which he must measure up, and she often disagrees with his "opinions and conclusions." Her criticism of his story "L'Amoroso" sets her gendered understanding of both English and Italian customs against his, and her critique of his conservative politics is equally authoritative. His story "The Politico" hints that the Piedmontese should have "waited a few years" (345) to mount their revolution—"as if," she scoffs, "the capacity of waiting did not engender a callousness to the evils of tyranny." Furthermore, he is "judging only from the apparent effects" of "this crushed revolt"; Shelley supports her judgment of the true, beneficial effects with a long paragraph of political analysis. A detailed description of agricultural Italy further evinces her Anglo-Italian political authority: "[I]t is in the country of Italy that you see most of the true Italian character" (348), Shelley writes, and her knowledge of this character justifies her claim that the Italians' "rich stores of talent" (351) will eventually lead to their emancipation.

A letter Mary Shelley wrote to *The Examiner* in June 1826 contains another affirmation of Anglo-Italian taste. Signed "Anglo-Italicus," the letter defends the Italian opera singer Velluti against a reviewer's lack of aesthetic taste.[14] The defects of Velluti's voice are "so glaring as to be evident to the coarsest ears" (*MWSL*, 1:517), she sniffs; to "the judicious and delicate," however, the singer's deficiencies are "annulled" by his acting. Moreover, Velluti's "patient sweetness" (*MWSL*, 1:518) inspires a "sentiment" that "the generous and the gentle must instinctively feel" but that cannot be "instil[led] into the coarse and vulgar." This language of class-specific taste not only distinguishes the "judicious" and "gentle" (as in "gentleman") from the "coarse and vulgar," it implies that the former group have an instinctive good taste that the latter group can never learn. Shelley's letter thus demonstrates "the social uses of culture" as "an instrument of symbolic domination."[15]

Other forms of distinction and taste appear in Mary Shelley's 1828 review of two travel books, Best's *Italy as it is* and Simonds's *A Tour in Italy and Sicily*. She begins with her own view of "Italy as it is," which establishes her distinction by the familiar mode of distaste. Finding "[t]he vile hut of an artificer" in the middle of an ancient temple, she states, checks one's "enthusiasm" for Rome.[16] Like much mid-century writing on travel to Egypt,[17] this review couples admiration of an

ancient civilization with distaste for its modern avatar. A "degenerate race" (130) of "modern usurpers" now occupies the city's "sacred soil"; to make Rome "really a Roman scene," then, "every inhabitant should be dismissed" from the "consecrated ground." Her distaste for modern Romans extends to Best's Catholicism. The "genial temper of ancient [Roman] philosophy" (129) stands in sharp contrast to modern Rome's "austere" Catholicism, and she is "disgusted" (131) that Catholics like Best prefer "the corruption, profligacy and imbecility of Papal Rome" to the city's "ancient glories." Moreover, Best considers Austria's despotism in Italy "the next best thing to the power of the Pope" (132). For all these reasons, his book will not appeal to "men of taste."

In the Simonds section of the review, Shelley emphasizes her Anglo-Italian knowledge and taste. As a "long sojourner" in Italy (135), she can "vouch for every part" of Simonds's descriptions of Italian "manners and morals" and for his view of the Italian character. But Simonds lacks both a "sense of the ills occasioned by tyranny" and Shelley's knowledge of Italian politics, so he fails to understand that "long freedom" created the "civilization enjoyed by the Tuscan republics." Simonds is also guilty of "bad taste" (137) for disliking Etruscan vases; in contrast, the Etruscan influence on English potters like Wedgwood shows that their "taste [was] educated in the pure school of graceful and simple antiquity." Another instance of Simonds's bad taste, his lack of admiration for the "great masters" of Italian painting (133), might have been avoided had he "sufficiently studied" them. The letter on Velluti had suggested that aesthetic appreciation cannot be learned; in this review, perceiving an artist's intention and "pass[ing] judgment" on it requires "refinement *and* education" (italics added). The new recognition that taste can be learned indicates a muting of Mary Shelley's earlier aesthetic elitism.

The differentiation of traveler from tourist took new forms in the 1840s. Steam-powered ships and trains made travel faster and cheaper and hence more accessible to the middle classes. Also facilitating travel were the guidebooks to the Continent that "proliferated" after the Napoleonic Wars (Buzard, 69) to aid first-time, middle-class travelers unfamiliar with the Grand Tour tradition. Mariana Starke's popular *Travels on the Continent* (1820) recommended routes for travelers; by 1833 it had gone into eight editions, and in 1843 Mary Shelley found it an "excellent guide" to parts of Italy.[18] The series of *Handbooks* issued by publisher John Murray not only listed routes and sights as well as distinctive features and attractions, they were the first guidebooks small

enough to be carried in the hand. With newly affordable travel and stock itineraries, however, came an anxiety over the upward mobility and "instant democratization" (Buzard, 83) they seemed to herald. Critics often represented tourists as an indistinguishable swarm, all jockeying for social position and some pretending a status to which they were not entitled. Such complaints about tourists became a "rhetorical strategy" for guaranteeing the traveler's difference (Buzard, 94). True travelers further distinguished themselves from this tourist ruck and its standard itinerary through a discourse of authenticity. By recognizing the sights and people that were authentically "native," and by recording a "personal impression" (Barrell, 100) rather than a guidebook-directed response to these experiences, authentic travelers were elevated above the indiscriminate crowd of tourists, and their authentic experience became a sign of distinction. In her last travel book, Mary Shelley uses several rhetorical strategies to create a narrative of authenticity and distinction.

Rambles in Germany and Italy, in 1840, 1842, and 1843 was published as a collection of letters in 1844. Part I, roughly half of the first volume, covers Mary Shelley's four-month trip in 1840 with her son, Percy, and his Cambridge friends Julian Robinson and George Deffell. Her fourteen-month journey with Percy and his friend Alexander Knox during 1842 and 1843 is recorded in two sections: Part II, which covers June through August 1842, concludes Volume I; and Part III, which covers the balance of the trip, constitutes Volume II. After her return to England in September 1843 she proposed to the publisher Edward Moxon that she write a travel book, promising to make it "as light—as personal to myself—& as amusing as I can" (*MWSL*, 3:96). The book's epistolary form contributes to its personal note by "reinforcing the valued sense of immediacy of witness" (Frow, 143). Unlike the *History*, which generally eschewed first-person reflections, *Rambles* is marked throughout by the "personal to myself," by "discourses of the self" that signal the traveler's authenticity.[19] The following discussion of those discourses is divided into two sections corresponding to the two journeys in *Rambles*—that of Part I and that of Parts II and III. A final section analyses the political concerns that unite the book.

In some ways, *Rambles* simply echoes standard discourses of travel. Mid-Victorian travelers frequently complained of crowds and noise (Buzard, 83). Mary Shelley is similarly distressed by the "throng" at Baden-Baden (1:37) and the "noise and turmoil," "confusion and crowd" (1:104) of the hotel at Como; she routinely finds *table d'hôte* din-

ing "tiresome and even disgusting" (1:38) because of its "noise and numbers" (1:5). Her mentions of work often replicate guidebook "descriptions," which were actually "a method of representing work while
deflecting attention away from the worker."[20] Such a deflection occurs
when Shelley focuses on the product rather than the laborers in a silk-
factory (1:111), or when she limits her discussion of Italian mill girls to
their good moral conduct (1:77), "well-tuned" singing (1:98), and "picturesque" dress; indeed, one reviewer's stated interest in the "condition
of the factory population of every country" was satisfied by this "cheerful" picture.[21] In its distancing of work, Part I is complicit in a "structural arrangement" (MacCannell, 68) of travel writing, one that creates
a "touristic relationship" to a social object and thus turns the *soi-disant*
traveler into a tourist.

More characteristically, Shelley consciously negotiates with familiar
discourses of travel. Bringing the authenticity of her own experience
into relief requires a recognizable background, so she positions her experiences sometimes within and sometimes against conventional travelers'
discourses. One that she works within is a discourse of the uses of travel.
The idea of travel as "an ameliorative *vacation*" (Buzard, 102) first
appeared in William Hazlitt's and Samuel Rogers's travel writings of the
1820s. *Rambles* is dedicated to Rogers and often cites his works; Shelley
may have borrowed from him her belief that the "novel and various
scenes" of travel (1:2) will "cure" her physical and nervous illnesses.
Another standard trope, that travel "legitimates the transgression of
one's static, stable, or fixed location" by enabling the "disavowing [of]
daily life" (Friedberg, 59) appears in Shelley's view of travel as escape:

> [I]n the every-day scenes of life . . . you are weighed with others accord-
> ing to your extrinsic possessions; your income, your connexions, your
> position. . . . But what are these to me now? My home is the readiest
> means of conveyance, . . . —my only acquaintance the companions of my
> wanderings—the single business of my life to enjoy the passing scene.
> (1:9–10)

If this lighthearted sense of freedom from the usual constraints of financial and social position is "a commonplace" of post-1815 travel books
(Buzard, 102), still Shelley's "me" sentences turn a standard trope into
an authentic experience. Part I often positions the authentic within the
conventional in this way. As she boards a steam-boat, her personal
"blessings" on steam travel (1:54) also become the "traveller's blessing"

of all who "love to roam far and free"; the fact that travelers are "always impatient of stoppages" (1:141) is attested by her own "grumbling."

In other ways, however, Shelley is careful to distinguish herself from the usual tourist, in part because she was in fact following in familiar footsteps. The route she takes through the Alps and many of her stops in Italy were staples of the Grand Tour;[22] the Alps had been further popularized by Romantic travel books like her own *History* and James Fenimore Cooper's *Excursions in Italy*. Sometimes she negotiates this "belatedness" (Buzard, 110) overtly. She concludes her short description of the Alps by quoting a long passage from Cooper (2:291), and the preface acknowledges that her journey followed "the common range of the tourist" (1:vii).

Other strategies of distinction are more covert. When the preface admits that *Rambles* "could tell nothing new, except as each individual's experience possesses novelty," Shelley subtly claims that distinction of "novelty." The success of this strategy appears in the reviews that praised *Rambles*'s "individuality"[23] and Shelley's "good judgment" in avoiding "threadbare" themes (*Tait's*, 730). Although she often cites the "inestimable" Murray *Handbooks* (1:30), she distinguishes her book from them by noting their misprints (1:49) and other errors. Another sign of distinction is the trope of indescribability by which Shelley shows her unique apprehension of familiar sights. Her "imperfect words" (1:67) cannot convey the "matchless scene" of the Alps, for example, and "words are vain" to describe the scenery along the Rhine. Most significant are Part I's expressions of disgust, for in *Rambles* as in the *History*, distaste signals distinction. The Prussian villages are "indescribably squalid" (1:17); rooms at one inn are "dirty" (1:21), and a "loathly reptile" (1:107) appears in another "squalid" inn; bathing accommodations at Baden-Baden are "inferior and dirty-looking" (1:40); the Swartzwald peasants are "dirty" (1:47) and "by no means attractive"; and so on.

The most distinctive, "personal to myself" element of Part I is her memories of her past in Italy with Percy Shelley. Because Sir Timothy Shelley's death in April 1844 had voided his ban on Mary's use of the family name, *Rambles* was published as "by Mrs. Shelley," and one reviewer commented that its "merit of saying something novel" arose from "Mrs. Shelley's . . . early reminiscences" (*Tait's*, 730). This past also marks the authenticity of her present Italian travels, as Part I constructs a unique narrative of her distinctive relations to Percy Shelley and to nature.

Part I begins with insistent memories of her husband and children and their deaths. When she reaches Italy, recollections of "young and

happy days" (1:61) with Percy Shelley alternate with memories of his death and the consequent fears of "wreck and danger" (1:38) that still "haunt [her] continually" (1:74). At one point, her "inexpressible sadness" (1:89) gives way to "ecstacy" (1:94), for "the sun of Italy has thawed the frozen stream." This trope of natural change marks a moment of Christian pantheism, of belief that the natural world is peopled by "loving spirits" (1:94) and of hope that her husband's is among them. But she cannot sustain this mood, and she compares the "unreal phantasmagoria" (1:140) of day-to-day life to "the soul's life, which I shall, I trust, hereafter rejoin." This dreary half-hope is Part I's final word on Mary Shelley's past relation to Italy, and it is all too authentic; only Mrs. Shelley could have had this experience of travel.

In Parts II and III, the most significant forms of authenticity and distinction are "touristic shame" and the "touristic critique of tourism." Touristic shame is the belief that one is not seeing everything "the way it 'ought' to be seen" (MacCannell, 10). In the 1840s that shame often centered around tropes of speed and superficiality, especially in relation to the new technologies of steam. While some commentators shared Mary Shelley's view that the "blessings of steam" extended the areas in which the traveler could "roam wild and free," others felt this new technology was turning travel into tourism. Travel by horse or stagecoach was necessarily slow and thus had given the traveler time to actively appreciate his surroundings. Travel by railroad, in contrast, "'transmutes a man from a traveller into a living parcel'" (quoted in Buzard, 33), into a passive and superficial tourist. Of course, such touristic shame is created by mystifying the fact that leisured travel is "the mark of the aristocrat" (Feifer, 166) who has wealth and no professional or commercial calls on his or her time.

Rambles's relation to touristic shame and its mystifications is complicated. Mary Shelley and her companions were "perforce economical travellers" during their 1840 journey (1:49), yet Part I focuses on "the pleasure of loitering" (1:36, 85) and "linger[ing]" (1:46, 84). The term "rambles" itself connotes leisure, and while the travelers sometimes proceed too rapidly to "indulge in extraneous rambles" (1:33), they linger at Baden-Baden not to gamble as tourists do but to "ramble" (1:41). The journey of 1842–43 was longer but only slightly better financed, and Shelley sometimes refuses touristic shame by baldly stating her lack of the money that "enables the tourist to loiter." Her greatest "regret" (2:22) is that her "narrow means" prevent her from hiring a carriage "to

drive about everywhere, and see everything," and she both "env[ies] and despise[s] the happy rich" (2:134) who do not use their carriages to "ramble." Yet Parts II and III are also suffused with touristic shame. With "no time to spare" (1:159) and too little money, Shelley pleads half-facetiously "do not despise us"; the phrase recurs when she must hurry through Cologne (1:167). Although she wants to "linger" and see more of the Rhine than "the steam-voyager sees," she must move "on, on" (1:170–71); nor can she fulfill her "dream" (2:136) of "rambl[ing]" through Italy to "see places untrod by the usual tourist." "We could not linger" in the Salzburg area (2:34) and had only a *"flash-of-lightning view"* of it (2:36). Such rapid and superficial journeys, she recognizes, lump her with tourists, "who travel only for the sake of saying that they have travelled" (1:265).

Rambles's complicated touristic shame results in part from its contradictory view of "the uses of travel" (1:158). On the one hand are "the exhaustless current of new ideas suggested by travelling" and the "wild adventures, that enliven the imagination" of the traveler. On the other hand are "knowledge," which "free[s] the mind" from prejudice, and a wider "sympathy with our fellow-creatures." Knowledge comes when the true traveler unites with what he or she sees, when we "go out from, and take some of the external into, ourselves" (1:265). Visiting one art gallery, Shelley desires "to make all [she] saw a part of [her]self," even if she must retain some sights at the "expense" of others (1:224); in the gallery at Rabenau she tries to store her mind with "the memory of a thousand objects" that will later be her "choicest treasures" (1:242). Her economic language is a reminder that a union with what one sees is a form of "tourist consumption" (Frow, 147); although her consumption is based in sympathy, it remains "predominantly a middle-class mode of appropriation."

Appropriative appreciation will sometimes "deliberately seek to control access to its preferred objects" (Frow, 147). This move is characteristic of the second form of authenticity and distinction that appears in Parts II and III, the touristic critique of tourism. In this strategy, the true traveler goes beyond "'mere' tourists to a more profound appreciation," controlling access to the objects of appreciation by categorizing as a tourist anyone who fails to see the object "the way it 'ought' to be seen" (MacCannell, 10). This form of distinction was particularly enabling for a woman traveler-writer; unlike the "staid and sober" Murray *Handbook*, said one reviewer, women's travel books "quicken our reflections," "excite our sympathies," and "give a tone and temper to our

feelings."[24] In *Rambles*, as in Mary Shelley's essays of the 1820s, a critique of tourism operates through taste, for "a more profound appreciation" of art attests to the traveler's distinction. *Rambles* distinguishes this taste from both "untaught instinct" (2:140) and the over-sophistication of the "connoisseur"; good taste is achieved by the "student" (2:14) of art, who joins "natural powers" to "familiarity with the best productions." Good taste can be learned, but it also *must* be learned; it is a distinction available only to the traveler, for it requires more study and work than the mere tourist would give it.

Mary Shelley's aesthetic judgments in Parts II and III constitute a many-sided discourse of taste and distinction. She dismisses a Jesuit church as "even in worse taste than usual" (2:97), the Basilica of San Marco as lacking "real taste" (2:123). She promises not to "detain" (2:151) the reader in the "beaten road of the public galleries," and she twice insists that she is not writing "a mere catalogue" of paintings (1:221, 245). A painting's "technical merits" (1:223) can be felt "even by those who cannot define, nor even point them out"; thus her own distinction comes from admiring not the painter's art but "his pure, exalted soul." Her access to authentic art is another sign of distinction; prints and copies become "very inefficient things . . . if you look at the originals" (1:237). To a "connoisseur" (1:244), the face of Christ in one Titian might lack dignity; to Mary Shelley, "it has as much as the human face, in sorrow, can express." Although she occasionally states her own "ignorance" of art (1:245), she subtly makes a claim to "enlightened criticism" (2:217) by drawing attention to the lack of it in the arrangement of paintings at the Vatican. Reviewers agreed that *Rambles* was a guide to aesthetic appreciation; *Tait's* felt that Shelley's descriptions of paintings were refreshingly "devoid of the slang and technicalities of criticism" (735), and both the *Athenaeum* (727) and the *Examiner*[25] praised her taste.

Despite the differences between Mary Shelley's accounts of her two journeys, *Rambles* is united by an overarching concern with Italian politics. She proposed the book to Moxon because she needed money to aid Ferdinando Gatteschi, an expatriate Italian revolutionary (*MWSL*, 3:96). Although by 1845 he was attempting to blackmail her, in 1843 Gatteschi wrote up his recollections of the 1831 Carbonari insurrection for *Rambles*, and she considered his contribution the "best part" of an otherwise "wretched piece of work" (*MWSL*, 3:144, 146). If this judgment is

overstated, still it points to the importance she attached to *Rambles*'s politics.

This importance first appears in the preface. Shelley points out that the "general tone" (1:viii) of travel books about Italy has been "contempt" for its people and their political "risings." Instead English readers "ought to sympathise" with those struggles, because England is the "source" of "the aspiration for free institutions all over the world" (1:x–xi). Furthermore, the English "enjoy the privilege of doing and saying whatever we please, [as long as] we infringe no law" (1:xii), and this is now an important model in Italian politics. In this sense, the new politics that *Rambles* hails becomes a form of distinction not only for modern Italians but for Shelley's readers. If *Rambles* induces its English readers to pay "greater attention" to (1:xvi) and "sympathize" with the struggle for Italian liberty, then it will have aided "the cause of civilisation and moral improvement" (1:xi). *Rambles* supports this Whiggish ideology of political gradualism through discourses on the educational, religious, and political improvement that attest distinction.

In politics as in taste, *Rambles* insists on the importance of education. Because the Austrian government denies "rich and high-born" Italians (1:122) an "enlightened education," they have "the faults of the oppressed" (1:87). "[H]ighly gifted with intellectual powers" (1:86), however, they are "made to be a free active, inquiring people," and they will develop the necessary "severer virtues" when "free institutions" (1:87) reward "intellectual activity." The poetry of modern Italy already shows that "the genius of the Italians survives the blighting influence of misrule and oppression" (1:86).

The prospect of religious improvement is less sure. In *Rambles* as in all her writings, Shelley veers between tolerance of Roman Catholicism and outright hostility to it. Dante's poetry and the "elevated piety" (2:91) of early Italian painting are "the sublimest achievement of Catholicism"; but she also praises the "independent and Protestant spirit" (2:2) of the reformers who "undermine[d]" Catholicism. In modern Florence, "the soul of man" (2:186) is captive to the priests who teach him to "obey the church, not God"; yet in modern Rome, Papal ceremonies serve as "aids and supports" (2:233) in "raising the soul from earth and linking it to Heaven." Moreover, the poor of Italy derive "real comfort" (2:272) from even a religion "hung round with falsehood," and the variety and extent of charities in modern Rome show that charity flourishes "wherever the Catholic religion prevails" (2:234). Finally, however, what is needed is

not "eleemosynary charity" (2:243) but "the spirit of improvement, just laws and an upright administration."

True improvement, then, is political, and it must come from a historical education. "History fails fearfully in its duty" (1:205) if it fails to record "cruelty and tyranny," for history wakens the reader's "imagination" to "abhorrence" of such acts. Shelley consistently uses historical sites to write political history. In one particularly striking passage, she compares the "cruelties" (2:230) of England's assault on Afghanistan in 1842 to the "revenge" politics of "old Rome" and its "disdain for human life and suffering" (2:229). Like Italy in the present, the Swiss Tyrol of the past was ruled by Austrian "despotism" (2:41), so Shelley often points out sights "rendered illustrious" by the Tyrolean "struggle for liberty" (2:44). Although English visitors find an "appearance of ease and equality" (2:181) in Florence, the city's history reveals a lack of "progress in the framework of society" (2:184); what appears to be "a sort of golden age" is in fact a history of "genius" crushed by "the jealousy of government" (2:185).

Letter 14 (written by Gatteschi) and Shelley's Letter 18 give an extended history of the revolutionary Carbonari movement and its successors. The early Carbonari lessened the divisive "spirit of local attachment" (2:179); as a secret association, however, they "lost their moral sense" (2:176) and turned to assassination. The Carbonari's successors "keep awake the spirit of national union" (2:178–79), and they "work by spreading knowledge and civilisation, instead of striking terror" (2:179). Still they are secret societies and therefore "must use falsehood as a shield, and terror as a weapon" (2:260). In contrast, "the real interests of the country" are served by "the improvement of the moral sense." Every Italian of "courage and genius" (2:261) now "consecrates his moral and intellectual faculties to this end," and so "the hour must and will come."

This is Rambles's final message—and call—to its British readers, the culmination of its lessons in distinction and improvement. The response was mixed. The Athenaeum thought that "hopes for Italy" lay in a continued "Austrian domination" (725). But the reviewer agreed with Shelley's condemnation of "old-fashioned" travel-book "complaints of Italian morals and Italian degeneracy" (726), and the Examiner fully endorsed her "great hope for the national regeneration" of Italy (468). For some readers, at least, Rambles fulfilled Mary Shelley's aim: as the narrative of a true traveler, it educated the mere tourist in politics as well as taste.

Notes and References

Chapter One

1. Betty T. Bennett, "Finding Mary Shelley in Her Letters," in *Romantic Revisions*, ed. Robert Brinkley and Keith Hanley (Cambridge: Cambridge University Press, 1992), 297.

2. Quoted in *First Feminists: British Women Writers 1578–1799*, ed. Moira Ferguson (Bloomington: Indiana University Press, 1985), 192.

3. Mary Wollstonecraft, *A Vindication of the Rights of Men* (1790; Gainesville, Fla.: Scholars' Facsimiles & Reprints, 1960), 151; hereafter cited in text.

4. David B. Pirie, *Shelley* (Milton Keynes, U.K.: Open University Press, 1988), 4.

5. Mary Wollstonecraft, *A Vindication of the Rights of Woman* (1792; New York: W. W. Norton, 1975), 147; hereafter cited in text.

6. Quoted in William Godwin, *Memoirs of the Author of A Vindication of the Rights of Woman* (1798); reprinted as *Memoirs of Mary Wollstonecraft* (New York: Haskell House, 1969), 319; hereafter cited in text.

7. Quoted in William St. Clair, *The Godwins and the Shelleys: A Biography of a Family* (Baltimore: Johns Hopkins University Press, 1989), 185; hereafter cited in text.

8. Quoted in C. Kegan Paul, *William Godwin: His Friends and Contemporaries*, 2 vols. (London: Henry S. King, 1876), 1:231; hereafter cited in text.

9. *The Letters of Mary Wollstonecraft Shelley*, ed. Betty T. Bennett, 3 vols. (Baltimore: Johns Hopkins University Press, 1980–1988), 1:376; hereafter cited in text as *MWSL*, by volume and page number.

10. *The Journals of Mary Shelley, 1814–1844*, ed. Paula R. Feldman and Diana Scott-Kilvert, 2 vols. (Oxford: Clarendon Press, 1987), 2:553, 554; hereafter cited in text as *MWSJ*, by volume and page number.

11. E. P. Thompson, *The Making of the English Working Class* (1963; London: Penguin, 1988), 117.

12. Quoted in Don Locke, *A Fantasy of Reason: The Life and Thought of William Godwin* (London: Routledge, 1980), 60; hereafter cited in text.

13. William Godwin, *Enquiry concerning Political Justice*, ed. K. Codell Carter (1793; Oxford: Clarendon Press, 1971), 125; hereafter cited in text as *PJ*.

14. Quoted in Emily W. Sunstein, *Mary Shelley: Romance and Reality* (Baltimore: Johns Hopkins University Press, 1989), 27; hereafter cited in text.

15. Quoted in Muriel Spark, *Mary Shelley*, rev. ed. (London: Sphere-Penguin, 1987), 14; hereafter cited in text.

16. Emily W. Sunstein, "A William Godwin Letter, and Young Mary Godwin's Part in *Mounseer Nongtongpaw*," forthcoming in *Keats-Shelley Journal*.

17. Mary Shelley, Author's Introduction, *Frankenstein* (1831); reprinted in *Mary Shelley: "Frankenstein,"* ed. Johanna M. Smith (Boston: Bedford-St. Martin's, 1992), 20; hereafter cited in text.

18. *The Letters of Percy Bysshe Shelley*, ed. Frederick L. Jones, 2 vols. (Oxford: Clarendon Press, 1964), 1:103, 402; hereafter cited in text as *PBSL*, by volume and page number.

19. Mary Jean Corbett, "Reading Mary Shelley's *Journals*: Romantic Subjectivity and Feminist Criticism," in *The Other Mary Shelley: Beyond "Frankenstein,"* ed. Audrey A. Fisch, Anne K. Mellor, and Esther H. Schor (New York: Oxford University Press, 1993), 81.

20. Jean de Palacio, "Mary Shelley's Latin Studies: Her Unpublished Translation of Apuleius," *Revue de Littérature Comparée* 38, no. 4 (1964): 564.

21. Mary Shelley, "Note on the Poems of 1818," in *The Works of Percy Bysshe Shelley*, ed. Mrs. Shelley (London: Edward Moxon, 1850), 230; hereafter cited in Notes as *Works*.

22. Jane Blumberg, *Mary Shelley's Early Novels: "This Child of Imagination and Misery"* (Iowa City: University of Iowa Press, 1993), 206–15.

23. See Betty T. Bennett, *Mary Diana Dods, a Gentleman and a Scholar* (1991; Baltimore: Johns Hopkins University Press, 1995).

24. Sunstein, *Mary Shelley: Romance and Reality*, 272, decodes the reference, which appears in *MWSL*, 1:573.

25. Percy Bysshe Shelley, *The Revolt of Islam*, in *Works*, 51.

26. Mary Poovey, *The Proper Lady and the Woman Writer: Ideology as Style in the Works of Mary Wollstonecraft, Mary Shelley, and Jane Austen* (Chicago: University of Chicago Press, 1984), 116.

27. Lee Sterrenburg, "Mary Shelley's Monster: Politics and Psyche in *Frankenstein*," in *The Endurance of "Frankenstein"*, ed. George Levine and U. C. Knoepflmacher (Berkeley: University of California Press, 1979), 143.

28. Elie Halevy, *A History of the English People in 1815* (1924; London: Ark-Routledge, 1987), 192–93.

29. John Foster, *Class Struggle and the Industrial Revolution: Early Industrial Capitalism in Three English Towns* (London: Methuen, 1974), 18–20.

30. Mary Shelley, "Note on *The Revolt of Islam*," in *Works*, 96.

31. The Feldman and Scott-Kilvert edition of the *Journals* reproduces Mary's revisions typographically.

Chapter Two

1. There are grounds for attributing "A Night-Scene," published in *The Keepsake* for 1831, to Mary; they are not entirely convincing, however, and the poem is not considered in this chapter. Another poem attributed to her, "Ode to Ignorance," in the *Metropolitan Magazine* (1834), is even less likely to be hers. Finally, I have not commented on Mary's translations from Italian and German because I do not know those languages.

2. Alan Richardson, "*Proserpine* and *Midas*: Gender, Genre, and Mythic Revisionism in Mary Shelley's Dramas," in *The Other Mary Shelley: Beyond "Frankenstein,"* ed. Audrey A. Fisch, Anne K. Mellor, and Esther H. Schor (New York: Oxford University Press, 1993), 124; hereafter cited in text.

3. Robert Graves, *The Greek Myths*, vol. 1 (Baltimore: Penguin, 1955), 93.

4. Mary Shelley, *Proserpine*, in *"Proserpine" and "Midas": Two Unpublished Mythological Dramas*, ed. A. H. Koszul (London: Humphrey Milford, 1922), 5; hereafter cited in text by page number. The book is hereafter cited in Notes as Koszul.

5. H. J. Rose, *A Handbook of Greek Mythology* (1928; London: Methuen, 1958), 60; hereafter cited in text.

6. Mary Shelley, *Midas*, in Koszul, 49; hereafter cited in text by page number.

7. Elizabeth Fox-Genovese, *The Origins of Physiocracy: Economic Revolution and Social Order in Eighteenth-Century France* (Ithaca: Cornell University Press, 1976), 50.

8. Mary Shelley, "The Choice," in *Mary Shelley: A Biography*, by R. Glynn Grylls (London: Oxford University Press, 1938), 297; hereafter cited in text by page number. The book is hereafter cited in text as Grylls.

9. "Absence," in *The Keepsake for MDCCCXXXI*, 39.

10. Mary Shelley, preface to *The Poetical Works of Percy Bysshe Shelley* (1839), in *The Works of Percy Bysshe Shelley*, ed. Mrs. Shelley (London: Edward Moxon, 1850), vi–vii.

11. Mary Shelley, *"La Vida es sueño,"* in Elizabeth Nitchie, *Mary Shelley, Author of "Frankenstein"* (New Brunswick, N.J.: Rutgers University Press, 1953), 233; hereafter cited in text by page number. The book is hereafter cited in text and Notes as Nitchie.

12. Mary Shelley, "Tempo é più di Morire/Io ho tardato più ch'i' non vorrei," in Nitchie, 231; hereafter cited in text by page number.

13. Mary Shelley, "Stanzas," in *Mary Shelley: Romance and Reality*, by Emily W. Sunstein (Baltimore: Johns Hopkins University Press, 1989), Appendix A; hereafter cited in text.

14. Mary Shelley, "O listen while I sing to thee," in Nitchie, 234; hereafter cited in text.

15. *The Keepsake for MDCCCXXXIX*, 179.

16. *The Keepsake for MDCCCXXXIX*, 201.

Chapter Three

1. Brian W. Aldiss, "Mary Wollstonecraft Shelley," in *Science Fiction Writers: Critical Studies of the Major Authors from the Early Nineteenth Century to the Present Day*, ed. E. F. Bleiler (New York: Scribner's, 1982), 3, 5.

2. Darko Suvin, *Metamorphoses of Science Fiction: On the Poetics and History of a Literary Genre* (New Haven: Yale University Press, 1979), 4; hereafter cited in text.

3. Carl Freedman, "Science Fiction and Critical Theory," *Science-Fiction Studies*, no. 42 (July 1987): 182.

4. Mary Shelley, "Valerius: The Reanimated Roman," in *Mary Shelley: Collected Tales and Stories*, ed. Charles E. Robinson (Baltimore: Johns Hopkins University Press, 1976), 333; hereafter cited in text. The book is hereafter cited in Notes as *Tales*.

5. Charles E. Robinson, "Mary Shelley and the Roger Dodsworth Hoax," *Keats-Shelley Journal* 2 (1975): 20–28.

6. Mary Shelley, "Roger Dodsworth: The Reanimated Englishman," in *Tales*, 45; hereafter cited in text.

7. Bradford Allen Booth, Introduction, *A Cabinet of Gems: Short Stories from the English Annuals* (Berkeley: University of California Press, 1938), 6–7.

8. Eleanore Jamieson, *English Embossed Bindings 1825–1850* (Cambridge: Cambridge University Press, 1972), 2–3.

9. Quoted in Alison Adburgham, *Women in Print: Writing Women and Women's Magazines from the Restoration to the Accession of Victoria* (London: Allen & Unwin, 1972), 262; hereafter cited in text.

10. Sonia Hofkosh, "Disfiguring Economies: Mary Shelley's Short Stories," in *The Other Mary Shelley: Beyond "Frankenstein,"* ed. Audrey A. Fisch, Anne K. Mellor, and Esther H. Schor (New York: Oxford University Press, 1993), 208; hereafter cited in text. The book is hereafter cited in Notes as *Other*.

11. Preface to *The Keepsake for MCMXXVIII*, vi.

12. Preface to *The Keepsake for MCMXXVIX*, iii, iv.

13. Ros Ballister, *Women's Worlds: Ideology, Femininity, and the Woman's Magazine* (London: Macmillan, 1991), 82; hereafter cited in text.

14. Anonymous, "The Annuals," *The Spirit and Manners of the Age; A Christian and Literary Miscellany*, NS 2 (December 1829): 881.

15. Laurie Langbauer, "Swayed by Contraries: Mary Shelley and the Everyday," in *Other*, 196.

16. Paul A. Cantor, "Mary Shelley and the Taming of the Bryonic Hero: 'Transformation' and *The Deformed Transformed*," in *Other*, 100; hereafter cited in text.

17. Mary Shelley, "Transformation," in *Tales*, 122–23; hereafter cited in text.

18. Mary Shelley, "The Mortal Immortal," in *Tales*, 220; hereafter cited in text.

19. Mary Shelley, *Frankenstein; or, the Modern Prometheus* (1831), in *Mary Shelley: "Frankenstein,"* ed. Johanna M. Smith (Boston: Bedford-St. Martin's, 1992), 29; hereafter cited in text. The collection is hereafter cited in Notes as Smith.

20. Lee E. Heller, "*Frankenstein* and the Cultural Uses of Gothic," in Smith, 331–38.

21. Kate Ellis, "Monsters in the Garden: Mary Shelley and the Bourgeois Family," in *The Endurance of "Frankenstein,"* ed. George Levine and U. C. Knoepflmacher (Berkeley: University of California Press, 1979), 123–42.

22. John A. Dussinger, "Kinship and Guilt in Mary Shelley's *Frankenstein,*" *Studies in the Novel* 8 (1976): 52.

23. Anca Vlasopolos, "*Frankenstein*'s Hidden Skeleton: The Psycho-Politics of Oppression," *Science-Fiction Studies* 10, no. 2 (July 1983): 126, 133.

24. Alan Rauch, "The Monstrous Body of Knowledge in Mary Shelley's *Frankenstein,*" *Studies in Romanticism* 34.2 (Summer 1995): 227–53.

25. Anne Cranny-Francis, "Feminist Futures: A Generic Study," in *Alien Zones: Cultural Theory and Contemporary Science Fiction Cinema,* ed. Annette Kuhn (London: Verso, 1990), 220.

26. Anne K. Mellor, *Mary Shelley: Her Life, Her Fiction, Her Monsters* (New York: Routledge, 1988), chapter 5.

27. Quoted in Anne McWhir, "Teaching the Monster to Read: Mary Shelley, Education, and *Frankenstein,*" in *The Educational Legacy of Romanticism,* ed. John Willinsky (Waterloo, Canada: Wilfrid Laurier University Press, 1990), 77; hereafter cited in text.

28. Laura Kranzler, "Frankenstein and the Technological Future," *Foundation* 44 (Winter 1988–89): 43.

29. William Veeder, *Mary Shelley and "Frankenstein": The Fate of Androgyny* (Chicago: University of Chicago Press, 1986), 190.

30. "On Frankenstein," in *The Works of Percy Bysshe Shelley in Verse and Prose,* 8 vols, ed. Henry Buxton Forman (London: Reeves and Turner, 1880), 7:12.

31. On Mary's rewriting of *Paradise Lost,* see Sandra M. Gilbert and Susan Gubar, *The Madwoman in the Attic: The Woman Writer and the Nineteenth-Century Literary Imagination* (New Haven: Yale University Press, 1979), 213–47.

32. Paul O'Flinn, "Production and Reproduction: The Case of *Frankenstein,*" *Literature and History* 9, no. 2 (1983): 194–213, and Warren Montag, "'The Workshop of Filthy Creation': A Marxist Reading of *Frankenstein,*" in Smith, 300–11.

33. Quoted in E. P. Thompson, *The Making of the English Working Class* (1963; London: Penguin, 1988), 894.

34. Anonymous review, *British Critic* 9 (April 1818): 436.

35. Mary Wollstonecraft, *A Vindication of the Rights of Woman,* ed. Carol H. Poston (1792; New York: Norton, 1975), 8.

36. William Godwin, *Enquiry Concerning Political Justice,* ed. F. E. L. Priestley, 3d ed., 3 vols. (1797; Toronto: University of Toronto Press, 1946), 1:27, 35; hereafter cited in text as *PJ*.

37. Chris Baldick, *In Frankenstein's Shadow: Myth, Monstrosity, and Nine-teenth-Century Writing* (Oxford: Clarendon Press, 1987), 17.

38. Hugh J. Luke Jr., "Introduction," *The Last Man*, by Mary Shelley (Lincoln: University of Nebraska Press, 1965), xi-xv; the novel is hereafter cited in text.

39. Anonymous review, *Panoramic Miscellany* 1 (March 1826): 386; reprinted in *The Romantics Reviewed: Contemporary Reviews of British Romantic Writers*, 8 vols., ed. Donald H. Reiman (New York: Garland, 1972), 7:748; hereafter cited in text as *Panoramic*.

40. Quoted in Morton D. Paley, "Mary Shelley's *The Last Man*: Apoca-lypse without Millenium," in *Other*, 3–4; hereafter cited in text.

41. Pamela Clemit, *The Godwinian Novel: The Rational Fictions of God-win, Brockden Brown, Mary Shelley* (Oxford: Clarendon Press, 1993), 189; here-after cited in text.

42. Jane Blumberg, *Mary Shelley's Early Novels: "This Child of Imagina-tion and Misery"* (Iowa City: University of Iowa Press, 1993), 129; hereafter cited in text.

43. Jean de Palacio, "Mary Shelley and the 'Last Man,' A Minor Romantic Theme," *Revue de Littérature Comparée* 42, no. 1 (1968): 37–49, and Paley, 107–23.

44. Robert Lance Snyder, "Apocalypse and Indeterminacy in Mary Shelley's *The Last Man*," *Studies in Romanticism* 17 (Fall 1978): 442–43.

45. Audrey A. Fisch, "Plaguing Politics: AIDS, Deconstruction, and *The Last Man*," in *Other*, 270.

46. Gregory O'Dea, "Prophetic History and Textuality in Mary Shelley's *The Last Man*," *Papers on Language and Literature* 28 (Summer 1992): 283–304.

47. Jane Aaron, "The Return of the Repressed: Reading Mary Shelley's *The Last Man*," in *Feminist Criticism: Theory and Practice*, ed. Susan Sellers (Toronto: University of Toronto Press, 1991), 17.

48. Steven Goldsmith, *Unbuilding Jerusalem: Apocalypse and Romantic Rep-resentation* (Ithaca: Cornell University Press, 1993), 290; hereafter cited in text.

49. Lee Sterrenburg, "*The Last Man*: Anatomy of Failed Revolutions," *Nineteenth-Century Fiction* 33, no. 3 (December 1978): 329.

Chapter Four

1. Ina Ferris, *The Achievement of Literary Authority: Gender, History, and the Waverly Novels* (Ithaca: Cornell University Press, 1991), 2; hereafter cited in text.

2. Thomas Walter Laqueur, *Religion and Respectability: Sunday Schools and Working-Class Culture, 1780–1850* (New Haven: Yale University Press, 1976), 170, 187–240.

3. George Moir, "Modern Romance and Novel" (1842), in *Victorian Criticism of the Novel*, ed. Edwin M. Eigner and George J. Worth (Cambridge: Cambridge University Press, 1985), 40; hereafter cited in text.

4. Mary Poovey, *The Proper Lady and the Woman Writer: Ideology as Style in the Works of Mary Wollstonecraft, Mary Shelley, and Jane Austen* (Chicago: University of Chicago Press, 1984), 38.

5. Quoted in Ian Duncan, *Modern Romance and Transformations of the Novel: The Gothic, Scott, Dickens* (Cambridge: Cambridge University Press, 1992), 10; hereafter cited in text.

6. Anonymous review, *The Examiner*, no. 788 (2 March 1823): 154.

7. Anonymous review, *Blackwood's Magazine* vol. 13, no. 74 (March 1823): 284, 283; hereafter cited in text as *Blackwood's*.

8. Walter Scott, general preface (1829) of *The Waverly Novels*, 25 vols. (Edinburgh: Robert Cadell, 1842), 1:11.

9. Anonymous review, *The Athenaeum* 135 (29 May 1830): 323; hereafter cited in text as *Athenaeum*.

10. David Punter, "Social Relations of Gothic Fiction," in *Romanticism and Ideology: Studies in English Writing 1765–1830*, ed. David Aers, Jonathan Cook, and David Punter (London: Routledge & Kegan Paul, 1981), 106; hereafter cited in text.

11. Robert Miles, *Gothic Writing, 1750–1820: A Genealogy* (London: Routledge, 1993) 31; hereafter cited in text.

12. Gary Kelly, *The English Jacobin Novel 1780–1805* (Oxford: Clarendon Press, 1976), 14; hereafter cited in text.

13. William Godwin, *Enquiry Concerning Political Justice*, ed. F. E. L. Priestley, 3d ed., 3 vols. (1797; Toronto: University of Toronto Press, 1946), 1:24.

14. Georg Lukács, *The Historical Novel*, trans. Hannah and Stanley Mitchell (1937; Lincoln: University of Nebraska Press, 1983), 26; hereafter cited in text.

15. Nicola J. Watson, *Revolution and the Form of the British Novel, 1790–1825: Intercepted Letters, Interrupted Seductions* (Oxford: Clarendon Press, 1994), 110.

16. Mary Shelley, "A Tale of the Passions," in *Tales*, 1; hereafter cited in text.

17. Robinson, note to "The Heir of Mondolfo," in *Tales*, 395.

18. Mary Shelley, "The Heir of Mondolfo," in *Tales*, 308; hereafter cited in text.

19. Mary Shelley, "The False Rhyme," in *Tales*, 119; hereafter cited in text.

20. Sonia Hofkosh, "Disfiguring Economies: Mary Shelley's Short Stories," in *Other*, 209.

21. Mary Shelley, "The Swiss Peasant," in *Tales*, 137; hereafter cited in text.

22. Laurie Langbauer, "Swayed by Contraries: Mary Shelley and the Everyday," in *Other*, 194; hereafter cited in text.

23. Mary Shelley, "The Dream," in *Tales*, 153; hereafter cited in text.

24. Mary Shelley, "The Brother and Sister," in *Tales*, 166; hereafter cited in text.

25. Mary Shelley, "The Invisible Girl," in *Tales*, 190; hereafter cited in text.

26. Mary Shelley, *Valperga*, 3 vols. (London: G. and W. B. Whittaker, 1823), 1:iii; hereafter cited in text.

27. Ronald L. Meek, *The Economics of Physiocracy* (Cambridge: Harvard University Press, 1963), 20.

28. Joseph W. Lew, "God's Sister: History and Ideology in *Valperga*," in *Other*, 162; hereafter cited in text.

29. Barbara Jane O'Sullivan, "Beatrice in *Valperga*: A New Cassandra," in *Other*, 144; hereafter cited in text.

30. Pamela Clemit, *The Godwinian Novel: The Rational Fictions of Godwin, Brockden Brown, Mary Shelley* (Oxford: Clarendon Press, 1993), 182; hereafter cited in text.

31. Marlon Ross, "Romantic Quest and Conquest: Troping Masculine Power in the Crisis of Poetic Identity," in *Romanticism and Feminism*, ed. Anne K. Mellor (Bloomington: Indiana University Press, 1988), 40, 42.

32. Kate Ferguson Ellis, "Subversive Surfaces: The Limits of Domestic Affection in Mary Shelley's Later Fiction," in *Other*, 225.

33. Edward Said, *Orientalism* (New York: Pantheon, 1978), 63.

34. Nigel Leask, *British Romantic Writers and the East: Anxieties of Empire* (Cambridge: Cambridge University Press, 1992), 18; hereafter cited in text.

35. John Drew, "'In Vishnu-land what Avatar?': Sir William Jones, India, and the English Romantic Imagination," in *Tropic Crucible: Self and Theory in Language and Literature*, ed. Ranjit Chatterjee and Colin Nicholson (Singapore: Singapore University Press, 1984), 221.

36. Mary Shelley, "The Evil Eye," in *Tales*, 100; hereafter cited in text.

37. Mary Shelley, "Euphrasia: A Tale of Greece," in *Tales*, 295; hereafter cited in text.

38. Mary Shelley, *The Fortunes of Perkin Warbeck*, 3 vols. (1830; np: Norwood, 1976), 1:v; hereafter cited in text.

39. Mark Girouard, *The Return to Camelot: Chivalry and the English Gentleman* (New Haven: Yale University Press, 1981), 54.

40. Antony E. Simpson, "Dandelions on the Field of Honor: Dueling, the Middle Classes, and the Law in Nineteenth-Century England," *Criminal Justice History* 9 (1988): 104; hereafter cited in text.

41. David Hume, *The History of England, from the Invasion of Julius Caesar to the Revolution in 1688*, 10 vols. (1753–61; London: J. Wallis, 1803), 4:124; hereafter cited in text as *History*.

42. Eve Kosofsky Sedgwick, *Between Men: English Literature and Male Homosocial Desire* (New York: Columbia University Press, 1985), 25.

Chapter Five

1. Laurie Langbauer, "Swayed by Contraries: Mary Shelley and the Everyday," in *Other*, 187; hereafter cited in text.

2. Vineta Colby, *Yesterday's Woman: Domestic Realism in the English Novel* (Princeton: Princeton University Press, 1974), 4; hereafter cited in text.

3. Nancy Armstrong, *Desire and Domestic Fiction: A Political History of the Novel* (New York: Oxford University Press, 1987), 23; hereafter cited in text.

4. Eleanor Ty, *Unsex'd Revolutionaries: Five Women Novelists of the 1790s* (Toronto: University of Toronto Press, 1993), xi.

5. Terry Lovell, *Consuming Fiction* (London: Verso, 1987), 57.

6. Beth Kowalski-Wallace, "Home Economics: Domestic Ideology in Maria Edgeworth's *Belinda*," *The Eighteenth Century* 29 (Fall 1988): 242–43.

7. Mary Poovey, *The Proper Lady and the Woman Writer: Ideology as Style in the Works of Mary Wollstonecraft, Mary Shelley, and Jane Austen* (Chicago: University of Chicago Press, 1984), 38.

8. Janet Todd, *The Sign of Angellica: Women, Writing, and Fiction, 1660–1800* (New York: Columbia University Press, 1989), 228.

9. Alison Adburgham, *Silver Fork Society: Fashionable Life and Literature from 1814 to 1840* (London: Constable, 1983), 1; hereafter cited in text.

10. Quoted in Emily W. Sunstein, *Mary Shelley: Romance and Reality* (Baltimore: Johns Hopkins University Press, 1989), 179.

11. Linda Zwinger, *Daughters, Fathers, and the Novel: The Sentimental Romance of Heterosexuality* (Madison: University of Wisconsin Press, 1991), 4; hereafter cited in text.

12. Mary Shelley, *Mathilda*, in *The Mary Shelley Reader*, ed. Betty T. Bennett and Charles E. Robinson (New York: Oxford University Press, 1990), 175; hereafter cited in text.

13. Tilottama Rajan, "Mary Shelley's *Mathilda*: Melancholy and the Political Economy of Romanticism," *Studies in the Novel* 26 (Summer 1994): 44.

14. Terence Harpold, "'Did you get Mathilda from Papa?': Seduction Fantasy and the Circulation of Mary Shelley's *Mathilda*," *Studies in Romanticism* 28 (Spring 1989): 49–67.

15. Mary Shelley, "The Bride of Modern Italy," in *Tales*, 34; hereafter cited in text.

16. Mary Shelley, "The Sisters of Albano," in *Tales*, 53; hereafter cited in text.

17. Mary Shelley, "The Smuggler and His Family," in *Tales*, 203; hereafter cited in text.

18. Mary Shelley, "Ferdinando Eboli: A Tale," in *Tales*, 65; hereafter cited in text.

19. Mary Shelley, "The Elder Son," in *Tales*, 245; hereafter cited in text.

20. Mary Shelley, "The Trial of Love," in *Tales*, 232; hereafter cited in text.

21. Mary Shelley, "The Mourner," in *Tales*, 85; hereafter cited in text.

22. Kate Ferguson Ellis, "Subversive Surfaces: The Limits of Domestic Affection in Mary Shelley's Later Fiction," in *Other*, 230.

23. Burton R. Pollin, "Mary Shelley as the Parvenue," *A Review of English Literature* 8, no. 3 (1967): 21; hereafter cited in text.

24. Mary Shelley, "The Parvenue," in *Tales*, 266, 267; hereafter cited in text.

25. Anonymous review, *New Monthly Magazine* 44 (June 1835): 237.

26. Anonymous review, *Athenaeum* 484 (4 February 1837): 74.

27. Mary Shelley, *Lodore*, 3 vols. (London: Richard Bentley, 1835), 1:20; hereafter cited in text.

28. George Eliot, *The Mill on the Floss*, ed. Gordon S. Haight (1860; Boston: Riverside-Houghton, 1961), 237–38.

29. Celia Morris Eckhardt, *Fanny Wright: Rebel in America* (Cambridge: Harvard University Press, 1984).

30. Jean-Jacques Rousseau, *Emile or Treatise on Education* (1762), abridged and trans. William H. Payne (New York: Appleton, 1926), 59; hereafter cited in text as *Emile*.

31. Richard Holmes, *Shelley: The Pursuit* (New York: Dutton, 1975), 18–32.

32. Mary Wollstonecraft, *A Vindication of the Rights of Woman*, ed. Carol H. Poston (1792; New York: Norton, 1975), 19.

33. Sarah Stickney Ellis, *The Women of England: Their Social Duties and Domestic Habits* (1838), in *The Select Works of Mrs. Ellis* (New York: Langley, 1854), 48, 16.

34. Frances Wright, *Views of Society and Manners in America*, ed. Paul R. Baker (1821; Cambridge, Mass.: Belknap Press, 1963), 130.

35. *Letters of John Keats*, ed. Hyder Edward Rollins, 2 vols. (Cambridge: Harvard University Press, 1958), 1:184.

36. Mary Shelley, *Falkner*, 3 vols. (London: Sanders and Otley, 1837), 1:149; hereafter cited in text.

37. "The Rime of the Ancient Mariner," in *The Poetical Works of Samuel Taylor Coleridge*, ed. Ernest Hartley Coleridge (London: Henry Frowde, 1912), part V, ll.408–09.

38. William Wordsworth, "Ode: Intimations of Immortality," in *Wordsworth: Poetical Works*, ed. Thomas Hutchinson (Oxford: Oxford University Press, 1989), p. 460, l.64.

39. Anonymous review, *The Metropolitan* 18 (March 1837): 65.

40. Anonymous review, *Examiner* (12 February 1837): 101.

41. Mary Lyndon Shanley, *Feminism, Marriage, and the Law in Victorian England, 1850–1895* (Princeton: Princeton University Press, 1989), 24–25.

Chapter Six

1. The term gained currency with Robert Metcalf Smith's *The Shelley Legend* (New York: Scribner's, 1945).

2. Patrick Parrinder, *Authors and Authority: A Study of English Literary Criticism and its Relation to Culture 1750–1900* (London: Routledge and Kegan Paul, 1977), 21; hereafter cited in text.

3. Trevor Ross, "Copyright and the Invention of Tradition," *Eighteenth-Century Studies* 26, no. 1 (Fall 1992): 20–21; hereafter cited in text.

4. Marilyn Butler, "Culture's medium: the role of the review," in *British Romanticism*, ed. Stuart Curran (Cambridge: Cambridge University Press, 1993), 125; hereafter cited in text.

5. Chris Baldick, *The Social Mission of English Criticism, 1848–1932* (Oxford: Clarendon Press, 1983), 9.

6. Emily W. Sunstein, *Mary Shelley: Romance and Reality* (Baltimore: Johns Hopkins University Press, 1989), 51.

7. Nigel Cross, *The Common Writer: Life in Nineteenth-Century Grub Street* (Cambridge: Cambridge University Press, 1985), 179; hereafter cited in text.

8. "On Ghosts," *London Magazine* 9 (March 1823): 253. Reprinted in *The Mary Shelley Reader*, ed. Betty T. Bennett and Charles E. Robinson (New York: Oxford University Press), 334; hereafter cited in text. The book is hereafter cited in Notes as *Reader*.

9. Alvin Sullivan, ed., *British Literary Magazines*, 4 vols. (Westport, Conn.: Greenwood Press, 1984): 2:221–23.

10. "Madame d'Houtetôt," *The Liberal: Verse and Prose from the South* 2, no. 3 (1823): 68, 67; hereafter cited in text.

11. "Living Literary Characters, no. 2. The Honourable Mrs. Norton," *New Monthly Magazine* 33 (February 1831): 180; hereafter cited in text.

12. "Living Literary Characters, no. 4. James Fenimore Cooper," *New Monthly Magazine* 33 (April 1831): 360; hereafter cited in text.

13. "Memoirs of William Godwin," in Godwin, *Caleb Williams* (London: Colburn & Bentley, 1831), vi; hereafter cited in text.

14. Quoted in C. Kegan Paul, *William Godwin: His Friends and Contemporaries*, 2 vols. (London: Henry S. King, 1876), 1:120, 129, 130; hereafter cited in text as Paul, by volume and page number.

15. Review of *The Italian Novelists*, *Westminster Review* 7 (January 1827): 116; hereafter cited in text.

16. "Illyrian Poems—Feudal Scenes," *Westminster Review* 10 (January 1829): 72; hereafter cited in text.

17. Review of *The Loves of the Poets*, *Westminster Review* 11 (October 1829): 472. Reprinted in *Reader*, 366; hereafter cited in text.

18. Review of *1572 Chronique du Temps de Charles IX*, *Westminster Review* 13 (October 1830): 495; hereafter cited in text.

19. Review of *Cloudesley; A Tale, Blackwood's Edinburgh Magazine* vol. 27, no. 166 (May 1830): 711; hereafter cited in text.

20. Review of *The Bravo, Westminster Review* 16 (January 1832): 183; hereafter cited in text.

21. "Giovanni Villani," *The Liberal: Verse and Prose from the South* vol. 2, no. 4 (1823): 282; hereafter cited in text.

22. Review of *Life and Death of Lord Edward Fitzgerald, Westminster Review* 31 (January 1832): 110; hereafter cited in text.

23. Review of *Richard the Third, as Duke of Gloucester and King of England, Athenaeum*, no. 875 (3 August 1844): 707; and no. 876 (10 August 1844): 731; hereafter cited in text by volume and page number.

24. Olivia Smith, *The Politics of Language, 1791–1819* (Oxford: Clarendon Press, 1986), 161; hereafter cited in text.

25. Michael Sanderson, *Education, Economic Change, and Society in England, 1780–1870* (London: Macmillan, 1983), 13; hereafter cited in text.

26. Alan Rauch, *Moral Responsibility and the Growth of Knowledge: Science in the British Novel, 1818–1860*, forthcoming from Duke University Press.

27. A. Dwight Culler, *The Imperial Intellect: A Study of Newman's Intellectual Ideal* (New Haven: Yale University Press, 1955), 175.

28. Morse Peckham, "Dr. Lardner's *Cabinet Cyclopaedia*," *Papers of the Bibliographical Society of America* 45 (1951): 50; hereafter cited in text.

29. Quoted in Elizabeth Nitchie, *Mary Shelley, Author of "Frankenstein"* (New Brunswick: Rutgers University Press, 1953), 161.

30. William Thackeray, *The Memoirs of Mr. C. J. Yellowplush*, in *The Works of William Makepeace Thackeray*, 24 vols. (London: Smith Elder, 1892), 17:120, 128.

31. Anonymous review, *Monthly Review*, no. 138 (November 1835): 332; anonymous review, *Monthly Review*, no. 136 (March 1835): 300; hereafter cited in text by volume and page number.

32. Anonymous review, *Monthly Review*, no. 135 (December 1834): 445–46; hereafter cited in text by volume and page number.

33. J. C. L. de Sismondi, *A History of the Italian Republics, being a View of the Origin Progress and Fall of Italian Freedom* (London: Longman & Co., 1832), v.

34. Mary Shelley with David Brewster, James Montgomery, and others, *Lives of the Most Eminent Literary and Scientific Men of Italy, Spain, and Portugal*, 3 vols. (London: Longman & Co., 1835–37), 1:256; hereafter cited in text by volume and page number.

35. Mary Shelley, *Lives of the Most Eminent French Writers*, 2 vols. (Philadelphia: Lea and Blanchard, 1840), 2:124–25; hereafter cited in text by page number.

36. James O'Rourke, "'Nothing More Unnatural': Mary Shelley's Revision of Rousseau," *ELH* 56, no. 3 (Fall 1989): 545.

37. Neil Hertz, "Medusa's Head: Male Hysteria under Political Pressure," in *The End of the Line: Essays on Psychoanalysis and the Sublime*, by Hertz (New York: Columbia University Press, 1985), 161–94.

38. Mary Shelley, "Preface to the Volume of *Posthumous Poems* published in 1824," in *The Works of Percy Bysshe Shelley*, ed. Mrs. Shelley (London: Edward Moxon, 1850), 328; hereafter cited in text as *WPBS*. All further citations of *Posthumous Poems* and the 1839 *Poetical Works* are to this edition.

39. Joseph Raben, "Shelley's 'Invocation to Misery': An Expanded Text," *Journal of English and German Philology* 65 (January 1966): 65.

40. Michael Henry Scrivener, *Radical Shelley: The Philosophical Anarchism and Utopian Thought of Percy Bysshe Shelley* (Princeton: Princeton University Press, 1982), 257.

41. Irving Massey, *Posthumous Poems of Shelley: Mary Shelley's Fair Copy Book* (Montreal: McGill-Queen's University Press, 1969), 8; hereafter cited in text.

42. Quoted in *The Romantics Reviewed: Contemporary Reviews of British Romantic Writers*, ed. Donald H. Reiman, 8 vols. (New York: Garland, 1972), part C, vol. 2, p. 503; hereafter cited in text as Reiman by part, volume, and page number.

43. Sylva Norman, *Flight of the Skylark: The Development of Shelley's Reputation* (Norman: University of Oklahoma Press, 1954), 86; hereafter cited in text.

44. Kenneth S. Cameron, *The Young Shelley: Genesis of a Radical* (New York: Macmillan, 1950), 274.

45. Neil Fraistat, "Illegitimate Shelley: Radical Piracy and the Textual Edition as Cultural Performance," *PMLA* 109, no. 3 (May 1994): 415; hereafter cited in text.

46. Donald H. Reiman, "Shelley in the Encyclopedias," *Keats-Shelley Journal* 12 (Winter 1963): 55, 57.

47. William St. Clair, *The Godwins and the Shelleys: A Biography of a Family* (Baltimore: Johns Hopkins University Press, 1989), 516.

48. Quoted in Morag Shiach, *Discourse on Popular Culture: Class, Gender, and History in Cultural Analysis, 1730 to the Present* (Stanford: Stanford University Press, 1989), 27.

49. Susan J. Wolfson, "Editorial Privilege: Mary Shelley and Percy Shelley's Audiences," in *Other*, 45; hereafter cited in text.

50. Paula R. Feldman, "Biography and the Literary Executor: The Case of Mary Shelley," *Papers of the Bibliographical Society of America* 72, no. 3 (1978): 295.

51. T. N. Talfourd, *Speech for the Defendant, in the Prosecution of The Queen vs. Moxon, for the Publication of Shelley's Works* (London: Edward Moxon, 1841), 32, 19. I am indebted to Rick Swartz for this reference.

52. Karsten Engelberg, "The Sentimental Appeal in Criticism of Shelley, 1822–1860," in *The Romantic Heritage: A Collection of Critical Essays*, ed.

Engelberg (Copenhagen: University of Copenhagen English Department, 1983), 167.

53. Mary Favret, "Mary Shelley's Sympathy and Irony: The Editor and Her Corpus," in *Other*, 20; hereafter cited in text.

54. Mary Shelley, "Preface," *Essays, Letters from Abroad, Translations and Fragments by Percy Bysshe Shelley* (Philadelphia: Lea and Blanchard, 1840), 13; hereafter cited in text.

Chapter Seven

1. "Note on the Poems of 1820," *The Poetical Works of Percy Bysshe Shelley*, in *The Works of Percy Bysshe Shelley*, ed. Mrs. Shelley (London: Edward Moxon, 1850), 279.

2. This chapter omits the essays "Rome in the First and Nineteenth Centuries" and "Recollections of the Lake of Geneva"; although both have been attributed to Mary Shelley, internal evidence suggests that she did not write them. I have not been able to consult her "Narrative of a Tour round the Lake of Geneva" or "A Visit to Brighton."

3. Judith Adler, "Origins of Sightseeing," *Annals of Tourism Research* 16 (1989): 9; hereafter cited in text.

4. John Frow, "Tourism and the Semiotics of Nostalgia," *October* 57 (Summer 1991): 143; hereafter cited in text.

5. Thomas M. Curley, *Samuel Johnson and the Age of Travel* (Athens: University of Georgia Press, 1976), 53; hereafter cited in text.

6. Margaret Hunt, "Racism, Imperialism, and the Traveler's Gaze in Eighteenth-Century England," *Journal of British Studies* 32 (October 1993): 348.

7. James Buzard, *The Beaten Track: European Tourism, Literature, and the Ways to "Culture" 1800–1918* (Oxford: Clarendon Press, 1993), 99; hereafter cited in text.

8. Anne Friedberg, *Window Shopping: Cinema and the Postmodern* (Berkeley: University of California Press, 1993), 59; hereafter cited in text.

9. Pierre Bourdieu, *Distinction: A Social Critique of the Judgement of Taste*, trans. Richard Nice (Cambridge: Harvard University Press, 1984), 56; hereafter cited in text.

10. Mary Shelley, The *History of a Six Weeks' Tour through a part of France, Switzerland, Germany, and Holland; with Letters, descriptive of a sail round the Lake of Geneva, and of the glaciers of Chamouni*, in *Essays, Letters from Abroad, Translations and Fragments by Percy Bysshe Shelley* (Philadelphia: Lea and Blanchard, 1840), 11; hereafter cited in text.

11. Anonymous review, *Blackwood's Magazine* 3 (July 1818): 412, 416.

12. Mary Shelley, "Recollections of Italy," in *Tales*, 28; hereafter cited in text.

13. Anonymous review, *Westminster Review* 6 (October 1826). Reprinted in *The Mary Shelley Reader*, ed. Betty T. Bennett and Charles E. Robinson (New York: Oxford University Press, 1990), 341; hereafter cited in text from *Reader*.

14. Mary Shelley, "Velluti," *The Examiner*, no. 958 (11 June 1826): 372. Reprinted in *MWSL* 1:517–19; hereafter cited in text from *MWSL*.

15. Pierre Bourdieu and Loïc Wacquant, *An Invitation to Reflexive Sociology* (Chicago: University of Chicago Press, 1992), 154.

16. *Westminster Review* 11 (July 1829): 129; hereafter cited in text.

17. John Barrell, "Death on the Nile: Fantasy and the Literature of Tourism, 1840–1860," *Essays in Criticism* 41, no. 2 (April 1991): 97; hereafter cited in text.

18. Mary Shelley, *Rambles in Germany and Italy, in 1840, 1842, and 1843*, 2 vols. (1844; Folcroft, Pa.: Folcroft Library Editions, 1975), 2:266; hereafter cited in text by volume and page number.

19. Esther H. Schor, "Mary Shelley in Transit," in *Other*, 236; hereafter cited in text.

20. Dean MacCannell, *The Tourist: A New Theory of the Leisure Class* (New York: Schocken, 1976), 67; hereafter cited in text.

21. Anonymous review, *Tait's Edinburgh Magazine* vol. 11, no. 81 (November 1844): 731; hereafter cited in text.

22. Maxine Feifer, *Going Places: The Ways of the Tourist from Imperial Rome to the Present Day* (London: Macmillan, 1985), 107; hereafter cited in text.

23. Anonymous review, *Athenaeum*, no. 876 (10 August 1844): 727; hereafter cited in text.

24. "Lady Travellers in Italy and Germany," *New Monthly Magazine* vol. 72, no. 3 (October 1844): 285.

25. Anonymous review, *The Examiner*, no. 1904 (27 July 1844): 467; hereafter cited in text.

Selected Bibliography

Primary sources cited singly are listed chronologically; secondary sources are listed alphabetically.

PRIMARY SOURCES
Published Works

Novels

Frankenstein; or, The Modern Prometheus. 3 vols. London: Lackington & Co., 1818.
Valperga. 3 vols. London: G. and W. B. Whittaker, 1823.
The Last Man. 3 vols. London: Henry Colburn, 1826.
The Fortunes of Perkin Warbeck, A Romance. 3 vols. London: Colburn & Bentley, 1830.
Frankenstein; or, The Modern Prometheus. Rev. ed. London: Colburn & Bentley, 1831.
Lodore. 3 vols. London: Richard Bentley, 1835.
Falkner. 3 vols. London: Sanders and Otley, 1837.

Short Fiction

Mathilda. Edited by Elizabeth Nitchie. Chapel Hill: University of North Carolina, 1959. Reprinted in *The Mary Shelley Reader.* Edited by Betty T. Bennett and Charles E. Robinson. New York: Oxford University Press, 1990, 173–246. Hereafter cited in bibliography as *Reader.*
Mary Shelley: Collected Tales and Stories. Edited by Charles E. Robinson. Baltimore: Johns Hopkins University Press, 1976. Includes all the stories and fragments, "The Pole" (a story written by Claire Clairmont and corrected by Mary Shelley), and the essay "Recollections of Italy."

Nonfiction Books, Journals, and Letters

History of a Six Weeks' Tour through a part of France, Switzerland, Germany, and Holland; with Letters, descriptive of a sail round the Lake of Geneva, and of the glaciers of Chamouni. London: Thomas J. Hookham, 1817.
Preface. *Posthumous Poems of Percy Bysshe Shelley.* London: John and Henry Hunt, 1824.
Lives of the Most Eminent Literary and Scientific Men of Italy, Spain, and Portugal. 3 vols. London: Longman & Co., 1835–37. Vols. 86–88 of Lardner's Cabinet Cyclopedia.

Lives of the Most Eminent Literary and Scientific Men of France. 2 vols. London: Longman & Co., 1838–39. Vols. 102 and 103 of Lardner's Cabinet Cyclopedia. Reprinted as *Lives of the Most Eminent French Writers,* 1840.

Preface and Notes. *The Poetical Works of Percy Bysshe Shelley.* 4 vols. London: Edward Moxon, 1839. One–volume edition with added postscript published in 1840. Preface reprinted in *Reader,* 377–81.

Preface and Notes. *Essays, Letters from Abroad, Translations and Fragments by Percy Bysshe Shelley.* 2 vols. London: Edward Moxon, 1840.

Rambles in Germany and Italy, in 1840, 1842, and 1843. 2 vols. London: Edward Moxon, 1844. Preface reprinted in *Reader,* 382–86.

The Journals of Mary Shelley, 1814–1844. Edited by Paula R. Feldman and Diana Scott-Kilvert. 2 vols. Oxford: Clarendon, 1987. Hereafter cited in bibliography as *MWSJ,* by volume and page number.

The Letters of Mary Wollstonecraft Shelley. Edited by Betty T. Bennett. 3 vols. Baltimore: Johns Hopkins University Press, 1980–1988. Hereafter cited in bibliography as *MWSL,* by volume and page number.

Nonfiction Articles

"Madame d'Houtetôt." *The Liberal: Verse and Prose from the South* 2, no. 3 (1823): 67–83.

"Giovanni Villani." *The Liberal: Verse and Prose from the South* 2, no. 4 (1823): 281–97. Partial reprint, in *Reader,* 329–33.

"Recollections of Italy." *London Magazine* 9 (January 1824): 21–26.

"On Ghosts." *London Magazine* 9 (March 1824): 253–56. Reprint, in *Reader,* 334–40.

"Defense of Velluti." *The Examiner* 958 (11 June 1826): 372–73. Reprint, in *MWSL,* 1:517–18.

"The English in Italy." *Westminster Review* 6 (October 1826): 325–41. Reprint, in *Reader,* 341–57.

"A Visit to Brighton." *London Magazine* 16 (December 1826): 460–66.

Review of *The Italian Novelists. Westminster Review* 7 (January 1827): 115–16.

"Illyrian Poems—Feudal Scenes." *Westminster Review* 10 (January 1829): 71–81.

"Modern Italy." *Westminster Review* 11 (July 1829): 127–40. Partial reprint, in *Reader,* 358–64.

Review of *The Loves of the Poets. Westminster Review* 11 (October 1829): 472–77. Reprint, in *Reader,* 365–71.

Review of *Cloudesley; A Tale. Blackwood's Edinburgh Magazine* 27:166 (May 1830): 711–16. Partial reprint, in *Reader,* 372–76.

Review of *1572 Chronique du Temps de Charles IX. Westminster Review* 13 (October 1830): 495–502.

"Living Literary Characters. No. II. The Honourable Mrs. Norton." *New Monthly Magazine* 33 (February 1831): 180–83.

"Living Literary Characters. No. IV. James Fenimore Cooper." *New Monthly Magazine* 33 (April 1831): 356–62.
"Memoirs of William Godwin." In Godwin, *Caleb Williams*, iii–xiii. London: Colburn & Bentley, 1831.
Review of *Life and Death of Lord Edward Fitzgerald*. *Westminster Review* 16 (January 1832): 110–21.
Review of *The Bravo*. *Westminster Review* 16 (January 1832): 180–92.
Review of *Richard the Third, as Duke of Gloucester and King of England*. *Athenaeum*, no. 875 (3 August 1844): 707–08 and no. 876 (10 August 1844): 728–31.

Poetry

"The Choice" (written 1823). In *MWSJ*, 2:490–94, and in *Mary Shelley: A Biography*, by R. Glynn Grylls. London: Oxford University Press, 1938. 297–301. Hereafter cited in bibliography as Grylls.
"On Reading Wordsworth's Lines on Peel Castle" (written 1825). In *MWSJ*, 2:494–95 and Grylls, 302–03.
"Fragment: To Jane" (written 1826). In *MWSJ*, 2:495 and Grylls, 303.
"Absence." *The Keepsake for MDCCCXXXI* (1830): 39.
"A Dirge." *The Keepsake for MDCCCXXXI* (1830): 85. Revised reprint, in *The Poetical Works of Percy Bysshe Shelley* (1839).
"Alas I weep my life away" (written 1831). In *MWSJ*, 2:522 and *Mary Shelley, Author of "Frankenstein,"* by Elizabeth Nitchie. New Brunswick, N. J.: Rutgers University Press, 1953. 235. Hereafter cited in bibliography as Nitchie.
"Struggle no more, my soul" (written 1831). In *MWSJ*, 2:523 and Nitchie, 235.
"Stanzas [I must forget]." *The Keepsake for MDCCCXXXIII* (1832). Reprint, in *Mary Shelley: Romance and Reality*, by Emily W. Sunstein, Appendix A. Baltimore: Johns Hopkins University Press, 1989. 52.
"La Vida es sueño" (written 1833). In Nitchie, 233–34.
"Tempo é più di Morire/Io ho tardato più ch'i' non vorrei" (written 1833). In Nitchie, 231–33.
"O listen while I sing to thee" (written 1838). In Nitchie, 234. Revised version published as canzonet in 1842.
"Stanzas [How like a star]." *The Keepsake for MDCCCXXXIX* (1838): 179. Reprinted in this book.
"Stanzas [O come to me]." *The Keepsake for MDCCCXXXIX* (1838): 201. Reprinted in this book.

Translations

"The Stars," from Schiller (written 1823). In *MWSJ*, 1:271.
"Guidiccioni's 'Sonnet to Italy.'" *New Monthly Magazine and Literary Journal* 10 (March 1824): 222.

"'The Divysion of The Earth'," from Schiller. *The Bijou for 1829* (1828): 164–65.
"'The Song of the Sword'," from Korner. *The Bijou for 1829* (1828): 174–77.
"Ritratto di Ugo Foscolo." *The Bijou for 1830* (1829): 40–41.
"To Glory," from Ciapetti. *The Bijou for 1830* (1829): 98.
"Ode," from Klopstock. *The Bijou for 1830* (1829): 225–26.

Drama

Midas (written 1820). In *"Proserpine" and "Midas": Two Unpublished Mythological Dramas.* Edited by A. H. Koszul, 45–89. London: Humphrey Milford, 1922. Hereafter cited in bibliography as Koszul.
Proserpine (written 1820). *The Winter's Wreath for 1832* (1831): 1–20. Reprint, in Koszul, 3–44.

Unpublished Works

Notes for a biography of William Godwin. In *William Godwin: His Friends and Contemporaries*, by C. Kegan Paul, 1:25–26, 36–37, 47, 64, 73–74, 76, 78–83, 120–25, 129–35, 161–62, 231–32, 238–39, 332–33. 2 vols. London: Henry S. King, 1876.
The Frankenstein Manuscripts: The Drafts for Mary Shelley's Novel in Lord Abinger's Collection (Bodleian Abinger dep. c. 534 and dep. c. 477/1. Transcribed and edited by Charles E. Robinson. New York: Garland, 1995.

SECONDARY SOURCES
Bibliographies

Lyles, W. H. *Mary Shelley: An Annotated Bibliography.* New York: Garland, 1975. Now outdated, but still an essential guide to reprints and movies of *Frankenstein* and to contemporary reviews of Mary Shelley's works.

Books and Parts of Books

Baldick, Chris. *In Frankenstein's Shadow: Myth, Monstrosity, and Nineteenth-Century Writing.* Oxford: Clarendon, 1987. Comprehensive and fascinating study of the permutations of the "Frankenstein's monster" trope.
Bennett, Betty T. "Finding Mary Shelley in her Letters." In *Romantic Revisions.* Edited by Robert Brinkley and Keith Hanley. Cambridge: Cambridge University Press, 1992. 291–306. Helpful introduction to Mary Shelley's interests as revealed in her letters.
Blumberg, Jane. *Mary Shelley's Early Novels: "This Child of Imagination and Misery."* Iowa City: University of Iowa Press, 1993. Study of Mary Shelley's first three novels and her editions of Shelley; illuminating on her relations with Byron.

Clemit, Pamela. *The Godwinian Novel: The Rational Fictions of Godwin, Brockden Brown, Mary Shelley.* Oxford: Clarendon, 1993. Places *Frankenstein* and *Valperga* in the radical literary tradition practiced by Mary Shelley's father.

Fisch, Audrey A., Anne K. Mellor, and Esther H. Schor, eds. *The Other Mary Shelley: Beyond "Frankenstein."* New York: Oxford University Press, 1993. Valuable collection of essays; see especially Corbett, Ellis, Favret, Hofkosh, Paley, and Schor.

Gilbert, Sandra M. and Susan Gubar. *The Madwoman in the Attic: The Woman Writer and the Nineteenth-Century Literary Imagination.* New Haven: Yale University Press, 1979. 213–47. Early and still useful feminist reading of *Frankenstein.*

Levine, George, and U. C. Knoepflmacher, eds. *The Endurance of "Frankenstein."* Berkeley: University of California Press, 1979. The first scholarly collection of essays on *Frankenstein*; fine essays by Brooks, Ellis, LaValley (on film adaptations), Moers, Owen, and Sterrenburg.

McWhir, Anne. "Teaching the Monster to Read: Mary Shelley, Education, and *Frankenstein.*" In *The Educational Legacy of Romanticism.* Edited by John Willinsky. Waterloo, Canada: Wilfrid Laurier University Press, 1990. The broadest treatment of reading and education in *Frankenstein.*

Mellor, Anne K. *Mary Shelley: her Life, her Fiction, her Monsters.* New York: Routledge, 1988. Sometimes overstated, but essential on *Frankenstein*'s science and on Percy Shelley's contributions to the novel.

Poovey, Mary. *The Proper Lady and the Woman Writer: Ideology as Style in the Works of Mary Wollstonecraft, Mary Shelley, and Jane Austen.* Chicago: University of Chicago Press, 1984. Especially valuable on Mary Shelley's revisions of *Frankenstein* for the 1831 edition.

St. Clair, William. *The Godwins and the Shelleys: A Biography of a Family.* Baltimore: Johns Hopkins University Press, 1989. More on the Godwins than the Shelleys, but good coverage of Mary Shelley's radical heritage.

Smith, Johanna M., ed. *Mary Shelley: "Frankenstein."* Boston: Bedford-St. Martin's, 1992. Contains *Frankenstein*, essays on its biographical and historical contexts and its critical reception, and five essays exemplifying contemporary critical methodologies.

Spark, Muriel. *Mary Shelley.* London: Penguin, 1987. The best brief life.

Sunstein, Emily W. *Mary Shelley: Romance and Reality.* Baltimore: Johns Hopkins University Press, 1989. Essential; the most complete life.

Articles

Bewell, Alan. "An Issue of Monstrous Desire: *Frankenstein* and Obstetrics." *Yale Journal of Criticism* 2, no. 1 (Fall 1988): 105–28. Fascinating cultural-studies reading of *Frankenstein* in terms of midwifery manuals.

Carson, James B. "Bringing the Author Forward: *Frankenstein* through Mary Shelley's Letters." *Criticism* 30, no. 4 (Fall 1988): 431–53. Interesting reading of the feminine voice.

Crafts, Stephen. "*Frankenstein*: Camp Curiosity or Premonition?" *Catalyst* 3 (Summer 1967): 96–103. Good example of political criticism of the 1960s.

Dussinger, John A. "Kinship and Guilt in Mary Shelley's *Frankenstein*." *Studies in the Novel* 8 (1976): 38–55. Most enlightening on alchemy.

Favret, Mary. "A Woman Writes the Fiction of Science: The Body in *Frankenstein*." *Genders* 14 (Fall 1992): 50–65. Fascinating analysis of forms of reproduction.

Goodwin, Sarah Webster. "Domesticity and Uncanny Kitsch in 'The Rime of the Ancient Mariner' and *Frankenstein*." *Tulsa Studies in Women's Literature* 10, no. 1 (Spring 1991): 93–108. Interesting on the vexing question of Mary Shelley's attitudes toward domesticity.

Harpold, Terence. "'Did you get Mathilda from Papa?': Seduction Fantasy and the Circulation of Mary Shelley's *Mathilda*." *Studies in Romanticism* 28, no. 1 (Spring 1989): 49–67. Dense but intriguing exploration of the novella and its circulation between Mary and Godwin.

Kranzler, Laura. "Frankenstein and the Technological Future." *Foundation* 44 (Winter 1988–89): 42–49. Fine example of science-fiction readings of *Frankenstein*.

London, Bette. "Mary Shelley, *Frankenstein*, and the Spectacle of Masculinity." *PMLA* 108, no. 2 (March 1993): 253–67. Interesting revisionist point of view on gender issues.

Manson, Michael, and Robert Scott Stewart. "Heroes and Hideousness: *Frankenstein* and Failed Unity." *SubStance* 71/72 (1993): 228–42. Very useful on Romantic science.

May, Marilyn. "Publish and Perish: William Godwin, Mary Shelley, and the Public Appetite for Scandal." *Papers on Language and Literature* 26, no. 4 (Fall 1990): 489–512. Very interesting material on Godwin's and Mary Shelley's relations to their audiences.

Michie, Elsie B. "Production Replaces Creation: Market Forces and *Frankenstein* as Critique of Romanticism." *Nineteenth-Century Contexts* 12, no. 1 (1988): 27–33. Rich Marxist analysis.

O'Dea, Gregory. "Prophetic History and Textuality in Mary Shelley's *The Last Man*." *Papers on Language and Literature* 28.3 (Summer 1992): 283–304. Very interesting on concept of prophetic history.

O'Flinn, Paul. "Production and Reproduction: The Case of *Frankenstein*." *Literature and History* 9.2 (1983): 194–213. Marxist reading, and particularly interesting analysis of two *Frankenstein* movies.

O'Rourke, James. "'Nothing More Unnatural': Mary Shelley's Revision of Rousseau." *ELH* 56, no. 3 (Fall 1989): 543–69. Good introduction to Mary Shelley's views of Rousseau.

Rajan, Tilottama. "Mary Shelley's *Mathilda*: Melancholy and the Political Economy of Romanticism." *Studies in the Novel* 26, no. 2 (Summer 1994): 43–68. Rigorous Lacanian and Kristevan analysis.

Snyder, Robert Lance. "Apocalypse and Indeterminacy in Mary Shelley's *The Last Man.*" *Studies in Romanticism* 17, no. 4 (Fall 1978): 442–43. Especially interesting on early-nineteenth-century theories of apocalypse.

Spivak, Gayatri Chakravorty. "Three Women's Texts and a Critique of Imperialism." *Critical Inquiry* 12, no. 1 (1985): 243–61; reprint, in *"Race," Writing, and Difference*, edited by Henry Louis Gates, Jr. Chicago: University of Chicago Press, 1986. 262–80. Includes reading of *Frankenstein* in its response to liberal-feminist analyses of women's texts.

Sterrenburg, Lee. *"The Last Man*: Anatomy of Failed Revolutions," *Nineteenth Century Fiction* 33, no. 3 (December 1978): 324–47. Thorough analysis of the novel's relation to revolutionary politics.

Vlasopolos, Anca. *"Frankenstein's* Hidden Skeleton: The Psycho-Politics of Oppression." *Science-Fiction Studies* 10, no. 2 (July 1983): 125–35. Essential on the politics of *Frankenstein.*

Winnett, Susan. "Coming Unstrung: Women, Men, Narrative, and Principles of Pleasure." *PMLA* 105, no. 3 (May 1990): 505–18. Interesting on the gendering of narrative strategies in *Frankenstein.*

Zonana, Joyce. "'They Will Prove the Truth of My Tale': Safie's Letters as the Feminist Core of Mary Shelley's *Frankenstein.*" *Journal of Narrative Technique* 21, no. 2 (Spring 1991): 170–84. Unique reading of Safie's role.

Index

Alfieri, Vittorio, 133–36
America, 105, 111, 122, 126
Anglo-Italian, 124, 160–62
annuals, 36–37; *Forget-Me-Not,* 36; *Heath's Book of Beauty,* 101; *Juvenile Forget-Me-Not,* 22; *Keepsake, The,* 36–37, 80; Shelley's work in, 28, 29, 31, 39, 61, 62, 67, 78, 79, 98, 102, 103, 104; *New Year's Gift and Juvenile Souvenir,* 22; *Winter's Wreath,* 19; and woman reader, 37, 39, 62, 80, 101, 104
Ariosto, 131–32
Astell, Mary, 1
Aurora Leigh, 38
Austen, Jane, 68, 105

Baxter, William, 7
Beauclerk, Aubrey, 13
bed trick, 100
Berni, Francesco, 131–32
Blessington, Countess of, 37
Boccaccio, Giovanni, 131–32
Bojardo, Matteo, 131, 133
Boscan, Mosen, 136, 137
Brewster, Sir David, 130, 133
Bulwer, Edward, 126
Burke, Edmund, 1–2
Burr, Aaron, 6
Byron, Allegra, 8, 10
Byron, Lord (George Gordon), 8–11, 15, 37, 48; friendship with Mary Shelley, 78, 113; and *The Liberal,* 59, 121; works of, 77, 111, 112

Cabinet Cyclopedia, 13, 119, 124, 128, 130–31
Calderon, Pedro, 136
Camoens, Luis, 136, 139
capital, cultural, 121, 157
Carter, Elizabeth, 1
cavalier servente, 133, 135–36, 142
Cervantes, Miguel de, 136–39
chartism, 16
Chiabrera, Gabriello, 133

chivalry, 57, 62, 66, 82, 84–92
cholera, 48
Clairmont, Charles, 6
Clairmont, Claire (Jane), 6–10, 14, 15, 146, 157
Colburn & Bentley, 122–23
Colburn, Henry, 120
Coleridge, Samuel Taylor, 6, 112, 120
Colonna, Vittoria, 133, 135
Condorcet, Marquis de, 140–42
Cooper, James Fenimore, 123–24, 126, 165
criminality, 101–102, 115–16

Dante, 71, 131, 132, 169
Davy, Humphry, 6, 43
Deffell, George, 163
de la Vega, Garcilaso, 136, 138
de Leon, Luis, 136
de Medici, Lorenzo, 131–32
de Stael, Mme Germaine, 140, 144, 157
de Vega, Lope, 136–37
Dickens, Charles, 112, 144
Dods, Mary Diana, 12
Douglas, Isabel Robinson, 12
Dunciad, The (Pope), 156

Edgeworth, Maria, 6
education, 55, 129, 143, 155, 169; in "Euphrasia," 79–80; in *Frankenstein,* 40, 45; in *Lodore,* 105, 109–10; in "The Mourner," 103; in *Valperga,* 69–71, 73
Eliot, George, 107
Ellis, Sarah, 110
Elstob, Elizabeth, 1
encyclopedias, 130
Ercilla, Alonso de, 136–38
Espinel, Vicente, 136, 138

fairy tale, 67–68
Faust, 38, 43
Fiction: domestic/sentimental, 92–93, 96–99, 103, 105, 112–13, 118;

193

fashionable, 92–93, 105; Gothic, 57, 60–61, 67–68, 72–76, 84, 96; historical, 58–59, 68–69, 76; Jacobin, 57–58, 62, 68, 76, 144; Newgate, 107; realistic, 56, 76, 92; romance, 56–58, 62–63, 67, 81–82, 98; science fiction, 33 ; and cognitive estrangement, 36, 40, 48
Filicaja, Vincenzo da, 133
Foscolo, Ugo, 133–34, 136

Galileo, 133
Gatteschi, Ferdinando, 14, 167, 169
genius, 127, 134, 138–39
Godwin, M. J. & Co., 6
Godwin, Mary Jane Clairmont, 6–7, 13
Godwin, William, 1, 3, 4–6, 8–9, 11, 13, 16, 47, 53, 57, 123, 157; *Caleb Williams,* 4, 56, 112, 123; *Enquiry concerning Political Justice,* 4–5, 46, 71, 123; and Mary Shelley's writing, 9, 68, 94; works of, 3, 123, 126
Godwin, William, Jr., 6
Goldoni, Carlo, 133–34
Gongora, Luis de, 136
Gore, Catherine, 93
Graham, Catherine Macaulay, 1
Grand Tour, 155–57, 160, 162, 165
Guarini, Battista, 133
Guicciardini, Francesco, 133–34

Hamilton, Mary, 1
Hawthorne, Nathaniel, 97
Hays, Mary, 1
Hazlitt, William, 120, 146, 164
Hermsprong (Bage), 57
Holbach, Ludwig, 43
Hume, David, 53, 81, 83–84, 90–91
Hunt, Leigh, 8, 9, 11, 17, 25, 47, 153; and *The Liberal,* 59, 121
Hunt, Marianne, 11, 25

ideology: of domesticity, 41–44, 92; of gender, 15, 18, 40, 42, 49, 58–59, 64, 92–93, 107–8, 142; of imperialism, 79, 84; of Orientalism, 77, 79–80, 86, 124

imagination, 69–70, 72–73, 75, 84, 121, 124–25, 167
Imlay, Fanny, 6, 8
Imlay, Gilbert, 3, 6
improvvisatore, 133
incest, 94, 96, 103, 110, 112–13, 124–25. *See also* League of Incest
Industrial Revolution, 17
Ireland, 86, 89, 127–28

Jacobins, 2, 4, 16, 55, 57
Jameson, Anna, 125, 160
Jane Eyre, 38
Johnson, Samuel, 120, 133, 156

Keats, John, 112
Knox, Alexander, 163

Lardner, Dionysius, 13, 119, 130–31
Lawrence, Sir Thomas, 6
League of Incest, 9, 13
Lee, Harriet, 6
Liberal, The, 59, 119, 121, 127
liberalism, 17–18
literacy, 55, 128–29
literary biography, 136–37; educative function of, 132–33, 144
literary criticism, 119–22, 125, 131, 154; educative function of, 125–26, 132–33, 140–41; politico-literary criticism, 134–35, 137

Macaulay, Thomas, 149
Machiavelli, Niccolò, 69–70, 131–32
Man of Mode, The (Etherege), 156
Marini, Giambatista, 133
Mavrocordato, Prince Alexander, 9, 78, 113
Medwin, Thomas, 15, 148
Mendoza, Diego de, 136
Mérimée, Prosper, 12, 124–26
Metastasio, Pietro, 133
Milton, John, 45, 110
Mirabeau, Honore-Gabriele, 140, 142
Montagu, Lady Mary Wortley, 1, 156
Montgomery, Sir James, 131, 133
Monti, Vincenzo, 133–35

Moore, Thomas, 127–28, 130
Moxon, Edward, 147–49, 163, 168

Napoleonic Wars, 17, 58, 64, 135, 156,
    160, 162
necessity, philosophy of, 53–54, 58
Norfolk, Lord (Henry Charles), 17–18
Norton, Lady Caroline, 16, 37, 117–18,
    122

orientalism. *See* ideology
Owen, Robert Dale, 46

Paine, Thomas, 4
Payne, John Howard, 12
Peake, Richard Brinsley, 11
Petrarch, Francesco, 131–33
physiocracy, 70
Polidori, John William, 8
Pulci, Luigi, 132

Quevedo, Francisco de, 136

radicalism, 1–2, 4–5, 16, 18, 123, 149,
    158–59
reform, 5, 17, 146, 154
Reform Bill of 1832, 2, 17, 46–47, 127,
    149
Reveley, Maria, 6
revolution, 5; American, 1; French, 1, 4,
    16, 39, 48, 58, 63–64, 92, 127, 135,
    142, 144, 158; Greek, 9, 77, 79–80,
    113, 150; Italian, 9, 14, 58, 98, 134,
    150, 161, 168–69
Robinson, Julian, 163
Rogers, Samuel,
Roland, Mme Manon, 140, 142–44
Rousseau, Jean-Jacques, 71, 109, 121,
    140–43, 158

science, 40–41, 43–46
Scotland, 7, 88
Scott, Sarah, 1
Scott, Sir Walter, 56, 81, 126, 130
Shelley, Clara, 8, 10, 26
Shelley, Harriet, 7, 8
Shelley, Ianthe, 7

Shelley, Jane St. John, 15
Shelley, Mary Wollstonecraft: and
    Catholicism, 97, 141, 162, 169; child-
    hood, 6; and class, 22, 24, 61; death,
    13, 15

DRAMA
Midas, 19, 22–24
Proserpine, 19–22

EDITIONS
*Essays, Letters from Abroad, Translations and
    Fragments by Percy Bysshe Shelley*, 13,
    152–54
Poetical Works of Percy Bysshe Shelley, 13,
    148–52
Posthumous Poems of Percy Bysshe Shelley, 11,
    145–47

NON-FICTION
History of a Six Weeks' Tour, 7, 152, 155,
    157–59, 163, 165
*Lives of the Most Eminent Literary and Scien-
    tific Men of France*, 139–44
*Lives of the most Eminent Literary and Scien-
    tific Men of Italy, Spain, and Portugal*,
    128, 131–39, 141, 149
Rambles in Germany and Italy, 14, 163–70

NOVELS
Falkner, 13, 92, 94, 97, 100, 102, 104,
    111–18
Frankenstein, 8, 11, 13, 27, 33, 40, 50,
    53–54, 68, 85, 100, 108, 111, 114, 123
Last Man, The, 11, 27, 33, 48–54, 100,
    108, 113
Lodore, 13, 92, 96, 105–12
Mathilda, 9, 94–96, 103, 112;
Perkin Warbeck, 12, 81–91, 128
Valperga, 9, 50, 68–76, 108

POETRY
"Absence," 28
"Alas I weep my life away," 28
"Choice, The," 10, 25–27, 30
"Dirge, A," 28–29
"Fragment: To Jane," 27

"Mounseer Nongtongpaw," 6
"O listen while I sing to thee," 31
"On Reading Wordsworth's Lines on Peel Castle," 27, 29–30
"Stanzas [How like a star]," 31–32
"Stanzas [I must forget]," 30–31
"Stanzas [O, come to me]," 32
"Struggle no more, my soul," 28
"Tempo é piu di Morire/Io ho tardato piu ch'i' non vorrei," 30

SHORT FICTION
"Bride of Modern Italy, The," 68, 96–97, 107
"Brother and Sister, The," 65–67
"Dream, The," 64–66
"Elder Son, The," 101–102
"Euphrasia," 77, 79–80, 113
"Evil Eye, The," 77–79
"False Rhyme, The," 61–62, 64–65
"Ferdinando Eboli," 99–101
"Hate," 7
"Heir of Mondolfo, The," 60–61, 67
"Invisible Girl, The," 67–68
"Mortal Immortal, The," 33, 39–40, 54
"Mourner, The," 102–3
"Parvenue, The," 104–5
"Roger Dodsworth: The Reanimated Englishman," 33, 35–36
"Sisters of Albano, The," 98–99, 101
"Smuggler and his Family, The," 99, 101–2
"Swiss Peasant, The," 62–65, 67
"Tale of the Passions, A," 59–60, 64
"Transformation," 33, 37–39
"Trial of Love, The," 102
"Valerius: The Reanimated Roman," 33–35

SHORT NONFICTION
"Defense of Velluti," 161–62
"English in Italy, The," 160
"Giovanni Villani," 127
"Illyrian Poems—Feudal Scenes," 124–25
"Living Literary Characters. No. II. The Honourable Caroline Norton," 122

"Living Literary Characters. No. IV. James Fenimore Cooper," 123–24
"Madame d'Houtetot," 121–22
"Memoirs of William Godwin," 123
"Modern Italy," 161–62
"On Ghosts," 121, 124
"Recollections of Italy," 159–60
Review, The Bravo, 126
Review, Cloudesley, 126
Review, The Italian Novelists, 124
Review, Life and Death of Lord Edward Fitzgerald, 127–28
Review, The Loves of the Poets, 125
Review, Richard the Third, as Duke of Gloucester and King of England, 128

Shelley, Percy Florence, 9, 11–14, 163;
Shelley, Percy Bysshe, 1, 7–11, 13, 15, 18, 68, 107, 109, 125, 157; and Frankenstein, 16; in The Last Man, 48; in Mary Shelley's poetry, 26–29; in Rambles in Germany and Italy, 165–66; "Shelley legend," 119, 145–46, 148; works of, 19, 48, 145–54
Shelley, Sir Timothy, 7, 11–14, 112, 147–49, 165
Shelley, William, 8, 10, 26
Sismondi, Simonde de, 69, 130–31
Smith, Maria, 6
Sorrows of Young Werther, (Goethe), 45
Starke, Mariana, 162

Tasso, Torquato, 133
Tassoni, Alessandro, 133
Tennyson, Lord Alfred, 154
Thackeray, William, 131
tourism, 155–57, 162–63; and Murray Handbooks, 162, 165, 167; touristic critique of, 167–68; touristic shame, 166–67
travel: and distinction, 157, 163, 165, 168–69; and taste, 157–58, 168
Trelawny, Edward, 16, 78
Tristan, Flora, 16

Villegas, Esteban de, 136

Viviani, Emilia, 10, 96
Volney, Comte de, 45, 47–48
Voltaire, 140–43

Williams, Edward, 10–11, 27, 152
Williams, Helen Maria, 1

Williams, Jane, 11–12, 26–27
Wollstonecraft, Mary, 1–3, 16, 47, 110,
    112, 123
Wordsworth, William, 27, 112
Wortley, Lady Emeline Stuart, 37
Wright, Fanny, 15, 46, 109, 111
Wuthering Heights, (E. Bronte), 112

About the Author

Johanna M. Smith is an associate professor of English at the University of Texas–Arlington, where she teaches eighteenth- and nineteenth-century British literature, women's literature, and critical theory. Her previous work on Mary Shelley includes editing a collection of essays, *Mary Shelley: "Frankenstein"*, and two articles, "'Cooped up': Feminine Domesticity in *Frankenstein*" and "'Hideous Progenies': The Texts of *Frankenstein*." She is writing *Interventions: British Women's Social and Political Action, 1750–1850* and coediting the anthology *Autobiographical Writings by Eighteenth-Century Englishwomen*. Her articles on nineteenth-century texts and issues include "A Marxist/Feminist Reading of *Pride and Prejudice*," "'My only sister now': Incest in *Mansfield Park*," "'Too beautiful altogether': Patriarchal Ideology in *Heart of Darkness*," "Sherlock Holmes, Jack the Ripper, and the New Woman," and "Feminism and Family in Nineteenth-Century Studies." Professor Smith is on the advisory board of her university's women's studies program and on the executive board of the Interdisciplinary Nineteenth-Century Studies Association.

ISBN-10: 0-8057-7045-3
ISBN-13: 978-0-8057-7045-2